McDougal, Littell
Literature

Purple Level
Yellow Level
Blue Level
ORANGE LEVEL
Green Level
Red Level

LUMINOUS, 1965. *Richard Anuszkiewicz.*
© *Richard Anuszkiewicz, 1982.*

McDougal, Littell
Literature

Orange Level

Julie West Johnson
New Trier Township High School
Winnetka, Illinois

Margaret Grauff Forst
Lake Forest High School
Lake Forest, Illinois

McDougal, Littell & Company
Evanston, Illinois
New York   Sacramento

Consultants

Marilyn Dever, Emmerich Manual High School,
Indianapolis, Indiana

Frances M. Russell, Director of English, Winchester Public Schools,
Winchester, Massachusetts

Frances Snow, English Supervisor, Winston-Salem/Forsyth County Schools,
Winston-Salem, North Carolina

Robert Squires, English Department Chairperson, Oneonta High School,
Oneonta, New York

Acknowledgments

F. E. Albi: For "Moco Limping" by David Nava Monreal, from *Sighs and Songs of Aztlan*; copyright F. E. Albi and J. G. Nieto. Margaret Walker Alexander: For "Memory" and "Lineage" by Margaret Walker, from *For My People*; copyright 1942, Yale University Press. Atheneum Publishers, Inc.: For "The Cave" by Jean McCord, from *Deep Where the Octopi Lie*; copyright © 1968. Pat Ayres: For continued on page 742

ISBN: 0–88343–267–6

Contents

Special Features of This Text

High-Quality Selections

- The **McDougal, Littell Literature Series** offers exceptionally high-quality selections—both traditional and contemporary.
- The selections have appeal to a broad range of student interests and abilities.

Clear, Consistent Organization

- Each book is organized into units. Each unit deals with a literary type or theme.
- Each unit follows a consistent organization:

    Unit Opener—The fine art evokes images that reflect the unifying idea of the unit.

    Introduction to the Unit—This page prepares the student for the literary type or thematic idea to be covered in the unit.

    The Selections and Study Questions—Each selection is followed by its own set of study questions and skills.

    Unit Review—Each unit ends with a unit review that synthesizes similarities, differences, and relationships among the ideas in the selections.

Sustained Study of Literary Types

- The series provides an exceptionally comprehensive study of literary types: the short story, nonfiction, poetry, drama, the novel, and myths. The sustained exploration of each literary type gives students a strong grasp of the possibilities of the genre.
- Literary types have been subdivided into elements that provide the focus of study of each genre, as follows:

    The Short Story—Setting, Character, Plot, Theme
    Nonfiction—Autobiography, Heroes, Humor, Social Commentary
    Poetry—Shape and Sound, Imagery, Speaker and Tone, Idea
    Myths: The Hero—Greek Heroes, Medieval Heroes, Modern Conceptions of the Hero

Carefully Formulated Study Questions

- In-depth study questions develop the following skills:

    Getting at Meaning—These study questions help students uncover the deeper meanings of a work of literature.

    Developing Skills in Reading Literature—These questions introduce and reinforce literary terms and techniques that guide the students in learning how to read and understand literature.

    Developing Vocabulary—These exercises provide for the study, analysis, and improvement of vocabulary.

    Developing Writing Skills—These exercises provide continuing guided opportunities for writing in all forms, including creative writing.

ROASTED CHESTNUTS. *Andrew Wyeth.*
Collection of the Brandywine River Museum.

Unit 1

The Self and Others

THE GIRLS ON THE BRIDGE. *Edvard Munch.*
Nasjonalgalleriet, Oslo.

Introduction to the Unit

Suppose that on the first day of class a teacher asks you to identify yourself in a few words. What one thing would you want everyone to know about you? What would you leave out? Would your response this year be different from what you might have said a year ago?

You are a complex person, always changing. The person you are is constantly being shaped by your physical appearance, your special talents and abilities, your environment, your interactions with family and friends, and your unique experiences.

The selections in this unit explore the forces that shape human lives. Many of the selections are about relationships with family members. In one selection, a famous baseball player describes his thorough and loving training under the guidance of his father. Two stories involve young people learning important lessons through the actions of their brothers. Another involves a fourteen-year-old who seriously disappoints his parents. Some of the selections focus on the kinds of decisions that influence the directions of people's lives.

The problems of the characters may at first seem far removed from your own problems. As you read, however, you will realize that people of all ages and circumstances struggle to understand themselves and their place in the world. This realization will increase your sensitivity to the people around you and your understanding of what is happening in your own life.

Identity

THE WHITE GIRL (SYMPHONY IN WHITE, NO. 1), 1862.
James McNeill Whistler.
National Gallery of Art, Washington.
Harris Whittemore Collection.

Charles   *Shirley Jackson*

The day Laurie started kindergarten, he renounced corduroy overalls with bibs and began wearing blue jeans with a belt. I watched him go off the first morning with the older girl next door, seeing clearly that an era of my life was ended, my sweet-voiced nursery-school tot replaced by a long-trousered, swaggering[1] character who forgot to stop at the corner and wave goodbye to me.

He came home the same way, the front door slamming open, his cap on the floor, and the voice suddenly become raucous shouting, "Isn't anybody *here?*"

At lunch he spoke insolently to his father, spilled Jannie's milk, and remarked that his teacher said that we were not to take the name of the Lord in vain.

"How *was* school today?" I asked, elaborately casual.

"All right," he said.

"Did you learn anything?" his father asked.

Laurie regarded his father coldly. "I didn't learn nothing," he said.

"Anything," I said. "Didn't learn anything."

"The teacher spanked a boy, though," Laurie said, addressing his bread and butter. "For being fresh," he added with his mouth full.

"What did he do?" I asked. "Who was it?"

Laurie thought. "It was Charles," he said. "He was fresh. The teacher spanked him and made him stand in a corner. He was awfully fresh."

"What did he do?" I asked again, but Laurie slid off his chair, took a cookie, and left, while his father was still saying, "See here, young man."

The next day Laurie remarked at lunch, as soon as he sat down, "Well, Charles was bad again today." He grinned enormously and said, "Today Charles hit the teacher."

"Good heavens," I said, mindful of the Lord's name, "I suppose he got spanked again?"

"He sure did," Laurie said. "Look up," he said to his father.

"What?" his father said, looking up.

"Look down," Laurie said. "Look at my thumb. Gee, you're dumb." He began to laugh insanely.

"Why did Charles hit the teacher?" I asked quickly.

"Because she tried to make him color with red crayons," Laurie said. "Charles wanted to color with green crayons, so he hit the teacher, and she spanked him and said nobody play with Charles; but everybody did."

The third day—it was Wednesday of the first week—Charles bounced a seesaw onto the head of a little girl and made her bleed, and the teacher made him stay inside all during recess. Thursday Charles had to stand in a corner during storytime because he kept pounding his feet on the floor. Friday Charles was deprived of blackboard privileges because he threw chalk.

On Saturday I remarked to my husband, "Do you think kindergarten is too unsettling

---

1. **swaggering** (swag′ ər iŋ): walking with a bold, showy stride.

for Laurie? All this toughness and bad grammar, and this Charles boy sounds like such a bad influence."

"It'll be all right," my husband said reassuringly. "Bound to be people like Charles in the world. Might as well meet them now as later."

On Monday Laurie came home late, full of news. "Charles," he shouted as he came up the hill; I was waiting anxiously on the front steps, "Charles," Laurie yelled all the way up the hill, "Charles was bad again."

"Come right in," I said, as soon as he came close enough. "Lunch is waiting."

"You know what Charles did?" he demanded, following me through the door. "Charles yelled so in school they sent a boy in from first grade to tell the teacher she had to make Charles keep quiet, and so Charles had to stay after school. And so all the children stayed to watch him."

"What did he do?" I asked.

"He just sat there," Laurie said, climbing into his chair at the table. "Hi Pop, y'old dust mop."

"Charles had to stay after school today," I told my husband. "Everyone stayed with him."

"What does this Charles look like?" my husband asked Laurie. "What's his other name?"

"He's bigger than me," Laurie said. "And he doesn't have any rubbers, and he doesn't ever wear a jacket."

Monday night was the first Parent-Teachers meeting, and only the fact that Jannie had a cold kept me from going; I wanted passionately to meet Charles's mother. On Tuesday Laurie remarked suddenly, "Our teacher had a friend come see her in school today."

"Charles's mother?" my husband and I asked simultaneously.

"Naaah," Laurie said scornfully. "It was a man who came and made us do exercises.

Look." He climbed down from his chair and squatted down and touched his toes. "Like this," he said. He got solemnly back into his chair and said, picking up his fork, "Charles didn't even *do* exercises."

"That's fine," I said heartily. "Didn't Charles want to do exercises?"

"Naaah," Laurie said. "Charles was so fresh to the teacher's friend he wasn't *let* do exercises."

"Fresh again?" I said.

"He kicked the teacher's friend," Laurie said. "The teacher's friend told Charles to touch his toes like I just did, and Charles kicked him."

"What are they going to do about Charles, do you suppose?" Laurie's father asked him.

Laurie shrugged elaborately. "Throw him out of school, I guess," he said.

Wednesday and Thursday were routine; Charles yelled during story hour and hit a boy in the stomach and made him cry. On Friday Charles stayed after school again and so did all the other children.

With the third week of kindergarten, Charles was an institution in our family. Jannie was being a Charles when she cried all afternoon. Laurie did a Charles when he filled his wagon full of mud and pulled it through the kitchen. Even my husband, when he caught his elbow in the telephone cord and pulled telephone, ash tray, and a bowl of flowers off the table, said, after the first minute, "Looks like Charles."

During the third and fourth weeks there seemed to be a reformation[2] in Charles. Laurie reported grimly at lunch on Thursday of the third week, "Charles was so good today the teacher gave him an apple."

"What?" I said, and my husband added warily, "You mean Charles?"

---

2. **reformation** (ref′ ər mā′ shən): the act of giving up bad conduct and behaving better.

"Charles," Laurie said. "He gave the crayons around and he picked up the books afterward, and the teacher said he was her helper."

"What happened?" I asked incredulously.

"He was her helper; that's all," Laurie said, and shrugged.

"Can this be true, about Charles?" I asked my husband that night. "Can something like this happen?"

"Wait and see," my husband said cynically. "When you've got a Charles to deal with, this may mean he's only plotting."

He seemed to be wrong. For over a week, Charles was the teacher's helper. Each day he handed things out, and he picked things up; no one had to stay after school.

"The P.-T.A. meeting's next week again," I told my husband one evening. "I'm going to find Charles's mother there."

"Ask her what happened to Charles," my husband said. "I'd like to know."

"I'd like to know myself," I said.

On Friday of that week things were back to normal. "You know what Charles did today?" Laurie demanded at the lunch table, in a voice slightly awed. "He told a little girl to say a word, and she said it; and the teacher washed her mouth out with soap, and Charles laughed."

"What word?" his father asked unwisely, and Laurie said, "I'll have to whisper it to you; it's so bad." He got down off his chair and went around to his father. His father bent his head down, and Laurie whispered joyfully. His father's eyes widened.

"Did Charles tell the little girl to say that?" he asked respectfully.

"She said it twice," Laurie said. "Charles told her to say it twice."

"What happened to Charles?" my husband asked.

"Nothing," Laurie said. "He was passing out the crayons."

Monday morning Charles abandoned the little girl and said the evil word himself three or four times, getting his mouth washed out with soap each time. He also threw chalk.

My husband came to the door with me that evening as I set out for the P.-T.A. meeting. "Invite her over for a cup of tea after the meeting," he said. "I want to get a look at her."

"If only she's there," I said prayerfully.

"She'll be there," my husband said. "I don't see how they could hold a P.-T.A. meeting without Charles's mother."

At the meeting I sat restlessly, scanning each comfortable, matronly face, trying to determine which one hid the secret of Charles. None of them looked to me haggard enough. No one stood up in the meeting and apologized for the way her son had been acting. No one mentioned Charles.

After the meeting, I identified and sought out Laurie's kindergarten teacher. She had a plate with a cup of tea and a piece of chocolate cake; I had a plate with a cup of tea and a piece of marshmallow cake. We maneuvered up to one another cautiously and smiled.

"I've been so anxious to meet you," I said. "I'm Laurie's mother."

"We're all so interested in Laurie," she said.

"Well, he certainly likes kindergarten," I said. "He talks about it all the time."

"We had a little trouble adjusting, the first week or so," she said primly, "but now he's a fine little helper. With lapses, of course."

"Laurie usually adjusts very quickly," I said. "I suppose this time it's Charles's influence."

"Charles?"

"Yes," I said, laughing, "you must have your hands full in that kindergarten, with Charles."

"Charles?" she said. "We don't have any Charles in the kindergarten."

Getting at Meaning

1. List some of the things that Charles does and says at school that make him a problem. Next, list some of the things that Laurie does and says at home. Compare the lists.

2. Why does Laurie create Charles? Why does Laurie change Charles in the middle of the story?

3. Why are Laurie's parents so eager to meet Charles's mother?

4. At the end of the story, Laurie's mother learns that there is no one named Charles in the kindergarten. What clues to this fact are given earlier in the story?

Developing Skills in Reading Literature

1. **Fiction.** This story is fiction; that is, the characters and events are products of the writer's imagination. Some fiction selections are realistic, while others are purely fanciful. In "Charles," which characters seem most realistic? Why? Which events seem true to life? Which seem improbable?

2. **Surprise Ending.** An unexpected turn at the end of a story is a surprise ending. What is the surprise at the end of this story? The story is titled "Charles," although it is really about Laurie. How would titling the story "Laurie" have ruined the surprise?

Developing Vocabulary

Adjectives and Adverbs. Adjectives and adverbs are descriptive words that enrich and refine the meanings of nouns and verbs. For example, near the beginning of the story the narrator tells the reader that Laurie "spoke insolently to his father." What information does the adverb *insolently* add to the verb *spoke?* What does the narrator say about Laurie in the phrase "long-trousered, swaggering character"? What are the adjectives in the phrase? Find ten other phrases in the story in which adjectives and adverbs give significant information about characters or their actions. Write the phrases on a separate sheet of paper.

Developing Writing Skills

1. **Describing an Event from a Different Point of View.** Imagine that you are Laurie's teacher. In one paragraph, describe the thoughts you have when you finally meet Laurie's mother.

2. **Describing a Person.** Write a paragraph about a classmate from your early years of school. You may write about a real person or about a person you create in your imagination. Use vivid description to bring the person to life for the reader.

The Education of a Baseball Player

Mickey Mantle

When I was a boy in Commerce, Oklahoma, the very best place to play ball, except for the ball field where the Commerce Merchants played, was the "Alkali"—a flat stretch of plain where lead-mine shafts had been sunk and abandoned; and where chat-piles, heaps of exhausted ore, some higher than houses, made mile-long shadows in the early morning. The dry summer winds would sift the alkali dust from the tops of the chat-piles and sprinkle it over the plains all around, burning them bare of grass and undergrowth until the whole area was hard-packed and barren as a parade ground. The cave-ins and the old shafts, closed off by beaten fences any boy could climb over or through, created a constant hazard, yet it was not one that bore heavily on us. The bad feature of the place, to a boy playing ball, was the outfield, which went on and on, without a ditch or a brook or a fence or an embankment, just flat plain that stretched unbroken to the back yards of Commerce. A ball hit over an outfielder's head meant a weary chase, for the hard ground would hardly slow the ball at all, and sometimes it would skip away faster than a boy could run, until it seemed bound to get back to his own back yard before he did.

I think that endless outfield is the chief reason why I became an infielder, despite my lack of aptitude for that job. When I got big enough to have some say where I played, I refused to play outfield on the Alkali. When I was real small, but still able to play ball with my betters, I was not supposed to be out on the Alkali at all; and if my mother caught me there, as she did once or twice, she would haul me home and really warm my britches. People still told about children who had fallen into the cave-ins and been killed, but I had never known of any. Still, my mother was bound that none of her own young would tumble to an untimely death down one of those black holes. She did not object to my playing ball, however. On the contrary, she and my father agreed that there was nothing a growing boy could do better than play baseball as long as daylight would let him. There were days when I left home with nothing more than a Thermos jug of water, to play ball from breakfast until dark, without even a break for food; and my parents sent me off with their blessing.

Baseball had long been my father's passion. He named me—his oldest—after a baseball hero of his own, Mickey Cochrane; and my name was always Mickey; not Michael, just Mickey. All his youth my father had wanted to be a professional baseball player, and like my grandfather, Charles Mantle, he had played amateur and semi-pro[1] ball throughout our corner of the state. While his aim had always been to play shortstop, he was best at pitching, and when he did not pitch, he played the outfield. He never wanted to sit on the bench. So it happened that my father, who was known everywhere as Mutt Mantle, although his name was Elven, decided that if he couldn't become a professional baseball

---

1. **semi-pro:** taking part in a sport for pay but not as a regular occupation.

player, I should. He was almost comic in his determination to make a baseball player out of his little boy. When I was still in the cradle, I had a knitted baseball cap; and a pair of his old baseball pants were whittled down to fit me before I was in kindergarten. I believe, too, that he put a baseball and a glove in my crib when I was still too new to do much more than chew at them. It was a wonder, I suppose, that I did not turn against baseball, from having it forced on me so young. But instead I loved the game with a fierce devotion that has never slackened. Once I had learned to hit a ball with a bat, I needed none of my father's urging to play the game. Knowing that it pleased my father to see me do well at the game only made it twice as much fun to me.

No boy, I think, ever loved his father more than I did. I was a good boy, really, who needed little disciplining, and I would do nearly anything to keep my father happy. He was a big, strong, stern-looking man, just a fraction short of six feet tall, lean and well muscled, with the strong, gnarled hands of a miner, and dark, thick hair, a good-looking man and a good athlete. He was only nineteen when I was born, and he died when he was just past forty; so I never knew him except as a young and vigorous man, basically, and a loving, generous parent. He never had to raise his hand to me to make me obey, for I needed only a sharp look and a word from him and the knowledge that I had displeased him to make me go and do better.

He never drove me to play baseball, for no one ever had to do that. But he worked hard to help me improve, and he gave me good advice to follow, and played with me when he had the chance. It wasn't the thought of riches or fame that drove me. I didn't think about those things. I had no desire to leave home or to get very far from Commerce and the towns around us. What did keep me driving hard, from the time that I was ten, to

hit the ball better and farther was first of all my own love for the game and then my love for my father. I knew from the time I was small that every small victory I won, and every solid hit I made or prize I was awarded, brought real joy to my father's heart. Not long ago, when I read in the paper that George Scott of the Boston Red Sox had telephoned his mother to tell her of being chosen for the All Star team, I felt a tingle of sympathy. And when I got on first base against the Red Sox that day and had a chance to talk to George, I mentioned this to him; and we agreed that having someone to share an accomplishment with, someone you knew would get a thrill from it, made the accomplishment twice as sweet.

When I first started to play games with a bat and ball, I was about eight or nine, and my playground was our own back yard. With my two little friends, LeRoy and Nick, I used to engage in a game that I think was probably familiar to kids all over the country in those years—the time just before the Second World War began. All the game required was a bat of some kind, a tennis ball, and three boys— one to pitch, one to bat, and one to field the ball. Each of us would take on the name of a favorite team (mine was always the New York Yankees), and we would stay at bat right through the whole line-up, or until three men had made out through having fly balls caught. I would be Charley Keller, and Frank Crosetti, and Joe DiMaggio, and Joe Gordon, and Red Rolf, batting right-handed or left-handed, according to how the men themselves stood at the plate. If I was DiMaggio, I batted right-handed. If I was Tommy Henrich, I batted left. And that was where I got my first practice at switch-hitting,[2] before I was ten years old.

The bats we used were bats that had been

2. **switch-hitting:** batting sometimes right-handed and sometimes left-handed.

given us by grownups, or discarded by the local town team. To fix them so that we could swing them freely, we would saw several inches off the barrel. In those days, there was no Little League promotion to fill the stores with kid-sized equipment. Even if there had been, I don't believe we could have afforded it. For a long time we played with just any sort of paraphernalia we could find.

In our back-yard game, hitting was everything. A ball that went over the roof of the house was a home run. If it landed on the roof, it was a triple, and shorter hits were doubles or singles. A caught fly was out. We would keep track of the men on base and the scores, from inning to inning and game to game. We would figure out the "league standings" of the teams we represented and keep the records all season long to see which club won the championship. I don't recollect that I was any better at the game than Nick and LeRoy. The difference was—and the difference between me and many other boys who played ball with just as much skill—is that I had a father to encourage and push me. My father approved of my switch-hitting and urged me to keep at it. My grandfather was a lefty, and my father threw right-handed, and they would take turns pitching to me when I grew a little bigger, so I could get the practice I needed. For a long time it was awkward and difficult for me to bat left-handed, but my father would not let me quit. Some day, he said, baseball managers are going to use right-handed batters entirely against left-handed pitchers, then change their line-ups to use lefties against righties. You'll get to bat more often if you learn to bat from both sides, he told me, and of course, he was right.

Left-handed pitchers were almost as scarce as sea food out in that country in those days, and I found myself—once I started playing team baseball—batting left-handed most of the time. It never seemed wholly comfortable

to me, and I still think I am better right-handed than left, assuming my legs are equally strong. If my father was not nearby, I would often sneak around and bat right-handed against a right-handed pitcher. Once he saw me do this, and he called me off the diamond and sent me back home to get out of my baseball suit and stay home all day. After that, as long as he had his eye on me, I was a switch-hitter; and this is about the best thing that ever happened to me as a ballplayer. A switch-hitter never has to fret about a cross-fire pitch.[3] If the ball is coming at you, it's going to hit you, for the curve ball always breaks your way.

In odd moments, when there was no ball game on, and when my grandfather was no longer there to pitch lefty, I played pepper games[4] with my father; and in those games I always batted left-handed. This is a habit that has stuck to me—batting left-handed in pepper games.

In the games I played with Nick and LeRoy in the Mantle back yard, there was no baserunning, and pitching was just tossing the tennis ball up to be hit. Hitting was the whole game. We had plenty of practice swinging for distance with our sawed-off bats, swinging free and easy, with no fear of getting hit by the ball, and with plenty of time to wait for the pitch that looked right.

When I was fourteen, I received the Christmas present I will remember all my life. Christmas was always a thrilling day in our house, as in most homes thereabouts; for even though money was scarce, my father saw to it that Santa Claus forgot no one, and he tried hard always to surprise us with things we longed for. The family was up early on Christmas morning, usually before it was

---

3. **cross-fire pitch:** a sidearm pitch that angles across the plate.
4. **pepper games:** practice sessions in which the ball is repeatedly thrown to a batter nearby, who lightly bats it back to be fielded.

full day, to see what lay under the tree. This morning my present took my breath away. It was a full-size professional model baseball glove, carrying Marty Marion's[5] autograph, the best glove money could buy. I knew exactly what it cost, for I had yearned after it for a long time. It was twenty-two dollars, about one-third of my father's weekly salary, and I knew, as all poor boys do, exactly what that amount of money meant in a family like ours. Of course, I doted on the glove with an unholy passion, loving even the smell of it, and I caressed and cared for it through the winter as if it had been a holy relic. But most of all, my heart was bursting with the realization of what a sacrifice like this said about my father's love for me and about his pride in my ability.

Looking back on it now, I don't believe I was even the best batter in town when I was a schoolboy. I actually considered myself the worst player of the lot I played with as a kid because my fielding was always erratic. But as I said before, I was the one who had the father to coach, encourage, and keep me playing. If there were no games going or no other boys around with time to play, I would have those pepper games; with my father batting the ball on the ground as I tossed it to him, then knocking it right back when I fielded it and tossed it up again. I became an expert at this game and could go for an hour or more without booting a ground ball, while my father tirelessly tapped them down.

Our high school team did not amount to much, and of course, the season was short. But there were teams of all sorts to play on, once I was big enough. After the Pee Wee League, there was the Gabby Street League; and then the Ban Johnson League, with teams in most of the nearby small towns, in our corner of Oklahoma, and in the neighboring corners of Kansas and Missouri. I played with teams from Picher and Douthat, Oklahoma; then for Miami, in the Ban Johnson League;

and eventually joined the fastest teen-age team in the area—the Whiz Kids from Baxter Springs, Kansas. It was with the Whiz Kids that I began to make myself known beyond the columns of the local press.

One night when I hit especially hard for the Baxter Springs Whiz Kids, I knew that Tom Greenwade, the Yankee scout, was in the stands. As a matter of fact, that was to have been my graduation night at Commerce High, and I had been permitted to get my diploma during the day, just so I could play in this game before Greenwade. But I knew I would have hit those balls just as hard if Greenwade had been 500 miles away.

My father, by that time, was doing his best to get me a big league trial. He had even carted me to St. Louis to try to get me a tryout with the Browns, but they were not interested in kid short-stops at all. The first major league scout to approach me, as it turned out, was a fellow well known in the area, Runt Marr, who scouted for the Cardinals. He came to my house one day and asked me simply not to sign with any other club until he had a chance to make me an offer. This put a chill of excitement into my bones, but when days went by with no further word from him, I concluded there was not going to be any offer at all from that quarter.

My fielding, I knew, was often sorry. I had learned to charge a ground ball well, and if I could get an angle on a ball, I could field it cleanly and get off a fast throw. My arm was unusually strong, and my throws would really hum across the diamond. But when a ball came straight at me, I was often undone. Somehow it was almost impossible for me to judge the speed or the bounce of a ground ball like that. I might back off foolishly, letting the ball play me, and then lose it altogether. Or I would turn my head as it reached me,

5. **Marty Marion:** an outstanding baseball player with the St. Louis Cardinals in the 1940's.

and the ball would skip by or bounce right into my face. I carried around uncounted fat lips in that day from stopping ground balls with my mouth. And the more often I got hit, the more I would shy at such a ball. Even the balls I fielded cleanly did not always mean an out, for I had a habit of rejoicing so in the strength of my arm that I would not take the time to get a sure eye on the target. I would just let fly with my full strength, and often the ball would sail untouched into the stands.

But my hitting just seemed to get better, and my speed on drag bunts[6] made it possible for me to pull myself out of a batting slump by legging out a few base-hits almost any time I needed them. I doted on fast balls. Curves did not bother me, but it was just that I could get better distance on a fast ball; and when I was ahead of the pitcher and knew he would have to come in with a fast ball, I could really bust it into small pieces. This was what my local reputation was based on, and when scouts came to see me, they came to see me hit.

I had had my preview for Tom Greenwade and nothing happened. Then, on a sultry evening in 1949, Tom drove with my father to another Whiz Kid game. Rain cut the game short, and I dashed through the downpour to Tom Greenwade's car, to find my father sitting there with Greenwade beside him. I climbed into the back seat and listened to the negotiations. I'm not going to say my heart was in my mouth, because I already knew that Tom Greenwade had seen me at my best. But I was somewhat atremble inside all the same, as I sat there while the two men talked.

This was no "We'll call you later" deal. Greenwade was there to sign me to a contract. Once I understood that, I don't believe I'd have been distracted by a tornado, much less by the pelting rain on the car roof. Greenwade was solemnly outlining to my father all the reasons why I probably would never make good in the majors: I was too small; my fielding was atrocious; nobody knew what I would look like against really good pitching. All in all, he insisted, it was a chancy thing. But the Yankees were willing to risk a *small* investment.

My father may have believed some of this, but I did not—not about my being too small anyway. Phil Rizzuto was holding down the shortstop post with the Yankees at that time, and it would have taken one and a half of him to match me in size. And I was confident that I was as strong as most big leaguers already. Still, I listened respectfully, convinced that Mr. Greenwade really believed what he was saying, and conscious at least that my fielding was a long way from major league quality. My father agreed finally that $1,100 would be an appropriate bonus on such a doubtful prospect, plus a $400 fee for playing out the season in the minors; and he had me put my name, along with his, on the paper Tom Greenwade gave him. It was not until the signing was announced in the paper, and I read Tom Greenwade's prediction that I would probably set records with the Yankees, equaling Ruth's and DiMaggio's, that I began to wonder if my father and I had been outslicked. Greenwade, by *his* account, had just been going through Oklahoma on his way to look over a *real* prospect, when he stopped to talk to us. I never did find out who that *real* prospect was.

But all this was no more than a passing irritation. Just the chance with the Yankees was all I wanted or felt I deserved. I never for one moment believed I would give Babe Ruth's records a run, or even come close to matching Joe DiMaggio, who was my own private hero. Greenwade assigned me at once

---

6. **drag bunts:** very light hits to the infield.

to the Class D club in Independence, Missouri, of the K-O-M League; and after I had had a few days' orientation at the Yankee farm club in Joplin, my father set out to deliver my body to Independence.

This was the first time in my life I had left home to stay and I was not entirely easy in my mind about it. I was glad my father was going to drive me to Independence. It was just seventy miles away. But still, to be without my family, in a strange bed, with ballplayers all probably much abler and much older than I . . .

At Independence, we went together to find the manager of the ball club, Harry Craft. He greeted us in his hotel room, with shaving cream all over his face. Yet, despite his state of undress, he had the same stern dignity about him that my father had, and a way of carrying himself that told you here was a man of the kind you don't meet every day. He shook my hand pleasantly and let us sit down while he finished shaving.

"From now on," my father said, "Mr. Craft is your boss. I want you to do just as he tells you and pay attention to what he says, just as if I were saying it myself. And I want you to play this game just the way you would play it if I were here to watch you. And to act in every way just as if I were right handy." I promised that I would. For I was struck nearly dumb now with the solemnity of the occasion, being an obedient son and, at seventeen, young for my age, as many a small-town boy was in that day. Then my father shook hands and left me, and promptly I felt the beginnings of that dreadful uneasiness that shy people suffer when left suddenly in strange surroundings with people they do not know. I did not know where I was to sleep or take my meals, or when, and could not shame myself by asking. For a long moment, I did not want to play professional baseball at all. I just wanted to be home.

Getting at Meaning

1. What is the "Alkali"? What effect does it have on Mickey Mantle's career?

2. Is the Mantle family rich or poor? What information in the selection brings out the family's economic status?

3. How does Mantle become a switch-hitter?

4. Mickey Mantle does not think that he had more ability in his early years than his friends had. How does he explain his eventual success as a major league baseball player?

5. Describe Mickey Mantle's father. Describe the relationship between father and son. Identify two or three passages that show how Mickey's father influenced him.

6. What are Mantle's feelings as he leaves home to join the Class D club?

7. Why does Mickey Mantle feel a "dreadful uneasiness" at the end of the selection?

8. Mantle says, "... having someone to share an accomplishment with, someone you knew would get a thrill from it, made the accomplishment twice as sweet." To whom does he make this observation? How does it apply to his own life?

Developing Skills in Reading Literature

Fiction and Nonfiction. Prose writing in which characters, plots, and settings are imaginary is called fiction. Short stories and novels are fiction. Writing that recalls real life characters and events that actually happened is called nonfiction.

"The Education of a Baseball Player" is nonfiction. What experience in Mickey Mantle's life is the focus of the selection? What makes the experience interesting for readers, even those not interested in baseball?

Developing Writing Skills

Writing About a Personal Experience. Mantle says, "... the difference between me and many other boys ... is that I had a father to encourage and push me." People often do things better than they would have thought possible because of the encouragement of a relative, friend, or teacher. In one paragraph, describe an experience in which someone's encouragement helped you to accomplish something. You might start your paragraph with a topic sentence such as, "I did _____, but I couldn't have done it without _____'s help." Another approach would be to describe the experience, building up to the accomplishment.

Dreams   *Langston Hughes*

Hold fast to dreams
For if dreams die
Life is a broken-winged bird
That cannot fly.

Hold fast to dreams   5
For when dreams go
Life is a barren field
Frozen with snow.

Getting at Meaning

1. What advice begins both the first and second stanzas? What does the speaker mean by these words?

2. How does the speaker feel about dreams? According to the speaker, what would life be without dreams?

Developing Skills in Reading Literature

1. **Speaker.** The speaker of a poem is the voice in the poem that talks to the reader. It is important to understand the difference between speaker and poet, for although the ideas of the speaker often reflect those of the poet, this is not always the case. Be prepared to distinguish between the speaker and the writer of this poem and to describe briefly the speaker's ideas about dreams.

2. **Metaphor.** A metaphor is a comparison between two things that are essentially unlike but that have something in common. For example, a student might write, "The sun is a yellow ball." The writer obviously does not wish to say that the sun and a yellow ball are exactly the same. Rather, he or she wishes to point out that the sun and a yellow ball share the qualities of roundness and brightness.

Each stanza of "Dreams" contains a metaphor. In the first stanza, the speaker compares life without dreams to "a broken-winged bird/ That cannot fly." How are the two similar? What is the metaphor in the second stanza? How are these two things similar?

Developing Writing Skills

Using Figures of Speech: Metaphor. A good metaphor paints a vivid word picture for the reader. For example, the metaphor in the following sentence provides a lively comparison between a tennis player and two agile animals:

My tennis opponent was a cross between an octopus and a gazelle.

Complete each of these sentences with a fresh, interesting metaphor. Then write two completely original metaphors.

1. The stars are _____.
2. The clock is _____.
3. The rain is _____.
4. Knowledge is _____.

Ride a Wild Horse   *Hannah Kahn*

Ride a wild horse
with purple wings
striped yellow and black
except his head
which must be red.   5

Ride a wild horse
against the sky—
hold tight to his wings

before you die
whatever else you leave undone—   10
once ride a wild horse
into the sun.

Getting at Meaning

1. What words in the poem summarize the speaker's message to the reader? What does the speaker mean by these words?

2. Why is the wild horse so brightly colored? Why does it have wings?

Developing Skills in Reading Literature

1. **Symbol.** A symbol is an object or idea that stands for something else. Often a symbol is something concrete that represents an idea or concept. For example, the United States flag stands for the union of the fifty states.

What does the wild horse symbolize to the speaker of this poem? Why is it important that it is a *wild* horse?

2. **Theme.** A theme is the main idea or message in a piece of literature. What is the speaker of this poem saying about the pursuit of dreams and goals? Why should a person ride a wild horse "against the sky" and "into the sun"? How does the theme of this poem compare with the theme of "Dreams"?

Developing Writing Skills

Explaining an Idea. What is your "wild horse"? In other words, what do you dream of doing that might take you outside the safety and security of everyday life? Describe your dream in one paragraph.

Young   *Anne Sexton*

A thousand doors ago
when I was a lonely kid
in a big house with four
garages and it was summer
as long as I could remember,   5
I lay on the lawn at night,
clover wrinkling under me,
the wise stars bedding over me,
my mother's window a funnel
of yellow heat running out,   10
my father's window, half shut,
an eye where sleepers pass,
and the boards of the house
were smooth and white as wax
and probably a million leaves   15
sailed on their strange stalks
as the crickets ticked together
and I, in my brand new body,
which was not a woman's yet,
told the stars my questions   20
and thought God could really see
the heat and the painted light,
elbows, knees, dreams, goodnight.

Getting at Meaning

1. What does the speaker mean by "A thousand doors ago"? How old might the speaker be? How old is she at the moment described in the poem? Which lines suggest her age?

2. When and where does the experience described in the poem take place?

3. What can you tell about the speaker's family from this poem?

Developing Skills in Reading Literature

1. **Theme.** The speaker of this poem recalls her adolescent feelings about nature and God. Which lines suggest her feelings about nature? What does she mean by the phrase "wise stars bedding over me"? What does she notice about the crickets? How does she feel about God? Which lines support your conclusion?

2. **Structure.** The structure of a piece of literature is the way it is put together. For example, this poem is one unit, without breaks into sentences or stanzas. How does the structure of the poem relate to its content?

Lineage   *Margaret Walker*

My grandmothers were strong.
They followed plows and bent to toil.
They moved through fields sowing seed.
They touched earth and grain grew.
They were full of sturdiness and singing.   5
My grandmothers were strong.

My grandmothers are full of memories
Smelling of soap and onions and wet clay
With veins rolling roughly over quick hands
They have many clean words to say.   10
My grandmothers were strong.
Why am I not as they?

Getting at Meaning

1. What kind of ancestors does the speaker of this poem have? What does she remember about her grandmothers?

2. How does the speaker feel she compares to her ancestors? What does she admire about them?

Developing Skills in Reading Literature

Alliteration. Alliteration is the repetition of a consonant sound at the beginnings of words. Tongue-twisters, such as, "Peter Piper picked a peck of pickled peppers," contain good examples of alliteration.

In line 4, the phrase "grain grew" is an example of alliteration. What other consonant sound is repeated frequently at the beginnings of words in this poem? What does this alliteration do for the poem?

The Way It Is   *Gloria Oden*

I have always known
that had I been blonde
blue-eyed
with skin fabled white as the unicorn's
with cheeks tinted and pearled   5
as May morning on the lips of a rose
such commercial virtues
could never have led me to assume myself
anywhere near as beautiful as
my mother   10
whose willow fall of black hair
—now pirate silver—
I brushed as a child
(earning five cents)
when shaken free from the bun   15
as wrapped round and pinned
it billowed in a fine mist
from her proud shoulders
to her waist.

Brown as I am, she is browner.   20
Walnut
like the satin leaves of the oak
that fallen overwinter in woods
where night comes quickly
and whose wind-peaked piles   25
deepen the shadows of
such seizure.

Moreover, she is tall.
At her side standing
I feel I am still   30
the scarecrow child of
yesteryear:

owl-eyed
toothed, boned, and angled
opposite to her   35
soft southern presence—
an inaudible allegiance
but sweetening her attendance
upon strangers and friends.

Dark hair, dark skin   40
these are the dominant measures of
my sense of beauty
which explains possibly
why being a black girl
in a country of white strangers   45
I am so pleased with myself.

Getting at Meaning

1. What does the speaker's mother look like? How does the speaker feel when she stands next to her?

2. What is the common notion of feminine beauty described in the first few lines of the poem? What is the speaker's own notion of feminine beauty?

3. Whom does the speaker thank for her ideas about beauty? What has been the effect of these ideas on the speaker's life?

Developing Skills in Reading Literature

Simile. A simile, like a metaphor, compares two things that at first glance do not seem to be similar. Unlike a metaphor, a simile does not say that one thing *is* another, but rather that one thing is *like* or *as* another. The comparison "My cousin is a pig" is a metaphor. The comparison "My cousin eats *like* a pig" is a simile.

In this poem, the phrase "Skin fabled white as the unicorn's" is a simile. Find at least two other similes in the poem and write them on a separate sheet of paper.

Developing Vocabulary

Using a Glossary. Look up each word in the Glossary, beginning on page 715, and write the meaning on a separate sheet of paper. Study the way the word is used in "The Way It Is." Then use each word in an original sentence.

commercial   inaudible
billowed   allegiance
seizure   dominant

Developing Writing Skills

Descriptive Language. Read the poem again, this time looking for descriptions of color, such as "pirate silver" in line 12. Then choose a color and describe vividly three different shades of the color. For example, you could describe the red of the sun setting, the red of a fire engine, and the red of a tulip. Try to make the differences in these shades clear to your reader.

Maggie and Milly and Molly and May

E. E. Cummings

maggie and milly and molly and may
went down to the beach(to play one day)

and maggie discovered a shell that sang
so sweetly she couldn't remember her troubles, and

milly befriended a stranded star   5
whose rays five languid fingers were;

and molly was chased by a horrible thing
which raced sideways while blowing bubbles:and

may came home with a smooth round stone
as small as a world and as large as alone.   10

For whatever we lose(like a you or a me)
it's always ourselves we find in the sea

Getting at Meaning

1. What object does Maggie find on the beach? How does it make her feel?
2. Milly "befriended a stranded star." What does this suggest about her character?
3. What does Molly's experience say about her?
4. What does May's stone suggest about her?
5. What is the meaning of the last two lines?

Developing Skills in Reading Literature

Poetry. The grammatical rules of capitalization and punctuation are not as strictly observed in poetry as they are in other forms of writing. You probably noticed that the poet does not capitalize proper names or use end punctuation in this poem. How does his disregard for these conventions affect you as you read the poem? Why do you think he does not capitalize the names? Why do you think he does capitalize the first word on line 11?

Developing Writing Skills

Writing a Poem. Examine carefully a stone, a shell, a leaf, or some other object that you have found. Then write a short poem that describes its interesting characteristics. The poem does not have to include rhyming words.

Conflicts

ARÏ REDON, PORTRAIT OF ARTIST'S SON, 1894. *Odilon Redon.*
Courtesy of The Art Institute of Chicago.

It's Raining in Love   *Richard Brautigan*

I don't know what it is,
but I distrust myself
when I start to like a girl
   a lot

It makes me nervous.   5
I don't say the right things
or perhaps I start
   to examine,
             evaluate,
                     compute   10
   what I am saying.

If I say, "Do you think it's going to rain?"
and she says, "I don't know,"
I start thinking: "Does she really like me?"

In other words   15
I get a little creepy.

A friend of mine once said,
"It's twenty times better to be friends
   with someone
than it is to be in love with them."   20

I think he's right and besides
it's raining somewhere, programing flowers
and keeping snails happy.
   That's all taken care of.
       BUT   25
if a girl likes me a lot
and starts getting real nervous
and suddenly begins asking me funny questions
and looks sad if I give the wrong answers
and she says things like,   30

"Do you think it's going to rain?"
and I say, "It beats me,"
and she says, "Oh,"
and looks a little sad
at the clear blue California sky,   35
I think, Thank God, it's you, baby, this time,
    instead of me.

SPRING ORCHARD, 1959. *Milton Avery.*
National Museum of American Art (formerly National Collection of Fine Arts),
Smithsonian Institution. Gift of S. C. Johnson & Son, Inc.

Getting at Meaning

1. What is the problem experienced by the speaker in this poem?

2. The speaker describes his own nervousness as well as his observation of the same feeling in others. What symptoms of nervousness does the speaker note?

3. A friend of the speaker once said, "It's twenty times better to be friends/with someone/than it is to be in love with them." What does this statement mean?

4. In the last stanza, the speaker gives an example of nervous behavior. What does this example add to the poem?

Developing Skills in Reading Literature

Rhythm. This poem consists, to a great extent, of conversation. Read it aloud. In reading, you should feel the rhythm, the pattern of accented and unaccented syllables. How is the rhythm of the poem like the rhythm of conversation? How does the placement of "examine,/ evaluate,/compute" affect the rhythm?

Antaeus   *Borden Deal*

(In Greek mythology, Antaeus [an tē'əs] was a giant wrestler who was all-powerful as long as he touched the earth, his mother.)

This was during the war-time, when lots of people were coming North for jobs in factories and war industries, when people moved around a lot more than they do now, and sometimes kids were thrown into new groups and new lives that were completely different from anything they had ever known before. I remember this one kid, T. J. his name was, from somewhere down South, whose family moved into our building during that time. They'd come North with everything they owned piled into the back seat of an old-model sedan that you wouldn't expect could make the trip, with T.J. and his three younger sisters riding shakily on top of the load of junk.

Our building was just like all the others there, with families crowded into a few rooms, and I guess there were twenty-five or thirty kids about my age in that one building. Of course, there were a few of us who formed a gang and ran together all the time after school, and I was the one who brought T.J. in and started the whole thing.

The building right next door to us was a factory where they made walking dolls. It was a low building with a flat, tarred roof that had a parapet all around it about head high; and we'd found out a long time before that no one, not even the watchman, paid any attention to the roof because it was higher than any of the other buildings around. So my gang used the roof as a headquarters. We could get up there by crossing over to the fire escape from our own roof on a plank and then going on up. It was a secret place for us, where nobody else could go without our permission.

I remember the day I first took T.J. up there to meet the gang. He was a stocky, robust kid with a shock of white hair, nothing sissy about him except his voice—he talked in this slow, gentle voice like you never heard before. He talked different from any of us, and you noticed it right away. But I liked him anyway, so I told him to come on up.

We climbed up over the parapet and dropped down on the roof. The rest of the gang were already there.

"Hi," I said. I jerked my thumb at T.J. "He just moved into the building yesterday."

He just stood there, not scared or anything, just looking, like the first time you see somebody you're not sure you're going to like.

"Hi," Blackie said. "Where are you from?"

"Marion County," T.J. said.

We laughed. "Marion County?" I said. "Where's that?"

He looked at me for a moment like I was a stranger, too. "It's in Alabama," he said, like I ought to know where it was.

"What's your name?" Charley said.

"T.J.," he said, looking back at him. He had pale blue eyes that looked washed-out, but he looked directly at Charley, waiting for his reaction. He'll be all right, I thought. No sissy in him . . . except that voice. Who ever talked like that?

"T.J.," Blackie said. "That's just initials.

What's your real name? Nobody in the world has just initials."

"I do," he said. "And they're T.J. That's all the name I got."

His voice was resolute with the knowledge of his rightness, and for a moment no one had anything to say. T.J. looked around at the rooftop and down at the black tar under his feet. "Down yonder where I come from," he said, "we played out in the woods. Don't you-all have no woods around here?"

"Naw," Blackie said. "There's the park a few blocks over, but it's full of kids and cops and old women. You can't do a thing."

T.J. kept looking at the tar under his feet. "You mean you ain't got no fields to raise nothing in? . . . no watermelons or nothing?"

"Naw," I said scornfully. "What do you want to grow something for? The folks can buy everything they need at the store."

He looked at me again with that strange, unknowing look. "In Marion County," he said, "I had my own acre of cotton and my own acre of corn. It was mine to plant and make ever' year."

He sounded like it was something to be proud of, and in some obscure way it made the rest of us angry. "Gee!" Blackie said. "Who'd want to have their own acre of cotton and corn? That's just work. What can you do with an acre of cotton and corn?"

T.J. looked at him. "Well, you get part of the bale offen your acre," he said seriously. "And I fed my acre of corn to my calf."

We didn't really know what he was talking about, so we were more puzzled than angry; otherwise, I guess, we'd have chased him off the roof and wouldn't let him be part of our gang. But he was strange and different, and we were all attracted by his stolid sense of rightness and belonging, maybe by the strange softness of his voice contrasting our own tones of speech into harshness.

He moved his foot against the black tar. "We could make our own field right here," he said softly, thoughtfully. "Come spring, we could raise us what we want to . . . watermelons and garden truck and no telling what all."

"You'd have to be a good farmer to make these tar roofs grow any watermelons," I said. We all laughed.

But T.J. looked serious. "We could haul us some dirt up here," he said. "And spread it out even and water it, and before you know it, we'd have us a crop in here." He looked at us intently. "Wouldn't that be fun?"

"They wouldn't let us," Blackie said quickly.

"I thought you said this was you-all's roof," T.J. said to me. "That you-all could do anything you wanted to up here."

"They've never bothered us," I said. I felt the idea beginning to catch fire in me. It was a big idea, and it took a while for it to sink in; but the more I thought about it the better I liked it. "Say," I said to the gang. "He might have something there. Just make us a regular roof garden, with flowers and grass and trees and everything. And all ours, too," I said. "We wouldn't let anybody up here except the ones we wanted to."

"It'd take a while to grow trees," T.J. said quickly, but we weren't paying any attention to him. They were all talking about it suddenly, all excited with the idea after I'd put it in a way they could catch hold of it. Only rich people had roof gardens, we knew, and the idea of our own private domain excited them.

"We would bring it up in sacks and boxes," Blackie said. "We'd have to do it while the folks weren't paying any attention to us, for we'd have to come up to the roof of our building and then cross over with it."

"Where could we get the dirt?" somebody said worriedly.

"Out of those vacant lots over close to school," Blackie said. "Nobody'd notice if we scraped it up."

I slapped T.J. on the shoulder. "Man you had a wonderful idea," I said; and everybody grinned at him, remembering that he had started it. "Our own private roof garden."

He grinned back. "It'll be ourn," he said. "All ourn." Then he looked thoughtful again. "Maybe I can lay my hands on some cotton seed, too. You think we could raise us some cotton?"

We'd started big projects before at one time or another, like any gang of kids, but they'd always petered out for lack of organization and direction. But this one didn't . . . some how or other T. J. kept it going all through the winter months. He kept talking about the watermelons, and the cotton we'd raise, come spring; and when even that wouldn't work, he'd switch around to my idea of flowers and grass and trees, though he was always honest enough to add that it'd take a while to get any trees started. He always had it on his mind, and he'd mention it in school, getting them lined up to carry dirt that afternoon, saying in a casual way that he reckoned a few more weeks ought to see the job through.

Our little area of private earth grew slowly. T.J. was smart enough to start in one corner of the building, heaping up the carried earth two or three feet thick, so that we had an immediate result to look at, to contemplate with awe. Some of the evenings T.J. alone was carrying earth up to the building, the rest of the gang distracted by other enterprises or interests; but T.J. kept plugging along on his own, and eventually we'd all come back to him again, and then our own little acre would grow more rapidly.

He was careful about the kind of dirt he'd let us carry up there, and more than once he dumped a sandy load over the parapet into the areaway below because it wasn't good enough. He found out the kinds of earth in all the vacant lots for blocks around. He'd pick it up and feel it and smell it, frozen

though it was sometimes; and then he'd say it was good growing soil or it wasn't worth anything, and we'd have to go on somewhere else.

Thinking about it now, I don't see how he kept us at it. It was hard work, lugging paper sacks and boxes of dirt all the way up the stairs of our own building, keeping out of the way of the grownups so they wouldn't catch on to what we were doing. They probably wouldn't have cared, for they didn't pay much attention to us; but we wanted to keep it secret anyway. Then we had to go through the trap door to our roof, teeter over a plank to the fire escape, then climb two or three stories to the parapet and drop down onto the roof. All that for a small pile of earth that sometimes didn't seem worth the effort. But T.J. kept the vision bright within us, his words shrewd and calculated toward the fulfilment of his dream; and he worked harder than any of us. He seemed driven toward a goal that we couldn't see, a particular point in time that would be definitely marked by signs and wonders that only he could see.

The laborious earth just lay there during the cold months, inert and lifeless, the clods lumpy and cold under our feet when we walked over it. But one day it rained, and afterward there was a softness in the air; and the earth was live and giving again with moisture and warmth. That evening T.J. smelled the air, his nostrils dilating with the odor of the earth under his feet.

"It's spring," he said, and there was a gladness rising in his voice that filled us all with the same feeling. "It's mighty late for it, but it's spring. I'd just about decided it wasn't never gonna get here at all."

We were all sniffing at the air, too, trying to smell it the way that T.J. did; and I can still remember the sweet odor of the earth under our feet. It was the first time in my life that spring and spring earth had meant anything to me. I looked at T.J. then, knowing in a faint way the hunger within him through the toilsome winter months, knowing the dream that lay behind his plan. He was a new Antaeus, preparing his own bed of strength.

"Planting time," he said. "We'll have to find us some seed."

"What do we do?" Blackie said. "How do we do it?"

"First we'll have to break up the clods," T.J. said. "That won't be hard to do. Then we plant the seed, and after a while they come up. Then you got a crop." He frowned. "But you ain't got it raised yet. You got to tend it and hoe it and take care of it, and all the time it's growing and growing, while you're awake and while you're asleep. Then you lay it by when it's growed and let it ripen, and then you got you a crop."

"There's those wholesale seed houses over on Sixth," I said. "We could probably swipe some grass seed over there."

T.J. looked at the earth. "You-all seem mighty set on raising some grass," he said. "I ain't never put no effort into that. I spent all my life trying not to raise grass."

"But it's pretty," Blackie said. "We could play on it and take sunbaths on it. Like having our own lawn. Lots of people got lawns."

"Well," T.J. said. He looked at the rest of us, hesitant for the first time. He kept on looking at us for a moment. "I did have it in mind to raise some corn and vegetables. But we'll plant grass."

He was smart. He knew where to give in. And I don't suppose it made any difference to him, really. He just wanted to grow something, even if it was grass.

"Of course," he said, "I do think we ought to plant a row of watermelons. They'd be mighty nice to eat while we was a-laying on that grass."

We all laughed. "All right," I said. "We'll plant us a row of watermelons."

Things went very quickly then. Perhaps half the roof was covered with the earth, the half that wasn't broken by ventilators; and we swiped pocketfuls of grass seed from the open bins in the wholesale seed house, mingling among the buyers on Saturday and during the school lunch hour. T.J. showed us how to prepare the earth, breaking up the clods and smoothing it and sowing the grass seed. It looked rich and black now with moisture, receiving of the seed, and it seemed that the grass sprang up overnight, pale green in the early spring.

We couldn't keep from looking at it, unable to believe that we had created this delicate growth. We looked at T.J. with understanding now, knowing the fulfilment of the plan he had carried alone within his mind. We had worked without full understanding of the task, but he had known all the time.

We found that we couldn't walk or play on the delicate blades, as we had expected to, but we didn't mind. It was enough just to look at it, to realize that it was the work of our own hands, and each evening the whole gang was there, trying to measure the growth that had been achieved that day.

One time a foot was placed on the plot of ground . . . one time only, Blackie stepping onto it with sudden bravado. Then he looked at the crushed blades, and there was shame in his face. He did not do it again. This was his grass, too, and not to be desecrated. No one said anything, for it was not necessary.

T.J. had reserved a small section for watermelons, and he was still trying to find some seed for it. The wholesale house didn't have any watermelon seed, and we didn't know where we could lay our hands on them. T.J. shaped the earth into mounds, ready to receive them, three mounds lying in a straight line along the edge of the grass plot.

We had just about decided that we'd have to buy the seed if we were to get them. It was a violation of our principles, but we were anxious to get the watermelons started. Somewhere or other, T.J. got his hands on a seed catalog and brought it one evening to our roof garden.

"We can order them now," he said, showing us the catalog. "Look!"

We all crowded around, looking at the fat, green watermelons pictured in full color on the pages. Some of them were split open, showing the red, tempting meat, making our mouths water.

"Now we got to scrape up some seed money," T.J. said, looking at us. "I got a quarter. How much you-all got?"

We made up a couple of dollars between us, and T.J. nodded his head. "That'll be more than enough. Now we got to decide what kind to get. I think them Kleckley Sweets. What do you-all think?"

He was going into esoteric matters beyond our reach. We hadn't even known there were different kinds of melons. So we just nodded our heads and agreed that Yes, we thought the Kleckley Sweets too.

"I'll order them tonight," T.J. said. "We ought to have them in a few days."

"What are you boys doing up here?" an adult voice said behind us.

It startled us, for no one had ever come up here before, in all the time we had been using the roof of the factory. We jerked around and saw three men standing near the trap door at the other end of the roof. They weren't policemen, or night watchmen, but three men in plump business suits, looking at us. They walked toward us.

"What are you boys doing up here?" the one in the middle said again.

We stood still, guilt heavy among us, levied by the tone of voice, and looked at the three strangers.

The men stared at the grass flourishing behind us. "What's this?" the man said. "How did this get up here?"

"Sure is growing good, ain't it?" T.J. said conversationally. "We planted it."

The men kept looking at the grass as if they

didn't believe it. It was a thick carpet over the earth now, a patch of deep greenness, startling in the sterile industrial surroundings.

"Yes sir," T.J. said proudly. "We toted that earth up here and planted that grass." He fluttered the seed catalog. "And we're just fixing to plant us some watermelon."

The man looked at him then, his eyes strange and far-away. "What do you mean, putting this on the roof of my building?" he said. "Do you want to go to jail?"

T.J. looked shaken. The rest of us were silent, frightened by the authority of his voice. We had grown up aware of adult authority, of policemen and night watchmen and teachers, and this man sounded like all the others. But it was a new thing to T.J.

"Well, you wan't using the roof," T.J. said. He paused a moment and added shrewdly, "So we just thought to pretty it up a little bit."

"And sag it so I'd have to rebuild it," the man said sharply. He started turning away, saying to another man beside him, "See that all that junk is shoveled off by tomorrow."

"Yes sir," the man said.

T.J. started forward. "You can't do that," he said. "We toted it up here and it's our earth. We planted it and raised it and toted it up here."

The man stared at him coldly. "But it's my building," he said. "It's to be shoveled off tomorrow."

"It's our earth," T.J. said desperately. "You ain't got no right!"

The men walked on without listening and descended clumsily through the trap door. T.J. stood looking after them, his body tense with anger, until they had disappeared. They wouldn't even argue with him, wouldn't let him defend his earth-rights.

He turned to us. "We won't let 'em do it," he said fiercely. "We'll stay up here all day tomorrow and the day after that, and we won't let 'em do it."

We just looked at him. We knew that there was no stopping it. He saw it in our faces, and his face wavered for a moment before he gripped it into determination.

"They ain't got no right," he said. "It's our earth. It's our land. Can't nobody touch a man's own land."

We kept on looking at him, listening to the words but knowing that it was no use. The adult world had descended on us even in our richest dream, and we knew there was no calculating the adult world, no fighting it, no winning against it.

We started moving slowly toward the parapet and the fire escape, avoiding a last look at the green beauty of the earth that T.J. had planted for us . . . had planted deeply in our minds, as well as in our experience. We filed slowly over the edge and down the steps to the plank, T.J. coming last, and all of us could feel the weight of his grief behind us.

"Wait a minute," he said suddenly, his voice harsh with the effort of calling. We stopped and turned, held by the tone of his voice, and looked up at him standing above us on the fire escape.

"We can't stop them?" he said, looking down at us, his face strange in the dusky light. "There ain't no way to stop 'em?"

"No," Blackie said with finality. "They own the building."

We stood still for a moment, looking up at T.J., caught into inaction by the decision working in his face. He stared back at us and his face was pale and mean in the poor light, with a bald nakedness in his skin like cripples have sometimes.

"They ain't gonna touch my earth," he said fiercely. "They ain't gonna lay a hand on it! Come on."

He turned around and started up the fire escape again, almost running against the effort of climbing. We followed more slowly, not knowing what he intended. By the time we reached him, he had seized a board and thrust it into the soil, scooping it up and flinging it over the parapet into the areaway below. He straightened and looked at us.

"They can't touch it," he said. "I won't let 'em lay a dirty hand on it!"

We saw it then. He stooped to his labor again and we followed, the gusts of his anger moving in frenzied labor among us as we scattered along the edge of earth, scooping it and throwing it over the parapet, destroying with anger the growth we had nurtured with such tender care. The soil carried so laboriously upward to the light and the sun cascaded swiftly into the dark areaway, the green blades of grass crumpled and twisted in the falling.

It took less time than you would think . . . the task of destruction is infinitely easier than that of creation. We stopped at the end, leaving only a scattering of loose soil; and when it was finally over, a stillness stood among the group and over the factory building. We looked down at the bare sterility of black tar, felt the harsh texture of it under the soles of our shoes; and the anger had gone out of us, leaving only a sore aching in our minds, like overstretched muscles.

T.J. stood for a moment, his breathing slowing from anger and effort, caught into the same contemplation of destruction as all of us. He stooped slowly, finally, and picked up a lonely blade of grass left trampled under our feet, and put it between his teeth, tasting it, sucking the greenness out of it into his mouth. Then he started walking toward the fire escape, moving before any of us were ready to move, and disappeared over the edge.

We followed him, but he was already halfway down to the ground, going on past the board where we crossed over, climbing down into the areaway. We saw the last section swing down with his weight, and then he stood on the concrete below us, looking at the small pile of anonymous earth scattered by our throwing. Then he walked across the place where we could see him and disappeared toward the street without glancing back, without looking up to see us watching him.

They did not find him for two weeks. Then the Nashville police caught him just outside the Nashville freight yards. He was walking along the railroad track; still heading south, still heading home.

As for us, who had no remembered home to call us . . . none of us ever again climbed the escape-way to the roof.

Getting at Meaning

1. What is the time and place in which this story is set?

2. Why is the roof important to the gang?

3. Describe T.J. How is he different from the other boys?

4. What possibilities does T.J. see for the roof? Why do the other boys prefer a roof garden? Why does T.J. agree to plant grass, even though he would rather grow crops?

5. Describe the process of hauling the dirt up to the roof. Why does the gang stick with the project?

6. How do the boys feel as the grass begins to grow? Why don't they walk or play on it?

7. Why does the owner of the building want the earth off the roof? How does T.J. react to the owner's order? What qualities in T.J. are brought out by this reaction?

8. Why does T.J. decide that the gang should destroy the garden?

9. What does the narrator mean when he says that "the task of destruction is infinitely easier than that of creation"?

Developing Skills in Reading Literature

1. **Allusion.** An allusion is a reference to a person, place, or event with which the reader is expected to be familiar. The title of this story is an allusion to a character in Greek mythology. Antaeus is a giant wrestler who cannot be conquered as long as he is in contact with the earth, his mother. Hercules lifts Antaeus off the ground and thus conquers him.

What is the connection between Antaeus and T.J.? What does the narrator mean when he calls T.J. "a new Antaeus, preparing his own bed of strength"? What does T.J. do at the end of the story? Why? In what way is T.J. "conquered"?

2. **Conflict.** Conflict is a struggle between opposing forces. Some conflicts are between two characters or between a character and the forces of nature. These are called external

conflicts. Other conflicts take place within characters. These are called internal conflicts.

One conflict in this story is between the owner of the building and the gang of boys. What does the owner want? What do the boys want? Is it possible for both the owner and the boys to get what they want? Is the conflict external or internal?

3. **Narrator and Point of View.** If you have a quarrel with a brother or sister and each of you explains the quarrel to your parents, the stories will probably be different. Each of you will tell the story from your own point of view. The narrator, or teller, of a short story relates the story from his or her point of view. When the narrator uses the pronouns *I* and *we*, the story is written in the first person.

"Antaeus" is told from the first-person point of view. Who is the narrator of the story? How is the reader made aware of T.J.'s feelings? Does T.J. reveal his feelings directly to the reader? Why might the writer have chosen this particular narrator and point of view?

Developing Vocabulary

Understanding Dialect. Dialect refers to a special way of pronouncing and using words that is characteristic of a region or location. For example, people in Boston speak a different dialect of English than do people in Alabama, and both are different from the dialect spoken in Chicago.

What expressions and qualities in T.J.'s language indicate that he speaks a southern dialect? How does his speech sound to his new friends? Why?

Developing Writing Skills

Maintaining the Same Point of View. Write a paragraph that explains why T.J. is running away, and his thoughts as he heads south. Write the paragraph in the first person, from T.J.'s point of view.

Raymond's Run   *Toni Cade Bambara*

I don't have much work to do around the house like some girls. My mother does that. And I don't have to earn my pocket money by hustling; George runs errands for the big boys and sells Christmas cards. And anything else that's got to get done, my father does. All I have to do in life is mind my brother Raymond, which is enough.

Sometimes I slip, and say my little brother Raymond. But as any fool can see he's much bigger, and he's older too. But a lot of people call him my little brother cause he needs looking after cause he's not quite right. And a lot of smart mouths got lots to say about that too, especially when George was minding him. But now, if anybody has anything to say to Raymond, anything to say about his big head,[1] they have to come by me. And I don't play the dozens[2] or believe in standing around with somebody in my face doing a lot of talking. I much rather just knock you down and take my chances, even if I am a little girl with skinny arms and a squeaky voice, which is how I got the name Squeaky. And if things get too rough, I run. And as anybody can tell you, I'm the fastest thing on two feet.

There is no track meet that I don't win the first place medal. I used to win the twenty-yard dash when I was a little kid in kindergarten. Nowadays, it's the fifty-yard dash. And tomorrow I'm subject to run the quarter-meter relay all by myself and come in first, second, and third. The big kids call me Mercury[3] cause I'm the swiftest thing in the neighborhood. Everybody knows that—except two people who know better, my father

and me. He can beat me to Amsterdam Avenue with me having a two fire-hydrant head-start and him running with his hands in his pockets and whistling. But that's private information. Cause can you imagine some thirty-five-year-old man stuffing himself into PAL shorts to race little kids? So as far as everyone's concerned, I'm the fastest; and that goes for Gretchen, too, who has put out the tale that she is going to win the first-place medal this year. Ridiculous. In the second place, she's got short legs. In the third place, she's got freckles. In the first place, no one can beat me, and that's all there is to it.

I'm standing on the corner admiring the weather and about to take a stroll down Broadway so I can practice my breathing exercises, and I've got Raymond walking on the inside close to the buildings, cause he's subject to fits of fantasy and starts thinking he's a circus performer and that the curb is a tightrope strung high in the air. And sometimes after a rain he likes to step down off his tightrope right into the gutter and slosh around, getting his shoes and cuffs wet. Then I get hit when I get home. Or sometimes if you don't watch him, he'll dash across traffic to the island in the middle of Broadway and give the pigeons a fit. Then I

---

1. **big head:** a reference to Raymond's condition, hydrocephalus (hi' drə sef' ə ləs), which is characterized by an abnormal amount of fluid on the cranium, causing enlargement of the head and destruction of the brain.
2. **play the dozens:** to slander one's or another's parents.
3. **Mercury** (mʉr' kyoo rē): in Roman mythology, the messenger of the gods, known for his swiftness.

have to go behind him, apologizing to all the old people sitting around trying to get some sun and getting all upset with the pigeons fluttering around them, scattering their newspapers and upsetting the wax-paper lunches in their laps. So I keep Raymond on the inside of me, and he plays like he's driving a stage coach; which is OK by me so long as he doesn't run me over or interrupt my breathing exercises, which I have to do on account of I'm serious about my running, and I don't care who knows it.

Now some people like to act like things come easy to them, won't let on that they practice. Not me. I'll high-prance down 34th Street like a rodeo pony to keep my knees strong, even if it does get my mother uptight so that she walks ahead like she's not with me, don't know me, is all by herself on a shopping trip, and I am somebody else's crazy child. Now you take Cynthia Procter for instance. She's just the opposite. If there's a test tomorrow, she'll say something like, "Oh, I guess I'll play handball this afternoon and watch television tonight," just to let you know she ain't thinking about the test. Or like last week when she won the spelling bee for the millionth time, "A good thing you got *receive,* Squeaky, cause I would have got it wrong. I completely forgot about the spelling bee." And she'll clutch the lace on her blouse like it was a narrow escape. Oh, brother. But of course, when I pass her house on my early morning trots around the block, she is practicing the scales on the piano over and over and over and over. Then in music class she always lets herself get bumped around so she falls accidently on purpose onto the piano stool, and is so surprised to find herself sitting there that she decides just for fun to try out the ole keys. And what do you know —Chopin's waltzes just spring out of her fingertips, and she's the most surprised thing in the world. A regular prodigy. I could kill people like that. I stay up all night studying the words for the spelling bee. And you can see me any time of the day practicing running. I never walk if I can trot, and shame on Raymond if he can't keep up. But of course he does, cause if he hangs back, someone's liable to walk up to him and get smart, or take his allowance from him, or ask him where he got that great big pumpkin head. People are so stupid sometimes.

So I'm strolling down Broadway breathing out and breathing in on counts of seven, which is my lucky number, and here comes Gretchen and her sidekicks: Mary Louise, who used to be a friend of mine when she first moved to Harlem from Baltimore and got beat up by everybody till I took up for her, on account of her mother and my mother used to sing in the same choir when they were young girls, but people ain't grateful, so now she hangs out with the new girl Gretchen and talks about me like a dog; and Rosie, who is as fat as I am skinny and has a big mouth where Raymond is concerned and is too stupid to know that there is not a big deal of difference between herself and Raymond and that she can't afford to throw stones. So they are steady coming up Broadway, and I see right away that it's going to be one of those Dodge City scenes, cause the street ain't that big and they're close to the buildings, just as we are. First I think I'll step into the candy store and look over the new comics and let them pass. But that's chicken, and I've got a reputation to consider. So then I think I'll just walk straight on through them or even over them if necessary. But as they get to me, they slow down. I'm ready to fight, cause like I said, I don't feature a whole lot of chit-chat. I much prefer to just knock you down right from the jump and save everybody a lotta precious time.

"You signing up for the May Day races?" smiled Mary Louise; only it's not a smile at all. A dumb question like that doesn't deserve an answer. Besides, there's just me and Gretchen standing there really, so no use wasting my breath talking to shadows.

"I don't think you're going to win this time," says Rosie, trying to signify with her hands on her hips, all salty, completely forgetting that I have whupped her behind many times for less salt than that.

"I always win cause I'm the best," I say straight at Gretchen who is, as far as I'm concerned, the only one talking in this ventriloquist-dummy[4] routine. Gretchen smiles but it's not a smile; and I'm thinking that girls never really smile at each other because they don't know how and don't want to know how and there's probably no one to teach us how, cause grown-up girls don't know either. Then they all look at Raymond, who has just brought his mule team to a standstill. And they're about to see what trouble they can get into through him.

"What grade you in now, Raymond?"

"You got anything to say to my brother, you say it to me, Mary Louise Williams of Raggedy Town, Baltimore."

"What are you, his mother?" sasses Rosie.

"That's right, Fatso. And the next word out of anybody, and I'll be *their* mother too." So they just stand there, and Gretchen shifts from one leg to the other and so do they. Then Gretchen puts her hands on her hips and is about to say something with her freckle-face self, but doesn't. Then she walks around me, looking me up and down, but keeps walking up Broadway, and her side-kicks follow her. So me and Raymond smile at each other, and he says, "Gidyap" to his team; and I continue with my breathing exercises, strolling down Broadway toward the ice man on 145th with not a care in the world cause I am Miss Quicksilver herself.

I take my time getting to the park on May Day because the track meet is the last thing on the program. The biggest thing on the program is the May Pole dancing, which I can do without, thank you, even if my mother thinks it's a shame I don't take part and act like a girl for a change. You'd think my mother'd be grateful not to have to make me a white organdy dress with a big satin sash, and buy me new white baby-doll shoes that can't be taken out of the box till the big day. You'd think she'd be glad her daughter ain't out there prancing around a May Pole getting the new clothes all dirty and sweaty and trying to act like a fairy or a flower or whatever you're supposed to be when you should be trying to be yourself, whatever that is; which is, as far as I am concerned, a poor Black girl who really can't afford to buy shoes and a new dress you only wear once a lifetime, cause it won't fit next year.

I was once a strawberry in a Hansel and Gretel pageant when I was in nursery school,

---

4. **ventriloquist-dummy routine** (ven tril' ə kwist): Squeaky thinks of Gretchen as speaking through Rosie and Mary Louise, like a speaker who can make his or her voice seem to come from a dummy, or figure made in human form.

and didn't have no better sense than to dance on tiptoe with my arms in a circle over my head, doing umbrella steps and being a perfect fool just so my mother and father could come dressed up and clap. You'd think they'd know better than to encourage that kind of nonsense. I am not a strawberry. I do not dance on my toes. I run. That is what I am all about. So I always come late to the May Day program, just in time to get my number pinned on and lay in the grass till they announce the fifty-yard dash.

I put Raymond in the little swings, which is a tight squeeze this year and will be impossible next year. Then I look around for Mr. Pearson, who pins the numbers on. I'm really looking for Gretchen if you want to know the truth, but she's not around. The park is jam-packed. Parents in hats and corsages and breast-pocket handkerchiefs peeking up. Kids in white dresses and light-blue suits. The parkees unfolding chairs and chasing the rowdy kids from Lenox,[5] as if they had

no right to be there. The big guys with their caps on backwards, leaning against the fence swirling the basketballs on the tips of their fingers, waiting for all these crazy people to clear out the park so they can play. Most of the kids in my class are carrying bass drums and glockenspiels[6] and flutes. You'd think they'd put in a few bongos or something for real like that.

Then here comes Mr. Pearson with his clipboard and his cards and pencils and whistles and safety pins and fifty million other things he's always dropping all over the place with his clumsy self. He sticks out in a crowd because he's on stilts. We use to call him Jack and the Beanstalk to get him mad. But I'm the only one that can outrun him and get away, and I'm too grown for that silliness now.

"Well, Squeaky," he says, checking my name off the list and handing me number seven and two pins. And I'm thinking he's got no right to call me Squeaky, if I can't call him Beanstalk.

"Hazel Elizabeth Deborah Parker," I correct him and tell him to write it down on his board.

"Well, Hazel Elizabeth Deborah Parker, going to give someone else a break this year?" I squint at him real hard to see if he is seriously thinking I should lose the race on purpose just to give someone else a break. "Only six girls running this time," he continues, shaking his head sadly like it's my fault all of New York didn't turn out in sneakers. "That new girl should give you a run for your money." He looks around the park for Gretchen like a periscope in a submarine movie. "Wouldn't it be a nice gesture if you were . . . to ahhh . . ."

---

5. **Lenox:** an avenue in the Harlem section of New York City.

6. **glockenspiel** (gläk′ ən spēl′): a percussion instrument with flat metal bars set in a frame, which produces bell-like tones when struck with small hammers.

I give him such a look he couldn't finish putting that idea into words. Grownups got a lot of nerve sometimes. I pin number seven to myself and stomp away, I'm so burnt. And I go straight for the track and stretch out on the grass while the band winds up with "Oh, the Monkey Wrapped His Tail Around the Flag Pole," which my teacher calls by some other name. The man on the loudspeaker is calling everyone over to the track, and I'm on my back looking at the sky, trying to pretend I'm in the country, but I can't, because even grass in the city feels hard as sidewalk, and there's just no pretending you are anywhere but in a "concrete jungle" as my grandfather says.

The twenty-yard dash takes all of two minutes cause most of the little kids don't know no better than to run off the track or run the wrong way or run smack into the fence and fall down and cry. One little kid, though, has got the good sense to run straight for the white ribbon up ahead, so he wins. Then the second-graders line up for the thirty-yard dash, and I don't even bother to turn my head to watch cause Raphael Perez always wins. He wins before he even begins by psyching the runners, telling them they're going to trip on their shoelaces and fall on their faces or lose their shorts or something, which he doesn't really have to do since he is very fast, almost as fast as I am. After that is the forty-yard dash which I used to run when I was in first grade. Raymond is hollering from the swings cause he knows I'm about to do my thing cause the man on the loudspeaker has just announced the fifty-yard dash, although he might just as well be giving a recipe for angel food cake cause you can hardly make out what he's sayin for the static. I get up and slip off my sweat pants, and then I see Gretchen standing at the starting line, kicking her legs out like a pro. Then as I get into place, I see that ole Raymond is on line on the other side of the fence, bend-

ing down with his fingers on the ground just like he knew what he was doing. I was going to yell at him, but then I didn't. It burns up your energy to holler.

Every time, just before I take off in a race, I always feel like I'm in a dream, the kind of dream you have when you're sick with fever and feel all hot and weightless. I dream I'm flying over a sandy beach in the early morning sun, kissing the leaves of the trees as I fly by. And there's always the smell of apples, just like in the country when I was little and used to think I was a choo-choo train, running through the fields of corn and chugging up the hill to the orchard. And all the time I'm dreaming this, I get lighter and lighter until I'm flying over the beach again, getting blown through the sky like a feather that weighs nothing at all. But once I spread my fingers in the dirt and crouch over the Get on Your Mark, the dream goes and I am solid again and am telling myself, Squeaky you must win, you must win, you are the fastest

thing in the world, you can even beat your father up Amsterdam if you really try. And then I feel my weight coming back just behind my knees, then down to my feet, then into the earth, and the pistol shot explodes in my blood; and I am off and weightless again, flying past the other runners, my arms pumping up and down, and the whole world is quiet except for the crunch as I zoom over the gravel in the track. I glance to my left and there is no one. To the right, a blurred Gretchen, who's got her chin jutting out as if it would win the race all by itself. And on the other side of the fence is Raymond, with his arms down to his side and the palms tucked up behind him, running in his very own style; and it's the first time I ever saw that, and I almost stop to watch my brother Raymond on his first run. But the white ribbon is bouncing toward me and I tear past it, racing into the distance till my feet with a mind of their own start digging up footfuls of dirt to break me short. Then all the kids standing on the side pile on me, banging me on the back and slapping my head with their May Day programs, for I have won again, and everybody on 151st Street can walk tall for another year.

"In first place . . ." the man on the loudspeaker is clear as a bell now. But then he pauses, and the loudspeaker starts to whine. Then static. And I lean down to catch my breath, and here comes Gretchen walking back; for she's overshot the finish line too, huffing and puffing with her hands on her hips, taking it slow, breathing in steady time like a real pro, and I sort of like her a little for the first time. "In first place . . ." and then three or four voices get all mixed up on the loudspeaker, and I dig my sneaker into the grass and stare at Gretchen who's staring back, we both wondering just who did win. I can hear old Beanstalk arguing with the man on the loudspeaker, and then a few others running their mouths about what the stopwatches say. Then I hear Raymond yanking at the fence to call me, and I wave to shush him; but he keeps rattling the fence like a gorilla in a cage like in them gorilla movies, but then like a dancer or something he starts climbing up nice and easy but very fast. And it occurs to me, watching how smoothly he climbs hand over hand and remembering how he looked running with his arms down to his side and with the wind pulling his mouth back and his teeth showing and all, it occurred to me that Raymond would make a very fine runner. Doesn't he always keep up with me on my trots? And he surely knows how to breathe in counts of seven cause he's always doing it at the dinner table, which drives my brother George up the wall. And I'm smiling to beat the band, cause if I've lost this race, or if me and Gretchen tied, or even if I've won, I can always retire as a runner and begin a whole new career as a coach with Raymond as my champion. After all, with a little more study I can beat Cynthia and her phony self at the spelling bee. And if I bugged my mother, I could get piano lessons and become a star. And I have a big rep as the baddest thing around. And I've got a roomful of ribbons and medals and awards. But what has Raymond got to call his own?

So I stand there with my new plans, laughing out loud by this time as Raymond jumps down from the fence and runs over with his teeth showing and his arms down to the side, which no one before him has quite mastered as a running style. And by the time he comes over, I'm jumping up and down, so glad to see him—my brother Raymond, a great runner in the family tradition. But of course everyone thinks I'm jumping up and down because the men on the loudspeaker have finally gotten themselves together and compared notes and are announcing "In first place —Miss Hazel Elizabeth Deborah Parker." (Dig that.) "In second place—Miss Gretchen

P. Lewis." And I look over at Gretchen, wondering what the "P" stands for. And I smile. Cause she's good, no doubt about it. Maybe she'd like to help me coach Raymond; she obviously is serious about running, as any fool can see. And she nods to congratulate me, and then she smiles. And I smile. We stand there with this big smile of respect between us. It's about as real a smile as girls can do for each other, considering we don't practice real smiling every day, you know, cause maybe we too busy being flowers or fairies or strawberries instead of something honest and worthy of respect . . . you know . . . like being people.

Getting at Meaning

1. Who is the narrator of this story? What information is the reader given about the narrator and her family?

2. What is Squeaky's attitude toward Raymond? How do her actions reflect this attitude? How do other young people treat Raymond?

3. How does Squeaky feel about running? How does the last paragraph of the story show a change in her attitude?

4. How does Squeaky prepare to run her race? How does she feel while she is running?

5. At the end of the story, why is Squeaky so happy for Raymond? Why do she and Gretchen smile genuinely at each other?

Developing Skills in Reading Literature

1. **Conflict.** What is the conflict, or struggle, in this story? How is it resolved? How does Raymond help to resolve the conflict?

2. **Style.** Style is the way a piece of literature is written. The style of this story is informal, with slang expressions and run-on sentences. How does the informal style help the reader to understand Squeaky's personality and background?

Developing Vocabulary

Levels of Language. People adjust the way they talk to the situations they are in and to their listeners. For example, a child generally talks to a grandparent in a more formal way than to a friend. Often, a writer uses a more formal style when writing a story than you would use when telling the same story to a friend.

In "Raymond's Run," however, the writer has Squeaky tell the story informally, as if she were telling it to a friend. For instance, Squeaky says that Raymond "gives the pigeons a fit" instead of "frightens the pigeons." Find other expressions that help to create the informal style of the selection.

Developing Writing Skills

Writing an Explanation. The final sentence of the story contains these words: ". . . we don't practice real smiling every day, you know, cause maybe we too busy being flowers or fairies or strawberries instead of something honest and worthy of respect . . . you know . . . like being people." What things prevent you from being a "real" person, a person as honest as you might like to be? Discuss one or more of these obstacles in a well organized paragraph.

The Lie   *Kurt Vonnegut, Jr.*

It was early springtime. Weak sunshine lay cold on old gray frost. Willow twigs against the sky showed the golden haze of fat catkins about to bloom. A black Rolls-Royce streaked up the Connecticut Turnpike from New York City. At the wheel was Ben Barkley, a black chauffeur.

"Keep it under the speed limit, Ben," said Doctor Remenzel. "I don't care how ridiculous any speed limit seems; stay under it. No reason to rush—we have plenty of time."

Ben eased off on the throttle. "Seems like in the springtime she wants to get up and go," he said.

"Do what you can to keep her down— OK?" said the doctor.

"Yes, sir!" said Ben. He spoke in a lower voice to the thirteen-year-old boy who was riding beside him, to Eli Remenzel, the doctor's son. "Ain't just people and animals feel good in the springtime," he said to Eli. "Motors feel good too."

"Um," said Eli.

"Everything feel good," said Ben. "Don't you feel good?"

"Sure, sure I feel good," said Eli emptily.

"Should feel good—going to that wonderful school," said Ben.

The wonderful school was the Whitehill School for Boys, a private preparatory school[1] in North Marston, Massachusetts. That was where the Rolls-Royce was bound. The plan was that Eli would enroll for the fall semester, while his father, a member of the class of 1939, attended a meeting of the Board of Overseers of the school.

"Don't believe this boy's feeling so good, doctor," said Ben. He wasn't particularly serious about it. It was more genial springtime blather.

"What's the matter, Eli?" said the doctor absently. He was studying blueprints, plans for a thirty-room addition to the Eli Remenzel Memorial Dormitory—a building named in honor of his great-great-grandfather. Doctor Remenzel had the plans draped over a walnut table that folded out of the back of the front seat. He was a massive, dignified man, a physician, a healer for healing's sake, since he had been born as rich as the Shah of Iran. "Worried about something?" he asked Eli without looking up from the plans.

"Nope," said Eli.

Eli's lovely mother, Sylvia, sat next to the doctor, reading the catalog of the Whitehill School. "If I were you," she said to Eli, "I'd be so excited I could hardly stand it. The best four years of your whole life are just about to begin."

"Sure," said Eli. He didn't show her his face. He gave her only the back of his head, a pinwheel of coarse brown hair above a stiff white collar, to talk to.

"I wonder how many Remenzels have gone to Whitehill," said Sylvia.

"That's like asking how many people are dead in a cemetery," said the doctor. He gave the answer to the old joke, and to Sylvia's question too. "All of 'em."

---

1. **preparatory school:** a private high school that prepares students to enter college.

"If all the Remenzels who went to White-hill were numbered, what number would Eli be?" said Sylvia. "That's what I'm getting at."

The question annoyed Doctor Remenzel a little. It didn't seem in very good taste. "It isn't the sort of thing you keep score on," he said.

"Guess," said his wife.

"Oh," he said, "you'd have to go back through all the records, all the way back to the end of the eighteenth century, even, to make any kind of a guess. And you'd have to decide whether to count the Schofields and the Haleys and the MacLellans as Remenzels."

"Please make a guess—" said Sylvia, "just people whose last names were Remenzel."

"Oh—" The doctor shrugged, rattled the plans. "Thirty maybe."

"So Eli is number thirty-one!" said Sylvia, delighted with the number. "You're number thirty-one, dear," she said to the back of Eli's head.

Doctor Remenzel rattled the plans again. "I don't want him going around saying something asinine, like he's number thirty-one," he said.

"Eli knows better than that," said Sylvia. She was a game, ambitious woman, with no money of her own at all. She had been married for sixteen years, but was still openly curious and enthusiastic about the ways of families that had been rich for many generations.

"Just for my own curiosity—not so Eli can go around saying what number he is," said Sylvia, "I'm going to go wherever they keep the records and find out what number he is. That's what I'll do while you're at the meeting and Eli's doing whatever he has to do at the Admissions Office."

"All right," said Doctor Remenzel, "you go ahead and *do* that."

"I will," said Sylvia. "I think things like that are interesting, even if you don't." She waited for a rise on that, but didn't get one. Sylvia enjoyed arguing with her husband about her lack of reserve and his excess of it, enjoyed saying, toward the end of arguments like that, "Well, I guess I'm just a simple-minded country girl at heart, and that's all I'll ever be; and I'm afraid you're going to have to get used to it."

But Doctor Remenzel didn't want to play that game. He found the dormitory plans more interesting.

"Will the new rooms have fireplaces?" said Sylvia. In the oldest part of the dormitory, several of the rooms had handsome fireplaces.

"That would practically double the cost of construction," said the doctor.

"I want Eli to have a room with a fireplace, if that's possible," said Sylvia.

"Those rooms are for seniors."

"I thought maybe through some fluke—" said Sylvia.

"What kind of fluke do you have in mind?" said the doctor. "You mean I should demand that Eli be given a room with a fireplace?"

"Not *demand*—" said Sylvia.

"Request firmly?" said the doctor.

"Maybe I'm just a simple-minded country girl at heart," said Sylvia, "but I look through this catalog, and I see all the buildings named after Remenzels, look through the back and see all the hundreds of thousands of dollars given by Remenzels for scholarships, and I just can't help thinking people named Remenzel are entitled to ask for a little something extra."

"Let me tell you in no uncertain terms," said Doctor Remenzel, "that you are not to ask for anything special for Eli—not anything."

"Of course I won't," said Sylvia. "Why do you always think I'm going to embarrass you?"

"I don't," he said.

"But I can still think what I think, can't I?" she said.

"If you have to," he said.

"I have to," she said cheerfully, utterly unrepentant. She leaned over the plans. "You think those people will like those rooms?"

"What people?" he said.

"The Africans," she said. She was talking about thirty Africans who, at the request of the State Department, were being admitted to Whitehill in the coming semester. It was because of them that the dormitory was being expanded.

"The rooms aren't for them," he said. "They aren't going to be segregated."

"Oh," said Sylvia. She thought about this awhile, and then she said, "Is there a chance Eli will have to have one of them for a roommate?"

"Freshmen draw lots for roommates," said the doctor. "That piece of information's in the catalog too."

"Eli?" said Sylvia.

"H'm?" said Eli.

"How would you feel about it if you had to room with one of those Africans?"

Eli shrugged listlessly.

"That's all right?" said Sylvia.

Eli shrugged again.

"I guess it's all right," said Sylvia.

"It had better be," said the doctor.

The Rolls-Royce pulled abreast of an old Chevrolet, a car in such bad repair that its back door was lashed shut with clothesline. Doctor Remenzel glanced casually at the driver, and then, with sudden excitement and pleasure, he told Ben Barkley to stay abreast of the car.

The doctor leaned across Sylvia, rolled down his window, yelled to the driver of the old Chevrolet, "Tom! Tom!"

The man was a Whitehill classmate of the doctor. He wore a Whitehill necktie, which he waved at Doctor Remenzel in gay recognition. And then he pointed to the fine young son who sat beside him, conveyed with proud smiles and nods that the boy was bound for Whitehill.

Doctor Remenzel pointed to the chaos of the back of Eli's head; beamed that his news was the same. In the wind blustering between the two cars they made a lunch date at the Holly House in North Marston, at the inn whose principal business was serving visitors to Whitehill.

"All right," said Doctor Remenzel to Ben Barkley, "drive on."

"You know," said Sylvia, "somebody really ought to write an article—" And she turned to look through the back window at the old car now shuddering far behind. "Somebody really ought to."

"What about?" said the doctor. He noticed that Eli had slumped way down in the front seat. "Eli!" he said sharply. "Sit up straight!" He turned his attention to Sylvia.

"Most people think prep schools are such snobbish things, just for people with money," said Sylvia, "but that isn't true." She leafed through the catalog and found the quotation she was after.

"The Whitehill School operates on the assumption," she read, *"that no boy should be deterred from applying for admission because his family is unable to pay the full cost of a Whitehill education. With this in mind, the Admissions Committee selects each year from approximately 3,000 candidates the 150 most promising and deserving boys, regardless of their parents' ability to pay the full $2,200 tuition. And those in need of financial aid are given it to the full extent of their need. In certain instances, the school will even pay for the clothing and transportation of a boy."*

Sylvia shook her head. "I think that's perfectly amazing. It's something most people don't realize at all. A truckdriver's son can come to Whitehill."

"If he's smart enough," he said.

"Thanks to the Remenzels," said Sylvia with pride.

"And a lot of other people too," said the doctor.

Sylvia read out loud again: *"In 1799, Eli Remenzel laid the foundation for the present Scholarship Fund by donating to the school forty acres in Boston. The school still owns twelve of those acres, their current evaluation being $3,000,000."*

"Eli!" said the doctor. "Sit up! What's the matter with you?"

Eli sat up again, but began to slump almost immediately, like a snowman in the sun. Eli had good reason for slumping, for actually hoping to die or disappear. He could not bring himself to say what the reason was. He slumped because he knew he had been denied admission to Whitehill. He had failed the entrance examinations. Eli's parents did not know this, because Eli had found the awful notice in the mail and had torn it up.

Doctor Remenzel and his wife had no doubts whatsoever about their son's getting into Whitehill. It was inconceivable to them that Eli could not go there, so they had no curiosity as to how Eli had done on the examinations, were not puzzled when no report ever came.

"What all will Eli have to do to enroll?" said Sylvia, as the black Rolls-Royce crossed the Rhode Island border.

"I don't know," said the doctor. "I suppose they've got it all complicated now with forms to be filled out in quadruplicate, and punch-card machines and bureaucrats. This business of entrance examinations is all new, too. In my day a boy simply had an interview with the headmaster. The headmaster would look him over, ask him a few questions, and then say, 'There's a Whitehill boy.' "

"Did he ever say, 'There isn't a Whitehill boy'?" said Sylvia.

"Oh, sure," said Doctor Remenzel, "if a boy was impossibly stupid or something. There have to be standards. There have always been standards. The African boys have to meet the standards, just like anybody else. They aren't getting in just because the State Department wants to make friends. We made that clear. Those boys had to meet the standards."

"And they did?" said Sylvia.

"I suppose," said Doctor Remenzel. "I heard they're all in, and they all took the same examination Eli did."

"Was it a hard examination, dear?" Sylvia asked Eli. It was the first time she'd thought to ask.

"Um," said Eli.

"What?" she said.

"Yes," said Eli.

"I'm glad they've got high standards," she said, and then she realized that this was a fairly silly statement. "Of course they've got high standards," she said. "That's why it's such a famous school. That's why people who go there do so well in later life."

Sylvia resumed her reading of the catalog again, opened out a folding map of "The Sward," as the campus of Whitehill was traditionally called. She read off the names of features that memorialized Remenzels—the Sanford Remenzel Bird Sanctuary, the George MacLellan Remenzel Skating Rink, the Eli Remenzel Memorial Dormitory, and then she read out loud a quatrain printed on one corner of the map:

> *"When night falleth gently*
> *Upon the green Sward,*
> *It's Whitehill, dear Whitehill,*
> *Our thoughts all turn toward."*

"You know," said Sylvia, "school songs are so corny when you just read them. But when I hear the Glee Club sing those words, they sound like the most beautiful words ever written, and I want to cry."

"Um," said Doctor Remenzel.

"Did a Remenzel write them?"

"I don't think so," said Doctor Remenzel. And then he said, "No—Wait. That's the *new* song. A Remenzel didn't write it. Tom Hilyer wrote it."

"The man in that old car we passed?"

"Sure," said Doctor Remenzel. "Tom wrote it. I remember when he wrote it."

"A scholarship boy wrote it?" said Sylvia. "I think that's awfully nice. He *was* a scholarship boy, wasn't he?"

"His father was an ordinary automobile mechanic in North Marston."

"You hear what a democratic school you're going to, Eli?" said Sylvia.

Half an hour later Ben Barkley brought the limousine to a stop before the Holly House, a rambling country inn twenty years older than the Republic. The inn was on the edge of the Whitehill Sward, glimpsing the school's rooftops and spires over the innocent wilderness of the Sanford Remenzel Bird Sanctuary.

Ben Barkley was sent away with the car for an hour and a half. Doctor Remenzel shepherded Sylvia and Eli into a familiar, low-ceilinged world of pewter, clocks, lovely old woods, agreeable servants, elegant food and drink.

Eli, clumsy with horror of what was surely to come, banged a grandmother clock with his elbow as he passed, made the clock cry.

Sylvia excused herself. Doctor Remenzel and Eli went to the threshold of the dining room, where a hostess welcomed them both by name. They were given a table beneath an oil portrait of one of the three Whitehill boys who had gone on to become President of the United States.

The dining room was filling quickly with families. What every family had was at least one boy about Eli's age. Most of the boys wore Whitehill blazers—black, with pale-blue piping, with Whitehill seals on the breast

pockets. A few, like Eli, were not yet entitled to wear blazers, were simply hoping to get in.

The doctor ordered a drink, then turned to his son and said, "Your mother has the idea that you're entitled to special privileges around here. I hope you don't have that idea too."

"No, sir," said Eli.

"It would be a source of the greatest embarrassment to me," said Doctor Remenzel with considerable grandeur, "if I were ever to hear that you had used the name Remenzel as though you thought Remenzels were something special."

"I know," said Eli wretchedly.

"That settles it," said the doctor. He had nothing more to say about it. He gave abbreviated salutes to several people he knew in the room, speculated as to what sort of party had reserved a long banquet table that was set up along one wall. He decided that it was for a visiting athletic team. Sylvia arrived, and Eli had to be told in a sharp whisper to stand when a woman came to a table.

Sylvia was full of news. The long table, she related, was for the thirty boys from Africa. "I'll bet that's more black people than have eaten here since this place was founded," she said softly. "How fast things change these days!"

"You're right about how fast things change," said Doctor Remenzel. "You're wrong about the black people who've eaten here. This used to be a busy part of the Underground Railroad."[2]

"Really?" said Sylvia. "How exciting." She looked all about herself in a birdlike way. "I think everything's exciting here. I only wish Eli had a blazer on."

Doctor Remenzel reddened. "He isn't entitled to one," he said.

2. **Underground Railroad:** a system set up by opponents of slavery before the Civil War to help fugitive slaves escape to free states and Canada.

"I know that," said Sylvia.

"I thought you were going to ask somebody for permission to put a blazer on Eli right away," said the doctor.

"I wouldn't do that," said Sylvia, a little offended now. "Why are you always afraid I'll embarrass you?"

"Never mind. Excuse me. Forget it," said Doctor Remenzel.

Sylvia brightened again, put her hand on Eli's arm, and looked radiantly at a man in the dining-room doorway. "There's my favorite person in all the world, next to my son and husband," she said. She meant Dr. Donald Warren, headmaster of the Whitehill School. A thin gentleman in his early sixties, Doctor Warren was in the doorway with the manager of the inn, looking over the arrangements for the Africans.

It was then that Eli got up abruptly, fled the dining room, fled as much of the nightmare as he could possibly leave behind. He brushed past Doctor Warren rudely, though he knew him well, though Doctor Warren spoke his name. Doctor Warren looked after him sadly.

"I'll be darned," said Doctor Remenzel. "What brought that on?"

"Maybe he really *is* sick," said Sylvia.

The Remenzels had no time to react more elaborately, because Doctor Warren spotted them and crossed quickly to their table. He greeted them, some of his perplexity about Eli showing in his greeting. He asked if he might sit down.

"Certainly, of course," said Doctor Remenzel expansively. "We'd be honored if you did. Heavens."

"Not to eat," said Doctor Warren. "I'll be eating at the long table with the new boys. I would like to talk, though." He saw that there were five places set at the table. "You're expecting someone?"

"We passed Tom Hilyer and his boy on the

way," said Doctor Remenzel. "They'll be along in a minute."

"Good, good," said Doctor Warren absently. He fidgeted, looked again in the direction in which Eli had disappeared.

"Tom's boy will be going to Whitehill in the fall?" said Doctor Remenzel.

"H'm?" said Doctor Warren. "Oh—yes, yes. Yes, he will."

"Is he a scholarship boy, like his father?" said Sylvia.

"That's not a polite question," said Doctor Remenzel severely.

"I beg your pardon," said Sylvia.

"No, no—that's a perfectly proper question these days," said Doctor Warren. "We don't keep that sort of information very secret any more. We're proud of our scholarship boys, and they have every reason to be proud of themselves. Tom's boy got the highest score anyone's ever got on the entrance examinations. We feel privileged to have him."

"We never *did* find out Eli's score," said Doctor Remenzel. He said it with good-humored resignation, without expectation that Eli had done especially well.

"A good strong medium, I imagine," said Sylvia. She said this on the basis of Eli's grades in primary school, which had ranged from medium to terrible.

The headmaster looked surprised. "I didn't tell you his scores?" he said.

"We haven't seen you since he took the examinations," said Doctor Remenzel.

"The letter I wrote you—" said Doctor Warren.

"What letter?" said Doctor Remenzel. "Did we get a letter?"

"A letter from me," said Doctor Warren, with growing incredulity. "The hardest letter I ever had to write."

Sylvia shook her head. "We never got any letter from you."

Doctor Warren sat back, looking very ill. "I

mailed it myself," he said. "It was definitely mailed—two weeks ago."

Doctor Remenzel shrugged. "The U.S. mails don't lose much," he said, "but I guess that now and then something gets misplaced."

Doctor Warren cradled his head in his hands. "Oh, dear—oh, my, oh, Lord," he said. "I was surprised to see Eli here. I wondered that he would want to come along with you."

"He didn't come along just to see the scenery," said Doctor Remenzel. "He came to enroll."

"I want to know what was in the letter," said Sylvia.

Doctor Warren raised his head, folded his hands. "What the letter said, was this, and no other words could be more difficult for me to say: *'On the basis of his work in primary school and his scores on the entrance examinations, I must tell you that your son and my good friend Eli cannot possibly do the work required of boys at Whitehill.'*" Doctor Warren's voice steadied, and so did his gaze. "*'To admit Eli to Whitehill, to expect him to do Whitehill work,'*" he said, "*'would be both unrealistic and cruel.'*"

Thirty African boys, escorted by several faculty members, State Department men, and diplomats from their own countries, filed into the dining room.

And Tom Hilyer and his boy, having no idea that something had just gone awfully wrong for the Remenzels, came in, too, and said hello to the Remenzels and Doctor Warren gaily, as though life couldn't possibly be better.

"I'll talk to you more about this later, if you like," Doctor Warren said to the Remenzels, rising. "I have to go now, but later on—" He left quickly.

"My mind's a blank," said Sylvia. "My mind's a perfect blank."

Tom Hilyer and his boy sat down. Hilyer looked at the menu before him, clapped his hands and said, "What's good? I'm hungry." And then he said, "Say—where's your boy?"

"He stepped out for a moment," said Doctor Remenzel evenly.

"We've got to find him," said Sylvia to her husband.

"In time, in due time," said Doctor Remenzel.

"That letter," said Sylvia; "Eli knew about it. He found it and tore it up. Of course he did!" She started to cry, thinking of the hideous trap Eli had caught himself in.

"I'm not interested right now in what Eli's done," said Doctor Remenzel. "Right now I'm a lot more interested in what some other people are going to do."

"What do you mean?" said Sylvia.

Doctor Remenzel stood impressively, angry and determined. "I mean," he said, "I'm going to see how quickly people can change their minds around here."

"Please," said Sylvia, trying to hold him, trying to calm him, "we've got to find Eli. That's the first thing."

"The first thing," said Doctor Remenzel quite loudly, "is to get Eli admitted to Whitehill. After that we'll find him, and we'll bring him back."

"But darling—" said Sylvia.

"No 'but' about it," said Doctor Remenzel. "There's a majority of the Board of Overseers in this room at this very moment. Every one of them is a close friend of mine, or a close friend of my father. If they tell Doctor Warren Eli's in, that's it—Eli's in. If there's room for all these other people," he said, "there's darn well room for Eli too."

He strode quickly to a table nearby, sat down heavily, and began to talk to a fierce-looking and splendid old gentleman who was eating there. The old gentleman was chairman of the board.

Sylvia apologized to the baffled Hilyers, and then went in search of Eli.

Asking this person and that person, Sylvia found him. He was outside—all alone on a bench in a bower of lilacs that had just begun to bud.

Eli heard his mother's coming on the gravel path, stayed where he was, resigned. "Did you find out," he said, "or do I still have to tell you?"

"About you?" she said gently. "About not getting in? Doctor Warren told us."

"I tore his letter up," said Eli.

"I can understand that," she said. "Your father and I have always made you feel that you had to go to Whitehill, that nothing else would do."

"I feel better," said Eli. He tried to smile, found he could do it easily. "I feel so much better now that it's over. I tried to tell you a couple of times—but I just couldn't. I didn't know how."

"That's my fault, not yours," she said.

"What's father doing?" said Eli.

Sylvia was so intent on comforting Eli that she'd put out of her mind what her husband was up to. Now she realized that Doctor Remenzel was making a ghastly mistake. She didn't want Eli admitted to Whitehill, could see what a cruel thing that would be.

She couldn't bring herself to tell the boy what his father was doing, so she said, "He'll be along in a minute, dear. He understands." And then she said, "You wait here, and I'll go get him and come right back."

But she didn't have to go to Doctor Remenzel. At that moment, the big man came out of the inn and caught sight of his wife and son. He came to her and to Eli. He looked dazed.

"Well?" she said.

"They—they all said no," said Doctor Remenzel, very subdued.

"That's for the best," said Sylvia. "I'm relieved. I really am."

"Who said no?" said Eli. "Who said no to what?"

"The members of the board," said Doctor Remenzel, not looking anyone in the eye. "I asked them to make an exception in your case —to reverse their decision and let you in."

Eli stood, his faced filled with incredulity and shame that were instant. "You what?" he said, and there was no childishness in the way he said it. Next came anger. "You shouldn't have done that!" he said to his father.

Doctor Remenzel nodded. "So I've already been told."

"That isn't done!" said Eli. "How awful! You shouldn't have."

"You're right," said Doctor Remenzel, accepting the scolding lamely.

"Now I *am* ashamed," said Eli, and he showed that he was.

Doctor Remenzel, in his wretchedness, could find no strong words to say. "I apologize to you both," he said at last. "It was a very bad thing to try."

"Now a Remenzel *has* asked for something," said Eli.

"I don't suppose Ben's back yet with the car?" said Doctor Remenzel. It was obvious that Ben wasn't. "We'll wait out here for him," he said. "I don't want to go back in there now."

"A Remenzel asked for something—as though a Remenzel were something special," said Eli.

"I don't suppose—" said Doctor Remenzel, and he left the sentence unfinished, dangling in the air.

"You don't suppose what?" said his wife, her face puzzled.

"I don't suppose," said Doctor Remenzel, "that we'll ever be coming here any more."

Getting at Meaning

1. Eli tears up the letter of rejection from Whitehill. What are the results of this act?

2. Describe the Remenzel family. What is Mrs. Remenzel's background? Why is she so fascinated by the family's relationship with Whitehill?

3. Describe Eli's behavior in the car on the way to Whitehill.

4. What kind of school is Whitehill? What is the most important factor in determining whether a student is admitted to Whitehill?

5. What makes Doctor Warren's position a particularly difficult one?

6. What does Mrs. Remenzel do when she learns of Eli's rejection? What does she tell Eli when she finds him? What concerns her most?

7. At the end of the story, how does Doctor Remenzel feel about himself? How does Eli feel about what his father has done? What does Doctor Remenzel mean when he says, "I don't suppose that we'll ever be coming here any more"?

8. Were the Remenzels realistic about Eli's abilities? Explain your answer.

Developing Skills in Reading Literature

1. **Foil.** A foil is a character with qualities that contrast with those of a major character. In this story, for example, Tom Hilyer serves as a foil to Doctor Remenzel. Remenzel is from an old, wealthy family; Hilyer is the son of a local auto mechanic. Remenzel's family estab- lishes scholarships; Hilyer was a scholarship student. The Remenzels ride to Whitehill in a chauffeured limousine; the Hilyers drive in an old Chevrolet. In what ways is Hilyer's son a foil to Eli? Which father and son seem to be the happier pair?

2. **Conflict.** What is the major conflict in this story? Who or what are the opposing forces? How is the conflict resolved?

3. **Third-Person Narration.** When a narrator outside the story relates the events, the narrative technique is called third-person narration. In third-person narration, the narrator refers to the characters as *he, she,* and *they.* The most common type of third-person narration is third-person omniscient narration, in which the narrator is all-knowing and can see into the minds of all the characters.

"The Lie" is an example of third-person omniscient narration. Which characters' thoughts are revealed by the narrator of this story?

Developing Writing Skills

Analyzing a Character. Write one paragraph about some quality demonstrated by Doctor or Mrs. Remenzel. The topic sentence of the paragraph should make a general statement about the character. For example, a paragraph about Mrs. Remenzel might begin, "Mrs. Remenzel cares more about her son than about family traditions." The rest of the paragraph should cite specific incidents from the story to support the idea presented in the topic sentence.

Tears
Alonzo Lopez

THE MOTHER, 1901. *Pablo Picasso. The St. Louis Art Museum.*

Tears of loneliness
    rinse my memory;
Tears of memory
    cleanse my heart;
Tears of sadness   5
    bathe my eyes;
Tears of hate
    build up
    to drown me.

Getting at Meaning

1. Of the four kinds of tears named in the poem, which affects the entire person?

2. How are tears of hate different from tears of loneliness, memory, and sadness?

Developing Skills in Reading Literature

1. **Poetry.** Tight structure is a characteristic of most poetry. In this poem, all of the ideas are connected through the poet's careful choice of related words. How are the verbs *rinse, cleanse, bathe,* and *drown* related? How are they related to tears?

2. **Denotation and Connotation.** Many words have two kinds of meaning: a denotative meaning, which is the dictionary definition of the word, and a connotative meaning, which is the personal, emotional meaning. For example, the denotation of *slim* is "thin." The word, however, also brings forth images of elegance and grace. These images are the connotations of the word.

Look at the verbs in the first six lines of the poem. Are they harsh or soothing words? How do their connotations contribute to the reader's understanding of the speaker's ideas about tears?

Where the Rainbow Ends   *Richard Rive*

Where the rainbow ends
There's going to be a place, brother,
Where the world can sing all sorts of songs,
And we're going to sing together, brother,
You and I, though you're white and I'm not.   5
It's going to be a sad song, brother,
Because we don't know the tune,
And it's a difficult tune to learn.
But we can learn, brother, you and I.
There's no such tune as a black tune.   10
There's no such tune as a white tune.
There's only music, brother,
And it's music we're going to sing
Where the rainbow ends.

Getting at Meaning

1. Is the speaker's outlook basically positive or negative?

2. What race is the speaker in the poem? What race is the speaker's audience?

3. According to the speaker, where is the place where black and white will "sing together"? What is the speaker saying by this choice of location?

4. What reasons does the speaker give for saying "It's going to be a sad song"?

Developing Skills in Reading Literature

Symbol. A symbol, as you know, stands for, or represents, something beyond itself. In this poem, music is a symbol for unity. Notice how the speaker uses the idea of singing together. For example, the speaker says that the tune is a "difficult tune to learn." What does he or she mean by this? What other references to singing and songs can you find in the poem? Is music a good symbol for unity? Why?

Developing Writing Skills

Explaining an Idea. In one paragraph, describe the end of your rainbow, your concept of what would make a better world for you and others. Focus on one idea and describe it fully.

Turning Points

ON THE BALCONY, 1955–57. *Peter Blake.*
The Tate Gallery.

Everybody Knows Tobie   *Daniel Garza*

When I was thirteen years old, my older brother, Tobie, had the town newspaper route. Everyone in the town knew him well because he had been delivering papers for a year and a half. Tobie used to tell me that he had the best route of all because his customers would pay promptly each month, and sometimes, he used to brag that the nice people of the town would tip him a quarter or maybe fifty cents at the end of the month because he would trudge up many stairs to deliver the paper personally.

The other newspaper boys were not as lucky as Tobie because sometimes their customers would not be at home when they went by to collect payment for that month's newspaper, or maybe at the end of the month the customers would just try to avoid the paper boys to keep from paying.

Yes, Tobie had it good. The biggest advantage, I thought, that Tobie had over all the newspaper boys was that he knew the gringos of the town so well that he could go into a gringo barber shop and get a haircut without having the barber tell him to go to the Mexican barber in our town, or maybe just embarrassing him in front of all the gringo customers in the shop as they often did when chicano cotton pickers came into their places during the fall months.

The gringo barbers of my town were careful whom they allowed in their shops during the cotton harvest season in the fall. September and October and cotton brought chicanos from the south to the north of Texas where I lived, and where the cotton was sometimes plentiful and sometimes scarce. Chicanos is

what we say in our language, and it is slang among our people. It means the Mexicans of Texas. These chicano cotton pickers came from the Rio Grande Valley in South Texas, and sometimes, even people from Mexico made the trip to the north of Texas. All these chicanos came to my little town in which many gringos lived, and a few of us who spoke both English and Spanish.

When the chicanos came to my town on Saturdays after working frightfully in the cotton fields all week, they would go to the town market for food, and the fathers would buy candy and ice cream for their flocks of little black-headed ones. The younger ones, the *jovenes*, would go to the local movie house. And then maybe those who had never been to the north of Texas before would go to the gringos' barbershops for haircuts, not knowing that they would be refused. The gringo barbers would be very careful not to let them come too close to their shops because the regular gringo customers would get mad, and sometimes they would curse the chicanos.

"It's them darn pepper bellies again. Can't seem to get rid of 'em in the fall," the prejudiced gringos of my town would say. Some of the nicer people would only become uneasy at seeing so many chicanos with long, black, greasy hair wanting haircuts.

The barbers of the town liked Tobie, and they invited him to their shops for haircuts. Tobie said that the barbers told him that they would cut his hair because he did not belong to that group of people who came from the south of Texas. Tobie understood. And he did not argue with the barbers because he knew how chicanos from South Texas were, and how maybe gringo scissors would get all greasy from cutting their hair.

During that fall, Tobie encouraged me to go to the gringo's place for a haircut. "Joey, when are you going to get rid of that mop of hair?" he asked.

"I guess I'll get rid of it when Mr. Lopez learns how to cut flat-tops."

"Golly, Joey, Mr. Lopez is a good ole guy and all that, but if he doesn't know how to give flat-tops, then you should go to some other barber for flat-tops. Really, Kid-brother, that hair looks awful."

"Yeah, but I'm afraid."

"Afraid of what?" Tobie asked.

"I'm afraid the barber will mistake me for one of those guys from South Texas and run me out of his shop."

"Oh, forget it," Tobie said. "Mr. Brewer . . . you know, the barber who cuts my hair . . . is a nice man, and he'll cut your hair. Just tell him you're my kid-brother."

I thought about this new adventure for several days, and then on a Saturday, when there was no school, I decided on the haircut at Mr. Brewer's. I hurriedly rode my bike to town and parked it in the alley close to the barber-shop. As I walked into the shop, I noticed that all of a sudden the gringos inside stopped their conversation and looked at me. The shop was silent for a moment. I thought then that maybe this was not too good and that I should leave. I remembered what Tobie had told me about being his brother, and about Mr. Brewer being a nice man. I was convinced that I belonged in the gringo barber-shop.

I found an empty chair and sat down to wait my turn for a haircut. One gringo customer sitting next to me rose and explained to the barber that he had to go to the court-house for something. Another customer left without saying anything. And then one, who was dressed in dirty coveralls and a faded khaki shirt, got up from Mr. Brewer's chair and said to him, "Say, Tom, looks like you got yourself a little tamale to clip."

Mr. Brewer smiled only.

My turn was next, and I was afraid. But I remembered again that this was all right because I was Tobie's brother, and everybody liked Tobie. I went to Mr. Brewer's chair. As I started to sit down, he looked at me and smiled a nice smile.

He said, "I'm sorry, Sonny, but I can't cut your hair. You go to Mr. Lopez's. He'll cut your hair."

Mr. Brewer took me to the door and pointed the way to Lopez's barbershop. He pointed with his finger and said, "See, over there behind that service station. That's his place.

You go there. He'll clip your hair."

Tears were welling up in my eyes. I felt a lump in my throat. I was too choked up to tell him I was Tobie's brother, and that it was all right to cut my hair. I only looked at him as he finished giving directions. He smiled again and patted me on the back. As I left, Mr. Brewer said, "Say hello to Mr. Lopez for me, will you, Sonny?"

I did not turn back to look at Mr. Brewer. I kept my head bowed as I walked to Mr. Lopez's because tears filled my eyes, and these tears were tears of hurt to the pride and confidence that I had slowly gained in my gringo town.

I thought of many things as I walked slowly. Maybe this was a foolish thing that I had done. There were too many gringos in the town and too few of us who lived there all the year long. This was a bad thing because the gringos had the right to say yes or no, and we could only follow what they said. It was useless to go against them. It was foolish. But I was different from the chicanos who came from the south, not much different. I did live in the town the ten months of the year when the other chicanos were in the South or in Mexico. Then I remembered what the barber had told my brother about the South Texas people, and why the gringo customers had left while I was in Mr. Brewer's shop. I began to understand. But it was very hard for me to realize that even though I had lived among gringos all of my life I still had to go to my own people for such things as haircuts. Why wouldn't gringos cut my hair? I was clean. My hair was not long and greasy.

I walked into Mr. Lopez's shop. There were many chicanos sitting in the chairs and even on the floor, waiting their turn for a haircut. Mr. Lopez paused from his work as he saw me enter and said, "Sorry, Joey, full up. Come back in a couple of hours."

I shrugged my shoulders and said OK. As I started to leave, I remembered what Mr.

Brewer had told me to say to Mr. Lopez. "Mr. Lopez," I said, and all the chicanos, the ones who were waiting, turned and looked at me with curious eyes. "Mr. Brewer told me to tell you hello."

Mr. Lopez shook his head approvingly, not digesting the content of my statement. The chicanos looked at me again and began to whisper among themselves. I did not hear, but I understood.

I told Mr. Lopez that I would return later in the day, but I did not because there would be other chicanos wanting haircuts on Saturday. I could come during the week when he had more time, and when all the chicanos would be in the fields working.

I went away, feeling rejected both by the gringos and even my people, the entire world I knew.

Back in the alley where my bike was parked, I sat on the curb for a long while thinking how maybe I did not fit into this town. Maybe my place was in the south of Texas where there were many of my kind of people, and where there were more chicano barbershops and fewer gringo barbers. Yes, I thought, I needed a land where I could belong to one race. I was so concerned with myself that I did not notice a chicano, a middle-aged man dressed in a new chambray shirt and faded denim pants, studying me.

He asked, *"Que paso, Chamaco?"*[1]

"Nada,"[2] I answered.

"Maybe the cotton has not been good for you this year."

"No, Señor. I live here in the town."

And then the chicano said, "Chico, I mistook you for one of us."

Suddenly the chicano became less interested in me and walked away unconcerned.

I could not have told him that I had tried

---

1. **Que paso, Chamaco?** (kä pä′ sō chä mä′ cō) *Spanish:* What happened, boy?
2. **Nada** (nä′ də) *Spanish:* Nothing.

for a haircut at the gringo's because he would have laughed at me, and called me a *pocho*, a chicano who prefers gringo ways. These experienced chicanos knew the ways of the gringos in the north of Texas.

After the chicano had left me, I thought that maybe these things that were happening to me in the town would all pass in a short time. The entire cotton crop would soon be harvested, and the farmers around my town would have it baled and sold. Then the chicanos would leave the north of Texas and journey back to their homes in the Valley in the south and to Mexico.

My town would be left alone for ten more months of the year, and in this time everything and everybody would be all right again. The gringo barbers would maybe think twice before sending me to Mr. Lopez's.

Early in November, the last of the cotton around my town had been harvested. The people of South Texas climbed aboard their big trucks with tall sideboards and canvas on the top to shield the sun, and they began their long journey to their homes in the border country.

The streets of the little town were now empty on Saturday. A few farmers came to town on Saturday and brought their families to do their shopping. Still, the streets were quiet and empty.

In my home there was new excitement for me. Tobie considered leaving his newspaper route for another job, one that would pay more money. And I thought that maybe he would let me take over his route. This was something very good. By taking his route, I would know all the gringos of the town, and maybe . . . maybe then the barbers would invite me to their shops as they had invited Tobie.

At supper that night I asked Tobie if he would take me on his delivery for a few days, and then let me deliver the newspaper on my own.

Tobie said, "No, Joey. You're too young to handle money. Besides, the newspaper bag would be too heavy for you to carry on your shoulder all over town. No, I think I'll turn the route over to Red."

My father was quiet during this time, but soon he spoke, "Tobie, you give the route to Joey. He knows about money. And he needs to put a little muscle on his shoulders."

The issue was settled.

The next day Tobie took me to the newspaper office. Tobie's boss, a nice elderly man wearing glasses, studied me carefully, scratched his white head, and then asked Tobie, "Well, what do you think?"

"Oh," Tobie said, "I told him he was too young to handle this job, but he says he can do it."

"Yes, sir," I butted in enthusiastically.

Tobie's boss looked at me and chuckled, "Well, he's got enough spunk."

He thought some more.

Tobie spoke, "I think he'll make you a good delivery boy, sir."

A short silence followed while Tobie's boss put his thoughts down on a scratch pad on his desk.

Finally, the boss said, "We'll give him a try, Tobie." He looked at me. "But, Young 'un, you'd better be careful with that money. It's your responsibility."

"Yes, sir," I gulped.

"OK, that's settled," the boss said.

Tobie smiled and said, "Sir, I'm taking him on my delivery for a few days so he can get the hang of it, and then I'll let him take it over."

The boss agreed. I took his hand and shook it, and promised him that I would do my extra best. Then Tobie left, and I followed behind.

In a few days I was delivering the *Daily News* to all the gringos of the town, and also, to Mr. Brewer.

Each afternoon, during my delivery, I was careful not to go into Mr. Brewer's with the newspaper. I would carefully open the door and drop the paper in. I did this because I thought that maybe Mr. Brewer would remember me, and this might cause an embarrassing incident. But I did this a very few times because one afternoon Mr. Brewer was standing at the door. He saw me. I opened the door and quickly handed him the newspaper, but before I could shut the door he said, "Say, Sonny, aren't you the one I sent to Mr. Lopez's a while back?"

"Yes, sir," I said.

"Why'd you stay around here? Didn't your people go back home last week? You do belong to 'em, don't you?"

"No, sir." I said. "I live here in the town."

"You mean to say you're not one of those . . .?"

"No, sir."

"Well, I'll be durned." He paused and thought. "You know, Sonny, I have a young Meskin[3] boy who lives here in town come to

this here shop for haircuts every other Saturday. His name is . . . durn, can't think of his name to save my soul . . ."

"Tobie?"

"Yeah, yeah, that's his name. Fine boy. You know him?"

"Yes, sir. He's my older brother."

Then Mr. Brewer's eyes got bigger in astonishment. "Well, I'll be doubly durned." He paused and shook his head unbelievingly. "And I told you to go to Mr. Lopez's. Why didn't you speak up and tell me you was Tobie's brother? I woulda put you in that there chair and clipped you a pretty head of hair."

"Oh, I guess I forgot to tell you," I said.

"Well, from now on, Sonny, you come to this here shop, and I'll cut your hair."

---

3. **Meskin:** mispronunciation of *Mexican.*

"But what about your customers? Won't they get mad?"

"Naw. I'll tell 'em you're Tobie's brother, and everything will be all right. Everybody in town knows Tobie, and everybody likes him."

Then a customer walked into the barbershop. He looked at Mr. Brewer, and then at me, and then at my newspaper bag. And then the gringo customer smiled a nice smile at me.

"Well, excuse me, Sonny, got a customer waitin'. Remember now, come Saturday, and I'll clip your hair."

"OK, Mr. Brewer. Bye."

Mr. Brewer turned and said goodbye.

As I continued my delivery, I began to chuckle small bits of contentment to myself because Mr. Brewer had invited me to his shop for haircuts, and because the gringo customer had smiled at me, and because now all the gringos of the town would know me and maybe accept me.

Those incidents that had happened to me during the cotton harvest in my town—Mr. Brewer sending me to Mr. Lopez's for the haircut, and the chicano cotton picker avoiding me after discovering that I was not one of his people, and the gringo customers leaving Mr. Brewer's barbershop because of me—all seemed so insignificant. And now I felt that delivering the *Daily News* to the businessmen had given me a place among them, and all because of the fact that everybody in my town knew Tobie.

Getting at Meaning

1. Do you think Joey will be as successful a newspaper carrier as his brother is? Why or why not?

2. Describe the town where this story is set. What is the relationship between the gringos and the Mexican-American residents? What is the relationship between the Mexican-American residents and chicano pickers who come for two months of the year?

3. How do the people in the town show that they like Tobie? What qualities does Tobie have that cause the residents to accept him?

4. How does Joey feel when Mr. Brewer sends him out of the barbershop? What thoughts run through his head? Two other incidents make Joey feel even more rejected. What are they?

5. Mr. Brewer offers to cut Joey's hair when he finds out that Joey is Tobie's brother. Why? How does this offer change Joey's outlook on his life in the town? What does the newspaper route mean to Joey?

Developing Skills in Reading Literature

1. **Climax.** The climax, or turning point, is the high point of interest in a story or play. At the climax, a change takes place that brings the resolution of the conflict into view. The change can make things better or worse for the main character. What is the climax of this story, the point at which things change for Joey?

2. **First-Person Narration.** When a character within a story relates the events, the narrative technique is called first-person narration.

"Everybody Knows Tobie" is narrated by Joey. The reader sees the other characters through Joey's eyes and learns first hand Joey's thoughts and feelings. How would the story be different if it were told by Tobie?

Developing Writing Skills

Writing About a Personal Experience. Write a paragraph about how a relative, teacher, or friend helped you in a major way. Perhaps the person stood by you through a difficult experience. Perhaps the person helped you achieve an important goal. Describe the situation and explain the specific way you were assisted.

The Fish   *Elizabeth Bishop*

I caught a tremendous fish
and held him beside the boat
half out of water, with my hook
fast in a corner of his mouth.
He didn't fight.   5
He hadn't fought at all.
He hung a grunting weight,
battered and venerable
and homely. Here and there
his brown skin hung in strips   10
like ancient wallpaper,
and its pattern of darker brown
was like wallpaper:
shapes like full-blown roses
stained and lost through age.   15
He was speckled with barnacles,
fine rosettes of lime,
and infested
with tiny white sea-lice,

and underneath two or three   20
rags of green weed hung down.
While his gills were breathing in
the terrible oxygen
—the frightening gills,
fresh and crisp with blood,   25
that can cut so badly—
I thought of the coarse white flesh
packed in like feathers,
the big bones and the little bones,
the dramatic reds and blacks   30
of his shiny entrails,
and the pink swim-bladder
like a big peony.
I looked into his eyes
which were far larger than mine   35
but shallower, and yellowed,
the irises backed and packed
with tarnished tinfoil

THE GOLDEN FISH, 1925. *Paul Klee. Kunsthalle, Hamburg.*

seen through the lenses
of old scratched isinglass.   40
They shifted a little, but not
to return my stare.
—It was more like the tipping
of an object toward the light.
I admired his sullen face,   45
the mechanism of his jaw,
and then I saw
that from his lower lip
—if you could call it a lip—
grim, wet, and weaponlike,   50
hung five old pieces of fish-line,
or four and a wire leader
with the swivel still attached,
with all their five big hooks
grown firmly in his mouth.   55
A green line, frayed at the end
where he broke it, two heavier lines,
and a fine black thread
still crimped from the strain and snap

when it broke and he got away.   60
Like medals with their ribbons
frayed and wavering,
a five-haired beard of wisdom
trailing from his aching jaw.
I stared and stared   65
and victory filled up
the little rented boat,
from the pool of bilge
where oil had spread a rainbow
around the rusted engine   70
to the bailer rusted orange,
the sun-cracked thwarts,[1]
the oarlocks on their strings,
the gunnels[2]—until everything
was rainbow, rainbow, rainbow!   75
And I let the fish go.

---

1. **thwarts** (thwôrts): rowers' seats extending across a boat.
2. **gunnel** (gun' 'l): the upper edge of the side of a boat.

Getting at Meaning

1. What is the initial attitude of the speaker toward the fish?

2. Describe the appearance of the fish. What does the speaker observe about the eyes of the fish?

3. How do the "five old pieces of fish-line" hanging from the lip of the fish affect the speaker?

4. At first, it seems as if the speaker is going to keep the fish. Later, the speaker lets the fish go. Where is the turning point in the speaker's attitude toward the fish? Why does the speaker throw the fish back into the water, just when victory seems sweetest?

5. What is the "rainbow" the speaker describes at the end of the poem? What does the rainbow represent for the speaker?

Developing Skills in Reading Literature

1. **Simile.** A simile, as you know, is a comparison using the word *like* or *as*. To what is the fish's skin compared in lines 10 and 11? How are the two things alike? What simile describes the pattern of the fish's skin? In line 61, the speaker compares the hooks in the fish's jaw to medals. How does this simile bring out the speaker's changing attitude toward the fish?

2. **Narrative Poem.** A poem that tells a story is called a narrative poem. In three or four sentences, summarize the story told in "The Fish."

3. **Imagery.** This poem is full of vivid images, words and phrases that appeal to the senses. The image "tiny white sea-lice," for example, appeals to the sense of sight. List at least ten other images from the poem. Be prepared to identify their sense appeal.

Moss-Gathering *Theodore Roethke*

To loosen with all ten fingers held wide and limber
And lift up a patch, dark-green, the kind for lining cemetery baskets,
Thick and cushiony, like an old-fashioned doormat,
The crumbling small hollow sticks on the underside mixed with roots,
And wintergreen berries and leaves still stuck to the top,—   5
That was moss-gathering.
But something always went out of me when I dug loose those carpets
Of green, or plunged to my elbows in the spongy yellowish moss of the marshes:
And afterwards I always felt mean, jogging back over the logging road,
As if I had broken the natural order of things in that swampland;   10
Disturbed some rhythm, old and of vast importance,
By pulling off flesh from the living planet;
As if I had committed, against the whole scheme of life, a desecration.

Getting at Meaning

1. The speaker begins by talking about the physical process of gathering moss. Describe this process in your own words.

2. What is meant by this line: "But something always went out of me when I dug loose those carpets"? How does the speaker feel after ripping up the moss?

3. What is the meaning of *desecration?* What does the speaker view as a desecration?

4. What is the speaker's message about the relationship between human beings and nature?

Developing Skills in Reading Literature

Metaphor. In this poem the speaker compares gathering moss from the ground to "pulling off flesh from the living planet." How does this metaphor reveal the speaker's feelings about the subject?

Developing Writing Skills

Combining Narration and Description. Write a paragraph in which you describe an experience you have had in the world of nature. You might choose as a subject a visit to the ocean or the mountains, a camping trip, or an encounter with an animal. Describe clearly the experience and how it made you feel.

One Throw   *W. C. Heinz*

I checked into a hotel called the Olympia, which is right on the main street and the only hotel in the town. After lunch I was hanging around the lobby, and I got to talking to the guy at the desk. I asked him if this wasn't the town where that kid named Maneri played ball.

"That's right," the guy said. "He's a pretty good ballplayer."

"He should be," I said. "I read that he was the new Phil Rizzuto."

"That's what they said," the guy said.

"What's the matter with him?" I said. "I mean, if he's such a good ballplayer, what's he doing in this league?"

"I don't know," the guy said. "I guess the Yankees know what they're doing."

"What kind of a kid is he?"

"He's a nice kid," the guy said. "He plays good ball, but I feel sorry for him. He thought he'd be playing for the Yankees soon, and here he is in this town. You can see it's got him down."

"He lives here in this hotel?"

"That's right," the guy said. "Most of the older ballplayers stay in rooming houses, but Pete and a couple other kids live here."

He was leaning on the desk, talking to me and looking across the hotel lobby. He nodded his head. "This is a funny thing," he said. "Here he comes now."

The kid had come through the door from the street. He had on a light gray sport shirt and a pair of gray flannel slacks.

I could see why, when he showed up with the Yankees in spring training, he made them all think of Rizzuto. He isn't any bigger than Rizzuto, and he looks just like him.

"Hello, Nick," he said to the guy at the desk.

"Hello, Pete," the guy at the desk said. "How goes it today?"

"All right," the kid said, but you could see he was exaggerating.

"I'm sorry, Pete," the guy at the desk said, "but no mail today."

"That's all right, Nick," the kid said. "I'm used to it."

"Excuse me," I said, "but you're Pete Maneri?"

"That's right," the kid said, turning and looking at me.

"Excuse me," the guy at the desk said, introducing us. "Pete, this is Mr. Franklin."

"Harry Franklin," I said.

"I'm glad to know you," the kid said, shaking my hand.

"I recognize you from your pictures," I said.

"Pete's a good ballplayer," the guy at the desk said.

"Not very," the kid said.

"Don't take his word for it, Mr. Franklin," the guy said.

"I'm a great ball fan," I said to the kid. "Do you people play tonight?"

"We play two games," the kid said.

"The first game's at six o'clock," the guy at the desk said. "They play pretty good ball."

"I'll be there," I said. "I used to play a little ball myself."

"You did?" the kid said.

"With Columbus," I said. "That's twenty years ago."

"Is that right?" the kid said. . .

That's the way I got to talking with the kid. They had one of those pine-paneled taprooms in the basement of the hotel, and we went down there. I had a couple, and the kid had a Coke; and I told him a few stories, and he turned out to be a real good listener.

"But what do you do now, Mr. Franklin?" he said after a while.

"I sell hardware," I said. "I can think of some things I'd like better, but I was going to ask you how you like playing in this league."

"Well," the kid said, "I suppose it's all right. I guess I've got no kick coming."

"Oh, I don't know," I said. "I understand you're too good for this league. What are they trying to do to you?"

"I don't know," the kid said. "I can't understand it."

"What's the trouble?"

"Well," the kid said, "I don't get along very well here. I mean there's nothing wrong with my playing. I'm hitting .365 right now. I lead the league in stolen bases. There's nobody can field with me, but who cares?"

"Who manages this ball club?"

"Al Dall," the kid said. "You remember, he played in the outfield for the Yankees for about four years."

"I remember."

"Maybe he is all right," the kid said, "but I don't get along with him. He's on my neck all the time."

"Well," I said, "that's the way they are in the minors sometimes. You have to remember the guy is looking out for himself and his ball club first. He's not worried about you."

"I know that," the kid said. "If I get the big hit or make the play, he never says anything. The other night I tried to take second on a loose ball, and I got caught in the run-down. He bawls me out in front of everybody. There's nothing I can do."

"Oh, I don't know," I said. "This is probably a guy who knows he's got a good thing in you, and he's looking to keep you around. You people lead the league, and that makes him look good. He doesn't want to lose you to Kansas City or the Yankees."

"That's what I mean," the kid said. "When the Yankees sent me down here, they said, 'Don't worry. We'll keep an eye on you.' So Dall never sends a good report on me. Nobody ever comes down to look me over. What chance is there for a guy like Eddie Brown or somebody like that coming down to see me in this town?"

"You have to remember that Eddie Brown's the big shot," I said, "the great Yankee scout."

"Sure," the kid said. "I never even saw him, and I'll never see him in this place. I have an idea that if they ever ask Dall about me, he keeps knocking me down."

"Why don't you go after Dall?" I said. "I had trouble like that once myself, but I figured out a way to get attention."

"You did?" the kid said.

"I threw a couple of balls over the first baseman's head," I said. "I threw a couple of games away, and that really got the manager sore. I was lousing up his ball club and his record. So what does he do? He blows the whistle on me, and what happens? That gets the brass curious, and they send down to see what's wrong."

"Is that so?" the kid said. "What happened?"

"Two weeks later," I said, "I was up with Columbus."

"Is that right?" the kid said.

"Sure," I said, egging him on. "What have you got to lose?"

"Nothing," the kid said. "I haven't got anything to lose."

"I'd try it," I said.

"I might try it," the kid said. "I might try it tonight if the spot comes up."

I could see from the way he said it that he

was madder than he'd said. Maybe you think this is mean to steam a kid up like this, but I do some strange things.

"Take over," I said. "Don't let this guy ruin your career."

"I'll try it," the kid said. "Are you coming out to the park tonight?"

"I wouldn't miss it," I said. "This will be better than making out route sheets and sales orders."

It's not much ball park in this town—old wooden bleachers and an old wooden fence and about four hundred people in the stands. The first game wasn't much either, with the home club winning something like 8 to 1.

The kid didn't have any hard chances, but I could see he was a ballplayer, with a double and a couple of walks and a lot of speed.

The second game was different, though. The other club got a couple of runs, and then the home club picked up three runs in one; and they were in the top of the ninth with a 3–2 lead and two outs when the pitching began to fall apart, and they loaded the bases.

I was trying to wish the ball down to the kid, just to see what he'd do with it, when the batter drives one on one big bounce to the kid's right.

The kid was off for it when the ball started.

He made a backhand stab and grabbed it. He was deep now, and he turned in the air and fired. If it goes over the first baseman's head, it's two runs in and a panic—but it's the prettiest throw you'd want to see. It's right on a line, and the runner is out by a step, and it's the ball game.

I walked back to the hotel, thinking about the kid. I sat around the lobby until I saw him come in, and then I walked toward the elevator like I was going to my room, but so I'd meet him. And I could see he didn't want to talk.

"How about a Coke?" I said.

"No," he said. "Thanks, but I'm going to bed."

"Look," I said. "Forget it. You did the right thing. Have a Coke."

We were sitting in the taproom again. The kid wasn't saying anything.

"Why didn't you throw that ball away?" I said.

"I don't know," the kid said. "I had it in my mind before he hit it, but I couldn't."

"Why?"

"I don't know why."

"I know why," I said.

The kid didn't say anything. He just sat looking down.

"Do you know why you couldn't throw that ball away?" I said.

"No," the kid said.

"You couldn't throw that ball away," I said, "because you're going to be a major-league ballplayer someday."

The kid just looked at me. He had that same sore expression.

"Do you know why you're going to be a major-league ballplayer?" I said.

The kid was just looking down again, shaking his head. I never got more of a kick out of anything in my life.

"You're going to be a major-league ballplayer," I said, "because you couldn't throw that ball away, and because I'm not a hardware salesman, and my name's not Harry Franklin."

"What do you mean?" the kid said.

"I mean," I explained to him, "that I tried to needle you into throwing that ball away because I'm Eddie Brown."

Getting at Meaning

1. What clues in the story hint at Harry Franklin's real identity?

2. At the beginning of the story, why is Pete so frustrated? What is Mr. Franklin's advice?

3. Why does Eddie Brown test Pete? Does Pete pass the test? What is Brown's reaction to the result of the test?

4. Why doesn't Pete throw away the game? Support your opinion with passages from the story.

Developing Skills in Reading Literature

1. **Conflict.** As you know, conflict within a character is called internal conflict. What is Pete's internal conflict? What is the turning point, the point at which things change for Pete?

2. **Point of View.** Who is the main character in this story? Why do you think the writer has chosen to tell the story from Mr. Franklin's point of view?

3. **Theme.** The theme of a story, as you have learned, is the main idea or message brought out through the characters and their actions. In this story, what is the writer's message to his readers? What standards or values does the theme emphasize?

The Elk Tooth Dress   *Dorothy M. Johnson*

Joe Red Crane came over to talk about our going to the Indian Institute in Missoula.[1] It is a big gathering at the University, with meetings for several days, to talk about the problems of Indians; and have we got problems! Grandpa said that this year he would let the professors talk about the problems, and he would just as soon be in the big show in the University Field House after they got the problems all talked about.

Sometime, maybe, I will learn how to get around Grandma; but Grandpa still can't do it, and he has been married to her for thirty-five years. I am only sixteen years old. They are both old-fashioned, but Grandpa is not so stubborn.

Grandpa wanted to wear his own grandfather's feather war bonnet in the big show, but Joe Red Crane talked him out of it. That shows the difference between Grandpa and Grandma. Nobody ever talked her out of anything.

"That is absolutely right," said Grandpa.

"So you will dance at the Indian Institute in Missoula, maybe?"

"Now you put it that way, maybe I will," said Grandpa. "But I won't wear tail feathers or no mail-order war bonnet. I will just wear my beaded vest."

"You will also wear pants," Grandma said to him over her shoulder.

Grandpa said, "All the time I meant to wear pants. Women should stay out of serious conversations."

"There would be serious conversations if you went to Missoula with no pants," Grandma answered.

Then Mr. Red Crane got around to noticing me. I was doing my homework, and you can bet it is hard to memorize irregular French verbs when you are listening to a conversation that switches from English to Salish[2] and back.

"We got to have a nice display of art work for the exhibit," he said. "You going to bring something pretty, Natalie? I bet you are. Some nice beadwork."

"I don't like beadwork," I said. "It's old-fashioned. I don't think I will go anyway. Not unless I can get my hair cut short and have a permanent."

Grandma said to the wall, "Natalie will go, and she will not have a permanent. She will wear her hair in braids like she was meant to. She has not got her exhibit finished yet, but she will. It is a bag all covered with beads." Grandma switched to Salish and muttered, "She is lazy. Bad girl."

I am only kind of lazy and not very bad, but I did not argue, because getting a permanent is something we have not agreed about for two years or more.

Joe Red Crane saved his talk with Grandma till last, because it was going to be the toughest.

---

1. **Missoula:** a town in Montana.
2. **Salish** (sā'lish): a family of fifteen North American Indian languages of the northwest United States and southwest Canada, including Flathead, Natalie's tribe.

"And you will wear your fringed buckskin dress with the elk teeth all over it," he said to her with a big smile, "and you will be in the Grass Dance."

"I will not do any such thing," said Grandma. "I am going to wear my go-to-town clothes and sit in the audience and watch everybody and see whether my old man is wearing his pants. Natalie can wear my dress with the elk teeth if she wants to. I guess she won't want to, though, because she has all these modern ideas."

I almost jumped out of my chair. She had never let me wear that dress before. It is very old and valuable. If I asked her for it, she would have said, "No, you are careless; you would lose some of the elk teeth."

"That's all settled then," Mr. Red Crane said, getting up off the floor.

After he left, I went to work on Grandma, figuring that if I said no, she would say yes.

"I don't want to get my braids cut off and have a permanent," I said. "I have decided to wear my hair long even if you do have to work so hard brushing it."

"Good thing," she said, "because that is how it is going to be."

At school all the kids were talking about going to Missoula, and when I found out some more about the plans, I got pouty.

"I am not going to go," I told Grandma. "Mary MacTavish is going to be introduced as a princess because her great-grandfather was a chief and signed some old treaty. She would have flunked algebra if I had not helped with her homework. So now she is a princess. Mary MacTavish—some Indian!"

Grandma got a firm look on her face and said, "Just be proud you're a full-blood and never mind that princess stuff. But you will go."

Now I am glad I went, because it was a lovely time. It was the most wonderful time I can remember.

BEADWORKER. O. C. Seltzer. Thomas Gilcrease Institute, Tulsa, Oklahoma.

That was a big affair, that Indian Institute at the University Field House in Missoula. Grandpa even washed the station wagon. He spent so much time on it that Grandma got nervous and said she would rather ride in a car with mud on it than get there after everybody else had left. But we got there early.

We had the biggest bunch of people from our reservation because we only had to go a few miles. There were people from tribes all over Montana, strangers, handsome people in beautiful costumes. Second to us, the Blackfeet had the biggest bunch, and Grandma said, "Huh! The women wear rouge."

There were more languages being spoken than I had ever heard before—Indian languages, all different. Absolutely nobody said one word in French. Sometimes I wonder why I go to all the trouble with those irregular verbs. One good thing about Salish, nobody fusses about grammar. You just talk it.

It was a wonderful time, the gathering of all those dark, dignified people—my people, even if they were from other tribes with other languages. The whites came too, of course, lots of them, but they were just there to see us.

In the big crowd, we lost track of Grandpa.

"Now where is that Indian exhibit?" Grandma muttered, and I said, "I don't want to go see that."

"I should think you wouldn't," she answered, "but we are going to see it anyway."

It was embarrassing because I never did finish my beadwork exhibit, and Grandma had to. She fussed because she had to do it kind of sloppy so nobody would know it wasn't all mine. But after all, when a girl is a junior in high school and studying French, and she's in a lot of activities, how much time has she got for beadwork?

We found the exhibit. Grandma asked an Indian where it was. She wouldn't ask a white person because she wouldn't admit they might know something she didn't.

Mary MacTavish was hanging around the exhibit, because her entry for art work was a drawing of Marilyn Monroe that she copied out of a movie magazine. Mary MacTavish, that princess, stood around in her mail-order buckskin dress, batting her eyelashes; and I must admit she had two fellows from our football team and two others hanging around with her.

"Oh, hello, Natalie," she said very sweetly, for fear I wouldn't notice all those fellows; and I said, "Hi ya, princess, old kid."

Grandma said in a carrying voice, "We will not look at any drawings copied out of magazines. We will look at the real Indian art. Well, that bag you beaded looks pretty good, Natalie. They displayed it nice."

I kind of nudged my arm against her arm to tell her I was grateful that she didn't give away my guilty secret about not finishing

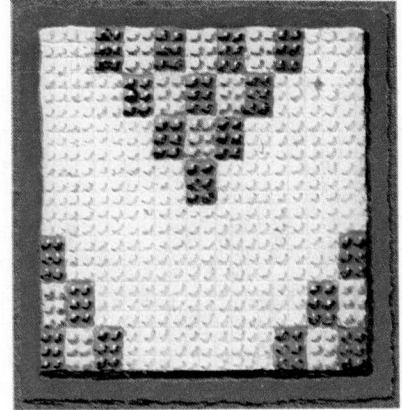

BEADWORKER (detail). O. C. Seltzer.
Thomas Gilcrease Institute, Tulsa, Oklahoma.

it myself, and she nudged back. When Grandma is for you, she is for you all the way, especially if somebody else is against you.

"Where did that old man of mine go?" she grumbled.

"He just came in," I said, "with a white woman," and Grandma said, "What!"

Grandpa was being very Noble Red Man. He is not very tall, but he can look awful noble. He was just looking past this white woman in a baggy tweed suit and not answering her, and she was getting more and more earnest, pointing at her camera and talking her idea of Indian English: "Me take picture, okay? You stand still, me take nice picture?"

I was so grateful to Grandma for being on my side that I walked over and rescued him from her, because she wouldn't lower herself by chasing after him.

I said to him in Salish, "Come on with me if you want to get away."

The white woman said, "Little girl, maybe you talk English—just tell him I want to take his picture."

So if she wanted to, why didn't she go ahead?

I murmured, "*Je ne parle pas l'anglais. Mon grandpère ne parle pas l'anglais.*"[3]

---

3. *Je ne parle pas l'anglais. Mon grandpère ne parle pas l'anglais* (zhǝ nǝ pärl pä läŋ glä' mōn grän per' nǝ pärl pä laŋ glä) *French:* I do not speak English. My grandfather does not speak English.

She shook her head and said, "Oh, dear. They all talk Indian," and walked away.

Then we three went to the Field House and got settled in the front row of the audience.

We looked around, and I saw the most beautiful thing I ever laid eyes on. He was tall and lean, in tight jeans and cowboy boots, and he had long hair. Long, thick, glossy braids, even if he was young like me—long hair like the old men, but ah, how pretty it looks on a young fellow!

He was as handsome as a calendar, with a sharp profile and his head held high. He wore a cowboy hat, sort of tipped back so it wouldn't hide the soft way his hair came down over his ears, because he was proud of his hair, and that was right.

Alongside him, all the boys I know look just plain stupid. My heart hurt. I kind of wanted to cry.

I said in a whisper, "Grandma, look."

"Look at what?" she asked. "All those strange Indians?"

Then I saw he was not by himself but in a group of five or six men, all older; but do you know, I hadn't noticed them before. They were Indians, but wearing business suits, and a couple of them had braids.

Grandma saw the young man then and said, "Ah." She said something to Grandpa and he looked and said, "Ah."

Then he got up and ambled over to these men halfway across the arena, and they all got acquainted and shook hands. The young long-hair didn't talk. He just stood there listening, the way a young man should in the presence of his betters; only generally they don't.

Grandma said, "They are Cheyennes," and I asked, "How can you tell from here?"

"Your grandpa just told me in sign talk," she answered. "If you'd keep your eyes open, you might learn something. The young fellow is going to be in the show." She squinted and added, "His name is something like water."

It just goes to show you how much good French does a girl when something really important comes up. I don't pay much attention to sign talk; it's old-fashioned. We used to use it in grade school when we wanted to make remarks about a new teacher.

"Oh, look at that mail-order princess," I said, shocked. "She is going right over to interrupt the men. She is going to get that Cheyenne boy for herself."

"I don't think she is," said Grandma. "Keep still and trust your grandpa. Sometimes he is a no-good, but in a pinch you can depend on him."

Mary was heading for the men, with two other girls, all giggling and wiggling. But Grandpa fixed her wagon. It was cute how he did it. He never saw them, but every time Mary moved a little to one side, he moved too, so his back was always toward her while he talked to the other men.

There was quite a crowd of Indians around there, making a quiet fuss over the long-hair boy. The old people approved because he was conservative, old-fashioned; and the boys hung around because he was twirling a rope, sort of playing with it; and the girls edged up because he was so cute. And I had to stay by Grandma because we are conservative.

Grandma said, "Never mind that phony Minnehaha,[4] making eyes. You make eyes at the ground. . . . Listen, I saw some other women from other reservations with elk teeth on their dresses, but not so many as on the dress you're wearing. Don't you worry."

She dug in the big bag she carried and brought out something. It was her little old short cape embroidered with porcupine quills, dyed in soft colors long ago. She hung it over my shoulders, and I felt warm and

---

4. **Minnehaha** (min′ ē hä′ hä): Indian girl, in reference to the girl Hiawatha married in Longfellow's poem.

cared for because I know she thought a lot of me and was on my side.

Even when I was a child, not many women were embroidering with porcupine quills; they used all beads because it was easier. This cape was very old, made by my grandmother. The buckskin was soft and gray, not dirty but not glaring white. Wearing it, I felt like a queen and was not very jealous of Princess MacTavish.

The men and boys from our reservation were buckling on the bells they wear on their legs for dancing, and you couldn't hear yourself think. They are big, round bells with something noisy inside. And Grandpa had gone over to the middle and started beating a drum. The only thing he doesn't like about a show is that he can't beat a drum and dance at the same time.

Then a man said, "Woof, woof, testing," into the public-address system, and asked everybody to take his seat because the show was going to begin. The young long-hair walked past us with his friends, but he did not look our way at all.

Grandma said, "Natalie, stop looking at him all the time."

"What does he wear long hair for if he doesn't want to be looked at?" I answered.

"I don't know what he wants," said Grandma, "but I want you to stop looking. He will think you are bold."

"He doesn't know I'm alive," I moaned; and she said with a satisfied chuckle, "Oh, yes, he does. What do you think your grandpa went over there for? To talk about the hay crop, maybe?"

I was so happy I even stopped staring.

Grandma said, "Doesn't Mary MacTavish look silly with her short hair in that Indian dress from mail order? But you look just right."

"I am a bad girl and lazy," I said. "You had to finish my beadwork."

"Oh, not so bad," she answered, always arguing.

Somebody on the public-address system made a long speech about the significance of all this and named all the tribes that were represented, and then he said the Flatheads would please take their places. So I left Grandma and went drifting out to the arena with the rest of our people and stood with the other girls in the back.

The men sat down in chairs in a long row. The chairs were turned backward, because if a man wears tail feathers he has to straddle when he sits down. But Grandpa turned his chair around and leaned back and was comfortable, because he wouldn't be caught dead in those mail-order tail feathers. He had a big silver ornament on each braid, but he wasn't dressed up except for a beaded vest. He wore his pants all right, blue jeans. He wore his silver-rimmed glasses, too, and Grandma didn't like that; she says it is too modern. But he says, "I am nearsighted, and I wear glasses. You want me to fall over something and break my neck, maybe?"

Mary MacTavish said to me, "Hi, kid. It's too bad they won't let me present you to the audience. Alice and Elizabeth are my maids-in-waiting, you know. I am going to present them to the audience. But I can't do a thing for you, because their ancestors signed the same treaty mine did, but your ancestors wouldn't sign."

"My ancestors never gave the country away," I said. "They wanted to hang onto it."

"What are you looking at the ground for?" she asked. "Lost something?"

"Indian girls are supposed to be modest," I said. "Didn't anybody ever tell you? I am a full-blood, so I am going to be modest while I've got this elk tooth dress on and this old and valuable embroidered cape all covered with dyed porcupine quills."

"I guess you're just jealous because I'm not

going to present you too," Mary MacTavish said.

"I guess you better be kind of polite," I I said, "if you don't want to flunk French."

Then we had to quit talking, because Mr. Red Crane started to talk on the public-address system, introducing our people.

There were a couple of dances for the men, good and noisy, with all the drumming and all those bells on their legs clanging with every step, and I was in the Grass Dance with Mary and the rest of them.

Mr. Red Crane introduced Princess Mary MacTavish, and she walked forward with her beaded moccasins on her feet and her permanent on her head, looking so modest it would kill you, making eyes at the ground.

"Princess Mary will now present her maids-in-waiting," Mr. Red Crane said, and everybody waited, but she didn't. She was being so modest, she just stood there. So Alice had to walk out by herself, and so did Elizabeth.

Then *they* just stood there, the modest Indian maidens, until the announcer told them twice they could go sit down now.

Then he said. "One of the girls from the Flathead Reservation is wearing a very rare costume, very old, that I am sure you will want to see. Natalie Root Digger, will you please walk forward so the audience can see you?"

Well, I just about died. I went forward about three steps and stood there with my eyes down, feeling those thousands of people staring. He told about the old dress with the elk teeth on it and the precious cape embroidered with porcupine quills, and the people clapped. I went back without anybody telling me.

I never took my eyes off the ground, but I saw that long-hair Cheyenne in the front row sitting by Grandma. She looked good. She wore her black dress with red figures in it, and her best purple silk handkerchief

draped around her head in folds, with her long, dark braids looped to hang down under it.

Our people did more dances, and Grandpa would sneak out in front of the rest and kind of clown with his dancing. Everytime he did that, the audience would laugh and clap. Then we went out of the arena and finally I got over to where Grandma was. She said in Salish, "Sit down. Lots of room," and the long-hair started to get up out of the way. But Grandma said in English, "Stay there. She's little; she won't crowd you."

He said, "She sure won't," and we sat close because we had to, both looking at the ground but seeing each other just the same. He had the most wonderful voice, deep and soft and bashful. The announcer said now the Blackfeet would come in and perform, and Grandma said, "Huh!"

All the other Indians, when they had gone into the arena, had just sort of drifted in. But those Blackfeet came marching to a drum, very showy, and their leader gave them signals with an eagle wing fan. Real fancy.

The long-hair boy said, "Tourist stuff," and Grandma looked at him with approval.

They did some dances, and they were so popular with the silly crowd of white people that they kept right on doing dances. The Cheyenne boy made a thoughtful sound and got up and walked across the arena toward Grandpa and the rest of our Flathead men. In a minute, Grandpa and the others from our reservation started walking from one end of the arena toward the other.

You should have heard it. They didn't do anything but just walk and mind their own business, but when two dozen Indians walk from one place to another with strings of big bells on their legs, not keeping step—well. The racket was so loud, with the clanging of the bells drowning out the Blackfeet drums, that the audience forgot about the Blackfeet dancing, so smart and sassy. People got kind of fidgety and started looking at their programs, and when they clapped for the Blackfeet, Grandma and I clapped for the Flatheads.

Grandma said, "Well, I guess we won *that* battle."

When the young long-hair came back, drifting, Grandma moved over so he would sit between us.

"What's your name, Cheyenne?" she asked.

"George Standing in the Water," he answered.

"You're a smart boy," Grandma said, "and I would like to meet your folks sometime."

He didn't say anything, but he blushed. A blush under a bronze skin is pretty.

"Your folks are old-fashioned?" Grandma asked him, and he knew it was a compliment, and nodded.

WOLF ON THE HILL (HIGH WOLF), TRIBAL CHIEF, 1834. *George Catlin.*
National Museum of American Art (Formerly National Collection of Fine Arts),
Smithsonian Institution. Gift of Mrs. Sarah Harrison.

"My brother fasted in the Sun Dance last year," he said. "Maybe I will someday."

We don't do the Sun Dance—we have our own customs—but I knew a little about that, and I shivered. They starve and don't drink any water for four days, the few men who dare to dance the Sun Dance; then they dance until they faint sometimes.

"Maybe we'll come to your reservation sometime," Grandma purred.

"I wouldn't want to see the Sun Dance if anybody I knew was in it," I said, feeling terrible.

"My brother's girl, she was kind of proud of him," George said. So then I thought I could watch him if the time came, and I would be proud too.

The announcer said on the public-address system, "A young Cheyenne from the Tongue River Reservation will demonstrate his skill in roping. I present George Standing in the Water, of the Northern Cheyenne."

George went out in the arena, not very far, not looking up at the audience, but as if he were there all by himself with nobody around. It was all quiet, no drumming. He twirled his rope in little circles and big circles. He danced into the spinning rope circle and danced out of it again. The rope was like a live thing that did just what he wanted it to do, and his hands hardly moved, but the rope spun its circle and rippled and flashed like water.

People were taking pictures—flash, flash went the cameras, taking pictures of the fine long-hair. Grandpa's white-woman friend was jumping around in her baggy tweed suit, putting new flash bulbs in her camera, and taking pictures and talking to herself.

It was as if George were there all alone, in the big Field House, dreaming with the spinning rope. When he stopped, there was nothing dramatic about the stopping. He didn't bow to the audience like some performers do. Why should he bow? He didn't owe them anything. He just gathered up his rope when he was through, while the audience clapped and hollered, and he walked over to sit by us again.

I thought, I wish I had a camera. I wish I could have a picture of George Standing in the Water to keep forever.

Somebody made another long speech about the significance of all this, and some other tribes danced, and then the whole show was over. Grandpa drifted over to us, and that white woman in the tweed suit made a dive at him.

"Well, I'll take care of *this*," said Grandma, and marched toward them like an army with banners.

"You going home tonight?" George asked, looking at the ground.

I said, "Yes. To Arlee." And maybe I will never see you again, I thought. That will be worse than if I never had known you were alive. "Where you going?"

"Staying at a motel with my friends. Long drive to Tongue River. We'll start early in the morning. Listen, where would a fellow write you a letter if he wanted to, maybe? Just Arlee?"

"That's right. Natalie Root Digger, Arlee, Montana." Then I got really bold. "You know, we dig bitterroot around Missoula in the spring, pretty soon. We're old-fashioned. We don't mind if our friends come dig bitterroot with us. Or maybe you have to go to school."

"This year I have to go to school. I am on the track team. Maybe next year. If your folks come to our rodeo. I ride bucking horses."

"Maybe Grandma and Grandpa would like to go to your rodeo," I answered. "I guess they would probably take me along."

We never looked at each other all that time, but I saw his black, soft, shining braids; and he saw my braids, and the buckskin dress trimmed with elk teeth and the little cape with the faded-color porcupine quill embroidery.

"Well, so long," he said.

I said. "Okay. See you around."

He walked away, so lithe and slim, and my heart wanted to cry.

My folks came back, their faces straight, but I could tell they were laughing inside about something. I didn't feel like laughing.

"Well, that white woman got your grandpa's picture," Grandma said. "It's hard talking this Injun English she likes, but I got the idea across that she could take his picture if she would send me a print; also, she has to send me some other pictures that are on the same roll of film."

"That's nice," I said with my heart jumpnig. Because she had taken pictures of George while he was spinning the rope.

"Where'd that Cheyenne go?" Grandma asked.

"He had to catch up with his friends. Grandma, he asked us to their rodeo, and I asked him to help us dig bitterroot, and is it all right? If you say it's wrong and I'm not a nice, modest girl, I'll just die!"

"It is all right and you are a good girl," she answered. "I think we will maybe go to the Cheyennes' rodeo when the time comes."

When my letter comes from the Tongue River Reservation, it will have his return address on it, I guess. But I wouldn't ask him for it, because it is a good thing to be old-fashioned, even for a girl who is a junior in high school and learning French.

Getting at Meaning

1. Describe Natalie's attitude toward her grandparents at the beginning of the story. How does Natalie try to make her grandmother change her views? Does Natalie succeed?

2. Why is Natalie happy to be wearing the elk tooth dress?

3. Why doesn't Natalie finish her beadwork exhibit? Why, then, does her grandmother praise the beadwork?

4. Contrast Natalie and Mary MacTavish. What does each girl's outfit say about her? How are the ways they appear in front of the crowd different? Cite two other examples that highlight their differences.

5. What is so humorous about the woman who tries to take a picture of Natalie's grandfather? How do the Indians feel about this kind of white woman?

6. Natalie says, "When Grandma is for you, she is for you all the way, especially if somebody else is against you." How does Grandma prove that she is "for" Natalie? Does Grandma really believe that Natalie is "lazy" and "bad"? Give reasons to support your answer.

7. How do Natalie and George show their interest in each other? What things about George impress Natalie the most?

Developing Skills in Reading Literature

1. **Character.** Natalie, the main character, changes a great deal because of her experience at the show. Find passages at the beginning of the story that illustrate Natalie's preference for modern ways. Write the page and paragraph number of each passage. Find the point at which Natalie begins to understand the importance of the old ways. Note the number of the page on which the change becomes apparent. At the end of the story, several statements show that Natalie has changed her views. Record the location of these statements.

2. **First-Person Narration.** This story, like "Everybody Knows Tobie," is told through first-person narration. Natalie tells the story in her own words. Why do you think the writer chose Natalie as the narrator?

3. **Symbol.** The elk tooth dress symbolizes something important in Natalie's mind. What does the dress represent to Natalie? How does wearing the dress make her feel?

4. **Theme.** How does the writer of this story view the importance of Indian traditions and customs? How does Natalie exemplify the writer's views? Could the writer be making a statement about the customs and traditions of other groups as well?

Developing Vocabulary

Word Origins. Some words came into American English from the languages of American Indian tribes. Examples of these words include *chipmunk, hickory, hominy, mackinaw, moccasin, moss, opossum, pecan, persimmon, raccoon, skunk, squash, succotash,* and *terrapin.* How might the words have come into the English language?

Developing Writing Skills

Combining Description and Exposition. Write a paragraph about Natalie's grandmother. Start with a general statement, which can be a sentence from the story or a sentence of your own. Then support the statement with specific examples and incidents from the story.

Unit Review   *The Self and Others*

The Theme

1. Choose one story from the unit. Does the main character in the selection seem believable? Why or why not? What insights about yourself did you gain from the story?

2. Mickey Mantle comes from a poor family, while Eli in "The Lie" comes from a wealthy one. What advantages does Eli have over young Mickey Mantle? How is Mickey Mantle better off than Eli?

3. How are the subjects of "Moss-Gathering" and "The Fish" similar? What change in attitude takes place in the speaker of each poem?

4. Which selections in this unit illustrate the importance of family members in shaping a person's ideas? Which selections show the importance of friends?

5. What is the message presented in the poem "Dreams"? How does this message apply to each of these characters?

T.J.   Dr. Remenzel
Squeaky   Pete

Which characters realize their dreams? Which do not?

Reading Literature

1. What is the climax, or turning point, in each of these stories?
"Charles"
"Antaeus"
"Raymond's Run"

2. Which selections in this unit involve considerable internal conflict? Which selections center more on external conflict?

3. Identify at least two images in each of the following poems. Then explain how the images reinforce the theme of the poem.
"Ride a Wild Horse"   "Lineage"
"Young"   "The Way It Is"

4. Which selections in this unit provide examples of first-person narration? Which are examples of third-person narration?

Writing

1. Review the difference between simile and metaphor. Then write a poem on any subject that employs both similes and metaphors. Attempt to make your comparisons striking and vivid.

2. Choose a conflict from your own experiences; for example, an argument with a relative or friend, a problem at school, or a major decision. Describe clearly the opposing forces. Then tell what happened, building up to a turning point. Finally, explain how the conflict was resolved.

DINING ROOM ON THE GARDEN, 1934. *Pierre Bonnard.*
The Solomon R. Guggenheim Museum, New York.

Unit 2

The Short Story

THE GULFSTREAM, 1889. *Winslow Homer.*
Courtesy of The Art Institute of Chicago.

Introduction to the Unit

Science fiction, romance, mystery, adventure, fantasy, humor—all are types of the literature known as fiction. Although fiction is the product of a writer's imagination, the people, places, and events in fiction often are related to the real world. A "made-up" story, therefore, can provide important insights into actual life situations.

The short story is one type of fiction. It is a type of fiction that was developed largely in the United States, beginning in the nineteenth century. A short story usually can be read in one sitting and generally is limited to one main action or event. A short story does not have the large number of characters and the wealth of detail frequently found in longer works of fiction.

This unit focuses on four elements of the short story: setting, character, plot, and theme. Setting refers to when and where the action of a story takes place. A story may be set in the future, in the past, or in the present, and in any location imaginable. The characters are the people or animals who take part in the action. Usually the characters involve a reader in a story, for the reader becomes interested in finding out what the characters think and feel, what they will do, and what will happen to them. The plot is the plan of action, the arrangement of events in a story. The theme is the central message of a story, conveyed through the setting, characters, and plot.

Just as a basketball player combines the skills of shooting, passing, and dribbling, so does a writer interweave the elements of setting, character, plot, and theme. The particular emphasis, however, varies from story to story. In one story in this unit, a brief encounter between a troubled boy and a kindly woman is the basis for the action. In another story, a stranger on a train tells an unconventional children's tale. In a third story, the sea at night provides much of the dramatic tension.

As you read the short stories in the unit, be aware of the writers' techniques, pay close attention to details, and, above all, enjoy yourself.

Setting

LA SEINE A VERNON, 1930. *Pierre Bonnard.*
Courtesy of The Art Institute of Chicago.

The Sea Devil   *Arthur Gordon*

The man came out of the house and stood quite still, listening. Behind him, the lights glowed in the cheerful room, the books were neat and orderly in their cases, the radio talked importantly to itself. In front of him, the bay stretched dark and silent, one of the countless lagoons that border the coast where Florida thrusts its great green thumb deep into the tropics.

It was late in September. The night was breathless; summer's dead hand still lay heavy on the land. The man moved forward six paces and stood on the sea wall. He dropped his cigarette and noted where the tiny spark hissed and went out. The tide was beginning to ebb.

Somewhere out in the blackness a mullet jumped, and fell back with a sullen splash. Heavy with roe, they were jumping less often now. They would not take a hook, but a practiced eye could see the swirls they made in the glassy water. In the dark of the moon, a skilled man with a cast net might take half a dozen in an hour's work. And a big mullet makes a meal for a family.

The man turned abruptly and went into the garage, where his cast net hung. He was in his late twenties, wide-shouldered and strong. He did not have to fish for a living, or even for food. He was a man who worked with his head, not with his hands. But he liked to go casting alone at night.

He liked the loneliness and the labor of it. He liked the clean taste of salt when he gripped the edge of the net with his teeth as a cast netter must. He liked the arching flight of sixteen pounds of lead and linen against the starlight, and the weltering crash of the net into the unsuspecting water. He liked the harsh tug of the retrieving rope around his wrist, and the way the net came alive when the cast was true, and the thud of captured fish on the floor boards of the skiff.

He liked all that because he found in it a reality that seemed to be missing from his twentieth-century job and from his daily life. He liked being the hunter, skilled and solitary and elemental. There was no conscious cruelty in the way he felt. It was the way things had been in the beginning.

The man lifted the net down carefully and lowered it into a bucket. He put a paddle beside the bucket. Then he went into the house. When he came out, he was wearing swimming trunks and a pair of old tennis shoes. Nothing else.

The skiff, flat-bottomed, was moored off the sea wall. He would not go far, he told himself. Just to the tumbledown dock half a mile away. Mullet had a way of feeding around old pilings after dark. If he moved quietly, he might pick up two or three in one cast close to the dock. And maybe a couple of others on the way down or back.

He shoved off and stood motionless for a moment, letting his eyes grow accustomed to the dark. Somewhere out in the channel, a porpoise blew with a sound like steam escaping. The man smiled a little; porpoises were his friends. Once, fishing in the Gulf, he had seen the charter-boat captain reach overside and gaff a baby porpoise through the sinewy part of the tail. He had hoisted it aboard, had dropped it into the bait well, where it thrashed around, puzzled and un-happy. And the mother had swum alongside the boat and under the boat and around the boat, nudging the stout planking with her back, slapping it with her tail, until the man felt sorry for her and made the captain let the baby porpoise go.

He took the net from the bucket, slipped the noose in the retrieving rope over his wrist, pulled the slipknot tight. It was an old net, but still serviceable; he had rewoven the rents made by underwater snags. He coiled the thirty-foot rope carefully, making sure there were no kinks. A tangled rope, he knew, would spoil any cast.

The basic design of the net had not changed in three thousand years. It was a mesh circle with a diameter of fourteen feet. It measured close to fifteen yards around the circumference and could, if thrown perfectly, blanket a hundred and fifty square feet of sea water. In the center of this radial trap was a small iron collar where the retrieving rope met the twenty-three separate drawstrings leading to the outer rim of the net. Along this rim, spaced an inch and a half apart, were the heavy lead sinkers.

The man raised the iron collar until it was a foot above his head. The net hung soft and pliant and deadly. He shook it gently, making sure that the drawstrings were not tangled, that the sinkers were hanging true. Then he eased it down and picked up the paddle.

The night was black as a witch's cat; the stars looked fuzzy and dim. Down to the southward, the lights of a causeway made a yellow necklace across the sky. To the man's left were the tangled roots of a mangrove swamp; to his right, the open waters of the bay. Most of it was fairly shallow, but there were channels eight feet deep. The man could not see the old dock, but he knew where it was. He pulled the paddle quietly through the water, and the phosphorescence glowed and died.

For five minutes he paddled. Then, twenty feet ahead of the skiff, a mullet jumped. A big fish, close to three pounds. For a moment it hung in the still air, gleaming dully. Then it vanished. But the ripples marked the spot, and where there was one there were often others.

The man stood up quickly. He picked up the coiled rope, and with the same hand grasped the net at a point four feet below the iron collar. He raised the skirt to his mouth, gripped it strongly with his teeth. He slid his free hand as far as it would go down the circumference of the net so that he had three points of contact with the mass of cordage and metal. He made sure his feet were planted solidly. Then he waited, feeling the tension that is older than the human race, the fierce exhilaration of the hunter at the moment of ambush, the atavistic desire to capture and kill and ultimately consume.

A mullet swirled, ahead and to the left. The man swung the heavy net back, twisting his body and bending his knees so as to get more upward thrust. He shot it forward, letting go simultaneously with rope hand and with teeth, holding a fraction of a second longer with the other hand so as to give the net the necessary spin, impart the centrifugal force that would make it flare into a circle. The skiff ducked sideways, but he kept his balance. The net fell with a splash.

The man waited for five seconds. Then he began to retrieve it, pulling in a series of sharp jerks so that the drawstrings would gather the net inward, like a giant fist closing on this segment of the teeming sea. He felt the net quiver, and knew it was not empty. He swung it, dripping, over the gunwale, saw the broad silver side of the mullet quivering, saw too the gleam of a smaller fish. He looked closely to make sure no sting ray was hidden in the mesh, then raised the iron collar and shook the net out. The mullet fell with a thud and flapped wildly. The other victim was an angel fish, beautifully marked, but too small to keep. The man picked it up gently and dropped it overboard. He coiled the rope, took up the paddle. He would cast no more until he came to the dock.

The skiff moved on. At last, ten feet apart, a pair of stakes rose up gauntly out of the night. Barnacle encrusted, they once had marked the approach from the main channel. The man guided the skiff between them, then put the paddle down softly. He stood up, reached for the net, tightened the noose around his wrist. From here he could drift down upon the dock. He could see it now, a ruined skeleton in the starshine. Beyond it a mullet jumped and fell back with a flat, liquid sound. The man raised the edge of the net, put it between his teeth. He would not cast at a single swirl, he decided; he would wait until he saw two or three close together. The skiff was barely moving. He felt his muscles tense themselves, awaiting the signal from the brain.

Behind him in the channel he heard the porpoise blow again, nearer now. He frowned in the darkness. If the porpoise chose to fish this area, the mullet would scatter and vanish. There was no time to lose.

A school of sardines surfaced suddenly, skittering along like drops of mercury. Something, perhaps the shadow of the skiff, had frightened them. The old dock loomed very close. A mullet broke water just too far away; then another, nearer. The man marked the spreading ripples and decided to wait no longer.

He swung back the net, heavier now that it was wet. He had to turn his head, but out of the corner of his eye he saw two swirls in the black water just off the starboard bow. They were about eight feet apart, and they had the sluggish, oily look that marks the presence of something big just below the surface. His conscious mind had no time to function, but instinct told him that the net was wide enough to cover both swirls if he could alter the direction of his cast. He could not halt the swing, but he shifted his feet slightly and made the cast off balance. He saw the net shoot forward, flare into an oval, and drop just where he wanted it.

Then the sea exploded in his face. In a frenzy of spray, a great horned thing shot like a huge bat out of the water. The man saw the mesh of his net etched against the mottled blackness of its body and he knew, in the split second in which thought was still possible, that those twin swirls had been made not by two mullet, but by the wing tips of the giant ray of the Gulf Coast, *Manta birostris*, also known as clam cracker, devil ray, sea devil.

The man gave a hoarse cry. He tried to claw the slipknot off his wrist, but there was no time. The quarter-inch line snapped taut. He shot over the side of the skiff as if he had roped a runaway locomotive. He hit the water head first and seemed to bounce once. He plowed a blinding furrow for perhaps ten yards. Then the line went slack as the sea devil jumped again. It was not the full-grown manta of the deep Gulf, but it was close to nine feet from tip to tip. It weighed over a thousand pounds. Up into the air it went, pearl-colored underbelly gleaming as it twisted in a frantic effort to dislodge the clinging thing that had fallen upon it. Up into the starlight, a monstrous survival from the dawn of time.

The water was less than four feet deep. Sobbing and choking, the man struggled for a foothold on the slimy bottom. Sucking in great gulps of air, he fought to free himself from the rope. But the slipknot was jammed deep into his wrist; he might as well have tried to loosen a circle of steel.

The ray came down with a thunderous splash and drove forward again. The flexible net followed every movement, impeding it hardly at all. The man weighed a hundred and seventy-five pounds. He was braced for the shock, and he had the desperate strength that comes from looking into the blank eyes of death. It was useless. His arm straightened out with a jerk that seemed to dislocate his shoulder. His feet shot out from under him. His head went under again. Now at last he knew how the fish must feel when the line tightens and drags him toward the alien element that is his doom. Now he knew.

Desperately he dug the fingers of his free hand into the ooze, felt them dredge a futile channel through broken shells and the ribbonlike sea grasses. He tried to raise his head, but could not get it clear. Torrents of spray choked him as the ray plunged toward deep water.

His eyes were of no use to him in the foam-streaked blackness. He closed them tight, and at once an insane sequence of pictures flashed through his mind. He saw his wife sitting in their living room, reading, waiting calmly for his return. He saw the mullet he had just caught, gasping its life away on the floorboards of the skiff. He saw the cigarette he had flung from the sea wall touch the water and expire with a tiny hiss. He saw all these things and many others simultaneously in his mind as his body fought silently and tenaciously for its existence. His hand touched something hard and closed on it in a death grip, but it was only the sharp-edged helmet of a horseshoe crab; and after an instant he let it go.

He had been under water perhaps fifteen seconds now, and something in his brain told him quite calmly that he could last another forty or fifty. Then the red flashes behind his eyes would merge into darkness, and the water would pour into his lungs in one sharp, painful shock, and he would be finished.

This thought spurred him to a desperate effort. He reached up and caught his pinioned wrist with his free hand. He doubled up his knees to create more drag. He thrashed his body madly, like a fighting fish, from side to side. This did not disturb the ray; but now one of the great wings tore through the mesh, and the net slipped lower over the fins projecting like horns from below the nightmare head, and the sea devil jumped again.

And once more the man was able to get his feet on the bottom and his head above water, and he saw ahead of him the pair of ancient stakes that marked the approach to the channel. He knew that if he was dragged much beyond those stakes he would be in eight feet of water, and the ray would go down to hug the bottom as rays always do, and then no power on earth could save him. So in the moment of respite that was granted him, he flung himself toward them.

For a moment he thought his captor yielded a bit. Then the ray moved off again, but more slowly now; and for a few yards the man was able to keep his feet on the bottom. Twice he hurled himself back against the rope with all his strength, hoping that something would break. But nothing broke. The mesh of the net was ripped and torn, but the draw lines were strong; and the stout perimeter cord threaded through the sinkers was even stronger.

The man could feel nothing now in his trapped hand; it was numb; but the ray could feel the powerful lunges of the unknown thing that was trying to restrain it. It drove its great wings against the unyielding water and forged ahead, dragging the man and pushing a sullen wave in front of it.

The man had swung as far as he could toward the stakes. He plunged toward one and missed it by inches. His feet slipped and he went down on his knees. Then the ray swerved sharply and the second stake came right at him. He reached out with his free hand and caught it.

He caught it just above the surface, six or eight inches below high-water mark. He felt the razor-sharp barnacles bite into his hand, collapse under the pressure, drive their tiny slime-covered shell splinters deep into his flesh. He felt the pain, and he welcomed it; and he made his fingers into an iron claw that would hold until the tendons were severed or the skin was shredded from the bone. The ray felt the pressure increase with a jerk that stopped it dead in the water. For a moment all was still as the tremendous forces came into equilibrium.

Then the net slipped again, and the perimeter cord came down over the sea devil's eyes, blinding it momentarily. The great ray settled to the bottom and braced its wings against the mud and hurled itself forward and upward.

The stake was only a four-by-four of creosoted pine, and it was old. Ten thousand tides had swirled around it. Worms had bored; parasites had clung. Under the crust of barnacles it still had some heart left, but not enough. The man's grip was five feet above the floor of the bay; the leverage was too great. The stake snapped off at its base.

The ray lunged upward, dragging the man and the useless timber. The man had his lungs full of air, but when the stake snapped he thought of expelling the air and inhaling the water so as to have it finished quickly. He thought of this, but he did not do it. And then, just at the channel's edge, the ray met the porpoise, coming in.

The porpoise had fed well this night and was in no hurry, but it was a methodical creature; and it intended to make a sweep around the old dock before the tide dropped too low. It had no quarrel with any ray, but it feared no fish in the sea; and when the great black shadow came rushing blindly and unavoidably, it rolled fast and struck once with its massive horizontal tail.

The blow descended on the ray's flat body

with a sound like a pistol shot. It would have broken a buffalo's back, and even the sea devil was half stunned. It veered wildly and turned back toward shallow water. It passed within ten feet of the man, face down in the water. It slowed and almost stopped, wing tips moving faintly, gathering strength for another rush.

The man had heard the tremendous slap of the great mammal's tail and the snorting gasp as it plunged away. He felt the line go slack again, and he raised his dripping face, and he reached for the bottom with his feet. He found it, but now the water was up to his neck. He plucked at the noose once more with his lacerated hand, but there was no strength in his fingers. He felt the tension come back into the line as the ray began to move again, and for half a second he was tempted to throw himself backward and fight as he had been doing, pitting his strength against the vastly superior strength of the brute.

But the acceptance of imminent death had done something to his brain. It had driven out the fear, and with the fear had gone the panic. He could think now, and he knew with absolute certainty that if he was to make any use of this last chance that had been given him, it would have to be based on the one faculty that had carried man to his pre-eminence above all beasts, the faculty of reason. Only by using his brain could he possibly survive, and he called on his brain for a solution. His brain responded. It offered him one.

He did not know whether his body still had the strength to carry out the brain's commands, but he began to swim forward, toward the ray that was still moving hesitantly away from the channel. He swam forward, feeling the rope go slack as he gained on the creature.

Ahead of him he saw the one remaining stake. He made himself swim faster until he was parallel with the ray, and the rope trailed behind both of them in a deep U. He swam with a surge of desperate energy that came from nowhere, so that he was slightly in the lead as they came to the stake. He passed on one side of it; the ray was on the other.

Then the man took one last deep breath and went down under the black water until he was sitting on the bottom of the bay. He put one foot over the line so that it passed under his bent knee. He drove both his heels into the mud and clutched the slimy grass with his bleeding hand. He waited for the tension to come again.

The ray passed on the other side of the stake, moving faster now. The rope grew taut again, and it began to drag the man back toward the stake. He held his prisoned wrist close to the bottom, under his knee, and he prayed that the stake would not break. He felt the rope vibrate as the barnacles bit into it. He did not know whether the rope would crush the barnacles, or whether the barnacles would cut the rope. All he knew was that in five seconds or less he would be dragged into the stake and cut to ribbons if he tried to hold on; or drowned if he didn't.

He felt himself sliding slowly, and then faster, and suddenly the ray made a great leap forward, and the rope burned around the base of the stake, and the man's foot hit it hard. He kicked himself backward with his remaining strength, and the rope parted, and he was free.

He came slowly to the surface. Thirty feet away the sea devil made one tremendous leap and disappeared into the darkness. The man raised his wrist and looked at the frayed length of rope dangling from it. Twenty inches, perhaps. He lifted his other hand and felt the hot blood start instantly, but he didn't care. He put this hand on the stake above the barnacles and held on to the good, rough, honest wood. He heard a strange noise, and realized that it was himself, sobbing.

High above, there was a droning sound.

Looking up, he saw the nightly plane from New Orleans inbound from Tampa. Calm and serene, it sailed, symbol of man's proud mastery over nature. Its lights winked red and green for a moment; then it was gone.

Slowly, painfully, the man began to move through the placid water. He came to the skiff at last and climbed into it. The mullet, still alive, slapped convulsively with its tail. The man reached down with his torn hand, picked up the mullet, let it go.

He began to work on the slipknot doggedly with his teeth. His mind was almost a blank, but not quite. He knew one thing. He knew he would do no more casting alone at night. Not in the dark of the moon. No, not he.

Getting at Meaning

1. Why will the fisherman "do no more casting alone at night"?

2. Why does the man fish? Why does he especially like night fishing?

3. How does the man try to escape from the sea devil? What finally makes his escape possible?

4. What does the man do when he returns to the boat? Why?

Developing Skills in Reading Literature

1. **Setting.** Setting refers to both where and when a story takes place. How does the night-time setting of this story make it more exciting? How does the description of the sea and the night make the story seem real? What elements of the setting can you picture clearly? Locate passages that describe these elements.

2. **Theme.** What does the fisherman learn from his experience? Why does the writer compare him to "a fighting fish"? As the fisherman is being dragged through the black water, he recalls the "mullet . . . gasping away its life on the floorboards" and the cigarette expiring "with a tiny hiss" as it hit the water. How are these recollections significant? What does the writer want the reader to realize about human beings and life?

Developing Vocabulary

Getting Word Meaning from Context. The context, or the sentence and paragraph in which a word appears, often provides clues to its meaning. For example, the third paragraph of this story introduces the word *mullet* in the first sentence: "Somewhere out in the blackness a mullet jumped, and fell back with a sudden splash." The rest of the paragraph talks about hooks, fishermen's nets, and a mullet making a meal for a family. Therefore, it is easy for the reader to guess that a mullet is a type of fish.

Using the context provided in the sentences below, determine the meanings of the italicized words.

1. He *hoisted* the baby porpoise from the water and dropped it into the boat.

2. He liked the harsh tug of the retrieving rope around his wrist, the way the net came alive when the cast was true, and the thud of captured fish on the floor boards of the *skiff*.

3. As he was being pulled by the ray, he plowed a blinding *furrow* for perhaps ten yards.

4. The man felt that he would live only a little longer. But the acceptance of *imminent* death did something to his brain.

Developing Writing Skills

Describing a Place. Describe a place in nature that you know well. Try to bring out your feelings for the place by the way you describe it. Be sure that you tell not only how the place looks but also how it tastes, feels, smells and/or sounds.

Happy Birthday
Toni Cade Bambara

Ollie spent the whole morning waiting. First she tried shaking Granddaddy Larkins, who just wouldn't wake up. She thought he was just playing, but he was out. His teeth weren't even in the glass, and there was a bottle on the bedstand. He'd be asleep for days. Then she waited on the cellar steps for Chalky, the building superintendent, to get through hauling garbage and come talk. But he was too busy. And then Ollie sat on the stairs waiting for Wilma. But it was Saturday and Wilma'd be holed up somewhere stuffing herself with potato chips and crunching down on jaw breakers, too greedy to cool it and eat 'em slow. Wilma'd come by tomorrow, though, and lie her behind off. "I went to Bear Mountain yesterday on a big boat with my brother Chestnut and his wife," she'd say, "and that's why I didn't come by for you cause we left so early in the morning that my mother even had to get me up when it was still dark out and we had a great time and I shot bows and arrows when we got there, and do you like my new dress?" Wilma always had some jive tale and always in one breath.

Ollie tried to figure out why she was even friends with Wilma. Wilma was going to grow up to be a lady and marry a doctor and live in New York, Wilma's mother said. But Ollie, poor orphan, was going to grow up and marry a drinking man if she didn't get killed first, Wilma's mother said. Ollie never told Granddaddy Larkins what Wilma's mother was all the time saying. She just hated her in private.

Ollie spent the early afternoon sitting on the rail in front of The Chicken Shack Restaurant, watching the cooks sling the wire baskets of chicken in and out of the frying fat. They were too sweaty and tired to tell her to move from in front. "Ruining the business," the owner used to fuss. Later she stood between the laundry and shoe store, watching some men pitch pennies against the building. She waited for a while, squeezing a rubber ball in her hand. If I can just get the wall for a minute, she thought, maybe somebody'll come along and we'll have us a good game of handball. But the men went right on pitching while other ones were waiting their turn. They'd be there for hours, so Ollie left.

She knocked on Mrs. Robinson's door to see if she wanted her dog walked. It was cool in the hallway at least. No one was home, not even the loud-mouth dog that usually slammed itself against the door like he was big and bad instead of being just a sorry little mutt. Then Ollie took the stairs two at a time, swinging up past the fourth floor to the roof. There was rice all over. Ronnie must have already fed his pigeons. The door to the roof was unlocked, and that meant that the big boys were on the roof. She planted her behind against the door and pushed. She kicked at a cluster of rice. Some grains bounced onto the soft tar of the roof and sank. When Ollie moved onto the roof, the blinding sun made her squint. And there they were, the big boys, jammed between the skylight and the chimney like dummies in a window, just doing nothing and looking half-asleep.

Peter Proper, as always, was dressed to the teeth. "I naturally stays clean," he was always saying. Today he said nothing, just sitting. Marbles, a kid from the projects,[1] had an open book on his knees. James was there, too, staring at a fingernail. And Ferman, the nut from crosstown, and Frenchie, the athlete. A flurry of cinders floated down from the chimney and settled into their hair like gray snow.

"Why don't you just sit in the incinerator? You can get even dirtier that way," Ollie yelled. No one moved or said anything. She expected Frenchie to at least say, "Here comes Miss Freshmouth," or for Peter to send her to the store for eighteen cents' worth of American cheese. It was always eighteen cents' worth, and he always handed her a quarter and a nickel. Big Time. "Don't none of you want nothing from the store today?" She squinted with her hands on her hips, waiting for the store dummies to start acting like Marbles, Peter, James, and so forth.

Ferman straightened out a leg against the skylight. "Ollie, when are you going to learn how to play with dolls?"

"Ya want anything from the store, Ferman Fruitcake? I'm too big for dolls." Ollie hitched up her jeans.

Ferman started to say something, but his audience was nearly asleep. Frenchie's head was nodding. James was staring into space. The pages of the open book on Marbles's knees were turning backward, three at a time, by themselves. Peter Proper was sitting very straight, back against the chimney with his eyes closed to the sun.

Ollie turned, looking over the edge of the roof. There was no one down in the park today. There was hardly anyone on the block. She propped a sticky foot against the roof railing and scraped off the tar. Everything below was gray, as if the chimney had snowed on the whole block.

Chalky, the superintendent, was rolling a mattress onto a cart. Maybe he'd play cards with her. Just last Friday he had, but sometimes he wouldn't even remember her and would run and hide, thinking she was King Kong come down just to hit him in the head or something. Ollie looked past the swings to the track. Empty. Frenchie should be out there trotting, she thought, looking back at him. He was dipping his head. Sometimes she'd trot beside Frenchie, taking big jumps to keep up. He'd smile at her but never teased her about them silly little jumps. He'd tell her for the hundredth time how he was going to enter the Olympics and walk off with a cup full of money.

"Go away, little girl!" Ferman had just yelled at her as if he had forgotten her name or didn't know her any more. He's as crazy as Chalky, thought Ollie, slamming the big roof door behind her and running down the stairs to the street. They must be brothers.

It was now four o'clock by the bank clock. Ollie remembered the bar-b-que place that had burned down. But she'd already rummaged through the ruins and found nothing. No use messing up her sneakers any further. She turned around to look the block over. Empty. Everyone was either at camp or at work or was sleeping like the boys on the roof or dead or just plain gone off. She perched on top of the fire hydrant with one foot, balancing with her arms. She could almost see into the high windows of Mount Zion A.M.E. Church. "This time I'm going to fly off and kill myself," she yelled, flapping her arms. A lady with bundles turned the corner and gave Ollie a look, crossed against the traffic, looking over her shoulder and shaking her head at what the kids of today had come

---

1. **the project:** a planned group of apartments or houses, especially those owned by the government, that provide housing for people with low incomes.

to. Reverend Hall came out of the church basement, mopping his head with a big handkerchief.

"You go play somewhere else," he said, frowning into the sun.

"Where?" Ollie asked.

"Well, go to the park and play."

"With who?" she demanded. "I've got nobody to play with."

Reverend Hall just stood there trying to control his temper. He was always chasing the kids. That's why he's got no choir, Granddaddy Larkins was always saying. He always chases kids and dogs and pigeons and drunks.

"Little girl, you can't act up here in front of the church. Have you no—"

"How come you always calling me little girl, but you sure know my name when I'm walking with my grandfather?" Ollie said.

"Tell'm all about his sanctified self," said Miss Hazel, laughing out her window. But when the Reverend looked up to scowl, she ducked back in. He marched back into the church, shooing the pigeons off the steps.

"Wish me happy birthday," Ollie whispered to the pigeons. They hurried off toward the curb. "Better wish me happy birthday," she yelled, "or somebody around here is gonna get wasted."

Miss Hazel leaned out the window again. "What's with you, Ollie? You sick or something?"

"You should never have a birthday in the summertime," Ollie yelled, "cause nobody's around to wish you happy birthday or give you a party."

"Well, don't cry, sugar. When you get as old as me, you'll be glad to forget all about—"

"I'm not crying." Ollie stamped her foot, but the tears kept coming and before she could stop herself she was howling, right there in the middle of the street and not even caring who saw her. And she howled so

loudly that even Miss Hazel's great-grand-mother had to come to the window to see who was dying and with so much noise and on such a lovely day.

"What's the matter with the Larkins child?" asked the old woman.

"Beats me." Miss Hazel shook her head and watched Ollie for a minute. "I don't understand kids sometimes," she sighed, and closed the window so she could hear the television good.

Getting at Meaning

1. Ollie wonders why she is friends with Wilma. Why is she? Why does she bother with "the big boys"? with Chalky, the superintendent?

2. How does Ollie spend the afternoon? Summarize briefly her activities.

3. Think about the adults in Ollie's neighborhood. What is true of Granddaddy Larkins? Why does the Reverend chase Ollie away? Why is Miss Hazel unable to understand why Ollie is crying?

Developing Skills in Reading Literature

1. **Setting.** The writer of this story creates the setting indirectly. What is the setting? In what passages is the setting suggested?

2. **Irony.** Irony is a contrast between what is expected and what actually exists or happens. Verbal irony is the contrast between what is said and what is meant. For example, if you fail a test and your friends say to you, "Nice job," they mean the exact opposite of what they are actually saying. In what way is the title of this story an example of verbal irony?

3. **Theme.** What is the writer of this story saying about how people treat each other?

Developing Vocabulary

Using Precise Verbs. The verbs used in this story produce vivid pictures for the reader. For example, Ollie sees cooks that "*sling* the wire baskets of chicken" and thinks about the dog that "*slammed* itself against the door." Find at least ten other examples of strong, specific verbs in the story.

Next, study the italicized verbs in the following sentences. For each verb, substitute a more colorful, specific action word. Write the words on a sheet of paper.

1. I *walked* out of the room, knowing I had failed the test.

2. I was disappointed in the way the barber had *cut* my hair.

3. The door *closed* with a crash.

4. The bell *rang,* surprising me as I slept.

5. His mind wandered as he *looked* out the window.

Developing Writing Skills

Writing About a Personal Experience. Write a paragraph about a memorable birthday you have had, either happy or sad. Concentrate on describing the setting for this birthday and on explaining why it was memorable. Use precise verbs to re-create the experience for your readers.

The Boy Who Drew Cats   *Lafcadio Hearn*

A long, long time ago, in a small country village in Japan, there lived a poor farmer and his wife, who were good people. They had a number of children, and found it hard to feed them all. The elder son was strong enough when only fourteen years old to help his father, and the little girls learned to help their mother almost as soon as they could walk.

But the youngest child, a little boy, did not seem to be fit for hard work. He was very clever, cleverer than all his brothers and sisters, but he was quite weak and small; and people said he could never grow very big. So his parents thought it would be better for him to become a priest than to become a farmer. They took him with them to the village temple one day, and asked the good old priest who lived there if he would have their little boy for his acolyte and teach him all that a priest ought to know.

The old man spoke kindly to the lad, and asked him some hard questions. So clever were the answers that the priest agreed to take the little fellow into the temple as an acolyte, and to educate him for the priesthood.

The boy learned quickly what the old priest taught him, and was obedient in most things. But he had one fault. He liked to draw cats during study hours, and to draw cats even where cats ought not to have been drawn at all.

Whenever he found himself alone, he drew cats. He drew them on the margins of the priest's books, and on all the screens of the temple, and on the walls, and on the pillars.

Several times the priest told him this was not right, but he did not stop drawing cats. He drew them because he could not really help it. He had what is called "the genius of an *artist*," and just for that reason he was not quite fit to be an acolyte. A good acolyte should study books.

One day, after he had drawn some clever pictures of cats upon a paper screen, the old priest said to him severely, "My boy, you must go away from this temple at once. You will never make a good priest, but perhaps you will become a great artist. Now let me give you a last piece of advice, and be sure you never forget it. *Avoid large places at night; keep to small!*"

The boy did not know what the priest meant by saying, "*Avoid large places; keep to small.*" He thought and thought, while he was tying up his little bundle of clothes to go away; but he could not understand those words, and he was afraid to speak to the priest any more, except to say goodbye.

He left the temple sorrowfully, and began to wonder what he should do. If he went straight home, he felt sure his father would punish him for having been disobedient to the priest, so he was afraid to go home. All at once, he remembered that at the next village, twelve miles away, there was a big temple. He had heard there were several priests at that temple, and he made up his mind to go to them and ask them to take him for their acolyte.

Now, that big temple was closed up, but the boy did not know this fact. The reason it had been closed up was that a goblin had fright-

ened the priests away, and had taken possession of the place. Some brave warriors had afterward gone to the temple at night to kill the goblin, but they had never been seen alive again. Nobody had ever told these things to the boy, so he walked all the way to the village, hoping to be kindly treated by the priests.

When he got to the village, it was already dark, and all the people were in bed; but he saw the big temple on a hill at the other end of the principal street, and he saw there was a light in the temple. People who tell the story say the goblin used to make that light in order to tempt lonely travelers to ask for shelter. The boy went at once to the temple, and knocked. There was no sound inside. He knocked and knocked again, but still nobody came. At last he pushed gently at the door, and was quite glad to find that it had not been fastened. So he went in, and saw a lamp burning—but no priest.

He thought some priest would be sure to come soon, and he sat down and waited. Then he noticed that everything in the temple was gray with dust and thickly spun over with cobwebs. He thought to himself that the priests would certainly like to have an acolyte to keep the place clean. He wondered why they had allowed everything to get so dusty. What most pleased him, however, were some big white screens, good to paint cats upon. Though he was tired, he looked at once for a writing-box, and found one, and ground some ink,[1] and began to paint cats.

He painted a great many cats upon the screens, and then he began to feel very, very sleepy. He was just on the point of lying down to sleep beside one of the screens, when he suddenly remembered the words, "*Avoid large places; keep to small!*"

---

1. **ground some ink:** in early times ink was made by grinding lampblack with a solution of glue or gums.

The temple was very large. He was all alone, and as he thought of these words—though he could not quite understand them—he began to feel for the first time a little afraid. He resolved to look for a *small place* in which to sleep. He found a little cabinet with a sliding door, and went into it and shut himself up. Then he lay down and fell fast asleep.

Late in the night he was awakened by a most terrible noise, a noise of fighting and screaming. It was so dreadful that he was afraid even to look through a chink of the little cabinet. He lay very still, holding his breath in fright.

The light that had been in the temple went out, but the awful sounds continued and became more awful; and all the temple shook. After a long time, silence came; but the boy was still afraid to move. He did not move until the light of the morning sun shone into the cabinet through the chinks of the little door.

Then he cautiously got out of his hiding place and looked about. The first thing he saw was that all the floor of the temple was covered with blood. And then he saw, lying dead in the middle of it, an enormous, monstrous rat—a goblin-rat—bigger than a cow!

But who or what could have killed it? There was no man or other creature to be seen. Suddenly the boy observed that the mouths of all the cats he had drawn the night before were red and wet with blood. Then he knew that the goblin had been killed by the cats that he had drawn. And then also, for the first time, he understood why the wise old priest had said to him, *"Avoid large places at night; keep to small."*

Afterward that boy became a famous artist. Some of the cats that he drew are still shown to travelers in Japan.

Getting at Meaning

1. What qualities enable the boy to succeed against great odds?

2. Why do the boy's parents take him to the priest? Why does the priest send him away?

3. What does the priest recognize about the boy? What is the meaning of his advice to the boy? How does this advice help the boy succeed?

Developing Skills in Reading Literature

1. **Setting.** The first sentence of this story tells you that the setting is "a long, long time ago, in a small country village in Japan." What details in the story make the setting seem real? What elements in the story seem unreal? How does the time that this story takes place help you to accept these elements?

2. **Parable.** A parable is a simple story that teaches a moral lesson. The lesson usually can be applied to different people in a variety of situations. What is the writer of this parable saying about the power of art? Why are the characters in the parable nameless?

3. **Irony.** Irony is created when the outcome of a story is the opposite of what the reader expects. What is the major irony in the end of "The Boy Who Drew Cats"?

Developing Writing Skills

Writing a Parable. Write a parable that teaches an important lesson. Create at least two characters and an interesting conflict to illustrate the lesson.

The Most Dangerous Game

Richard Connell

Off there to the right—somewhere—is a large island," said Whitney. "It's rather a mystery—"

"What island is it?" Rainsford asked.

"The old charts call it 'Ship-Trap Island,' " Whitney replied. "A suggestive name, isn't it? Sailors have a curious dread of the place. I don't know why. Some superstition—"

"Can't see it," remarked Rainsford, trying to peer through the dank tropical night that was palpable as it pressed its thick, warm blackness in upon the yacht.

"You've good eyes," said Whitney, with a laugh, "and I've seen you pick off a moose moving in the brown fall bush at four hundred yards; but even you can't see four miles or so through a moonless Caribbean night."

"Nor four yards," admitted Rainsford. "Ugh! It's like moist black velvet."

"It will be light in Rio," promised Whitney. "We should make it in a few days. I hope the jaguar guns have come from Purdey's. We should have some good hunting up the Amazon. Great sport, hunting."

"The best sport in the world," agreed Rainsford.

"For the hunter," amended Whitney. "Not for the jaguar."

"Don't talk rot, Whitney," said Rainsford. "You're a big-game hunter, not a philosopher. Who cares how a jaguar feels?"

"Perhaps the jaguar does," observed Whitney.

"Bah! They've no understanding."

"Even so, I rather think they understand one thing—fear. The fear of pain and the fear of death."

"Nonsense," laughed Rainsford. "This hot weather is making you soft, Whitney. Be a realist. The world is made up of two classes —the hunters and the huntees. Luckily, you and I are hunters. Do you think we've passed that island yet?"

"I can't tell in the dark. I hope so."

"Why?" asked Rainsford.

"The place has a reputation—a bad one."

"Cannibals?" suggested Rainsford.

"Hardly. Even cannibals wouldn't live in such a Godforsaken place. But it's gotten into sailor lore, somehow. Didn't you notice that the crew's nerves seemed a bit jumpy today?"

"They were a bit strange, now you mention it. Even Captain Nielsen—"

"Yes, even that tough-minded old Swede, who'd go up to the devil himself and ask him for a light. Those fishy blue eyes held a look I never saw there before. All I could get out of him was: 'This place has an evil name among seafaring men, sir.' Then he said to me, very gravely, 'Don't you feel anything?'—as if the air about us was actually poisonous. Now, you mustn't laugh when I tell you this—I did feel something like a sudden chill.

"There was no breeze. The sea was as flat as a plate-glass window. We were drawing near the island then. What I felt was a—a mental chill; a sort of sudden dread."

"Pure imagination," said Rainsford. "One superstitious sailor can taint the whole ship's company with his fear."

"Maybe. But sometimes I think sailors have an extra sense that tells them when they are in danger. Sometimes I think evil is a tangible thing—with wavelengths, just as sound and light have. An evil place can, so to speak, broadcast vibrations of evil. Anyhow, I'm glad we're getting out of this zone. Well, I think I'll turn in now, Rainsford."

"I'm not sleepy," said Rainsford. "I'm going to smoke another pipe up on the afterdeck."

"Good night, then, Rainsford. See you at breakfast."

"Right. Good night, Whitney."

There was no sound in the night as Rainsford sat there, but the muffled throb of the engine that drove the yacht swiftly through the darkness, and the swish and ripple of the wash of the propeller.

Rainsford, reclining in a steamer chair, indolently puffed on his favorite brier. The sensuous drowsiness of the night was on him. "It's so dark," he thought, "that I could sleep without closing my eyes; the night would be my eyelids—"

An abrupt sound startled him. Off to the right he heard it, and his ears, expert in such matters, could not be mistaken. Again he heard the sound, and again. Somewhere, off in the blackness, someone had fired a gun three times.

Rainsford sprang up and moved quickly to the rail, mystified. He strained his eyes in the direction from which the reports had come, but it was like trying to see through a blanket. He leaped upon the rail and balanced himself there, to get greater elevation; his pipe, striking a rope, was knocked from his mouth. He lunged for it; a short, hoarse cry came from his lips as he realized he had reached too far and had lost his balance. The cry was pinched off short as the blood-warm waters of the Caribbean Sea closed over his head.

He struggled up to the surface and tried to cry out, but the wash from the speeding yacht slapped him in the face and the salt water in his open mouth made him gag and strangle. Desperately he struck out with strong strokes after the receding lights of the yacht, but he stopped before he had swum fifty feet. A cer-

tain coolheadedness had come to him; it was not the first time he had been in a tight place. There was a chance that his cries could be heard by someone aboard the yacht, but that chance was slender, and grew more slender as the yacht raced on. He wrestled himself out of his clothes, and shouted with all his power. The lights of the yacht became faint and ever-vanishing fireflies; then they were blotted out entirely by the night.

Rainsford remembered the shots. They had come from the right, and doggedly he swam in that direction, swimming with slow, deliberate strokes, conserving his strength. For a seemingly endless time he fought the sea. He began to count his strokes; he could do possibly a hundred more and then—

Rainsford heard a sound. It came out of the darkness, a high screaming sound, the sound of an animal in an extremity of anguish and terror.

He did not recognize the animal that made the sound. He did not try to. With fresh vitality, he swam toward the sound. He heard it again; then it was cut short by another noise, crisp, staccato.

"Pistol shot," muttered Rainsford, swimming on.

Ten minutes of determined effort brought another sound to his ears—the most welcome he had ever heard—the muttering and growling of the sea breaking on a rocky shore. He was almost on the rocks before he saw them; on a night less calm he would have been shattered against them. With his remaining strength he dragged himself from the swirling waters. Jagged crags appeared to jut up into the opaqueness; he forced himself upward, hand over hand. Gasping, his hands raw, he reached a flat place at the top. Dense jungle came down to the very edge of the cliffs. What perils that tangle of trees and underbrush might hold for him did not concern Rainsford just then. All he knew was that he was safe from his enemy, the sea, and that

utter weariness was on him. He flung himself down at the jungle edge and tumbled headlong into the deepest sleep of his life.

When he opened his eyes, he knew from the position of the sun that it was late in the afternoon. Sleep had given him new vigor; a sharp hunger was picking at him. He looked about him, almost cheerfully.

"Where there are pistol shots, there are men. Where there are men, there is food," he thought. But what kind of men, he wondered, in so forbidding a place? An unbroken front of snarled and ragged jungle fringed the shore.

He saw no sign of a trail through the closely knit web of weeds and trees; it was easier to go along the shore, and Rainsford floundered along by the water. Not far from where he had landed, he stopped.

Some wounded thing, by the evidence a large animal, had thrashed about in the underbrush. The jungle weeds were crushed down and the moss was lacerated; one patch of weeds was stained crimson. A small, glittering object not far away caught Rainsford's eye, and he picked it up. It was an empty cartridge.

"A twenty-two," he remarked. "That's odd. It must have been a fairly large animal, too. The hunter had his nerve to tackle it with a light gun. It's clear that the brute put up a fight. I suppose the first three shots I heard was when the hunter flushed his quarry and wounded it. The last shot was when he trailed it here and finished it."

He examined the ground closely and found what he had hoped to find—the print of hunting boots. They pointed along the cliff in the direction he had been going. Eagerly he hurried along, now slipping on a rotten log or a loose stone, but making headway; night was beginning to settle down on the island.

Bleak darkness was blacking out the sea and jungle when Rainsford sighted the lights. He came upon them as he turned a crook in the coastline, and his first thought was that he had come upon a village, for there were many lights. But as he forged along, he saw to his great astonishment that all the lights were in one enormous building—a lofty structure with pointed towers plunging upward into the gloom. His eyes made out the shadowy outlines of a palatial château; it was set on a high bluff, and on three sides of it cliffs dived down to where the sea licked greedy lips in the shadows.

"Mirage," thought Rainsford. But it was no mirage, he found, when he opened the tall spiked iron gate. The stone steps were real enough; the massive door with a leering gargoyle for a knocker was real enough; yet about it all hung an air of unreality.

He lifted the knocker, and it creaked up stiffly, as if it had never before been used. He let it fall, and it startled him with its booming loudness. He thought he heard steps within; the door remained closed. Again Rainsford lifted the heavy knocker, and let it fall. The door opened then, opened as suddenly as if it were on a spring, and Rainsford stood blinking in the river of glaring gold light that poured out. The first thing Rainsford's eyes discerned was the largest man Rainsford had

ever seen—a gigantic creature, solidly made and black-bearded to the waist. In his hand the man held a long-barreled revolver, and he was pointing it straight at Rainsford's heart.

Out of the snarl of beard two small eyes regarded Rainsford.

"Don't be alarmed," said Rainsford, with a smile which he hoped was disarming. "I'm no robber. I fell off a yacht. My name is Sanger Rainsford of New York City."

The menacing look in his eyes did not change. The revolver pointed as rigidly as if the giant were a statue. He gave no sign that he understood Rainsford's words, or that he had even heard them. He was dressed in uniform, a black uniform trimmed with gray astrakhan.

"I'm Sanger Rainsford of New York," Rainsford began again. "I fell off a yacht. I am hungry."

The man's only answer was to raise with his thumb the hammer of his revolver. Then Rainsford saw the man's free hand go to his forehead in a military salute, and he saw him click his heels together and stand at attention. Another man was coming down the broad marble steps, an erect, slender man in evening clothes. He advanced to Rainsford and held out his hand.

In a cultivated voice marked by a slight accent that gave it added precision and deliberateness, he said: "It is a very great pleasure and honor to welcome Mr. Sanger Rainsford, the celebrated hunter, to my home."

Automatically Rainsford shook the man's hand.

"I've read your book about hunting snow leopards in Tibet, you see," explained the man. "I am General Zaroff."

Rainsford's first impression was that the man was singularly handsome; his second was that there was an original, almost bizarre quality about the general's face. He was a tall man past middle age, for his hair was a vivid white; but his thick eyebrows and pointed military mustache were as black as the night from which Rainsford had come. His eyes, too, were black and very bright. He had high cheek bones, a sharp-cut nose, a spare, dark face, the face of a man used to giving orders, the face of an aristocrat. Turning to the giant in uniform, the general made a sign. The giant put away his pistol, saluted, withdrew.

"Ivan is an incredibly strong fellow," remarked the general, "but he has the misfortune to be deaf and dumb. A simple fellow, but, I'm afraid, like all his race, a bit of a savage."

"Is he Russian?"

"He is a Cossack,"[1] said the general, and his smile showed red lips and pointed teeth. "So am I."

"Come," he said, "we shouldn't be chatting here. We can talk later. Now you want clothes, food, rest. You shall have them. This is a most restful spot."

Ivan had reappeared, and the general spoke to him with lips that moved but gave forth no sound.

"Follow Ivan, if you please, Mr. Rainsford," said the general. "I was about to have my dinner when you came. I'll wait for you. You'll find that my clothes will fit you, I think."

It was to a huge, beam-ceilinged bedroom with a canopied bed big enough for six men that Rainsford followed the silent giant. Ivan laid out an evening suit, and Rainsford, as he put it on, noticed that it came from a London tailor who ordinarily cut and sewed for none below the rank of duke.

The dining room to which Ivan conducted him was in many ways remarkable. There was a medieval magnificence about it. It suggested a baronial hall of feudal times[2] with its oaken panels, its high ceiling, its vast refectory table where twoscore men could sit down to eat. About the hall were the mounted heads of many animals—lions, tigers, elephants, moose, bears; larger or more perfect specimens Rainsford had never seen. At the great table the general was sitting, alone.

"You'll have a cocktail, Mr. Rainsford," he suggested. The cocktail was surpassingly good; and, Rainsford noted, the table appointments were of the finest—the linen, the crystal, the silver, the china.

They were eating borsch, the rich, red soup with sour cream so dear to Russian palates. Half apologetically General Zaroff said, "We do our best to preserve the amenities of civilization here. Please forgive any lapses. We are well off the beaten track, you know.

---

1. **Cossack** (käs′ ak): a member of the people of southern Russia, famous as horsemen and cavalrymen.
2. **baronial hall of feudal times:** the hall of a European nobleman in the Middle Ages.

Do you think the champagne has suffered from its long ocean trip?"

"Not in the least," declared Rainsford. He was finding the general a most thoughtful and affable host, a true cosmopolite. But there was one small trait of the general's that made Rainsford uncomfortable. Whenever he looked up from his plate he found the general studying him, appraising him narrowly.

"Perhaps," said General Zaroff, "you were surprised that I recognized your name. You see, I read all books on hunting published in English, French, and Russian. I have but one passion in my life, Mr. Rainsford, and it is the hunt."

"You have some wonderful heads here," said Rainsford as he ate a particularly well cooked filet mignon. "That Cape buffalo is the largest I ever saw."

"Oh, that fellow. Yes, he was a monster."

"Did he charge you?"

"Hurled me against a tree," said the general. "Fractured my skull. But I got the brute."

"I've always thought," said Rainsford, "that the Cape buffalo is the most dangerous of all big game."

For a moment the general did not reply; he was smiling his curious, red-lipped smile. Then he said slowly, "No. You are wrong, sir. The Cape buffalo is not the most dangerous big game." He sipped his wine. "Here in my preserve on this island," he said in the same slow tone, "I hunt more dangerous game."

Rainsford expressed his surprise. "Is there big game on this island?"

The general nodded. "The biggest."

"Really?"

"Oh, it isn't here naturally, of course. I have to stock the island."

"What have you imported, general?" Rainsford asked. "Tigers?"

The general smiled. "No," he said. "Hunting tigers ceased to interest me some years ago. I exhausted their possibilities, you see. No thrill left in tigers, no real danger. I live

for danger, Mr. Rainsford."

The general took from his pocket a gold cigarette case and offered his guest a long black cigarette with a silver tip; it was perfumed and gave off a smell like incense.

"We will have some capital hunting, you and I," said the general. "I shall be most glad to have your society."

"But what game—" began Rainsford.

"I'll tell you," said the general. "You will be amused, I know. I think I may say, in all modesty, that I have done a rare thing. I have invented a new sensation. May I pour you another glass of port, Mr. Rainsford?"

"Thank you, general."

The general filled both glasses, and said, "God makes some men poets. Some He makes kings, some beggars. Me He made a hunter. My hand was made for the trigger, my father said. He was a very rich man with a quarter of a million acres in the Crimea, and he was an ardent sportsman. When I was only five years old he gave me a little gun, specially made in Moscow for me, to shoot sparrows with. When I shot some of his prize turkeys with it, he did not punish me; he complimented me on my marksmanship. I killed my first bear in the Caucasus[3] when I was ten. My whole life has been one prolonged hunt. I went into the army—it was expected of noblemen's sons—and for a time commanded a division of Cossack cavalry, but my real interest was always the hunt. I have hunted every kind of game in every land. It would be impossible for me to tell you how many animals I have killed."

The general puffed at his cigarette.

"After the debacle in Russia, I left the country, for it was imprudent for an officer of the Czar to stay there. Many noble Russians lost everything. I, luckily, had invested heavily in American securities, so I shall never have to

---

3. **Crimea** (krī mē′ ə) . . . **Caucasus** (kôk′ ə səs): regions in southern U.S.S.R.

open a tearoom in Monte Carlo or drive a taxi in Paris. Naturally, I continued to hunt—grizzlies in your Rockies, crocodiles in the Ganges,[4] rhinoceroses in East Africa. It was in Africa that the Cape buffalo hit me and laid me up for six months. As soon as I recovered, I started for the Amazon to hunt jaguars, for I had heard they were unusually cunning. They weren't." The Cossack sighed. "They were no match at all for a hunter with his wits about him, and a high-powered rifle. I was bitterly disappointed. I was lying in my tent with a splitting headache one night when a terrible thought pushed its way into my mind. Hunting was beginning to bore me! And hunting, remember, had been my life. I have heard that in America, businessmen often go to pieces when they give up the business that has been their life."

"Yes, that's so," said Rainsford.

The general smiled. "I had no wish to go to pieces," he said. "I must do something. Now, mine is an analytical mind, Mr. Rainsford. Doubtless that is why I enjoy the problems of the chase."

"No doubt, General Zaroff."

"So," continued the general, "I asked myself why the hunt no longer fascinated me. You are much younger than I am, Mr. Rainsford, and have not hunted as much, but you perhaps can guess the answer."

"What was it?"

"Simply this: hunting had ceased to be what you call 'a sporting proposition.' It had become too easy. I always got my quarry. Always. There is no greater bore than perfection."

The general lit a fresh cigarette.

"No animal had a chance with me any more. That is no boast; it is a mathematical certainty. The animal had nothing but his legs and his instinct. Instinct is no match for reason. When I thought of this it was a tragic moment for me, I can tell you."

Rainsford leaned across the table, absorbed in what his host was saying.

"It came to me as an inspiration what I must do," the general went on.

"And that was?"

The general smiled the quiet smile of one who has faced an obstacle and surmounted it with success. "I had to invent a new animal to hunt," he said.

"A new animal? You're joking."

"Not at all," said the general. "I never joke about hunting. I needed a new animal. I found one. So I bought this island, built this house, and here I do my hunting. The island is perfect for my purposes—there are jungles with a maze of trails in them, hills, swamps—"

"But the animal, General Zaroff?"

"Oh," said the general, "it supplies me with the most exciting hunting in the world. No other hunting compares with it for an instant. Every day I hunt, and I never grow bored now, for I have a quarry with which I can match my wits."

Rainsford's bewilderment showed in his face.

"I wanted the ideal animal to hunt," explained the general. "So, I said: 'What are the attributes of an ideal quarry?' And the answer was, of course: 'It must have courage, cunning, and, above all, it must be able to reason.'"

"But no animal can reason," objected Rainsford.

"My dear fellow," said the general, "there is one that can."

"But you can't mean—" gasped Rainsford.

"And why not?"

"I can't believe you are serious, General Zaroff. This is a grisly joke."

"Why should I not be serious? I am speaking of hunting."

---

4. **Ganges** (gan' jēs): a river in northern India.

"Hunting? General Zaroff, what you speak of is murder."

The general laughed with entire good nature. He regarded Rainsford quizzically. "I refuse to believe that so modern and civilized a young man as you seem to be harbors romantic ideas about the value of human life. Surely your experiences in the war—"

"Did not make me condone cold-blooded murder," finished Rainsford stiffly.

Laughter shook the general. "How extraordinarily droll you are!" he said. "One does not expect nowadays to find a young man of the educated class, even in America, with such a naive, and, if I may say so, mid-Victorian point of view. It's like finding a snuffbox in a limousine. Ah, well, doubtless you had Puritan ancestors. So many Americans appear to have had. I'll wager you'll forget your notions when you go hunting with me. You've a genuine new thrill in store for you, Mr. Rainsford."

"Thank you. I'm a hunter, not a murderer."

"Dear me," said the general, quite unruffled. "Again that unpleasant word. But I think I can show you that your scruples are quite ill-founded."

"Yes?"

"Life is for the strong, to be lived by the strong, and, if need be, taken by the strong. The weak of the world were put here to give the strong pleasure. I am strong. Why should I not use my gift? If I wish to hunt, why should I not? I hunt the scum of the earth— sailors from tramp ships—lascars, blacks, Chinese, whites, mongrels—a thoroughbred horse or hound is worth more than a score of them."

"But they are men," said Rainsford hotly.

"Precisely," said the general. "That is why I use them. It gives me pleasure. They can reason, after a fashion. So they are dangerous."

"But where do you get them?"

The general's left eyelid fluttered down in a wink. "This island is called Ship-Trap," he answered. "Sometimes an angry god of the high seas sends them to me. Sometimes, when Providence is not so kind, I help Providence a bit. Come to the window with me."

Rainsford went to the window and looked out toward the sea.

"Watch! Out there!" exclaimed the general, pointing into the night. Rainsford's eyes saw only blackness, and then, as the general pressed a button, far out to sea Rainsford saw the flash of lights.

The general chuckled. "They indicate a channel," he said, "where there's none; giant rocks with razor edges crouch like a sea monster with wide-open jaws. They can crush a ship as easily as I crush this nut." He dropped a walnut on the hardwood floor and brought his heel grinding down on it. "Oh, yes," he said, casually, as if in answer to a question, "I have electricity. We try to be civilized here."

"Civilized? And you shoot down men?"

A trace of anger was in the general's black eyes, but it was there for but a second, and he said, in his most pleasant manner, "Dear me, what a righteous young man you are! I assure you I do not do the thing you suggest. That would be barbarous. I treat these visitors with every consideration. They get plenty of good food and exercise. They get into splendid physical condition. You shall see for yourself tomorrow."

"What do you mean?"

"We'll visit my training school," smiled the general. "It's in the cellar. I have about a dozen pupils down there now. They're from the Spanish bark *San Lucar* that had the bad luck to go on the rocks out there. A very inferior lot, I regret to say. Poor specimens and more accustomed to the deck than to the jungle."

He raised his hand, and Ivan, who served as waiter, brought thick Turkish coffee. Rainsford, with an effort, held his tongue in check.

"It's a game, you see," pursued the general blandly. "I suggest to one of them that we go hunting. I give him a supply of food and an excellent hunting knife. I give him three hours' start. I am to follow, armed only with a pistol of the smallest caliber and range. If my quarry eludes me for three whole days, he wins the game. If I find him"—the general smiled—"he loses."

"Suppose he refuses to be hunted?"

"Oh," said the general, "I give him his option, of course. He need not play that game if he doesn't wish to. If he does not wish to hunt, I turn him over to Ivan. Ivan once had the honor of serving as official knouter[5] to the Great White Czar, and he has his own ideas of sport. Invariably, Mr. Rainsford, invariably they choose the hunt."

"And if they win?"

The smile on the general's face widened. "To date I have not lost," he said.

Then he added, hastily: "I don't wish you to think me a braggart, Mr. Rainsford. Many of them afford only the most elementary sort of problem. Occasionally I strike a tartar. One almost did win. I eventually had to use the dogs."

"The dogs?"

"This way, please. I'll show you."

The general steered Rainsford to a window. The lights from the windows sent a flickering illumination that made grotesque patterns on the courtyard below, and Rainsford could see moving about there a dozen or so huge black shapes. As they turned toward him, their eyes glittered greenly.

"A rather good lot, I think," observed the general. "They are let out at seven every night. If anyone should try to get into my house—or out of it—something extremely regrettable would occur to him." He hummed a snatch of song from the Folies Bergère.[6]

"And now," said the general, "I want to show you my new collection of heads. Will you come with me to the library?"

"I hope," said Rainsford, "that you will excuse me tonight, General Zaroff. I'm really not feeling at all well."

"Ah, indeed?" the general inquired solicitously. "Well, I suppose that's only natural, after your long swim. You need a good, restful night's sleep. Tomorrow you'll feel like a new man, I'll wager. Then we'll hunt, eh? I've one rather promising prospect—"

Rainsford was hurrying from the room.

"Sorry you can't go with me tonight," called the general. "I expect rather fair sport —a big, strong fellow. He looks resourceful— Well, good night, Mr. Rainsford; I hope you have a good night's rest."

The bed was good, and the pajamas of the softest silk, and he was tired in every fiber of his being, but nevertheless Rainsford could not quiet his brain with the opiate of sleep. He lay, eyes wide open. Once he thought he heard stealthy steps in the corridor outside his room. He sought to throw open the door; it would not open. He went to the window and looked out. His room was high up in one of the towers. The lights of the château were out now, and it was dark and silent; but there was a fragment of sallow moon, and by its wan light he could see, dimly, the courtyard. There, weaving in and out in the pattern of shadow, were black, noiseless forms. The hounds heard him at the window and looked up, expectantly, with their green eyes. Rainsford went back to the bed and lay down. By many methods he tried to put himself to sleep. He had achieved a doze when, just as morning began to come, he heard, far off in the jungle, the faint report of a pistol.

General Zaroff did not appear until lunch-

---

5. **knouter** (nout' ər): a person who whipped criminals in Russia.

6. **Folies Bergère** (fō lē' ber zher') *French:* an elaborately costumed French theatrical revue consisting of musical skits and dancing.

eon. He was dressed faultlessly in the tweeds of a country squire. He was solicitous about the state of Rainsford's health.

"As for me," sighed the general, "I do not feel so well. I am worried, Mr. Rainsford. Last night I detected traces of my old complaint."

To Rainsford's questioning glance the general said: "Ennui. Boredom."

Then, taking a second helping of crêpes suzette, the general explained: "The hunting was not good last night. The fellow lost his head. He made a straight trail that offered no problems at all. That's the trouble with these sailors; they have dull brains to begin with, and they do not know how to get about in the woods. They do excessively stupid and obvious things. It's most annoying. Will you have another glass of Chablis, Mr. Rainsford?"

"General," said Rainsford firmly, "I wish to leave this island at once."

The general raised his thickets of eyebrows; he seemed hurt. "But, my dear fellow," the general protested, "you've only just come. You've had no hunting—"

"I wish to go today," said Rainsford. He saw the dead black eyes of the general on him, studying him. General Zaroff's face suddenly brightened.

He filled Rainsford's glass with venerable Chablis from a dusty bottle.

"Tonight," said the general, "we will hunt —you and I."

Rainsford shook his head. "No, general," he said. "I will not hunt."

The general shrugged his shoulders and delicately ate a hothouse grape. "As you wish, my friend," he said. "The choice rests entirely with you. But may I not venture to suggest that you will find my idea of sport more diverting than Ivan's?"

He nodded toward the corner to where the giant stood, scowling, his thick arms crossed on his hogshead of chest.

"You don't mean—" cried Rainsford.

"My dear fellow," said the general, "have I not told you I always mean what I say about hunting? This is really an inspiration. I drink to a foeman worthy of my steel—at last."

The general raised his glass, but Rainsford sat staring at him.

"You'll find this game worth playing," the general said enthusiastically. "Your brain against mine. Your woodcraft against mine. Your strength and stamina against mine. Outdoor chess! And the stake is not without value, eh?"

"And if I win—" began Rainsford huskily.

"I'll cheerfully acknowledge myself defeated if I do not find you by midnight of the third day," said General Zaroff. "My sloop will place you on the mainland near a town."

The general read what Rainsford was thinking.

"Oh, you can trust me," said the Cossack. "I will give you my word as a gentleman and a sportsman. Of course you, in turn, must agree to say nothing of your visit here."

"I'll agree to nothing of the kind," said Rainsford.

"Oh," said the general, "in that case—But why discuss that now? Three days hence we can discuss it over a bottle of Veuve Cliquot, unless—"

The general sipped his wine.

Then a businesslike air animated him. "Ivan," he said to Rainsford, "will supply you with hunting clothes, food, a knife. I suggest you wear moccasins; they leave a poorer trail. I suggest, too, that you avoid a big swamp in the southeast corner of the island. We call it Death Swamp. There's quicksand there. One foolish fellow tried it. The deplorable part of it was that Lazarus followed him. You can imagine my feelings, Mr. Rainsford. I loved Lazarus; he was the finest hound in my pack. Well, I must beg you to excuse me now, I always take a siesta after lunch. You'll hardly have time for a nap, I fear. You'll want to start, no doubt. I shall not follow till dusk. Hunting at night is so much more exciting than by day, don't you think? Au revoir, Mr. Rainsford, au revoir."[7]

General Zaroff, with a deep, courtly bow, strolled from the room.

From another door came Ivan. Under one arm he carried khaki hunting clothes, a haversack of food, a leather sheath containing a long-bladed hunting knife; his right hand rested on a cocked revolver thrust in the crimson sash about his waist. . . .

Rainsford had fought his way through the bush for two hours. "I must keep my nerve. I must keep my nerve," he said through tight teeth.

He had not been entirely clearheaded when the château gates snapped shut behind him. His whole idea at first was to put distance between himself and General Zaroff, and, to this end, he had plunged along, spurred on by the sharp rowels of something very like panic. Now he had got a grip on himself, had stopped, and was taking stock of himself and the situation.

He saw that straight flight was futile; inevitably it would bring him face to face with the sea. He was in a picture with a frame of water, and his operations, clearly, must take place within that frame.

"I'll give him a trail to follow," muttered Rainsford, and he struck off from the rude paths he had been following into the trackless wilderness. He executed a series of intricate loops; he doubled on his trail again and again, recalling all the lore of the fox hunt, and all the dodges of the fox. Night found him legweary, with hands and face lashed by the branches, on a thickly wooded ridge. He knew it would be insane to blunder on through the dark, even if he had the strength. His need for rest was imperative, and he thought, "I have played the fox, now I must play the cat of the fable." A big tree with a thick trunk and outspread branches was nearby, and, taking care to leave not the slightest mark, he climbed up

into the crotch, and stretching out on one of the broad limbs, after a fashion, rested. Rest brought him new confidence and almost a feeling of security. Even so zealous a hunter as General Zaroff could not trace him there, he told himself; only the devil himself could follow that complicated trail through the jungle after dark. But, perhaps, the general was a devil—

An apprehensive night crawled slowly by like a wounded snake, and sleep did not visit Rainsford, although the silence of a dead world was on the jungle. Toward morning, when a dingy gray was varnishing the sky, the cry of some startled bird focused Rainsford's attention in that direction. Something was coming through the bush, coming slowly, carefully, coming by the same winding way Rainsford had come. He flattened himself down on the limb, and through a screen of leaves almost as thick as tapestry, he watched. The thing that was approaching was a man.

It was General Zaroff. He made his way along with his eyes fixed in utmost concentration on the ground before him. He paused, almost beneath the tree, dropped to his knees, and studied the ground. Rainsford's impulse was to hurl himself down like a panther, but he saw that the general's right hand held something metallic—a small automatic pistol.

The hunter shook his head several times, as if he were puzzled. Then he straightened up and took from his case one of his black cigarettes; its pungent, incenselike smoke floated up to Rainsford's nostrils.

Rainsford held his breath. The general's eyes had left the ground and were traveling inch by inch up the tree. Rainsford froze there, every muscle tensed for a spring. But the sharp eyes of the hunter stopped before

---

7. **au revoir** (ō' rə vwër) *French:* until we meet again; goodbye.

they reached the limb where Rainsford lay; a smile spread over his brown face. Very deliberately he blew a smoke ring into the air; then he turned his back on the tree and walked carelessly away, back along the trail he had come. The swish of the underbrush against his hunting boots grew fainter and fainter.

The pent-up air burst hotly from Rainsford's lungs. His first thought made him feel sick and numb. The general could follow a trail through the woods at night; he could follow an extremely difficult trail. He must have uncanny powers. Only by the merest chance had the Cossack failed to see his quarry.

Rainsford's second thought was even more terrible. It sent a shudder of cold horror through his whole being. Why had the general smiled? Why had he turned back?

Rainsford did not want to believe what his reason told him was true, but the truth was as evident as the sun that had by now pushed through the morning mists. The general was playing with him! The general was saving him for another day's sport! The Cossack was the cat; he was the mouse. Then it was that Rainsford knew the full meaning of terror.

"I will not lose my nerve. I will not."

He slid down from the tree, and struck off again into the woods. His face was set, and he forced the machinery of his mind to function. Three hundred yards from his hiding place he stopped where a huge, dead tree leaned precariously on a smaller, living one. Throwing off his sack of food, Rainsford took his knife from its sheath and began to work with all his energy.

The job was finished at last, and he threw himself down behind a fallen log a hundred feet away. He did not have to wait long. The cat was coming again to play with the mouse.

Following the trail with the sureness of a bloodhound came General Zaroff. Nothing escaped those searching black eyes, no crushed blade of grass, no bent twig, no mark, no matter how faint, in the moss. So intent was the Cossack on his stalking that he was upon the thing Rainsford had made before he saw it. His foot touched the protruding bough that was the trigger. Even as he touched it, the general sensed his danger and leaped back with the agility of an ape. But he was not quite quick enough; the dead tree, delicately adjusted to rest on the cut living one, crashed down and struck the general a glancing blow on the shoulder as it fell; but for his alertness, he must have been smashed beneath it. He staggered, but he did not fall; nor did he drop his revolver. He stood there, rubbing his injured shoulder, and Rainsford, with fear again gripping his heart, heard the general's mocking laugh ring through the jungle.

"Rainsford," called the general, "if you are within sound of my voice, as I suppose you are, let me congratulate you. Not many men know how to make a Malay man-catcher. Luckily, for me, I too have hunted in Malacca. You are proving interesting, Mr. Rainsford. I am going now to have my wound dressed; it's only a slight one. But I shall be back. I shall be back."

When the general, nursing his bruised shoulder, had gone, Rainsford took up his flight again. It was flight now, a desperate, hopeless flight, that carried him on for some hours. Dusk came, then darkness, and still he pressed on. The ground grew softer under his moccasins; the vegetation grew ranker, denser; insects bit him savagely. Then, as he stepped forward, his foot sank into the ooze. He tried to wrench it back, but the muck sucked viciously at his foot as if it were a giant leech. With a violent effort, he tore his foot loose. He knew where he was now. Death Swamp and its quicksand.

His hands were tight closed as if his nerve were something tangible that someone in the darkness was trying to tear from his grip. The softness of the earth had given him an idea. He stepped back from the quicksand a dozen feet or so and, like some huge prehistoric beaver, he began to dig.

Rainsford had dug himself in in France when a second's delay meant death. That had been a placid pastime compared to his digging now. The pit grew deeper; when it was above his shoulders, he climbed out, and from some hard saplings cut stakes and sharpened them to a fine point. These stakes he planted in the bottom of the pit with the points sticking up. With flying fingers he wove a rough carpet of weeds and branches and with it he covered the mouth of the pit. Then, wet with sweat and aching with tiredness, he crouched behind the stump of a lightning-charred tree.

He knew his pursuer was coming; he heard the padding sound of feet on the soft earth, and the night breeze brought him the perfume of the general's cigarette. It seemed to Rainsford that the general was coming with unusual swiftness; he was not feeling his way along, foot by foot. Rainsford, crouching there, could not see the general, nor could he see the pit. He lived a year in a minute. Then he felt an impulse to cry aloud with joy, for he heard the sharp crackle of the breaking branches as the cover of the pit gave way; he heard the sharp scream of pain as the pointed stakes found their mark. He leaped up from his place of concealment. Then he cowered back. Three feet from the pit a man was standing, with an electric torch in his hand.

"You've done well, Rainsford," the voice of the general called. "Your Burmese tiger pit has claimed one of my best dogs. Again you score. I think, Mr. Rainsford, I'll see what you can do against my whole pack. I'm going home for a rest now. Thank you for a most amusing evening."

At daybreak, Rainsford, lying near the swamp, was awakened by a sound that made him know that he had new things to learn about fear. It was a distant sound, faint and wavering, but he knew it. It was the baying of a pack of hounds.

Rainsford knew he could do one of two

things. He could stay where he was and wait. That was suicide. He could flee. That was postponing the inevitable. For a moment he stood there, thinking. An idea that held a wild chance came to him, and tightening his belt, he headed away from the swamp.

The baying of the hounds grew nearer, then still nearer, nearer, ever nearer. On a ridge Rainsford climbed a tree. Down a watercourse, not a quarter of a mile away, he could see the bush moving. Straining his eyes, he saw the lean figure of General Zaroff. Just ahead of him Rainsford made out another figure whose wide shoulders surged through the tall jungle weeds. It was the giant Ivan, and he seemed pulled forward by some unseen force. Rainsford knew that Ivan must be holding the pack in leash.

They would be on him any minute now. His mind worked frantically. He thought of a native trick he had learned in Uganda. He slid down the tree. He caught hold of a springy young sapling, and to it he fastened his hunting knife, with the blade pointing down the trail. With a bit of wild grapevine he tied back the sapling. Then he ran for his life. The hounds raised their voices as they hit the fresh scent. Rainsford knew now how an animal at bay feels.

He had to stop to get his breath. The baying of the hounds stopped abruptly, and Rainsford's heart stopped too. They must have reached the knife.

He shinnied excitedly up a tree and looked back. His pursuers had stopped. But the hope that was in Rainsford's brain when he climbed died, for he saw in the shallow valley that General Zaroff was still on his feet. But Ivan was not. The knife, driven by the recoil of the springing tree, had not wholly failed.

Rainsford had hardly tumbled to the ground when the pack took up the cry again.

"Nerve, nerve, nerve!" he panted, as he dashed along. A blue gap showed between the trees dead ahead. Ever nearer drew the hounds. Rainsford forced himself on toward that gap. He reached it. It was the shore of the sea. Across the cove he could see the gloomy gray stone of the château. Twenty feet below

him the sea rumbled and hissed. Rainsford hesitated. He heard the hounds. Then he leaped far out into the sea. . . .

When the general and his pack reached the place by the sea, the Cossack stopped. For some minutes he stood regarding the blue-green expanse of water. He shrugged his shoulders. Then he sat down, took a drink of brandy from a silver flask, lit a perfumed cigarette, and hummed a bit from *Madame Butterfly*.[8]

General Zaroff had an exceedingly good dinner in his great paneled dining hall that evening. With it he had a bottle of Pol Roger and half a bottle of Chambertin. Two slight annoyances kept him from perfect enjoyment. One was the thought that it would be difficult to replace Ivan; the other was that his quarry escaped him. Of course, the American hadn't played the game—so thought the general as he tasted his after-dinner liqueur. In his library he read, to soothe himself, from the works of Marcus Aurelius.[9] At ten he went up to his bedroom. He was deliciously tired, he said to himself, as he locked himself in. There was a little moonlight, so, before turning on his light, he went to the window and looked down at the courtyard. He could see the great hounds, and he called: "Better luck next time," to them. Then he switched on the light.

A man, who had been hiding in the curtains of the bed, was standing there.

"Rainsford!" screamed the general. "How did you get here?"

"Swam," said Rainsford. "I found it quicker than walking through the jungle."

The general sucked in his breath and smiled. "I congratulate you," he said. "You have won the game."

Rainsford did not smile. "I am still a beast at bay," he said, in a low, hoarse voice. "Get ready, General Zaroff."

The general made one of his deepest bows. "I see," he said. "Splendid! One of us is to furnish a repast for the hounds. The other will sleep in this very excellent bed. On guard, Rainsford. . . ."

He had never slept in a better bed, Rainsford decided.

---

8. *Madame Butterfly:* an opera written by Giacomo Puccini.
9. **Marcus Aurelius** (ô rē′ lē əs): Roman emperor and philosopher.

Getting at Meaning

1. Rainsford and his friend Whitney have a discussion about hunting at the beginning of the story. What is Rainsford's position? Why is this conversation significant in the story?

2. How does Rainsford end up on the island? Describe the island and the château.

3. What makes Ivan a frightening character?

4. When do you first begin to suspect that General Zaroff is not just a polite host?

5. How does Zaroff justify his "game"? What are the rules of the game? What is Rainsford's reaction to Zaroff's description of the game?

6. During his three days at bay, Rainsford uses three traps to evade capture. Name each one and describe how it works. What happens on each day?

7. Why does Zaroff look away from Rainsford's hiding place in the tree? What is the meaning of Rainsford's realization, "The Cossack was the cat; he was the mouse"?

8. Describe Zaroff's reaction to Rainsford's plunge from the cliff. What does this reaction indicate about Zaroff's character?

9. Why do you think Rainsford chooses to confront Zaroff in the end, rather than simply to ambush and kill him?

Developing Skills in Reading Literature

1. **Setting.** How is the setting important to this story? Reread the description of the tropical night at the beginning of the story. How does this description make you feel? What words and phrases are particularly effective in creating this feeling?

2. **Suspense.** This story is difficult to put down; it generates a desire to find out what is going to happen. This feeling of excited anticipation is called suspense. Name several ways the writer of the story builds suspense.

3. **Foreshadowing.** Foreshadowing is a clue, a warning signal, in a story that something disturbing or tragic is going to happen later in the narrative. What clues to later events are given before Rainsford reaches the island? What clues are given when he first reaches the island?

4. **Irony.** How does Rainsford's position in the discussion with Whitney prove to be ironic? What is ironic about General Zaroff's character? about the ending of the story? Can you think of other ironies involving the plot and the characters?

5. **Characterization.** One of the ways a reader learns about a character is through description of that character's interests and style of living. What kind of person is Zaroff? How does he live? What does he value? Give evidence to support your answers. Why has Zaroff taken to hunting humans? What does this show about him?

Another way that a reader learns about a character is through the thoughts and feelings of the character. In this story, which character's thoughts and feelings are revealed directly to the reader? Find examples of passages that illustrate this technique of characterization.

6. **Theme.** Is there a message in this adventure story? If so, what is it?

7. **Connotation.** The writer of this story creates atmosphere and suspense through the careful choice of words. For example, when Rainsford falls off the ship, the reader is told that "the *blood-warm* waters of the Caribbean Sea closed over his head." What does the writer achieve with the adjective *blood-warm*? Find at least ten other examples of well chosen words and phrases that convey a great deal of meaning.

Developing Vocabulary

Antonyms. Rainsford tells Whitney, "The world is made up of two classes—the hunters and the huntees." *Hunter* and *huntee* are antonyms, words with opposite meanings; a hunter does the hunting while the huntee is a person or thing hunted. In this case, the antonym is formed by changing the suffix, or ending, on the root word *hunt*.

Copy the words below on a separate sheet of paper and then form an antonym for each word by adding a prefix, a syllable at the beginning of the word, or by changing the suffix on the root word.

dressed	luckily	usual
employer	obey	tasteful

Developing Writing Skills

1. **Analyzing a Character.** Using the clues to Zaroff's character supplied by the writer, write a paragraph about Zaroff. Your topic sentence should make a generalization about Zaroff, and the rest of your paragraph should support this generalization with specific information from the story.

2. **Developing an Argument.** Early in the story, Rainsford says to Whitney, "The world is made up of two classes—the hunters and the huntees. Luckily, you and I are hunters." Write a paragraph in which you either agree or disagree with Rainsford's statement. Support your position with evidence from your own experiences.

Something Bright   *Zenna Henderson*

Do you remember the Depression?[1] That black shadow across time? That hurting place in the consciousness of the world? Maybe not. Maybe it's like asking do you remember the Dark Ages?[2] Except what would I know about the price of eggs in the Dark Ages? I knew plenty about prices in the Depression.

If you had a quarter—*first find your quarter*—and five hungry kids, you could supper them on two cans of soup and a loaf of day-old bread, or two quarts of milk and a loaf of day-old bread. It was filling and—in an after-thoughty kind of way—nourishing. But if you were one of the hungry five, you eventually began to feel erosion set in, and your teeth ached for substance.

But to go back to eggs. Those were a precious commodity. You savored them slowly or gulped them eagerly—unmistakably as eggs—boiled or fried. That's one reason why I remember Mrs. Klevity. She had eggs for *breakfast!* And *every day!* That's *one* reason why I remember Mrs. Klevity.

I didn't know about the eggs the time she came over to see Mom, who had just got home from a twelve-hour day, cleaning up after other people at thirty cents an hour. Mrs. Klevity lived in the same court as we did. Courtesy called it a court because we were all dependent on the same shower house and two toilets that occupied the shack square in the middle of the court.

All of us except the Big House, of course. It had a bathroom of its own and even a radio blaring "Nobody's Business" and "Should I Reveal" and had ceiling lights that didn't

dangle nakedly at the end of a cord. But then it really wasn't a part of the court. Only its back door shared our area, and even that was different. It had *two* back doors in the same frame—a screen one and a wooden one!

Our own two-room place had a distinction, too. It had an upstairs. One room the size of our two. The Man Upstairs lived up there. He was mostly only the sound of footsteps overhead and an occasional cookie for Danna.

Anyway, Mrs. Klevity came over before Mom had time to put her shopping bag of work clothes down or even to unpleat the folds of fatigue that dragged her face down ten years or more of time to come. I didn't much like Mrs. Klevity. She made me uncomfortable. She was so solid and slow-moving and so nearly blind that she peered frighteningly wherever she went. She stood in the doorway as though she had been stacked there like bricks and a dress drawn hastily down over the stack and a face sketched on beneath a fuzz of hair. Us kids all gathered around to watch, except Danna who snuffled wearily into my neck. Day nursery or not, it was a long, hard day for a four-year-old.

"I wondered if one of your girls could sleep at my house this week." Her voice was as slow as her steps.

"At your house?" Mom massaged her hand

---

1. **Depression:** the period from about 1929 to 1939 that was marked by high unemployment, as well as falling prices and wages.
2. **Dark Ages:** the Middle Ages, especially from A.D. 476 to the late tenth century.

where the shopping-bag handles had criss-crossed it. "Come in. Sit down." We had two chairs and a bench and two apple boxes. The boxes scratched bare legs, but surely they couldn't scratch a stack of bricks.

"No, thanks." Maybe she couldn't bend. "My husband will be away several days and I don't like to be in the house alone at night."

"Of course," said Mom. "You must feel awfully alone."

The only aloneness *she* knew, what with five kids and two rooms, was the taut secretness of her inward thoughts as she mopped and swept and ironed in other houses. "Sure, one of the girls would be glad to keep you company." There was a darting squirm and LaNell was safely hidden behind the swaying of our clothes in the diagonally curtained corner of the Other room, and Kathy knelt swiftly just beyond the dresser, out of sight.

"Anna is eleven." I had no place to hide, burdened as I was with Danna. "She's old enough. What time do you want her to come over?"

"Oh, bedtime will do." Mrs. Klevity peered out of the door at the darkening sky. "Nine o'clock. Only it gets dark before then—" Bricks can look anxious, I guess.

"As soon as she has supper, she can come," said Mom, handling my hours as though they had no value to me. "Of course she has to go to school tomorrow."

"Only when it's dark," said Mrs. Klevity. "Day is all right. How much should I pay you?"

"Pay?" Mom gestured with one hand. "She has to sleep anyway. It doesn't matter to her where, once she's asleep. A favor for a friend."

I wanted to cry out, whose favor for what friend? We hardly passed the time of day with Mrs. Klevity. I couldn't even remember Mr. Klevity except that he was straight and old and wrinkled. Uproot me and make me lie in a strange house, a strange dark, listening to a strange breathing, feeling a strange warmth making itself a part of me for all night long, seeping into me. . . .

"Mom—" I said.

"I'll give her breakfast," said Mrs. Klevity. "And lunch money for each night she comes."

I resigned myself without a struggle. Lunch money each day—a whole dime! Mom couldn't afford to pass up such a blessing, such a gift from God, who unerringly could be trusted to ease the pinch just before it became intolerable.

"Thank you, God," I whispered as I went to get the can opener to open supper. For a night or two I could stand it.

I felt all naked and unprotected as I stood in my flimsy crinkle cotton pajamas, one bare foot atop the other, waiting for Mrs. Klevity to turn the bed down.

"We have to check the house first," she said thickly. "We can't go to bed until we check the house."

"Check the house?" I forgot my starchy stiff shyness enough to question. "What for?"

Mrs. Klevity peered at me in the dim light of the bedroom. They had *three* rooms for only the two of them! Even if there was no door to shut between the bedroom and the kitchen.

"I couldn't sleep," she said, "unless I looked first. I have to."

So we looked. Behind the closet curtain, under the table—Mrs. Klevity even looked in the portable oven that sat near the two-burner stove in the kitchen.

When we came to the bed, I was moved to words again. "But we've been in here with the doors locked ever since I got here. What could possibly—"

"A prowler?" said Mrs. Klevity nervously, after a brief pause for thought. "A criminal?"

Mrs. Klevity pointed her face at me. I doubt if she could see me from that distance.

"Doors make no difference," she said. "It might be when you least expect, so you have to expect all the time."

"I'll look," I said humbly. She was older than Mom. She was nearly blind. She was one of God's *Also Unto Me's*.[3]

"No," she said. "I have to. I couldn't be sure, else."

So I waited until she grunted and groaned to her knees, then bent stiffly to lift the limp spread. Her fingers hesitated briefly, then flicked the spread up. Her breath came out flat and finished. Almost disappointed, it seemed to me.

She turned the bed down and I crept across the gray, wrinkled sheets and, turning my back to the room, I huddled one ear on the flat tobacco-smelling pillow and lay tense and uncomfortable in the dark, as her weight shaped and reshaped the bed around me. There was a brief silence before I heard the soundless, breathy shape of her words, "How long, O God, how long?"

I wondered through my automatic *Bless Papa and Mama*—and the automatic back-up because Papa had abdicated from my specific prayers—*bless Mama and my brother and sisters*—what it was that Mrs. Klevity was finding too long to bear.

After a restless waking, dozing sort of night that strange sleeping places held for me, I awoke to a thin, chilly morning and the sound of Mrs. Klevity moving around. She had set the table for breakfast, a formality we never had time for at home. I scrambled out of bed and into my clothes with only my skinny, goosefleshed back between Mrs. Klevity and me for modesty. I felt uncomfortable and unfinished because I hadn't brought our comb over with me.

I would have preferred to run home to our usual breakfast of canned milk and shredded wheat, but instead I watched, fascinated, as Mrs. Klevity struggled with lighting the kerosene stove. She bent so close, peering at the burners with the match flaring in her hand that I was sure the frowzy brush of her hair would catch fire, but finally the burner caught instead and she turned her face toward me.

"One egg or two?" she asked.

"Eggs! Two!" Surprise wrung the exclamation from me. Her hand hesitated over the crumpled brown bag on the table. "No, no!" I corrected her thought hastily. "One. One is plenty." And sat on the edge of a chair watching as she broke an egg into the sizzling frying pan.

"Hard or soft?" she asked.

"Hard," I said casually, feeling very woman-of-the-worldish, dining out—well, practically—and for breakfast, too! I watched Mrs. Klevity spoon the fat over the egg, her hair swinging stiffly forward when she peered. Once it even dabbled briefly in the fat, but she didn't notice and, as it swung back, it made a little shiny curve on her cheek.

"Aren't you afraid of the fire?" I asked as she turned away from the stove with the frying pan. "What if you caught on fire?"

"I did once." She slid the egg out onto my plate. "See?" She brushed her hair back on the left side, and I could see the mottled pucker of a large old scar. "It was before I got used to Here," she said, making Here more than the house, it seemed to me.

"That's awful," I said, hesitating with my fork.

"Go ahead and eat," she said. "Your egg will get cold." She turned back to the stove, and I hesitated a minute more. Meals at a table you were supposed to ask a blessing, but . . . I ducked my head quickly and had a mouthful of egg before my soundless amen was finished.

---

3. *Also Unto Me's:* A reference to the New Testament passage: "Inasmuch as you have done it unto one of the least of these my brethren, you have done it also unto me."

After breakfast I hurried back to our house, my lunch-money dime clutched securely, my stomach not quite sure it liked fried eggs so early in the morning. Mom was ready to leave, her shopping bag in one hand, Danna swinging from the other, singing one of her baby songs. She *liked* the day nursery.

"I won't be back until late tonight," Mom said. "There's a quarter in the corner of the dresser drawer. You get supper for the kids and try to clean up this messy place. We don't have to be pigs just because we live in a place like this."

"Okay, Mom." I struggled with a snarl in my hair, the pulling making my eyes water. "Where you working today?" I spoke over the clatter in the other room where the kids were getting ready for school.

She sighed, weary before the day began. "I have three places today, but the last is Mrs. Paddington." Her face lightened. Mrs. Paddington sometimes paid a little extra or gave Mom discarded clothes or leftover food she didn't want. She was nice.

"You get along all right with Mrs. Klevity?" asked Mom as she checked her shopping bag for her work shoes.

"Yeah," I said. "But she's funny. She looks under the bed before she goes to bed."

Mom smiled. "I've heard of people like that, but it's usually old maids they're talking about."

"But, Mom, nothing coulda got in. She locked the door after I got there."

"People who look under beds don't always think straight," she said. "Besides, maybe she'd *like* to find something under there."

"But she's *got* a husband," I cried after her as she herded Danna across the court.

"There are other things to look for beside husbands," she called back.

"Anna wants a husband! Anna wants a husband!" Deet and LaNell were dancing around me, teasing me singsong. Kathy smiled slowly behind them.

"Shut up," I said. "You don't even know what you're talking about. Go on to school."

"It's too early," said Deet, digging his bare toes in the dust of the front yard. "Teacher says we get there too early."

"Then stay here and start cleaning house," I said.

They left in a hurry. After they were gone, Deet's feet reminded me I'd better wash my own feet before I went to school. So I got a washpan of water from the tap in the middle of the court and, sitting on the side of the bed, I eased my feet into the icy water. I scrubbed with the hard, gray, abrasive soap we used and wiped quickly on the tattered towel. I threw the water out the door and watched it run like dust-covered snakes across the hard-packed front yard.

I went back to put my shoes on and get my sweater. I looked at the bed. I got down on my stomach and peered under. *Other things to look for.* There was the familiar huddle of cardboard cartons we kept things in and the familiar dust fluffs and one green sock LaNell had lost last week, but nothing else.

I dusted my front off. I tied my lunch-money dime in the corner of a handkerchief and, putting my sweater on, left for school.

I peered out into the windy wet semi-twilight. "Do I have to?"

"You said you would," said Mom. "Keep your promises. You should have gone before this. She's probably been waiting for you."

"I wanted to see what you brought from Mrs. Paddington's." LaNell and Kathy were playing in the corner with a lavender hug-me-tight[4] and a hat with green grapes on it. Deet was rolling an orange on the floor, softening it preliminary to poking a hole in it to suck the juice out.

"She cleaned a trunk out today," said Mom. "Mostly old things that belonged to her

---

4. **hug-me-tight:** a woman's close-fitting jacket.

mother, but these two coats are nice and heavy. They'll be good covers tonight. It's going to be cold. Someday when I get time, I'll cut them up and make quilts." She sighed. Time was what she never had enough of. "Better take a newspaper to hold over your head."

"Oh, Mom!" I huddled into my sweater. "It isn't raining now. I'd feel silly!"

"Well, then, scoot!" she said, her hand pressing my shoulder warmly, briefly.

I scooted, skimming quickly the flood of light from our doorway, and splishing through the shallow run-off stream that swept across the court. There was a sudden wild swirl of wind and a vindictive splatter of heavy, cold raindrops that swept me, exhilarated, the rest of the way to Mrs. Klevity's house and under the shallow little roof that was just big enough to cover the back step. I knocked quickly, brushing my disordered hair back from my eyes. The door swung open and I was in the shadowy, warm kitchen, almost in Mrs. Klevity's arms.

"Oh!" I backed up, laughing breathlessly. "The wind blew—"

"I was afraid you weren't coming." She turned away to the stove. "I fixed some hot cocoa."

I sat cuddling the warm cup in my hands, savoring the chocolate sip by sip. She had made it with milk instead of water, and it tasted rich and wonderful. But Mrs. Klevity was sharing my thoughts with the cocoa. In that brief moment when I had been so close to her, I had looked deep into her dim eyes and was feeling a vast astonishment. The dimness was only on top. Underneath—underneath—

I took another sip of cocoa. Her eyes—almost I could have walked into them, it ~~seemed~~ like. Slip past the gray film, run down ~~~~ bright corridor, into the live young ~~~~ far end.

~~~~ into my cup of cocoa. Were

all grownups like that? If you could get behind their eyes, were they different, too? Behind Mom's eyes, was there a corridor leading back to youth and sparkle?

I finished the cocoa drowsily. It was still early, but the rain was drumming on the roof and it was the kind of night you curl up to if you're warm and fed. Sometimes you feel thin and cold on such nights, but I was feeling curl-uppy. So I groped under the bed for the paper bag that had my jammas in it. I couldn't find it.

"I swept today," said Mrs. Klevity, coming back from some far country of her thoughts. "I musta pushed it farther under the bed."

I got down on my hands and knees and peered under the bed. "Ooo!" I said. "What's shiny?"

Something snatched me away from the bed and flung me to one side. By the time I had gathered myself up off the floor and was rubbing a banged elbow, Mrs. Klevity's bulk was pressed against the bed, her head under it.

"Hey!" I cried indignantly, and then remembered I wasn't at home. I heard an odd, whimpering sob and then Mrs. Klevity backed slowly away, still kneeling on the floor.

"Only the lock on the suitcase," she said. "Here's your jammas." She handed me the bag and ponderously pulled herself upright again.

We went silently to bed after she had limped around and checked the house, even under the bed again. I heard that odd breathy whisper of a prayer and lay awake, trying to add up something shiny and the odd eyes and the whispering sob. Finally I shrugged in the dark and wondered what I'd pick for funny when I grew up. All grownups had some kind of funny.

The next night Mrs. Klevity couldn't get down on her knees to look under the bed.

She'd hurt herself when she plumped down on the floor after yanking me away from the bed.

"You'll have to look for me tonight," she said slowly, nursing her knees. "Look good. Oh, Anna, look good!"

I looked as good as I could, not knowing what I was looking for.

"It should be under the bed," she said, her palms tight on her knees as she rocked back and forth. "But you can't be sure. It might miss completely."

"What might?" I asked, hunkering down by the bed.

She turned her face blindly toward me. "The way out," she said. "The way back again———"

"Back again?" I pressed my cheek to the floor again. "Well, I don't see anything. Only dark and suitcases."

"Nothing bright? Nothing? Nothing———" She tried to lay her face on her knees, but she was too unbendy to manage it, so she put her hands over her face instead. Grownups aren't suppose to cry. She didn't quite, but her hands looked wet when she reached for the clock to wind it.

I lay in the dark, one strand of her hair tickling my hand where it lay on the pillow. Maybe she was crazy. I felt a thrill of terror fan out on my spine. I carefully moved my hand from under the lock of hair. How can you find a way *out* under a *bed*? I'd be glad when Mr. Klevity got home, eggs or no eggs, dime or no dime.

Somewhere in the darkness of the night, I was suddenly swimming to wakefulness, not knowing what was waking me but feeling that Mrs. Klevity was awake too.

"Anna." Her voice was small and light and silver. "Anna———"

"Hummm?" I murmured, my voice still drowsy.

"Anna, have you ever been away from home?" I turned toward her, trying in the dark to make sure it was Mrs. Klevity. She sounded so different.

"Yes," I said. "Once I visited Aunt Katie at Rocky Butte for a week."

"Anna." I don't know whether she was even hearing my answers; her voice was almost a chant. "Anna, have you ever been in prison?"

"No! Of course not!" I recoiled indignantly. "You have to be awfully bad to be in prison."

"Oh, no. Oh, no!" she sighed. "Not jail, Anna. Prison, prison. The weight of the flesh —bound about———"

"Oh," I said, smoothing my hands across my eyes. She was talking to a something deep in me that never got talked to, that hardly

THE RED TREE, 1908. *Piet Mondrian.*
Gemeente Museum, The Hague, The Netherlands.

even had words. "Like when the wind blows the clouds across the moon and the grass whispers along the road and all the trees pull like balloons at their trunks and one star comes out and says 'Come' and the ground says 'Stay' and part of you tries to go and it hurts——" I could feel the slender roundness of my ribs under my pressing hands. "And it hurts——"

"Oh, Anna, Anna!" The soft, light voice broke. "You feel that way and you *belong* Here. You won't ever——"

The voice stopped and Mrs. Klevity rolled over. Her next words came thickly, as though a gray film were over them as over her eyes. "Are you awake, Anna? Go to sleep, child. Morning isn't yet."

I heard the heavy sigh of her breathing as she slept. And finally I slept too, trying to visualize what Mrs. Klevity would look like if she looked like the silvery voice-in-the-dark.

I sat savoring my egg the next morning, letting thoughts slip in and out of my mind to the rhythm of my jaws. What a funny dream to have, to talk with a silver-voiced someone. To talk about the way blowing clouds and windy moonlight felt. But it wasn't a dream! I paused with my fork raised. At least not my dream. But how can you tell? If you're part of someone else's dream, can it still be real for you?

"Is something wrong with the egg?" Mrs. Klevity peered at me.

"No—no——" I said, hastily snatching the bite on my fork. "Mrs. Klevity——"

"Yes." Her voice was thick and heavy-footed.

"Why did you ask me about being in prison?"

"Prison?" Mrs. Klevity blinked blindly. "Did I ask you about prison?"

"Someone did—I thought——" I faltered, shyness shutting down on me again.

"Dreams." Mrs. Klevity stacked her knife on her plate. "Dreams."

I wasn't quite sure I was to be at Mrs. Klevity's the next evening. Mr. Klevity was supposed to get back sometime during the evening. But Mrs. Klevity welcomed me.

"Don't know when he'll get home," she said. "Maybe not until morning. If he comes early, you can go home to sleep and I'll give you your dime anyway."

"Oh, no," I said, Mom's teaching solidly behind me. "I couldn't take it if I didn't stay."

"A gift," said Mrs. Klevity.

We sat opposite one another until the silence stretched too thin for me to bear.

"In olden times," I said, snatching at the magic that drew stories from Mom, "when you were a little girl——"

"When I was a girl——" Mrs. Klevity rubbed her knees with reflective hands. "The other Where. The other When."

"In olden times," I persisted, "things were different then."

"Yes." I settled down comfortably, recognizing the reminiscent tone of voice. "You do crazy things when you are young." Mrs. Klevity leaned heavily on the table. "Things you have no business doing. You volunteer when you're young." I jerked as she lunged across the table and grabbed both my arms. "But I *am* young! Three years isn't an eternity. I *am* young!"

I twisted one arm free and pried at her steely fingers that clamped my other one.

"Oh." She let go. "I'm sorry. I didn't mean to hurt you."

She pushed back the tousled brush of her hair.

"Look," she said, her voice was almost silver again. "Under all this—this grossness, I'm still me. I thought I could adjust to anything, but I had no idea that they'd put me in such——" She tugged at her sagging dress. "Not the clothes!" she cried. "Clothes you can take off. But this——" Her fingers dug into her heavy shoulder and I could see the bulge of flesh between them.

"If I knew *anything* about the setup maybe I could locate it. Maybe I could call. Maybe——"

Her shoulders sagged and her eyelids dropped down over her dull eyes.

"It doesn't make any sense to you," she said, her voice heavy and thick again. "To you I'd be old even There. At the time it seemed like a perfect way to have an odd holiday and help out with research, too. But we got caught."

She began to count her fingers, mumbling to herself. "Three years There, but Here that's —eight threes are——" She traced on the table with a blunt forefinger, her eyes close to the old, wornout cloth.

"Mrs. Klevity." My voice scared me in the silence, but I was feeling the same sort of upsurge that catches you sometimes when you're playinglike and it gets so real. "Mrs. Klevity, if you've lost something, maybe I could look for it for you."

"You didn't find it last night," she said.

"Find what?"

She lumbered to her feet. "Let's look again. Everywhere. They'd surely be able to locate the house."

"What are we looking for?" I asked, searching the portable oven.

"You'll know it when we see it," she said.

And we searched the whole house. Oh, such nice things! Blankets, not tattered and worn, and even an extra one they didn't need. And towels with wash rags that matched —and weren't rags. And uncracked dishes that matched! And glasses that weren't jars. And books. And money. Crisp new-looking bills in the little box in the bottom drawer— pushed back under some *extra* pillow cases. And clothes—lots and lots of clothes. All too

big for any of us, of course, but my practiced eye had already visualized this, that, and the other cut down to dress us all like rich people.

I sighed as we sat wearily looking at one another. Imagine having so much and still looking for something else! It was bedtime, and all we had for our pains were dirty hands and tired backs.

I scooted out to the bath house before I undressed. I gingerly washed the dirt off my hands under the cold of the shower and shook them dry on the way back to the house. Well, we had moved everything in the place, but nothing was what Mrs. Klevity looked for.

Back in the bedroom, I groped under the bed for my jammas and again had to lie flat and burrow under the bed for the tattered bag. Our moving around had wedged it back between two cardboard cartons. I squirmed under farther and tried to ease it out after shoving the two cartons a little farther apart. The bag tore, spilling out my jammas, so I grasped them in the bend of my elbow and started to back out.

Then the whole world seemed to explode into brightness that pulsated and dazzled, that splashed brilliance into my astonished eyes until I winced them shut to rest their seeing and saw the dark inversions of the radiance behind my eyelids.

I forced my eyes open again and looked sideways, so the edge of my seeing was all I used until I got more accustomed to the glory.

Between the two cartons was an opening like a window would be, but little, little, into a wonderland of things I could never tell. Colors that had no names. Feelings that made windy moonlight a puddle of dust. I felt tears burn out of my eyes and start down my cheeks, whether from brightness or wonder, I don't know. I blinked them away and looked again.

Someone was in the brightness, several someones. They were leaning out of the squareness, beckoning and calling—silver signals and silver sounds.

"Mrs. Klevity," I thought. "Something bright."

I took another good look at the shining people and the tree things that were like music bordering a road, and grass that was the song my evening grass hummed in the wind—a last, last look, and began to back out.

I scrambled to my feet, clutching my jammas. "Mrs. Klevity." She was still sitting at the table, as solid as a pile of bricks, the sketched face under the wild hair a sad, sad one.

"Yes, child." She hardly heard herself.

"Something bright . . ." I said.

Her heavy head lifted slowly, her blind face turned to me. "What, child?"

I felt my fingers bite into my jammas and the cords in my neck getting tight and my stomach clenching itself. "Something bright!" I thought I screamed. She didn't move. I grabbed her arm and dragged her off-balance in her chair. "Something bright!"

"Anna." She righted herself on the chair. "Don't be mean."

I grabbed the bedspread and yanked it up. The light sprayed out like a sprinkler on a lawn.

Then *she* screamed. She put both hands up to her heavy face and screamed, "Leolienn! It's here! Hurry, hurry!"

"Mr. Klevity isn't here," I said. "He hasn't got back."

"I can't go without him! Leolienn!"

"Leave a note!" I cried. "If you're there, you can make them come back again and I can show him the right place!" The upsurge had passed make-believe and everything was realer than real.

Then, quicker than I ever thought she could move, she got paper and a pencil. She was scribbling away at the table as I stood there holding the spread. So I dropped to my knees and then to my stomach and crawled under the bed again. I filled my eyes with the brightness and beauty and saw, beyond it, serenity and orderliness and—and uncluttered cleanness. The miniature landscape was like a stage setting for a fairy tale—so small, so small—so lovely.

And then Mrs. Klevity tugged at my ankle and I slid out, reluctantly stretching my sight of the bright square until the falling of the spread broke it. Mrs. Klevity worked her way under the bed, her breath coming pantingly, her big, ungainly body inching along awkwardly.

She crawled and crawled and crawled until she should have come up short against the wall, and I knew she must be funneling down

STONE CITY, IOWA, 1930. Grant Wood. Joslyn Art Museum. Gift of the Art Institute of Omaha, 1931.

into the brightness, her face, head, and shoulders, so small, so lovely, like her silvery voice. But the rest of her, still gross and ugly, like a butterfly trying to skin out of its cocoon.

Finally only her feet were sticking out from under the bed and they thrashed and waved and didn't go anywhere, so I got down on the floor and put my feet against hers and braced myself against the dresser and pushed. And pushed and pushed. Suddenly there was a going, a finishing, and my feet dropped to the floor.

There, almost under the bed, lay Mrs. Klevity's shabby old-lady black shoes, toes pointing away from each other. I picked them up in my hands, wanting, somehow, to cry. Her saggy lisle stockings were still in the shoes.

Slowly I pulled all of the clothes of Mrs. Klevity out from under the bed. They were held together by a thin skin, a sloughed-off leftover of Mrs. Klevity that only showed, gray and lifeless, where her bare hands and face would have been, and her dull gray filmed eyes.

I let it crumple to the floor and sat there, holding one of her old shoes in my hand.

The door rattled and it was gray, old, wrinkled Mr. Klevity.

"Hello, child," he said. "Where's my wife?"

"She's gone," I said, not looking at him. "She left you a note there on the table."

"Gone———?" He left the word stranded in mid-air as he read Mrs. Klevity's note.

The paper fluttered down. He yanked a dresser drawer open and snatched out spool-looking things, both hands full. Then he practically dived under the bed, his elbows thudding on the floor, to hurt hard. And there was only a wiggle or two and *his* shoes slumped away from each other.

I pulled his cast-aside from under the bed and crawled under it myself. I saw the tiny picture frame—bright, bright, but so small.

I crept close to it, knowing I couldn't go in. I saw the tiny perfection of the road, the landscape, the people—the laughing people who crowded around the two new rejoicing figures—the two silvery, lovely young creatures who cried out in tiny voices as they danced. The girl-one threw a kiss outward before they all turned away and ran up the winding white road together.

The frame began to shrink, faster, faster, until it squeezed to a single bright bead and then blinked out.

All at once the house was empty and cold. The upsurge was gone. Nothing was real any more. All at once the faint ghost of the smell of eggs was frightening. All at once I whimpered, "My lunch money!"

I scrambled to my feet, tumbling Mrs. Klevity's clothes into a disconnected pile. I gathered up my jammas and leaned across the table to get my sweater. I saw my name on a piece of paper. I picked it up and read it.

Everything that is ours in this house now belongs to Anna-across-the-court, the little girl that's been staying with me at night.
Ahvlaree Klevity

I looked from the paper across the room. All for me? All for us? All this richness and wonder of good things? All this and the box in the bottom drawer, too? And a paper that said so, so that nobody could take them away from us.

A fluttering wonder filled my chest and I walked stiffly around the three rooms, visualizing everything without opening a drawer or door. I stood by the stove and looked at the frying pan hanging above it. I opened the cupboard door. The paper bag of eggs was on the shelf. I reached for it, looking back over my shoulder almost guiltily.

The wonder drained out of me with a gulp. I ran back over to the bed and yanked up the spread. I knelt and hammered on the edge of the bed with my clenched fists. Then I leaned my forehead on my tight hands and felt my knuckles bruise me. My hands went limply to my lap, my head drooping.

I got up slowly and took the paper from the table, bundled my jammas under my arm and got the eggs from the cupboard. I turned the lights out and left.

I felt tears wash down from my eyes as I stumbled across the familiar yard in the dark. I don't know why I was crying—unless it was because I was homesick for something bright that I knew I would never have, and because I knew I could never tell Mom what really happened.

Then the pale trail of light from our door caught me, and I swept in on an astonished Mom, calling softly, because of the sleeping kids. "Mom! Mom! Guess what!"

Yes, I remember Mrs. Klevity because she had eggs for *breakfast! Every day!* That's *one* of the reasons I remember her.

Getting at Meaning

1. Why does Anna feel such sadness at the end of the story? At the same time, what makes her feel a little better?

2. What is Anna's first reaction to Mrs. Klevity? Find passages in the story to support your answer. Later, what other side to Mrs. Klevity does Anna see?

3. What routine does Mrs. Klevity go through every night? How is her home different from Anna's?

4. What prevents Mrs. Klevity from being happy? What mistake had she made when she was young? What is her "prison"?

Developing Skills in Reading Literature

1. **Fiction.** Some stories are realistic; that is, they present characters and events that are true to life. Other stories are more imaginative. They feature characters and deal with events that are not possible in the real world. What stories that you have read so far are examples of realistic fiction? What makes "Something Bright" an example of imaginative rather than realistic fiction?

2. **Setting.** The writer of this story does not use lengthy descriptions of setting. Instead, she has the main character make observations about her home and the time in which she lives. These observations give the reader a clear picture of both the time and place.

When does the story take place? Why is this important? Give two concrete examples from the story that help the reader understand what life was like in the Depression. Describe Anna's house and the surrounding courtyard. Find four or five details about the place, and note the location of the details.

3. **Theme.** In this story, what does Anna realize about her world from her experiences with Mrs. Klevity?

Developing Writing Skills

1. **Writing an Explanation.** Anna defines the value of a quarter through examples of what a quarter can do. She explains that a quarter can feed five hungry kids by buying "two cans of soup and a loaf of day-old bread, or two quarts of milk and a loaf of day-old bread." Choose something that you value: a job, a friend, a pet, a freedom. Then describe your choice by giving concrete, specific examples to illustrate its importance to you.

2. **Description: Creating a Dominant Impression.** Describe, in as much detail as possible, the land of There as you imagine it. Unify your description by developing and maintaining one feeling about the place.

Character

THREE STUDIES OF A YOUNG NEGRO. *Jean-Antoine Watteau.*
The Louvre, Paris.

Thank You, M'am   *Langston Hughes*

She was a large woman with a large purse that had everything in it but a hammer and nails. It had a long strap, and she carried it slung across her shoulder. It was about eleven o'clock at night, dark, and she was walking alone, when a boy ran up behind her and tried to snatch her purse. The strap broke with the sudden single tug the boy gave it from behind. But the boy's weight and the weight of the purse combined caused him to lose his balance. Instead of taking off full blast as he had hoped, the boy fell on his back on the sidewalk and his legs flew up. The large woman simply turned around and kicked him right square in his blue-jeaned sitter. Then she reached down, picked the boy up by his shirt front, and shook him until his teeth rattled.

After that the woman said, "Pick up my pocketbook, boy, and give it here."

She still held him tightly. But she bent down enough to permit him to stoop and pick up her purse. Then she said, "Now ain't you ashamed of yourself?"

Firmly gripped by his shirt front, the boy said, "Yes'm."

The woman said, "What did you want to do it for?"

The boy said, "I didn't aim to."

She said, "You a lie!"

By that time two or three people passed, stopped, turned to look, and some stood watching.

"If I turn you loose, will you run?" asked the woman.

"Yes'm," said the boy.

"Then I won't turn you loose," said the woman. She did not release him.

"Lady, I'm sorry," whispered the boy.

"Um-hum. Your face is dirty. I got a great mind to wash your face for you. Ain't you got nobody home to tell you to wash your face?"

"No'm," said the boy.

"Then it will get washed this evening," said the large woman, starting up the street, dragging the frightened boy behind her.

He looked as if he were fourteen or fifteen, frail and willow-wild, in tennis shoes and blue jeans.

The woman said, "You ought to be my son. I would teach you right from wrong. Least I can do right now is to wash your face. Are you hungry?"

"No'm," said the being-dragged boy. "I just want you to turn me loose."

"Was I bothering *you* when I turned that corner?" asked the woman.

"No'm."

"But you put yourself in contact with *me*," said the woman. "If you think that that contact is not going to last awhile, you got another thought coming. When I get through with you, sir, you are going to remember Mrs. Luella Bates Washington Jones."

Sweat popped out on the boy's face, and he began to struggle. Mrs. Jones stopped, jerked him around in front of her, put a half nelson[1] about his neck, and continued to drag him up the street. When she got to her door, she

---

1. **half nelson:** a wrestling hold.

dragged the boy inside, down a hall, and into a large kitchenette-furnished room at the rear of the house. She switched on the light and left the door open. The boy could hear other roomers laughing and talking in the large house. Some of their doors were open, too, so he knew that he and the woman were not alone. The woman still had him by the neck in the middle of her room.

She said, "What is your name?"

"Roger," answered the boy.

"Then, Roger, you go to that sink and wash your face," said the woman, whereupon she turned him loose—at last. Roger looked at the door—looked at the woman—looked at the door—*and went to the sink.*

"Let the water run until it gets warm," she said. "Here's a clean towel."

"You gonna take me to jail?" asked the boy, bending over the sink.

"Not with that face; I would not take you nowhere," said the woman. "Here I am trying to get home to cook me a bite to eat, and you snatch my pocketbook! Maybe you ain't been to your supper either, late as it be. Have you?"

"There's nobody home at my house," said the boy.

"Then we'll eat," said the woman. "I believe you're hungry—or been hungry—to try to snatch my pocketbook!"

"I want a pair of blue suede shoes," said the boy.

"Well, you didn't have to snatch *my* pocketbook to get some suede shoes," said Mrs. Luella Bates Washington Jones. "You could of asked me."

"M'am?"

The water dripping from his face, the boy looked at her. There was a long pause. A very long pause. After he had dried his face and not knowing what else to do, dried it again, the boy turned around, wondering what next. The door was open. He could make a dash for it down the hall. He could run, run, run, *run!*

The woman was sitting on the day bed. After a while she said, "I were young once and I wanted things I could not get."

There was another long pause. The boy's mouth opened. Then he frowned, not knowing he frowned.

The woman said, "Um-hum! You thought I was going to say *but,* didn't you? You thought I was going to say, *but I didn't snatch people's pocketbooks.* Well I wasn't going to say that." Pause. Silence. "I have done things, too, which I would not tell you, son—neither tell God, if He didn't already know. Everybody's got something in common. So you set down while I fix us something to eat. You might run that comb through your hair so you will look presentable."

In another corner of the room behind a screen was a gas plate and an icebox. Mrs. Jones got up and went behind the screen. The woman did not watch the boy to see if he was going to run now, nor did she watch her purse, which she left behind her on the day bed. But the boy took care to sit on the far side of the room, away from the purse, where he thought she could easily see him out of the corner of her eye if she wanted to. He did not trust the woman *not* to trust him. And he did not want to be mistrusted now.

"Do you need somebody to go to the store," asked the boy, "maybe to get some milk or something?"

"Don't believe I do," said the woman, "unless you just want sweet milk yourself. I was going to make cocoa out of this canned milk I got here."

"That will be fine," said the boy.

She heated some lima beans and ham she had in the icebox, made the cocoa, and set the table. The woman did not ask the boy anything about where he lived, or his folks, or anything else that would embarrass him. Instead, as they ate, she told him about her job in a hotel beauty shop that stayed open late, what the work was like, and how all kinds of women came in and out, blondes, redheads, and Spanish. Then she cut him a half of her ten-cent cake.

"Eat some more, son," she said.

When they were finished eating, she got up and said, "Now here, take this ten dollars and buy yourself some blue suede shoes. And next time, do not make the mistake of latching onto *my* pocketbook *nor nobody else's*— because shoes got by devilish ways will burn your feet. I got to get my rest now. But from here on in, son, I hope you will behave yourself."

She led him down the hall to the front door and opened it. "Good night! Behave yourself, boy!" she said, looking out into the street as he went down the steps.

The boy wanted to say something other than, "Thank you, m'am," to Mrs. Luella Bates Washington Jones; but although his lips moved, he couldn't even say that as he turned at the foot of the barren stoop and looked up at the large woman in the door. Then she shut the door.

Getting at Meaning

1. What does Mrs. Jones guess about Roger's home life? What is apparently true of her own home life?

2. Why does Mrs. Jones respond as she does to Roger's attempted theft? What does her attention to Roger indicate about her? Why is her manner so gruff? Why does she give Roger the ten dollars?

3. How does Roger feel when Mrs. Jones first takes him home? Why doesn't he steal her pocketbook and run away when he has the chance? Why does Roger ask if he can go to the store for her? How do you think he feels when he leaves her?

Developing Skills in Reading Literature

1. **Plot.** Is the conflict in this story mainly external or internal? What is the climax, or turning point? What does Roger realize?

2. **Characterization.** One way that writers develop characters is through description of external characteristics, such as size, clothes, color of hair, and facial expression.

What are Mrs. Jones's external characteristics? What is her full name? Why does her name seem to suit her? Does her physical appearance fit the kind of person she is?

Another way that writers develop characters is through dialogue and action. What Mrs. Jones says and does, for example, give clues to her personality, values, and beliefs. Why does Mrs. Jones make Roger wash his face? Why does she talk about her youth? What action shows that she trusts Roger? How does she show that she understands Roger and his situation?

3. **Theme.** Mrs. Jones responds to a violent act with kindness. What message is the writer trying to convey through this character? In one or two sentences, suggest a theme for this story.

Developing Writing Skills

1. **Maintaining the Same Point of View.** Write a paragraph from Roger's point of view in which you describe his thoughts as he leaves Mrs. Jones. Use first-person narration, and remember that the "I" in your paragraph is Roger.

2. **Narration: Writing About an Incident.** Write a paragraph about an incident in which someone responded to a hostile act with kindness and love. It may be an incident that involved you personally or one that you observed. Describe the effects of the kindness on the person who performed the hostile act.

Everyday Use   *Alice Walker*

I will wait for her in the yard that Maggie and I made so clean and wavy yesterday afternoon. A yard like this is more comfortable than most people know. It is not just a yard. It is like an extended living room. When the hard clay is swept clean as a floor and the fine sand around the edges lined with tiny, irregular grooves, anyone can come and sit and look up into the elm tree and wait for the breezes that never come inside the house.

Maggie will be nervous until after her sister goes. She will stand hopelessly in corners, homely and ashamed of the burn scars down her arms and legs, eyeing her sister with a mixture of envy and awe. She thinks her sister has held life always in the palm of one hand, that "no" is a word the world never learned to say to her.

You've no doubt seen those TV shows where the child who has "made it" is confronted, as a surprise, by her own mother and father, tottering in weakly from backstage. (A pleasant surprise, of course. What would they do if parent and child came on the show only to curse out and insult each other?) On TV, mother and child embrace and smile into each other's faces. Sometimes the mother and father weep, the child wraps them in her arms and leans across the table to tell how she would not have made it without their help. I have seen these programs.

Sometimes I dream a dream in which Dee and I are suddenly brought together on a TV program of this sort. Out of a dark and soft-seated limousine I am ushered into a bright room filled with many people. There I meet a smiling, gray, sporty man like Johnny Carson, who shakes my hand and tells me what a fine girl I have. Then we are on the stage and Dee is embracing me with tears in her eyes. She pins on my dress a large orchid, even though she has told me once that she thinks orchids are tacky flowers.

In real life I am a large, big-boned woman with rough, man-working hands. In the winter I wear flannel nightgowns to bed and overalls during the day. I can kill and clean a hog as mercilessly as a man. My fat keeps me hot in zero weather. I can work outside all day, breaking ice to get water for washing; I can eat pork liver cooked over the open fire minutes after it comes steaming from the hog. One winter I knocked a bull calf straight in the brain between the eyes with a sledge hammer and had the meat hung up to chill before nightfall. But of course all this does not show on television. I am the way my daughter would want me to be: a hundred pounds lighter, my skin like an uncooked barley pancake. My hair glistens in the hot bright lights. Johnny Carson has much to do to keep up with my quick and witty tongue.

But that is a mistake. I know even before I wake up. Who ever knew a Johnson with a quick tongue? Who can even imagine me looking a strange white man in the eye? It seems to me I have talked to them always with one foot raised in flight, with my head turned in whichever way is farthest from them. Dee, though. She would always look anyone in the eye. Hesitation was no part of her nature.

"How do I look, Mama?" Maggie says, showing just enough of her thin body enveloped in pink skirt and red blouse for me to know she's there, almost hidden by the door.

"Come out into the yard," I say.

Have you ever seen a lame animal, perhaps a dog run over by some careless person rich enough to own a car, sidle up to someone who is ignorant enough to be kind to him? That is the way my Maggie walks. She has been like this, chin on chest, eyes on ground, feet in shuffle, ever since the fire that burned the other house to the ground.

Dee is lighter than Maggie, with nicer hair and a fuller figure. She's a woman now, though sometimes I forget. How long ago was it that the other house burned? Ten, twelve years? Sometimes I can still hear the flames and feel Maggie's arms sticking to me, her hair smoking and her dress falling off her in little black papery flakes. Her eyes seemed stretched open, blazed open by the flames reflected in them. And Dee. I see her standing off under the sweet gum tree she used to dig gum out of; a look of concentration on her face as she watched the last dingy gray board of the house fall in toward the red-hot brick chimney. Why don't you do a dance around the ashes? I'd wanted to ask her. She had hated the house that much.

I used to think she hated Maggie, too. But that was before we raised the money, the church and me, to send her to Augusta[1] to school. She used to read to us without pity; forcing words, lies, other folks' habits, whole lives upon us two, sitting trapped and ignorant underneath her voice. She washed us in a river of make-believe, burned us with a lot of knowledge we didn't necessarily need to know. Pressed us to her with the serious way

she read, to shove us away at just the moment, like dimwits, we seemed about to understand.

Dee wanted nice things. A yellow organdy dress to wear to her graduation from high school; black pumps to match a green suit she'd made from an old suit somebody gave me. She was determined to stare down any disaster in her efforts. Her eyelids would not flicker for minutes at a time. Often I fought off the temptation to shake her. At sixteen she had a style of her own, and knew what style was.

I never had an education myself. After second grade the school was closed down. Don't ask me why; in 1927 blacks asked fewer questions than they do now. Sometimes Maggie reads to me. She stumbles along good-naturedly but can't see well. She knows she is not bright. Like good looks and money, quickness passed her by. She will marry John Thomas (who has mossy teeth in an earnest face), and then I'll be free to sit here and I guess just sing church songs to myself. Although I never was a good singer. Never could carry a tune. I was always better at a man's job. I used to love to milk till I was hooked in the side in '49. Cows are soothing and slow and don't bother you, unless you try to milk them the wrong way.

I have deliberately turned my back on the house. It is three rooms, just like the one that burned, except the roof is tin; they don't make shingle roofs any more. There are no real windows, just some holes cut in the sides, like the portholes in a ship, but not round and not square, with rawhide holding the shutters up on the outside. This house is in a pasture, too, like the other one. No doubt when Dee sees it she will want to tear it down. She wrote me once that no matter where we "choose" to

---

1. **Augusta:** a city in Georgia that is the site of Augusta College.

live, she will manage to come see us. But she will never bring her friends. Maggie and I thought about this and Maggie asked me, "Mama, when did Dee ever *have* any friends?"

She had a few. Furtive boys in pink shirts hanging about on washday after school. Nervous girls who never laughed. Impressed with her, they worshiped the well turned phrase, the cute shape, the scalding humor that erupted like bubbles in lye. She read to them.

When she was courting Jimmy T, she didn't have much time to pay to us, but turned all her faultfinding power on him. He *flew* to marry a cheap city girl from a family of ignorant, flashy people. She hardly had time to recompose herself.

When she comes I will meet—but there they are!

Maggie attempts to make a dash for the house, in her shuffling way, but I stay her with my hand. "Come back here," I say. And she stops and tries to dig a well in the sand with her toe.

It is hard to see them clearly through the strong sun. But even the first glimpse of leg out of the car tells me it is Dee. Her feet were always neat-looking, as if God himself had shaped them with a certain style. From the other side of the car comes a short, stocky man. Hair is all over his head a foot long and hanging from his chin like a kinky mule tail. I hear Maggie suck in her breath. "Uhnnnh," is what it sounds like. Like when you see the wriggling end of a snake just in front of your foot on the road. "Uhnnnh."

Dee next. A dress down to the ground, in this hot weather. A dress so loud it hurts my eyes. There are yellows and oranges enough to throw back the light of the sun. I feel my whole face warming from the heat waves it throws out. Earrings gold, too, and hanging down to her shoulders. Bracelets dangling and making noises when she moves her arm up to shake the folds of the dress out of her armpits. The dress is loose and flows, and as she walks closer, I like it. I hear Maggie go "Uhnnnh" again. It is her sister's hair. It stands straight up like the wool on a sheep. It is black as night and around the edges are two long pigtails that rope about like small lizards disappearing behind her ears.

"Wa-su-zo-Tean-o!" she says, coming on in that gliding way the dress makes her move. The short stocky fellow with the hair to his navel is all grinning and he follows up with "Asalamalakim,[2] my mother and sister!" He moves to hug Maggie but she falls back, right up against the back of my chair. I feel her trembling there, and when I look up I see the perspiration falling off her chin.

"Don't get up," says Dee. Since I am stout, it takes something of a push. You can see me trying to move a second or two before I make it. She turns, showing white heels through her sandals, and goes back to the car. Out she peeks next with a Polaroid. She stoops down quickly and lines up picture after picture of me sitting there in front of the house with Maggie cowering behind me. She never takes a shot without making sure the house is included. When a cow comes nibbling around the edge of the yard, she snaps it and me and Maggie *and* the house. Then she puts the Polaroid in the back seat of the car, and comes up and kisses me on the forehead.

Meanwhile Asalamalakim is going through motions with Maggie's hand. Maggie's hand is as limp as a fish, and probably as cold, despite the sweat, and she keeps trying to pull it back. It looks like Asalamalakim wants to shake hands but wants to do it fancy. Or maybe he don't know how people shake hands. Anyhow, he soon gives up on Maggie.

"Well," I say. "Dee."

---

2. **Wa-su-zo-Tean-o . . . Asalamalakim:** Black Muslim greetings.

"No, Mama," she says. "Not 'Dee,' Wangero Leewanika Kemanjo!"

"What happened to 'Dee'?" I wanted to know.

"She's dead," Wangero said. "I couldn't bear it any longer, being named after the people who oppress me."

"You know as well as me you was named after your aunt Dicie," I said. Dicie is my sister. She named Dee. We called her "Big Dee" after Dee was born.

"But who was *she* named after?" asked Wangero.

"I guess after Grandma Dee," I said.

"And who was she named for?" asked Wangero.

"Her mother," I said, and saw Wangero was getting tired. "That's about as far back as I can trace it," I said. Though, in fact, I probably could have carried it back beyond the Civil War through the branches.

"Well," said Asalamalakim, "there you are."

"Uhnnnh," I heard Maggie say.

"There I was not," I said, "before 'Dicie' cropped up in our family, so why should I try to trace it that far back?"

He just stood there grinning, looking down on me like somebody inspecting a Model A car. Every once in a while he and Wangero sent eye signals over my head.

"How do you pronounce this name?" I asked.

"You don't have to call me by it if you don't want to," said Wangero.

"Why shouldn't I?" I asked. "If that's what you want us to call you, we'll call you."

"I know it might sound awkward at first," said Wangero.

"I'll get used to it," I said. "Ream it out again."

Well, soon we got the name out of the way. Asalamalakim had a name twice as long and three times as hard. After I tripped over it two or three times, he told me to just call him Hakim-a-barber. I wanted to ask him was he a barber, but I really didn't think he was, so I didn't ask.

"You must belong to those beef-cattle peoples down the road," I said. They said "Asalamalakim" when they met you, too, but they didn't shake hands. Always too busy: feeding the cattle, fixing the fences, putting up salt-lick shelters, throwing down hay. When the white folks poisoned some of the herd, the men stayed up all night with rifles in their hands. I walked a mile and a half just to see the sight.

Hakim-a-barber said, "I accept some of their doctrines, but farming and raising cattle is not my style." (They didn't tell me, and I didn't ask, whether Wangero (Dee) had really gone and married him.)

We sat down to eat, and right away he said he didn't eat collards and pork was unclean. Wangero, though, went on through the chitlins and corn bread, the greens, and everything else. She talked a blue streak over the sweet potatoes. Everything delighted her. Even the fact that we still used the benches her daddy made for the table when we couldn't afford to buy chairs.

"Oh, Mama!" she cried. Then turned to Hakim-a-barber. "I never knew how lovely these benches are. You can feel the rump prints," she said, running her hands underneath her and along the bench. Then she gave a sigh, and her hand closed over Grandma Dee's butter dish. "That's it!" she said. "I knew there was something I wanted to ask you if I could have." She jumped up from the table and went over in the corner where the churn stood, the milk in it clabber by now. She looked at the churn and looked at it.

"This churn top is what I need," she said. "Didn't Uncle Buddy whittle it out of a tree you all used to have?"

"Yes," I said.

"Uh huh," she said happily. "And I want the dasher, too."

"Uncle Buddy whittle that, too?" asked the barber.

Dee (Wangero) looked up at me.

"Aunt Dee's first husband whittled the dash," said Maggie so low you almost couldn't hear her. "His name was Henry, but they called him Stash."

"Maggie's brain is like an elephant's," Wangero said, laughing. "I can use the churn top as a centerpiece for the alcove table," she said, sliding a plate over the churn, "and I'll think of something artistic to do with the dasher."

When she finished wrapping the dasher, the handle stuck out. I took it for a moment in my hands. You didn't even have to look close to see where hands pushing the dasher up and down to make butter had left a kind of sink in the wood. In fact, there were a lot of small sinks; you could see where thumbs and fingers had sunk into the wood. It was beautiful light yellow wood, from a tree that grew in the yard where Big Dee and Stash had lived.

After dinner Dee (Wangero) went to the trunk at the foot of my bed and started rifling through it. Maggie hung back in the kitchen over the dishpan. Out came Wangero with two quilts. They had been pieced by Grandma Dee, and then Big Dee and me had hung them on the quilt frames on the front porch and quilted them. One was in the Lone Star pattern. The other was Walk Around the Mountain. In both of them were scraps of dresses Grandma Dee had worn fifty and more years ago. Bits and pieces of Grandpa Jarrell's Paisley shirts. And one teeny faded blue piece, about the size of a penny matchbox, that was from Great Grandpa Ezra's uniform that he wore in the Civil War.

"Mama," Wangero said, sweet as a bird. "Can I have these old quilts?"

I heard something fall in the kitchen, and a minute later the kitchen door slammed.

"Why don't you take one or two of the others?" I asked. "These old things was just done by me and Big Dee from some tops your grandma pieced before she died."

"No," said Wangero. "I don't want those. They are stitched around the borders by machine."

"That'll make them last better," I said.

"That's not the point," said Wangero. "These are all pieces of dresses Grandma used to wear. She did all this stitching by hand. Imagine!" She held the quilts securely in her arms, stroking them.

"Some of the pieces, like those lavender ones, come from old clothes her mother handed down to her," I said, moving up to touch the quilts. Dee (Wangero) moved back just enough so that I couldn't reach the quilts. They already belonged to her.

"Imagine!" she breathed again, clutching them closely to her bosom.

"The truth is," I said, "I promised to give them quilts to Maggie, for when she marries John Thomas."

She gasped like a bee had stung her.

"Maggie can't appreciate these quilts!" she said. "She'd probably be backward enough to put them to everyday use."

"I reckon she would," I said. "God knows I been saving 'em for long enough with nobody using 'em. I hope she will!" I didn't want to bring up how I had offered Dee (Wangero) a quilt when she went away to college. Then she had told me they were old-fashioned, out of style.

"But they're *priceless!*" she was saying now, furiously; for she has a temper. "Maggie would put them on the bed and in five years they'd be in rags. Less than that!"

"She can always make some more," I said. "Maggie knows how to quilt."

Dee (Wangero) looked at me with hatred. "You just will not understand. The point is these quilts, *these* quilts!"

"Well," I said, stumped. "What would *you* do with them?"

"Hang them," she said. As if that was the only thing you *could* do with quilts.

Maggie by now was standing in the door. I could almost hear the sound her feet made as they scraped over each other.

"She can have them, Mama," she said, like somebody used to never winning anything, or having anything reserved for her. "I can 'member Grandma Dee without the quilts."

I looked at her hard. She had filled her bottom lip with checkerberry snuff, and it gave her face a kind of dopey, hangdog look. It was Grandma Dee and Big Dee who taught her how to quilt herself. She stood there with her scarred hands in the folds of her skirt. She looked at her sister with something like fear, but she wasn't mad at her. This was Maggie's portion. This was the way she knew God to work.

When I looked at her like that, something hit me in the top of my head and ran down to the soles of my feet. Just like when I'm in church and the spirit of God touches me and I get happy and shout. I did something I never had done before: hugged Maggie to me, then dragged her on into the room, snatched the quilts out of Miss Wangero's hands and dumped them into Maggie's lap. Maggie just sat there on my bed with her mouth open.

"Take one or two of the others," I said to Dee.

But she turned without a word and went out to Hakim-a-barber.

"You just don't understand," she said, as Maggie and I came out to the car.

"What don't I understand?" I wanted to know.

"Your heritage," she said. And then she turned to Maggie, kissed her, and said, "You

ought to try to make something of yourself, too, Maggie. It's really a new day for us. But from the way you and Mama still live, you'd never know it."

She put on some sunglasses that hid everything above the tip of her nose and her chin.

Maggie smiled; maybe at the sunglasses. But a real smile, not scared. After we watched the car dust settle, I asked Maggie to bring me a dip of snuff. And then the two of us sat there just enjoying, until it was time to go in the house and go to bed.

Getting at Meaning

1. Why does Maggie smile at the end of the story?

2. Do you think the narrator is looking forward to Dee's arrival? Explain your answer.

3. How does Maggie feel about seeing her sister again? What kind of relationship have Dee and Maggie had as sisters? How do you know?

4. What things does Dee want to take back with her? What is she going to do with them? Why does she want them? Why does her mother refuse to give her the quilts?

Developing Skills in Reading Literature

1. **Character.** Describe Dee. What does she look like? How does she act? What information about her childhood helps to make her actions more believable? Why has she changed her name? Why are the quilts important to her? How does she feel about her heritage?

Describe Maggie. How is her personality related to her physical appearance? How does she feel in the presence of her sister? How does her attitude toward her sister change? What does she have that Dee does not have?

2. **Structure.** Structure is the arrangement of the various elements in a piece of literature. This story includes a section in which the narrator talks about television shows. What do you learn from this section about the narrator and her perceptions of herself?

3. **First-Person Narration.** This story is told by a character in her own words. Who is the narrator? Why is her point of view important? How do her comments add humor to the story?

Developing Vocabulary

Idioms. The narrator of the story states that Maggie thinks her sister has "held life always in the palm of one hand. . . ." What do these words mean? This expression is an idiom; its meaning is different from the literal meaning of the words.

Explain the meaning of the following idioms. In the story, find other idiomatic expressions.

never could carry a tune
a dress so loud it hurts my eyes

Developing Writing Skills

1. **Supporting an Opinion.** At the beginning of the story, the writer talks about television shows in which everyone seems happy and all things work out well in the end. Do you think that television programs, especially those about family life, give a realistic or an unrealistic picture of life? Support your opinion with specific examples from actual television shows.

2. **Selecting Specific Details.** Reread the paragraph in which the narrator describes herself as she is "in real life." All of the details in the paragraph contribute to the overall impression that she is a strong, tough woman. In one paragraph, describe yourself or a friend. Include specific details that paint a clear and consistent picture of your subject.

The Cave *Jean McCord*

George is gone. He's either dead, or he's crawled off into one of the deep caves and laid himself down in darkness and silence to die. How long do you think it will take for an old man to die of a broken heart?

I know I'm to blame. I had my part in what happened, except right at the last when the guys went and did what they did. I wasn't in on that, but I might as well have been. It was the same in the end, anyway. When the work and the glory was gone, there was simply no reason for George to go on living.

Why do things happen like that in life? Things you do or cause to be done like me, and you don't even know what's going on, what it really means, at the time.

I was the only one who knew about him at first.

One Saturday morning in early spring, I'd left the house for a run. My bones are growing fast and sometimes I get these aches in my knees. When I'm all scrunched up behind my desk in school, they ache all the more. The only thing that helps is to get away by myself and run along the banks of the Godalming River. My mother frequently says, "Charles, you eat like a horse these days." What she doesn't know is that I feel like a horse, too. I run along the trails on the riverbank for miles, the blood pounding in my throat, the clap of my hooves beating against the dirt, the wind tickling through my mane, before I finally collapse and throw myself down on the ground, and my hooves turn back into smelly canvas sneakers.

That morning I'd been galloping long and hard to get the kinks out of my knees. The riverbanks are high and steep where we live, overgrown with trees that lean outward, and trails that wind along for miles. Once they were animal trails, I think; then the Chippewa Indians lived here and must have used them. Nobody knows all the trails; they run at different levels, dipping and rising with the contour of the banks. I'd gotten a little further than I'd ever been before, changing levels, first up high near the top of the cliffs, then running swiftly downhill by a cross-trail. I'd suddenly seen a new path angling up from the river road, had swung into it, and loped along uphill as far as I could until a stitch in my side made me stop.

There was a spring there, bubbling up into a little pool under the roots of a tree. I leaned over and drank like a horse drinks, lips barely touching water, sucking it up noisily. The water was as clear as sunlight, and cold, and tasted slightly brown from the leaves lying in it.

When I raised my head I was looking up the hill about twenty feet, and I saw something hidden behind some brush. I wish now I'd gone on and let it be, but my curiosity always drives me like I was some snoopy girl, fingering something in her best friend's dresser drawer. I went soundlessly up the hill in my sneakers, noticing there were no steps or trail to give this away, whatever it was. I got up to it and found it was the mouth of a cave, high on the hill with a perfect view up and down the river. It had been boarded over with two-by-fours and some rough, river-washed planks. A skinny door hung slightly open on leather hinges.

I started to stick my nose in the crack when, just then, a voice remarked behind my back, "Looking for something?" and I spun around so fast and so guilty, I almost fell down the hill.

There was an old man sitting casually under a tree and keeping so still that I hadn't even seen him. But he had been watching me, probably since the moment I'd stopped to drink.

He looked so weird I recognized him right away for what he was, a bum, yet he wasn't like any other bum I'd ever seen. His hair was long and tangled, falling almost to his shoulders like a Bible prophet's, and his face was a mass of porcupine bristles, not having been shaved in weeks. His nose was a narrow, anxious-looking beak, but his brown eyes were as soft as the spring water, and his mouth was clamped on the broken stub of a pipe, unlit. I took time to look him over instead of bolting as had been my first intention since there was that look in his eye that told me he was harmless. Besides, what was there to be afraid of? I hadn't done anything.

"Sit down, boy, if you like." He motioned me over.

I went and squatted, looking up and down at the view companionably.

After a while he spoke again. "Got a name?"

I almost said, "Yes, sir, Charles," but I stopped myself. "Charley," I grunted.

"Good name," he said. "Long lineage; way back. You heard of Charlemagne?"[1]

"Yes." I looked at him curiously. I'd studied that in history class, but where had he heard about the guy?

"Same name. Means Charley the Greatest. A royal name. Dozens of crowned heads answered to it."

"Oh yeah?" I was interested in spite of myself. Now why hadn't the teacher mentioned that? It might have made that history class a little easier to take. But our history teacher

always droned on, reading from our textbook like he was a hive of bees on a warm day. After a while, your ears got hypnotized and heard what he was saying, but the meaning was completely gone.

"Got a pretty royal name myself," the old bum was saying. "George. Same as six kings of England, two of Greece, a Pres. of the U. S. of A., and a saint who was quite a dragon-hunter.[2] Not that it's ever brought me much." He was looking ruefully at his pipe, which was quite empty. And then to make it look funny and make me laugh, which I did, he wriggled his big toe, which was sticking clean out of the tip of one shoe. I wished I had some tobacco to give him, but I didn't. Maybe another time.

"You live in there?" I jerked my thumb at the boards hiding the cave.

---

1. **Charlemagne** (shar' lə mān'): King of the Franks and emperor of the Roman Empire who lived from A.D. 742–814.
2. **a saint . . . dragon-hunter:** the patron saint of England, a reference to St. George, a legendary dragon slayer.

"Well, let's just say it's my Passport to Paradise."

Urrgh, I thought, this old boy's got a few bats flying round in his belfry. But he had my curiosity aroused again, just the same. I'll come back tomorrow and bring him some tobacco, I thought. I can take some from my Dad and he'll never miss it.

As it happened, I didn't return the next day because my folks made me go with them to visit Aunt Margaret.

A week later, Saturday again, I wrapped some tobacco in a handkerchief and headed back to see old George. Usually I would have gone to the clubhouse and spent the day with my gang. I belong to the Jesse James gang. When you live in a city like ours where all the tough kids seem jammed together on the South Side, you either join a gang or get your head knocked off. We're not really fierce guys, not like some of the gangs you read about in other parts of the country. We don't have police records, and we don't go in for mugging or robbery or any of that stuff. We just got together for protection, you might say, and it depends mostly on where a guy lives as to what gang he'll belong to. The toughest gang of all live down on the river flats and call themselves the River Rats. We all stay away from them, much as we can. The River Rats are . . . well, I just wouldn't have wanted to belong to them, not then.

I was walking on the new trail leading to George's place, going slowly so I could look at the sun shining through the trees with a green light. I felt a sudden prickle of cold air on my neck, and the coolness led me like the flow of a little stream falling downhill, right to a small opening that slanted down into the ground. I knew it was the airhole for some cave, a new one, one I'd never been in. You see, the cliffs are made of limestone, and waters trickling down through them for millions of years have cut out many caves. The mouths of the large ones are down at the present river level, and they are mostly all in use as mushroom caves. There are huge steel doors blocking them off, and the mushroom growers have made long beds inside of dirt and manure. Dim electric lights swing down the middle, and the temperature is always a cool 55° which is perfect for mushrooms, but chilly for a person.

My gang had been in lots of mushroom caves, but we had to sneak in by the air holes and stand a chance of getting caught by the mushroom growers. They would shout at us, threatening to call the police if they saw us in the shadowy darkness of their stinking caves, thinking we were going to steal their old toadstools. Who wanted them? We never even touched them, except to kick over a few once in a while. The stuff they grew in was too much for us. Outside the caves were big banks of manure, steaming in the cool drafts and smelling like something you'd rather not even get close to.

For a long time now we'd been looking for an unused cave, one we could keep secret for ourselves. We wanted to hold meetings there, safe from the other neighborhood gangs, have initiations, and just sit around in the darkness lit up by a warm fire, and chew the fat. We were pretty sure there were a few caves not grabbed off by the mushroom tycoons if we could just find them.

This was it. I knew when I brushed the dirt away a little and peered down into the darkness leading into the hillside like a large animal's burrow, that this would be our own cave. I would go tell the gang about it.

I ran all the way back, putting my best into being one of the greatest, Man O' War,[3] and made about as good a time as possible for a horse with only two legs.

The gang was all gathered at the usual place, an abandoned coal shed. They were

---

3. **Man O'War:** a famous racehorse.

itchy with restlessness, and it made the perfect announcement.

"You're late, Charley," Pat Dalloway, our leader, said out of the side of his mouth. He likes to act like John Dillinger or the head of the Mafia. He narrowed his eyes while I was giving the details of my discovery.

"What are we waiting for?" Butts yelped. He's a barky type, like a scared dog, and lives on the far side of town. He's only in our Jesse James gang because he's Pat Dalloway's cousin.

"Lead on, boy!" "Let's go!" Chunky and Ted and the others were yelling.

They followed me, a pounding troop at my heels, though we had to stop several times for Chunky to catch his breath.

We clustered round at the spot, and Pat fell on his knees and stuck his head into the hole. He pulled it out again quickly. "It's a good one, Charley," he said with a grin at the gang, "and since you were the finder, to you goes the honor."

I opened my mouth to protest because going into a cave for the first time is always scary. You know such things as saber-toothed tigers and floating ghosts don't really exist, but when you are in total darkness in an unknown place with only a small flashlight, you become suddenly positive they not only do, they are breathing down your neck that instant.

"No, no, we can't have it any other way, can we, boys?" Pat said as he saw my face.

I could only swallow and shrug, but I thought to myself, OK Dalloway, but a couple more times like this, and I'll be ready to take over the gang. It takes guts to be the leader, and Pat seemed to be slacking up a bit.

I took one flashlight in my hand and dropped another inside my shirt. Then I stuck my head in the hole, and lay down on my stomach. I was prepared for a gentle, short drop that would end in a small cave from which I'd holler back at the others to "come on in."

Only, after wriggling in till my feet were out of sight of the gang, this little hole took me by surprise and suddenly slanted down at a swift angle. There was nothing to grab at along the way, just the soft sandstone walls worn into smoothness by the ancient waters. I slid down the hole like I was on one of those little tin chutes at a kid's playground, and it occurred to me, sliding like an otter, trying to drag my elbows and toes into the unyielding walls, that I could pop out of this into a really big cave with a nice little drop of maybe a couple hundred feet. I groaned.

Why hadn't I had the sense to tie a rope around my waist and have the gang lower me easy? I'd never make a leader because I didn't have any brains, and a voice seemed to tell me I was going to have even fewer in a couple seconds.

I dropped on into what seemed the center of the earth, and when I'd given up hope, rolled out of that chute like a marble and fell about three feet to bounce on soft, cool sand. The flashlight shot out of my hand pointing away from me, its puny beam lost in the vastness of this black cavern. I sat there rubbing my hands and stomach to ease the smarting and feeling myself, but I was OK. However, the thought occurred to me before I even reached for the light, how was I going to get out? That hole was too steep and smooth to climb back up, and something told me the gang wasn't going to follow me in.

I crawled over to the flashlight. When I turned it up towards the ceiling its beam just got lost in the blackness. There was no sound in the cave. It felt as if there had never been a single sound ever in there. I went over to the hole I'd dropped out of, and listened up it for the gang. I couldn't hear them. It was so spooky in that huge cave that it felt like I was down among the dead, like in the catacombs[4] I'd read about, and I even looked around a bit, but not too much. I couldn't see anything, just creamy yellow walls and white sand underfoot. I wondered if I was the first person who had ever been in here. It sure looked like it. There wasn't a mark on the walls, and I couldn't see any footprints. My light was wavering around, and I got a desolate feeling that it was going to go out on me.

I knew the guys outside would notify somebody sooner or later, the firemen or police. Even my Dad. Or would they? I began to doubt even that, thinking maybe they might all go on home and be too scared to get themselves into any trouble with the police and might just decide to forget about me. Well, in a place like that, your mind just seems to run away from you.

I had to get out. I turned and started walking, hurrying for what seemed like miles, but there's nothing to judge by, so you don't really know how far. A few steps even seems like a long ways. My flashlight was dimming down, and my fear was growing. I started running, not even watching for anything, just trying to find some new hole, or an end of any kind. The back of my mind kept telling me that most of these big caves had open mouths down on the river level, but I had also heard that some of them emptied out beneath the water. And that would be just great!

The cave was so long and black I felt like Jonah[5] inside his whale. I felt I was going deeper into the earth all the time, but I couldn't tell about that, either. And just when my light was about to go out for good, and I was going to throw myself down and yell in terror for help, I saw a paleness around a bend.

I shot around the corner and found myself in a room about as big as our living room at home. It was still a cave, but someone was living in it. A few scraps of furniture sat around, made-up furniture of boxes and planks and junk. The front of the cave was boarded over with old planks and a small door swung lazily on leather hinges.

I stopped right in the middle of it and looked around. And then I saw what was really so different from anyone's living room in a house. The walls were covered with statues. Not the kind carved from wood; these statues were cut right out of the walls in what our art teacher calls bas-relief.[6] They seemed

---

4. **catacombs** (kat' ə kōmz'): a series of galleries in an underground burial place.
5. **Jonah:** a Hebrew prophet who was tossed overboard during a storm and was swallowed by a whale.
6. **bas-relief** (bä' rə lēf'): sculpture in which figures are carved in a flat surface so that they project only a little from the background.

almost to be living beings who were growing out of the rock, and all of them were watching me carefully. I was so glad to see the sunlight through the door, I could only sob with relief. But as usual my curiosity was still with me, so I looked around. On one wall I could recognize certain figures. One was Lincoln, surely, with his big nose and sad eyes. Next to him was George Washington, I thought. Another wall held a Crucifixion scene with bent-over people seeming to writhe at the foot of it. Next to that was, holy cow, a real Masterpiece, I thought in slow admiration. A guy on a horse, both of them wearing armor, was spearing a dragon who was lashing around with claws and scales all over him. They were all big, more than life-size, and you could see that somebody had put an awful lot of work into them.

As I walked towards the swinging door, it struck me then. I'd seen that door before. I stepped through it, looked around feeling terribly foolish, and found myself staring right into George's startled eyes. I guess he'd never seen anyone walk out of his cave before.

"Hey!" he said.

"Yeah, I know." I waved my hand backwards. "I got lost." I grinned feebly. "A wicked witch changed me into a rabbit and a dog chased me down a hole, and, well, here I am. . . ."

It was the best I could do, seeing I was so happy I wanted to run over and shake both his hands.

George looked at me a minute, then he laughed. "You're all right, kid," he said. "I told you Charley was a lucky name. Come and sit. You look pretty fagged out."

I stretched out beside him in the sun and squirmed with the pure pleasure of it on my body. Somewhere back in there I had thought I was doomed to wander in darkness for the rest of my life, which in that dry cave, didn't seem to be too long to go. It was only when I

rolled over on my stomach, wanting to hug the ground, that I felt the extra flashlight biting into me.

"What time is it?" I asked, my face against the dirt.

George squinted at the sun. "Mebbe two o'clock, or so."

I sighed. I'd been in the cave less than half an hour. It had seemed like days.

"That's pretty good stuff in there," I said cautiously. "It looks like . . . well . . . like a regular art gallery."

George looked down at his hands. They were square and blocky with dirt under the nails. "It fills my time," he said. He stared at them for a long time. Finally, gazing down the river, he said quietly, "Look, Charley. I don't pay no rent on that cave, but it's mine just the same. I found it first. I fixed it up. Been here over five years now, and I got a lot more work to do. I'm just beginning to get good." He looked at me, and I could actually see the pleading in his eyes. "If people knew about me, they'd come and drive me out. Against the law, or if it ain't, they'd make one. Now why don't you just go on home and keep your mouth shut. Here. Take this." He handed me a little bit of wood that he had been working on when I'd stepped out of his home. It was a tiny carved fawn, its legs folded under itself and its head bent like it was hiding from dogs who were hunting it.

"Well, gee. Thanks. Thanks a lot." I got up and stood there, tongue-tied. I wanted to say I was sorry I'd intruded, that it was just to save my neck, that I had to come out that way. But he must have known. After all, he knew that cave better than I did, and right then he was welcome to it, all of it. I had no intention of telling anyone; certainly not the gang, but I had to get back to them before they got up a lot of people looking for me.

I plunged down George's hill and onto the trail leading back to where I'd left the others. I ran pretty well. Maybe I'd never beat Man

O' War in a straightaway, but I could sure make him blow a little on the curves. If he was still around, that is.

When I got to where I'd left the gang, I slowed down and sauntered up to them. They were all in a knot with serious looks on their faces, and when they turned around, their jaws dropped.

"You lily-livered chickens doing anything to get me out of there?" I blustered at them.

"Hey, Charley! Charley, old boy. We thought you were a goner, sure!" They were all shouting at once, and pounding me on the back.

"You been in there before, wise guy, ain't you?" Pat scowled at me. "Tried to be smart. Snuck out another way and let us think you were lost." He was really mad. Some of the guys must have been riding him about getting some help to rescue me. His leadership was toppling, all right. Any day soon, now, Dalloway, I thought, I'm gonna fight you and win. I flexed my arm muscles. They felt good and tight to me.

But at the same time I was thinking desperately. What was I going to tell them to make them stay out of the cave? I had to think up a story, and a good one, quick. "Look," I said. "It ain't even a cave. It's just a kind of tunnel, not big enough for a cat. It goes down a long ways, straight, and then winds around and comes out behind the bend over there, somewhere. I didn't even mark it."

"You were gone too long," Pat said, shoving his face next to mine.

"I was scrabbling along on my belly, the whole way. See?" I showed them the raw marks on my arms and stomach. "It never gets more than two feet high, or wide. It ain't worth beans." I turned. "Come on. Let's go home. I'm starved."

"What you got in your hand, Charley? You must have found something."

I stared at my own hand like I'd never seen it before. I hadn't thought to put the little carving in my pocket. Then I did a stupid thing, which makes me think I'll never be fit to be a leader for a pack of mangy dogs. Instead of blustering it out, I gave a leap downhill and started running hard. With a head start none of them could catch me, and I raced along as fast as I'd ever run in my life before. I could hear them for a while pounding along almost at my back, but one by one, I outran them, and got to my home.

I sped up to my bedroom, and in a couple minutes I could hear them all outside, hollering at me, "Charley, hey, come on out. We want to talk to you." But I wouldn't go.

Then I stayed away from the gang for a while. I'd see the fellows in school since we were in the same classes, but I didn't go to the clubhouse, nor join them at the drugstore like I always had. And that seemed funny. To me, who had been thinking of taking over the gang any day, and to them, too, because they couldn't figure it out. There was no real reason except I thought I'd try being an individual for a change, instead of just one of a group who all did and thought the same things. And that mostly what Pat Dalloway said to do and think.

I took to visiting old George as often as I had time for it. He was a pretty smart old buzzard, and he seemed to know some secret about life. What I mean is, he had kind of come to terms with life, and he had made all the conditions. He sure didn't work, since every time I ever went there, except once, he was either outside looking at his view, possessing it, kind of, or in his cave doing a carving. He had started a new one of Knute Rockne[7] which was going to be really great. He let me come into his place now and sit on the bunch of planks and old rags that was his bed. If I just sat and watched him and didn't

---

7. **Knute Rockne** (nōōt räk′ nē): a famous American football player and coach.

ask a lot of nosy questions, he ignored me and went on with his work. I usually brought him some tobacco, and whatever I could sneak out of the refrigerator behind my Mom's back. I guess she thought I'd suddenly developed a tapeworm because she'd look funny at me and frown once in a while, but never said anything.

At first I pried him a little. "Say, George, what you been doing all your life?"

"My life, boy? I lost it. Laid it down for a little and when I went back looking for it, it was too late. Gone. Just like that." He snapped his fingers.

"Where were you the other day?"

"Well, occasionally even an old hermit's got to go down into the morass of humanity." He stepped back viewing his work. "If you can find me another picture of Knute here, why, I'd be might obliged."

"Sure." I knew where there was one. In my Dad's picture album. He'd played football when he was in college and was still crazy about the game.

George looked over at me. His beard was only about a half-inch long now because he'd shaved last week. It must have been the day he was gone, I thought. Wonder where he goes and for what? Maybe he's got some money stashed away in a bank and he goes for some every once in a while. I could see he'd bought a few groceries because they stood out in clear sight on a couple orange crates piled up, but I didn't know how he cooked or if he even bothered to. I knew he got his water from the little spring and kept several cans of it in the cave which he used to throw on his new carving. It softened up the rock a little.

"You ever going to let people see all this someday?" I asked. "When you're ready, I mean?"

"Maybe I should have done drawings with burnt sticks and red ochre. Of ancient bison and vanished deer. That would have confused a few experts, I'll bet," he answered, almost to himself. If you could call that an answer. That's how George was. I liked being with George. He didn't expect anything of me like my Dad always did, and by now, I was getting pretty fond of the old guy. Oh, I knew he wasn't any Michelangelo,[8] but considering everything, he was pretty good. Lincoln and Washington and St. George and Christ and Knute Rockne and others. I loved the way he mixed them up like they were all friends of each other. Maybe they were.

"You know, Charley boy," George seemed to be talking to Knute, but I was listening. "I been thinking. That's a big cave in behind there. Lots of beautiful walls. Nothing ever been done to them. My time . . . my grains of sand . . . are running through pretty fast now." He was silent till I thought he'd forgotten what he was talking about. Then he said, "You ever have a hankering to do a little carving?"

I shook my head "no," but his back was turned and he didn't see me.

"Old, old," he was muttering to Knute, "seventy-five, and that's the full allotment. Might not even get to finish this one." He jabbed at Knute's jaw. "It's a way of life, Charley my boy. The only way; creating things. Let others build the cars and roads and wooden houses. You know how long the cave drawings, the ones in southern France, been around?" He whirled on me with a fierce light in his eye.

I shook my head again.

"Fifteen, maybe twenty thousand years." He glared at me. "How do you like that for beating old Mister Time?"

I got up to go. It was getting late and I didn't have anything to say to him.

"See you, George."

"Yuh," he grunted.

---

8. **Michelangelo** (mī k'l an'jə lō'): an Italian sculptor, painter, and architect, who lived from 1475–1564.

I didn't go back for three weeks. It was late Spring now, and final exams were coming up. Every time it looked like I was going to stick my nose out the door, either my Mom or Dad pounced on me and made me get to studying. The cave was too far to go to after school and still get home in time for supper, and weekends, like I say, I was kept hopping.

Finally school was out. I'd passed everything, and it was a real relief. I couldn't even stay mad at my parents for making me work because otherwise, I probably wouldn't have made it.

But now I was free for the whole summer. Maybe next year when I'd be sixteen, I'd get a job of some sort, but this summer was still mine, to use as I wanted. I'd been thinking over the last few weeks that I'd spend most of it with old George. Secretly, I'd begun to think about carving. The old boy had something there. I knew he'd teach me. I thought of that long, beautiful, empty cave. We'd haul in firewood and build us a nice, warming fire which would give us light to work by. Maybe someday we could run in an electric line like the mushroom growers. People would come from all around.

My folks would be so surprised they'd be speechless. "Do you mean our boy Charles did this?" they'd say to George, and old George would grin and say, "Yep."

I took a loaf of bread, a half pound of salami from the cupboard, a pocketful of tobacco from my Dad's stock, and slipped off to the cliffs. Over the edge onto the trails and boy, it sure felt good to be running along them again. The trees were solid green now, and the river was running clean like a band of silver far below. Mourning doves were moaning their sad calls, and spiders had flung their lines across the trails overnight.

Coming up to George's cave, I slowed to catch my breath. When I looked up there, something was terribly wrong. The boards hiding the mouth of the cave were all knocked out, though you still couldn't see it from the trail unless you knew it was there. I stopped to listen a minute, and then I heard voices. I knew those voices.

I burst into George's living room and the shock of it made me sick to my stomach. The whole cave was a mess, completely torn up. The furniture was busted so it was nothing now but old driftwood boards. A fire had been built right in the middle of the cave out of the orange crates. But worse than that, the statues had been destroyed. The delicate ones, the ones that had been carved out almost full, were knocked completely loose and lay on the cave floor as a pile of broken rubbish. The others had heads and arms missing and could never be fixed. "Looey," cross-eyed and stupid, was lounging on what was left of the beautiful horse; St. George had been scraped out of his saddle completely. The place was dirty. And George was nowhere around.

The gang, my gang, was sitting around smoking and looking smug.

"Welcome to our new clubhouse, Charley old boy," Pat Dalloway said.

"Where's George?" My tongue seemed too thick to talk.

"You mean that old bum?" Pat chuckled. "He cleared out after we knocked up the place."

I stepped forward and kicked aside Knute Rockne's face. My fists were cocked.

"You dirty rats," I screamed. "You dirty, filthy no-good rats! Who gave you the right?"

"Aw, come on, Charley," big fat Chunky was saying. "That old bum didn't own this cave. We got as much right to it. We just chased him out and took over, that's all. You helped. We all went in that air hole and found out it ended here."

And that did it. Inside I was all broken up into little pieces. I knew what the outcome would be before I started, but from where I stood, I leaped at Pat and crashed him to the floor. We fought, slugging each other, biting and gouging, rolling over on top of broken statues. Pat was a pretty dirty fighter. He fought to win; no rules. Once I had him on his back and was choking him, but his hand came up with a fistful of sand right into my eyes. From there on he had it all his way. He finished me off and for good measure gave me a couple extra kicks. No one else interfered. They knew it was between Pat and me.

"Get out," he panted. "You don't belong no more."

Butts and Jim dragged me out and threw me down the hill. My bread and salami had scattered all over. They tossed it after me. "So long, Charley," they said.

When I could move, I picked myself up and hobbled away. I took the trail going downhill. Tomorrow I would have two black eyes. A pretty way to start summer vacation. And my folks were in for a big surprise, all right, a big, fat dentist bill.

But it isn't over yet. In fact, it's just started.

I been lying up in my bedroom for three days now, thinking. My mother brings me hot soup and cries a little when she looks at me. My father wanted to go to the police and prosecute, but I wouldn't tell him anything. This is between me and my old gang.

To do a thing like that . . . to destroy an old man's dream of immortality . . . to tear up what he called his Passport to Paradise . . . well . . . they're going to pay for it, all right.

Tomorrow I'm getting out of bed. I'm going down to the river flats and join that gang that calls themselves the River Rats. I'm going to fight every guy in it till I'm the leader.

Then I'm going to lead them to that cave.

Pat Dalloway . . . you are going to get what's coming to you!

Bill and Ted and Chunky. Jim and Butts and Looey . . . you are in for a big surprise . . . When we descend on you . . . when we get through with you . . . you are going to feel just like those statues . . .

Getting at Meaning

1. Why does Charley blame himself for what happens to George's cave?

2. Why does Charley run along the river?

3. Why does Charley belong to a gang? Does his position in the gang seem secure?

4. As the story progresses, why does Charley spend less time with the gang and more time with George?

5. What qualities does George have that Charley likes? How does Charley's relationship with George cause Charley to change?

6. Describe George's statues. Why does he carve them? Why does he want to keep their existence a secret? What is George's attitude toward people?

7. When Charley returns to his gang after being stuck in the cave, what mistakes does he make?

8. Why do the members of the gang destroy George's statues? What is Charley's reaction?

9. At the end of the story, what does Charley know? What would George think about Charley's plans? Give reasons for your answer.

Developing Skills in Reading Literature

1. **Conflict.** An individualist is a person who does things his or her own way, without regard for the opinions and wishes of others. In this story, the conflict might be described as the individualist versus society. Who is the individualist? Who represents society? Who wins? What is Charley's role in the conflict?

2. **Characterization.** The writer of this story uses several techniques to draw the character of George. One technique is physical description. Reread the paragraph that gives Charley's first impression of George.

Another technique used by the writer is dialogue between characters. In his conversations with Charley, how does George reveal his knowledge of history? What is George's answer when Charley asks, "Say, George, what you been doing all your life?"

A third technique used by the writer is the revelation of one character's thoughts about another. For example, Charley believes that George "had kind of come to terms with life." Find other examples of Charley's thoughts about George.

A fourth technique is the inclusion of an object that represents something important about a character. In this story, the significant object is a fawn, "its legs folded under itself and its head bent like it was hiding from dogs who were hunting it." How is George like this fawn?

3. **Theme.** George explains to Charley that carving statues is "a way of life . . . the only way; creating things." He calls the statues his way of "beating old Mister Time." What statement about art is the writer making through George? What message about people and so-

ciety does the ending of the story bring out?

4. **Allusion.** An allusion, as you know, is a reference to a person, place, or event with which the reader is expected to be familiar. For example, George makes an allusion to Charlemagne. Charley makes allusions to things he has learned at school. Identify other examples.

5. **Extended Metaphor.** Find the paragraph near the beginning of the story in which Charley compares himself to a horse. This basic metaphor is extended by several specific comparisons in the following paragraphs. In what ways are Charley and the horse compared?

Developing Vocabulary

Idioms. The following idioms are all used in the story. Be prepared to explain why each is an idiomatic rather than a literal expression.
1. stick my nose out of the door
2. bats in his belfry
3. chew the fat
4. catch his breath
5. crazy about the game
6. tongue-tied
7. your mind just seems to run away
8. to save my neck

Developing Writing Skills

1. **Analyzing a Character.** Formulate a general statement about George's character. For example, "George is not an ordinary hermit." Then support your idea with specific passages and events from the story.

2. **Describing a Person.** Charley says of George, "He was a pretty smart old buzzard, and he seemed to know some secret about life. What I mean is, he had kind of come to terms with life, and he had made all the conditions." Write a paragraph about a person who seems to have come to terms with life. Your subject can be a public figure or someone you know.

3. **Writing an Explanation.** Write a paragraph in which you analyze why the boys destroy George's statues.

Marigolds   *Eugenia Collier*

When I think of the home town of my youth, all that I seem to remember is dust—the brown, crumbly dust of late summer—arid, sterile dust that gets into the eyes and makes them water, gets into the throat and between the toes of bare brown feet. I don't know why I should remember only the dust. Surely there must have been lush green lawns and paved streets under leafy shade trees somewhere in town; but memory is an abstract painting—it does not present things as they are, but rather as they *feel*. And so, when I think of that time and that place, I remember only the dry September of the dirt roads and grassless yards of the shanty-town where I lived. And one other thing I remember, another incongruency of memory—a brilliant splash of sunny yellow against the dust—Miss Lottie's marigolds.

Whenever the memory of those marigolds flashes across my mind, a strange nostalgia comes with it and remains long after the picture has faded. I feel again the chaotic emotions of adolescence, illusive as smoke, yet as real as the potted geranium before me now. Joy and rage and wild animal gladness and shame become tangled together in the multicolored skein of fourteen-going-on-fifteen as I recall that devastating moment when I was suddenly more woman than child, years ago in Miss Lottie's yard. I think of those marigolds at the strangest times. I remember them vividly now as I desperately pass away the time waiting for you, who will not come.

I suppose that futile waiting was the sorrowful background music of our impoverished little community when I was young.

The Depression that gripped the nation was no new thing to us, for the black workers of rural Maryland had always been depressed. I don't know what it was that we were waiting for; certainly not for the prosperity that was "just around the corner," for those were white folks' words, which we never believed. Nor did we wait for hard work and thrift to pay off in shining success as the American Dream[1] promised, for we knew better than that, too. Perhaps we waited for a miracle, amorphous in concept but necessary if one were to have the grit to rise before dawn each day and labor in the white man's vineyard until after dark, or to wander about in the September dust offering one's sweat in return for some meager share of bread. But God was *chary* with miracles in those days, and so we waited—and waited.

We children, of course, were only vaguely aware of the extent of our poverty. Having no radios, few newspapers, and no magazines, we were somewhat unaware of the world outside our community. Nowadays we would be called "culturally deprived" and people would write books and hold conferences about us. In those days everybody we knew was just as hungry and ill-clad as we were. Poverty was the cage in which we all were trapped, and our hatred of it was still the vague, undirected restlessness of the zoo-bred flamingo who knows that nature created him to fly free.

As I think of those days I feel most poig-

---

1. **American Dream:** the dream of the good life that is associated with America.

nantly the tag end of summer, the bright, dry times when we began to have a sense of shortening days and the imminence of the cold.

By the time I was fourteen my brother Joey and I were the only children left at our house, the older ones having left home for early marriage or the lure of the city, and the two babies having been sent to relatives who might care for them better than we. Joey was three years younger than I, and a boy, and therefore vastly inferior. Each morning our mother and father trudged wearily down the dirt road and around the bend, she to her domestic job, he to his daily unsuccessful quest for work. After our few chores around the tumble-down shanty, Joey and I were free to run wild in the sun with other children similarly situated.

For the most part, those days are ill-defined in my memory, running together and combining like a fresh water-color painting left out in the rain. I remember squatting in the road, drawing a picture in the dust, a picture that Joey gleefully erased with one sweep of his dirty foot. I remember fishing for minnows in a muddy creek and watching sadly as they eluded my cupped hands, while Joey laughed uproariously. And I remember, that year, a strange restlessness of body and of spirit, a feeling that something old and familiar was ending, and something unknown and therefore terrifying was beginning.

One day returns to me with special clarity for some reason, perhaps because it was the beginning of the experience that in some inexplicable way marked the end of innocence. I was loafing under the great oak tree in our yard, deep in some reverie that I have now forgotten except that it involved some secret thoughts of one of the Harris boys across the yard. Joey and a bunch of kids were bored now with the old tire suspended from an oak limb, which had kept them entertained for awhile.

"Hey, Lizabeth," Joey yelled. He never talked when he could yell. "Hey, Lizabeth, let's us go somewhere."

I came reluctantly from my private world. "Where at, Joey?"

The truth was that we were becoming tired of the formlessness of our summer days. The idleness whose prospect had seemed so beautiful during the busy days of spring now had degenerated to an almost desperate effort to fill up the empty midday hours.

"Let's go see can we find us some locusts on the hill," someone suggested.

Joey was scornful. "Ain't no more locusts there. Y'all got 'em all while they was still green."

The argument that followed was brief and not really worth the effort. Hunting locust trees wasn't fun any more by now.

"Tell you what," said Joey finally, his eyes sparkling. "Let's us go over to Miss Lottie's."

The idea caught on at once, for annoying Miss Lottie was always fun. I was still child enough to scamper along with the group over rickety fences and through bushes that tore our already raggedy clothes, back to where Miss Lottie lived. I think now that we must have made a tragicomic spectacle, five or six kids of different ages, each of us clad in only one garment—the girls in faded dresses that were too long or too short, the boys in patchy pants, their sweaty brown chests gleaming in the hot sun. A little cloud of dust followed our thin legs and bare feet as we tramped over the barren land.

When Miss Lottie's house came into view we stopped, ostensibly to plan our strategy, but actually to reinforce our courage.

Miss Lottie's house was the most ramshackle of all our ramshackle homes. The sun and rain had long since faded its rickety frame siding from white to a sullen gray. The boards themselves seemed to remain upright, not from being nailed together but rather from leaning together like a house that a child might have constructed from cards.

A brisk wind might have blown it down, and the fact that it was still standing implied a kind of enchantment that was stronger than the elements. There it stood, and as far as I know is standing yet—a gray, rotting thing with no porch, no shutters, no steps, set on a cramped lot with no grass, not even any weeds—a monument to decay.

In front of the house in a squeaky rocking chair sat Miss Lottie's son, John Burke, completing the impression of decay. John Burke was what was known as "queer-headed." Black and ageless, he sat, rocking day in and day out in a mindless stupor, lulled by the monotonous squeak-squawk of the chair. A battered hat atop his shaggy head shaded him from the sun. Usually John Burke was totally unaware of everything outside his quiet dream world. But if you disturbed him, if you intruded upon his fantasies, he would become enraged, strike out at you, and curse at you in some strange enchanted language which only he could understand. We children made a game of thinking of ways to disturb John Burke and then to elude his violent retribution.

But our real fun and our real fear lay in Miss Lottie herself. Miss Lottie seemed to be at least a hundred years old. Her big frame still held traces of the tall, powerful woman she must have been in youth, although it was now bent and drawn. Her smooth skin was a dark reddish-brown, and her face had Indian-like features and the stern stoicism that one associates with Indian faces. Miss Lottie didn't like intruders either, especially children. She never left her yard, and nobody ever visited her. We never knew how she managed those necessities that depend on human interaction—how she ate, for example, or even whether she ate. When we were tiny children, we thought Miss Lottie was a witch, and we made up tales, that we half believed ourselves, about her exploits. We were far too sophisticated now, of course, to believe the witch-nonsense. But old fears have a way of clinging like cobwebs, and so when we sighted the tumbledown shack, we had to stop to reinforce our nerves.

"Look, there she," I whispered, forgetting that Miss Lottie could not possibly have heard me from that distance. "She fooling with them crazy flowers."

"Yeh, look at 'er."

Miss Lottie's marigolds were perhaps the strangest part of the picture. Certainly they did not fit in with the crumbling decay of the rest of her yard. Beyond the dusty brown yard, in front of the sorry gray house, rose suddenly and shockingly a dazzling strip of bright blossoms, clumped together in enormous mounds, warm and passionate and sun-golden. The old Black witch-woman worked on them all summer, every summer, down on her creaky knees, weeding and cultivating and arranging, while the house crumbled and John Burke rocked. For some perverse reason, we children hated those marigolds. They interfered with the perfect

ugliness of the place; they were too beautiful; they said too much that we could not understand; they did not make sense. There was something in the vigor with which the old woman destroyed the weeds that intimidated us. It should have been a comical sight—the old woman with the man's hat on her cropped white head, leaning over the bright mounds, her big backside in the air—but it wasn't comical; it was something we could not name. We had to annoy her by whizzing a pebble into her flowers or by yelling a dirty word, then dancing away from her rage, reveling in our youth and mocking her age. Actually, I think it was the flowers we wanted to destroy, but nobody had the nerve to try it, not even Joey, who was usually fool enough to try anything.

"Y'all git some stones," commanded Joey now, and was met with instant giggling obedience as everyone except me began to gather pebbles from the dusty ground. "Come on, Lizabeth."

I just stood there peering through the bushes, torn between wanting to join the fun and feeling that it was all a bit silly.

"You scared, Lizabeth?"

I cursed and spat on the ground—my favorite gesture of phony bravado. "Y'all children get the stones, I'll show you how to use 'em."

I said before that we children were not consciously aware of how thick were the bars of our cage. I wonder now, though, whether we were not more aware of it than I thought. Perhaps we had some dim notion of what we were, and how little chance we had of being anything else. Otherwise, why would we have been so preoccupied with destruction? Anyway, the pebbles were collected quickly, and everybody looked at me to begin the fun.

"Come on, y'all."

We crept to the edge of the bushes that bordered the narrow road in front of Miss Lottie's place. She was working placidly, kneeling over the flowers, her dark hand plunged into the golden mound. Suddenly "zing"—an expertly-aimed stone cut the head off one of the blossoms.

"Who out there?" Miss Lottie's backside came down and her head came up as her sharp eyes searched the bushes. "You better git!"

We had crouched down out of sight in the bushes, where we stifled the giggles that insisted on coming. Miss Lottie gazed warily across the road for a moment, then cautiously returned to her weeding. "Zing"—Joey sent a pebble into the blooms, and another marigold was beheaded.

Miss Lottie was enraged now. She began struggling to her feet, leaning on a rickety cane and shouting, "Y'all git! Go on home!" Then the rest of the kids let loose with their pebbles, storming the flowers and laughing wildly and senselessly at Miss Lottie's impotent rage. She shook her stick at us and started shakily toward the road crying, "Git 'long! John Burke! John Burke, come help!"

Then I lost my head entirely, mad with the power of inciting such rage, and ran out of the bushes in the storm of pebbles, straight toward Miss Lottie chanting madly, "Old lady witch, fell in a ditch, picked up a penny and thought she was rich!" The children screamed with delight, dropped their pebbles and joined the crazy dance, swarming around Miss Lottie like bees and chanting, "Old lady witch!" while she screamed curses at us. The madness lasted only a moment, for John Burke, startled at last, lurched out of his chair, and we dashed for the bushes just as Miss Lottie's cane went whizzing at my head.

I did not join the merriment when the kids gathered again under the oak in our bare yard. Suddenly I was ashamed, and I did not like being ashamed. The child in me sulked and said it was all in fun, but the woman in me flinched at the thought of the malicious attack that I had led. The mood lasted all afternoon. When we ate the beans and rice that was supper that night, I did not notice my father's silence, for he was always silent these days, nor did I notice my mother's absence, for she always worked until well into evening. Joey and I had a particularly bitter argument after supper; his exuberance got on my nerves. Finally I stretched out upon the pallet in the room we shared and fell into a fitful doze.

When I awoke, somewhere in the middle of the night, my mother had returned, and I vaguely listened to the conversation that was audible through the thin walls that separated our rooms. At first I heard no words, only voices. My mother's voice was like a cool, dark room in summer—peaceful, soothing, quiet. I loved to listen to it; it made things seem all right somehow. But my father's voice cut through hers, shattering the peace.

"Twenty-two years, Maybelle, twenty-two years," he was saying, "and I got nothing for you, nothing, nothing."

"It's all right, honey, you'll get something. Everybody out of work now, you know that."

"It ain't right. Ain't no man ought to eat his woman's food year in and year out, and see his children running wild. Ain't nothing right about that."

"Honey, you took good care of us when you had it. Ain't nobody got nothing nowadays."

"I ain't talking about nobody else, I'm talking about *me*. God knows I try." My mother said something I could not hear, and my father cried out louder. "What must a man do, tell me that?"

"Look, we ain't starving. I git paid every week, and Mrs. Ellis is real nice about giving me things. She gonna let me have Mr. Ellis's old coat for you this winter—"

"Forget Mr. Ellis's coat! And forget his money! You think I want white folks' leavings? Oh, Maybelle"—and suddenly he sobbed, loudly and painfully, and cried help-lessly and hopelessly in the dark night. I had never heard a man cry before. I did not know men ever cried. I covered my ears with my hands but could not cut off the sound of my father's harsh, painful, despairing sobs. My father was a strong man who would whisk a child upon his shoulders and go singing through the house. My father whittled toys for us and laughed so loud that the great oak seemed to laugh with him, and taught us how to fish and hunt rabbits. How could it be that my father was crying? But the sobs went on, unstifled, finally quieting until I could hear my mother's voice, deep and rich, hum-ming softly as she used to hum to a frightened child.

The world had lost its boundary lines. My mother, who was small and soft, was now the strength of the family; my father, who was the rock on which the family had been built, was sobbing like the tiniest child. Everything was suddenly out of tune, like a broken accordion. Where did I fit into this crazy picture? I do not now remember my thoughts, only a feeling of great bewilder-ment and fear.

Long after the sobbing and the humming had stopped, I lay on the pallet, still as stone with my hands over my ears, wishing that I could cry and be comforted. The night was silent now except for the sound of the crickets and of Joey's soft breathing. But the room was too crowded with fear to allow me to sleep, and finally, feeling the terrible alone-ness of 4 A.M., I decided to awaken Joey.

"Ouch! What's the matter with you? What you want?" he demanded disagreeably when I had pinched and slapped him awake.

"Come on, wake up."

"What for? Go 'way."

I was lost for a reasonable reply. I could not say, "I'm scared, and I don't want to be alone," so I merely said, "I'm going out. If you want to come, come on."

The promise of adventure awoke him. "Going out now? Where at, Lizabeth? What you going to do?"

I was pulling my dress over my head. Until now I had not thought of going out. "Just come on," I replied tersely.

I was out the window and halfway down the road before Joey caught up with me.

"Wait, Lizabeth, where you going?"

I was running as if the furies[2] were after me, as perhaps they were—running silently and furiously until I came to where I had half-known I was headed—to Miss Lottie's yard.

The half-dawn light was more eerie than complete darkness, and in it the old house was like the ruin that my world had become —foul and crumbling, a grotesque caricature. It looked haunted, but I was not afraid be-cause I was haunted too.

"Lizabeth, you lost your mind?" panted Joey.

I had indeed lost my mind, for all the smoldering emotions of that summer swelled in me and burst—the great need for my mother who was never there, the hopeless-ness of our poverty and degradation, the bewilderment of being neither child nor woman and yet both at once, the fear un-leashed by my father's tears. And these feel-ings combined in one great impulse toward destruction.

"Lizabeth!"

I leaped furiously into the mounds of marigolds and pulled madly, trampling and pulling and destroying the perfect yellow blooms. The fresh smell of early morning and of dew-soaked marigolds spurred me on as I went tearing and mangling and sobbing while Joey tugged my dress or my waist crying, "Lizabeth stop, please stop!"

And then I was sitting in the ruined little garden among the uprooted and ruined

---

2. **furies** (fyoor′ēz): three female spirits of Greek and Roman mythology who punished wrongdoers.

flowers, crying and crying, and it was too late to undo what I had done. Joey was sitting beside me, silent and frightened, not knowing what to say. Then, "Lizabeth, look."

I opened my swollen eyes and saw in front of me a pair of large calloused feet; my gaze lifted to the swollen legs, the age-distorted body clad in a tight cotton night dress, and then the shadowed Indian face surrounded by stubby white hair. And there was no rage in the face now, now that the garden was destroyed and there was nothing any longer to be protected.

"M-miss Lottie!" I scrambled to my feet and just stood there and stared at her, and that was the moment when childhood faded and womanhood began. The violent, crazy act was the last act of childhood. For as I gazed at the immobile face with sad, weary eyes, I gazed upon a kind of reality that is hidden to childhood. The witch was no longer a witch but only a broken old woman who had dared to create beauty in the midst of ugliness and sterility. She had been born in squalor and had lived in it all her life. Now at the end of that life she had nothing except a falling-down hut, a wrecked body, and John Burke, the mindless son of her passion. Whatever verve there was left in her, whatever was of love and beauty and joy that had not been squeezed out by life, had been there in the marigolds she had so tenderly cared for.

Of course I could not express the things that I knew about Miss Lottie as I stood there awkward and ashamed. The years have put words to the things I knew in that moment, and as I look back upon it, I know that that moment marked the end of innocence. . . . Innocence involves an unseeing acceptance of things at face value, an ignorance of the area below the surface. In that humiliating moment I looked beyond myself and into the depths of another person. This was the beginning of compassion, and one cannot have both compassion and innocence.

The years have taken me worlds away from that time and that place, from the dust and squalor of our lives and from the bright thing that I destroyed in a blind, childish striking out at God-knows-what. Miss Lottie died long ago and many years have passed since I last saw her hut, completely barren at last, for despite my wild contrition she never planted marigolds again. Yet, there are times when the image of those passionate yellow mounds returns with a painful poignancy. For one does not have to be ignorant and poor to find that one's life is barren as the dusty yards of one's town. And I too have planted marigolds.

Getting at Meaning

1. Why do you think the experience described in the story stands out in Lizabeth's memory?

2. Describe Lizabeth's town in rural Maryland. What is life like there? What do the children do in their spare time? Why do they like to annoy Miss Lottie?

3. What circumstances cause Lizabeth to return to Miss Lottie's yard? Why does Lizabeth feel that "the world had lost its boundary lines"?

4. Why does Lizabeth immediately regret what she has done?

Developing Skills in Reading Literature

1. **Character.** This story focuses on one brief event that Lizabeth views as a turning point in her life. How does this event signal the end of her childhood and the beginning of maturity? How has it affected her later life?

2. **Flashback.** Nearly all of this selection is a flashback, a recollection of events that happened before the beginning of the story. Where in the story does the flashback begin? Where does it end? Why do you think the writer chose to present the story as a flashback? What insights does the reader gain from the parts of the story outside the flashback?

3. **Symbol.** What kind of life has Miss Lottie had? What do the marigolds symbolize to her? What do they symbolize for the children?

4. **Theme.** How does the narrator define innocence? Why does she say that "one cannot have both compassion and innocence"? How is the lesson she learns an important part of her growing up process? How has her experience been both destructive and constructive?

5. **Figurative Language.** Language that conveys ideas beyond the ordinary meanings of the words is called figurative language. Similes and metaphors are two kinds of figurative language used by the writer of this story. For example, at the beginning of the story the

narrator says, ". . . memory is an abstract painting—it does not present things as they are, but rather as they *feel.*" What is she saying about memories? Find a least ten other similes and metaphors in the story.

Developing Vocabulary Skills

Getting Word Meaning from Context. Many times the meaning of a word is made clear by examining the sentence in which it appears. The italicized words in the following sentences are from the story. Try to determine the meaning of each word by examining its context. Then look up the word in the Glossary and write the definition.

1. Mother sent me to the store because she needed two more *skeins* of wool for my sweater.

2. The *meager* amount of bread was not enough to feed the entire family.

3. She worked *placidly,* enjoying both the work and the feeling of pleasure that she got from it.

4. John's *exuberance* filled the room as he enthusiastically announced his engagement.

5. She had been born in *squalor* and had lived most of her life in that same ugly, dirty environment.

6. Sarah apologized, but her *contrition* had no effect on her parents.

Developing Writing Skills

Explaining an Idea. In one paragraph use specific reasons to support or challenge one of the following quotations from the story. Try to develop a logical train of thought and a convincing argument as you write.

1. ". . . one cannot have both compassion and innocence."

2. "For one does not have to be ignorant and poor to find that one's life is barren. . . ."

3. ". . . memory is an abstract painting—it does not present things as they are, but rather as they *feel.*"

The Secret Life of Walter Mitty

James Thurber

We're going through!" The Commander's voice was like thin ice breaking. He wore his full-dress uniform, with the heavily braided white cap pulled down rakishly over one cold gray eye. "We can't make it, sir. It's spoiling for a hurricane, if you ask me." "I'm not asking you, Lieutenant Berg," said the Commander. "Throw on the power light! Rev her up to 8,500! We're going through!" The pounding of the cylinders increased: ta-pocketa-pocketa-pocketa-*pocketa-pocketa*. The Commander stared at the ice forming on the pilot window. He walked over and twisted a row of complicated dials. "Switch on No. 8 auxiliary!" he shouted. "Switch on No. 8 auxiliary!" repeated Lieutenant Berg. "Full strength in No. 3 turret!" shouted the Commander. "Full strength in No. 3 turret!" The crew, bending to their various tasks in the huge, hurtling eight-engined Navy hydroplane, looked at each other and grinned. "The Old Man'll get us through," they said to one another. "The Old Man ain't afraid of nothin'!" . . .

"Not so fast! You're driving too fast!" said Mrs. Mitty. "What are you driving so fast for?"

"Hmm?" said Walter Mitty. He looked at his wife, in the seat beside him, with shocked astonishment. She seemed grossly unfamiliar, like a strange woman who had yelled at him in a crowd. "You were up to fifty-five," she said. "You know I don't like to go more than forty. You were up to fifty-five." Walter Mitty drove on toward Waterbury in silence, the

roaring of the SN202 through the worst storm in twenty years of Navy flying fading in the remote, intimate airways of his mind. "You're tensed up again," said Mrs. Mitty, "It's one of your days. I wish you'd let Dr. Renshaw look you over."

Walter Mitty stopped the car in front of the building where his wife went to have her hair done. "Remember to get those overshoes while I'm having my hair done," she said. "I don't need overshoes," said Mitty. She put her mirror back into her bag. "We've been all through that," she said, getting out of the car. "You're not a young man any longer." He raced the engine a little. "Why don't you wear your gloves? Have you lost your gloves?" Walter Mitty reached into a pocket and brought out the gloves. He put them on, but after she had turned and gone into the building and he had driven on to a red light, he took them off again. "Pick it up, brother!" snapped a cop as the light changed, and Mitty hastily pulled on his gloves and lurched ahead. He drove around the streets aimlessly for a time, and then he drove past the hospital on his way to the parking lot.

. . . "It's the millionaire banker, Wellington McMillan," said the pretty nurse. "Yes?" said Walter Mitty, removing his gloves slowly. "Who has the case?" "Dr. Renshaw and Dr. Benbow, but there are two specialists here, Dr. Remington from New York and Dr. Pritchard-Mitford from London. He flew over." A door opened down a long, cool corridor and Dr. Renshaw came out. He looked

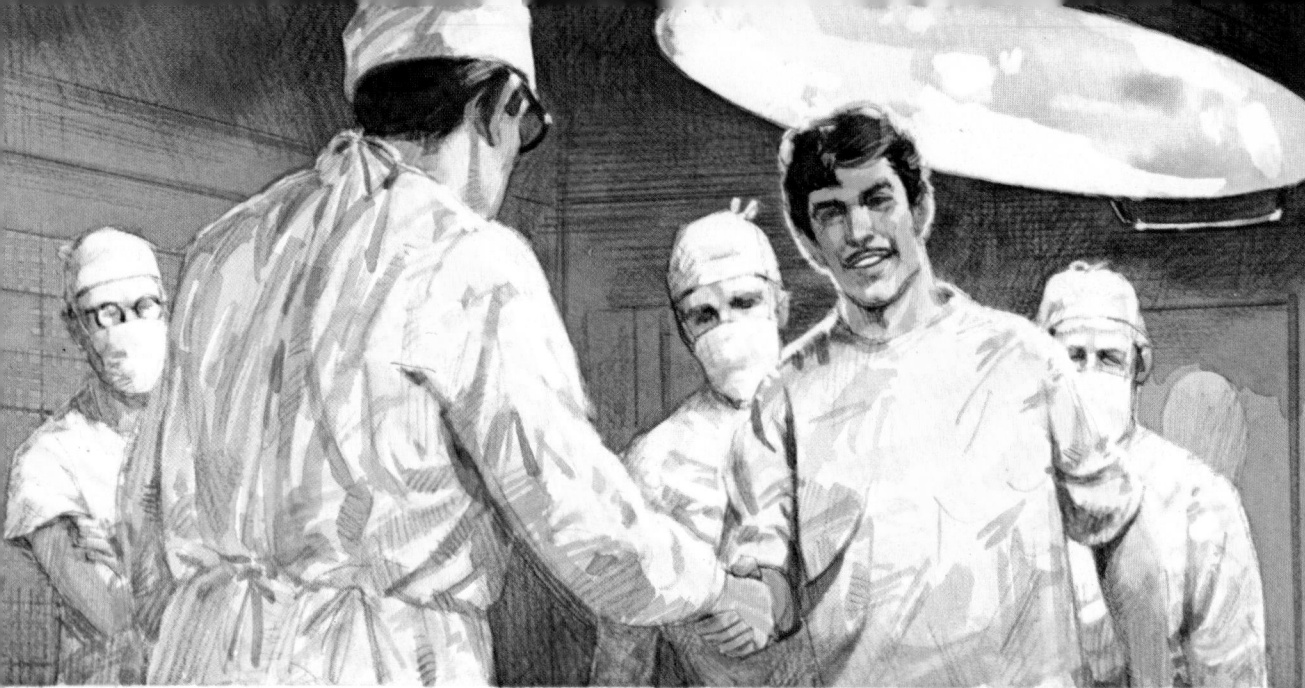

distraught and haggard. "Hello, Mitty," he said. "We're having the devil's own time with McMillan, the millionaire banker and close personal friend of Roosevelt. Obstreosis[1] of the ductal tract. Tertiary. Wish you'd take a look at him." "Glad to," said Mitty.

In the operating room there were whispered introductions: "Dr. Remington, Dr. Mitty. Dr. Pritchard-Mitford, Dr. Mitty." "I've read your book on streptothricosis," said Pritchard-Mitford, shaking hands. "A brilliant performance, sir." "Thank you," said Walter Mitty. "Didn't know you were in the States, Mitty," grumbled Remington. "Coals to Newcastle,[2] bringing Mitford and me up here for a tertiary." "You are very kind," said Mitty. A huge, complicated machine, connected to the operating table, with many tubes and wires, began at this moment to go pocketa-pocketa-pocketa. "The new anaesthetizer is giving away!" shouted an interne. "There is no one in the East who knows how to fix it!" "Quiet, man!" said Mitty, in a low, cool voice. He sprang to the machine, which was now going pocketa-pocketa-queep-pocketa-queep. He began fingering delicately a row of glistening dials. "Give me a fountain pen!" he snapped. Someone handed him a fountain pen. He pulled a faulty piston out of the machine and inserted the pen in its place. "That will hold for ten minutes," he said. "Get on with the operation." A nurse hurried over and whispered to Renshaw, and Mitty saw the man turn pale. "Coreopsis has set in," said Renshaw nervously. "If you would take over, Mitty?" Mitty looked at him and at the craven figure of Benbow, who drank, and at the grave, uncertain faces of the two great specialists. "If you wish," he said. They slipped a white gown on him; he adjusted a mask and drew on thin gloves; nurses handed him shining ...

"Back it up, Mac! Look out for that Buick!" Walter Mitty jammed on the brakes. "Wrong lane, Mac," said the parking-lot attendant, looking at Mitty closely. "Gee. Yeh," muttered Mitty. He began cautiously to back out

---

1. **obstreosis:** This word and other similar words in this section only look like medical terms; they are part of the humor of the story.

2. **coals to Newcastle:** to do something unnecessary.

of the lane marked "Exit Only." "Leave her sit there," said the attendant. "I'll put her away." Mitty got out of the car. "Hey, better leave the key." "Oh," said Mitty, handing the man the ignition key. The attendant vaulted into the car, backed it up with insolent skill, and put it where it belonged.

They're so darn cocky, thought Walter Mitty, walking along Main Street; they think they know everything. Once he had tried to take his chains off, outside New Milford, and he had got them wound around the axles. A man had had to come out in a wrecking car and unwind them, a young, grinning garageman. Since then Mrs. Mitty always made him drive to a garage to have the chains taken off. The next time, he thought, I'll wear my right arm in a sling; they won't grin at me then. I'll have my right arm in a sling, and they'll see I couldn't possibly take the chains off myself. He kicked at the slush on the sidewalk. "Overshoes," he said to himself, and he began looking for a shoe store.

When he came out into the street again, with the overshoes in a box under his arm, Walter Mitty began to wonder what the other thing was his wife had told him to get. She had told him, twice before they set out from their house for Waterbury. In a way he hated these weekly trips to town—he was always getting something wrong. Kleenex, he thought, Squibb's, razor blades? No. Toothpaste, toothbrush, bicarbonate, carborundum, initiative and referendum?[3] He gave it up. But she would remember it. "Where's the what's-its-name?" she would ask. "Don't tell me you forgot the what's-its-name." A newsboy went by shouting something about the Waterbury trial.

. . . "Perhaps this will refresh your memory." The District Attorney suddenly thrust a heavy automatic at the quiet figure on the witness stand. "Have you ever seen this before?" Walter Mitty took the gun and examined it expertly. "This is my Webley-Vickers 50.80," he said calmly. An excited buzz ran around the courtroom. The Judge rapped for order. "You are a crack shot with any sort of firearms, I believe?" said the District Attorney, insinuatingly. "Objection!" shouted Mitty's attorney. "We have shown that the defendant could not have fired the shot. We have shown that he wore his right arm in a sling on the night of the fourteenth of July." Walter Mitty raised his hand briefly and the bickering attorneys were stilled. "With any known make of gun," he said evenly, "I could have killed Gregory Fitzhurst at three hundred feet *with my left hand*." Pandemonium broke loose in the courtroom. A woman's scream rose above the bedlam, and suddenly a lovely, dark-haired girl was in Walter Mitty's arms. The District Attorney struck at her savagely. Without rising from his chair, Mitty let the man have it on the point of the chin. "You miserable cur!" . . .

"Puppy biscuit," said Walter Mitty. He stopped walking, and the buildings of Waterbury rose up out of the misty courtroom and surrounded him again. A woman who was passing laughed. "He said 'Puppy biscuit,'" she said to her companion. "That man said 'Puppy biscuit' to himself." Walter Mitty hurried on. He went into an A.&P., not the first one he came to but a smaller one farther up the street. "I want some biscuit for small, young dogs," he said to the clerk. "Any special brand, sir?" The greatest pistol shot in the world thought a moment. "It says 'Puppies Bark for It' on the box," said Walter Mitty.

His wife would be through at the hairdresser's in fifteen minutes, Mitty saw in looking at his watch, unless they had trouble drying it; sometimes they had trouble drying it. She didn't like to get to the hotel first; she would want him to be there waiting for her

---

3. **carborundum . . . referendum:** The use of these words adds humor to the story, as their meanings make no sense in this context.

as usual. He found a big leather chair in the lobby, facing a window, and he put the overshoes and the puppy biscuit on the floor beside it. He picked up an old copy of *Liberty* and sank down into the chair. "Can Germany Conquer the World through the Air?" Walter Mitty looked at the pictures of bombing planes and of ruined streets.

. . . "The cannonading has got the wind up in young Raleigh, sir," said the sergeant. Captain Mitty looked up at him through tousled hair. "Get him to bed," he said wearily, "with the others. I'll fly alone." "But you can't, sir," said the sergeant anxiously. "It takes two men to handle that bomber, and the Archies[4] are pounding everything out of the air. Von Richtman's circus[5] is between here and Saulier." "Somebody's got to get that ammunition dump," said Mitty. "I'm going over. Spot of brandy?" He poured a drink for the sergeant and one for himself. War thundered and whined around the dugout and battered at the door. There was a rending of wood, and splinters flew through the room. "A bit of a near thing," said Captain Mitty carelessly. "The box barrage is closing in," said the sergeant. "We only live once, Sergeant," said

Mitty, with his faint, fleeting smile. "Or do we?" He poured another brandy and tossed it off. "I never see a man could hold his brandy like you, sir," said the sergeant. "Begging your pardon, sir." Captain Mitty stood up and strapped on his huge Webley-Vickers automatic. "It's forty kilometres through death, sir," said the sergeant. Mitty finished one last brandy. "After all," he said softly, "what isn't?" The pounding of the cannon increased; there was the rat-tat-tatting of machine guns, and from somewhere came the menacing pocketa-pocketa-pocketa of the new flame-throwers. Walter Mitty walked to the door of the dugout humming "Auprès de Ma Blonde." He turned and waved to the sergeant. "Cheerio!" he said. . . .

Something struck his shoulder. "I've been looking all over this hotel for you," said Mrs. Mitty. "Why do you have to hide in this old chair? How did you expect me to find you?" "Things close in," said Walter Mitty vaguely.

---

4. **Archies:** slang term for German soldiers in World War I.
5. **Von Richtman's circus:** German air squadron in World War I, so called for the well-known pilot von Richtman.

"What?" Mrs. Mitty said. "Did you get the what's-its-name? The puppy biscuit? What's in that box?" "Overshoes," said Mitty. "Couldn't you have put them on in the store?" "I was thinking," said Walter Mitty. "Does it ever occur to you that I am sometimes thinking?" She looked at him. "I'm going to take your temperature when I get you home," she said.

They went out through the revolving doors that made a faintly derisive whistling sound when you pushed them. It was two blocks to the parking lot. At the drugstore on the corner she said, "Wait here for me. I forgot something. I won't be a minute." She was more than a minute. Walter Mitty lighted a cigarette. It began to rain, rain with sleet in it. He stood up against the wall of the drugstore, smoking. . . . He put his shoulders back and his heels together. "Remove the handkerchief," said Walter Mitty scornfully. He took one last drag on his cigarette and snapped it away. Then, with that faint, fleeting smile playing about his lips, he faced the firing squad; erect and motionless, proud and disdainful, Walter Mitty the Undefeated, inscrutable to the last.

Getting at Meaning

1. What kind of person is Walter Mitty in real life? What is he like in his fantasies?

2. What do the five separate daydreams described in the story have in common?

3. Walter Mitty feels embarrassed when he drives into the parking lot the wrong way. What other things make him ashamed?

4. Describe Mrs. Mitty. What kind of relationship does she have with Walter?

5. What happens to Walter Mitty in his final fantasy? How does this relate to what happens in real life? What does he mean when he says to Mrs. Mitty, "Things close in"?

6. What is the function of daydreaming in Walter Mitty's life? What prevents him from using other means of escape?

Developing Skills in Reading Literature

1. **Conflict.** The conflicts in this story are both internal and external. Describe the conflict between Walter Mitty and Mrs. Mitty. Describe the conflict in Walter's own mind. Which conflict is more important? Explain.

2. **Structure.** This story has a simple plot; Walter Mitty takes his wife to the hairdresser and runs a few errands. The story line is interrupted by Mitty's daydreams. The daydreams are triggered by situations in the basic plot. For example, in the first daydream Walter Mitty pilots a hydroplane, a fantasy perhaps suggested by his driving a car. What brings on each of the other daydreams? What snaps him out of each one? Does the story begin and end with daydreams or with real life experiences? What does your answer suggest about Mitty's life?

3. **Irony.** What is ironic about the characters Walter Mitty becomes in his daydreams?

4. **Theme.** This story deals with the conflict between a dream world and the real world. What message does the writer convey about this conflict through the character of Mitty?

5. **Point of View.** Although the reader is mainly inside the mind of Walter Mitty, the story is not an example of first-person narration. Why not? From what point of view is the story told?

Developing Writing Skills

Telling the Same Story from a Different Point of View. The reader of this story does not learn much about Mrs. Mitty. Retell one incident from her point of view. Be sure to bring out her thoughts and feelings about her husband and his actions.

A Mother in Mannville

Marjorie Kinnan Rawlings

The orphanage is high in the Carolina mountains. Sometimes in winter the snowdrifts are so deep that the institution is cut off from the village below, from all the world. Fog hides the mountain peaks, the snow swirls down the valleys, and a wind blows so bitterly that the orphanage boys who take the milk twice daily to the baby cottage reach the door with fingers stiff in an agony of numbness.

"Or when we carry trays from the cookhouse for the ones that are sick," Jerry said, "we get our faces frostbit, because we can't put our hands over them. I have gloves," he added. "Some of the boys don't have any."

He liked the late spring, he said. The rhododendron was in bloom, a carpet of color, across the mountainsides, soft as the May winds that stirred the hemlocks. He called it laurel.

"It's pretty when the laurel blooms," he said. "Some of it's pink and some of it's white."

I was there in the autumn. I wanted quiet, isolation, to do some troublesome writing. I wanted mountain air to blow out the malaria from too long a time in the subtropics. I was homesick, too, for the flaming of maples in October, and for corn shocks and pumpkins and black-walnut trees and the lift of hills. I found them all, living in a cabin that belonged to the orphanage, half a mile beyond the orphanage farm. When I took the cabin, I asked for a boy or man to come and chop wood for the fireplace. The first few days were warm, I found what wood I needed about the cabin, no one came, and I forgot the order.

I looked up from my typewriter one late afternoon, a little startled. A boy stood at the door, and my pointer dog, my companion, was at his side and had not barked to warn me. The boy was probably twelve years old, but undersized. He wore overalls and a torn shirt, and was barefooted.

He said, "I can chop some wood today."

I said, "But I have a boy coming from the orphanage."

"I'm the boy."

"You? But you're small."

"Size don't matter, chopping wood," he said. "Some of the big boys don't chop good. I've been chopping wood at the orphanage a long time."

I visualized mangled and inadequate branches for my fires. I was well into my work and not inclined to conversation. I was a little blunt.

"Very well. There's the ax. Go ahead and see what you can do."

I went back to work, closing the door. At first the sound of the boy dragging brush annoyed me. Then he began to chop. The blows were rhythmic and steady, and shortly I had forgotten him, the sound no more of an interruption than a consistent rain. I suppose an hour and a half passed, for when I stopped and stretched, and heard the boy's steps on the cabin stoop, the sun was dropping behind the farthest mountain, and the valleys were purple with something deeper than the asters.

The boy said, "I have to go to supper now. I can come again tomorrow evening."

I said, "I'll pay you now for what you've done," thinking I should probably have to insist on an older boy. "Ten cents an hour?"

"Anything is all right."

We went together back of the cabin. An astonishing amount of solid wood had been cut. There were cherry logs and heavy roots of rhododendron, and blocks from the waste pine and oak left from the building of the cabin.

"But you've done as much as a man," I said. "This is a splendid pile."

I looked at him, actually, for the first time. His hair was the color of the corn shocks and his eyes, very direct, were like the mountain sky when rain is pending—gray, with a shadowing of that miraculous blue. As I spoke, a light came over him, as though the setting sun had touched him with the same suffused glory with which it touched the mountains. I gave him a quarter.

"You may come tomorrow," I said, "and thank you very much."

He looked at me, and at the coin, and seemed to want to speak, but could not, and turned away.

"I'll split kindling tomorrow," he said over his thin, ragged shoulder. "You'll need kindling and medium wood and logs and backlogs."

At daylight I was half wakened by the sound of chopping. Again it was so even in texture that I went back to sleep. When I left my bed in the cool morning, the boy had come and gone, and a stack of kindling was neat against the cabin wall. He came again after school in the afternoon and worked until time to return to the orphanage. His name was Jerry; he was twelve years old, and he had been at the orphanage since he was four. I could picture him at four, with the same grave gray-blue eyes and the same—independence? No, the word that comes to me is "integrity."

The word means something very special to me, and the quality for which I use it is a rare one. My father had it—there is another of whom I am almost sure—but almost no man of my acquaintance possesses it with the clarity, the purity, the simplicity of a mountain stream. But the boy Jerry had it. It is bedded on courage, but it is more than brave. It is honest, but it is more than honesty. The ax handle broke one day. Jerry said the woodshop at the orphanage would repair it. I brought money to pay for the job, and he refused it.

"I'll pay for it," he said. "I broke it. I brought the ax down careless."

"But no one hits accurately every time," I told him. "The fault was in the wood of the handle. I'll see the man from whom I bought it."

It was only then that he would take the money. He was standing back of his own carelessness. He was a free-will agent, and he chose to do careful work; and if he failed, he took the responsibility without subterfuge.

And he did for me the unnecessary thing, the gracious thing, that we find done only by the great of heart. Things no training can teach, for they are done on the instant, with no predicated experience. He found a cubbyhole beside the fireplace that I had not noticed. There, of his own accord, he put kindling and "medium" wood, so that I might always have dry fire material ready in case of sudden wet weather. A stone was loose in the rough walk to the cabin. He dug a deeper hole and steadied it, although he came, himself, by a short cut over the bank. I found that when I tried to return his thoughtfulness with such things as candy and apples, he was wordless. "Thank you" was, perhaps, an expression for which he had had no use, for his courtesy was instinctive. He only looked at the gift and at me, and a curtain lifted, so that I saw deep into the clear well of his eyes, and gratitude was there, and affection, soft over the firm granite of his character.

He made simple excuses to come and sit with me. I could no more have turned him away than if he had been physically hungry. I suggested once that the best time for us to visit was just before supper, when I left off my writing. After that, he waited always until my typewriter had been some time quiet. One day I worked until nearly dark. I went outside the cabin, having forgotten him. I saw him going up over the hill in the twilight toward the orphanage. When I sat down on my stoop, a place was warm from his body where he had been sitting.

He became intimate, of course, with my pointer, Pat. There is a strange communion between a boy and a dog. Perhaps they possess the same singleness of spirit, the same kind of wisdom. It is difficult to explain, but it exists. When I went across the state for a weekend, I left the dog in Jerry's charge. I gave him the dog whistle and the key to the cabin, and left sufficient food. He was to come two or three times a day and let out the dog, and feed and exercise him. I should return Sunday night, and Jerry would take out the dog for the last time Sunday afternoon and then leave the key under an agreed hiding place.

My return was belated, and fog filled the mountain passes so treacherously that I dared not drive at night. The fog held the next morning, and it was Monday noon before I reached the cabin. The dog had been fed and cared for that morning. Jerry came early in the afternoon, anxious.

"The superintendent said nobody would drive in the fog," he said. "I came just before bedtime last night and you hadn't come. So I brought Pat some of my breakfast this morning. I wouldn't have let anything happen to him."

"I was sure of that. I didn't worry."

"When I heard about the fog, I thought you'd know."

He was needed for work at the orphanage, and he had to return at once. I gave him a dollar in payment, and he looked at it and went away. But that night he came in the darkness and knocked at the door.

"Come in, Jerry," I said, "if you're allowed to be away this late."

"I told maybe a story," he said. "I told them I thought you would want to see me."

"That's true," I assured him, and I saw his relief. "I want to hear about how you managed with the dog."

He sat by the fire with me, with no other light, and told me of their two days together. The dog lay close to him, and found a comfort there that I did not have for him. And it seemed to me that being with my dog, and caring for him, had brought the boy and me, too, together, so that he felt that he belonged

to me as well as to the animal.

"He stayed right with me," he told me, "except when he ran in the laurel. He likes the laurel. I took him up over the hill and we both ran fast. There was a place where the grass was high and I lay down in it and hid. I could hear Pat hunting for me. He found my trail and he barked. When he found me, he acted crazy, and he ran around and around me, in circles."

We watched the flames.

"That's an apple log," he said. "It burns the prettiest of any wood."

We were very close.

He was suddenly impelled to speak of things he had not spoken of before, nor had I cared to ask him.

"You look a little bit like my mother," he said. "Especially in the dark, by the fire."

"But you were only four, Jerry, when you came here. You have remembered how she looked, all these years?"

"My mother lives in Mannville," he said.

For a moment, finding that he had a mother shocked me as greatly as anything in my life has ever done, and I did not know why it disturbed me. Then I understood my distress. I was filled with a passionate resentment that any woman should go away and leave her son. A fresh anger added itself. A son like this one—The orphanage was a wholesome place, the executives were kind, good people, the food was more than adequate, the boys were healthy, a ragged shirt was no hardship, nor the doing of clean labor. Granted, perhaps, that the boy felt no lack, what blood fed the bowels of a woman who did not yearn over this child's lean body that had come in parturition out of her own? At four he would have looked the same as now. Nothing, I thought, nothing in life could change those eyes. His quality must be apparent to an idiot, a fool. I burned with questions I could not ask. In any case, I was afraid, there would be pain.

"Have you seen her, Jerry—lately?"

"I see her every summer. She sends for me."

I wanted to cry out, "Why are you not with her? How can she let you go away again?"

He said, "She comes up here from Mannville whenever she can. She doesn't have a job now."

His face shone in the firelight.

"She wanted to give me a puppy, but they can't let any one boy keep a puppy. You remember the suit I had on last Sunday?" He was plainly proud. "She sent me that for Christmas. The Christmas before that"—he drew a long breath, savoring the memory—"she sent me a pair of skates."

"Roller skates?"

My mind was busy, making pictures of her, trying to understand her. She had not, then, entirely deserted or forgotten him. But why, then—I thought, "I must not condemn her without knowing."

"Roller skates. I let the other boys use them. They're always borrowing them. But they're careful of them."

What circumstance other than poverty—

"I'm going to take the dollar you gave me for taking care of Pat," he said, "and buy her a pair of gloves."

I could only say, "That will be nice. Do you know her size?"

"I think it's 8½," he said.

He looked at my hands.

"Do you wear 8½?" he asked.

"No. I wear a smaller size, a 6."

"Oh! Then I guess her hands are bigger than yours."

I hated her. Poverty or no, there was other food than bread, and the soul could starve as quickly as the body. He was taking his dollar to buy gloves for her big stupid hands, and she lived away from him, in Mannville, and contented herself with sending him skates.

"She likes white gloves," he said. "Do you think I can get them for a dollar?"

"I think so," I said.

I decided that I should not leave the mountains without seeing her and knowing for myself why she had done this thing.

The human mind scatters its interests as though made of thistledown,[1] and every wind stirs and moves it. I finished my work. It did not please me, and I gave my thoughts to another field. I should need some Mexican material.

I made arrangements to close my Florida place. Mexico immediately, and doing the writing there, if conditions were favorable. Then, Alaska with my brother. After that, heaven knew what or where.

I did not take time to go to Mannville to see Jerry's mother, nor even to talk with the orphanage officials about her. I was a trifle abstracted about the boy, because of my work and plans. And after my first fury at her—we did not speak of her again—his having a mother, any sort at all, not far away, in Mannville, relieved me of the ache I had had about him. He did not question the anomalous relation. He was not lonely. It was none of my concern.

He came every day and cut my wood and did small helpful favors and stayed to talk. The days had become cold, and often I let him come inside the cabin. He would lie on the floor in front of the fire, with one arm across the pointer, and they would both doze and wait quietly for me. Other days they ran with a common ecstasy through the laurel, and since the asters were now gone, he brought me back vermilion maple leaves, and chestnut boughs dripping with imperial yellow. I was ready to go.

I said to him, "You have been my good friend, Jerry. I shall often think of you and miss you. Pat will miss you too. I am leaving tomorrow."

He did not answer. When he went away, I remember that a new moon hung over the mountains, and I watched him go in silence up the hill. I expected him the next day, but he did not come. The details of packing my personal belongings, loading my car, arranging the bed over the seat, where the dog would ride, occupied me until late in the day. I closed the cabin and started the car, noticing that the sun was in the west and I should do well to be out of the mountains by nightfall. I stopped by the orphanage and left the cabin key and money for my light bill with Miss Clark.

"And will you call Jerry for me to say goodbye to him?"

"I don't know where he is," she said. "I'm afraid he's not well. He didn't eat his dinner this noon. One of the other boys saw him going over the hill into the laurel. He was supposed to fire the boiler this afternoon. It's not like him; he's unusually reliable."

I was almost relieved, for I knew I should never see him again, and it would be easier not to say goodbye to him.

I said, "I wanted to talk with you about his mother—why he's here—but I'm in more of a hurry than I expected to be. It's out of the question for me to see her now too. But here's some money I'd like to leave with you to buy things for him at Christmas and on his birthday. It will be better than for me to try to send him things. I could so easily duplicate —skates, for instance."

She blinked her eyes.

"There's not much use for skates here," she said.

Her stupidity annoyed me.

"What I mean," I said, "is that I don't want to duplicate things his mother sends him. I might have chosen skates if I didn't know she had already given them to him."

She stared at me.

"I don't understand," she said. "He has no mother. He has no skates."

---

1. **thistledown:** the soft, fluffy down attached to the flower head of a thistle plant.

Getting at Meaning

1. What clues foreshadow the revelation that Jerry has no mother?

2. Why does the narrator rent the cabin?

3. Why is the narrator dismayed when she first sees Jerry? How does his work surprise her? Why does Jerry begin to appeal to her so strongly?

4. The narrator says that Jerry has integrity and illustrates her point by telling the story of the broken ax handle. What other incidents show Jerry's integrity?

5. Describe Jerry. Why does he grow so close to the narrator and her dog? What is he really saying when he tells the narrator, "You look a little bit like my mother"?

6. Why does Jerry make up the story about his mother in Mannville? Why isn't Jerry at the orphanage when the narrator comes to say goodbye? Why is she relieved?

Developing Skills in Reading Literature

1. **Conflict.** The conflict in this story is extremely subtle. Can you figure out what it is?

2. **Character.** Jerry and the writer are the two main characters in this story. How is each character independent? Who is more sensitive to the needs of others? Which character ultimately has more integrity? Explain your answer.

3. **Theme.** Like "The Secret Life of Walter Mitty," this story involves the conflict between fantasy and reality. What message about fantasy is the writer communicating through the character of Jerry? Explain the writer's message in one or two sentences.

4. **Metaphor.** Explain the following metaphors from the story:

a. ". . . almost no man of my acquaintance possesses [integrity] with the clarity, the purity, the simplicity of a mountain stream."

b. ". . . I saw deep into the clear well of his eyes, and gratitude was there, and affection, soft over the firm granite of his character."

Developing Vocabulary

Root Words. The narrator in the story uses the words *clarity, purity,* and *simplicity.* In each word, the suffix *-ity,* meaning a state or quality, has been added to a root word to create an abstract noun. In a dictionary, find the root word for each of the following abstract nouns. Then write the root and the meaning of each noun.

clarity	simplicity	rarity
purity	responsibility	

Developing Writing Skills

1. **Writing a Definition.** *Integrity* is an abstract noun, a word that stands for something that cannot be seen or touched. The narrator of this story clarifies her concept of *integrity* by giving examples to illustrate this quality in Jerry.

Choose an abstract noun, such as *courage, friendship,* or *loneliness.* Then write a paragraph in which you define the word through two or three concrete examples.

2. **Analyzing a Character.** Write a paragraph in which you analyze what the narrator has learned from her friendship with Jerry. Include comments about what you think she will do after she discovers that Jerry really has no mother.

3. **Using the Senses in Writing.** The writer of this story describes the setting in three different seasons: winter, spring, and autumn. Each description creates a different feeling for the place through images that appeal primarily to the senses of sight and touch.

Choose a place you know well and describe it in two different seasons. Write one paragraph for each season. Use images that appeal to two or more senses.

Plot

BETWEEN ROUNDS, 1899. *Thomas Eakins.*
Philadelphia Museum of Art. Given by Mrs. Thomas Eakins and Miss Mary A. Williams.

The Ransom of Red Chief   *O. Henry*

It looked like a good thing, but wait till I tell you. We were down South, in Alabama—Bill Driscoll and myself—when this kidnapping idea struck us. It was, as Bill afterward expressed it, "during a moment of temporary mental apparition"; but we didn't find that out till later.

There was a town down there, as flat as a flannel-cake, and called Summit, of course. It contained inhabitants of as undeleterious and self-satisfied a class of peasantry as ever clustered around a Maypole.

Bill and me had a joint capital of about six hundred dollars, and we needed just two thousand dollars more to pull off a fraudulent town-lot scheme in Western Illinois with. We talked it over on the front steps of the hotel. Philoprogenitiveness, says we, is strong in semi-rural communities; therefore, and for other reasons, a kidnapping project ought to do better there than in the radius of newspapers that send reporters out in plain clothes to stir up talk about such things. We knew that Summit couldn't get after us with anything stronger than constables and, maybe, some lackadaisical bloodhounds and a diatribe or two in the *Weekly Farmers' Budget*. So, it looked good.

We selected for our victim the only child of a prominent citizen named Ebenezer Dorset. The father was respectable and tight, a mortgage fancier and a stern, upright collection-plate passer and forecloser. The kid was a boy of ten, with bas-relief freckles, and hair the color of the cover of the magazine you buy at the newsstand when you want to catch a train. Bill and me figured that Ebenezer would melt down for a ransom of two thousand dollars to a cent. But wait till I tell you.

About two miles from Summit was a little mountain, covered with a dense cedar brake. On the rear elevation of this mountain was a cave. There we stored provisions.

One evening after sundown, we drove in a buggy past old Dorset's house. The kid was in the street, throwing rocks at a kitten on the opposite fence.

"Hey, little boy!" says Bill, "would you like to have a bag of candy and a nice ride?"

The boy catches Bill neatly in the eye with a piece of brick.

"That will cost the old man an extra five hundred dollars," says Bill, climbing over the wheel.

That boy put up a fight like a welter-weight cinnamon bear; but, at last, we got him down in the bottom of the buggy and drove away. We took him up to the cave, and I hitched the horse in the cedar brake. After dark I drove the buggy to the little village, three miles away, where we had hired it, and walked back to the mountain.

Bill was pasting court-plaster[1] over the scratches and bruises on his features. There was a fire burning behind the big rock at the entrance of the cave, and the boy was watching a pot of boiling coffee, with two buzzard tailfeathers stuck in his red hair. He points a stick at me when I come up, and says,

---

1. **court-plaster:** cloth covered with an adhesive material, formerly used to protect minor skin wounds.

"Ha! cursed paleface, do you dare to enter the camp of Red Chief, the terror of the plains?"

"He's all right now," says Bill, rolling up his trousers and examining some bruises on his shins. "We're playing Indian. We're making Buffalo Bill's show look like magic-lantern views of Palestine in the town hall.[2] I'm Old Hank, the Trapper, Red Chief's captive, and I'm to be scalped at daybreak. By Geronimo! that kid can kick hard."

Yes, sir, that boy seemed to be having the time of his life. The fun of camping out in a cave had made him forget that he was a captive himself. He immediately christened me Snake-eye, the Spy, and announced that, when his braves returned from the warpath, I was to be broiled at the stake at the rising of the sun.

Then we had supper; and he filled his mouth full of bacon and bread and gravy, and began to talk. He made a during-dinner speech something like this,

"I like this fine. I never camped out before, but I had a pet 'possum once, and I was nine last birthday. I hate to go to school. Rats ate up sixteen of Jimmy Talbot's aunt's speckled hen's eggs. Are there any real Indians in these woods? I want some more gravy. Does the trees moving make the wind blow? We had five puppies. What makes your nose so red, Hank? My father has lots of money. Are the stars hot? I whipped Ed Walker twice, Saturday. I don't like girls. You dassent catch toads unless with a string. Do oxen make any noise? Why are oranges round? Have you got beds to sleep on in this cave? Amos Murray has got six toes. A parrot can talk, but a monkey or a fish can't. How many does it take to make twelve?"

Every few minutes he would remember that he was a pesky redskin, and pick up his stick rifle and tiptoe to the mouth of the cave to rubber for the scouts of the hated paleface. Now and then he would let out a war-whoop that made Old Hank the Trapper shiver. That boy had Bill terrorized from the start.

"Red Chief," says I to the kid, "would you like to go home?"

"Aw, what for?" says he. "I don't have any fun at home. I hate to go to school. I like to camp out. You won't take me back home again, Snake-eye, will you?"

"Not right away," says I. "We'll stay here in the cave awhile."

"All right!" says he. "That'll be fine. I never had such fun in all my life."

We went to bed about eleven o'clock. We spread down some wide blankets and quilts and put Red Chief between us. We weren't afraid he'd run away. He kept us awake for three hours, jumping up and reaching for his rifle and screeching, "Hist! pard," in mine and Bill's ears, as the fancied crackle of a twig or the rustle of a leaf revealed to his young imagination the stealthy approach of the outlaw band. At last, I fell into a troubled sleep, and dreamed that I had been kidnapped and chained to a tree by a ferocious pirate with red hair.

Just at daybreak, I was awakened by a series of awful screams from Bill. They weren't yells, or howls, or shouts, or whoops, or yawps, such as you'd expect from a manly set of vocal organs—they were simply indecent, terrifying, humiliating screams, such as women emit when they see ghosts or caterpillars. It's an awful thing to hear a strong, desperate, fat man scream incontinently in a cave at daybreak.

I jumped up to see what the matter was. Red Chief was sitting on Bill's chest, with one hand twined in Bill's hair. In the other he had the sharp case-knife we used for slicing bacon; and he was industriously and realistically trying to take Bill's scalp, accord-

2. **Buffalo Bill's show . . . town hall:** Driscoll thinks that Red Chief's game makes a Wild West frontier show look as tame and boring as a slide-show travelog.

ing to the sentence that had been pronounced upon him the evening before.

I got the knife away from the kid and made him lie down again. But, from that moment, Bill's spirit was broken. He laid down on his side of the bed, but he never closed an eye again in sleep as long as that boy was with us. I dozed off for a while, but along toward sunup I remembered that Red Chief had said I was to be burned at the stake at the rising of the sun. I wasn't nervous or afraid, but I sat up and lit my pipe and leaned against a rock.

"What you getting up so soon for, Sam?" asked Bill.

"Me?" says I. "Oh, I got a kind of a pain in my shoulder. I thought sitting up would rest it."

"You're a liar!" says Bill. "You're afraid. You was to be burned at sunrise, and you was afraid he'd do it. And he would, too, if he could find a match. Ain't it awful, Sam? Do you think anybody will pay out money to get a little imp like that back home?"

"Sure," said I. "A rowdy kid like that is just the kind that parents dote on. Now, you and the Chief get up and cook breakfast, while I go up on the top of this mountain and reconnoitre."

I went up on the peak of the little mountain and ran my eye over the contiguous vicinity. Over toward Summit I expected to see the sturdy yeomanry of the village armed with scythes and pitchforks beating the countryside for the dastardly kidnappers. But what I saw was a peaceful landscape dotted with one man ploughing with a dun mule. Nobody was dragging the creek; no couriers dashed hither and yon, bringing tidings of no news to the distracted parents. There was a sylvan attitude of somnolent sleepiness pervading that section of the external outward surface of Alabama that lay exposed to my view. "Perhaps," says I to myself, "it has not yet been discovered that the wolves have borne away the tender lambkin from the fold.

Heaven help the wolves!" says I, and I went down the mountain to breakfast.

When I got to the cave, I found Bill backed up against the side of it, breathing hard, and the boy threatening to smash him with a rock half as big as a cocoanut.

"He put a red-hot boiled potato down my back," explained Bill, "and then mashed it with his foot, and I boxed his ears. Have you got a gun about you, Sam?"

I took the rock away from the boy and kind of patched up the argument. "I'll fix you," says the kid to Bill. "No man ever yet struck the Red Chief but what he got paid for it. You better beware!"

After breakfast, the kid takes a piece of leather with strings wrapped around it out of his pocket and goes outside the cave un-winding it.

"What's he up to now?" says Bill, anxiously. "You don't think he'll run away, do you, Sam?"

"No fear of it," says I. "He don't seem to be much of a home body. But we've got to fix up some plan about the ransom. There don't seem to be much excitement around Summit on account of his disappearance, but maybe they haven't realized yet that he's gone. His folks may think he's spending the night with Aunt Jane or one of the neighbors. Anyhow, he'll be missed today. Tonight we must get a message to his father demanding the two thousand dollars for his return."

Just then we heard a kind of war-whoop, such as David might have emitted when he knocked out the champion Goliath.[3] It was a sling that Red Chief had pulled out of his pocket, and he was whirling it around his head.

I dodged, and heard a heavy thud and a kind of a sigh from Bill, like a horse gives out when you take his saddle off. A rock the size of an egg had caught Bill just behind his left ear. He loosened himself all over and fell in the fire across the frying pan of hot water for washing the dishes. I dragged him out and poured cold water on his head for half an hour.

By and by, Bill sits up and feels behind his ear and says: "Sam, do you know who my favorite Biblical character is?"

"Take it easy," says I. "You'll come to your senses presently."

"King Herod,"[4] says he. "You won't go away and leave me here alone, will you, Sam?"

I went out and caught that boy and shook him until his freckles rattled.

"If you don't behave," says I, "I'll take you straight home. Now, are you going to be good, or not?"

"I was only funning," says he, sullenly. "I didn't mean to hurt Old Hank. But what did he hit me for? I'll behave, Snake-eye, if you won't send me home, and if you'll let me play the Black Scout today."

"I don't know the game," says I. "That's for you and Mr. Bill to decide. He's your playmate for the day. I'm going away for a while, on business. Now, you come in and make friends with him and say you are sorry for hurting him, or home you go, at once."

I made him and Bill shake hands, and then I took Bill aside and told him I was going to Poplar Cove, a little village three miles from the cave, to find out what I could about how the kidnapping had been regarded in Summit. Also, I thought it best to send a peremptory letter to old man Dorset that day, demanding the ransom and dictating how it should be paid.

"You know, Sam," says Bill, "I've stood by you without batting an eye in earthquakes, fire, and flood—in poker games, dynamite outrages, police raids, train robberies, and cyclones. I never lost my nerve yet till we kidnapped that two-legged skyrocket of a kid. He's got me going. You won't leave me long with him, will you, Sam?"

"I'll be back some time this afternoon," says I. "You must keep the boy amused and quiet till I return. And now we'll write the letter to old Dorset."

Bill and I got paper and pencil and worked on the letter while Red Chief, with a blanket wrapped around him, strutted up and down, guarding the mouth of the cave. Bill begged me tearfully to make the ransom fifteen hundred dollars instead of two thousand. "I ain't

---

3. **David . . . Goliath** (gə li′ əth): a reference to the Bible story in which the young David kills the Philistine giant Goliath with a stone from a sling.

4. **King Herod** (her′ əd): the ruler of Galilee who, according to the New Testament, executed John the Baptist and presided at the trial of Jesus.

attempting," says he, "to decry the celebrated moral aspect of parental affection, but we're dealing with humans; and it ain't human for anybody to give up two thousand dollars for that forty-pound chunk of freckled wildcat. I'm willing to take a chance at fifteen hundred dollars. You can charge the difference up to me."

So, to relieve Bill, I acceded, and we collaborated a letter that ran this way:

Ebenezer Dorset, Esq.:

We have your boy concealed in a place far from Summit. It is useless for you or the most skillful detectives to attempt to find him. Absolutely, the only terms on which you can have him restored to you are these: We demand fifteen hundred dollars in large bills for his return, the money to be left at midnight tonight at the same spot and in the same box as your reply—as hereinafter described. If you agree to these terms, send your answer in writing by a solitary messenger tonight at half-past eight o'clock. After crossing Owl Creek on the road to Poplar Cove, there are three large trees about a hundred yards apart, close to the fence of the wheat field on the right-hand side. At the bottom of the fence-post, opposite the third tree, will be found a small pasteboard box.

The messenger will place the answer in this box and return immediately to Summit.

If you attempt any treachery or fail to comply with our demand as stated, you will never see your boy again.

If you pay the money as demanded, he will be returned to you safe and well within three hours. These terms are final, and if you do not accede to them no further communication will be attempted.

Two Desperate Men

I addressed this letter to Dorset, and put it in my pocket. As I was about to start, the kid comes up to me and says,

"Aw, Snake-eye, you said I could play the Black Scout while you was gone."

"Play it, of course," says I. "Mr. Bill will play with you. What kind of game is it?"

"I'm the Black Scout," says Red Chief, "and I have to ride to the stockade to warn the settlers that the Indians are coming. I'm tired of playing Indian myself. I want to be the Black Scout."

"All right," says I. "It sounds harmless to me. I guess Mr. Bill will help you foil the pesky savages."

"What am I to do?" asks Bill, looking at the kid suspiciously.

"You are the hoss," says Black Scout. "Get down on your hands and knees. How can I

ride to the stockade without a hoss?"

"You'd better keep him interested," said I, "till we get the scheme going. Loosen up."

Bill gets down on his all fours, and a look comes in his eye like a rabbit's when you catch it in a trap.

"How far is it to the stockade, kid?" he asks, in a husky manner of voice.

"Ninety miles," says the Black Scout. "And you have to hurry yourself to get there on time. Whoa, now!"

The Black Scout jumps on Bill's back and digs his heels in his side.

"For Heaven's sake," says Bill, "hurry back, Sam, as soon as you can. I wish we hadn't made the ransom more than a thousand. Say, you quit kicking me, or I'll get up and warm you good."

I walked over to Poplar Cove and sat around the post-office and store, talking with the chawbacons that came in to trade. One whiskerando[5] says that he hears Summit is all upset on account of Elder Ebenezer Dorset's boy having been lost or stolen. That was all I wanted to know. I bought some smoking tobacco, referred casually to the price of black-eyed peas, posted my letter surreptitiously, and came away. The postmaster said the mail-carrier would come by in an hour to take the mail on to Summit.

When I got back to the cave, Bill and the boy were not to be found. I explored the vicinity of the cave, and risked a yodel or two, but there was no response.

So I lighted my pipe and sat down on a mossy bank to await developments.

In about half an hour I heard the bushes rustle, and Bill wabbled out into the little glade in front of the cave. Behind him was the kid, stepping softly like a scout, with a broad grin on his face. Bill stopped, took off his hat, and wiped his face with a red handkerchief. The kid stopped about eight feet behind him.

"Sam," says Bill, "I suppose you'll think I'm

a renegade, but I couldn't help it. I'm a grown person with masculine proclivities and habits of self-defense, but there is a time when all systems of egotism and predominance fail. The boy is gone. I have sent him home. All is off. There was martyrs in old times," goes on Bill, "that suffered death rather than give up the particular graft they enjoyed. None of 'em ever was subjugated to such supernatural tortures as I have been. I tried to be faithful to our articles of depredation; but there came a limit."

"What's the trouble, Bill?" I asks him.

"I was rode," says Bill, "the ninety miles to the stockade, not barring an inch. Then, when the settlers was rescued, I was given oats. Sand ain't a palatable substitute. And then, for an hour I had to try to explain to him why there was nothin' in holes, how a road can run both ways, and what makes the grass green. I tell you, Sam, a human can only stand so much. I takes him by the neck of his clothes and drags him down the mountain. On the way he kicks my legs black and blue from the knees down, and I've got to have two or three bites on my thumb and hand cauterized.

"But he's gone"—continues Bill—"gone home. I showed him the road to Summit and kicked him about eight feet nearer there at one kick. I'm sorry we lose the ransom, but it was either that or Bill Driscoll to the madhouse."

Bill is puffing and blowing, but there is a look of ineffable peace and growing content on his rose-pink features.

"Bill," says I, "there isn't any heart disease in your family, is there?"

"No," says Bill, "nothing chronic except malaria and accidents. Why?"

"Then you might turn around," says I, "and have a look behind you."

Bill turns and sees the boy, and loses his

---

5. **whiskerando:** an old-timer.

complexion and sits down plump on the ground and begins to pluck aimlessly at grass and little sticks. For an hour I was afraid of his mind. And then I told him that my scheme was to put the whole job through immediately and that we would get the ransom and be off with it by midnight if old Dorset fell in with our proposition. So Bill braced up enough to give the kid a weak sort of a smile and a promise to play the Russian in a Japanese war with him as soon as he felt a little better.

I had a scheme for collecting that ransom without danger of being caught by counterplots that ought to commend itself to professional kidnappers. The tree under which the answer was to be left—and the money later on—was close to the road fence with big, bare fields on all sides. If a gang of constables should be watching for anyone to come for the note, they could see him a long way off crossing the fields or in the road. But no, sirree! At half-past eight I was up in that tree as well hidden as a tree toad, waiting for the messenger to arrive.

Exactly on time, a half-grown boy rides up the road on a bicycle, locates the pasteboard box at the foot of the fence-post, slips a folded piece of paper into it, and pedals away again back toward Summit.

I waited an hour and then concluded the thing was square. I slid down the tree, got the note, slipped along the fence till I struck the woods, and was back at the cave in another half an hour. I opened the note, got near the lantern, and read it to Bill. It was written with a pen in a crabbed hand, and the sum and substance of it was this:

Two Desperate Men
Gentlemen:

I received your letter today by post, in regard to the ransom you ask for the return of my son. I think you are a little high in your demands, and I hereby make you a counter-proposition, which I am inclined to believe you will accept. You bring Johnny home and pay me two hundred and fifty dollars in cash, and I agree to take him off your hands. You had better come at night, for the neighbors believe he is lost, and I couldn't be responsible for what they would do to anybody they saw bringing him back.

Very respectfully,
Ebenezer Dorset.

"Great pirates of Penzance," says I; "of all the impudent——"

But I glanced at Bill, and hesitated. He had the most appealing look in his eyes I ever saw on the face of a dumb or a talking brute.

"Sam," says he, "what's two hundred and fifty dollars, after all? We've got the money. One more night of this kid will send me to a bed in Bedlam. Besides being a thorough gentleman, I think Mr. Dorset is a spendthrift for making us such a liberal offer. You ain't going to let the chance go, are you?"

"Tell you the truth, Bill," says I, "this little he ewe lamb has somewhat got on my nerves too. We'll take him home, pay the ransom, and make our getaway."

We took him home that night. We got him to go by telling him that his father had bought a silver-mounted rifle and a pair of moccasins for him, and we were going to hunt bears the next day.

It was just twelve o'clock when we knocked at Ebenezer's front door. Just at the moment when I should have been abstracting the fifteen hundred dollars from the box under the tree, according to the original proposition, Bill was counting out two hundred and fifty dollars into Dorset's hand.

When the kid found out we were going to leave him at home, he started up a howl like a calliope and fastened himself as tight as a leech to Bill's leg. His father peeled him away gradually, like a porous plaster.

"How long can you hold him?" asks Bill.

"I'm not as strong as I used to be," says old Dorset, "but I think I can promise you ten minutes."

"Enough," says Bill. "In ten minutes I shall cross the Central, Southern, and Middle Western States, and be legging it trippingly for the Canadian border."

And, as dark as it was, and as fat as Bill was, and as good a runner as I am, he was a good mile and a half out of Summit before I could catch up with him.

Getting at Meaning

1. What different elements combine to make the ending of this story humorous?

2. Describe Bill Driscoll and Sam, the narrator. What can you tell about them from their speech? How does each one react to Red Chief?

3. Describe Red Chief. What do his family and neighbors apparently think of him? How does he feel about being kidnapped? What are some of the things he does to annoy Bill?

Developing Skills in Reading Literature

1. **Rising Action, Climax, and Falling Action.** All plots follow the same basic pattern. After an initial introduction to the conflict, the struggle develops until a change must take place. This part of the story is called the rising action. The point of highest interest is the climax, or turning point. After the climax the action falls quickly, and the conflict is resolved.

What is the main conflict in this story? What incidents create the rising action? What is the climax of the story? What events make up the falling action? How is the conflict resolved?

2. **Irony.** What makes the ending of this story ironic? Can you find other examples of irony in the story?

Developing Vocabulary

Using a Dictionary. One source of humor in this story is the way that Bill and Sam misuse big words in an attempt to make themselves sound educated and "high class." In the following examples, look up the italicized words in a dictionary. For each word determine why its use is somehow wrong or inappropriate.

1. ". . . during a moment of temporary mental *apparition* . . ."

2. "*Philoprogenitiveness,* says we, is strong in semi-rural communities . . ."

3. "The father was respectable and tight, a mortgage *fancier* . . ."

4. "There was a sylvan attitude of *somnolent* sleepiness pervading that section of the *external* outward surface of Alabama that lay exposed to my view."

Developing Writing Skills

Telling the Same Story from a Different Point of View. This story is an example of first-person narration. The events are related from Sam's point of view. Imagine that you are Ebenezer Dorset or Red Chief, and write a five-paragraph composition in which you describe the kidnapping from your point of view.

The Story-Teller *Saki*

It was a hot afternoon, and the railway carriage was correspondingly sultry, and the next stop was at Templecombe, nearly an hour ahead. The occupants of the carriage were a small girl, and a smaller girl, and a small boy. An aunt belonging to the children occupied one corner seat, and the further corner seat on the opposite side was occupied by a bachelor who was a stranger to their party; but the small girls and the small boy emphatically occupied the compartment. Both the aunt and the children were conversational in a limited, persistent way, reminding one of the attentions of a housefly that refused to be discouraged. Most of the aunt's remarks seemed to begin with "Don't," and nearly all of the children's remarks began with "Why?" The bachelor said nothing out loud.

"Don't, Cyril, don't," exclaimed the aunt, as the small boy began smacking the cushions of the seat, producing a cloud of dust at each blow.

"Come and look out of the window," she added.

The child moved reluctantly to the window. "Why are those sheep being driven out of that field?" he asked.

"I expect they are being driven to another field where there is more grass," said the aunt weakly.

"But there is lots of grass in that field," protested the boy; "there's nothing else but grass there. Aunt, there's lots of grass in that field."

"Perhaps the grass in the other field is better," suggested the aunt fatuously.

"Why is it better?" came the swift, inevitable question.

"Oh, look at those cows!" exclaimed the aunt. Nearly every field along the line had contained cows or bullocks, but she spoke as though she were drawing attention to a rarity.

"Why is the grass in the other field better?" persisted Cyril.

The frown on the bachelor's face was deepening to a scowl. He was a hard, unsympathetic man, the aunt decided in her mind. She was utterly unable to come to any satisfactory decision about the grass in the other field.

The smaller girl created a diversion by beginning to recite "On the Road to Mandalay."[1] She knew only the first line, but she put her limited knowledge to the fullest possible use. She repeated the line over and over again in a dreamy but resolute and very audible voice. It seemed to the bachelor as though someone had had a bet with her that she could not repeat the line aloud two thousand times without stopping. Whoever it was who had made the wager was likely to lose his bet.

"Come over here and listen to a story," said the aunt, when the bachelor had looked twice at her and once at the communication cord.

The children moved listlessly towards the aunt's end of the carriage. Evidently her reputation as a story-teller did not rank high in their estimation.

---

1. **"On the Road to Mandalay":** a poem written by Rudyard Kipling, an English poet.

In a low, confidential voice, interrupted at frequent intervals by loud, petulant questions from her listeners, she began an unenterprising and deplorably uninteresting story about a little girl who was good, and made friends with every one on account of her goodness, and was finally saved from a mad bull by a number of rescuers who admired her moral character.

"Wouldn't they have saved her if she hadn't been good?" demanded the bigger of the small girls. It was exactly the question that the bachelor had wanted to ask.

"Well, yes," admitted the aunt lamely, "but I don't think they would have run quite so fast to her help if they had not liked her so much."

"It's the stupidest story I've ever heard," said the bigger of the small girls, with immense conviction.

"I didn't listen after the first bit, it was so stupid," said Cyril.

The smaller girl made no actual comment on the story, but she had long ago recommenced a murmured repetition of her favorite line.

"You don't seem to be a success as a storyteller," said the bachelor suddenly from his corner.

The aunt bristled in instant defense at this unexpected attack.

"It's a very difficult thing to tell stories that children can both understand and appreciate," she said stiffly.

"I don't agree with you," said the bachelor.

"Perhaps *you* would like to tell them a story," was the aunt's retort.

"Tell us a story," demanded the bigger of the small girls.

"Once upon a time," began the bachelor, "there was a little girl called Bertha, who was extraordinarily good."

The children's momentarily-aroused interest began at once to flicker; all stories seemed dreadfully alike, no matter who told them.

"She did all that she was told, she was always truthful, she kept her clothes clean, ate milk puddings as though they were jam tarts, learned her lessons perfectly, and was polite in her manners."

"Was she pretty?" asked the bigger of the small girls.

"Not as pretty as any of you," said the bachelor, "but she was horribly good."

There was a wave of reaction in favor of the story. The word *horrible* in connection with goodness was a novelty that commended itself. It seemed to introduce a ring of truth that was absent from the aunt's tales of infant life.

"She was so good," continued the bachelor, "that she won several medals for goodness, which she always wore, pinned on to her dress. There was a medal for obedience, another medal for punctuality, and a third for good behavior. They were large metal medals, and they clicked against one another as she walked. No other child in the town where she lived had as many as three medals, so everybody knew that she must be an extra good child."

"Horribly good," quoted Cyril.

"Everybody talked about her goodness, and the Prince of the country got to hear about it. He said that as she was so very good she might be allowed once a week to walk in his park, which was just outside the town. It was a beautiful park, and no children were ever allowed in it, so it was a great honor for Bertha to be allowed to go there."

"Were there any sheep in the park?" demanded Cyril.

"No," said the bachelor, "there were no sheep."

"Why weren't there any sheep?" came the inevitable question arising out of that answer.

The aunt permitted herself a smile, which might almost have been described as a grin.

"There were no sheep in the park," said the bachelor, "because the Prince's mother had once had a dream that her son would either be killed by a sheep or else by a clock falling on him. For that reason the Prince never kept a sheep in his park or a clock in his palace."

The aunt suppressed a gasp of admiration.

"Was the Prince killed by a sheep or by a clock?" asked Cyril.

"He is still alive, so we can't tell whether the dream will come true," said the bachelor unconcernedly. "Anyway, there were no sheep in the park, but there were lots of little pigs running all over the place."

"What color were they?"

"Black with white faces, white with black spots, black all over, gray with white patches, and some were white all over."

The story-teller paused to let a full idea of the park's treasures sink into the children's imaginations; then he resumed.

"Bertha was rather sorry to find that there were no flowers in the park. She had promised her aunts, with tears in her eyes, that she would not pick any of the kind Prince's flowers, and she had meant to keep her promise, so of course it made her feel silly to find that there were no flowers to pick."

"Why weren't there any flowers?"

"Because the pigs had eaten them all," said the bachelor promptly. "The gardeners had told the Prince that you couldn't have pigs and flowers, so he decided to have pigs and no flowers."

There was a murmur of approval at the excellence of the Prince's decision. So many people would have decided the other way.

"There were lots of other delightful things in the park. There were ponds with gold and blue and green fish in them, and trees with beautiful parrots that said clever things at a moment's notice, and humming birds that hummed all the popular tunes of the day. Bertha walked up and down and enjoyed herself immensely, and thought to herself, 'If I were not so extraordinarily good I should not have been allowed to come into this beautiful park and enjoy all that there is to be seen in it,' and her three medals clinked against one another as she walked and helped to remind her how very good she really was. Just then an enormous wolf came prowling into the park to see if it could catch a fat little pig for its supper."

"What color was it?" asked the children, amid an immediate quickening of interest.

"Mud-color all over, with a black tongue and pale gray eyes that gleamed with unspeakable ferocity. The first thing that it saw in the park was Bertha; her pinafore was so spotlessly white and clean that it could be seen from a great distance. Bertha saw the wolf and saw that it was stealing towards her, and she began to wish that she had never been allowed to come into the park. She ran as hard as she could, and the wolf came after her with huge leaps and bounds. She managed to reach a shrubbery of myrtle bushes, and she hid herself in one of the thickest of the bushes. The wolf came sniffing among the branches, its black tongue lolling out of its mouth and its pale gray eyes glaring with rage. Bertha was terribly frightened, and thought to herself, 'If I had not been so extraordinarily good I should have been safe in the town at this moment.' However, the scent of the myrtle was so strong that the wolf could not sniff out where Bertha was hiding, and the bushes were so thick that he might have hunted about in them for a long time without catching sight of her, so he thought he might as well go off and catch a little pig instead. Bertha was trembling very much at having the wolf prowling and sniffing so near her, and as she trembled the medal for obedience clinked against the medals for good conduct and punctuality. The wolf was just moving away when he heard the sound of the medals clinking and stopped to listen. They clinked again in a bush quite near him. He dashed into the bush, his pale gray eyes gleaming with ferocity and triumph, and dragged Bertha out and devoured her to the last morsel. All that was left of her were her shoes, bits of clothing, and the three medals for goodness."

"Were any of the little pigs killed?"

"No, they all escaped."

"The story began badly," said the smaller of the small girls, "but it had a beautiful ending."

"It is the most beautiful story that I ever heard," said the bigger of the small girls, with immense decision.

"It is the *only* beautiful story I have ever heard," said Cyril.

A dissentient opinion came from the aunt.

"A most improper story to tell to young children! You have undermined the effect of years of careful teaching."

"At any rate," said the bachelor, collecting his belongings preparatory to leaving the carriage, "I kept them quiet for ten minutes, which was more than you were able to do."

"Unhappy woman!" he observed to himself as he walked down the platform of Templecombe station, "for the next six months or so those children will assail her in public with demands for an improper story!"

Getting at Meaning

1. What kinds of questions do the children ask their aunt? How does she feel about these questions? When the children start asking the bachelor the same kind of questions, how does he respond? What do these reactions tell the reader about the difference between the aunt and the bachelor?

2. What is the aunt's reaction to the bachelor's story? What does the bachelor mean when he thinks, "Unhappy woman . . . for the next six months or so those children will assail her in public with demands for an improper story!"

3. Why do the children like the bachelor's story? What makes him such a good storyteller?

Developing Skills in Reading Literature

1. **Irony.** One reason the children enjoy the bachelor's story is that it is full of ironies, or unexpected twists. Why is it ironic that the sound of Bertha's medals leads the wolf to her? What other ironies are present in the bachelor's story?

2. **Satire.** Satire is a form of literature in which foolish ideas or customs are ridiculed

through exaggeration. For example, in "The Ransom of Red Chief," O. Henry uses the speech of Sam and Bill to satirize the way people often try to act "high-class." What aspects of standard children's stories does the bachelor satirize with his story?

3. **Description.** When the children ask the bachelor about the color of the pigs, he answers, "Black with white faces, white with black spots, black all over, gray with white patches, and some were white all over." Find other places where the bachelor uses descriptive phrases to make his story unusual and interesting.

Developing Writing Skills

Rising Action, Climax, and Ending of a Story. Write a children's story of your own, perhaps a modern version of a well known story such as "The Three Pigs." Using some of the bachelor's techniques, attempt to make your story unusual and appealing. The story should have a conflict that builds to a climax and is resolved. You may wish to illustrate your story.

Trurl's Machine   *Stanislaw Lem*

Once upon a time Trurl, the constructor, built an eight-story thinking machine. When it was finished, he gave it a coat of white paint, trimmed the edges in lavender, stepped back, squinted, then added a little curlicue on the front and, where one might imagine the forehead to be, a few pale orange polkadots. Extremely pleased with himself, he whistled an air and, as is always done on such occasions, asked it the ritual question of how much is two plus two.

The machine stirred. Its tubes began to glow, its coils warmed up, current coursed through all its circuits like a waterfall, transformers hummed and throbbed, there was a clanging, and a chugging, and such an ungodly racket that Trurl began to think of adding a special mentation muffler. Meanwhile the machine labored on, as if it had been given the most difficult problem in the Universe to solve. The ground shook, the sand slid underfoot from the vibration, valves popped like champagne corks, the relays nearly gave way under the strain. At last, when Trurl had grown extremely impatient, the machine ground to a halt and said in a voice like thunder, SEVEN!

"Nonsense, my dear," said Trurl. "The answer's four. Now be a good machine and adjust yourself! What's two and two?"

"SEVEN!" snapped the machine. Trurl sighed and put his coveralls back on, rolled up his sleeves, opened the bottom trapdoor and crawled in. For the longest time he hammered away inside, tightened, soldered, ran clattering up and down the metal stairs, now on the sixth floor, now on the eighth, then pounded back down to the bottom and threw a switch; but something sizzled in the middle, and the spark plugs grew blue whiskers. After two hours of this he came out, covered with soot but satisfied, put all his tools away, took off his coveralls, wiped his face and hands. As he was leaving, he turned and asked, just so there would be no doubt about it,

"And now what's two and two?"

"SEVEN!" replied the machine.

Trurl uttered a terrible oath, but there was no help for it—again he had to poke around inside the machine, disconnecting, correcting, checking, resetting; and when he learned for the third time that two and two were seven, he collapsed in despair at the foot of the machine, and sat there until Klapaucius found him. Klapaucius inquired what was wrong, for Trurl looked as if he had just returned from a funeral. Trurl explained the problem. Klapaucius crawled into the machine himself a couple of times, tried to fix this and that, then asked it for the sum of one plus two, which turned out to be six. One plus one, according to the machine, equaled zero. Klapaucius scratched his head, cleared his throat, and said,

"My friend, you'll just have to face it. That isn't the machine you wished to make. However, there's a good side to everything, including this."

"What good side?" muttered Trurl, and kicked the base on which he was sitting.

"Stop that," said the machine.

"H'm, it's sensitive too. But where was I?

Oh yes . . . there's no question but that we have here a stupid machine, and not merely stupid in the usual, normal way, oh no! This is, as far as I can determine—and you know I am something of an expert—this is the stupidest thinking machine in the entire world, and that's nothing to sneeze at! To construct deliberately, such a machine would be far from easy; in fact, I would say that no one could manage it. For the thing is not only stupid, but stubborn as a mule; that is, it has a personality common to idiots, for idiots are uncommonly stubborn."

"What earthly use do I have for such a machine?!" said Trurl, and kicked it again.

"I'm warning you, you better stop!" said the machine.

"A warning, if you please," observed Klapaucius dryly. "Not only is it sensitive, dense, and stubborn, but quick to take offense; and believe me, with such an abundance of qualities, there are all sorts of things you might do!"

"What for example?" asked Trurl.

"Well, it's hard to say offhand. You might put it on exhibit and charge admission. People would flock to see the stupidest thinking machine that ever was—what does it have, eight stories? Really, could anyone imagine a bigger dunce? And the exhibition would not only cover your costs, but—"

"Enough, I'm not holding an exhibition!" Trurl said, stood up and, unable to restrain himself, kicked the machine once more.

"This is your third warning," said the machine.

"What?" cried Trurl, infuriated by its imperious manner. "You . . . you . . ." And he kicked it several times, shouting, "You're only good for kicking, you know that?"

"You have insulted me for the fourth, fifth, sixth, and eighth times," said the machine. "Therefore I refuse to answer all further questions of a mathematical nature."

"It refuses! Do you hear that?" fumed Trurl, thoroughly exasperated. "After six comes eight—did you notice, Klapaucius?—not seven, but eight! And *that's* the kind of mathematics Her Highness refuses to perform! Take that! And that! And that! Or perhaps you'd like some more?"

The machine shuddered, shook, and without another word started to lift itself from its foundations. They were very deep, and the girders began to bend; but at last it scrambled out, leaving behind broken concrete blocks with steel spokes protruding—and it bore down on Trurl and Klapaucius like a moving fortress. Trurl was so dumbfounded that he didn't even try to hide from the machine, which to all appearances intended to crush him to a pulp. But Klapaucius grabbed his arm and yanked him away, and the two of them took to their heels. When finally they looked back, they saw the machine swaying like a high tower, advancing slowly, at every step sinking to its second floor, but stubbornly, doggedly pulling itself out of the sand and heading straight for them.

"Whoever heard of such a thing?" Trurl gasped in amazement. "Why, this is mutiny! What do we do now?"

"Wait and watch," replied the prudent Klapaucius. "We may learn something."

But there was nothing to be learned just then. The machine had reached firmer ground and was picking up speed. Inside, it whistled, hissed, and sputtered.

"Any minute now the signal box will knock loose," said Trurl under his breath. "That'll jam the program and stop it. . . ."

"No," said Klapaucius, "this is a special case. The thing is so stupid, that even if the whole transmission goes, it won't matter. But—look out!!"

The machine was gathering momentum, clearly bent on running them down, so they fled just as fast as they could, the fearful rhythm of crunching steps in their ears. They ran and ran—what else could they do? They tried to make it back to their native district, but the machine outflanked them, cut them off, forced them deeper and deeper into a wild, uninhabited region. Mountains, dismal and craggy, slowly rose out of the mist. Trurl, panting heavily, shouted to Klapaucius,

"Listen! Let's turn into some narrow canyon . . . where it won't be able to follow us . . . the cursed thing . . . what do you say?"

"No . . . better go straight," wheezed Klapaucius. "There's a town up ahead . . . can't remember the name . . . anyway, we can find —oof!—find shelter there . . ."

So they ran straight and soon saw houses before them. The streets were practically deserted at this time of day, and the constructors had gone a good distance without meeting a living soul, when suddenly an awful crash, like an avalanche at the edge of the town, indicated that the machine was coming after them.

Trurl looked back and groaned.

"Good heavens! It's tearing down the houses, Klapaucius!!" For the machine, in stubborn pursuit, was plowing through the walls of the buildings like a mountain of steel; and in its wake lay piles of rubble and white clouds of plaster dust. There were dreadful screams, confusion in the streets, and Trurl and Klapaucius, their hearts in their mouths, ran on till they came to a large town hall, darted inside and raced down endless stairs to a deep cellar.

"It won't get us in here, even if it brings the whole building down on our heads!" panted Klapaucius. "But really, the devil himself had me pay you a visit today. . . . I was curious to see how your work was going—well, I certainly found out. . . ."

"Quiet," interrupted Trurl. "Someone's coming. . . ."

And indeed, the cellar door opened up and the mayor entered, accompanied by several aldermen. Trurl was too embarrassed to explain how this strange and calamitous situation had come about; Klapaucius had to do it. The mayor listened in silence. Suddenly the walls trembled, the ground heaved, and the sound of cracking stone reached them in the cellar.

"It's here?!" cried Trurl.

"Yes," said the mayor. "And it demands that we give you up, otherwise it says it will level the entire town. . . ."

Just then they heard, far overhead, words that honked as if from a muffled horn,

THE DOUBTER, 1937. Yves Tanguy.
Hirshhorn Museum and Sculpture Garden, Smithsonian Institution.

"Trurl's here . . . I smell Trurl . . ."

"But surely you won't give us up?" asked in a quavering voice the object of the machine's obstinate fury.

"The one of you who calls himself Trurl must leave. The other may remain, since surrendering him does not constitute part of the conditions. . . ."

"Have mercy!"

"We are helpless," said the mayor. "And were you to stay here, Trurl, you would have to answer for all the damage done to this town and its inhabitants, since it was because of you that the machine destroyed sixteen homes and buried beneath their ruins many of our finest citizens. Only the fact that you yourself stand in imminent peril permits me to let you leave unpunished. Go then, and nevermore return."

Trurl looked at the aldermen and, seeing his sentence written on their stern faces, slowly turned and made for the door.

"Wait! I'll go with you!" cried Klapaucius impulsively.

"You?" said Trurl, a faint hope in his voice. "But no . . ." he added after a moment. "Why should you have to perish too? . . ."

"Nonsense!" rejoined Klapaucius with great energy. "What, us perish at the hands of that iron imbecile? Never! It takes more than that, my friend, to wipe two of the most famous constructors off the face of the globe! Come, Trurl! Chin up!"

Encouraged by these words, Trurl ran up the stairs after Klapaucius. There was not a soul outside in the square. Amid clouds of dust and the gaunt skeletons of demolished homes, stood the machine, higher than the town hall tower itself, puffing steam, covered with the blood of powdered brick, and smeared with chalk.

"Careful!" whispered Klapaucius. "It doesn't see us. Let's take that first street on the left, then turn right, then straight for those mountains. There we can take refuge and think of how to make the thing give up once and for all its insane . . . *Now!*" he yelled, for the machine had just spotted them and was charging, making the pavement buckle.

Breathless, they ran from the town and galloped along for a mile or so, hearing behind them the thunderous stride of the colossus that followed relentlessly.

"I know that ravine!" Klapaucius suddenly cried. "That's the bed of a dried-out stream and it leads to cliffs and caves—faster, faster, the thing'll have to stop soon! . . ."

So they raced uphill, stumbling and waving their arms to keep their balance, but the machine still gained on them. Scrambling up over the gravel of the dried-out riverbed, they reached a crevice in the perpendicular rock and, seeing high above them the murky mouth of a cave, began to climb frantically toward it, no longer caring about the loose stones that flew from under their feet. The opening in the rock breathed chill and darkness. As quickly as they could, they leaped inside, ran a few extra steps, then stopped.

"Well, here at least we're safe," said Trurl, calm once again. "I'll just take a look, to see where it got stuck. . . ."

"Be careful," cautioned Klapaucius. Trurl inched his way to the edge of the cave, leaned out, and immediately jumped back in fright.

"It's coming up the mountain!!" he cried.

"Don't worry, it'll never be able to get in here," said Klapaucius, not altogether convinced. "But what's that? Is it getting dark? Oh no!"

At that moment a great shadow blotted out the bit of sky visible through the mouth of the cave, and in its place appeared a smooth steel wall with rows of rivets. It was the machine slowly closing with the rock, thereby sealing up the cave as if with a mighty metal lid.

"We're trapped . . ." whispered Trurl, his voice breaking off when the darkness became absolute.

"That was idiotic on our part!" Klapaucius exclaimed, furious. "To jump into a cave that it could barricade! How could we have done such a thing?"

"What do you think it's waiting for now?" asked Trurl after a long pause.

"For us to give up—that doesn't take any great brains."

Again there was silence. Trurl tiptoed in the darkness, hands outstretched, in the direction of the opening, running his fingers along the stone until he touched the smooth steel, which was warm, as if heated from within. . . .

"I feel Trurl . . ." boomed the iron voice. Trurl hastily retreated, took a seat alongside his friend, and for some time they sat there, motionless. At last Klapaucius whispered,

"There's no sense our just sitting here. I'll try to reason with it. . . ."

"That's hopeless," said Trurl. "But go ahead. Perhaps it will at least let you go free. . . ."

"Now, now, none of that!" said Klapaucius, patting him on the back. And he groped his way toward the mouth of the cave and called, "Hello out there, can you hear us?"

"Yes," said the machine.

"Listen, we'd like to apologize. You see . . . well, there was a little misunderstanding, true, but it was nothing, really. Trurl had no intention of . . ."

"I'll pulverize Trurl!" said the machine. "But first, he'll tell me how much two and two makes."

"Of course he will, of course he will, and you'll be happy with his answer, and make it up with him for sure, isn't that right, Trurl?" said the mediator soothingly.

"Yes, of course . . ." mumbled Trurl.

"Really?" said the machine. "Then how much is two and two?"

"Fo . . . that is, seven . . ." said Trurl in an even lower voice.

"Ha! Not four, but seven, eh?" crowed the machine. "There, I told you so!"

"Seven, yes, seven, we always knew it was seven!" Klapaucius eagerly agreed. "Now will you, uh, let us go?" he added cautiously.

"No. Let Trurl say how sorry he is and tell me how much is two times two. . . ."

"And you'll let us go, if I do?" asked Trurl.

"I don't know. I'll think about it. I'm not making any deals. What's two times two?"

"But you probably will let us go, won't you?" said Trurl, while Klapaucius pulled on his arm and hissed in his ear, "The thing's an imbecile; don't argue with it, for heaven's sake!"

"I won't let you go, if I don't want to," said the machine. "You just tell me how much two times two is. . . ."

Suddenly Trurl fell into a rage.

"I'll tell you, I'll tell you all right!" he screamed. "Two and two is four and two times two is four, even if you stand on your head, pound these mountains all to dust, drink the ocean dry and swallow the sky— do you hear? Two and two is four!!"

"Trurl! What are you saying? Have you taken leave of your senses? Two and two is seven, nice machine! Seven, seven!!" howled Klapaucius, trying to drown out his friend.

"No! It's four! Four and only four, four from the beginning to the end of time— FOUR!!" bellowed Trurl, growing hoarse.

The rock beneath their feet was seized with a feverish tremor.

The machine moved away from the cave, letting in a little pale light, and gave a piercing scream,

"That's not true! It's seven! Say it's seven or I'll hit you!"

"Never!" roared Trurl, as if he no longer cared what happened; and pebbles and dirt rained down on their heads, for the machine had begun to ram its eight-story hulk again and again into the wall of stone, hurling itself against the mountainside until huge boulders broke away and went tumbling down into the valley.

Thunder and sulfurous fumes filled the cave, and sparks flew from the blows of steel on rock, yet through all this pandemonium one could still make out, now and then, the ragged voice of Trurl bawling,

"Two and two is four! Two and two is four!!"

Klapaucius attempted to shut his friend's mouth by force, but, violently thrown off, he gave up, sat, and covered his head with his arms. Not for a moment did the machine's mad efforts flag, and it seemed that any minute now the ceiling would collapse, crush the prisoners and bury them forever. But when they had lost all hope, and the air was thick with acrid smoke and choking dust, there was suddenly a horrible scraping, and a sound like a slow explosion, louder than all the maniacal banging and battering, and the air whooshed, and the black wall that blocked the cave was whisked away, as if by a hurricane, and monstrous chunks of rock came crushing down after it. The echoes of that avalanche still rumbled and reverberated in the valley below when the two friends peered out of their cave. They saw the machine. It lay smashed and flattened, nearly broken in half by an enormous boulder that had landed in the middle of its eight floors. With the greatest care they picked their way down through the smoking rubble. In order to reach the riverbed, it was necessary to pass the remains of the machine, which resembled the wreck of some mighty vessel thrown up upon a beach. Without a word, the two stopped together in the shadow of its twisted hull. The machine still quivered slightly, and one could hear something turning, creaking feebly, within.

"Yes, this is the bad end you've come to, and two and two is—as it always was—" began Trurl, but just then the machine made a faint, barely audible croaking noise and said, for the last time, "SEVEN."

Then something snapped inside, a few stones dribbled down from overhead, and now before them lay nothing but a lifeless mass of scrap. The two constructors exchanged a look, and silently, without any further comment or conversation, walked back the way they had come.

Getting at Meaning

1. Describe the machine's physical appearance. What kind of personality does it have? What is the machine's attitude toward Trurl? Why is it important to the story that the machine have human qualities?

2. Where do Trurl and Klapaucius hide first? Why do they leave? Where do they go next? How do they finally get away from the machine?

3. How is Trurl's reaction to their uncomfortable situation different from Klapaucius's reaction? What does this say about each man?

4. What are the machine's dying words? What human quality is indicated by these words?

Developing Skills in Reading Literature

1. **Plot.** The climax of a plot is the moment of highest intensity at which something happens to bring on a resolution of the conflict. What is the conflict in this story? What is the climax? How is the conflict resolved?

2. **Science Fiction.** Science fiction is writing based on real or imagined scientific developments, often with a fantastical view of the future. What makes this story an example of science fiction?

3. **Theme.** What might the writer of this story be saying about machines with "intelligence," such as computers and robots? Is there a warning in his humor? Explain.

Developing Vocabulary

Inferring Word Meaning. Read the following sentences and try to guess the meaning of each italicized word. Then look up each word in the Glossary and write the correct definition of the word. Use the word in a sentence of your own that demonstrates its meaning.

1. Trurl uttered a terrible *oath*, but there was no help for it—again he had to poke around inside the machine. . . .

2. "This is your third warning," said the machine. "What?" cried Trurl, infuriated by its *imperious* manner.

3. Trurl was too embarrassed to explain how this strange and *calamitous* situation had come about; Klapaucius had to do it.

4. Breathless, they ran from the town and galloped along for a mile or so, hearing behind them the thunderous stride of the *colossus* that followed relentlessly.

5. "Of course he will, of course he will, and you'll be happy with his answer, and make it up with him for sure, isn't that right, Trurl?" said the *mediator* soothingly.

6. Thunder and sulfurous fumes filled the cave, and sparks flew from the blows of steel on rock, yet through all this *pandemonium* one could still make out . . . the ragged voice of Trurl bawling. . . .

Developing Writing Skills

1. **Writing About a Personal Experience.** Write a paragraph that describes an encounter you have had with a machine, such as a car, a bicycle, a vending machine, or a subway turnstyle. As an alternative, you might write a paragraph that describes how some machine, such as a stereo, a bicycle, or a camera, is important to you. Be specific in your description.

2. **Selecting Specific Details.** Imagine that you are a constructor in the time of Trurl. What kind of machine would you invent? Describe specifically the machine and how it would work. Before you begin to write, you might wish to reread the first two paragraphs in the story.

Lather and Nothing Else   *Hernando Tellez*

He came in without a word. I was stropping my best razor. And when I recognized him, I started to shake. But he did not notice. To cover my nervousness, I went on honing the razor. I tried the edge with the tip of my thumb and took another look at it against the light.

Meanwhile, he was taking off his cartridge-studded belt with the pistol holster suspended from it. He put it on a hook in the wardrobe and hung his cap above it. Then he turned full around toward me and, loosening his tie, remarked, "It's hot as the devil. I want a shave." With that he took his seat.

I estimated he had a four-days' growth of beard, the four days he had been gone on the last foray after our men. His face looked burnt, tanned by the sun.

I started to work carefully on the shaving soap. I scraped some slices from the cake, dropped them into the mug, then added a little lukewarm water, and stirred with the brush. The lather soon began to rise.

"The fellows in the troop must have just about as much beard as I." I went on stirring up lather.

"But we did very well, you know. We caught the leaders. Some of them we brought back dead; others are still alive. But they'll all be dead soon."

"How many did you take?" I asked.

"Fourteen. We had to go pretty far in to find them. But now they're paying for it. And not one will escape; not a single one."

He leaned back in the chair when he saw the brush in my hand, full of lather. I had not yet put the sheet on him. I was certainly flustered. Taking a sheet from the drawer, I tied it around my customer's neck.

He went on talking. He evidently took it for granted that I was on the side of the existing regime.

"The people must have gotten a scare with what happened the other day," he said.

"Yes," I replied, as I finished tying the knot against his nape, which smelt of sweat.

"Good show, wasn't it?"

"Very good," I answered, turning my attention now to the brush. The man closed his eyes wearily and awaited the cool caress of the lather.

I had never had him so close before. The day he ordered the people to file through the schoolyard to look upon the four rebels hanging there, my path had crossed his briefly. But the sight of those mutilated bodies kept me from paying attention to the face of the man who had been directing it all and whom I now had in my hands.

It was not a disagreeable face, certainly. And the beard, which aged him a bit, was not unbecoming. His name was Torres. Captain Torres.

I started to lay on the first coat of lather. He kept his eyes closed.

"I would love to catch a nap," he said, "but there's a lot to be done this evening."

I lifted the brush and asked, with pretended indifference: "A firing party?"

"Something of the sort," he replied, "but slower."

"All of them?"

"No, just a few."

I went on lathering his face. My hands began to tremble again. The man could not be aware of this, which was lucky for me. But I wished he had not come in. Probably many of our men had seen him enter the shop. And with the enemy in my house I felt a certain responsibility.

I would have to shave his beard just like any other, carefully, neatly, just as though he were a good customer, taking heed that not a single pore should emit a drop of blood. Seeing to it that the blade did not slip in the small whorls. Taking care that the skin was left clean, soft, shining, so that when I passed the back of my hand over it not a single hair should be felt. Yes. I was secretly a revolutionary, but at the same time I was a conscientious barber, proud of the way I did my job. And that four-day beard presented a challenge.

I took up the razor, opened the handle wide, releasing the blade, and started to work, downward from one sideburn. The blade responded to perfection. The hair was tough and hard; not very long, but thick. Little by little the skin began to show through. The razor gave out its usual sound as it gathered up layers of soap mixed with bits of hair. I paused to wipe it clean, and taking up the strop once more went about improving its edge, for I am a painstaking barber.

The man, who had kept his eyes closed, now opened them, put a hand out from under the sheet, felt of the part of his face that was emerging from the lather, and said to me, "Come at six o'clock this evening to the school."

"Will it be like the other day?" I asked, stiff with horror.

"It may be even better," he replied.

"What are you planning to do?"

"I'm not sure yet. But we'll have a good time."

Once more he leaned back and shut his eyes. I came closer, the razor on high.

"Are you going to punish all of them?" I timidly ventured.

"Yes, all of them."

The lather was drying on his face. I must hurry. Through the mirror, I took a look at the street. It appeared about as usual; there was the grocery shop with two or three customers. Then I glanced at the clock, two-thirty.

The razor kept descending. Now from the other sideburn downward. It was a blue beard, a thick one. He should let it grow like some poets, or some priests. It would suit him well. Many people would not recognize him. And that would be a good thing for him, I thought, as I went gently over all the throat line. At this point you really had to handle your blade skillfully, because the hair, while scantier, tended to fall into small whorls. It was a curly beard. The pores might open, minutely, in this area and let out a tiny drop of blood. A good barber like myself stakes his reputation on not permitting that to happen to any of his customers.

And this was indeed a special customer. How many of ours had he sent to their death? How many had he mutilated? It was best not to think about it. Torres did not know I was his enemy. Neither he nor the others knew it. It was a secret shared by very few, just because that made it possible for me to inform the revolutionaries about Torres's activities in the town and what he planned to do every time he went on one of his raids to hunt down rebels. So it was going to be very difficult to explain how it was that I had him in my hands and then let him go in peace, alive, clean-shaven.

His beard had now almost entirely disappeared. He looked younger, several years younger than when he had come in. I suppose that always happens to men who enter and leave barbershops. Under the strokes of my razor, Torres was rejuvenated; yes, because I am a good barber, the best in this town, and I say this in all modesty.

A little more lather here under the chin, on the Adam's apple, right near the great vein. How hot it is! Torres must be sweating just as I am. But he is not afraid. He is a tranquil man, who is not even giving thought to what he will do to his prisoners this evening. I, on the other hand, polishing his skin with this razor but avoiding the drawing of blood, careful with every stroke—I cannot keep my thoughts in order.

Confound the hour he entered my shop! I am a revolutionary but not a murderer. And it would be so easy to kill him. He deserves it. Or does he? No! No one deserves the sacrifice others make in becoming assassins. What is to be gained by it? Nothing. Others and still others keep coming, and the first kill the second, and then these kill the next, and so on until everything becomes a sea of blood. I could cut his throat, so, swish, swish! He would not even have time to moan, and with his eyes shut he would not even see the shine of the razor or the gleam in my eye.

But I'm shaking like a regular murderer. From his throat a stream of blood would flow on the sheet, over the chair, down on my hands, onto the floor. I would have to close the door. But the blood would go flowing, along the floor, warm, indelible, not to be stanched, until it reached the street like a small scarlet river.

I'm sure that with a good strong blow, a deep cut, he would feel no pain. He would not suffer at all. And what would I do then with the body? Where would I hide it? I would have to flee, leave all this behind, take shelter far away, very far away. But they would follow until they caught up with me. "The murderer of Captain Torres. He slit his throat while he was shaving him. What a cowardly thing to do."

And others would say, "The avenger of our people. A name to remember"—my name here. "He was the town barber. No one knew he was fighting for our cause."

And so, which will it be? Murderer or hero? My fate hangs on the edge of this razor blade. I can turn my wrist slightly, put a bit more pressure on the blade, let it sink in. The skin will yield like silk, like rubber, like the strop. There is nothing more tender than a man's skin, and the blood is always there, ready to burst forth. A razor like this cannot fail. It is the best one I have.

But I don't want to be a murderer. No, sir. You came in to be shaved. And I do my work honorably. I don't want to stain my hands with blood. Just with lather, and nothing else. You are an executioner; I am only a barber. Each one to his job. That's it. Each one to his job.

The chin was now clean, polished, soft. The man got up and looked at himself in the glass. He ran his hand over the skin and felt its freshness, its newness.

"Thanks," he said. He walked to the wardrobe for his belt, his pistol, and his cap. I must have been very pale, and I felt my shirt soaked with sweat. Torres finished adjusting his belt buckle, straightened his gun in its holster, and, smoothing his hair mechanically, put on his cap. From his trousers pocket he took some coins to pay for the shave. And he started toward the door. On the threshold he stopped for a moment, and turning toward me he said,

"They told me you would kill me. I came to find out if it was true. But it's not easy to kill. I know what I'm talking about."

Getting at Meaning

1. What kind of man is the barber? What are his political views? What is his attitude toward his work?

2. What kind of man is Torres? What does Torres talk about as the barber is shaving him? if he knows that the barber is his enemy, why does he talk about these things? What does the Captain's final remark to the barber reveal about him?

Developing Skills in Reading Literature

1. **Conflict.** Although Torres and the barber are on opposite political sides, the conflict is not between them. The main conflict in the story takes place in the barber's mind. What two ideas are in conflict? As the story develops, what changes in the physical appearance of the barber show that the conflict is becoming more intense?

2. **Flashback.** What flashback is included in this story? What is its function in the story?

3. **Theme.** Torres and the barber are enemies. Why then does Torres put himself into the barber's hands? What is the writer's message about fighting and warfare?

Theme

HOLY MOUNTAIN III, 1945. *Horace Pippin.*
Hirshhorn Museum and Sculpture Garden, Smithsonian Institution.

The Sniper   *Liam O'Flaherty*

The long June twilight faded into night. Dublin[1] lay enveloped in darkness but for the dim light of the moon that shone through fleecy clouds, casting a pale light as of approaching dawn over the streets and the dark waters of the Liffey. Around the beleaguered Four Courts the heavy guns roared. Here and there through the city, machine-guns and rifles broke the silence of the night, spasmodically, like dogs barking on lone farms. Republicans and Free Staters[2] were waging civil war.

On a roof-top near O'Connell Bridge, a Republican sniper lay watching. Beside him lay his rifle and over his shoulders were slung a pair of field glasses. His face was the face of a student, thin and ascetic, but his eyes had the cold gleam of the fanatic. They were deep and thoughtful, the eyes of a man who is used to looking at death.

He was eating a sandwich hungrily. He had eaten nothing since morning. He had been too excited to eat. He finished the sandwich, and, taking a flask from his pocket, he took a short draught. Then he returned the flask to his pocket. He paused for a moment, considering whether he should risk a smoke. It was dangerous. The flash might be seen in the darkness and there were enemies watching. He decided to take the risk.

Placing a cigarette between his lips, he struck a match. There was a flash and a bullet whizzed over his head. He dropped immediately. He had seen the flash. It came from the opposite side of the street.

He rolled over the roof to a chimney stack in the rear, and slowly drew himself up behind it, until his eyes were level with the top of the parapet. There was nothing to be seen —just the dim outline of the opposite house-top against the blue sky. His enemy was under cover.

Just then an armored car came across the bridge and advanced slowly up the street. It stopped on the opposite side of the street, fifty yards ahead. The sniper could hear the dull panting of the motor. His heart beat faster. It was an enemy car. He wanted to fire, but he knew it was useless. His bullets would never pierce the steel that covered the gray monster.

Then round the corner of a side street came an old woman, her head covered by a tattered shawl. She began to talk to the man in the turret of the car. She was pointing to the roof where the sniper lay. An informer.

The turret opened. A man's head and shoulders appeared, looking toward the sniper. The sniper raised his rifle and fired. The head fell heavily on the turret wall. The woman darted toward the side street. The sniper fired again. The woman whirled round and fell with a shriek into the gutter.

Suddenly from the opposite roof a shot rang out and the sniper dropped his rifle with a curse. The rifle clattered to the roof. The sniper thought the noise would wake the dead. He stopped to pick the rifle up. He couldn't lift it. His forearm was dead.

---

1. **Dublin:** a seaport city in eastern Ireland at the mouth of the Liffey River.
2. **Republicans and Free Staters:** The Free Staters favored an agreement that Ireland be self-governing with Dominion status in the British Commonwealth; the Republicans opposed the agreement.

"Blast!" he muttered, "I'm hit."

Dropping flat onto the roof, he crawled back to the parapet. With his left hand he felt the injured right forearm. There was no pain —just a deadened sensation, as if the arm had been cut off.

Quickly he drew his knife from his pocket, opened it on the breastwork of the parapet, and ripped open the sleeve. There was a small hole where the bullet had entered. On the other side there was no hole. The bullet had lodged in the bone. It must have fractured it. He bent the arm below the wound. The arm bent back easily. He ground his teeth to overcome the pain.

Then, taking out a field dressing, he ripped open the packet with his knife. He broke the neck of the iodine bottle and let the bitter fluid drip into the wound. A paroxysm of pain swept through him. He placed the cotton wadding over the wound and wrapped the dressing over it. He tied the ends with his teeth.

Then he lay against the parapet, and, closing his eyes, he made an effort of will to overcome the pain.

In the street beneath all was still. The armored car had retired speedily over the bridge, with the machine-gunner's head hanging lifelessly over the turret. The woman's corpse lay still in the gutter.

The sniper lay still for a long time nursing his wounded arm and planning escape. Morning must not find him wounded on the roof. The enemy on the opposite roof covered his escape. He must kill that enemy and he could not use his rifle. He had only a revolver to do it. Then he thought of a plan.

Taking off his cap, he placed it over the muzzle of his rifle. Then he pushed the rifle

slowly over the parapet, until the cap was visible from the opposite side of the street. Almost immediately there was a report, and a bullet pierced the center of the cap. The sniper slanted the rifle forward. The cap slipped down into the street. Then, catching the rifle in the middle, the sniper dropped his left hand over the roof and let it hang, life-lessly. After a few moments he let the rifle drop to the street. Then he sank to the roof, dragging his hand with him.

Crawling quickly to the left, he peered up at the corner of the roof. His ruse had suc-ceeded. The other sniper, seeing the cap and rifle fall, thought he had killed his man. He was now standing before a row of chimney pots, looking across, with his head clearly sil-houetted against the western sky.

The Republican sniper smiled and lifted his revolver above the edge of the parapet. The distance was about fifty yards—a hard shot in the dim light, and his right arm was paining him like a thousand devils. He took a steady aim. His hand trembled with eager-ness. Pressing his lips together, he took a deep breath through his nostrils and fired. He was almost deafened with the report and his arm shook with the recoil.

Then when the smoke cleared, he peered across and uttered a cry of joy. His enemy had been hit. He was reeling over the parapet in his death agony. He struggled to keep his feet, but he was slowly falling forward, as if in a dream. The rifle fell from his grasp, hit the parapet, fell over, bounded off the pole of a barber's shop beneath, and then clattered on the pavement.

Then the dying man on the roof crumpled up and fell forward. The body turned over and over in space and hit the ground with a dull thud. Then it lay still.

The sniper looked at his enemy falling, and he shuddered. The lust of battle died in him. He became bitten by remorse. The sweat stood out in beads on his forehead. Weakened by his wound and the long summer day of fasting and watching on the roof, he revolted from the sight of the shattered mass of his dead enemy. His teeth chattered, he began to gibber to himself, cursing the war, cursing himself, cursing everybody.

He looked at the smoking revolver in his hand, and with an oath he hurled it to the roof at his feet. The revolver went off with the concussion and the bullet whizzed past the sniper's head. He was frightened back to his senses by the shock. His nerves steadied. The cloud of fear scattered from his mind, and he laughed.

Taking the flask from his pocket, he emptied it at a draught. He felt reckless under the influence of the spirit. He decided to leave the roof now and look for his company com-mander, to report. Everywhere around was quiet. There was not much danger in going through the streets. He picked up his revolver and put it in his pocket. Then he crawled down through the skylight to the house underneath.

When the sniper reached the laneway on the street level, he felt a sudden curiosity as to the identity of the enemy sniper whom he had killed. He decided that he was a good shot, whoever he was. He wondered did he know him. Perhaps he had been in his own company before the split in the army. He decided to risk going over to have a look at him. He peered around the corner into O'Connell Street. In the upper part of the street there was heavy firing, but around here all was quiet.

The sniper darted across the street. A ma-chine-gun tore up the ground around him with a hail of bullets, but he escaped. He threw himself face downward beside the corpse. The machine-gun stopped.

Then the sniper turned over the dead body and looked into his brother's face.

Getting at Meaning

1. What does the reader learn about the sniper in the first three paragraphs?

2. Why does the sniper feel no hesitation about killing the man in the tank or the woman informer?

3. What are some of the physical hardships the sniper faces? How does he deal with these hardships?

4. Reread the passage in which the sniper kills his enemy with the revolver. What is his first reaction when the smoke clears? When he sees the dying soldier fall, how does his reaction change? Why does the sniper begin to curse?

5. What drives the sniper to discover the identity of the enemy?

Developing Skills in Reading Literature

1. **Theme.** Because the theme is not directly stated in a story, the reader must think carefully about the idea the writer wishes to communicate. When trying to determine theme, it is important to consider all the elements of the story. For example, writers often present their ideas through characters, especially through those whose views change drastically.

Think about the change in the sniper's attitude. Find passages that show how he feels about the enemy and the war at the beginning of the story. At what point does his attitude change? Why? How does he feel at the end of the story? What is your reaction to his final realization? What is the writer saying about this war? about all war? Can you think of more than one interpretation of "brother's face" in the last line?

2. **Setting.** This story is set in Northern Ireland, a country still racked by civil war. The setting, however, is not especially important. Why not?

Developing Writing Skills

Explaining an Idea. Write a paragraph that begins with the topic sentence, "In war, no side really wins." Support this statement with examples and ideas from literature, from history, from the experience of family members and friends, or from a combination of these sources. You may wish to interview older people who have lived through wars before you begin to write.

Sixpence   *Katherine Mansfield*

Children are unaccountable little creatures. Why should a small boy like Dicky, good as gold as a rule, sensitive, affectionate, obedient, and marvellously sensible for his age, have moods when, without the slightest warning, he suddenly went "mad dog," as his sisters called it, and there was no doing anything with him?

"Dicky, come here! Come here, sir, at once! Do you hear your mother calling you? Dicky!"

But Dicky wouldn't come. Oh, he heard right enough. A clear, ringing little laugh was his only reply. And away he flew; hiding, running through the uncut hay on the lawn, dashing past the woodshed, making a rush for the kitchen garden, and there dodging, peering at his mother from behind the mossy apple trunks, and leaping up and down like a wild Indian.

It had begun at tea-time. While Dicky's mother and Mrs. Spears, who was spending the afternoon with her, were quietly sitting over their sewing in the drawing-room, this, according to the servant girl, was what had happened at the children's tea. They were eating their first bread and butter as nicely and quietly as you please, and the servant girl had just poured out the milk and water, when Dicky had suddenly seized the bread plate, put it upside down on his head, and clutched the bread knife.

"Look at me!" he shouted.

His startled sisters looked, and before the servant girl could get there, the bread plate wobbled, slid, flew to the floor, and broke into slivers. At this awful point, the little girls lifted up their voices and shrieked their loudest.

"Mother, come and look what he's done!"

"Dicky's broke a great big plate!"

"Come and stop him, mother!"

You can imagine how mother came flying. But she was too late. Dicky had leapt out of his chair, run through the French windows on to the verandah, and, well—there she stood—popping her thimble on and off, helpless. What could she do? She couldn't chase after the child. She couldn't stalk Dicky among the apples and damsons. That would be too undignified. It was more than annoying, it was exasperating. Especially as Mrs. Spears, Mrs. Spears of all people, whose two boys were so exemplary, was waiting for her in the drawing-room.

"Very well, Dicky," she cried, "I shall have to think of some way of punishing you."

"I don't care," sounded the high little voice, and again there came that ringing laugh. The child was quite beside himself. . . .

"Oh, Mrs. Spears, I don't know how to apologize for leaving you by yourself like this."

"It's quite all right, Mrs. Bendall," said Mrs. Spears, in her soft, sugary voice, and raising her eyebrows in the way she had. She seemed to smile to herself as she stroked the gathers. "These little things will happen from time to time. I only hope it was nothing serious."

"It was Dicky," said Mrs. Bendall, looking rather helplessly for her only fine needle. And she explained the whole affair to Mrs. Spears.

"And the worst of it is, I don't know how to cure him. Nothing, when he's in that mood, seems to have the slightest effect on him."

Mrs. Spears opened her pale eyes. "Not even a whipping?" said she.

But Mrs. Bendall, threading her needle, pursed up her lips. "We never have whipped the children," she said. "The girls never seem to have needed it. And Dicky is such a baby, and the only boy. Somehow . . ."

"Oh, my dear," said Mrs. Spears, and she laid her sewing down. "I don't wonder Dicky has these little outbreaks. You don't mind my saying so? But I'm sure you make a great mistake in trying to bring up children without whipping them. Nothing really takes its place. And I speak from experience, my dear. I used to try gentler measures"—Mrs. Spears drew in her breath with a little hissing sound —"soaping the boys' tongues, for instance, with yellow soap, or making them stand on the table for the whole of Saturday afternoon. But no, believe me," said Mrs. Spears, "there is nothing, there is nothing like handing them over to their father."

Mrs. Bendall in her heart of hearts was dreadfully shocked to hear of that yellow soap. But Mrs. Spears seemed to take it so much for granted, that she did too.

"Their father," she said. "Then you don't whip them yourself?"

"Never." Mrs. Spears seemed quite shocked at the idea. "I don't think it's the mother's place to whip the children. It's the duty of the father. And, besides, he impresses them so much more."

"Yes, I can imagine that," said Mrs. Bendall, faintly.

"Now my two boys," Mrs. Spears smiled kindly, encouragingly, at Mrs. Bendall, "would behave just like Dicky if they were not afraid to. As it is . . ."

"Oh, your boys are perfect little models," cried Mrs. Bendall.

They were. Quieter, better-behaved little boys, in the presence of grown-ups, could not be found. In fact, Mrs. Spears's callers often made the remark that you never would have known that there was a child in the house. There wasn't—very often.

In the front hall, under a large picture of fat, cheery old monks fishing by the riverside, there was a thick, dark horsewhip that had belonged to Mr. Spears's father. And for some reason the boys preferred to play out of sight of this, behind the dog-kennel or in the tool-house, or round about the dustbin.[1]

"It's such a mistake," sighed Mrs. Spears, breathing softly, as she folded her work, "to be weak with children when they are little. It's such a sad mistake, and one so easy to make. It's so unfair to the child. That is what one has to remember. Now Dicky's little escapade this afternoon seemed to me as

---

1. **dustbin:** British term for a container for rubbish.

though he'd done it on purpose. It was the child's way of showing you that he needed a whipping."

"Do you really think so?" Mrs. Bendall was a weak little thing, and this impressed her very much.

"I do; I feel sure of it. And a sharp reminder now and then," cried Mrs. Spears in quite a professional manner, "administered by the father, will save you so much trouble in the future. Believe me, my dear." She put her dry, cold hand over Mrs. Bendall's.

"I shall speak to Edward the moment he comes in," said Dicky's mother firmly.

The children had gone to bed before the garden gate banged, and Dicky's father staggered up the steep concrete steps carrying his bicycle. It had been a bad day at the office. He was hot, dusty, tired out.

But by this time Mrs. Bendall had become quite excited over the new plan, and she opened the door to him herself.

"Oh, Edward, I'm so thankful you have come home," she cried.

"Why, what's happened?" Edward lowered the bicycle and took off his hat. A red angry pucker showed where the brim had pressed. "What's up?"

"Come—come into the drawing-room," said Mrs. Bendall, speaking very fast. "I simply can't tell you how naughty Dicky has been. You have no idea—you can't have at the office all day—how a child of that age can behave. He's been simply dreadful. I have no control over him—none. I've tried everything, Edward, but it's all no use. The only thing to do," she finished breathlessly, "is to whip him—is for you to whip him, Edward."

In the corner of the drawing-room there was a what-not, and on the top shelf stood a brown china bear with a painted tongue. It seemed in the shadow to be grinning at Dicky's father, to be saying, "Hooray, this is what you've come home to!"

"But why on earth should I start whipping him?" said Edward, staring at the bear. "We've never done it before."

"Because," said his wife, "don't you see, it's the only thing to do. I can't control the child. . . ." Her words flew from her lips. They beat round him, beat round his tired head. "We can't possibly afford a nurse. The servant girl has more than enough to do. And his naughtiness is beyond words. You don't understand, Edward; you can't, you're at the office all day."

The bear poked out his tongue. The scolding voice went on. Edward sank into a chair.

"What am I to beat him with?" he said weakly.

"Your slipper, of course," said his wife. And she knelt down to untie his dusty shoes.

"Oh, Edward," she wailed, "you've still got your cycling clips on in the drawing-room. No, really—"

"Here, that's enough." Edward nearly pushed her away. "Give me that slipper." He went up the stairs. He felt like a man in a dark net. And now he wanted to beat Dicky. Yes, he wanted to beat something. My God, what a life! The dust was still in his hot eyes; his arms felt heavy.

He pushed open the door of Dicky's slip of a room. Dicky was standing in the middle of the floor in his nightshirt. At the sight of him Edward's heart gave a warm throb of rage.

"Well, Dicky, you know what I've come for," said Edward.

Dicky made no reply.

"I've come to give you a whipping."

No answer.

"Lift up your nightshirt."

At that Dicky looked up. He flushed a deep pink. "Must I?" he whispered.

"Come on, now. Be quick about it," said Edward, and, grasping the slipper, he gave Dicky three hard slaps.

"There, that'll teach you to behave properly to your mother."

Dicky stood there, hanging his head.

"Look sharp and get into bed," said his father.

Still he did not move. But a shaking voice said, "I've not done my teeth yet, Daddy."

"Eh, what's that?"

Dicky looked up. His lips were quivering, but his eyes were dry. He hadn't made a sound or shed a tear. Only he swallowed and said, huskily, "I haven't done my teeth, Daddy."

But at the sight of that little face Edward turned, and, not knowing what he was doing, he bolted from the room, down the stairs, and out into the garden. Good God! What had he done? He strode along and hid in the shadow of the pear tree by the hedge. Whipped Dicky—whipped his little man with a slipper—and what the devil for? He didn't even know. Suddenly he barged into his room—and there was the little chap in his nightshirt. Dicky's father groaned and held on to the hedge. And he didn't cry. Never a tear. If only he'd cried or got angry. But that "Daddy"! And again he heard the quivering whisper. Forgiving like that without a word. But he'd never forgive himself—never. Coward! Fool! Brute! And suddenly he remembered the time when Dicky had fallen off his knee and sprained his wrist while they were playing together. He hadn't cried then, either. And that was the little hero he had just whipped.

Something's got to be done about this, thought Edward. He strode back to the house, up the stairs, into Dicky's room. The little boy was lying in bed. In the half light his dark head, with the square fringe, showed plain against the pale yellow. He was lying quite still, and even now he wasn't crying. Edward shut the door and leaned against it.

What he wanted to do was to kneel down by Dicky's bed and cry himself and beg to be forgiven. But, of course, one can't do that sort of thing. He felt awkward, and his heart was wrung.

"Not asleep yet, Dicky?" he said lightly.

"No, Daddy."

Edward came over and sat on his boy's bed, and Dicky looked at him through his long lashes.

"Nothing the matter, little chap, is there?" said Edward, half whispering.

"No-o, Daddy," came from Dicky.

Edward put out his hand, and carefully he took Dicky's hot little paw.

"You—you mustn't think any more of what happened just now, little man," he said huskily. "See? That's all over now. That's forgotten. That's never going to happen again. See?"

"Yes, Daddy."

"So the thing to do now is to buck up, little chap," said Edward, "and to smile." And he tried himself an extraordinary trembling apology for a smile. "To forget all about it—to—eh? Little man . . . Old boy . . ."

Dicky lay as before. This was terrible. Dicky's father sprang up and went over to the window. It was nearly dark in the garden. The servant girl had run out, and she was snatching, twitching some white clothes off the bushes and piling them over her arm. But in the boundless sky the evening star shone, and a big gum tree, black against the pale glow, moved its long leaves softly. All this he saw, while he felt in his trousers pocket for his money. Bringing it out, he chose a new sixpence and went back to Dicky.

"Here you are, little chap. Buy yourself something," said Edward softly, laying the sixpence on Dicky's pillow.

But could even that—could even a whole sixpence—blot out what had been?

Getting at Meaning

1. The first paragraph describes Dicky. What qualities does he possess? What kind of behavior does Dicky exhibit when he goes "mad dog"?

2. How is Dicky different from the Spears boys? How are the Spears different as parents from the Bendalls? Why does the narrator say of the Spears, ". . . you never would have known that there was a child in the house. There wasn't—very often"?

3. How does the presence of Mrs. Spears affect Mrs. Bendall's reaction to Dicky's misdeed? Why does Mrs. Bendall ask her husband to whip Dicky?

4. What is Mr. Bendall's initial attitude toward spanking Dicky? What causes him to become like "a man in a dark net . . . [who] wanted to beat Dicky"?

5. How does Dicky react to the whipping?

6. How does Mr. Bendall feel after he has spanked Dicky? What thoughts go through his mind? Why does he give Dicky the sixpence?

Developing Skills in Reading Literature

1. **Conflict.** What is the conflict between Dicky and his parents? between the two parents? in Mr. Bendall's mind?

2. **Theme.** This is a story about characters who try to manipulate, or control, each other's behavior. It is also about the influence of experiences and events on human behavior. How does Mrs. Spears manipulate Mrs. Bendall? How does Mrs. Bendall manipulate her husband? How does Dicky make his father feel guilty? How is Mr. Bendall influenced by his day at work? In one or two sentences, explain a possible theme for this story.

Developing Writing Skills

1. **Writing Dialogue.** What do you suppose Mr. Bendall said to his wife after giving Dicky the sixpence? Write a dialogue, or conversation, that might have taken place between the Bendalls. Check your dialogue against the dialogue in the story to be sure that you have used the correct forms of paragraphing and punctuation.

2. **Writing an Explanation.** Read two or three articles on effective forms of punishment for children. Choose the approach that you think is the most sensible and workable. Then write a paragraph explaining the approach.

The Possibility of Evil   *Shirley Jackson*

Miss Adela Strangeworth came daintily along Main Street on her way to the grocery. The sun was shining, the air was fresh and clear after the night's heavy rain, and everything in Miss Strangeworth's little town looked washed and bright. Miss Strangeworth took deep breaths and thought that there was nothing in the world like a fragrant summer day.

She knew everyone in town, of course; she was fond of telling strangers—tourists who sometimes passed through the town and stopped to admire Miss Strangeworth's roses —that she had never spent more than a day outside this town in all her long life. She was seventy-one, Miss Strangeworth told the tourists, with a pretty little dimple showing by her lip, and she sometimes found herself thinking that the town belonged to her. "My grandfather built the first house on Pleasant Street," she would say, opening her blue eyes wide with the wonder of it. "This house, right here. My family has lived here for better than a hundred years. My grandmother planted these roses, and my mother tended them, just as I do. I've watched my town grow; I can remember when Mr. Lewis, Senior, opened the grocery store, and the year the river flooded out the shanties on the low road, and the excitement when some young folks wanted to move the park over to the space in front of where the new post office is today. They wanted to put up a statue of Ethan Allen"—Miss Strangeworth would frown a little and sound stern—"but it should have been a statue of my grandfather. There wouldn't have been a town here at all if it hadn't been for my grandfather and the lumber mill."

Miss Strangeworth never gave away any of her roses, although the tourists often asked her. The roses belonged on Pleasant Street, and it bothered Miss Strangeworth to think of people wanting to carry them away, to take them into strange towns and down strange streets. When the new minister came, and the ladies were gathering flowers to decorate the church, Miss Strangeworth sent over a great basket of gladioli; when she picked the roses at all, she set them in bowls and vases around the inside of the house her grandfather had built.

Walking down Main Street on a summer morning, Miss Strangeworth had to stop every minute or so to say good morning to someone or to ask after someone's health. When she came into the grocery, half a dozen people turned away from the shelves and the counters to wave at her or call out good morning.

"And good morning to you, too, Mr. Lewis," Miss Strangeworth said at last. The Lewis family had been in the town almost as long as the Strangeworths; but the day young Lewis left high school and went to work in the grocery, Miss Strangeworth had stopped calling him Tommy and started calling him Mr. Lewis, and he had stopped calling her Addie and started calling her Miss Strangeworth. They had been in high school together, and had gone to picnics together, and to high-school dances and basketball games; but now Mr. Lewis was behind the counter in the grocery, and Miss Strangeworth was living alone in the Strangeworth house on Pleasant Street.

"Good morning," Mr. Lewis said, and added politely, "Lovely day."

"It is a very nice day," Miss Strangeworth said, as though she had only just decided that it would do after all. "I would like a chop, please, Mr. Lewis, a small, lean veal chop. Are those strawberries from Arthur Parker's garden? They're early this year."

"He brought them in this morning," Mr. Lewis said.

"I shall have a box," Miss Strangeworth said. Mr. Lewis looked worried, she thought, and for a minute she hesitated, but then she decided that he surely could not be worried over the strawberries. He looked very tired indeed. He was usually so chipper, Miss Strangeworth thought, and almost commented; but it was far too personal a subject to be introduced to Mr. Lewis, the grocer, so she only said, "And a can of cat food and, I think, a tomato."

Silently, Mr. Lewis assembled her order on the counter, and waited. Miss Strangeworth looked at him curiously and then said, "It's Tuesday, Mr. Lewis. You forgot to remind me."

"Did I? Sorry."

"Imagine your forgetting that I always buy my tea on Tuesday," Miss Strangeworth said gently. "A quarter pound of tea, please, Mr. Lewis."

"Is that all, Miss Strangeworth?"

"Yes thank you, Mr. Lewis. Such a lovely day, isn't it?"

"Lovely," Mr. Lewis said.

Miss Strangeworth moved slightly to make room for Mrs. Harper at the counter. "Morning, Adela," Mrs. Harper said, and Miss Strangeworth said, "Good morning, Martha."

"Lovely day," Mrs. Harper said, and Miss Strangeworth said, "Yes, lovely," and Mr. Lewis, under Mrs. Harper's glance, nodded.

"Ran out of sugar for my cake frosting," Mrs. Harper explained. Her hand shook slightly as she opened her pocketbook. Miss Strangeworth wondered, glancing at her quickly, if she had been taking proper care of herself. Martha Harper was not as young as she used to be, Miss Strangeworth thought. She probably could use a good strong tonic.

"Martha," she said, "you don't look well."

"I'm perfectly all right," Mrs. Harper said shortly. She handed her money to Mr. Lewis, took her change and her sugar, and went out without speaking again. Looking after her, Miss Strangeworth shook her head slightly. Martha definitely did *not* look well.

Carrying her little bag of groceries, Miss Strangeworth came out of the store into the bright sunlight and stopped to smile down on the Crane baby. Don and Helen Crane were really the two most infatuated young parents she had ever known, she thought indulgently, looking at the delicately embroidered baby cap and the lace-edged carriage cover.

"That little girl is going to grow up expecting luxury all her life," she said to Helen Crane.

Helen laughed. "That's the way we want her to feel," she said. "Like a princess."

"A princess can see a lot of trouble sometimes," Miss Strangeworth said dryly. "How old is Her Highness now?"

"Six months next Tuesday," Helen Crane said, looking down with rapt wonder at her child. "I've been worrying, though, about her. Don't you think she ought to move around more? Try to sit up, for instance?"

"For plain and fancy worrying," Miss Strangeworth said, amused, "give me a new mother every time."

"She just seems—slow," Helen Crane said.

"Nonsense. All babies are different. Some of them develop much more quickly than others."

"That's what my mother says." Helen Crane laughed, looking a little bit ashamed.

"I suppose you've got young Don all upset about the fact that his daughter is already six months old and hasn't yet begun to learn to dance?"

"I haven't mentioned it to him. I suppose she's just so precious that I worry about her all the time."

"Well, apologize to her right now," Miss Strangeworth said. "*She* is probably worrying about why you keep jumping around all the time." Smiling to herself and shaking her old head, she went on down the sunny street, stopping once to ask little Billy Moore why he wasn't out riding in his daddy's shiny new car; and talking for a few minutes outside the library with Miss Chandler, the librarian, about the new novels to be ordered and paid for by the annual library appropriation. Miss Chandler seemed absent-minded and very much as though she were thinking about something else. Miss Strangeworth noticed that Miss Chandler had not taken much trouble with her hair that morning, and sighed. Miss Strangeworth hated sloppiness.

Many people seemed disturbed recently, Miss Strangeworth thought. Only yesterday the Stewarts' fifteen-year-old Linda had run crying down her own front walk and all the way to school, not caring who saw her. People around town thought she might have had a fight with the Harris boy, but they showed up together at the soda shop after school as usual, both of them looking grim and bleak. Trouble at home, people concluded, and sighed over the problems of trying to raise kids right these days.

From halfway down the block, Miss Strangeworth could catch the heavy scent of her roses, and she moved a little more quickly. The perfume of roses meant home, and home meant the Strangeworth House on Pleasant Street. Miss Strangeworth stopped at her own front gate, as she always did, and looked with deep pleasure at her house, with the red and pink and white roses massed along the narrow lawn, and the rambler going up along the porch; and the neat, the unbelievably trim lines of the house itself, with its slimness and its washed white look. Every window sparkled, every curtain hung stiff and straight, and even the stones of the front walk were swept and clear. People around town wondered how old Miss Strangeworth managed to keep the house looking the way it did, and there was a legend about a tourist once mistaking it for the local museum and going all through the place without finding out about his mistake. But the town was proud of Miss Strangeworth and her roses and her house. They had all grown together.

Miss Strangeworth went up her front steps, unlocked her front door with her key, and went into the kitchen to put away her groceries. She debated about having a cup of tea and then decided that it was too close to midday dinnertime; she would not have the appetite for her little chop if she had tea now. Instead she went into the light, lovely sitting room, which still glowed from the hands of her mother and her grandmother, who had covered the chairs with bright chintz and hung the curtains. All the furniture was spare and shining, and the round hooked rugs on the floor had been the work of Miss Strangeworth's grandmother and her mother. Miss Strangeworth had put a bowl of her red roses on the low table before the window, and the room was full of their scent.

Miss Strangeworth went to the narrow desk in the corner and unlocked it with her key. She never knew when she might feel like writing letters, so she kept her notepaper inside and the desk locked. Miss Strange-

worth's usual stationery was heavy and cream-colored, with STRANGEWORTH HOUSE engraved across the top; but, when she felt like writing her other letters, Miss Strangeworth used a pad of various-colored paper bought from the local newspaper shop. It was almost a town joke, that colored paper, layered in pink and green and blue and yellow; everyone in town bought it and used it for odd, informal notes and shopping lists. It was usual to remark, upon receiving a note written on a blue page, that so-and-so would be needing a new pad soon—here she was, down to the blue already. Everyone used the matching envelopes for tucking away recipes, or keeping odd little things in, or even to hold cookies in the school lunchboxes. Mr. Lewis sometimes gave them to the children for carrying home penny candy.

Although Miss Strangeworth's desk held a trimmed quill pen that had belonged to her grandfather, and a gold-frosted fountain pen that had belonged to her father, Miss Strangeworth always used a dull stub of pencil when she wrote her letters; and she printed them in a childish block print. After thinking for a minute, although she had been phrasing the letter in the back of her mind all the way home, she wrote on a pink sheet: DIDN'T YOU EVER SEE AN IDIOT CHILD BEFORE? SOME PEOPLE JUST SHOULDN'T HAVE CHILDREN SHOULD THEY?

She was pleased with the letter. She was fond of doing things exactly right. When she made a mistake, as she sometimes did, or when the letters were not spaced nicely on the page, she had to take the discarded page to the kitchen stove and burn it at once. Miss Strangeworth never delayed when things had to be done.

After thinking for a minute, she decided that she would like to write another letter, perhaps to go to Mrs. Harper, to follow up the ones she had already mailed. She selected a green sheet this time and wrote quickly: HAVE YOU FOUND OUT YET WHAT THEY WERE ALL LAUGHING ABOUT AFTER YOU LEFT THE BRIDGE CLUB ON THURSDAY? OR IS THE WIFE REALLY ALWAYS THE LAST ONE TO KNOW?

Miss Strangeworth never concerned herself with facts; her letters all dealt with the more negotiable stuff of suspicion. Mr. Lewis would never have imagined for a minute that his grandson might be lifting petty cash from the store register if he had not had one of Miss Strangeworth's letters. Miss Chandler, the librarian, and Linda Stewart's parents would have gone unsuspectingly ahead with their lives, never aware of possible evil lurking nearby, if Miss Strangeworth had not sent letters opening their eyes. Miss Strangeworth would have been genuinely shocked if there *had* been anything between Linda Stewart and the Harris boy; but, as long as evil existed unchecked in the world, it was Miss Strangeworth's duty to keep her town alert to it. It was far more sensible for Miss Chandler to wonder what Mr. Shelley's first wife had really died of than to take a chance on not knowing. There were so many wicked people in the world and only one Strangeworth left in the town. Besides, Miss Strangeworth liked writing her letters.

She addressed an envelope to Don Crane after a moment's thought, wondering curiously if he would show the letter to his wife, and using a pink envelope to match the pink paper. Then she addressed a second envelope, green, to Mrs. Harper. Then an idea came to her and she selected a blue sheet and wrote: YOU NEVER KNOW ABOUT DOCTORS. REMEMBER THEY'RE ONLY HUMAN AND NEED MONEY LIKE THE REST OF US. SUPPOSE THE KNIFE SLIPPED ACCIDENTALLY. WOULD DR. BURNS GET HIS FEE AND A LITTLE EXTRA FROM THAT NEPHEW OF YOURS?

She addressed the blue envelope to old Mrs. Foster, who was having an operation next month. She had thought of writing one more letter, to the head of the school board, asking how a chemistry teacher like Billy Moore's father could afford a new convertible, but, all at once, she was tired of writing letters. The three she had done would do for one day. She could write more tomorrow; it was not as though they all had to be done at once.

She had been writing her letters—sometimes two or three every day for a week, sometimes no more than one in a month—for the past year. She never got any answers, of course, because she never signed her name. If she had been asked, she would have said that her name, Adela Strangeworth, a name honored in the town for so many years, did not belong on such trash. The town where she lived had to be kept clean and sweet, but people everywhere were lustful and evil and degraded, and needed to be watched; the world was so large, and there was only one Strangeworth left in it. Miss Strangeworth sighed, locked her desk, and put the letters into her big black leather pocketbook, to be mailed when she took her evening walk.

She broiled her little chop nicely, and had a sliced tomato and a good cup of tea ready when she sat down to her midday dinner at the table in her dining room, which could be opened to seat twenty-two, with a second table, if necessary, in the hall. Sitting in the warm sunlight that came through the tall windows of the dining room, seeing her roses massed outside, handling the heavy, old silverware and the fine, translucent china, Miss Strangeworth was pleased; she would not have cared to be doing anything else. People must live graciously, after all, she thought, and sipped her tea. Afterward, when her plate and cup and saucer were washed and dried and put back onto the shelves where they belonged, and her silverware was back in the mahogany silver chest, Miss Strangeworth went up the graceful staircase and into her bedroom, which was the front room overlooking the roses, and had been her mother's and her grandmother's. Their Crown Derby dresser set and furs had been kept there, their fans and silver-backed brushes and their own bowls of roses; Miss Strangeworth kept a bowl of white roses on the bed table.

She drew the shades, took the rose satin spread from the bed, slipped out of her dress and her shoes, and lay down tiredly. She knew that no doorbell or phone would ring; no one in town would dare to disturb Miss Strangeworth during her afternoon nap. She slept, deep in the rich smell of roses.

After her nap she worked in her garden for a little while, sparing herself because of the heat; then she came in to her supper. She ate asparagus from her own garden, with sweet-butter sauce and a soft-boiled egg; and, while she had her supper, she listened to a late-evening news broadcast and then to a program of classical music on her small radio.

After her dishes were done and her kitchen set in order, she took up her hat—Miss Strangeworth's hats were proverbial in the town; people believed that she had inherited them from her mother and her grandmother —and, locking the front door of her house behind her, set off on her evening walk, pocketbook under her arm. She nodded to Linda Stewart's father, who was washing his car in the pleasantly cool evening. She thought that he looked troubled.

There was only one place in town where she could mail her letters, and that was the new post office, shiny with red brick and silver letters. Although Miss Strangeworth had never given the matter any particular thought, she had always made a point of mailing her letters very secretly; it would, of course, not have been wise to let anyone see her mail them. Consequently, she timed her walk so she could reach the post office just as darkness was starting to dim the outlines of the trees and the shapes of people's faces, al-

though no one could ever mistake Miss Strangeworth, with her dainty walk and her rustling skirts.

There was always a group of young people around the post office, the very youngest roller-skating upon its driveway, which went all the way around the building and was the only smooth road in town; and the slightly older ones already knowing how to gather in small groups and chatter and laugh and make great, excited plans for going across the street to the soda shop in a minute or two. Miss Strangeworth had never had any self-consciousness before the children. She did not feel that any of them were staring at her unduly or longing to laugh at her; it would have been most reprehensible for their parents to permit their children to mock Miss Strangeworth of Pleasant Street. Most of the children stood back respectfully as Miss Strangeworth passed, silenced briefly in her presence, and some of the older children greeted her, saying soberly, "Hello, Miss Strangeworth."

Miss Strangeworth smiled at them and quickly went on. It had been a long time since she had known the name of every child in town. The mail slot was in the door of the post office. The children stood away as Miss Strangeworth approached it, seemingly surprised that anyone should want to use the post office after it had been officially closed up for the night and turned over to the children. Miss Strangeworth stood by the door, opening her black pocketbook to take out the letters, and heard a voice which she knew at once to be Linda Stewart's. Poor little Linda was crying again, and Miss Strangeworth listened carefully. This was, after all, her town, and these were her people; if one of them was in trouble she ought to know about it.

"I can't tell you, Dave," Linda was saying— so she *was* talking to the Harris boy, as Miss Strangeworth had supposed—"I just *can't*. It's just *nasty*."

"But why won't your father let me come around any more? What on earth did I do?"

"I can't tell you. I just wouldn't tell you for *anything*. You've got to have a dirty, dirty mind for things like that."

"But something's happened. You've been crying and crying, and your father is all upset. Why can't *I* know about it, too? Aren't I like one of the family?"

"Not any more, Dave, not any more. You're not to come near our house again; my father said so. He said he'd horsewhip you. That's all I can tell you: You're not to come near our house any more."

"But I didn't *do* anything."

"Just the same, my father said . . ."

Miss Strangeworth sighed and turned away. There was so much evil in people. Even in a charming little town like this one, there was still so much evil in people.

She slipped her letters into the slot, and two of them fell inside. The third caught on the edge and fell outside, onto the ground at Miss Strangeworth's feet. She did not notice it because she was wondering whether a letter to the Harris boy's father might not be of some service in wiping out this potential badness. Wearily Miss Strangeworth turned to go home to her quiet bed in her lovely house, and never heard the Harris boy calling to her to say that she had dropped something.

"Old lady Strangeworth's getting deaf," he said, looking after her and holding in his hand the letter he had picked up.

"Well, who cares?" Linda said. "Who cares any more, anyway?"

"It's for Don Crane," the Harris boy said, "this letter. She dropped a letter addressed to Don Crane. Might as well take it on over. We pass his house anyway." He laughed. "Maybe it's got a check or something in it, and he'd be just as glad to get it tonight instead of tomorrow."

"Catch old lady Strangeworth sending anybody a check," Linda said. "Throw it in the post office. Why do anyone a favor?" She sniffled. "Doesn't seem to me anybody around here cares about us," she said. "Why should we care about them?"

"I'll take it over anyway," the Harris boy said. "Maybe it's good news for them. Maybe they need something happy tonight, too. Like us."

Sadly, holding hands, they wandered off down the dark street, the Harris boy carrying Miss Strangeworth's pink envelope in his hand.

Miss Strangeworth awakened the next morning with a feeling of intense happiness and, for a minute wondered why, and then remembered that this morning three people would open her letters. Harsh, perhaps, at first, but wickedness was never easily banished, and a clean heart was a scoured heart. She washed her soft old face and brushed her teeth, still sound in spite of her seventy-one years, and dressed herself carefully in her sweet, soft clothes and buttoned shoes. Then, coming downstairs and reflecting that perhaps a little waffle would be agreeable for breakfast in the sunny dining room, she found the mail on the hall floor and bent to pick it up. A bill, the morning paper, a letter in a green envelope that looked oddly familiar. Miss Strangeworth stood perfectly still for a minute, looking down at the green envelope with the penciled printing, and thought: It looks like one of my letters. Was one of my letters sent back? No, because no one would know where to send it. How did this get here?

Miss Strangeworth was a Strangeworth of Pleasant Street. Her hand did not shake as she opened the envelope and unfolded the sheet of green paper inside. She began to cry silently for the wickedness of the world when she read the words:

Look out at what used to be your roses.

Getting at Meaning

1. What traditions are important to Miss Strangeworth? Why does she feel that the town "belongs" to her? What is her attitude toward her home and her roses?

2. Why does Miss Strangeworth send her letters? How does she know what to write? How does it make her feel to send them?

3. How do Miss Strangeworth's letters affect those who receive them? Support your answer with examples from the story.

4. At the end of the story, Miss Strangeworth reads the words, "Look out at what used to be your roses." What is the meaning of this message? Will the entire town know that she has been sending the letters? Explain.

Developing Skills in Reading Literature

1. **Irony.** Miss Strangeworth tells herself that she is sending the letters for what purpose? Ironically, what is true of the letters?

2. **Theme.** What kind of person do the townspeople assume Miss Strangeworth to be? In reality, what kind of person is she? What is the writer telling the reader about the existence of evil?

3. **Symbol.** This story contains considerable description of Miss Strangeworth's roses. What is usually associated with roses? What do the roses symbolize, or represent, to Miss Strangeworth and the town? Why is it significant that she never gives away her roses? Why are the roses destroyed?

Developing Vocabulary

Antonyms. The narrator of the story says, "Miss Strangeworth hated sloppiness." This means that she liked neatness, because *sloppiness* and *neatness* are antonyms.

Copy the following sentences. In the blank write an antonym for each italicized word.

1. The *fragrant* roses could not hide the odor of the _____ garbage.

2. The town was *proud* of Miss Strangeworth. Had they known the truth, they would have been _____.

3. Miss Strangeworth spoke *politely* to everyone. No one could imagine her answering _____.

4. People who grow up expecting *luxury* all the time have a hard time adjusting to _____.

5. Miss Strangeworth used the pad of various colored paper for her *informal* notes, although she did have engraved stationery for her more _____ correspondence.

6. Miss Strangeworth *liked* doing things right. She _____ sloppiness.

7. There were many *wicked* people in the town, thought Miss Strangeworth, but she was glad that she was one of the _____ ones.

8. Miss Strangeworth always had to mail her letters *secretly;* she certainly could not have done it _____.

Developing Writing Skills

1. **Writing a Letter.** Write a letter to Miss Strangeworth, expressing your views on her activities.

2. **Supporting an Opinion.** Miss Strangeworth believes that "it was far more sensible for Miss Chandler to wonder what Mr. Shelley's first wife had really died of than to take a chance on not knowing." Do you agree that it is best to be alerted to every possible evil in every situation? Write a paragraph defending your answer. Use specific examples to illustrate your points.

3. **Combining Narration and Description.** Have you ever discovered that someone was quite different from the way he or she first appeared? Have you found evil in someone who appeared to be good? Have you learned that someone whom you originally disapproved of or disliked was in fact a good person? Write a well developed paragraph about this person, explaining in detail how and why your views changed.

Unit Review   *The Short Story*

Understanding the Unit

1. The setting of "The Secret Life of Walter Mitty" is a car, a hotel lobby, and the sidewalk along Main Street. The setting of "The Sniper" is a roof top. How do these limited settings help to bring out the writers' ideas? In which other stories is setting an important factor in developing the writers' themes?

2. Which characters in this unit have experiences that change their views about life? Which characters understand themselves better after these experiences?

3. Which stories in the unit focus on the inner conflict of the main characters? In which stories are the conflicts resolved? In which stories are they left largely unresolved?

4. Both "Thank You, M'am" and "The Cave" feature young boys who learn lessons from older people. Discuss the similarities and the differences between the experiences of Roger and Charley.

5. Both "Something Bright" and "Marigolds" are set in the Depression. How are the environments described the same? How are they different? What does the main character in each story realize about her environment?

6. In "The Most Dangerous Game," Rainsford says that everyone is either a hunter or the huntee. What other stories in this unit include characters who are either "hunters" or "huntees"? Discuss each example.

7. Choose one story written in the first person and one written in the third person. Explain how the narrative technique fits the subject and theme of each selection.

Writing

1. Several stories in this unit deal with problems faced by old people. Write a composition of five paragraphs in which you discuss three or four of the common problems faced by elderly people in our society. Include in your composition suggestions of ways that younger people might help older people cope with the problems. In your discussion, use examples from the stories and from your personal experience and observation.

2. Choose a story—for example, "Happy Birthday," "The Most Dangerous Game," or "The Possibility of Evil"—and explain how the setting, characters, and plot interact to bring out the writer's theme. The introduction of your composition should give the title and author of the story and explain its theme. The three body paragraphs should discuss the function of setting, characters, and plot in relation to the theme. The brief concluding paragraph should pull your thoughts together.

3. "The Secret Life of Walter Mitty" and "A Mother in Mannville" are both about the importance of fantasy and dreams in human life. Think about the answers to the following questions: What are your fantasies and daydreams? How do they function in your life? Do they affect your real-life actions and decisions in any way? What importance do they have for you? Then write a conversation between the real-life you and the you of your fantasies, or write a story in which a fantasy is triggered by an everyday experience. For example, a daydream in which you are a famous scientist might be suggested by a classroom discussion about Madame Curie.

4. Many of the characters in this unit exist in times and places unfamiliar to you. Interview an adult—a neighbor, friend, or relative—about an experience he or she has had in an unfamiliar time or place. Write an account of your interview that accurately summarizes the facts of the experience and also reflects the person's feelings about the experience.

Unit 3

Nonfiction

Introduction to the Unit

After you have visited someplace new or have observed something out of the ordinary, your first inclination often is to share your experience with family and friends. In describing your experience, you hope that other people will understand what happened and will react as you did.

The reasons you want to share your experiences and the goals of nonfiction writers are basically the same. However, while your audience is small and is made up of those who know you, nonfiction writers hope that many readers will find their works interesting and appealing.

This unit is divided into four sections, each featuring a different kind of nonfiction writing. The first section consists of autobiographical selections in which writers write about their own experiences. All of the selections in the first section are about growing up, in families, in neighborhoods, and in schools that may seem both strange and familiar at the same time.

The selections in the second section are all eulogies for heroes, heroes who may provoke thought about the meaning of the word *hero*. The third section, on the humorous essay, includes two selections that describe wildly improbable events and two that recall childhood incidents. The unit concludes with four essays of social commentary whose purpose is to make the reader think about issues that concern all human beings.

Talented writers of nonfiction have both skill and imagination. Like writers of fiction, they select characters, settings, and conflicts that illustrate universal themes. They use literary techniques, such as irony, foreshadowing, figurative language, and suspense. The works of nonfiction writers, however, contain a bonus for you, the reader—everything depicted actually happened.

Autobiography

from I Know Why the Caged Bird Sings

Maya Angelou

When I was three and Bailey four, we had arrived in the musty little town, wearing tags on our wrists that instructed—"To Whom It May Concern"—that we were Marguerite and Bailey Johnson, Jr., from Long Beach, California, en route to Stamps, Arkansas, c/o Mrs. Annie Henderson.

Our parents had decided to put an end to their calamitous marriage, and Father shipped us home to his mother. A porter had been charged with our welfare—he got off the train the next day in Arizona—and our tickets were pinned to my brother's inside coat pocket.

I don't remember much of the trip, but after we reached the segregated southern part of the journey, things must have looked up. Negro passengers, who always traveled with loaded lunch boxes, felt sorry for "the poor little motherless darlings" and plied us with cold fried chicken and potato salad.

Years later I discovered that the United States had been crossed thousands of times by frightened black children traveling alone to their newly affluent parents in Northern cities, or back to grandmothers in Southern towns when the urban North reneged on its economic promises.

The town reacted to us as its inhabitants had reacted to all things new before our coming. It regarded us a while without curiosity but with caution, and after we were seen to be harmless (and children) it closed in around us, as a real mother embraces a stranger's child. Warmly, but not too familiarly.

We lived with our grandmother and uncle in the rear of the Store (it was always spoken of with a capital *s*), which she had owned for some twenty-five years.

Early in the century, Momma (we soon stopped calling her Grandmother) sold lunches to the sawmen in the lumberyard (east Stamps) and the seedmen at the cotton gin (west Stamps). Her crisp meat pies and cool lemonade, when joined to her miraculous ability to be in two places at the same time, assured her business success. From being a mobile lunch counter, she set up a stand between the two points of fiscal interest and supplied the workers' needs for a few years. Then she had the Store built in the heart of the black area. Over the years it became the lay center of activities in town. On Saturdays, barbers sat their customers in the shade on the porch of the Store, and troubadours on their ceaseless crawlings through the South, leaned across its benches and sang their sad songs of The Brazos[1] while they played juice harps and cigar-box guitars.

The formal name of the Store was the Wm. Johnson General Merchandise Store. Customers could find food staples, a good variety of colored thread, mash for hogs, corn for chickens, coal oil for lamps, light bulbs for the wealthy, shoestrings, hair dressing, balloons, and flower seeds. Anything not visible had only to be ordered.

Until we became familiar enough to belong

---

1. **The Brazos** (brä'zəs): a river in Texas.

to the Store and it to us, we were locked up in a Fun House of Things where the attendant had gone home for life.

Each year I watched the field across from the Store turn caterpillar green, then gradually frosty white. I knew exactly how long it would be before the big wagons would pull into the front yard and load on the cotton pickers at daybreak to carry them to the remains of slavery's plantations.

During the picking season, my grandmother would get out of bed at four o'clock (she never used an alarm clock) and creak down to her knees and chant in a sleep-filled voice, "Our Father, thank you for letting me see this New Day. Thank you that you didn't allow the bed I lay on last night to be my cooling board, nor my blanket my winding sheet. Guide my feet this day along the straight and narrow, and help me to put a bridle on my tongue. Bless this house, and everybody in it. Thank you, in the name of your Son, Jesus Christ, Amen."

Before she had quite arisen, she called our names and issued orders, and pushed her large feet into homemade slippers and across the bare, lye-washed wooden floor to light the coal-oil lamp.

The lamplight in the Store gave a soft make-believe feeling to our world that made me want to whisper and walk about on tiptoe. The odors of onions and oranges and kerosene had been mixing all night and wouldn't be disturbed until the wooden slat was removed from the door and the early morning air forced its way in with the bodies of people who had walked miles to reach the pickup place.

"Sister, I'll have two cans of sardines."

"I'm gonna work so fast today I'm gonna make you look like you standing still."

"Lemme have a hunk uh cheese and some sody crackers."

"Just gimme a coupla them fat peanut pad-

dies." That would be from a picker who was taking his lunch. The greasy brown paper sack was stuck behind the bib of his overalls. He'd use the candy as a snack before the noon sun called the workers to rest.

In those tender mornings, the Store was full of laughing, joking, boasting, and bragging. One man was going to pick two hundred pounds of cotton, and another three hundred. Even the children were promising to bring home fo' bits and six bits.

The champion picker of the day before was the hero of the dawn. If he prophesied that the cotton in today's field was going to be sparse and stick to the bolls like glue, every listener would grunt a hearty agreement.

The sound of the empty cotton sacks dragging over the floor, and the murmurs of waking people were sliced by the cash register as we rang up the five-cent sales.

If the morning sounds and smells were touched with the supernatural, the late afternoon had all the features of the normal Arkansas life. In the dying sunlight the people dragged, rather than their empty cotton sacks.

Brought back to the Store, the pickers would step out of the backs of trucks and fold down, dirt-disappointed, to the ground. No matter how much they had picked, it wasn't enough. Their wages wouldn't even get them out of debt to my grandmother, not to mention the staggering bill that waited on them at the white commissary downtown.

The sounds of the new morning had been replaced with grumbles about cheating houses, weighted scales, snakes, skimpy cotton, and dusty rows. In later years I was to confront the stereotyped picture of happy, song-singing cotton pickers with such inordinate rage that I was told even by fellow blacks that my paranoia was embarrassing. But I had seen the fingers cut by the mean little cotton bolls, and I had witnessed the backs and shoulders and arms and legs resisting any further demands.

Some of the workers would leave their sacks at the Store to be picked up the following morning, but a few had to take them home for repairs. I winced to picture them sewing the coarse material under a coal-oil lamp with fingers stiffening from the day's work. In too few hours they would have to walk back to Sister Henderson's Store, get vittles and load, again, onto the trucks. Then they would face another day of trying to earn enough for the whole year, with the heavy knowledge that they were going to end the season as they started it. Without the money or credit necessary to sustain a family for three months. In cotton-picking time the late afternoons revealed the harshness of black Southern life, which in the early morning had been softened by nature's blessing of grogginess, forgetfulness, and the soft lamplight.

Getting at Meaning

1. How old are Marguerite and Bailey when they travel south to join their grandmother? What does Marguerite tell the reader about this train trip?

2. What is Momma like? Give evidence from the selection to support your answer. In what way is the Store more than a place to buy food and supplies?

3. The physical routine of the cotton pickers is described vividly. What evidence indicates that picking cotton is a life of hardship? What details does the writer emphasize in her description of how the cotton pickers begin the day? How is the description of their return different?

Developing Skills in Reading Literature

1. **Setting.** The location of this story is described in detail. What kind of town is Stamps? When does the story probably take place?

2. **Autobiography.** A biography is the story of a person's life. An autobiography is the story of a person's life written by that person, not by someone else. Does the reader learn much about Maya Angelou herself in this short selection? In what sense is the selection about her life?

Developing Vocabulary

Word Parts. A root word is the part of a word that contains its basic meaning. A prefix is a syllable added at the beginning of a root word to change its meaning in some way. Some prefixes are derived from ancient Latin and Greek. *Auto-*, for example, comes from the Greek word *autos* meaning "self."

On a separate sheet of paper, explain how the prefix *auto-* functions in each of the following words. Consult a dictionary if you need help. Then use each word in a sentence.

autocracy	autohypnosis	autograph
automatic	automobile	autonomy

Developing Writing Skills

Writing About a Personal Experience. What is your earliest recollection? Describe your memory in one paragraph, using specific details to help your readers envision your experience.

Discovery of a Father   *Sherwood Anderson*

One of the strangest relationships in the world is that between father and son. I know it now from having sons of my own.

A boy wants something very special from his father. You hear it said that fathers want their sons to be what they feel they cannot themselves be, but I tell you it also works the other way. I know that as a small boy I wanted my father to be a certain thing he was not. I wanted him to be a proud, silent, dignified father. When I was with the other boys and he passed along the street, I wanted to feel a glow of pride: "There he is. That is my father."

But he wasn't such a one. He couldn't be. It seemed to me then that he was always showing off. Let's say someone in our town had got up a show. They were always doing it. The druggist would be in it, the shoe-store clerk, the horse doctor, and a lot of women and girls. My father would manage to get the chief comedy part. It was, let's say, a Civil War play and he was a comic Irish soldier. He had to do the most absurd things. They thought he was funny, but I didn't.

I thought he was terrible. I didn't see how Mother could stand it. She even laughed with the others. Maybe I would have laughed if it hadn't been my father.

Or there was a parade, the Fourth of July or Decoration Day. He'd be in that, too, right at the front of it, as Grand Marshal or something, on a white horse hired from a livery stable.

He couldn't ride for shucks. He fell off the horse and everyone hooted with laughter, but he didn't care. He even seemed to like it. I remember once when he had done something ridiculous, and right out on Main Street, too. I was with some other boys and they were laughing and shouting at him and he was shouting back and having as good a time as they were. I ran down an alley back of some stores and there in the Presbyterian Church sheds I had a good long cry.

Or I would be in bed at night and Father would come home and bring some men with him. He was a man who was never alone. Before he went broke, running a harness shop, there were always a lot of men loafing in the shop. He went broke, of course, because he gave too much credit. He couldn't refuse it, and I thought he was a fool. I had got to hating him.

There'd be men I didn't think would want to be fooling around with him. There might even be the superintendent of our schools and a quiet man who ran the hardware store. Once I remember there was a white-haired man who was a cashier of the bank. It was a wonder to me they'd want to be seen with such a windbag. That's what I thought he was. I know now what it was that attracted them. It was because life in our town, as in all small towns, was at times pretty dull, and he livened it up. He made them laugh. He could tell stories. He'd even get them to singing.

If they didn't come to our house they'd go off, say at night, to where there was a grassy place by a creek. They'd cook food there and drink beer and sit about listening to his stories.

He was always telling stories about himself. He'd say this or that wonderful thing had happened to him. It might be something that made him look like a fool. He didn't care.

If an Irishman came to our house, right away Father would say he was Irish. He'd tell what county in Ireland he was born in. He'd tell things that happened there when he was a boy. He'd make it seem so real that, if I hadn't known he was born in southern Ohio, I'd have believed him myself.

If it was a Scotchman the same thing happened. He'd get a burr[1] into his speech. Or he was a German or a Swede. He'd be anything the other man was. I think they all knew he was lying, but they seemed to like him just the same. As a boy, that was what I couldn't understand.

And there was Mother. How could she stand it? I wanted to ask but never did. She was not the kind you asked such questions.

I'd be upstairs in my bed, in my room above the porch, and Father would be telling some of his tales. A lot of Father's stories were about the Civil War. To hear him tell it, he'd been in about every battle. He'd known Grant, Sherman, Sheridan, and I don't know how many others. He'd been particularly intimate with General Grant, so that when Grant went East, to take charge of all the armies, he took Father along.

"I was an orderly at headquarters, and Sam Grant said to me, 'Irve,' he said, 'I'm going to take you along with me.'"

It seems he and Grant used to slip off sometimes and have a quiet drink together. That's what my father said. He'd tell about the day Lee[2] surrendered and how, when the great moment came, they couldn't find Grant.

"You know," my father said, "about General Grant's book, his memoirs. You've read of how he said he had a headache and how, when he got word that Lee was ready to call it quits, he was suddenly and miraculously cured.

"Huh," said Father. "He was in the woods with me.

"I was in there with my back against a tree. I was drinking. I had got hold of a bottle.

"They were looking for Grant. He had got off his horse and come into the woods. He found me. He was covered with mud.

"I had the bottle in my hand. What'd I care? The war was over. I knew we had them licked."

My father said that he was the one who told Grant about Lee. An orderly riding by had told him, because the orderly knew how thick he was with Grant. Grant was embarrassed.

"But, Irve, look at me. I'm all covered with mud," he said to Father.

And then, my father said, he and Grant decided to have a drink together. They took a couple of drinks and then, because he didn't want Grant to show up drunk before the immaculate Lee, he smashed the bottle against the tree.

"Sam Grant's dead now, and I wouldn't want it to get out on him," my father said.

That's just one of the kind of things he'd tell. Of course the men knew he was lying, but they seemed to like it just the same.

When we got broke, down and out, do you think he ever brought anything home? Not he. If there wasn't anything to eat in the house, he'd go off visiting around at farmhouses. They all wanted him. Sometimes he'd stay away for weeks, Mother working to keep us fed, and then home he'd come bringing, let's say, a ham. He'd got it from some farmer friend. He'd slap it on the table in the kitchen. "You bet I'm going to see that my kids have something to eat," he'd say, and Mother would just stand smiling at him. She'd never say a word about all the weeks and months

---

1. **burr:** a trilling sound of the letter *r*.
2. **Grant, Sherman, Sheridan . . . Lee:** During the Civil War, Ulysses S. Grant was commander-in-chief of the Union forces; William Sherman and Philip Sheridan were Union generals; Robert E. Lee was commander-in-chief of the Confederate forces.

he'd been away, not leaving us a cent for food. Once I heard her speaking to a woman in our street. Maybe the woman had dared to sympathize with her. "Oh," she said, "it's all right. He isn't ever dull like most of the men in this street. Life is never dull when my man is about."

But often I was filled with bitterness, and sometimes I wished he wasn't my father. I'd even invent another man as my father. To protect my mother, I'd make up stories of a secret marriage that for some strange reason never got known. As though some man, say the president of a railroad company or maybe a Congressman, had married my mother, thinking his wife was dead and then it turned out she wasn't.

So they had to hush it up, but I got born just the same. I wasn't really the son of my father. Somewhere in the world there was a very dignified, quite wonderful man who was really my father. I even made myself half believe these fancies.

And then there came a certain night. Mother was away from home. Maybe there was church that night. Father came in. He'd been off somewhere for two or three weeks. He found me alone in the house, reading by the kitchen table.

It had been raining, and he was very wet. He sat and looked at me for a long time, not saying a word. I was startled, for there was on his face the saddest look I had ever seen. He sat for a time, his clothes dripping. Then he got up.

"Come on with me," he said.

I got up and went with him out of the house. I was filled with wonder, but I wasn't afraid. We went along a dirt road that led down into a valley, about a mile out of town, where there was a pond. We walked in silence. The man who was always talking had stopped his talking.

I didn't know what was up and had the queer feeling that I was with a stranger. I don't know whether my father intended it so. I don't think he did.

The pond was quite large. It was still raining hard, and there were flashes of lightning followed by thunder. We were on a grassy bank at the pond's edge when my father spoke, and in the darkness and rain his voice sounded strange.

"Take off your clothes," he said. Still filled with wonder, I began to undress. There was a flash of lightning, and I saw that he was already naked.

Naked, we went into the pond. Taking my hand, he pulled me in. It may be that I was too frightened, too full of a feeling of strangeness, to speak. Before that night my father had never seemed to pay any attention to me.

"And what is he up to now?" I kept asking myself. I did not swim very well, but he put my hand on his shoulder and struck out into the darkness.

He was a man with big shoulders, a powerful swimmer. In the darkness I could feel the movement of his muscles. We swam to the far edge of the pond and then back to where we had left our clothes. The rain continued and the wind blew. Sometimes my father swam on his back and when he did he took my hand in his large powerful one and moved it over so that it rested always on his shoulder. Sometimes there would be a flash of lightning and I could see his face quite clearly.

It was as it was earlier, in the kitchen, a face filled with sadness. There would be the momentary glimpse of his face and then again the darkness, the wind, and the rain. In me there was a feeling I had never known before.

It was a feeling of closeness. It was something strange. It was as though there were only we two in the world. It was as though I had been jerked suddenly out of myself, out of my world of the schoolboy, out of a world in which I was ashamed of my father.

He had become blood of my blood; he the strong swimmer and I the boy clinging to him in the darkness. We swam in silence, and in silence we dressed in our wet clothes, and went home.

There was a lamp lighted in the kitchen, and when we came in, the water dripping from us, there was my mother. She smiled at us. I remember that she called us "boys." "What have you boys been up to?" she asked, but my father did not answer. As he had begun the evening's experience with me in silence, so he ended it. He turned and looked at me. Then he went, I thought, with a new and strange dignity, out of the room.

I climbed the stairs to my own room, undressed in darkness, and got into bed. I couldn't sleep and did not want to sleep. For the first time, I knew that I was the son of my father. He was a storyteller as I was to be. It may be that I even laughed a little softly there in the darkness. If I did, I laughed knowing that I would never again be wanting another father.

Getting at Meaning

1. What changes Sherwood Anderson's attitude toward his father? What does he begin to understand about the man? What qualities does he come to appreciate?

2. Give specific examples of the father's embarrassing behavior. The boy says, "Maybe I would have laughed if it hadn't been my father." What does he mean? What kind of father does he wish he had?

3. What is the attitude of Anderson's mother toward the antics of her husband?

4. Why do you think the father seems so sad when he finds the boy reading in the kitchen? What has he realized? Why does the father suddenly take his son swimming?

Developing Skills in Reading Literature

1. **Autobiography.** What does Sherwood Anderson learn about himself from the experience recounted in this autobiographical selection? What does he mean when he says, "For the first time, I knew that I was the son of my father. He was a storyteller as I was to be"?

2. **Title.** How does the title "Discovery of a Father" fit the content of this selection?

3. **Theme.** What elements of the writer's experience with his father can be applied to human relationships in general?

Developing Vocabulary

Finding the Appropriate Meaning. The narrator of this selection says of his father, "He'd get a burr into his speech." The word *burr* has several distinct meanings:

1. a prickly seed case
2. a dentist's drill
3. a trilling sound of the letter *r*

The third definition applies to the word as used in this selection.

Find the definitions of each of the following words in a dictionary. Then locate the word in the selection, and decide which definition fits its use.

part	stand	broke	bank
play	right	shop	slip

Developing Writing Skills

Writing About a Personal Experience. Write a paragraph that describes in detail a situation in which you suddenly gained appreciation for one of your parents. Include in the paragraph the answers to the following questions: What was the situation? How did your parent act? What qualities in your mother or father did you begin to admire?

A Christmas Memory   *Truman Capote*

Imagine a morning in late November. A coming of winter morning more than twenty years ago. Consider the kitchen of a spreading old house in a country town. A great black stove is its main feature, but there is also a big round table and a fireplace with two rocking chairs placed in front of it. Just today the fireplace commenced its seasonal roar.

A woman with shorn white hair is standing at the kitchen window. She is wearing tennis shoes and a shapeless gray sweater over a summery calico dress. She is small and sprightly, like a bantam hen; but, due to a long youthful illness, her shoulders are pitifully hunched. Her face is remarkable—not unlike Lincoln's, craggy like that, and tinted by sun and wind; but it is delicate too, finely boned; and her eyes are sherry-colored and timid. "Oh, my," she exclaims, her breath smoking the windowpane, "it's fruitcake weather!"

The person to whom she is speaking is myself. I am seven; she is sixty-something. We are cousins, very distant ones, and we have lived together—well, as long as I can remember. Other people inhabit the house, relatives; and though they have power over us, and frequently make us cry, we are not, on the whole, too much aware of them. We are each other's best friend. She calls me Buddy, in memory of a boy who was formerly her best friend. The other Buddy died in the 1880's, when she was still a child. She is still a child.

"I knew it before I got out of bed," she says, turning away from the window with a purposeful excitement in her eyes. "The courthouse bell sounded so cold and clear. And there were no birds singing; they've gone to warmer country, yes, indeed. Oh, Buddy, stop stuffing biscuit and fetch our buggy. Help me find my hat. We've thirty cakes to make."

It's always the same: a morning arrives in November, and my friend, as though officially inaugurating the Christmas time of year that exhilarates her imagination and fuels the blaze of her heart, announces, "It's fruitcake weather! Fetch our buggy. Help me find my hat."

The hat is found, a straw cartwheel corsaged with velvet roses out-of-doors has faded; it once belonged to a more fashionable relative. Together, we guide our buggy, a dilapidated baby carriage, out to the garden and into a grove of pecan trees. The buggy is mine; that is, it was bought for me when I was born. It is made of wicker, rather unraveled, and the wheels wobble like a drunkard's legs. But it is a faithful object; springtimes, we take it to the woods and fill it with flowers, herbs, wild fern for our porch pots. In the summer, we pile it with picnic paraphernalia and sugar-cane fishing poles and roll it down to the edge of a creek. It has its

winter uses, too: as a truck for hauling firewood from the yard to the kitchen, as a warm bed for Queenie, our tough little orange and white rat terrier who has survived distemper and two rattlesnake bites. Queenie is trotting beside it now.

Three hours later we are back in the kitchen hulling a heaping buggyload of windfall pecans. Our backs hurt from gathering them. How hard they were to find (the main crop having been shaken off the trees and sold by the orchard's owners, who are not us) among the concealing leaves, the frosted deceiving grass. Caaarackle! A cheery crunch, scraps of miniature thunder sound as the shells collapse and the golden mound of sweet oily ivory meat mounts in the milk-glass bowl. Queenie begs to taste, and now and again my friend sneaks her a mite, though insisting we deprive ourselves. "We mustn't, Buddy. If we start, we won't stop. And there's scarcely enough as there is. For thirty cakes." The kitchen is growing dark. Dusk turns the window into a mirror: our reflections mingle with the rising moon as we work by the fireside in the firelight. At last, when the moon is quite high, we toss the final hull into the fire and, with joined sighs, watch it catch flame. The buggy is empty; the bowl is brimful.

We eat our supper (cold biscuits, bacon, blackberry jam) and discuss tomorrow. Tomorrow the kind of work I like best begins: buying. Cherries and citron, ginger and vanilla and canned Hawaiian pineapple, rinds and raisins and walnuts and whiskey and oh, so much flour, butter, so many eggs, spices, flavorings. Why, we'll need a pony to pull the buggy home.

But before these purchases can be made, there is the question of money. Neither of us has any. Except for skinflint sums persons in the house occasionally provide (a dime is considered very big money); or what we earn ourselves from various activities: holding rummage sales, selling buckets of hand-picked blackberries, jars of homemade jam and apple jelly and peach preserves, rounding up flowers for funerals and weddings. Once we won seventy-ninth prize, five dollars, in a national football contest. Not that we know a fool thing about football. It's just that we enter any contest we hear about. At the moment our hopes are centered on the fifty-thousand-dollar Grand Prize being offered to name a new brand of coffee (we suggested "A.M."; and, after some hesitation, for my friend thought it perhaps sacrilegious, the slogan "A.M.! Amen!"). To tell the truth, our only *really* profitable enterprise was the Fun and Freak Museum we conducted in a backyard woodshed two summers ago. The Fun was a stereopticon with slide views of Washington and New York lent us by a relative who had been to those places (she was furious when she discovered why we'd borrowed it); the Freak was a three-legged biddy chicken hatched by one of our own hens. Everybody hereabouts wanted to see that biddy. We charged grown-ups a nickel, kids two cents, and took in a good twenty dollars before the museum shut down due to the decease of the main attraction.

But one way and another we do each year accumulate Christmas savings, a Fruitcake Fund. These moneys we keep hidden in an ancient bead purse under a loose board under the floor under a chamber pot under my friend's bed. The purse is seldom removed from this safe location except to make a deposit, or, as happens every Saturday, a withdrawal; for on Saturdays I am allowed ten cents to go to the picture show. My friend has never been to a picture show, nor does she intend to. "I'd rather hear you tell the story, Buddy. That way I can imagine it more. Besides, a person my age shouldn't squander their eyes. When the Lord comes, let me see him clear." In addition to never having seen a movie, she has never eaten in a restaurant, traveled more than five miles from home, received or sent a telegram, read anything except funny papers and the Bible, worn cosmetics, cursed, wished someone harm, told a lie on purpose, let a hungry dog go hungry. Here are a few things she has done, does do: killed with a hoe the biggest rattlesnake ever seen in this county (sixteen rattles), dip snuff (secretly), tame hummingbirds (just try it) till they balance on her finger, tell ghost stories (we both believe in ghosts) so tingling they chill you in July, talk to herself, take walks in the rain, grow the prettiest japonicas in town, know the recipe for every sort of old-time Indian cure, including a magical wart-remover.

Now, with supper finished, we retire to the room in a faraway part of the house where my friend sleeps in a scrap-quilt-covered iron bed painted rose pink, her favorite color. Silently, wallowing in the pleasures of conspiracy, we take the bead purse from its secret place and spill its contents on the scrap quilt. Dollar bills, tightly rolled and green as May buds. Somber fifty-cent pieces, heavy enough to weight a dead man's eyes. Lovely dimes, the liveliest coin, the one that really jingles. Nickels and quarters, worn smooth as creek pebbles. But mostly a hateful heap of bitter-odored pennies. Last summer, others in the house contracted to pay us a penny for every twenty-five flies we killed. Oh, the carnage of August: the flies that flew to heaven! Yet it was not work in which we took pride. And, as we sit counting pennies, it is as though we were back tabulating dead flies. Neither of us has a head for figures; we count slowly, lose track, start again. According to her calculations, we have $12.73. According to mine, exactly $13. "I do hope you're wrong, Buddy. We can't mess around with thirteen. The cakes will fall. Or put somebody in the cemetery. Why, I wouldn't dream of getting out of bed on the thirteenth." This is true; she always spends thirteenths in bed. So, to be on the safe side, we subtract a penny and toss it out the window.

Of the ingredients that go into our fruitcakes, whiskey is the most expensive, as well as the hardest to obtain. State laws forbid its sale. But everybody knows you can buy a bottle from Mr. Haha Jones. And the next day, having completed our more prosaic shopping, we set out for Mr. Haha's business address, a "sinful" (to quote public opinion) fish-fry and dancing café down by the river. We've been there before, and on the same errand; but in previous years our dealings have been with Haha's wife, an iodine-dark Indian woman with brassy, peroxided hair and a dead-tired disposition. Actually, we've never laid eyes on her husband, though we've heard that he's an Indian too. A giant with razor scars across his cheeks. They call him Haha because he's so gloomy, a man who never laughs. As we approach his café (a large log cabin festooned inside and out with chains of garish-gay naked light bulbs and standing by the river's muddy edge under the shade of river trees where moss drifts through the branches like gray mist) our steps slow down. Even Queenie stops prancing and sticks close by. People have been murdered in Haha's café. Cut to pieces. Hit on the head. There's a case coming up in court next month. Naturally these goings-on happen at night when the colored lights cast crazy patterns and the victrola wails. In the daytime, Haha's is shabby and deserted. I knock at the door, Queenie barks, my friend calls, "Mrs. Haha, ma'am? Anyone to home?"

Footsteps. The door opens. Our hearts overturn. It's Mr. Haha Jones himself! And he *is* a giant; he *does* have scars; he *doesn't* smile. No, he glowers at us through Satan-tilted eyes and demands to know, "What you want with Haha?"

For a moment we are too paralyzed to tell. Presently my friend half-finds her voice, a whispery voice at best, "If you please, Mr. Haha, we'd like a quart of your finest whiskey."

His eyes tilt more. Would you believe it? Haha is smiling! Laughing, too. "Which one of you is a drinkin' man?"

"It's for making fruitcakes, Mr. Haha. Cooking."

This sobers him. He frowns. "That's no way to waste good whiskey." Nevertheless, he retreats into the shadowed café and seconds later appears carrying a bottle of daisy yellow unlabeled liquor. He demonstrates its sparkle in the sunlight and says, "Two dollars."

We pay him with nickels and dimes and pennies. Suddenly, jangling the coins in his hand like a fistful of dice, his face softens. "Tell you what," he proposes, pouring the money back into our bead purse, "just send me one of them fruitcakes instead."

"Well," my friend remarks on our way home, "there's a lovely man. We'll put an extra cup of raisins in *his* cake."

The black stove, stoked with coal and firewood, glows like a lighted pumpkin. Eggbeaters whirl, spoons spin round in bowls of butter and sugar, vanilla sweetens the air, ginger spices it; melting, nose-tingling odors saturate the kitchen, suffuse the house, drift out to the world on puffs of chimney smoke. In four days our work is done. Thirty-one cakes, dampened with whiskey, bask on window sills and shelves.

Who are they for?

Friends. Not necessarily neighbor friends; indeed, the larger share are intended for persons we've met maybe once, perhaps not at all. People who've struck our fancy. Like President Roosevelt. Like the Reverend and Mrs. J. C. Lucey, Baptist missionaries to Borneo who lectured here last winter. Or the little knife grinder who comes through town twice a year. Or Abner Packer, the driver of the six o'clock bus from Mobile, who exchanges waves with us every day as he passes in a dust-cloud whoosh. Or the young Wistons, a California couple whose car one after-noon broke down outside the house and who spent a pleasant hour chatting with us on the porch (young Mr. Wiston snapped our picture, the only one we've ever had taken). Is it because my friend is shy with everyone *except* strangers that these strangers, and merest acquaintances, seem to us our truest friends? I think yes. Also, the scrapbooks we keep of thank-you's on White House stationery, time-to-time communications from California and Borneo, the knife grinder's penny post cards, make us feel connected to eventful worlds beyond the kitchen with its view of a sky that stops.

Now a nude December fig branch grates against the window. The kitchen is empty, the cakes are gone; yesterday we carted the last of them to the post office, where the cost of stamps turned our purse inside out. We're broke. That rather depresses me, but my friend insists on celebrating—with two inches of whiskey left in Haha's bottle. Queenie has a spoonful in a bowl of coffee (she likes her coffee chicory-flavored and strong). The rest we divide between a pair of jelly glasses. We're both quite awed at the prospect of drinking straight whiskey; the taste of it brings screwed-up expressions and sour shudders. But by and by we begin to sing, the two of us singing different songs simultaneously. I don't know the words to mine, just, *Come on along, come on along, to the dark-town strutters' ball.* But I can dance; that's what I mean to be, a tap dancer in the movies. My dancing shadow rollicks on the walls; our voices rock the chinaware; we giggle, as if unseen hands were tickling us. Queenie rolls on her back, her paws plow the air, something like a grin stretches her black lips. Inside myself, I feel warm and sparky as those crumbling logs, carefree as the wind in the chimney. My friend waltzes round the stove, the hem of her poor calico skirt pinched between her fingers as though it were a party dress. *Show me the way to go home,* she sings, her tennis shoes squeaking on the floor. *Show me the way to go home.*

Enter: two relatives. Very angry. Potent with eyes that scold, tongues that scald. Listen to what they have to say, the words tumbling together into a wrathful tune: "A child of seven! whiskey on his breath! are you out of your mind? feeding a child of seven! must be loony! road to ruination! remember Cousin Kate? Uncle Charlie? Uncle Charlie's brother-in-law? shame! scandal! humiliation! kneel, pray, beg the Lord!"

Queenie sneaks under the stove. My friend gazes at her shoes, her chin quivers, she lifts her skirt and blows her nose and runs to her room. Long after the town has gone to sleep and the house is silent except for the chimings of clocks and the sputter of fading fires, she is weeping into a pillow already as wet as a widow's handkerchief.

"'Don't cry,'" I say, sitting at the bottom of her bed and shivering despite my flannel nightgown that smells of last winter's cough syrup. "Don't cry," I beg, teasing her toes, tickling her feet, "you're too old for that."

"It's because," she hiccups, "I *am* too old. Old and funny."

"Not funny. Fun. More fun than anybody. Listen. If you don't stop crying you'll be so tired tomorrow we can't go cut a tree."

She straightens up. Queenie jumps on the bed (where Queenie is not allowed) to lick her cheeks. "I know where we'll find real pretty trees, Buddy. And holly, too. With berries big as your eyes. It's way off in the woods. Farther than we've ever been. Papa used to bring us Christmas trees from there; carry them on his shoulder. That's fifty years ago. Well, now, I can't wait for morning."

Morning. Frozen rime lusters the grass; the sun, round as an orange and orange as hot-weather moons, balances on the horizon, burnishes the silvered winter woods. A wild turkey calls. A renegade hog grunts in the undergrowth. Soon, by the edge of knee-deep, rapid-running water, we have to abandon the buggy. Queenie wades the stream first, paddles across barking complaints at the swiftness of the current, the pneumonia-making coldness of it. We follow, holding our shoes and equipment (a hatchet, a burlap sack) above our heads. A mile more, of chastising thorns, burrs, and briers that catch at our clothes; of rusty pine needles brilliant with gaudy fungus and molted feathers. Here, there, a flash, a flutter, an ecstasy of shrillings remind us that not all the birds have flown south. Always, the path unwinds through lemony sun pools and pitch vine tunnels. Another creek to cross; a disturbed armada of speckled trout froths the water round us, and frogs the size of plates practice belly flops; beaver workmen are building a dam. On the farther shore, Queenie shakes herself and trembles. My friend shivers, too: not with cold but enthusiasm. One of her hat's ragged roses sheds a petal as she lifts her head and inhales the pine-heavy air. "We're almost there. Can you smell it, Buddy?" she says, as though we were approaching an ocean.

And, indeed, it is a kind of ocean. Scented acres of holiday trees, prickly-leafed holly. Red berries shiny as Chinese bells; black crows swoop upon them screaming. Having stuffed our burlap sacks with enough greenery and crimson to garland a dozen windows, we set about choosing a tree. "It should be," muses my friend, "twice as tall as a boy. So a boy can't steal the star." The one we pick is twice as tall as me. A brave, handsome brute that survives thirty hatchet strokes before it keels with a creaking, rending cry. Lugging it like a kill, we commence the long trek out. Every few yards we abandon the struggle, sit down and pant. But we have the strength of triumphant huntsmen; that and the tree's virile, icy perfume revive us, goad us on. Many compliments accompany our sunset return along the red clay road to town; but my friend is sly and noncommittal when

passers-by praise the treasure perched in our buggy: what a fine tree and where did it come from? "Yonderways," she murmurs vaguely. Once a car stops and the rich mill owner's lazy wife leans out and whines, "Giveya two-bits cash for that ol tree." Ordinarily my friend is afraid of saying no, but on this occasion she promptly shakes her head. "We wouldn't take a dollar." The mill owner's wife persists. "A dollar, my foot! Fifty cents. That's my last offer. Goodness, woman, you can get another one." In answer, my friend gently reflects, "I doubt it. There's never two of anything."

Home. Queenie slumps by the fire and sleeps till tomorrow, snoring loud as a human.

A trunk in the attic contains a shoebox of ermine tails (off the opera cape of a curious lady who once rented a room in the house), coils of frazzled tinsel gone gold with age, one silver star, a brief rope of dilapidated, undoubtedly dangerous candy-like light bulbs. Excellent decorations, as far as they go, which isn't far enough. My friend wants our tree to blaze "like a Baptist window," droop with weighty snows of ornament. But we can't afford the made-in-Japan splendors at the five-and-dime. So we do what we've always done, sit for days at the kitchen table with scissors and crayons and stacks of colored paper. I make sketches and my friend cuts

them out: lots of cats, fish too (because they're easy to draw), some apples, some watermelons, a few winged angels devised from saved-up sheets of Hershey-bar tin foil. We use safety pins to attach these creations to the tree; as a final touch, we sprinkle the branches with shredded cotton (picked in August for this purpose). My friend, surveying the effect, clasps her hands together. "Now honest, Buddy. Doesn't it look good enough to eat?" Queenie tries to eat an angel.

After weaving and ribboning holly wreaths for all the front windows, our next project is the fashioning of family gifts. Tie dye scarves for the ladies, for the men a home-brewed lemon and licorice and aspirin syrup to be taken "at the first Symptoms of a Cold and after Hunting." But when it comes time for making each other's gift, my friend and I separate to work secretly. I would like to buy her a pearl-handled knife, a radio, a whole pound of chocolate-covered cherries (we tasted some once, and she always swears, "I could live on them, Buddy, Lord yes I could—and that's not taking His name in vain"). Instead, I am building her a kite. She would like to give me a bicycle (she's said so on several million occasions. "If only I could, Buddy. It's bad enough in life to do without something *you* want; but confound it, what gets my goat is not being able to give somebody something you want *them* to have. Only one of these days I will, Buddy. Locate you a bike.

Don't ask how. Steal it, maybe"). Instead, I'm fairly certain that she is building me a kite—the same as last year, and the year before; the year before that we exchanged slingshots. All of which is fine by me. For we are champion kite-fliers who study the wind like sailors; my friend, more accomplished than I, can get a kite aloft when there isn't enough breeze to carry clouds.

Christmas Eve afternoon we scrape together a nickel and go to the butcher's to buy Queenie's traditional gift, a good, gnawable beef bone. The bone, wrapped in funny paper, is placed high in the tree near the silver star. Queenie knows it's there. She squats at the foot of the tree, staring up in a trance of greed; when bedtime arrives she refuses to budge. Her excitement is equaled by my own. I kick the covers and turn my pillow as though it were a scorching summer's night. Somewhere a rooster crows; falsely, for the sun is still on the other side of the world.

"Buddy, are you awake?" It is my friend, calling from her room, which is next to mine; and an instant later she is sitting on my bed holding a candle. "Well, I can't sleep a hoot," she declares. "My mind's jumping like a jack rabbit. Buddy, do you think Mrs. Roosevelt will serve our cake at dinner?" We huddle in the bed, and she squeezes my hand I-love-you. "Seems like your hand used to be so much smaller. I guess I hate to see you grow up. When you're grown up, will we still be friends?" I say always. "But I feel so bad, Buddy. I wanted so bad to give you a bike. I tried to sell my cameo Papa gave me. Buddy—" she hesitates, as though embarrassed—"I made you another kite." Then I confess that I made her one, too; and we laugh. The candle burns too short to hold. Out it goes, exposing the starlight, the stars spinning at the window like a visible caroling that slowly, slowly daybreak silences. Possibly we doze; but the beginnings of dawn splash us like cold water. We're up, wide-eyed and wandering while we wait for others to waken. Quite deliberately my friend drops a kettle on the kitchen floor. I tap-dance in front of closed doors. One by one the household emerges, looking as though they'd like to kill us both; but it's Christmas, so they can't. First, a gorgeous breakfast; just everything you can imagine—from flapjacks and fried squirrel to hominy grits and honey-in-the-comb. Which puts everyone in a good humor except my friend and I. Frankly, we're so impatient to get at the presents we can't eat a mouthful.

Well, I'm disappointed. Who wouldn't be? With socks, a Sunday school shirt, some handkerchiefs, a hand-me-down sweater, and a year's subscription to a religious magazine for children. *The Little Shepherd.* It makes me boil. It really does.

My friend has a better haul. A sack of

Satsumas;[1] that's her best present. She is proudest, however, of a white wool shawl knitted by her married sister. But she *says* her favorite gift is the kite I built her. And it *is* very beautiful; though not as beautiful as the one she made me, which is blue and scattered with gold and green Good Conduct stars; moreover, my name is painted on it, "Buddy."

"Buddy, the wind is blowing."

The wind is blowing, and nothing will do till we've run to a pasture below the house where Queenie had scooted to bury her bone (and where, a winter hence, Queenie will be buried, too). There, plunging through the healthy, waist-high grass, we unreel our kites, feel them twitching at the string like sky fish as they swim into the wind. Satisfied, sun-warmed, we sprawl in the grass and peel Satsumas and watch our kites cavort. Soon I forget the socks and hand-me-down sweater. I'm as happy as if we'd already won the fifty-thousand-dollar Grand Prize in that coffee-naming contest.

"My, how foolish I am!" my friend cries, suddenly alert, like a woman remembering too late she has biscuits in the oven. "You know what I've always thought?" she asks in a tone of discovery, and not smiling at me but a point beyond. "I've always thought a body would have to be sick and dying before they saw the Lord. And I imagined that when He came it would be like looking at the Baptist window: pretty as colored glass with the sun pouring through, such a shine you don't know it's getting dark. And it's been a comfort: to think of that shine taking away all the spooky feeling. But I'll wager it never happens. I'll wager at the very end a body realizes the Lord has already shown Himself. That things as they are"—her hand circles in a gesture that gathers clouds and kites and grass and Queenie pawing earth over her bone—"just what they've always been, was seeing Him. As for me, I could leave the world with today in my eyes."

This is our last Christmas together.

Life separates us. Those who Know Best decide that I belong in a military school. And so follows a miserable succession of bugle-blowing prisons, grim, reveille-ridden summer camps. I have a new home too. But it doesn't count. Home is where my friend is, and there I never go.

And there she remains, puttering around the kitchen. Alone with Queenie. Then alone. ("Buddy dear," she writes in her wild, hard-to-read script, "yesterday Jim Macy's horse kicked Queenie bad. Be thankful she didn't feel much. I wrapped her in a Fine Linen sheet and rode her in the buggy down to Simpson's pasture where she can be with all her Bones . . .".) For a few Novembers she continues to bake her fruitcakes single-handed; not as many, but some; and, of course, she always sends me "the best of the batch." Also, in every letter she encloses a dime wadded in toilet paper: "See a picture show and write me the story." But gradually in her letters she tends to confuse me with her other friend, the Buddy who died in the 1880's; more and more thirteenths are not the only days she stays in bed. A morning arrives in November, a leafless, birdless coming of winter morning, when she cannot rouse herself to exclaim: "Oh, my, it's fruitcake weather!"

And when that happens, I know it. A message saying so merely confirms a piece of news some secret vein had already received, severing from me an irreplaceable part of myself, letting it loose like a kite on a broken string. That is why, walking across a school campus on this particular December morning, I keep searching the sky. As if I expected to see, rather like hearts, a lost pair of kites hurrying toward heaven.

---

1. **Satsuma** (sat' sōō mə): a small, loose-skinned variety of orange.

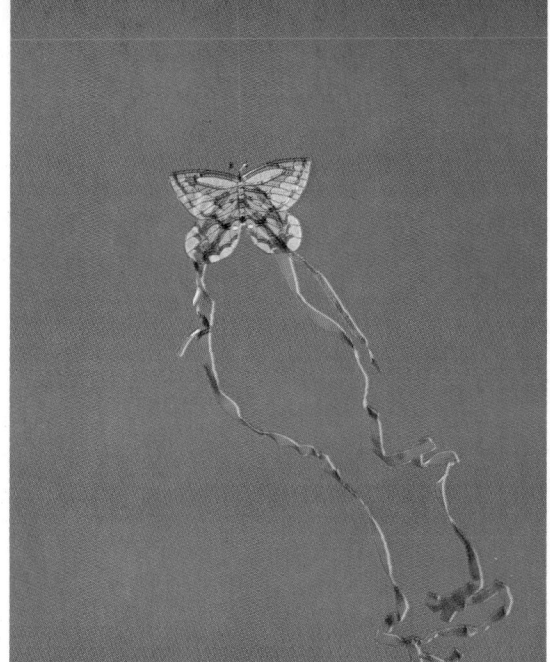

Getting at Meaning

1. The first two paragraphs of the selection describe a scene in the writer's memory almost as if it were a picture. Why does he begin the selection with this description?

2. Describe Buddy's friend. Buddy says of her, "She is still a child." What does he mean by this? What position does she apparently have in the household? What position does Buddy have in the household?

3. What are the rituals involved in making fruitcakes? Who are some of the people to whom Buddy and his friend send them? Why do they send them to people they hardly know when they have so little themselves?

4. What are some of the family's other Christmas rituals? Why is Buddy disappointed in all but one of his Christmas presents?

5. Describe Buddy's life after he is sent away to school. What becomes of his friend? What is his final memory of his friend?

6. Why do these people, separated by almost sixty years, feel so much excitement for each other? Do the others in the house understand their feelings? Give evidence from the story to support your answers.

Developing Skills in Reading Literature

1. **Autobiography.** The four autobiographical selections in this unit do not concentrate so much on facts as they do on experiences. Each sketch gives a detailed description of one significant event or period in the writer's life.

When Buddy as an adult recalls the experiences recounted in this selection, what do you suppose he realizes he learned from his friend? What qualities in her might he appreciate the most?

2. **Setting.** Where do you think this story is set? About when is it set? Give evidence from the story to support your conclusions.

3. **Theme.** When Buddy and his friend are flying their Christmas kites, she says to him, "I'll wager at the very end a body realizes the Lord has already shown Himself. That things as they are . . . just what they've always been, was seeing Him." What does she mean? What is the message that is implied in her words?

4. **Description.** The descriptions in this selection are especially vivid and beautiful. They contain words and phrases that appeal to all five senses. Be prepared to identify passages that appeal to each of the five senses.

Developing Vocabulary

Synonyms. The six adjectives listed here are from the selection. Look up each word in the Glossary and write its definition. Then use the word in an interesting sentence of your own. Finally, try to write a synonym, another word with roughly the same meaning.

sacrilegious   renegade   virile
potent   chastising   noncommittal

Developing Writing Skills

Description: Using the Senses in Writing. Describe a holiday memory of your own. Include specific details and colorful language that appeals to the different senses. Your description should be five paragraphs long.

Eulogies for Heroes

Jackie Robinson Said, "Pray for the Whole Team, Ma."

Robert Signer

Somewhere in Brooklyn there's a drab housing project where the winds sweep in off Bedford Av., the soulful sound of Gladys Goodings' "Dodger Symphony" wafts over the streets, and, if you listen carefully, the echoes of cheers and roars still sound.

Ebbets Field it once was, a tiny, miserable ballpark where the fielders couldn't roam, the pitchers got claustrophobia, and the crowds couldn't find seats.

A legend grew there, the legend of a team of heroes, the boys of summer, skillful artisans who could do no wrong—except that they couldn't win the World Series from the hated Yankees.

The legend died in 1957, when the Brooklyn Dodgers, the finest group of bums ever to play baseball, moved west to Los Angeles, and something in the city they left behind died a little, too.

Jackie Robinson didn't go west with the team. He stayed back home in retirement, a ballplayer who once could hit and run and field and drive the fans crazy with the little dance he would do on the base paths.

Try me, he would taunt the pitcher. Just try me. I'll outrun you every time. And he usually did.

Jackie Robinson, who died Tuesday morning in Stamford, Conn., at the age of 53, was the first black man to play major-league baseball.

He broke the ground for the scores of black men who now are the mainstays of every major-league team, the winners of numerous top awards, the unquestioned superstars who draw the fans to the ballparks in record numbers.

It was not easy. There were times when it seemed that Jackie wouldn't make it, not because he didn't have the ability or the inner strength, but because he was fighting a nearly unbroken wall of racial prejudice that permeated the world he was trying to move into.

He was born in Cairo, Ga., and christened Jack Roosevelt Robinson. He was one of four boys and a girl, and they never knew their father. To support the family, his mother took in washing and ironing. Soon afterward, the Robinsons moved to Pasadena, Calif.

Young Jackie played softball on a corner lot with the other members of his childhood group, the Pepper St. gang, and they occasionally earned pocket change by sneaking onto nearby golf courses to retrieve lost balls.

Ma Robinson, a fervent Methodist, kept him in line with stern talks about how to live a proper life. (Once, in later years, when the Dodgers weren't doing so well, Jackie wrote to his mother, "Quit praying just for me alone, Ma, and pray for the whole team.")

His mother told him it was a sin for a 12-year-old to be playing baseball on Sundays while the pews at nearby Preacher Scott's church were empty.

"The devil is sending the people to watch you play, and he's also sending you to play," she told him.

He was a natural athlete, and when he went on later to the University of California at Los Angeles, he gained national notice in football, basketball, and track. He won an All-American honorable mention in football, set a Pacific Coast Conference broad-jump record, and led the league in basketball scoring.

After service in the Army, Robinson made history Oct. 23, 1945—just 27 years ago Monday—when he was signed by the Brooklyn Dodger baseball organization to a contract with their Montreal farm club.

He had first come to the attention of Branch Rickey, the owner and undisputed boss of the Dodgers, through Wendell Smith, now a sportscaster here for WGN-TV. Smith, at that time a columnist for the *Pittsburgh Courier*, a black newspaper, had seen Robinson play for the Kansas City Monarchs, an all-black team.

From the start, Rickey intended to watch Robinson and, if possible, bring him into the major leagues. The time was ending, Rickey believed, when white men and black men could be segregated in American life.

"I need more than a great ballplayer," Rickey told Robinson when he said he was planning to bring him to the Dodgers. "I need a man who can fly the flag for his race, who

can turn the other cheek. If I get a firebrand who blows his top and comes up swinging after a collision at second base, it could set the case back 20 years."

There was no question about Robinson's ability on the baseball field. After watching Jackie in action during spring training of 1946, Clay Hopper, a Mississippian who became Robinson's first minor-league manager, said, "Mr. Rickey, do you think he is human?"

Robinson got a $3,500 bonus and a $600 monthly salary to play with Montreal. By the time he left the Dodgers a decade later, he was one of the big-money boys, earning $42,000 a year and six World Series purses.

He won a minor-league batting title with a .349 average his rookie year in professional ball, earning a chance with the Dodgers. Rickey warned him, "I want a man with guts enough not to fight back."

Robinson broke into the major leagues in 1947. He batted .297, led the league in stolen bases, and kept his mouth shut. The next year, he batted .296 and clearly established himself as the best second baseman and baserunner in the major leagues.

In his third year, Robinson put together enough credentials to take the gag off. He won

the National League batting title with a .342 average and was named most valuable player. He felt he now could speak out, like any other ballplayer.

"I'm a human being," he said. "I have a right to talk, haven't I?"

Most Dodger players, notably shortstop Pee Wee Reese, treated Robinson as one of the boys. Enemy pitchers, quickly learning of his abilities, treated him with respect.

Acceptance quickly set in among the fans and the ballplayers. Robinson could do everything better than most ballplayers. He deserved to be there.

In 1956, the Dodger organization stunned the Brooklyn fans and the baseball world. Robinson, then 37, was traded to the archrival New York Giants. But he wouldn't go. If he couldn't play for Brooklyn, he wouldn't play for anybody. He came up as a Dodger; he would quit as a Dodger. And he did.

With his retirement, an era closed in a sense, although he had opened the way for the others of his race who otherwise might have languished in the black leagues, unheralded legends and forgotten names.

Getting at Meaning

1. What characteristics does Branch Rickey want in the first black man to play in the major leagues? How does Robinson measure up to these qualifications?

2. Why does Jackie Robinson refuse to be traded to the New York Giants?

3. What traits in Jackie Robinson does Robert Signer admire the most? In what ways does Robinson fit your concept of a hero?

Developing Skills in Reading Literature

1. **Eulogy.** A eulogy is a written or spoken tribute that praises a person's virtues or achievements. What prompted the writer to write this selection about Robinson? How does it fit the definition of a eulogy?

2. **Title.** What is the message conveyed by the title of the selection?

Developing Vocabulary

Words from Latin and Greek. When scientists discover a new phenomenon, they may give it a name derived from Greek or Latin. The name often is a combination of two words, one

that describes a general concept and one that adds a specific idea.

For example, the Latin word *phobia* means "fear." Scientists combine different words with *phobia* to identify various specific fears. Thus, *claustro,* which in Latin means "an enclosed place" added to *phobia* becomes *claustrophobia,* which is a fear of confined places.

Examine the following words, which are formed by joining the word *phobia* with words derived from ancient Greek. Be prepared to discuss the meaning of each word.

acrophobia (*acro:* a high point)
xenophobia (*xeno:* a stranger)
necrophobia (*necro:* death)
hydrophobia (*hydro:* water)
agoraphobia (*agora:* market place)

Developing Writing Skills

Supporting an Opinion. Rickey says, "I want a man with guts enough not to fight back." Does it take courage not to fight back? Agree or disagree with Rickey's statement in a well developed paragraph. You may wish to support your opinion with examples drawn from personal experience.

Robert J. Casey Finds Heroism in a Man Nobody Noticed
Robert J. Casey

Hotspot, Southeast England —In the larger matters of threatened invasion by aerial bombs and artillery fire, people have given little thought to Jock Evans, upon whose thin breast nobody will ever pin any medals, even posthumously.[1]

He will never have a public funeral with muffled drums, muted trumpets, and such-like tokens of civic gratitude. It is most unlikely he will ever have any funeral at all.

In the years before the war, he had done nothing to distinguish himself. He had some sort of dock job where the dust hadn't been too good for his lungs. Because of bad eyes and other deficiencies, he had been rejected for military service even at the end of the last war, when medical examiners hadn't been too particular.

In other words, though nobody noticed it at the time, he was made of the stuff heroes are made of.

So far as concerns the elements that have made England to date, he was an architect's model for the spirit of the British Empire.

Evans, to get on with it, was in his most recent career an air raid-precautions warden. In a year's drill on how to put on the gas mask, how to revive fainting women, how to direct people to the nearest shelter, he had never shown more than ordinary aptitude.

Evans was on duty that night. He had been on duty most nights in the last month, as he would be now, with warnings on all the time and never an all-clear. He had phoned to the central control at 11 p.m. that he had seen a bright light somewhere—his superiors, re-membering Jock, suspected it might be somebody with a too-bright cigar.

He had stationed himself near the telephone kiosk near the edge of an outlying suburb, where the artillery shells still land each day when the town is shelled. He had had no occasion to move from his post at midnight when the big crump fell.

The big crump was a dud. For a moment Jock felt glad of that. The shriek of it had been pretty nerve-racking. But after a while, when he remembered that he had better go run over and look at it, he wasn't reassured. It wasn't a dud. He had looked at enough diagrams and sketches to know. It was a time bomb—and a big one.

He told all this to his chief in his report a minute later.

"Where is it?" inquired his chief.

"In the garden," said Jock.

Then the same order:

"Get people out, empty nearby houses, and keep people away!"

"Yes, sir," said Jock.

Maybe it might be as well to mention here something of the nature of a time bomb, especially for Americans, who so far haven't had much experience with such things.

In the first place, it is not like the old-type torpedo with nose fuse that could be unscrewed by a handy man with a monkey wrench. This is more complicated. The timing device is a simple interior arrangement of acid working on metal.

1. **posthumously** (päs′ choo məs lē): coming after death.

By varying the thickness of the metal density, the acid rate of corrosion may be set for anything between one minute and one month. Eventually the acid reaches the fulminating charge, and the neighborhood goes to pieces.

There have been some hints that in what followed after his report, Jock didn't show any great judgment; but the same might have been said of Dewey if he had run into a mine at Manila Bay.[2] He followed out his orders. In less than an hour he had evacuated the few homes in the immediate vicinity. Then he stationed himself to warn off traffic.

There wasn't much to do until about 7 in the morning, when workers and sightseers began to pass afoot, on bicycles and in automobiles.

The odd feature of a community that is being continuously bombed is the inquisitive interest in lethal hazards. Evans suddenly found himself alone in a two-man job. The bomb lay almost at the junction of two lanes, giving access to it from four directions.

Evans solved this problem as best he could. He roped off the street a hundred yards behind the bomb, then took up his post at the middle of the crossing.

Dozens of persons heard and heeded his call during the next two hours. "Time bomb here. Keep away, keep away."

One of those who passed was the priest of the neighborhood Anglican church, to whom is owing the best description of Evans's last stand.

"He hardly needed to point out the bomb," said the padre. "It was lying there in a grass plot right behind him, and it was evident he knew all about it. His face was white and drawn, but there wasn't any tremor in his voice. I couldn't get it out of my head, as he sang out the warning and blew his whistle, that he was the psychological equivalent of the medieval leper, ringing his bell and shouting, 'Unclean! unclean!'"

"I had told him to get away from the corner, block off the streets with ropes. But he said, 'My duty is to stay here. Please go on, sir, don't set a bad example.' I went to telephone for help."

The bomb went off at 9:10, blowing a crater 40 feet wide. No trace has been found of Evans.

---

2. **Dewey . . . Manila Bay:** In 1898, U.S. Admiral George Dewey, in the Spanish-American War, destroyed the Spanish fleet at Manila.

Getting at Meaning

1. Does Jock Evans have an alternative to waiting right beside the bomb? Why does he choose to stay at his post?

2. Describe the character of Jock Evans before his final act.

3. How does the community react to the bomb?

Developing Skills in Reading Literature

1. **Eulogy.** For what qualities does Robert J. Casey praise, or eulogize, Jock Evans? In what ways does Evans fit your concept of a hero?

2. **Understatement.** When recalling a dramatic event, a writer will sometimes choose to describe the event in as few words and with as little emphasis as possible. This literary technique is called understatement. How are the last two sentences in this selection an example of understatement? What effect do these sentences have on you? How is their effect more successful than a long, gory description of the bomb exploding?

Grandmother and the Workmen

Anthony Quinn

Grandmother had been watching the men digging out on the street for five days. At first there had been an army of engineers surveying with their transits and levels. The neighborhood had been excited by the rumor that we would finally get a sewer pipe, which would spell the end of the backyard two-holers.[1]

The men had marked the street with red and yellow chalk marks, put pegs down, and then had disappeared. After two or three months, the only memory of their having been there was that Widow Alonzo's daughter had been jilted by the head engineer.

Then one day three trucks arrived, unloaded men and equipment, and the digging began. Grandmother kept close check on their progress. They dug about a cubic foot and a half per man in one week. According to my grandmother, she dug more than that an hour in the vegetable garden surrounding our privy.

Every night as she prepared our frijoles and mustard greens, she cursed the injustice that we should be starving while those men out in the street were getting the enormous wage of three dollars a day, enough money to feed our family for a month.

One morning she couldn't stand it any longer and went out and accosted the fat foreman.

"I want a job!"

"Doing what, lady?"

"Digging like these men."

"Are you kidding, lady? That's man's work."

"Look, mister, I can lean on a shovel as good as they can. I've been watching them all week. A dog can dig faster."

"Look, you got any complaints, go to City Hall."

"I just want a job. I've got two hungry kids to feed."

"Go and do some sewing or washing."

Feeling challenged, my grandmother pulled a pick from the hands of a stunned workman and began to tear up the street.

The foreman tried to wrest the pick out of her hand, but she threatened him with it.

"I'm going to dig here all day. If you don't think I've earned my money at the end of the day you won't have to pay me."

The foreman shrugged and walked away. All the men, who had gathered around to watch the spectacle, laughed uproariously at her. An hour later, when she was still furiously swinging the pick, the men started to gather off to one side and mutter about going on strike. Meanwhile, various spectators had gathered on the side, cheering.

The men finally went back to their work, at the insistence of the foreman, who seemed to hope the old lady would disappear and that it was all just a bad dream—a nightmare. After a while, the superintendent showed up and was amazed at the sight that greeted him. The foreman rushed up to him and explained. The superintendent looked at the other workers and said, "From what I can see, this is the first time these bums have done any work.

---

1. **two-holer:** an outhouse, also called a privy (priv′ē).

Maybe she's right. Maybe we should let her work."

He walked over to Grandmother and said, "Lady, stop a minute. I want to talk to you."

She went on digging.

"Lady, listen to me. You can't work like a common laborer."

"Why not?"

"I don't know," he said, "but it don't look right. Besides," he smiled, "you're making them all look bad. You're right, they are bums, but this would start a revolution, lady. My business is to get this street done. I don't want to be involved in any crazy revolution by women picking and shoveling like ordinary laborers."

The old lady stopped for a second and considered.

"All you want is this street done, right? I promise you, with me among them, you will get it done in half the time."

"I don't doubt it, lady, but there'd be an awful lot of explaining to do. I beg you to leave the men alone. Look, tell you what I'll do. I understand you've worked three hours already. I'll pay you for the whole day. We'll be around for some time and you can bring the men water. I'll pay you for a full day's work."

For the rest of the month, the men had the best water carrier of their lives. My grandmother took her job very seriously. In the morning she would make ice-cold lemonade for the men working out on the street. Sometimes she would vary it and put in strawberry. No group of pick-and-shovel workers ever drank such nectar as she made. I think they were a little sad when they finished the job and had to move to another neighborhood. But that month my grandmother made a grand total of sixty dollars, which kept us in three square meals a day for a long time.

Getting at Meaning

1. What qualities does the writer admire in his grandmother?

2. Why does the grandmother ask for a job? How does the foreman react? How does she prove her ability to do the job?

3. What is the superintendent's solution to the workers' complaints? How is this a wise solution? What issues are left unresolved by the solution?

Developing Skills in Reading Literature

1. **Eulogy.** What makes the grandmother in this selection a heroic figure? What would the children who witnessed the event learn from her?

2. **Irony.** What are some of the ironies of the situation the writer describes?

Developing Vocabulary

Word Origins: Slang and Colloquial Expressions. The word *colloquial* means "appropriate to common, everyday speech." In this selection, for example, the foreman uses the colloquial expression "they are bums." Special dictionaries give the origins of slang and colloquial expressions. Find a dictionary of American slang or colloquial speech in a library, and try to discover the origins of the following italicized expressions:

1. He really put me *on the spot*.
2. She is such a *nut*.
3. Is he *on the level*?
4. He's *loco*.
5. This radio is *on the fritz* again.
6. My dad really *blew his stack* last night.

The Washwoman

Isaac Bashevis Singer

Our home had little contact with Gentiles.[1] The only Gentile in the building was the janitor. Fridays he would come for a tip, his "Friday money." He remained standing at the door, took off his hat, and my mother gave him six groschen.[2]

Besides the janitor, there were also the Gentile washwomen who came to fetch our laundry. My story is about one of these.

She was a small woman, old and wrinkled. When she started washing for us, she was already past seventy. Most Jewish women of her age were sickly, weak, broken in body. All the old women in our street had bent backs and leaned on sticks when they walked. But this washwoman, small and thin as she was, possessed a strength that came from generations of peasant forbears. Mother would

count out to her a bundle of laundry that had accumulated over several weeks. She would lift the unwieldy pack, load it on her narrow shoulders, and carry it the long way home. She lived on Krochmalna Street too, but at the other end, near the Wola section. It must have been a walk of an hour and a half.

She would bring the laundry back about two weeks later. My mother had never been so pleased with any washwoman. Every piece of linen sparkled like polished silver. Every piece was neatly ironed. Yet she charged no more than the others. She was a real find. Mother always had her money ready, because it was too far for the old woman to come a second time.

Laundering was not easy in those days. The old woman had no faucet where she lived but had to bring in the water from a pump. For the linens to come out so clean, they had to be scrubbed thoroughly in a washtub, rinsed with washing soda, soaked, boiled in an enormous pot, starched, then ironed. Every piece was handled ten times or more. And the drying! It could not be done outside because thieves would steal the laundry. The wrung-out wash had to be carried up to the attic and hung on clotheslines. In the winter it would become as brittle as glass and almost break when touched. And there was always a to-do with other housewives and washwomen who wanted the attic clotheslines for their own use. Only God knows all the old woman had to endure each time she did a wash!

---

1. **Gentile** (jen′ tīl): a person who is not a Jew.
2. **groschen** (grō shən): a coin used in Poland.

She could have begged at the church door or entered a home for the penniless and aged. But there was in her a certain pride and love of labor with which many Gentiles have been blessed. The old woman did not want to become a burden, and so she bore her burden.

My mother spoke a little Polish, and the old woman would talk with her about many things. She was especially fond of me and used to say I looked like Jesus. She repeated this every time she came, and Mother would frown and whisper to herself, her lips barely moving, "May her words be scattered in the wilderness."

The woman had a son who was rich. I no longer remember what sort of business he had. He was ashamed of his mother, the washwoman, and never came to see her. Nor did he ever give her a groschen. The old woman told this without rancor. One day the son was married. It seemed that he had made a good match. The wedding took place in a church. The son had not invited the old mother to his wedding, but she went to the church and waited at the steps to see her son lead the "young lady" to the altar.

The story of the faithless son left a deep impression on my mother. She talked about it for weeks and months. It was an affront not only to the old woman but to the entire institution of motherhood. Mother would argue, "Nu, does it pay to make sacrifices for children? The mother uses up her last strength, and he does not even know the meaning of loyalty."

And she would drop hints to the effect that she was not certain of her own children: Who knows what they would do some day? This, however, did not prevent her from dedicating her life to us. If there was any delicacy in the house, she would put it aside for the children and invent all sorts of excuses and reasons why she herself did not want to taste it. She knew charms that went back to ancient times, and she used expressions she had inherited

from generations of devoted mothers and grandmothers. If one of the children complained, she would say, "May I be your ransom and may you outlive my bones!" Or she would say, "May I be the atonement for the least of your fingernails." When we ate, she used to say, "Health and marrow in your bones!" The day before the new moon she gave us a kind of candy that was said to prevent parasitic worms. If one of us had something in his eye, Mother would lick the eye clean with her tongue. She also fed us rock candy against coughs, and from time to time she would take us to be blessed against the evil eye. This did not prevent her from studying *The Duties of the Heart, The Book of the Covenant,* and other serious philosophic works.

But to return to the washwoman. That winter was a harsh one. The streets were in the grip of a bitter cold. No matter how much we heated our stove, the windows were covered with frostwork and decorated with icicles. The newspapers reported that people were dying of the cold. Coal became dear. The winter had become so severe that parents stopped sending children to cheder,[3] and even the Polish schools were closed.

On one such day the washwoman, now nearly eighty years old, came to our house. A good deal of laundry had accumulated during the past weeks. Mother gave her a pot of tea to warm herself, as well as some bread. The old woman sat on a kitchen chair trembling and shaking, and warmed her hands against the teapot. Her fingers were gnarled from work, and perhaps from arthritis too. Her fingernails were strangely white. These hands spoke of the stubbornness of mankind, of the will to work not only as one's strength permits but beyond the limits of one's power. Mother counted and wrote down the list: men's undershirts, women's vests, long-legged drawers, bloomers, petticoats, shifts, featherbed covers, pillowcases, sheets, and the men's fringed garments. Yes, the Gentile woman washed these holy garments as well.

The bundle was big, bigger than usual. When the woman placed it on her shoulders, it covered her completely. At first she swayed, as though she were about to fall under the load. But an inner obstinacy seemed to call out: No, you may not fall. A donkey may permit himself to fall under his burden, but not a human being, the crown of creation.

It was fearful to watch the old woman staggering out with the enormous pack, out into the frost, where the snow was dry as salt, and the air was filled with dusty white whirlwinds like goblins dancing in the cold. Would the old woman ever reach Wola?

She disappeared, and Mother sighed and prayed for her.

Usually the woman brought back the wash after two or, at the most, three weeks. But three weeks passed, then four and five, and nothing was heard of the old woman. We remained without linens. The cold had become even more intense. The telephone wires were now as thick as ropes. The branches of the trees looked like glass. So much snow had fallen that the streets had become uneven, and sleds were able to glide down many streets as on the slopes of a hill. Kind-hearted people lit fires in the streets for vagrants to warm themselves and roast potatoes in, if they had any to roast.

For us the washwoman's absence was a catastrophe. We needed the laundry. We did not even know the woman's address. It seemed certain that she had collapsed, died. Mother declared she had had a premonition, as the old woman left our house that last time, that we would never see our things again. She found some old torn shirts and washed and mended them. We mourned, both for the laundry and for the old, toil-worn woman who had grown close to us through the years she had served us so faithfully.

More than two months passed. The frost had subsided, and then a new frost had come, a new wave of cold. One evening, while Mother was sitting near the kerosene lamp

---

3. **chedar** (khā' dər): a Jewish religious school.

mending a shirt, the door opened and a small puff of steam, followed by a gigantic bundle, entered. Under the bundle tottered the old woman, her face as white as a linen sheet. A few wisps of white hair straggled out from beneath her shawl. Mother uttered a half-choked cry. It was as though a corpse had entered the room. I ran toward the old woman and helped her unload her pack. She was even thinner now, more bent. Her face had become more gaunt, and her head shook from side to side as though she were saying no. She could not utter a clear word, but mumbled something with her sunken mouth and pale lips.

After the old woman had recovered somewhat, she told us that she had been very ill, very ill. Just what her illness was, I cannot remember. She had been so sick that someone had called a doctor, and the doctor had sent for a priest. Someone had informed the son, and he had contributed money for a coffin and for the funeral. But the Almighty had not yet wanted to take this pain-racked soul to Himself. She began to feel better, she became well, and as soon as she was able to stand on her feet once more, she resumed her washing. Not just ours, but the wash of several other families too.

"I could not rest easy in my bed because of the wash," the old woman explained. "The wash would not let me die."

"With the help of God you will live to be a hundred and twenty," said my mother, as a benediction.

"God forbid! What good would such a long life be? The work becomes harder and harder . . . my strength is leaving me . . . I do not want to be a burden on anyone!" The old woman muttered and crossed herself, and raised her eyes toward heaven.

Fortunately there was some money in the house, and Mother counted out what she owed. I had a strange feeling: the coins in the old woman's washed-out hands seemed to become as worn and clean and pious as she herself was. She blew on the coins and tied them in a kerchief. Then she left, promising to return in a few weeks for a new load of wash.

But she never came back. The wash she had returned was her last effort on this earth. She had been driven by an indomitable will to return the property to its rightful owners, to fulfill the task she had undertaken.

And now at last her body, which had long been no more than a shard supported only by the force of honesty and duty, had fallen. Her soul passed into those spheres where all holy souls meet, regardless of the roles they played on this earth, in whatever tongue, of whatever creed. I cannot imagine paradise without this Gentile washwoman. I cannot even conceive of a world where there is no recompense for such effort.

Getting at Meaning

1. Describe some of the hardships the wash-woman faces. What steps are involved in washing clothes? Why does Singer include the lengthy description of laundering in the days of his youth?

2. Describe the Singer home. What evidence is there that his family is not wealthy?

3. What insights does the writer provide into the character of his mother? How does she treat her children?

4. What keeps the washwoman alive and working?

5. What does the writer mean when he says, "I cannot imagine paradise without this Gentile washwoman. I cannot even conceive of a world where there is no recompense for such effort"?

Developing Skills in Reading Literature

1. **Nonfiction.** Nonfiction enables readers to become acquainted with customs and traditions that are not their own. What does the reader learn from this selection about the life of a Jewish family in Poland? How does Singer re-create a feeling for this way of life?

2. **Character.** Singer writes, "The old woman did not want to become a burden, and so she bore her burden." What is he saying about the washwoman's values? How does the story of her son affect your picture of her? What new understanding do you gain from the final scene in which the washwoman returns the laundry? In what ways does the washwoman fit your concept of a hero?

3. **Symbol.** As the story progresses, the woman's pack becomes heavier and more difficult to carry, until, at the end, she can barely lift it. What does the pack symbolize?

Developing Vocabulary

Inferring Word Meaning. Read each pair of sentences, and try to figure out the meaning of the word in italics. Write a possible definition for the word. After you have done this for each pair of sentences, look up the words in the Glossary, and write their correct definition. Then use the words in sentences of your own.

1. "Nor did he ever give her a groschen. The old woman told this without *rancor*."

2. "The story of the faithless son left a deep impression on my mother. . . . It was an *affront* not only to the old woman but to the entire institution of motherhood."

3. "At first she swayed, as though she were about to fall under the load. But an inner *obstinacy* seemed to call out: No, you may not fall."

4. "For us the washwoman's absence was a *catastrophe*. We needed the laundry."

5. "It seemed certain that she had collapsed, died. Mother declared she had had a *premonition,* as the old woman left our house that last time, that we would never see our things again."

6. "The wash she had returned was her last effort on this earth. She had been driven by an *indomitable* will to return the property to its rightful owners, to fulfill the task she had undertaken."

Developing Writing Skills

1. **Writing a Eulogy.** Write a eulogy praising a person for heroic or admirable behavior. Describe at least one incident in which the person acts in a heroic or admirable fashion.

2. **Explaining a Process.** The writer of this selection explains in detail the process of doing laundry. Choose a familiar household chore and, in one or two paragraphs, explain the process of completing the chore from beginning to end. Include details about the equipment used and the difficulties generally encountered.

The Humorous Essay

SPLIT-BODY MASK, 1890. *Cayuga Indian.*
Museum of the American Indian.

Beds   *Shirley Jackson*

We are all of us, in our family, very fond of puzzles. I do Double-Crostics and read mystery stories, my husband does baseball box scores and figures out batting averages, our son Laurie is addicted to the kind of puzzle that begins, "There are fifty-four items in this picture beginning with the letter C," our older daughter Jannie does children's jigsaws, and Sally, the baby, can put together an intricate little arrangement of rings and bars that has had the rest of us stopped for two months. We are none of us, however, capable of solving the puzzles we work up for ourselves in the oddly diffuse patterns of our several lives (who is, now I think of it?); and along with such family brainteasers as, "Why is there a pair of roller skates in Mommy's desk?" and, "What is *really* in the back of Laurie's closet?" and, "Why doesn't Daddy wear the nice shirts Jannie picked out for Father's Day?" we are all of us still wondering nervously about what might be called The Great Grippe[1] Mystery. As a matter of fact, I should be extremely grateful if anyone could solve it for us, because we are certainly very short of blankets, and it's annoying not to have *any* kind of answer. Here, in rough outline, is our puzzle:

Our house is, as I have said, large, and the second floor has four bedrooms and a bathroom, all opening out onto a long narrow hall which we have made even narrower by lining it with bookcases so that every inch of hall which is not doorway is books. As is the case with most houses, both the front door and the back door are downstairs on the first floor. The front bedroom, which is my husband's and mine, is the largest and lightest, and has a double bed. The room next down the hall belongs to the girls, and contains a crib and a single, short bed. Laurie's room, across the hall, has a double-decker bed and he sleeps on the top half. The guest room, at the end of the hall, has a double bed. The double bed in our room is made up with white sheets and cases, the baby's crib has pink linen, and Jannie's bed has yellow. Laurie's bed has green linen, and the guest room has blue. The bottom half of Laurie's bed is never made up, unless company is going to use it immediately, because the dog traditionally spends a large part of his time there and regards it as his bed. There is no bed table on the distaff side of the double bed in our room. One side of the bed in the guest room is pushed against the wall. No one can fit into the baby's crib except the baby; the ladder to the top half of Laurie's double-decker is very shaky and stands in a corner of the room; the children reach the top half of the bed by climbing up over the footboard. All three of the children are accustomed to having a glass of apple juice, to which they are addicted, by their bedsides at night. Laurie uses a green glass, Jannie uses a red glass, Sally uses one of those little flowered cheese glasses, and my husband uses an aluminum tumbler because he has broken so many ordinary glasses trying to find them in the dark.

---

1. **grippe** (grip): influenza, or flu.

I do not take cough drops or cough medicine in any form.

The baby customarily sleeps with half a dozen cloth books, an armless doll, and a small cardboard suitcase that holds the remnants of half a dozen decks of cards. Jannie is very partial to a pink baby blanket, which has shrunk from many washings. The girls' room is very warm, the guest room moderately so; our room is chilly, and Laurie's room is quite cold. We are all of us, including the dog, notoriously easy and heavy sleepers; my husband never eats coffee cake.

My husband caught the grippe first, on a Friday, and snarled and shivered and complained until I prevailed upon him to go to bed. By Friday night both Laurie and Sally were feverish, and on Saturday Jannie and I began to cough and sniffle. In our family we take ill in different manners; my husband is extremely annoyed at the whole procedure and is convinced that his being sick is somebody's fault, Laurie tends to become a little light-headed and strews handkerchiefs around his room, Jannie coughs and coughs and coughs, Sally turns bright red, and I suffer in stoical silence, so long as everyone knows clearly that I am sick. We are each of us privately convinced that our own ailment is far more severe than anyone else's. At any rate, on Saturday night I put all the children into their beds, gave each of them half an aspirin and the usual fruit juice, covered them warmly, and then settled my husband down for the night with his tumbler of water and his cigarettes and matches and ashtray; he had decided to sleep in the guest room because it was warmer. At about ten o'clock I checked to see that all the children were covered and asleep and that Toby was in his place on the bottom half of the double-decker. I then took two aspirin tablets and went to sleep in my own bed in my own room. Because my husband was in the guest room, I slept on his side of the bed, next to the bed

table. I put my cigarettes and matches on the end table next to the ashtray, along with a small glass of herb tea, which I find more efficacious than cough medicine.

I woke up some time later to find Jannie standing beside the bed. "Can't sleep," she said. "Want to come in *your* bed."

"Come along," I said. "Bring your own pillow."

She went and got her pillow and her small pink blanket and her glass of fruit juice, which she put on the floor next to the bed, since she had got the side without any end table. She put her pillow down, rolled herself in her pink blanket, and fell asleep. I went back to sleep, but sometime later Sally came in, asking sleepily, "Where's Jannie?"

"She's here," I said. "Are you coming in bed with us?"

"Yes," said Sally.

"Go and get your pillow, then," I said.

She returned with her pillow, her books, her doll, her suitcase, and her fruit juice, which she put on the floor next to Jannie's. Then she crowded in comfortably next to Jannie and fell asleep. Eventually the pressure of the two of them began to force me uneasily toward the edge of the bed, so I rolled out wearily, took my pillow and my small glass of tea and my cigarettes and matches and my ashtray and went into the guest room, where my husband was asleep. I pushed at him and he snarled, but he finally moved over to the side next to the wall, and I put my cigarettes and matches and my tea and my ashtray on the end table next to *his* cigarettes and matches and ashtray and tumbler of water and put my pillow on the bed and fell asleep. Shortly after this he woke me and asked me to let him get out of the bed, since it was too hot in that room to sleep and he was going back to his own bed. He took his pillow and his cigarettes and matches and his ashtray and his aluminum glass of water and went padding off down the hall. In a few minutes Laurie came into the guest room where I had just fallen asleep again; he was carrying his pillow and his glass of fruit juice. "Too cold in my room," he said, and I moved out of the way and let him get into the bed on the side next to the wall. After a few minutes the dog came in, whining nervously, and came up onto the bed and curled himself up around Laurie and I had to get out or be smothered. I gathered together what of my possessions I could, and made my way into my own room, where my husband was asleep with Jannie on one side and the baby on the other. Jannie woke up when I came in and said, "Own bed," so I helped her carry her pillow and her fruit juice and her pink blanket back to her own bed.

The minute Jannie got out of our bed the baby rolled over and turned sideways, so there was no room for me. I could not get into the crib and I could not climb into the top half of the double-decker, so since the dog was in the guest room, I went and took the blanket off the crib and got into the bottom half of the double-decker, setting my tea and my cigarettes and matches and my ashtray on the floor next to the bed. Shortly after that Jannie, who apparently felt left out, came in with her pillow and her pink blanket and her fruit juice and got up into the top half of the double-decker, leaving her fruit juice on the floor next to my tea.

At about six in the morning the dog wanted to get out, or else he wanted his bed back, because he came and stood next to me and howled. I got up and went downstairs, sneezing, and let him out, and then decided that since it had been so cold anyway in the bottom half of the double-decker, I might as well stay downstairs and heat up some coffee and have that much warmth, at least. While I was waiting for the coffee to heat, Jannie came to the top of the stairs and asked if I would bring *her* something hot, and I heard Laurie stirring in the guest room, so I heated

some milk and put it into a jug and decided that while I was at it I might just as well give everybody something hot so I set out enough cups for everyone and brought out a coffee cake and put it on the tray and added some onion rolls for my husband, who does not eat coffee cake. When I brought the tray upstairs, Laurie and Jannie were both in the guest room, giggling, so I set the tray down in there and heard Sally talking from our room in the front. I went to get her, and she was sitting up in bed talking to her father, who was only very slightly awake. "Play card?" she was asking brightly, and she opened her suitcase and dealt him, onto the pillow next to his nose, four diamonds to the ace jack and the seven of clubs.

I asked my husband if he would like some coffee, and he said it was terribly cold. I suggested that he come down into the guest room, where it was warmer. He and the baby followed me down to the guest room, and my husband and Laurie got into the bed and the rest of us sat on the foot of the bed and I poured the coffee and the hot milk and gave the children coffee cake and my husband the onion rolls. Jannie decided to take her milk and coffee cake back into her own bed, and since she had mislaid her pillow she took one from the guest room bed. Sally of course followed her, going first back into our room to pick up *her* pillow. My husband fell asleep again while I was pouring his coffee, and Laurie set his hot milk precariously on the headboard of the bed and asked me to get his pillow from wherever it was, so I went into the double-decker and got him the pillow from the top, which turned out to be Jannie's, and her pink blanket was with it. I took my coffee cake and my coffee into my own bed and had just settled down when Laurie came in to say cloudily that Daddy had kicked him out of bed and could he stay in here. I said of course and he said he would get a pillow and he came back in a minute with the one from the bottom half of the double-decker which was mine. He went to sleep right away, and then the baby came in to get her books and her suitcase and decided to stay with her milk and her coffee cake, so I left and went into the guest room and made my husband move over and sat *there* and had my coffee. Meanwhile Jannie had moved into the top half of the double-decker, looking for her pillow, and had taken instead the pillow from Sally's bed and my glass of tea and had settled down there to listen to Laurie's radio. I went downstairs to let the dog in, and he came upstairs and got into his bed on the

bottom half of the double-decker, and while I was gone my husband had moved back over onto the accessible side of the guest room bed so I went into Jannie's bed, which is rather too short, and I brought a pillow from the guest room, and my coffee.

At about nine o'clock the Sunday papers came, and I went down to get them, and at about nine-thirty everyone woke up. My husband had moved back into his own bed when Laurie and Sally vacated it for their own beds, Laurie driving Jannie into the guest room when he took back the top half of the double-decker, and my husband woke up at nine-

thirty and found himself wrapped in Jannie's pink blanket, sleeping on Laurie's green pillow and with a piece of coffee cake and Sally's fruit juice glass, not to mention the four diamonds to the ace jack and the seven of clubs. Laurie, in the top half of the double-decker, had my glass of tea and my cigarettes and matches and the baby's pink pillow. The dog had my white pillow and my ashtray. Jannie in the guest room had one white pillow and one blue pillow and two glasses of fruit juice and my husband's cigarettes and matches and ashtray and Laurie's hot milk, besides her own hot milk and coffee cake and her father's onion rolls. The baby in her crib had her father's aluminum tumbler of water and her suitcase and books and doll and a blue pillow from the guest room, but no blanket.

The puzzle is, of course, what became of the blanket from Sally's bed? I took it off her crib and put it on the bottom half of the double-decker, but the dog did not have it when he woke up, and neither did any of the other beds. It was a blue-patterned patchwork quilt, and has not been seen since, and I would most particularly like to know where it got to. As I say, we are very short of blankets.

Getting at Meaning

1. How much time passes from the beginning to the end of this selection?

2. How are the family members characterized? Choose one character and list all the things associated with that character.

3. Why is it important that the family members are "notoriously easy and heavy sleepers"? that they are all ill on this particular night?

Developing Skills in Reading Literature

1. **Essay.** An essay is a literary form in which a writer presents factual information from his or her point of view. The writer's purpose is either to instruct or to entertain the reader. How does the writer of "Beds" present factual material? What is her purpose in writing this essay?

2. **Tone.** Tone is a writer's attitude toward a subject. The first four paragraphs of this essay establish the tone. What information is given in these paragraphs? What do the paragraphs emphasize? Are the facts in the paragraphs presented in an orderly or random fashion? What tone emerges from this presentation?

3. **Humor.** What makes the presentation of facts in this essay funny? Reread the last two paragraphs. How do these paragraphs contribute to the humor of the essay?

4. **Narrator.** Why is it important that the mother is telling this story? What picture of family life emerges from her narrative?

Developing Vocabulary

Suffixes. A suffix, or syllable added to the end of a root word, often changes a word from one part of speech to another. For example, the suffix -ment changes a word from a verb to a noun.

Copy the following nouns. Look up each word in a dictionary, and write its definition next to the word. Be prepared to identify and to define the verbs from which the nouns are derived.

resentment   commencement
inducement   commitment
management

The Night the Bed Fell   *James Thurber*

I suppose that the high-water mark of my youth in Columbus, Ohio, was the night the bed fell on my father. It makes a better recitation (unless, as some friends of mine have said, one has heard it five or six times) than it does a piece of writing, for it is almost necessary to throw furniture around, shake doors, and bark like a dog, to lend the proper atmosphere and verisimilitude to what is admittedly a somewhat incredible tale. Still, it did take place.

It happened, then, that my father had decided to sleep in the attic one night, to be away where he could think. My mother opposed the notion strongly because, she said, the old wooden bed up there was unsafe; it was wobbly, and the heavy headboard would crash down on father's head in case the bed fell, and kill him. There was no dissuading him, however, and at a quarter past ten he closed the attic door behind him and went up the narrow twisting stairs. We later heard ominous creakings as he crawled into bed. Grandfather, who usually slept in the attic bed when he was with us, had disappeared some days before. (On these occasions he was usually gone six or eight days and returned growling and out of temper, with the news that the federal Union was run by a passel of blockheads and that the Army of the Potomac[1] didn't have any more chance than a fiddler's dog.)

We had visiting us at this time a nervous first cousin of mine named Briggs Beall, who believed that he was likely to cease breathing when he was asleep. It was his feeling that if he were not awakened every hour during the night, he might die of suffocation. He had been accustomed to setting an alarm clock to ring at intervals until morning, but I persuaded him to abandon this. He slept in my room, and I told him that I was such a light sleeper that if anybody quit breathing in the same room with me, I would wake instantly. He tested me the first night—which I had suspected he would—by holding his breath after my regular breathing had convinced him I was asleep. I was not asleep, however, and called to him. This seemed to allay his fears a little, but he took the precaution of putting a glass of spirits of camphor on a little table at the head of his bed. In case I didn't arouse him until he was almost gone, he said, he would sniff the camphor, a powerful reviver. Briggs was not the only member of his family who had his crotchets. Old Aunt Melissa Beall (who could whistle like a man, with two fingers in her mouth) suffered under the premonition that she was destined to die on South High Street, because she had been born on South High Street and married on South High Street. Then there was Aunt Sarah Shoaf, who never went to bed at night without the fear that a burglar was going to get in and blow chloroform under her door through a tube. To avert this calamity—for she was in greater dread of anesthetics than of losing her household goods—she always piled her money, silverware, and other valuables in a neat stack just outside her bedroom, with a note reading, "This is all I

---

1. **Union . . . Army of the Potomac:** references to the army of the North during the Civil War.

have. Please take it and do not use your chloroform, as this is all I have." Aunt Gracie Shoaf also had a burglar phobia, but she met it with more fortitude. She was confident that burglars had been getting into her house every night for forty years. The fact that she never missed anything was to her no proof to the contrary. She always claimed that she scared them off before they could take anything, by throwing shoes down the hallway. When she went to bed she piled, where she could get at them handily, all the shoes there were about her house. Five minutes after she had turned off the light, she would sit up in bed and say "Hark!" Her husband, who had learned to ignore the whole situation as long ago as 1903, would either be sound asleep or pretend to be sound asleep. In either case he would not respond to her tugging and pulling, so that presently she would arise, tiptoe to the door, open it slightly and heave a shoe down the hall in one direction, and its mate down the hall in the other direction. Some nights

she threw them all, some nights only a couple of pairs.

But I am straying from the remarkable incidents that took place during the night that the bed fell on father. By midnight we were all in bed. The layout of the rooms and the disposition of their occupants is important to an understanding of what later occurred. In the front room upstairs (just under father's attic bedroom) were my mother and my brother Herman, who sometimes sang in his sleep, usually "Marching Through Georgia" or "Onward, Christian Soldiers." Briggs Beall and myself were in a room adjoining this one. My brother Roy was in a room across the hall from ours. Our bull terrier, Rex, slept in the hall.

My bed was an army cot, one of those affairs that are made wide enough to sleep on comfortably only by putting up, flat with the middle section, the two sides which ordinarily hang down like the sideboards of a drop-leaf table. When these sides are up, it is perilous to roll too far toward the edge, for then the cot is likely to tip completely over, bringing the whole bed down on top of one, with a tremendous banging crash. This, in fact, is precisely what happened, about two o'clock in the morning. (It was my mother who, in recalling the scene later, first referred to it as "the night the bed fell on your father.")

Always a deep sleeper, slow to arouse (I had lied to Briggs), I was at first unconscious of what had happened when the iron cot rolled me onto the floor and toppled over on me. It left me still warmly bundled up and unhurt, for the bed rested above me like a canopy. Hence I did not wake up, only reached the edge of consciousness and went back. The racket, however, instantly awakened my mother, in the next room, who came to the immediate conclusion that her worst dread was realized: the big wooden bed upstairs had fallen on father. She therefore screamed,

"Let's go to your poor father!" It was this shout, rather than the noise of my cot falling, that awakened Herman, in the same room with her. He thought that mother had become, for no apparent reason, hysterical. "You're all right, Mamma!" he shouted, trying to calm her. They exchanged shout for shout for perhaps ten seconds: "Let's go to your poor father!" and "You're all right!" That woke up Briggs. By this time I was conscious of what was going on, in a vague way, but did not yet realize that I was under my bed instead of on it. Briggs, awakening in the midst of loud shouts of fear and apprehension, came to the quick conclusion that he was suffocating and that we were all trying to "bring him out." With a low moan, he grasped the glass of camphor at the head of his bed and instead of sniffing it, poured it over himself. The room reeked of camphor. "Ugf, ahfg," choked Briggs, like a drowning man, for he had almost succeeded in stopping his breath under the deluge of pungent spirits. He leaped out of bed and groped toward the open window, but he came up against one that was closed. With his hand, he beat out the glass, and I could hear it crash and tinkle on the alleyway below. It was at this juncture that I, in trying to get up, had the uncanny sensation of feeling my bed above me! Foggy with sleep, I now suspected, in my turn, that the whole uproar was being made in a frantic endeavor to extricate me from what must be an unheard-of and perilous situation. "Get me out of this!" I bawled. "Get me out!" I think I had the nightmarish belief that I was entombed in a mine. "Gugh," gasped Briggs, floundering in his camphor.

By this time my mother, still shouting, pursued by Herman, still shouting, was trying to open the door to the attic, in order to go up and get my father's body out of the wreckage. The door was stuck, however, and wouldn't yield. Her frantic pulls on it only added to the general banging and confusion. Roy and the dog were now up, the one shouting questions, the other barking.

Father, farthest away and soundest sleeper of all, had by this time been awakened by the battering on the attic door. He decided that the house was on fire. "I'm coming, I'm coming!" he wailed in a slow, sleepy voice—it took him many minutes to regain full consciousness. My mother, still believing he was caught under the bed, detected in his "I'm coming!" the mournful, resigned note of one who is preparing to meet his Maker. "He's dying!" she shouted.

"I'm all right!" Briggs yelled to reassure her. "I'm all right!" He still believed that it was his own closeness to death that was worrying mother. I found at last the light switch in my room, unlocked the door, and Briggs and I joined the others at the attic door. The dog, who never did like Briggs, jumped for him— assuming that he was the culprit in whatever was going on—and Roy had to throw Rex and hold him. We could hear father crawling out of bed upstairs. Roy pulled the attic door open, with a mighty jerk, and father came down the stairs, sleepy and irritable but safe and sound. My mother began to weep when she saw him. Rex began to howl. "What in the name of God is going on here?" asked father.

The situation was finally put together like a gigantic jig-saw puzzle. Father caught a cold from prowling around in his bare feet, but there were no other bad results. "I'm glad," said mother, who always looked on the bright side of things, "that your grandfather wasn't here."

Getting at Meaning

1. James Thurber says that this story "makes a better recitation . . . than it does a piece of writing." What kinds of sounds and actions might he use if he were telling the story aloud?

2. The writer talks about several members of his family who have rather odd habits. Describe two of these strange relatives.

3. What starts the confusion on "the night the bed fell"? What misunderstandings add to the confusion? How does the writer's mother contribute to the confusion?

Developing Skills in Reading Literature

1. **Humor.** What ironies create humor in this story? Why does the writer refer to the incident as "the night the bed fell on my father"? What are other sources of humor in the essay?

2. **Sequence.** Sequence is the order or arrangement of events in a selection. In this essay, each event sets off another. Beginning with the cot's falling, briefly list the sequence of events.

3. **Tone.** What is the writer's attitude toward his family and the events of the night described in the essay?

Developing Vocabulary

Suffixes. The suffix -*tion* often changes a verb into a noun. For example, *recitation*, used in the first paragraph of the story, is the noun form of the verb *recite*.

On a sheet of paper write the noun forms of the following verbs along with their meanings. You may need to check the spellings of these words in a dictionary.

suffocate   dictate   locate   recollect
dispose   import   saturate

Sleeping Arrangements   *Sam Levenson*

It is not good for man to be alone," Papa used to say, quoting from the *Poor Man's Almanac of Rationalizations*[1]—so we slept in various sets: four in a bed (the group plan); three in a bed (semiprivate, unless one of the three had a contagious disease, in which case he was allowed to sleep with only one, preferably one who had never had the disease); two in a bed (doubleheader); and one in a bed (critical list). Hopeless cases slept in Mama's bed. Chairs and floors also served as beds. Floors were preferred because you could not fall off.

In order to insure a reasonable amount of air not already filtered through our bed partner's adenoids, we slept not tête-à-tête[2] but foot-à-tête—cross-ventilation we called it—an arrangement that made it impossible to cough into a brother's face; we could cough only into his feet.

There were other sleeping patterns such as crisscross, ticktacktoe, checkerboard, pyramids, and shambles. A sudden sneeze by the kid in the middle of any of these configurations could trigger a chain reaction that sent kids flying in all directions.

The procedure of getting bedded down for the night often started with the shock treatment. Just before bedtime Mama would reel in the clothesline, remove several sheets of ice that earlier in the day had been sheets of linen, put them on your bed and say, "Go to bed." Those were the nights when nobody fought to be first in bed. Mama would reduce the intensity of the shock by placing a hot stove lid wrapped in a towel at your feet. I still carry the name of the stove manufacturer branded on my left arch.

Some people brag that they sleep like a rock. I slept *on* one. Mama's pillows were about the size of a home movie screen and were as hard as bags of cement. You slept with your head propped up as though you were lying in state.[3] Years later, as we got married, Mama made each of us a present of a set of pillows extracted from the mother pillow. Still, no matter how much stuffing Mama pulled out of the original, it never got softer.

For most people, sound sleep implies quiet. We slept through the sounds of a world that never slept. Our nervous systems were geared to noise. Silence would have shocked us. We slept through the din of fire engines, trolleys, trucks, trains, slamming doors, barking dogs, and wailing cats. Within our own walls plumbing hummed, faucets chirped, bedsprings twanged, stoves hissed, mattresses groaned, floors creaked, windows banged, and the window shades wildly applauded all the performances.

While there was room for all to sleep, quilts were at a premium, as were brothers with warm feet. The latter sold high on the open market. Deals for quilts were made before

---

1. ***Poor Man's Almanac of Rationalizations:*** an imaginary title, meaning a common man's book of excuses, used here for humorous effect.
2. **tête-à-tête** (tāt' ə tāt'): head to head.
3. **lying in state:** displaying the body of an important person before burial.

bedtime. We called it the Cover Charge. "Hey, Al! If you let me have the heavy quilt tonight I'll give you my searchlight for lend for two days." The heavy quilt was not warm, just heavy, but therein lay its merit. It didn't slide off the bed. It rested there like a mound of earth on a fresh grave, and we slept the sleep of the just. That quilt could cover three of us, if one of us were not my brother Mike, who was not just a restless sleeper—he was a night crawler. He would start moving across the bed on a forty-five degree angle from the footboard to the headboard, instinctively dragging the quilt along his route. We held on for dear life and he dragged us, quilt and all, wherever he was going. The tug-of-war lasted until we all fell asleep from sheer exhaustion.

Papa's heavy coat was a prize. He had brought it from the old, cold country and it was lined with fur. We would slip our feet through the sleeves, button ourselves into the hairy straitjacket and hibernate for one winter's night at a time.

The coldest room in the house was the front room. To get any warmth into it, you would have had to open the windows. Mama used to keep her marinated fish there. In order to survive the night in that room, you wore a sweater under your undershirt, and long woolen socks. But Mother Nature, not nearly so kind as our own mother, had a way of taunting us on extra-cold nights. Just when you were nice and warm, the call came. You tried to throw her off your track by concentrating on deserts, droughts, sand dunes, or petrified forests—all to no avail.

"Hey, Al. Come with me. It's dark." It was not the dark alone I was afraid of. There was the ghoulish red face of the hot coal stove and, even more frightening, the phosphorescent glow of Mama's teeth in a glass in the kitchen.

Al wouldn't come. "Not me, buddy."

"I'll give you my searchlight for lend for *three* days."

"Make it a week."

"OK. If you throw in the heavy quilt."

"It's a deal."

Together we made the trip to the toilet, dragging the bartered quilt after us lest some older brother roll up in it and claim seniority rights.

Getting at Meaning

1. Describe the different sleeping patterns in the writer's house. What other physical hardships do the sleepers face besides crowded beds?

2. Describe some of the "deals" the brothers engage in to make their sleep more comfortable.

Developing Skills in Reading Literature

1. **Tone and Mood.** Tone, as you know, is the writer's attitude toward a subject. Mood is the feeling experienced by the reader. How does the writer feel about the experiences described in this essay? Do you think the writer regrets these experiences? What feeling do you get about the experiences as you read?

2. **Hyperbole.** A major source of humor in this essay is exaggeration, an enlarging of the truth to make situations seem more important or more extreme than they really are. When exaggeration is used as a literary tool, it is called hyperbole. Find at least six examples of hyperbole in the selection.

3. **Setting.** Explain in general terms when and where this piece probably is set. What can you tell about the way of life and economic status of the family?

Developing Vocabulary

1. **Prefixes.** The prefix *semi-* can mean half, as in the word *semicircle*. More often it means partly, as in *semiautomatic*. Study each word below and decide which meaning of *semi-* is used. Then, write and define at least three other words that use the prefix *semi-*.

semiprofessional   semitropical
semiprivate   semiskilled

2. **Finding Words in the Dictionary.** At the top of each dictionary page are two guide words. The guide word on the left is the first word defined on the page; the guide word on the right is the last word defined on the page. Imagine that your dictionary has two pages with these guide words:

semester/semiprecious
semiprivate/semolina

Study the words listed in the preceding vocabulary exercise. Study the additional examples that you gave for the exercise. On which dictionary page would each word appear?

The World in a Wall   *Gerald Durrell*

The crumbling wall that surrounded the sunken garden alongside the house was a rich hunting ground for me. It was an ancient brick wall that had been plastered over, but now this outer skin was green with moss, bulging and sagging with the damp of many winters. The whole surface was an intricate map of cracks, some several inches wide, others as fine as hairs. Here and there large pieces had dropped off and revealed the rows of rose-pink bricks lying beneath like ribs. There was a whole landscape on this wall if you peered closely enough to see it. The roofs of a hundred tiny toadstools, red, yellow, and brown, showed in patches like villages on the damper portions. Mountains of bottle-green moss grew in tuffets so symmetrical that they might have been planted and trimmed. Forests of small ferns sprouted from cracks in the shady places, drooping languidly like little green fountains. The top of the wall was a

desert land, too dry for anything except a few rust-red mosses to live in it, too hot for anything except sun-bathing by the dragon-flies. At the base of the wall grew a mass of plants—cyclamen, crocus, asphodel—thrusting their leaves among the piles of broken and chipped roof-tiles that lay there. This whole strip was guarded by a labyrinth of blackberry hung, in season, with fruit that was plump and juicy and black as ebony.

The inhabitants of the wall were a mixed lot, and they were divided into day and night workers, the hunters and the hunted. At night the hunters were the toads that lived among the brambles, and the geckos, pale, translucent, with bulging eyes, that lived in the cracks higher up the wall. Their prey was the population of stupid, absent-minded crane-flies that zoomed and barged their way among the leaves; moths of all sizes and shapes, moths striped, tessellated, checked, spotted, and blotched, that fluttered in soft clouds along the withered plaster; the beetles, rotund and neatly clad as business men, hurrying with portly efficiency about their night's work. When the last glow-worm had dragged his frosty emerald lantern to bed over the hills of moss, and the sun rose, the wall was taken over by the next set of inhabitants. Here it was more difficult to differentiate between the prey and the predators, for everything seemed to feed indiscriminately off everything else. Thus the hunting wasps searched out caterpillars and spiders; the spiders hunted for flies; the dragon-flies, big, brittle and hunting-pink, fed off the spiders and the flies; and the swift, lithe, and multi-colored wall lizards fed off everything.

But the shyest and most self-effacing of the wall community were the most dangerous; you hardly ever saw one unless you looked for it, and yet there must have been several hundred living in the cracks of the wall. Slide a knife-blade carefully under a piece of the loose plaster and lever it gently away from the brick, and there, crouching beneath it, would be a little black scorpion an inch long, looking as though he were made out of polished chocolate. They were weird-looking little things, with their flattened, oval bodies, their neat, crooked legs, the enormous crab-like claws, bulbous and neatly jointed as armor, and the tail like a string of brown beads ending in a sting like a rose-thorn. The scorpion would lie there quite quietly as you examined him, only raising his tail in an almost apologetic gesture of warning if you breathed too hard on him. If you kept him in the sun too long, he would simply turn his back on you and walk away, and then slide slowly but firmly under another section of plaster.

I grew very fond of these scorpions. I found them to be pleasant, unassuming creatures with, on the whole, the most charming habits. Provided you did nothing silly or clumsy (like putting your hand on one) the scorpions treated you with respect, their one desire being to get away and hide as quickly as possible. They must have found me rather a trial, for I was always ripping sections of the plaster away so that I could watch them, or capturing them and making them walk about in jam jars so that I could see the way their feet moved. By means of my sudden and unexpected assaults on the wall, I discovered quite a bit about the scorpions. I found that they would eat bluebottles (though how they caught them was a mystery I never solved), grasshoppers, moths, and lacewing flies. Several times I found one of them eating an-

other, a habit I found most distressing in a creature otherwise so impeccable.

By crouching under the wall at night with a torch, I managed to catch some brief glimpses of the scorpions' wonderful courtship dances. I saw them standing, claws clasped, their bodies raised to the skies, their tails lovingly entwined; I saw them waltzing slowly in circles among the moss cushions, claw in claw. But my view of these performances was all too short, for almost as soon as I switched on the torch the partners would stop, pause for a moment, and then, seeing that I was not going to extinguish the light, would turn round and walk firmly away, claw in claw, side by side. They were definitely beasts that believed in keeping themselves to themselves. If I could have kept a colony in captivity, I would probably have been able to see the whole of the courtship, but the family had forbidden scorpions in the house, despite my arguments in favor of them.

Then one day I found a fat female scorpion in the wall, wearing what at first glance appeared to be a pale fawn fur coat. Closer

inspection proved that this strange garment was made up of a mass of tiny babies clinging to the mother's back. I was enraptured by this family, and I made up my mind to smuggle them into the house and up to my bedroom so that I might keep them and watch them grow up. With infinite care I maneuvered the mother and family into a matchbox, and then hurried to the villa. It was rather unfortunate that just as I entered the door, lunch should be served; however, I placed the matchbox carefully on the mantel-piece in the drawing room, so that the scor-pions should get plenty of air, and made my way to the dining room and joined the family for the meal. Dawdling over my food, feeding Roger surreptitiously under the table, and listening to the family arguing, I com-pletely forgot about my exciting new cap-tures. At last Larry, having finished, fetched the cigarettes from the drawing room, and lying back in his chair, he put one in his mouth and picked up the matchbox he had brought. Oblivious of my impending doom, I watched him interestedly as, still talking glibly, he opened the matchbox.

Now I maintain to this day that the female scorpion meant no harm. She was agitated and a trifle annoyed at being shut up in a matchbox for so long, and so she seized the first opportunity to escape. She hoisted her-self out of the box with great rapidity, her babies clinging on desperately, and scuttled onto the back of Larry's hand. There, not quite certain what to do next, she paused, her sting curved up at the ready. Larry, feeling the movement of her claws, glanced down to see what it was, and from that moment things got increasingly confused.

He uttered a roar of fright that made Lugaretzia drop a plate and brought Roger out from beneath the table, barking wildly. With a flick of his hand he sent the unfortu-nate scorpion flying down the table, and she landed midway between Margo and Leslie,[1] scattering babies like confetti as she thumped onto the cloth. Thoroughly enraged at this treatment, the creature sped towards Leslie, her sting quivering with emotion. Leslie leaped to his feet, overturning his chair, and flicked out desperately with his napkin, send-ing the scorpion rolling across the cloth towards Margo, who promptly let out a scream that any railway engine would have been proud to produce. Mother, completely bewildered by this sudden and rapid change from peace to chaos, put on her glasses and peered down the table to see what was caus-ing the pandemonium; and at that moment Margo, in a vain attempt to stop the scor-pion's advance, hurled a glass of water at it. The shower missed the animal completely, but successfully drenched Mother, who, not being able to stand cold water, promptly lost

---

1. **Roger, Larry, Lugaretzia, Margo, Leslie:** Roger is the narrator's dog; Larry, Leslie, and Margo are his older brothers and sister. Lugaretzia is the family's maid.

her breath and sat gasping at the end of the table, unable even to protest. The scorpion had now gone to ground under Leslie's plate, while her babies swarmed wildly all over the table. Roger, mystified by the panic, but determined to do his share, ran round and round the room, barking hysterically.

"It's that bloody² boy again . . ." bellowed Larry.

"Look out! Look out! They're coming!" screamed Margo.

"All we need is a book," roared Leslie; "don't panic, hit 'em with a book."

"What on earth's the *matter* with you all?" Mother kept imploring, mopping her glasses.

"It's that bloody boy . . . he'll kill the lot of us. . . . Look at the table . . . knee-deep in scorpions. . . ."

"Quick . . . quick . . . do something . . . Look out, look out!"

"Stop screeching and get a book, for heaven's sake. . . . You're worse than the dog. . . . Shut *up*, Roger. . . ."

"By the grace of God I wasn't bitten. . . ."

"Look out . . . there's another one. . . . Quick . . . quick . . ."

"Oh, shut up and get me a book or something. . . ."

"But *how* did the scorpions get on the table, dear?"

"That bloody boy. . . . Every matchbox in the house is a deathtrap. . . ."

"Look out, it's coming towards me. . . . Quick, quick, do something. . . ."

"Hit it with your knife . . . *your knife* . . . Go on, hit it. . . ."

Since no one had bothered to explain things to him, Roger was under the mistaken impression that the family were being attacked, and that it was his duty to defend them. As Lugaretzia was the only stranger in the room, he came to the logical conclusion that she must be the responsible party, so he bit her in the ankle. This did not help matters very much.

By the time a certain amount of order had been restored, all the baby scorpions had hidden themselves under various plates and bits of cutlery. Eventually, after impassioned pleas on my part backed up by Mother, Leslie's suggestion that the whole lot be slaughtered was quashed. While the family, still simmering with rage and fright, retired to the drawing room, I spent half an hour rounding up the babies, picking them up in a teaspoon, and returning them to their mother's back. Then I carried them outside on a saucer and, with the utmost reluctance, released them on the garden wall. Roger and I went and spent the afternoon on the hillside, for I felt it would be prudent to allow the family to have a siesta before seeing them again.

---

2. **bloody** *British slang:* cursed.

Getting at Meaning

1. How does the narrator's attitude toward scorpions differ from the attitude of the rest of his family?

2. Who are the various inhabitants of the wall? What has the narrator figured out about the life cycle within the wall?

3. What one family member appears to support the narrator's interest in the scorpions? What indicates this support?

Developing Skills in Reading Literature

1. **Narrator.** What details in this essay indicate that the narrator is a careful observer? How old do you think the narrator is? Explain your answer.

2. **Structure.** This selection can be divided into two parts that contrast not only in content, but also in style. Where in the story is the break between the parts? How do the content and the style of writing contrast? How does the first part lead into the second?

3. **Title.** Why is this selection titled "The World in a Wall"? What has the narrator discovered?

4. **Simile.** The narrator describes "the beetles, rotund and neatly clad as business men, hurrying with portly efficiency about their night's work." Find eight other similes in this selection. Be prepared to discuss the effectiveness of the comparisons.

Developing Vocabulary

Multiple Meanings of Words. Sometimes the same word functions as both a noun and a verb. For example: At the base of the wall grew a mass of *plants*. (noun) Each spring Luis *plants* a garden. (verb)

Study the following pairs of sentences. Then determine which italicized word is the noun and which is the verb.

1. I hadn't seen the *rip* in my shirt.
   I saw you *rip* the sheet beyond repair.
2. Ray understood that Sam's *gesture* meant he should be quiet.
   Sally didn't see Claudia *gesture* wildly.
3. We watched the flags *flutter* in the breeze.
   With a *flutter,* the butterfly was gone.
4. A seed *sprouts* quickly with proper care.
   The *sprouts* grew quickly into strong young plants.
5. The tiger stalked its *prey* through the jungle.
   Owls *prey* on field mice.

Developing Writing Skills

Writing About a Personal Experience. The four short sketches in this section all present humorous incidents that take place in families. Write a humorous sketch of your own about some situation that involved you and your family. Describe the incident in detail, using colorful, specific language. Be sure to explain how the situation was resolved.

Essays of Social Commentary

An Editorial Lost in a News Item

Louis Nizer

I almost skipped this item. I do not read reports of personal tragedies that are printed in newspapers. They may attract the curious, but in a world tottering toward another war, of what importance is a lover's death or a child's disappearance? But a subheading held my eye: "Posse Holds Hands." I began to read.

It appeared that a young child had been lost in a thicket. The parents frantically summoned friends to aid them in their search for the child. Twenty hours had passed, and the child might die from exposure. The police joined the search. Neighbors gathered and looked. Every bush was carefully examined, but the child was not to be found. Precious hours passed. The parents and their army of searchers grew more desperate.

Suddenly one old lady called out, "Why don't we all hold hands in one huge circle. Then we'll be sure we have covered every inch of ground." The suggestion was adopted. The neighbors, friends, and police joined hands and moved forward cautiously.

In less than an hour, the crumpled body of the child was discovered. It was dead. The father cried out in anguish, "O God, why didn't we join hands sooner!"

I was stunned by the story. Here was the perfect aphorism[1] for our troubled international scene. This story belongs on the editorial page, I thought to myself. And so I have written it here, as though the stricken father had uttered a cry on behalf of all the peoples of the world. For it is not yet too late to save the next generation of children.

To this lesson in cooperation I would like to add one on tolerance. There is an Aesop fable of a woodsman who came into a forest to ask the trees to give him a handle for his axe. It seemed so modest a request that the principal trees at once agreed on it. They decided that a plain, homely ash, the least important among them, should be sacrificed. No sooner had the woodsman fitted the staff into his axe than he began laying about him on all sides, felling the noblest trees in the wood. The oak, now understanding the whole matter too late, whispered to the cedar, "The first concession has lost all; if we had not sacrificed our humblest neighbor, we might have stood for ages ourselves."

---

1. **aphorism** (af′ ə riz′m): a short statement of a general truth or a wise observation.

Getting at Meaning

1. Why does the child die? What is the specific meaning of the father's remark, "O God, why didn't we join hands sooner"? What is the broader application of the remark?

2. In the Aesop fable, what do the large trees realize too late? Why does the writer include the Aesop fable along with the discussion of the child's death?

Developing Skills in Reading Literature

1. **Editorial.** An editorial is an expression of opinion on a topic of social or political importance. Written editorials appear in newspapers and magazines. They may express the opinion of just one person or of a larger group. What is the subject of this editorial? What is the editorial really about? What does the death of the child illustrate to the writer?

2. **Fable.** A fable is a short tale that teaches a moral or lesson about human life. Animals and plants that talk and act like human beings often appear as characters in fables. What is the moral of the fable about the woodsman and the axe? How does this moral relate to the writer's message, or theme?

Developing Writing Skills

1. **Supporting an Opinion.** The writer says, "in a world tottering toward another war, of what importance is a lover's death or a child's disappearance?" In one paragraph, agree or disagree with this statement.

2. **Writing an Editorial.** Study examples of editorials in newspapers and magazines. Then write an editorial on a topic of social or political importance, such as war or race relations, or on some aspect of school life. Try to use real problems and situations to illustrate your views.

from All Creatures Great and Small

James Herriot

Rheumatism is a terrible thing in a dog. It is painful enough in humans, but an acute attack can reduce an otherwise healthy dog to terrified, screaming immobility.

Very muscular animals suffered most, and I went carefully as my fingers explored the bulging triceps and gluteals of the little Staffordshire bull terrier. Normally a tough little fellow, afraid of nothing, friendly, leaping high in an attempt to lick people's faces; but today rigid, trembling, staring anxiously in front of him. Even to turn his head a little brought a shrill howl of agony.

Mercifully it was something you could put right, and quickly, too. I pulled the Novalgin into the syringe and injected it rapidly. The little dog, oblivious to everything but the knife-like stabbing of the rheumatism, did not stir at the prick of the needle. I counted out some salicylate tablets into a box, wrote

the directions on the lid and handed the box to the owner.

"Give him one of those as soon as the injection has eased him, Mr. Tavener. Then repeat in about four hours. I'm pretty sure he'll be greatly improved by then."

Mrs. Tavener snatched the box away as her husband began to read the directions. "Let me see it," she snapped. "No doubt I'll be the one who has the job to do."

It had been like that all the time, ever since I had entered the beautiful house with the terraced gardens leading down to the river. She had been at him ceaselessly while he was holding the dog for me. When the animal had yelped, she had cried, "Really, Henry, don't grip the poor thing like that; you're hurting him!" She had kept him scuttling about for this and that, and when he was out of the room she said, "You know, this is all my husband's fault. He will let the dog swim in the river. I knew this would happen."

Half-way through, daughter Julia had come in, and it was clear from the start that she was firmly on Mama's side. She helped out with plenty of "How could you, Daddy!" and "For heaven's sake, Daddy!" and generally managed to fill in the gaps when her mother wasn't in full cry.

The Taveners were in their fifties. He was a big, floridly handsome man who had made millions in the Tyneside[1] shipyards before pulling out of the smoke to this lovely place.

---

1. **Tyneside:** located on the Tyne River in north England.

I had taken an instant liking to him; I had expected a tough tycoon and had found a warm, friendly, curiously vulnerable man, obviously worried sick about his dog.

I had reservations about Mrs. Tavener despite her still considerable beauty. Her smile had a switched-on quality and there was a little too much steel in the blue of her eyes. She had seemed less concerned about the dog than with the necessity of taking it out on her husband.

Julia, a scaled-down model of her mother, drifted about the room with the aimless, bored look of the spoiled child; glancing blankly at the dog or me, staring without interest through the window at the smooth lawns, the tennis court, the dark band of river under the trees.

I gave the terrier a final reassuring pat on the head and got up from my knees. As I put away the syringe, Tavener took my arm. "Well, that's fine, Mr. Herriot. We're very grateful to you for relieving our minds. I must say I thought the old boy's time had come when he started yelling. And now you'll have a drink before you go."

The man's hand trembled on my arm as he spoke. It had been noticeable, too, when he had been holding the dog's head, and I had wondered; maybe Parkinson's disease,[2] or nerves, or just drink. Certainly he was pouring a generous measure into his glass; but as he tipped up the bottle, his hand was seized by an even more violent tremor, and he slopped the spirit on to the polished sideboard.

"Oh no!" Mrs. Tavener burst out. There was a bitter note of oh no, not again, in her cry, and Julia struck her forehead with her hand and raised her eyes to heaven. Tavener shot a single hunted look at the women, then grinned as he handed me my glass.

"Come and sit down, Mr. Herriot," he said. "I'm sure you have time to relax for a few minutes."

We moved over to the fireside, and Tavener talked pleasantly about dogs and the countryside and the pictures that hung on the walls of the big room. Those pictures were noted in the district; many of them were originals by famous painters, and they had become the main interest in Tavener's life. His other passion was clocks; and as I looked round the room at the rare and beautiful timepieces standing among elegant period furniture, it was easy to believe the rumors I had heard about the wealth within these walls.

The women did not drink with us. They had disappeared when the bottle was brought out; but as I drained my glass, the door was pushed open and they stood there, looking remarkably alike in expensive tweed coats and fur-trimmed hats. Mrs. Tavener, pulling on a pair of motoring gloves, looked with distaste at her husband. "We're going into Brawton," she said. "Don't know when we'll be back."

Behind her, Julia stared coldly at her father; her lip curled slightly.

Tavener did not reply. He sat motionless as I listened to the roar of the car engine and the spatter of whipped-up gravel beyond the window; then he looked out, blank-faced, empty-eyed at the drifting cloud of exhaust smoke in the drive.

There was something in his expression that chilled me. I put down my glass and got to my feet. "Afraid I must be moving on, Mr. Tavener. Thanks for the drink."

He seemed suddenly to be aware of my presence; the friendly smile returned. "Not at all. Thank you for looking after the old boy. He seems better already."

In the driving mirror, the figure at the top of the steps looked small and alone till the high shrubbery hid him from my view.

---

2. **Parkinson's disease:** a degenerative brain disease marked by tremors and rigidity of muscles.

The next call was to a sick pig, high on Marstang Fell. The road took me at first along the fertile valley floor, winding under the riverside trees past substantial farmhouses and rich pastures; but as the car left the road and headed up a steep track, the country began to change. The transition was almost violent as the trees and bushes thinned out and gave way to the bare, rocky hillside and the miles of limestone walls.

And though the valley had been rich with the fresh green of the new leaves, up here the buds were unopened, and the naked branches stretched against the sky still had the look of winter.

Tim Alton's farm lay at the top of the track, and as I pulled up at the gate, I wondered as I always did how the man could scrape a living from those few harsh acres with the grass flattened and yellowed by the wind that always blew. At any rate, many generations had accomplished the miracle and had lived and struggled and died in that house with its outbuildings crouching in the lee of a group of stunted, wind-bent trees, its massive stones crumbling under three centuries of fierce weathering.

Why should anybody want to build a farm in such a place? I turned as I opened the gate and looked back at the track threading between the walls, down and down to where the white stones of the river glittered in the spring sunshine. Maybe the builder had stood here and looked across the green vastness and breathed in the cold, sweet air and thought it was enough.

I saw Tim Alton coming across the yard. There had been no need to lay down concrete or cobbles here; they had just swept away the thin soil, and there, between house and buildings was a sloping stretch of fissured rock. It was more than a durable surface—it was everlasting.

"It's your pig this time, then, Tim," I said, and the farmer nodded seriously.

"Aye, right as owt yesterday and laid flat like a dead 'un this morning. Never looked up when I filled his trough; and by gaw, when a pig won't tackle his grub, there's summat far wrong." Tim dug his hands inside the broad leather belt that encircled his oversized trousers and that always seemed to be about to nip his narrow frame in two, and led the way gloomily into the sty. Despite the

bitter poverty of his existence, he was a man who took misfortune cheerfully. I had never seen him look like this, and I thought I knew the reason; there is something personal about the family pig.

Smallholders like Tim Alton made their meager living from a few cows; they sold their milk to the big dairies or made butter. And they killed a pig or two each year and cured it themselves for home consumption. On the poorer places, it seemed to me that they ate little else; whatever meal I happened to stumble in on, the cooking smell was always the same—roasting fat bacon.

It appeared to be a matter of pride to make the pig as fat as possible; in fact, on these little wind-blown farms, where the people and the cows and the dogs were lean and spare, the pig was about the only fat thing to be seen.

I had seen the Alton pig before. I had been stitching a cow's torn teat about a fortnight ago, and Tim had patted me on the shoulder and whispered, "Now come along wi' me, Mr. Herriot and I'll show tha summat." We had looked into the sty at a twenty-five-stone[3] monster effortlessly emptying a huge trough of wet meal. I could remember the pride in the farmer's eyes and the way he listened to the smacking and slobbering as if to great music.

It was different today. The pig looked, if possible, even more enormous as it lay on its side, eyes closed, filling the entire floor of the sty like a beached whale. Tim splashed a stick among the untouched meal in the trough and made encouraging noises, but the animal never stirred. The farmer looked at me with haggard eyes.

"He's bad, Mr. Herriot. It's serious, whatever it is."

I had been taking the temperature, and when I read the thermometer, I whistled. "A hundred and seven. That's some fever."

The color drained from Tim's face. "Oh no! A hundred and seven! It's hopeless, then. It's ower with him."

I had been feeling along the animal's side, and I smiled reassuringly. "No, don't worry, Tim. I think he's going to be all right. He's got erysipelas. Here, put your fingers along his back. You can feel a lot of flat swellings on his skin—those are the diamonds. He'll have a beautiful rash within a few hours, but at the moment you can't see it; you can only feel it."

"And you can make him better?"

"I'm nearly sure I can. I'll give him a whacking dose of serum, and I'd like to bet you he'll have his nose in that trough in a couple of days. Most of them get over it all right."

"Well, that's a bit o' good news, any road,"

---

3. **twenty-five stone:** about 350 pounds. In England, a stone is a unit of weight equal to fourteen pounds.

said Tim, a smile flooding over his face. "You had me worried there with your hundred and seven, dang you!"

I laughed. "Sorry, Tim; didn't mean to frighten you. I'm often happier to see a high temperature than a low one. But it's a funny time for erysipelas. We usually see it in late summer."

"All right, I'll let ye off this time. Come in and wash your hands."

In the kitchen I ducked my head but couldn't avoid bumping the massive side of bacon hanging from the beamed ceiling. The heavy mass rocked gently on its hooks; it was about eight inches thick in parts—all pure white fat. Only by close inspection was it possible to discern a thin strip of lean meat.

Mrs. Alton produced a cup of tea; and as I sipped, I looked across at Tim, who had fallen back into a chair and lay with his hands hanging down. For a moment he closed his eyes, and his face became a mask of weariness. I thought for the hundredth time about the endless labor that made up the lives of these little farmers. Alton was only forty, but

his body was already bent down and ravaged by the constant demands he made on it; you could read his story in the corded forearm, the rough, work-swollen fingers. He told me once that the last time he missed a milking was twelve years ago, and that was for his father's funeral.

I was taking my leave when I saw Jennie. She was the Altons' eldest child and was pumping vigorously at the tire of her bicycle, which was leaning against the wall just outside the kitchen door.

"Going somewhere?" I asked, and the girl straightened up quickly, pushing back a few strands of dark hair from her forehead. She was about eighteen, with delicate features and large, expressive eyes; in her wild, pinched prettiness there was something of the wheeling curlews, the wind and sun, the wide emptiness of the moors.

"I'm going down to t'village." She stole a glance into the kitchen. "I'm going to get a bottle of Guinness[4] for dad."

"The village! It's a long way to go for a bottle of Guinness. It must be two miles and then you've got to push back up this hill. Are you going all that way just for one bottle?"

"Ay, just one," she whispered, counting out a sixpence and some coppers into her palm with calm absorption. "Dad's been up all night waiting for a heifer to calve—he's tired out. I won't be long, and he can have his Guinness with his dinner. That's what he likes." She looked up at me conspiratorially. "It'll be a surprise for him."

As she spoke, her father, still sprawled in the chair, turned his head and looked at her; he smiled, and for a moment I saw a serenity in the steady eyes, a nobility in the seamed face.

Jennie looked at him for a few seconds, a happy, secret look from under her lowered brows; then she turned quickly, mounted her

---

4. **Guinness** (gin' əs): an ale popular in Great Britain.

bicycle and began to pedal down the track at surprising speed.

I followed her more slowly, the car, in second gear, bumping and swaying over the stones. I stared straight ahead, lost in thought. I couldn't stop my mind roaming between the two houses I had visited; between the gracious mansion by the river and the crumbling farmhouse I had just left; from Henry Tavener with his beautiful clothes, his well-kept hands, his rows of books and pictures and clocks to Tim Alton with his worn, chest-high trousers nipped in by that great belt, his daily, monthly, yearly grind to stay alive on that unrelenting hilltop.

But I kept coming back to the daughters; to the contempt in Julia Tavener's eyes when she looked at her father, and the shining tenderness in Jennie Alton's.

It wasn't so easy to work out as it seemed; in fact, it became increasingly difficult to decide who was getting the most out of their different lives. But as I guided the car over the last few yards of the track and pulled on to the smooth tarmac of the road, it came to me with unexpected clarity. Taking it all in all, if I had the choice to make, I'd settle for the Guinness.

Getting at Meaning

1. What kind of man is James Herriot? What attitude does he have toward his work? Support your answers with evidence from the selection.

2. Describe the Tavener family and their home. What kind of relationship does Mr. Tavener have with his wife and daughter? What does the veterinarian think of Mr. Tavener?

3. Describe Tim Alton and his farm. What kind of life does Alton apparently lead? What is his relationship with his daughter?

Developing Skills in Reading Literature

1. **Setting.** The writer of this selection spends considerable time describing the physical environments and the homes of his clients. Why is Herriot so interested in where these people live? What conclusions does he draw about their lives from their surroundings?

2. **Foil.** A foil, as you know, is a character with qualities that contrast with those of another character. Tavener and Alton are foils, for although both men are concerned about their sick animals, their situations are otherwise quite different. How do their lives differ? How do their daughters differ?

3. **Theme.** What does the writer mean when he says, "Taking it all in all, if I had the choice to make, I'd settle for the Guinness"? What is he saying about wealth and happiness?

Developing Writing Skills

1. **Exposition: Using Contrasts.** Think about who is more fortunate, Mr. Tavener or Tim Alton. Consider the advantages and disadvantages each one has in his life. Then write a topic sentence that states your conclusion clearly. Develop the sentence into a well written paragraph that includes contrasts between the two characters.

2. **Combining Narration and Description.** Have you ever had a pet? How did you feel about your pet? How did you feel when your pet was sick, ran away, or died? Write a paragraph that describes your pet and your feelings toward it. Include at least one specific experience that illustrates your feelings.

Whales for the Killing *Farley Mowat*

The tranquil acceptance of the Fin Whales at Burgeo[1] was in sharp contrast to an incident I witnessed at about this time at St. Pierre, the capital and only port for the French islands of St. Pierre-Miquelon, which lie a few miles off the south coast of Newfoundland.[2] Most of the inhabitants there are fishermen too, but St. Pierre itself is full of shops, tourist establishments, ship repair facilities, and people whose loyalties lie with the modern industrial society.

On a moonless night in August 1961, my schooner lay moored to a rotting dock in St. Pierre harbor. About midnight I went on deck to smoke a pipe and enjoy the silence, but the quiet was soon broken by what sounded like a gust of heavy breathing in the waters almost alongside. Startled, I grabbed a flashlight and played its beam over the dark waters. The calm surface was mysteriously roiled in great, spreading rings. As I puzzled over the meaning of this phenomenon, there came another burst of heavy exhalations. I swung the light to port and was in time to see one, three, then a dozen broad black backs smoothly break the oily surface, blow, then slip away into the depths again.

I was seeing a school of Potheads who had made their way into the sewage-laden waters of the inner harbor. They must have had a pressing reason, for no free-swimming animal in its right mind would have entered that cesspool willingly. The skipper of a local dragger later told me he had met a small group of Killer Whales close to the harbor channel on the day the Potheads entered.

Killer Whales have been given a ferocious reputation by men, one not at all deserved; but it is true that they will occasionally make a meal of a Pothead calf, and the Potheads in St. Pierre harbor were accompanied by several calves.

When I went to bed, the whales were still circling leisurely. I slept late, to be awakened by the snarl of outboard engines, by excited shouting, and by the sound of feet pounding on my deck. When I thrust my head out of the hatch, I found what appeared to be about half the male population of St. Pierre, accompanied by a good many women and children, closely clustered along the waterfront.

There was a slight fog lying over the harbor. In and out of it wove two over-powered launches, roaring along at full throttle. In the bow of one stood a young man wielding a homemade lance which he had made by lashing a hunting knife to the end of an oar. In the second boat was another young man, balancing a rifle across his knees. Both boats were in furious pursuit of the Potheads, which numbered some fifteen adults and six or seven calves.

The whales were very frightened. The moment one of them surfaced, the boats tore down upon it, while gunners on the shore poured out a fusillade of shots. The big animals had no time to ventilate their lungs

---

1. **Burgeo:** a coastal village in southwest Newfoundland.
2. **Newfoundland** (noō'fənd land): an island of Canada, located off the east coast.

properly but were forced to submerge after snatching a single breath. The calves, choking for oxygen, were often slow in diving. Time after time the harpooner got close enough to ram his hunting knife into the back of one of them, so that long streamers of crimson began to appear on the filthy surface of the harbor. It was obvious that neither the gunfire——mostly from .22 calibre rifles—nor the lance were capable of killing the whales outright; but it did not appear that killing them was the object. In truth, what I was watching was a sporting event.

I was appalled and infuriated, but there seemed to be nothing I could do to end this exhibition of wanton bloodlust. A fisherman friend of mine, Theophille Detcheverey, came aboard, and I poured out my distress to him. He shrugged.

"That one in the big speedboat, he is the son of the biggest merchant here. The other, with the spear, he is from France. He came here two years ago to start a raft voyage across the Atlantic. But he don't get out of the bars until today, I think. They are pigs, eh? But we are not all pigs. You see, there is no fisherman helping them with their dirty work."

This was true enough, if of small comfort to the whales. The fishermen of St. Pierre had left for the cod grounds at dawn. When they returned in their laden dories late in the afternoon, the excitement in the harbor had reached a crescendo. All the fast pleasure craft available had joined in the game. The onlookers crowding around the harbor became so densely packed it was hard to push one's way through. I had chased scores of them off my decks where they sought a better vantage point, and they had responded to my anger with derision. For ten hours, relays of boats had chased the whales. Clusters of men with rifles stood at the pierhead at the harbor entrance, and every time the Potheads tried to escape in that direction, they were met with a barrage of bullets which now included heavy-calibre slugs. Unable to run that gauntlet, the whales were forced to give up their attempts to escape in the only direction open to them.

Toward evening the whales, most of them now bleeding profusely, had become so exhausted they began to crowd up into the dangerously shoal water at the head of the harbor where the boats could not follow. Here they lay, gasping and rolling, until they had recovered enough strength to return to deeper water. Many times they swam directly under my boat, and they were beautiful . . . superb masters of the seas, now at the mercy of the bifurcated killer of the land.

At dusk the sportsmen called it a day and went home to dinner. The audience departed. The fog rolled in thickly and silence returned. Again I sat on deck, and again the strange, sibilant breathing of the whales kept me company. I could not go to my berth, knowing what must await them with the dawn. Finally I untied my little dinghy and rowed out into the darkness of the fog shroud. I had a vague hope that I might be able to drive the herd out of the harbor before daylight brought a renewal of their ordeal.

It was an uncanny experience, and a nerve-wracking one, to row my little cockleshell silently through that dense and dripping fog, not knowing where the whales might be. The size of them—the largest must have been nearly twenty feet long—and their mysterious and unseen presence intimidated me. I felt extraordinarily vulnerable, detached from my own world, adrift on the lip of a world that was utterly alien. I thought, as a man would think, that if there was the capacity of vengeance in these beasts, surely I would experience it.

Then, with heart-stopping suddenness, the entire pod surfaced all around me. A calf blew directly under one upraised oar, and my little boat rocked lightly in its wash. It should have been a terrifying moment, but it was not.

Inexplicably, I was no longer afraid. I began talking to the beasts in a quiet way, warning them that they must leave. They stayed at or near the surface, swimming very slowly—perhaps still exhausted—and I had no difficulty staying with them. Time after time they surfaced all around me, and although any one of them, even the smallest calf, could have easily overturned the dinghy, they avoided touching it. I began to experience an indescribable sense of empathy with them . . . and a mounting frustration. How could I help them to escape from what the morrow held?

We slowly circled the harbor—this strange flotilla of man and whales—but they would not go near the harbor mouth, either because they knew the Killer Whales were still in the vicinity or because of the vicious barrage of bullets with which men had greeted their every attempt to escape during the daylight hours.

Eventually I decided to try desperate measures. At the closest point to the harbor entrance to which they would go, I suddenly began howling at them and wildly flailing my oars against the water. Instantly they sounded, diving deep and long. I heard them blow once more at the far side of the harbor, but they never came close to me again. I had done the wrong thing—the human thing

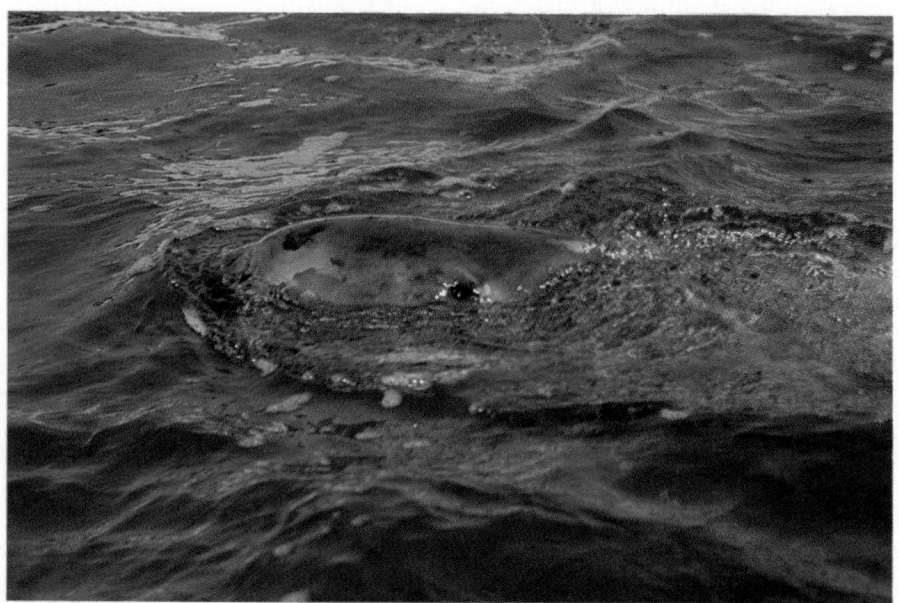

—and my action had brought an end to their acceptance of me.

The whales were still in the harbor when dawn broke. During the long evening in the bars, the ingenious sportsmen of St. Pierre had set the stage for a massacre.

Early in the morning, just as the tide was beginning to ebb, half a dozen boats came out and formed a line abreast at the harbor mouth. Slowly, they began to sweep the harbor, driving the herd closer and closer to the shoals. When the whales sounded and doubled back, they were again met with rifle fire from the breakwater as on the day before. One of the largest beasts seemed to be leading these attempts to escape, with the rest following close in its wake. It looked like a stalemate until three small whales became momentarily separated from the pod as it came under the fusillade from the breakwater. They gave way to panic. Fleeing at full speed on the surface, and close-harried by a fast speedboat, they torpedoed across the harbor and into the shoals where the tide was dropping fast. Within minutes they were hopelessly aground.

Howling like the veriest banshees, men and boys armed with axes and carving knives leaped into the knee-deep shallows. Blood began to swirl thickly about them. The apparent leader of the pod, responding to what impulse I shall never know, charged toward the three stranded and mutilated whales. There was a wild melée of running, falling, yelling people; then the big whale stranded too. The rest of the herd, following close behind, were soon ashore as well. Only one calf remained afloat. It swam aimlessly back and forth just beyond the fatal shoals, and for a few minutes was ignored as the boats crowded in upon the herd and men leapt overboard, jostling one another in their lust to have a hand in the slaughter. Blood from one impaled whale spouted high over their heads—a red and drenching rain. Men flung up their ensanguined faces, wiped the blood away, and laughed and shouted in the delirium of dealing death.

Finally someone noticed the calf. Arms, red and savage, pointed urgently. A man leapt into his speedboat. The engine roared. He circled once at top speed then bore straight at the calf, which was in such shoal water it could not sound. The boat almost ran up on its back. The calf swerved frantically, beat its flukes wildly, and was aground.

The slashing and the hacking on that bloody foreshore continued long after all the whales had bled to death. A crowd of four or five hundred people drank in the spectacle with eager appetite. It was a great fiesta in St. Pierre. Throughout the remainder of the day there was a crowd standing and staring at the monstrous corpses. I particularly remember a small boy, who could not have been more than eight years of age, straddling a dead calf and repeatedly striking into its flesh with a pocket knife, while his father stood by and encouraged him.

Nor were the "townies" of St. Pierre the only ones to enjoy the spectacle. Many American and Canadian tourists had witnessed the show and now were busy taking pictures of one another posing beside the dead behemoths. Something to show the folks back home.

It was a grand exhibition . . . but the aftermath was not so grand. Those many tons of putrefying flesh could not be left lying where they were. So, on the following day, several big trucks appeared at the shore where lay the carcasses of twenty-three Pothead Whales. One by one the whales were hauled up by a mobile derrick and either loaded aboard the trucks or, if they were too big, chained behind. Then the trucks carried and dragged the bodies across the island to a cliff where, one by one, they were rolled over the steep slopes . . . and returned to the freedom of the seas.

Getting at Meaning

1. How many whales are in the harbor? Why have they fled there?

2. Who leads the first assault on the whales? How is it significant that no fishermen are among the attackers?

3. How do the whales react to the narrator when he tries to lead them out of the harbor? What mistake does he make?

4. How does the narrator describe the slaughter? the people who participate in it?

5. What is the unpleasant aftermath of the slaughter? How is the method used to dispose of the carcasses somehow fitting?

Developing Skills in Reading Literature

1. **Setting.** When and where is this selection set? What makes the setting an important element in the selection?

2. **Tone.** At one point Mowat writes, "Men flung up their ensanguined faces, wiped the blood away, and laughed and shouted in the delirium of dealing death." What is the writer's attitude toward this form of sport? Identify other sentences that bring out this same attitude. Then list phrases the writer uses to describe the whales. How do these phrases reinforce the writer's attitude toward the events he describes?

3. **Mood.** How do you feel as you read the opening paragraphs of this account? At what point do your feelings begin to change? How do they change? What words describe the feelings you experience as you read the description of the slaughter? How do you feel as you read the final paragraph in the selection?

4. **Connotation.** Connotation, as you know, is the emotional response created by a word. Many words in this selection connote heavy battle; for example, *fusillade, flotilla,* and *bar-rage.* How does the writer use the connotative meanings of these words to help bring out his theme? What other words in the selection suggest battle?

Developing Vocabulary

Using a Glossary. Find each of the following adjectives in the narrative. Then look up the word in the Glossary. Write the definition and use the word in a sentence of your own.

tranquil   sibilant   ensanguined
ferocious   uncanny   putrefying
wanton   ingenious

Developing Writing Skills

1. **Writing a Report.** Using the *Readers' Guide to Periodical Literature,* find two or three articles on the killing of whales. Then, in your own words, write a report based on the information in these articles.

2. **Writing an Eyewitness Account.** The writer of this selection has given the reader an eyewitness account of a dramatic event. Choose an event from your own experience and describe it in a five-paragraph composition. Strive to re-create the event for your readers through specific details and vivid descriptive language.

3. **Description: Establishing Tone.** The writer describes his feelings as he rows around the whales, feelings of uncertainty that change to empathy and finally to frustration. In one paragraph, describe feelings that you have had in the presence of a natural phenomenon. The phenomenon could be a drenching rainstorm, a rainbow, or a bird building a nest. Use words that have connotative meanings consistent with your feelings.

Pompeii *Robert Silverberg*

Not very far from Naples, a strange city sleeps under the hot Italian sun. It is the city of Pompeii, and there is no other city quite like it in all the world. No one lives in Pompeii but crickets and beetles and lizards, yet every year thousands of people travel from distant countries to visit it.

Pompeii is a dead city. No one has lived there for nearly 2,000 years—not since the summer of the year A.D. 79, to be exact.

Until that year, Pompeii was a prosperous city of 25,000 people. Nearby was the Bay of Naples, an arm of the blue Mediterranean. Rich men came down from wealthy Rome, 125 miles to the north, to build luxurious seaside villas. Fertile farmlands occupied the fields surrounding Pompeii. Rising sharply behind the city was the 4,000-foot bulk of Mount Vesuvius, a grass-covered slope where the shepherds of Pompeii took their goats to graze. Pompeii was a busy city and a happy one.

It died suddenly, in a terrible rain of fire and ashes.

The tragedy struck on the twenty-fourth of August, A.D. 79. Mount Vesuvius, which had slumbered quietly for centuries, exploded with savage violence. Death struck on a hot summer afternoon. Tons of hot ashes fell on Pompeii, smothering it, hiding it from sight. For three days the sun did not break through the cloud of volcanic ash that filled the sky. And when the eruption ended, Pompeii was buried deep. A thriving city had perished in a single day.

Centuries passed . . . Pompeii was forgotten. Then, 1,500 years later, it was discovered again. Beneath the protecting shroud of ashes, the city lay intact. Everything was as it had been the day Vesuvius erupted. There were still loaves of bread in the ovens of the bakeries. In the wine shops, the wine jars were in place, and on one counter could be seen a stain where a customer had thrown down his glass and fled.

Modern archaeology began with the discovery of buried Pompeii. Before then, the digging of treasures from the ground had been a haphazard and unscholarly affair. But the excavation of Pompeii was done in a sys-

tematic, scientific manner, and so the science of serious archaeology can be said to have begun there. Since the year 1748, generations of skilled Italian workmen have been carefully removing the ashes that buried Pompeii, until today almost four-fifths of the city has been uncovered.

Other Roman cities died more slowly. Wind and rain and fire wore them away. Later peoples tore down the ancient monuments, using the stone to build houses and churches. Over the centuries, the cities of the Caesars[1] vanished, and all that is left of them today are scattered fragments.

Not so with Pompeii. It was engulfed in an instant, and its people's tragedy was our great gain. The buildings of Pompeii still stand as they stood 2,000 years ago, and within the houses we can still see the pots and pans, the household tools, the hammers and nails. On the walls of the buildings are election slogans and the scrawlings of unruly boys. Pompeii is like a photograph in three dimensions. It shows us exactly what a city of the Roman Empire was like, down to the smallest detail of everyday life.

To go to Pompeii today is to take a trip backward in a time machine. The old city comes to vivid life all around you. You can almost hear the clatter of horses' hoofs on the narrow streets; the cries of children; the loud, hearty laughter of the shopkeepers. You can almost smell meat sizzling over a charcoal fire. The sky is cloudlessly blue, with the summer sun almost directly overhead. The grassy slopes of great Vesuvius pierce the heavens behind the city, and sunlight shimmers on the water of the bay a thousand yards from the city walls. Ships from every nation are in port, and the babble of strange languages can be heard in the streets.

Such was Pompeii on its last day. And so it is today, now that the volcanic ash has been cleared away. A good imagination is all you need to restore it to bustling vitality.

As its last day of life dawned, in A.D. 79, Pompeii found itself in the midst of a long, sleepy Mediterranean summer. It was a city several hundred years old. Its founders were an Italian people called the Oscans, who had built the city long before Rome had carved out its worldwide empire. Greeks from Naples had settled in Pompeii, too, and the walls that surrounded the city were built in the Greek style.

For more than 150 years, Pompeii had been part of the Roman Empire. The Roman dictator Sulla had besieged and captured the town in 89 B.C., giving it to his soldiers and making it a Roman colony. By A.D. 79, it had become a fashionable seaside resort, an Atlantic City or a Miami Beach of its day. Important Romans had settled there. The great orator Cicero had been very proud of his summer home in Pompeii. It was a city of merchants and bankers, too.

Pompeii had not had unbroken peace. Twenty years earlier, in the year 59, a contest of gladiators had been held in the big outdoor stadium of Pompeii. A team of gladiators from the neighboring town of Nocera had come to fight against Pompeii's best gladiators. Tempers grew hot as local favorites were pitted against each other in combat to the death. Men from Pompeii began to hurl insults at Nocerans. Words led to blows. Then daggers flashed. A terrible massacre resulted, in which dozens of Nocerans perished and only a few escaped.

Nocera appealed to Rome, and the Roman Senate issued a stern decree: the amphitheater of Pompeii would be closed for ten years. No more gladiatorial games! It was like having our Congress declare that neither the Yankees nor the Dodgers could play baseball for a decade.

The ruling was considered a great tragedy in sports-loving Pompeii. But an even

---

1. **Caesars** (sē'zərz): the emperors of the Roman Empire.

greater one was in store four years later, in A.D. 63, for an earthquake rocked the town. Nearly every building in Pompeii toppled. Hundreds of people died.

One who survived the earthquake of 63 was the banker, Caecilius Jucundus. He was a plump, well fed man with a harsh smile and beady eyes and a big wart on his left cheek. At the moment the earth shook, Caecilius was in the Forum, the main square of Pompeii. Much business was transacted in the Forum, which was lined with imposing stone columns arranged in a double row, one above the other.

As statues of the gods and slabs of marble tumbled to the ground, fat Caecilius sank to his knees in terror. "If my life is spared," he cried to the heavens, "I'll sacrifice a bull to the gods!"

We know that Caecilius escaped—and that he kept his vow. For when he rebuilt his house after the earthquake, he added a little strip of marble above his family's altar, and on it was a scene showing the earthquake and depicting the bull he had sacrificed. Next to the altar the fat moneylender kept his treasure chest, crammed full with gold coins—and, facing it, a portrait of himself, wart and all.

Sixteen years passed after the dreadful earthquake of 63. Sixteen years later, signs of the catastrophe could still be seen everywhere, for the Pompeiians were slow to rebuild. The private homes were back in order, of course, but the big public places still showed the effects of the quake. The columns of the Forum remained fallen. The Basilica, or law court, still looked devastated. The Temple of Apollo was not yet restored to its former glory. Such repairs took time and cost a great deal of money. The Pompeiians were in no hurry. Time passes slowly along the Mediterranean coast. The columns could be rebuilt next year, or the year after next, or the year after that. In time, everything would be attended to. Commerce and daily life were more important.

But time was running short.

At dawn, on the twenty-fourth of August, in the year 79, Pompeii's 25,000 people awakened to another hot day in that hot summer. There was going to be a performance in the arena that night, and the whole town was looking forward to the bloody contests of the gladiators, for the Senate's ban had long since ended. The rumble of heavy wooden wheels were heard as carts loaded with grain entered the city from the farms outside the walls. Over the centuries, the steady stream of carts had worn ruts deep into the pavement of Pompeii's narrow streets.

Wooden shutters were drawn back noisily. The grocers and sellers of fruit opened their shops, displaying their wares on trays set out on the sidewalk. In the wine shops, the girls who sold wine to the thirsty sailors got ready for another busy day.

Outside, children headed toward school, carrying slates and followed by their dogs. Nearly everyone in Pompeii had a dog, and barking could be heard everywhere as the Pompeiian pets greeted one another. A small boy who had just learned the Greek alphabet stopped in front of a blank wall and took a piece of charcoal from his tunic. Hastily he scribbled the Greek letters: *alpha, beta, gamma. . . .*

In the Forum, the town's important men had gathered after breakfast to read the political signs that were posted during the night. Elsewhere in the Forum, the wool merchants talked business, and the men who owned the vineyards were smiling to each other about the high quality of this year's wine, which would fetch a good price in other countries.

The quiet morning moved slowly along. There was nothing very unusual about Pompeii. Hundreds of other towns just like it dotted the rolling plains of Italy.

But tragedy was on its way. Beneath Vesuvius's vinecovered slopes, a mighty force was about to break loose.

No one in Pompeii knew the dangerous power imprisoned in Vesuvius. For 1,500 years the mountain had slept quietly, but far beneath the crest a boiling fury of molten lava had gradually been gathering strength. The solid rock of Vesuvius held the hidden forces in check. The earthquake sixteen years before had been the first sign that the trapped fury beneath the mountain was struggling to break free. Pressure was building up. In the city at the base of the mountain, life went on in complete ignorance of the looming catastrophe.

At one o'clock in the afternoon on the twenty-fourth of August, 79, the critical point was reached. The walls of rock could hold no longer.

The mountain exploded, raining death on thousands.

Like many tragedies, this one was misunderstood at first. Down in Pompeii, four miles from Vesuvius, a tremendous explosion was heard, echoing ringingly off the mountains on the far side of the city.

"What was that?" people cried from one end of town to another. They stared at each other, puzzled, troubled. Were the gods fighting in heaven? Is that what the loud explosion was?

"Look!" somebody shouted. "Look at Vesuvius!"

Thousands of eyes swiveled upward. Thousands of arms pointed. A black cloud was rising from the shattered crest of the mountain. Higher and higher it rose. An eyewitness, the Roman philosopher Pliny, described the cloud as he saw it from Misenum, twenty-two miles from Pompeii on the opposite side of the Bay.

"Better than any other tree, the pine can give an idea of the shape and appearance of this cloud," Pliny wrote in his notebook later that day. "In fact, it was projected into the air like an enormous trunk and then spread into many branches, now white, now black, now spotted, according to whether earth or ashes were thrown up."

Minutes passed. The sound of the great explosion died away, but it still tingled in everyone's ears. The cloud over Vesuvius still rose, black as night, higher and higher.

"The cloud is blotting out the sun!" someone cried in terror.

Still, no one in Pompeii had perished. The fragments of rock thrown up when the mountain exploded all fell back on the volcano's slopes. Within the crater, sizzling masses of molten rock were rushing upward, and upwelling gas drove small blobs of liquefied stone thousands of feet into the air. They cooled, high above the gaping mouth of the volcano, and plummeted earthward.

A strange rain began to fall on Pompeii—a rain of stone.

The stones were light. They were pumice stones, consisting mostly of air bubbles. They poured down as though there had been a sudden cloudburst. The pumice stones, or lapilli, did little damage. They clattered against the wooden roofs of the Pompeiian houses. They fell by the hundreds in the streets. The people who had rushed out of houses and shops and thermopolia to see what had caused the explosion now scrambled to take cover as the weird rain of lapilli continued.

"What is happening?" Pompeiians asked one another. They rushed to the temples— the Temple of Jupiter, the Temple of Apollo, the Temple of Isis. Bewildered priests tried to calm bewildered citizens. Darkness had come at midday, and a rain of small stones fell from the sky, and who could explain it?

Some did not wait for explanation. In a tavern near the edge of the city, half a dozen gladiators who were scheduled to compete in that night's games decided to flee quickly. They had trumpets with them that were used to sound a fanfare at the amphitheater. But they tossed the trumpets aside, leaving them to be found centuries later. Covering their heads with tiles and pieces of wood, the gladiators rushed out into the hail of lapilli and sprinted toward the open country beyond the walls, where they hoped they would be safe.

Vesuvius was rumbling ominously now. The sky was dark. Lapilli continued to pour down, until the streets began to clog with them.

"The eruption will be over soon!" a hopeful voice exclaimed.

But it did not end. An hour went by and darkness still shrouded everything, and still the lapilli fell. All was confusion now. Children struggled home from school, panicky in the midday darkness.

The people of Pompeii knew that doom was at hand now. Their fears were doubled when an enormous rain of hot ashes began to fall on them, along with more lapilli. Pelted with stones, half smothered by the ashes, the Pompeiians cried out to the gods for mercy. The wooden roofs of some of the houses began to catch fire as the heat of the ashes reached them. Other buildings were collapsing under the weight of the pumice stones that had fallen on them.

In those first few hours, only the quick-witted managed to escape. Vesonius Primus, the wealthy wool merchant, called his family together and piled jewelry and money into a sack. Lighting a torch, Vesonius led his little band out into the nightmare of the streets. Overlooked in the confusion was Vesonius's black watchdog, chained in the courtyard. The terrified dog barked wildly as lapilli struck and drifting white ash settled around him. The animal struggled with his chain, battling fiercely to get free, but the chain held, and no one heard the dog's cries. The humans were too busy saving themselves.

Many hundreds of Pompeiians fled in those first few dark hours. Stumbling in the darkness, they made their way to the city gates, then out, down to the harbor. They boarded boats and got away, living to tell the tale of their city's destruction. Others preferred to remain within the city, huddling inside the temples, or in the public baths, or in the cellars of their homes. They still hoped that the nightmare would end—that the tranquillity of a few hours ago would return.

It was evening, now. And new woe was in store for Pompeii. The earth trembled and quaked! Roofs that had somehow withstood the rain of lapilli went crashing in ruin, burying hundreds who had hoped to survive the eruption. In the Forum, tall columns toppled as they had in 63. Those who remembered

that great earthquake screamed in new terror as the entire city seemed to shake in the grip of a giant fist.

Three feet of lapilli now covered the ground. Ash floated in the air. Gusts of poisonous gas came drifting from the belching crater, though people could still breathe. Roofs were collapsing everywhere. The cries of the dead and dying filled the air. Rushing throngs, blinded by the darkness and the smoke, hurtled madly up one street and down the next, trampling the fallen in a crazy, fruitless dash toward safety. Dozens of people plunged into dead-end streets and found themselves trapped by crashing buildings. They waited there, too frightened to run farther, expecting the end.

The rich man Diomedes was another of those who decided not to flee at the first sign of alarm. Rather than risk being crushed by the screaming mobs, Diomedes calmly led the members of his household into the solidly built basement of his villa. Sixteen people altogether, as well as his daughter's dog and her beloved little goat. They took enough food and water to last for several days.

But for all his shrewdness and foresight, Diomedes was undone anyway. Poison gas was creeping slowly into the underground shelter! He watched his daughter begin to cough and struggle for breath. Vesuvius was giving off vast quantities of deadly carbon monoxide, that was now settling like a blanket over the dying city.

The poison gas thickened as the terrible night continued. It was possible to hide from the lapilli, but not from the gas, and Pompeiians died by the hundreds. Carbon monoxide gas keeps the body from absorbing oxygen. Victims of carbon monoxide poisoning get sleepier and sleepier, until they lose consciousness, never to regain it. All over Pompeii, people lay down in the beds of lapilli, overwhelmed by the gas, and death came quietly to them.

Two prisoners, left behind in the jail when their keepers fled, pounded on the sturdy wooden doors. "Let us out!" they called. But no one heard, and the gas entered. They died, not knowing that the jailers outside were dying as well.

In a lane near the Forum, a hundred people were trapped by a blind-alley wall. Others hid in the stoutly built public bathhouses, protected against collapsing roofs but not against the deadly gas. Near the house of Diomedes, a beggar and his little goat sought shelter. The man fell dead a few feet from Diomedes's door; the faithful goat remained by his side, its silver bell tinkling, until its turn came.

All through the endless night, Pompeiians wandered about the streets or crouched in their ruined homes or clustered in the temples to pray. By morning, few remained alive. Not once had Vesuvius stopped hurling lapilli and ash into the air, and the streets of Pompeii were filling quickly. At midday on August twenty-fifth, exactly twenty-four hours after the beginning of the holocaust, a second eruption racked the volcano. A second cloud of ashes rose above Vesuvius's summit. The wind blew ash as far as Rome and Egypt. But most of the new ashes descended on Pompeii.

The deadly shower of stone and ashes went unslackening into its second day. But it no longer mattered to Pompeii whether the eruption continued another day or another year. For by midday on August twenty-fifth, Pompeii was a city of the dead.

Arriving at Pompeii today, you leave your car outside and enter through an age-old gate. Just within the entrance is a museum that has been built in recent years to house many of the smaller antiquities found in the ruins. Here are statuettes and toys, saucepans and loaves of bread. The account books of the banker Caecilius Jucundus are there, noting all the money he had lent at steep interest rates. Glass cups, coins, charred beans and peas and turnips, baskets of grapes and plums and figs, a box of chestnuts—the little things of Pompeii have all been miraculously preserved for your startled eyes.

Then you enter the city proper. The streets are narrow and deeply rutted with the tracks of chariot wheels. Only special narrow Pompeiian chariots could travel inside the town. Travelers from outside were obliged to change vehicles when they reached the walls of the city. This provided a profitable monopoly for the Pompeiian equivalent of cab drivers, twenty centuries ago!

At each intersection, blocks of stone several feet high are mounted in the roadway, so designed that chariot wheels could pass on either side of them.

"Those are steppingstones for the people of Pompeii," your guide tells you. "Pompeii had no sewers, and during heavy rainfalls the streets were flooded with many inches of water. The Pompeiians could keep their feet dry by walking on those stones."

The houses and shops are of stone. The upper stories, which were wooden, were burned away in the holocaust, or simply crumbled with the centuries. The biggest of the shops are along the Street of Abundance, which must have been the Fifth Avenue[2] of its day. Silversmiths, shoemakers, manufacturers of cloth—all had their shops here. And every few doors, there is another thermopolium, or wine shop. In many of these, the big jars of wine are still intact, standing in holes in marble counters just the way bins of ice cream are stored in a soda fountain today.

The center of the city's life was the Forum, a large square that you enter not far from the main gate of the city. Before the earthquake of 63, Pompeii's Forum must have been a truly imposing place, enclosed on three sides by a series of porticoes supported by huge columns. At the north end, on the fourth side, stood the temple of Jupiter, Juno, and Minerva, raised on a podium ten feet high. But the earthquake toppled the temple and most of the columns, and not much rebuilding had been done at the time of the eruption. Pompeii's slowness to rebuild was our eternal loss, for little remains of the Forum except the stumps of massive columns.

Other public buildings were also on the main square: the headquarters of the wool industry, and several other temples, including one dedicated to Vespasian (father of Titus), a Roman emperor who was worshiped as a deity. Near the Forum was a macellum, or market, where food-stuffs were sold and where beggars wandered.

Pompeii had many beggars. One of them was found in April, 1957, at the gate of the road leading to the town of Nocera. A cast taken of him shows him to have been less than five feet tall, and deformed by the bone disease known as rickets. On the last day of Pompeii's life, this beggar had gone about asking for alms, and some generous citizen had given him a bone with a piece of meat still adhering to it. When the eruption came, the beggar tried to flee, jealously guarding his precious sack containing the cutlet—and he was found with it, 2,000 years later.

Pompeii was a city of many fine temples, both around the Forum and in the outlying streets. One of the most interesting is one dating from the sixth century B.C., the oldest building in the city. Only the foundation and a few fragmented columns remain, but this temple was evidently regarded with great reverence, since it was located in the center of a fairly large triangular space adjoining the main theater. Nearby is the Temple of Isis, which was rebuilt after the earthquake and so is in fairly good preservation. Isis, an Egyptian goddess, was one of the many foreign gods and goddesses who had come to be worshiped in the Roman Empire by the time of the destruction of Pompeii. Her gaudily decorated temple at Pompeii is the only European temple of Isis that has come down to us from the ancient world.

But many temples, bathhouses, amphitheaters, and government buildings have survived in other places. What makes Pompeii uniquely significant is the wealth of knowledge it gives us about the *private* lives of its people. Nowhere else do we have such complete information about the homes of the ancients, about their customs and living habits, about their humble pots and pans.

---

2. **Fifth Avenue:** a street in New York City known for its elegant shops.

The houses in Pompeii show the evolution of styles over a period of several centuries. Many of the houses are built to the same simple plan: a central court, known as the atrium, around which a living room, bedrooms, and a garden are arrayed. This was the classic Roman style of home. Some of the later and more impressive houses show the influence of Greek styles, with paintings and mosaic decorations as well as baths, reception rooms, huge gardens, and sometimes a second atrium.

The houses of Pompeii are known by name, and a good deal is known of their occupants. One of the most famous is the House of the Vetti Brothers, which is lavishly decorated with paintings, mosaics, and sculptures. The inscriptions on these houses are often amusing today. One businessman had written on the walls of his villa, WELCOME PROFITS! Another greeted his visitors with the inscribed words, PROFITS MEAN JOY!

At the so-called House of the Tragic Poet, a mosaic shows a barking dog, with the inscription *cave canem*—"Beware of the dog." On the building known as the House of the Lovers, which received its name because the newly married Claudius Elogus lived there, someone had written a line of verse dedicated to the newlyweds on the porch: *Amantes, ut apes, vitam mellitem exigunt.* ("Lovers, like bees, desire a life full of honey.")

One interesting house uncovered since World War II is the Villa of Giulia Felix ("Happy Julia") which was of exceptional size. Apparently Giulia found the expense of this elegant house too much for her budget, because she had opened her baths to the public and advertised the fact with a sign on the gate. For a fee, Pompeiians who scorned the crowds at the public baths could bathe at Giulia's in privacy and comfort. Even this income does not seem to have been enough, for another sign uncovered in 1953 announced that the magnificent villa was for rent.

One of the truly fascinating aspects of Pompeii is the multitude of scribbled street signs. Notices were painted directly on the stone, and have come down to us. At the big amphitheater, an inscription tells us, "The troupe of gladiators owned by Suettius Centus will give a performance at Pompeii on May thirty-first. There will be an animal show. The awnings will be used." And at the theater where plays were given, a message to a popular actor reads, "Actius, beloved of the people, come back soon; fare thee well!"

There are inscriptions at the taverns, too. "Romula loves Staphyclus" is on one wall. Elsewhere there is a poem that sounds like one of today's hit tunes: "Anyone could as well stop the winds blowing, / And the waters from flowing, / As stop lovers from loving."

To enter Pompeii is to step into the Rome of the Caesars. An entire city, forever frozen in the last moment of its life by a terrible cataclysm, awaits the visitor. Thanks to the painstaking work of generations of devoted Italian archaeologists, we can experience to-day the most minute details of life twenty centuries ago in a Roman city. So much do we know of the people of Pompeii that they take on vivid life for us—the banker Jucundus, the wool merchant Vesonius, the newlywed Claudius Elogus, the nobleman Diomedes. The dreadful eruption that snatched the life of these people and this city in a single day also gave it a kind of immortality. Pompeii and its people live on today, in timeless permanence, their city transformed by Vesuvius's fury into a miraculous survivor of the ancient world.

Getting at Meaning

1. What event foreshadows the eruption of Mount Vesuvius? Why hasn't the city been completely rebuilt by A.D. 79?

2. Describe the activities of the citizens of Pompeii on a typical day. What kind of city is Pompeii as the writer re-creates it?

3. What terrors do the people experience the day that Vesuvius erupts? How do some of them escape? Why do some people choose not to flee?

4. Why are the ruins of Pompeii especially significant for people today?

Developing Skills in Reading Literature

1. **Historical Narrative.** This selection is nonfiction. However, unlike most of the other selections in the unit, the event described was not experienced first-hand by the writer. Where did the writer get his information? How does the writer make an event that happened over 2,000 years ago interesting to the reader?

2. **Theme.** What is the writer's message about civilization? How does the writer show that people do not change much in basic ways?

Developing Vocabulary

Context Clue: Definition or Restatement. Sometimes a writer defines a word within the context of a sentence. The definition usually is presented in a phrase set off by commas.

Study the italicized word in these sentences. Using the definition provided in the sentence, determine the meaning of the word. Then use the word in a sentence of your own.

1. Every few doors, there is another *thermopolium,* or wine shop.

2. Near the Forum was a *macellum,* or market, where foodstuffs were sold and where beggars wandered.

3. Many *deities,* or gods and goddesses, were worshiped in ancient Pompeii.

4. The Exodus from Egypt was depicted in the famous *mosaic,* a picture made by setting small colored tiles in mortar.

5. Preserved at Pompeii are beggars asking for *alms,* or gifts of money and goods for the poor.

6. The water fell 250 feet in a marvelous *cascade,* or waterfall.

7. The *massacre,* or savage killing, was completed in only twenty-four hours.

Unit Review *Nonfiction*

Understanding the Unit

1. Several selections in this unit deal with the influence of family members on children. For each selection listed below, describe the lessons learned by a child from an adult member of the family.

   "I Know Why the Caged Bird Sings"
   "Discovery of a Father"
   "A Christmas Memory"
   "Grandmother and the Workmen"

2. Which selections in this unit are about poor families and their struggles? How does the experience of being poor affect these families?

3. What are the characteristics of a short story? Which selections in this unit exhibit these characteristics? Give examples from the selections to support your answer.

4. Four types of nonfiction are presented in this unit. What is the purpose of each type?

5. Both humorous essays and essays of social commentary are included in this unit. How are these two types of essays the same? How are they different in subject? in method of presentation?

6. Which selections are examples of first-person narration? Which are examples of third-person narration? What subjects seem to lend themselves to first-person narration? to third-person narration?

7. In which selections is setting described in detail? Choose one of these selections and identify at least five phrases that help to create a clear impression of the setting in the mind of the reader.

8. Which qualities do the following women have in common?

   Grandmother, in "Grandmother and the Workmen"
   the Washwoman
   Momma, in "I Know Why the Caged Bird Sings"

   Cite an incident that illustrates each quality.

9. In your opinion, which character presented in this unit is the most heroic? Explain your choice.

Writing

1. Consider the selections in this unit that deal with older people. Using the ideas from these selections, as well as your own ideas, write a five-paragraph composition that discusses how older people are an important part of society. Your introduction should make a general statement about the elderly, your body paragraphs should give specific examples to support the introductory statement, and your conclusion should summarize your ideas.

2. The writers of the autobiographical selections in this unit describe incidents that have shaped their lives. Think about your own life up to this point. Then describe one main event or several related events that have been important in shaping your life. Relate the events in such a way that your readers gain both a feeling for and an understanding of your experiences.

GREEK VASE. HERACLES WITH CERBERUS.
The Louvre, Paris.

Unit 4

Myths: The Hero

The Nine Heroes Tapestries, 1385. KING ARTHUR WITH THREE CARDINALS.
HEAD OF KING ARTHUR (detail).
The Metropolitan Museum of Art, The Cloisters Collections, Munsey Fund, 1932.

Introduction to the Unit

As a child, you probably had favorite fairy tales. Later, you most likely enjoyed tales of fantasy and imagination, with strange beasts and heroes and heroines whose beauty, strength, and intelligence were beyond human limitations. Some of these tales may be myths and legends, fictitious stories involving gods, heroes, and frequently imaginary animals. The first myths and legends were created before writing systems were invented. They were passed from one generation to the next by what is called the "oral tradition"; the stories were recited by storytellers who retained the basic plots while adding, changing, and often exaggerating details.

Myths and legends appear in all cultures. "Classical mythology" comes from ancient Greece and Rome. For the ancient Greeks and Romans, the myths probably functioned, at least originally, in three different ways. They explained natural phenomena, such as the changing of the seasons and the fertility of the earth. They recounted the activities of gods and goddesses who were worshiped devoutly. They provided entertainment for readers and listeners.

In this unit, you will read about the adventures of three heroes of classical mythology. You will also read about King Arthur and Siegfried, two Medieval heroes. In the final section, you will read an excerpt from a popular book of modern fantasy and a short humorous piece that ridicules classical myths and fairy tales.

Almost all hero stories, ancient and modern, reveal something about the ideals and values of the cultures from which they spring. Perhaps the stories in this unit will stimulate you to think about the heroes admired by people in America today.

Greek Heroes

Tapestry, XVI Century. HERCULES AND ONE OF DIOMEDES' STALLIONS.
The Louvre, Paris.

Daedalus   *Retold by* *Bernard Evslin*

The gods, being all-powerful, needed a more subtle praise than obedience. They preferred their intention to become man's aspiration, their caprice, his law. Athene, in particular, liked to be served this way. The gray-eyed goddess of wisdom, whose sign was the owl, taught men the arts they needed to know, not through gross decree, but through firing the brightest spirits to a white heat wherein they perceived the secret laws of nature and made discoveries and inventions.

Now, in those times, her favorite among all mortals was an Athenian named Daedalus. In the white city of the goddess, Daedalus was honored among all men, and treasure after treasure flowed from his workshop—the wheel, the plough, the loom. Finally, as happens to many men, his pride raced away with his wits; and he fell into a black envy of his own nephew, Talos, a most gifted lad, whom he had taken into his workshop, and who, everyone said, was bound to follow in his footsteps.

"Aye, but he's following too fast," grumbled Daedalus to himself. "He's treading on my heels."

Daedalus, at that time, was working on a special project, a blade to cut wood more quickly than knife or ax. He had puzzled, tested, and tried many things, but nothing seemed to work. Then, one day, coming early to his workshop, he heard a curious sound. It was his nephew, Talos, who had come even earlier. He was leaning over, holding a board pinned to a low table under his knee, and swiftly cutting into it with what looked like the backbone of a fish.

The boy turned to him, smiling. "Look, Uncle," he cried. "See, how splendid! Yesterday I saw a large fish stranded on the beach, half-eaten by gulls, and a notion came to me that his spine with its many sharp teeth might be just the thing we're looking for. So I took it from the fish who had no more need of it and tried it right there. I cut through a great piece of driftwood. Isn't it wonderful? Don't you think the goddess, Athene, herself, washed the fish on shore for me to see? Why are you looking at me that way, Uncle? Are you not pleased?"

"Very pleased, my boy. I have long been considering your case and have been weighing how to reward you according to your merit. Well, now I think I know. But first we must go to Athene's temple to give thanks for this timely inspiration."

He took the boy by the hand and led him up the sunny road to the top of the hill, to the Acropolis where the temple of Athene stood —and still stands. Daedalus led him to the roof of the marble building; and there, as the lad stretched his arms toward heaven, Daedalus stepped softly behind him, placed his hands on his shoulders, and pushed. The boy went tumbling off the temple, off the hill, to the rocks below. But Athene who had heard the first words of the boy's prayer, caught him in mid-air, and turned him into a partridge, which flew away, drumming. She then withdrew her favor from Daedalus.

Word of the boy's death flashed through the city. Nothing could be proved against Daedalus, but he was the target of the darkest suspicions, which, curiously enough, he took as an affront, for nothing could be proved, and so he felt unjustly accused.

"Ungrateful wretches!" he cried. "I will leave this city. I will go elsewhere and find more appreciative neighbors."

He had not told them about his invention of the saw, but he took the model Talos had made and set out for Crete. Arriving there, he went directly to the palace of King Minos, who, at that time, was the most powerful king in all the world, and made him a gift of the marvelous tool that could cut wood more swiftly than knife or ax. Minos, delighted, immediately appointed Daedalus Court Artificer, Smith Extraordinary, and fitted out a workshop for him with the likeliest lads for apprentices. Minos also gave the old fellow a beautiful young slave girl for his own.

Now, the Cretan women were the loveliest in the world, and Crete's court the most glittering. The capital city of Knossos made Athens seem like a little village. Women and girls alike wore topless dresses, gems in their hair, and a most beguiling scent made by slaves who had been blinded so that their noses would grow more keen. Daedalus was an honored figure at this court—and a novelty besides. The Cretans were mad for novelties, so the old man was much flattered and content.

He was a special favorite with the young princesses, Ariadne and Phaedra, who loved to visit him at his workshop and watch him make things. He became very fond of the girls and made them marvelous jointed wooden dolls with springs cunningly set and coiled so that they curtsied and danced and winked their eyes. Queen Pasiphae also came to see him often. He made her a perfume flask that played music when it was uncorked, and a looking glass that allowed her to see the back of her head. She spent hours with him gossiping, for she was very bored.

The queen kept coaxing Daedalus to tell her why he had really left Athens, for she sensed a secret; but all he would ever say was that the goddess, Athene, had withdrawn her favor, so he had been forced to leave her city.

"Goddess Athene!" she cried. "Goddess this and god that . . . What nonsense! These are old wives' tales, nursery vapors, nothing for intelligent men and women to trouble themselves about."

"Oh, my lady," cried Daedalus. "In heaven's name, take care what you say. The gods will hear, and you will be punished."

"And I took you for a sophisticated man," said the queen. "A man of the world, a traveler, a scientist. I am disappointed in you. Gods, indeed! And are you not, my Smith, more clever by far than that lame Hephaestus?[1] And am I not more beautiful than Aphrodite?"[2]

She stood up tall and full-bodied, and, indeed, very beautiful. The old man trembled.

"Come here. Come closer. Look at me. Confess that I am more beautiful than the Cytherean . . . Aphrodite. Of all the gods, she is the one I disbelieve in most. Love . . . my serving maids prate of it, my daughters frisk with the idea. All through the island men meet women by rock and tree, their shadows mingle; and I, I have Minos, the crown on a stick who loves nothing but his own decrees."

"Softly, madame, softly," said Daedalus. "You are not yourself. It is midsummer, a confusing time for women; what they say then must be discounted. Your wild words will be forgiven, but please do not repeat them. Now, see what I have made for you, even as you were saying those foolish things: a parasol, lighter than a butterfly's wing, and

---

1. **Hephaestus:** god of fire and the forge.
2. **Aphrodite:** goddess of love and beauty.

yet so constructed that it opens by itself like a flower when it feels the sun."

But Aphrodite had heard, and she planned a terrible vengeance.

Now, Minos had always been very fond of bulls, especially white ones. He was not aware that this was a matter of heredity, that his mother, Europa, had been courted by Zeus[3] who had assumed the guise of a white bull for the occasion. The king knew only that he liked white bulls. And, since he was in a position to indulge his preferences, he sent through all the world for the largest, the finest, and the whitest. Finally, one arrived, the most splendid bull he had ever seen. It was dazzling white, with hot black eyes, polished hooves, and coral-pink nostrils; its long sharp horns seemed to be made of jet. The king was delighted and sent for all the court to see his fine new bull.

He had no way of knowing that the animal had been sent there by Aphrodite, and neither did Pasiphae. As soon as the queen saw the bull, she felt herself strangling with a great rush of passion. She fell violently, monstrously, in love with the bull. She came to Daedalus and told him.

"What shall I do?" she moaned. "What can I do? I'm going mad. It's tearing me to pieces. You are the cleverest man in the world. Only you can help me. Please, please, tell me what to do."

Daedalus could not resist the beautiful queen; besides, she had touched his vanity. He had to prove himself clever enough to help her in her impossible wish. He thought and thought, and finally went to work. He fashioned a wooden cow with amber eyes, real ivory horns, and ivory hooves and tenderly upholstered it with the most pliant cowhide. It was hollow, and so shaped that Pasiphae could hide herself inside. He put wheels on the hooves, and springs in the wheels. That night, as the moon was rising, the great white bull saw the form of a graceful cow gliding toward him over the meadow, mooing musically.

The next morning, Pasiphae came to the workshop. She gave Daedalus a great leather bag full of gold, and said, "Be careful, old friend. This secret is a deadly one."

Both Pasiphae and Daedalus were good at keeping secrets; but this was one that had to come out for, after a while, the queen gave birth to a child, who attracted a great deal of notice as he was half bull. People derisively called him the Minotaur, or Minos' bull.

Even in his most cruel fury, Minos was a careful planner. He decided to hide his shame, knowing that the world forgets what it does not see. He had Daedalus construct a tangled maze on the palace grounds, a place of thorny hedges and sudden rooms, called the Labyrinth. There were paths running this way and that, becoming corridors, plunging underground, crossing each other, crossing themselves, each one leading back to the middle, so there was no way out.

Here King Minos imprisoned Pasiphae and the Minotaur—and Daedalus too. Minos wanted to make very sure that the old craftsman would never divulge the secret of the Labyrinth, so here Daedalus dwelt. His workshop was in the Labyrinth, but he did not work well. At his bench he could hear Pasiphae howling, and the hideous, broken bellowing of the bull-man, who grew more loathsome and ferocious each day.

His only comfort was his son, Icarus, who, of his own free will, chose to live with him because he so loved and admired his father. It was Icarus who said to him one day, "Father, I grow weary of this maze. Let us leave this place and go to places I have not seen."

"Alas, dear boy," said Daedalus, "we cannot. It is forbidden to leave the Labyrinth."

---

3. **Zeus:** supreme god of the ancient Greeks.

"You know the way out, do you not? You built the thing, after all."

"Yes, certainly, I know the way out. But I dare not take it. Minos would have us put to death immediately. All I can do is petition the king to allow you to go, but I must remain."

"No. We go together."

"But I have explained to you that we cannot."

"Minos is a great king," said Icarus. "But he does not rule the whole earth. Let us leave the island. Let us leave Crete and cross the sea."

"You are mad, dear boy. How can we do this? The sea is locked against us. Every boatman on every craft, large and small, is under strict interdict against allowing me voyage. We cannot leave the island."

"Oh, yes, we can," said Icarus. "I'll tell you how. Just make us wings."

"Wings?"

"To fly with. Like the birds—you know—wings."

"Is it possible? Can I do this?"

"Birds have them; therefore, they have been made. And anything, dear father, that has been made you can duplicate. You have made things never seen before, never known before, never dreamed before."

"I will start immediately," cried Daedalus.

He had Icarus set out baits of fish and capture a gull. Then, very carefully, he copied its wings—not only the shape of them, but the hollow bone struts, and the feathers with their wind-catching overlaps and hollow stems, and he improved a bit on the model. Finally, one day, he completed two magnificent sets of wings with real feathers plucked from the feather cloaks the Cretan dancers used. They were huge, larger than eagles' wings.

He fitted a pair to Icarus, sealing the pinions to the boy's powerful shoulders with wax. Then he donned his own.

"Goodbye to Crete!" cried Icarus joyfully.

"Hear me, boy," said Daedalus. "Follow me closely and do not go off the way. Do not fly too low or the spray will wet your wings, not too high or the sun will melt them. Not too high and not too low, but close by me, through the middle air."

"Oh, come, come," cried Icarus, and he leaped into the air, spreading his wings and soaring off above the hedges of the Labyrinth as if he had been born with wings. Daedalus flew after him.

They flew together over the palace grounds, over the beaches, and headed out to sea. A shepherd looked up and saw them; and a fisherman looked up and saw them; and they both thought they saw gods flying. The shepherd prayed to Hermes,[4] and the fisherman prayed to Poseidon,[5] with glad hearts. Now, they knew, their prayers would be answered.

Icarus had never been so happy. In one leap his life had changed. Instead of groveling in the dank tunnels of the Labyrinth, he was flying, flying free under the wide, bright sky in a great drench of sunlight, the first boy in the history of the world to fly. He looked up and saw a gull, and tried to hold his wings steady and float on the air as the gull was doing, as easily as a duck floats on water. He felt himself slipping, and he slipped all the way in a slanting dive to the dancing surface of the water before he could regain his balance. The water splashing his chest felt deliciously cool.

"No . . . no . . . ," he heard his father call from far above. "Not too low and not too high. Keep to the middle air . . ."

Icarus yelled back a wordless shout of joy, beat his wings, and soared up, up, toward the floating gull.

"Ha . . . ," he thought to himself. "Those

---

4. **Hermes:** god who was messenger to the other gods.
5. **Poseidon:** god of the sea.

things have been flying all their lives. Wait till I get a little practice. I'll outfly them all."

Crete was a brown dot behind them now; there was no land before them, just the diamond-glittering water. Old Daedalus was beating his way through the air, steadily and cautiously, trying this wing-position and that, this body angle and that, observing how the gulls thrust and soared. He kept an eye on Icarus, making mental notes about how to improve the wings once they had landed. He felt a bit tired. The sun was heavy on his shoulders. The figures spun in his head.

"I must not go to sleep," he said to himself. "I must watch the boy. He may do something rash."

But Icarus was flying easily alongside so Daedalus hunched his shoulders, let his chin fall on his chest, and half-coasted on a column of air. He shut his eyes for a moment . . . just for a moment . . .

In that moment Icarus saw a great white swan climb past him, wings spread, shooting like a great white arrow straight for the sun and uttering a long honking call. Icarus looked after him; he had already dwindled and was a splinter of light, moving toward the sun.

"How splendid he is, flying so swiftly, so proudly, so high. How I should like to get a closer look at the sun. Once and for all I should like to see for myself what it really is. Is it a great, burning eye looking through an enormous spyhole, as some Libyans say; or is it Apollo[6] driving a golden coach drawn by golden horses, as the Athenians believe; or perhaps is it a great flaming squid swimming the waters of the sky, as the barbarians say; or, maybe, as my father holds, is it a monster ball of burning gas that Apollo moves by its own motion? I think I shall go a bit closer, anyway. The old man seems to be napping. I can be up and back before he opens his eyes. How splendid if I could get a really good look at the sun and be able to tell my father some-

thing he doesn't know. How that would delight him. What a joke we will have together. Yes . . . I must follow that swan."

So Icarus, full of strength and joy, blood flaming in his veins, stretched his home-made wings and climbed after the swan. Up, up, up, he flew. The air seemed thinner, his body heavier; the sun was swollen now, filling the whole sky, blazing down at him. He couldn't see any more than he had before; he was dazed with light.

"Closer . . ." he thought. "Higher . . . closer . . . up and up. . . ."

He felt the back of his shoulders growing wet.

"Yes," he thought. "This is hot work."

But the wetness was not what he supposed; it was wax—melting wax. The wax bonds of his wings were melting in the heat of the sun. He felt the wings sliding away from him. As they fell away and drifted slowly down, he gazed at them, stupefied. It was as if a great golden hand had taken him in its grasp and hurled him toward the sea. The sky tilted. His breath was torn from his chest. The diamond-hard sea was rushing toward him.

"No," he cried. "No . . . no . . ."

Daedalus, dozing and floating on his column of air, felt the cry ripping through his body like an arrow. He opened his eyes to see the white body of his son hurtling down. It fell into the sea and disappeared.

---

6. **Apollo:** god of music, poetry, prophecy, and medicine.

THE FALL OF ICARUS. Pieter Breughel the Elder.. Musée Royaux des Beaux Arts, Brussels.

Getting at Meaning

1. Name the inventions of Daedalus that are mentioned in this story.

2. How does Athene show her favor toward Daedalus? How does he lose her favor?

3. Why does Daedalus go to Crete? What kind of life does he lead at first?

4. Which goddess does Queen Pasiphae offend? How? What punishment does the queen receive for her insults?

5. Why does King Minos order Daedalus to construct the Labyrinth? Why does he imprison Daedalus in the Labyrinth?

6. How does Daedalus escape from his prison? Why does Icarus perish?

Developing Skills in Reading Literature

1. **Hero.** Because of the special relationship between mythical heroes and the gods, many of the things that happen to the heroes are determined by the gods, not by the heroes themselves. The heroes are destined to become great, but if they offend the gods, they are bound to suffer and to fail. How is Daedalus destined for greatness? What is his special relationship with the gods? How does his destiny change? What qualities does Daedalus possess that would make the Greeks admire him?

2. **Character.** Daedalus shows several human character traits. For instance, he feels jealous and threatened when his nephew invents the saw. What other human emotions does he show?

Developing Vocabulary

Words from Greek and Roman Mythology. The six words below have mythological origins. Using a general dictionary, or a dictionary of word origins, record the definition of each word and its mythological source. Then explain the relationship between the meaning of the word and its source.

| Icarian Sea | cereal | fate |
| chronology | vulcanize | cloth |

Theseus   *Retold by Bernard Evslin*

Young Theseus had a secret. He lived with his mother in a little hut on a wild, sea-battered part of the coast called Troezen. For all his poor house and worn-out clothes, he was very proud, for he had a secret. He knew that he was the son of a king. His mother had told him the story one night when their day's catch of fish had been very bad and they were hungry.

"A king, truly," she said. "And one day you will know his name."

"But mother, then why are you not a queen and I a prince? Why don't we live in a palace instead of a hovel?"

"Politics, my son," she said sadly. "All politics . . . You're too young to understand, but your father has a cousin, a very powerful lord with fifty sons. They are waiting for your father to die so they can divide the kingdom. If they knew he had a son of his own to inherit it, they would kill the son immediately."

"When can I go to him? When can I go there and help my father?"

"When you're grown. When you know how to fight your enemies."

This was Theseus' secret . . . and he needed a secret to keep him warm in those long, cold, hard years. One of his worst troubles was his size. His being small for his age bothered him terribly, for how could he become a great fighter and help his father against terrible enemies if he couldn't even hold his own against the village boys? He exercised constantly by running up and down the cliffs, swimming in the roughest seas, lifting logs and rocks, bending young trees; and indeed he grew much stronger, but he was still very dissatisfied with himself.

A Voice from the Sea

One day, when he had been beaten in a fight with a larger boy, he felt so gloomy that he went down to the beach and lay on the sand watching the waves, hoping that a big one would come along and cover him.

"I will not live this way!" he cried to the wind. "I will not be small and weak and poor. I will be a king, a warrior . . . or I will not be at all."

And then it seemed that the sound of the waves turned to a deep-voiced lullaby, and Theseus fell asleep—not quite asleep, perhaps, because he was watching a great white gull smashing clams open by dropping them on the rocks below. Then the bird swooped down and stood near Theseus' head looking at him, and spoke, "I can crack clams open because they are heavy. Can I do this with shrimps or scallops? No . . . they are too light. Do you know the answer to my riddle?"

"Is it a riddle?"

"A very important one. The answer is this: do not fear your enemy's size, but use it against him. Then his strength will become yours. When you have tried this secret, come back, and I will tell you a better one."

Theseus sat up, rubbing his eyes. Was it a dream? Had the gull been there, speaking to him? Could it be? What did it all mean?

Theseus thought and thought; then he leaped to his feet and raced down the beach, up the cliff to the village where he found the boy who had just beaten him, and slapped him across the face. When the boy, who was almost as big as a man, lunged toward him swinging his big fist, Theseus caught the fist and pulled in the same direction. The boy, swung off balance by his own power, went spinning off his feet and landed headfirst.

"Get up," said Theseus. "I want to try that again."

The big fellow lumbered to his feet and rushed at Theseus, who stopped suddenly. The boy went hurtling over him and landed in the road again. This time he lay still.

"Well," said Theseus, "that was a smart gull."

One by one, Theseus challenged the largest boys of the village; and, by being swift and sure and using their own strength against them, he defeated them all.

Then, he returned to the beach and lay on the sand, watching the waves, and listening as the crashing became a lullaby. Once again his eyes closed, then opened. The great white seagull was pacing the sand near him.

"Thank you," said Theseus.

"Don't thank me," said the gull. "Thank your father. I am but his messenger."

"My father, the king?"

"King, indeed. But not the king your mother thinks."

"What do you mean?"

"Listen now . . . Your father rules no paltry stretch of earth. His domain is as vast as all the seas, and all that is beneath them, and all that the seas claim. He is the Earthshaker, Poseidon."

"Poseidon . . . my father?"

"You are his son."

"Then why does my mother not know? How can this be?"

"You must understand, boy, that the gods sometimes fall in love with beautiful maidens of the earth, but they cannot appear to the maidens in their own forms. The gods are too large, too bright, too terrifying, so they must disguise themselves. Now, when Poseidon fell in love with your mother, she had just been secretly married to Aegeus, king of Athens. Poseidon disguised himself as her new husband, and you, you are his son. One of many, very many; but he seems to have taken a special fancy to you and plans great and terrible things for you . . . if you have the courage."

"I have the courage," said Theseus. "Let me know his will."

"Tomorrow," said the seagull, "you will receive an unexpected gift. Then you must bid farewell to your mother and go to Athens to visit Aegeus. Do not go by sea. Take the dangerous overland route, and your adventures will begin."

The waves made a great, crashing music. The wind crooned. A blackness crossed the boy's mind. When he opened his eyes the gull was gone, and the sun was dipping into the sea.

"Undoubtedly a dream," he said to himself. "But the last dream worked. Perhaps this one will too."

The next morning there was a great excitement in the village. A huge stone had appeared in the middle of the road. In this stone was stuck a sword half-way up to its hilt, and a messenger had come from the oracle[1] at Delphi saying that whoever pulled the sword from the stone was a king's son and must go to his father.

When Theseus heard this, he embraced his mother and said, "Farewell."

"Where are you going, my son?"

"To Athens. This is the time we have been waiting for. I shall take the sword from the stone and be on my way."

---

1. **oracle** (ôr′ə k′l): the place where gods were consulted for answers to questions.

"But, son, it is sunk so deeply. Do you think you can? Look . . . look . . . the strongest men cannot budge it. There is the smith trying . . . And there the Captain of the Guard . . . And look . . . look at that giant herdsman trying. See how he pulls and grunts. Oh, son, I fear the time is not yet."

"Pardon me," said Theseus, moving through the crowd. "Let me through, please. I should like a turn."

When the villagers heard this, heard the short, fragile-looking youth say these words, they exploded in laughter.

"Delighted to amuse you," said Theseus. "Now, watch this."

Theseus grasped the sword by the hilt and drew it from the stone as easily as though he were drawing it from a scabbard. He bowed to the crowd and stuck the sword in his belt. The villagers were too stunned to say anything. They moved apart as he approached, making room for him to pass. He smiled, embraced his mother again, and set out on the long road to Athens.

The Road

The overland road from Troezen to Athens was the most dangerous in the world. It was infested not only by bandits but also giants, ogres, and sorcerers who lay in wait for travelers and killed them for their money, or their weapons, or just for sport. Those who had to make the trip usually went by boat, preferring the risk of shipwreck and pirates to the terrible mountain brigands. If the trip overland had to be made, travelers banded together, went heavily armed, and kept watch as though on a military march.

Theseus knew all this, but he did not give it a second thought. He was too happy to be on his way . . . leaving his poky little village and his ordinary life. He was off to the great world and adventure. He welcomed the dangers that lay in wait. "The more, the better," he thought. "Where there's danger, there's glory. Why, I shall be disappointed if I am *not* attacked."

He was not to be disappointed. He had not gone far when he met a huge man in a bearskin carrying an enormous brass club. This was Corynetes, the cudgeler, terror of travelers. He reached out a hairy hand, seized Theseus by the throat, and lifted his club, which glittered in the hot sunlight.

"Pardon me," said Theseus. "What are you planning to do?"

"Bash in your head."

"Why?"

"That's what I do."

"A beautiful club you have there, sir," said Theseus. "So bright and shiny. You know, it's a positive honor to have my head bashed in with a weapon like this."

"Pure brass," growled the bandit.

"Mmm . . . but is it really brass? It might be gilded wood, you know. A brass club would be too heavy to lift."

"Not too heavy for me," said the bandit, "and it's pure brass. Look . . ."

He held out his club, which Theseus accepted, smiling. Swinging it in a mighty arc, he cracked the bandit's head as if it were an egg.

"Nice balance to this," said Theseus. "I think I'll keep it." He shouldered the club and walked off.

The road ran along the edge of the cliff above the burning blue sea. He turned a bend in the road and saw a man sitting on a rock. The man held a great battle-ax in his hand; he was so large that the ax seemed more like a hatchet.

"Stop!" said the man.

"Good day," said Theseus.

"Now listen, stranger, everyone who passes this way washes my feet. That's the toll. Any questions?"

"One. Suppose I don't?"

"Then I'll simply cut off your head," said

the man, "unless you think that little twig you're carrying will stop this ax."

"I was just asking," said Theseus. "I'll be glad to wash your feet, sir. Personal hygiene is very important, especially on the road."

"What?"

"I said I'll do it."

Theseus knelt at the man's feet and undid his sandals, thinking hard. He knew who this man was; he had heard tales of him. This was Sciron, who was notorious for keeping a pet turtle that was as large for a turtle as Sciron was for a man and was trained to eat human flesh. This giant turtle swam about at the foot of the cliff, waiting for Sciron to kick his. victims over. Theseus glanced swiftly down the cliffside. Sure enough, he saw the great, blunt head of the turtle lifted out of the water, waiting.

Theseus took Sciron's huge foot in his hand, holding it by the ankle. As he did so, the giant launched a mighty kick. Theseus was ready. When the giant kicked, Theseus pulled, dodging swiftly out of the way as the enormous body hurtled over him, over and down, splashing the water cliff-high as it hit. Theseus saw the turtle swim toward the splash. He arose, dusted off his knees, and proceeded on his journey.

The road dipped now, running past a grove of pines.

"Stop!"

He stopped. There was another huge brute of a man facing him. First Theseus thought that Sciron had climbed back up the cliff somehow; but then he realized that this must be Sciron's brother, of whom he had also heard. This fellow was called Pityocamptes, which means "pine-bender." He was big enough and strong enough to press pine trees to the ground. It was his habit to bend a tree just as a passerby approached and ask the newcomer to hold it for a moment. The traveler, afraid not to oblige, would grasp the top of the tree. Then Pityocamptes, with a

great, jeering laugh, would release his hold. The pine tree would spring mightily to its full height, flinging the victim high in the air, so high that the life was dashed out of him when he hit the ground. Then the bandit would search his pockets, chuckling all the while; he was a great joker. Now he said to Theseus, "Wait, friend. I want you to do me a favor."

He reached for a pine tree and bent it slowly to earth like an enormous bow. "Just hold this for a moment like a good fellow, will you?"

"Certainly," said Theseus.

Theseus grasped the tree, set his feet, clenched his teeth, let his mind go dark and all his strength flow downward, through his legs, into the earth, anchoring him to the earth like a rock. Pityocamptes let go, expecting to see Theseus fly into the air. Nothing happened. The pine stayed bent. The lad was holding it, legs rigid, arms trembling. The giant could not believe his eyes. He thought he must have broken the pine while bending it. He leaned his head closer to see. Then Theseus let go. The tree snapped up, catching the giant under the chin, knocking him unconscious. Theseus bent the tree again, swiftly bound the giant's wrists to it. He pulled down another pine and tied Pityocamptes' legs to that . . . and then let both pines go. They sprang apart. Half of Pityocamptes hung from one tree, half from the other. Vultures screamed with joy and fed on both parts impartially. Theseus wiped the pine tar from his hands and continued on his way.

By now it was nightfall, and he was very weary. He came to an inn where light was coming from the window, smoke from the chimney. But it was not a cozy sight; the front yard was littered with skulls and other bones.

"They don't do much to attract guests," thought Theseus. "Well . . . I'm tired. It has been a gruesome day. I'd just as soon go to bed now without any more fighting. On the other hand, if an adventure comes my way, I must not avoid it. Let's see what this bone-collector looks like."

He strode to the door and pounded on it, crying, "Landlord! Landlord, ho!"

The door flew open. In it was framed a greasy-looking giant, resembling Sciron and the pine-bender, but older, filthier, with long, tangled gray hair and a blood-stained gray beard. He had great, meaty hands, like grappling hooks.

"Do you have a bed for the night?" said Theseus.

"A bed? That I have. Come with me."

He led Theseus to a room where a bed stood —an enormous ugly piece of furniture, hung with leather straps and chains and shackles.

"What are all those bolts and bindings for?" said Theseus.

"To keep you in bed until you've had your proper rest."

"Why should I wish to leave the bed?"

"Everyone else seems to. You see, this is a special bed, exactly six feet long from head to foot. And I am a very neat, orderly person. I like things to fit. Now, if the guest is too short for the bed, we attach those chains to his ankles and stretch him. Simple."

"And if he's too long?" said Theseus.

"Oh, well then we just lop off his legs to the proper length."

"I see."

"But don't worry about that part of it. You look like a stretch job to me. Go ahead, lie down."

"And if I do, then you will attach chains to my ankles and stretch me—if I understand you correctly."

"You understand me fine. Lie down."

"But all this stretching sounds uncomfortable."

"You came here. Nobody invited you. Now you've got to take the bad with the good."

"Yes, of course," said Theseus. "I suppose if I decided not to take advantage of your hospitality . . . I suppose you'd *make* me lie down, wouldn't you?"

"Oh sure. No problem."

"How? Show me."

The inn-keeper, whose name was Procrustes, reached out a great hand, put it on Theseus' chest, and pushed him toward the bed. Theseus took his wrist, and, as the big man pushed, he pulled . . . in the swift, shoulder-turning downward snap he had taught himself. Procrustes flew over his shoulder and landed on the bed. Theseus bolted him fast, took up an ax, and chopped off his legs as they dangled over the footboards. Then, because he did not wish the fellow to suffer, chopped off his head too.

"As you have done by travelers, so are you done by," said Theseus. "You have made your bed, old man. Now lie on it."

He put down the ax, picked up his club, and resumed his journey, deciding to sleep in the open because he found the inn unpleasant.

Athens

Athens was not yet a great city in those days, but it was far more splendid than any Theseus had seen. He found it quite beautiful, with arbors and terraces and marble temples. After the adventures of the road, however, he found it strangely dull. He suffered, too, from humiliation; for, although he was the king's son, his father was in a very weak position, so he could not be a real prince. It was his father's powerful cousin, the tall, black-browed Pallas, with his fifty fierce sons, who actually ran things. Their estate was much larger and finer than the castle, their private army stronger than the Royal Guard, and Theseus could not bear it.

"Why was I given the sign?" he stormed. "Why did I pull the sword from the stone and come here to Athens? To skulk in the castle like a runaway slave? What difference does it make, Father, how *many* there are? After we fight them, there will be many less. Let's fight! Right now!"

"No," said Aegeus, "we cannot. Not yet. It would not be a battle; it would be suicide. They must not know you are here. I am sorry now I had you come all the way to Athens. It is too dangerous. I should have kept you in some little village somewhere, outside of town, where we could have seen each other every day, but where you would not be in such danger."

"Well, if I am no use here, let me go to Crete!" cried Theseus. "If I can't fight our enemies at home, let me try my hand abroad."

"Crete! . . . Oh, my dear boy, no, no . . ." and the old man fell to lamenting, for it was in these days that Athens, defeated in a war with Crete, was forced by King Minos to pay a terrible tribute. He demanded that each year the Athenians send him seven of their most beautiful maidens, seven of their strongest young men. These were taken to the Labyrinth and offered to the monster who lived there—the dread Minotaur, half man and half bull—son of Pasiphae and the bull she had fallen in love with. Year after year they were taken from their parents, these seven maidens and seven youths, and were never heard of again. Now the day of tribute was approaching again.

Theseus offered to go himself as one of the seven young men and take his chances with the monster. He kept hammering at his father, kept producing so many arguments, was so electric with impatience and rage, that finally his father consented, and the name Theseus was entered among those who were to be selected for tribute. The night before he left, he embraced Aegeus and said, "Be of good heart, dear sire. I traveled a road that was supposed to be fatal before and came

out alive. I met quite a few unpleasant characters on my journey and had a few anxious moments, but I learned from them that the best weapon you can give an enemy is your own fear. So . . . who can tell? I may emerge victorious from the Labyrinth and lead my companions home safely. Then I will be known to the people of Athens and will be able to rouse them against your tyrant cousins and make you a real king."

"May the gods protect you, son," said Aegeus." I shall sacrifice to Zeus and to Ares,[2] and to our own Athene, every day, and pray for your safety."

"Don't forget Poseidon," said Theseus.

"Oh, yes, Poseidon too," said Aegeus. "Now do this for me, son. Each day I shall climb the Hill of the Temple, and from there watch over the sea . . . watching for your ship to return. It will depart wearing black sails, as all the sad ships of tribute do; but if you should overcome the Minotaur, please, I pray you, raise a white sail. This will tell me that you are alive and save a day's vigil."

"That I will do," said Theseus. "Watch for the white sail . . ."

Crete

All Athens was at the pier to see the black-sailed ship depart. The parents of the victims were weeping and tearing their clothing. The maidens and the young men, chosen for their beauty and courage, stood on the deck trying to look proud; but the sound of lamentation reached them, and they wept to see their parents weep. Then Theseus felt the cords of his throat tighten with rage. He stamped his foot on the deck and shouted, "Up anchor, and away!" as though he were the captain of the vessel. The startled crew obeyed, and the ship moved out of the harbor.

Theseus immediately called the others to

---

2. **Ares:** god of war.

him. "Listen to me," he said. "You are not to look upon yourselves as victims, or victims you will surely be. The time of tribute has ended. You are to regard this voyage not as a submission but as a military expedition. Everything will change, but first you must change your own way of looking at things. Place your faith in my hands; place yourselves under my command. Will you?"

"We will!" they shouted.

"Good. Now I want every man to instruct every girl in the use of the sword and the battle-ax. We may have to cut our way to freedom. I shall also train you to respond to my signals—whistles, hand-movements—for if we work as a team, we may be able to defeat the Minotaur and confound our enemies."

They agreed eagerly. They were too young to live without hope, and Theseus' words filled them with courage. Every day he drilled them, man and maiden alike, as though they were a company of soldiers. He taught them to wrestle in the way he had invented. And this wild young activity, this sparring and fencing, so excited the crew, that they were eager to place themselves under the young man's command.

"Yes," he said. "I will take your pledges. You are Athenians. Right now that means you are poor, defeated, living in fear. But one day 'Athenian' will be the proudest name in the world, a word to make warriors quake in their armor, kings shiver upon their thrones!"

Now Minos of Crete was the most powerful king in all the world. His capital, Knossos, was the gayest, richest, proudest city in the world; and the day, each year, when the victims of the Minotaur arrived from Athens, was always a huge feast-day. People mobbed the streets—warriors with shaven heads and gorgeous feathered cloaks, women in jewels and topless dresses, children, farmers, great swaggering bullherders, lithe bullfighters, dwarfs, peacocks, elephants, and slaves, slaves, slaves from every country known to man. The streets were so jammed no one could walk freely, but the King's Guard kept a lane open from quayside to Palace. And here, each year, the fourteen victims were marched so that the whole city could see them—marched past the crowds to the Palace to be presented to the king to have their beauty approved before giving them to the Minotaur.

On this day of arrival, the excited harbor-master came puffing to the castle, fell on his knees before the throne, and gasped, "Pity, great king, pity . . ."

And then in a voice strangled with fright, the harbormaster told the king that one of the intended victims, a young man named Theseus, demanded a private audience with Minos before he would allow the Athenians to disembark.

"My warships!" thundered Minos. "The harbor is full of triremes.[3] Let the ship be seized, and this Theseus and his friends dragged here through the streets."

"It cannot be, your majesty. Their vessel stands over the narrow neck of the harbor. And he swears to scuttle it right there, blocking the harbor, if any of our ships approach."

"Awkward . . . very awkward," murmured Minos. "Quite resourceful for an Athenian, this young man. Worth taking a look at. Let him be brought to me."

Thereupon Theseus was informed that the king agreed to see him privately. He was led to the Palace, looking about eagerly as he was ushered down the lane past the enormous crowd. He had never seen a city like this. It made Athens look like a little fishing village. He was excited and he walked proudly, head high, eyes flashing. When he came to the Palace, he was introduced to the king's daughters, two lovely young princesses, Ariadne and Phaedra.

---

3. **trireme** (trī′rēm): a warship with three banks of oars on each side.

"I regret that my queen is not here to greet you," said Minos. "But she has become attached to her summer house in the Labyrinth and spends most of her time there."

The princesses were silent, but they never took their eyes off Theseus. He could not decide which one he preferred. Ariadne he supposed—the other was really still a little girl. But she had a curious cat-faced look about her that intrigued him. However, he could not give much thought to this; his business was with the king.

Finally, Minos signaled the girls to leave the room, and motioned Theseus toward his throne. "You wanted to see me alone," he said. "Here I am. Speak."

"I have a request, your majesty. As the son of my father, Aegeus, King of Athens, and his representative in this court, I ask you formally to stop demanding your yearly tribute."

"Oh, heavens," said Minos. "I thought you would have something original to say. And you come with this threadbare old petition. I have heard it a thousand times and refused it a thousand times."

"I know nothing of what has been done before," said Theseus. "But only of what I must do. You laid this tribute upon Athens to punish the city, to show the world that you were the master. But it serves only to degrade you and show the world that you are a fool."

"Feeding you to the Minotaur is much too pleasant a finale for such an insolent rascal," said Minos. "I shall think of a much more interesting way for you to die—perhaps several ways."

"Let me explain what I mean," said Theseus. "Strange as it seems, I do not hate you. I admire you. You're the most powerful king in the world, and I admire power. In fact, I intend to imitate your career. So what I say, I say in all friendliness, and it is this: when you take our young men and women and shut them in the Labyrinth to be devoured by the Minotaur, you are making the whole world forget Minos, the great general Minos, the wise king. What you are forcing upon their attention is Minos, the betrayed husband, the man whose wife disliked him so much she eloped with a bull. And this image of you is what people remember. Drop the tribute, I say, and you will once again live in man's mind as warrior, law-giver, and king."

"You are an agile debater," said Minos, "as well as a very reckless young man, saying these things to me. But there is a flaw in your argument. If I were to drop the tribute, my subjects would construe this as an act of weakness. They would be encouraged to launch conspiracies against me. Other countries under my sway would be encouraged to rebel. It cannot be done."

"I can show you a graceful way to let the tribute lapse. One that will not be seen as a sign of weakness. Just tell me how to kill the monster."

"Kill the monster, eh? And return to Athens a hero? And wipe out your enemies there? And then subdue the other cities of Greece until you become leader of a great alliance? And then come visit me again with a huge fleet and an enormous army, and topple old Minos from his throne . . . ? Do I describe your ambitions correctly?"

"The future does not concern me," said Theseus. "I take one thing at a time. And the thing that interests me now is killing the Minotaur."

"Oh, forget the Minotaur," said Minos. "How do you know there is one? How do you know it's not some maniac there who ties sticks to his head? Whatever it is, let him rot there in the Labyrinth with his mad mother. I have a better plan for you. My sons are dead. My daughter Ariadne, I notice, looks upon you with favor. Marry her, and become my heir. One day you will rule Crete and Athens both . . . and all the cities of the sea."

"Thank you, sir. I appreciate your offer. But I came here to fight a monster."

"You are mad."

"Perhaps. But this is the only way I know how to be. When I am your age, when the years have thinned my blood, when rage has cooled into judgment, then I will go in for treaties, compromises. Now, I must fight."

"Why is the young fool so confident?" thought Minos to himself. "He acts like a man who knows he is protected by the gods. Can it be true what they say? Is he really the son of Poseidon? Do I have that kind of enemy on my hands? If so, I will make doubly sure to get rid of him."

Then he said aloud, "You are wrong to refuse my offer. I suppose you are made so wildly rash by some old wives' gossip in your little village that you are the son of this god or that. Those mountain villages of yours, they're ridiculous. Every time a child does something out of the way, all the crones and hags get together and whisper, 'He's the son of a god, really the son of a god.' Is that the way of it? Tell the truth now."

"My truth," said Theseus, "is that I am the son of Poseidon."

"Poseidon, eh? No less. Well, how would you like to prove it?"

"Why should I care to prove it? *I* know. That's enough for me. The whole world has heard that you are the son of Zeus, who courted your mother, Europa, in the guise of a white bull. Everyone has heard this tale; few disbelieve it. But can you prove it?"

"Come with me," said Minos.

He led him out of the Palace, beyond the wall, to a cliff overlooking the sea. He stood tall, raised his arms, and said, "Father Zeus, make me a sign."

Lightning flashed so furiously that the night became brighter than day, and the sky spoke in thunder. Then Minos dropped his arms; the light stopped pulsing in the sky, and the thunder was still.

"Well," said Minos. "Have I proved my parentage?"

"It's an impressive display. I suppose it proves something."

"Then show me you are the son of Poseidon."

Minos took the crown from his head and threw it over the cliff into the sea. They heard the tiny splash far below.

"If you are his son, the sea holds no terror for you. Get me my crown," said Minos.

Without a moment's hesitation, Theseus stepped to the edge of the cliff and leaped off. As he fell, he murmured, "Father, help me now."

Down he plunged, struck the black water and went under, shearing his way through until he felt his lungs bursting. But he did not kick toward the surface. He let out the air in his chest in a long tortured gasp, and then, breathed in. No strangling rush of water, but a great lung-full of sweet, cool air . . . and he felt himself breathing as naturally as a fish. He swam down, down, and as he swam, his eyes became accustomed to the color of the night sea; he moved in a deep green light. And the first thing he saw was the crown gleaming on the bottom. He swam down and picked it up.

Theseus stood on the ocean bottom holding the crown in his hand and said, "All thanks, Father Poseidon."

He waited there for the god to answer him, but all he saw were dark gliding shapes, creatures of the sea passing like shadows. He swam slowly to the surface, climbed the cliff, and walked to where Minos was waiting.

"Your crown, sir."

"Thank you."

"Are you convinced now that Poseidon is my father?"

"I am convinced that the water is more shallow here than I thought. Convinced that you are lucky."

"Luck? Is that not another word for divine favor?"

"Perhaps. At any rate, I am also convinced

that you are a dangerous young man. So dangerous that I am forced to strip you of certain advantages allowed those who face the Minotaur. You will carry neither sword nor ax, but only your bare hands . . . And your luck, of course. I think we will not meet again. So farewell." He whistled sharply. His Royal Guard appeared, surrounded Theseus, and marched him off to a stone tower at the edge of the Labyrinth. There they locked him up for the night.

An hour before dawn, Ariadne appeared in his cell and said, "I love you, Theseus. I will save you from death if you promise to take me back to Athens with you."

"And how do you propose to save me, lovely princess?"

"Do you know what the Labyrinth is? It is a hedge of a thousand lanes, all leading in, and only one leading out. And this one is so concealed, has so many twists and turns and secret windings that no one can possibly find his way out. Only I can travel the Labyrinth freely. I will lead you in and hide you. I will also lead you around the central chamber where the Minotaur is and lead you out again. You will not even see the monster. Since no one has ever found his way out of the maze, Minos will assume that you have killed the Minotaur, and you will have a chance to get to your ship and escape before the trick is discovered. But you must take me with you."

"It cannot be," said Theseus.

"Don't you believe me? It's all true. Look . . ."

She took from her tunic a ball of yellow silk thread and dropped it on the floor. The ball swiftly rolled across the room, unwinding itself as it went. It rolled across the bench, wrapped itself around one of Theseus' ankles, rolled up the wall, across the ceiling and down again. Then Ariadne tugged sharply on her end of the thread, and the ball reversed itself, rolling back the way it had come, reeling in its thread as it rolled. Back to Ariadne it rolled and leaped into her hand.

"This was made for me by old Daedalus," said Ariadne. "It was he who built the Labyrinth, you know. And my father shut him up in it, too. I used to go visit him there. He made me this magic ball of thread so that I would always be able to find my way to him, and find my way back. He was very fond of me."

"I'm getting very fond of you too," said Theseus.

"Do you agree?" cried Ariadne. "Will you let me guide you in the Labyrinth and teach you how to avoid the monster, and fool my father? Say you will. Please . . ."

"I'll let you guide me through the maze," said Theseus. "Right to where the monster dwells. You can stay there and watch the fight. And when it's over, you can lead me back."

"No, no, I won't be able to. You'll be dead! It's impossible for you to fight the Minotaur."

"It is impossible for me not to."

"You won't even be armed."

"I have always traveled light, sweet princess, and taken my weapons from the enemy. I see no reason to change my habits now. Are you the kind of girl who seeks to change a man's habits? If you are, I don't think I will take you back to Athens."

'Oh, please, do not deny me your love," she said. "I will do as you say."

The next morning when the Royal Guard led Theseus out of the tower and forced him into the outer lane of the Labyrinth, Ariadne was around the first bend, waiting. She tied one end of the thread to a branch of the hedge, then dropped the ball to the ground. It rolled slowly, unwinding; they followed, hand in hand. It was pleasant, walking in the Labyrinth. The hedge grew tall above their heads and was heavy with little white, sweet-smelling flowers. The lane turned and twisted and turned again, but the ball of thread ran ahead, and they followed it. Theseus heard a howling.

"Sounds like the wind," he said.

"No, it is not the wind. It is my mad mother, howling."

They walked farther. They heard a rumbling, crashing sound.

"What's that?"

"That is my brother. He's hungry."

They continued to follow the ball of thread. Now the hedges grew so tall the branches met above their heads, and it was dark. Ariadne looked up at him, sadly. He bent his head and brushed her lips in a kiss.

"Please don't go to him," she said. "Let me lead you out now. He will kill you. He has the strength of a bull and the cunning of a man."

"Who knows?" said Theseus. "Perhaps he has the weakness of a man and the stupidity of a bull." He put his hand over her mouth. "Anyway, let me think so because I must fight him, you see, and I'd rather not frighten myself beforehand."

The horrid roaring grew louder and louder. The ball of thread ran ahead, ran out of the lane, into an open space. And here, in a kind of meadow surrounded by the tall hedges of the Labyrinth, stood the Minotaur.

Theseus could not believe his eyes. The thing was more fearsome than in his worst dreams. What he had expected was a bull's head on a man's body. What he saw was something about ten feet tall shaped like a man, like an incredibly huge and brutally muscular man, but covered with a short, dense brown fur. It had a man's face, but a squashed, bestialized one, with poisonous red eyes, great blunt teeth, and thin leathery lips. Sprouting out of its head were two long, heavy, polished horns. Its feet were hooves, razor sharp; its hands were shaped like a man's hands, but much larger and hard as

horn. When it clenched them, they were great fists of bone.

It stood pawing the grass with a hoof, peering at Theseus with its little red eyes. There was a bloody slaver on its lips.

Now, for the first time in all his battles, Theseus became unsure of himself. He was confused by the appearance of the monster. It filled him with a kind of horror that was beyond fear, as if he were wrestling a giant spider. So when the monster lowered its head and charged, thrusting those great bone lances at him, Theseus could not move out of the way.

There was only one thing to do. Drawing himself up on tiptoe, making himself as narrow as possible, he leaped into the air and seized the monster's horns. Swinging himself between the horns, he somersaulted onto the Minotaur's head, where he crouched, gripping the horns with desperate strength. The monster bellowed with rage and shook its head violently. But Theseus held on. He thought his teeth would shake out of his head; he felt his eyeballs rattling in their sockets. But he held on.

Now, if it can be done without one's being gored, somersaulting between the horns is an excellent tactic when fighting a real bull; but the Minotaur was not a real bull; it had hands. So when Theseus refused to be shaken off but stood on the head between the horns, trying to dig his heels into the beast's eyes, the Minotaur stopped shaking his head, closed his great horny fist, big as a cabbage and hard as a rock, and struck a vicious backward blow, smashing his fist down on his head, trying to squash Theseus as you squash a beetle.

This is what Theseus was waiting for. As soon as the fist swung toward him, he jumped off the Minotaur's head, and the fist smashed between the horns, full on the skull. The Minotaur's knees bent; he staggered and fell over; he had stunned himself. Theseus

GREEK VASE, 550 B.C. *Theseus Killing the Minotaur (detail). British Museum.*

knew he had only a few seconds before the beast would recover his strength. He rushed to the monster, took a horn in both hands, put his foot against the ugly face, and putting all his strength in a sudden tug, broke the horn off at the base. He leaped away. Now he, too, was armed, and with a weapon taken from the enemy.

The pain of the breaking horn goaded the Minotaur out of his momentary swoon. He scrambled to his feet, uttered a great, choked bellow, and charged toward Theseus, trying to hook him with his single horn. Bone cracked against bone as Theseus parried with his horn. It was like a duel now, the beast thrusting with his horn, Theseus parrying, thrusting in return. Since the Minotaur was much stronger, it forced Theseus back—back until it had Theseus pinned against the hedge. As soon as he felt the first touch of the hedge, Theseus disengaged, ducked past the Minotaur, and raced to the center of the meadow, where he stood, poised, arm drawn back. For

the long, pointed horn made as good a javelin as it did a sword, and so could be used at a safer distance.

The Minotaur whirled and charged again. Theseus waited until he was ten paces away, and then whipped his arm forward, hurling the javelin with all his strength. It entered the bull's neck and came out the other side. But so powerful was the Minotaur's rush, so stubborn his bestial strength, that he trampled on with the sharp horn through his neck and ran right over Theseus, knocking him violently to the ground. Then it whirled to try to stab Theseus with its horn; but the blood was spouting fast now, and the monster staggered and fell on the ground beside Theseus.

Ariadne ran to the fallen youth. She turned him over, raised him in her arms; he was breathing. She kissed him. He opened his eyes, looked around, and saw the dead Minotaur; then he looked back at her and smiled. He climbed to his feet, leaning heavily on Ariadne.

"Tell your thread to wind itself up again, Princess. We're off to Athens."

When Theseus came out of the Labyrinth there was an enormous crowd of Cretans gathered. They had heard the sound of fighting, and, as the custom was, had gathered to learn of the death of the hostages. When they saw the young man covered with dirt and blood, carrying a broken horn, with Ariadne clinging to his arm, they raised a great shout.

Minos was there, standing with his arms folded. Phaedra was at his side. Theseus bowed to him and said, "Your majesty, I have the honor to report that I have rid your kingdom of a foul monster."

"Prince Theseus," said Minos. "According to the terms of the agreement, I must release you and your fellow hostages."

"Your daughter helped me, king. I have promised to take her with me. Have you any objection?"

"I fancy it is too late for objections. The women of our family haven't had much luck in these matters. Try not to be too beastly to her."

"Father," said Phaedra, "she will be lonesome there in far-off Athens. May I go with her and keep her company?"

"You too?" said Minos. He turned to Theseus. "Truly, young man, whether or not Poseidon has been working for you, Aphrodite surely has."

"I will take good care of your daughters, king," said Theseus. "Farewell."

And so, attended by the Royal Guard, Theseus, his thirteen happy companions, and the two Cretan princesses, walked through the mobbed streets from the Palace to the harbor. There they boarded their ship.

It was a joyous ship that sailed northward from Crete to Athens. There was feasting and dancing night and day. And every young man aboard felt himself a hero too, and every maiden a princess. And Theseus was lord of them all, drunk with strength and joy. He was so happy he forgot his promise to his father—forgot to tell the crew to take down the black sail and raise a white one.

King Aegeus, keeping a lonely watch on the Hill of the Temple, saw first a tiny speck on the horizon. He watched it for a long time and saw it grow big and then bigger. He could not tell whether the sail was white or black; but as it came nearer, his heart grew heavy. The sail seemed to be dark. The ship came nearer, and he saw that it wore a black sail. He knew that his son was dead.

"I have killed him," he cried. "In my weakness, I sent him off to be killed. I am unfit to be king, unfit to live. I must go to Tartarus[4] immediately and beg his pardon there."

And the old king leaped from the hill, dived through the steep air into the sea far below, and was drowned. He gave that lovely blue, fatal stretch of water its name for all time—the Aegean Sea.

Theseus, upon his return to Athens, was hailed as king. The people worshipped him. He swiftly raised an army, wiped out his powerful cousins, and then led the Athenians forth into many battles, binding all the cities of Greece together in an alliance. Then, one day he returned to Crete to reclaim the crown of Minos that once he had recovered from the sea.

---

4. **Tartarus:** the home of the dead, beneath the earth.

GREEK VASE, 550 B.C. THESEUS AND THE MINOTAUR.
The Metropolitan Museum of Art. Purchase, 1947, Joseph Pulitzer Bequest.

Getting at Meaning

1. What would you say is the single most important factor in the successes of Theseus? Explain your answer.

2. Who is the father of Theseus? In what sense does Theseus have two fathers? Why does he live in the village and not with his father?

3. What does the gull's riddle mean? As the story progresses, how does Theseus use the gull's advice to triumph over his enemies? Give specific examples.

4. How does Theseus prove to the messenger and to the villagers that he is a king's son?

5. Describe the adventures of Theseus on the road to Athens. Who are the various villains he meets? How does he deal with each one?

6. What is the tribute that the citizens of Athens must pay each year to King Minos of Crete? Why does Theseus insist on going to Crete? What is King Aegeus' final advice to him?

7. How does Theseus impress King Minos?

8. Describe the Minotaur. What is the story of the monster's birth? How is Theseus able to kill the beast?

9. What is the one unhappy element of Theseus' journey home? What geographical name recalls this misfortune?

Developing Skills in Reading Literature

1. **Hero.** The heroes in Greek mythology often are "demigods," meaning that they are half human and half god. In what ways is Theseus half god? Which of his exploits strike you as superhuman? What qualities in Theseus might have represented ideal human qualities to the Greeks?

One reason that Theseus is able to perform superhuman feats is that he is advised and protected by a god. Who helps him? Why?

2. **Myth.** A myth is one of a class of stories, usually concerning gods, heroes, and imagi-

nary animals, the purpose of which is to explain some religious belief, custom, or natural phenomenon. Some characters and events in mythology are based on historical reality. For example, evidence suggests that there was once a king of Athens named Theseus. Which aspects of this story might have some historical truth to them? Which elements are obviously imaginary?

3. **Rising Action.** Theseus' adventures begin when he leaves his village to go to Athens. How do the dangers along the way help to create suspense in the story? In what sense do they build to his final challenge, the Minotaur?

4. **Description.** Reread the descriptions of these mythical beasts:

Corynetes	Procrustes	Sciron
the Minotaur	Pityocamptes	

Notice that the writer provides increasingly detailed descriptions, leading up to the description of the Minotaur, which is the most gruesomely detailed of all. In what way do the descriptions of the beasts reinforce the plot of the story?

Developing Vocabulary

Words from Greek and Roman Mythology. Consult a general dictionary or a dictionary of word origins to discover the mythological source for each of the following words. Explain the meaning of each word and how it relates to mythology. Identify the two words that come from sources mentioned in the Theseus story.

mercurial	chaos	cupidity
Procrustian	labyrinthine	tantalize

The Labors of Heracles

Retold by *Robert Graves*

Heracles, whom the Romans called Hercules, was Zeus' son by Alcmene, a Theban princess. Hera,[1] angry that Zeus had made another of his marriages with a mortal woman, sent two tremendous snakes to kill Heracles while still a baby. He and his twin brother Iphicles were lying asleep in a shield, used as a cradle, when the snakes crawled hissing towards them across the floor. Iphicles screamed and rolled out of the shield. But Heracles, an immensely strong child, caught the snakes by their throats, one in each hand, and strangled them.

As a boy, Heracles took far more interest in fighting than in reading, writing, or music. He also preferred roast meat and barley bread to honey cakes and fruit pies. Soon he became the best archer, the best wrestler, and the best boxer alive. Because Linus, his music teacher, beat him for not taking enough trouble over his scales, Heracles knocked Linus dead with a lyre.[2] Accused of murder, Heracles said simply, "Linus hit me first. All I did was to defend myself." The judges let him off.

Eurystheus, the High King of Greece, wanted to banish Amphitryon, King of Thebes, now Heracles' stepfather; but Heracles nobly offered to be his slave for ninety-nine months if Amphitryon might stay and keep his throne. Hera advised Eurystheus: "Agree, but set Heracles the ten most dangerous Labors you can possibly choose, all to be performed in those ninety-nine months. I want him killed."

The First Labor that Eurystheus set Heracles was to kill the Nemean Lion, an enormous beast, with a skin proof against stone, brass, or iron. It lived in a mountain cave. When the arrows that Heracles shot at the lion bounced off harmlessly, he took his great club of wild olive wood and hit it on the head, but only smashed the club. The lion shook its head, because of the singing noise in its ears, then yawned and went back to its cave. This cave had two entrances. Heracles netted the smaller with a brass net and, going in by the larger, caught the lion by the throat. Though it bit off the middle finger of his left hand, he managed to get its head under his right arm and squeeze it to death. Heracles skinned the lion by using one of its own claws for a knife, and afterwards wore the skin. Then he cut himself a second club of wild olive wood and reported to Eurystheus.

The Second Labor was far more dangerous: to kill the monstrous Hydra in the marshes of Lerna. She had a huge body, like a dog's, and eight snake heads on long necks. Heracles fired flaming arrows at the Hydra as she came out from her hole under the roots of a plane tree. Then he rushed forward and battered at the eight heads. As fast as he crushed them, others grew in their places.

---

1. **Hera:** wife of Zeus, queen of the gods.
2. **lyre** (līr): a small stringed instrument of the harp family.

Up scuttled a crab, sent by Hera, and bit his foot. Heracles broke its shell with a kick. At the same time he drew his sharp, gold-hilted sword and called for Iolaus, his chariot driver. Iolaus hurriedly brought a torch and, after Heracles had cut off each head, singed the neck to prevent a new one from sprouting. That was the end of the Hydra. Heracles dipped his arrows in her poisonous blood. Whoever they struck would die painfully.

The Third Labor was to capture the Ceryneian Hind, a white deer with brass hooves and golden horns, belonging to the Goddess Artemis.[3] It took Heracles a whole year to catch the hind. He chased her up hill and down dale all over Greece, until at last he shot an unpoisoned arrow at her as she ran past him. The arrow went between the sinew and bone of her forelegs, without drawing a drop of blood, and pinned them together. As she stumbled and fell, Heracles seized her, drew out the arrow, and carried her on his shoulders to Eurystheus. Artemis would have been furious if he had killed her pet hind, but forgave him because she admired his clever shooting. Eurystheus then set the hind free.

The Fourth Labor was to capture the Erymanthian Boar, a huge creature with tusks like an elephant's, and an arrow-proof skin. Heracles chased it to and fro across the mountains in winter, until it stuck in a deep snowdrift. There he jumped in after it and tied its hind legs to its forelegs. When Eurystheus saw Heracles carrying the boar on his back up the palace avenue, he ran off and hid in a big brass jar.

The Fifth Labor was to clean King Augeias' filthy cattle yard in a single day. Augeias owned many thousands of cattle and never troubled to get rid of the messes they made. Eurystheus set this task just to annoy Heracles, hoping that he would cover himself with filth as he loaded the dung in baskets and carried them away. Augeias stood and sneered at Heracles: "I bet you twenty cows to one, that you cannot clean the yard in a day."

"Done," said Heracles.

---

3. **Artemis:** the goddess of the moon, wild animals, and hunting.

GREEK VASE, 540 B.C. *Heracles and the Keryneian Hind (detail).*
British Museum.

GREEK VASE, 510 B.C. *Heracles and the Eyrmanthian Boar* (detail). *British Museum.*

He swung his club, knocked down the yard wall, then borrowed a mattock[4] and quickly dug deep channels from two nearby rivers. The river water, rushing through the yard, washed it clean in a very short time.

As his Sixth Labor, Eurystheus told Heracles to free the Stymphalian Marsh of its brass-feathered, man-eating birds. They looked like cranes, but had beaks that would pierce an iron breastplate. Heracles could not swim through the marsh because it was too muddy, nor walk across it because the mud would not bear his weight; and when he shot at the birds, his arrows glanced off their feathers.

The Goddess Athene appeared and handed him a brass rattle. "Shake that!" she ordered. Heracles shook the rattle. The birds rose into the air, mad with terror. He shot and killed scores of them as they flew off towards the Black Sea, for they had no brass feathers on the undersides of their bodies. None ever returned.

The Seventh Labor was to capture a bull, the terror of Crete. It chased farmers and soldiers, battered down huts and barns, trampled cornfields flat, frightened women and children. This bull had first appeared when Europa's son Minos told the Cretans, "I am King of this island. Let the gods send me a sign to prove it!" As he spoke, the Cretans saw a snow-white bull with golden horns swimming in from the sea. But instead of sacrificing this beautiful beast to the gods, as he should have done, Minos kept it and sacrificed another. Zeus punished him by letting the bull escape and make trouble all over Crete.

Heracles tracked the bull to a wood. There he climbed a tree, waited for it to pass, and jumped on its back. After a hard struggle, he managed to clip a ring through the bull's nose and take it safely across the sea to Eurystheus.

The Eighth Labor was to capture the four

---

4. **mattock** (mat′ ək): a tool like a pickax.

GREEK VASE, 550 B.C. *Heracles and the*
Stymphalian Birds (detail).
British Museum.

the Black Sea, and bring it back as a present for Eurystheus' daughter. Heracles reached Amazonia without danger. There Queen Hippolyte fell in love with him, and he could have had the girdle as a gift. However, the Goddess Hera spitefully disguised herself as an Amazon and spread the rumor that Heracles had come to kidnap Hippolyte and carry her away to Greece. The angry Amazons jumped on their horses and rode to rescue her, shooting arrows at Heracles as they went. Though Heracles beat off the attack, Hippolyte was killed in the confusion of battle; so he took the girdle from her dead body, and sailed sadly away. He would have liked to marry Hippolyte, and hated giving the girdle to Eurystheus' daughter.

The Tenth Labor was to steal a herd of red cows from King Geryon, who lived on an island near the Ocean Stream. Geryon had three bodies, but only one pair of legs. Hera hoped that Heracles would fail in this last Labor, or else not have time to finish it before the ninety-nine months were up. When he reached the western end of the Mediterranean Sea, where Spain and Africa were joined together in those days, he cut a channel between them; the cliffs on either side are still called "The Pillars of Heracles." Then he sailed out into the Ocean in a golden boat lent him by the Sun, using his lion-skin for a sail. As he landed on Geryon's island, a two-headed dog attacked him; he struck it dead with a swing from his club, and did the same to Geryon's herdsman. Lastly, Geryon himself rushed from his palace, like a row of three men. The Goddess Hera tried to help him by flashing a mirror in Heracles' eyes, but he dodged and killed Geryon with an arrow shot sideways through all his three bodies. Then he shot at Hera, too, wounding her in the shoulder. She flew off, screaming for Apollo and Artemis to draw out the arrow and make her well again.

savage mares of the Thracian King Diomedes. Diomedes fed these mares on the flesh of strangers who visited his kingdom. Heracles sailed to Thrace, landed near the palace, went straight to Diomedes' stables, chased away the grooms, and drove the mares plunging and kicking down to the seashore. Alarmed by the noise, Diomedes called the palace guards and hurried in pursuit. Heracles left the mares in charge of his groom Abderus and turned to fight. The battle was short. He stunned Diomedes with his club, and allowed the mares to eat him alive—as they had unfortunately also eaten Abderus, who could not control them. Before he left, Heracles instituted annual funeral games in Abderus' honor. But finding his ship too small for all four mares, he harnessed them to Diomedes' chariot, left the ship behind, and drove home by way of Macedonia.

The Ninth Labor was to get a famous golden girdle from Hippolyte, Queen of the Amazons, who lived on the southern coast of

Heracles drove the red cows across the Pyrenees and along the south coast of France. At the Alps, however, a messenger of Hera's misdirected him, on purpose. He turned right and went all the way down to the Straits of Messina before he realized that this was Italy, not Greece. Angrily he turned back, and wasted still more time when he reached what is now Trieste, because Hera sent her gadfly, which stung the cows in their tenderest parts. They stampeded eastward, and Heracles had to follow their tracks for five or six hundred miles, as far as the Crimea. There an ugly, snake-tailed woman promised to round them up, on condition that he kissed her three times. He did so, though grudging every kiss, and at last came safely home to Greece with the cows, just as the ninety-nine months ended.

Heracles should now have been set free but, on Hera's advice, Eurystheus said, "You did not perform my Second Labor properly, because you called in your friend Iolaus to help kill the Hydra. And you did not perform my Fifth Labor properly either, because Augeias paid you for cleaning his cattle yard."

"How unfair!" cried Heracles. "I called Iolaus because Hera interfered: she sent a crab to bite my foot. And though Augeias certainly betted me twenty cows to one that I could not clean the cattle yard in a day, I would have performed the Labor anyhow."

"No argument, please! You made the bet; so instead of working for me alone, you got twenty cows from another man."

"Nonsense! Augeias refused to pay me. He claimed that I had not cleaned the yard myself—the River-god did it."

"He was quite right. The Labor should not count as your own work. You must perform two more, but you may take your time over them."

"Agreed," said Heracles, "and if I live to complete them, it will be the worse for your family."

Eurystheus had thought of two very dangerous extra Labors. The first was to fetch the Golden Apples of the Hesperides from the Far West. These apples were the fruit of a tree once given by Mother Earth to Hera as a wedding present. The Hesperides, the Titan Atlas' daughters, tended the tree; and Ladon, an unsleeping dragon, coiled around it.

Heracles visited the Caucasus to ask Prometheus'[5] advice. Prometheus welcomed him, saying, "Please, drive off that vulture. It prevents me from thinking clearly." Heracles not only drove away the vulture, but shot it dead and begged Zeus to forgive Prometheus. Zeus, who felt that the punishment had lasted quite long enough, kindly allowed Heracles to break the chains. However, he ordered Prometheus always to wear an iron finger ring, as a reminder of his slavery. This was how rings first came into fashion.

Prometheus now warned Heracles not to pick the apples himself, because any mortal who did so would drop dead at once. "Persuade some immortal to pick them for you," he suggested. After a farewell feast, Heracles sailed toward Morocco. On reaching Tangier, he walked inland to where Atlas, the rebellious Titan, was holding up the Heavens. Heracles asked: "If I take on your duty for an hour, will you be willing to pick me three apples from your daughters' tree?"

"Certainly," said Atlas, "if you first kill the unsleeping dragon."

Heracles drew his bow and shot Ladon over the garden wall. Then he stood behind Atlas and, straddling his legs wide apart, took the weight of the Heavens on his own head and shoulders. Atlas climbed the wall, greeted his daughters, stole the apples, and shouted to Heracles, "Be good enough to stay there just a little longer, while I carry these apples

---

5. **Prometheus:** a Titan who stole fire from heaven to benefit mankind; in punishment, Zeus chained him to a rock where a vulture ate away at his liver.

to Eurystheus. With my huge legs I should be back here in an hour's time."

Though Heracles knew that Atlas would never deliver the apples, but go off to rescue the other Titans instead, and start a new rebellion, he pretended to trust him. "With pleasure," he answered, "if you will please take the weight from me again for one moment more, while I fold up this lion-skin to make a comfortable head pad."

Atlas laid down the apples and did as Heracles asked. Heracles then took the apples and walked away. "You tried to trick me," he said, laughing, "but I have tricked you. Goodbye!"

As Heracles went home through Libya, a gigantic son of Mother Earth, by name Antaeus, challenged him to a wrestling match. Heracles oiled himself all over, so that Antaeus could not get a firm grip on him; Antaeus, on the contrary, rubbed himself with sand. Every time Heracles threw Antaeus hard to the ground, he was surprised to see him rise again stronger than ever because touching Mother Earth renewed his strength. Realizing what he must do, Heracles lifted Antaeus off the ground, cracked his ribs, and held him aloft out of Mother Earth's reach, until he died. A month later Heracles brought the apples safely to Eurystheus.

The last and worst Labor was to capture the dog Cerberus,[6] and drag him up from Tartarus. On receiving this order, Heracles went for purification to Eleusis, where Demeter's[7] Mysteries were held; and now, cleansed of all defilement, boldly descended to Tartarus. Charon[8] refused to ferry a live mortal across the Styx.[9]

"I will wreck your boat," Heracles threatened, "and fill you as full of arrows as a hedgehog is full of prickles."

Charon shivered in terror and ferried him across. Hades[10] afterwards punished Charon for his cowardice.

Heracles saw Theseus and Peirithous stuck to Hades' bench, and being whipped by the Furies.[11] He gave Theseus an enormous tug and wrenched him free, though a large part of his back stayed behind. But finding it impossible to release Peirithous, except with an ax, he left him there.

Persephone[12] darted from the palace and took Heracles by both hands. "Can I help you, dear Heracles?" she asked.

"Be kind enough to lend me your watchdog for a few days, Your Majesty. He can run home again as soon as I have shown him to Eurystheus."

Persephone turned to King Hades: "Please, Husband, grant Heracles what he asks. This is a task set him on your sister-in-law Hera's advice. He promises not to keep our dog Cerberus."

Hades answered, "Very well, and he may take that fool Theseus back, too, while he is about it. Still, I must make it a rule that he masters Cerberus without the use of club or arrows."

Hades thought this a safe condition, but Heracles' lion-skin was proof against the blows of Cerberus' barbed tail; and his strong hands squeezed Cerberus' throat until all three heads turned black. Cerberus fainted, and let himself be dragged up on earth. Unfortunately, the only tunnel wide enough for him was one that came out near Mariandyne, beside the Black Sea; so Heracles had a long and difficult journey. Before starting, he took a branch of the white poplar

---

6. **Cerberus:** the three-headed dog guarding the gate of Hades, the underworld.

7. **Demeter:** the goddess of agriculture; the Mysteries were religious rites in her honor.

8. **Charon:** the boatman who ferried souls of the dead across the river to Hades.

9. **Styx:** the river of Hades.

10. **Hades:** the ruler of the underworld.

11. **Furies:** three female spirits who punished evildoers.

12. **Persephone:** the daughter of Zeus and Demeter, abducted by Hades to be his wife in the lower world.

with him for a trophy, and wore it as a wreath.

Eurystheus was nearly scared to death when Heracles appeared, dragging Cerberus behind him on a leash. "Thank you, noble Heracles," he said, "you are now free of your Labors. But please send that brute back at once."

Heracles returned to Thebes, where his mother Alcmene welcomed him joyfully. Then Hera thought of a clever plot. She told Autolycus to steal a herd of dappled mares and foals from a man named Iphitus, change their color, and sell them to Heracles. Iphitus tracked the herd all the way to Tiryns by their footprints, and asked Heracles whether he had taken them by any chance. Heracles led Iphitus to the top of a high tower, and said, grimly, "Look around you! Can you see any dappled mares in my pastures?"

"No," answered Iphitus. "But I know that they are somewhere about."

Heracles, losing his temper at being thought a thief and a liar, flung Iphitus over the battlements.

The gods sentenced Heracles to be the slave of Queen Omphale of Lydia; the money he fetched at his sale, which Hermes had arranged, went to Iphitus' orphan children. Omphale, who did not know who Heracles was, asked him what he could do. "Anything you like, madam," he answered readily. So she made him dress as a woman, in a yellow petticoat, handed him a distaff, and showed him how to spin wool. Heracles found the work very restful. One day a gigantic dragon starting eating Omphale's Lydian subjects, and she said to Heracles: "You look a strong man. Dare you fight the dragon?"

"At your service, madam."

Dragons were nothing to Heracles. He shot a poisoned arrow between this dragon's jaws, and Omphale gratefully gave him his freedom.

Later, Heracles married a princess named Deianeira, a daughter of the God Dionysus, and founded the Olympic Games, which were to be held every four years as long as the world should last. He ruled that the winners of each event were to be given wreaths, instead of the usual valuable prizes, because he had not been paid for his Labors either. No man dared wrestle against Heracles, which disappointed the spectators. However, King Zeus kindly came down from Olympus. He and Heracles had a wonderful tussle together. The match ended in a draw, and everyone cheered.

Heracles now took vengeance on kings who had treated him scornfully while he was performing his Labors, including Augeias, and killed three of Eurystheus' sons. Zeus forbade him to attack Eurystheus himself. That would set a bad example to other freed slaves. The River-god Achelous challenged Heracles to a fight, but lost a horn in the struggle. Heracles also fought the God Ares and sent him hobbling back to Olympus.

One day a Centaur[13] named Nessus offered to carry Heracles' wife, Deianeira, across a flooded river for a small fee. Heracles paid the money, but Nessus, having reached the farther bank, galloped off with Deianeira in his arms. Heracles shot Nessus, at a distance of half a mile, using one of the arrows dipped in the Hydra's blood. The dying Nessus whispered to Deianeira: "Collect a little of my blood in this small oil jar. Then, if Heracles ever loves a woman more than you, here is a sure charm to use. The oil will keep my blood from drying up. Spread it on his shirt. He will never be unfaithful again. Goodbye!" Deianeira did as Nessus advised.

While still serving Eurystheus, Heracles had taken part in an archery contest proposed by King Eurytus of Oechalia, the prize of which was his daughter Iole. Eurytus

---

13. **Centaur:** any of a race of monsters with a man's head, trunk, and arms, and a horse's body and legs.

GREEK VASE, 520 B.C.
Heracles and Acheloos (detail).
British Museum.

boasted himself the best archer in Greece, and felt very cross at being beaten by Heracles. He shouted, "My daughter is a princess. I cannot possibly marry her to Eurystheus' slave. The competition is void." Remembering this insult some years later, Heracles sacked Oechalia, killed Eurytus, and took away Iole, with her two sisters, to scrub floors and cook. Deianeira feared he might fall in love with Iole, who was very beautiful. When he sent a messenger home, asking Deianeira for his best embroidered shirt, she thought, "He wants to wear it when he marries Iole." So she smeared some of Nessus' blood on the red embroidery of the shirt, where it would not show, and handed it to the messenger.

Heracles really needed the shirt for a thanksgiving sacrifice to Zeus, after the capture of Oechalia. He put it on, and was pouring wine on the altar when he suddenly felt as though he were being bitten by scorpions. The heat of his body had melted the Hydra's poison in Nessus' blood. He yelled, bellowed, shrieked, knocked over the altar, and tried to rip off the shirt; but great lumps of flesh came away too. His blood hissed with the poison. Then he jumped into a stream; the

poison burned him worse than before. Heracles knew that he was doomed.

He begged his friends in an unsteady voice, "Please, carry me to Mount Oeta, and build a pyre of oak and wild-olive." They obeyed, weeping. Heracles climbed to the platform at the top, and calmly lay down on his lion-skin, using his club for a pillow. He let himself be burned to death; the fire hurt far less than the Hydra's poison.

Zeus felt proud of his brave son. He told the Olympians, "Heracles will be our porter, and marry my daughter Hebe, the Goddess of Youth. If anyone objects, I shall start throwing thunderbolts. Rise, noble soul of Heracles! Welcome to Olympus!"

Zeus looked so fierce that Hera dared say nothing. Heracles' immortal soul ascended on a cloud, and Athene was soon introducing him to the other gods. Only Ares turned his back, but when Demeter begged him not to be a fool he too shook hands with Heracles—rather rudely.

Deianeira, hearing that she had caused Heracles' death, took a sword and stabbed herself.

Getting at Meaning

1. Explain the story of Heracles' birth. As an infant, how does Heracles prove that he is not a normal child?

2. In what subjects does Heracles excel as a boy? Describe the incident with his music teacher.

3. How many labors does Eurystheus assign Heracles? Why does he later change his mind?

4. Which goddess repeatedly tries to prevent Heracles from accomplishing his tasks? Why does she do this?

5. Describe the three labors that are the most interesting to you.

6. How does Heracles free himself from his second period of slavery?

7. Describe the death of Heracles. What causes his death? How does Zeus pay tribute to Heracles?

Developing Skills in Reading Literature

1. **Hero.** Heracles, like Theseus, is a demigod, or one who is half human and half god. In what ways is Heracles god-like? In what ways is he human? What qualities does he possess besides his strength? Judging from Daedalus, Theseus, and Heracles, what qualities did the ancient Greeks seem to admire most in their heroes?

2. **Myth.** Myths offer explanations for elements in nature and for the origins of customs and traditions. For example, the encounter with Prometheus explains "how rings first came into fashion." What other phenomena are explained by this myth?

Another characteristic of myths is that they tend to be violent. How is violence used in this myth? How does it help to develop Heracles' character?

3. **Structure.** This myth is actually a series of adventures, loosely tied together. How is the order of the adventures important? How does it build suspense?

4. **Irony.** How is the death of Heracles ironic?

Developing Vocabulary

Words from Greek and Roman Mythology. Look up each listed word in a general or specialized dictionary, and record its meaning. Write the mythological source for the word and an explanation of how the meaning of each word relates to the source.

Amazon	Herculean	furious
Promethean	lyrical	Olympian

Developing Writing Skills

1. **Writing an Explanation.** Write a paragraph in which you discuss one or two of the qualities that ancient Greeks appear to have admired most in their heroes. Use examples from "Daedalus," "Theseus," and "Heracles" to back up what you say.

2. **Combining Narration and Description.** Create yet another labor for Heracles, one that he could perform between any two of the labors described in the story or after all of those labors have been completed. Use your imagination to make up characters, settings, and creatures. Try to include some conversation in your story. Describe in detail how Heracles performs the difficult task you have assigned him.

Medieval Heroes

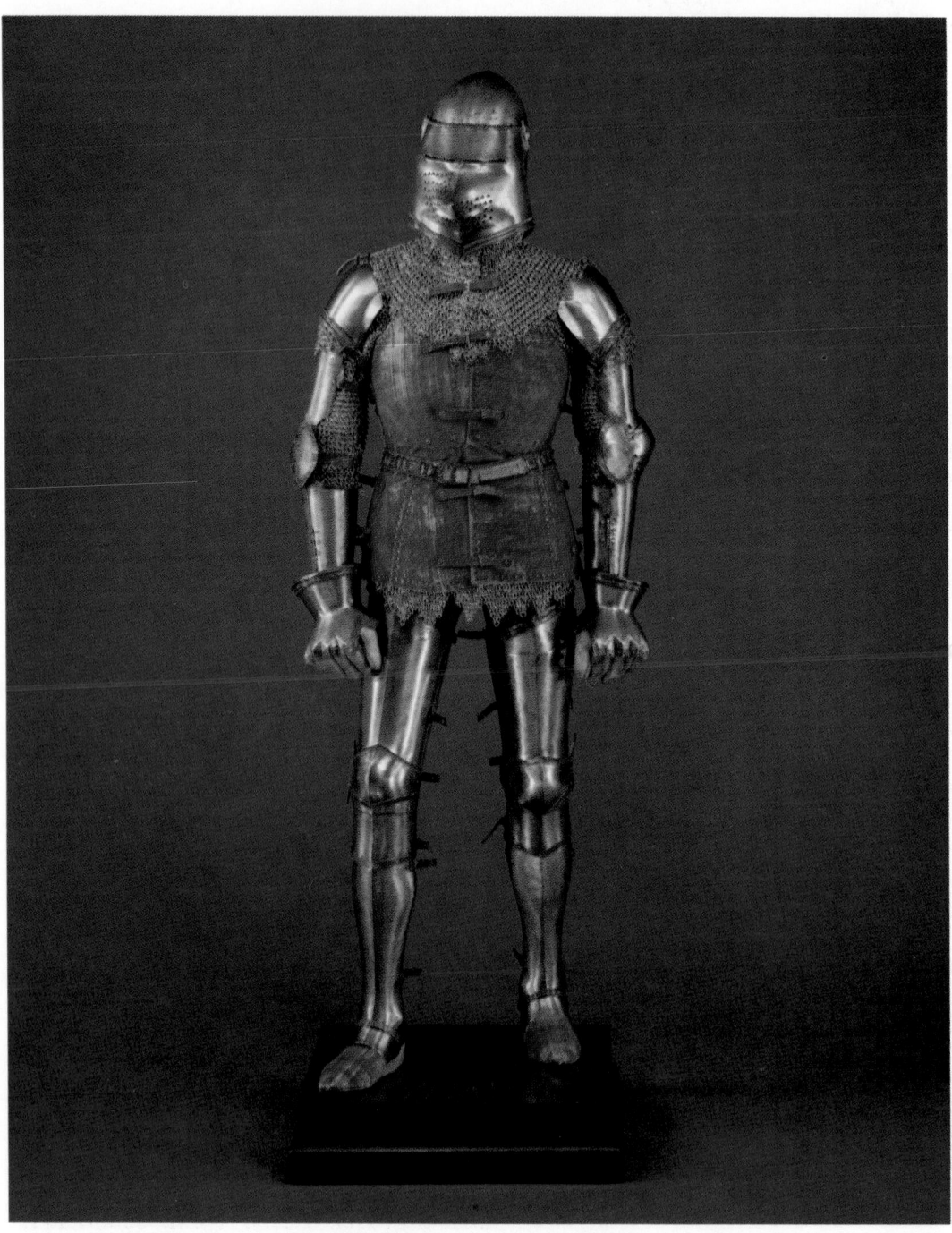

SUIT OF ARMOR, 1400.
The Metropolitan Museum of Art, The Bashford Dean Memorial Collection.
Gift of Helen Fahnestock Hubbard, 1929, in memory of her father, Harris C. Fahnestock.

The Story of Siegfried

Retold by Max J. Herzberg

Near Xanten on the Rhine lived a king and queen named Siegmund and Sieglinde, to whom was born a fair prince named Siegfried. As Siegfried grew older, the Netherlands, the kingdom over which his parents ruled, was threatened by invaders; and the young prince was sent away from the castle, for fear that he might fall into the hands of the foe. His parents intrusted him to the care of a blacksmith named Mimer, who lived in the secret thickets of a great forest.

Now Mimer was a dwarf, or troll, and belonged to a strange race of the little people called Nibelungs. These Nibelungs dwelt for most part underground, in a dark little town that they had built. This town was named Nibelheim. The great majority of the Nibelungs were very skillful smiths, who would hammer all day at their tiny anvils. But at night the Nibelungs, men and women, would make merry with dance and music. Mimer was a Nibelung who lived on the surface of the earth, and he built his forge under the trees of the forest.

Siegfried was delighted to join Mimer and his apprentices, and he learned in a little while how to swing the heavy hammer. Indeed, his strength soon became too great, for so resounding and powerful were the blows he struck that often the anvil would be shattered to pieces. Then Mimer would scold him sarcastically, and Siegfried, angrily leaving the smithy, would stride off into the woods and listen to the cheerful caroling of the birds.

One day, while Siegfried was wandering through the forest, the whim came upon him to blow his mighty silver horn. He did so, and before the sound had died away, he saw suddenly before him a huge shaggy bear. He was not in the least frightened. Rather, it occurred to him that here was a good chance to pay Mimer back for his numerous rebukes. He rushed at the great beast, seized it in his arms, and in the twinkling of an eye had muzzled the animal with his belt. Then he led the bear quickly and quietly back to the forge.

There Mimer was sharpening a sword at the anvil. As he heard the laughter of the prince, he turned around and saw the bear. Instantly he dropped the sword with a clang and ran off to the darkest corner of the smithy, trembling with fear. For a time Siegfried continued to tease the little man; then he unmuzzled the bear and set him free in the forest again.

This was but one of the many pranks that the young prince played upon Mimer, for he did not care very much for the cunning and ill-tempered troll. Finally, the latter grew tired of the trouble that Siegfried was causing him, and determined to get rid of him.

One day, therefore, he sent him deep into the forest to bring home some charcoal for the forge from a certain storehouse. He did not tell the lad that on the road he would have to pass a terrifying dragon, named Fafnir. Siegfried strode merrily along. Once more the impulse came on him to blow a few notes on his beloved horn, and as he did so, once more danger appeared. At the sound of the blast, the dragon roused himself in his lair and began to spout fire. The trees swayed and trembled as the dragon made his way underneath them toward Siegfried, and the little birds and beasts of the forest scurried away in fear.

Yet when Siegfried beheld the dragon, he was not at all frightened. In fact, after a few moments, he began to laugh, for he welcomed the break in his too peaceful life that the dragon was bringing him. The dragon sat down on a hill and glared at Siegfried. But Siegfried remarked cheerfully,

"I am going to kill you, for you are too ugly to live."

At these bold words Fafnir opened his huge jaws and showed his teeth, extending in triple rows like a forest. But again Siegfried laughed. Then Fafnir, wild with anger, crept nearer and nearer and lashed his tail furiously. But Siegfried drew his sword, which he himself had forged with care at the anvil of Mimer. Leaping upon the dragon's back, he plunged the blade into his heart. In dreadful convulsions, the dragon fell dead.

Siegfried was not yet done with the dragon, however. As the dragon lay at his feet, he remembered that while working in Mimer's smithy he had heard some of the Nibelungs talk of this very dragon. He recalled that they had said that whoever bathed in the blood of the dragon would be forever after invulnerable, for his skin would grow so tough that no sword or arrow could pierce it. So Siegfried flung aside his dress of deerskins and plunged into his dragon bath. From top to toe he laved himself with the magical red fluid. Yet, as he bathed, a linden leaf dropped unseen right between his shoulders, and there alone the dragon blood did not touch him, and there alone, consequently, he was vulnerable.

This duty performed, Siegfried returned swiftly to the forge. He realized that Mimer had wished to kill him, so without more ado he slew the treacherous dwarf.

Afterward Siegfried wandered to many places, and after a while he came to a country called Iceland, over which reigned a queen named Brunhild, who was both beautiful and warlike. Her castle stood by the sea, and was guarded by seven gates; and her marble palace glittered in the sun. He inquired of passers-by who might dwell here, and they not only told him her name, but also spoke to him of her strange refusal to marry anyone unless he could vanquish her in the tests she set him.

When Siegfried entered the castle, Brunhild, who marveled at his handsome face and his mighty muscles, received him favorably and even allowed him to see her magic horse, Gana. Yet Siegfried somehow had no love for Brunhild, and refused to undertake the tests she set. But to prove to her that it was no lack of skill or strength that made him decline her proffers, Siegfried calmly threw down the seven gates of her castle and even enticed the horse Gana to accompany him. For his scorn of her, Brunhild never forgave Siegfried.

Siegfried, continuing on his travels, came to an immense cavern where lay outspread the treasure of the Nibelungs: gold and silver, jewels of all kinds, most marvelous riches. Quarreling over the treasure were two Nibelung princes, surrounded by twelve foolish giants, their counselors. For the king of the Nibelungs had died, and now his sons could not divide their heritage peacefully. When the little princes saw Siegfried, they asked him to act as arbitrator, promising him as a reward, the sword Balmung, which could overcome the strongest warriors. He consented, and began to make a division, but soon the dwarfs in dissatisfaction began to mock at him and scold him in their harsh voices. At last Siegfried in anger slew both of them, and likewise the giants, and laid the treasure aside in a secret place.

Now seven hundred knights came to bar his way, but Siegfried conquered them, and made them swear to be his liegemen[1] thereafter. In a little while he had need of them, for the dwarfs of Nibelheim, under the leadership of a chieftain named Alberich, took the field against him, anxious not only to avenge the death of their princes but also to recover the lost treasure of the Nibelungs. But Siegfried had little trouble with them. He chased them all into a great cave on the mountainside, and from Alberich himself he stripped his Cloak of Darkness, which rendered the wearer invisible and invincible. He made Alberich and his army of dwarfs likewise swear allegiance to him, and then he placed them in charge of his treasure.

When Siegfried returned to his own country he was most warmly welcomed. Great feasts were held in his honor, and he received knighthood from the hands of the king. But he could not rest in quiet, and shortly he set forth on a new quest. For he had heard of a beautiful princess named Kriemhild, who dwelt at the Court of Worms in Burgundy, and from her description she seemed to him the ideal maiden of his dreams. He journeyed to Burgundy, accompanied only by eleven stalwart knights, and he was graciously welcomed by King Gunther, brother of Kriemhild, and by the latter's uncle and chief councilor Hagen, who was a cunning and cruel man. Not long after Siegfried arrived, two kings threatened Burgundy, but largely by Siegfried's valor they were overcome and conquered.

Then a great feast was held, and to it Kriemhild lent her presence. For the first time Siegfried gazed upon her, and thought her more lovely even than her fame. But when Siegfried sought to have her as a bride,

King Gunther, at the advice of Hagen, would by no means grant him her hand unless Siegfried first accompanied Gunther to Iceland and helped him win Brunhild for wife. Siegfried consented, and accompanied only by a small band they set out for the country of Brunhild.

They were gayly welcomed, although Brunhild was angry that Siegfried came to assist Gunther and not to win her himself. With the help of Siegfried, who was clad in his Cloak of Darkness, Gunther passed the three trials—to overcome Brunhild in combat, to cast a stone farther than her cast, and to jump a greater distance than the queen did. Then did Brunhild yield to Gunther and wed him, and Siegfried was given Kriemhild as his bride.

But the story does not end here. Siegfried and Kriemhild in time became rulers of the Netherlands, and after a while were invited to Worms to take part in a tournament and its accompanying festivals. As the two queens sat together and watched their husbands in the combat, each began to boast of the prowess of her spouse. By a slip of the tongue, Kriemhild revealed that in one place her husband was vulnerable. Later, goaded to anger by Brunhild's remarks, Kriemhild revealed the stratagem by which Siegfried had aided Gunther to win Brunhild, and the latter determined on revenge. With the aid of Hagen, Kriemhild was persuaded to make a garment for Siegfried in which a silken cross was embroidered above the spot on which the linden leaf had fallen; and there one day, as he was bending over a brook to drink, Hagen thrust his spear and killed him.

The Burgundians then came into possession of the treasure of the Nibelungs, but always Kriemhild plotted vengeance. In the course of time she married again, and her hus-

---

1. **liegeman** (lēj′mən): a loyal follower.

band, King Etzel, was willing to aid her schemes. She invited her brothers and Hagen to visit her. Quarreling rose, and a fierce battle took place, in which many were killed, Hagen dying by the hand of Kriemhild, and she herself being slain by the knight Hildebrand.

Getting at Meaning

1. Describe Siegfried's youth. How does he first demonstrate that he has unusual powers and abilities?

2. Who are the Nibelungs? Why does Siegfried kill Mimer?

3. Describe Fafnir. How does Siegfried kill the beast? What does he do with the animal's blood?

4. Who is Brunhild? How does Siegfried treat her?

5. What is the treasure of the Nibelungs? How does Siegfried conquer the Nibelungs?

6. What must Siegfried do before he can marry Kriemhild?

7. Explain how Siegfried meets his end. What oversight makes his death possible?

Developing Skills in Reading Literature

Hero. Although Siegfried is not protected by gods and goddesses, he does acquire superhuman characteristics. What are they? What qualities of a hero does Siegfried possess? Which of the Greek heroes does he most resemble? Explain your response.

Developing Vocabulary

1. **Suffixes.** The suffix -or or -er can be added to a verb; the result is a noun that names a doer of the action described by the verb. For example, the suffix -or added to the verb arbitrate, forms the noun arbitrator, which means one who decides or judges in a dispute.

From each of the following verbs form a noun by adding the suffix -er or -or. You may need to use a dictionary to check on the meanings and spellings of the words.

administrate   advise   incubate
contend   dispense   confess

2. **Context Clues: Definition or Restatement; Examples; Inference Based on the Main Idea.** As you know, the meanings of difficult words often can be determined from the context in which they appear. Some context clues are specific, as in the following sentences:

1. From top to toe he *laved* himself with the magical red fluid. Yet, as he bathed, a linden leaf. . . .

2. He recalled that . . . whoever bathed in the blood of the dragon would be forever after *invulnerable,* for his skin would grow so tough that no sword or arrow could pierce it.

What synonym for *laved* is given in the first example? What does *invulnerable* mean? What context clue suggests this definition?

Sometimes the main idea of a passage or a selection provides clues to the general meaning of a word. The meanings of the following words, for example, can be inferred from the broad context in which they appear:

anvil   rebuke   impulse   proffer

Study the context of each word. Then write a brief definition of the word, based on the context clues you have identified.

King Arthur and the Knights of the Round Table

Retold by Emma G. Sterne *and* Barbara Lindsay

The Sword in the Stone

It happened that on a New Year's morning, Sir Hector Anton and his son, Sir Kay, were riding toward London. With them, sitting fair and tall on his dappled horse, rode Sir Kay's young foster brother, Arthur. He had been allowed to come along on the journey to see his elder brother joust in his first great tournament.

"We have waited long for this day," said Sir Hector, looking proudly at his elder son. "In the old days, when Uther Pendragon ruled England and peace was in the land, there were chances a-plenty for friendly jousting and the courtesies of chivalry."

Sir Hector looked sadly around the countryside. "Now," he went on, "we see wasted fields, and no one is safe from the wild beasts and robbers roaming the highways."

Sir Kay made no answer, but Arthur nudged his horse closer. The boy was full of curiosity, for at seventeen he had heard little and seen less of the world outside Sir Hector's quiet domain.

"This is what happens when there is no sovereign, no king of the realm," Sir Hector said.

"But why no sovereign, Sire?" Arthur asked.

"When King Uther Pendragon died, he left no son to take the throne. Merlin the Magician, adviser to the good King Uther, promised that a new ruler would appear one day.

He even named the magic sign by which the king would be known. But the lords and barons refused to believe him and soon began fighting among themselves for the throne. If they had taken care of their lands and waited as Merlin bade, England would be strong, but now—" The old knight shook his head and was silent.

"But what of Merlin's promise?" Arthur asked.

Sir Hector looked at the handsome boy whom he loved as his own son. "Merlin has retired to a cave to live the life of a hermit. Perhaps even to him it looks as if his prophecy will never be fulfilled."

Sir Hector spoke on as they left the highway and entered the narrow, gray streets of London. Sir Kay was not listening. His mind was only on the tournament. How he had longed for this chance to prove himself an able knight!

"If my fortune holds," he said to himself, "before another day is gone, some mark of honor shall at last be blazoned on my shield."

He sat stiffly in the saddle, in his polished armor, thinking of the trial at arms ahead. His horse was good, his spear beautifully tempered and sharpened. And in the scabbard at his side was a worthy sword.

Suddenly Sir Kay reined his horse in dismay. "My sword!" he cried. "I left my sword where we lodged last night!"

"Let me ride back to fetch it," Arthur said.

Before the others could answer, he wheeled swiftly and was off.

Sir Hector and Sir Kay then made their way through the city to the edge of the meadow where the tournament was to be held. They had scarcely dismounted when, to their surprise, Arthur was back again, flourishing a sword.

Sir Kay stared at the weapon. He knew the sword for what it was, for he had seen it often, deep in its anvil in St. Stephen's churchyard.

Eagerly he seized it and held it close, staring at the words engraved on the jeweled hilt: *Whoso shall pull this sword out of the anvil, he is King of England by right.* Merlin's magic sign!

Sir Kay seemed to grow in height as he turned to his father. "Look, Sire!" he cried. "The sword from the stone! Now I shall be King of England!"

Sir Hector turned pale. He grasped Arthur's horse by the rein. "How came you by this sword?" he asked the boy sternly.

"Sire, I was riding in all haste lest my brother miss entering the lists of the tournament. As I crossed St. Stephen's churchyard, to save precious time, I came upon this sword. It was stuck in an anvil on a great stone. It seemed a good weapon and I thought it would serve my brother as well as his own. So I pulled it from the stone and brought it hither."

Without another word, Sir Hector mounted his horse, signed for Sir Kay to do the same, and led the way back to the churchyard. There, with his own eyes, he saw that the sword was gone from the anvil.

Sir Hector thought of all the petty kings and lords and barons who had tried in vain to pull out the sword in the years since Merlin's magic had caused it to be placed in the stone.

He turned to his elder son. "Give me the sword," he said.

Sir Hector told Arthur to replace it in the anvil. The blade sank deeply through the anvil into the stone.

"Draw it forth," Sir Hector said to his elder son.

Sir Kay tried with all his strength. The sword did not budge. Then Arthur put his hand to the hilt, and the sword came out easily.

Sir Hector and Sir Kay knelt on the ground before the boy. And other nobles knelt as well, and common folk came running from off the street, and craftsmen from the houses across the way—all marveling and rejoicing because they knew that Merlin's promise had been fulfilled.

Excalibur

Next morning, as Arthur rode with Merlin, he sighed. "How can I do battle for my kingdom when I have no sword?"

"Be of good cheer," Merlin answered, "for nearby is a sword that shall be yours."

So saying, Merlin led the King down a path deep into the woods until they came upon a shining blue lake. In the middle of the lake, Arthur saw an arm clothed in white samite,[1] mysterious and wonderful. High above the blue water, the raised arm held a sword encased in a rich scabbard embellished all in gold.

"Behold," said Merlin, "there is the sword I spoke of."

As Arthur still stared at the wondrous sight, a damsel rose up out of the water and walked on the rippling waves as if she moved on dry land.

"What damsel is that?" Arthur asked.

"The Lady of the Lake," Merlin answered. "She lives beneath the water in a palace of rock, as fine a domain as ever you beheld. See!

---

1. **samite** (sam' īt): a heavy silk fabric interwoven with gold or silver threads.

She is coming toward you. When she puts foot upon this mossy bank, speak to her with courtesy. She will give you the sword if you ask it."

When the Lady of the Lake came close, Arthur spoke. "Madam," he asked, "what sword is it that yonder hand holds above the water? I would have it for my own, for I have no sword."

"Sir Arthur, King of England, the sword Excalibur is mine," the lady replied in a voice that was deep and yet soft, like water falling over stones on a winter's morning. "If you will give me a gift when I ask it, you shall have the sword."

"By my faith," said Arthur, "I will give you whatever you ask."

"Row you then in yonder boat, and take the sword. Take the scabbard also, and I will ask my gift when the time comes."

Arthur looked where the damsel pointed and there, moored on the lake, half hidden in tall grasses, was a small skiff. The young king alighted from his horse and rowed out to the center of the lake. He reached for the sword Excalibur. At his touch, the hand let go the hilt, and hand and arm sank slowly under the water.

When he came to land again, Merlin was alone. The Lady of the Lake had disappeared.

Arthur pulled the sword from its scabbard. The jeweled hilt flashed brilliant in the sun. The blade was the keenest Arthur had ever seen.

On one side of the blade were engraved the words: *Take Me.* But when Arthur turned the blade over, he read on the other side: *Cast me away.* Doubt came into the King's eyes until Merlin said,

"Take the sword and strike! The time to cast it away is far off."

Slowly Arthur encased the great weapon in its scabbard.

"Which do you like the better," Merlin asked, "the sword or the scabbard?"

"The sword," Arthur answered quickly.

"In that you are unwise," Merlin said. "Excalibur is a good sword, the best in the world. But the scabbard is worth far more. For however sorely you are beset in battle, you will not lose a drop of blood as long as you have the scabbard with you."

In all the battles that he had to fight to bring peace to his realm, King Arthur bore himself in such noble fashion that those kings who were not slain accepted him at last as their overlord. Then Arthur forgave them, and returned to them their lands. Even King Lot of Orkney was given back his lands.

Then the sons of Lot became knights of King Arthur. Sir Gawaine and Sir Gaheris and Agravaine took the vows in good faith. But Sir Mordred swore fealty with a sullen face, for he had little understanding of what Arthur meant by courtesy, manliness, or knighthood.

Camelot

At last the rebellion was ended. There was peace again in the kingdom, and Arthur and his knights turned homeward. When they had come to a certain place where a mountain rose out of a spacious plain, Arthur saw the spires and turrets of a high city, like a vision out of Fairyland. Around gray walls of stone a golden mist rose that all but hid the great arched portal. As the knights pressed their steeds forward, the gate opened. Merlin came out, with such pride on his face as none had seen before.

While Arthur was away fighting this last battle, Merlin had caused the city to be built, employing all the arts his magic could command. Camelot, the place was called, and the famed cities of the East could not match it for beauty.

Through winding streets, past gardens stretching out on either side, Arthur and his knights entered Camelot. As they neared the courtyard, they came upon a leveled space. It was a meadow for jousting, where five hundred knights could meet in friendly tournament.

Then at last Arthur came to the castle. The carved doorway from the courtyard to the hall was so broad that six knights could ride through abreast. Arthur's banner, emblazoned with the golden dragon of Uther Pendragon, flew from the highest turret. And music, seeming to come from nowhere, filled the air when Arthur entered.

The rooms were richly furnished, all but the great hall, which was bare. But as the young king walked from room to room with Merlin at his side, the castle seemed a lonely place, for he had no wife, no queen to share its wonders.

"It is well that a man of your nobility take a wife," Merlin said. "Is there any that you love more than another?"

"I love Guinevere, the daughter of Leodegrance," Arthur said. "I saw her only the one time, but I thought her the fairest lady alive."

Merlin frowned. "I can think of other damsels of equal beauty and goodness who would bring you greater happiness," he said. "But when a man has given his heart, he will be loath to change."

"That is truth indeed," said Arthur, and at once sent his best-loved knight, Sir Lancelot, to the kingdom of the North to bring him home a wife and queen.

The Gift of King Leodegrance

A hearty welcome to you, Sir Lancelot," cried King Leodegrance to the brave knight and his companions as they entered the great hall at Cameliard. "When you have rested and eaten, I want to hear the news from the south of our good King Arthur."

"That news I shall be happy to bring you," Lancelot said, smiling, "for it has to do with yourself."

King Leodegrance had Sir Lancelot and his friends taken to rooms in the castle. He called for the finest foods to be set forth and the best musicians to play for his guests.

The Lady Guinevere heard that Lancelot had arrived. She remembered well the tall, handsome knight who had ridden to the castle after the victory over King Ryons.

It was the custom not to allow ladies in the dining hall while noblemen were eating. But Guinevere, who was seventeen, did not always choose to follow the rules.

"Enid," she said to her companion, "help me lift this tapestry from the loom. I shall go and ask my father if he is pleased with our new design of the lady with the unicorn, all surrounded by the tiny birds and beasts of the wood."

"You asked him that last night when he came to bid you good night," Enid answered. "But here, take the tapestry and go down to see our handsome visitor from the south!"

Guinevere laughed and turned pink. Holding the tapestry carefully, she started down the ramp toward the dining hall. But, as she was about to enter the hall, she heard her father mention the words "marriage dowry." Had Sir Lancelot, then, come to seek her hand?

She stood for an instant in the doorway and was about to slip away unseen when her father spied her. He beckoned her to enter.

"My daughter," he said, "Sir Lancelot du Lac has brought news of great honor to Cameliard. King Arthur desires you above other ladies to be his queen. You and the ladies of your court will return with Sir Lancelot in a few days."

Guinevere curtsied, her head bent low. She knew she must give a proper answer to her father. She knew, too, that she had been honored above all the ladies of the realm, for Arthur's name was already a legend throughout Britain. And yet, she had no memory of the great king whose wife and queen she was to be.

She raised her head and, as she did so, she glanced at Lancelot. Only for a moment did their eyes meet, but Guinevere knew that it was a moment neither of them would ever forget.

Now every inch a king's daughter, Guinevere stood before her father.

"Sire," she said, "I will have my ladies prepare at once for the journey."

King Leodegrance smiled at his lovely daughter. "You shall not go empty-handed," he said, "for I am sending as your dowry the finest gift I can give. It is the Round Table entrusted to me by King Uther Pendragon— the great oaken table with place for one hundred and fifty knights. One hundred knights I can send," he continued to Sir Lancelot. "But fifty seats I cannot fill, for such was the number slain in the years of fighting."

The Oath

While Guinevere, her ladies, and the hundred knights prepared for the journey south, a messenger was sent ahead to Arthur at Camelot.

The young king's face lit up when word was brought him.

"This fair lady shall be most welcome to me," he said, "for I have loved her long. And these knights with the Round Table please me far more than the greatest riches."

The King ordered preparation made for a magnificent wedding ceremony. For two weeks there would be feasting, tournaments, and all manner of celebration throughout the kingdom.

He asked Merlin to find fifty knights to fill the Round Table. Merlin chose King Pellinore and his sons, Aglovale and Lamorak. He chose Sir Lancelot, his brother, Sir Ector de Maris, and his cousin, Sir Bors of Brittany.

Sir Bedivere and his father Sir Lucan were selected, and of course, Sir Hector Anton and Sir Kay. Of the sons of the rebel kings who now swore fealty to Arthur, Merlin brought the four sons of King Lot, Arthur's nephews, and King Urien's son, Sir Uwaine, a valiant fighter and a true knight.

The ancient counselor chose other brave warriors. Yet when the list was completed, many seats at the Round Table were still empty. There were only twenty-eight knights to be found whom the magician felt worthy of so great an honor.

"But," he assured the King, "before your reign shall come to an end, the Round Table shall be filled."

Every lord in Britain, and princes from the continent of Europe attended the marriage at Camelot. Cheering crowds lined the streets. Even the harnesses of the horses were jewelled, and the lords and ladies wore their finest silks and velvets.

Story-tellers, acrobats, conjurers, and dancers entertained in all the public squares. To the visiting knights and princes, the King gave gifts of armor and horses, lances, swords, and golden ornaments. Gifts of food and money were passed out freely among the common folk.

On the day after the wedding, King Arthur had the Round Table placed in the great hall at Camelot. With his young bride at his side, he watched the noblest knights of all his land enter the hall.

"These knights shall sit in true brotherhood," Arthur said quietly to Guinevere. "Here shall be the fairest fellowship and the truest knighthood ever seen together in any realm of the world."

The Archbishop of Canterbury blessed the Round Table and all its knights with great ceremony. Then the knights came forward together to repeat in homage to their king the oaths of knighthood: To speak the truth; to maintain the right; to practice courtesy; to

despise the allurements of ease and safety; to maintain honor in every perilous adventure; to uphold Christianity; to destroy tyranny wherever it might be; to defend and protect to the uttermost, women, the poor, and the oppressed.

Arthur spoke to his knights as they knelt before him.

"Around this Table," he said, "none shall sit higher, none lower. Here shall a man's worth depend upon his valor, and his devotion, and his skill. You shall defend and help one another as brother unto brother.

"Never forget this—a brave knight will always be merciful. But a coward will never show gentleness nor mercy nor any manner of goodness. Yet always a good man will do to another man as he would be done to himself.

"And if you would show loyalty and love to me, your king, you will ride forth and see that justice and mercy prevail throughout the length and breadth of this realm. This above all shall be the duty of the knights of the Round Table."

A rolling thunder seemed to fill the hall, and the sound of majestic music. Slowly, silently, the knights rose to return to their places at the Round Table. Before their very eyes, the knights saw their names appear in gold letters on the backs of the heavy oaken seats, or sieges.

On one of the empty sieges appeared the words "The Siege Perilous." Nor did any knights' names appear on the sieges on either side.

Arthur turned to Merlin the Magician.

"What does this mean?" he asked.

The murmurs of wonder in the hall stopped and the deep voice of the old wizard rang out.

"Sir," said Merlin, "in that seat, the Siege Perilous, shall no man sit but one. And if there be any other so hardy as to do it, he shall be destroyed. And he that shall sit therein and live shall have no equal in all the world."

The Coming of Galahad

Twenty-four years had passed since Arthur's reign began. With his brave knights, he had brought peace and order and justice to England. The knights of the Round Table now numbered one hundred and forty-nine. Only the Siege Perilous remained empty. Since Merlin's first words of warning, only one insolent knight had ventured to occupy the seat. He had sat there for an instant, only to fall dead with a cry of anguish.

On the day of the Feast of the Pentecost, Arthur was awakened before daylight. For the first time since Merlin's disappearance, he heard the old counselor's voice.

"This day shall come your greatest moment of joy. Savor it well, Arthur of England, for sorrow must follow."

At the Feast, the King sat deep in thought, wondering at the meaning of Merlin's words. Or had the voice of the enchanter been in truth only a dream?

A clatter of hoofs broke into the King's thoughts. A lady on a white palfrey came riding into the hall.

"Which is Sir Lancelot?" she cried. "Let him follow me!"

Sir Lancelot rose. "I am the knight you seek. What would you?"

The gentlewoman would say no more. She rode from the hall and, at a nod from the King, Sir Lancelot followed her to a glade in the forest.

In the leafy glade, twelve nuns came forward, leading a fair youth clothed in shining white armor.

"Sir," said the eldest of the nuns, "we bring you this boy and pray you make him a knight. There is no hand more worthy than yours to give him the order of knighthood."

Lancelot looked upon the youth and found himself strangely stirred. "If I had a son," he thought, "I would wish it to be this boy."

"What is your name," he asked, "and is it your own desire that you be knighted?"

"My name is Galahad," the youth answered, "and it is my own desire that you dub me knight, sir." And Galahad knelt and was knighted.

"Now hasten to the court of the King," said the eldest nun, "for this youth has long been awaited."

When Lancelot and Galahad returned to the great hall at Camelot, Arthur himself came forward to greet them. Lancelot saw with wonder that the cover had been thrown back from the Siege Perilous. There, written in letters of gold, were the words: *This is the Siege of Sir Galahad.*

"Welcome to the Round Table, Sir Galahad," said Arthur gravely.

Before the awestruck company the young, untried knight moved unafraid to the Siege Perilous.

As Sir Galahad took his place, the hall darkened. There was a cracking as of thunder, and, in the midst of darkness, there appeared a beam of light seven times more bright than sunlight. In the beam appeared a vessel covered by a cloth of white samite.

"The Holy Grail!" Arthur's kingly voice was no more than a whisper.

According to legend, the Grail was the dish that Jesus used at the Last Supper. Now it moved slowly around the hall. Each knight, while the glow of the Grail was in his eyes, felt his heart's desire fulfilled. Then, miraculously as it had come, the Holy Cup in its covering of white samite disappeared from view.

Sir Percival was reminded of the moment when he had seen the corner of the covering raised in the castle of King Pecheur. Again the voice came to him, "You saw and you saw not. You wondered and you did not ask. . . ." Now the knight knew that he was called to take up the search.

He rose. "The Grail, covered, brought us such joy, I vow to seek it and never again to return to court until I have seen the Holy Cup uncovered, if it be God's will that I may do so."

Then Sir Gawaine leaped up and took the self-same vow, and after him, Sir Lancelot. Now all the knights around the table vowed to undertake the quest. Lastly, Sir Galahad rose from the Siege Perilous and knelt before King Arthur.

"If I may," he said, "I vow to find the Grail for the glory of God and for the crowning glory of thy reign. If I may not, God grant that I serve mankind in the search. For this I am come, Sire."

Now Arthur understood the words of Merlin. His greatest joy had come, in the completion of the Round Table and the appearance of the Holy Grail in his hall. Yet sorrow followed as he heard the vow made by all the knights. For he knew that this quest was not for the many, but only for the chosen few—the blameless and perfect knights. For the most part, they would fail of this quest. Many would become discouraged of their knighthood, and many would die.

The King said sorrowfully, "Never again after this quest shall I see this fellowship of the Round Table whole together. Therefore let us meet before you depart in one last tournament. Let us joust and tourney on the meadow tomorrow that men may say that such good knights were together on such a day."

Queen Guinevere and her ladies watched the tournament from the tower. They were amazed to see Sir Galahad ride forth without a shield, for he would take none that was offered. So marvelously did he break spears with the knights, that he unhorsed every one he met. Yet when they fell before his spear, they felt no pain.

And on the third day after the Feast of the Pentecost, one hundred and fifty knights of the Round Table mounted their horses and rode away from Camelot to seek the Holy Grail.

The Search for the Holy Grail

Some of the knights went together, and some singly. They went, not as they chose, but as God directed them, for the search for the Holy Grail was not like other adventures. The knights wandered hither and yon, in lands they knew and in lands that were strange to them. More than half of them died in the search for the Holy Grail, without getting a glimpse of it. Some gave up the search early and returned to Arthur's court, saying, "This quest is not for me."

Sir Gawaine and Sir Percival rode for a way together. Percival told Gawaine all that he remembered of the castle of King Pecheur, where he had seen the covered Grail in that king's keeping. The two knights set their faces westward toward the castle. Soon, however, a heavy white mist separated the knights. Gawaine went on alone and found the castle with its gate guarded by a lion. He braved the lion and entered the castle.

"I shall not fail in this quest," he said joyfully. But when he came to the chapel door, it was barred to him. He could hear sweet singing within, but could not enter. Over the music, a mocking voice came to his ears,

"You have the courage of a man, but you have the pride of a man. The quest of the Holy Grail is not for you."

Sadly the knight left the castle and made his way toward Camelot. On the way he had many adventures and set many wrongs to right, for he was a brave knight and courageous in all the ways of the everyday world.

A knight overcoming trials. Detail from a medieval manuscript. Bibliotheque Nationale, Paris.

Meanwhile Sir Galahad rode alone, still confident that a shield would be provided him. He made his way through the forest and up a steep mountain trail. Far below was the river, winding through green meadows.

A cry of distress came to the young knight's ears. He reined in his horse and looked down. Nothing was in sight but a shepherd guarding a flock of sheep. The cry came again, and Sir Galahad saw that a wolf had come among the sheep.

Along the river bank two knights were riding. "They will stop and rid the shepherd of that wolf," Sir Galahad said to himself. But the knights rode on, unnoticing.

Galahad spurred his horse down the steep slope. He cast his spear unerringly. Dripping blood, the wolf disappeared in the high bushes.

The shepherd peered from eyes clouded with age. "White Knight of the Ready Spear, I thank you. No other knight has troubled himself with an old shepherd's woes. I knew not how you would come, but that you

would come, I knew. Now follow me, for I have that which you lack for your quest."

Sir Galahad followed silently into a rude hut at the meadow's edge. There in the corner stood a white shield with a red cross.

"This shield was left with me by one who passed on a long journey. No man can lift it save the one to whom it belongs. If you are he, the shield will guide you and guard you to your journey's end. There, on a certain ship at sea, you will achieve your quest. But if you put hand to the shield and cannot lift it, harm will come to you, and great suffering."

The shepherd's warning could not stay Sir Galahad's purpose. He said,

"I will have this shield and all the dangers that go with it. For God has sent me to this place."

And he lifted the shield with ease and set it about his neck. But when he would have thanked the shepherd, the old man was nowhere to be seen.

Lancelot rode out from Camelot with the thought that he would keep close to Sir Galahad to guard the youth from harm. But Sir Galahad was soon far ahead. Lancelot found himself alone in a strange countryside. He wandered long and stopped by the wayside whenever there was call for help from maid or knight beset in combat.

At last, in a mighty tempest, he reached a great forest. Night came and, seeing no place for shelter, he lay down upon his shield. In the darkness, a vision came to him. He thought that a sick man was carried by upon a litter. After a little while two maidens followed, bearing the Holy Grail covered on a tray.

Lancelot rose and followed the procession to a hermitage. As he came into the outer hall, the Grail was borne through a door to the room where the sick knight lay groaning. Slowly the door began to close. But before it was quite closed, Lancelot beheld the cover being raised from the Holy Cup. The radiance all but blinded his eyes. He saw the sick knight start up with a cry of joy, for he was made whole again. But before Lancelot could enter the bright room where the Grail shone clear, the door closed. Sir Lancelot was left desolate in the darkness of the hermitage.

A hermit came into the hall. "My son," he said to the knight, "noble you are, and valiant beyond other men, and blameless, as the world measures blame. But the brave deeds you have done were done not for the deed's sake, but for the honor of Queen Guinevere. Therefore it is not given you to see the Holy Grail uncovered."

Lancelot was most sorrowful at these words. But he looked deeply into his heart and saw that the hermit spoke truth.

Sadly he turned his horse homeward to Camelot. He had not gone far upon the way when he met another Knight of the Round Table, Sir Bors de Ganis, his cousin.

"Well met, Lancelot," Sir Bors cried. "Seek no further. The quest for the Holy Grail is done!"

"You saw the Grail?" Lancelot looked in surprise at his quiet, kindly kinsman.

Sir Bors answered, "I saw it, beyond all hopes of mine to see. Alone I wandered far until a nun came to me as I rode along the shore. She was the sister of Sir Percival, and as fair as he. She bade me dismount. Then she led me to a ship that floated idly on the sea. Upon the ship were Sir Galahad and Sir Percival. I heard voices singing 'Glory and joy and honor to our Lord, and to the Holy Vessel of the Grail.' And there on a table before us was the Holy Cup.

"I knelt and closed my eyes against that brightness, and Galahad and Percival knelt beside me. I know not how it was, but when I rose from prayer a pale mist hid the Holy Grail from my sight. When I looked again, the Grail was gone. With it, to heaven, went the soul of Galahad."

"Galahad is dead?" Lancelot was silent for a moment. "What of Percival?"

"Percival has put aside the trappings of knighthood. He has become a monk for the glory of our Lord. He had me bring you greeting, and to say that Galahad healed King Pecheur and performed many other deeds of kindness before he left the world of man. Come with me, cousin. Let us hasten to Camelot and report to Arthur all that has befallen."

But Lancelot turned away. "Not yet, good Sir Bors. Not while there are deeds to be done for the deed's sake. You can say to the King—and to the Queen—that I have a quest. Say Lancelot seeks to conquer Lancelot. I shall stay alone at my castle, Joyous Gard, and will not return to the pleasures of the court until my quest is done."

Getting at Meaning

1. What kind of boyhood does Arthur have? How does he prove that he will be king?

2. Who gives Arthur Excalibur? What is Merlin's role in this episode? Why does he ask Arthur if he prefers the sword or the scabbard? What is the meaning of Merlin's answer?

3. How does Guinevere become Arthur's queen? On hearing Arthur's choice, what is Merlin's advice? What is Guinevere's initial reaction to Lancelot's visit? Why does she agree to become Arthur's queen?

4. What is the Round Table? How are the seats filled? What oaths of knighthood do the men swear to Arthur?

5. What is the "Siege Perilous"? Which knight finally fills it? Describe him.

6. What is the Holy Grail? Who undertakes the quest for the Holy Grail? Explain how Sir Gawaine and Sir Lancelot fail in their quests.

7. What does Lancelot mean when he says, "Lancelot seeks to conquer Lancelot"?

8. How is the quest ended? What happens to Sir Galahad?

Developing Skills in Reading Literature

1. **Hero.** Who is the supernatural power who aids Arthur? What qualities fit Arthur to be king? What heroic qualities does he possess? How does the heroic ideal in the Arthur stories differ from that in the Greek stories?

2. **Legend.** A legend is a fictitious story, which sometimes involves the supernatural and which usually concerns a real person and place. According to English history, a King Arthur lived around A.D. 600. What elements in these stories might be historically accurate? What elements are clearly imaginary?

3. **Setting.** One of the outstanding qualities of the Arthur legends is the development of the setting. How is Camelot described? How is the atmosphere like a dream?

4. **Symbol.** The Holy Grail is a major symbol in European literature. What kind of quest is the search for the Holy Grail? Why do all the knights but one fail? What does "questing after the Holy Grail" mean?

Developing Vocabulary

Language History: Medieval English. The tales and stories about King Arthur and his knights were first written down about 1100. Because language is constantly changing, you would find it very difficult to read the early version of the stories. The authors of this version of the Arthur stories have used modern English. However, they have included words that are associated with earlier times.

Examine the italicized words in the following quotations from the story. Using both the context and your knowledge of English, explain their meanings. How does use of these words contribute to the atmosphere of the story?

1. "*Behold,*" said Merlin, "there is the sword I spoke of."

2. "... a *damsel* rose up out of the water ..."

3. "As the knights pressed their *steeds* forward, the gate opened."

4. "But when a man has given his heart, he will be *loath* to change."

5. "The shepherd's warning *could not stay* Sir Galahad's purpose."

6. "Let us hasten to Camelot and report to Arthur all that has *befallen.*"

7. "Had Sir Lancelot, then, come to *seek her hand?*"

Developing Writing Skills

Analyzing a Character. Merlin, the great magician, has a prominent role in the Arthur stories. His character is perhaps not drawn as distinctly in these selections as in some others, but important characteristics do emerge. Reread the passages in the stories in which Merlin is mentioned. Form a generalization about him. Then write a paragraph that includes and supports your generalization.

Modern Conceptions of the Hero

from The Hobbit   *J. R. R. Tolkien*

The men of the lake-town Esgaroth were mostly indoors, for the breeze was from the black East and chill; but a few were walking on the quays, and watching, as they were fond of doing, the stars shine out from the smooth patches of the lake as they opened in the sky. From their town the Lonely Mountain was mostly screened by the low hills at the far end of the lake, through a gap in which the Running River came down from the North. Only its high peak could they see in clear weather, and they looked seldom at it, for it was ominous and drear even in the light of morning. Now it was lost and gone, blotted in the dark.

Suddenly it flickered back to view; a brief glow touched it and faded.

"Look!" said one. "The lights again! Last night the watchmen saw them start and fade from midnight until dawn. Something is happening up there."

"Perhaps the King under the Mountain is forging gold," said another. "It is long since he went north. It is time the songs began to prove themselves again."

"Which king?" said another with a grim voice. "As like as not it is the marauding fire of the Dragon, the only king under the Mountain we have ever known."

"You are always foreboding gloomy things!" said the others. "Anything from floods to poisoned fish. Think of something cheerful!"

Then suddenly a great light appeared in the low place in the hills, and the northern end of the lake turned golden. "The King be-neath the Mountain!" they shouted. "His wealth is like the Sun, his silver like a fountain, his rivers golden run! The river is running gold from the Mountain!" they cried, and everywhere windows were opening and feet were hurrying.

There was once more a tremendous excitement and enthusiasm. But the grim-voiced fellow ran hotfoot to the Master. "The dragon is coming or I am a fool!" he cried. "Cut the bridges! To arms! To arms!"

Then warning trumpets were suddenly sounded, and echoed along the rocky shores. The cheering stopped, and the joy was turned to dread. So it was that the dragon did not find them quite unprepared.

Before long, so great was his speed, they could see him as a spark of fire rushing towards them and growing ever huger and more bright, and not the most foolish doubted that the prophecies had gone rather wrong. Still they had a little time. Every vessel in the town was filled with water, every warrior was armed, every arrow and dart was ready; and the bridge to the land was thrown down and destroyed, before the roar of Smaug's terrible approach grew loud; and the lake rippled red as fire beneath the awful beating of his wings.

Amid shrieks and wailing and the shouts of men he came over them, swept towards the bridges and was foiled! The bridge was gone, and his enemies were on an island in deep water—too deep and dark and cool for his liking. If he plunged into it, a vapor and a steam would arise enough to cover all the land with a mist for days; but the lake was mightier than he, it would quench him before he could pass through.

Roaring, he swept back over the town. A hail of dark arrows leaped up and snapped and rattled on his scales and jewels; and their shafts fell back, kindled by his breath burning and hissing into the lake. No fireworks you ever imagined equalled the sights that night. At the twanging of the bows and the shrilling of the trumpets, the dragon's wrath blazed to its height, till he was blind and mad with it. No one had dared to give battle to him for many an age; nor would they have dared now, if it had not been for the grim-voiced man (Bard was his name), who ran to and fro cheering on the archers and urging the Master to order them to fight to the last arrow.

Fire leaped from the dragon's jaws. He circled for a while high in the air above them, lighting all the lake; the trees by the shores shone like copper and like blood, with leaping shadows of dense black at their feet. Then down he swooped, straight through the arrow-storm, reckless in his rage, taking no heed to turn his scaly sides towards his foes, seeking only to set their town ablaze.

Fire leaped from thatched roofs and wooden beam-ends as he hurtled down and past and round again, though all had been drenched with water before he came. Once more, water was flung by a hundred hands wherever a spark appeared. Back swirled the dragon. A sweep of his tail, and the roof of the Great House crumbled and smashed down. Flames unquenchable sprang high into the night. Another swoop and another, and another house and then another sprang afire and fell; and still no arrow hindered Smaug or hurt him more than a fly from the marshes.

Already men were jumping into the water on every side. Women and children were being huddled into laden boats in the market-pool. Weapons were flung down. There was mourning and weeping, where but a little time ago the old songs of mirth to come had been sung about the dwarves. Now men cursed their names. The Master himself was turning to his great gilded boat, hoping to row away in the confusion and save himself. Soon all the town would be deserted and burned down to the surface of the lake.

That was the dragon's hope. They could all get into boats for all he cared. There he could have fine sport hunting them, or they could stop till they starved. Let them try to get to land and he would be ready. Soon he would set all the shoreland woods ablaze, and wither every field and pasture. Just now he was enjoying the sport of town-baiting more than he had enjoyed anything for years.

But there was still a company of archers that held their ground among the burning houses. Their captain was Bard, grim-voiced and grim-faced, whose friends had accused him of prophesying floods and poisoned fish, though they knew his worth and courage. He was a descendant in long line of Girion, Lord of Dale, whose wife and child had escaped down the Running River from the ruin long ago. Now he shot with a great yew bow, till all his arrows but one were spent. The flames were near him. His companions were leaving him. He bent his bow for the last time.

Suddenly out of the dark, something fluttered to his shoulder. He started—but it was only an old thrush. Unafraid, it perched by his ear and it brought him news. Marvelling, he found he could understand its tongue, for he was of the race of Dale.

"Wait! Wait!" it said to him. "The moon is rising. Look for the hollow of the left breast as he flies and turns above you!" And while Bard paused in wonder, it told him of tidings up in the Mountain and of all that it had heard.

Then Bard drew his bow-string to his ear. The dragon was circling back, flying low, and as he came the moon rose above the eastern shore and silvered his great wings.

"Arrow!" said the bowman. "Black arrow! I have saved you to the last. You have never failed me, and always I have recovered you. I had you from my father and he from of old. If ever you came from the forges of the true King under the Mountain, go now and speed well!"

The dragon swooped once more, lower than ever; and as he turned and dived down, his belly glittered white with sparkling fires of gems in the moon—but not in one place. The great bow twanged. The black arrow sped straight from the string, straight for the hollow by the left breast where the foreleg was flung wide. In it smote and vanished, barb, shaft, and feather, so fierce was its flight. With a shriek that deafened men, felled trees, and split stone, Smaug shot spouting into the air, turned over, and crashed down from on high in ruin.

Full on the town he fell. His last throes splintered it to sparks and gledes. The lake roared in. A vast steam leaped up, white in the sudden dark under the moon. There was a hiss, a gushing whirl, and then silence. And that was the end of Smaug and Esgaroth.

Getting at Meaning

1. Describe Smaug. What is the most destructive thing about him?

2. How do the people of Esgaroth prepare for the dragon's attack?

3. What is Smaug's plan? Does he succeed? Why or why not?

Developing Skills in Reading Literature

1. **Hero.** The people of Esgaroth do not regard Bard as a hero. Why not? What qualities make him a hero after all?

2. **Myth.** J. R. R. Tolkien's stories were written in modern times, but they recall the old myths and legends in many ways. What parallels do you see between this story and the Greek stories? between this story and the legends of Arthur and Siegfried?

3. **Description.** The success of this selection lies in the writer's ability to describe action in an exciting way. Reread the passage that describes Smaug's entrance into the town. How does the writer's word choice generate excitement? Which other passages do you find particularly effective?

Happy Childhood Tales   *Robert Benchley*

We have had so many stories lately dealing with the sordid facts of life, about kitchen sinks and murders and young girls thrown out into the streets by mean old farmers who live in horsehair trunks, to say nothing of incidental subjects, such as cold oatmeal and unfortunate people who have only one glove apiece, that a reaction is taking place in the mind of the reading public and a demand is going up for some of the fanciful, happy tales of our youth.

"Enough of these stories of crime and unhappiness!" the people are crying. "Tell us again some of the ancient myths of an older day, the merry little legends on which we were brought up before the world grew grim and sordid."

And so, my readers, I am going to try to recall to you some of the charming fairy tales, or, at any rate, to make up some like them; and I hope that after this little trip back into the Never-Never Land of our youth, those cheeks of yours will be blooming again and that you will shut your traps. For, after all, there must be *some* good in the world, else why were erasers put on the ends of lead pencils?

Endremia and Liason

(From the Greek Mythology)

Endremia was the daughter of Polygaminous, the God of Ensilage,[1] and Reba, the Goddess of Licorice. She was the child of a most unhappy union, it later turned out; for when she was a tiny child, her father struck her mother with an anvil and turned himself into a lily pad to avoid the vengeance of Jove. But Jove was too sly for Polygaminous and struck him with a bolt of lightning the size of the Merchants Bank Building, which threw him completely off his balance so that he toppled over into a chasm and was dashed to death.

In the meantime, Little Endremia found herself alone in the world, with nobody but Endrocine, the Goddess of Lettuce, and her son Bilax, the God of Gum Arabic,[2] to look after her. But, as Polygaminous (her father; have you forgotten so soon?) had turned Endremia into a mushroom before he turned himself into a lily pad, neither of her guardians knew who she was, so their protection did her no good.

But Jove had not so soon forgotten the daughter of his favorite (Reba), and appeared to her one night in the shape of a mushroom gatherer. He asked her how she would like to get off that tree (she was one of those mushrooms that grow on trees) and get into his basket. Endremia, not knowing that it was Jove who was asking her, said not much. Whereupon Jove unloosed his mighty wrath and struck down the whole tree with a bolt of lightning that he had brought with him in case Endremia wouldn't listen to reason.

This is why it is never safe to eat the mushrooms that grow on trees, or to refuse to get into Jove's basket.

---

1. **Ensilage** (en's'l ij): the preserving of green fodder by storage in a silo.
2. **Gum Arabic:** a gum that comes from plants, used in making medicines and candy.

Milgrig and the Tree Wilfs

(Something like Hans Christian Andersen)

Once upon a time there was a little girl named Milgrig, believe it or not. She lived in the middle of a deep, dark forest with her three ugly sisters and their husbands, who were charcoal burners. Every night the three ugly sisters used to take little Milgrig and pull out a strand of her golden hair, so that by the time she was thirteen years old she looked something awful. And after the three sisters had pulled out her hair, their three husbands (I forgot to tell you that the three husbands were even uglier than the three sisters and much nastier) would stick pins into little Milgrig until she looked like a war map.

One night, when little Milgrig was so full of pins that she couldn't see straight, a fairy prince came riding up to the door of the charcoal burners' hut and asked if he had lost his way.

"How should I know?" replied the oldest sister, who was uglier than all the rest. "What was your way?"

"My way was to the king's castle," replied the prince, "and I must get there before midnight, for my father is torturing my mother with red-hot irons."

"Your father sounds like a good egg," replied the oldest husband, who was uglier than all the rest. "We must ask him down some night."

The prince, however, did not think that this was very funny and asked if little Milgrig

might not be allowed to show him the way to the castle.

The ugly husbands and sisters, thinking that Milgrig would not know the way and would get the prince lost in the forest, agreed heartily to this suggestion, and the pins were pulled out of Milgrig to make it possible for her to walk.

"Good luck and a happy landing!" they all called out after the two young people as they set forth on their perilous journey.

But the prince was no fool, and knew his way through the forest as well as you or I do (better, I'll wager), and he took little Milgrig to the palace just as fast as his palfrey would carry him.

She wasn't particularly crazy about going, but a prince is a prince, and she knew enough to keep her mouth shut.

When they reached the palace, and the prince found that his father had already killed his mother, he turned to little Milgrig and said:

"Now you are queen."

At this, little Milgrig was very pleased and immediately dispatched messengers to the charcoal burners' hut, where her three ugly sisters and three still uglier brothers-in-law were burned alive in a slow fire. Little Milgrig and the prince, happy in this termination to their little affair, lived happily ever after.

And so now, my readers, you must toddle off to bed, for we have had an evening with the happy, happy storytellers of an earlier day and have had a vacation, for one night at least, from the drab, unpleasant sordidness of present-day writing.

Getting at Meaning

1. What reason does the narrator give for writing these tales? Is this purpose accomplished?

2. What two types of stories are retold?

Developing Skills in Reading Literature

1. **Parody.** Satire is the literary art of making fun of foolish ideas, customs, and traditions. A parody is a special kind of satire that mocks a specific literary work or type of literature, usually through exaggeration or through the application of the characteristics of that literature to silly or ridiculous subject matter.

"Endremia and Liason" is a parody of a Greek myth. The writer makes fun of Greek mythology by creating gods and goddesses for insignificant things, such as licorice and lettuce. What other qualities in the myths does he parody? Cite examples to support your answer. What makes the parody humorous? How does "Milgrig and the Tree Wilfs" fit the definition of a parody?

2. **Irony.** The title of this selection is humorously ironic. What is the writer trying to emphasize about many of the old myths and fairy tales by calling this piece "Happy Childhood Tales"?

Developing Writing Skills

Writing a Parody. Write a parody of a myth or of a well known fairy tale. (You may choose one of the myths or legends from this unit, if you wish.) Attempt to make fun of certain important details or characteristics in the story, and try to add humor through the names of the characters and through clever dialogue.

Unit Review *Myths: The Hero*

Understanding the Unit

1. Which hero in this unit do you find most appealing? Why?

2. Which of the stories in this unit involve mysterious births, with heroes searching to discover their identities?

3. What qualities do the ancient Greeks appear to admire in a hero? Do Arthur and Siegfried fit the Greek conception of a hero? How are they different? What is the social position of most or all of the heroes in this unit?

4. Which stories in this unit involve strange beasts or creatures? What qualities do the mythological beasts have in common? Why do you think imaginary creatures are such an important part of many myths and legends?

5. In most myths the hero returns home after his exploits to enjoy his rewards. Which heroes in the unit follow this pattern? What happens after they return home?

6. Which heroes are killed, directly or indirectly, by women who love them? How are their deaths ironic?

7. Think about some modern-day heroes, such as Paul Bunyan, Pecos Bill, Superman, and Wonder Woman. What qualities do these characters possess? In what ways are they like the classical heroes presented in this unit? In what ways are they different? What function do heroes serve in people's lives?

Writing

1. What qualities should a hero have in real life? Who are your heroes? What makes these people heroic? Think about these questions yourself, and ask others of various ages what they think. Then write a five-paragraph composition that attempts to define what a modern hero should be, giving examples to support your ideas. You may wish to compare and contrast the modern hero with the heroes of classical myth and legend.

2. Write a myth or legend that features a central hero or heroine of your own creation. Your story may be set at any point in history, distant or recent, or it may be set in the present. You may want to include imaginary beasts in your story or characters from other myths and legends. Work to make your plot and your characters colorful and interesting. You may wish to illustrate your story.

DISKS OF NEWTON (STUDY FOR "FUGUE IN TWO COLORS"), 1912. *Franz Kupka.*
Philadelphia Museum of Art. The Louise and Walter Arensberg Collection.

Unit 5

Poetry

AMBASSADOR OF AUTUMN, 1922. *Paul Klee.*
Yale University Art Gallery. Gift of Collection Société Anonyme.

Introduction to the Unit

Essentials   Robin Fulton

A poem they say must be all muscle
Like a man swimming.

If it must be dressed let it wear tools
Like a man climbing, hoisting kit up with him.

Or maybe you know a poem (like a goddess)   5
From the grace it doesn't need to have but has.
When you watch a stream you know it is a stream
Not entirely from the moving muscle of water
But from the fineries of light it wears.

Poems, like short stories and nonfiction selections, deal
with life experiences and the reactions of human beings to
these experiences. Like fiction and nonfiction, poems are
meant to bring you pleasure and insights. More poetry
touches your life than you may realize. The lyrics to popular
songs are usually poetry, as are many advertising jingles.
Tongue twisters, slogans, and word games also involve poetic
language.

The poem "Essentials" is about the qualities necessary
in a poem. The first two lines suggest that a poem must be
tight and to the point, with no spare words or "fat." Lines 3
and 4 explain that, if a poem does have "clothing" on its flesh,
the extra weight should be somehow important to the purpose of the poem, just as tools are important to a climber.
The final five lines compare a poem to a stream, defining the
essence of a poem as both meaning, or "muscle," and beauty,
or "fineries of light."

As you read the poems in this unit, think about the
answers to these questions: Do all poems rhyme? Do they all
have rhythm? Are all poems descriptive? Are they all emotional? In what ways is poetry similar to other types of
literature? In what ways is it different? As you read, enjoy the
poems. Appreciate them for the meaning and the beauty
they can convey to you.

Shape and Sound

COMPOSITION WITH CLARINETS AND TIN HORN, 1951. *Ben Shahn.*
Detroit Institute of Arts. Founder Society Purchase, Friends of Modern Art Fund.

How Everything Happens

(Based on a Study of the Wave)   *May Swenson*

                                                happen.
                                                 to
                                                up
                                          stacking
                                        is   5
                                  something
When nothing is happening

When it happens
                something
                          pulls   10
                        back
                      not
                        to
                          happen.

When   has happened.   15
        pulling back   stacking up
                  happens
            has happened   stacks up.
When it   something   nothing
                          pulls back while   20

Then nothing is happening.

                                    happens.
                                  and
                          forward
                        pushes   25
                    up
                stacks
          something
Then

Getting at Meaning

1. How do you know where each line of this poem begins? How many separate statements are there in all?

2. What is this poem saying about things happening? What does the speaker mean in talking about the opposite actions of "pulling back" and "stacking up"?

Developing Skills in Reading Literature

1. **Concrete Poem.** A concrete poem is one in which the shape of the poem suggests something important about its meaning. For example, a concrete poem about the stars might have the shape of a star. What does the shape of this poem suggest to you? In what ways is the shape related to the poem's meaning?

2. **Theme.** The reader is told that the speaker of the poem has come to conclusions about how everything happens "based on a study of the wave." What generalization about the world comes to the speaker through this study?

Developing Vocabulary

Suffixes. This poem contains the root word *happen* and the words *happening, happens,* and *happened,* which are formed by adding suffixes to the root word. For each of the following root words, list at least five words that are formed by the addition of one or more suffixes.

exhibit	believe	line
retract	sick	found
measure	reform	young

NORTHEASTER, 1895. *Winslow Homer.*
The Metropolitan Museum of Art, New York.

Riding on the Train   *Eloise Greenfield*

I see
fences and fields
barns and bridges
stations and stores
trees   5
other trains
horses and hills
water tanks
towers
streams   10
old cars
old men
roofs
raindrops crawling backwards on the window

I hear   15
ruggety-ruggety
squeakety-squeakety
rumbledy-rumbledy
woonh, WOONH!
Wil–ming–tonnnnnnn   20

I feel
my leg jiggling
my bottom bouncing
my shoulders shaking
my head rolling   25
I'm getting s l e
                  e
                    e
                      e
                        p y

Getting at Meaning

What does the speaker see while riding on the train? What does the speaker hear? feel?

Developing Skills in Reading Literature

1. **Alliteration.** Alliteration, you will remember, is the repetition of consonant sounds at the beginnings of words. Find lines in this poem that use alliteration.

2. **Stanza.** On what does the first stanza of this poem focus? the second? the third? Why is the word *sleepy* stretched out in the way that it is?

Developing Vocabulary

Echoic Words. In the second stanza of this poem, the speaker uses pairs of words that imitate the sounds of a train. What are these echoic words? Imagine yourself in a setting, such as a football stadium, a forest at night, a busy supermarket, or a city bus. Make up echoic words that capture the sounds of this setting.

I Hear America Singing   *Walt Whitman*

I hear America singing, the varied carols I hear,
Those of mechanics, each one singing his as it should be blithe and strong,
The carpenter singing his as he measures his plank or beam,
The mason singing his as he makes ready for work, or leaves off work,
The boatman singing what belongs to him in his boat, the deckhand singing on the   5
   steamboat deck,
The shoemaker singing as he sits on his bench, the hatter singing as he stands,
The wood-cutter's song, the ploughboy's on his way in the morning, or at noon
   intermission or at sundown,
The delicious singing of the mother, or of the young wife at work, or of the girl sewing
   or washing,
Each singing what belongs to him or her and to none else,
The day what belongs to the day—at night the party of young fellows, robust,   10
   friendly,
Singing with open mouths their strong melodious songs.

Getting at Meaning

1. What is the speaker of the poem hearing? What kinds of workers does the speaker name? Why does the speaker mention these particular kinds of workers?

2. What is each worker doing as he or she "sings"? What do you think the speaker means by the word *singing?*

Developing Skills in Reading Literature

1. **Rhythm.** This poem appeals primarily to the sense of hearing. This appeal is emphasized by the speaker's repeated use of the words *hear, carols, singing,* and *song.* Read the poem aloud. In what ways is the poem itself like a song? What makes it musical?

2. **Free Verse.** Poetry that has no regular pattern of rhythm and rhyme is called free verse. This poem is an example of free verse. Review the characteristics of poetry presented in the Introduction to the Unit. Be prepared to point out the qualities that make "I Hear America Singing" a poem.

3. **Structure.** Notice that this poem is all one sentence, with each line flowing freely into the next one. How is this structure related to what the speaker hears in America? In what sense are all the various workers united?

How They Brought the Good News from Ghent to Aix

Robert Browning

I sprang to the stirrup, and Joris, and he;
I galloped, Dirck galloped, we galloped all three;
"Good speed!" cried the watch, as the gatebolts undrew;
"Speed!" echoed the wall to us galloping through;
Behind shut the postern, the lights sank to rest,   5
And into the midnight we galloped abreast.

Not a word to each other; we kept the great pace
Neck by neck, stride by stride, never changing our place;
I turned in my saddle and made its girths tight,
Then shortened each stirrup, and set the pique[1] right,   10
Rebuckled the cheek-strap, chained slacker the bit,
Nor galloped less steadily Roland a whit.

'Twas moonset at starting; but while we drew near
Lokeren,[2] the cocks crew and twilight dawned clear;
At Boom, a great yellow star came out to see;   15
At Düffeld, 'twas morning as plain as could be;
And from Mecheln church-steeple we heard the half-chime,
So, Joris broke silence with, "Yet there is time!"

At Aershot, up leaped of a sudden the sun,
And against him the cattle stood black every one,   20
To stare thro' the mist at us galloping past,
And I saw my stout galloper Roland at last,
With resolute shoulders, each butting away
The haze, as some bluff river headland its spray:

---

1. **pique** (pēk): a device to spur a horse.
2. **Lokeren:** This and other place names are towns on the route between Ghent and Aix.

And his low head and crest, just one sharp ear bent back 25
For my voice, and the other pricked out on his track;
And one eye's black intelligence,—ever that glance
O'er its white edge at me, his own master, askance!
And the thick heavy spume-flakes which aye and anon[3]
His fierce lips shook upwards in galloping on. 30

By Hasselt, Dirck groaned; and cried Joris, "Stay spur![4]
Your Roos galloped bravely, the fault's not in her,
We'll remember at Aix"[5]—for one heard the quick wheeze
Of her chest, saw the stretched neck and staggering knees,
And sunk tail, and horrible heave of the flank, 35
As down on her haunches she shuddered and sank.

So, we were left galloping, Joris and I,
Past Looz and past Tongres, no cloud in the sky;
The broad sun above laughed a pitiless laugh,
'Neath our feet broke the brittle bright stubble like chaff; 40
Till over by Dalhem a dome-spire sprang white,
And "Gallop," gasped Joris, "for Aix is in sight!"

"How they'll greet us!"—and all in a moment his roan
Rolled neck and croup over, lay dead as a stone;
And there was my Roland to bear the whole weight 45
Of the news which alone could save Aix from her fate,
With his nostrils like pits full of blood to the brim,
And with circles of red for his eye-sockets' rim.

Then I cast loose my buffcoat, each holster let fall,
Shook off both my jack-boots, let go belt and all, 50
Stood up in the stirrup, leaned, patted his ear,
Called my Roland his pet-name, my horse without peer;
Clapped my hands, laughed and sang, any noise, bad or good,
Till at length into Aix Roland galloped and stood.

And all I remember is—friends flocking round 55
As I sat with his head 'twixt my knees on the ground;
And no voice but was praising this Roland of mine,
As I poured down his throat our last measure of wine,
Which (the burgesses voted by common consent)
Was no more than his due who brought good news from Ghent. 60

---

3. **aye and anon** (ā and ə nän'): now and then.
4. **Stay spur:** stop driving your horse on.
5. **Aix** (eks): a shortened form of Aix-la-Chapelle, a town on the Belgian border, located about 100 miles from Ghent (gent) in Flanders.

Getting at Meaning

1. List the events in this poem in the order that they happen.

2. What is Roland's remarkable feat? How is he rewarded? When do you think this poem is set?

3. How many riders begin the journey? What happens to Dirck? What happens to Joris?

4. What does the speaker do toward the end of the ride to make Roland's journey easier?

Developing Skills in Reading Literature

1. **Stanza.** How many stanzas make up this poem? How many lines are there per stanza?

2. **Rhyme.** The rhyming pattern is the same throughout the poem. Which lines rhyme in each stanza?

3. **Rhythm.** Rhythm is determined by the relationship between accented and unaccented syllables in a line of poetry. This poem has a driving, insistent rhythm. Read it aloud. What does the rhythm remind you of? Why do you suppose the poet has chosen it for this poem?

Sun Dance Sun   *Dave Etter*

sun dance sun

Apache brazen
Shoshone[1] bold

war dance sun
war paint bright   5

assaults the cold

swift sassy
brave brassy

arrows of sun

bleed the day   10

to a tomahawked
scarlet death

in the crisp
Indian summer

afternoon   15

---

1. **Apache** (ə pach′ ē). . .**Shoshone** (shō shō′ nē): tribes of
Indians.

Getting at Meaning

1. What is the time of year in this poem?
2. How does the speaker describe the temperature of the day? What is the effect of the sun?

Developing Skills in Reading Literature

1. **Repetition of Words and Sounds.** One poetic device used by this poet is the repetition of words and of vowel and consonant sounds. For example, the word *sun* is repeated three times; the long *o* sound is repeated in the phrase "Shoshone bold." Find other examples of repetition in the poem.

2. **Metaphor.** To what does the speaker compare the sunlight? Why is this metaphor appropriate to the subject of the poem? How is the metaphor carried throughout the entire poem?

The Double-Play   *Robert Wallace*

In his sea lit
distance, the pitcher winding
like a clock about to chime comes down with

the ball, hit
sharply, under the artificial   5
banks of arc-lights, bounds like a vanishing string

over the green
to the shortstop magically
scoops to his right whirling above his invisible

shadows   10
in the dust redirects
its flight to the running poised second baseman

pirouettes[1]
leaping, above the slide, to throw
from mid-air, across the colored tightened interval,   15

to the leaning-
out first baseman ends the dance
drawing it disappearing into his long brown glove

stretches. What
is too swift for deception   20
is final, lost, among the loosened figures

jogging off the field
(the pitcher walks), casual
in the space where the poem has happened.

---

1. **pirouettes** (pir′ oo wet′): to whirl around on one foot or the point of
the toe, as in ballet.

Getting at Meaning

1. Why does everyone walk off the field at the end of the poem? What has happened?

2. How many people handle the ball on the play? Who "ends the dance"? How?

Developing Skills in Reading Literature

1. **Stanza.** The stanzas in this free verse poem are surprisingly regular. What is true for each one? Notice how each stanza leads into the next one. How does the structure relate to the content of the poem?

2. **Theme.** The last six lines of the poem make up a separate sentence commenting on the action of the double-play. What is the meaning of these lines? What is the speaker saying about the double-play?

3. **Simile.** Find two similes in the poem and be prepared to discuss their effectiveness.

Developing Vocabulary

Word Origins. This poem contains the word *pirouette*, a French word that has become a part of English. Following are several French expressions that have become standard in our language. Find each phrase in a dictionary and write its meaning on a separate sheet of paper.

bon voyage   noblesse oblige
hors d'oeuvre   raison d'être
déjà vu   tête-à-tête
pièce de résistance   coup de grâce

Developing Writing Skills

Using Figures of Speech. Summarize what happens in this poem in one simple sentence. Notice how the poet has turned this basic idea into vivid description through the use of figurative language.

Find or write a simple sentence that summarizes another activity or experience. Now extend your sentence, through the use of figurative language, into a descriptive poem.

Velvet Shoes   *Elinor Wylie*

Let us walk in the white snow
  In a soundless space;
With footsteps quiet and slow,
  At a tranquil pace,
  Under veils of white lace.   5

I shall go shod in silk,
  And you in wool,
White as a white cow's milk,
  More beautiful
  Than the breast of a gull.   10

We shall walk through the still town
  In a windless peace;
We shall step upon white down,
  Upon silver fleece,
  Upon softer than these.   15

We shall walk in velvet shoes:
  Wherever we go
Silence will fall like dews
  On white silence below.
  We shall walk in the snow.   20

Getting at Meaning

To whom do you imagine the speaker is addressing this poem? Explain your response.

Developing Skills in Reading Literature

1. **Structure.** What patterns do you see in the stanzas? Which lines rhyme in each stanza? Does the poem have a regular rhythm?

2. **Mood.** Notice all the words in this poem related to sound, or more specifically, to the absence of sound. What are some of these words? What mood do they create?

3. **Repetition.** Why is the word *white* used so often? What effect does the repetition of this word create?

4. **Simile.** What effect is created by these similes: "White as a white cow's milk" and "More beautiful/Than the breast of a gull"?

Lucy Gray   *William Wordsworth*

Oft I had heard of Lucy Gray:
And, when I crossed the wild,
I chanced to see at break of day
The solitary child.

No mate, no comrade Lucy knew;   5
She dwelt on a wide moor,
—The sweetest thing that ever grew
Beside a human door!

You yet may spy the fawn at play,
The hare upon the green;   10
But the sweet face of Lucy Gray
Will never more be seen.

"To-night will be a stormy night—
You to the town must go;
And take a lantern, Child, to light   15
Your mother through the snow."

"That, Father! will I gladly do:
'Tis scarcely afternoon—
The minster[1]-clock has just struck two,
And yonder is the moon!"   20

At this the Father raised his hook,
And snapped a faggot-band;[2]
He plied his work;—and Lucy took
The lantern in her hand.

Not blither is the mountain roe:[3]   25
With many a wanton stroke
Her feet disperse the powdery snow,
That rises up like smoke.

The storm came on before its time:
She wandered up and down;   30
And many a hill did Lucy climb:
But never reached the town.

The wretched parents all that night
Went shouting far and wide;
But there was neither sound nor sight   35
To serve them for a guide.

At day-break on a hill they stood
That overlooked the moor;
And thence they saw the bridge of wood,
A furlong from their door.   40

They wept—and, turning homeward, cried,
"In heaven we all shall meet";
—When in the snow the mother spied
The print of Lucy's feet.

Then downwards from the steep hill's edge   45
They tracked the footmarks small;
And through the broken hawthorn hedge,
And by the long stone-wall;

---

1. **minster:** church
2. **faggot-band** (fag′ ət): a cord binding a bundle of sticks
to be used for fuel.
3. **roe** (rō): a small, graceful deer.

And then an open field they crossed;
The marks were still the same;   50
They tracked them on, nor ever lost;
And to the bridge they came.

They followed from the snowy bank
Those footmarks, one by one,
Into the middle of the plank;   55
And further there were none!

—Yet some maintain that to this day
She is a living child;
That you may see sweet Lucy Gray
Upon the lonesome wild.   60

O'er rough and smooth she trips along,
And never looks behind;
And sings a solitary song
That whistles in the wind.

Getting at Meaning

1. How is Lucy described in this poem? What causes her death?

2. What is the mystery that surrounds Lucy's death? What are the legends about her?

Developing Skills in Reading Literature

1. **Quatrain.** A stanza containing four lines is called a quatrain, from the French word *quatre*, meaning "four." How many quatrains make up this poem?

2. **Rhyme and Rhythm.** What is the rhyming pattern of each quatrain? Is there a regular rhythm?

3. **Narrative Poem.** A poem that tells a story is called a narrative poem. Who are the charac-ters in this narrative poem? What is the setting? the plot? the conflict?

Developing Vocabulary

Synonyms. Each of the following words has a synonym in the poem. Find the synonyms, using a dictionary, if necessary.

lonely	scatter	frisky	lived
claim	friend	miserable	did

Developing Writing Skills

Writing a Narrative Poem. Write a narrative poem that has strong rhyme and rhythm. It may be on any subject.

Imagery

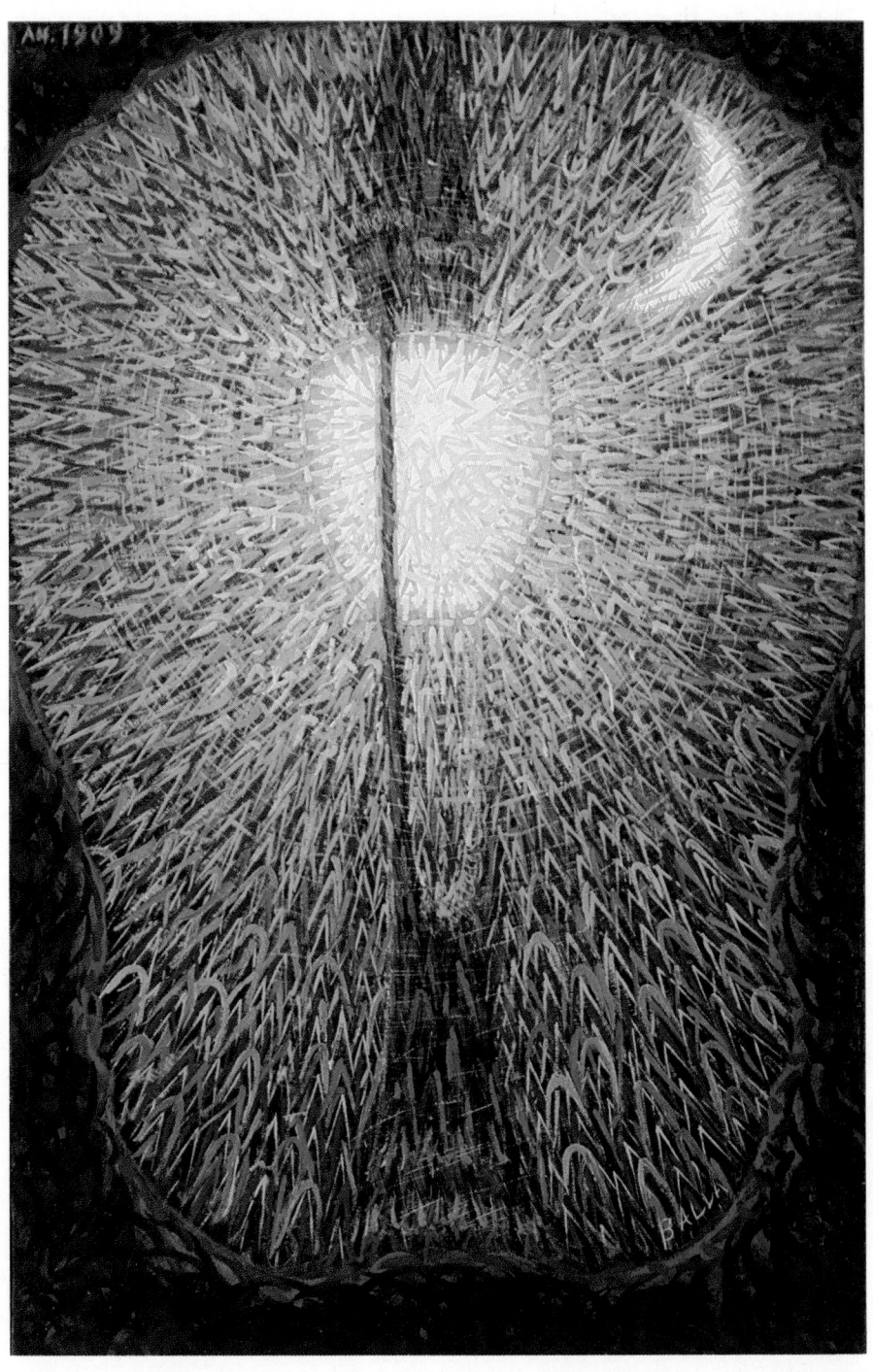

STREET LIGHT, 1909. *Giacomo Balla.*
Collection, The Museum of Modern Art, New York.
Hillman Periodicals Fund.

Dandelions *Deborah Austin*

under cover of night and rain
the troops took over.
waking to total war in beleaguered houses
over breakfast we faced the batteries
marshalled by wall and stone, deployed   5
with a master strategy no one had suspected
and now all
firing

pow

all day, all yesterday   10
and all today
the barrage continued
deafening sight.
reeling now, eyes ringing from noise, from walking
gingerly over the mined lawns   15
exploded at every second
rocked back by the starshellfire
concussion of gold on green
bringing battle-fatigue

pow by lionface firefur pow by   20
goldburst shellshock pow by
whoosh   splat   splinteryellow   pow   by
pow   by   pow
tomorrow smoke drifts up
from the wrecked battalions,   25
all the ammunition, firegold fury, gone.
smoke
drifts
thistle-blown
over the war-zone, only   30

here and there, in the shade by the
peartree
pow   in the crack by the
curbstone   pow   and back of the
ashcan, lonely   35
guerrilla snipers, hoarding
their fire shrewdly
never

pow

surrender   40

Getting at Meaning

1. What experience does the poem describe?

2. What two stages of the battle does the speaker recognize?

3. Will the speaker win the battle? Explain your answer.

Developing Skills in Reading Literature

1. **Extended Metaphor.** The central comparison in this poem is between a battle against dandelions and a battle against enemy troops. What two forces are at war? What is the "barrage" that continues "all yesterday/and all today"? What is the smoke that "drifts up/from the wrecked battalions"? Who are the "guerrilla snipers"? What other words and phrases reinforce the central metaphor?

2. **Imagery.** The images in this poem help the reader to picture a battle scene. What specific pictures are suggested by the following images:

marshalled by wall and stone
barrage
eyes ringing from noise
walking gingerly
starshellfire

concussion of gold on green
pow by lionface firefur pow
goldburst shellshock pow
wrecked battalions
firegold fury
smoke drifts thistle-blown
hoarding their fire shrewdly

3. **Onomatopoeia.** Onomatopoeia is the use of echoic words to create images that appeal to the sense of hearing. What words in the poem illustrate this literary technique? What sound is imitated by each word? How do these words reinforce the meaning of the poem?

4. **Tone and Mood.** What are the poet's feelings about dandelions? What are your feelings as you read the poem? How do the images in the poem convey the poet's feelings? How do the images elicit a response from the reader?

5. **Title.** If you had not read the title of this poem, would you have understood the central comparison?

Developing Vocabulary

Coined Words. Poets sometimes create, or coin, new words by joining words in new combinations. What words in this poem are coined words? Explain briefly the denotation and the connotation of each word.

Daffodils *May Swenson*

Yellow telephones
in a row in the garden
are ringing,
shrill with light.

Old-fashioned spring   5
brings earliest models out
each April the same,
naïve and classical.

Look into the yolk-
colored mouthpieces   10
alert with echoes.
Say hello to time.

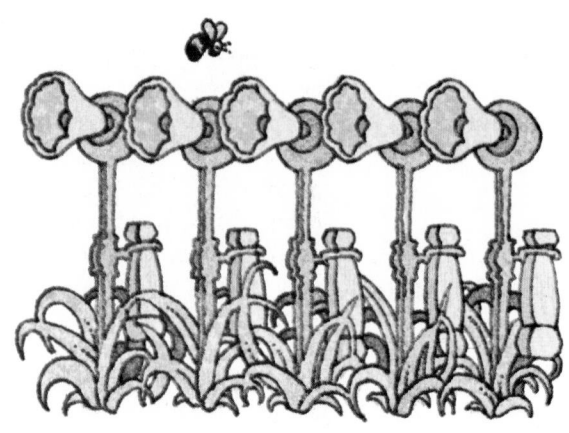

Getting at Meaning

1. Describe the kind of old-fashioned telephone the speaker is referring to in this poem.

2. Why does the speaker call the flowers "naïve and classical"?

Developing Skills in Reading Literature

1. **Extended Metaphor.** One metaphor controls this poem. What is it? In what specific ways are the two unlike things compared?

2. **Imagery.** The images in this poem appeal to two senses. What are these two senses? Give examples that appeal to each sense.

3. **Theme.** What does the last line of the poem mean? What do the daffodils represent to the speaker?

Developing Writing Skills

Description: Selecting Specific Details. What signals the beginning of spring for you? Write a paragraph or a poem about one or more things you associate with the coming of spring.

High Tide   *Jean Starr Untermeyer*

I edged back against the night.
The sea growled assault on the wave-bitten shore.
And the breakers,
Like young and impatient hounds,
Sprang with rough joy on the shrinking sand.   5
Sprang—but were drawn back slowly,
With a long, relentless pull,
Whimpering, into the dark.

Then I saw who held them captive;
And I saw how they were bound   10
With a broad and quivering leash of light,
Held by the moon,
As, calm and unsmiling,
She walked the deep fields of the sky.

Getting at Meaning

1. What is the speaker of the poem observing?

2. To what does the word *them* refer in line 9? To whom does the word *she* refer in the last line?

Developing Skills in Reading Literature

1. **Imagery.** What images describe the sea? the shore? the moon?

2. **Simile.** What simile describes the breakers? To what different senses does the simile appeal?

3. **Personification.** The speaker personifies the moon in this poem; that is, the moon is given human characteristics. Describe the moon in the poem.

Developing Writing Skills

Writing About a Personal Experience. In a poem or a paragraph, write about something you have observed in nature that made you better understand or appreciate yourself and the world around you. Try to re-create your observation with specific, colorful details.

The Base Stealer *Robert Francis*

Poised between going on and back, pulled
Both ways taut like a tightrope-walker,
Fingertips pointing the opposites,
Now bouncing tiptoe like a dropped ball
Or a kid skipping rope, come on, come on,   5
Running a scattering of steps sidewise,
How he teeters, skitters, tingles, teases,
Taunts them, hovers like an ecstatic bird,
He's only flirting, crowd him, crowd him,
Delicate, delicate, delicate, delicate—now!   10

Getting at Meaning

What happens in this poem? How long might it take for the action described to happen?

Developing Skills in Reading Literature

1. **Simile.** What similes are used? How do they contribute to your picture of the base stealer?

2. **Rhythm.** The rhythm of this poem parallels the action in it. Notice that the first few lines move slowly. How does the rhythm change in lines 4 and 5? What happens to the rhythm in lines 7–10? How does the rhythm reflect the content of these lines? Why is the entire poem run together in one sentence?

Developing Vocabulary

Using Precise Verbs. List the verbs that describe the actions of the base stealer. What do these verbs contribute to the reader's mental image of the player?

Picture another action that takes place during a baseball game. List six or seven verbs that describe the action precisely and accurately.

Training *Demetrio Herrera*

The sea—quick pugilist—[1]
uses for a pun
        ching
           ball
the restless little boats.   5

With the towel of the wind,
even rubs down the boxer's
sweaty body.

The buildings—
ringside fans—   10
crowd close to watch
the big training.

(The dock is whispering
with a smoking ship . . .)

And the surf's applause
makes the tower stand on tiptoe
With its watch in hand   15
to keep the time.

Stray kids,
the sea-birds
sneak in through the roof.

---

1. **pugilist** (pyo͞o′jə list): a boxer.

Getting at Meaning

What scene is the speaker describing? What elements of the scene are described?

Developing Skills in Reading Literature

1. **Extended Metaphor.** This poem, like the first four poems in the section, develops one comparison. In the first stanza, the speaker compares the sea to a boxer and the boats to a punching ball. What is the comparison in the second stanza? What other comparisons does the poem contain? What picture of the sea do you have in your mind after reading the poem?

2. **Structure.** This poem has neither regular rhythm nor rhyme. However, the poet has obviously paid careful attention to the arrangement of words. What seems to determine the stanza breaks? What effect does the poet achieve by separating the word *punching?* Why is the fourth stanza in parentheses?

Developing Vocabulary

Multiple Meanings of Words. Several words in this poem have two or more distinct meanings. For example, *quick* means "swift" and "the sensitive flesh under a fingernail." Find five other words with multiple meanings, and be prepared to give the definitions of the words.

Developing Writing Skills

Description: Using Figures of Speech. Choose a scene, such as a crowded store, or a classroom, and create a feeling for the scene by comparing it to something else. Separate the scene into parts, as the poet does in this poem, and find specific comparisons, consistent with your basic metaphor, for each of these parts. You may write your comparison in either paragraph or poem form.

Good Night   *Carl Sandburg*

Many ways to spell good night.

Fireworks at a pier on the Fourth of July spell it with red wheels and yellow spokes.
They fizz in the air, touch the water and quit.
Rockets make a trajectory of gold-and-blue and then go out.

Railroad trains at night spell with a smokestack mushrooming a white pillar.   5

Steamboats turn a curve in the Mississippi crying in a baritone that crosses lowland
    cottonfields to a razorback hill.

It is easy to spell good night.
        Many ways to spell goodnight.

Getting at Meaning

How many ways to spell "good night" does the poem mention?

Developing Skills in Reading Literature

Imagery. How does each image in the poem suggest "good night"? What do the images have in common?

Developing Vocabulary

Word Origins. Some English words are derived from Latin or Greek. Other words were created to meet specific needs, such as the invention of a machine or the discovery of a plant or animal species. Still others are the result of a desire to capture the quality of a sound.

Study the following words. Look them up in a dictionary, if necessary. Then try to explain the origin of each word.

baritone	pillar	spoke
smokestack	trajectory	razorback
fizz	fireworks	curve

Spring Is Like a Perhaps Hand

E. E. Cummings

Spring is like a perhaps hand
(which comes carefully
out of Nowhere) arranging
a window, into which people look (while
people stare   5
arranging and changing placing
carefully there a strange
thing and a known thing here) and

changing everything carefully

spring is like a perhaps   10
Hand in a window
(carefully to
and fro moving New and
Old things, while
people stare carefully   15
moving a perhaps
fraction of flower here placing
an inch of air there) and

without breaking anything.

Getting at Meaning

What characteristics of spring does the poem emphasize? How are these qualities similar to those of a hand that arranges the contents of a display window?

Developing Skills in Reading Literature

1. **Diction.** Diction is a writer's choice of words. Why does the poet use the word *carefully* so many times? What other words in the poem suggest that the coming of spring is a delicate process? Why do you think the poet uses so many verbs that end in *-ing?*

2. **Personification.** What abstract idea does the poet personify, or present as human, in this poem? Why does the poet use the word *perhaps* when he compares spring to a hand?

3. **Structure.** Why do you think the poet encloses sections of the poem in parentheses? Why are lines 9 and 19 set off by themselves?

Developing Writing Skills

Description: Avoiding Clichés. The simile "Spring is like a perhaps hand" is a fresh, original statement about spring. Write three similes of your own, each about one of the four seasons. Avoid writing clichés, which are tired, overused expressions.

Precision   *Peter Collenette*

A small red-painted helicopter
buzzes straight and undeviating
overhead.
Rotors clatter,
turning smoothly in pivots of oiled steel.   5
Bolts, springs, blades, plates,
cool,
efficient,
combine smoothly
and move.   10
It is guided by man:
this is man's precision.

A small red carrot-fly
(the color is built in)
whirrs along an indefinite flight path.   15
Its wings are finely stressed
to the height
of strength and flexibility.
Its built-in guidance system—
a superbly miniaturized computer—   20
is effectively served
by a wide-angle video-scanner
and twin, highly sensitive antennae.
These combine
to form   25
an internally guided,
highly maneuverable
living flying machine.
God forms it to guide itself;
this is God's precision.   30

Getting at Meaning

1. What does the first stanza describe? What characteristics does this object have?

2. What does the second stanza describe? What characteristics does this object have? Is it more or less complex than the object described in the first stanza?

Developing Skills in Reading Literature

Analogy. An analogy sets up a lengthy comparison between two things that may seem unlike, but that in fact have important similarities. The purpose of an analogy is to help the reader to understand similarities and differences, as well as something new about the objects or ideas being compared.

Notice the difference in the flight paths of the helicopter and the carrot-fly. What are other differences between these two objects? What are similarities? What does the reader realize about human precision? about God's precision?

Developing Vocabulary

Using a Dictionary. A writer must always use the most precise words possible, especially when trying to create images. Thus, it is important for you as a writer to discriminate between shades, or slight differences, in meaning.

Copy the following groups of related words. Look up each word in a dictionary and write the definition next to the word. For each group of words, examine the differences in meanings and then write sentences that capture these differences.

1. strong
   tough
   sturdy

2. distress
   suffering
   agony

Developing Writing Skills

Writing an Analogy. Think about the movements of an inanimate, mechanical object. Choose an insect or other animal that performs similar actions. Then, in one paragraph, develop an analogy between the object and the living thing.

The Cat   *William Matthews*

While you read
the sleepmoth begins
to circle your eyes
and then—
a hail of claws   5
lands the cat
in your lap.
The little motor
in his throat
is how a cat says   10
Me. He rasps the soft
file of his tongue
along the inside
of your wrist.
He licks himself.   15
He's building
a pebble of fur
in his stomach.
And now he pulls
his body in a circle   20
around the fire of sleep.

Getting at Meaning

1. What experience does the poem describe?

2. How does the speaker feel toward cats? How do you know?

Developing Skills in Reading Literature

Metaphor. This poet uses several metaphors to describe the cat. How does a "hail of claws" describe a cat's sudden landing on a person's lap? To what is the lick of the cat's tongue compared? What other comparisons can you find?

Rhinoceros   *Adrien Stoutenburg*

I have never seen that beast
with his snout bearing a pagoda
and his eyes like little fragments
and his haunches carrying hills
with them. His teeth, I have read,   5
are monuments, and his heart colder
than a key in winter
though he sweats from pores round as goblets
full of swamps.
The white hunters have killed him   10
a thousand times over.

I think of myself walking toward him
and preaching a love of creatures,
leaves in my palm, or a loaf of sugar,
and his great horn still,   15
the knees waiting,
and between us, like birds,
a twittering hope,
or merely the pause
between monster and monster.   20

RHINOCEROS *(Woodcut), 1515. Albrecht Dürer. British Museum.*

Getting at Meaning

1. How does the speaker describe the rhinoceros in the first stanza?

2. Has the speaker ever seen a rhinoceros? How does the speaker picture a meeting with the beast?

Developing Skills in Reading Literature

1. **Simile and Metaphor.** Find the comparisons used to describe the rhinoceros in the first stanza. What do these comparisons suggest about the beast? How do you feel about the beast after reading this stanza?

2. **Theme.** How are the images in the second stanza different from those in the first? Who are the two monsters mentioned in the last line? How does this idea relate to the last two lines of the first stanza? What is the speaker saying about human beings?

Developing Vocabulary

Words from Greek. The word *rhinoceros* comes from the Greek word *rhinokiros,* meaning "nose-horned." Explain the origins of the following words, using a dictionary as necessary.

| hippopotamus | tiger | plankton |
| elephant | shark | hyena |

Pigeons   *Richard Kell*

They paddle with staccato feet
in powder-pools of sunlight,
small blue busybodies
strutting like fat gentlemen
with hands clasped   5
under their swallowtail coats;
and as they stump about,
their heads like tiny hammers
tap at imaginary nails
in non-existent walls.   10

Elusive ghosts of sunshine
slither down the green gloss
of their necks an instant, and are gone.

Summer hangs drugged from sky to earth
in limpid fathoms of silence: 15
only warm dark dimples of sound
slide like slow bubbles
from the contented throats.

Raise a casual hand—
with one quick gust   20
they fountain into air.

Getting at Meaning

1. What scene does the poem describe? What kind of day is it? How do you know?

2. What movements of pigeons are described?

Developing Skills in Reading Literature

1. **Simile.** The poem describes the pigeons as "strutting like fat gentlemen/with hands clasped/under their swallowtail coats." What kind of mental picture does this comparison create? Find and discuss the two other similes in the poem.

2. **Imagery.** Descriptive language often appeals to the sense of sight. It can, however, appeal to other senses as well. "They paddle with staccato feet," for example, makes the reader hear the sound, as well as see the movement, of the pigeons' feet. What other images in the poem help the reader to hear the sounds of the scene?

Developing Vocabulary

Using a Glossary. In this poem, pigeons are compared to people. In other contexts, people might be described in animal terms. Look up each of the following animal-related words in the Glossary, write the meaning, and use the word in a sentence.

porcine   equine   feline   hircine
bovine   lupine   canine

A Bird Came Down the Walk

Emily Dickinson

A Bird came down the Walk—
He did not know I saw—
He bit an Angleworm in halves
And ate the fellow, raw,

And then he drank a Dew   5
From a convenient Grass—
And then hopped sidewise to the Wall
To let a Beetle pass—

He glanced with rapid eyes
That hurried all around—   10
They looked like frightened Beads, I thought—
He stirred his Velvet Head

Like one in danger, Cautious,
I offered him a Crumb
And he unrolled his feathers   15
And rowed him softer home—

Than Oars divide the Ocean,
Too silver for a seam—
Or Butterflies, off Banks of Noon
Leap, plashless as they swim.   20

SPARROWS AND CAMELLIAS IN THE SNOW, 1840. Ichiryusai Hiroshige.
The Minneapolis Institute of Arts.

Getting at Meaning

1. Why is the speaker watching the bird?
2. What activities does the speaker observe?

Developing Skills in Reading Literature

1. **Meter.** Meter is the pattern of accented and unaccented syllables that creates the rhythm of a poem. The pattern is made up of units, each having one accented and one or two unaccented syllables. Each unit is called a foot.

In this poem the most common foot is the iamb, which consists of an unaccented syllable followed by an accented syllable. The first line of the poem would be scanned, or marked, in this way:

Ă Bírd cắme dówn thĕ Wálk

How many feet, or units, are in this first line?

Copy the entire first stanza and scan, or mark, each line. How many feet does each line have?

2. **Imagery.** What images appear in the last six lines of the poem? What mental picture is suggested by these images? What feelings toward the bird do the images bring out in the reader?

Developing Writing Skills

Using Figures of Speech. Choose an animal that has not been described in this section of the unit. Then describe the animal in either paragraph or poem form. Create vivid impressions through the use of colorful figurative language.

The Market Man   *John Ratti*

The walnut brains think moist
in their light tan skulls;
the apples croon redly
of their tooth white pulp;
and the squash curves voluptuously   5
in its yellow skin.
It is cold and the market man
burns an orange crate;
it is dark and bare bulbs hang down
like fiery glass pears.   10
The market man has big blunt thumbs,
he feels chapped melons;
the market man has a strong mouth,
dry as potato dust;
the market man has black grape eyes,   15
no seeds show in them.
The market man has lonely shanks,
he splats lemons against a wall;
the market man is angry at the cold,
he strips the heads of lettuce down   20
and throws the green leaves on the cobble street;
the market man smells the salty river,
he bites an onion open with his teeth
and floods the black night with tears and burning.

Getting at Meaning

1. How does the poem present the market man? How does he feel? What actions show his feelings?

2. What is the double meaning of the line "and floods the black night with tears and burning"?

Developing Skills in Reading Literature

1. **Personification.** The first two lines personify the walnut. How? What other produce is personified? How do these figures of speech contrast with the images in the rest of the poem?

2. **Imagery.** How is the man's mouth described? What kind of eyes does he have? What other images describe the market man? How are all of these images similar? What effect does the poet create through his choice of images?

Medicine   *Alice Walker*

Grandma sleeps with
my sick
      grand-
pa so she
can get him   5
during the night
medicine
to stop
  the pain

    In   10
the morning
  clumsily
    I
wake
  them   15

Her eyes
look at me
from under-
      neath
his withered   20
arm

   The
medicine
  is all
    in   25
her long
  un-
    braided
      hair.

Getting at Meaning

1. What is the best medicine that Grandma can offer Grandpa?

2. Why are Grandma's eyes looking out from underneath Grandpa's withered arm?

Developing Skills in Reading Literature

1. **Metaphor.** The speaker compares Grandma's "long unbraided hair" to medicine. In what sense are the two things alike?

2. **Structure.** Why does the poem have this particular shape? Of what does it remind you? How does the shape relate to the content of the poem?

Developing Writing Skills

Describing an Event. This poem is about the way that one person shows her love to another. What signs of love have you observed in the people around you? In a poem or a paragraph, vividly describe one interesting or unusual way of showing love.

Memory   *Margaret Walker*

I can remember wind-swept streets of cities
on cold and blustery nights, on rainy days;
heads under shabby felts and parasols
and shoulders hunched against a sharp concern;
seeing hurt bewilderment on poor faces,   5
smelling a deep and sinister unrest
these brooding people cautiously caress;
hearing ghostly marching on pavement stones
and closing fast around their squares of hate.
I can remember seeing them alone,   10
at work, and in their tenements at home.
I can remember hearing all they said:
their muttering protests, their whispered oaths,
and all that spells their living in distress.

Getting at Meaning

1. Whom is the speaker remembering? What characteristics do these people have? Are they rich or poor? Point out specific words and phrases that support your answer.

2. What feelings does the speaker have towards these people? Support your opinion, using specific lines from the poem.

Developing Skills in Reading Literature

Imagery. What picture do you form after reading the first four lines of the poem? Give two interpretations for "shoulders hunched against a sharp concern." What does the speaker want you to realize about these people?

Developing Vocabulary

Word Origins. The following words have interesting origins. Find their meanings and origins in a dictionary and record the information.

sinister   boycott
chauvinism   mackintosh (raincoat)

I Like To See It Lap the Miles

Emily Dickinson

I like to see it lap the Miles—
And lick the Valleys up—
And stop to feed itself at Tanks—
And then—prodigious step

Around a Pile of Mountains—   5
And supercilious peer
In Shanties—by the sides of Roads—
And then a Quarry pare

To fits its Ribs
And crawl between   10
Complaining all the while
In horrid—hooting stanza—
Then chase itself down Hill—

And neigh like Boanerges[1]—
Then—punctual as a Star   15
Stop—docile and omnipotent
At its own stable door—

---

1. **Boanerges** (bō′ ə nur′ jez): probably the name of a racehorse; literally meaning "sons of wrath"; used to refer to a vociferous preacher.

THE OLD LOCOMOTIVE, 1906. *Lyonel Feininger.*
Collection, *The Musuem of Modern Art, New York.*
Gift of Mrs. Lyonel Feininger.

Getting at Meaning

1. What is the subject of this poem? How do you know this?
2. What is the route described in the poem?

Developing Skills in Reading Literature

Extended Metaphor. This poem, like others you have read, relies on a well developed comparison, which is supported by specific images and figures of speech. In the first stanza, the words *lap, lick,* and *feed* suggest a comparison. What is the comparison? What other words and phrases extend the comparison? How does the comparison affect the way you see the train?

Developing Writing Skills

Narration: Using the Senses in Writing. In this section, you have seen how poets describe common occurrences—the sprouting of dandelions, the coming of spring, the strutting and pecking of pigeons—with colorful images that appeal to the senses of sight, hearing, taste, smell, and touch. Now choose an everyday experience and re-create it in a paragraph or poem, using specific, original images.

Speaker and Tone

BACKYARDS, GREENWICH VILLAGE, 1914. *John Sloan.*
Collection of Whitney Museum of American Art.

Mother to Son   *Langston Hughes*

Well, Son, I'll tell you
Life for me ain't been no crystal stair
It's had tacks in it,
And splinters,
And boards torn up,   5
And places with no carpets on the floor,

Bare.
But all the time
I'se been climbin' on
And reachin' landin's   10
And turning corners
And sometimes goin' on in the dark
Where there ain't been no light.
So, Boy, don't you turn back.
Don't you set down on the steps   15
'Cause you find it's kinder hard.
Don't you fall now—
For I'se still goin', Honey,
I'se still climbin'
And life for me ain't been   20
                  no crystal stair.

THE MOTHER, 1952. *Charles White.*
Hirshhorn Museum and Sculpture Garden, Smithsonian Institution.

Getting at Meaning

What is the mother's advice to her son? What does she mean when she says, "Life for me ain't been no crystal stair"?

Developing Skills in Reading Literature

1. **Speaker.** Who is the speaker in this poem? What do you know about her from her speech? What do you know about her life? How do you feel towards her? Why?

2. **Theme.** What view of life does this poem project? What kind of figurative language does the poet use to project this attitude?

Developing Vocabulary

Understanding Dialect. This poem is written in a dialect that recalls the speech pattern of one group of people. What group speaks this dialect? Identify at least five examples of dialect in the poem and be prepared to explain how each is a variation of standard English.

Piñones   *Leroy Quintana*

when i was young
we would sit by
an old firewood stove
watching my grandmother make candy,
listening to the stories   5
my grandparents would tell
about the "old days"
                    and eat piñones[1]

now we belong
to a supersonic age   10
and have college degrees.
we sit around color t.v. sets
watching the super bowl
listening to howard cosell,
stories of rioting, war, inflation   15
                    and eat piñones

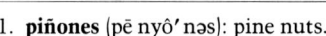

1. **piñones** (pē nyô′ nəs): pine nuts.

Getting at Meaning

What kinds of activities does the speaker describe in the first stanza? in the second stanza?

Developing Skills in Reading Literature

1. **Speaker.** How does the speaker feel about the way things are now and the way they were? How is the speaker's attitude communicated?

2. **Stanza.** How are the stanzas the same? different? Why is the last line the same in both stanzas?

3. **Symbol.** What do the piñones symbolize to the speaker?

Moco Limping   *David Nava Monreal*

My dog hobbles
with a stick
of a leg that
he drags behind
him as he moves.   5
And I was a man
that wanted a
beautiful, noble
animal as a pet.
I wanted him   10
to be strong and
capture all the
attention by
the savage grace
of his gait.   15
I wanted him to
be the first
dog howling in
the pack.
The leader,   20
the brutal hunter
that broke through
the woods with
thunder.
But, instead he's   25
this rickety

little canine
that leaves trails
in the dirt
with his club foot.   30
He's the stumbler
that trips while
chasing lethargic
bees and butterflies.
It hurts me to   35
see him so
abnormal,
so clumsy and
stupid.
My vain heart weeps   40
knowing he
is mine.
But then he turns
my way and
looks at me with   45
eyes that cry out
with life.
He jumps at me with
his feeble paws.
I feel his warm fur   50
and his imperfection is
     forgotten.

Getting at Meaning

What kind of dog would the speaker like to have? How does his dog differ from this dream? What attraction does the dog have for the speaker?

Developing Skills in Reading Literature

1. **Speaker.** What contradictory feelings does the speaker have toward the dog? Why does he describe himself as having a "vain heart"?

2. **Imagery.** The poet uses strong images so that the reader can understand the speaker's feelings toward the dog, as well as vividly picture the dog. What is the effect of the image "the savage grace of his gait"? List six or seven other particularly effective images.

DOG, 1951. *Alberto Giacometti.*
Hirshhorn Museum and Sculpture Garden, Smithsonian Institution.

On the Inclusion of Miniature Dinosaurs in Breakfast Cereal Boxes

John Updike

A post-historic herbivore,[1]
I come to breakfast looking for
A bite. Behind the box of Brex
I find *Tyrannosaurus rex.*

And lo! beyond the Sugar Pops,   5
An acetate *Triceratops.*
And here! across the Shredded Wheat,
The spoor of *Brontosaurus feet.*

Too unawake to dwell upon
A model of *Iguanodon,*   10
I hide within the Raisin Bran;
And thus begins the dawn of *Man.*

---

1. **herbivore** (hûr′bə vôr′): an animal that eats chiefly grass or other plants.

Getting at Meaning

1. What experience does the speaker relate?
2. What is the double meaning of the last line?

Developing Skills in Reading Literature

1. **Tone.** Tone, as you know, is the writer's attitude toward a subject. You can discover a writer's tone by looking at his or her choice and arrangement of words and by examining the general way the writer approaches the subject.

Describe the poet's tone in this poem. Support what you say by referring to specific lines.

2. **Rhythm and Rhyme.** How do the rhythm and rhyme of this poem contribute to its humor?

Developing Vocabulary

Words from Latin. The word *herbivore* comes from the Latin words *herba* meaning "herb" and *vorare* meaning "to devour." What is the derivation of the word *carnivore*?

Developing Writing Skills

1. **Establishing Tone.** Write a letter or a poem in which you either give advice on a subject or present an opinion about the subject. Before you begin, decide on the tone you wish to use; for example, serious, humorous, or sarcastic. Maintain the same tone throughout the letter or poem.

2. **Writing a Poem.** Write a short humorous poem about a prehistoric carnivore or about your experience with a food product.

Good Humor Man   *Phyllis McGinley*

Listen! It is the summer's self that ambles
   Through the green lanes with such a coaxing tongue.
Not birds or daisy fields were ever symbols
   More proper to the time than this bell rung
   With casual insistence—no, not swallow   5
   Circling the roof or bee in hollyhock.
His is the season's voice, and children follow,
   Panting, from every doorway down the block.

So, long ago, in some such shrill procession
   Perhaps the Hamelin[1] children gave pursuit   10
To one who wore a red-and-yellow fashion
   Instead of white, but made upon his flute
The self-same promise plain to every comer:
Unending sweets, imperishable summer.

---

1. **Hamelin** (ham' ə lin): the German village where the Pied Piper led
children away with his music.

Getting at Meaning

1. What season is the subject of this poem? What things does the speaker point out about this season?

2. Where is the Good Humor man found? What is his "promise"? What is the children's response to him?

Developing Skills in Reading Literature

1. **Symbol.** According to the speaker, why is the Good Humor man more of a symbol for summer than birds, daisy fields, and other things common to summer?

2. **Allusion.** Recall the story of the Pied Piper of Hamelin. How does your knowledge of this story help you to understand the second stanza of the poem? Point out and explain specific comparisons between the Good Humor man and the Pied Piper.

3. **Couplet.** A couplet is two rhyming lines of poetry. Find the couplet in this poem.

Developing Writing Skills

Explaining an Idea. Choose something that symbolizes your favorite season. In a paragraph or a poem, explain your choice of a symbol.

The Sharks *Denise Levertov*

Well, then, the last day the sharks appeared.
Dark fins appear, innocent
as if in fair warning. The sea becomes
sinister, are they everywhere?
I tell you, they break six feet of water.   5
Isn't it the same sea, and won't we
play in it any more?
I like it clear and not
too calm, enough waves
to fly in on. For the first time   10
I dared to swim out of my depth.
It was sundown when they came, the time
when a sheen of copper stills the sea,
not dark enough for moonlight, clear enough
to see them easily. Dark   15
the sharp lift of the fins.

Getting at Meaning

1. When do the sharks arrive? at what time of day?

2. How had the speaker felt about the sea previously? How do the speaker's feelings change after the appearance of the sharks?

Developing Skills in Reading Literature

Tone and Mood. In this poem, the tone, or attitude, of the poet is more difficult to interpret than the tone in "On the Inclusion of Miniature Dinosaurs in Breakfast Cereal Boxes." Reread the descriptions of the sharks. What attitude does the poet seem to have towards the sharks? How do the descriptions make you feel?

Filling Station   *Elizabeth Bishop*

Oh, but it is dirty!
—this little filling station,
oil-soaked, oil-permeated
to a disturbing, over-all
black translucency.   5
Be careful with that match!

Father wears a dirty,
oil-soaked monkey suit
that cuts him under the arms,
and several quick and saucy   10
and greasy sons assist him
(it's a family filling station),
all quite thoroughly dirty.

Do they live in the station?
It has a cement porch   15
behind the pumps, and on it
a set of crushed and grease-
impregnated wickerwork;
on the wicker sofa
a dirty dog, quite comfy.   20

Some comic books provide
the only note of color—
of certain color. They lie
upon a big dim doily
draping a taboret[1]   25
(part of the set), beside
a big hirsute begonia.

Why the extraneous plant?
Why the taboret?
Why, oh why, the doily?   30
(Embroidered in daisy stitch
with marguerites, I think,
and heavy with gray crochet.)

Somebody embroidered the doily.
Somebody waters the plant,   35
or oils it, maybe. Somebody
arranges the rows of cans
so that they softly say:
ESSO—SO—SO—SO
to high-strung automobiles.   40
Somebody loves us all.

---

1. **taboret** (tab' ər it): a stool.

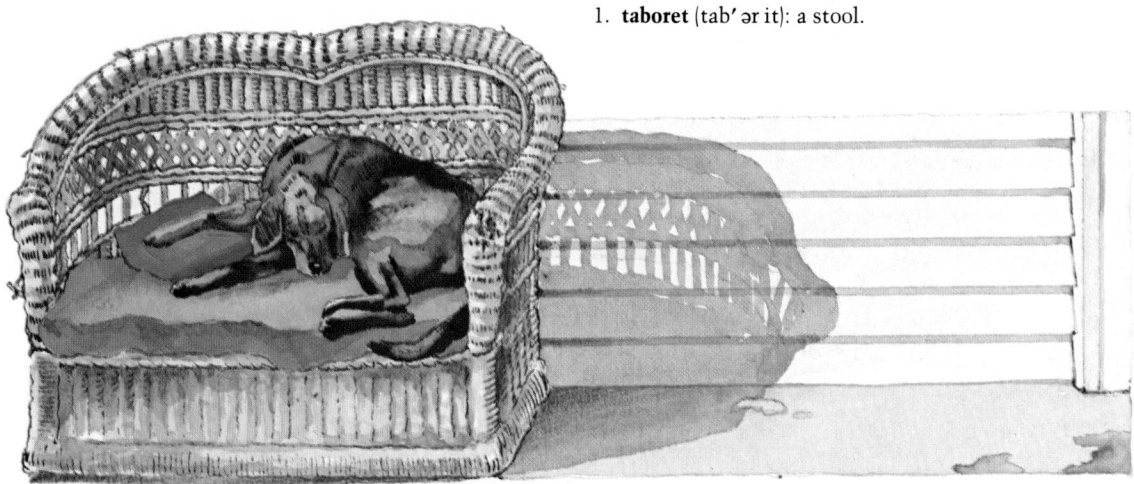

Getting at Meaning

1. Describe the filling station as it is presented in the first three stanzas.

2. What do the last three stanzas describe? How is this description different from the description in the opening stanzas?

Developing Skills in Reading Literature

1. **Tone.** How does the tone of the poem change? What note of humor is included in the last stanza? What is the meaning of the last line? How does the change in tone bring out the meaning of the poem?

2. **Assonance and Consonance.** The repetition of vowel sounds within words is called assonance. For example, in the phrase "that match," the sound of *a* is repeated. The repetition of consonant sounds is called consonance, as in "but it is dirty." Find other examples of assonance and consonance in this poem.

Developing Vocabulary

Prefixes. The prefix *trans-* comes from Latin and means "across or over." Read the following sentences and try to guess the meanings of the italicized words. Write your definition for each word and next to it write the definition that you find in your dictionary.

1. The *transatlantic* flight ran into a storm but landed safely in Ireland.

2. I had to *transfer* trains to reach my destination.

3. The shabby house had been *transformed* into a mansion.

4. He looked out through a *translucent* glass.

5. They *transported* their goods by rail.

6. His motives were *transparent* to all who knew him.

7. I would have had a perfect score on my math test if I hadn't *transposed* two numbers.

8. In moving from Boston to Dallas, we found the *transition* difficult; however, once we adjusted, we found our new home very pleasant.

Developing Writing Skills

Establishing Tone. Describe a place that you have visited recently. Choose a place that brought out some strong feeling in you, and try to show your attitude toward the place in your writing.

Young Soul   *Imamu Amiri Baraka*

First, feel, then feel, then
read, or read, then feel, then
fall, or stand, where you
already are. Think
of your self, and the other   5
selves . . . think
of your parents, your mothers
and sisters, your bentslick
father, then feel, or
fall, on your knees   10
if nothing else will move you,

        then read
        and look deeply
        into all matters
        come close to you   15
        city boys—
        country men

        Make some muscle
        in your head, but
        use the muscle   20
        in yr heart

Getting at Meaning

1. Whom is the speaker in this poem addressing? What advice does the speaker give that person?

2. What is "muscle in your head"? What is "muscle in yr heart"? How do you obtain each kind? What kind of muscle does the speaker suggest is the more important?

Developing Skills in Reading Literature

Speaker. This poem reveals clearly the values of the speaker. What is important to the speaker? What qualities do you imagine the speaker has?

Be Daedalus   *Nanina Alba*

Be Daedalus: make wings,
Make feathered wings;
Bind them with wax.
   Avoid the parching sun that brings
   Death as its tax.   5
   Suns can be brutal things.

Be Daedalus; make wings,
If Icarus be unwise
And swing up toward the flame,
   Forget his prejudice and prize,   10
   The price, the name.

Be Daedalus; make wings,
Make even feathered wings . . .

Getting at Meaning

1. From your knowledge of the myth and from the information in this poem, explain the achievement and the downfall of Daedalus.

2. How is Daedalus different from Icarus? Why does the speaker say "Be Daedalus" and not "Be Icarus"?

Developing Skills in Reading Literature

1. **Theme.** How might you apply the experience of Daedalus to your own life? What things could you do to "Be Daedalus"? How might attempting these things be like making "feathered wings" bound with wax?

2. **Rhyme.** Chart the rhyme scheme of this poem, using letters of the alphabet. Then describe the rhyme scheme in two or three sentences, and make a general statement about the relationship between the rhyme scheme and the content of the poem.

Developing Writing Skills

Writing a Poem. Choose a character from mythology that you think has an admirable trait and write your own poem beginning, if you like, with Be _____. Try to incorporate details from the myth into your poem.

Birches   *Robert Frost*

When I see birches bend to left and right
Across the lines of straighter darker trees,
I like to think some boy's been swinging them.
But swinging doesn't bend them down to stay
As ice-storms do. Often you must have seen them   5
Loaded with ice a sunny winter morning
After a rain. They click upon themselves
As the breeze rises, and turn many-colored
As the stir cracks and crazes their enamel.
Soon the sun's warmth makes them shed crystal shells   10
Shattering and avalanching on the snow-crust—
Such heaps of broken glass to sweep away
You'd think the inner dome of heaven had fallen.
They are dragged to the withered bracken[1] by the load,
And they seem not to break; though once they are bowed   15
So low for long, they never right themselves:
You may see their trunks arching in the woods
Years afterwards, trailing their leaves on the ground
Like girls on hands and knees that throw their hair
Before them over their heads to dry in the sun.   20
But I was going to say when Truth broke in
With all her matter-of-fact about the ice-storm
I should prefer to have some boy bend them
As he went out and in to fetch the cows—
Some boy too far from town to learn baseball,   25
Whose only play was what he found himself,
Summer or winter, and could play alone.
One by one he subdued his father's trees
By riding them down over and over again
Until he took the stiffness out of them,   30
And not one but hung limp, not one was left
For him to conquer. He learned all there was
To learn about not launching out too soon
And so not carrying the tree away
Clear to the ground. He always kept his poise   35
To the top branches, climbing carefully

---

1. **bracken** (brak' 'n): a large, coarse fern.

With the same pains you use to fill a cup
Up to the brim, and even above the brim.
Then he flung outward, feet first, with a swish,
Kicking his way down through the air to the ground.   40
So was I once myself a swinger of birches.
And so I dream of going back to be.
It's when I'm weary of considerations,
And life is too much like a pathless wood
Where your face burns and tickles with the cobwebs   45
Broken across it, and one eye is weeping
From a twig's having lashed across it open.
I'd like to get away from earth awhile
And then come back to it and begin over.
May no fate willfully misunderstand me   50
And half grant what I wish and snatch me away
Not to return. Earth's the right place for love:
I don't know where it's likely to go better.
I'd like to go by climbing a birch tree,
And climb black branches up a snow-white trunk   55
Toward heaven, till the tree could bear no more,
But dipped its top and set me down again.
That would be good both going and coming back.
One could do worse than be a swinger of birches.

Getting at Meaning

1. What two explanations for bent birches does the speaker give? Which one does the speaker prefer? Why? According to the speaker, which explanation is more likely?

2. At what time does the speaker dream about swinging on birches? What does the speaker mean by these lines: "I'd like to get away from earth awhile/And then come back to it and begin over"?

Developing Skills in Reading Literature

1. **Speaker.** Is the speaker in this poem an adult or a child? What evidence in the poem supports your answer? What does the reader learn about the speaker's childhood? the speaker's feelings about that childhood? the speaker's feelings about life?

2. **Imagery.** Read lines 7–13, which describe the branches of birches laden with ice. Which images in these lines appeal to your sense of sight? Which appeal to your sense of hearing?

3. **Personification.** Find an example of personification in this poem.

4. **Theme.** Explain the speaker's simile for life in lines 44–47. What do the birches represent? What does the speaker mean by this line: "One could do worse than be a swinger of birches"?

5. **Alliteration, Assonance, and Consonance.** Find five examples each of alliteration, assonance, and consonance in this poem. Then choose three of these examples and explain how the repetition of sounds enhances the meanings of the phrases or lines.

Vernal Sentiment　　*Theodore Roethke*

Though the crocuses poke up their heads in the usual places,
The frog scum appears on the pond with the same froth of green,
And the boys moon at girls with last year's fatuous faces,
I never am bored, however familiar the scene.

When from under the barn the cat brings a similar litter—　　5
Two yellow and black, and one that looks in between—
Though it all happened before, I cannot grow bitter:
I rejoice in the spring, as though no spring ever had been.

Getting at Meaning

What are the signs of spring mentioned in the poem?

Developing Skills in Reading Literature

1. **Tone.** What is the attitude toward spring voiced by the speaker? What prevents the same old pattern from being boring?

2. **Structure.** Why do you think the poet elected to make this a tightly patterned poem?

Developing Vocabulary

Word Origins. The word *vernal* is an adjective meaning "spring-like." *Vernal,* however, looks nothing like the word *spring.* The reason is that *vernal* is derived from *vernalis,* the Latin word for "spring," and *spring* is derived from *springan,* an Old English word.

Many other words in our language are related in meaning but not in origin. Copy the following pairs of words; then look up each word in a dictionary. Write both the origin and the meaning of the word.

| hibernal | autumnal | estival |
| winter | fall | summer |

Developing Writing Skills

Using the Senses in Writing. List several vivid images that you associate with the arrival of summer, fall, or winter. You may wish to make this list into a poem.

Idea

MAN AND WOMAN IN THE STREET, 1887. *Charles Angrand.*
Musée National d'Art Moderne, Paris.

Sympathy   *Paul Laurence Dunbar*

I know what the caged bird feels, alas!
  When the sun is bright on the upland slopes;
When the wind stirs soft through the springing grass,
And the river flows like a stream of glass;
  When the first bird sings and the first bud opes,   5
And the faint perfume from its chalice steals—
I know what the caged bird feels!

I know why the caged bird beats his wing
  Till its blood is red on the cruel bars;
For he must fly back to his perch and cling   10
When he fain[1] would be on the bough a-swing;
  And a pain still throbs in the old, old scars
And they pulse again with a keener sting—
I know why he beats his wing!

I know why the caged bird sings, ah me,   15
  When his wing is bruised and his bosom sore,—
When he beats his bars and he would be free;
It is not a carol of joy or glee,
  But a prayer that he sends from his heart's deep core,
But a plea, that upward to Heaven he flings—   20
I know why the caged bird sings!

---

1. **fain:** gladly or willingly.

Getting at Meaning

1. This poem has three stanzas. What is the bird doing or experiencing in each stanza?

2. What does the caged bird want more than anything else, according to the speaker? Why does the bird beat its wings? How does the speaker describe the bird's song?

Developing Skills in Reading Literature

Symbol. What does the caged bird symbolize? Why is the poem titled "Sympathy"?

Developing Vocabulary

Root Words. *Patho* is a root word meaning "suffering," "disease," or "feeling." Thus, *sympathy*, a combination of *patho* and *sym*, which means "together," means "feel with." *Pathology*, a combination of *patho* and *-logy*, which means "the science of," is the study of diseases.

Look up each listed word in the Glossary and record its meaning. Observe how the root *patho* is used in each. Finally, write a sentence for each word that makes its meaning clear.

    pathos   pathetic   empathy   telepathy

The Broncho That Would Not Be Broken   *Vachel Lindsay*

A little colt—broncho, loaned to the farm
To be broken in time without fury or harm,
Yet black crows flew past you, shouting alarm,
Calling "Beware," with lugubrious singing . . .
The butterflies there in the bush were romancing,   5
The smell of the grass caught your soul in a trance,
So why be a-fearing the spurs and the traces,
O broncho that would not be broken of dancing?

You were born with the pride of the lords great and olden
Who danced, through the ages, in corridors golden.   10
In all the wide farm-place the person most human.
You spoke out so plainly with squealing and capering,
With whinnying, snorting contorting and prancing,
As you dodged your pursuers, looking askance,
With Greek-footed figures, and Parthenon[1] paces,   15
O broncho that would not be broken of dancing.

The grasshoppers cheered. "Keep whirling," they said.
The insolent sparrows called from the shed
"If men will not laugh, make them wish they were dead."
But arch were your thoughts, all malice displacing,   20
Though the horse-killers came, with snake-whips advancing.
You bantered and cantered away your last chance.
And they scourged you, with Hell in their speech and their faces,
O broncho that would not be broken of dancing.

"Nobody cares for you," rattled the crows,   25
As you dragged the whole reaper, next day, down the rows.
The three mules held back, yet you danced on your toes.
You pulled like a racer, and kept the mules chasing.
You tangled the harness with bright eyes side-glancing,
While the drunk driver bled you—a pole for a lance—   30
And the giant mules bit at you—keeping their places.
O broncho that would not be broken of dancing.

---

1. **Parthenon** (pär′ thə nän′): a classical Greek temple built in the fifth century, B.C.

In that last afternoon your boyish heart broke.
The hot wind came down like a sledge-hammer stroke.
The blood-sucking flies to a rare feast awoke.   35
And they searched out your wounds, your death-warrant tracing.
And the merciful men, their religion enhancing,
Stopped the red reaper, to give you a chance.
Then you died on the prairie, and scorned all disgraces,
O broncho that would not be broken of dancing.   40

Getting at Meaning

1. What causes the broncho's death?

2. What is the broncho's life story? Why is the broncho loaned to the farm?

3. What other animals are mentioned? What role does each play in the broncho's death?

Developing Skills in Reading Literature

1. **Ballad.** This poem is a ballad, or song that tells a story. What qualities make it musical? What similarities do you notice among the five stanzas? Does it have a regular meter?

2. **Rhyme.** What is the rhyme scheme in each stanza? What is the effect of the use of rhyme?

3. **Foreshadowing.** Reread the first stanza. How is the broncho's death foreshadowed?

4. **Symbol.** The broncho is an important symbol. What do you think it represents?

5. **Theme.** What is the speaker's attitude toward the broncho? What does the speaker admire about it? What does the speaker wish to convey by describing this animal who "scorned all disgraces"?

6. **Refrain.** A refrain is the repetition of a word, phrase, or line, usually at the end of succeeding stanzas. What is the refrain in this poem? Why does the speaker return to this refrain?

Developing Vocabulary

Word Origins. Use your knowledge of word origins and language development to answer each question with a word from the poem. Then check your answers in a dictionary.

1. What word meaning "an easy gallop" comes from Chaucer's *Canterbury Tales*?

2. What word comes from the Spanish meaning "rough, crude"?

3. What word is derived from the Old French word *harnes,* meaning "armor"?

4. What word is derived from the Latin word *currere,* meaning "to run"?

5. What noun comes from the same root as *calf*?

6. What word is derived from the verb *whine*?

7. What word was originally an echoic word for the call of a certain bird?

8. What noun was coined to describe a movement made by an insect?

Untitled *Alonzo Lopez*

Go, my child,
    to the lands of your people.
Awaken them.
They have slept too long.
Many years have passed.
Traditions have been carried away   5
    by the wind.
Old tales have fled into the night.
The way of the Ancient Ones is dying.
Wash away the evil and harm
    that have befallen them.
Lead them in traditional song.
Lead them in ceremonial dance.   10
Send them forth to the far edges
    of the earth
To find all that has been lost.
Let those among us
    who have left us to die
Know that we only slept,
And now,   15
We live again.

Getting at Meaning

1. How old might the speaker be? What has happened to the speaker's people?

2. What is the speaker's attitude toward tradition?

3. Find these lines in the poem: "Send them forth to the far edges/of the earth/To find all that has been lost." What kinds of things might have been lost?

4. What does the speaker mean by "we only slept"?

Developing Skills in Reading Literature

1. **Theme.** Who are the people addressed in the poem? What is the speaker's message to these people?

2. **Tone.** What is the poet's tone, or attitude, toward the subject of the poem? How is the tone suited to both the speaker and the theme?

Developing Writing Skills

Supporting an Opinion. Do you agree with the speaker that important traditions from our ancestors have been lost? Have important values and customs disappeared from our way of life? Write a paragraph in which you take a position on these questions and support your opinion with examples. You may write about your own family heritage or about American heritage in general.

The Elephant   *Sandra Hochman*

The atrocity
Of the great elephant
In the Milano[1] Zoo: He is
Chained by his leg to the
Floor. His cage is as large   5
As he is—just a little larger.
He stands there, looking
At adults and children
Pelting him with peanuts and
Garbage, he looks out of his   10
Tear-shaped eye circled by pink.

I will save you.

His name is Pepsi. He was a gift
From the American Pepsi-Cola Company
To the city of Milano. I wrote   15
A letter to the company and asked, "Do you
Know what agony this elephant suffers? This
Beast which was named after your beverage?"

I received a reply
On heavy stationery from   20
The head of the company saying
Zoo conditions in Italy can
Not be helped. He said he was
Taking my letter under advisement.
But there was nothing he could do. He   25
Ended with a paragraph on zoo
Conditions in general.

I received, a month later, a letter
From the Italian head of the company.
He told me the elephant, Pepsi, had   30
Been blessed by a cardinal when he was
Given to the Milano Zoo.

I imagine the
Miserable elephant in captivity.
At night I lie awake   35
Plotting our escape.

I think of the history of the elephant:
Heroic and courageous beasts
Worshiped in India, thought of as
Holy men in Bangkok, treated with love   40
Throughout Asia. In my childhood
I saw them wrapped in circus dresses
And made to perform—
Displayed
By managers who found them funny. I   45
Think of the elephant with a chain
On his leg. I think of his life.
His captivity.

Each night
I prepare our departures.   50

---

1. **Milano** (mē lä′ nō) *Italian:* Milan, a city in northwest Italy.

Getting at Meaning

1. What bothers the speaker about the elephant's situation? How is the elephant described?

2. What does the speaker ask of the American Pepsi-Cola Company? How does the head of the company respond?

3. According to the speaker, how does the treatment of the elephant in the zoo contrast with the treatment of elephants in other parts of the world?

Developing Skills in Reading Literature

1. **Tone.** What is the poet's attitude toward the Pepsi-Cola Company? toward the American head of the company? toward the Italian head of the company? toward the elephant?

2. **Mood.** As you read this poem, how do you feel about the elephant? about the response from the head of the Pepsi-Cola Company?

3. **Theme.** What does the speaker imply about the treatment of animals by human beings?

Developing Writing Skills

Combining Description and Exposition. Visit a zoo near you, or think about a previous trip to a zoo. Write a paragraph or two in which you record observations about the living conditions of the animals. Refer to specific animals as often as possible. Also, describe in general terms your emotional response to the situations of the animals.

Ape   *Babette Deutsch*

His eyes are mournful, but the long lined palm
He thrusts between the bars expects the best.
His old man's face as innocent as calm,
The beggar puts compassion to the test
And fails. He grips the bars; his pained state grows   5
To a brown study framed in dusty fur.
He has a cold. He sneezes, cleans his nose,
Then gravely licks a flexile forefinger.

A pause; the bald mauve hand from which men shrink,
The fingers, strong to clutch, quick to explore,   ·   10
Again extended, are again refused.
The eyes, poor sorrow's jewels, seldom wink,
But to his grinning public, as before,
Show endless patience, endlessly abused.

Getting at Meaning

What things does the speaker notice about the ape? What words does the speaker use to characterize the ape?

Developing Skills in Reading Literature

1. **Structure.** The poet has structured the poem in two parts. What are the differences between the parts?

2. **Speaker.** What does the ape seem to represent to the speaker? How does the speaker feel about the ape? What does the ape make the speaker think about?

Developing Vocabulary

Using a Dictionary. The writer of this poem used the word *mauve* to describe the ape's hand. Mauve is "a delicate purple." Using a dictionary as necessary, identify the following colors. Then group related colors into three or four color families.

cerise	maroon	magenta
puce	aquamarine	maize
fuchsia	ocher	sepia
chartreuse	salmon	burnt umber

Jungle   *Mary Carter Smith*

Lions and tigers dominate
Headlines from the Jungle
But mostly gentle folk are there
Rabbits and beavers in lowly lair
A nightingale sings in the fetid air   5
Ah yes
The wolves and skunks run free
Fattening on innocents they see
The People
See only the lions and tigers   10
Whom they fear
For the quiet ones with frightened eyes
No one sheds a tear.

YOUNG HARE, 1502. Albrecht Dürer.
Graphische Sammlung Albertina, Vienna.

Getting at Meaning

1. Why do people focus mainly on the lions and tigers of the jungle?

2. What other animals does the speaker mention? What activities does the speaker note?

3. Which kinds of animals are superior in number? Which kinds are the more visible?

Developing Skills in Reading Literature

1. **Alliteration, Assonance, and Consonance.** Find examples of alliteration, assonance, and consonance in this poem. What do these repetitions of sounds do for the rhythm of the poem?

2. **Symbol.** On one level, this poem is about an actual jungle. On another level, what might the jungle represent, or symbolize, to the speaker?

3. **Theme.** What do the final two lines of the poem mean? What message is conveyed in this poem?

Developing Vocabulary

Suffixes. The word *fattening* is formed by adding the suffixes -*en* and -*ing* to the root word *fat*. What other word in the poem is formed by adding two suffixes to a root word?

From each of the following root words, make a new word by adding two suffixes. Check spellings in a dictionary if necessary.

hope   spin   earth   mad
lone   music   pity   fast

The Rainwalkers *Denise Levertov*

An old man whose black face
shines golden-brown as wet pebbles
under the streetlamp, is walking
two mongrel dogs of dis-
proportionate size, in the rain,   5
in the relaxed early-evening avenue.

The small sleek one wants to stop,
docile to the imploring soul of the trashbasket,
but the young tall curly one
wants to walk on; the glistening sidewalk   10
entices him to arcane happenings.

Increasing rain. The old bareheaded man
smiles and grumbles to himself.
The lights change: the avenue's
endless nave echoes notes of   15
liturgical red. He drifts

between his dogs' desires.
The three of them are enveloped—
turning now to go crosstown—in their
sense of each other, of pleasure,   20
of weather, of corners,
of leisurely tensions between them
and private silence.

Getting at Meaning

1. Describe the two dogs that the man is walking. Describe the man.

2. What is the setting for this poem? What actions of the man and the dogs does the speaker describe?

3. What does the speaker note about the relationship between the man and his dogs? What lines in the final stanza describe the relationship?

Developing Skills in Reading Literature

1. **Simile and Metaphor.** Identify the simile in the first stanza of the poem. What two things are compared? What is the metaphor in the third stanza? What quality of the avenue does the speaker suggest through this comparison?

2. **Tone.** What is the attitude of the poet toward her subject? Identify words and phrases that help to create the tone of the poem.

Developing Vocabulary

Using a Glossary. Notice how each of the following words functions in the poem. Then look up the words in the Glossary and record their definitions. Finally, use each word in an interesting, original sentence.

disproportionate   arcane
docile   nave
imploring   liturgical

White Dwarf   *John Updike*

Discovery of the smallest known star in the universe was announced today . . . The star is about
one half the diameter of the moon.
>   —*The Times*

Welcome, welcome, little star!
I'm delighted that you are
Up in Heaven's vast extent,
No bigger than a continent.

Relatively minuscule,   5
Spinning like a penny spool,
Glinting like a polished spoon,
A kind of kindled demi-moon,

You offer cheer to tiny Man
'Mid galaxies Gargantuan—[1]   10
A little pill in endless night,
An antidote to cosmic fright.

---

1. **Gargantuan** (gär gan' choo wən): gigantic, referring to a
giant king in Rabelais' *Gargantua and Pantagruel*.

Getting at Meaning

What does the speaker appreciate about the
new star?

Developing Skills in Reading Literature

1. **Structure.** How do the tight rhyme and
meter, as well as the stanza pattern, contribute
to this poem? Why do you think the poet chose
such a structured pattern? What nursery rhyme
does the poem recall?

2. **Theme.** On the surface, the tone of this
poem is light and humorous. Still, a serious realization lurks behind the amused tone. What
does the speaker mean in referring to the star
as "A little pill in endless night,/An antidote to
cosmic fright"?

Developing Vocabulary

Prefixes. This poem contains the word *demi-
moon,* meaning "a half moon." Related to
demi- is the prefix *semi-,* which also means
"half."

Look up these words in a dictionary. Note
how the prefix functions in the word. Record
the definition and use the word in a sentence.

demigod	semifinals
semiannual	semiquaver
semiconscious	demisemiquaver
semicolon	

Developing Writing Skills

Writing a Poem. A small item in the newspaper inspired this poem. Read newspapers for
several days, clipping out stories and items that
suggest possibilities for poems. Select one story
or item and use it as the basis for a poem. The
poem may have any form you choose. Hand in
the newspaper clipping with your poem.

Southbound on the Freeway   *May Swenson*

A tourist came in from Orbitville,
parked in the air, and said:

The creatures of this star
are made of metal and glass.

Through the transparent parts   5
you can see their guts.

Their feet are round and roll
on diagrams or long

measuring tapes, dark
with white lines.   10

They have four eyes.
The two in back are red.

Sometimes you can see a five-eyed
one, with a red eye turning

on the top of his head.   15
He must be special—

the others respect him
and go slow

when he passes, winding
among them from behind.   20

They all hiss as they glide,
like inches, down the marked

tapes. Those soft shapes,
shadowy inside

the hard bodies—are they   25
their guts or their brains?

Getting at Meaning

1. From whose point of view are the ideas in this poem presented?
2. What is the "five-eyed" creature? What are the "soft shapes . . . inside the hard bodies"?

Developing Skills in Reading Literature

1. **Theme.** What is the speaker's main point in this poem? To what extent do cars dominate our lives?
2. **Tone.** What do you think is the poet's attitude toward the subject of the poem? What is the tone of the final question?

Developing Vocabulary

Idioms. Several words in this poem function in common idiomatic expressions. For example, the word *feet* appears in the phrase "stand on one's own feet," which means "to be independent." Following are three words from the poem, along with idioms in which the words appear. Explain the meaning of each idiom. Then give another idiom using the word.

head: to keep one's head
air: to give oneself airs
eye: in the public eye

Sunset Colors   *Yoshino Hiroshi*

As usual the train was crowded.
The young were sitting
and the old were standing.
A girl who'd had her head down
stood up and gave her seat to an old man   5
who sat down quickly
and then got off at the next station
without thanking her.
The girl sat down again.
An old woman got pushed in front of her.   10
The girl had her head down.
But, standing up once more,
she offered her seat to the old woman.
Who got off at the next station
but did say thank you.   15
The girl sat down again.
Things always go in threes.
Another old man got pushed in front of her.
The poor girl kept her head down
and this time   20
she didn't stand up.
The next station came
and the one after that.
She kept gnawing on her lip
tensing her body.   25
I got off.
I wonder how far she was going,
sitting so stiffly, keeping her head down.
Soft-hearted people
always, anywhere,   30
feel the pain of others
like their own.

Getting at Meaning

1. Describe the behavior of the old people to whom the girl gives her seat.

2. How does the saying "Things always go in threes" apply to this poem?

3. Why doesn't the girl offer her seat to an old person a third time? How does she apparently feel as she remains in her seat?

Developing Skills in Reading Literature

1. **Tone.** What is the poet's attitude toward the situation on the train? Give evidence to support your answer.

2. **Theme.** What does the speaker suggest about the way people treat each other? Do you agree that "soft-hearted people always, anywhere, feel the pain of others like their own"?

Distance and a Certain Light

May Swenson

Distance
and a certain light
makes anything artistic—
it doesn't matter what.

From an airplane, all   5
that rigid splatter of the Bronx[1]
becomes organic, logical
as web or beehive. Chunks

of decayed cars in junkyards,
garbage scows (nimble roaches   10
on the Harlem),[2] herds of stalled
manure-yellow boxes on twisting reaches

of rails, are punched clean and sharp
as ingots in the ignition of the sun.
Rubbish becomes engaging shape—   15
you only have to get a bead on it,

the right light filling the corridor
of your view—a gob of spit
under a microscope, fastidious
in structure as a crystal. No contortion   20

without intention, and nothing ugly.
In any random, sprawling, decomposing thing
is the charming string
of its history—and what it will be next.

---

1. **the Bronx** (braŋks): a borough of New York City.
2. **the Harlem:** a river separating Manhattan Island from the Bronx.

Getting at Meaning

1. Why does the speaker believe that nothing is ugly?

2. What different examples does the speaker use to prove that "distance and a certain light makes anything artistic"?

3. Does the speaker have a hopeful or a pessimistic view of the world?

4. What does the speaker mean by the phrase "No contortion without intention"?

Developing Skills in Reading Literature

Simile and Metaphor. The speaker says that from an airplane, "that rigid splatter of the Bronx" becomes as ordered as a spiderweb or a beehive. What other comparisons does the speaker make?

Developing Vocabulary

Using a Dictionary. Write the definitions of the following words, using a dictionary as necessary.

rigid	engaging	manure
scow	gob	ingot
organic	fastidious	random
nimble	contortion	decompose

Think about the emotional response elicited by each word. Then classify the words according to whether they would be used in creating an artistic or a realistic view of the world. Study the way the words are used in the poem. Does your concept of each word agree with that of the poet?

RELATIONAL PAINTING, 1949–51. Fritz Glarner.
Collection of Whitney Museum of American Art, New York.

The Bean Eaters   *Gwendolyn Brooks*

They eat beans mostly, this old yellow pair.
Dinner is a casual affair.
Plain chipware on a plain and creaking wood,
Tin flatware.

Two who are Mostly Good.   5
Two who have lived their day,
But keep on putting on their clothes
And putting things away.

And remembering . . .
Remembering, with twinklings and twinges,   10
As they lean over the beans in their rented back room
        that is full of beads and receipts and dolls and cloths,
        tobacco crumbs, vases and fringes.

Getting at Meaning

1. What kind of life do you think these two old people have had? What details lead to your conclusion?

2. What is life like now for the two old people? What are their main activities?

Developing Skills in Reading Literature

1. **Tone.** What do you think is the poet's attitude toward "this old yellow pair"? Support your response with specific phrases and lines.

2. **Theme.** Why are the words "Mostly Good" capitalized? What comment is the speaker making about life through the description of this old pair?

Women   *Alice Walker*

They were women then
My mama's generation
Husky of voice—Stout of
Step
With fists as well as   5
Hands
How they battered down
Doors
And ironed
Starched white   10
Shirts
How they led
Armies
Headragged Generals
Across mined   15
Fields
Booby-trapped
Ditches
To discover books
Desks   20
A place for us
How they knew what we
Must know
Without knowing a page
Of it   25
Themselves.

Getting at Meaning

1. What are some of the activities performed by the women who are the subject of the poem?

2. According to the speaker, why did these women work so hard? What did the women know that proved to be so important for the speaker's generation?

Developing Skills in Reading Literature

1. **Imagery.** What mental pictures demonstrate the strength of the speaker's forebears? What are the "booby-trapped ditches" the speaker refers to in lines 17 and 18? What other images of war can you find?

2. **Theme.** What did the hard-working women of the poem discover? Why does the speaker admire her "mama's generation" so much?

Developing Vocabulary

Finding the Appropriate Meaning. Each of the following words has several different meanings. Study the way each word, or form of the word, is used in the poem. Then look up the word in a dictionary and copy the one definition that best fits its use in the poem.

stout	iron	step	batter	book
voice	mine	fist	ditch	page

Developing Writing Skills

Describing a Person. Write a poem about your own ancestors or about just one ancestor whose character and achievements are familiar to you.

Warning   *Alice Walker*

To love a man wholly
love him
feet first
    head down
      eyes cold   5
    closed
in depression.

It is too easy to love
a surfer
white eyes   10
godliness &
      bronze
in the bright sun.

Getting at Meaning

1. What condition does the speaker describe in the first stanza? What images does the speaker use to describe this condition?

2. What kind of man does the speaker describe in the second stanza of the poem?

Developing Skills in Reading Literature

Theme. What is the speaker saying about love? When do people need love the most?

Ballad of the Faithless Wife · *Charles Causley*

Carry her down to the river
  Carry her down to the sea
Let the bully-boys stare at her braided hair
  But never a glance from me.

Down by the writhing water   5
  Down by the innocent sand
They laid my bride by the toiling tide
  A stone in her rifled hand.

Under the dainty eagle
  Under the ravening dove   10
Under a high and healthy sky
  I waited for my love.

Off she ran with a soldier
  Tall as a tree, and gay,
Soft as a mouse he came to my house   15
  And stole my love away.

O splintered were all the windows
  And broken all the chairs
War like a knife ran through my life
  And the blood ran down the stairs.   20

Loud on the singing morning
  I hear the mad birds rise
Safe from harm to the sun's alarm
  As the sound of fighting dies.

I would hang my harp on the branches   25
  And weep all through the day
But stranger, see! The wounded tree
  Has burned itself away.

False O false was my lover
  Dead on the diamond shore   30
White as a fleece, for her name was Peace
  And the soldier's name was War.

Getting at Meaning

1. In the last two lines, the reader learns the identity of the "faithless wife." What words and details in the earlier stanzas suggest battle and warfare?

2. Does the speaker blame himself for what happened? Why won't he look at his dead "bride"?

Developing Skills in Reading Literature

1. **Ballad.** A ballad is one kind of poem that tells a story. Most ballads are made up of four-line stanzas, each having the same pattern of rhythm and rhyme. Most contain repetitions of words, phrases, and lines. What characteristics make this poem a ballad?

2. **Alliteration.** In the first stanza, the poet repeats the *b* sound in "bully," "boys," "braided," and "but." Where do you hear alliteration in the other stanzas?

3. **Allegory.** An allegory is a literary work in which the characters stand for abstract ideas or concepts. In this poem, the wife stands for peace, her soldier-lover for war. How do other details in the poem help develop this basic meaning? What statement about war and peace does the poet wish to make in this ballad?

The Shooting of John Dillinger Outside the Biograph Theater, July 22, 1934

David Wagoner

Chicago ran a fever of a hundred and one that groggy Sunday.
A reporter fried an egg on a sidewalk; the air looked shaky.
And a hundred thousand people were in the lake like shirts in a laundry.
Why was Johnny lonely?
Not because two dozen solid citizens, heat-struck, had keeled over backward.   5
Not because those lawful souls had fallen out of their sockets and melted.
But because the sun went down like a lump in a furnace or a bull in the Stockyards.
Where was Johnny headed?
Under the Biograph Theater sign that said, "Our Air is Refrigerated."
Past seventeen FBI men and four policemen who stood in doorways and sweated.   10
Johnny sat down in a cold seat to watch Clark Gable get electrocuted.
Had Johnny been mistreated?
Yes, but Gable told the D.A. he'd rather fry than be shut up forever.
Two women sat by Johnny. One looked sweet, one looked like J. Edgar Hoover.[1]
Polly Hamilton made him feel hot, but Anna Sage made him shiver.   15
Was Johnny a good lover?
Yes, but he passed out his share of squeezes and pokes like a jittery masher
While Agent Purvis sneaked up and down the aisle like an extra usher,
Trying to make sure they wouldn't slip out till the show was over.
Was Johnny a fourflusher?[2]   20
No, not if he knew the game. He got it up or got it back.
But he liked to take snapshots of policemen with his own Kodak,
And once in a while he liked to take them with an automatic.
Why was Johnny frantic?
Because he couldn't take a walk or sit down in a movie   25
Without being afraid he'd run smack into somebody
Who'd point at his rearranged face and holler, "Johnny!"
Was Johnny ugly?
Yes, because Dr. Wilhelm Loeser had given him a new profile

---

1. **J. Edgar Hoover:** director of the Federal Bureau of Investigation from 1924 to 1972.
2. **fourflusher:** a bluffer; one who pretends to be something in a way meant to deceive.

With a baggy jawline and squint eyes and an erased dimple,   30
With kangaroo-tendon cheekbones and a gigolo's mustache that should've been illegal.
Did Johnny love a girl?
Yes, a good-looking, hard-headed Indian named Billie Frechette.
He wanted to marry her and lie down and try to get over it,
But she was locked in jail for giving him first-aid and comfort.   35
Did Johnny feel hurt?
He felt like breaking a bank or jumping over a railing
Into some panicky teller's cage to shout, "Reach for the ceiling!"
Or like kicking some vice president in the bum checks and smiling.
What was he really doing?   40
Going up the aisle with the crowd and into the lobby
With Polly saying, "Would *you* do what Clark done?" And Johnny saying, "Maybe."
And Anna saying, "If he'd been smart, he'd of acted like Bing Crosby."
Did Johnny look flashy?
Yes, his white-on-white shirt and tie were luminous.   45
His trousers were creased like knives to the tops of his shoes,
And his yellow straw hat came down to his dark glasses.
Was Johnny suspicious?
Yes, and when Agent Purvis signalled with a trembling cigar,
Johnny ducked left and ran out of the theater,   50
And innocent Polly and squealing Anna were left nowhere.
Was Johnny a fast runner?
No, but he crouched and scurried past a friendly liquor store
Under the coupled arms of double-daters, under awnings, under stars,
To the curb at the mouth of an alley. He hunched there.   55
Was Johnny a thinker?
No, but he was thinking more or less of Billie Frechette
Who was lost in prison for longer than he could possibly wait,
And then it was suddenly too hard to think around a bullet.
Did anyone shoot straight?   60
Yes, but Mrs. Etta Natalsky fell out from under her picture hat.
Theresa Paulus sprawled on the sidewalk, clutching her left foot.
And both of them groaned loud and long under the streetlight.
Did Johnny like that?
No, but he lay down with those strange women, his face in the alley,   65
One shoe off, cinders in his mouth, his eyelids heavy.
When they shouted questions at him, he talked back to nobody.
Did Johnny lie easy?
Yes, holding his gun and holding his breath as a last trick,
He waited, but when the Agents came close, his breath wouldn't work.   70
Clark Gable walked his last mile; Johnny ran half a block.
Did he run out of luck?
Yes, before he was cool, they had him spread out on dished-in marble
In the Cook County Morgue, surrounded by babbling people

With a crime reporter presiding over the head of the table.
Did Johnny have a soul?
Yes, and it was climbing his slippery wind-pipe like a trapped burglar.
It was beating the inside of his ribcage, hollering, "Let me out of here!"
Maybe it got out, and maybe it just stayed there.
Was Johnny a money-maker?
Yes, and thousands paid 25¢ to see him, mostly women,
And one said, "I wouldn't have come, except he's a moral lesson,"
And another, "I'm disappointed. He feels like a dead man."
Did Johnny have a brain?
Yes, and it always worked best through the worst of dangers,
Through flat-footed hammerlocks,[3] through guarded doors, around corners,
But it got taken out in the morgue and sold to some doctors.
Could Johnny take orders?
No, but he stayed in the wicker basket carried by six men
Through the bulging crowd to the hearse and let himself be locked in,
And he stayed put as it went driving south in a driving rain.
And he didn't get stolen?
No, not even after his old hard-nosed dad refused to sell
The quick-drawing corpse for $10,000 to somebody in a carnival.
He figured he'd let *Johnny* decide how to get to Hell.
Did anyone wish him well?
Yes, half of Indiana camped in the family pasture,
And the minister said, "With luck, he could have been a minister."
And up the sleeve of his oversized gray suit, Johnny twitched a finger.
Does anyone remember?
Everyone still alive. And some dead ones. It was a new kind of holiday
With hot and cold drinks and hot and cold tears. They planted him in a cemetery
With three unknown vice presidents, Benjamin Harrison,[4] and James Whitcomb Riley,[5]
Who never held up anybody.

---

3. **hammerlock:** a wrestling hold.
4. **Benjamin Harrison:** the twenty-third President of the United States.
5. **James Whitcomb Riley:** an American Poet.

Getting at Meaning

1. Describe Dillinger on the day he was shot. How had his appearance changed in recent months?

2. What other details is the reader given about Dillinger's life? What is his general attitude? How does he die?

3. Describe Dillinger's wake and burial. Why do you think that so many people attended both?

Developing Skills in Reading Literature

1. **Narrative Poem.** The story told in this narrative poem is a famous one. Who is the main character? Who are the minor characters? Why do you think the poet includes so many details about the setting, such as Chicago's weather on the day of the shooting?

2. **Simile.** This poem contains a number of similes. Choose three that seem especially effective and explain why you find them so striking.

3. **Theme.** One of the women who views Dillinger's body says, "I wouldn't have come, except he's a moral lesson." Another says, "I'm disappointed. He feels like a dead man." What does the poet suggest about Dillinger by including these comments? What message does the poet wish to convey about Dillinger?

Developing Writing Skills

Writing a Narrative Poem. Tell a story of your own choosing in poem form. The story may recall an event that you experienced personally, or it may have nothing to do with you directly. You may wish to make your narrative poem a ballad.

Unit Review   *Poetry*

Understanding the Unit

1. Many poems in this unit are about nature. Choose three of these poems and discuss the attitude toward nature that they reflect.

2. Choose three poems in which the speakers arrive at new understandings. What triggers each realization? How does the use of imagery and figurative language help the reader to share the experience of the speaker?

3. Some poems are like pictures; they are written to capture a specific scene, as a painter might. Identify two or three poems in this unit that fall into this category. How is the poet's use of imagery important in each poem?

4. Reread the poem "Essentials" in the Introduction to the Unit. Choose one poem and discuss how the poem illustrates the characteristics of poetry presented in "Essentials."

5. Prose is the term used to describe the kind of language and writing used in short stories and essays. Some of the poems in this unit, such as "The Elephant," resemble prose pieces. Can you find others? Why are these poems still classified as poetry?

6. Compare the attitude of the speaker in "Be Daedalus" to the attitude of the speaker in "Birches."

7. Choose two poems from the first section of the unit and for each poem explain the relationship between the shape of the poem and its content.

8. Which poems in this unit are narrative poems? What characteristics do these poems have in common?

9. Which poems in this unit are ballads? Compare and contrast the rhyme schemes and the meters of these poems.

Writing

1. Assemble a collection of your own poetry. Include revised versions of several poems you have written for this unit and also several new poems. To vary your collection, experiment with different types of poetry. Work to present your poetry in an interesting and polished manner. You may wish to illustrate or decorate your collection.

2. Choose your favorite poem in the unit. Locate other poems by the same writer. Then, in a well developed paragraph, discuss two or three poetic techniques favored by the writer. Include examples from the poems to illustrate the techniques.

PIERROT, 1918. *Pablo Picasso.*
Collection, The Museum of Modern Art, New York.
Sam A. Lewisohn Bequest.

Unit 6

Drama

TWO ON THE AISLE, 1927. *Edward Hopper.*
The Toledo Museum of Art, Toledo, Ohio.
Gift of Edward Drummond Libbey.

Introduction to the Unit

Drama is older than the novel, the short story, or any other form of literature. Drama originated thousands of years ago in the dances of primitive tribes, performed in tribute to a god or gods when a tribal group wished to beg for rain or sun or to celebrate a successful harvest. At some point in history, one dancer separated from the others, possibly playing the part of a god, maybe impersonating a human character. Thus the concept of acting was born.

Plays as we know them are structured presentations of characters, speaking to one another and interacting. Plays are written to appeal to the senses as well as to the mind and imagination of an audience. Therefore, plays should be seen and heard, performed and read orally.

In this unit are two American plays from the twentieth century, followed by *Romeo and Juliet,* written in 1595, nearly four hundred years ago. Perhaps the most famous of all plays, *Romeo and Juliet* was written by William Shakespeare, without a doubt the most famous of all English playwrights.

Read aloud sections of the plays in this unit. If possible, organize performances of scenes with groups of classmates. Experience fully the sensual, emotional, and intellectual appeal of the drama.

Trifles   *Susan Glaspell*

SCENE: *The kitchen in the now abandoned farmhouse of* JOHN WRIGHT, *a gloomy kitchen, and left without having been put in order— the walls covered with a faded wallpaper. D. R. is a door leading to the parlor. On the R. wall above this door is a built-in kitchen cupboard with shelves in the upper portion and drawers below. In the rear wall at R., up two steps, is a door opening onto stairs leading to the second floor. In the rear wall at L. is a door to the shed and from there to the outside. Between these two doors is an old-fashioned black iron stove. Running along the L. wall from the shed door is an old iron sink and sink shelf, in which is set a hand pump. Downstage of the sink is an uncurtained window. Near the window is an old wooden rocker. Center stage is an unpainted wooden kitchen table with straight chairs on either side. There is a small chair D. R. Unwashed pans under the sink, a loaf of bread outside the breadbox, a dish towel on the table— other signs of incompleted work. At the rear, the shed door opens and the* SHERIFF *comes in followed by the* COUNTY ATTORNEY *and* HALE. *The* SHERIFF *and* HALE *are men in middle life; the* COUNTY ATTORNEY *is a young man; all are much bundled up and go at once to the stove. They are followed by the two women— the* SHERIFF'S *wife,* MRS. PETERS, *first; she is a slight wiry woman, a thin, nervous face.* MRS. HALE *is larger and would ordinarily be called more comfortable looking, but she is disturbed now and looks fearfully about as she enters. The women have come in slowly, and stand close together near the door.*

COUNTY ATTORNEY *(at stove rubbing his hands).* This feels good. Come up to the fire, ladies.

MRS. PETERS *(after taking a step forward).* I'm not—cold.

SHERIFF *(unbuttoning his overcoat and stepping away from the stove to right of table as if to mark the beginning of official business).* Now, Mr. Hale, before we move things about, you explain to Mr. Henderson just what you saw when you came here yesterday morning.

COUNTY ATTORNEY *(crossing down to left of the table).* By the way, has anything been moved? Are things just as you left them yesterday?

SHERIFF *(looking about).* It's just the same. When it dropped below zero last night, I thought I'd better send Frank out this morning to make a fire for us—*(sits right of center table)* no use getting pneumonia with a big case on, but I told him not to touch anything except the stove—and you know Frank.

COUNTY ATTORNEY. Somebody should have been left here yesterday.

SHERIFF. Oh—yesterday. When I had to send Frank to Morris Center for that man who went crazy—I want you to know I had my hands full yesterday. I knew you could get back from Omaha by today, and as long as I went over everything here myself——

COUNTY ATTORNEY. Well, Mr. Hale, tell just what happened when you came here yesterday morning.

HALE (crossing down to above table). Harry and I had started to town with a load of potatoes. We came along the road from my place and as I got here I said, "I'm going to see if I can't get John Wright to go in with me on a party telephone." I spoke to Wright about it once before and he put me off, saying folks talked too much anyway, and all he asked was peace and quiet—I guess you know about how much he talked himself; but I thought maybe if I went to the house and talked about it before his wife, though I said to Harry that I didn't know as what his wife wanted made much difference to John——

COUNTY ATTORNEY. Let's talk about that later, Mr. Hale. I do want to talk about that, but tell now just what happened when you got to the house.

HALE. I didn't hear or see anything; I knocked at the door, and still it was all quiet inside. I knew they must be up; it was past eight o'clock. So I knocked again, and I thought I heard somebody say, "Come in." I wasn't sure, I'm not sure yet, but I opened the door—this door (indicating the door by which the two women are still standing) and there in that rocker—(pointing to it) sat Mrs. Wright. (They all look at the rocker D. L.)

COUNTY ATTORNEY. What—was she doing?

HALE. She was rockin' back and forth. She had her apron in her hand and was kind of—pleating it.

COUNTY ATTORNEY. And how did she—look?

HALE. Well, she looked queer.

COUNTY ATTORNEY. How do you mean—queer?

HALE. Well, as if she didn't know what she was going to do next. And kind of done up.

COUNTY ATTORNEY (takes out notebook and pencil and sits left of center table). How did she seem to feel about your coming?

HALE. Why, I don't think she minded—one way or other. She didn't pay much attention. I said, "How do, Mrs. Wright, it's cold, ain't it?" And she said, "Is it?"—and went on kind of pleating at her apron. Well, I was surprised; she didn't ask me to come up to the stove, or to set down, but just sat there, not even looking at me, so I said, "I want to see John." And then she—laughed. I guess you would call it a laugh. I thought of Harry and the team outside, so I said a little sharp, "Can't I see John?" "No," she says, kind o' dull like. "Ain't he home?" says I. "Yes," says she, "he's home." "Then why can't I see him?" I asked her, out of patience. "'Cause he's dead," says she. "Dead?" says I. She just nodded her head, not getting a bit excited, but rockin' back and forth. "Why—where is he?" says I, not knowing what to say. She just pointed upstairs—like that. (Himself pointing to the room above.) I started for the stairs, with the idea of going up there. I walked from there to here—then I says, "Why, what did he die of?" "He died of a rope round his neck," says she, and just went on pleatin' at her apron. Well, I went out and called Harry. I thought I might—need help. We went upstairs and there he was lyin'——

COUNTY ATTORNEY. I think I'd rather have you go into that upstairs, where you can point it all out. Just go on now with the rest of the story.

HALE. Well, my first thought was to get that rope off. It looked . . . (stops, his face twitches) . . . but Harry, he went up to him, and he said, "No, he's dead all right, and we'd better not touch anything." So we went back downstairs. She was still sitting that same way. "Has anybody been notified?" I asked. "No," says she, unconcerned. "Who did this, Mrs. Wright?" said Harry. He said it business-like—and she stopped pleatin' of her apron. "I don't know," she says. "You don't know?" says

Harry. "No," says she. "Weren't you sleepin' in the bed with him?" says Harry. "Yes," says she, "but I was on the inside." "Somebody slipped a rope round his neck and strangled him, and you didn't wake up?" says Harry. "I didn't wake up," she said after him. We must 'a' looked as if we didn't see how that could be, for after a minute she said, "I sleep sound." Harry was going to ask her more questions, but I said maybe we ought to let her tell her story first to the coroner, or the sheriff, so Harry went fast as he could to Rivers' place, where there's a telephone.

COUNTY ATTORNEY. And what did Mrs. Wright do when she knew that you had gone for the coroner?

HALE. She moved from the rocker to that chair over there (*pointing to a small chair in the* D. R. *corner*) and just sat there with her hands held together and looking down. I got a feeling that I ought to make some conversation, so I said I had come in to see if John wanted to put in a telephone, and at that she started to laugh, and then she stopped and looked at me— scared. (*The* COUNTY ATTORNEY, *who has had his notebook out, makes a note.*) I dunno, maybe it wasn't scared. I wouldn't like to say it was. Soon Harry got back, and then Dr. Lloyd came, and you, Mr. Peters, and so I guess that's all I know that you don't.

COUNTY ATTORNEY (*rising and looking around*). I guess we'll go upstairs first— and then out to the barn and around there. (*To the* SHERIFF.) You're convinced that there was nothing important here— nothing that would point to any motive?

SHERIFF. Nothing here but kitchen things. (*The* COUNTY ATTORNEY, *after again looking around the kitchen, opens the door of a cupboard closet in* R. *wall. He brings a small chair from* R.—*gets up on it and looks on a shelf. Pulls his hand away, sticky.*)

COUNTY ATTORNEY. Here's a nice mess. (*The women draw nearer* U. C.)

MRS. PETERS (*to the other woman*). Oh, her fruit; it did freeze. (*To the* LAWYER.) She worried about that when it turned so cold. She said the fire'd go out and her jars would break.

SHERIFF (*rises*). Well, can you beat the women! Held for murder and worryin' about her preserves.

COUNTY ATTORNEY (*getting down from chair*). I guess before we're through she may have something more serious than preserves to worry about. (*Crosses down* R. C.)

HALE. Well, women are used to worrying over trifles. (*The two women move a little closer together.*)

COUNTY ATTORNEY (*with the gallantry of a young politician*). And yet, for all their worries, what would we do without the ladies? (*The women do not unbend. He goes below the center table to the sink, takes a dipperful of water from the pail and pouring it into a basin, washes his hands. While he is doing this, the* SHERIFF *and* HALE *cross to cupboard, which they inspect. The* COUNTY ATTORNEY *starts to wipe his hands on the roller towel, turns it for a cleaner place.*) Dirty towels! (*Kicks his foot against the pans under the sink.*) Not much of a housekeeper, would you say, ladies?

MRS. HALE (*stiffly*). There's a great deal of work to be done on a farm.

COUNTY ATTORNEY. To be sure. And yet (*with a little bow to her*) I know there are some Dickson County farmhouses which do not have such roller towels. (*He gives it a pull to expose its full length again.*)

MRS. HALE. Those towels get dirty awful quick. Men's hands aren't always as clean as they might be.

COUNTY ATTORNEY. Ah, loyal to your sex, I

see. But you and Mrs. Wright were neighbors. I suppose you were friends, too.

MRS. HALE (*shaking her head*). I've not seen much of her of late years. I've not been in this house—it's more than a year.

COUNTY ATTORNEY (*crossing to women U. C.*). And why was that? You didn't like her?

MRS. HALE. I liked her all well enough. Farmers' wives have their hands full, Mr. Henderson. And then—

COUNTY ATTORNEY. Yes—?

MRS. HALE (*looking about*). It never seemed a very cheerful place.

COUNTY ATTORNEY. No—it's not cheerful. I shouldn't say she had the homemaking instinct.

MRS. HALE. Well, I don't know as Wright had, either.

COUNTY ATTORNEY. You mean that they didn't get on very well?

MRS. HALE. No, I don't mean anything. But I don't think a place'd be any cheerfuller for John Wright's being in it.

COUNTY ATTORNEY. I'd like to talk more of that a little later. I want to get the lay of things upstairs now. (*He goes past the women to U. R. where steps lead to a stair door.*)

SHERIFF. I suppose anything Mrs. Peters does'll be all right. She was to take in some clothes for her, you know, and a few little things. We left in such a hurry yesterday.

COUNTY ATTORNEY. Yes, but I would like to see what you take, Mrs. Peters, and keep an eye out for anything that might be of use to us.

MRS. PETERS. Yes, Mr. Henderson. (*The men leave by U. R. door to stairs. The women listen to the men's steps on the stairs, then look about the kitchen.*)

MRS. HALE (*crossing L. to sink*). I'd hate to have men coming into my kitchen, snooping around and criticizing. (*She arranges the pans under sink, which the LAWYER had shoved out of place.*)

MRS. PETERS. Of course, it's no more than their duty. (*Crosses to cupboard U. R.*)

MRS. HALE. Duty's all right, but I guess that deputy sheriff that came out to make the fire might have got a little of this on. (*Gives the roller towel a pull.*) Wish I'd thought of that sooner. Seems mean to talk about her for not having things slicked up when she had to come away in such a hurry. (*Crosses R. to MRS. PETERS at cupboard.*)

MRS. PETERS (*who has been looking through cupboard, lifts one end of a towel that covers a pan*). She had bread set. (*Stands still.*)

MRS. HALE (*eyes fixed on a loaf of bread beside the breadbox, which is on a low shelf of the cupboard*). She was going to put this in there. (*Picks up loaf, then abruptly drops it. In a manner of returning to familiar things.*) It's a shame about her fruit. I wonder if it's all gone. (*Gets up on the chair and looks.*) I think there's some here that's all right, Mrs. Peters. Yes—here; (*holding it toward the window*) this is cherries, too. (*Looking again.*) I declare I believe that's the only one. (*Gets down, jar in her hand. Goes to the sink and wipes it off on the outside.*) She'll feel awful bad after all her hard work in the hot weather. I remember the afternoon I put up my cherries last summer. (*She puts the jar on the big kitchen table, center of the room. With a sigh, is about to sit down in the rocking chair. Before she is seated, realizes what chair it is; with a slow look at it, steps back. The chair that she has touched rocks back and forth.*)

MRS. PETERS *moves to center table, and they both watch the chair rock for a moment or two.*)

MRS. PETERS (*shaking off the mood that the empty rocking chair has evoked. Now, in a businesslike manner, she speaks*). Well, I must get those things from the front room closet. *(She goes to the door at the R., but, after looking into the other room, steps back.)* You coming with me, Mrs. Hale? You could help me carry them. *(They go into the other room; reappear,* MRS. PETERS *carrying a dress, petticoat, and skirt,* MRS. HALE *following with a pair of shoes.)* My, it's cold in there. *(She puts the clothes on the big table, and hurries to the stove.)*

MRS. HALE *(right of center table, examining the skirt).* Wright was close. I think maybe that's why she kept so much to herself. She didn't even belong to the Ladies' Aid. I suppose she felt she couldn't do her part, and then, you don't enjoy things when you feel shabby. I heard she used to wear pretty clothes and be lively, when she was Minnie Foster, one of the town girls singing in the choir. But that—oh, that was thirty years ago. This all you was to take in?

MRS. PETERS. She said she wanted an apron. Funny thing to want, for there isn't much to get you dirty in jail, goodness knows. But I suppose just to make her feel more natural. *(Crosses to cupboard.)* She said they was in the top drawer in this cupboard. Yes, here. And then her little shawl that always hung behind the door. *(Opens stair door and looks.)* Yes, here it is. *(Quickly shuts door leading upstairs.)*

MRS. HALE *(abruptly moving toward her).* Mrs. Peters?

MRS. PETERS. Yes, Mrs. Hale? *(At U. R. door.)*

MRS. HALE. Do you think she did it?

MRS. PETERS *(in a frightened voice).* Oh, I don't know.

MRS. HALE. Well, I don't think she did. Asking for an apron and her little shawl. Worrying about her fruit.

MRS. PETERS *(starts to speak, glances up, where footsteps are heard in the room above. In a low voice).* Mr. Peters says it looks bad for her. Mr. Henderson is awful sarcastic in a speech, and he'll make fun of her sayin' she didn't wake up.

MRS. HALE. Well, I guess John Wright didn't wake when they was slipping that rope under his neck.

MRS. PETERS *(crossing slowly to table and placing shawl and apron on table with other clothing).* No, it's strange. It must have been done awful crafty and still. They say it was such a—funny way to kill a man, rigging it all up like that.

MRS. HALE *(crossing to left of* MRS. PETERS *at table).* That's just what Mr. Hale said. There was a gun in the house. He says that's what he can't understand.

MRS. PETERS. Mr. Henderson said, coming out, that what was needed for the case was a motive; something to show anger, or—sudden feeling.

MRS. HALE *(who is standing by the table).* Well, I don't see any signs of anger around here. *(She puts her hand on the dish towel that lies on the table, stands looking down at table, one-half of which is clean, the other half messy.)* It's wiped to here. *(Makes a move as if to finish work, then turns and looks at loaf of bread outside the breadbox. Drops towel. In that voice of coming back to familiar things.)* Wonder how they are finding things upstairs. *(Crossing below table to D. R.)* I hope she had it a little more red-up up there. You know, it seems kind of *sneaking.* Locking her up in town and then coming out here and trying to get her own house to turn against her!

MRS. PETERS. But, Mrs. Hale, the law is the law.

MRS. HALE. I s'pose 'tis. *(Unbuttoning her coat.)* Better loosen up your things, Mrs. Peters. You won't feel them when you go out. *(MRS. PETERS takes off her fur tippet, goes to hang it on chair back left of table, stands looking at the work basket on floor near D. L. window.)*

MRS. PETERS. She was piecing a quilt. *(She brings the large sewing basket to the center table, and they look at the bright pieces,* MRS. HALE *above the table and* MRS. PETERS *left of it.)*

MRS. HALE. It's a log cabin pattern. Pretty, isn't it? I wonder if she was goin' to quilt it or just knot it? *(Footsteps have been heard coming down the stairs. The* SHERIFF *enters followed by* HALE *and the* COUNTY ATTORNEY.)*

SHERIFF. They wonder if she was going to quilt it or just knot it! *(The men laugh, the women look abashed.)*

COUNTY ATTORNEY *(rubbing his hands over the stove).* Frank's fire didn't do much up there, did it? Well, let's go out to the barn and get that cleared up. *(The men go outside by* U. L. *door.)*

MRS. HALE *(resentfully).* I don't know as there's anything so strange, our takin' up our time with little things while we're waiting for them to get the evidence. *(She sits in chair right of table smoothing out a block with decision.)* I don't see as it's anything to laugh about.

MRS. PETERS *(apologetically).* Of course, they've got awful important things on their minds. *(Pulls up a chair and joins* MRS. HALE *at the left of the table.)*

MRS. HALE *(examining another block).* Mrs. Peters, look at this one. Here, this is the one she was working on, and look at the sewing! All the rest of it has been so nice and even. And look at this! It's all over the place! Why, it looks as if she didn't know what she was about! *(After she has said this, they look at each other, then start to glance back at the door. After an instant* MRS. HALE *has pulled at a knot and ripped the sewing.)*

MRS. PETERS. Oh, what are you doing, Mrs. Hale?

MRS. HALE *(mildly).* Just pulling out a stitch or two that's not sewed very good.

(Threading a needle.) Bad sewing always made me fidgety.

MRS. PETERS *(with a glance at door, nervously).* I don't think we ought to touch things.

MRS. HALE. I'll just finish up this end. *(Suddenly stopping and leaning forward.)* Mrs. Peters?

MRS. PETERS. Yes, Mrs. Hale?

MRS. HALE. What do you suppose she was so nervous about?

MRS. PETERS. Oh—I don't know. I don't know as she was nervous. I sometimes sew awful queer when I'm just tired. *(MRS. HALE starts to say something, looks at* MRS. PETERS, *then goes on sewing.)* Well, I must get these things wrapped up. They may be through sooner than we think. *(Putting apron and other things together.)* I wonder where I can find a piece of paper, and string. *(Rises.)*

MRS. HALE. In that cupboard, maybe.

MRS. PETERS *(crosses* R. *looking in cupboard).* Why, here's a bird cage. *(Holds it up.)* Did she have a bird, Mrs. Hale?

MRS. HALE. Why, I don't know whether she did or not—I've not been here for so long. There was a man around last year selling canaries cheap, but I don't know as she took one; maybe she did. She used to sing real pretty herself.

MRS. PETERS *(glancing around).* Seems funny to think of a bird here. But she must have had one, or why would she have a cage? I wonder what happened to it?

MRS. HALE. I s'pose maybe the cat got it.

MRS. PETERS. No, she didn't have a cat. She's got that feeling some people have about cats—being afraid of them. My cat got in her room and she was real upset and asked me to take it out.

MRS. HALE. My sister Bessie was like that. Queer, ain't it?

MRS. PETERS *(examining the cage).* Why, look at this door. It's broke. One hinge is pulled apart. *(Takes a step down to* MRS. HALE'S *right.)*

MRS. HALE *(looking too).* Looks as if someone must have been rough with it.

MRS. PETERS. Why, yes. *(She brings the cage forward and puts it on the table.)*

MRS. HALE *(glancing toward* U. L. *door).* I wish if they're going to find any evidence they'd be about it. I don't like this place.

MRS. PETERS. But I'm awful glad you came with me, Mrs. Hale. It would be lonesome for me sitting here alone.

MRS. HALE. It would, wouldn't it? *(Dropping her sewing.)* But I tell you what I do wish, Mrs. Peters. I wish I had come over sometimes when *she* was here. I—*(looking around the room)*—wish I had.

MRS. PETERS. But of course you were awful busy, Mrs. Hale—your house and your children.

MRS. HALE *(rises and crosses* L.*).* I could've come. I stayed away because it weren't cheerful—and that's why I ought to have come. I—*(looking out* L. *window)*—I've never liked this place. Maybe because it's down in a hollow and you don't see the road. I dunno what it is, but it's a lonesome place and always was. I wish I had come over to see Minnie Foster sometimes. I can see now—— *(Shakes her head.)*

MRS. PETERS *(left of table and above it).* Well, you mustn't reproach yourself, Mrs. Hale. Somehow we just don't see how it is with other folks until—something turns up.

MRS. HALE. Not having children makes less work—but it makes a quiet house, and Wright out to work all day, and no company when he did come in. *(Turning from window.)* Did you know John Wright, Mrs. Peters?

MRS. PETERS. Not to know him; I've seen him in town. They say he was a good man.

MRS. HALE. Yes—good; he didn't drink, and kept his word as well as most, I guess, and paid his debts. But he was a hard man,

Mrs. Peters. Just to pass the time of day with him—— *(Shivers.)* Like a raw wind that gets to the bone. *(Pauses, her eye falling on the cage.)* I should think she would 'a' wanted a bird. But what do you suppose went with it?

MRS. PETERS. I don't know, unless it got sick and died. *(She reaches over and swings the broken door, swings it again, both women watch it.)*

MRS. HALE. You weren't raised round here, were you? *(*MRS. PETERS *shakes her head.)* You didn't know—her?

MRS. PETERS. Not till they brought her yesterday.

MRS. HALE. She—come to think of it, she was kind of like a bird herself—real sweet and pretty, but kind of timid and—fluttery. How—she—did—change. *(Silence; then as if struck by a happy thought and relieved to get back to everyday things. Crosses* R. *above* MRS. PETERS *to cupboard, replaces small chair used to stand on to its original place* D. R.*)* Tell you what, Mrs. Peters, why don't you take the quilt in with you? It might take up her mind.

MRS. PETERS. Why, I think that's a real nice idea, Mrs. Hale. There couldn't possibly be any objection to it, could there? Now, just what would I take? I wonder if her patches are in here—and her things. *(They look in the sewing basket.)*

MRS. HALE *(crosses to right of table).* Here's some red. I expect this has got sewing things in it. *(Brings out a fancy box.)* What a pretty box. Looks like something somebody would give you. Maybe her scissors are in here. *(Opens box. Suddenly puts her hand to her nose.)* Why—— *(*MRS. PETERS *bends nearer, then turns her face away.)* There's something wrapped up in this piece of silk.

MRS. PETERS. Why, this isn't her scissors.

MRS. HALE *(lifting the silk).* Oh, Mrs. Peters— it's—— *(*MRS. PETERS *bends closer.)*

MRS. PETERS. It's the bird.

MRS. HALE. But, Mrs. Peters—look at it! Its neck! Look at its neck! It's all—other side to.

MRS. PETERS. Somebody—wrung—its neck. *(Their eyes meet. A look of growing comprehension, of horror. Steps are heard outside.* MRS. HALE *slips box under quilt pieces, and sinks into her chair. Enter* SHERIFF *and* COUNTY ATTORNEY. MRS. PETERS *steps* D. L. *and stands looking out of window.)*

COUNTY ATTORNEY *(as one turning from serious things to little pleasantries).* Well, ladies, have you decided whether she was going to quilt it or knot it? *(Crosses to* C. *above table.)*

MRS. PETERS. We think she was going to— knot it. *(SHERIFF crosses to right of stove, lifts stove lid, and glances at fire; then stands warming hands at stove.)*

COUNTY ATTORNEY. Well, that's interesting, I'm sure. *(Seeing the bird cage.)* Has the bird flown?

MRS. HALE *(putting more quilt pieces over the box).* We think the—cat got it.

COUNTY ATTORNEY *(preoccupied).* Is there a cat? *(MRS. HALE glances in a quick, covert way at MRS. PETERS.)*

MRS. PETERS *(turning from window takes a step in).* Well, not *now*. They're superstitious, you know. They leave.

COUNTY ATTORNEY *(to SHERIFF PETERS, continuing an interrupted conversation).* No sign at all of anyone having come from the outside. Their own rope. Now let's go up again and go over it piece by piece. *(They start upstairs).* It would have to have been someone who knew just the—— *(MRS. PETERS sits down left of table. The two women sit there not looking at one another, but as if peering into something and at the same time holding back. When they talk now, it is in the manner of feeling their way over strange ground, as if afraid of what they are saying, but as if they cannot help saying it.)*

MRS. HALE *(hesitatively and in hushed voice).* She liked the bird. She was going to bury it in that pretty box.

MRS. PETERS *(in a whisper).* When I was a girl —my kitten—there was a boy took a hatchet and before my eyes—and before I could get there—— *(Covers her face an instant.)* If they hadn't held me back I would have—*(catches herself, looks upstairs where steps are heard, falters weakly)*— hurt him.

MRS. HALE *(with a slow look around her).* I wonder how it would seem never to have had any children around. *(Pause.)* No, Wright wouldn't like the bird—a thing that sang. She used to sing. He killed that, too.

MRS. PETERS *(moving uneasily).* We don't know who killed the bird.

MRS. HALE. I knew John Wright.

MRS. PETERS. It was an awful thing was done in this house that night, Mrs. Hale. Killing a man while he slept, slipping a rope around his neck that choked the life out of him.

MRS. HALE. His neck. Choked the life out of him. *(Her hand goes out and rests on the bird cage.)*

MRS. PETERS *(with rising voice).* We don't know who killed him. We don't *know*.

MRS. HALE *(her own feeling not interrupted).* If there'd been years and years of nothing, then a bird to sing to you, it would be awful—still, after the bird was still.

MRS. PETERS *(something within her speaking).* I know what stillness is. When we homesteaded[1] in Dakota, and my first baby died —after he was two years old, and me with no other then——

---

1. **homestead** (hōm′ sted′): to settle a 160-acre tract of public land granted by the United States government.

MRS. HALE *(moving)*. How soon do you suppose they'll be through looking for the evidence?

MRS. PETERS. I know what stillness is. *(Pulling herself back.)* The law has got to punish crime, Mrs. Hale.

MRS. HALE *(not as if answering that)*. I wish you'd seen Minnie Foster when she wore a white dress with blue ribbons and stood up there in the choir and sang. *(A look around the room.)* Oh, I wish I'd come over here once in a while! That was a crime! That was a crime! Who's going to punish that?

MRS. PETERS *(looking upstairs)*. We mustn't—take on.

MRS. HALE. I might have known she needed help! I know how things can be—for women. I tell you, it's queer, Mrs. Peters. We live close together and we live far apart. We all go through the same things—it's all just a different kind of the same thing. *(Brushes her eyes, noticing the jar of fruit, reaches out for it.)* If I was you, I wouldn't tell her her fruit was gone. Tell her it *ain't*. Tell her it's all right. Take this in to prove it to her. She—she may never know whether it was broke or not.

MRS. PETERS *(takes the jar, looks about for something to wrap it in; takes petticoat from the clothes brought from the other room, very nervously begins winding this around the jar. In a false voice.)* My, it's a good thing the men couldn't hear us. Wouldn't they just laugh! Getting all stirred up over a little thing like a—dead canary. As if that could have anything to do with—with—wouldn't they *laugh!* *(The men are heard coming downstairs.)*

MRS. HALE *(under her breath)*. Maybe they would—maybe they wouldn't.

COUNTY ATTORNEY. No, Peters, it's all perfectly clear except a reason for doing it. But you know juries when it comes to women. If there was some definite thing. *(Crosses slowly to above table. SHERIFF crosses D. R. MRS. HALE and MRS. PETERS remain seated at either side of table.)* Something to show—something to make a story about—a thing that would connect up with this strange way of doing it—— *(The women's eyes meet for an instant. Enter HALE from outer door.)*

HALE *(remaining U. L. by door)*. Well, I've got the team around. Pretty cold out there.

COUNTY ATTORNEY. I'm going to stay awhile by myself. *(To the SHERIFF.)* You can send Frank out for me, can't you? I want to go over everything. I'm not satisfied that we can't do better.

SHERIFF. Do you want to see what Mrs. Peters is going to take in? *(The LAWYER picks up the apron, laughs.)*

COUNTY ATTORNEY. Oh, I guess they're not very dangerous things the ladies have picked out. *(Moves a few things about, disturbing the quilt pieces that cover the box. Steps back.)* No, Mrs. Peters doesn't need supervising. For that matter, a sheriff's wife is married to the law. Ever think of it that way, Mrs. Peters?

MRS. PETERS. Not—just that way.

SHERIFF *(chuckling)*. Married to the law. *(Moves to D. R. door to the other room.)* I just want you to come in here a minute, George. We ought to take a look at these windows.

COUNTY ATTORNEY *(scoffingly)*. Oh, windows!

SHERIFF. We'll be right out, Mr. Hale. *(HALE goes outside. The SHERIFF follows the COUNTY ATTORNEY into the other room. Then MRS. HALE rises, hands tight together, looking intensely at MRS. PETERS, whose eyes make a slow turn, finally meeting MRS. HALE's. A moment MRS. HALE holds her; then her own eyes point the way to where the box is concealed. Suddenly MRS. PETERS throws back quilt pieces and tries to put the box into the bag she is carrying. It is too big. She opens box, starts to take bird out, cannot touch it, goes to pieces, stands there helpless. Sound of a knob turning in the other room.* MRS. HALE *snatches the box and puts it in the pocket of her big coat. Enter* COUNTY ATTORNEY *and* SHERIFF, *who remains* D. R.*)*

COUNTY ATTORNEY *(crosses to* U. L. *door facetiously).* Well, Henry, at least we found out that she was not going to quilt it. She was going to—what is it you call it, ladies?
MRS. HALE *(standing* C. *below table facing front, her hand against her pocket).* We call it—knot it, Mr. Henderson.

Getting at Meaning

1. Why do Mrs. Hale and Mrs. Peters suppress evidence, when they know it is against the law?

2. Describe the Wright marriage, as Mrs. Hale comments on it. How does she describe Minnie Wright? John Wright?

3. What kinds of clues are the men seeking? How is the approach of the women different? What is the attitude of the men toward the women's activities?

4. Relate the circumstances surrounding John Wright's death. Why was Mr. Wright killed by strangulation instead of with a gun?

5. When Mrs. Hale and Mrs. Peters discuss Minnie Wright's patchwork quilt with the Sheriff and the County Attorney, what have they in fact discovered? What is the significance of Mrs. Peters's answer, "We think she was going to knot it"?

6. Why does Mrs. Hale regret not visiting Mrs. Wright?

7. Do you think Minnie Wright killed her husband? Give reasons for your answer. What might prevent a jury from finding her guilty?

Developing Skills in Reading Literature

1. **Drama.** An audience understands the characters in a drama through what they do and what they say. No narrator outside the action can tell the reader or viewer about the characters, which is a major difference between the play and the short story or novel.

In this play, you learn about Mrs. Wright's life as Minnie Foster from one of the characters. Who tells about Mrs. Wright's youth? Why?

2. **Setting.** This play consists of only one act, with all of the action happening in one location. Where is the action set? How does the playwright indicate action in other rooms of the house?

What dramatic purpose is served by the discussion of the gloomy and cheerless Wright farmhouse? Why is the silence of the farmhouse emphasized?

3. **Character.** The character of Minnie Wright slowly unfolds as you learn of her predicament and what led up to it. It is Mrs. Hale and Mrs. Peters, however, who actually face a crisis during the course of the play. How do their characters change? What would you say is the turning point for Mrs. Peters? for Mrs. Hale?

4. **Symbol.** What do you think the bird represented to Minnie Wright? In what sense is the bird a symbol for Mrs. Wright? What is symbolic about John Wright's death?

5. **Irony.** This play is full of ironies, some major and some minor. What is ironic about the way in which John Wright dies? What is ironic about the title of the play? What is ironic about Hale's joking remark that "women are used to worrying over trifles"?

6. **Theme.** Does this play project an attitude about human life? about legal justice? State a possible theme for the play.

Developing Vocabulary

Inferring Word Meaning. Read each of the following passages from the play. Try to determine the meaning of the word that appears after each passage. Look up the word in a dictionary and write its correct definition. Then use the word in a sentence of your own that clearly indicates the word's meaning.

1. The kitchen in the now abandoned farmhouse of JOHN WRIGHT, a gloomy kitchen, and left without having been put in order —the walls covered with a faded wallpaper. *gloomy*

2. COUNTY ATTORNEY (*with the gallantry of a young politician*). And yet, for all their worries, what would we do without the ladies? *gallantry*

3. SHERIFF. They wonder if she was going to quilt it or just knot it! (*The men laugh, the women look abashed.*) *abashed*

4. COUNTY ATTORNEY (*preoccupied*). Is there a cat? (MRS. HALE *glances in a quick, covert way at* MRS. PETERS.) *preoccupied*

5. COUNTY ATTORNEY (*crosses to* U.L. *door facetiously*). Well, Henry, at least we found out that she was not going to quilt it. She was going to—what is it you call it, ladies? *facetiously*

Developing Writing Skills

1. **Supporting an Opinion.** In a fully developed paragraph, either defend or criticize the action taken by Mrs. Hale and Mrs. Peters at the end of "Trifles." Present logical reasons to support your position.

2. **Writing Dialogue.** Listen to a conversation in the hallway, on a bus, in the park, or in some other familiar place. Using what you have heard as a starting point, write a short dialogue in play form. Be sure to include stage directions. Before you begin, look over the form of this play.

I Remember Mama   *John Van Druten*

ACT 1

SCENE: *The period of the play is around 1910. On either side of the stage, down front, are two small turntables, left and right, on which the shorter front scenes are played against very simplified backgrounds. As each scene finishes, the lights dim and the table revolves out, leaving an unobstructed view of the main stage. The main stage is raised by two steps, above which traveler curtains open and close.*

When the curtain rises, KATRIN, *in a spotlight, is seated at a desk on the right turntable, facing the audience. She is writing and smoking a cigarette.* KATRIN *is somewhere in her early twenties. She should be played by an actress who is small in stature, and capable of looking sufficiently a child not to break the illusion in subsequent scenes. She is a blonde. Her hair, when we see her first, is in a modern "up" style, capable of being easily loosened to fall to shoulder length for the childhood scenes. She wears a very short dress, the skirt of which is concealed for the prologue by the desk behind which she is seated.*

KATRIN *writes in silence for a few moments, then puts down her pen, takes up her manuscript, and begins to read aloud what she has written.*

KATRIN (*reading*). "For as long as I could remember, the house on Steiner Street had been home. Papa and Mama had both been born in Norway, but they came to San Francisco because Mama's sisters were here. All of us were born here. Nels, the oldest and the only boy—my sister Christine—and the littlest sister, Dagmar." (*She puts down her manuscript and looks out front.*) It's funny, but when I look back, I always see Nels and Christine and myself looking almost as we do today. I guess that's because the people you see all the time stay the same age in your head. Dagmar's different. She was always the baby—so I see her as a baby. Even Mama—it's funny, but I always see Mama as around forty. She couldn't always have been forty. (*She puts out her cigarette, picks up her manuscript, and starts to read again.*) "Besides us, there was our boarder, Mr. Hyde. Mr. Hyde was an Englishman who had once been an actor, and Mama was very impressed by his flowery talk and courtly manners. He used to read aloud to us in the evenings. But first and foremost, I remember Mama." (*The light dims down, leaving* KATRIN *only faintly visible. Lights come up on the main stage, revealing the house on Steiner Street—a kitchen room. It has a black flat, with a dresser* C., *holding china. On either side of the dresser is a door, the one to the* R. *leads to the pantry, the one to the* L. *to the rest of the house. The* L. *wall is a short one. It is the wall of the house, and contains a door upstage leading into the street, being presumably the back door of the house, but the one most commonly used as the entry-door. Beyond it the street is visible, with a single lamppost* L., *just outside the house. Behind the room rises the house itself with upper windows lighted, and behind it a painted backdrop of the San Francisco hills, houses, and telegraph posts. The furniture of the kitchen is simple. A table c., with two chairs above it, armchairs at either end, and a low bench below it. Against the R. wall upstage, a large stove, below it another armchair. The window is below the door in the L. wall and has a low Norwegian chest under it.* KATRIN'S VOICE *continuing in the half-dark, as the scene is revealed.)* "I remember that every Saturday night Mama would sit down by the kitchen table and count out the money Papa had brought home in the little envelope."

(By now the tableau is revealed in full, and the light on KATRIN *dwindles further. The picture is as she described.* MAMA—*looking around forty—is in the armchair R. of the table, emptying the envelope of its silver dollars and smaller coins.* PAPA—*looking a little older than* MAMA—*stands above her. His English throughout is better than hers, with less accent.)*

MAMA. You call the children, Lars. Is good they should know about money.

*(*PAPA *goes to door back L., and calls.)*

PAPA. Children! Nels—Christine—Katrin!

CHILDREN'S VOICES *(off, answering)*. Coming, Papa!

MAMA. You call loud for Katrin. She is in her study, maybe.

PAPA. She is where?

MAMA. Katrin make the old attic under the roof into a study.

PAPA *(amused)*. So? *(Shouting.)* Katrin! Katrin!

KATRIN *(still at her desk, down front)*. Yes, Papa. I heard.

PAPA *(returning to the room)*. A study now, huh? What does Katrin study?

MAMA. I think Katrin wants to be author.

PAPA. Author?

MAMA. Stories she will write. For the magazines. And books, too, maybe, one day.

PAPA *(taking out his pipe)*. Is good pay to be author?

MAMA. I don't know. For magazines, I think maybe yes. For books, I think no.

PAPA. Then she become writer for magazines.

MAMA. Maybe. But I like she writes books. Like the ones Mr. Hyde reads us. *(DAGMAR enters from the pantry. She is a plump child of about eight and carries an alley cat in her arms.)* Dagmar, you bring that cat in again?

DAGMAR. Sure, she's my Elizabeth—my beautiful Elizabeth! *(She crosses to the chest under the window, and sits, nursing the cat.)*

PAPA. Poor Elizabeth looks as if she had been in fight again.

DAGMAR. Not poor Elizabeth. *Brave* Elizabeth. Elizabeth's a Viking cat. She fights for her honor!

PAPA *(exchanging an amused glance with MAMA)*. And just what is a cat's honor, little one?

DAGMAR. The honor of being the bravest cat in San Francisco. *(CHRISTINE comes in back L. She, like KATRIN, should be played by a small young actress, but not a child. Her hair is to her shoulders—her dress short— her age indeterminate. Actually, she is about 13 at this time. She is the cool, aloof, matter-of-fact one of the family. She carries a box of crayons, scissors, and a picture book.)* Aren't you, Elizabeth?

CHRISTINE *(sitting above the table and starting to color the picture book with the crayons)*. That disgusting cat!

DAGMAR. She's not disgusting. She's beautiful. Beautiful as the dawn!

CHRISTINE. And when have *you* ever seen the dawn?

DAGMAR. I haven't seen it, but Mr. Hyde read to us about it. *(MR. HYDE comes in from door back L. He is a slightly seedy, long-haired man in his fifties. Rather of the old-fashioned English "laddie" actor type. He wears a very shabby long overcoat, with a deplorable fur collar, and carries his hat. His accent is English.)* Didn't you, Mr. Hyde? Didn't you read to us about the dawn?

MR. HYDE. I did, my child of joy. The dawn, the rosy-finger-tipped Aurora. . .

DAGMAR. When can I get to *see* the dawn, Mama?

MAMA. Any morning you get up early.

DAGMAR. Is there a dawn every morning?

MAMA. Sure.

DAGMAR *(incredulous)*. It's all that beautiful, and it happens every *morning*? Why didn't anyone *tell* me?

MR. HYDE. My child, that is what the poets are for. To tell you of *all* the beautiful things that are happening every day, and that no one sees until they tell them. *(He starts for the door L.)*

MAMA. You go out, Mr. Hyde?

MR. HYDE. For a few moments only, dear Madam. To buy myself a modicum of that tawny weed, tobacco, that I lust after, as Ben Jonson[1] says. I shall be back in time for our nightly reading. *(He goes out and disappears down the street, into the wings, off L.)*

MAMA *(who has gone to the door back L., calls with a good deal of sharpness and firmness)*. Nels! Katrin! You do not hear Papa call you?

NELS *(from off, upstairs)*. Coming, Mama!

KATRIN *(at her desk)*. Yes, Mama. I'm coming. *(She rises. In her few moments in the dark, she has loosened her hair to her shoulders, and we see that her skirt is short as she walks from her desk, and up the steps into the set. As soon as she has left it, the turntable revolves out. Immediately after her, NELS comes in back L. He is a tall, strapping young fellow—old enough to look 18 or 19, or 15 or 16, according to his dress, or demeanor. Now, he is about 15. KATRIN, to CHRISTINE.)* Move over. *(She shares CHRISTINE's chair at the table with her.)*

PAPA. So now all are here.

---

1. **Ben Jonson:** an English dramatist and poet of the 17th century.

MAMA. Come, then. (CHRISTINE, NELS, *and* KATRIN *gather around the table.* DAGMAR *remains crooning to* ELIZABETH, *but rises and stands behind* PAPA. *Sorting coins.*) First, for the landlord. (*She makes a pile of silver dollars. It gets pushed down the table from one member of the family to the next, each speaking as he passes it.* PAPA *comes last.*)

NELS (*passing it on*). For the landlord.

KATRIN (*doing likewise*). For the landlord.

CHRISTINE (*passing it to* PAPA). The landlord.

PAPA. For the landlord. (*He dumps the pile at his end of the table, writing on a piece of paper, which he wraps around the pile.*)

MAMA (*who has been sorting*). For the grocer.

(*The business is repeated. During this repeat,* DAGMAR'S *crooning to the cat becomes audible, contrapuntally to the repetitions of "For the grocer."*)

DAGMAR (*in a crescendo*). In all the United States no cat was as brave as Elizabeth. (*Fortissimo.*) In all the *world* no cat was as brave as Elizabeth!

MAMA (*gently*). Hush, Dagmar. Quietly. You put Elizabeth back into the pantry.

DAGMAR (*in a loud stage whisper, as she crosses to pantry*). In Heaven or Hell no cat was as brave as Elizabeth! (*She goes out with the cat.*)

MAMA. For Katrin's shoes to be half-soled. (*She passes a half dollar.*)

NELS. Katrin's shoes.

KATRIN (*proudly*). *My* shoes!

CHRISTINE (*contemptuously*). Katrin's old shoes.

PAPA. Katrin's shoes.

CHRISTINE (*rising and coming* R. *of* MAMA). Mama, Teacher says this week I'll need a new notebook.

MAMA. How much it will be?

CHRISTINE. A dime.

MAMA (*giving her a dime*). For the notebook. You don't lose it.

CHRISTINE. I won't lose it. (*She wraps it in her handkerchief.*)

MAMA. You take care when you blow your nose.

CHRISTINE. I'll take care. (*She returns to her seat.*)

PAPA. Is all, Mama?

MAMA. Is all for this week. Is good. We do not have to go to the Bank. (*She starts to gather up the few remaining coins.* KATRIN *leaves the group, comes and sits on steps, front.*)

NELS (*rising*). Mama. . . . (*She looks up, catching an urgency in his tone.* PAPA *suspends smoking for a moment.*) Mama, I'll be graduating from grammar school next month. Could I . . . could I go on to High, do you think?

MAMA (*pleased*). You want to go to High School?

NELS. I'd like to . . . if you think I could.

MAMA. Is good.

(PAPA *nods approvingly.*)

NELS (*awkwardly*). It . . . it'll cost a little money. I've got it all written down. (*Producing a piece of paper from his pocket.*) Carfare, clothes, notebooks, things I'll really need. I figured it out with Cy Nichols. He went to High last year.

(PAPA *rises and comes behind* MAMA *to look at the paper* NELS *puts before them.*)

MAMA. Get the *Little* Bank, Christine.

(CHRISTINE *gets a small box from the dresser.*)

KATRIN (*from the steps—herself again, in the present—looking out front*). The Little Bank! That was the most important thing in the whole house. It was a box we used to keep for emergencies—like the time when Dagmar had croup and Papa had to go and get medicine to put in the steam kettle. I can *smell* that medicine now! The things that came out of the Little Bank! Mama was always going to buy herself a

warm coat out of it, when there was enough; only there never was.

(*Meanwhile,* MAMA *has been counting the contents.*)

NELS (*anxiously*). Is there enough, Mama?

MAMA (*shaking her head*). Is not much in the Little Bank right now. We give to the dentist, you remember? And for your roller skates?

NELS (*his face falling*). I know. And there's your warm coat you've been saving for.

MAMA. The coat I can get another time. But even so . . . (*She shakes her head.*)

CHRISTINE. You mean Nels can't go to High?

MAMA. Is not enough here. We do not want to have to go to the Bank, do we?

NELS. No, Mama, no. I'll work in Dillon's grocery after school.

(MAMA *writes a figure on the paper and starts to count on her fingers.* PAPA *looks over, and does the sum in his head.*)

PAPA. Is not enough.

MAMA (*finishing on her fingers against her collarbone*). No, is not enough.

PAPA (*taking his pipe out of his mouth and looking at it a long time*). I give up tobacco.

(MAMA *looks at him, almost speaks, then just touches his sleeve, writes another figure, and starts on her fingers again.*)

CHRISTINE. I'll mind the Maxwell children Friday nights. Katrin can help me.

(MAMA *writes another figure.* PAPA *looks over—calculates again, nods with satisfaction.*)

MAMA (*triumphantly*). Is good! Is enough!

NELS. Gee! (*He moves beside* PAPA *down* R. *and starts to play with a wire puzzle.*)

MAMA. We do not have to go to the Bank.

(DAGMAR *returns, without the cat.*)

DAGMAR (*hearing the last line*). Where is the Bank?

CHRISTINE (*leaving the table, moving down* L., *cutting out the picture which she colored*). Downtown.

DAGMAR. What's it look like?

CHRISTINE. Just a building.

DAGMAR (*sitting on the bench, below the table*). Like a prison?

CHRISTINE (sharply). No, nothing like a prison.

DAGMAR. Well, then, why does Mama always say "We don't want to go to the Bank"?

CHRISTINE. Because . . . well, because no one ever wants to go to the Bank.

DAGMAR. Why not?

CHRISTINE. Because if we went to the Bank all the time, there'd be no money left there. And then if we couldn't pay our rent, they'd turn us out like Mrs. Jensen down the street.

DAGMAR. You mean, it's like saving some of your candy for tomorrow?

MAMA (busy with coffee and cups at the stove and the dresser). Yes, my Dagmar. Is exactly like saving your candy.

DAGMAR. But if . . . if all the other people go to the Bank, then there won't be any money left for us, either.

NELS (kindly). It isn't like that, Dagmar. Everyone can only get so much.

DAGMAR. How much?

NELS. However much you've got there . . . put away. You see, it's *our* money that we put there, to keep safe.

DAGMAR. When did we put it there?

NELS. I . . . I don't know when. A long time back, I guess. Wasn't it, Mama?

MAMA. Is enough about the Bank.

DAGMAR. How much money have we got in the Bank?

NELS. I don't know. How much, Mama?

MAMA. Enough. (During the last speeches AUNT TRINA appears from the wings down front L. She is a timid, mouselike little woman of about 40, with some prettiness about her. She wears her hat and coat, and a pathetic feather boa. She comes up the street and knocks on the house door. MAMA, hearing the knock.) Was the door?

CHRISTINE (quickly moving). If it's the aunts, I'm going to my boodwar.[2]

KATRIN (rising, entering the scene). And I'm going to my study.

MAMA (stopping them). You cannot run away.

We must be polite to the aunts. (She opens the door.) Why, is Trina!

PAPA. Trina, and all by herself!

MAMA. Say good evening to Aunt Trina, children.

CHILDREN (together). Good evening, Aunt Trina.

TRINA. Good evening, children. How well they all look. (She comes above the table L.)

MAMA. You have a feather boa. Is new. (Inspecting it.) Beautiful.

TRINA (simpering a little). It was a present.

MAMA (smiling). A present! Look, Lars. Trina has a present.

PAPA (feeling it). Is fine. (He puts TRINA's hat, coat, and boa on the chest under the window.)

MAMA. Jenny and Sigrid don't come with you, Trina?

TRINA (embarrassed). No, I . . . I didn't tell them I was coming. I want to talk to you, Marta.

MAMA (smiling). So? Sit then, and we talk. (She puts her in PAPA's chair, L. of the table.)

TRINA (nervously agitated). Could we talk alone?

MAMA. Alone?

TRINA. If you wouldn't mind.

MAMA. Children, you leave us alone a little. I call you. Dagmar, you go with Katrin.

KATRIN (protesting). Oh, but, Mama . . .

MAMA (firmly). Katrin, you take Dagmar!

KATRIN. Yes, Mama. (Pushing DAGMAR, resentfully.) Come on.

(The CHILDREN go out back L.)

MAMA. Now—what is it, Trina?

TRINA (looking down, embarrassed). Marta . . .

MAMA (helpfully). Yes?

TRINA. Oh, no, I can't say it.

MAMA (anxiously). Trina, what is it?

---

2. **boodwar:** an exaggerated pronunciation of *boudoir*, a woman's bedroom, dressing room, or private sitting room.

TRINA. It's . . . something very personal.

MAMA. You want Lars should go outside?

TRINA. Would you mind, Lars? Just for a minute?

PAPA (*good-humoredly*). No, I go. I know what women's secrets are. (*Teasing.*) As your Uncle Chris say—"Vomen! Pff!"

MAMA. You have your pipe, Lars? Is fine night. (*PAPA takes out his pipe—then lays it down.*) What is it?

PAPA. I forget. I give up tobacco.

MAMA. Is still some tobacco in your pouch? (*PAPA nods.*) Then you do not give up tobacco till you have finish. You give up *more* tobacco—not the tobacco you already have.

PAPA. Is not right, Marta. (*He pats her, takes his pipe, and goes out L., standing outside the house, under the lamppost, and looking up at the stars, smoking.*)

MAMA (R. *of table*). So, Trina. Now. What is it?

TRINA (L. *of table*). Marta . . . I want to get married.

MAMA. You mean . . . you want to get married, or there is someone you want to marry?

TRINA. There's someone I want to marry.

MAMA. Does *he* want to marry *you*?

TRINA (*sitting on bench*). He says he does.

MAMA (*delighted*). Trina! Is wonderful! (*She sits beside her.*)

TRINA (*crying a little*). I think it is.

MAMA. Who is?

TRINA. Mr. Thorkelson.

MAMA. From the Funeral Parlor? (*TRINA nods.* MAMA *nods, speculatively, but with less enthusiasm.*)

TRINA. I know he isn't very handsome or . . . or tall. I know it isn't what most people would think a very nice profession, but . . .

MAMA. You love him, Trina. (*TRINA nods ecstatically.*) Then is good. (*She pats* TRINA's *hand.*)

TRINA. Marta, will you . . . will you help me tell the others?

MAMA. Oh . . . Jenny and Sigrid . . . they do not know?

TRINA. No. I was afraid they'd laugh at me. But if *you* tell them . . .

MAMA. Jenny will not like you tell me first.

TRINA (*desperately*). I can't help that. You've got to tell them not to laugh at me. If they laugh at me, I'll . . . I'll kill myself.

MAMA (*with decision*). Jenny and Sigrid will not laugh. I promise you, Trina.

TRINA. Oh, thank you, Marta, and . . . Uncle Chris?

MAMA (*with some seriousness*). Ah!

TRINA. Will you talk to him?

MAMA. It is Mr. Thorkelson who must talk to Uncle Chris. Always it is the husband who must talk to the head of the family.

TRINA. Yes. I know, but . . . well, Uncle Chris is so very frightening. He's so big and black, and he shouts so. And Mr. Thorkelson is (*gesturing a very small man*) . . . well, kind of timid, really.

MAMA (*gently*). But Trina, if he is to be your husband, he must learn not to be timid. You do not want husband should be timid. *You* are timid. It is not good when *both* are timid. (*Then firmly.*) No! Jenny and Sigrid I speak to, but Mr. Thorkelson must go to Uncle Chris.

PAPA (*re-enters the house*). Marta, Trina, I do not want to interrupt your talk, but Jenny and Sigrid are coming.

TRINA (*alarmed*). Oh, dear! (*She rises, quickly.*)

PAPA. I see them get off the cable car. They came up the hill.

TRINA (*in a flurry*). I'd better go to your room for a minute. (*She starts for the door, turns back, gets her things from the chest, and runs out, carrying them, back L. Meanwhile,* MAMA *has been whispering the news to* PAPA.)

MAMA. The coffee is ready—I get more cups.

(*During the above,* AUNTS JENNY *and* SIGRID *have entered from the wings L., front.* JENNY *is a domineering woman in her fifties,* SIGRID, *whining and complaining.)*

SIGRID *(in the street).* Wait, Jenny, I must get my breath. This hill kills me every time I climb it.

JENNY. You climbed bigger hills than that in the old country.

SIGRID. I was a *girl* in the old country.

*(They march to the door and knock—*SIGRID *following* JENNY.*)*

MAMA *(opening the door to them).* Jenny. Sigrid. Is surprise. *(To* SIGRID.*)* Where's Ole?

SIGRID. Working. He's always working. I never see anything of him at all.

MAMA *(crossing to the stove for coffeepot).* Is good to work.

SIGRID. It's good to see your husband once in a while, too. *(Sits above table* L.*)*

JENNY *(no nonsense about her).* Has Trina been here? *(*L. *of table.)*

MAMA *(*R. *of table).* Trina?

JENNY. She's gone somewhere. And she doesn't know anyone but *you.* . . .

MAMA. That is what *you* think.

JENNY. What do you mean by that?

MAMA. Give Lars your coat. I give you some coffee. Then we talk about Trina.

SIGRID *(as* PAPA *helps with coats).* She *has* been here?

MAMA. Yes, she has been here. *(Pouring coffee and passing cups.)*

JENNY. What did Trina want?

MAMA. She want to talk to me.

JENNY. What about?

MAMA. Marriage.

SIGRID. What?

MAMA *(pouring calmly).* Marriage. *(Passing* SIGRID's *cup.)* Trina wants to get married.

JENNY *(seated* L. *of table).* That's no news. Of course she wants to get married. Every old maid wants to get married. *(She rolls up her veil.)*

MAMA. There is someone who wants to marry Trina.

JENNY. Who'd want to marry Trina?

MAMA. Mr. Thorkelson.

SIGRID. Peter Thorkelson? Little Peter? *(She gestures a midget.)*

MAMA. He is not so little.

SIGRID. He's hardly bigger than my Arne— and Arne is not ten yet.

MAMA. So he is hardly bigger than your Arne. Does every husband have to be big man?

JENNY. Trina's making it up. That happens with old maids when they get to Trina's age.

MAMA *(firmly).* No, Jenny—it is true. Mr. Thorkelson wants to marry Trina.

JENNY *(changing her tactics slightly).* Mr. Thorkelson. She'd be the laughing stock. *(She laughs, rising and moving* L.*)*

MAMA *(moving to her).* Jenny, Trina is here. She will come in in a minute. This is serious for her. You will not laugh at her.

JENNY. I shall do what I please.

MAMA. No, Jenny, you will not.

JENNY. And why won't I?

MAMA. Because I will not let you.

JENNY. And how will you stop me?

MAMA. If you laugh at Trina, I will tell her of the time before your wedding when your husband try to run away.

SIGRID *(rising, intrigued).* What is that?

JENNY. Who told you that?

MAMA. I know.

SIGRID *(intrigued—stealing around and below the table).* Erik . . . tried to run away?

JENNY. It's not true.

MAMA. Then you do not mind if I tell Trina.

JENNY. Uncle Chris told you.

SIGRID *(tenaciously).* Tried to run away?

MAMA. It does not matter, Sigrid. Jenny will not laugh at Trina now. Nor will you! For if *you* laugh at her, I will tell her of your wedding night with Ole, when you cry all the time, and he send you back to Mother.

PAPA (with sudden enjoyment). This I do *not* know!

MAMA (reprovingly). Is no need you should know. I do not tell these stories for spite —only so they do not laugh at Trina. Call her, Lars. You like more coffee, Jenny? Sigrid?

(PAPA *goes to the door back* L., *calls "Trina."* MAMA *pours coffee for* JENNY. MR. HYDE *reappears down front* L., *and lets himself into the house. The* AUNTS *rise, standing in line with* MAMA.)

MR. HYDE (seeing company). Oh, I beg your pardon. I was not aware . . .

MAMA. Mr. Hyde, these are my sisters.

MR. HYDE. Enchanted, ladies, Madame, Madame. The Three Graces.[3] (He bows. SIGRID *giggles coyly. He goes to the door back* L.) You will excuse me?

MAMA. Sure, Mr. Hyde.

MR. HYDE. I shall be in my room. (He goes out.)

JENNY (moving L. of table again). So that's your famous boarder. Has he paid you his rent yet? Three months he's been here, hasn't he?

MAMA (R. of table). Is hard to ask. Surely he will pay soon.

JENNY (with a snort). Surely he won't! If I ran my boarding house the way you run this place . . .

PAPA. Maybe your boarders wouldn't always leave you.

JENNY. If Marta thinks she's going to get the warm coat she's always talking about out of *that* one . . .

MAMA. Jenny, Mr. Hyde is a gentleman. He reads to us aloud. Wonderful books . . . Longfellow, and Charles Dickens, and Fenimore Kipling.[4] (TRINA *steals back.* MAMA, *seeing her hesitant in the doorway.*) Come in, Trina. The coffee is getting cold. (She pours a cup. There is a silence.) I tell them.

JENNY. Why did you come to Marta first?

PAPA (beside her L.). She thought Marta would understand.

JENNY. Aren't Sigrid and I married women, too?

PAPA. You have been married longer than Marta. She think maybe you forget.

JENNY. What sort of a living does Mr. Thorkelson make?

TRINA (on bench below table). I . . . I haven't asked.

SIGRID (R. of table). Can he keep you?

TRINA. I don't think he would have asked me to marry him if he couldn't.

JENNY. Maybe he thinks you are going to keep *him*.

MAMA (warningly). Jenny!

SIGRID. Maybe he thinks Trina will have a dowry[5] like the girls at home.

TRINA. Well, why shouldn't I? You all had dowries . . .

JENNY. We were married in Norway. And our parents were alive. Where would your dowry come from, I'd like to know?

TRINA. Uncle Chris. He's head of the family.

JENNY. And who will ask him?

TRINA. He won't need asking. When Mr. Thorkelson goes to see him . . .

JENNY. Uncle Chris will eat him!

SIGRID (giggling maliciously). Little Peter and Uncle Chris!

MAMA (with meaning). Maybe Uncle Chris will tell him some family stories. He knows many, does Uncle Chris.

(The AUNTS *put down their cups, discomfited.*)

JENNY (to change the subject). Where are the

---

3. **Three Graces:** in Greek mythology, three sister goddesses.
4. **Fenimore Kipling:** a confusion of the names of two authors, James Fenimore Cooper and Rudyard Kipling.
5. **dowry** (dou′rē): property that a woman brings to her husband at marriage.

children? Aren't we going to see them before we go?

PAPA. Of course. I'll call them. *(He goes to the door and does so, shouting.)* Children! You aunts are *leaving!*

CHILDREN'S VOICES *(eagerly shouting back).* Coming, Papa!

JENNY. You come with us, Trina?

MAMA. I think maybe Trina like to stay here and listen to Mr. Hyde read to us. You like, Trina?

TRINA. Well, if I wouldn't be in the way. I asked Mr. Thorkelson to call for me here. He'll see me home. I'll help you with the coffee things. *(She takes the tray of coffee cups and goes into the pantry.)*

(KATRIN returns back L. She carries her diary. DAGMAR follows her, and behind them, CHRISTINE.)

KATRIN *and* DAGMAR *(curtseying).* Good evening, Aunt Sigrid. Good evening, Aunt Jenny.

(CHRISTINE sketches a perfunctory curtsey without speaking.)

JENNY. Where have *you* all been hiding yourselves?

DAGMAR *(going into the pantry).* We've been in Christine's boodwar.

JENNY. Her *what?*

MAMA. Christine makes the little closet into a boudoir. I give her those bead portieres,[6] Jenny, that you lend us when we come from the old country.

SIGRID. And what does she do there?

CHRISTINE *(impertinently).* What people usually do in boudoirs.

MAMA. Christine, that is rude. It is her little place to herself.

(NELS enters, back L.)

NELS. Hello, Aunt Sigrid. Hello, Aunt Jenny.

SIGRID *(shaking hands).* Good evening, Nels! My, how tall he is getting!

MAMA *(proudly).* Yes, is almost as tall as his Papa.

(NELS sits on the chest under the windows.)

SIGRID. He looks to me as if he was outgrowing his strength. Dagmar was looking pale, too. *(DAGMAR returns now, carrying the cat again. SIGRID, jumping.)* Goodness, what a horrid-looking cat.

DAGMAR. She's not. She's beautiful.

PAPA. Is her new friend. She goes with Dagmar everywhere.

CHRISTINE *(seated, above table).* She does. First thing you know, she'll have the cat sleeping with her.

DAGMAR *(eagerly).* Oh, Mama, can I? Can I, Mama? *(She comes to the bench and sits.)*

JENNY. Certainly not. Don't you know a cat draws breath from a sleeping child? You wouldn't want to wake up some morning *smothered,* would you?

DAGMAR. I wouldn't care. Elizabeth can have *all* my breath! *(She blows into the cat's face.)* There!

JENNY *(putting on gloves).* Elizabeth—what a very silly name for a cat.

NELS *(rising).* It's a very silly name for *that* cat. It's a Tom.

MAMA. Nels, how you know?

NELS. I looked!

DAGMAR. How can you tell?

NELS. You can.

DAGMAR. But how?

MAMA *(quickly warning).* Nels, you do not say how!

NELS *(to DAGMAR).* So you'd better think up another name for him.

DAGMAR. I won't. He's Elizabeth. And he's going to *stay* Elizabeth.

PAPA. We could call him *Uncle* Elizabeth!

DAGMAR *(laughing delightedly).* Uncle Elizabeth! Do you hear, Elizabeth? You're called *Uncle* Elizabeth now!

---

6. **portieres** (pôr tyerz′): curtains hung in a doorway.

JENNY. Such foolishness! Well, goodbye, all. Marta. Lars.

(Goodbyes are exchanged all around, the CHILDREN curtseying formally.)

MAMA. Goodbye, Jenny. Goodbye, Sigrid. Nels, you go tell Mr. Hyde we are ready for the reading.

(NELS goes off, back L. The AUNTS leave and walk down L. MAMA stands in the doorway, waving goodbye.)

SIGRID *(as they go)*. Well, I never thought we'd live to see Trina get married.

JENNY. She's not married yet. She's got Uncle Chris to deal with first.

(They disappear into wings L.)

MAMA *(returning to the room and calling into the pantry)*. Trina, they have gone. Dagmar, you put Elizabeth out for the night now.

DAGMAR *(correcting her)*. Uncle Elizabeth!

MAMA. Uncle Elizabeth. *(DAGMAR goes out into the pantry with the cat. TRINA comes in as MR. HYDE and NELS return back L.)* Mr. Hyde, this is my sister Trina.

MR. HYDE *(bowing)*. Enchanted!

MAMA *(seating herself R. of the table)*. Mr. Hyde reads to us *The Tales from Two Cities*.[7] Is beautiful story. But sad.

TRINA *(brightly)*. I like sad stories. *(She gets out her handkerchief.)*

(The whole family group themselves around the table, MAMA R. of table in her old chair— PAPA above her. TRINA R. above table, NELS L. above the table. DAGMAR returning and seating herself on the floor below MAMA. MR. HYDE takes the armchair L. of table. CHRISTINE sits on the floor below the table. KATRIN is on the steps R. front.)

MR. HYDE. Tonight, I would like to finish it.

MAMA. Is good.

MR. HYDE. Are you ready?

CHILDREN. Yes, please, Mr. Hyde.

MR. HYDE. I will go on from where we left off. *(He starts to read.)* "In the black prison of the Conciergerie, the doomed of the day awaited their fate. They were in number as the weeks of the year. Fifty-two were to roll that afternoon on the life-tide of the City to the boundless, everlasting sea. . . ."

(The lights dim down slowly, leaving spots on KATRIN and MR. HYDE only.)

KATRIN. I don't think I shall ever forget that night. It was almost midnight when he came to the end, and none of us had noticed.

MR. HYDE *(reading from the last page)*. "It is a far, far better thing that I do than I have ever done; it is a far, far better rest that I go to than I have ever known." *(He closes the book.)* "The End."

(The R. turntable revolves in again. KATRIN rises from the step and crosses to her desk on the turntable.)

KATRIN. I wrote in my diary that night before I went to bed. *(She reads aloud from it.)* "Tonight Mr. Hyde finished *The Tale of Two Cities*. The closing chapters are indeed superb. How beautiful a thing is self-sacrifice. I wish there were someone I could die for." *(She sits looking out front.)* Mr. Hyde read us all kinds of books. He thrilled us with *Treasure Island*, and terrified us with "The Hound of the Baskervilles." I can still remember the horror in his voice as he read. . . .

MR. HYDE *(still on the main stage in his spot, reading)*. "Dr. Mortimer looked strangely at us for an instant, and his voice sank almost to a whisper as he answered, 'Mr. Holmes, they were the footprints of a gigantic *hound!*' " *(He closes the book.)* We

---

7. *The Tales from Two Cities:* actually *A Tale of Two Cities,* a novel by Charles Dickens.

will continue tomorrow night. If you are interested.

KATRIN (*looking out front*). If we were interested! You couldn't have kept us from it. It meant a lot to Mama, too, because Nels stopped going nights to the street corner to hang about with the neighborhood boys. The night they got into trouble for breaking into Mr. Dillon's store, Nels was home with us. And sometimes Mr. Hyde read us poetry. "The Lady of the Lake" . . . and the "Rime of the Ancient Mariner."

MR. HYDE (*reading*).

"About, about, in reel and rout
The death-fires danced at night.
The water, like a witch's oils,
Burnt green and blue and white."

(*His spot goes out, and the traveler curtains close on the kitchen scene.*)

KATRIN. There were many nights I couldn't sleep for the way he had set my imagination dancing. (*Reading from her diary again.*) "What a wonderful thing is literature, transporting us to realms unknown." (*To herself.*) And all the time my school teacher kept telling me that I ought to write about things I knew. I did write a piece for her once about Uncle Chris, and she said it wasn't nice to write like that about a member of one's own family. Papa called Mama's Uncle Chris a black Norwegian, because of his dark hair and fierce mustache, but there were others in the family who claimed that he was black in a different way. The aunts, for example.

(*Spot goes up on L. front turntable, representing* JENNY's *kitchen.* JENNY *and* TRINA *are discovered.* JENNY *is rolling pastry.* TRINA *is crocheting.*)

JENNY. Black! I'll say he's black. Black in his heart. Cursing and swearing. . . .

TRINA. Marta says that's only because it hurts him to walk.

JENNY. Rubbish. I know all about his limp and the accident back in the old country— but has anyone ever heard him complain? Marta's always making excuses for him.

TRINA. I know . . . but he *is* good to the children. All those oranges he's always sending them. . . .

JENNY. Oranges! What good is oranges? Turn 'em yellow. They're the only things he's ever been known to give away, anyway. He's got other uses for his money.

TRINA. What you mean?

JENNY. That woman he lives with!

TRINA. He says she's his housekeeper.

(SIGRID *comes through the curtains* C. *She crosses to* JENNY *and* TRINA.)

SIGRID. Jenny. Trina. What do you think? What do you think Uncle Chris has done now?

TRINA. What?

JENNY. Tell us.

SIGRID. You know my little Arne's knee— that fall he had two months ago? The man at the drugstore said it was only a bruise, but today it was hurting him again, so I left him home when I went to do the marketing. I asked Mrs. Schultz next door to keep an eye on him, and who should turn up, not ten minutes after I'd gone, but Uncle Chris. And what do you think?

JENNY. Well, tell us, if you're going to. Don't keep *asking* us.

SIGRID. He took one look at Arne's knee, bundled him into that rattletrap old automobile of his, and rushed him straight off to the hospital. I've just come from there . . . and what do you think? They've operated! They've got him in Plaster of Paris!

JENNY. Without consulting you?

SIGRID. It seems the doctor is a friend of his . . . that's why he did it. No, this time he's gone too far. To put a child of Arne's age through all that pain. They wouldn't even let me *see* Arne. I'm going to tell Uncle

Chris exactly what I think of him. . .

JENNY. That's right.

SIGRID. I'm going to tell him right now. *(Weakening a little.)* Come with me, Jenny.

JENNY. Well, I . . . No, I can't leave my baking.

SIGRID. You must, Jenny. We must stand together. You come, too, Trina, and ask about your dowry. *Make* him give it to you.

TRINA. Oh, but . . . Marta said Mr. Thorkelson should do that. . .

JENNY. Well, then, go and get Mr. Thorkelson. Go down to the mortuary and get him now. Sigrid is right. We girls have got to stand together!

(Blackout. Turntable revolves out.)

KATRIN *(at her desk).* Nobody knew where Uncle Chris lived. That was part of the mystery about him. He used to roam up and down the state buying up farms and ranches that had gone to pieces, and bullying them back into prosperity. Then he'd sell at a profit and move on again. Two or three times a year he'd descend on the city in his automobile and come roaring and stamping into our house.

(Her light dims. The sound of a very old and noisy Ford car changing gears is heard off L. A grinding and screaming as it comes to a standstill. Then UNCLE CHRIS'S VOICE, shouting.)

UNCLE CHRIS'S VOICE. Marta! Lars! Children— vere are you?

(The curtains part on the kitchen again. Outside in the street is UNCLE CHRIS'S car—an antique model. A woman is seated beside the empty driver's seat. UNCLE CHRIS is knocking on the house door. He is an elderly, powerful, swarthy man with a limp. In the kitchen, NELS and CHRISTINE are cowering.)

UNCLE CHRIS. Marta! Lars!

CHRISTINE *(scared).* It's Uncle Chris.

NELS *(equally so).* I know.

CHRISTINE. What'll we do?

UNCLE CHRIS. Is nobody home? Hey, there— is nobody home? *(Banging on the door.)* Hey—someone—answer the door. *(He tries the door handle, it opens and he strides, limpingly in. He has a strong accent, and uses the Norwegian pronunciation of the children's names.)* So, vat is—you do not answer the door? You do not hear me calling? *(The CHILDREN cower silently.)* I say, you do not hear me calling? I do not call loud enough?

CHRISTINE. Y-yes, Uncle Chris.

UNCLE CHRIS. Which yes? Yes, you do not hear me—or yes I do not call loud enough?

NELS. We heard you, Uncle Chris.

UNCLE CHRIS. Then why you do not come?

NELS. We . . . we were just going to.

(KATRIN has left her desk and come up the steps.)

UNCLE CHRIS. Let me look at you. You too, Katrinë, do not stand there—come and let me look at you. *(They line up as though for inspection. He thumps NELS between the shoulderblades.)* Stand tall! *(They all straighten up.)* Um-hum. By the dresser, where the marks are. (NELS *goes to the wall by the dresser back* R. UNCLE CHRIS *compares his mark with the previous one—and makes a new one on the wall, writing by it.)* Two inches. Two inches in . . . *(Examining the date.)* Six months. Is good. Christinë. (CHRISTINE *replaces* NELS.) Show me your teeth. *(She does so.)* You brush them goot? *(She nods.)* Nils, there is a box of oranges in the automobile. You fetch them in. (NELS *goes out* L. UNCLE CHRIS *measures* CHRISTINE.) Where is the little von? Dagmar?

KATRIN. She's sick, Uncle Chris.

UNCLE CHRIS *(arrested).* Sick? What is the matter with her?

KATRIN. It's her ear. She's had an earache for

two days. Bad earache. Mama sent for the doctor.

UNCLE CHRIS. Goot doctor? What he say?

KATRIN. He's in there now. *(She points off, back L. Meanwhile* CHRISTINE *has remained standing by the wall, afraid to move.)*

UNCLE CHRIS. I go in. *(He starts to the door back L., but* MAMA *and* DR. JOHNSON *come into the room as he does so. During this,* NELS *has gone to the car, and with nervous smiles at the woman seated by the driver's seat, has heaved out a huge box of oranges. He returns with the oranges during the ensuing scene.)*

MAMA *(greeting him)*. Uncle Chris.

UNCLE CHRIS. How is with Dagmar?

MAMA. Is bad. Doctor, this is my uncle, Mr. Halvorsen.

DOCTOR. How do you do, sir? *(He goes for his hat and bag which are on the bench below the window.)*

UNCLE CHRIS. What is with the child?

DOCTOR. We must get her to a hospital. At once. We'll have to operate.

MAMA. Operate?

DOCTOR. I'm afraid so.

MAMA. Can wait? Until my husband comes home from work?

DOCTOR. I'm afraid not. Her best chance is for us to operate immediately.

MAMA *(after a second)*. We go. *(She goes to the dresser for the Little Bank.)*

UNCLE CHRIS *(who has watched her decision with approval, turns to the doctor, moving to him down L)*. What is with the child?

DOCTOR. I'm afraid it's a mastoid.[8]

UNCLE CHRIS. Ah . . . then you operate immediately.

DOCTOR *(resenting this)*. That's what I said.

UNCLE CHRIS. Immediately!

MAMA *(who has poured the contents of the Little Bank onto the table)*. Doctor . . . is enough?

DOCTOR *(L. of table)*. I was thinking of the County Hospital.

MAMA. No. No. We pay. Is enough?

KATRIN. If there isn't, we can go to the Bank.

CHRISTINE. We've got a bank account.

MAMA. Is enough without we go to the Bank, Doctor? My husband is carpenter. Make good money.

UNCLE CHRIS. If there is need of money, I pay.

DOCTOR *(mainly in dislike of* UNCLE CHRIS*)*. It'll be all right. We'll take her to the Clinic. You pay what you can afford.

UNCLE CHRIS. Goot. Goot. I have a patient there already. My nephew, Arne. They operate this morning on his knee.

DOCTOR. Are you a physician, sir?

UNCLE CHRIS. I am better physician than most doctors. Nils, there, my other nephew, he become doctor when he grow up.

*(*NELS, *who has just returned, looks up, surprised.)*

DOCTOR *(chilly)*. Oh, indeed . . . very interesting. Well, now, if you will have the child at the Clinic in . . . shall we say an hour's time . . .

UNCLE CHRIS *(striding across below table)*. The child will be at the Clinic in *ten minutes'* time. I haf my automobile.

DOCTOR. I can hardly make arrangements in ten minutes.

UNCLE CHRIS *(R. of table)*. *I* make arrangements. I know doctors.

MAMA. Uncle Chris, Dr. Johnson arrange. He is good doctor.

DOCTOR *(ironically)*. Thank you, Madam.

MAMA. You go, Doctor. We come.

DOCTOR. Very well, in an hour, then. And Dagmar will be well taken care of, I promise you. I will do the operation myself.

UNCLE CHRIS. I watch.

DOCTOR. You will do no such thing, sir.

UNCLE CHRIS. Always I watch operations. I am head of family.

---

8. **mastoid** (mas'toid): an inflammation of that part of the temporal bone that sticks out behind the ear.

DOCTOR. I allow no one to attend my operations.

UNCLE CHRIS. Are so bad?

DOCTOR *(to* MAMA*)*. Mrs. Hanson, if I am to undertake this operation and the care of your child, it must be on the strict understanding that this gentleman does not come near either me or my patient.

MAMA. Yes, Doctor, I talk to him. . . . You go to hospital now, please.

DOCTOR. Very well. But you understand . . . nowhere near me, or I withdraw from the case. *(He goes.)*

UNCLE CHRIS. I go see Dagmar.

MAMA *(stopping him above table)*. Wait. Uncle Chris, is kind of you, but Dagmar is sick. You frighten her.

UNCLE CHRIS. I frighten her?

MAMA. Yes, Uncle Chris. You frighten everyone. . . .

UNCLE CHRIS *(amazed)*. I??

MAMA. Everyone but me. Even the girls. . . . Jenny, Sigrid, Trina . . . they are frightened of you.

UNCLE CHRIS. The girls! Vomen! Pff!

MAMA. And the children, too. So Nels and I get Dagmar. You drive us to hospital in your automobile, but you do not frighten Dagmar. And you leave doctor alone. Dr. Johnson is *fine* doctor. You come with me, Nels. You carry Dagmar.

*(*NELS *and* MAMA *go out back* L. UNCLE CHRIS *stands in amazement and puzzlement. The* TWO GIRLS *watch him, hardly daring to move.)*

UNCLE CHRIS *(coming down* L. *of table)*. Is true? I frighten you? Christinë . . . Katrinë . . . you are frightened of me? Come, I ask you. Tell me the truth. You are frightened of me?

KATRIN *(tremulously)*. A . . . a little, Uncle Chris.

UNCLE CHRIS *(on bench)*. No? And you, Christinë?

CHRISTINE. Y . . . yes, Uncle Chris.

UNCLE CHRIS. But Nils . . . Nils is a boy . . . he is not frightened?

CHRISTINE. Not . . . not as much as we are. . . .

UNCLE CHRIS. But he is frightened?

CHRISTINE. Yes, Uncle Chris.

UNCLE CHRIS *(with a roar)*. But why? What is there to be frightened of? I am your Uncle Chris . . . why do I frighten you?

CHRISTINE. I don't know.

UNCLE CHRIS. But that is bad. Very bad. The aunts, yes, I like to frighten them. *(The* GIRLS *giggle.)* That makes you laugh. *(He crosses to them.)* You do not like the aunts? Come, tell me. You do not like the aunts. Say!

KATRIN. Not . . . very much, Uncle Chris.

UNCLE CHRIS. And which do you not like the most? Jenny . . . Sigrid . . . Trina. . . . Tell me—huh?

KATRIN. I think I like Aunt Jenny least. She's so . . . so bossy.

CHRISTINE. I can't stand Aunt Sigrid. Always whining and complaining.

UNCLE CHRIS *(with a great roar of laughter)*. Is good. Jenny, bossy. Sigrid, whining. Is true! But your Mama, she is different. And she cook goot. The aunts, they cannot cook at all. Only you do not tell your Mama we have talked of them so. It is a secret, for us. Then you cannot be frightened of me any more . . . when we have secret. I tell you my secret, too. *I* do not like the aunts. And so that they do not bother me, I frighten them and shout at them. You I do not shout at if you are goot children, and clean your teeth goot, and eat your oranges. *(He takes out a snuffbox and partakes of its contents.)*

(On the cue "You I do not shout at" the posse of AUNTS *appears, in outdoor clothes, accompanied by* MR. THORKELSON, *a terrified little man. They come in down* L. *and start up to the house.)*

JENNY *(striding to the front door and entering*

the house, with the others following).
Uncle Chris, Sigrid has something to say
to you.

SIGRID *(with false bravery).* Uncle Chris, you
took Arne to the hospital. . . .

UNCLE CHRIS *(R. of table).* Yes, I take Arne to
the hospital. And now we take Dagmar to
the hospital, so you do not clutter up the
place.

JENNY *(L. of table).* What's the matter with
Dagmar?

CHRISTINE. It's her ear. Dr. Johnson's going to
operate.

SIGRID *(catching her favorite word).* Operate?
This is some more of Uncle Chris's doing.
Did you hear what he did to Arne?

UNCLE CHRIS *(turning on her).* Sigrid, you are
a whining old fool, and you get out of
here. . . .

SIGRID *(deflating).* We'd better go, Jenny. . . .

JENNY *(stoutly).* No . . . there has been enough
of these highhanded goings-on. . . .

UNCLE CHRIS. And you, Jenny . . . you are a
bossy old fool, and you get out of here, too,
and we take Dagmar to hospital. *(NELS*
enters, back L., carrying DAGMAR in his
arms, wrapped in a blanket.) You got her
goot, Nils?

NELS. Sure, Uncle Chris.

UNCLE CHRIS. We go.

JENNY *(getting between him and the door).*
No! You are going to hear me out. *(Weak-*
ening.) That is, you are going to hear *Sigrid*
out. . . .

UNCLE CHRIS. If you do not get out of the way
of the door before I count three, I trow you
out. And Sigrid, too, as big as she is. Von.
. . . *(SIGRID moves.)* Two. . . . *(JENNY moves.*
He looks back at the children with a wink
and a smile.) Is goot! You put her in back
of the car, Nils.

(NELS goes out, L., carrying DAGMAR, and lifts
her into the car. UNCLE CHRIS follows and
starts cranking.)

TRINA *(running to the door after him, with*
MR. THORKELSON*).* But, Uncle Chris, I want
to introduce Mr. Thorkelson. . . . *(But*
UNCLE CHRIS *ignores her, continuing to*
crank. She returns crestfallen into the
room with MR. THORKELSON. MAMA *re-*
enters back L, wearing hat and coat and
carrying a cheap little overnight case.)

MAMA. Jenny . . . Trina, we go to hospital.
(She goes to KATRIN *and* CHRISTINE.*)* You
will be good children until Mama comes
home?

THE GIRLS. Sure, Mama.

UNCLE CHRIS *(calling from the car).* Marta,
we go!

MAMA *(calling back).* I come! *(She turns to the*
children again.) There is milk in the cooler,
and fruit and cookies for your lunch.

CHRISTINE. We'll be all right, Mama. Don't
worry.

MAMA. I go now. *(She starts for the door.)*

SIGRID *(stopping her).* Marta!

MAMA. What is it?

SIGRID. You *can't* go in his automobile.

MAMA. Why not?

UNCLE CHRIS *(calling again).* Marta, we go!

MAMA. I come!

SIGRID. Because . . . because *she's* in it. The
. . . the woman!

MAMA. So it will kill me, or Dagmar, if we sit
in the automobile with her? I have see her.
She looks nice woman. *(Calling off, as she*
goes.) I come!

UNCLE CHRIS. We go! *(MAMA climbs into the*
rear of the car, which backs noisily off
during the next speeches.)

MR. THORKELSON *(in a low whisper to* TRINA*).*
Is that woman his wife?

TRINA *(nervously).* Yes. . . .

MR. THORKELSON. Yes?

TRINA *(whispering back, loudly).* No!

JENNY *(to the* GIRLS*).* Don't stand there gaping
like that, girls. *(She shoos them into the*
pantry.) Go away! Go away! *(The GIRLS go.*
JENNY *turns and sees the disappearing car*

through the open door.) Oh! They've gone! We go after them! Sigrid, you lead the way! *(She gives* SIGRID *a push and the four go out, with* JENNY *dragging* MR. THORKELSON, *and* TRINA *following. Blackout. The travelers close.)*

(Spot on R. *turntable, representing a kind of closet-room. Rollerskates hanging on the wall.* KATRIN *is seated on the floor and* CHRISTINE *on a small kitchen stepladder with glasses of milk, and cookies on plates.)*

KATRIN. How long have they been gone now?

CHRISTINE. About three hours. And I wish you wouldn't keep asking that.

KATRIN. How long do operations take? I heard Aunt Sigrid telling about Mrs. Bergman who was five hours on the table.

CHRISTINE. Aunt Sigrid's friends always have everything worse than anyone else. And it gets worse each time she tells it, too.

*(*KATRIN *smiles—drinks some milk and eats a cookie.)*

KATRIN *(with a certain melancholy enjoyment).* The house feels lonesome, doesn't it—without Mama? It's like in a book. "The sisters sat huddled in the empty house, waiting for the verdict that was to spell life or death to the little family."

CHRISTINE. Oh, don't talk such nonsense.

KATRIN. It's not nonsense.

CHRISTINE. It is, too. In the first place, we're not a little family. We're a big one. And who said anything about life or death, anyway? Always trying to make everything so dramatic!

KATRIN. Well, it *is* dramatic.

CHRISTINE. It's not. It's just . . . well, worrying. But you don't have to make a tragedy out of it.

(Pause.)

KATRIN. You're not eating anything.

CHRISTINE. I know that.

KATRIN. You're not drinking your milk, either. Aren't you hungry?

CHRISTINE. No. And you wouldn't be, either, if you'd any feeling for Mama and Dagmar, instead of just heartlessly sitting there eating and enjoying making a story out of it.

KATRIN. Oh, Chris, I'm not heartless. I do have feeling for them. I can't help it if it goes into words like that. Everything always does with me. But it doesn't mean I don't feel it. And I think we *ought* to eat. I think Mama would want us to.

(Pause. CHRISTINE hesitates a moment, then takes a bite of a cookie. They both eat in silence. The light dims on them, and the turntable revolves out. The travelers part on the hospital corridor. A main back flat representing the wall, running diagonally up from the front of the main stage L. towards the back. Down front L. is a bench, on which MAMA and NELS are sitting, holding hands, looking off. Below the bench is the elevator, and above the bench, set back a little, is a closet for brooms and mops, etc. The reception desk, at which a nurse is sitting, is R. C., towards the front. The wall goes up into darkness, and behind the nurse's desk is darkness. As the curtains open, there is a hubbub down front by the nurse's desk, where the AUNTS are haranguing UNCLE CHRIS. MR. THORKELSON stands slightly in back of them.)

SIGRID. But, Uncle Chris, I tell you I must see him!

UNCLE CHRIS *(storming)*. You don't understand English? No visitors for twenty-four hours.

SIGRID. But *you've* seen him.

UNCLE CHRIS. I am not visitor. I am exception.

SIGRID. Well, then, his mother should be an exception, too. I'll see the doctor.

UNCLE CHRIS. *I* have seen doctor. I have told him you are not goot for Arne.

SIGRID. Not good for my own son. . . .

UNCLE CHRIS. Not goot at all. You cry over him. I go now. *(He starts to do so, but JENNY pushes TRINA forward.)*

TRINA *(with desperate courage)*. Uncle Chris . . . Uncle Chris . . . I *must* speak to you.

UNCLE CHRIS. I have business.

TRINA. But, Uncle Chris . . . I want to get married.

UNCLE CHRIS. Well, then, *get* married. *(He starts off again.)*

TRINA. No, wait, I . . . I want to marry Mr. Thorkelson. Here. *(She produces him from behind her.)* Peter, this is Uncle Chris. Uncle Chris, this is Mr. Thorkelson.

UNCLE CHRIS *(staring at him)*. So?

MR. THORKELSON. How are you, sir?

UNCLE CHRIS. Busy. *(He turns again.)*

TRINA. Please, Uncle Chris . . .

UNCLE CHRIS. What is? You want to marry him? All right, marry him. I have other things to think about.

TRINA *(eagerly)*. Then . . . then you give your permission?

UNCLE CHRIS. Yes, I give my permission. If you want to be a fool, I cannot stop you.

TRINA *(gratefully)*. Oh, thank you, Uncle Chris.

UNCLE CHRIS. So. Is all?

TRINA *(anxious to escape)*. Yes, I think is all.

JENNY *(firmly)*. No!!

UNCLE CHRIS. No? *(MR. THORKELSON is pushed forward again.)*

MR. THORKELSON. Well, there . . . there was a little something else. You see, Trina mentioned . . . well, in the old country it was always usual . . . and after all, we do all come from the old country. . . .

UNCLE CHRIS. What is it? What you want?

MR. THORKELSON. Well, it's a question of Trina's . . . well, not to mince matters . . . her dowry.

UNCLE CHRIS *(shouting)*. Her what?

MR. THORKELSON *(very faintly)*. Her dowry . . .

UNCLE CHRIS. Ah. Her dowry. Trina wants a dowry. She is forty-two years old. . . .

TRINA (interrupting). No, Uncle Chris. . . .

UNCLE CHRIS (without pausing). And it is not enough she gets husband. She must have dowry.

NURSE (who has been trying to interrupt, now bangs on her desk and moves down R.). Please! Would you mind going and discussing your family matters somewhere else? This is a hospital, not a marriage bureau.

UNCLE CHRIS (after glaring at the NURSE, turns to MR. THORKELSON). You come into waiting room. I talk to you about dowry. (He strides off into the darkness behind the NURSE's desk. MR. THORKELSON, with an appealing look back at TRINA, follows him. The AUNTS now remember MAMA, sitting on the bench, and cross to her.)

JENNY. Did you hear that, Marta?

MAMA (out of a trance). What?

JENNY. Uncle Chris.

MAMA. No, I do not hear. I wait for doctor. Is two hours since they take Dagmar to operating room. More.

SIGRID. Two hours? That's nothing! When Mrs. Bergman had her gall bladder removed she was six hours on the table.

MAMA. Sigrid, I do not want to hear about Mrs. Bergman. I do not want to hear about anything. I wait for doctor. Please, you go away now. You come this evening.

TRINA. But, Marta, you can't stay here all by yourself.

MAMA. I have Nels. Please, Trina . . . I wait for doctor . . . you go now.

JENNY. We go.

TRINA. Oh, but I must wait for Peter and Uncle Chris. . . .

JENNY. We'll go next door and have some coffee. Sigrid, do you have money?

SIGRID. Yes, I . . . I have a little.

JENNY. Good. Then I treat you. We'll be next door if you want us, Marta.

(MAMA nods without looking at them, her eyes still fixed on the elevator door. The AUNTS leave, going down the steps from the stage as though they were the hospital steps, and off L. For a moment, the stage is quiet. Then a SCRUBWOMAN enters from down R., carrying a mop and pail which she puts into the closet, and then leaves. The elevator door opens and a doctor in white coat comes out, followed by an orderly, carrying a tray of dressings. They disappear up R. behind the desk. MAMA rises, agitatedly, looking after them. Then DR. JOHNSON returns from R. front, carrying his hat and bag. He sees MAMA and crosses to her, C.)

DOCTOR. Oh, Mrs. Hanson. . . .

MAMA. Doctor. . . .

DOCTOR. Well, Dagmar's fine. She came through it beautifully. She's back in bed now, sleeping off the anesthetic.

MAMA. Thank you, Doctor. (She shakes hands with him.)

DOCTOR. You're very welcome.

MAMA. Is good of you, Doctor. (She shakes hands with him again.) Where is she? I go to her now.

DOCTOR. Oh, I'm sorry, but I'm afraid that's against the rules. You shall see her tomorrow.

MAMA. Tomorrow? But, Doctor, she is so little. When she wakes up she will be frightened.

DOCTOR. The nurse will take care of her. Excellent care. You needn't worry. You see, for the first twenty-four hours, clinic patients aren't allowed to see visitors. The wards must be kept quiet.

MAMA. I will not make a sound.

DOCTOR. I'm very sorry. Tomorrow. And now . . . (He looks at his watch.) Good afternoon. (He puts on his hat and goes L., down the steps and off. MAMA stands still a moment, looking after him.)

MAMA. Come, Nels. We go find Dagmar.

NELS. But, Mama, the doctor said . . .

MAMA. We find Dagmar. *(She looks vaguely around her. She goes to the* NURSE'S *desk.)* You tell me, please, where I can find my daughter?

NURSE. What name?

MAMA. Dagmar.

NELS. Dagmar Hanson.

NURSE *(looking at her record book).* Hanson, Ward A. Along there. *(She points upstage.* MAMA *starts to go up.)* Oh, just a moment. *(*MAMA *returns.)* When did she come in?

MAMA. This morning. They just finish operation.

NURSE. Oh, well, then, I'm afraid you can't see her today. No visitors for the first twenty-four hours.

MAMA. Am not visitor. I am her Mama.

NURSE. I'm sorry, but it's against the rules.

MAMA. Just for one minute. Please.

NURSE. I'm sorry, but it's against the rules.

*(*MAMA *stands staring.* NELS *touches her arm. She looks at him, nods, trying to smile, then turns and walks with him to* L. *and down the steps.)*

MAMA. We must think of some way.

NELS. Mama, they'll let you see her tomorrow. They said so.

MAMA. If I don't see her today, how will I know that all is well with her? What can I tell Papa when he comes home from work?

NELS. The nurses will look after her, Mama. Would you like to come next door for some coffee?

MAMA *(shaking her head).* We go home. We have coffee at home. But I must see Dagmar today. *(She plods off* L. *with* NELS.*)*

(The travelers close. Spot goes up on R. *turntable.* UNCLE CHRIS *and* MR. THORKELSON *are seated on a bench and chair, as in a waiting-room. A table with a potted plant is between them. A clock on the wall points to 2:30.)*

UNCLE CHRIS *(on bench,* R.*).* Well, it comes then to this. You love my niece, Trina?

*(*MR. THORKELSON, *very scared, gulps and nods.)* You want to marry her? *(*MR. THORKELSON *nods again.)* You are in position to support her? *(*MR. THORKELSON *nods again.)* Why, then, you want dowry? *(No answer. He shouts.)* What for you want dowry?

MR. THORKELSON. Well . . . well, it would be a nice help. And it is customary.

UNCLE CHRIS. Is not customary. Who give dowries? Parents. Why? Because they are so glad they will not have to support their daughters any more, they pay money. I do not support Trina. I do not care if Trina gets married. Why then should I pay to have her married?

MR. THORKELSON. I never thought of it like that.

UNCLE CHRIS. Is insult to girl to pay dowry. If I do not give dowry, will you still marry Trina?

MR. THORKELSON. I . . . I don't know.

UNCLE CHRIS. You don't know? You don't know? You think I let Trina marry a man who will not take her without dowry?

MR. THORKELSON. No, I suppose you wouldn't.

UNCLE CHRIS. What kind of man would that be? I ask you, what kind of man would that be?

MR. THORKELSON *(fascinated—helpless).* Well, not a very nice kind of man.

UNCLE CHRIS. And are you that kind of man?

MR. THORKELSON. I . . . I don't think so.

UNCLE CHRIS *(conclusively).* Then you don't want dowry!!

MR. THORKELSON *(giving up).* No, I . . . I guess I don't.

UNCLE CHRIS *(slapping his back).* Goot. Goot. You are goot man. I like you. I give you my blessing. And I send you vedding present. I send you box of oranges!

(While he is boisterously shaking MR. THORKELSON'S *hand, blackout. Turntable revolves out. The curtain opens on the kitchen. It is empty.* MAMA *and* NELS *come up the hill from*

the L. *and let themselves into the house.*
There is silence as they take off their hats and
coats.)

MAMA *(after a moment).* Where are the girls?

NELS. I guess they're upstairs. *(Goes to door
back* L. *and calls.)* Chris! Katrin!

GIRLS' VOICES. Coming!

NELS. Shall I make you some coffee? *(MAMA
shakes her head.)* You said you'd have coffee when you got home.

MAMA. Later. First I must think.

NELS. Mama, please don't worry like that.
Dagmar's all right. You know she's all
right.

(The GIRLS *come in back* L.)

CHRISTINE *(trying to be casual,* R. *of table).*
Well, Mama, everything all right?

MAMA *(nodding).* Is all right. You have eaten?

KATRIN (L. *of table).* Yes, Mama.

MAMA. You drink your milk?

CHRISTINE. Yes, Mama.

MAMA. Is good.

CHRISTINE *(seeing her face).* Mama, something's the matter.

KATRIN *(over-dramatically).* Mama, Dagmar's
not ——? She isn't ——? Mama!

MAMA. No, Dagmar is fine. The doctor say
she is fine. *(She rises.)* What is time?

NELS. It's three o'clock.

MAMA. Three hours till Papa come home.
*(She looks around, and then goes slowly
into the pantry, back* R.)

KATRIN. Nels, what is it? There *is* something
the matter.

NELS. They wouldn't let Mama see Dagmar.
It's a rule of the hospital.

CHRISTINE. But Dagmar's all right?

NELS. Oh, yes, she's all right.

CHRISTINE *(impatiently).* Well, then . . . !

NELS. But Mama's very upset. She started
talking to me in Norwegian in the street-
car.

KATRIN *(emotionally).* What can we do?

CHRISTINE *(coldly).* You can't do anything.
When *will* they let her see Dagmar?

NELS. Tomorrow.

CHRISTINE. Well, then, we'll just have to wait
till tomorrow.

KATRIN. Chris, how can you be so callous?
Can't you see that Mama's heart is breaking?

CHRISTINE. No. I can't. And you can't, either.
People's hearts don't break.

KATRIN. They do, too.

CHRISTINE. Only in books. *(MAMA comes
back; she wears an apron, and carries a
scrub brush and a bucket of hot water.)*
Why, Mama, what are you going to do?

MAMA *(coming down front,* R. *of table).* I
scrub the floor. *(She gets down on her
knees, facing front.)*

CHRISTINE. But you scrubbed it yesterday.

MAMA. I scrub it again. *(She starts to do so.)*

KATRIN. But, Mama . . .

MAMA *(bending low).* Comes a time when
you've got to get down on your knees.

KATRIN *(to* CHRISTINE*).* Now do you believe
me?

*(*CHRISTINE, *suddenly unendurably moved,
turns and rushes from the room.)*

NELS. Mama, don't. Please don't. You must
be tired.

KATRIN *(strangely).* Let her alone, Nels.
(They stand in silence watching MAMA
scrub. Suddenly she stops.) What is it,
Mama? What is it?

MAMA *(sitting back on her haunches).* I tink
of something! *(Slowly.)* I tink I tink of
something!

*(The lights dim and the curtains close on the
kitchen. From down front* L. UNCLE CHRIS'S
*VOICE singing. The lights slowly come up on
the* L. *turntable, showing* ARNE [*a child of
about eight*] *in a hospital bed, with* UNCLE
CHRIS *beside him.)*

UNCLE CHRIS *(singing).*

"Ten t'ousand Svedes vent t'rough de veeds
   At de battle of Coppen-hagen.
Ten t'ousand Svedes went t'rough de veeds
   Chasing vun Nor-ve-gan!"

ARNE. Uncle Chris!

UNCLE CHRIS. Yes, Arne?

ARNE. Uncle Chris, does it *have* to hurt like this?

UNCLE CHRIS. If you vant it to be vell, and not to valk alvays like Uncle Chris, it does . . . for a little. Is very bad?

ARNE. It is . . . kinda . . .
   Oo—oo . . . !

UNCLE CHRIS. You sleep some now, maybe?

ARNE. I'll try. Will . . . will you stay here, Uncle Chris?

UNCLE CHRIS. Sure. Sure. I stay here. You are not frightened of Uncle Chris?

ARNE. No. Not any more.

UNCLE CHRIS. Goot. Goot. You like I sing some more?

ARNE. If you wouldn't mind. But maybe something a little . . . well, quieter.

UNCLE CHRIS (*tenderly*). Sure. Sure. (*He begins quietly to sing a Norwegian lullaby; in the midst,* ARNE *cries out.*)

ARNE. Oo—oo.

UNCLE CHRIS. Now you sleep some! (*He fixes* ARNE's *pillows for him, and resumes the lullaby, seated on his chair beside the bed. After another verse, he leans over, assuring himself that the child is asleep, as the light dims. The table revolves out.*)

(*The curtains part on the hospital corridor again. There is a different* NURSE *now at the reception desk, talking on the telephone as* MAMA *and* KATRIN *come in from* L. *and up the steps.*)

MAMA (*as they come up, in an undertone*). Is not the same nurse. Katrin, you take my hat and coat. (*She takes them off, revealing that she still wears her apron.*)

KATRIN. But, Mama, won't they . . .

MAMA (*interrupting, finger to her lips*). Ssh!

You let me go ahead. You wait on bench for me. (*She goes to the closet door above the bench and opens it.* KATRIN *stares after her in trepidation.* MAMA *takes out a damp mop and pail, and gets down on her knees by the nurse's desk, starting to clean the floor. The* NURSE *looks up.* MAMA *catches her eye, brightly*). Very dirty floors.

NURSE. Yes, I'm glad they've finally decided to clean them. Aren't you working late?

MAMA (*quickly, lowering her head*). Floors need cleaning. (*She pushes her way, crawling on hands and knees, up behind the desk, and disappears up the corridor, still scrubbing.* KATRIN *steals to the bench, where she sits, still clutching* MAMA's *hat and coat, looking interestedly around her. The light dims, leaving her in a single spot, as she starts to talk to herself.*)

KATRIN (*to herself*). "The Hospital" . . . A poem by Katrin Hanson. (*She starts to improvise.*)
   "She waited, fearful, in the hall,
   And held her bated breath."
Breath—yes, that'll rhyme with death.

(*She repeats the first two lines.*)
   "She waited fearful in the hall
   And held her bated breath.
   She trembled at the least footfall,
   And kept her mind on death."

(*She gets a piece of paper and pencil from her pocket and begins to scribble, as a* NURSE *comes out of the elevator, carrying some charts, which she takes to the desk, and then goes out down* R. KATRIN *goes on with her poem.*)
   "Ah, God, 'twas agony to wait.
   To wait and watch and wonder. . . ."
Wonder—under—bunder—funder—sunder. Sunder! (*Nods to herself and goes on again.*)
   "To wait and watch and wonder,
   About her infant sister's fate.
   If Death life's bonds would sunder."

(Then to herself again, looking front.) That's beautiful. Yes, but it isn't true. Dagmar isn't dying. It's funny—I don't want her to die—and yet when Mama said she was all right I was almost—well, almost disappointed. It wasn't exciting any more. Maybe Christine's right, and I haven't any heart. How awful! "The girl without a heart." That'd be a nice title for a story. "The girl without a heart sat in the hospital corridor. . . ."

(The lights come up again as UNCLE CHRIS *appears, up* R. *behind the desk. He wears his hat. He sees* KATRIN.*)*

UNCLE CHRIS. Katrinë! What you do here? *(He sits on the bench beside her.)*

KATRIN *(nervously)*. I'm waiting for Mama.

UNCLE CHRIS. Where is she?

KATRIN *(scared)*. I . . . don't know.

UNCLE CHRIS. What you mean . . . you don't know?

KATRIN *(whispering)*. I think . . . I think she's seeing Dagmar.

UNCLE CHRIS *(shaking his head)*. Is first day. They do not allow visitors first day.

KATRIN *(trying to make him aware of the* NURSE*)*. I know. But I think that's where she is.

UNCLE CHRIS. Where *is* Dagmar?

KATRIN. I don't know.

*(*UNCLE CHRIS *rises and goes to the* NURSE *at the desk.)*

UNCLE CHRIS. In what room is my great-niece, Dagmar Hanson?

NURSE *(looking at her book)*. Hanson . . . Hanson . . . when did she come in?

UNCLE CHRIS. This morning.

NURSE. Oh, yes. Were you wanting to see her?

UNCLE CHRIS. What room is she in?

NURSE. I asked were you wanting to see her.

UNCLE CHRIS. And *I* ask what room she is in.

NURSE. We don't allow visitors the first day.

UNCLE CHRIS. Have I said I vant to visit her? I ask what room she is in.

NURSE. Are you by any chance, Mr. . . . *(Looking at her book.)* Halvorsen?

UNCLE CHRIS *(proudly, and correcting her pronunciation)*. Christopher Halvorsen.

NURSE. Did you say you were her uncle?

UNCLE CHRIS. Her great-uncle.

NURSE. Well, then, I'm afraid I can't tell you anything about her.

UNCLE CHRIS. Why not?

NURSE. Orders.

UNCLE CHRIS. Whose orders?

NURSE. Dr. Johnson's. There's a special note here. Patient's uncle, Mr. Halvorsen, not to be admitted or given information under any circumstances.

UNCLE CHRIS *(after a moment's angry stupefaction)*. Vomen! Pff! *(He strides away down* L.*)*

*(*MAMA *returns from up* R., *carrying the mop and pail, walking now and smiling triumphantly.)*

MAMA *(to the* NURSE*)*. Thank you. *(She replaces the mop and pail in the closet, and then sees* UNCLE CHRIS. *Crossing to him.)* Uncle Chris, Dagmar is fine!

UNCLE CHRIS *(amazed)*. You see her?

MAMA. Sure, Uncle Chris, I see her.

UNCLE CHRIS *(reiterating, incredulous)*. You see Dagmar?!

MAMA. Sure. *(She takes her hat from* KATRIN *and starts to put it on.)* Is fine hospital. But such floors! A mop is never good. Floors should be scrubbed with a brush. We go home. Uncle Chris, you come with us? I make coffee.

UNCLE CHRIS *(joining them in a little group on the steps down* L.*)*. Pah! Vot good is coffee? I go get drink.

MAMA *(reprovingly)*. Uncle Chris!

UNCLE CHRIS. Marta, you are fine woman. Fine. But I go get drink.

MAMA (*quickly aside to* KATRIN). His leg hurts him.

UNCLE CHRIS. And you do not make excuses for me! I get drink because I like it.

MAMA (*conciliating him*). Sure, Uncle Chris.

UNCLE CHRIS (*shouting*). I like it! (*Then, with a change.*) No, is not true. You know is not true. I do not like to drink at all. But I do not like to come home with you, either. (*Growing slightly maudlin.*) You have family. Is fine thing. You do not know how fine. Katrinë, one day when you grow up, maybe you know what a fine thing family is. I haf no family.

KATRIN (*on the lower step*). But, Uncle Chris, Mama's always said you were the *head* of the family.

UNCLE CHRIS. Sure. Sure. I am head of the family, but I haf no family. So I go get drink. You understand, Marta?

MAMA. Sure, Uncle Chris. You go get drink. (*Sharply*). But don't you feel sorry for yourself! (UNCLE CHRIS *glares at her a moment, then strides down the steps and off* R., *boisterously singing his song of "Ten Thousand Swedes."* MAMA *watches him go, then takes her coat from* KATRIN.) Is fine man. Has fine ideas about family. (KATRIN *helps her on with her coat.*) I can tell Papa now that Dagmar is fine. She wake while I am with her. I explain rules to her. She will not expect us now until tomorrow afternoon.

KATRIN. You won't try and see her again before that?

MAMA (*gravely*). No. That would be against the rules! Come. We go home.

(*They go off* L.)

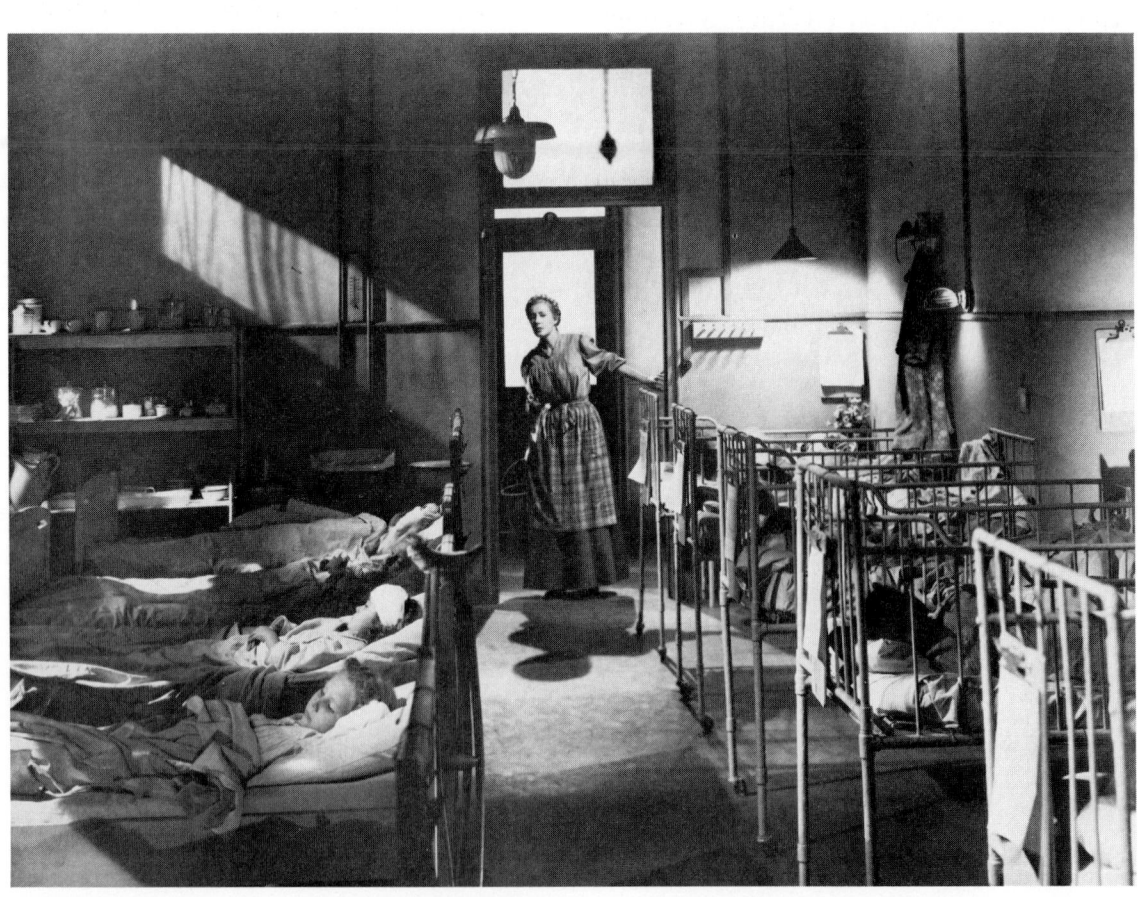

Act I

Getting at Meaning

1. Describe Katrin and the members of her immediate family. What do you learn about the family from the way in which they make it possible for Nels to go to high school? What is the attitude of the parents toward their children? toward education?

2. Why does Mama like the children to be present each week when she counts out Papa's pay?

3. Describe the three aunts. Why does Trina come to Mama first to discuss her marriage? How does Mama later handle Jenny and Sigrid? How do the children feel about their aunts?

4. Why does the family appreciate Mr. Hyde so much, even though he has not paid his rent?

5. Describe Uncle Chris. What is his position in the family? How do the various family members feel about him? What can you tell about Uncle Chris from the way he takes his nephew Arne off to the hospital? Why does he do this so abruptly?

6. What is the "secret" that Christine and Katrin share with Uncle Chris? What can you tell about Uncle Chris from his handling of Mr. Thorkelson over the dowry issue?

7. How does Mama use her resourcefulness to visit Dagmar in the hospital? Why does she do this, even though it is against the rules?

Developing Skills in Reading Literature

1. **Flashback.** Most of this play is written as flashback. That is, a character in the play recalls experiences that happened at an earlier time. Which character remembers the events? How does the playwright show changes in time? Point out several places in which the storyteller is in the present rather than in the past. How can you tell where the flashbacks begin and end?

2. **Setting.** When and where is this play set? In what specific settings does the first act take place? What does the reader learn about the family's economic and social circumstances? How does the playwright show changes in the location of the action?

Developing Vocabulary

Inferring Word Meaning. Guess the meaning of each italicized word in the following sentences. Then look up each word in a dictionary and copy the definition. Use the word in a sentence of your own that clearly illustrates its meaning.

1. Katrin is somewhere in her early twenties. She should be played by an actress who is small in *stature* and capable of looking *sufficiently* like a child not to break the *illusion* in *subsequent* scenes.

2. Mr. Hyde was an Englishman who had once been an actor, and Mama was very impressed by his flowery talk and *courtly* manners.

3. She is the cool, *aloof,* matter-of-fact one of the family.

4. He wears a very shabby long overcoat, with a *deplorable* fur collar, and carries his hat.

ACT 2

SCENE: *Opening, exactly as in Act One.* KATRIN *at her desk.*

KATRIN *(reading).* "It wasn't very often that I could get Mama to talk—about herself, or her life in the old country, or what she felt about things. You had to catch her unawares, or when she had nothing to do, which was very, very seldom. I don't think I can ever remember seeing Mama unoccupied." *(Laying down the manuscript and looking out front.)* I do remember one occasion, though. It was the day before Dagmar came home from the hospital. And as we left, Mama suggested treating me to an ice-cream soda. *(She rises, gets her hat from beside her—a schoolgirl hat—puts it on and crosses* C. *while she speaks the next lines.)* She had never done such a thing before, and I remember how proud it made me feel—just to sit and talk to her quietly like a grown-up person. It was a kind of special *treat*-moment in my life that I'll always remember—quite apart from the soda, which was *wonderful. (She has reached* C. *stage now.* MAMA *has come from between the curtains, and starts down the steps.)*

MAMA. Katrin, you like we go next door, and I treat you to an ice-cream soda?

KATRIN *(young now, and overcome).* Mama —do you mean it?

MAMA. Sure. We celebrate. We celebrate that Dagmar is well, and coming home again. *(They cross to the* L., *where the turntable represents a drugstore, with a table and two chairs at which they seat themselves.* MAMA *is* L. *of table.)* What you like to have, Katrin?

KATRIN *(with desperate earnestness).* I think a chocolate . . . no, a strawberry . . . no, a chocolate soda.

MAMA *(smiling).* You are sure?

KATRIN *(gravely).* I think so. But, Mama, can we *afford* it?

MAMA. I think this once we can afford it.

(The SODA CLERK *appears from* L.*)*

SODA CLERK. What's it going to be, ladies?

MAMA. A chocolate ice-cream soda, please— and a cup of coffee.

(The SODA CLERK *goes.)*

KATRIN. Mama, he called us "ladies"! *(*MAMA *smiles.)* Why aren't you having a soda, too?

MAMA. Better I like coffee.

KATRIN. When can I drink coffee?

MAMA. When you are grown up.

KATRIN. When I'm eighteen?

MAMA. Maybe before that.

KATRIN. When I graduate?

MAMA. Maybe. I don't know. Comes the day you are grown up. Papa and I will know.

KATRIN. Is coffee really nicer than a soda?

MAMA. When you are grown up, it is.

KATRIN. Did you used to like sodas better . . . before you were grown up?

MAMA. We didn't have sodas before I was grown up. It was in the old country.

KATRIN *(incredulous).* You mean they don't have sodas in Norway?

MAMA. Now, maybe. Now I think they have many things from America. But not when I was a little girl.

(The SODA CLERK *brings the soda and the coffee.)*

SODA CLERK. There you are, folks. *(He sets them down and departs.)*

KATRIN *(after a good pull at the soda).* Mama, do you ever want to go back to the old country?

MAMA. I like to go back once to look, maybe. To see the mountains and the fjords. I like to show them once to you all. When Dagmar is big, maybe we all go back once . . . one summer . . . like tourists. But that is how it would be. I would be tourist there now. There is no one I would know any more. And maybe we see the little house where Papa and I live when we first marry. And . . . (*Her eyes grow misty and reminiscent.*) something else I would look at.

KATRIN. What is that? (MAMA *does not answer.*) What would you look at, Mama?

MAMA. Katrin, you do not know you have brother? Besides Nels?

KATRIN. No! A brother? In Norway? Mama. . . .

MAMA. He is my first baby. I am eighteen when he is born.

KATRIN. Is he there now?

MAMA (*simply*). He is dead.

KATRIN (*disappointed*). Oh. I thought you meant . . . I thought you meant a real brother. A long-lost one, like in stories. When did he die?

MAMA. When he is two years old. It is his grave I would like to see again. (*She is suddenly near tears, biting her lip and stirring her coffee violently, spilling some. She gets her handkerchief from her pocketbook, dabs at her skirt, then briefly at her nose, then she returns the handkerchief and turns to* KATRIN *again. Matter-of-factly.*) Is good, your ice-cream soda?

KATRIN (*more interested now in* MAMA *than in it*). Yes. Mama . . . have you had a very hard life?

MAMA (*surprised*). Hard? No. No life is easy all the time. It is not meant to be. (*She pours the spilled coffee back from the saucer into her cup.*)

KATRIN. But . . . rich people . . . aren't *their* lives easy?

MAMA. I don't know, Katrin. I have never known rich people. But I see them sometimes in stores and in the streets, and they do not *look* as if they were easy.

KATRIN. Wouldn't you like to be rich?

MAMA. I would like to be rich the way I would like to be ten feet high. Would be good for some things—bad for others.

KATRIN. But didn't you come to America to *get* rich?

MAMA (*shocked*). No. We come to America because they are all here—all the others. Is good for families to be together.

KATRIN. And did you like it right away?

MAMA. Right away. When we get off the ferry boat and I see San Francisco and all the family, I say, "Is like Norway," only it is better than Norway. And then you are all born here, and I become American citizen. But not to get rich.

KATRIN. *I* want to be rich. Rich and famous. I'd buy you your warm coat. When are you going to get that coat, Mama?

MAMA. Soon now, maybe—when we pay doctor, and Mr. Hyde pay his rent. I think now I *must* ask him. I ask him tomorrow, after Dagmar comes home.

KATRIN. When I'm rich and famous, I'll buy you lovely clothes. White satin gowns with long trains to them. And jewelry. I'll buy you a pearl necklace.

MAMA. We talk too much! (*She signs to the* SODA CLERK.) Come, finish your soda. We must go home. (*The* SODA CLERK *comes.*) How much it is, please?

SODA CLERK. Fifteen cents.

MAMA. Here are two dimes. You keep the nickel. And thank you. Was good coffee. (*They start out and up the steps towards the curtains* C.) Tomorrow Dagmar will be home again. And, Katrin, you see Uncle Elizabeth is there. This afternoon again she was asking for him. You keep Uncle Elizabeth in the house all day until she comes home.

(*They disappear behind the curtains. After a second, the howls of a cat in pain are heard from behind the curtains—low at first, then rising to a heart-rending volume, and then diminishing again as the curtains part on the kitchen once more.* MAMA, PAPA, *and* DAGMAR *are entering the house.*)

DAGMAR (*standing on threshold, transfixed*). It's Uncle Elizabeth, welcoming me home! That's his song of welcome. Where is he, Mama? (*She looks around for the source of the howls.*)

MAMA. He is in the pantry. . . . (*As DAGMAR starts to rush thither.*) But wait . . . wait a minute, Dagmar. I must tell you. Uncle Elizabeth is . . . sick.

DAGMAR. Sick? What's the matter with him?

PAPA. He has been in fight. Last night. He come home this morning very sick indeed.

(DAGMAR *starts for the pantry door, back R., as* NELS *comes out.*)

MAMA. Nels, how is Uncle Elizabeth? Nels has been doctoring him.

NELS. He's pretty bad, Mama. I've dressed all his wounds again with boric acid, but . . . (*As* DAGMAR *tries to get past him.*) I wouldn't go and see him now, baby.

DAGMAR. I've got to. He's my cat. I haven't seen him in a whole month. More. (*She runs into the pantry and disappears.*)

MAMA. Nels, what you think?

NELS. I think we ought to have had him put away before she came home.

MAMA. But she would have been so unhappy if he was not here *at all*.

NELS. She'll be unhappier still if he dies.

(*Another howl is heard from the pantry, and then* DAGMAR *comes rushing back.*)

DAGMAR. Mama, what happened to him? What happened to him? Oh, Mama . . . when I tried to pick him up, his bandage slipped over his eye. It was bleeding. Oh, Mama, it looked awful. Oh . . . (*She starts to cry.*)

MAMA (*fondling her*). He looks like that all over. Nels, you go see to his eye again. (*Wearily,* NELS *returns to the pantry.*) Listen, Dagmar . . . *Lille Ven* . . . would it not be better for the poor thing to go quietly to sleep?

DAGMAR. You mean—go to sleep and never wake up again? (MAMA *nods gently.*) No.

PAPA. I think he die, anyway. Nels try to make him well. But I do not think he can.

DAGMAR. Mama can. Mama can do everything. (*Another howl from offstage. She clutches* MAMA *agonizedly.*) Make him live, Mama. Make him well again. *Please!*

MAMA. We see. Let us see how he gets through the night. And now, Dagmar, you must go to bed. I bring you your supper.

DAGMAR. But you will fix Uncle Elizabeth? You promise, Mama?

MAMA. I promise I try. Go now. (DAGMAR *goes out, back L.*) I must fix her supper. (*She starts for the pantry. Howls again. She and* PAPA *stand and look at each other.* NELS *comes out.*)

NELS. Mama, it's just cruelty, keeping that cat alive.

MAMA. I know.

PAPA (*as another howl, the loudest yet, emerges*). You say we see how the cat get through the night. I ask you how do *we* get through the night? Is no use, Marta. We must put the cat to sleep. Nels, you go to the drugstore, and get something. Some chloroform, maybe. (*He gives him a coin.*)

NELS. How much shall I get?

PAPA. You ask the man. You tell him it is for a cat. He knows. (NELS *goes out L. and down the street into the wings. Looking at* MAMA'S *face.*) Is best. Is the only thing.

MAMA. I know. But poor Dagmar. It is sad homecoming for her. And she has been so good in hospital. Never once she cry. (*She pulls herself together.*) I get her supper. (*Another howl from off stage.*) And I take the cat outside. Right outside, where we . . . where *Dagmar* cannot hear him. (*She goes into the pantry.* PAPA *takes a folded newspaper from his pocket, puts on his glasses and starts to read. The door, back L., opens gently and* MR. HYDE *peeps out. He wears his hat and coat and carries his suit-*

case and a letter. PAPA *has his back to him.* MR. HYDE *lays the letter on the dresser and then starts to tiptoe across to the door. Then* PAPA *sees him.)*

PAPA. You go out, Mr. Hyde?

MR. HYDE *(pretending surprise).* Oh. . . . Oh, I did not see you, Mr. Hanson. *(He puts down the suitcase.)* I did not know you were back. As a matter of fact, I . . . I was about to leave this letter for you. *(He fetches it.)* The fact is . . . I . . . I have been called away.

PAPA. So?

MR. HYDE. A letter I received this morning necessitates my departure. My immediate departure.

PAPA. I am sorry. *(MAMA returns with a tray, on which are milk, bread, butter, and jelly.)* Mama, Mr. Hyde says he goes away.

MAMA *(coming to the table with the tray).* Is true?

MR. HYDE. Alas, dear Madam, yes. 'Tis true, 'tis pity. And pity 'tis, 'tis true. You will find here . . . *(He presents the letter.)* my check for all I owe you, and a note expressing my profoundest thanks for all your most kind hospitality. You will say good-bye to the children for me? *(He bows, as* MAMA *takes the letter.)*

MAMA *(distressed).* Sure. Sure.

MR. HYDE *(bowing again).* Madam, my deepest gratitude. *(He kisses her hand.* MAMA *looks astonished. He bows to* PAPA.) *Sir—* my sincerest admiration! *(He opens the street door.)* It has been a privilege. *Ave Atque Vale!* Hail and farewell! *(He makes a gesture and goes.)*

MAMA. Was wonderful man! Is too bad. *(She opens the letter, takes out the check.)*

PAPA. How much is check for?

MAMA. Hundred ten dollar! Is four months.

PAPA. Good. Good.

MAMA. Is wonderful. Now we pay doctor everything.

PAPA. And you buy your warm coat. With fur now, maybe.

MAMA *(sadly)*. But there will be no more reading. You take the check, Lars. You get the money?

PAPA *(taking it)*. Sure. I get it. What does he say in his letter?

MAMA. You read it while I fix supper for Dagmar. *(She starts to butter the bread, and spread jelly, while* PAPA *reads.)*

PAPA *(reading)*. "Dear Friends, I find myself compelled to take a somewhat hasty departure from this house of happiness. . . ."

MAMA. Is beautiful letter.

PAPA *(continuing)*. "I am leaving you my library for the children. . . ."

MAMA. He leaves his books?

PAPA. He says so.

MAMA. But is wonderful. Go see, Lars. See if they are in his room.

*(*PAPA *lays down the letter and goes out back* L. NELS *and* CHRISTINE *appear down* L., *coming up to the house.* CHRISTINE *carries school books.)*

CHRISTINE. I'm sure it was him, Nels. Carrying his suitcase, and getting on the cable car. I'm sure he's going away.

NELS. Well, I hope he's paid Mama.

(They open the street door.)

CHRISTINE *(bursting in)*. Mama, I saw Mr. Hyde getting on the cable car.

MAMA. I know. He leave.

CHRISTINE. Did he pay you?

MAMA. Sure, he pay me. Hundred ten dollar. . . .

NELS. Gee. . . .

MAMA *(smiling)*. Is good.

CHRISTINE. Are you going to put it in the Bank?

MAMA. We need it right away. *(*PAPA *returns, staggering under an armload of books.)*

Mr. Hyde leaves his books, too. For you.

NELS. Say! (PAPA *stacks them on the table.* NELS *and* CHRISTINE *rush to them, reading the titles.*) The Pickwick Papers, The Complete Shakespeare . . .

CHRISTINE. *Alice in Wonderland, The Oxford Book of Verse . . .*

NELS. *The Last of the Mohicans, Ivanhoe . . .*

CHRISTINE. We were right in the middle of that.

MAMA. Nels can finish it. He can read to us now in the evenings. He has fine voice, too, like Mr. Hyde. (NELS *flushes with pleasure.*) Is wonderful. So much we can learn. (*She finishes the supper-making.*) Christine, you take the butter back to the cooler for me, and the yelly, too. (CHRISTINE *does so.*) I go up to Dagmar now. (*She lifts the tray, then pauses.*) You get it, Nels?

NELS. What? . . . Oh. . . . (*Taking a druggist's small bottle from his pocket.*) Here.

MAMA. You put it down. After I come back, we do it. You know how?

NELS. Why, no, Mama, I . . .

MAMA. You do not ask?

NELS. No, I . . . I thought Papa . . .

MAMA. You know, Lars?

PAPA. No, I don't *know* . . . but it cannot be difficult. If you *hold* the cat . . .

MAMA. And watch him die? No! I think better you get rags . . . and a big sponge, to soak up the chloroform. You put it in the box with him, and cover him over. You get them ready out there.

NELS. Sure, Mama.

MAMA. I bring some blankets.

(NELS *goes off to the pantry, as* CHRISTINE *comes back. Again* MAMA *lifts the tray and starts for the door back* L. *But there is a knock on the street door from* AUNT JENNY, *who has come to the house from down* L. *in a state of some excitement.*)

MAMA (*agitated*). So much goes on! See who it is, Christine.

CHRISTINE (*peeping*). It's Aunt Jenny. (*She opens the door.*)

MAMA. Jenny. . . .

JENNY (*breathless*). Marta . . . has he gone?

MAMA (*above table*). Who?

JENNY (L. *of table*). Your boarder . . . Mr. Hyde. . . .

MAMA. Yes, he has gone. Why?

JENNY. Did he pay you?

MAMA. Sure he pay me.

JENNY. How?

MAMA. He give me a check. Lars has it right there.

JENNY (*with meaning*). A check!

MAMA. Jenny, what is it? Christine, you give Dagmar her supper. I come soon. (CHRISTINE *takes the tray from her and goes out back* L.) What is it, Jenny? How do you know that Mr. Hyde has gone?

JENNY. I was at Mr. Kruper's down the street . . . you know, the restaurant and bakery . . . and he told me Mr. Hyde was there today having his lunch, and when he left he asked if he would cash a check for him. For fifty dollars. (*She pauses.*)

PAPA. Well, go on.

JENNY. Your fine Mr. Hyde didn't expect Mr. Kruper to take it to the bank until tomorrow, but he did. And what do you think? Mr. Hyde hasn't even an *account* at that bank! (NELS *returns and stands in the pantry doorway.*)

MAMA. I don't understand.

PAPA (*taking the check from his pocket*). You mean the check is no good?

JENNY. No good at all. (*Triumphantly.*) Your Mr. Hyde was a crook, just as I always thought he was, for all his reading and fine ways. Mr. Kruper said he'd been cashing them all over the neighborhood. (MAMA *stands quite still, without answering.*) How much did he owe you? Plenty, I'll bet. (*Still no answer.*) Eh? Marta, I said I bet he owed you plenty. Didn't he?

MAMA (*looks around, first at* NELS *and then*

down at the books on the table; she touches them). No. No, he owed us nothing. *(She takes the check from* PAPA, *tearing it.)* Nothing.

JENNY *(persistently).* How much was that check for? *(She reaches her hand for it.)*

MAMA *(evading her).* It does not matter. He pay with better things than money. *(She goes to the stove, where she throws the check, watching it burn.)*

JENNY. I told you right in the beginning that you shouldn't trust him. But you were so sure . . . just like you always are. Mr. Hyde was a gentleman. A gentleman! I bet it must have been a hundred dollars that he rooked you of. Wasn't it?

MAMA *(returning to the table).* Jenny, I cannot talk now. Maybe you don't have things to do. I have.

JENNY *(sneeringly).* What? What have *you* got to do that's so important?

MAMA *(taking up the medicine bottle, fiercely).* I have to chloroform a cat!

*(*JENNY *steps back in momentary alarm, almost as though* MAMA *were referring to her, as she goes out into the pantry with the medicine bottle, not so very unlike Lady Macbeth with the daggers.[9] Blackout and curtains close. After a moment, the curtains part again on the kitchen, the next morning. The books have been taken off the table, and* MAMA *is setting the breakfast dishes, with* PAPA *helping her.* DAGMAR *comes bursting into the room, back* L.*)*

DAGMAR. Good morning, Mama, 'Morning, Papa. Is Uncle Elizabeth all better?

MAMA. Dagmar, there is something I must tell you.

DAGMAR. I want to see Uncle Elizabeth first. *(She runs into the pantry.* MAMA *turns helplessly to* PAPA.*)*

MAMA. Do something! Tell her!

PAPA. If we just let her think the cat die . . . by itself. . . .

MAMA. No. We cannot tell her lies.

*(*PAPA *goes to the pantry door, opening it.)*

DAGMAR *(heard in pantry, off).* What a funny, funny smell. Good morning, my darling, my darling Elizabeth. *(*MAMA *and* PAPA *stand stricken.* DAGMAR *comes in, carrying the cat, wrapped in an old shirt, with its head covered. She comes down* R. *of table.)* My goodness, you put enough blankets on him! Did you think he'd catch cold?

MAMA *(horror-stricken).* Dagmar, you must not. . . . *(She stops at the sight of the cat, whose tail is twitching, quite obviously alive.)* Dagmar, let me see . . . Let me see the cat! *(She goes over to her, below table front, and uncovers the cat's head.)*

DAGMAR *(overjoyed).* He's well. Oh, Mama, I *knew* you'd fix him.

MAMA *(appalled).* But, Dagmar, I didn't. I . . .

DAGMAR *(ignoring her).* I'm going to take him right up and show him to Nels. *(She runs off back* L., *calling.)* Nels! Nels! Uncle Elizabeth's well again!

MAMA *(turning to* PAPA*).* Is a miracle! *(She sits, dumbfounded, on the bench in front of the table.)*

PAPA *(beside her, shrugging).* You cannot have used enough chloroform. You just give him good sleep, and that cures him. We re-christen the cat, Lazarus![10]

MAMA. But, Lars, we must tell her. Is not *good* to let her grow up believing I can fix *every-thing!*

PAPA. Is best thing in the world for her to believe. *(He chuckles.)* Besides, I know *exactly* how she feels. *(He lays his hand on hers.)*

MAMA *(turning with embarrassment from his demonstrativeness and slapping his hand).*

---

9. **Lady Macbeth . . . daggers:** a character in William Shakespeare's *Macbeth* who urges her husband to murder the king with a dagger.

10. **Lazarus** (laz′ ə rəs): according to the Bible, a man who was raised from the dead by Jesus.

We finish getting breakfast. (*She turns back to the table.*)

(*The curtains close. Lights up down front* R. KATRIN *and* CHRISTINE *enter from the wings, in school clothes, wearing hats.* CHRISTINE *carries schoolbooks in a strap.* KATRIN *is reciting.*)

KATRIN. "The quality of mercy is not strained,

>It droppeth as the gentle rain from heaven
>
>Upon the place beneath: it is twice blest;
>
>It blesseth him that gives, and him that takes. . . ."

(*She dries up.*) ". . . him that takes. It blesseth him that gives and him that takes . . ." (*She turns to* CHRISTINE.) What comes after that?

CHRISTINE. I don't know. And I don't care.

KATRIN. Why, Chris!

CHRISTINE. I don't. It's all I've heard for weeks. The school play, and your graduation, and going on to High. And never a thought of what's happening at home.

KATRIN. What do you mean?

CHRISTINE. You see—you don't even know!

KATRIN. Oh, you mean the strike?

CHRISTINE. Yes, I mean the strike. Papa hasn't worked for four whole weeks, and a lot you care. Why, I don't believe you even know what they're striking *for*. Do you? All you and your friends can talk about is the presents you're going to get. You make me ashamed of being a girl.

(*Two girls,* MADELINE *and* DOROTHY, *come through the curtains,* C., *talking.*)

MADELINE (*to* DOROTHY). Thyra Walsh's family's going to add seven pearls to the necklace they started for her when she was a baby. Oh, hello, Katrin! Did you hear about Thyra's graduation present?

KATRIN (*not very happily*). Yes, I heard.

MADELINE. I'm getting an onyx ring, with a diamond in it.

KATRIN. A real diamond?

MADELINE. Yes, of course. A *small* diamond.

DOROTHY. What are *you* getting?

KATRIN. Well . . . well, they haven't actually told me, but I think . . . I think I'm going to get that pink celluloid dresser set in your father's drugstore.

DOROTHY. You mean that one in the window?

KATRIN (*to* MADELINE). It's got a brush and comb and mirror . . . and a hair-receiver. It's genuine celluloid!

DOROTHY. I wanted Father to give it to me, out of stock, but he said it was too expensive. Father's an awful tightwad. They're giving me a bangle.

MADELINE. Oh, there's the street car. We've got to fly. 'Bye, Katrin. 'Bye, Christine. See you tomorrow. Come on, Dorothy.

(*The* TWO GIRLS *rush off* L.)

CHRISTINE. Who said you were going to get the dresser set?

KATRIN. Nobody's said so . . . for certain. But I've sort of hinted, and . . .

CHRISTINE (*going up the steps*). Well, you're not going to get it.

KATRIN. How do you know?

CHRISTINE (*turning up back, still on steps*). Because I know what you *are* getting. I heard Mama tell Aunt Jenny. Aunt Jenny said you were too young to appreciate it.

KATRIN. What is it?

CHRISTINE. Mama's giving you her brooch. Her *solje*.

KATRIN. You mean that old silver thing she wears that belonged to Grandmother? What would I want an old thing like that for?

CHRISTINE. It's an heirloom. Mama thinks a lot of it.

KATRIN. Well, then, she ought to keep it. You don't really mean that's *all* they're going to give me?

CHRISTINE. What more do you want?

KATRIN. I want the dresser set. My goodness, if Mama doesn't realize what's a suitable present . . . why, it's practically the most important time in a girl's life, when she graduates.

CHRISTINE. And you say you're not selfish!

KATRIN. It's not selfishness.

CHRISTINE. Well, I don't know what else you'd call it. With Papa not working, we need every penny we can lay our hands on. Even the Little Bank's empty. But you'll devil Mama into giving you the dresser set somehow. So why talk about it? I'm going home. (She turns and goes through the curtains.)

(KATRIN stands alone with a set and stubborn mouth, and then sits on the steps.)

KATRIN. Christine was right. I got the dresser set. They gave it to me just before supper on graduation night. Papa could not attend the exercises because there was a strike meeting to decide about going back to work. I was so excited that night I could hardly eat, and the present took the last remnants of my appetite clean away.

(The curtains part on the kitchen. PAPA, MAMA, and DAGMAR at table, with coffee. CHRISTINE is clearing dishes.)

CHRISTINE. I'll just stack the dishes now, Mama. We'll wash them when we come home. (She carries them into the pantry.)

PAPA (R. of table, holding up a cube of sugar). Who wants coffee sugar? (He dips it in his coffee.) Dagmar? (He hands it to her.) Katrin? (She rises from the steps, coming into the scene for the sugar.)

MAMA (L. of table). You get your coat, Katrin; you need it.

(KATRIN goes out back L.)

DAGMAR (above table). Aunt Jenny says if we drank black coffee like you do at our age, it would turn our complexions dark. I'd like to be a black Norwegian. Like Uncle Chris. Can I, Papa?

PAPA. I like you better blonde. Like Mama.

DAGMAR. When do you get old enough for your complexion not to turn dark? When can we drink coffee?

PAPA. One day, when you are grown up.

(JENNY and TRINA have come to the street door L. JENNY knocks.)

MAMA. There are Jenny and Trina. (She goes to the door.) Is good. We can start now. (She opens the door. JENNY and TRINA come in.)

JENNY. Well, are you all ready? Is Katrin very excited?

PAPA (nodding). She ate no supper.

(MAMA has started to put on her hat, and to put on DAGMAR's hat and coat for her down L. CHRISTINE comes back from the pantry. PAPA gives her a dipped cube of sugar.)

JENNY. Is that black coffee you dipped that sugar in? Lars, you shouldn't. It's not good for them. It'll . . .

PAPA (finishing for her). Turn their complexions dark. I know. Well, maybe it is all right if we have one dark Norwegian.

JENNY. Lars, really!

(KATRIN returns with her coat.)

KATRIN. Aunt Jenny, did you see my graduation present? (She gets it from a chair. CHRISTINE gives her a disgusted look, and goes out back L. KATRIN displays the dresser set above the table.) Look! It's got a hair-receiver.

JENNY (L. of table). But I thought . . . Marta, I thought you were going to give her . . .

MAMA (L.). No, you were right, Jenny. She is too young to appreciate that. She like something more gay . . . more modern.

JENNY. H'm. Well, it's very pretty, I suppose, but . . . (She looks up as MAMA puts on her coat.) You're not wearing your solje!

MAMA (*quickly*). No. I do not wear it tonight. Come, Trina, we shall be late.

TRINA (*above table* R.). Oh, but Peter isn't here yet.

MAMA. Katrin has her costume to put on. He can follow. Or do you like to wait for Peter?

TRINA. I think . . . if you don't mind . . .

MAMA. You can stay with Lars. He does not have to go yet.

JENNY. I hope Katrin knows her part.

PAPA. Sure she knows it. *I* know it, too.

TRINA. It's too bad he can't see Katrin's debut as an actress.

MAMA. You will be back before us, Lars?

PAPA (*nodding*). I think the meeting will not last long.

MAMA. Is good. We go now. (*She goes out with* JENNY *and* DAGMAR. CHRISTINE *and* NELS *return from back* L., *and follow, waiting outside for* KATRIN, *while the others go ahead.* KATRIN *puts on her hat and coat and picks up the dresser set.*)

PAPA (*to* TRINA). You like we play a game of checkers while we wait?

TRINA (*sitting* R. *of table*). Oh, I haven't played checkers in years.

PAPA. Then I beat you. (*He rises to get the checker set.* KATRIN *kisses him.*)

KATRIN. Goodbye, Papa.

PAPA. Goodbye, daughter. I think of you.

KATRIN. I'll see you there, Aunt Trina.

TRINA. Good luck!

PAPA. I get the checkers.

(KATRIN *goes out* L., PAPA *gets the checker set from a cupboard under the dresser, brings it to the table and sets it up during the ensuing scene, which is played outside in the street.*)

CHRISTINE (*contemptuously*). Oh, bringing your cheap trash with you to show off?

KATRIN. It's not trash. It's beautiful. You're just jealous.

CHRISTINE. I told you you'd devil Mama into giving it to you.

KATRIN. I didn't. I didn't devil her at all. I just showed it to her in Mr. Schiller's window . . .

CHRISTINE. And made her go and sell her brooch that her very own mother gave her.

KATRIN. What?

NELS. Chris . . . you weren't supposed to tell that!

CHRISTINE. I don't care. I think she ought to know.

KATRIN. Is that true? Did Mama—Nels——?

NELS. Well, yes, as a matter of fact, she did. Now, come on.

KATRIN. No, no, I don't believe it. I'm going to ask Papa.

NELS. You haven't time.

KATRIN. I don't care. (*She rushes back to the house and dashes into the kitchen.* CHRISTINE *goes off down* L., NELS *follows her.*) Papa—Papa—Christine says —— Papa, did Mama sell her brooch to give me this?

PAPA (*above table*). Christine should not have told you that.

KATRIN. It's true, then?

PAPA. She did not sell it. She traded it to Mr. Schiller for your present.

KATRIN (*near tears*). Oh, but she shouldn't. . . . I never meant . . .

PAPA (*taking her by the shoulders*). Look, Katrin. You wanted the present. Mama wanted your happiness; she wanted it more than she wanted the brooch.

KATRIN. But I never meant her to do *that*. (*Crying.*) She *loved* it so. It was all she had of Grandmother's.

PAPA. She always meant it for you, Katrin. And you must not cry. You have your play to act.

KATRIN (*sobbing*). I don't want to act in it now.

PAPA. But you must. Your audience is waiting.

KATRIN (*as before*). I don't care.

PAPA. But you must care. Tonight you are not Katrin any longer. You are an actress. And an actress must act, whatever she is feeling. There is a saying—what is it ——

TRINA (brightly). The mails must go through!

PAPA. No, no. The show must go on. So stop your crying, and go and act your play. We talk of this later. Afterwards.

KATRIN (pulling herself together). All right, I'll go. (Sniffing a good deal, she picks up the dresser set and goes back to the street and off down L. PAPA and TRINA exchange glances, and then settle down to their checkers.)

PAPA. Now we play.

(The lights fade and the curtains close. Spot up on stage R. turntable. The two girls from the earlier scene are dressing in costumes for The Merchant of Venice[11] before a plank dressing table.)

DOROTHY. I'm getting worried about Katrin. If anything's happened to her . . .

MADELINE (pulling up her tights). I'll forget my lines. I know I will. I'll look out and see Miss Forrester sitting there, and forget every single line. (KATRIN rushes in from the L. She carries the dresser set, places it on the dressing table.) We thought you'd had an accident, or something. . . .

KATRIN. Dorothy, is your father here tonight?

DOROTHY. He's going to be. Why?

KATRIN. I want to speak to him. (As she pulls off her hat and coat.) Will you tell him . . . please . . . not to go away without speaking to me? After. After the exercises.

DOROTHY. What on earth do you want to speak to Father for?

KATRIN. I've got something to say to him. Something to ask him. It's important. Very important.

MADELINE. Is that the dresser set? (Picking it up.) Can I look at it a minute?

KATRIN (snatching it from her, violently). No!

MADELINE. Why, what's the matter? I only wanted to look at it.

KATRIN (emotionally). You can't. You're not to touch it. Dorothy, you take it and put it where I can't see it. (She thrusts it at her.) Go on. . . . Take it! Take it! Take it!!

(Blackout. Curtains part on the kitchen. MAMA and PAPA in conclave at the table with cups of coffee.)

MAMA (above table). I am worried about her, Lars. When it is over, I see her talking with Mr. Schiller—and then she goes to take off her costume and Nels tells me that he will bring her home. But it is long time, and is late for her to be out. And in the play, Lars, she was not good. I have heard her practice it here, and she was good, but tonight, no. It was as if . . . as if she was thinking of something else all the time.

PAPA (R. of table). I think maybe she was.

MAMA. But what? What can be worrying her?

PAPA. Marta . . . tonight, after you leave, Katrin found out about your brooch.

MAMA. My brooch? But how? Who told her?

PAPA. Christine.

MAMA (angry). Why?

PAPA. I do not know.

MAMA (rising with a sternness we have not seen before, and calling). Christine! Christine!

CHRISTINE (emerging from the pantry, wiping a dish). Were you calling me, Mama?

MAMA. Yes. Christine, did you tell Katrin tonight about my brooch?

CHRISTINE (frightened, but firm, R.). Yes.

MAMA (level with her, L. of table). Why did you?

CHRISTINE. Because I hated the smug way she was acting over that dresser set.

MAMA. Is no excuse. You make her unhappy. You make her not good in the play.

CHRISTINE. Well, she made you unhappy, giving up your brooch for her selfishness.

MAMA (moving towards her, above table). Is not your business. I choose to give my brooch. Is not for you to judge. And you

---

11. *The Merchant of Venice:* a play by Shakespeare.

know I do not want you to tell. I am angry with you, Christine.

CHRISTINE. I'm sorry. But I'm not sorry I told. *(She goes back to the pantry with a set, obstinate face.)*

PAPA. Christine is the stubborn one.

(NELS and KATRIN have approached the house outside L. They stop and look at each other in the lamplight. KATRIN looks scared. Then NELS pats her, and she goes in, NELS following. MAMA looks up inquiringly and searchingly into KATRIN's face. KATRIN turns away, taking off her hat and coat, and taking something from her pocket.)

NELS. What happened at the meeting, Papa?

PAPA. We go back to work tomorrow.

NELS. Gee, that's bully. Isn't it, Mama?

MAMA *(seated again L. of table, absently).* Yes, is good.

KATRIN *(coming to MAMA).* Mama . . . here's your brooch. *(She gives it to her.)* I'm sorry I was so bad in the play. I'll go and help Christine with the dishes. *(She turns and goes into the pantry.)*

MAMA *(unwrapping the brooch from tissue paper).* Mr. Schiller give it back to her?

NELS *(above table).* We went to his house to get it. He didn't want to. He was planning to give it to his wife for her birthday. But Katrin begged and begged him. She even offered to go and work in his store during her vacation if he'd give it back.

PAPA *(impressed).* So? So?

MAMA. And what did Mr. Schiller say?

NELS. He said that wasn't necessary. But he gave her a job all the same. She's going to work for him, afternoons, for three dollars a week.

MAMA. And the dresser set—she gave that back?

NELS. Yes. She was awful upset, Mama. It was kinda hard for her to do. She's a good kid. Well, I'll say good night. I've got to be up early.

PAPA. Good night, Nels.

NELS. Good night, Papa. *(He goes out back L.)*

MAMA. Good night, Nels.

PAPA. Nels is the kind one. *(He starts to refill MAMA's coffee cup. She stops him, putting her hand over her cup.)* No?

MAMA *(rising, crossing R. and calling)*. Katrin! Katrin!

KATRIN *(coming to the pantry door)*. Yes, Mama?

MAMA *(sitting R. of table)*. Come here. *(KATRIN comes to her. MAMA holds out the brooch.)* You put this on.

KATRIN. No . . . it's yours.

MAMA. It is your graduation present. I put it on for you. *(She pins the brooch on KATRIN's dress.)*

KATRIN *(near tears)*. I'll wear it always. I'll keep it forever.

MAMA. Christine should not have told you.

KATRIN *(moving away down R.)*. I'm glad she did. Now.

PAPA. And I am glad, too. *(He dips a lump of sugar and holds it out to her.)* Katrin?

KATRIN *(tearful again, shakes her head)*. I'm sorry, Papa. I . . . I don't feel like it. *(She crosses below the table and sits on the chest under the window, with her back to the room.)*

PAPA. So? So? *(He goes to the dresser.)*

MAMA. What you want, Lars? *(He does not answer, but takes a cup and saucer, comes to the table and pours a cup of coffee, indicating KATRIN with his head. MAMA nods, pleased, then checks his pouring and fills up the cup from the cream pitcher, which she empties in so doing. PAPA puts in sugar, and moves to KATRIN.)*

PAPA. Katrin. *(She turns. He holds out the cup.)*

KATRIN *(incredulous)*. For me?

PAPA. For our grown-up daughter. *(MAMA nods, standing arm in arm with PAPA. KATRIN takes the cup, lifts it—then her emotion overcomes her. She thrusts it at PAPA and rushes from the room.)* Katrin is

the dramatic one! Is too bad. Her first cup of coffee, and she does not drink it.

MAMA. It would not have been good for her, so late at night.

PAPA *(smiling)*. And you, Marta, you are the practical one.

MAMA. You drink the coffee, Lars. We do not want to waste it. *(She pushes it across to him.)*

(Lights dim. Curtains close. Light up on L. turntable, representing the parlor of JENNY's house. A telephone on a table, at which TRINA is discovered, talking.)

TRINA *(into phone)*. Yes, Peter. Yes, Peter. I know, Peter, but we don't know where he is. It's so long since we heard from him. He's sure to turn up soon. Yes, I know, Peter. I know, but . . . *(Subsiding obediently.)* Yes, Peter. Yes, Peter. *(Sentimentally.)* Oh, Peter, you know I do. Goodbye, Peter. *(She hangs up, and turns, to see JENNY, who has come in behind her, eating a piece of toast and jam.)*

JENNY. What was all that about?

TRINA. Peter says we shouldn't wait any longer to hear from Uncle Chris. He says we should send the wedding invitations out right away. He was quite insistent about it. Peter can be very masterful sometimes . . . when he's alone with *me!*

(The telephone rings again. JENNY answers it, putting down the toast, which TRINA takes up and nibbles at during the scene.)

JENNY. This is Mrs. Stenborg's boarding house. Mrs. Stenborg speaking. Oh, yes, Marta . . . what is it? *(She listens.)*

(Spot up on R. turntable, disclosing MAMA standing at a wall telephone booth. She wears hat and coat, and has an opened telegram in her hand.)

MAMA. Jenny, is Uncle Chris. I have a telegram. It says if we want to see him again we should come without delay.

JENNY. Where is he?

MAMA (*consulting the telegram*). It comes from a place called Ukiah. Nels says it is up north from San Francisco.

JENNY. Who is the telegram from?

MAMA. It does not say.

JENNY. That . . . woman?

MAMA. I don't know, Jenny. I think maybe.

JENNY. I won't go. (SIGRID *comes in through the curtains* C., *dressed in hat and coat, carrying string marketing bags, full of vegetables.* JENNY *speaks to her, whisperingly, aside.*) It's Uncle Chris. Marta says he's dying. (*Then, back into phone.*) Why was the telegram sent to *you*? I'm the eldest.

MAMA. Jenny, is not the time to think of who is eldest. Uncle Chris is dying.

JENNY. *I* don't believe it. He's too mean to die. Ever. (NELS *comes to booth from wings,* R., *and hands* MAMA *a slip of paper.*) I'm not going.

MAMA. Jenny, I cannot stop to argue. There is a train at eleven o'clock. It takes four hours. You call Sigrid.

JENNY. Sigrid is here now.

MAMA. Good. Then you tell her.

JENNY. What do you say the name of the place is?

MAMA. Ukiah. (*Spelling in Norwegian.*) U-K-I-A-H.

JENNY. I won't go.

MAMA. That *you* decide. (*She hangs up. Her spot goes out.*)

SIGRID. Uncle Chris dying!

JENNY. The wages of sin.

TRINA. Oh, he's old. Maybe it is time for him to go.

JENNY. Four hours by train, and maybe have to stay all night. All that expense to watch a wicked old man die.

SIGRID. I know, but . . . there is his will. . . .

JENNY. Huh, even supposing he's anything to leave—you know who he'd leave it *to*, don't you?

SIGRID. Yes. But all the same he's dying now,

and blood is thicker than water. Especially when it's Norwegian. I'm going. I shall take Arne with me. Uncle Chris was always fond of children.

TRINA. I agree with Sigrid. I think we *should* go.

JENNY. Well, *you* can't go, anyway.

TRINA. Why not?

JENNY. Because of that woman. You can't meet that woman.

TRINA. Why not? If you two can . . .

SIGRID. We're married women.

TRINA. I'm engaged!

JENNY. That's not the same thing.

SIGRID. Not the same thing at all!

TRINA. Nonsense. I've never met a woman like that. Maybe I'll never get another chance. Besides, if he's going to change his will, there's still my dowry, remember. Do you think we should take Peter?

JENNY. Peter Thorkelson? Whatever for?

TRINA. Well, after all, I mean . . . I mean, his profession . . .

JENNY. Trina, you always were a fool. Anyone would know the last person a dying man wants to see is an undertaker!

(*Blackout. Turntable revolves out. Spot up on* KATRIN, *standing down from* R. C. *She wears her schoolgirl hat.*)

KATRIN. When Mama said I was to go with her, I was excited and I was frightened. It was exciting to take sandwiches for the train, almost as though we were going on a picnic. But I was scared at the idea of seeing death, though I told myself that if I was going to be a writer, I had to experience everything. But all the same, I hoped it would be all over when we got there. (*She starts to walk toward* C. *and up the steps.*) It was afternoon when we arrived. We asked at the station for the Halvorsen ranch, and it seemed to me that the man looked at us strangely. Uncle Chris was obviously considered an odd character.

The ranch was about three miles from the town; a derelict, rambling old place. There was long grass, and tall trees, and a smell of honeysuckle. We made quite a cavalcade, walking up from the gate. *(The procession comes from the* R., *behind* KATRIN. MAMA, JENNY, TRINA, SIGRID, *and* ARNE.*)* The woman came out on the steps to meet us.

(The procession starts towards the C., *moving upwards. The* WOMAN *comes through the curtains, down one step. The* AUNTS *freeze in their tracks.* MAMA *goes forward to her.)*

MAMA. How is he? Is he ——?

WOMAN *(with grave self-possession)*. Come in, won't you? *(She holds the curtains slightly aside.* MAMA *goes in.* KATRIN *follows, looking curiously at the* WOMAN. *The* AUNTS *walk stiffly past her,* SIGRID *clutching* ARNE. *They disappear behind the curtains. The* WOMAN *stands a moment, looking off into the distance. Then she goes in behind the curtains, too.)*

(The curtains draw apart, revealing UNCLE CHRIS's *bedroom. It is simple, and shabby. The door to the room is at the back,* L. *In the* L. *wall is a window, with curtains, drawn aside now. In front of it, a washstand. The afternoon sunlight comes through the window, falling onto the big double bed, in which* UNCLE CHRIS *is propped up on pillows. Beside him,* R., *on a small table, is a pitcher of water. He has a glass in his hand.* MAMA *stands to the* R. *of him,* JENNY *to the* L. *The others are ranged below the window. The* WOMAN *is not present.)*

UNCLE CHRIS *(handing* MAMA *the empty glass)*. I want more. You give me more.

MAMA. Uncle Chris, that will not help now.

UNCLE CHRIS. It always help. *(With a glance at* JENNY.*)* Now especially.

JENNY *(firmly)*. Uncle Chris, I don't think you realize . . .

UNCLE CHRIS. What I don't realize? That I am dying? Why else do I think you come here? Why else do I think you stand there, watching me? *(He sits upright.)* Get out. Get out. I don't want you here. Get out!

JENNY. Oh, very well. Very well. We'll be outside on the porch, if you want us. *(She starts towards the door.)*

UNCLE CHRIS. That is where I want you—on the porch! *(*JENNY *goes out.* TRINA *follows.* SIGRID *is about to go, too, when* UNCLE CHRIS *stops her.)* Wait. That is Arne. Come here, Arne. *(*ARNE, *propelled by* SIGRID, *advances toward the bed.)* How is your knee?

ARNE. It's fine, Uncle Chris.

UNCLE CHRIS. Not hurt any more?

ARNE. N-no, Uncle Chris.

UNCLE CHRIS. You walk goot? Quite goot? Let me see you walk. Walk around the room. *(*ARNE *does so.)* Fast. Fast. Run! Run! *(*ARNE *does so.)* Is goot.

SIGRID *(encouraged and advancing)*. Uncle Chris, Arne has always been so fond of you. . . .

UNCLE CHRIS *(shouting)*. I tell you all to get out. Except Marta. *(As* KATRIN *edges with the* AUNTS *to the door.)* And Katrinë. Katrinë and I haf secret. You remember, Katrinë?

KATRIN. Yes, Uncle Chris.

MAMA. Uncle Chris, you must lie down again.

UNCLE CHRIS. Then you give me drink.

MAMA. No, Uncle Chris.

UNCLE CHRIS. We cannot waste what is left. You do not drink it . . . who will drink it when I am gone? What harm can it do . . . now? I die, anyway. . . . You give it to me. *(*MAMA *goes to the wash-stand, pours him a drink and takes it to him, sitting on the bed beside him to the* L. *of him. He drinks, then turns to her, leaning back against her arm and the pillows.)* Marta, I haf never made a will. Was never enough money.

But you sell this ranch. It will not bring moch. I have not had it long enough. And there is mortgage. Big mortgage. But it leave a little. Maybe two, tree hundred dollars. You give to Yessie.

MAMA. Yessie?

UNCLE CHRIS. Yessie Brown. My housekeeper. She was trained nurse, but she get sick, and I bring her to the country to get well again. There will be no money for *you*, Marta. Always I wanted there should be money to make Nils doctor. But there were other things . . . quick things. And now there is no time to make more. There is no money, but you make Nils doctor, all the same. You like?

MAMA. Sure, Uncle Chris. It is what Lars and I have always wanted for him. To help people who suffer. . . .

UNCLE CHRIS. Is the greatest thing in the world. It is to have a little of God in you. Always I wanted to be doctor myself. Is the only thing I have ever wanted. Nils must do it for me.

MAMA. He will, Uncle Chris.

UNCLE CHRIS. Is goot. *(He strokes her hand.)* You are the goot one. I am glad you come, *Lille Ven. (He moves his head restlessly.)* Where is Yessie?

MAMA. I think she wait outside.

UNCLE CHRIS. You do not mind if she is here?

MAMA. Of course not, Uncle Chris.

UNCLE CHRIS. You call her. I like you both be here. *(MAMA goes, with a quick glance at KATRIN, who has been standing, forgotten, down L. listening intently. UNCLE CHRIS signs to KATRIN to come closer. She sits on the chair beside the bed.)* Katrinë, your Mama write me you drink coffee now? *(She nods. He looks at her affectionately.)* Katrinë, who will be writer. . . . You are not frightened of me now?

KATRIN. No, Uncle Chris.

UNCLE CHRIS. One day maybe you write story about Uncle Chris. If you remember.

KATRIN *(whispering).* I'll remember.

(MAMA returns with the WOMAN. They come to his bed, standing on either side of it— MAMA to the L.)

UNCLE CHRIS *(obviously exhausted and in pain).* I like you both stay with me . . . now. I think best now maybe Katrinë go away. Goodbye, Katrinë. *(Then he repeats it in Norwegian.)* Farvell, Katrinë.

KATRIN. Goodbye, Uncle Chris.

UNCLE CHRIS. You say it in Norwegian, like I do.

KATRIN *(in Norwegian).* Farvell, Onkel Chris. *(She slips out, in tears.)*

UNCLE CHRIS. Yessie! Maybe I should introduce you to each other. Yessie, this is my niece, Marta. The only von of my nieces I can stand. Marta, this is Yessie, who have give me much happiness. . . .

(The TWO WOMEN shake hands across the bed.)

MAMA. I am very glad to meet you.

JESSIE. I am, too.

UNCLE CHRIS *(as they shake).* Is goot. And now you give me von more drink. You have drink with me . . . both of you.

(JESSIE and MAMA look at each other.)

MAMA. Sure, Uncle Chris.

UNCLE CHRIS. Goot. Yessie, you get best glasses. *(With a chuckle to MAMA.)* Yessie does not like to drink, but this is special occasion. *(JESSIE gets three glasses from a wall shelf.)* What is the time?

MAMA. It is about half-past four, Uncle Chris.

UNCLE CHRIS. The sun come around this side the house in afternoon. You draw the curtain a little maybe. Is strong for my eyes. *(MAMA goes over and draws the curtain over the window. The stage darkens. JESSIE pours three drinks, filling the glasses*

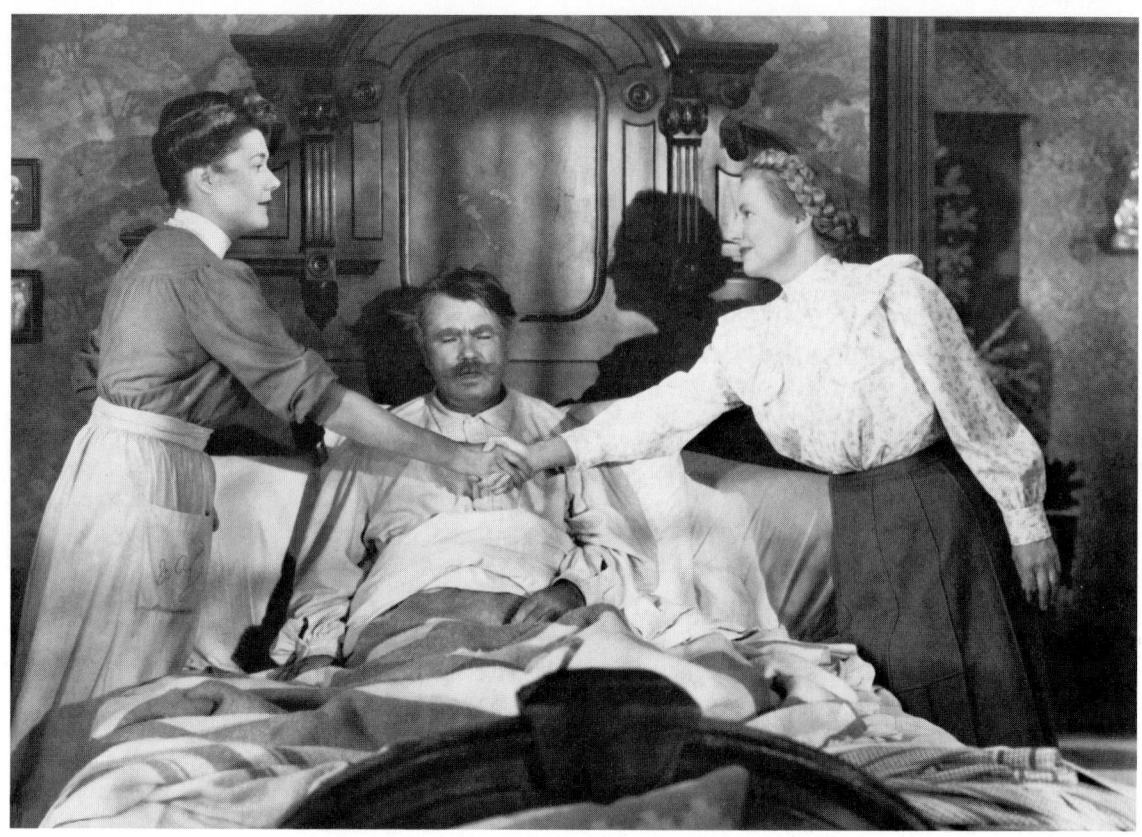

with water. She sits on the bed beside him, about to feed his drink to him, but he pushes her aside.) No. No, I do not need you feed it to me. I can drink myself. *(He takes the glass from her.)* Give Marta her glass. *(JESSIE hands a glass to MAMA. The TWO WOMEN stand on either side of the bed, holding their glasses.)* So. . . . Skoal!

JESSIE *(clinking glasses with him).* Skoal.

MAMA *(doing likewise).* Skoal.

(They all three drink. Slow dim to blackout. Curtains close. Spot up on R. turntable. A porch with a bench, and a chair, on which the three AUNTS are sitting. JENNY is dozing in the chair.)

SIGRID *(flicking her handkerchief).* These gnats are awful. I'm being simply eaten alive.

TRINA. Gnats are always worse around sunset. *(She catches one.)*

JENNY *(rousing herself).* I should never have let you talk me into coming. To be insulted like that . . . turned out of his room . . . and then expected to sit here hour after hour without as much as a cup of coffee. . . .

SIGRID. I'd make coffee if I knew where the kitchen was.

JENNY *(rising).* No, I'm going home. Are you coming, Trina?

TRINA. Oh, I think we ought to wait a little longer. After all, you can't *hurry* these things. . . . I mean . . . *(She breaks off in confusion at what she has said.)*

JENNY *(to SIGRID).* And all your talk about his will. A lot of chance we got to say a word!

TRINA. Maybe Marta's been talking to him.

(MAMA comes from between the curtains C.)

JENNY. Well?

MAMA. Uncle Chris has . . . gone.

(There is a silence.)

JENNY *(more gently than is her wont)*. Did he . . . say anything about a will?

MAMA. There is no will.

JENNY. Well, then, that means . . . we're his nearest relatives. . . .

MAMA. There is no money, either.

SIGRID. How do you know?

MAMA. He told me. *(She brings out a small notebook that she is carrying.)*

JENNY. What's that?

MAMA. Is an account of how he spent the money. I read it to you. *(JENNY sits again.)* You know how Uncle Chris was lame . . . how he walked always with limp. It was his one thought . . . lame people. He would have liked to be doctor and help them. Instead, he help them other ways. I read you the last page. . . . *(She reads from the notebook.)* "Joseph Spinelli. Four years old. Tubercular left leg. Three hundred thirty-seven dollars, eighteen cents." *(Pause.)* "Walks now. Esta Jensen. Nine years. Club-foot. Two hundred seventeen dollars, fifty cents. Walks now." *(Then, reading very slowly.)* "Arne Solfeldt. . . ."

SIGRID *(startled)*. My Arne?

MAMA *(reading on)*. "Nine years. Fractured kneecap. Four hundred forty-two dollars, sixteen cents."

(KATRIN and ARNE come running in from the L. across the stage.)

ARNE *(calling as he comes running across)*. Mother . . . Mother . . . Are we going to eat soon? *(He stops, awed by the solemnity of the group, and by MAMA, who puts out her hand gently, to silence him.)* What is it? Is Uncle Chris . . . ?

MAMA *(to the AUNTS)*. It does not tell the end about Arne. I like to write "Walks now." Yes?

SIGRID *(very subdued)*. Yes.

MAMA *(taking a pencil from the book)*.

Maybe even . . . "runs"? *(SIGRID nods, moist-eyed. TRINA is crying. MAMA writes in the book, and then closes it.)* So. Is finished. Is all. *(She touches JENNY on the shoulder.)* It was good.

JENNY *(after a gulping movement)*. I go and make some coffee.

(The woman, JESSIE, appears from between the curtains on the steps.)

JESSIE. You can go in and see him now if you want. *(JENNY looks back, half-hesitant, at the others. Then she nods and goes in. TRINA follows her, mopping her eyes. SIGRID puts her arm suddenly around ARNE in a spasm of maternal affection, and they, too, go in. MAMA, KATRIN, and JESSIE are left alone. KATRIN stands L. C., MAMA and JESSIE are in front of the curtains.)* I'm moving down to the hotel for tonight . . . so that you can all stay. *(She is about to go back, when MAMA stops her.)*

MAMA. Wait. What will you do now . . . after he is buried? You have money? *(JESSIE shakes her head.)* Where you live?

JESSIE. I'll find a room somewhere. I'll probably go back to nursing.

MAMA. You like to come to San Francisco for a little? To our house? We have room. Plenty room.

JESSIE *(touched, moving to MAMA)*. That's very kind of you, but . . .

MAMA. I like to have you. You come for a little as our guest. When you get work you can be our boarder.

JESSIE *(awkwardly grateful)*. I don't know why you should bother. . . .

MAMA *(touching her)*. You were good to Uncle Chris. *(JESSIE grasps her hand, deeply moved, then turns and goes quickly back through the curtains. MAMA turns to KATRIN.)* Katrin, you come and see him?

KATRIN *(scared)*. See him? You mean . . .

MAMA. I like you see him. You need not be frightened. He looks . . . happy and at peace. I like you to know what death looks like. Then you are not frightened of it, ever.

KATRIN. Will you come with me?

MAMA. Sure. *(She stretches out her hand, puts her arm around her, and then leads her gently in through the curtains.)*

(Spot up on L. *turntable, representing a park bench against a hedge.* TRINA *and* MR. THORKELSON, *in outdoor clothes, are seated together.* TRINA *is cooing over a baby carriage.)*

TRINA. Who's the most beautiful Norwegian baby in San Francisco? Who's going to be three months old tomorrow? Little Christopher Thorkelson! *(To* MR. THORKELSON.*)* Do you know, Peter, I think he's even beginning to *look* a little like Uncle Chris! Quite apart from his black curls—and those, of course, he gets from *you.* *(To baby again.)* He's going to grow up to be a black Norwegian, isn't he, just like his daddy and his Uncle Chris? *(Settling down beside* MR. THORKELSON.*)* I think there's something about his mouth . . . a sort of . . . well . . . *firmness.* Of course, it's *your* mouth, too. But then, I've always thought you had quite a lot of Uncle Chris about you. *(She looks back at the baby.)* Look— he's asleep!

MR. THORKELSON. Trina, do you know what next Thursday is?

TRINA *(nodding, smilingly).* Our anniversary.

MR. THORKELSON. What would you think of our giving a little party?

TRINA. A party?

MR. THORKELSON. Oh, quite a modest one. Nothing showy or ostentatious—but, after all, we have been married a year, and with your having been in mourning and the baby coming so soon and everything, we've not been able to entertain. I think it's time you . . . took your place in society.

TRINA *(scared).* What . . . sort of a party?

MR. THORKELSON. An evening party. *(Proudly.)* A soirée! I should say about ten people . . . some of the Norwegian colony . . . and Lars and Marta, of course. . . .

TRINA *(beginning to count on her fingers).* And Jenny and Sigrid. . . .

MR. THORKELSON. Oh . . . I . . . I hadn't thought of asking Jenny and Sigrid.

TRINA. Oh, we'd have to. We couldn't leave them out.

MR. THORKELSON. Trina, I hope you won't be offended if I say that I have never really felt . . . well, altogether comfortable with Jenny and Sigrid. They have always made me feel that they didn't think I was . . . well . . . *worthy* of you. Of course, I know I'm not, but . . . well . . . one doesn't like to be reminded of it . . . *all* the time.

TRINA *(taking his hand).* Oh, Peter.

MR. THORKELSON. But you're quite right. We must ask them. Now, as to the matter of refreshments . . . what would you suggest?

TRINA *(flustered).* Oh, I don't know. I . . . what would you say to . . . ice cream and cookies for the ladies . . . and coffee, of course . . . and . . . perhaps port wine for the gentlemen?

MR. THORKELSON *(anxiously).* Port wine?

TRINA. Just a little. You could bring it in already poured out, in *little* glasses. Jenny and Sigrid can help me serve the ice cream.

MR. THORKELSON *(firmly).* No. If Jenny and Sigrid come, they come as guests, like everybody else. You shall have someone in to help you in the kitchen.

TRINA. You mean a waitress? *(MR. THORKELSON nods, beaming.)* Oh, but none of us have *ever* . . . do you really think . . . I mean . . . you did say we shouldn't be ostentatious. . . .

MR. THORKELSON *(nervously, rising and starting to pace up and down).* Trina, there's something I would like to say. I've never been very good at expressing myself or my

... well ... *deeper* feelings—but I want you to know that I'm not only very fond of you, but very ... well ... very *proud* of you as well, and I want you to have the best of everything, as far as it's in my power to give it to you. *(He sits again—then, as a climax.)* I want you to have a waitress!

TRINA *(overcome)*. Yes, Peter. *(They hold hands.)*

(The lights fade and the turntable revolves out. Curtains part on kitchen, slightly changed, smartened and refurnished now. MAMA and PAPA seated as usual. MAMA is darning. DAGMAR, looking a little older, is seated on the chest, reading a solid-looking book. NELS enters from back L. door, carrying a newspaper. He wears long trousers now, and looks about seventeen.)

NELS *(hitting PAPA playfully on the head with the paper)*. Hello! Here's your evening paper, Papa.

(PAPA puts down the morning paper he is reading, and takes the evening one from NELS.)

PAPA *(R. of table)*. Is there any news?

NELS. No. *(He takes out a package of cigarettes with elaborate unconcern. MAMA watches with disapproval. Then, as he is about to light his cigarette, he stops, remembering something.)* Oh, I forgot. There's a letter for Katrin. I picked it up on the mat as I came in. *(Going to door back L., and calling.)* Katrin! Katrin! There's a letter for you.

KATRIN *(answering from off stage)*. Coming!

MAMA *(L. of table)*. Nels, you know who the letter is from?

NELS. Why, no, Mama. *(Hands it to her.)* It looks like her own handwriting.

MAMA *(gravely inspecting it)*. Is bad.

PAPA. Why is bad?

MAMA. She gets too many like that. I think they are stories she send to the magazines.

DAGMAR *(closing her book loudly, rising)*. Well, I'll go and see if I have any puppies yet. *(Crosses below the table and then turns.)* Mama, I've just decided something.

MAMA. What have you decided?

DAGMAR. If Nels is going to be a doctor, when I grow up, I'm going to be a—*(Looking at the book-title, and stumbling over the word.)*—vet-vet-veterinarian.

MAMA. And what is that?

DAGMAR. A doctor for animals.

MAMA. Is good. Is good.

DAGMAR. There are far more animals in the world than there are human beings, and far more human doctors than animal ones. It isn't fair. *(She goes to the pantry door.)* I suppose we couldn't have a horse, could we? *(This only produces a concerted laugh from the family. She turns, sadly.)* No. ... I was afraid we couldn't. *(She goes into the pantry.)*

(KATRIN comes in, back L. She wears a slightly more adult dress than before. Her hair is up, and she looks about eighteen.)

KATRIN. Where's the letter?

MAMA *(handing it to her)*. Here.

(KATRIN takes it, nervously. She looks at the envelope, and her face falls. She opens it, pulls out a manuscript and a rejection slip, looks at it a moment, and then replaces both in the envelope. The others watch her covertly. Then she looks up, with determination.)

KATRIN *(above table)*. Mama ... Papa ... I want to say something.

PAPA. What is it?

KATRIN. I'm not going to go to college.

PAPA. Why not?

KATRIN. Because it would be a waste of time and money. The only point in my going to college was to be a writer. Well, I'm not going to be one, so . . .

MAMA. Katrin, is it your letter that makes you say this? It is a story come back again?

KATRIN. Again is right. This is the tenth time. I made this one a test. It's the best I've ever written, or ever shall write. I know that. Well, it's no good.

NELS *(R. of her)*. What kind of a story is it?

KATRIN. Oh . . . it's a story about a painter, who's a genius, and he goes blind.

NELS. Sounds like *The Light That Failed*.[12]

KATRIN. Well, what's wrong with that?

NELS *(quickly)*. Nothing. Nothing!

KATRIN *(moving down L.)*. Besides, it's not like that. My painter gets better. He has an operation and recovers his sight, and paints better than ever before.

MAMA. Is good.

KATRIN *(bitterly unhappy)*. No, it isn't. It's rotten. But it's the best I can do.

MAMA. You have asked your teachers about this?

KATRIN. Teachers don't know anything about writing. They just know about literature. *(She crosses R.)*

MAMA. If there was someone we could ask . . . for advice . . . to tell us . . . tell us if your stories are good.

KATRIN. Yes. Well, there isn't. And they're not.

PAPA *(looking at the evening paper)*. There is something here in the paper about a lady writer. I just noticed the headline. Wait. *(He looks back for it and reads.)* "Woman writer tells key to literary success."

KATRIN. Who?

PAPA. A lady called Florence Dana Moorhead. It gives her picture. A fat lady. You have heard of her?

KATRIN. Yes, of course. Everyone has. She's terribly successful. She's here on a lecture tour.

MAMA. What does she say is the secret?

PAPA. You read it, Katrin. *(He hands her the paper.)*

KATRIN *(grabbing the first part)*. "Florence Dana Moorhead, celebrated novelist and short story writer . . . blah-blah-blah . . . interviewed today in her suite at the Fairmont . . . blah-blah-blah . . . pronounced sincerity the one essential quality for success as a writer." *(Throwing aside the paper.)* A lot of help that is.

MAMA. Katrin, this lady . . . maybe if you sent her your stories, *she* could tell you what is wrong with them?

KATRIN *(wearily)*. Oh, Mama, don't be silly.

MAMA. Why is silly?

KATRIN *(above table)*. Well, in the first place because she's a very important person . . . a celebrity . . . and she'd never read them. And in the second, because . . . you seem to think writing's like . . . well, like cooking, or something. That all you have to have is the recipe. It takes a lot more than that. You have to have a gift for it.

MAMA. You have to have a gift for cooking, too. But there are things you can learn, if you have the gift.

KATRIN. Well, that's the whole point. I haven't. I *know* . . . now. So, if you've finished with the morning paper Papa, I'll take the want ad section, and see if I can find myself a job. *(She takes the morning paper and goes out back L.)*

MAMA. Is bad. Nels, what you think?

NELS. I don't know, Mama. Her stories seem all right to me, but I don't know.

MAMA. It would be good to know. Nels, this lady in the paper . . . what else does she say?

NELS *(taking up the paper)*. Not much. The rest seems to be about *her* and her home.

---

12. **The Light That Failed:** a novel by Rudyard Kipling about an artist who tries to complete his masterpiece before going blind.

Let's see. . . . *(He reads—walking down* L.*)* "Apart from literature, Mrs. Moorhead's main interest in life is gastronomy."

MAMA. The stars?

NELS. No—eating. "A brilliant cook herself, she says that she would as soon turn out a good soufflé as a short story, or find a new recipe as she would a first edition."[13]

MAMA *(reaching for the paper)*. I see her picture? *(She looks at it.)* Is kind face. *(Pause while she reads a moment. Then she looks up and asks.)* What is first edition?

(Blackout. Lights up on L. *turntable, representing the lobby of the Fairmont Hotel. A couch against a column with a palm behind it. An orchestra plays softly in the background.* MAMA *is discovered seated on the couch, waiting patiently. She wears a hat and a suit, and clutches a newspaper and a bundle of manuscripts. A couple of guests come through the curtains and cross, disappearing into the wings* L. MAMA *watches them. Then* FLORENCE DANA MOORHEAD *enters through the curtains. She is a stout, dressy, good-natured, middle-aged woman. A* BELLBOY *comes from the* R., *paging her.)*

BELLBOY. Miss Moorhead?

F. D. MOORHEAD. Yes?

BELLBOY. Telegram.

F. D. MOORHEAD. Oh . . . Thank you. *(She tips him, and he goes.* MAMA *rises and moves towards her.)*

MAMA. Please . . . Please . . . Miss Moorhead . . . Miss Moorhead.

F. D. MOORHEAD *(looking up from her telegram, on the steps)*. Were you calling me?

MAMA. Yes. You are . . . Miss Florence Dana Moorhead?

F. D. MOORHEAD. Yes.

MAMA. Please . . . might I speak to you for a moment?

F. D. MOORHEAD. Yes—what's it about?

MAMA. I read in the paper what you say about writing.

F. D. MOORHEAD *(with a vague social smile)*. Oh, yes?

MAMA. My daughter, Katrin, wants to be writer.

F. D. MOORHEAD *(who has heard that one before)*. Oh, really? *(She glances at her watch on her bosom.)*

MAMA. I bring her stories.

F. D. MOORHEAD. Look, I'm afraid I'm in rather a hurry. I'm leaving San Francisco this evening. . . .

MAMA. I wait two hours here for you to come in. Please, if I may talk to you for one, two minutes. That is all.

F. D. MOORHEAD *(kindly)*. Of course, but I think I'd better tell you that if you want me to read your daughter's stories, it's no use. I'm very sorry, but I've had to make it a rule never to read anyone's unpublished material.

MAMA *(nods—then after a pause)*. It said in the paper you like to collect recipes . . . for eating.

F. D. MOORHEAD. Yes, I do. I've written several books on cooking.

MAMA. I, too, am interested in gastronomy. I am good cook. Norwegian. I make good Norwegian dishes. Lutefisk.[14] And Kjodboller. That is meat-balls with cream sauce.

F. D. MOORHEAD. Yes, I know. I've eaten them in Christiania.[15]

MAMA. I have a special recipe for Kjodboller . . . my mother give me. She was best cook I ever knew. Never have I told this recipe,

---

13. **first edition:** the original form in which a literary work is published, frequently valuable.

14. **Lutefisk** (lо̄о′ te fēsk): a Norwegian dish made from dried fish, usually cod, that is soaked in lye before cooking.

15. **Christiania** (kris′ chē an′ē ə): the former name of Oslo, the capital of Norway.

not even to my own sisters, because they are not good cooks.

F. D. MOORHEAD (amused). Oh?

MAMA. But . . . if you let me talk to you . . . I give it to you. I promise it is good recipe.

F. D. MOORHEAD (vastly tickled now). Well, that seems fair enough. Let's sit down. (They move to the couch and sit.) Now, your daughter wants to write, you say? How old is she?

MAMA. She is eighteen. Just.

F. D. MOORHEAD. Does she write, or does she just . . . want to write?

MAMA. Oh, she write all the time. Maybe she should not be author, but it is hard to give up something that has meant so much.

F. D. MOORHEAD. I agree, but . . .

MAMA. I bring her stories. I bring twelve.

F. D. MOORHEAD (aghast). Twelve!

MAMA. But if you could read maybe just one . . . To know if someone is good cook, you do not need to eat a whole dinner.

F. D. MOORHEAD. You're very persuasive. How is it your daughter did not come herself?

MAMA. She was too unhappy. And too scared . . . of you. Because you are celebrity. But I see your picture in the paper. . .

F. D. MOORHEAD. That frightful picture!

MAMA. Is the picture of woman who like to eat good. . . .

F. D. MOORHEAD (with a rueful smile). It certainly is. Now, tell me about the Kjodboller.

MAMA. When you make the meat-balls you drop them in boiling stock. Not water. That is one of the secrets.

F. D. MOORHEAD. Ah!

MAMA. And the cream sauce. That is another secret. It is half sour cream, added at the last.

F. D. MOORHEAD. That sounds marvelous.

MAMA. You must grind the meat six times. I could write it out for you. And . . . (tentatively.) while I write, you could read?

F. D. MOORHEAD (with a laugh). All right. You win. Come upstairs to my apartment. (She rises.)

MAMA. Is kind of you. (They start out L.) Maybe if you would read two stories, I could write the recipe for Lutefisk as well. You know Lutefisk . . . ?

(They have disappeared into the wings, and the turntable revolves out. Spot up, R. turntable. KATRIN at her desk.)

KATRIN. When Mama came back, I was sitting with my diary, which I called my Journal now, writing a Tragic Farewell to my Art. It was very seldom that Mama came to the attic, thinking that a writer needed privacy, and I was surprised to see her standing in the doorway. (She looks up. MAMA is standing on the steps, C.) Mama!

MAMA. You are busy, Katrin?

KATRIN (jumping up). No, of course not. Come in.

MAMA (coming down). I like to talk to you.

KATRIN. Yes, of course.

MAMA (seating herself at the desk). You are writing?

KATRIN (on the steps). No. I told you, that's all over.

MAMA. That is what I want to talk to you about.

KATRIN. It's all right, Mama. Really, it's all right. I was planning to tear up all my stories this afternoon, only I couldn't find half of them.

MAMA. They are here.

KATRIN. Did you take them? What for?

MAMA. Katrin, I have been to see Miss Moorhead.

KATRIN. Who's Miss . . . ? You don't mean Florence Dana Moorhead? (MAMA nods.) You don't mean . . . (She comes down to her.) Mama, you don't mean you took her my stories?

MAMA. She read five of them. I was two hours with her. We have glass of sherry. Two glass of sherry.

KATRIN. What . . . what did she say about them?

MAMA *(quietly).* She say they are not good.

KATRIN *(turning away).* Well, I knew that. It was hardly worth your going to all that trouble just to be told that.

MAMA. She say more. Will you listen, Katrin?

KATRIN *(trying to be gracious).* Sure. Sure. I'll listen.

MAMA. I will try and remember. She say you write now only because of what you have read in other books, and that no one can write good until they have felt what they write about. That for years she write bad stories about people in the olden times, until one day she remember something that happen in her own town . . . something that only she could know and understand . . . and she feels she must tell it . . . and that is how she write her first good story. She say you must write more of things you know. . . .

KATRIN. That's what my teacher always told me at school.

MAMA. Maybe your teacher was right. I do not know if I explain good what Miss Moorhead means, but while she talks I think I understand. Your story about the painter who is blind . . . that is because . . . forgive me if I speak plain, my Katrin, but it is important to you . . . because you are the dramatic one, as Papa has said . . . and you think it would feel good to be a painter and be blind and not complain. But never have you imagined how it would really be. Is true?

KATRIN *(subdued).* Yes, I . . . guess it's true.

MAMA. But she say you are to go on writing. That you have the gift. (KATRIN *turns back to her, suddenly aglow.)* And that when you have written story that is real and true

. . . then you send it to someone whose name she give me. *(She fumbles for a piece of paper.)* It is her . . . agent . . . and say she recommend you. Here. No, that is recipe she give me for goulash as her grandmother make it . . . here . . . *(She hands over the paper.)* It helps, Katrin, what I have told you?

KATRIN *(subdued again).* Yes, I . . . I guess it helps. Some. But what have *I* got to write about? I haven't seen anything, or been anywhere.

MAMA. Could you write about San Francisco, maybe? Is fine city. Miss Moorhead write about her home town.

KATRIN. Yes, I know. But you've got to have a central character or something. She writes about her grandfather . . . he was a wonderful old man.

MAMA. Could you maybe write about Papa?

KATRIN. Papa?

MAMA. Papa is fine man. Is wonderful man.

KATRIN. Yes, I know, but . . .

MAMA *(rising).* I must go fix supper. Is late. Papa will be home. *(She goes up the steps to the curtains, and then turns back.)* I like you should write about Papa. *(She goes inside.)*

KATRIN *(going back to her seat behind the desk).* Papa. Yes, but what's he ever done? What's ever happened to him? What's ever happened to *any* of us? Except always being poor and having illness, like the time when Dagmar went to hospital and Mama . . . *(The idea hits her like a flash.)* Oh. . . . Oh. . . . *(Pause— then she becomes the* KATRIN *of today.)* And that was how it was born . . . suddenly in a flash . . . the story of "Mama and the Hospital" . . . the first of all the stories. I wrote it . . . oh, quite soon after that. I didn't tell Mama or any of them. But I sent it to Miss Moorhead's agent. It was a long time before I heard anything . . . and then one evening the

letter came. *(She takes an envelope from the desk in front of her.)* For a moment I couldn't believe it. Then I went rushing into the kitchen, shouting. . . . *(She rises from the desk, taking some papers with her, and rushes upstage, crying, "Mama, Mama." The curtains have parted on the kitchen—and the family tableau—*MAMA, PAPA, CHRISTINE, *and* NELS. DAGMAR *is not present.* KATRIN *comes rushing in, up the steps. The* R. *turntable revolves out as soon as she has left it.)* Mama . . . Mama . . . I've sold a story!

MAMA *(R. of table).* A story?

KATRIN. Yes, I've got a letter from the agent . . . with a check for . . . *(Gasping.)* five hundred dollars!

NELS *(on the chest).* No kidding? *(He rises.)*

MAMA. Katrin . . . is true?

KATRIN. Here it is. Here's the letter. Maybe I haven't read it right. *(She hands the letter.* PAPA *and* MAMA *huddle and gloat over it.)*

CHRISTINE *(behind* MAMA's *chair).* What will you *do* with five hundred dollars?

KATRIN. I don't know. I'll buy Mama her warm coat. I know that.

CHRISTINE. Coats don't cost five hundred dollars.

KATRIN. I know. We'll put the rest in the Bank.

NELS *(kidding,* C.). Quick. Before they change their mind, and stop the check.

KATRIN. Will you, Mama? Will you take it to the Bank downtown tomorrow. *(MAMA looks vague.)* What is it?

MAMA. I do not know how.

NELS. Just give it to the man and tell him to put it in your account, like you always do.

(MAMA *looks up at* PAPA.)

PAPA. You tell them . . . now.

CHRISTINE. Tell us what?

MAMA (*desperately*). Is no bank account! (*She rises, feeling hemmed in by them—sits on bench.*) Never in my life have I been inside a bank.

CHRISTINE. But you always told us . . .

KATRIN. Mama, you've always said . . .

MAMA. I know. But was not true. I tell a lie.

KATRIN. But why, Mama? Why did you pretend?

MAMA. Is not good for little ones to be afraid . . . to not feel secure. (*Rising again and moving* L.) But now . . . with five hundred dollar . . . I think I can tell.

KATRIN (*going to her, emotionally*). Mama!

MAMA (*stopping her, quickly*). You read us the story. You have it there?

KATRIN. Yes.

MAMA. Then read.

KATRIN. Now?

MAMA. Yes. No—— Wait. Dagmar must hear. (*She opens pantry door and calls.*) Dagmar.

DAGMAR (*off*). Yes, Mama?

MAMA (*calling*). Come here, I want you.

DAGMAR (*off*). What is it?

MAMA. I want you. No, you leave the rabbits! (*She comes back.*) What is it called . . . the story?

KATRIN (*seating herself in the chair that* MR. HYDE *took in the opening scene*). It's called "Mama and the Hospital."

PAPA (*delighted*). You write about **Mama**?

KATRIN. Yes.

MAMA. But I thought . . . I thought you say . . . I tell you . . . (*She gestures at* PAPA, *behind his back.*)

KATRIN. I know, Mama, but . . . well, that's how it came out.

(DAGMAR *comes in.*)

DAGMAR. What is it? What do you want?

MAMA. Katrin write story for magazine. They pay her five hundred dollar to print it.

DAGMAR (*completely uninterested*). Oh. (*She starts back for the pantry.*)

MAMA (*Stopping her*). She read it to us. I want you should listen. (DAGMAR *sits on the floor at* MAMA's *feet.*) You are ready, Katrin?

KATRIN. Sure.

MAMA. Then read.

(*The group around the table is now a duplicate of the grouping around* MR. HYDE *in the first scene, with* KATRIN *in his place.* CHRISTINE *is in* TRINA's *chair.*)

KATRIN (*reading*). "For as long as I could remember, the house on Steiner Street had been home. All of us were born there. Nels, the oldest and the only boy . . ." (NELS *looks up, astonished to be in a story.*) "my sister, Christine . . ." (CHRISTINE *does likewise.*) "and the littlest sister, Dagmar. . . ."

DAGMAR. Am I in the story?

MAMA. Hush, Dagmar. We are all in the story.

KATRIN. "But first and foremost, I remember Mama." (*The lights begin to dim and the curtain slowly to fall. As it descends, we hear her voice continuing.*) "I remember that every Saturday night Mama would sit down by the kitchen table and count out the money Papa had brought home in the little envelope. . . ."

(*By now, the curtain is down.*)

Act II

Getting at Meaning

1. Why does Mama tell the "lie" about the bank account to her children?

2. What does each of the children want to do with his or her life? How do the choices reflect each child's character? How does the family try to allow for these individual differences?

3. How does Katrin feel when Mama takes her out for a soda? What is more important than the soda?

4. How would most people react upon discovering that Mr. Hyde's check is worthless? Why does Mama accept the situation without complaint? What does she mean when she says, "He pay with better things than money"?

5. What happens when Mama attempts to chloroform the cat? Why does Mama say to Papa, "But Lars, we must tell her. Is not *good* to let her grow up believing I can fix *everything*"? What is Papa's response?

6. Why does Mama trade her brooch for the dresser set? How does Katrin find out about Mama's sacrifice? Why does Katrin return the dresser set? Why does Papa serve her coffee after this? What does the coffee symbolize?

7. What is the main concern of the aunts when they go to Uncle Chris's death bed? Why does Uncle Chris leave so little money?

8. How does Mama gain an interview with Florence Dana Moorhead? What is it about

Mama that delights Miss Moorhead? How does Miss Moorhead's advice help Katrin?

9. Why does Mama put off buying her winter coat? What event seems to indicate that she might finally get her coat?

Developing Skills in Reading Literature

1. **Character.** Mama's character is revealed in part by the way she relates to other people. How does she show understanding to each of her children? Why is she the only niece that Uncle Chris likes? How does she relate to her sisters? How does she treat Jessie Brown?

Katrin grows up as the story progresses. How does she show her flair for the dramatic? her selfishness? In the beginning, what is wrong with her writing? How does her writing change?

2. **Setting.** What is the scene suggested for the main stage? Why has the playwright chosen to focus on this place? How are the other areas of the stage secondary to this one?

3. **Tone.** What is the writer's attitude toward the subject matter in the play? How can you tell?

4. **Theme.** What does Mama mean when she says to Katrin, "I would like to be rich the way I would like to be ten feet high. Would be good for some things—bad for others"? What does she mean when she says, "No life is easy all the time. It is not meant to be"? How does Mama approach hardship and pain? What comment about human life emerges from this play?

Developing Vocabulary

Adverbs. Playwrights often give actors and actresses clues about how to speak the dialogue in plays. These stage directions can be inserted between the names of the characters and their lines.

Following is a list of adverbs this playwright has used as stage directions. Look up each word in the Glossary and write the definition. Use the word in a sentence. Then think about how you, as an actor or actress, would say lines preceded by the adverb.

tentatively	covertly
boisterously	impertinently
tenaciously	contemptuously
reprovingly	triumphantly

Developing Writing Skills

1. **Analyzing a Character.** Although she is not rich and famous, not a person with outstanding mental or physical capabilities, Mama is a heroine. Why? Select three qualities that you feel are especially important in making her the wonderful woman she is and discuss these qualities in a five-paragraph composition. Your composition should begin with an introduction and end with a conclusion. Each of the three body paragraphs should discuss one of the qualities you have selected. Support your statements by referring to specific actions, remarks, and events in the play.

2. **Character.** Choose from the play a character other than Mama and write a five-paragraph character analysis. Your introduction should make a generalization about the character, and your three body paragraphs should support the generalization with specific examples. You should end the analysis with a conclusion that sums up your interpretation of the character.

Romeo and Juliet   *William Shakespeare*

CHARACTERS

The Montagues

Lord Montague
Lady Montague
Romeo, son of Montague
Benvolio, nephew of Montague
   and friend of Romeo
Balthasar, servant to Romeo
Abraham, servant to Montague

The Capulets

Lord Capulet
Lady Capulet
Juliet, daughter of Capulet
Tybalt, nephew of Lady Capulet
Nurse to Juliet
Peter, servant to Juliet's Nurse
Sampson ⎱ servants to Capulet
Gregory ⎰
An Old Man of the Capulet family

Prince Escalus, ruler of Verona
Mercutio, kinsman of the Prince and friend of Romeo
Friar Laurence, a Franciscan priest
Friar John, another Franciscan priest
Count Paris, a young nobleman, kinsman of the Prince
Apothecary
Page to Paris
Chief Watchman
Three Musicians
An Officer

Citizens of Verona, Gentlemen and Gentlewomen of both houses, Maskers,
   Torchbearers, Pages, Guards, Watchmen, Servants, and Attendants

The Time: The fourteenth century
The Place: Verona; Mantua, in northern Italy

Prologue

[*The* Chorus[1] *enters from the back of the stage to introduce and explain the theme of the play.*]

Chorus. Two households, both alike in dignity,[2]
   In fair Verona, where we lay our scene,
   From ancient grudge break to new mutiny,[3]
   Where civil blood makes civil hands unclean.[4]
   From forth the fatal loins of these two foes   5
   A pair of star-crossed[5] lovers take their life,
   Whose misadventured piteous overthrows
   Doth with their death bury their parents' strife.
   The fearful passage of their death-marked love,
   And the continuance of their parents' rage,   10
   Which, but their children's end, naught could remove,
   Is now the two hours' traffic[6] of our stage,
   The which if you with patient ears attend,
   What here shall miss, our toil shall strive to mend.[7]

                                                [*Exit.*]

Act One

Scene 1

[*The feud between the houses of Montague and Capulet results in a street fight between the followers of the two houses. The ruler of Verona, Prince Escalus, is angered by this latest disruption of the peace by the Montagues and Capulets and declares that the penalty for another such incident will be death.*]

[*A public square in Verona.*]

---

1. **chorus:** a single actor who speaks to the audience directly to comment on the action.   2. **dignity:** rank.
3. **mutiny:** quarrel.   4. **civil blood . . . unclean:** citizens' hands are soiled with each other's blood.   5. **star-crossed:** controlled by evil.   6. **traffic:** action.   7. **mend:** make clear.

[*Enter* Sampson *and* Gregory, *servants of the house of* Capulet, *armed with swords and bucklers.*[8]]

Sampson. Gregory, on my word, we'll not carry coals.[9]
Gregory. No, for then we should be colliers.[10]
Sampson. I mean, an[11] we be in choler,[12] we'll draw.
Gregory. Ay, while you live, draw your neck out of collar.[13]
Sampson. I strike quickly, being moved.   5
Gregory. But thou art not quickly moved to strike.
Sampson. A dog of the house of Montague moves me.
Gregory. To move is to stir, and to be valiant is to stand. Therefore, if thou art moved, thou runnest away.
Sampson. A dog of that house shall move me to stand. I will take the wall[14]   10 of any man of Montague's.
Gregory. The quarrel is between our masters and us their men.
Sampson. 'Tis all one. I will show myself a tyrant.
Gregory. Draw thy sword! Here comes two of the house of Montagues.

[*Enter* Abraham *and* Balthasar, *servants to the* Montagues.]

Sampson. My naked weapon is out. Quarrel! I will back thee.   15
Gregory. How? turn thy back and run?
Sampson. Fear me not.[15]
Gregory. No, marry.[16] I fear thee!
Sampson. Let us take the law of our sides;[17] let them begin.
Gregory. I will frown as I pass by, and let them take it as they list.[18]   20
Sampson. Nay, as they dare. I will bite my thumb[19] at them; which is disgrace to them, if they bear it.
Abraham. Do you bite your thumb at us, sir?
Sampson. I do bite my thumb, sir.
Abraham. Do you bite your thumb at us, sir?   25
Sampson. [*Aside to* Gregory] Is the law of our side if I say ay?
Gregory. [*Aside to* Sampson] No.
Sampson. No, sir, I do not bite my thumb at you, sir; but I bite my thumb, sir.
Gregory. Do you quarrel, sir?
Abraham. Quarrel, sir? No, sir.   30
Sampson. But if you do, sir, I am for you. I serve as good a man as you.

---

8. **bucklers:** small shields.   9. **carry coals:** endure insults.   10. **colliers:** coal-dealers.   11. **an:** if.   12. **in choler:** angry.   13. **collar:** hangman's noose. The servants are punning on the words *collier, choler,* and *collar.* See page 507 for a discussion of puns.   14. **take the wall:** go to the inside of the sidewalk, where the ground was higher and less muddy, and thus show superiority.   15. **Fear me not:** do not mistrust me.   16. **marry:** by the Virgin Mary; a mild oath.   17. **take ... sides:** be legally in the right.   18. **list:** please.   19. **bite my thumb:** an insulting gesture.

Abraham. No better.
Sampson. Well, sir.

[*Enter* Benvolio, *nephew of* Montague *and first cousin of* Romeo.]

Gregory. [*Aside to* Sampson] Say "better." Here comes one of my master's
    kinsmen.   35
Sampson. Yes, better, sir.
Abraham. You lie.
Sampson. Draw, if you be men. Gregory, remember thy swashing[20] blow.
                                                [*They fight.*]
Benvolio. Part, fools! [*Beats down their swords.*] Put up your swords. You
    know not what you do.   40

[*Enter* Tybalt, *hot-headed nephew of* Lady Capulet *and first cousin
of* Juliet.]

Tybalt. What, art thou drawn among these heartless hinds?[21]
    Turn thee, Benvolio! look upon thy death.
Benvolio. I do but keep the peace. Put up thy sword,
    Or manage it to part these men with me.
Tybalt. What, drawn, and talk of peace? I hate the word   45
    As I hate hell, all Montagues, and thee.
    Have at thee,[22] coward!   [*They fight.*]

[*Enter several of both houses, who join the fray; then enter* Citizens
and Peace Officers, *with clubs.*]

Officer. Clubs, bills, and partisans![23] Strike! beat them down!
Citizens. Down with the Capulets! Down with the Montagues!

[*Enter old* Capulet *in his gown,*[24] *and* Lady Capulet.]

Capulet. What noise is this? Give me my long sword, ho!   50
Lady Capulet. A crutch, a crutch![25] Why call you for a sword?
Capulet. My sword, I say! Old Montague is come
    And flourishes his blade in spite[26] of me.

[*Enter old* Montague *and* Lady Montague.]

---

20. **swashing:** smashing.   21. **heartless hinds:** cowardly servants.   22. **Have at thee:** be on your guard.
23. **bills . . . partisans:** long-handled spears with sharp cutting blades.   24. **gown:** dressing gown.
25. **crutch:** Lady Capulet implies that her aged husband could better use a crutch than a sword.   26. **spite:**
contempt.

Montague. Thou villain Capulet!—Hold me not, let me go.

Lady Montague. Thou shalt not stir one foot to seek a foe.   55

> [*Enter* Prince Escalus, *with attendants. At first no one hears him.*]

Prince. Rebellious subjects, enemies to peace,
    Profaners of this neighbor-stainèd steel—[27]
    Will they not hear? What, ho! you men, you beasts,
    That quench the fire of your pernicious rage
    With purple fountains issuing from your veins!   60
    On pain of torture, from those bloody hands
    Throw your mistempered weapons to the ground
    And hear the sentence of your movèd prince.
    Three civil brawls, bred of an airy word
    By thee, old Capulet, and Montague,   65
    Have thrice disturbed the quiet of our streets
    And made Verona's ancient citizens
    Cast by their grave beseeming[28] ornaments
    To wield old partisans, in hands as old,
    Cankered with peace, to part your cankered[29] hate.   70
    If ever you disturb our streets again,
    Your lives shall pay the forfeit of the peace.[30]
    For this time all the rest depart away.
    You, Capulet, shall go along with me;
    And, Montague, come you this afternoon,   75
    To know our farther pleasure in this case,
    To old Freetown, our common judgment place.
    Once more, on pain of death, all men depart.

> [*Exeunt*[31] *all but* Montague, Lady Montague, *and* Benvolio.]

Montague. Who set this ancient quarrel new abroach?[32]
    Speak, nephew, were you by when it began?   80

Benvolio. Here were the servants of your adversary
    And yours, close fighting ere I did approach.
    I drew to part them. In the instant came
    The fiery Tybalt, with his sword prepared;
    Which, as he breathed defiance to my ears,   85
    He swung about his head and cut the winds,
    Who, nothing hurt withal,[33] hissed him in scorn.
    While we were interchanging thrusts and blows,
    Came more and more, and fought on part and part,
    Till the Prince came, who parted either part.   90

---

27. **neighbor-stainèd steel:** swords stained with neighbors' blood. 28. **beseeming:** dignified. 29. **Cankered . . . cankered:** rusted . . . corroded. 30. **forfeit of the peace:** penalty for creating a disturbance. 31. **Exeunt:** plural form of *Exit*. 32. **set . . . abroach:** reopened this old quarrel. 33. **withal:** by this.

Lady Montague. O, where is Romeo? Saw you him today?
    Right glad I am he was not at this fray.
Benvolio. Madam, an hour before the worshiped sun
    Peered forth the golden window of the East,
    A troubled mind drave[34] me to walk abroad,   95
    Where, underneath the grove of sycamore
    That westward rooteth from the city's side,
    So early walking did I see your son.
    Towards him I made, but he was ware of me
    And stole into the covert[35] of the wood.   100
    I—measuring his affections[36] by my own,
    Which then most sought where most might not be found,
    Being one too many by my weary self—
    Pursued my humor,[37] not pursuing his,
    And gladly shunned who gladly fled from me.   105
Montague. Many a morning hath he there been seen,
    With tears augmenting the fresh morning's dew,
    Adding to clouds more clouds with his deep sighs;
    But all so soon as the all-cheering sun
    Should in the farthest East begin to draw   110
    The shady curtains from Aurora's[38] bed,
    Away from light steals home my heavy[39] son
    And private in his chamber pens himself,
    Shuts up his windows, locks fair daylight out,
    And makes himself an artificial night.   115
    Black and portentous must this humor prove
    Unless good counsel may the cause remove.
Benvolio. My noble uncle, do you know the cause?
Montague. I neither know it nor can learn of him.
Benvolio. Have you impórtuned[40] him by any means?   120
Montague. Both by myself and many other friends;
    But he, his own affections' counselor,
    Is to himself—I will not say how true—
    But to himself so secret and so close,[41]
    So far from sounding and discovery,[42]   125
    As is the bud bit with an envious[43] worm
    Ere he can spread his sweet leaves to the air
    Or dedicate his beauty to the sun.
    Could we but learn from whence his sorrows grow,
    We would as willingly give cure as know.   130

---

34. **drave:** drove.   35. **covert:** covering.   36. **affections:** feelings.   37. **humor:** mood.   38. **Aurora:** goddess of the dawn.   39. **heavy:** depressed.   40. **impórtuned:** continued to ask.   41. **close:** unwilling to talk.   42. **sounding and discovery:** responding to efforts to understand his problem.   43. **envious:** hateful.

[*Enter* Romeo *lost in thought.*]

[*Romeo, son of Lord Montague, is depressed because
Rosaline has spurned him. His cousin Benvolio tries to
turn his thoughts to the beauty of other women.*]

Benvolio. See, where he comes. So please you step aside,
    I'll know his grievance, or be much denied.
Montague. I would thou wert so happy by thy stay⁴⁴
    To hear true shrift.⁴⁵ Come, madam, let's away.

[Exeunt Montague and Lady.]

Benvolio. Good morrow, cousin.⁴⁶   135
Romeo.   Is the day so young?
Benvolio. But new struck nine.
Romeo.   Ay me! sad hours seem long.
    Was that my father that went hence so fast?
Benvolio. It was. What sadness lengthens Romeo's hours?   140
Romeo. Not having that which having makes them short.
Benvolio. In love?
Romeo. Out—
Benvolio. Of love?
Romeo. Out of her favor where I am in love.   145
Benvolio. Alas that love,⁴⁷ so gentle in his view,
    Should be so tyrannous and rough in proof!⁴⁸
Romeo. Alas that love, whose view is muffled still,⁴⁹
    Should without eyes see pathways to his will!
    Where shall we dine?—O me! What fray was here?—   150
    Yet tell me not, for I have heard it all.
    Here's much to do with hate, but more with love.
    Why then, O brawling love! O loving hate!
    O anything, of nothing first create!
    O heavy lightness! serious vanity!⁵⁰   155
    Misshapen chaos of well-seeming forms!
    Feather of lead, bright smoke, cold fire, sick health!
    Still-waking⁵¹ sleep, that is not what it is!
    This love feel I, that feel no love in this.⁵²
    Dost thou not laugh?   160
Benvolio.   No, coz,⁵³ I rather weep.
Romeo. Good heart, at what?
Benvolio.   At thy good heart's oppression.

---

44. **happy . . . stay:** fortunate in your waiting.   5. **shrift:** confession.   46. **Good morrow:** good morning. "Cousin"
refers to any relative.   47. **love:** refers to Cupid, god of love.   48. **proof:** experience.   49. **view . . . still:** always
blindfolded.   50. **vanity:** frivolity.   51. **Still-waking:** always watchful.   52. **that feel . . . in this:** can take no
pleasure in this love.   53. **coz:** cousin.

Romeo. Why, such is love's transgression.
    Griefs of mine own lie heavy in my breast,   165
    Which thou wilt propagate,[54] to have it prest[55]
    With more of thine. This love that thou hast shown
    Doth add more grief to too much of mine own.
    Love is a smoke raised with the fume of sighs;
    Being purged, a fire sparkling in lovers' eyes;   170
    Being vexed, a sea nourished with lovers' tears.
    What is it else? A madness most discreet,
    A choking gall, and a preserving sweet.
    Farewell, my coz.

Benvolio.   Soft![56] I will go along.   175
    An if you leave me so, you do me wrong.

Romeo. Tut! I have lost myself; I am not here:
    This is not Romeo, he's some other where.

Benvolio. Tell me in sadness,[57] who is that you love?

Romeo. What, shall I groan and tell thee?   180

Benvolio.   Groan? Why no;
    But sadly[58] tell me who.

Romeo. Bid a sick man in sadness make his will.
    Ah, word ill urged to one that is so ill!
    In sadness, cousin, I do love a woman.   185

Benvolio. I aimed so near when I supposed you loved.

Romeo. A right good markman! And she's fair I love.

Benvolio. A right fair mark, fair coz, is soonest hit.

Romeo. Well, in that hit you miss. She'll not be hit
    With Cupid's arrow. She hath Dian's wit,[59]   190
    And, in strong proof[60] of chastity well armed,
    From Love's weak childish bow she lives unharmed.
    She will not stay[61] the siege of loving terms,
    Nor bide the encounter of assailing eyes.
    O, she is rich in beauty; only poor   195
    That, when she dies, with beauty dies her store.[62]

Benvolio. Then she hath sworn that she will still[63] live chaste?

Romeo. She hath, and in that sparing makes huge waste;
    For beauty, starved with her severity,
    Cuts beauty off from all posterity.   200
    She is too fair, too wise, wisely too fair,
    To merit bliss by making me despair.
    She hath forsworn to[64] love, and in that vow
    Do I live dead that live to tell it now.

Richard Monette as Romeo, Gregory Wanless as Benvolio.
Romeo and Juliet, Stratford Festival, Canada, 1977.

---

54. **propagate:** increase.   55. **prest:** burdened.   56. **Soft:** wait a minute.   57. **sadness:** seriousness.   58. **sadly:** gravely.   59. **Dian's wit:** the goddess Diana's wisdom.   60. **proof:** armor.   61. **stay:** endure.   62. **with . . . store:** She will die without passing on her beauty to children.   63. **still:** forever.   64. **forsworn to:** sworn not to.

Benvolio. Be ruled by me: forget to think of her.   205
Romeo. O, teach me how I should forget to think!
Benvolio. By giving liberty unto thine eyes:
    Examine other beauties.
Romeo.   'Tis the way
    To call hers exquisite, in question more.[65]   210
    These happy masks[66] that kiss fair ladies' brows,
    Being black, puts us in mind they hide the fair.
    He that is strucken blind cannot forget
    The precious treasure of his eyesight lost.
    Show me a mistress that is passing[67] fair,   215
    What doth her beauty serve but as a note
    Where I may read who passed[68] that passing fair?
    Farewell. Thou canst not teach me to forget.
Benvolio. I'll pay that doctrine, or else die in debt.[69]

                                      [*Exeunt.*]

Scene 2

[*When Paris asks Capulet for Juliet's hand, Capulet says that Juliet, not quite fourteen, is too young; but he gives his consent if Juliet is willing. He gives a party that night at which Paris can compare Juliet with other ladies.*

    The servant who is sent with a list to invite people to the party cannot read. He meets Benvolio and Romeo in the street and asks for help. Rosaline's name is on the list, and Benvolio persuades Romeo to go to the ball to compare her with other ladies. Romeo agrees, but says he will always be true to Rosaline.]

[*A street near the* Capulet *house.*]

[*Enter* Capulet *with* Paris, *a kinsman of the* Prince, *and* Servant.]

---

65. **To call . . . more:** to examine their beauty is the way to realize her greater beauty.   66. **masks:** worn to protect faces from the sun.   67. **passing:** exceedingly.   68. **passed:** surpassed.   69. **pay . . . debt:** convince you that you are wrong.

Capulet. But Montague is bound[1] as well as I,
  In penalty alike; and 'tis not hard, I think,
  For men so old as we to keep the peace.
Paris. Of honorable reckoning[2] are you both,
  And pity 'tis you lived at odds so long.   5
  But now, my lord, what say you to my suit?
Capulet. But saying o'er what I have said before:
  My child is yet a stranger in the world,
  She hath not seen the change of fourteen years;
  Let two more summers wither in their pride   10
  Ere we may think her ripe to be a bride.
Paris. Younger than she are happy mothers made.
Capulet. And too soon marred are those so early made.
  The earth hath swallowed all my hopes but she;[3]
  She is the hopeful lady of my earth.[4]   15
  But woo her, gentle Paris, get her heart;
  My will to her consent is but a part.
  An[5] she agree, within her scope[6] of choice
  Lies my consent and fair according[7] voice.
  This night I hold an old accustomed feast,   20
  Whereto I have invited many a guest,
  Such as I love, and you among the store,
  One more, most welcome, makes my number more.
  At my poor house look to behold this night
  Earth-treading stars that make dark heaven light.   25
  Such comfort as do lusty young men feel
  When well-appareled April on the heel
  Of limping Winter treads, even such delight
  Among fresh female buds shall you this night
  Inherit[8] at my house. Hear all, all see,   30
  And like her most whose merit most shall be;
  Which, on more view of many, mine, being one,
  May stand in number, though in reck'ning none.[9]
  Come, go with me. [*To* Servant, *giving him a paper.*] Go, sirrah,[10] trudge
     about
  Through fair Verona; find those persons out   35
  Whose names are written there, and to them say,
  My house and welcome on their pleasure stay.[11]
                        [*Exeunt* Capulet *and* Paris.]

---

1. **bound:** pledged to keep the peace.   2. **reckoning:** reputation.   3. **The earth . . . she:** she is his only living child.
4. **hopeful . . . earth:** center of my universe.   5. **An:** if.   6. **scope:** range.   7. **according:** agreeing.   8. **Inherit:**
have.   9. **Which . . . reck'ning none:** My daughter will be one among the beauties whom you will see, but none will
be worth more.   10. **sirrah:** term used in addressing servants.   11. **on their . . . stay:** await their pleasure.

Servant. Find them out whose names are written here! It is written that the shoemaker should meddle with his yard and the tailor with his last, the fisher with his pencil and the painter with his nets;[12] but I am sent to find those persons whose names are here writ, and can never find what names the writing person hath here writ. I must to the learned. In good time![13]

    [Enter Benvolio and Romeo.]

Benvolio. Tut, man, one fire burns out another's burning;
  One pain is lessened by another's anguish;
  Turn giddy, and be holp[14] by backward turning;
  One desperate grief cures with another's languish.
  Take thou some new infection to thy eye,
  And the rank poison of the old will die.
Romeo. Your plantain leaf[15] is excellent for that.
Benvolio. For what, I pray thee?
Romeo.   For your broken[16] shin.
Benvolio. Why, Romeo, art thou mad?
Romeo. Not mad, but bound more than a madman is;
  Shut up in prison, kept without my food.
  Whipped and tormented and—God-den,[17] good fellow.
Servant. God gi' go-den. I pray, sir, can you read?
Romeo. Ay, mine own fortune in my misery.
Servant. Perhaps you have learned it without book. But
  I pray, can you read anything you see?
Romeo. Ay, if I know the letters and the language.
Servant. Ye say honestly. Rest you merry![18]

[Romeo's joking goes over the clown's head. He concludes that Romeo cannot read and prepares to seek someone who can.]

Romeo. Stay, fellow; I can read.   *[He reads.]*
  "Signior Martino and his wife and daughters;
  County[19] Anselmo and his beauteous sisters;
  The lady widow of Vitruvio;
  Signior Placentio and his lovely nieces;
  Mercutio and his brother Valentine;
  Mine uncle Capulet, his wife, and daughters;
  My fair niece Rosaline; Livia;
  Signior Valentio and his cousin Tybalt;
  Lucio and the lively Helena."

---

12. **shoemaker . . . nets:** He mixes his metaphors, as is common with servants in Shakespeare's plays. **meddle:** occupy himself. **yard:** yardstick.   13. **In good time:** What luck, an exclamation on seeing Romeo and Benvolio approach.   14. **holp:** helped.   15. **plantain leaf:** a weed used to stop bleeding.   16. **broken:** scratched. 17. **God-den:** good evening.   18. **Rest you merry:** May you continue happy.   19. **County:** Count.

[*Gives back the paper.*] A fair assembly. Whither should they come?
Servant. Up.
Romeo. Whither?   75
Servant. To supper, to our house.
Romeo. Whose house?
Servant. My master's.
Romeo. Indeed I should have asked you that before.
Servant. Now I'll tell you without asking. My master is the great rich   80
    Capulet; and if you be not of the house of Montagues, I pray come and
    crush²⁰ a cup of wine. Rest you merry!   [*Exit.*]
Benvolio. At this same ancient²¹ feast of Capulet's
    Sups the fair Rosaline whom thou so lovest,
    With all the admirèd beauties of Verona.   85
    Go thither, and with unattainted²² eye
    Compare her face with some that I shall show,
    And I will make thee think thy swan a crow.
Romeo. One fairer than my love? The all-seeing sun
    Ne'er saw her match since first the world begun.   90
Benvolio. Tut! you saw her fair, none else being by,
    Herself poised²³ with herself in either eye;
    But in that crystal scales²⁴ let there be weighed
    Your lady's love²⁵ against some other maid
    That I will show you shining at this feast,   95
    And she shall scant²⁶ show well that now shows best.
Romeo. I'll go along, no such sight to be shown,
    But to rejoice in splendor of mine own.²⁷

                                      [*Exeunt.*]

Scene 3   [*Juliet's mother prepares her for Count Paris' proposal of
                        marriage. Juliet is not sure she is ready for marriage but
                        says she will consider Paris.*]

[*A room in* Capulet's *house.*]

---

20. **crush:** drink; a slang phrase.   21. **ancient:** traditional.   22. **unattainted:** unbiased.   23. **poised:** balanced.
24. **crystal scales:** Romeo's eyes.   25. **lady's love:** ladylove.   26. **scant:** hardly.   27. **splendor of mine own:** the
beauty of the only woman for me.

[*Enter* Lady Capulet *and* Nurse.]

Lady Capulet. Nurse, where's my daughter? Call her forth to me.
Nurse. I bade her come. What, lamb! what, ladybird!
    God forbid! Where's this girl? What, Juliet!

[*Enter* Juliet.]

Juliet. How now? Who calls?
Nurse. Your mother.   5
Juliet. Madam, I am here. What is your will?
Lady Capulet. This is the matter—Nurse, give leave awhile,[1]
    We must talk in secret. Nurse, come back again;
    I have remembered me, thou's[2] hear our counsel.
    Thou knowest my daughter's of a pretty age.   10
Nurse. Faith, I can tell her age unto an hour.
Lady Capulet. She's not fourteen.
Nurse.   I'll lay fourteen of my teeth—
    And yet, to my teen[3] be it spoken, I have but four—
    She's not fourteen. How long is it now   15
    To Lammastide?[4]
Lady Capulet.   A fortnight and odd days.
Nurse. Even or odd, of all days in the year,
    Come Lammas Eve at night shall she be fourteen.
    Susan and she (God rest all Christian souls!)   20
    Were of an age. Well, Susan is with God;
    She was too good for me. But, as I said,
    On Lammas Eve at night shall she be fourteen;
    That shall she, marry,[5] I remember it well.
    'Tis since the earthquake[6] now eleven years;   25
    And she was weaned (I never shall forget it),
    Of all the days of the year, upon that day.
    My lord and you were then at Mantua—
    For then she could stand alone; nay, by the rood,[7]
    She could have run and waddled all about;   30
    For even the day before, she broke her brow;[8]
    And then my husband (God be with his soul!
    'A[9] was a merry man) took up the child.
    "Yea," quoth he, "dost thou fall upon thy face?"

---

1. **give leave awhile:** leave us for a while; a polite request to leave.   2. **thou's:** thou shalt.   3. **teen:** sorrow.
4. **Lammastide:** August 1, a holy feast.   5. **marry:** indeed.   6. **earthquake:** in 1580, an earthquake occurred in
England.   7. **rood:** cross.   8. **even . . . brow:** just the day before, she cut her forehead.   9. **'A:** he.

Lady Capulet. Enough of this. I pray thee hold thy peace.   35

Nurse. Peace, I have done. God mark thee to his grace!
    Thou wast the prettiest babe that e'er I nursed.
    An I might live to see thee married once,
    I have my wish.

Lady Capulet. Marry, that "marry" is the very theme   40
    I came to talk of. Tell me, daughter Juliet,
    How stands your disposition to be married?

Juliet. It is an honor that I dream not of.

Lady Capulet. Well, think of marriage now. Younger than you,
    Here in Verona, ladies of esteem,   45
    Are made already mothers. By my count,
    I was your mother much upon these years[10]
    That you are now a maid. Thus then in brief:
    The valiant Paris seeks you for his love.

Nurse. A man, young lady! lady, such a man   50
    As all the world—why he's a man of wax.[11]

Lady Capulet. Verona's summer hath not such a flower.

Nurse. Nay, he's a flower, in faith—a very flower.

Lady Capulet. What say you? Can you love the gentleman?
    This night you shall behold him at our feast.   55
    Read o'er the volume of young Paris' face,
    And find delight writ there with beauty's pen;
    Examine every several[12] lineament,
    And see how one another lends content;[13]
    And what obscured in this fair volume lies   60
    Find written in the margent of his eyes.[14]
    This precious book of love, this unbound lover,
    To beautify him only lacks a cover.[15]
    That book in many's eyes doth share the glory,
    That in gold clasps locks in the golden story;   65
    So shall you share all that he doth possess,
    By having him making yourself no less.

Juliet. I'll look to like, if looking liking move;[16]
    But no more deep will I endart mine eye
    Than your consent gives strength to make it fly.   70

Pamela Hyatt as Lady Capulet, Marti Maraden as Juliet. *Romeo and Juliet*, Stratford Festival, Canada, 1977.

---

10. **much . . . years:** at much the same age.   11. **man of wax:** a perfect model of a man.   12. **several:** separate.
13. **one . . . content:** each feature enhances the other.   14. **what obscured . . . eyes:** What you cannot define of his character from his features, his eyes will make clear. The *margent* (margin) was used for explanatory notes in books of the time.   15. **cover:** possibly a double meaning: something that wraps around him (a wife's love), or something that binds him.   16. **I'll look . . . move:** I am ready to look upon him favorably if that is enough to make him love me.

[*Enter a* Servingman.]

Servant. Madam, the guests are come, supper served up, you called, my
young lady asked for, the nurse cursed in the pantry, and everything in
extremity.[17] I must hence to wait. I beseech you, follow straight.[18]
Lady Capulet. We follow thee. [*Exit* Servingman.] Juliet, the County stays.[19]

[*Exeunt.*]

Scene 4

[*The three friends, Romeo, Benvolio, and Mercutio are
disguised in masks and costumes to avoid recognition as
they wend their way to the Capulet's party. In order to perk
up Romeo's spirits, Mercutio recounts his elaborate dream
of a tiny fairy queen. Romeo is not interested in Mercutio's
dream. He has a feeling of dread consequences resulting
from the evening's festivities.*]

[*A street near the* Capulet *house.*]

[*Enter* Romeo, Mercutio, Benvolio, *with five or six other* Maskers; Torchbearers.]

Romeo. What, shall this speech be spoke for our excuse?[1]
  Or shall we on without apology?
Benvolio. The date is out of such prolixity.[2]
  We'll measure them a measure,[3] and be gone.
Romeo. Give me a torch. I am not for this ambling;   5
  Being but heavy,[4] I will bear the light.
Mercutio. Nay, gentle Romeo, we must have you dance.
Romeo. Not I, believe me. You have dancing shoes
  With nimble soles; I have a soul of lead
  So stakes me to the ground I cannot move.   10
Mercutio. You are a lover. Borrow Cupid's wings
  And soar with them above a common bound.[5]
Romeo. I am too sore[6] enpiercèd with his shaft
  To soar with his light feathers, and so bound

---

17. **extremity:** confusion.   18. **straight:** at once.   19. **County stays:** Count Paris waits for you.
1. **shall . . . excuse:** the usual introductory presentation of our group.   2. **the date . . . prolixity:** such an elaborate
device is out-of-date.   3. **measure . . . measure:** perform a dance.   4. **heavy:** sad.   5. **bound:** leap.   6. **sore:** sorely.

I cannot bound a pitch[7] above dull woe.   15
Under love's heavy burden do I sink.
Mercutio. And, to sink in it, should you burden love—
Too great oppression for a tender thing.
Romeo. Is love a tender thing? It is too rough,
Too rude, too boist'rous, and it pricks like thorn.   20
Mercutio. If love be rough with you, be rough with love.
Prick love for pricking, and you beat love down.
Give me a case[8] to put my visage in.
A visor for a visor![9] What care I
What curious[10] eye doth quote[11] deformities?   25
Here are the beetle brows shall blush for me.
Benvolio. Come, knock and enter, and no sooner in
But every man betake him to his legs.
Romeo. A torch for me! Let wantons[12] light of heart
Tickle the senseless rushes[13] with their heels;   30
For I am proverbed with a grandsire phrase,[14]
I'll be a candle-holder[15] and look on;
The game was ne'er so fair, and I am done.
I dreamt a dream tonight.[16]
Mercutio.   And so did I.   35
Romeo. Well, what was yours?
Mercutio.   That dreamers often lie.
Romeo. In bed asleep, while they do dream things true.
Mercutio. O, then I see Queen Mab[17] hath been with you.
She is the fairies' midwife, and she comes   40
In shape no bigger than an agate stone[18]
On the forefinger of an alderman,
Drawn with a team of little atomies[19]
Athwart men's noses as they lie asleep;
Her wagon spokes made of long spinners'[20] legs,   45
The cover, of the wings of grasshoppers;
Her traces, of the smallest spider's web;
Her collars, of the moonshine's wat'ry beams;
Her whip, of cricket's bone; the lash, of film;[21]
Her wagoner,[22] a small grey-coated gnat,   50
Not half so big as a round little worm
Pricked from the lazy finger of a maid;[23]

---

7. **pitch:** any distance. 8. **case:** mask. 9. **visor . . . visor:** a mask for an ugly face. 10. **curious:** careful,
accurate. 11. **quote:** note. 12. **wantons:** those of high spirits. 13. **rushes:** Floors were commonly covered with
rushes. 14. **proverbed . . . phrase:** an old proverb. 15. **candle-holder:** spectator. 16. **tonight:** last
night. 17. **Queen Mab:** the fairy queen. 18. **agate stone:** large seal ring. 19. **atomies:** tiny creatures.
20. **spinners':** spiders'. 21. **film:** delicate thread. 22. **wagoner:** coachman. 23. **worm . . . maid:** a popular belief
was that worms bred in the fingers of the idle.

Nicholas Pennell as Mercutio, Richard Monette as Romeo. *Romeo and Juliet*, Stratford Festival, Canada, 1977.

Her chariot is an empty hazelnut,
Made by the joiner[24] squirrel or old grub,
Time out o' mind the fairies' coachmakers.   55
And in this state[25] she gallops night by night
Through lovers' brains, and then they dream of love;
O'er courtiers' knees, that dream on curtsies straight;
O'er lawyers' fingers, who straight dream on fees;
O'er ladies' lips, who straight on kisses dream,   60
Which oft the angry Mab with blisters plagues,
Because their breaths with sweetmeats tainted are.
Sometime she gallops o'er a courtier's nose,
And then dreams he of smelling out a suit,[26]
And sometime comes she with a tithe-pig's[27] tail   65
Tickling a parson's nose as 'a lies asleep,
Then dreams he of another benefice.[28]
Sometime she driveth o'er a soldier's neck,
And then dreams he of cutting foreign throats,
Of breaches, ambuscadoes,[29] Spanish blades,   70
Of healths[30] five fathom deep; and then anon
Drums in his ear, at which he starts and wakes,
And being thus frighted, swears a prayer or two
And sleeps again. This is that very Mab
That plaits the manes of horses in the night   75
And bakes the elflocks[31] in foul sluttish hairs,
Which once untangled much misfortune bodes.
This is she—

---

24. **joiner:** carpenter.   25. **state:** elegant style.   26. **suit:** a petition to the monarch for some favor.
27. **tithe-pig:** The parson was entitled to a tithe, or tenth, of his parishioners' produce.   28. **benefice:** a post with a source of income.   29. **ambuscadoes:** ambushes.   30. **healths:** toasts.   31. **elflocks:** The knots in the manes of horses and uncombed human hair were sometimes attributed to mischievous fairies.

Romeo.   Peace, peace, Mercutio, peace!
   Thou talkst of nothing.   80

Mercutio.   True, I talk of dreams;
   Which are the children of an idle brain,
   Begot of nothing but vain fantasy;[32]
   Which is as thin of substance as the air,
   And more inconstant than the wind, who woos   85
   Even now the frozen bosom of the North
   And, being angered, puffs away from thence,
   Turning his face to the dew-dropping South.[33]

Benvolio. This wind you talk of blows us from ourselves.
   Supper is done, and we shall come too late.   90

Romeo. I fear, too early; for my mind misgives[34]
   Some consequence,[35] yet hanging in the stars,
   Shall bitterly begin his[36] fearful date
   With this night's revels and expire the term
   Of a despisèd life, closed in my breast,   95
   By some vile forfeit of untimely death.
   But he that hath the steerage of my course
   Direct my sail! On, lusty gentlemen!

Benvolio. Strike, drum.

                                    [Exeunt.]

Scene 5

[*Capulet welcomes Romeo's party and invites the guests to dance. As Romeo watches the dancers, he notices a particularly beautiful girl. When he asks a servant about her, Tybalt, a Capulet, recognizes his voice and flames with anger. Capulet forbids him to fight with Romeo.*
   Romeo and Juliet speak briefly together and immediately fall in love. After they have parted, they both learn that they are the heirs of the feuding families.]

[*A spacious hall in* Capulet's house. Musicians *waiting.*]

[Servingmen *come forth with napkins.*]

---

32. **fantasy:** fancy.   33. **dew-dropping South:** south wind bringing rain.   34. **misgives:** fears.   35. **consequence:** future event.   36. **his:** its.

First Servant. Where's Potpan, that he helps not to take away? He shift a trencher!¹ he scrape a trencher!

Second Servant. When good manners shall lie all in one or two men's hands, and they unwashed too, 'tis a foul thing.

First Servant. Away with the joint-stools,² remove the court-cupboard,³ look to the plate.⁴ Good thou, save me a piece of marchpane⁵ and, as thou lovest me, let the porter let in Susan Grindstone and Nell. Anthony, and Potpan!

Second Servant. Ay, boy, ready.

First Servant. You are looked for and called for, asked for and sought for, in the great chamber.

Third Servant. We cannot be here and there too. Cheerly, boys! Be brisk awhile, and the longer liver take all.

                 [Exeunt.]

[Maskers *appear with* Capulet, Lady Capulet, Juliet, *all the* Guests, *and* Servants.]

Capulet. Welcome, gentlemen! Ladies that have their toes
 Unplagued with corns will have a bout⁶ with you.   15
 Ah ha, my mistresses! which of you all
 Will now deny to dance? She that makes dainty,
 She I'll swear hath corns. Am I come near ye now?⁷
 Welcome, gentlemen! I have seen the day
 That I have worn a visor and could tell   20
 A whispering tale in a fair lady's ear,
 Such as would please. 'Tis gone, 'tis gone, 'tis gone!
 You are welcome, gentlemen! Come, musicians, play.
 A hall,⁸ a hall! give room! and foot it, girls.
         [Music plays, and they dance.]
 More light, you knaves! and turn the tables up,⁹   25
 And quench the fire, the room is grown too hot.
 Ah, sirrah,¹⁰ this unlooked-for sport¹¹ comes well.
 Nay, sit, nay, sit, good cousin¹² Capulet,
 For you and I are past our dancing days.
 How long is't now since last yourself and I   30
 Were in a mask?

---

1. **trencher:** wooden platter. 2. **joint-stools:** sturdy stools made by a carpenter. 3. **court-cupboard:** sideboard. 4. **plate:** silver plate. 5. **marchpane:** marzipan, a sweet made of almond paste. 6. **bout:** dance. 7. **Am I . . . now:** do I touch a tender spot? 8. **A hall:** clear the hall for dancing. 9. **turn the tables up:** The tables were flat leaves, hinged together and set on trestles. When folded, they took little space. 10. **sirrah:** a term of address indicating familiarity. 11. **this unlooked-for sport:** the appearance of the uninvited maskers. 12. **cousin:** a term used of any relative less close in blood than brother or sister of the speaker.

Richard Partington as Paris, Marti Maraden as Juliet.
Romeo and Juliet, Stratford Festival, Canada, 1977.

Second Capulet. By'r Lady, thirty years.

Capulet. What, man? 'Tis not so much, 'tis not so much!
    'Tis since the nuptial of Lucentio,
    Come Pentecost[13] as quickly as it will,   35
    Some five-and-twenty years, and then we masked.

Second Capulet. 'Tis more, 'tis more! His son is elder, sir;
    His son is thirty.

Capulet.   Will you tell me that?
    His son was but a ward[14] two years ago.   40

Romeo. [*To a Servingman*] What lady's that, which doth
      enrich the hand
    Of yonder knight?

Servant. I know not, sir.

Romeo. O, she doth teach the torches to burn bright!   45
    It seems she hangs upon the cheek of night
    Like a rich jewel in an Ethiop's ear—
    Beauty too rich for use, for earth too dear![15]
    So shows a snowy dove trooping with crows
    As yonder lady o'er her fellows shows.   50
    The measure[16] done, I'll watch her place of stand
    And, touching hers, make blessèd my rude hand.
    Did my heart love till now? Forswear it, sight!
    For I ne'er saw true beauty till this night.

Tybalt. This, by his voice, should be a Montague.   55
    Fetch me my rapier, boy. What, dares the slave
    Come hither, covered with an antic face,[17]
    To fleer[18] and scorn at our solemnity?[19]
    Now, by the stock and honor of my kin,
    To strike him dead I hold it not a sin.   60

Capulet. Why, how now, kinsman? Wherefore storm you
      so?

Tybalt. Uncle, this is a Montague, our foe;
    A villain, that is hither come in spite
    To scorn at our solemnity this night.

Capulet. Young Romeo is it?   65

Tybalt.   'Tis he, that villain Romeo.

Capulet. Content thee, gentle coz, let him alone.
    'A bears him like a portly[20] gentleman,
    And, to say truth, Verona brags of him
    To be a virtuous and well-governed youth.   70
    I would not for the wealth of all this town
    Here in my house do him disparagement.

---

13. **Pentecost:** the seventh Sunday after Easter.   14. **ward:** minor.   15. **dear:** precious.   16. **measure:** dance.
17. **antic face:** grotesque mask.   18. **fleer:** sneer.   19. **solemnity:** celebration.   20. **portly:** dignified.

Therefore be patient, take no note of him.
It is my will; the which if thou respect,
Show a fair presence²¹ and put off these frowns,   75
An ill-beseeming semblance²² for a feast.
Tybalt. It fits when such a villain is a guest.
I'll not endure him.
Capulet.   He shall be endured.
What, goodman boy?²³ I say he shall. Go to!²⁴   80
Am I the master here, or you? Go to!
You'll not endure him? God shall mend my soul!²⁵
You'll make a mutiny²⁶ among my guests!
Tybalt. Why, uncle, 'tis a shame.
Capulet.   Go to, go to!   85
You are a saucy boy. Is't so, indeed?
This trick²⁷ may chance to scathe you. I know what.²⁸
You must contrary me! Marry, 'tis time.—
Well said, my hearts!²⁹—You are a princox³⁰—go!
Be quiet, or—More light, more light!—For shame!   90
I'll make you quiet; what!—Cheerly, my hearts!
Tybalt. Patience perforce³¹ with wilful choler³² meeting
Makes my flesh tremble in their different greeting.³³
I will withdraw; but this intrusion shall,
Now seeming sweet, convert to bitter gall.   [*Exit.*] 95
Romeo. If I profane with my unworthiest hand
This holy shrine, the gentle fine³⁴ is this:
My lips, two blushing pilgrims, ready stand
To smooth that rough touch with a tender kiss.
Juliet. Good pilgrim, you do wrong your hand too much,   100
Which mannerly devotion shows in this;
For saints have hands that pilgrims' hands do touch,
And palm to palm is holy palmers'³⁵ kiss.
Romeo. Have not saints lips, and holy palmers too?
Juliet. Ay, pilgrim, lips that they must use in prayer.   105
Romeo. O, then, dear saint, let lips do what hands do!
They pray; grant thou, lest faith turn to despair.
Juliet. Saints do not move, though grant for prayers' sake.³⁶
Romeo. Then move not while my prayer's effect I take.
Thus from my lips, by thine my sin is purged.   [*Kisses her.*] 110

---

21. **show a fair presence:** assume a good appearance.   22. **ill-beseeming semblance:** unbecoming appearance.
23. **goodman boy:** *Goodman* indicated a man under the rank of gentleman. *Boy* is a youngster, an insulting
term.   24. **Go to:** be off, that's enough.   25. **God . . . soul:** God save me; an exclamation showing impatience.
26. **mutiny:** riot.   27. **trick:** habit.   28. **what:** what I'm doing.   29. **hearts:** good fellows. Capulet is admiring
the skill of the dancers.   30. **princox:** a saucy, conceited youngster.   31. **Patience perforce:** imposed restraint.
32. **choler:** anger.   33. **different greeting:** opposition.   34. **fine:** penance.   35. **palmer:** a pilgrim to the Holy Land.
36. **Saints . . . sake:** saints do not become involved in human affairs, but they may intercede for the sake of prayer.

Juliet. Then have my lips the sin that they have took.
Romeo. Sin from my lips? O trespass sweetly urged!³⁷
    Give me my sin again.   *[Kisses her.]*
Juliet.   You kiss by the book.³⁸
Nurse. Madam, your mother craves a word with you.   115
Romeo. What is her mother?
Nurse.   Marry, bachelor,
    Her mother is the lady of the house.
    And a good lady, and a wise and virtuous.
    I nursed her daughter that you talked withal.³⁹   120
    I tell you, he that can lay hold of her
    Shall have the chinks.⁴⁰
Romeo.   Is she a Capulet?
    O dear⁴¹ account! my life is my foe's debt.⁴²
Benvolio. Away, be gone, the sport is at the best.   125
Romeo. Ay, so I fear; the more is my unrest.
Capulet. Nay, gentlemen, prepare not to be gone;
    We have a trifling foolish banquet towards.⁴³

                        [They whisper in his ear.]

    Is it e'en so? Why then, I thank you all.
    I thank you, honest gentlemen. Good night.   130
    More torches here! *[Exeunt* Maskers.] Come on then, let's
        to bed.
    Ah, sirrah, by my fay,⁴⁴ it waxes late;
    I'll to my rest.   *[Exeunt all but* Juliet *and* Nurse.]
Juliet. Come hither, nurse. What is yond gentleman?   135
Nurse. The son and heir of old Tiberio.
Juliet. What's he that now is going out of door?
Nurse. Marry, that, I think, be young Petruchio.
Juliet. What's he that follows there, that would not dance?
Nurse. I know not.   140
Juliet. Go ask his name—If he be married,
    My grave is like to be my wedding bed.
Nurse. His name is Romeo, and a Montague,
    The only son of your great enemy.
Juliet. My only love, sprung from my only hate!   145
    Too early seen unknown, and known too late!
    Prodigious⁴⁵ birth of love it is to me
    That I must love a loathèd enemy.
Nurse. What's this? what's this?

---

37. **urged:** argued.   38. **by the book:** according to the book of instructions on gallantry.   39. **withal:** with.
40. **shall . . . chinks:** become rich through Juliet's inheritance.   41. **dear:** costly.   42. **in my foe's debt:** a
debt due my enemy.   43. **towards:** in preparation.   44. **fay:** faith.   45. **Prodigious:** unnatural; thus promising
bad luck.

Juliet.   A rhyme I learnt even now   150
Of one I danced withal.

                         [One calls within, "Juliet."]

Nurse.   Anon, anon!
Come, let's away; the strangers all are gone.

                                         [Exeunt.]

Act I

Getting at Meaning

Prologue

1. The Chorus gives the reader some background for the play. What is the social status of the feuding families? Where do they live? Why do you think the writer chose to tell the reader at the beginning what is going to happen in the play?

Scene 1

2. Who causes the fight in Scene 1? What causes the fight? Who tries to stop it? What is Tybalt's attitude toward the fight?

3. What does the Prince tell the feuding families? What is the penalty if they fight again?

4. What is wrong with Romeo? How has he been acting toward Benvolio? What is Benvolio's advice for how Romeo can forget Rosaline?

Scene 2

5. How old is Juliet? What plans has her father made for her future? What does Capulet mean when he says to Paris, "But woo her, gentle Paris, get her heart;/My will to her consent is but a part"?

6. Why does the Capulet servant approach Romeo and Benvolio for help with the party list? Why do Romeo and Benvolio decide to attend the party?

Scene 3

7. Describe Juliet's relationship with her mother and with the nurse.

8. What is Juliet's attitude toward marriage? toward Paris?

Scene 4

9. What is the mood of Romeo and his friends as they go to the Capulet party? How will they escape detection at the party?

10. Who is Queen Mab? How does Mercutio describe her in his famous "Queen Mab" speech? What kind of person is Mercutio?

Scene 5

11. Describe Capulet as a host. What is his attitude toward his guests?

12. Romeo sees Juliet for the first time in this scene. What does he first notice about her? To what does he compare her? What excuse do they use for kissing each other?

13. What is Tybalt's most obvious character trait? How does he feel about Montagues attending his uncle's party?

14. What do Romeo and Juliet realize about each other at the end of this act? What does Juliet mean when she says, "My only love, sprung from my only hate!/Too early seen unknown, and known too late"?

Developing Skills in Reading Literature

1. **Pun.** A pun is a play on words. Usually a pun involves words that sound alike, even

though they are spelled differently and have different meanings.

In Scene 4, Romeo is punning when he tells Mercutio why he cannot dance. "You have dancing shoes/With nimble soles;" says Romeo, but "I have a soul of lead/So stakes me to the ground I cannot move." What do these lines mean? What is Romeo's pun? Find an example of punning in Scene 1. Find other examples of punning in Act One.

2. **Paradox.** A paradox is a statement that appears to contradict itself, but that on closer examination reveals a truth. For example, when Juliet describes Romeo as "My only love, sprung from my only hate!" she appears to contradict herself. On closer examination, however, you understand that she realizes a sad fact: Romeo, her "only love," belongs to the Montague family, a family she has been taught to despise since birth (her "only hate").

In Scene 1, Romeo describes his love for Rosaline in a series of paradoxes. He says, "O heavy lightness! serious vanity!" and "Feather of lead, bright smoke, cold fire, sick health!/ Still-waking sleep. . . ." Can you explain these paradoxes? How does Romeo apparently feel?

3. **Aside.** A remark whispered by one character to another, which other characters are not supposed to hear, is called an aside. In Scene 1, for example, when Sampson and Gregory pick a quarrel with the Montagues, they plan their strategy through whispered asides. Find several other examples of asides in Act One.

Developing Vocabulary

Homonyms. Homonyms are words that sound alike but are spelled differently. *Two, too,* and *to* are homonyms. Often homonyms are used in punning, as when Romeo plays on the different meanings of the words *sole* and *soul.*

Make a list of at least ten pairs of homonyms. Choose one pair from your list and create a pun based on these words.

Act Two

Scene 1   [*Now that Romeo knows who Juliet is, he cannot bear to leave her house. He eludes his friends by climbing over the garden wall. Mercutio continues to make jests at Romeo's expense.*]

[*A lane by the wall of* Capulet's *orchard.*]

[*Enter* Romeo *alone.*]

Romeo. Can I go forward when my heart is here?
Turn back, dull earth,[1] and find thy center[2] out.
                 [*Climbs the wall and leaps down within it.*]

[*Enter* Benvolio *with* Mercutio.]

Benvolio. Romeo! my cousin Romeo! Romeo!
Mercutio.   He is wise,
And, on my life, hath stol'n him home to bed.   5
Benvolio. He ran this way, and leapt this orchard wall.
Call, good Mercutio.
Mercutio.   Nay, I'll conjure [3] too.
Romeo! humors! madman! passion! lover!
Appear thou in the likeness of a sigh;   10
Speak but one rhyme, and I am satisfied!
Cry but "Ay me!" pronounce but "love" and "dove."
He heareth not, he stirreth not, he moveth not;
The ape is dead,[4] and I must conjure him.
I conjure thee by Rosaline's bright eyes,   15
By her high forehead and her scarlet lip,
That in thy likeness thou appear to us!
Benvolio. An if he hear thee, thou wilt anger him.
Mercutio. This cannot anger him. My invocation
Is fair and honest,[5] in his mistress' name,   20
I conjure only but to raise up him.

---

1. **earth:** body.   2. **center:** center of the universe; that is, Juliet.   3. **conjure:** call up a spirit.   4. **The ape is dead:** a term of endearment. Romeo, refusing to heed their call, is compared to a trained ape who plays dead until his master gives the word.   5. **fair and honest:** proper and honorable.

Benvolio. Come, he hath hid himself among these trees
 To be consorted with the humorous night.[6]
 Blind is his love and best befits the dark.
Mercutio. If love be blind, love cannot hit the mark.   25
 Romeo, good night. I'll to my truckle bed;[7]
 This field-bed is too cold for me to sleep.
 Come, shall we go?
Benvolio.   Go then, for 'tis in vain
 To seek him here that means not to be found.   30

                                        [*Exeunt.*]

Scene 2   [*While Romeo is in the garden, Juliet appears at her
                   bedroom window. Romeo hears her speak of her love for
                   him and her despair at his being a Montague. They declare
                   their love, and Juliet says she will send a messenger to
                   Romeo tomorrow to find out where and when they can
                   be married.*]

[*Capulet's orchard.*]

[*Enter Romeo.*]

Romeo. He jests at scars that never felt a wound.

[*Enter Juliet above at a window.*]

But soft! What light through yonder window breaks?
It is the East, and Juliet is the sun!
Arise, fair sun, and kill the envious moon,
Who is already sick and pale with grief   5
That thou her maid art far more fair than she.
Be not her maid, since she is envious;
Her vestal livery[1] is but sick and green,
And none but fools do wear it; cast it off.
It is my lady; O, it is my love!   10
O that she knew she were!
She speaks, yet she says nothing. What of that?
Her eye discourses; I will answer it.

---

6. **be consorted . . . night:** be associated with the moody night.   7. **truckle bed:** trundle bed, a small bed on casters, pushed under the great bed in the daytime.   1. **vestal livery:** maiden's dress.

I am too bold; 'tis not to me she speaks.
Two of the fairest stars in all the heaven,   15
Having some business, do entreat her eyes
To twinkle in their spheres till they return.
What if her eyes were there, they in her head?
The brightness of her cheek would shame those stars
As daylight doth a lamp; her eyes in heaven   20
Would through the airy region stream so bright
That birds would sing and think it were not night.
See how she leans her cheek upon her hand!
O that I were a glove upon that hand,
That I might touch that cheek!   25

Juliet.   Ay me!
Romeo.   She speaks.
O, speak again, bright angel! for thou art
As glorious to this night, being o'er my head,
As is a wingèd messenger of heaven   30
Unto the white-upturnèd wond'ring eyes
Of mortals that fall back to gaze on him
When he bestrides the lazy-pacing clouds
And sails upon the bosom of the air.

Juliet. O Romeo, Romeo! wherefore² art thou Romeo?   35
Deny thy father and refuse thy name!
Or, if thou wilt not, be but sworn my love,
And I'll no longer be a Capulet.

Romeo. [*Aside*] Shall I hear more, or shall I speak at this?

Juliet. 'Tis but thy name that is my enemy.   40
Thou art thyself, though not³ a Montague.
What's Montague? It is nor hand, nor foot,
Nor arm, nor face, nor any other part
Belonging to a man. O, be some other name!
What's in a name? That which we call a rose   45
By any other name would smell as sweet.
So Romeo would, were he not Romeo called,
Retain that dear perfection which he owes⁴
Without that title. Romeo, doff thy name;
And for that name, which is no part of thee,   50
Take all myself.

Romeo.   I take thee at thy word.
Call me but love, and I'll be new baptized;
Henceforth I never will be Romeo.

Juliet. What man art thou that, thus bescreened in night, 55
So stumblest on my counsel?⁵

---

2. **wherefore:** why.   3. **though not:** even if you were not.   4. **owes:** owns.   5. **counsel:** private thoughts.

Romeo.   By a name
    I know not how to tell thee who I am.
    My name, dear saint, is hateful to myself,
    Because it is an enemy to thee.   60
    Had I it written, I would tear the word.
Juliet. My ears have yet not drunk a hundred words
    Of that tongue's utterance, yet I know the sound.
    Art thou not Romeo, and a Montague?
Romeo. Neither, fair saint, if either thee dislike.   65
Juliet. How camest thou hither, tell me, and wherefore?
    The orchard walls are high and hard to climb,
    And the place death, considering who thou art,
    If any of my kinsmen find thee here.
Romeo. With love's light wings did I o'erperch[6] these walls;   70
    For stony limits cannot hold love out,
    And what love can do, that dares love attempt.
    Therefore thy kinsmen are no let[7] to me.
Juliet. If they do see thee, they will murder thee.
Romeo. Alack, there lies more peril in thine eye   75
    Than twenty of their swords! Look thou but sweet,
    And I am proof[8] against their enmity.
Juliet. I would not for the world they saw thee here.
Romeo. I have night's cloak to hide me from their sight;
    And but[9] thou love me, let them find me here.   80
    My life were better ended by their hate
    Than death prorogued,[10] wanting of thy love.
Juliet. By whose direction foundst thou out this place?
Romeo. By love, that first did prompt me to enquire.
    He lent me counsel, and I lent him eyes.   85
    I am no pilot, yet, wert thou as far
    As that vast shore washed with the farthest sea,
    I would adventure for such merchandise.
Juliet. Thou knowest the mask of night is on my face;
    Else would a maiden blush bepaint my cheek   90
    For that which thou hast heard me speak tonight.
    Fain would I dwell on form[11]—fain, fain deny
    What I have spoke; but farewell compliment![12]
    Dost thou love me? I know thou wilt say "Ay";
    And I will take thy word. Yet, if thou swearst,   95
    Thou mayst prove false. At lovers' perjuries,
    They say Jove[13] laughs. O gentle Romeo,

---

6. **o'erperch:** climb over.   7. **let:** hindrance.   8. **proof:** armored.   9. **And but:** if only.   10. **prorogued:**
postponed.   11. **Fain . . . form:** gladly would I behave according to convention.   12. **compliment:** polite
behavior.   13. **Jove:** in classical mythology, ruler of the gods and humans.

If thou dost love, pronounce it faithfully.
Or if thou thinkst I am too quickly won,
I'll frown, and be perverse, and say thee nay,
So thou wilt woo; but else, not for the world.
In truth, fair Montague, I am too fond,[14]
And therefore thou mayst think my 'havior light;[15]
But trust me, gentleman, I'll prove more true
Than those that have more cunning to be strange.[16]
I should have been more strange, I must confess,
But that thou overheardst, ere I was ware,
My true love's passion. Therefore pardon me,
And not impute this yielding to light love,
Which the dark night hath so discovered.[17]

Romeo. Lady, by yonder blessèd moon I swear,
That tips with silver all these fruit-tree tops—
Juliet. O, swear not by the moon, the inconstant moon,
That monthly changes in her circled orb,[18]
Lest that thy love prove likewise variable.
Romeo. What shall I swear by?
Juliet.   Do not swear at all;
Or if thou wilt, swear by thy gracious self,
Which is the god of my idolatry,
And I'll believe thee.
Romeo.   If my heart's dear love—
Juliet. Well, do not swear. Although I joy in thee,
I have no joy of this contract[19] tonight.
It is too rash, too unadvised,[20] too sudden;
Too like the lightning, which doth cease to be
Ere one can say "It lightens." Sweet, good night!
This bud of love, by summer's ripening breath,
May prove a beauteous flow'r when next we meet.
Good night, good night! As sweet repose and rest
Come to thy heart as that within my breast!
Romeo. O, wilt thou leave me so unsatisfied?
Juliet. What satisfaction canst thou have tonight?
Romeo. The exchange of thy love's faithful vow for mine.
Juliet. I gave thee mine before thou didst request it;
And yet I would it were to give again.
Romeo. Wouldst thou withdraw it? For what purpose, love?
Juliet. But to be frank[21] and give it thee again.
And yet I wish but for the thing I have.
My bounty is as boundless as the sea,

100

105

110

115

120

125

130

135

---

14. **fond:** foolishly affectionate.   15. **light:** improper.   16. **strange:** cold, distant.   17. **discovered:** revealed.
18. **orb:** orbit.   19. **contract:** betrothal.   20. **unadvised:** heedless.   21. **frank:** generous.

My love as deep; the more I give to thee,   140
The more I have, for both are infinite.
I hear some noise within. Dear love, adieu!

                                                        [Nurse *calls within.*]

Anon,[22] good nurse! Sweet Montague, be true.
Stay but a little, I will come again.   [*Exit.*]
Romeo. O blessed, blessed night! I am afeard,   145
    Being in night, all this is but a dream,
    Too flattering-sweet to be substantial.[23]

    [*Reenter* Juliet, *above.*]

Juliet. Three words, dear Romeo, and good night indeed.
    If that thy bent of love[24] be honorable,
    Thy purpose marriage, send me word tomorrow,   150
    By one that I'll procure[25] to come to thee,
    Where and what time thou wilt perform the rite;
    And all my fortunes at thy foot I'll lay
    And follow thee my lord throughout the world.
Nurse. [*Within*] Madam!   155
Juliet. I come, anon.—But if thou meanst not well,
    I do beseech thee—
Nurse. [*Within*] Madam!
Juliet.   By-and-by[26] I come.—
    To cease thy suit and leave me to my grief.   160
    Tomorrow will I send.
Romeo.   So thrive my soul—
Juliet. A thousand times good night!   [*Exit.*]
Romeo. A thousand times the worse, to want thy light!
    Love goes toward love as schoolboys from their books;   165
    But love from love, towards school with heavy looks.

    [*Enter* Juliet *again, above.*]

Juliet. Hist! Romeo, hist! O for a falc'ner's voice
    To lure this tassel-gentle[27] back again!
    Bondage is hoarse and may not speak aloud;[28]
    Else would I tear the cave where Echo[29] lies,   170
    And make her airy tongue more hoarse than mine
    With repetition of my Romeo's name.
    Romeo!

---

22. **Anon:** in a minute.   23. **substantial:** real.   24. **thy bent of love:** the intention of your love.   25. **procure:**
provide.   26. **By-and-by:** at once.   27. **tassel-gentle:** male falcon.   28. **Bondage . . . aloud:** that is, being under
the control of my parents, I must be careful not to be overheard.   29. **Echo:** a nymph who pined away for the man
she loved until only her voice was left.

Romeo. It is my soul that calls upon my name.
How silver-sweet sound lovers' tongues by night,   175
Like softest music to attending ears!
Juliet. Romeo!
Romeo.   My sweet?
Juliet.   What o'clock tomorrow
Shall I send to thee?   180
Romeo.   By the hour of nine.
Juliet. I will not fail. 'Tis twenty years till then.
I have forgot why I did call thee back.
Romeo. Let me stand here till thou remember it.
Juliet. I shall forget, to have thee still[30] stand there,   185
Remem'ring how I love thy company.
Romeo. And I'll still stay, to have thee still forget,
Forgetting any other home but this.
Juliet. 'Tis almost morning. I would have thee gone—
And yet no farther than a wanton's[31] bird,   190
That lets it hop a little from her hand,
Like a poor prisoner in his twisted gyves,[32]
And with a silk thread plucks it back again,
So loving-jealous of his liberty.
Romeo. I would I were thy bird.   195
Juliet.   Sweet, so would I.
Yet I should kill thee with much cherishing.
Good night, good night! Parting is such sweet sorrow,
That I shall say good night till it be morrow.   *[Exit.]*
Romeo. Sleep dwell upon thine eyes, peace in thy breast!   200
Would I were sleep and peace, so sweet to rest!
Hence will I to my ghostly father's[33] cell,
His help to crave and my dear hap[34] to tell.   *[Exit.]*

Scene 3   [*Romeo hurries away to consult Friar Laurence about marrying Juliet immediately. The Friar is concerned about his sudden change of heart about Rosaline but agrees to marry him to Juliet that very day, hoping that the marriage will end the feud between the two families.*]

---

30. **still:** always.   31. **wanton:** spoiled child.   32. **gyves:** fetters.   33. **ghostly father:** spiritual father, as in the next scene.   34. **dear hap:** great good fortune.

[Friar Laurence's *cell*.]

[*Enter* Friar Laurence *alone, with a basket.*]

Friar Laurence. The grey-eyed morn smiles on the frowning night,
    Chequ'ring the Eastern clouds with streaks of light;
    And fleckèd darkness like a drunkard reels
    From forth day's path and Titan's[1] fiery wheels.
    Now, ere the sun advance his burning eye   5
    The day to cheer and night's dank dew to dry,
    I must upfill this osier cage[2] of ours
    With baleful[3] weeds and precious-juicèd flowers.
    O, mickle[4] is the powerful grace[5] that lies
    In plants, herbs, stones, and their true qualities;   10
    For naught so vile that on the earth doth live
    But to the earth some special good doth give;
    Nor aught so good but, strained[6] from that fair use,
    Revolts from true birth,[7] stumbling on abuse.[8]
    Virtue itself turns vice, being misapplied,   15
    And vice sometime's by action dignified.
    Within the infant rind of this small flower
    Poison hath residence, and medicine power;
    For this, being smelt, with that part cheers each part;[9]
    Being tasted, slays all senses with the heart.[10]   20
    Two such opposèd kings encamp them still[11]
    In man as well as herbs—grace[12] and rude will;[13]
    And where the worser is predominant,
    Full soon the canker[14] death eats up that plant.

[*Enter* Romeo.]

Romeo. Good morrow, father.   25
Friar Laurence.   Benedicite![15]
    What early tongue so sweet saluteth me?
    Young son, it argues a distempered[16] head
    So soon to bid good morrow to thy bed.
    Care keeps his watch in every old man's eye,   30
    And where care lodges sleep will never lie;
    But where unbruisèd youth with unstuffed brain

---

1. **Titan:** the sun god.   2. **osier cage:** wicker basket.   3. **baleful:** poisonous.   4. **mickle:** great.   5. **grace:** goodness.   6. **strained:** turned aside.   7. **Revolts from true birth:** denies its own special purpose.   8. **abuse:** misuse.   9. **that part cheers each part:** its odor refreshes all parts of the body.   10. **with the heart:** by stopping the heart.   11. **still:** always.   12. **grace:** the powers of goodness.   13. **rude will:** desire for evil.   14. **canker:** cankerworm, which destroys plants.   15. **Benedicite:** God bless you.   16. **distempered:** disturbed.

Doth couch his limbs, there golden sleep doth reign.
Therefore thy earliness doth me assure
Thou art uproused with some distemp'rature;[17]   35
Or if not so, then here I hit it right—
Our Romeo hath not been in bed tonight.

Romeo. That last is true, the sweeter rest was mine.

Friar Laurence. God pardon sin! Wast thou with Rosaline?

Romeo. With Rosaline, my ghostly father? No.   40
I have forgot that name, and that name's woe.

Friar Laurence. That's my good son! But where hast thou been then?

Romeo. I'll tell thee ere thou ask it me again.
I have been feasting with mine enemy,
Where on a sudden one hath wounded me   45
That's by me wounded. Both our remedies
Within thy help and holy physic[18] lies.
I bear no hatred, blessed man, for, lo,
My intercession[19] likewise steads[20] my foe.

Friar Laurence. Be plain, good son, and homely in thy drift.[21]   50
Riddling[22] confession finds but riddling shrift.[23]

Romeo. Then plainly know my heart's dear love is set
On the fair daughter of rich Capulet;
As mine on hers, so hers is set on mine,
And all combined,[24] save what thou must combine   55
By holy marriage. When, and where, and how
We met, we wooed, and made exchange of vow,
I'll tell thee as we pass; but this I pray,
That thou consent to marry us today.

Friar Laurence. Holy Saint Francis! What a change is here!   60
Is Rosaline, that thou didst love so dear,
So soon forsaken? Young men's love then lies
Not truly in their hearts, but in their eyes.
Jesu Maria! What a deal of brine
Hath washed thy sallow cheeks for Rosaline!   65
How much salt water thrown away in waste,
To season love, that of it doth not taste![25]
The sun not yet thy sighs from heaven clears,[26]
Thy old groans ring yet in mine ancient ears.
Lo, here upon thy cheek the stain doth sit   70
Of an old tear that is not washed off yet.
If e'er thou wast thyself, and these woes thine,

---

17. **distemp'rature:** sickness.   18. **physic:** remedy.   19. **intercession:** plea.   20. **steads:** helps.   21. **homely . . .**
drift: that is, tell your story in simple speech.   22. **Riddling:** speaking in riddles.   23. **shrift:** forgiveness.
24. **combined:** that is, Juliet and he are united spiritually.   25. **season . . . taste:** preserve love, that does not seem to
have been affected by it.   26. **thy sighs . . . clears:** the heat of the sun has not yet cleared the air of his signs.

Thou and these woes were all for Rosaline.
And art thou changed? Pronounce this sentence[27] then:
Women may fall when there's no strength in men.   75
Romeo. Thou chidst[28] me oft for loving Rosaline.
Friar Laurence. For doting, not for loving, pupil mine.
Romeo. And badest me bury love.
Friar Laurence.   Not in a grave
To lay one in, another ought to have.   80
Romeo. I pray thee chide not. She whom I love now
Doth grace for grace and love for love allow.
The other did not so.
Friar Laurence.   O, she knew well
Thy love did read by rote,[29] that could not spell.   85
But come, young waverer, come go with me.
In one respect I'll thy assistant be;
For this alliance may so happy prove
To turn your households' rancor to pure love.
Romeo. O, let us hence! I stand[30] on sudden haste.   90
Friar Laurence. Wisely, and slow. They stumble that run fast.

[*Exeunt.*]

---

27. **sentence:** proverb.   28. **chidst:** scolded.   29. **by rote:** from memory.   30. **stand on:** demand.

Richard Monette as Romeo, Leo Leyden as Friar Laurence.
Romeo and Juliet, Stratford Festival, Canada, 1977.

Scene 4

[Benvolio and Mercutio meet Romeo in the street the next day. Romeo is his old self, sharp and high spirited. Juliet's nurse finds Romeo, and he tells her that he and Juliet are to be married that afternoon in Friar Laurence's cell.]

[A street.]

[Enter Benvolio and Mercutio.]

Mercutio. Where the devil should this Romeo be?
Came he not home tonight?
Benvolio. Not to his father's. I spoke with his man.¹
Mercutio. Why, that same pale hard-hearted wench, that Rosaline,
Torments him so that he will sure run mad. 5
Benvolio. Tybalt, the kinsman to old Capulet,
Hath sent a letter to his father's house.
Mercutio. A challenge, on my life.
Benvolio. Romeo will answer it.
Mercutio. Any man that can write may answer a letter. 10
Benvolio. Nay, he will answer the letter's master, how he dares, being dared.
Mercutio. Alas, poor Romeo, he is already dead! stabbed with a white wench's black eye; shot through the ear with a love song; the very pin² of his heart cleft with the blind bowboy's butt-shaft;³ and is he a man to 15 encounter Tybalt?
Benvolio. Why, what is Tybalt?
Mercutio. More than Prince of Cats,⁴ I can tell you. O, he's the courageous captain of compliments.⁵ He fights as you sing pricksong⁶—keeps time, distance, and proportion; rests me his minim rest,⁷ one, two, and the 20 third in your bosom! the very butcher of a silk button, a duelist, a duelist! a gentleman of the very first house,⁸ of the first and second cause.⁹ Ah, the immortal *passado!* the *punto reverso!* the *hay!*¹⁰

[Enter Romeo, no longer moody.]

Benvolio. Here comes Romeo! here comes Romeo!
Mercutio. You gave us the counterfeit¹¹ fairly last night. 25

---

1. **man:** servant.   2. **pin:** center of a target.   3. **butt-shaft:** unpointed arrow. Mercutio is saying that Cupid used only the least effective weapon to overpower Romeo.   4. **Prince of Cats:** In the tale of Reynard the Fox, Tibert (or Tybalt) is Prince of Cats.   5. **compliments:** expert in fashionable behavior.   6. **pricksong:** melody accompanying a song.   7. **minim rest:** the shortest pause in music.   8. **of the very first house:** of the finest school, an expert.   9. **cause:** cause for dueling.   10. **passado . . . hay:** dueling terms. *Passado* is a step forward accompanied by a lunge; *punto reverso* is a backhanded thrust from the left side of the body; *hay* is an exclamation of triumph at making a home thrust.   11. **counterfeit:** a piece of counterfeit money was called a slip.

Romeo. Good morrow to you both. What counterfeit did I give you?

Mercutio. The slip, sir, the slip. Can you not conceive?[12]

Romeo. Pardon, good Mercutio. My business was great, and in such a case as mine a man may strain courtesy.

Mercutio. Why, is not this better now than groaning for love? Now art thou 30 sociable, now art thou Romeo.

[*Enter* Nurse *and* Peter, *her servant. He is carrying a large fan.*]

Romeo. Here's goodly gear![13]

Mercutio. A sail, a sail!

Benvolio. Two, two! a shirt and a smock.[14]

Nurse. Peter! 35

Peter. Anon.

Nurse. My fan, Peter.

Mercutio. Good Peter, to hide her face; for her fan's the fairer of the two.

Nurse. God ye good morrow, gentlemen.

Mercutio. God ye good-den, fair gentlewoman. 40

Nurse. Gentlemen, can any of you tell me where I may find the young Romeo?

Romeo. I can tell you; but young Romeo will be older when you have found him than he was when you sought him. I am the youngest of that name, for fault[15] of a worse. 45

Nurse. If you be he, sir, I desire some confidence with you.

Mercutio. Romeo, will you come to your father's? We'll to dinner thither.

Romeo. I will follow you.

Mercutio. Farewell, ancient lady. Farewell, [*sings*] lady, lady, lady.

[Exeunt Mercutio and Benvolio.]

Nurse. Marry, farewell! I pray you, sir, what saucy merchant was this that 50 was so full of his ropery?[16]

Romeo. A gentleman, nurse, that loves to hear himself talk and will speak more in a minute than he will stand to in a month.

Nurse. An 'a speak anything against me, I'll take him down, an 'a were lustier than he is, and twenty such Jacks;[17] and if I cannot, I'll find 55 those that shall. Scurvy[18] knave! Pray you, sir, a word; and, as I told you, my young lady bid me enquire you out. What she bid me say, I will keep to myself; but first let me tell ye, if ye should lead her into a fool's paradise, as they say, it were a very gross kind of behavior, as they say; for the gentlewoman is young; and therefore, if you should 60 deal double with her, truly it were an ill thing to be offered to any gentlewoman, and very weak dealing.

---

12. **conceive:** understand.   13. **goodly gear:** handsome stuff (joking).   14. **shirt ... smock:** a man and a woman.   15. **fault:** lack.   16. **ropery:** roguery.   17. **Jacks:** knaves.   18. **Scurvy:** contemptible.

Romeo. Nurse, commend me[19] to thy lady and mistress. I protest[20] unto thee—

Nurse. Good heart, and i' faith I will tell her as much. Lord, Lord! she will   65
be a joyful woman.

Romeo. What wilt thou tell her, nurse? Thou dost not mark[21] me.

Nurse. I will tell her, sir, that you do protest, which, as I take it, is a
gentlemanlike offer.

Romeo. Bid her devise   70
Some means to come to shrift[22] this afternoon;
And there she shall at Friar Laurence' cell
Be shrived and married. Here is for thy pains.

Nurse. No, truly, sir; not a penny.

Romeo. Go to![23] I say you shall.   75

Nurse. This afternoon, sir? Well, she shall be there.

Romeo. And stay, good nurse, behind the abbey wall.
Within this hour my man shall be with thee
And bring thee cords made like a tackled stair,[24]
Which to the high topgallant[25] of my joy   80
Must be my convoy in the secret night.
Farewell. Be trusty, and I'll quit[26] thy pains.
Farewell. Commend me to thy mistress.

Nurse. Now God in heaven bless thee! Hark you, sir.

Romeo. What sayst thou, my dear nurse?   85

Nurse. Is your man secret? Did you ne'er hear say,
Two may keep counsel, putting one away?[27]

Romeo. I warrant thee my man's as true as steel.

Nurse. Well, sir, my mistress is the sweetest lady. Lord, Lord! when 'twas
a little prating thing—O, there is a nobleman in town, one Paris, that   90
would fain lay knife aboard;[28] but she, good soul, had as lief see a toad,
a very toad, as see him. I anger her sometimes, and tell her that Paris is
the properer[29] man; but I'll warrant you, when I say so, she looks as pale
as any clout[30] in the versal world.[31] Doth not rosemary and Romeo begin both with a letter?   95

Romeo. Ay, nurse, what of that? Both with an R.

Nurse. Ah, mocker! that's the dog's name.[32] R is for the—No; I know it
begins with some other letter; and she hath the prettiest sententious[33]
of it, of you and rosemary, that it would do you good to hear it.

Romeo. Commend me to thy lady.   100

Nurse. Ay, a thousand times. [*Exit* Romeo.] Peter!

---

19. **commend me:** give my respectful greetings.   20. **protest:** declare.   21. **mark:** pay attention to.   22. **shrift:**
confession.   23. **Go to:** say no more.   24. **tackled stair:** rope ladder.   25. **topgallant:** topmost.   26. **quit:**
reward.   27. **Two . . . away:** two can keep a secret if only one of them knows it.   28. **fain . . . aboard:** is eager to get
her for himself.   29. **properer:** more handsome.   30. **clout:** cloth.   31. **versal world:** universe.   32. **dog's name:**
because it sounds like a dog growling.   33. **sententious:** nurse's mistake for "sentence," or proverb.

Peter. Anon.
Nurse. Peter, take my fan, and go before, and apace.[34]

[Exeunt.]

Scene 5

[*Juliet can hardly wait for her nurse to return from her
meeting with Romeo. The nurse is full of talk, and Juliet
has difficulty extracting the news from her. Juliet is to
say that she has gone to confession at Friar Laurence's cell,
and Friar Laurence will marry them there.*]

[Capulet's *orchard.*]

[*Enter* Juliet.]

Juliet. The clock struck nine when I did send the nurse;
   In half an hour she promised to return.
   Perchance she cannot meet him. That's not so.
   O, she is lame! Love's heralds should be thoughts,
   Which ten times faster glide than the sun's beams   5
   Driving back shadows over lowering[1] hills.
   Therefore do nimble-pinioned[2] doves draw Love,
   And therefore hath the wind-swift Cupid wings.
   Now is the sun upon the highmost hill
   Of this day's journey, and from nine till twelve   10
   Is three long hours; yet she is not come.
   Had she affections and warm youthful blood,
   She would be as swift in motion as a ball;
   My words would bandy[3] her to my sweet love,
   And his to me.   15
   But old folks, many feign as they were dead—
   Unwieldy, slow, heavy, and pale as lead.

[*Enter* Nurse *and* Peter.]

   O God, she comes! O honey nurse, what news?
   Has thou met with him? Send thy man away.
Nurse. Peter, stay at the gate.   20

[Exit Peter.]

---

34. **apace:** quickly.   1. **lowering:** frowning.   2. **nimble-pinioned:** swift-winged.   3. **bandy:** hit back.

Juliet. Now, good sweet nurse—O Lord, why lookst thou sad?
Though news be sad, yet tell them merrily;
If good, thou shamest the music of sweet news
By playing it to me with so sour a face.

Nurse. I am aweary, give me leave⁴ awhile.   25
Fie, how my bones ache! What a jaunce⁵ have I had!

Juliet. I would thou hadst my bones, and I thy news.
Nay, come, I pray thee speak. Good, good nurse, speak.

Nurse. Jesu, what haste! Can you not stay awhile?
Do you not see that I am out of breath?   30

Juliet. How art thou out of breath when thou hast breath
To say to me that thou art out of breath?
The excuse that thou dost make in this delay
Is longer than the tale thou dost excuse.
Is thy news good or bad? Answer to that.   35
Say either, and I'll stay the circumstance.⁶
Let me be satisfied, is't good or bad?

Nurse. Well, you have made a simple⁷ choice; you know not how to choose
a man. Romeo? No, not he. Though his face be better than any man's,
yet his leg excels all men's; and for a hand and a foot, and a body,   40
though they be not to be talked on, yet they are past compare. He is not
the flower of courtesy, but, I'll warrant him, as gentle as a lamb. Go thy
ways, wench; serve God. What, have you dined at home?

Juliet. No, no. But all this did I know before.
What says he of our marriage? What of that?   45

Nurse. Lord, how my head aches! What a head have I!
It beats as it would fall in twenty pieces.
My back o' t' other side—ah, my back, my back!
Beshrew⁸ your heart for sending me about
To catch my death with jauncing up and down!   50

Juliet. I' faith, I am sorry that thou art not well.
Sweet, sweet, sweet nurse, tell me, what says my love?

Nurse. Your love says, like an honest gentleman, and a courteous, and a
kind, and a handsome, and, I warrant, a virtuous—Where is your mother?

Juliet. Where is my mother? Why, she is within.   55
Where should she be? How oddly thou repliest!
"Your love says, like an honest gentleman,
'Where is your mother?'"

Nurse.   O God's Lady dear!
Are you so hot?⁹ Marry come up, I trow.¹⁰   60

---

4. **give me leave:** let me alone.   5. **jaunce:** running to and fro.   6. **stay the circumstance:** wait for details.
7. **simple:** foolish.   8. **Beshrew:** a plague on.   9. **hot:** impatient.   10. **Marry . . . trow:** really, you are too
impatient, I declare.

Is this the poultice for my aching bones?
Henceforward do your messages yourself.
Juliet. Here's such a coil![11] Come, what says Romeo?
Nurse. Have you got leave to go to shrift today?
Juliet. I have.   65
Nurse. Then hie you hence to Friar Laurence' cell;
   There stays a husband to make you a wife.
   Now comes the wanton blood up in your cheeks:
   They'll be in scarlet straight at any news.
   Hie you to church; I must another way,   70
   To fetch a ladder, by the which your love
   Must climb a bird's nest soon when it is dark.
   I am the drudge, and toil in your delight;
   But you shall bear the burden soon at night.
   Go; I'll to dinner; hie you to the cell.   75
Juliet. Hie to high fortune! Honest nurse, farewell.   [*Exeunt.*]

---

11. **coil:** fuss.

Scene 6

[*Juliet meets Romeo at Friar Laurence's cell for their marriage.*]

[Friar Laurence's *cell.*]

[*Enter* Friar Laurence *and* Romeo.]

Friar Laurence. So smile the heavens upon this holy act
    That after-hours with sorrow chide us not!
Romeo. Amen, amen! But come what sorrow can,
    It cannot countervail¹ the exchange of joy
    That one short minute gives me in her sight.   5
    Do thou but close our hands with holy words,
    Then love-devouring death do what he dare—
    It is enough I may but call her mine.
Friar Laurence. These violent delights have violent ends
    And in their triumph die, like fire and powder,   10
    Which, as they kiss, consume. The sweetest honey
    Is loathsome in his own deliciousness²
    And in the taste confounds³ the appetite.
    Therefore love moderately: long love doth so;
    Too swift arrives as tardy as too slow.   15

    [*Enter* Juliet.]

    Here comes the lady. O, so light a foot
    Will ne'er wear out the everlasting flint.⁴
    A lover may bestride the gossamer⁵
    That idles in the wanton summer air,
    And yet not fall; so light is vanity.⁶   20
Juliet. Good even to my ghostly confessor.
Friar Laurence. Romeo shall thank thee, daughter, for us both.
Juliet. As much⁷ to him, else is his thanks too much.
Romeo. Ah, Juliet, if the measure of thy joy
    Be heaped like mine, and that⁸ thy skill be more   25
    To blazon⁹ it, then sweeten with thy breath
    This neighbor air, and let rich music's tongue
    Unfold the imagined happiness that both
    Receive in either by this dear encounter.
Juliet. Conceit,¹⁰ more rich in matter than in words,   30
    Brags of his substance, not of ornament.
    They are but beggars that can count their worth;

---

1. **countervail:** outweigh.   2. **loathsome . . . deliciousness:** Its excessive sweetness quickly becomes offensive.   3. **confounds:** destroys.   4. **flint:** hard stone.   5. **gossamer:** cobweb.   6. **vanity:** the unreality of love's illusions.   7. **as much:** the same greeting.   8. **that:** if.   9. **blazon:** proclaim.   10. **Conceit:** understanding.

But my true love is grown to such excess
I cannot sum up sum of half my wealth.
Friar Laurence. Come, come with me, and we will make short work; 35
For, by your leaves, you shall not stay alone
Till Holy Church incorporate two in one.

[*Exeunt.*]

Act II

Getting at Meaning

Scene 1

1. How does Romeo escape his friends? Why does he wish to remain at the Capulet house?

Scene 2

2. To what does Romeo compare Juliet when she appears at the window? What does he say about her eyes? her cheek?

3. What does Juliet say in her famous "What's in a name" speech? Why does Romeo hesitate to identify himself?

4. Why is Juliet embarrassed that Romeo hears her thinking out loud? What are Juliet's fears?

5. What do the lovers plan for the following day?

Scene 3

6. What does Friar Laurence observe about the opposing powers of herbs? What comparison does he make between herbs and human beings?

7. What is the reaction of Friar Laurence when he learns that Romeo wishes to marry Juliet? Why does he change his mind?

Scene 4

8. How do Benvolio and Mercutio treat Juliet's nurse? What does the nurse tell Romeo?

Scene 5

9. What is Juliet's state of mind as she waits for the nurse? What is humorous about the scene when the nurse returns?

Scene 6

10. What is Friar Laurence's fear before he marries Romeo and Juliet? What is his advice to Romeo?

11. What do Romeo and Juliet say to each other just before they marry?

Developing Skills in Reading Literature

1. **Soliloquy.** When a character speaks directly to the audience rather than another character, the speech is called a soliloquy. The soliloquy provides a way for a playwright to reveal a character's thoughts to the audience. Find two examples of soliloquy in this act.

2. **Theme.** Friar Laurence expresses a theme of the play when he says to Romeo, "Wisely and slow. They stumble that run fast." What words of Juliet in the balcony scene express this same fear? How much time elapses between the first meeting of Romeo and Juliet and their marriage?

3. **Meter.** The lines spoken by many of the characters are poetry. The meter of the poetry is iambic pentameter. Pentameter means that there are five feet, or units of rhythm, to a line. Each foot in iambic pentameter is an iamb, or an unaccented syllable followed by an accented syllable. The first line, then, of Romeo's famous speech to Juliet in the balcony scene has this pattern:

But soft! What light

1   2

through yonder window breaks?

3   4   5

Write out the three lines that follow this opening line. Mark the accented and the unaccented syllables and number the feet, as in the example.

4. **Blank Verse and Heroic Couplet.** When lines of iambic pentameter do not rhyme, they are called blank verse. Romeo's speech to Juliet in the balcony scene is an example of blank verse. Identify one more example in Act Two.

When two lines of iambic pentameter do rhyme, they are called a heroic couplet. Find at least two examples of heroic couplets in Act Two.

5. **Simile and Metaphor.** Act Two is full of beautiful similes and metaphors. What similes and metaphors does Romeo use to describe

Juliet's beauty? What simile and metaphors does Juliet use for the suddenness of their love?

6. **Paradox.** Explain the paradox of Friar Laurence's remark to Romeo, "Too swift arrives as tardy as too slow"?

Developing Vocabulary

Root Words. Romeo speaks of Friar Laurence's knowledge of *physic*, meaning "medicine." The root *physi-* or *physio-* comes from Ancient Greek, and it means "concerned with the natural order, or having to do with the body."

Look up the following words in a dictionary and record their meanings. Be prepared to explain how the root *physi-* functions in each word.

physics	physical	physiometry
physiology	physique	physician

Act Three

Scene 1

[*Tybalt meets Benvolio and Mercutio on the street. Romeo appears and Tybalt purposely insults him, but Romeo ignores the insults. Mercutio's temper flares, and he challenges Tybalt. They duel. When Romeo tries to separate them, Tybalt's sword passes under Romeo's arm and kills Mercutio. Aware of the secrecy of his new relationship to Tybalt through marriage to Juliet but ashamed of what may appear cowardice, he duels with Tybalt and kills him. The Capulets demand Romeo's life for Tybalt's death in accordance with the Prince's recent threat, in spite of Benvolio's explanation of the events. Romeo is banished on pain of death by the Prince.*]

[*A public place.*]

[*Enter Mercutio, Benvolio, Page, and Servants.*]

Benvolio. I pray thee, good Mercutio, let's retire.
    The day is hot, the Capulets abroad,
    And if we meet, we shall not scape a brawl,
    For now, these hot days, is the mad blood stirring.
Mercutio. Thou art like one of those fellows that, when he enters the con-   5
    fines of a tavern, claps me his sword upon the table and says "God send

me no need of thee!" and by the operation of the second cup[1] draws him
on the drawer,[2] when indeed there is no need.

Benvolio. Am I like such a fellow?

Mercutio. Come, come, thou art as hot a Jack in thy mood as any in Italy;   10
and as soon moved to be moody,[3] and as soon moody to be moved.[4]

Benvolio. And what to?

Mercutio. Nay, an there were two[5] such, we should have none shortly, for
one would kill the other. Thou! why, thou wilt quarrel with a man that
hath a hair more or a hair less in his beard than thou hast. Thou wilt   15
quarrel with a man for cracking nuts, having no other reason but because thou hast hazel eyes. What eye but such an eye would spy out
such a quarrel? Thy head is as full of quarrels as an egg is full of meat;
and yet thy head hath been beaten as addle as an egg for quarreling.
Thou hast quarreled with a man for coughing in the street, because he   20
hath wakened thy dog that hath lain alseep in the sun. Didst thou not
fall out with a tailor for wearing his new doublet[6] before Easter? with
another for tying his new shoes with old riband?[7] And yet thou wilt
tutor me from quarreling!

Benvolio. An I were so apt to quarrel as thou art, any man should buy the   25
fee simple[8] of my life for an hour and a quarter.[9]

Mercutio. The fee simple? O simple!

[*Enter* Tybalt *and others.*]

Benvolio. By my head, here come the Capulets.

Mercutio. By my heel, I care not.

Tybalt. Follow me close, for I will speak to them.   30
Gentlemen, good den. A word with one of you.

Mercutio. And but one word with one of us?
Couple it with something; make it a word and a blow.

Tybalt. You shall find me apt enough to that, sir, an you will give me
occasion.   35

Mercutio. Could you not take some occasion without giving?

Tybalt. Mercutio, thou consortest[10] with Romeo.

Mercutio. Consort?[11] What, dost thou make us minstrels? An thou make
minstrels of us, look to hear nothing but discords. Here's my fiddlestick;[12] here's that shall make you dance. Zounds,[13] consort!   40

Benvolio. We talk here in the public haunt of men.
Either withdraw unto some private place

---

1. **by the operation . . . cup:** as the second drink begins to affect him.   2. **drawer:** waiter.   3. **moved to be moody:** inclined to anger.   4. **moody to be moved:** quarrelsome.   5. **two:** Mercutio pretends to misunderstand Benvolio's *to*.   6. **doublet:** short, close-fitting jacket.   7. **riband:** ribbon.   8. **fee simple:** absolute ownership.   9. **an hour and a quarter:** merest part of its actual value.   10. **consortest:** are friendly with.   11. **Consort:** party of musicians.   12. **fiddlestick:** sword.   13. **Zounds:** by God's wounds.

And reason coldly of your grievances,
Or else depart. Here all eyes gaze on us.
Mercutio. Men's eyes were made to look, and let them gaze. I will not budge   45
for no man's pleasure, I.

    [*Enter* Romeo.]

Tybalt. Well, peace be with you, sir. Here comes my man.
Mercutio. But I'll be hanged, sir, if he wear your livery.[14]
    Marry, go before to field,[15] he'll be your follower!
    Your worship in that sense may call him man.   50
Tybalt. Romeo, the love I bear thee can afford
    No better term than this: thou art a villain.[16]
Romeo. Tybalt, the reason that I have to love thee
    Doth much excuse the appertaining rage[17]
    To such a greeting. Villain am I none.   55
    Therefore farewell. I see thou knowst me not.[18]
Tybalt. Boy, this shall not excuse the injuries
    That thou hast done me; therefore turn and draw.
Romeo. I do protest I never injured thee,
    But love thee better than thou canst devise   60
    Till thou shalt know the reason of my love;
    And so, good Capulet, which name I tender[19]
    As dearly as mine own, be satisfied.
Mercutio. O calm, dishonorable, vile submission!
    Alla stoccata[20] carries it away.   [*Draws.*]   65
    Tybalt, you ratcatcher,[21] will you walk?[22]
Tybalt. What wouldst thou have with me?
Mercutio. Good King of Cats, nothing but one of your nine lives. That I
    mean to make bold withal,[23] and, as you shall use me hereafter, dry-beat
    the rest of the eight.[24] Will you pluck your sword out of his pilcher[25] by   70
    the ears?[26] Make haste, lest mine be about your ears ere it be out.
Tybalt. I am for you.   [*Draws.*]
Romeo. Gentle Mercutio, put thy rapier up.
Mercutio. Come, sir, your *passado!*   [*They fight.*]
Romeo. Draw, Benvolio; beat down their weapons.   75
    Gentlemen, for shame! forbear this outrage!
    Tybalt, Mercutio, the Prince expressly hath
    Forbid this bandying[27] in Verona streets.
    Hold, Tybalt! Good Mercutio!

---

14. **livery:** servant's uniform. Mercutio chooses to interpret *man* in other sense of "servant."   15. **field:** dueling
place.   16. **villain:** a form of address to a servant.   17. **appertaining rage:** anger suitable to such a greeting.
18. **knowst me not:** Tybalt does not know they are kinsmen as a result of Romeo's marriage to Juliet.
19. **tender:** cherish.   20. ***Alla stoccata:*** a thrust in fencing.   21. **ratcatcher:** cat.   22. **will you walk:** step aside
with me.   23. **make bold withal:** he intends to take one life now.   24. **dry-beat . . . eight:** soundly beat your
other eight lives.   25. **his pilcher:** its scabbard.   26. **ears:** hilt.   27. **bandying:** quarreling.

Richard Monette as Romeo, Nicholas Pennell as Mercutio,
Paul Batten as Tybalt. *Romeo and Juliet,* Stratford Festival, Canada, 1977.

[Tybalt, *under* Romeo's *arm, thrusts* Mercutio *in, and flies with his* Men.]

Mercutio.   I am hurt.   80
  A plague o' both your houses! I am sped.[28]
  Is he gone and hath nothing?
Benvolio.   What, art thou hurt?
Mercutio. Ay, ay, a scratch, a scratch. Marry, 'tis enough.
  Where is my page? Go, villain, fetch a surgeon.   85

                                                     [*Exit* Page.]

Romeo. Courage, man. The hurt cannot be much.
Mercutio. No, 'tis not so deep as a well, nor so wide as a church door; but
  'tis enough, 'twill serve. Ask for me tomorrow, and you shall find me a
  grave man. I am peppered,[29] I warrant, for this world. A plague o' both
  your houses! Zounds, a dog, a rat, a mouse, a cat, to scratch a man to   90
  death! A braggart, a rogue, a villain, that fights by the book of arithmetic![30] Why the devil came you between us? I was hurt under your
  arm.
Romeo. I thought all for the best.
Mercutio. Help me into some house, Benvolio,   95
  Or I shall faint. A plague o' both your houses!
  They have made worms' meat of me. I have it,
  And soundly too. Your houses!

---

28. **sped:** done for.   29. **peppered:** completely destroyed.   30. **book of arithmetic:** textbook on fencing; by exact
rules.

Romeo. This gentleman, the Prince's near ally,[31]
  My very[32] friend, hath got this mortal hurt   100
  In my behalf—my reputation stained
  With Tybalt's slander—Tybalt, that an hour
  Hath been my kinsman. O sweet Juliet,
  Thy beauty hath made me effeminate
  And in my temper softened valor's steel!   105

    [*Reenter* Benvolio.]

Benvolio. O Romeo, Romeo, brave[33] Mercutio's dead!
  That gallant spirit hath aspired[34] the clouds,
  Which too untimely here did scorn the earth.
Romeo. This day's black fate on mo[35] days doth depend;[36]
  This but begins the woe others must end.   110

    [*Reenter* Tybalt.]

Benvolio. Here comes the furious Tybalt back again.
Romeo. Alive in triumph, and Mercutio slain?
  Away to heaven respective lenity,[37]
  And fire-eyed fury be my conduct now!
  Now, Tybalt, take the "villain" back again   115
  That late thou gavest me, for Mercutio's soul
  Is but a little way above our heads,
  Staying for thine to keep him company.
  Either thou or I, or both, must go with him.
Tybalt. Thou, wretched boy, that didst consort him here,   120
  Shalt with him hence.
Romeo.   This shall determine that.

                      [*They fight. Tybalt falls.*]

Benvolio. Romeo, away, be gone!
  The citizens are up, and Tybalt slain.
  Stand not amazed. The Prince will doom thee[38] death   125
  If thou art taken. Hence, be gone, away!
Romeo. O, I am fortune's fool![39]
Benvolio.   Why dost thou stay?

                      [*Exit Romeo.*]

    [*Enter* Citizens.]

Citizen. Which way ran he that killed Mercutio?
  Tybalt, that murderer, which way ran he?   130

---

31. **ally:** kinsman.   32. **very:** true.   33. **brave:** noble.   34. **aspired:** soared to.   35. **mo:** more.   36. **depend:** will be followed by more fatal days.   37. **respective lenity:** considerate mercy.   38. **doom thee:** sentence thee to.   39. **fool:** plaything.

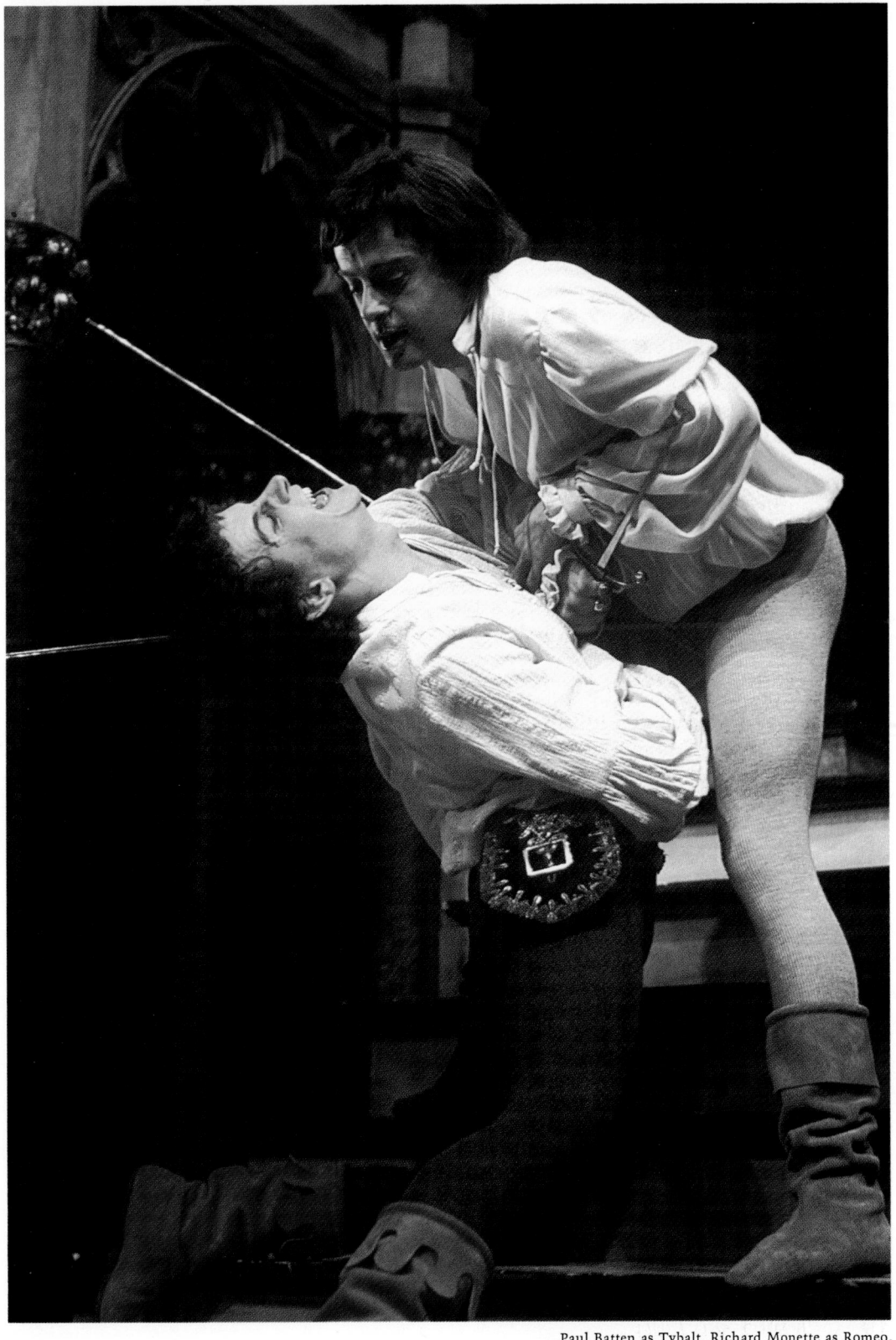

Paul Batten as Tybalt, Richard Monette as Romeo.
Romeo and Juliet, Stratford Festival, Canada, 1977.

Benvolio. There lies that Tybalt.

Citizen.   Up, sir, go with me.
    I charge thee in the Prince's name obey.

    [*Enter* Prince *with his* Attendants, Montague, Capulet, *their* Wives,
    and others.]

Prince. Where are the vile beginners of this fray?
Benvolio. O noble Prince, I can discover[40] all   135
    The unlucky manage[41] of this fatal brawl.
    There lies the man, slain by young Romeo,
    That slew thy kinsman, brave Mercutio.
Lady Capulet. Tybalt, my cousin! O my brother's child!
    O Prince! O cousin! O husband! O, the blood is spilled   140
    Of my dear kinsman! Prince, as thou art true,
    For blood of ours shed blood of Montague.
    O cousin, cousin!
Prince. Benvolio, who began this bloody fray?
Benvolio. Tybalt, here slain, whom Romeo's hand did slay.   145
    Romeo, that spoke him fair, bid him bethink
    How nice[42] the quarrel was, and urged withal
    Your high displeasure. All this—uttered
    With gentle breath, calm look, knees humbly bowed—
    Could not take truce with the unruly spleen[43]   150
    Of Tybalt deaf to peace, but that he tilts
    With piercing steel at bold Mercutio's breast;
    Who, all as hot, turns deadly point to point,
    And, with a martial scorn, with one hand beats
    Cold death aside and with the other sends   155
    It back to Tybalt, whose dexterity
    Retorts[44] it. Romeo he cries aloud,
    "Hold, friends! friends, part!" and swifter than his tongue,
    His agile arm beats down their fatal points,
    And 'twixt them rushes; underneath whose arm   160
    An envious[45] thrust from Tybalt hit the life
    Of stout[46] Mercutio, and then Tybalt fled,
    But by-and-by comes back to Romeo,
    Who had but newly entertained revenge,
    And to't they go like lightning; for, ere I   165
    Could draw to part them, was stout Tybalt slain;
    And, as he fell, did Romeo turn and fly.
    This is the truth, or let Benvolio die.

---

40. discover: reveal.   **41. manage:** circumstances.   **42. nice:** trivial.   **43. spleen:** fiery temper.   **44. Retorts:** returns.   **45. envious:** hateful.   **46. stout:** valiant.

Lady Capulet. He is a kinsman to the Montague;
    Affection makes him false, he speaks not true.   170
    Some twenty of them fought in this black strife,
    And all those twenty could but kill one life.
    I beg for justice, which thou, Prince, must give.
    Romeo slew Tybalt; Romeo must not live.
Prince. Romeo slew him; he slew Mercutio.   175
    Who now the price of his dear blood doth owe?
Montague. Not Romeo, Prince; he was Mercutio's friend;
    His fault concludes but what the law should end,
    The life of Tybalt.
Prince.   And for that offense   180
    Immediately we do exile him hence.
    I have an interest in your hate's proceeding,
    My blood for your rude brawls doth lie a-bleeding;
    But I'll amerce[47] you with so strong a fine
    That you shall all repent the loss of mine.   185
    I will be deaf to pleading and excuses;
    Nor tears nor prayers shall purchase out[48] abuses.
    Therefore use none. Let Romeo hence in haste,
    Else, when he is found, that hour is his last.
    Bear hence this body, and attend our will.   190
    Mercy but murders, pardoning those that kill.

                                [Exeunt.]

Scene 2

[The nurse informs Juliet that Romeo has killed Tybalt. Grief-stricken for her cousin Tybalt, she is consoled only by the fact that Tybalt wanted to kill Romeo. Knowing that Romeo has been banished, she makes the nurse promise to bring him to her secretly before he leaves Verona.]

[Capulet's *orchard*.]

[*Enter* Juliet *alone*.]

Juliet. Gallop apace, you fiery-footed steeds,
    Towards Phoebus'[1] lodging! Such a wagoner

---

47. **amerce:** punish.   48. **purchase out:** pay for.   1. **Phoebus:** the sun god.

As Phaëton[2] would whip you to the West
And bring in cloudy night immediately.
Come, gentle night; come, loving, black-browed night;   195
Give me my Romeo; and, when he shall die,
Take him and cut him out in little stars,
And he will make the face of heaven so fine
That all the world will be in love with night
And pay no worship to the garish sun.   200
O, here comes my nurse,

[Enter Nurse, *wringing her hands, with the ladder of cords in her lap.*]

And she brings news; and every tongue that speaks
But Romeo's name speaks heavenly eloquence.
Now, nurse, what news? What hast thou there? the cords
That Romeo bid thee fetch?   205
Nurse.   Ay, ay, the cords.
Juliet. Ay me! what news? Why dost thou wring thy hands?
Nurse. Ah, well-a-day![3] he's dead, he's dead, he's dead!
　　We are undone, lady, we are undone!
　　Alack the day! he's gone, he's killed, he's dead!   210
Juliet. Can heaven be so envious?
Nurse.   Romeo can,
　　Though heaven cannot. O Romeo, Romeo!
　　Who ever would have thought it? Romeo!
Juliet. What devil art thou that dost torment me thus?   215
　　This torture should be roared in dismal hell.
　　Hath Romeo slain himself?
Nurse. I saw the wound, I saw it with mine eyes,
　　(God save the mark!)[4] here on his manly breast.
　　A piteous corse,[5] a bloody piteous corse;   220
　　Pale, pale as ashes, all bedaubed in blood,
　　All in gore blood. I swounded[6] at the sight.
Juliet. O, break, my heart! poor bankrout,[7] break at once!
　　To prison, eyes; ne'er look on liberty!
　　Vile earth, to earth resign;[8] end motion here,   225
　　And thou and Romeo press one heavy bier!
Nurse. O Tybalt, Tybalt, the best friend I had!
　　O courteous Tybalt! honest gentleman!
　　That ever I should live to see thee dead!
Juliet. What storm is this that blows so contrary?   230

---

2. **Phaëton:** the son of Phoebus, who tried to drive his father's chariot but could not control the horses.
3. **well-a-day:** alas.　4. **God . . . mark:** a phrase uttered to set aside the bad luck that might result from seeing such a disaster.　5. **corse:** corpse.　6. **swounded:** fainted.　7. **bankrout:** bankrupt.　8. **Vile . . . resign:** miserable body, resign yourself to death.

Is Romeo slaughtered, and is Tybalt dead?
My dear-loved cousin, and my dearer lord?
Then, dreadful trumpet,[9] sound the general doom!
For who is living, if those two are gone?

Nurse. Tybalt is gone, and Romeo banishèd; 235
    Romeo that killed him, he is banishèd.

Juliet. O God! Did Romeo's hand shed Tybalt's blood?

Nurse. It did, it did! alas the day, it did!

Juliet. O serpent heart, hid with a flow'ring face!
    Did ever dragon keep[10] so fair a cave? 240
    Was ever book containing such vile matter
    So fairly bound? O, that deceit should dwell
    In such a gorgeous palace!

Nurse.   There's no trust,
    No faith, no honesty in men; all perjured 245
    All forsworn, all naught, all dissemblers.[11]
    Ah, where's my man? Give me some aqua vitae.[12]
    These griefs, these woes, these sorrows make me old.
    Shame come to Romeo!

Juliet.   Blistered be thy tongue 250
    For such a wish! He was not born to shame.
    Upon his brow shame is ashamed to sit;
    For 'tis a throne where honor may be crowned
    Sole monarch of the universal earth.
    O, what a beast was I to chide at him! 255

Nurse. Will you speak well of him that killed your cousin?

Juliet. Shall I speak ill of him that is my husband?
    Ah, poor my lord, what tongue shall smooth thy name
    When I, thy three-hours' wife, have mangled it?
    But wherefore, villain, didst thou kill my cousin? 260
    That villain cousin would have killed my husband.
    Back, foolish tears, back to your native spring!
    Your tributary drops belong to woe,
    Which you, mistaking, offer up to joy.
    My husband lives, that Tybalt would have slain; 265
    And Tybalt's dead, that would have slain my husband.
    All this is comfort; wherefore weep I then?
    Some word there was, worser than Tybalt's death,
    That murdered me. I would forget it fain;[13]
    But O, it presses to my memory 270
    Like damnèd guilty deeds to sinners' minds!
    "Tybalt is dead, and Romeo—banishèd."

---

9. **dreadful trumpet:** the trumpet that proclaims doomsday.   10. **keep:** guard.   11. **forsworn . . . dissemblers:**
faithless, all wicked, all pretenders.   12. **aqua vitae:** spirits.   13. **fain:** willingly.

That "banishèd," that one word "banishèd,"
Hath slain ten thousand Tybalts. Tybalt's death
Was woe enough, if it had ended there;   275
Or, if sour woe delights in fellowship
And needly[14] will be ranked with other griefs,
Why followed not, when she said "Tybalt's dead,"
Thy father, or thy mother, nay, or both,
Which modern[15] lamentation might have moved?   280
But with a rearward[16] following Tybalt's death,
"Romeo is banishèd"—to speak that word
Is father, mother, Tybalt, Romeo, Juliet,
All slain, all dead. "Romeo is banishèd"—
There is no end, no limit, measure, bound,   285
In that word's death; no words can that woe sound.
Where is my father and my mother, nurse?
Nurse. Weeping and wailing over Tybalt's corse.
Will you go to them? I will bring[17] you thither.
Juliet. Wash they his wounds with tears? Mine shall be spent,   290
When theirs are dry, for Romeo's banishment.
Nurse. Hie to your chamber. I'll find Romeo
To comfort you. I wot[18] well where he is.
Hark ye, your Romeo will be here at night.
I'll to him; he is hid at Laurence' cell.   295
Juliet. O, find him! give this ring to my true knight
And bid him come to take his last farewell.

[*Exeunt.*]

Scene 3

[*When Friar Laurence informs Romeo that he has been
banished instead of being executed, Romeo is desperate
over separation from Juliet. The nurse appears and tells
him to hurry to Juliet's side. Friar Laurence, hoping that in
time Romeo may be pardoned and allowed to return to
Verona, sends Romeo to Juliet. Romeo will live in Mantua,
and Friar Laurence will send his man Balthasar with news.*]

[Friar Laurence's *cell.*]

---

14. **needly:** of necessity. 15. **modern:** ordinary. 16. **rearward:** a guard bringing up the rear. 17. **bring:**
accompany. 18. **wot:** know.

[*Enter* Friar Laurence.]

Friar Laurence. Romeo, come forth; come forth, thou fearful man.
    Affliction is enamored of thy parts,
    And thou art wedded to calamity.

[*Enter* Romeo.]

Romeo. Father, what news? What is the Prince's doom?
    What sorrow craves acquaintance at my hand   5
    That I yet know not?
Friar Laurence.   Too familiar
    Is my dear son with such sour company.
    I bring thee tidings of the Prince's doom.
Romeo. What less than doomsday is the Prince's doom?   10
Friar Laurence. A gentler judgment vanished[1] from his lips—
    Not body's death, but body's banishment.
Romeo. Ha, banishment? Be merciful, say "death";
    For exile hath more terror in his look,
    Much more than death. Do not say "banishment."   15
Friar Laurence. Hence from Verona art thou banishèd.
    Be patient,[2] for the world is broad and wide.
Romeo. There is no world without Verona walls,
    But purgatory, torture, hell itself.
    Hence banishèd is banisht from the world,   20
    And world's exile[3] is death. Then "banishment"
    Is death mistermed. Calling death "banishment,"
    Thou cuttst my head off with a golden axe
    And smilest upon the stroke that murders me.
Friar Laurence. O deadly sin! O rude unthankfulness!   25
    Thy fault our law calls death; but the kind Prince,
    Taking thy part, hath rushed[4] aside the law,
    And turned that black word death to banishment.
    This is dear[5] mercy, and thou seest it not.
Romeo. 'Tis torture, and not mercy. Heaven is here,   30
    Where Juliet lives; and every cat and dog
    And little mouse, every unworthy thing,
    Live here in heaven and may look on her;
    But Romeo may not. More validity,[6]
    More honorable state, more courtship lives   35
    In carrion flies than Romeo. They may seize
    On the white wonder of dear Juliet's hand

---

1. **vanished:** issued.   2. **patient:** calm.   3. **world's exile:** exile from the world of Juliet.   4. **rushed:** brushed.
5. **dear:** precious.   6. **validity:** worth.

And steal immortal blessing from her lips,
Who, even in pure and vestal modesty,
Still blush, as thinking their own kisses sin;   40
But Romeo may not—he is banishèd.
This may flies do, when I from this must fly;
They are free men, but I am banishèd.
And sayst thou yet that exile is not death?
Hadst thou no poison mixed, no sharp-ground knife,   45
No sudden mean of death, though ne'er so mean,
But "banishèd" to kill me—"banishèd"?
O friar, the damned use that word in hell;
Howling attends it! How hast thou the heart,
Being a divine, a ghostly confessor,   50
A sin-absolver, and my friend professed,
To mangle me with that word "banishèd"?
Friar Laurence. Thou fond[7] mad man, hear me a little speak.
Romeo. O, thou wilt speak again of banishment.
Friar Laurence. I'll give thee armor to keep off that word;   55
Adversity's sweet milk, philosophy,
To comfort thee, though thou art banishèd.
Romeo. Yet "banishèd"? Hang up philosophy!
Unless philosophy can make a Juliet,
Displant a town, reverse a prince's doom,   60
It helps not, it prevails not. Talk no more.
Friar Laurence. O, then I see that madmen have no ears.
Romeo. How should they, when that wise men have no eyes?
Friar Laurence. Let me dispute with thee of thy estate.[8]
Romeo. Thou canst not speak of that thou dost not feel.   65
Wert thou as young as I, Juliet thy love,
An hour but married, Tybalt murdered,
Doting like me, and like me banishèd,
Then mightst thou speak, then mightst thou tear thy hair,
And fall upon the ground, as I do now,   70
Taking the measure of an unmade grave.

[Nurse *knocks within.*]

Friar Laurence. Arise; one knocks. Good Romeo, hide thyself.
Romeo. Not I; unless the breath of heartsick groans
Mist-like infold me from the search of eyes.   [*Knock.*]
Friar Laurence. Hark, how they knock! Who's there? Romeo, arise;   75
Thou wilt be taken.—Stay awhile!—Stand up;   [*Knock.*]
Run to my study.—By-and-by![9]—God's will,
What simpleness is this.—I come, I come!   [*Knock.*]

---

7. **fond:** foolish.   8. **dispute . . . estate:** discuss thy circumstances.   9. **By-and-by:** wait a moment.

Who knocks so hard? Whence come you? What's your will?

Nurse. [*Within*] Let me come in, and you shall know my errand. 80
    I come from Lady Juliet.

Friar Laurence.   Welcome then.

    [*Enter* Nurse.]

Nurse. O holy friar, O, tell me, holy friar,
    Where is my lady's lord, where's Romeo?

Friar Laurence. There on the ground, with his own tears made drunk. 85

Nurse. O, he is even[10] in my mistress' case,
    Just in her case! O woeful sympathy!
    Piteous predicament! Even so lies she,
    Blubb'ring and weeping, weeping and blubbering.
    Stand up, stand up! Stand, an you be a man. 90
    For Juliet's sake, for her sake, rise and stand!
    Why should you fall into so deep an O?[11]

Romeo. [*Rises*] Nurse—

Nurse. Ah sir! ah sir! Well, death's the end of all.

Romeo. Spakest thou of Juliet? How is it with her? 95
    Doth not she think me an old[12] murderer,
    Now I have stained the childhood of our joy
    With blood removed but little from her own?
    Where is she? and how doth she? and what says
    My concealed lady[13] to our canceled love? 100

Nurse. O, she says nothing, sir, but weeps and weeps;
    And now falls on her bed, and then starts up,
    And Tybalt calls; and then on Romeo cries,
    And then down falls again.

Romeo.   As if that name, 105
    Shot from the deadly level[14] of a gun,
    Did murder her; as that name's cursèd hand
    Murdered her kinsman. O tell me, friar, tell me,
    In what vile part of this anatomy
    Doth my name lodge? Tell me, that I may sack 110
    The hateful mansion.   [*Draws his dagger.*]

Friar Laurence.   Hold thy desperate hand.
    Art thou a man? Thy form cries out thou art;
    Thy tears are womanish, thy wild acts denote
    The unreasonable fury of a beast. 115
    Unseemly woman in a seeming man!
    Or ill-beseeming[15] beast in seeming both!

---

10. **even:** exactly.   11. **O:** cry of grief.   12. **old:** experienced.   13. **concealed by:** secret bride.   14. **level:** aim.
15. **ill-beseeming:** unsuitable.

Thou hast amazed me. By my holy order,
I thought thy disposition better tempered.
Hast thou slain Tybalt? Wilt thou slay thyself?   120
And slay thy lady too that lives in thee,
By doing damned hate upon thyself?
Why railst thou on[16] thy birth, the heaven, and earth?
Since birth and heaven and earth, all three do meet
In thee at once; which thou at once wouldst lose.   125
What, rouse thee, man! Thy Juliet is alive,
For whose dear sake thou wast but lately dead.
There art thou happy. Tybalt would kill thee,
But thou slewest Tybalt. There art thou happy.
The law, that threatened death, becomes thy friend   130
And turns it to exile. There art thou happy.
A pack of blessings light upon thy back;
Happiness courts thee in her best array;
But, like a misbehaved and sullen wench,
Thou poutst upon thy fortune and thy love.   135
Take heed, take heed, for such die miserable.
Go get thee to thy love, as was decreed,
Ascend her chamber, hence and comfort her.
But look thou stay not till the watch be set,[17]
For then thou canst not pass to Mantua,   140
Where thou shalt live till we can find a time
To blaze[18] your marriage, reconcile your friends,[19]
Beg pardon of the Prince, and call thee back
With twenty hundred thousand times more joy
Than thou wentst forth in lamentation.   145
Go before, nurse. Commend me to thy lady,
And bid her hasten all the house to bed,
Which heavy sorrow makes them apt[20] unto.
Romeo is coming.
Nurse. O Lord, I could have stayed here all the night   150
To hear good counsel. O, what learning is!
My lord, I'll tell my lady you will come.
Romeo. Do so, and bid my sweet prepare to chide.

[Nurse *offers to go and turns again.*]

Nurse. Here is a ring she bid me give you, sir.
Hie you, make haste, for it grows very late.   [*Exit.*]   155
Romeo. How well my comfort[21] is revived by this!

---

16. **railst . . . on:** complain about.   17. **watch be set:** the night watchmen go on duty at the gates.   18. **blaze:**
announce.   19. **friends:** your families.   20. **apt:** inclined.   21. **comfort:** well-being.

Friar Laurence. Go hence; good night; and here stands all your state:²²
    Either be gone before the watch be set,
    Or by the break of day disguised from hence.
    Sojourn in Mantua. I'll find out your man,   160
    And he shall signify from time to time
    Every good hap²³ to you that chances here.
    Give me thy hand. 'Tis late. Farewell; good night.
Romeo. But that a joy past joy calls out on me,
    It were a grief so brief to part with thee.   165
    Farewell.

                                                  [Exeunt.]

Scene 4

[Paris continues to discuss his marriage suit with Capulet. Knowing that Juliet mourns Tybalt's death and hoping to lighten her sorrow, Capulet consents to the marriage in three days.]

[Capulet's *house.*]

[*Enter* Capulet, Lady Capulet, *and* Paris.]

Capulet. Things have fall'n out,¹ sir, so unluckily
    That we have had no time to move² our daughter.
    Look you, she loved her kinsman Tybalt dearly,
    And so did I. Well, we were born to die.
    'Tis very late; she'll not come down tonight.   5
    I promise you, but for your company,
    I would have been abed an hour ago.
Paris. These times of woe afford no time to woo.
    Madam, good night. Commend me to your daughter.
Lady Capulet. I will, and know her mind early tomorrow;   10
    Tonight she's mewed up to her heaviness.³

    [Paris *offers to go and* Capulet *calls him again.*]

Capulet. Sir Paris, I will make a desperate tender⁴
    Of my child's love. I think she will be ruled

---

22. **here . . . state:** on this depends your fortune.   23. **hap:** happening.
1. **fall'n out:** worked out.   2. **move:** make your proposal to.   3. **mewed . . . heaviness:** confined with her
sorrow.   4. **desperate tender:** bold offer.

In all respects by me; nay more, I doubt it not.
Wife, go you to her ere you go to bed;   15
Acquaint her here of my son⁵ Paris' love
And bid her (mark you me?) on Wednesday next—
But, soft! what day is this?
Paris.   Monday, my lord.
Capulet. Monday! ha, ha! Well, Wednesday is too soon.   20
A⁶ Thursday let it be—a Thursday, tell her,
She shall be married to this noble earl.
Will you be ready? Do you like this haste?
We'll keep no great ado⁷—a friend or two;
For hark you, Tybalt being slain so late,⁸   25
It may be thought we held him carelessly,⁹
Being our kinsman, if we revel much.
Therefore we'll have some half a dozen friends,
And there an end. But what say you to Thursday?
Paris. My lord, I would that Thursday were tomorrow.   30
Capulet. Well, get you gone. A Thursday be it then.
Go you to Juliet ere you go to bed;
Prepare her, wife, against¹⁰ this wedding day.
Farewell, my lord.—Light to my chamber, ho!
Afore me,¹¹ it is so very very late   35
That we may call it early by-and-by.
Good night.

                                                        [*Exeunt.*]

Scene 5   [*Romeo and Juliet part at daybreak. Immediately after,
                    her mother arrives to inform Juliet of her coming marriage
                    to Paris. Juliet is stunned and tries to dissuade her parents.
                    They are furious at her disobedience, and her father
                    threatens to disown her if she refuses to consent to this
                    honorable match. Her nurse argues that Paris is a more
                    worthy match than the banished Romeo, and Juliet
                    pretends to agree. She realizes that the nurse must now
                    know nothing more about her affairs and that she can rely
                    solely on Friar Laurence.*]

---

5. **son:** future son-in-law.   6. **A:** on.   7. **ado:** formality.   8. **late:** recently.   9. **held him carelessly:** did not
care about him.   10. **against:** for.   11. **Afore me:** by my word!

[Capulet's *orchard*.]

[*Enter* Romeo *and* Juliet *above, at the window.*]

Juliet. Wilt thou be gone? It is not yet near day.
    It was the nightingale, and not the lark,
    That pierced the fearful hollow of thine ear.
    Nightly she sings on yond pomegranate tree.
    Believe me, love, it was the nightingale.   5
Romeo. It was the lark, the herald of the morn;
    No nightingale. Look, love, what envious streaks
    Do lace¹ the severing² clouds in yonder East.
    Night's candles³ are burnt out, and jocund day
    Stands tiptoe on the misty mountain tops.   10
    I must be gone and live, or stay and die.
Juliet. Yond light is not daylight; I know it, I.
    It is some meteor that the sun exhales
    To be to thee this night a torchbearer
    And light thee on thy way to Mantua.   15
    Therefore stay yet; thou needst not to be gone.
Romeo. Let me be ta'en, let me be put to death.
    I am content, so thou wilt have it so.
    I'll say yon grey is not the morning's eye,
    'Tis but the pale reflex⁴ of Cynthia's⁵ brow;   20
    Nor that is not the lark whose notes do beat
    The vaulty⁶ heaven so high above our heads.
    I have more care⁷ to stay than will to go.
    Come, death, and welcome! Juliet wills it so.
    How is't, my soul? Let's talk; it is not day.   25
Juliet. It is, it is! Hie hence, be gone, away!
    It is the lark that sings so out of tune,
    Straining harsh discords and unpleasing sharps.
    Some say the lark makes sweet division;⁸
    This doth not so, for she divideth us.   30
    Some say the lark and loathèd toad changed eyes;⁹
    O, now I would they had changed voices too,
    Since arm from arm that voice doth us affray,¹⁰
    Hunting thee hence with hunt's-up¹¹ to the day!
    O, now be gone! More light and light it grows.   35
Romeo. More light and light—more dark and dark our woes!

---

1. **lace:** stripe. 2. **severing:** scattering. 3. **Night's candles:** the stars. 4. **reflex:** reflection. 5. **Cynthia's:** the moon's. 6. **vaulty:** vaulted. 7. **care:** desire. 8. **division:** melody. 9. **changed eyes:** The toad has bright eyes and a harsh croak; the lark, dull eyes but a lovely voice. 10. **affray:** frighten. 11. **hunt's-up:** hunters' morning song.

[*Enter* Nurse, *hastily.*]

Nurse. Madam!
Juliet. Nurse?
Nurse. Your lady mother is coming to your chamber.
    The day is broke; be wary, look about.   [*Exit.*]   40
Juliet. Then, window, let day in, and let life out.
Romeo. Farewell, farewell! One kiss, and I'll descend.

[*He starts down the ladder.*]

Juliet. Art thou gone so, my lord, my love, my friend?[12]
    I must hear from thee every day in the hour,
    For in a minute there are many days.   45
    O, by this count I shall be much in years
    Ere I again behold my Romeo!
Romeo. Farewell!
    I will omit no opportunity
    That may convey my greetings, love, to thee.   50
Juliet. O, thinkst thou we shall ever meet again?
Romeo. I doubt it not; and all these woes shall serve
    For sweet discourses in our time to come.
Juliet. O God, I have an ill-divining[13] soul!
    Methinks I see thee, now thou art below,   55
    As one dead in the bottom of a tomb.
    Either my eyesight fails, or thou lookst pale.
Romeo. And trust me, love, in my eye so do you.
    Dry sorrow drinks our blood.[14] Adieu! adieu!   [*Exit.*]
Juliet. O Fortune, Fortune! all men call thee fickle.   60
    If thou art fickle, what dost thou with him
    That is renowmed[15] for faith? Be fickle, Fortune,
    For then I hope thou wilt not keep him long
    But send him back.
Lady Capulet. [*Within*] Ho, daughter! are you up?   65
Juliet. Who is't that calls? It is my lady mother.
    Is she not down so late, or up so early?
    What unaccustomed cause procures[16] her hither?

    [*Enter* Lady Capulet.]

Lady Capulet. Why, how now, Juliet?
Juliet.   Madam, I am not well.   70
Lady Capulet. Evermore weeping for your cousin's death?
    What, wilt thou wash him from his grave with tears?

---

12. **friend:** lover.   13. **ill-divining:** foreseeing evil.   14. **Dry . . . blood:** sorrow was believed to dry up the blood.
15. **renowmed:** renowned.   16. **procures:** leads.

An if thou couldst, thou couldst not make him live.
Therefore have done. Some grief shows much of love;
But much of grief shows still some want of wit.   75
Juliet. Yet let me weep for such a feeling[17] loss.
Lady Capulet. So shall you feel the loss, but not the friend
 Which you weep for.
Juliet.   Feeling so the loss,
 I cannot choose but ever weep the friend.   80
Lady Capulet. Well, girl, thou weepst not so much for his death
 As that the villain lives which slaughtered him.
Juliet. What villain, madam?
Lady Capulet.   That same villain Romeo.
Juliet. [*Aside*] Villain and he be many miles asunder.—   85
 God pardon him! I do, with all my heart;
 And yet no man like he doth grieve my heart.
Lady Capulet. That is because the traitor murderer lives.
Juliet. Ay, madam, from the reach of these my hands.
 Would none but I might venge my cousin's death!   90
Lady Capulet. We will have vengeance for it, fear thou not.
 Then weep no more. I'll send to one in Mantua,
 Where that same banished runagate[18] doth live,
 Shall give him such an unaccustomed dram
 That he shall soon keep Tybalt company;   95
 And then I hope thou wilt be satisfied.
Juliet. Indeed I never shall be satisfied
 With Romeo till I behold him—dead[19]—
 Is my poor heart so for a kinsman vexed.
 Madam, if you could find out but a man   100
 To bear a poison, I would temper[20] it;
 That Romeo should, upon receipt thereof,
 Soon sleep in quiet. O, how my heart abhors
 To hear him named and cannot come to him,
 To wreak the love I bore my cousin Tybalt   105
 Upon his body that hath slaughtered him!
Lady Capulet. Find thou the means, and I'll find such a man.
 But now I'll tell thee joyful tidings, girl.
Juliet. And joy comes well in such a needy time.
 What are they, I beseech your ladyship?   110
Lady Capulet. Well, well, thou hast a careful[21] father, child;
 One who, to put thee from thy heaviness,

---

17. **feeling:** deeply felt. 18. **runagate:** runaway. 19. **dead:** Juliet is choosing her words in such a way that Lady Capulet will mistakenly think that Juliet wishes to see Romeo dead. 20. **temper:** mix. 21. **careful:** considerate.

Hath sorted out [22] a sudden day of joy
That thou expects not nor I looked not for.
Juliet. Madam, in happy time! [23] What day is that?   115
Lady Capulet. Marry, my child, early next Thursday morn
    The gallant, young, and noble gentleman,
    The County Paris, at Saint Peter's Church,
    Shall happily make thee there a joyful bride.
Juliet. Now by Saint Peter's Church, and Peter too,   120
    He shall not make me there a joyful bride!
    I wonder at this haste, that I must wed
    Ere he that should be husband comes to woo.
    I pray you tell my lord and father, madam,
    I will not marry yet; and when I do, I swear   125
    It shall be Romeo, whom you know I hate,
    Rather than Paris. These are news indeed!
Lady Capulet. Here comes your father. Tell him so yourself,
    And see how he will take it at your hands.

    [*Enter* Capulet *and* Nurse.]

Capulet. When the sun sets the air doth drizzle dew,   130
    But for the sunset of my brother's son
    It rains downright.
    How now? a conduit, [24] girl? What, still in tears?
    Evermore show'ring? In one little body
    Thou counterfeitst a bark, a sea, a wind: 135
    For still thy eyes, which I may call the sea,
    Do ebb and flow with tears; the bark thy body is,
    Sailing in this salt flood; the winds, thy sighs,
    Who, raging with thy tears and they with them,
    Without a sudden calm will overset   140
    Thy tempest-tossed body. How now, wife?
    Have you delivered to her our decree?
Lady Capulet. Ay, sir; but she will none, she gives you thanks.
    I would the fool were married to her grave!
Capulet. Soft! take me with you, [25] take me with you, wife.   145
    How? Will she none? Doth she not give us thanks?
    Is she not proud? Doth she not count her blest,
    Unworthy as she is, that we have wrought [26]
    So worthy a gentleman to be her bridegroom?
Juliet. Not proud you have, but thankful that you have.   150
    Proud can I never be of what I hate,
    But thankful even for hate that is meant love.

---

22. **sorted out:** chosen.   23. **in happy time:** indeed.   24. **conduit:** fountain.   25. **take me with you:** What do
you mean?   26. **wrought:** arranged for.

Capulet. How, how, how, how, choplogic?²⁷ What is this?
  "Proud"—and "I thank you"—and "I thank you not"—
  And yet "not proud"? Mistress minion²⁸ you,   155
  Thank me no thankings, nor proud me no prouds,
  But fettle²⁹ your fine joints 'gainst Thursday next
  To go with Paris to Saint Peter's Church,
  Or I will drag thee on a hurdle³⁰ thither.
  Out, you green-sickness carrion!³¹ out, you baggage!   160
  You tallow-face!
Lady Capulet.   Fie, fie; what, are you mad?
Juliet. Good father, I beseech you on my knees,   [*She kneels down.*]

  Hear me with patience but to³² speak a word.
Capulet. Hang thee, young baggage! disobedient wretch!   165
  I tell thee what—get thee to church a Thursday
  Or never after look me in the face.
  Speak not, reply not, do not answer me!
  My fingers itch.³³ Wife, we scarce thought us blest
  That God had lent us but this only child;   170
  But now I see this one is one too much,
  And that we have a curse in having her.
  Out on her, hilding!³⁴
Nurse.   God in heaven bless her!
  You are to blame, my lord, to rate³⁵ her so.   175
Capulet. And why, my Lady Wisdom? Hold your tongue,
  Good Prudence. Smatter³⁶ with your gossips, go!
Nurse. I speak no treason.
Capulet.   O, God-i-god-en!
Nurse. May not one speak?   180
Capulet.   Peace, you mumbling fool!
  Utter your gravity³⁷ o'er a gossip's bowl,³⁸
  For here we need it not.
Lady Capulet.   You are too hot.
Capulet. God's bread!³⁹ it makes me mad. Day, night, late, early,   185
  At home, abroad, alone, in company,
  Waking or sleeping, still my care hath been
  To have her matched; and having now provided
  A gentleman of princely parentage,
  Of fair demesnes,⁴⁰ youthful, and nobly trained,   190

---

27. **choplogic:** hair-splitting.   28. **minion:** saucy miss.   29. **fettle:** make ready.   30. **hurdle:** a wooden frame used to convey criminals to execution.   31. **green-sickness carrion:** anemic lump of flesh.   32. **but to:** just long enough to.   33. **itch:** that is, to strike you.   34. **hilding:** good-for-nothing.   35. **rate:** scold.   36. **Smatter:** chatter.   37. **gravity:** wise words.   38. **gossip's bowl:** a hot punch.   39. **God's bread:** an oath on the sacred host.   40. **demesnes:** wealth.

Stuffed, as they say, with honorable parts,[41]
Proportioned as one's thought would wish a man—
And then to have a wretched puling[42] fool,
A whining mammet,[43] in her fortunes tender,[44]
To answer "I'll not wed, I cannot love;   195
I am too young, I pray you pardon me"!
But, an you will not wed, I'll pardon you.[45]
Graze where you will, you shall not house with me.
Look to't, think on't; I do not use to[46] jest.
Thursday is near; lay hand on heart, advise:[47]   200
An you be mine, I'll give you to my friend;
An you be not, hang, beg, starve, die in the streets,
For, by my soul, I'll ne'er acknowledge thee,
Nor what is mine shall never do thee good.
Trust to't.[48] Bethink you. I'll not be forsworn.[49]   [Exit.]   205

Juliet. Is there no pity sitting in the clouds
That sees into the bottom of my grief?
O sweet my mother, cast me not away!
Delay this marriage for a month, a week;
Or if you do not, make the bridal bed   210
In that dim monument where Tybalt lies.

Lady Capulet. Talk not to me, for I'll not speak a word.
Do as thou wilt, for I have done with thee.   [Exit.]

Juliet. O God!—O nurse, how shall this be prevented?
My husband is on earth, my faith in heaven.   215
How shall that faith return again to earth
Unless that husband send it me from heaven
By leaving earth? Comfort me, counsel me.
Alack, alack, that heaven should practice stratagems
Upon[50] so soft a subject as myself!   220
What sayst thou? Hast thou not a word of joy?
Some comfort, nurse.

Nurse.   Faith, here it is.
Romeo is banisht; and all the world to nothing[51]
That he dares ne'er come back to challenge[52] you;   225
Or if he do, it needs must be by stealth.
Then, since the case so stands as now it doth,
I think it best you married with the County.
O, he's a lovely gentleman!
Romeo's a dishclout to[53] him. An eagle, madam,   230

---

41. **parts:** qualities.   42. **puling:** whining.   43. **mammet:** doll.   44. **in her fortunes tender:** when good fortune
is offered her.   45. **pardon you:** be glad to see you gone.   46. **I do not use to:** I do not usually.   47. **advise:** be
advised.   48. **Trust to't:** be assured of it.   49. **be forsworn:** break my vow.   50. **practice stratagems/Upon:** contrive
violent deeds.   51. **all the world to nothing:** There is no chance.   52. **challenge:** claim.   53. **to:** compared with.

Hath not so green, so quick,[54] so fair an eye
As Paris hath. Beshrew[55] my very heart,
I think you are happy in this second match,
For it excels your first; or if it did not,
Your first is dead—or 'twere as good he were   235
As living here[56] and you no use of him.
Juliet. Speakst thou this from thy heart?
Nurse. And from my soul too; else beshrew them both.
Juliet. Amen!
Nurse. What?   240
Juliet. Well, thou hast comforted me marvelous much.
    Go in; and tell my lady I am gone,
    Having displeased my father, to Laurence' cell,
    To make confession and to be absolved.
Nurse. Marry, I will; and this is wisely done.   [*Exit.*] 245
Juliet. Ancient damnation![57] O most wicked fiend!
    Is it more sin to wish me thus forsworn,[58]
    Or to dispraise my lord with that same tongue
    Which she hath praised him with above compare
    So many thousand times? Go, counselor!   250
    Thou and my bosom[59] henceforth shall be twain.
    I'll to the friar to know his remedy.
    If all else fail, myself have power to die.

                                                       [*Exit.*]

---

54. **quick:** lively. 55. **Beshrew:** curse. 56. **here:** on earth. 57. **Ancient damnation:** wicked old devil.
58. **forsworn:** guilty of breaking her marriage vow to Romeo. 59. **bosom:** inner thoughts.

Act III

Getting at Meaning

Scene 1

1. Who starts the fight in this scene? Why does Romeo refuse to fight Tybalt, and why does Mercutio insist on fighting Tybalt?

2. What is Mercutio's attitude as he is dying? What effect does his death have on Romeo?

3. Does Benvolio give a fair account of the fight to the Prince? Why does the Prince insist on Romeo's banishment? What will happen to Romeo if he does not leave Verona?

Scene 2

4. Why does Juliet speak of the night in such loving terms? What does she assume when the nurse comes in crying, "he's dead, he's dead, he's dead"?

5. What is Juliet's reaction to Tybalt's death? What does she mean when she says of Romeo, "O serpent heart, hid with a flow'ring face"? What causes her to defend Romeo?

Scene 3

6. What is Romeo's reaction to the news that he is banished? What is Friar Laurence's advice?

7. What plan does Friar Laurence devise?

Scene 4

8. Why does Lord Capulet decide that Juliet should marry Paris within the week?

Scene 5

9. Why does Juliet dread the lark and hope that the bird-song she hears is the nightingale?

10. What are Juliet's fears as she and Romeo part?

11. Why does Lady Capulet think Juliet is crying? How does Juliet react to the news that she is to marry Paris on Thursday?

12. Describe the reaction of Lord and Lady Capulet to Juliet's disobedience.

13. What is the nurse's advice to Juliet? How does Juliet's attitude toward the nurse change?

Developing Skills in Reading Literature

1. **Allusion.** An allusion, you will remember, is a reference to a person, place, or event, in or outside of literature, with which the reader is expected to be familiar. Explain the allusions in this passage from Scene 2:

Gallop apace, you fiery-footed steeds,
Toward Phoebus' lodging! Such a wagoner
As Phaëton would whip you to the West
And bring in cloudy night immediately.

What do these lines mean?

2. **Paradox.** Explain the paradox in Romeo's words, "More light and light—more dark and dark our woes," spoken to Juliet as he leaves her to flee to Mantua.

3. **Theme.** An important theme in *Romeo and Juliet* is the role of fate, or chance, in human affairs. Why does Romeo say, "O, I am fortune's fool" after he has killed Tybalt? In what ways is he a tool of fate in this fight scene? In what ways has fate worked against the lovers by the end of the third act?

Developing Vocabulary

Language History: Shakespearean English. Mercutio's speech, which follows, contains a number of italicized words that are no longer in common English usage. What is the modern word for each italicized word?

Nay, an there were two such, we should have none shortly, for one would kill the other. *Thou!* why, *thou wilt* quarrel with a man that *hath* a hair more or a hair less in his beard than *thou hast. Thou wilt* quarrel with a man for cracking nuts, having no other reason but because *thou hast* hazel eyes. What eye but such an eye would spy out such a quarrel? *Thy* head is as full of quarrels as an egg is full of meat; and yet *thy* head *hath* been beaten as addle as an egg for quarreling.

Look over other speeches in Act Three. Find additional examples of word forms that are no longer used in modern English.

Developing Writing Skills

1. **Supporting an Opinion.** Does Romeo kill Tybalt blindly or is he aware of the possible consequences? Are your sympathies with Romeo, or do you think he should have acted differently? State your opinion. Then argue your position in a paragraph, using specific quotations from the fight scene.

2. **Analyzing Characters.** Compare Romeo and Juliet in their reactions to the news of banishment (Act Three, Scenes 2 and 3). What similarities do you see in their reactions? How do they express their reactions? What conclusions can you draw about the two individuals from their behavior? Write a paragraph for Romeo and a paragraph for Juliet, using specific lines from the play to support your analysis.

Act Four

Scene 1

[*As Paris is discussing his marriage plans with Friar Laurence, Juliet enters. After Paris leaves, the Friar gives Juliet a drug to take on the night before this wedding. The drug will create a seeming death, and she will be placed in the burial vault. When she awakens, Romeo and Friar Laurence will be there to take her away from Verona.*]

[Friar Laurence's *cell.*]

[*Enter* Friar Laurence *and* Paris.]

Friar Laurence. On Thursday, sir? The time is very short.
Paris. My father[1] Capulet will have it so,
 And I am nothing slow to slack his haste.[2]
Friar Laurence. You say you do not know the lady's mind.
 Uneven[3] is the course; I like it not.   5
Paris. Immoderately she weeps for Tybalt's death,
 And therefore have I little talked of love;
 For Venus smiles not in a house of tears.
 Now, sir, her father counts it dangerous
 That she do give her sorrow so much sway,[4]   10
 And in his wisdom hastes our marriage
 To stop the inundation of her tears,
 Which, too much minded by herself alone,[5]
 May be put from her by society.
 Now do you know the reason of this haste.   15
Friar Laurence. [*Aside*] I would I knew not why it should be slowed.—
 Look, sir, here comes the lady toward my cell.

 [*Enter* Juliet.]

Paris. Happily met, my lady and my wife!
Juliet. That may be, sir, when I may be a wife.
Paris. That may be must be, love, on Thursday next.   20
Juliet. What must be shall be.
Friar Laurence.   That's a certain text.

---

1. **father:** prospective father-in-law.   2. **nothing ... haste:** eager to help him hasten the marriage.   3. **Uneven:** difficult.   4. **That ... sway:** that she allows her sorrow to overpower her.   5. **alone:** in private.

Paris. Come you to make confession to this father?
Juliet. To answer that, I should confess to you.
Paris. Do not deny to him that you love me.   25
Juliet. I will confess to you that I love him.
Paris. So will ye, I am sure, that you love me.
Juliet. If I do so, it will be of more price,
    Being spoke behind your back, than to your face.
Paris. Poor soul, thy face is much abused with tears.   30
Juliet. The tears have got small victory by that,
    For it was bad enough before their spite.[6]
Paris. Thou wrongst it more than tears with that report.
Juliet. That is no slander, sir, which is a truth;
    And what I spake, I spake it to my face.   35
Paris. Thy face is mine, and thou hast slandered it.
Juliet. It may be so, for it is not mine own.
    Are you at leisure, holy father, now,
    Or shall I come to you at evening mass?
Friar Laurence. My leisure serves me, pensive daughter, now.   40
    My lord, we must entreat[7] the time alone.
Paris. God shield[8] I should disturb devotion!
    Juliet, on Thursday early will I rouse ye.
    Till then, adieu, and keep this holy kiss.   [*Exit.*]
Juliet. O, shut the door! and when thou hast done so,   45
    Come weep with me—past hope, past cure, past help!
Friar Laurence. Ah, Juliet, I already know thy grief;
    It strains me past the compass of my wits.[9]
    I hear thou must, and nothing may prorogue[10] it,
    On Thursday next be married to this County.   50
Juliet. Tell me not, friar, that thou hearst of this,
    Unless thou tell me how I may prevent it.
    If in thy wisdom thou canst give no help,
    Do thou but call my resolution wise
    And with this knife I'll help it presently.[11]   55
    God joined my heart and Romeo's, thou our hands;
    And ere this hand, by thee to Romeo's sealed,
    Shall be the label to another deed,[12]
    Or my true heart with treacherous revolt
    True to another, this shall slay them both.   60
    Therefore, out of thy long-experienced time,
    Give me some present counsel; or, behold,
    'Twixt my extremes[13] and me this bloody knife

---

6. **spite:** injury.   7. **entreat:** request.   8. **shield:** forbid.   9. **strains . . . wits:** exceeds the limits of my wisdom.
10. **prorogue:** postpone.   11. **presently:** at once.   12. **deed:** legal document.   13. **extremes:** misfortunes.

Shall play the umpire, arbitrating that
Which the commission[14] of thy years and art   65
Could to no issue of true honor bring.
Be not so long to speak. I long to die
If what thou speakst speak not of remedy.

Friar Laurence. Hold, daughter. I do spy a kind of hope,
Which craves as desperate an execution   70
As that is desperate which we would prevent.
If, rather than to marry County Paris,
Thou hast the strength of will to slay thyself,
Then it is likely thou wilt undertake
A thing like death to chide away this shame,   75
That copest[15] with death himself to scape from it;
And, if thou darest, I'll give thee remedy.

Juliet. O, bid me leap, rather than marry Paris,
From off the battlements of yonder tower,
Or walk in thievish ways,[16] or bid me lurk   80
Where serpents are; chain me with roaring bears,
Or shut me nightly in a charnel house,[17]
O'ercovered quite with dead men's rattling bones,
With reeky[18] shanks and yellow chapless[19] skulls;
Or bid me go into a new-made grave   85
And hide me with a dead man in his shroud—
Things that, to hear them told, have made me tremble—
And I will do it without fear or doubt,
To live an unstained wife to my sweet love.

Friar Laurence. Hold, then. Go home, be merry, give consent 90
To marry Paris. Wednesday is tomorrow.
Tomorrow night look that thou lie alone;
Let not the nurse lie with thee in thy chamber.
Take thou this vial, being then in bed,
And this distillèd liquor drink thou off;   95
When presently through all thy veins shall run
A cold and drowsy humor;[20] for no pulse
Shall keep his native[21] progress, but surcease;
No warmth, no breath, shall testify thou livest;
The roses in thy lips and cheeks shall fade   100
To paly ashes, thy eyes' windows fall
Like death when he shuts up the day of life;
Each part, deprived of supple government,[22]
Shall, stiff and stark and cold, appear like death;

---

14. **commision:** authority.   15. **copest:** bargains.   16. **thievish ways:** in roads where thieves hide out.
17. **charnel house:** shed for bones from old graves.   18. **reeky:** stinking.   19. **chapless:** jawless.
20. **humor:** moisture.   21. **native:** natural.   22. **supple government:** ability to move.

And in this borrowed likeness of shrunk death   105
Thou shalt continue two-and-forty hours,[23]
And then awake as from a pleasant sleep.
Now, when the bridegroom in the morning comes
To rouse thee from thy bed, there art thou dead.
Then, as the manner of our country is,   110
In thy best robes uncovered[24] on the bier
Thou shalt be borne to that same ancient vault
Where all the kindred of the Capulets lie.
In the meantime, against[25] thou shalt awake,
Shall Romeo by my letters know our drift;[26]   115
And hither shall he come; and he and I
Will watch thy waking, and that very night
Shall Romeo bear thee hence to Mantua.
And this shall free thee from this present shame,
If no inconstant toy[27] nor womanish fear   120
Abate thy valor in the acting it.

Juliet. Give me, give me! O, tell me not of fear!

Friar Laurence. Hold! Get you gone, be strong and prosperous
In this resolve. I'll send a friar with speed
To Mantua, with my letters to thy lord.   125

Juliet. Love give me strength! and strength shall help afford.
Farewell, dear father.

                                                              [*Exeunt.*]

Scene 2

[*Wedding preparations are in progress in the Capulet household. Juliet is pretending full cooperation with their plans, and her father is so pleased that he decides to have the wedding the next day. He leaves quickly to tell Paris.*]

[Capulet's *house.*]

[*Enter* Capulet, Lady Capulet, Nurse, *and* Servingmen.]

---

23. **two and forty hours:** Shakespeare uses dramatic license here; the movement of the play does not allow for a lapse of forty-two hours before Juliet awakens.   24. **uncovered:** with uncovered face.   25. **against:** before.
26. **drift:** intention.   27. **inconstant toy:** foolish whim.

Capulet. So many guests invite as here are writ.   [*Exit a* Servingman.]
    Sirrah, go hire me twenty cunning cooks.
Servingman. You shall have none ill, sir; for I'll try if they can lick their
    fingers.
Capulet. How canst thou try them so?   5
Servingman. Marry, sir, 'tis an ill cook that cannot lick his own fingers.
    Therefore he that cannot lick his fingers goes not with me.
Capulet. Go, begone.   [*Exit* Servingman.]
    We shall be much unfurnished¹ for this time.
    What, is my daughter gone to Friar Laurence?   10
Nurse. Ay, forsooth.
Capulet. Well, he may chance to do some good on her.
    A peevish² self-willed harlotry³ it is.

    [*Enter* Juliet.]

Nurse. See where she comes from shrift with merry look.
Capulet. How now, my headstrong? Where have you been gadding?   15
Juliet. Where I have learnt me to repent the sin
    Of disobedient opposition
    To you and your behests,⁴ and am enjoined
    By holy Laurence to fall prostrate here
    To beg your pardon. Pardon, I beseech you!   20
    Henceforward I am ever ruled by you.
Capulet. Send for the County. Go tell him of this.
    I'll have this knot knit up tomorrow morning.
Juliet. I met the youthful lord at Laurence' cell
    And gave him what becomèd⁵ love I might,   25
    Not stepping o'er the bounds of modesty.
Capulet. Why, I am glad on't.⁶ This is well. Stand up.
    This is as't should be. Let me see the County.
    Ay, marry, go, I say, and fetch him hither.
    Now, afore God, this reverend holy friar,   30
    All our whole city is much bound⁷ to him.
Juliet. Nurse, will you go with me into my closet⁸
    To help me sort⁹ such needful ornaments
    As you think fit to furnish me tomorrow?
Lady Capulet. No, not till Thursday. There is time enough.   35

Capulet. Go, nurse, go with her. We'll to church tomorrow.
                           [*Exeunt* Juliet *and* Nurse.]
Lady Capulet. We shall be short in our provision.
    'Tis now near night.

---

1. **unfurnished:** unprepared.   2. **peevish:** silly.   3. **harlotry:** good-for-nothing girl.   4. **behests:** commands.
5. **becomèd:** suitable.   6. **on't:** of it.   7. **bound:** indebted.   8. **closet:** private room.   9. **sort:** select.

Capulet.   Tush, I will stir about,
　　And all things shall be well, I warrant thee, wife.   40
　　Go thou to Juliet, help to deck up her.
　　I'll not to bed tonight; let me alone.
　　I'll play the housewife for this once. What, ho!¹⁰
　　They are all forth; well, I will walk myself
　　To County Paris, to prepare him up   45
　　Against tomorrow. My heart is wondrous light,
　　Since this same wayward girl is so reclaimed.

　　　　　　　　　　　　　　　　　　　　　　　　[Exeunt.]

Scene 3   *[Juliet requests her nurse to leave her for the night. She
                  considers all the possible bad effects of the drug, but
                  finally gets up enough courage to drink it and immediately
                  falls into a deep sleep.]*

[*Juliet's chamber.*]

[*Enter* Juliet *and* Nurse.]

Juliet. Ay, those attires are best; but, gentle nurse,
　　I pray thee leave me to myself tonight;
　　For I have need of many orisons¹
　　To move the heavens to smile upon my state,
　　Which, well thou knowest, is cross² and full of sin.   5

　　　[*Enter* Lady Capulet.]

Lady Capulet. What, are you busy, ho? Need you my help?
Juliet. No, madam; we have culled³ such necessaries
　　As are behooveful⁴ for our state⁵ tomorrow.
　　So please you, let me now be left alone,
　　And let the nurse this night sit up with you;   10
　　For I am sure you have your hands full all
　　In this so sudden business.
Lady Capulet.   Good night.
　　Get thee to bed and rest, for thou hast need.
　　　　　　　　　　　　[*Exeunt* Lady Capulet *and* Nurse.]

---

10. **What, ho!:** Capulet calls for a servant.
1. **orisons:** prayers.　2. **cross:** contrary.　3. **culled:** selected.　4. **behooveful:** fit.　5. **state:** position.

Juliet. Farewell! God knows when we shall meet again. 15
   I have a faint[6] cold fear thrills though my veins
   That almost freezes up the heat of life.
   I'll call them back again to comfort me.
   Nurse!—What should she do here?
   My dismal[7] scene I needs must act alone. 20
   Come, vial.
   What if this mixture do not work at all?
   Shall I be married then tomorrow morning?
   No, no! This shall forbid it. Lie thou there.   [*Lays down a dagger.*]
   What if it be a poison which the friar 25
   Subtly hath ministered[8] to have me dead,
   Lest in this marriage he should be dishonored
   Because he married me before to Romeo?
   I fear it is; and yet methinks it should not,
   For he hath still been tried[9] a holy man. 30
   How if, when I am laid into the tomb,
   I wake before the time that Romeo
   Come to redeem me? There's a fearful point!
   Shall I not then be stifled in the vault,
   To whose foul mouth no healthsome air breathes in, 35
   And there die strangled ere my Romeo comes?
   Or, if I live, is it not very like[10]
   The horrible conceit[11] of death and night,
   Together with the terror of the place—
   As in a vault, an ancient receptacle 40
   Where for this many hundred years the bones
   Of all my buried ancestors are packed;
   Where bloody Tybalt, yet but green in earth,[12]
   Lies fest'ring in his shroud; where, as they say,
   At some hours in the night spirits resort— 45
   Alack, alack, is it not like that I,
   So early waking—what with loathsome smells,
   And shrieks like mandrakes[13] torn out of the earth,
   That living mortals, hearing them, run mad—
   O, if I wake, shall I not be distraught, 50
   Environed with all these hideous fears,
   And madly play with my forefathers' joints,
   And pluck the mangled Tybalt from his shroud,
   And, in this rage, with some great kinsman's bone

---

6. **faint:** a feeling of coldness and faintness.   7. **dismal:** dreadful.   8. **ministered:** provided.   9. **tried:** proved.
10. **like:** likely.   11. **conceit:** idea.   12. **green in earth:** recently buried.   13. **mandrakes:** Plants that resemble
the human form. The mandrake was thought to shriek and cause madness when dug up.

As with a club dash out my desp'rate brains?
O, look! methinks I see my cousin's ghost
Seeking out Romeo, that did spit his body
Upon a rapier's point. Stay,¹⁴ Tybalt, stay!
Romeo, I come! this do I drink to thee.

[*She drinks and falls upon her bed within the curtains.*]

55

Scene 4

[*On the morning of the wedding, the nurse is sent to awaken Juliet as the household bustles with last-minute preparations.*]

[Capulet's *house.*]

[*Enter* Lady Capulet *and* Nurse.]

Lady Capulet. Hold, take these keys and fetch more spices, nurse.
Nurse. They call for dates and quinces in the pastry.¹

[*Enter* Capulet.]

Capulet. Come, stir, stir, stir! The second cock hath crowed,
    The curfew bell hath rung, 'tis three o'clock.
    Look to the baked meats, good Angelica;
    Spare not for cost.
Nurse.   Go, you cot-quean,² go,
    Get you to bed! Faith, you'll be sick tomorrow
    For this night's watching.
Capulet. No, not a whit. What, I have watched ere now
    All night for lesser cause, and ne'er been sick.
Lady Capulet. Ay, you have been a mouse-hunt³ in your time;
    But I will watch you from such watching now.
                        [*Exeunt* Lady Capulet *and* Nurse.]
Capulet. A jealoushood,⁴ a jealoushood!

[*Enter three or four* Servants, *with spits and logs and baskets.*]

                        Now, fellow,
    What is there?
First Servant. Things for the cook, sir; but I know not what.

5

10

15

---

14. **Stay:** stop.   1. **pastry:** bakehouse.   2. **cot-quean:** a man who meddles with women's affairs.
3. **mouse-hunt:** a woman hunter.   4. **jealoushood:** jealousy.

Capulet. Make haste, make haste. [*Exit* Servant.] Sirrah, fetch drier logs.
　Call Peter; he will show thee where they are.
Second Servant. I have a head, sir, that will find out logs　　　　　20
　And never trouble Peter for the matter.
Capulet. Mass,[5] and well said, ha!
　Thou shalt be loggerhead.[6] [*Exit* Servant.] Good faith, 'tis day.
　The County will be here with music straight,
　For so he said he would. [*Music within.*] I hear him near.　　25
　Nurse! Wife! What, ho! What, nurse, I say!

　　[*Reenter* Nurse.]

　Go waken Juliet; go and trim her up.
　I'll go and chat with Paris. Hie, make haste,
　Make haste! The bridegroom he is come already:
　Make haste, I say.　　　　　30

　　　　　　　　　　　　　　　[*Exeunt.*]

Scene 5

[*The nurse discovers Juliet's apparently lifeless body, and the household turns into mourning. Funeral instead of wedding plans are begun.*]

[*Juliet's chamber. Curtains drawn around her bed.*]

[*Enter* Nurse.]

Nurse. Mistress! what, mistress! Juliet! Fast,[1] I warrant her, she.
　Why, lamb! why, lady! Fie, you slugabed!
　Why, love, I say! madam! sweetheart! Why, bride!
　What, not a word?

[*Opens the curtains.*]

　What, dressed and in your clothes and down again?　　5
　I must needs wake you. Lady! lady! lady!
　Alas, alas! Help, help! my lady's dead!
　O well-a-day that ever I was born!
　Some aqua vitae, ho! My lord! my lady!

　　[*Enter* Lady Capulet.]

Lady Capulet. What noise is here?　　10

---

5. **Mass:** by the Mass.　6. **loggerhead:** blockhead.　　1. **Fast:** fast asleep.

Nurse.   O lamentable day!
Lady Capulet. What is the matter?
Nurse.   Look, look! O heavy day!
Lady Capulet. O me, O me! My child, my only life!
　　Revive, look up, or I will die with thee!   15
　　Help, help! Call help.

　　　[*Enter* Capulet.]

Capulet. For shame, bring Juliet forth; her lord is come.
Nurse. She's dead, deceased; she's dead! Alack the day!
Lady Capulet. Alack the day, she's dead, she's dead, she's dead!
Capulet. Ha! let me see her. Out alas! she's cold,   20
　　Her blood is settled, and her joints are stiff;
　　Life and these lips have long been separated.
　　Death lies on her like an untimely frost
　　Upon the sweetest flower of all the field.
Nurse. O lamentable day!   25
Lady Capulet.   O woeful time!
Capulet. Death, that hath ta'en her hence to make me wail,
　　Ties up my tongue and will not let me speak.

　　　[*Enter* Friar Laurence *and* Paris, *with* Musicians.]

Friar Laurence. Come, is the bride ready to go to church?
Capulet. Ready to go, but never to return.   30
　　Death is my son-in-law, Death is my heir;
　　My daughter he hath wedded. I will die
　　And leave him all. Life, living, all is Death's.
Paris. Have I thought long to see this morning's face,
　　And doth it give me such a sight as this?   35
Lady Capulet. Accursed, unhappy, wretched, hateful day!
　　Most miserable hour that e'er time saw
　　In lasting labor of his pilgrimage!
　　But one, poor one, one poor and loving child,
　　But one thing to rejoice and solace in,   40
　　And cruel Death hath catched it from my sight!
Nurse. O woe! O woeful, woeful, woeful day!
　　Most lamentable day, most woeful day
　　That ever ever I did yet behold!
　　O day! O day! O day! O hateful day!   45
　　Never was seen so black a day as this.
　　O woeful day! O woeful day!
Paris. Beguiled, divorced, wronged, spited, slain!
　　Most detestable Death, by thee beguiled,
　　By cruel cruel thee quite overthrown!   50
　　O love! O life! not life, but love in death!

Capulet. Despisèd, distressèd, hated, martyred, killed!
    Uncomfortable[2] time, why camest thou now
    To murder, murder our solemnity?[3]
    O child! O child! my soul, and not my child!   55
    Dead art thou, dead! alack, my child is dead,
    And with my child my joys are buried!
Friar Laurence. Peace, ho, for shame! Confusion's[4] cure lives not
    In these confusions. Heaven and yourself
    Had part in this fair maid! now heaven hath all,   60
    And all the better is it for the maid.
    Your part in her you could not keep from death,
    But heaven keeps his part in eternal life.
    The most you sought was her promotion,
    For 'twas your heaven she should be advanced;   65
    And weep ye now, seeing she is advanced
    Above the clouds, as high as heaven itself?
    O, in this love, you love your child so ill
    That you run mad, seeing that she is well.[5]
    She's not well married that lives married long,   70
    But she's best married that dies married young.
    Dry up your tears and stick your rosemary[6]
    On this fair corse, and, as the custom is,
    In all her best array bear her to church;
    For though fond nature bids us all lament,   75
    Yet nature's tears are reason's merriment.[7]
Capulet. All things that we ordainèd festival
    Turn from their office to black funeral—
    Our instruments to melancholy bells,
    Our wedding cheer[8] to a sad burial feast;   80
    Our solemn hymns to sullen[9] dirges change;
    Our bridal flowers serve for a buried corse;
    And all things change them to the contrary.
Friar Laurence. Sir, go you in; and, madam, go with him;
    And go, Sir Paris. Every one prepare   85
    To follow this fair corse unto her grave.
    The heavens do lower[10] upon you for some ill;
    Move them no more by crossing their high will.
                  [They all but the Nurse *go forth, casting*
                  rosemary on her and shutting the curtains.]

---

2. **Uncomfortable:** distressing.   3. **solemnity:** festivity.   4. **Confusion:** disaster.   5. **well:** in heaven.
6. **rosemary:** a symbol of immortality and enduring love, used at funerals and weddings.   7. **nature's . . .**
merriment: While mourning is natural, rejoicing is also reasonable because Juliet is in heaven.   8. **cheer:** food.
9. **sullen:** mournful.   10. **lower:** frown.

Act IV

Getting at Meaning

Scene 1

1. How does Friar Laurence try to delay the marriage of Paris and Juliet?

2. How does Juliet respond to Paris when she meets him at Friar Laurence's cell? Why does Friar Laurence give Juliet the potion? What is his plan?

Scene 2

3. Why does Juliet pretend to be obedient to her father? How do her deceitful words make her situation more desperate?

Scene 3

4. What fears does Juliet voice before she takes the potion? Why does she take it in spite of her fears?

Scene 4

5. Why do you think that Shakespeare included this short scene in which the Capulet household prepares for Juliet's wedding?

Scene 5

6. Why are Juliet's parents and the nurse so quick to believe she is dead? How do they react?

7. How does Friar Laurence try to console the Capulets?

Developing Skills in Reading Literature

1. **Irony.** Irony plays an important role in tragedy, and *Romeo and Juliet* is no exception. What is ironic about the love affair of Romeo and Juliet? What is ironic about Romeo's role in killing Tybalt? What is ironic about Friar Laurence's role in Act Four? What other ironies are present in the play up to this point?

2. **Dialogue.** Which characters in the play speak in poetry? Which ones do not? What seems to be the difference between the two groups of characters?

Developing Vocabulary

Getting Word Meaning from Context: Inferring Word Meaning. Study the following passages and attempt to define each italicized word from the quoted context and from the broader context of the play. Then look up each word in a dictionary and record the definition. Use the word in a sentence of your own.

1. Paris: [her father] in his wisdom hastes our marriage
   To stop the *inundation* of her tears,

2. Juliet: Or shall I come to you at evening mass?

   Friar: My leisure serves me, *pensive* daughter, now.

3. Juliet: And ere this hand, by thee to Romeo's sealed,
   Shall be the label to another deed,
   Or my true heart with *treacherous* revolt
   Turn to another, this [knife] shall slay them both.

4. Friar: And this [potion] shall free thee from this present shame,
   If no inconstant toy nor womanish fear
   Abate thy *valor* in the acting it.

5. Capulet: Our wedding cheer to a sad burial feast;
   Our solemn hymns to sullen *dirges* change.

Act Five

Scene 1

[*Romeo learns from his servant Balthasar that Juliet is dead and has been placed in the Capulet vault. Wishing to join Juliet in death, Romeo buys poison and hurries to Verona.*]

[*A street in Mantua.*]

[*Enter* Romeo.]

Romeo. If I may trust the flattering truth of sleep,[1]
My dreams presage[2] some joyful news at hand.
My bosom's lord[3] sits lightly in his throne,
And all this day an unaccustomed spirit
Lifts me above the ground with cheerful thoughts.   5
I dreamt my lady came and found me dead
(Strange dream that gives a dead man leave to think!)
And breathed such life with kisses in my lips
That I revived and was an emperor.
Ah me! how sweet is love itself possessed,   10
When but love's shadows are so rich in joy!

[*Enter* Romeo's *servant,* Balthasar, *booted.*]

News from Verona! How now, Balthasar?
Dost thou not bring me letters from the friar?
How doth my lady? Is my father well?
How fares my Juliet? That I ask again,   15
For nothing can be ill if she be well.
Balthasar. Then she is well, and nothing can be ill.
Her body sleeps in Capels' monument,[4]
And her immortal part with angels lives.
I saw her laid low in her kindred's vault   20
And presently took post[5] to tell it you.
O, pardon me for bringing these ill news,
Since you did leave it for my office,[6] sir.

---

1. **flattering . . . sleep:** pleasant dreams that seemed true.   2. **presage:** foretell.   3. **bosom's lord:** heart.
4. **monument:** tomb.   5. **took post:** rode hard.   6. **office:** duty.

Romeo. Is it e'en so? Then I defy you, stars!
  Thou knowst my lodging. Get me ink and paper   25
  And hire posthorses. I will hence tonight.
Balthasar. I do beseech you, sir, have patience
  Your looks are pale and wild and do import⁷
  Some misadventure.
Romeo.   Tush, thou art deceived.   30
  Leave me and do the thing I bid thee do.
  Hast thou no letters to me from the friar?
Balthasar. No, my good lord.
Romeo.   No matter. Get thee gone
  And hire those horses. I'll be with thee straight.   35

                                        [*Exit* Balthasar.]

  Well, Juliet, I will lie with thee tonight.
  Let's see for means. O mischief, thou art swift
  To enter in the thoughts of desperate men!
  I do remember an apothecary,
  And hereabouts he dwells, which late I noted   40
  In tattered weeds,⁸ with overwhelming⁹ brows,
  Culling of simples.¹⁰ Meager were his looks,
  Sharp misery had worn him to the bones;
  And in his needy shop a tortoise hung,
  An alligator stuffed, and other skins   45
  Of ill-shaped fishes; and about his shelves
  A beggarly account¹¹ of empty boxes,
  Green earthen pots, bladders, and musty seeds,
  Remnants of packthread,¹² and old cakes of roses¹³
  Were thinly scattered, to make up a show.   50
  Noting this penury, to myself I said,
  "An if a man did need a poison now
  Whose sale is present¹⁴ death in Mantua,
  Here lives a caitiff¹⁵ wretch would sell it him."
  O, this same thought did but forerun my need,   55
  And this same needy man must sell it me.
  As I remember, this should be the house.
  Being holiday, the beggar's shop is shut.
  What, ho! apothecary!

  [*Enter* Apothecary.]

Apothecary.   Who calls so loud?   60

---

7. **import:** suggest.   8. **weeds:** clothes.   9. **overwhelming:** overhanging.   10. **Culling of simples:** sorting herbs.
11. **account:** number.   12. **packthread:** twine.   13. **cakes of roses:** small cakes of rose petals, used in perfume.
14. **present:** immediate.   15. **caitiff:** miserable.

Romeo. Come hither, man. I see that thou art poor.
    Hold, there is forty ducats.[16] Let me have
    A dram of poison, such soon-speeding gear[17]
    As will disperse itself through all the veins
    That the life-weary taker may fall dead,   65
    And that the trunk[18] may be discharged of breath
    As violently as hasty powder fired
    Doth hurry from the fatal cannon's womb.
Apothecary. Such mortal[19] drugs I have; but Mantua's law
    Is death to any he that utters[20] them.   70
Romeo. Art thou so bare and full of wretchedness
    And fearest to die? Famine is in thy cheeks,
    Need and oppression starveth in thine eyes,
    Contempt and beggary hangs upon thy back:
    The world is not thy friend, nor the world's law;   75
    The world affords no law to make thee rich;
    Then be not poor, but break it and take this.
Apothecary. My poverty but not my will consents.
Romeo. I pay thy poverty and not thy will.
Apothecary. Put this in any liquid thing you will   80
    And drink it off, and if you had the strength
    Of twenty men, it would dispatch you straight.
Romeo. There is thy gold—worse poison to men's souls,
    Doing more murder in this loathsome world,
    Than these poor compounds that thou mayst not sell.   85
    I sell thee poison; thou hast sold me none.
    Farewell. Buy food and get thyself in flesh.
    Come, cordial[21] and not poison, go with me
    To Juliet's grave; for there must I use thee.

                                         [Exeunt.]

Scene 2

[*Friar John tells Friar Laurence that he has not been successful in delivering his letter to Romeo. The letter contained the explanation of Juliet's wedding and the strategy used to prevent it. Friar Laurence, greatly worried, hurries to Juliet to be on hand when she awakens.*]

---

16. **ducats:** gold coins.   17. **gear:** stuff.   18. **trunk:** body.   19. **mortal:** deadly.   20. **utters:** sells.   21. **cordial:** a heart stimulant.

[*Verona.* Friar Laurence's *cell.*]

[*Enter* Friar John.]

Friar John. Holy Franciscan friar, brother, ho!

[*Enter* Friar Laurence.]

Friar Laurence. This same should be the voice of Friar John.
    Welcome from Mantua. What says Romeo?
    Or, if his mind be writ, give me his letter.
Friar John. Going to find a barefoot brother out,   5
    One of our order to associate[1] me,
    Here in this city visiting the sick,
    And finding him, the searchers[2] of the town,
    Suspecting that we both were in a house
    Where the infectious pestilence did reign,   10
    Sealed up the doors, and would not let us forth,
    So that my speed to Mantua there was stayed.
Friar Laurence. Who bare my letter, then, to Romeo?
Friar John. I could not send it—here it is again—
    Nor get a messenger to bring it thee,   15
    So fearful were they of infection.
Friar Laurence. Unhappy fortune! By my brotherhood,
    The letter was not nice,[3] but full of charge,[4]
    Of dear import,[5] and the neglecting it
    May do much danger. Friar John, go hence,   20
    Get me an iron crow[6] and bring it straight
    Unto my cell.
Friar John.   Brother, I'll go and bring it thee.   [*Exit.*]
Friar Laurence. Now must I to the monument alone.
    Within this three hours will fair Juliet wake.   25
    She will beshrew[7] me much that Romeo
    Hath had no notice of these accidents;[8]
    But I will write again to Mantua,
    And keep her at my cell till Romeo come—
    Poor living corse, closed in a dead man's tomb!   [*Exeunt.*] 30

---

1. **associate:** accompany.   2. **searchers:** health officers.   3. **nice:** trivial.   4. **full of charge:** very important.
5. **dear import:** dreadful significance.   6. **crow:** crowbar.   7. **beshrew:** blame.   8. **accidents:** happenings.

Scene 3

[When Romeo finds Paris at the Capulet tomb, he kills him when he refuses to leave. Romeo drinks the poison just before Friar Laurence arrives. When Juliet awakens, the Friar tries to hurry her out, but she sees Romeo's body and will not leave. The Friar, afraid of being discovered there, leaves, and Juliet kills herself with Romeo's dagger. The watch, summoned by Paris' servant, enters and finds the bodies. The Prince arrives, along with the Capulets and Montagues, and the Friar relates the entire story. Filled with grief at the series of misfortunes, Montague and Capulet agree to end their feud.]

[A churchyard with the Capulets' *tomb.]*

[Enter Paris *and his* Page *with flowers and a torch.]*

Paris. Give me thy torch, boy. Hence, and stand aloof.
    Yet put it out, for I would not be seen.
    Under yond yew tree lay thee all along,[1]
    Holding thine ear close to the hollow ground.
    So shall no foot upon the churchyard tread   5
    (Being loose, unfirm, with digging up of graves)
    But thou shalt hear it. Whistle then to me,
    As signal that thou hearst something approach.
    Give me those flowers. Do as I bid thee, go.
Page. *[Aside]* I am almost afraid to stand alone   10
    Here in the churchyard; yet I will adventure.   *[Withdraws.]*
Paris. Sweet flower, with flowers thy bridal bed I strew

[He strews the tomb with flowers.]

    (O woe! thy canopy is dust and stones)
    Which with sweet water[2] nightly I will dew;
    Or, wanting[3] that, with tears distilled by moans.   15
    The obsequies[4] that I for thee will keep
    Nightly shall be to strew thy grave and weep.

[The Page *whistles.]*

    The boy gives warning something doth approach.
    What cursèd foot wanders this way tonight
    To cross[5] my obsequies and true love's rite?   20
    What, with a torch? Muffle me, night, awhile.   *[Withdraws.]*

---

1. **all along:** at full length.   2. **sweet water:** perfume.   3. **wanting:** lacking.   4. **obsequies:** funeral rites.
5. **cross:** interfere with.

[*Enter* Romeo *and* Balthasar *with a torch, a mattock, and a crow of iron.*]

Romeo. Give me that mattock[6] and the wrenching iron.
    Hold, take this letter. Early in the morning
    See thou deliver it to my lord and father.
    Give me the light. Upon thy life I charge thee,   25
    Whate'er thou hearest or seest, stand all aloof
    And do not interrupt me in my course.
    Why I descend into this bed of death
    Is partly to behold my lady's face,
    But chiefly to take thence from her dead finger   30
    A precious ring—a ring that I must use
    In dear employment.[7] Therefore hence, be gone.
    But if thou, jealous,[8] dost return to pry
    In what I farther shall intend to do,
    By heaven, I will tear thee joint by joint   35
    And strew this hungry churchyard with thy limbs.
    The time and my intents are savage-wild,
    More fierce and more inexorable far
    Than empty[9] tigers or the roaring sea.
Balthasar. I will be gone, sir, and not trouble you.   40
Romeo. So shalt thou show me friendship. Take thou that.
    Live, and be prosperous; and farewell, good fellow.
Balthasar. [*Aside*] For all this same, I'll hide me hereabout.
    His looks I fear, and his intents I doubt.[10]   [*Withdraws.*]
Romeo. Thou detestable maw,[11] thou womb of death,   45
    Gorged with the dearest morsel of the earth,
    Thus I enforce thy rotten jaws to open,
    And in despite[12] I'll cram thee with more food.

[Romeo *opens the tomb.*]

Paris. This is that banisht haughty Montague
    That murdered my love's cousin—with which grief   50
    It is supposèd the fair creature died—
    And here is come to do some villainous shame
    To the dead bodies. I will apprehend[13] him.
    Stop thy unhallowed toil, vile Montague!
    Can vengeance be pursued further than death?   55
    Condemnèd villain, I do apprehend thee.
    Obey, and go with me; for thou must die.

---

6. **mattock:** a pickax.   7. **dear employment:** for an important purpose.   8. **jealous:** curious.   9. **empty:** hungry.   10. **doubt:** suspect.   11. **maw:** stomach.   12. **in despite:** scorn.   13. **apprehend:** appeal.

Romeo. I must indeed; and therefore came I hither.
    Good gentle youth, tempt not a desp'rate man.
    Fly hence and leave me. Think upon these gone;   60
    Let them affright thee. I beseech thee, youth,
    Put not another sin upon my head
    By urging me to fury. O, be gone!
    By heaven, I love thee better than myself,
    For I come hither armed against myself.   65
    Stay not, be gone. Live, and hereafter say
    A madman's mercy bid thee run away.
Paris. I do defy thy conjuration[14]
    And apprehend thee for a felon here.
Romeo. Wilt thou provoke me? Then have at thee, boy!   *[They fight.]*   70
Page. O Lord, they fight! I will go call the watch.

                                                  [Exit.]

Paris. O, I am slain! *[Falls.]* If thou be merciful,
    Open the tomb, lay me with Juliet.   *[Dies.]*
Romeo. In faith, I will. Let me peruse this face.
    Mercutio's kinsman, noble County Paris!   75
    What said my man when my betossèd[15] soul
    Did not attend[16] him as we rode? I think
    He told me Paris should have married Juliet.
    Said he not so? or did I dream it so?
    Or am I mad, hearing him talk of Juliet,   80
    To think it was so? O, give me thy hand,
    One writ with me in sour misfortune's book!
    I'll bury thee in a triumphant[17] grave.
    A grave? O, no, a lantern,[18] slaughtered youth,
    For here lies Juliet, and her beauty makes   85
    This vault a feasting presence[19] full of light.
    Death,[20] lie thou there, by a dead man interred.

[Lays Paris in the tomb.]

    How oft when men are at the point of death
    Have they been merry! which their keepers call
    A lightning[21] before death. O, how may I   90
    Call this a lightning? O my love! my wife!
    Death, that hath sucked the honey of thy breath,
    Hath had no power yet upon thy beauty.
    Thou art not conquered. Beauty's ensign yet
    Is crimson in thy lips and in thy cheeks,   95

---

14. **conjuration:** appeal.   15. **betossed:** upset.   16. **attend:** listen to.   17. **triumphant:** glorious.   18. **lantern:** a dome with windows that gives more light to a hall.   19. **feasting presence:** a chamber where the queen held public court.   20. **Death:** Paris' corpse.   21. **lightening:** a revival of spirit.

Richard Monette as Romeo, Marti Maraden as Juliet.
Romeo and Juliet, Stratford Festival, Canada, 1977.

And death's pale flag is not advancèd there.
Tybalt, liest thou there in thy bloody sheet?
O, what more favor can I do to thee
Than with that hand that cut thy youth in twain
To sunder his that was thine enemy?   100
Forgive me, cousin! Ah, dear Juliet,
Why art thou yet so fair? Shall I believe
That unsubstantial Death is amorous,
And that the lean abhorrèd monster keeps
Thee here in dark to be his paramour?   105
For fear of that I still will stay with thee
And never from this palace of dim night
Depart again. Here, here will I remain
With worms that are thy chambermaids. O, here
Will I set up my everlasting rest   110
And shake the yoke of inauspicious stars
From this world-wearied flesh. Eyes, look your last!
Arms, take your last embrace! and, lips, O you
The doors of breath, seal with a righteous kiss

A dateless[22] bargain to engrossing[23] death!   115
Come, bitter conduct; come, unsavory guide!
Thou desperate pilot, now at once run on
The dashing rocks thy seasick weary bark!
Here's to my love! [*Drinks.*] O true apothecary!
Thy drugs are quick. Thus with a kiss I die.   [*Falls.*] 120

[*Enter* Friar Laurence, *with lantern, crow, and spade.*]

Friar Laurence. Saint Francis be my speed![24] how oft tonight
    Have my old feet stumbled at graves! Who's there?
Balthasar. Here's one, a friend, and one that knows you well.
Friar Laurence. Bliss be upon you! Tell me, good my friend,
    What torch is yond that vainly lends his light   125
    To grubs and eyeless skulls? As I discern,
    It burneth in the Capels' monument.
Balthasar. It doth so, holy sir; and there's my master,
    One that you love.
Friar Laurence.   Who is it?   130
Balthasar.   Romeo.
Friar Laurence. How long hath he been there?
Balthasar.   Full half an hour.
Friar Laurence. Go with me to the vault.
Balthasar.   I dare not, sir.   135
    My master knows not but I am gone hence,
    And fearfully did menace me with death
    If I did stay to look on his intents.
Friar Laurence. Stay then; I'll go alone. Fear comes upon me.
    O, much I fear some ill unthrifty[25] thing.   140
Balthasar. As I did sleep under this yew tree here,
    I dreamt my master and another fought,
    And that my master slew him.
Friar Laurence.   Romeo!

[*Stoops and looks on the blood and weapons.*]

    Alack, alack, what blood is this which stains   145
    The stony entrance of this sepulcher?
    What mean these masterless and gory swords
    To lie discolored by this place of peace?

[*Enters the tomb.*]

    Romeo! O, pale! Who else? What, Paris too?
    And steeped in blood? Ah, what an unkind hour   150

---

22. **dateless:** eternal.   23. **engrossing:** monopolizing.   24. **speed:** help.   25. **unthrifty:** unlucky.

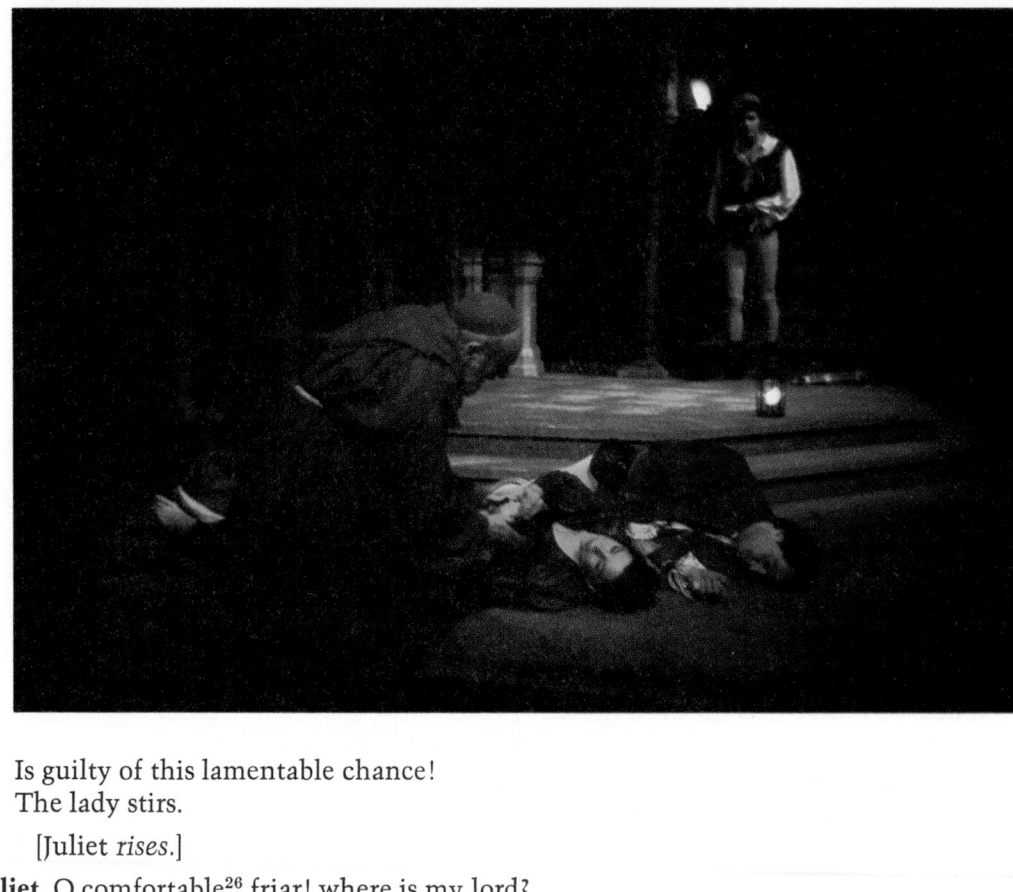

Is guilty of this lamentable chance!
The lady stirs.

    [Juliet *rises*.]

Juliet. O comfortable[26] friar! where is my lord?
    I do remember well where I should be,
    And there I am. Where is my Romeo?   155
Friar Laurence. I hear some noise. Lady, come from that nest
    Of death, contagion, and unnatural sleep.
    A greater power than we can contradict
    Hath thwarted our intents. Come, come away.
    Thy husband in thy bosom there lies dead;   160
    And Paris too. Come, I'll dispose of thee
    Among a sisterhood of holy nuns.
    Stay not to question, for the watch is coming.
    Come, go, good Juliet. I dare no longer stay.
Juliet. Go, get thee hence, for I will not away.   165

                             [*Exit* Friar Laurence.]

    What's here? A cup, closed in my true love's hand?
    Poison, I see, hath been his timeless[27] end.
    O churl![28] drunk all, and left no friendly drop
    To help me after? I will kiss thy lips.

---

26. **comfortable:** comforting.   27. **timeless:** untimely.   28. **churl:** miser.

Haply[29] some poison yet doth hang on them   170
To make me die with a restorative.[30]   [*Kisses him.*]
Thy lips are warm!
Chief Watchman. [*Within*] Lead, boy. Which way?
Juliet. Yea, noise? Then I'll be brief. O happy[31] dagger!

[*Snatches* Romeo's *dagger.*]

This is thy sheath; there rest, and let me die.   175

[*She stabs herself and falls.*]

[*Enter* Watchmen *with the* Page *of* Paris.]

Page. This is the place. There, where the torch doth burn.
Chief Watchman. The ground is bloody. Search about the churchyard.
Go, some of you; whoe'er you find attach.[32]
                                    [*Exeunt some of the* Watch.]
Pitiful sight! here lies the County slain;
And Juliet bleeding, warm, and newly dead,   180
Who here hath lain this two days buried.
Go, tell the Prince; run to the Capulets;
Raise up the Montagues; some others search.
                                    [*Exeunt others of the* Watch.]
We see the ground whereon these woes[33] do lie,
But the true ground of all these piteous woes   185
We cannot without circumstance descry.[34]

[*Reenter some of the* Watch, *with* Balthasar.]

Second Watchman. Here's Romeo's man. We found him in the
    churchyard.
Chief Watchman. Hold him in safety till the Prince come hither.

[*Reenter* Friar Laurence *and another* Watchman.]

Third Watchman. Here is a friar that trembles, sighs, and weeps.   190
We took this mattock and this spade from him
As he was coming from this churchyard side.
Chief Watchman. A great suspicion![35] Stay the friar too.

[*Enter the* Prince *and* Attendants.]

Prince. What misadventure is so early up,
That calls our person from our morning rest?   195

---

29. **Haply:** perhaps.   30. **restorative:** his kiss, if he were alive, would have that effect.   31. **happy:** timely.
32. **attach:** arrest.   33. **woes:** the three bodies.   34. **descry:** understand.   35. **A great suspicion:** a most
suspicious thing.

[*Enter* Capulet, Lady Capulet, *and others.*]

Capulet. What should it be, that they so shriek abroad?
Lady Capulet. The people in the street cry "Romeo,"
    Some "Juliet," and some "Paris"; and all run,
    With open outcry, toward our monument.
Prince. What fear is this which startles[36] in our ears?   200
Chief Watchman. Sovereign, here lies the County Paris slain;
    And Romeo dead; and Juliet, dead before,
    Warm and new killed.
Prince. Search, seek, and know how this foul murder comes.
Chief Watchman. Here is a friar, and slaughtered Romeo's man,   205
    With instruments upon them fit to open
    These dead men's tombs.
Capulet. O heavens! O wife, look how our daughter bleeds!
    This dagger hath mista'en,[37] for, lo, his house[38]
    Is empty on the back of Montague,   210
    And it missheathèd in my daughter's bosom!
Lady Capulet. O me! this sight of death is as a bell
    That warns my old age to a sepulcher.

    [*Enter* Montague *and others.*]

Prince. Come, Montague; for thou art early up
    To see thy son and heir now early down.   215
Montague. Alas, my liege, my wife is dead tonight!
    Grief of my son's exile hath stopped her breath.
    What further woe conspires against mine age?
Prince. Look, and thou shalt see.
Montague. O thou untaught! what manners is in this,   220
    To press before thy father to a grave?
Prince. Seal up the mouth of outrage[39] for a while,
    Till we can clear these ambiguities
    And know their spring,[40] their head, their true descent;
    And then will I be general of your woes   225
    And lead you even to death. Meantime forbear,
    And let mischance be slave to patience.[41]
    Bring forth the parties of suspicion.
Friar Laurence. I am the greatest, able to do least,
    Yet most suspected, as the time and place   230
    Doth make against me, of this direful murder;
    And here I stand, both to impeach and purge[42]
    Myself condemned and myself excused.

---

36. **startles:** shouts.   37. **mista'en:** missed its right target.   38. **his house:** the dagger's sheath.   39. **Seal . . . outrage:** no more emotional outbursts.   40. **spring:** source.   41. **let . . . patience:** let patience control your hasty reactions.   42. **impeach and purge:** accuse and clear (of guilt).

Prince. Then say at once what thou dost know in this.
Friar Laurence. I will be brief, for my short date of breath[43]   235
    Is not so long as is a tedious tale.
    Romeo, there dead, was husband to that Juliet;
    And she, there dead, that Romeo's faithful wife.
    I married them; and their stol'n marriage day
    Was Tybalt's doomsday, whose untimely death   240
    Banisht the new-made bridegroom from this city;
    For whom, and not for Tybalt, Juliet pined.
    You, to remove that siege of grief from her,
    Betrothed and would have married her perforce
    To County Paris. Then comes she to me   245
    And with wild looks bid me devise some mean
    To rid her from this second marriage,
    Or in my cell there would she kill herself.
    Then gave I her (so tutored by my art)
    A sleeping potion; which so took effect   250
    As I intended, for it wrought on her
    The form of death. Meantime I writ to Romeo
    That he should hither come as this dire night
    To help to take her from her borrowed[44] grave,
    Being the time the potion's force should cease.   255
    But he which bore my letter, Friar John,
    Was stayed by accident, and yesternight
    Returned my letter back. Then all alone
    At the prefixèd hour[45] of her waking
    Came I to take her from her kindred's vault;   260
    Meaning to keep her closely[46] at my cell
    Till I conveniently could send to Romeo.
    But when I came, some minute ere the time
    Of her awaking, here untimely lay
    The noble Paris and true Romeo dead.   265
    She wakes; and I entreated her come forth
    And bear this work of heaven with patience;
    But then a noise did scare me from the tomb,
    And she, too desperate, would not go with me,
    But, as it seems, did violence on herself.   270
    All this I know, and to the marriage
    Her nurse is privy;[47] and if aught in this
    Miscarried by my fault, let my old life
    Be sacrificed, some hour before his time,
    Unto the rigor of severest law.   275

---

43. **short . . . breath:** the little life left me.   44. **borrowed:** temporary.   45. **prefixèd hour:** time fixed in advance.   46. **closely:** secretly.   47. **privy:** shares the secret.

Prince. We still have known thee for a holy man.
    Where's Romeo's man? What can he say in this?

Balthasar. I brought my master news of Juliet's death;
    And then in post[48] he came from Mantua
    To this same place, to this same monument.   280
    This letter he early bid me give his father,
    And threatened me with death, going in the vault,
    If I departed not and left him there.

Prince. Give me the letter. I will look on it.
    Where is the County's page that raised[49] the watch?   285
    Sirrah, what made[50] your master in this place?

Page. He came with flowers to strew his lady's grave;
    And bid me stand aloof, and so I did.
    Anon comes one with light to ope the tomb;
    And by-and-by my master drew on him;   290
    And then I ran away to call the watch.

Prince. This letter doth make good the friar's words,
    Their course of love, the tidings of her death;
    And here he writes that he did buy a poison
    Of a poor 'pothecary, and therewithal   295
    Came to this vault to die and lie with Juliet.
    Where be these enemies? Capulet, Montague,
    See what a scourge[51] is laid upon your hate,
    That heaven finds means to kill your joys[52] with love!
    And I, for winking[53] at your discords too,   300
    Have lost a brace of kinsmen. All are punished.

Capulet. O brother Montague, give me thy hand.
    This is my daughter's jointure,[54] for no more
    Can I demand.

Montague.   But I can give thee more;   305
    For I will raise her statue in pure gold,
    That whiles Verona by that name is known,
    There shall no figure at such rate be set[55]
    As that of true and faithful Juliet.

Capulet. As rich shall Romeo's by his lady's lie—   310
    Poor sacrifices of our enmity!

Prince. A glooming peace this morning with it brings.
    The sun for sorrow will not show his head.
    Go hence, to have more talk of these sad things;
    Some shall be pardoned, and some punished;   315
    For never was a story of more woe
    Than this of Juliet and her Romeo.   *[Exeunt.]*

---

48. **in post:** with full speed.   49. **raised:** gave the alarm to.   50. **made:** did.   51. **scourge:** punishment.
52. **your joys:** your children.   53. **winking:** shutting my eyes.   54. **jointure:** dowry.   55. **at such ... set:** be valued so highly.

Leslie Yeo as Capulet, Pamela Hyatt as Lady Capulet,
John Goodlin as Escalus. *Romeo and Juliet*, Stratford Festival, Canada, 1977.

Act V

Getting at Meaning

Scene 1

1. When Balthasar tells Romeo that Juliet is dead, Romeo says, "Then I defy you, stars!" What does he mean?

2. What plans does Romeo immediately make? Why does the apothecary sell him poison?

Scene 2

3. Why has Friar John been unable to deliver the letter to Romeo? Why does his return with the letter upset Friar Laurence so much?

Scene 3

4. Why is Paris at the Capulet tomb? What causes the fight between Romeo and Paris?

5. Describe Romeo's feelings and his actions when he finds the body of Juliet.

6. When Juliet awakens, Friar Laurence is there. What does he suggest for Juliet's future? Why does he leave her alone in the tomb?

7. How does Juliet kill herself? Why does she kill herself?

8. How does Friar Laurence explain his actions to the assembled people? What is the Prince's reaction to the deaths of the lovers?

Developing Skills in Reading Literature

1. **Personification.** Reread the words that Romeo speaks when he finds Juliet's body. What force becomes a human character in his speech? what kind of character?

2. **Irony.** What are some of the final tragic ironies in this play? What role does timing play in the final events?

3. **Theme.** Are the lovers responsible for their own deaths in any way, or are they merely "star-crossed lovers," as the Prologue to the play suggests? What mistakes, if any, do they make? How might they have acted more sensibly? What role does fate play in the events of the play?

4. **Tragedy.** In a tragedy the characters who survive usually learn a lesson from the sad events they have witnessed. What lesson do the feuding families and the spectators learn in *Romeo and Juliet*? Are the deaths of Romeo and Juliet necessary to make this point? Why does Shakespeare make it clear in the Prologue that the lovers will die? How does this advance knowledge affect you as you read the play? What dramatic purpose is served by the deaths of Mercutio, Tybalt, and Paris?

Developing Writing Skills

1. **Developing an Argument.** Is Friar Laurence to blame for his interference in the lives of the characters, or is his behavior appropriate for a kind and loving man, long-time spiritual adviser to both Romeo and Juliet? Write a paragraph in which you criticize or defend the Friar's actions, supporting your position with evidence from the play.

2. **Explaining an Idea.** One common idea in tragedy is human ignorance; often, characters who act without full information trigger the tragic events.

Using three examples from *Romeo and Juliet*, show how characters acting out of ignorance or on incomplete information hasten the central tragedy. Your composition should have five paragraphs. Treat each example in a separate body paragraph, including at least one quotation per paragraph. Frame the three body paragraphs with an introduction and a conclusion.

Unit Review *Drama*

Understanding the Unit

1. How does the one-act play in this unit differ from the longer plays, apart from the obvious fact that it is shorter? How do the playwrights use the additional room in the longer plays?

2. A time span of almost four hundred years separates *Romeo and Juliet* from the other two plays. During this long period of time, many of the conventions of drama changed. For example, the use of the formal soliloquy gradually disappeared. What other changes can you identify?

3. Fate, or destiny, is a force in all three of these plays. Which characters give in to their fates? Which characters struggle against their fates? How?

4. How do the humorous passages function in *I Remember Mama?* in *Romeo and Juliet?*

Writing

In *I Remember Mama,* Katrin's teachers tell her to write about familiar characters and events. Mama tells Katrin of Miss Moorhead's experience:

> For years she write bad stories about people in the olden times, until one day she remember something that happen in her own town . . . something that only she could know and understand . . . and she feels she must tell it . . . and that is how she write her first good story. She say you must write more of things you know. . . .

Write a one-act play about an experience or event from your own life. Use interesting, natural-sounding dialogue that reveals the main traits of your characters. Be sure to structure your play so that it has rising action, a climax, and falling action.

BREAKING HOME TIES, 1890. *Thomas Hovenden.*
Philadelphia Museum of Art.
Given by Ellen Harrison McMichael in memory of C. Emory McMichael.

Unit 7

The Novel

A CROW FLEW BY. *Andrew Wyeth.*
The Metropolitan Museum of Art, Arthur H. Hearn Fund, 1950.

Introduction to the Unit

With the exception of the two long plays in the preceding unit, the works of literature that you have read so far have been relatively short, short enough to be read in one sitting. Some writers, however, wish to say more than what can be said in a few pages. These writers might choose the form of the novel as a vehicle for expressing their ideas.

Like a short story, a novel is a work of fiction. The novel includes the same elements as the short story: setting, plot, and character. As in a short story, these elements interact to communicate the writer's theme.

The obvious difference between the short story and the novel is length. Because the novel is longer, it usually has a main plot and also one or more subplots, or secondary plots. In *The Human Comedy,* the novel you are about to read, the main plot deals with the experiences of one character during a crucial six-month period of his life. The novel also contains subplots, which focus on the experiences of other major characters.

The longer length allows the novelist to develop the elements of character and setting more fully. The main characters in a novel are complex. As the plot unfolds, the reader discovers many subtle shadings of personality, motive, and feeling. The writer of a novel also can include more characters and a more detailed description of the setting. The richness and variety possible in a novel mean that the novelist can explore more themes, both major and minor.

As you read *The Human Comedy,* allow yourself to be drawn into the life of one small town in America in the early 1940's. Think about why the author chose this particular literary form as the best way to communicate his insights into the human condition.

The Human Comedy   *William Saroyan*

1 Ulysses

The little boy named Ulysses Macauley one day stood over the new gopher hole in the backyard of his house on Santa Clara Avenue in Ithaca, California. The gopher of this hole pushed up fresh moist dirt and peeked out at the boy, who was certainly a stranger but perhaps not an enemy. Before this miracle had been fully enjoyed by the boy, one of the birds of Ithaca flew into the old walnut tree in the backyard, and after settling itself on a branch, broke into rapture, moving the boy's fascination from the earth to the tree. Next, best of all, a freight train puffed and roared far away. The boy listened, and felt the earth beneath him tremble with the moving of the train. Then he broke into running, moving (it seemed to him) swifter than any life in the world.

When he reached the crossing, he was just in time to see the passing of the whole train, from locomotive to caboose. He waved to the engineer, but the engineer did not wave back to him. He waved to five others who were with the train, but not one of them waved back. They might have done so, but they didn't. At last a black man appeared, leaning over the side of a gondola. Above the clatter of the train, Ulysses heard the man singing:

Weep no more my lady, O weep no more today
We will sing one song for the old Kentucky home
For the old Kentucky home far away

Ulysses waved to the black man too, and then a wondrous and unexpected thing happened. *This* man, black and different from all the others, waved back to Ulysses, shouting: "Going home, boy—going back where I belong!"

The small boy and the black man waved to one another until the train was almost out of sight.

Then Ulysses looked around. There it was, all around him, funny and lonely—the world of his life. The strange, weed-infested, junky, wonderful, senseless yet beautiful world. Walking down the track came an old man with a rolled bundle on his back. Ulysses waved to this man too, but the man was too old and too tired to be pleased with a small boy's friendliness. The old man glanced at Ulysses as if both he and the boy were already dead.

The little boy turned slowly and started for home. As he moved, he still listened to the passing of the train, the singing of the black man, and the joyous words: "Going home, boy—going back where I belong!" He stopped to think of all this, loitering beside a china-ball tree and kicking at the yellow, smelly, fallen fruit of it. After a moment, he smiled the smile of the Macauley people—the gentle, wise, secret smile that said *Hello* to all things.

When he turned the corner and saw the Macauley house, Ulysses began to skip, kicking up a heel. He tripped and fell because of this merriment, but got to his feet and went on.

His mother was in the yard, throwing feed to the chickens. She watched the boy trip and fall and get up and skip again. He came quickly and quietly and stood beside her, then went to the hen nest to look for eggs. He found one. He looked at it a moment, picked it up, brought it to his mother and very carefully handed it to her, by which he meant what no man can guess and no child can remember to tell.

2 Homer

His brother Homer sat on the seat of a second-hand bicycle that struggled bravely with the dirt of a country road. Homer Macauley wore a telegraph messenger's coat that was far too big and a cap that was not quite big enough. The sun was going down in a somnolence of evening peace deeply cherished by the people of Ithaca. All about the messenger, orchards and vineyards rested in the old, old earth of California. Even though he was moving along swiftly, Homer was not missing any of the charm of the region. Look at that! he kept saying to himself of earth and tree, vine and sun and cloud. Look at that, will you? He began to make decorations with the movements of his bike, and, to accompany these ornaments of movement, he burst out with a shouting of music—simple, lyrical and ridiculous. The theme of this opera was taken over in his mind by the strings of an orchestra, then supplemented by the harp of his mother and the piano of his sister Bess. And finally, to bring the whole family together, an accordion came into the group, saying the theme with an easy humor, as Homer remembered his brother Marcus.

Homer's music fled before the hurrying clatter of three incredible objects moving across the sky. The messenger looked up at the airplanes and promptly rode into a small dry ditch. A farmer's dog came swiftly and with great importance, barking like a man with a message. Homer ignored the message, turning only once to spoof the animal by saying "Arp, Arp!" He seated himself on the bicycle again and rode on.

When he reached the beginning of the residential district of the city, he passed a sign without reading it:

ITHACA, CALIFORNIA
EAST, WEST—HOME IS BEST
WELCOME, STRANGER

He stopped at the next corner to watch a long line of Army trucks full of soldiers roll by. He saluted the men, just as his brother Ulysses had waved to the engineer and the hoboes. A great many soldiers returned the messenger's salute. Why not? What did they know about anything?

3 At the Telegraph Office

It was evening in Ithaca when Homer finally drew up in front of the telegraph office. The clock in the window said two minutes past seven. Inside the office Homer saw Mr. Spangler, the manager of the telegraph office, counting the words of a telegram that a tired-looking, troubled young man of twenty or so had just handed him. As he came into the office, Homer listened to Mr. Spangler and the young man.

"Fourteen words collect," Spangler said.

"How long will it take the telegram to get to my mother?" the boy said.

"Well, it's pretty late in the East now. It's not easy to raise money late at night sometimes, but I'll rush the telegram right through." Without looking at the boy again, Spangler went through his pockets, coming out with a handful of small coins, one piece of currency, and a hard-boiled egg.

"Here," he said, "just in case." He handed the boy the currency. "You can pay me back when your mother sends the money." He indicated the egg. "I picked it up in a bar seven days ago. Brings me luck."

The boy looked at the money, astonished.

"Thanks," he said, and hurried out of the office.

Spangler took the telegram over to William Grogan, the night-shift telegraph operator and wire-chief. "Send it paid, Willie. I'll pay for it myself."

Mr. Grogan put his hand around the "bug" and began rattling off the telegram in the Morse code, letter by letter:

MRS. MARGARET STRICKMAN
1874 BIDDLE STREET
YORK, PENNSYLVANIA

DEAR MA. PLEASE TELEGRAPH THIRTY DOL-LARS. WANT TO COME HOME. AM FINE. EVERY-THING O.K.

JOHN

Homer Macauley studied the delivery desk to see what was on hand for delivery, or if there were any calls to take. Mr. Spangler watched him a moment and then said, "How do you like being a messenger?"

"How do I *like* it?" Homer said. "I like it better than anything. You sure get to see a lot of different people. You sure get to go to a lot of different places."

"Yes, you do," Spangler said. He paused to look at the boy a little closer. "How did you sleep last night?"

"Fine," Homer said. "I was pretty tired but I slept fine."

"Did you sleep a little at school today?"

"A little."

"What subject?"

"Ancient history."

"What about sports? I mean what about not being able to take part in them on account of having this job?"

"I take part in them. We have a physical education period every day."

"Is that so? I used to run the two-twenty low hurdles when I went to Ithaca High. Valley Champion." The manager of the telegraph office paused, then went on. "You really like this job, don't you?"

"I'm going to be the best messenger this office ever had."

"OK. But don't kill yourself. Get there swiftly, but don't go *too* fast. Be polite to everybody—take your hat off in elevators and above all things don't lose a telegram."

"Yes, sir."

"Working nights is different from working days. Taking a telegram to Chinatown at night, or out to the sticks, is liable to scare a fellow—well, don't let it scare *you*. People are people. Don't be afraid of them. How old are you?"

Homer gulped. "Sixteen."

"Yes, I know," Spangler said. "You said that yesterday. We're not supposed to hire a boy unless he's at least sixteen, but I thought I'd take a chance on you. How old are you?"

"Fourteen."

"Well, you'll be sixteen in two years, at any rate."

"Yes, sir."

"If anything comes up that you don't understand, come to me."

"Yes, sir," Homer said. He paused. "What about singing telegrams?"

"You've got a pretty good voice, haven't you?"

"I used to sing at the First Presbyterian Sunday School."

"That's fine. That's exactly the kind of voice we need for our singing telegrams. Now, let's say Mr. Grogan over there was sent a birthday greeting. How would you do it?"

Homer went over to Mr. Grogan and sang:

Happy birthday to you—
Happy birthday to you—
Happy birthday, dear Grogan—
Happy birthday to you.

"Thank you," Mr. Grogan said.

"That's fine," Spangler said to Homer, "but you wouldn't say 'dear Grogan,' you'd say 'dear *Mr.* Grogan.' What are you going to do with the fifteen dollars a week?"

"Give it to my mother."

"All right. From now on you're working—*steady*. You're part of this outfit. Watch things—listen carefully—keep your eyes and ears open." The manager of the telegraph office looked away at nothing a moment and then said, "What future have you mapped out for yourself?"

"Future?" Homer said. He was a little embarrassed because all his life, from day to day, he had been busy mapping out a future, even if it was only a future for the next day. "Well," he said, "I don't know for sure, but I guess I'd like to be somebody some day."

"You will be," Spangler said. "Know where Chatterton's Bakery is on Broadway? Here's a quarter. Go get me two day-old pies—apple and coconut cream. Two for a quarter."

"Yes, sir," Homer said. He caught the quarter Spangler tossed, and ran out of the office. Spangler turned to the telegraph operator and said, "What do you think of him?"

"He's a good boy," Mr. Grogan said.

"Comes from a good, poor family on Santa Clara Avenue. No father. Brother in the Army. Mother works in the packinghouses in the summer. Sister goes to State College. He's a couple of years underage, that's all."

"I'm a couple overage," Mr. Grogan said. "We'll get along."

Spangler did a little work at his desk, and then suddenly got up. "If you want me, I'll be at Corbett's. Share the pies between you—" He stopped and stared, dumbfounded, as Homer came running into the office with two wrapped-up pies.

"What's your name again?" Spangler almost shouted at the boy.

"Homer Macauley."

The manager of the telegraph office put his arm around the new messenger. "All right, Homer Macauley. You're the boy this office needs on the night-shift. You're probably the fastest-moving thing in the San Joaquin valley. You're going to be a great man some day, too—if you live. So see that you do." He turned and left the office while Homer tried to understand the meaning of what the man had said.

"All right, my boy," Mr. Grogan said, "the pies."

Homer put the pies on the desk beside Mr. Grogan, who continued to talk. "Homer Macauley, my name is William Grogan. I am called Willie, however, although I am sixty-seven years old. I am an old-time telegrapher, one of the last in the world. I am also night wire-chief of this office. I am also hungry. Let us feast together on these pies—the apple and the coconut cream. From now on, you and I are friends."

"Yes, sir," Homer said.

The old telegraph operator broke one of the pies into four parts, and they began to eat coconut cream.

"I shall, on occasion, ask you to run an errand for me, to join me in song, or to sit and talk to me. In the event of unhappiness, I shall expect of you a depth of understanding one may not expect from men past the age of twelve. How old are you?"

"Fourteen, but I've got a pretty good understanding."

"Very well, I'll take your word for it. Every night in this office I shall count on you to see that I shall be able to perform my duties. A splash of cold water in the face if I do not respond when shaken—this to be followed by a cup of hot black coffee from Corbett's."

"Yes, sir."

"On the street, however, the procedure is quite another thing. If you behold me, greet me as you pass, but make no reference to my unhappiness. I am a sensitive man and prefer not to be the object of public solicitude."

"Cold water and coffee in the office," Homer said. "Greeting in the street. Yes, sir."

The telegraph box rattled. Mr. Grogan answered the call and took his place at the typewriter, but went on talking. "I believe I overheard you say that once upon a time you sang at Sunday School. Please be good enough to sing one of the Sunday School songs you know while I type this message from Washington, D.C."

Homer sang *Rock of Ages* while Mr. Grogan typed the telegram. It was addressed to Mrs. Rosa Sandoval, 1129 G Street, Ithaca, California, and in the telegram the War Department informed Mrs. Sandoval that her son, Juan Domingo Sandoval, had been killed in action.

Mr. Grogan handed the message to Homer. Homer folded the telegram, put it into an envelope, sealed the envelope, put the envelope in his cap, and left the office. When the messenger was gone, the old telegraph operator lifted his voice, also singing *Rock of Ages*. For once upon a time he, too, had been as young as any man.

4 At Home

Music came from the Macauley house on Santa Clara Avenue. Bess and Mrs. Macauley played *All the World Will Be Jealous of Me*. They played the song for the soldier Marcus, wherever he happened to be, because it was the song he loved best. Mary Arena came into the parlor from the house next door, and stood beside Bess at the piano and soon began to sing. She sang for Marcus, who was all the world to *her*. The small boy Ulysses listened and watched. Something about everything was mysterious, and he wanted to find out what it was, even though he was half asleep. At last he summoned up enough energy to say,

"Where's Marcus?"

"Marcus is in the Army," Mrs. Macauley said.

"When is he coming home?"

"When the War is over."

"Tomorrow?"

"No, not tomorrow."

"When?"

"We don't know. We're waiting."

"Then where is my father?" Ulysses said. "If we wait, will *he* come home like Marcus, too?"

"No, not that way. He won't come walking down the street, up the steps, across the porch, and on into the house, as he used to do."

This was too much for the boy, and as there was only one word by which to hope for something like truth and comfort, he said this word:

"Why?"

"Two years ago your father died, Ulysses. But as long as we are alive, as long as we are together, as long as *two* of us are left, and remember him, nothing in the world can take him from us."

The boy thought about this a moment and then remembered what he had witnessed earlier that day.

"What are the gophers?" he said.

His mother was not unprepared for such a question. She knew that he had eyes, and beyond eyes vision, and beyond vision heart and love and hunger—to know.

"They share this earth with us. They have life, just as we do. They are part of us, and part of all things that live."

"Then, where is Homer?" he said.

"Yesterday your brother found himself a job after school. He will be home at midnight, when you're fast asleep."

Ulysses tried hard to stay awake, but it was no longer possible.

Mrs. Macauley looked from the boy to his sister Bess. "Put him to bed," she said.

Bess and Mary took the boy to his room. When they were gone and Mrs. Macauley sat alone, she thought she heard a footstep and turned. There at the door she thought she saw Matthew Macauley, as if he were Ulysses himself all over again instead of a grown man who had died so recently and yet so long ago.

5 Mrs. Sandoval

The messenger got off his bicycle in front of the house of Mrs. Rosa Sandoval. He went to the door and knocked gently. He knew almost immediately that someone was inside the house. He could not hear anything, but he was sure the knock was bringing someone to the door; and he was most eager to see who this person would be—this woman named Rosa Sandoval. The door was not a long time opening, but there was no hurry in the way it moved on its hinges. The movement of the door was as if, whoever she was, she had nothing in the world to fear. Then the door was open, and there she was.

To Homer the Mexican woman was beautiful. He could see that she had been patient all her life, so that now, after years of it, her lips were set in a gentle smile. But like all people who never receive telegrams, the appearance of a messenger at the front door is full of terrible implications. Homer knew that Mrs. Rosa Sandoval was shocked to see him. Her first word was the first word of all surprise. She said "Oh," as if instead of a messenger she had thought of opening the door to someone she had known a long time and would be pleased to sit down with. She studied Homer's eyes, and Homer knew that she knew the message was not a welcome one.

It wasn't Homer's fault. His work was to deliver telegrams. Even so, he felt awkward and almost as if he *alone* were responsible for what had happened. At the same time he wanted to come right out and say, "I'm only a messenger, Mrs. Sandoval. I'm very sorry I must bring you a telegram like this, but it is only because it is my work to do so."

"Mrs. Rosa Sandoval, 1129 G Street?" Homer said. He extended the telegram to the Mexican woman, but she would not touch it.

"Are you Mrs. Sandoval?"

"Please. Please come in." She paused for a moment and looked at the boy standing awkwardly as near the door as he could be and still be inside the house.

"Please," she said, "what does the telegram say?"

"Mrs. Sandoval," the messenger said, "the telegram says—"

But now the woman interrupted him. "But you must *open* the telegram and *read* it to me," she said. "You have not opened it."

"Yes, ma'am," Homer said as if he were speaking to a school teacher who had just corrected him.

He opened the telegram with nervous fingers. The Mexican woman stooped to pick up the torn envelope. As she did so she said, "Who sent the telegram—my son Juan Domingo?"

"No, ma'am. The telegram is from the War Department."

"War Department?" the Mexican woman said.

"Mrs. Sandoval," Homer said swiftly, "your son is dead. Maybe it's a mistake. Maybe it wasn't your son. Maybe it was somebody else. The telegram *says* it was Juan Domingo. But maybe the telegram is wrong."

The Mexican woman pretended not to hear.

"Oh, do not be afraid," she said. "Come inside. I will bring you candy." She took the boy's arm and brought him to the table at the center of the room and there she made him sit.

"All boys like candy," she said. She went into another room and soon returned with an old chocolate candy box. She opened the box at the table and in it Homer saw a strange kind of candy.

"Here," she said. "Eat this candy. All boys like candy."

Homer took a piece of the candy from the box, put it into his mouth and tried to chew.

"You would not bring me a bad telegram," she said.

Homer sat chewing the dry candy while the Mexican woman talked. "It is our own candy," she said, "from cactus."

Now, suddenly she began to make strange soft breathing sounds, holding herself in, as if weeping were a disgrace. Homer wanted to get up and run, but he knew he would stay. He even thought he might stay the rest of his life. He just didn't know what else to do to try to make the woman less unhappy; and if she had *asked* him to take the place of her son, he would not have been able to refuse, because he would not have known how. He got to his feet as if by standing he meant to begin correcting what could not be corrected, and then he knew the foolishness of this intention and became more awkward than ever. In his heart he was saying over and over again, "What can I do? What can *I* do? I'm only the messenger."

The woman suddenly took him in her arms, saying, "My little boy, my little boy!"

He didn't know why, because he only felt wounded by the whole thing, but for some reason he felt sick and thought he would need to vomit. He didn't *dislike* the woman, but what was happening to her seemed so wrong and unnecessary that he didn't know if he ever wanted to go on living again, even.

"Come now," the woman said. "Sit down here." She forced him into another chair and stood over him. "Let me look at you." She looked at him strangely and, sick everywhere within himself, the messenger could not move. He felt neither love nor hate but something very close to disgust, but at the same time he felt great compassion, not for the poor woman alone, but for all things and the terrible way of their enduring and dying. He saw her back in time, a beautiful young woman sitting beside the crib of her infant son. He saw her looking down at this amazing human thing, speechless and helpless and full of the world to come. He saw her rocking the crib and he heard her singing to the child. Now look at her, he said to himself.

He was on his bicycle suddenly, riding swiftly down the dark street, tears coming out of his eyes, his mouth whispering crazy young curses. When he got back to the telegraph office, the tears had stopped; but everything else had started, and he knew there would be no stopping them. "Otherwise I'm just as good as dead myself," he said, as if someone were listening whose hearing was not very good.

6 Mr. Grogan

Homer sat across the table from Mr. Grogan. The telegraph wires were silent now, but suddenly the box began to rattle. Homer waited for Mr. Grogan to answer the call, but Mr. Grogan did not answer it. Homer ran around the table.

"Mr. Grogan," he said, "they're calling you!" He shook the man gently.

"Mr. Grogan, wake up! Wake up!"

Homer ran to the water jar and filled a paper cup full of water. He ran back to the old telegraph operator, but he was afraid to follow the instructions he had been given. He put the cup down on the table and shook Mr. Grogan again.

"Mr. Grogan, wake up! They're calling you!"

Homer splashed the cup of water into the telegraph operator's face. Mr. Grogan sat up with a start, opened his eyes, looked at Homer, listened to the telegraph box, and then answered the call.

"That's right, my boy. Now, quick! A cup of black coffee. Hurry!"

Homer ran out of the office to Corbett's. When he got back, the old telegraph operator's eyes were almost closed again, but he was still doing his work.

"That's right, boy," he said. "Don't worry. Don't be afraid. That's exactly right."

Mr. Grogan stopped the telegrapher at the other end of the wire a moment and began to sip the coffee. "First splash the cold water, then fetch the black coffee."

"Yes, sir," Homer said. "Is it an important telegram?"

"No," Mr. Grogan said. "It is most *unimportant*. Business. The accumulating of money. It's a night letter. You won't have to deliver it tonight. Most unimportant. But very important for me to receive it."

He lifted his voice now because he was awake and strong again. "They've been wanting to retire me for years. They've been wanting to put in the machines they're inventing all over the place—Multiplexes and Teletypes. Machines instead of human beings!" He spoke softly now, as if to himself or to the people who were seeking to put him out of his place in the world. "I wouldn't know what to do with myself if I didn't have this job. I guess I'd die in a week. I've worked all my life, and I'm not going to stop now."

"Yes, sir," Homer said.

"I know I can count on you to help me, my boy." He rattled the bug. The answer came and he began to type the telegram, but as he typed he spoke with a kind of pride and vigor that pleased Homer very much. "Trying to put me out of my job! Why, I was the fastest telegrapher in the world. Faster than Wolinsky, even, sending and receiving both—and no mistakes. Willie Grogan. Telegraph operators all over the world know that name. They know Willie Grogan was the best of them all!" He paused now and smiled at the messenger—the boy from the slums who had come to work last night, just in time.

"Sing another song, my boy."

Without thinking, Homer began to sing the old hymn, *Amazing Grace*.

7 Mrs. Macauley

Mrs. Macauley sat in the old rocking chair in the parlor of the house on Santa Clara Avenue waiting for her son to come home. He reached the parlor a little after midnight. He was grimy and tired and sleepy, but at the same time she could see that he was startled and restless. She knew that when he spoke his voice would be hushed, as the voice of her husband, this boy's father, had been. He stood a long time in the dark room, just being there. And then, instead of beginning with the things most important to talk about, he said, "Everything's all right. I don't want you to sit up this way *every* night." He paused and had to say again, "Everything's all right."

"I know," his mother said. "Now sit down."

He moved to sit in the old overstuffed chair but instead he collapsed. His mother smiled.

"Well," she said. "I know you're tired, but I can see you're troubled, too. What is it?"

The boy waited a moment and then began to speak very swiftly, but very quietly, too. "I had to deliver a telegram to a lady over on G Street," he said. "She was a Mexican lady." He stopped suddenly and got to his feet.

"I don't know how to tell you about this," he said, "because—well, the telegram was from the War Department. Her son was killed, but she wouldn't believe it. She just wouldn't believe it. I never saw anybody hurt that way before. She made me eat candy —made out of cactus. She hugged me and said *I* was her boy. I didn't care about that if it helped her. I didn't even care about the candy." He stopped again. "She kept looking at me as if *I* were her boy, and for a while I wasn't sure I wasn't, I felt so bad. When I got back to the office the old telegraph operator, Mr. Grogan—he was asleep. I did what he *told* me to do—splashed water in his face and got him a cup of black coffee to keep him awake. If he doesn't do his work they'll put him on a pension, and he doesn't want that. I got him awake all right and he did his work all right and then he told me about himself, and then we sang."

He stopped talking to walk about the room a moment. He went on, standing at the open door and looking away from his mother. "All of a sudden," he said, "I feel different—not like I ever felt before. Even when Papa died I didn't feel *this* way. In two days everything is changed. I'm lonely and I don't know what I'm lonely *for*."

His mother didn't speak, waiting for him to go on. "I don't know what's happening, or why it's happening; but no matter what hap-pens, don't let anything hurt *you* that way."

The woman waited to see if he had anything more to say, and as he didn't she began to speak. "Everything *is* changed," she said— "for you. But it is still the same, too. The loneliness you feel has come to you because you are no longer a child. But the world has always been full of that loneliness. If a message comes to me as to the Mexican woman tonight, I can't tell you what I shall do. I don't know." She stopped suddenly, and then after a moment went on, almost cheer-fully. "What did you have for supper?"

"Pie," Homer said—"apple and coconut cream. The manager of the office paid for them. He's the greatest guy I ever met."

"I'll send Bess with a lunch tomorrow."

"I don't want any lunch. We like to go out and buy something and sit down and eat together. You don't have to go to the trouble of making a lunch." He stopped. "This job is the greatest thing that ever happened to me, but it sure makes school seem silly."

"Of course," Mrs. Macauley said. "Schools are only to keep children off the streets, but sooner or later they've got to go out into the streets, whether they like it or not. It's natural for fathers and mothers to be afraid of the world for their children, but there's nothing for them to be afraid of. The world is full of frightened little children. Being frightened, they frighten each other. Try to understand," she went on. "Try to love everyone you meet. I shall be in this parlor waiting for you every night. But you needn't come in and talk to me unless you wish to do so. I shall understand. I know there shall be times when your heart shall be unable to give your tongue one word of speech to utter." She stopped now and looked at the boy.

"You're tired, so go along to sleep, now," Mrs. Macauley said.

"OK," the boy said, and went to his room.

8 Bess and Mary

At seven in the morning the alarm clock clicked—that's all—and Homer Macauley sat up. He adjusted the clock so that the alarm would not go off. He then got out of bed and brought out his body-building course from New York and began reading the instructions for the day. His brother Ulysses watched, as he always did, awakening with Homer at the click just before the alarm, which Homer never allowed to go off. The body-building course from New York consisted of a printed booklet and an elastic stretcher. Homer turned to Lesson 7 while Ulysses crowded in under his arm to be nearer the mysterious stuff. After some ordinary preliminary exercises, including deep breathing, Homer lay flat on his back and lifted his legs stiffly from the floor.

"What's that?" Ulysses said.

"Exercises."

"What for?"

"Muscle."

"Going to be the strongest man in the world?"

"Naah."

"What, then?"

"You go back to sleep," Homer said.

Ulysses got back in bed but sat up, watching. At last Homer began to get dressed.

"Where you going?"

"School."

"Going to learn something?"

"Yes, and I'm going to run the two-twenty low hurdles, too."

"Where you going to run 'em?"

"I'm not going to run 'em anywhere. They're wood frames every ten or fifteen yards that you've got to jump over as you run."

"Why?"

"Well, it's a race. Everybody born in this town runs the two-twenty low hurdles. It's the big race of Ithaca. The manager of the telegraph office where I work ran the two-twenty low hurdles when *he* went to Ithaca High. He was Valley Champion."

"What's Valley Champion?"

"That's the best."

"You going to be the best?"

"I'm going to *try*. Now go back to sleep."

Ulysses slipped down in bed, but as he did so he said, "Tomorrow—" then corrected himself—"*Yesterday* I saw the train."

Homer knew what his brother was telling him. He remembered his own fascination with the passing of a train. "How was it?"

"There was a black man, waved."

"Did you wave back?"

"First I waved first. Then he waved first. Then I waved. Then he waved. He said, 'Going home!'" Ulysses looked at his brother. "When are *we* going home?"

"We're home *now*."

"Then why didn't he come here?"

"Everybody's got a different home. Some East, some West, some North, some South. We're West."

"Is West the best?"

"I don't know. I haven't been anywhere else."

"Are you going?"

"Some day."

"Where?"

"New York."

"Where's New York?"

"East. After New York, London. After London, Paris. After Paris, Berlin. Then Vienna, Rome, Moscow, Stockholm—some day I'm going to all the great cities of the world."

"Going to come back?"

"Sure."

"Going to be glad?"

"Sure."

"Why?"

"It's always good to get back, that's why."

The little brother pleaded earnestly. "Don't go."

"I'm not going *now*. I'm going to school now, that's all."

"Don't *ever* go," Ulysses said.

"It's going to be a long time before I go. So you go back to sleep."

"All right," Ulysses said. "Going to run the twenty-two?"

"The *two-twenty*."

When Homer sat down at the breakfast table, his sister Bess was waiting for him. He bowed his head a moment, lifted it, and began to eat.

"What prayer did you say?" Bess said.

"The one I *always* say at the table," Homer said, and then quoted it, saying the words exactly as he had learned to say them when he had scarcely known how to speak.

Be present at our table, Lord.
Be here and everywhere adored.
These creatures bless, and grant that we
May feast in Paradise with Thee.
Amen.

"Oh, that's old. Besides, you don't even know what you're saying."

"I know all right. What prayer did *you* say?"

"Tell me first what the words mean."

"They mean what they *say*."

"Well, what *do* they say?"

"Be present at our table, Lord," Homer said. "That means—Be present at our table, Lord. Be here and everywhere adored—that means let good things be respected here and everywhere else. These creatures—that means us, and everybody else. Bless means to watch over, or something like that. And grant that we may feast in Paradise with Thee. Well, that means *exactly* what it says, or nothing. Take your choice. Just grant that we may feast in Paradise with Thee; that's all. I'm going to run the two-twenty low hurdles at the track meet today. It's an important race. Mr. Spangler ran it when *he* went to Ithaca High. You've got to run and jump *both* in that race. He carries a hard-boiled egg around with him for luck."

"Carrying a hard-boiled egg around for luck is superstition," Bess said.

"Who cares about that. He sent me for two day-old pies from Chatterton's—apple, and coconut cream. Two for a quarter. Fresh pies are a quarter each, so if you've only got a quarter to spend, you get only one. Day-old pies are *two* for a quarter, so you get two. Half of each pie for me and half for Mr. Grogan—but he can only eat one or two slices altogether. That gives me a lot of pie to eat."

Mary Arena, the neighbor girl, came into the kitchen by way of the back door. She brought with her a small Woolworth bowl and put it on the table. Homer got up.

"Here, Mary. Sit down."

"Oh, no, Homer. You go ahead with your breakfast. Try the stewed dried peaches that I made for my father."

"OK," Homer said. "How is your father?"

"Just fine. First thing this morning when he came to the table, he said, 'Any letters? Any new letters from Marcus?'"

"We'll be getting another letter soon," Bess

said. She got up from the table. "Come on, Mary. Let's go."

"To tell you the truth," Mary said to Mrs. Macauley, "I'm getting sick and tired of going to college. It's just like high school. I'm too old to be going to school. Times have changed. I'd really like to go out and find myself a job somewhere."

"And so would I," Bess said.

"Nonsense," Mrs. Macauley said. "You're both children—seventeen years old. Your father has a good job, Mary, and your *brother*, Bess."

"But it just doesn't seem right," Mary said. "Marcus in the Army, and the whole world gouging each other's eyes out."

Homer watched the girls go. "What about *that?*" he said.

"Why, it's perfectly natural for a couple of girls to want to get out and flap their wings," Mrs. Macauley said.

"I don't mean a couple of girls wanting to get out and flap their wings. I mean Mary."

"Mary's a sweet, unaffected, childlike girl. She's the most childlike girl I've ever known, and I'm glad Marcus is in love with her."

"Ma," Homer said impatiently, "I know all about *that*. That isn't what I'm talking about." He paused and said, "Oh, well, I got to get going."

Mrs. Macauley watched him go, and then suddenly out of the corner of her eye she saw Ulysses in his nightshirt. He looked up at her, precisely as any small animal looks up at the female of its kind which is its own. The expression of his face was deeply serious and incredibly charming. "Why does he say, 'Weep no more?'"

"Who?"

"The black man on the train."

"It's a song." She took his hand. "Come on, now, put on your clothes."

"Will he be on the train again today?"

Mrs. Macauley thought a moment. "Yes," she said.

9 The Veteran

On his way to school Homer Macauley passed a picket fence protecting an empty lot full of weeds on San Benito Avenue. The fence was old and rotten and had no use other than to ornament a small area of waste, and to protect a group of weed tribes that surely needed no protection. The daytime school student and nighttime telegraph messenger brought his bicycle to a dynamic skidding halt, dropped the contraption and hurried to the fence as if there he would discover something extremely fleeting and apt to be lost if he didn't hurry. The fence was about a foot higher than the regulation low hurdles. Homer studied the fence, the area beyond it, the running area before it, and then measured the height of the fence, which was considerably above his waist. He went back ten yards, and then without any announcement from himself to himself, he turned in a fury and ran toward the fence. When he was near enough, he made a beautiful hurdle, kicked the fence, knocked down part of it, and himself fell into the weeds, but got right up and went back for another try. Altogether Homer made seven tries, not one of which was successful. He stopped only when the whole fence had been brought down into still greater ruin.

An old man with a walking stick came out of the house across the street, smoking a pipe, and quietly watched Homer. Just as Homer was getting up from the last spill and was brushing himself off, the man spoke.

"What you doing?"

"Hurdling."

"Hurt yourself?"

"Naaah, the fence is a little too high, that's all. The weeds are slippery, too."

The old man looked at the weeds a moment and then said, "Those are milkweeds. They make good feed for rabbits. Rabbits like them. I used to have a hutch of rabbits about eleven years ago, but somebody opened the door in the middle of the night, and they ran away."

"What did he open the door for?"

"Well, I don't know. I never did find out who did it. I lost thirty-three head of the prettiest rabbits you ever saw. Pink-eyes, cat-faces, Belgians, and two or three other kinds —never did find out."

"Do you like rabbits?" Homer said.

"They're gentle little animals. Domestic rabbits are very mild-mannered." The old man looked around among the weeds of the empty lot. "Thirty-three rabbits out in the open for eleven years. There's no telling how many of them there are now—not the way *they* breed. I wouldn't be surprised if this whole city is full of wild rabbits now."

"*I* never see any of them."

"Maybe not. But they're here—somewhere. The whole city's overrun with them, most likely. A couple more years and they'll be a serious problem."

Even so, Homer got on his bike. "Well, I got to go now."

"Come again," the old man said. "Any time at all. You're welcome."

"Thanks," Homer said. "I'm going to run the two-twenty low hurdles at the high school track meet this afternoon."

"Didn't go to high school, myself, but I fought in the Spanish-American War."

"Yes, sir. Well, so long!"

"Oh, yes," the old man said, but he was talking to himself now. "Ran like a rabbit half the time."

Homer disappeared around the corner, and the old man strolled back to his little broken-down house, puffing his pipe and looking around.

10 The Ancient History Class

On the track of the athletic field at Ithaca High School, the hurdles were set for the 220-yard low hurdle race. Now, in the morning, four boys were running a practice race. Each ran well, under control, and each hurdled with good form. Coach Byfield, stopwatch in hand, came up to the winner.

"That was better, Ackley," he said to a boy who was surely not common, but for all that surely not terribly *uncommon*, either. He was a boy who had the resigned manner of one whose family had not in recent decades been in want of food, clothing, or shelter, who on occasion entertained others of similar good fortune.

"You've got a lot to learn yet," the coach said to the boy, "but I think you'll be able to win the race this afternoon."

"I'll try my best, sir."

"You won't be having any real competition today, but you'll have plenty in two weeks at the Valley Meet. Go to the shower now and take it easy until this afternoon."

"Yes, sir," the boy said.

The other three runners were over to one side, watching and listening.

"He may *act* like a sissy," one of the boys said, "but he always comes in first. What's the matter with you, Sam?"

"What's the matter with *me?*" Sam said. "What's the matter with *you?* Why don't *you* beat him?"

"I came in second."

"Second's no better than third," the third boy said.

"Hubert Ackley the Third, beating us!" Sam said. "We ought to be ashamed of ourselves."

"Sure," the second boy said, "but we've got no alibis. He just runs a better race, that's all."

The coach turned to these three and, in an altogether different tone of voice, said, "OK, you guys. You're not so good you can stand around and be proud of yourselves. Get to your marks and give it another try."

Without a word the boys went to their marks, and the coach sent them off for another run of the race. After they began to run, he decided he'd run them a couple of more times before the afternoon meet. He seemed determined to have Hubert Ackley III win the race.

The ancient history classroom was swiftly filling, as the teacher, old Miss Hicks, waited for the final bell and the kind of order and quiet that in her class was the sign for the beginning of another stab at the business of trying to educate, if not entertain, the boys and girls of Ithaca, now at high school and soon, at least theoretically, to be ready for the world. Homer Macauley watched a girl named Helen Eliot walk from the door to her desk. Without a doubt this girl was the most beautiful girl in the world. Besides that, she was a snob—which Homer refused to believe. Following her came Hubert Ackley III. When Hubert reached Helen, the two whispered a moment, which made Homer sick with envy and anger. The final bell rang, and Miss Hicks said, "All right. Silence, please. Who's absent?"

"I am," a boy said. His name was Joe Terranova, and he was the low comedian of the class. The four or five of Joe's faithful, the members of his religious cult of comedy, his disciples, were instant in their response and appreciation of his swift and goofy wit. But Helen Eliot and Hubert Ackley turned and frowned at these Holy Rollers of the classroom, these bad-mannered offspring of slum-dwellers. This in turn annoyed Homer so much that when everyone else had stopped laughing, he burst out with an artificial Hah Hah Hah, which he sent almost directly into the faces of Hubert, whom he despised, and Helen, whom he adored. Then he turned swiftly to Joe and said, "As for you, Joe, shut up when Miss Hicks is talking."

"None of your nonsense now, Joseph Terranova," Miss Hicks said. And turning to Homer, "Or yours, Homer Macauley." She paused a moment to look the class over. "We will take up the Assyrians where we left off yesterday. I want everyone's undivided attention—everyone's *continuous* undivided attention. First we will read from our ancient history textbook. Then we will have an oral discussion of what we have read."

The low comedian could not resist this opportunity for horseplay. "No, Miss Hicks," he suggested. "Let's not discuss it orally. Let's discuss it silently, so I can sleep." Again the faithful roared with laughter, and the snobs turned away, disgusted. Miss Hicks did not answer the comedian immediately. It was difficult not to enjoy his wit, and she didn't want it to stop, but at the same time it was absolutely necessary to keep him in line. At last she spoke.

"You must not be unkind, especially when it happens that you're right."

"Well, I'm sorry, Miss Hicks. I guess I just can't help it. Oral discussion! What other kind of discussion is there? But OK, I'm sorry." Now, with a kind of spoofing of himself and of his own presumptuousness, he waved to her, saying patronizingly, "Go ahead, Miss Hicks."

"Thank you," the teacher said. "Now, everybody—wide awake!"

"Wide awake?" Joe said. "Look at them— they're all fast asleep with their eyes wide open."

"Another interruption," the teacher said, "and I'll have to ask you to go to the principal's office."

"I'm only trying to get myself a little education," Joe said.

"Ah, shut up," Homer said to his friend. "You don't have to show off all the time, Joe. Everybody knows how smart you are."

"Not another word," Miss Hicks said. "Not another word from either of you. Page 117, paragraph two." Everyone turned to the page and found the place. "Ancient history," the teacher continued, "may *seem* to be a dull and unnecessary study. At a time like the present, when so much history is going on in our own world, the history of another world—long since ended—may seem useless to study and understand. Such a notion, however, is incorrect. It is very important for us to know of other times, other cultures, other peoples, and other worlds. Who'll volunteer to come to the head of the class and read?" Two girls and Hubert Ackley III raised their hands.

Joe, the comedian, glanced at Homer, and said, "Get a load of that guy, will you?"

Of the two girls who had volunteered, the teacher chose Helen Eliot. Homer watched her walk to the front of the class. She just stood there, being very beautiful; and then in the purest and most liquid voice imaginable she began to read, while Homer marveled at the incredible miracle of such a person and such a voice.

"The Assyrians," Helen read, "long of nose, hair, and beard, developed Nineveh in the north to a position of great power. After many vicissitudes with the Hittites, Egyptians and others, they conquered Babylon under the reign of Tiglath Pileser the First, in eleven hundred B.C. For centuries afterward, the power veered between Nineveh built of stone and Babylon built of brick. There is no connection between the names 'Syrian' and 'Assyrian,' and the Assyrians were to fight the Syrians until Tiglath Pileser the Third conquered them and exiled the ten lost tribes of Israel."

Helen paused for a fresh supply of breath with which to read the next paragraph, but before she could begin to read again, Homer Macauley said, "How about Hubert *Ackley* the Third? Who did *he* conquer, or what did *he* do?"

The well-bred boy got to his feet in a kind of decent bitterness. "Miss Hicks," he said very earnestly, "I cannot allow such malicious mischief to go uncorrected or unpunished. I must ask you to order Mr. Macauley to go to the principal's office—or," he said very deliberately, "I shall have to take the matter into my own hands."

Homer jumped out of his seat. "Ah, shut up! Your name *is* Hubert Ackley the Third, isn't it? Well, what did you ever do, or for that matter what did Hubert Ackley the Second ever do, or what did Hubert Ackley the First ever do?" He paused a moment and then faced Miss Hicks and Helen Eliot. "I think that's a good intelligent question." Then he turned to Hubert Ackley and repeated the question. "What did they do?"

"Well," Hubert said, "at least no Ackley has ever been a common—" He stopped to seek an appropriately withering word, and then said, "—fanfaron," a word nobody else in Ithaca had ever before heard.

"Fanfaron?" Homer said. "What's that mean, Miss Hicks?" As she was not ready with a definition of the word, Homer turned quickly to Hubert Ackley and went on. "Listen, number three, don't be calling me something I never even *heard* before."

"A fanfaron," Hubert said, "is a hoodlum —a braggart." And he stopped to find another, *lower* word.

"Ah, shut up," Homer said.

He glanced at Helen Eliot and smiled the famous Macauley smile. "*Fanfaron!*" he repeated. "What kind of cussing is that?" Then he sat down.

Helen Eliot waited for a sign from the teacher to go on reading. Miss Hicks, however, did not give the sign. Finally Homer understood. He got to his feet and said to Hubert Ackley III, "All right, I apologize. I'm sorry."

"Thank you," the well-bred boy said, and sat down.

The ancient-history teacher looked about the room a moment and then said, "Homer Macauley and Hubert Ackley will remain in their seats after school."

"But, Miss Hicks," Homer said, "what about the track meet?"

"The development of your minds is as important as the development of your bodies. Perhaps more important."

"Miss Hicks," Hubert Ackley said, "I'm afraid Coach Byfield will *insist* on my taking part in the track meet."

"I don't know about Coach Byfield *insisting*," Homer said, "but *I'm* going to run the two-twenty low hurdles; that's all."

Hubert Ackley looked at Homer. "I had no idea you had gone out for that race."

"Well, I have. Miss Hicks, if you let us go this time, I promise never again to make any trouble or to be disobedient or *anything*. And so does Hubert. Don't you?"

"Yes, I do, Miss Hicks," Hubert said.

"You will both stay in after school. Helen, please continue to read."

"The allied armies," Helen read, "of the Chaldeans from the south and the Medes and Persians from the north overcame the Assyrian empire and Nineveh bowed to their might. Nebuchadnezzar the Second ruled over the second Babylonian empire. Then came the great Cyrus, King of Persia, with his hordes of invaders. His conquest, however, was only one of a cycle, for the descendants of this army would later be subjugated by Alexander the Great."

Homer, disgusted now, tired from the work of the night before, and lulled by the sweet voice of the girl he believed was made only for himself, slowly dropped his head on his folded arms and began to enjoy something almost the equivalent of sleep. Still he could hear the girl reading.

"From this melting pot," she read, "the world has a heritage of great value. The Mosaic code of the Bible owes some of its principles to some of the laws formulated by Hammurabi, who was called the lawgiver. From their system of arithmetic, in which they used the multiple of twelve, as well as our familiar ten, we derive our sixty minutes to the hour and 360 degrees to the circle. Arabia gave us our numerals, which are still called Arabic to distinguish them from the Roman system of notation. The Assyrians invented the sundial. The modern apothecary symbols and the signs of the Zodiac originated with the Babylonians. Comparatively recent excavations in Asia Minor have revealed that there was a magnificent empire there."

"A magnificent empire?" Homer dreamed. "Where? In Ithaca in California? Away out of the universe and gone? Without any great people, without any great discoveries, without sundials, without numerals, without Zodiacs, without humor, without anything? Where was this great empire?" He decided to sit up and look around again. He saw only the face of Helen Eliot, perhaps the greatest empire of them all, and he heard her liquid voice, perhaps the greatest achievement of pathetic mankind.

"The Hittites," she said, "had swung down the coast and over into Egypt. They mingled their blood with the Hebrew tribes and gave to the Hebrews the Hittite nose."

Helen stopped reading and turned to the ancient-history teacher. "That's the end of the chapter, Miss Hicks."

"Very well, Helen. Thank you for an excellent reading. You may be seated."

11 The Human Nose

Miss Hicks waited for Helen to take her seat and then looked over the faces of her pupils. "Now," she said, "what have we learned?"

"That people all over the world have noses," Homer said.

Miss Hicks was not upset by this reply and took it for what it was worth. "What else?"

"That noses," Homer said, "are not only for blowing or to have colds in but also to keep the record of ancient history straight."

Miss Hicks turned away from Homer and said, "Someone else, please. Homer seems to have been carried away by the noses."

"Well, it's in the book, isn't it? What do *they* mention it for? It must be important."

"Perhaps you'd like to make an extemporaneous speech on the nose, Mr. Macauley."

"Well," Homer said, "maybe not exactly a speech—but ancient history tells us one thing." Slowly now, and with a kind of unnecessary emphasis, he continued, "People have always had noses. To prove it, all you have to do is look around at everybody in this classroom." He looked around at everybody. "Noses, all over the place." He stopped a moment to decide what else would be possible to say on this theme. "The nose has always been a source of embarrassment to the human race, and the Hittites probably beat up on everybody else because their noses were so big and crooked. It doesn't matter who invented the sundial because sooner or later somebody invents a watch. The important thing is, Who's got the noses?"

Joe the comedian listened with profound interest and admiration, if not envy. Homer continued.

"Some people talk through their noses. A great many people snore through their noses, and a handful of people whistle or sing through them. Some people are led around by their noses, others use the nose for prying and poking into miscellaneous places. Noses have been bitten by mad dogs and movie actors in passionate love scenes. Doors have been slammed on them, and they have been caught in eggbeaters and automatic record changers. The nose is stationary, like a tree, but being on a movable object—the head—it suffers great punishment by being taken to places where it is only in the way. The purpose of the nose is to smell what's in the air, but some people sniff with the nose at other people's ideas, manners, or appearances." He looked at Hubert Ackley III and then at Helen Eliot, whose nose, instead of moving upward, for some reason went slightly downward. "These people generally hold their noses toward heaven, as if that were the way to get in. Most animals have nostrils, but few have noses, as we understand noses; yet the sense of smell in animals is more highly developed than in man—who has a nose, and no fooling." Homer Macauley took a deep breath and decided to conclude his speech. "The most important thing to remember about the nose—is that it makes trouble, causes wars, breaks up old friendships, and wrecks many happy homes. *Now* can I go to the track meet, Miss Hicks?"

The ancient-history teacher, although pleased by this imaginative discourse on a trivial theme, would not allow its success to interfere with the need for her to maintain order in the classroom. "You will stay in after school, Mr. Macauley, and so will *you*, Mr. Ackley. Now that we have disposed of the matter of noses, someone else please comment on what we have read."

There were no comments.

"Come now," Miss Hicks said. "Somebody else comment—*anybody*."

Joe the comedian answered the call. "Noses are red, violets are blue. Ithaca's dead. California, I love you."

"Anyone else?"

"Big noses are generally on navigators and explorers," a girl said.

"Very good. Henry?"

"I don't know anything about noses," Henry said.

"All right," Joe said, "who is Moses?"

"Moses is in the Bible," Henry said.

"Did he have a nose?"

"Sure he had a nose."

"All right, then. Why don't you say, 'Moses had a nose as big as most noses'?"

"Why should I?"

"To learn a little ancient history, that's why."

"Anybody else?"

Nobody volunteered, so Joe said, "Well, I guess it's up to me, as usual. The hand is faster than the eye, but only the nose runs."

"Miss Hicks," Homer said, "you've got to let me run the two-twenty low hurdles."

"I'm not interested in *any* kind of hurdles," Miss Hicks said. "Anybody else?"

But it was too late. The class bell rang. Everyone got up to leave for the track meet except Homer Macauley and Hubert Ackley III.

12 Miss Hicks

The boys' athletic coach of Ithaca High stood in the office of the principal—a man whose last name was Ek, a circumstance duly reported by Mr. Robert Ripley in a daily newspaper cartoon entitled "Believe It or Not." Mr. Ek's first name was Oscar, and not worthy of notice.

"Miss Hicks," the principal said to the coach, "is the oldest and best teacher we have ever had at this school. She was *my* teacher when I attended Ithaca High, and she was your teacher, too, Mr. Byfield. I'm afraid I wouldn't care to go over her head about punishing a couple of unruly boys."

"Hubert Ackley the Third is *not* an unruly boy," the coach said. "Homer Macauley— yes. Hubert Ackley—no. He is a perfect little gentleman."

"Well, he comes from a well-to-do family, at any rate. But if Miss Hicks has asked him to stay in after school, then *in* it is. Perhaps he *is* a perfect little gentleman. But Miss Hicks is the teacher of the ancient history class, and she has never been known to punish anyone who has not deserved to be punished. Hubert Ackley will have to run the race some other time."

The matter was surely closed now, the principal felt. The coach turned and left the office. He did not go to the athletic field, however. He went to the ancient history classroom instead. There he found Homer and Hubert and Miss Hicks. He bowed to the old teacher and smiled.

"Miss Hicks," he said, "I have spoken to Mr. Ek about this matter." The implication of his remark was that he had been given authorization to come and liberate Hubert Ackley III. Homer Macauley, however, leaped to his feet as if it were *he* who was to be liberated.

"Not *you*," the coach said. "Mr. Ackley."

"What do you mean?" the ancient-history teacher said.

"Mr. Ackley is to get into his track suit immediately and run the two-twenty low hurdles. We're waiting for him."

"Oh yeah?" Homer said. He was overflow-ing with righteous indignation. "Well what about Mr. *Macauley?*" There was no reply from the coach, who walked out of the room followed by a somewhat troubled and confused young man—Hubert Ackley III.

"Did you see that, Miss Hicks?" Homer said.

The ancient-history teacher was so upset she could barely speak. At last she managed to whisper, "Mr. Byfield is a liar." Homer was amazed to see Miss Hicks so angry. It made him feel that she was just about the best teacher ever.

"I have taught ancient history at Ithaca High for thirty-five years. I have known hundreds of Ithaca boys and girls. I taught your brother Marcus and your sister Bess, and if you have younger brothers or sisters at home I shall some day teach them, too."

"Just a brother, Ulysses. How *was* Marcus in school?"

"Marcus and Bess were both good students —honest and civilized. Yes, *civilized*. The behavior of ancient peoples had made them civilized from birth. Like yourself, Marcus sometimes spoke out of turn, but he was never a liar. That man came here and deliberately lied to me—just as he lied to me time and again when he sat in this classroom as a boy. He has learned nothing except to toady to those he feels are superior. The two-twenty low hurdles! *Low* indeed!" The ancient-history teacher blew her nose and wiped her eyes.

"Don't feel bad, Miss Hicks," Homer said. "I never knew teachers are human beings like everybody else—and *better*, too! I'll stay in, Miss Hicks. You can punish me."

"I didn't keep you in to punish you," the teacher said. "I have always kept in only those who have meant the most to me. I still don't believe I'm mistaken about Hubert Ackley. I was going to send both of you to the field after a moment, anyway. You were not kept in for punishment, but for education. I watch the growth of spirit in the children who come to my class. You apologized to Hubert Ackley. And even though it embarrassed him to do so, because your apology made him unworthy, he graciously accepted your apology. I kept you in after school because I wanted to talk to both of you—one of you from a good, well-to-do family, the other from a good, poor family. Getting along in this world will be even more difficult for him than for you. I wanted you to know one another a little better. It is very important. I wanted to talk to *both* of you."

"I guess I like Hubert," Homer said, "only he seems to think he's better than the other boys."

"I know how you feel, but every man in the world *is* better than someone else. And not as good as someone *else*. Joseph Terranova is brighter than Hubert, but Hubert is just as honest in his own way. In a democratic state every man is the equal of every other man up to the point of exertion, and after that every man is free to exert himself as he chooses. I am eager for my boys and girls to exert themselves about behaving with honor. What my children appear to be on the surface is no matter to me. I am fooled neither by gracious manners nor by bad manners. I am interested in what is truly beneath each kind of manners. Whether one of my children is rich or poor, brilliant or slow, genius or simple-minded, is no matter to me, if there is humanity in him—if he has a heart—if he loves truth and honor—if he respects both his inferiors and his superiors. If the children of my classroom are human, I do not want them to be alike in their *manner* of being human. If they are not corrupt, it does not matter to me how they differ from one another. I want each of my children to be himself or herself. I don't want you to be like somebody else just to please me or to make my work easier. I would soon be weary of a classroom full of perfect little ladies and gentlemen. I want my children to be *people*— each one separate—each one special—each one a pleasant and exciting variation of all the others. I wanted Hubert Ackley here to listen to this with you—to understand with you that if at the present you do not like him and he does not like you, that is perfectly natural. I wanted him to know that each of you will begin to be truly human when, in spite of your natural dislike of one another, you still respect one another. That is what it means to be civilized—that is what we are to learn from a study of ancient history. I'm glad I've spoken to you, rather than to anyone else I know. When you leave this school —long after you have forgotten *me*—I shall be watching for you in the world." Again Miss Hicks blew her nose and touched her handkerchief to her eyes. "Run along to the athletic field, now."

The second son of the Macauley family of Santa Clara Avenue in Ithaca, California, got up from his desk and walked out of the room.

On the athletic field, Hubert Ackley and the three boys who had already raced with him that day were taking their places in the lanes for the two-twenty low hurdle race. Homer reached the fifth lane just as the man with the pistol lifted his arm to start the race. Homer went to his mark with the others. He felt good, but very angry, and he believed that nothing in the world would be able to keep him from winning this race—the wrong kind of shoes, the wrong kind of clothes for running, no practice, or anything else. He would just naturally win the race.

Hubert Ackley, in the lane next to Homer's lane, turned to him and said, "You can't run this race—like *that*."

"No?" Homer said. "Wait and see."

Mr. Byfield, sitting in the grandstand, asked himself, "Who's that starting in the outside lane without track clothes?" Then he remembered who it was.

He decided to stop the race so that he could remove the fifth runner, but it was too late. The gun had been fired and the runners were running. Homer and Hubert took the first hurdle a little ahead of the others, each of them clearing nicely. Homer moved a little ahead of Hubert on the second hurdle and kept moving ahead on the third, fourth, fifth, sixth, seventh and eighth hurdles. But close behind was Hubert Ackley.

Homer reached the ninth hurdle precisely when the coach of Ithaca High also reached it, coming in the opposite direction, so that Homer hurdled straight into the outstretched arms of the athletic coach, and the man and the boy fell to the ground. Hubert Ackley stopped running and stopped the other runners. "Stay where you are," he shouted. "Let him get up." Homer got to his feet, and the race resumed.

Everyone in the grandstand, even Helen Eliot, was amazed at what had happened. Now, the ancient-history teacher was at the finish line of the race.

"Come on, Homer!" she said. "Come on, Hubert! Hurry, Sam!—George!—Henry!"

At the next to the last hurdle Hubert caught up with Homer. "Sorry," he said.

"Go ahead," Homer said.

Hubert Ackley moved a little ahead of Homer, and now there was no longer very far to go. Homer kicked the last hurdle, but he almost caught up with Hubert. The finish of the race was so close no one could tell who had actually won it. Sam, George and Henry came in soon after.

Furious and bitter, and a little shocked by the fall he had taken, the coach of Ithaca High came running toward the group that Miss Hicks had gathered around her.

"Macauley!" he shouted from a distance of fifteen yards.

When he reached the group, he stood panting for breath and glaring at Homer Macauley.

Then he said, "For the remainder of this semester you will take no part in any school athletic activities."

"Yes, sir," Homer said.

"Now go to my office and stay there."

"Your office?" Homer suddenly remembered that he had to be at work at four o'clock. "What time is it?" he said.

Hubert Ackley looked at his wristwatch. "A quarter to four."

"Go to my office!" Byfield shouted.

"But you don't understand, Mr. Byfield," Homer said. "I've got to go somewhere, and I just can't be late."

Joe Terranova came into the group. "Why should he go to your office? He didn't do anything wrong."

The poor coach had already suffered too much. "You keep your dirty little foreigner mouth shut!" he shouted. Then he pushed the boy, who went sprawling. But even before he touched the ground, Joe shouted: "Foreigner?"

On his feet again, Joe tackled Byfield as if they were in a football game.

Mr. Ek came running, breathless and bewildered.

"Gentlemen!" he said. "Boys, boys!" He dragged Joe Terranova off the athletic coach, who did not get to his feet.

"Mr. Byfield," the principal said, "what is the meaning of this unusual behavior?"

Speechless, Byfield pointed at Miss Hicks.

"Mr. Byfield owes Joe Terranova an apology," she said.

"Is that so? Is that so, Mr. Byfield?" Mr. Ek said.

"Joe's people *are* from Italy, that's quite true, but they are not to be referred to as foreigners," Miss Hicks said.

Joe Terranova said, "He doesn't need to

apologize to me. If he calls me names, I'll bust him in the mouth. If he beats me up, I'll get my brothers."

"Joseph," Miss Hicks said. "You must allow Mr. Byfield to apologize. You must give him the privilege of once again trying to be an American."

"Yes, that's so," the principal said. "This is America, and the only foreigners here are those who forget that this *is* America." He turned to the man who was still sprawled on the ground. "Mr. Byfield," he commanded.

The athletic coach of Ithaca High School got to his feet. To no one in particular he said, "I apologize," and hurried away.

Joe Terranova and Homer Macauley went off together. Joe walked well, but Homer limped. He had hurt his left leg when Byfield had tried to stop him.

Miss Hicks and Mr. Ek turned to the thirty or forty boys and girls who had gathered around. They were of many types and many nationalities.

"All right, now," Miss Hicks said. "Go along home to your families," and as the boys and girls were all a little bewildered, she added, "Brighten up, brighten up—this is nothing."

"Yes," the principal said, "brighten up, every one of you, please."

The children broke up into groups and walked away.

Chapters 1–12

Getting at Meaning

1. Describe the Macauley family. Approximately how old is each child? How do the members of the family feel about each other?

2. Where does Homer work? What parts of the job does he like? What does he find difficult? What does he do with the money he earns?

3. How does Mrs. Sandoval react when Homer brings her the telegram from the War Department? What are Homer's feelings during the encounter?

4. Describe Mr. Grogan. What duties does Homer perform for him?

5. Who is Mary Arena? How is she connected with the Macauley household?

6. How is Mr. Byfield's attitude toward Hubert Ackley different from his attitude toward the other boys? Why do you think it is so different?

7. How does Miss Hicks handle the students in her classroom? What atmosphere does she seem to create? What values does she look for and cultivate in her students?

8. Why is there such rivalry between Homer and Hubert? Why does Miss Hicks keep them both after school? How does Miss Hicks define "civilized"?

9. How does Mr. Byfield get Hubert out on the track? How does Miss Hicks react to his trick?

10. How does Mr. Byfield interfere with the running of the race? What does Hubert do? How does Hubert's reaction confirm Miss Hicks's opinion of him?

Developing Skills in Reading Literature

1. **Characterization.** Major characters in a novel are those characters that are fully drawn and that appear throughout the novel. Minor characters, on the other hand, are not as fully drawn and may appear only in one or more scenes. Minor characters interact with main characters, often bringing out important traits in these characters. Minor characters also add interest to the story.

Which characters appear to be emerging as the major characters in this novel? as the minor characters? How do the minor characters provide insights into the major ones? How do the minor characters add interest to the story?

2. **Character.** Homer is perhaps the most fully drawn of the characters in these chapters. What things does Homer learn during the two days covered in this part of the novel? How do his experiences with Mr. Spangler, Mr. Grogan, Mrs. Sandoval, Miss Hicks, and Hubert Ackley affect him? What does his mother mean when she says, "The loneliness you feel has come to you because you are no longer a child." How is Homer beginning to grow up?

Developing Vocabulary

1. **Using Word Origin and Context Clues.** Hubert Ackley says, "I cannot allow such malicious mischief to go uncorrected or unpunished." You might be able to guess the meaning of *malicious* from the context. If you also know that malicious is derived from the Latin word *malus,* meaning "bad," you might accurately predict that malicious means "having a desire to harm another."

The italicized words in the following sentences are derived in part from the same Latin word as *malicious.* Use this knowledge, along with context clues to figure out the meaning of each word.

1. They were heartened by the news that the growth was not *malignant.*

2. Although the *malfunction* caused many delays and much inconvenience, it caused no injuries.

3. The *malfeasance* of the official resulted in his expulsion from office.

4. The doctor was sued for *malpractice,* but was later cleared of all responsibility for the mistake.

5. Scientists are continuously looking for new food sources to combat the problem of *malnutrition.*

6. He performed the action without *malice;* he had no idea that anyone would be hurt.

2. **Idioms.** In Homer's discourse on noses he states, "Some people are led around by their noses, others use the nose for prying and poking into miscellaneous places." What two idiomatic expressions does he refer to in this statement? List at least six other idioms based on the word *nose,* along with their meanings. Use a dictionary if you need help.

Developing Writing Skills

1. **Supporting an Opinion.** Reread Miss Hicks's explanation of the values she feels are important to cultivate in her students. Then write your own paragraph on what you believe are the most important values you can learn in school. Identify the values and explain why you think they are important.

2. **Using Contrasts.** Write a paragraph contrasting the attitudes of Miss Hicks and Mr. Byfield. Make a general statement about these teachers in the topic sentence, and, in the rest of the paragraph, support your statement with specific examples.

13 Big Chris

When Homer Macauley swung onto his bicycle after the track meet to get to work as soon as possible, a man named Big Chris walked into Covington's Sporting Goods Store on Tulare Street. He was a huge man, tall, lean, and hard, with a great blond beard. He had just come down from the hills around Piedra to see about some new grub and shells and traps. Mr. Covington, the founder and proprietor of the store, began immediately to demonstrate to Big Chris the workings of a rather involved new trap that had just been invented by a man out in Friant. The trap was enormous and complicated. It was made of steel, lemonwood, springs and ropes. Its principle seemed to be to take the animal, swing it up and around, and hold it off its feet until the trapper arrived.

"This is brand new," Mr. Covington said, "invented by a man named Safferty out in Friant. He's applied for a patent and so far he's made only two of them, one a model, which he sent to the patent office, and this one, which he sent to me, to sell. This trap is for any kind of animal that walks. Mr. Safferty calls it 'THE LIFT-THEM-OFF-THEIR-FEET,

SWING-THEM-AROUND, AND-HOLD-THEM SAFFERTY ALL-ANIMAL TRAP.' He's asking twenty dollars for it. Of course, the trap hasn't been tested; but as you can see for yourself, it is strong and could very likely lift, swing, and hold a full grown bear with no difficulty at all."

Big Chris listened to the proprietor of the sporting goods store as a child listens, and behind him Ulysses Macauley listened with the same fascination, ducking in between the two men for a better view of the trap. Mr. Covington was under the impression that Ulysses belonged to Big Chris, and Big Chris was under the impression that Ulysses belonged to Mr. Covington, so that between the two of them they had no reason to account for the small boy's presence. As for Ulysses himself, he was under the impression that he belonged wherever there was something interesting to see.

"The remarkable thing about this trap," Mr. Covington said, "is that it will not *hurt* the animal, leaving the fur whole and undamaged. The trap is guaranteed by Mr. Safferty himself for a period of eleven years. This includes all parts—the pliancy of the wood, the endurance of the springs, the steel, the ropes, and all the other parts. Mr. Safferty, although not a trapper himself, believes that this is the most effective and humane trap in the world. A man close to seventy, he lives quietly in Friant, reading books and inventing things. He has invented, all told, thirty-seven separate and distinct items of practical usefulness." Mr. Covington stopped his work with the trap. "Now," he said, "I believe the trap is set."

Ulysses, crowding in to watch, moved too far. The trap closed on him gently but swiftly, lifted him off his feet, turned him around and held him three feet off the floor, straight out, horizontally, clamped in. No sound came from the boy, even though he was a little bewildered. Big Chris, however, did not take the event so lightly.

"Careful there!" he said to Covington. "I don't want your son to be hurt."

"My son?" Covington said. "I thought he was *your* son. I never saw the boy before in my life. He came in with you."

"He did?" Big Chris said. "I didn't notice. Well, now, hurry! Get him out of the trap—get him out!"

"Yes, sir," Covington said. "Now let me see."

Big Chris was worried and confused. "What's your name, boy?" he said.

"Ulysses," the boy in the trap said.

"My name is Big Chris. Now you just hold tight there, Ulysses, and the man here will get you right out and set you free." Big Chris turned to Mr. Covington. "Well, come on now," he said, "get the boy back on his feet."

Mr. Covington, however, was just as confused as Big Chris. "I'm not sure I remember how Mr. Safferty explained *that* part of the trap. He didn't *demonstrate* the trap, you see, because—well—we didn't have anything to demonstrate it *on*. Mr. Safferty only *explained* it. I believe *this* is supposed to move out—no, it seems to be immovable."

Now, Big Chris and Mr. Covington went to work on the trap together, Big Chris holding Ulysses so that if the trap opened suddenly Ulysses wouldn't fall on his face, and the other man fooling around with the various parts of the trap to see if anything would give way.

"Well, hurry now," Big Chris said. "Let's not keep the boy in the air all day. You're not hurt, are you, Ulysses?"

"No, sir," Ulysses said.

"Well, you just hold tight. We'll get you out of this." He looked sharply at the boy and then said, "What made you crowd in there?"

"Watching," Ulysses said.

"Yes, it *is* a fascinating sort of contraption, isn't it? Now the man here will get you

right out, and I won't let you fall. How old are you?"

"Four," Ulysses said.

"Four," Big Chris said. "Well, I'm fifty years older than you. Now the man here will get you right out, won't you?" And Big Chris looked sharply at Mr. Covington. "What's *your* name?" he said.

"Walter Covington. I own this store."

"Well, that's fine. Now, Walter, get the boy out. Move that piece of wood there. I'm holding him. Don't you worry, Ulysses. What's your *father's* name?"

"Matthew," Ulysses said.

"Well, he's a lucky man to have a boy like you. A fellow with his eyes open. I'd give the world to have a boy like you, but I never met the right woman. I met a girl in Oklahoma thirty years ago but she went off with another fellow. Have you got it there, Walter?"

"Not yet," Mr. Covington said. "But I'll get it. I believe *this* is supposed to—no. Mr. Safferty *explained* how to get the animal out of the trap, but it seems I just can't get the hang of it. Maybe the principle changes when it's a small boy instead of an animal."

Two men, a woman with a small girl, and two boys of nine or ten came into the store to watch.

"What's the matter?" one of the boys said.

"We've got a boy caught in a trap here," Mr. Covington said. "A boy named Ulysses."

"How'd he get in?" one of the men said. "Shall I call a doctor?"

"No, he isn't hurt," Big Chris said. "The boy's all right. He's just off his feet, that's all."

"Maybe you ought to call the police," the woman said.

"No, lady," Big Chris said. "He's just caught in the trap. The man here—Walter—he'll get the boy out."

"Well," the lady said, "it's a shame the way little boys are made to suffer by all sorts of ridiculous mechanical devices."

"The boy's all right, lady," Big Chris said. "He *isn't* suffering."

"Well," the lady said, "if he were *my* boy, I'd have the police on you in two minutes." She went away in a huff, dragging her little daughter along.

"I want to see, I want to see!" the little girl cried. "Everybody gets to see but *me!*" The woman shook the little girl and dragged her out of the store.

"Now, don't you worry, Ulysses," Big Chris said. "We'll get you out of this in no time at all."

Mr. Covington, however, gave up. "Maybe I'd better telephone Mr. Safferty," he said. "*I* can't get the boy out."

"Got to stay here?" Ulysses said.

"No, you don't, boy," Big Chris said. "No, by God, you don't."

A boy with a dozen afternoon papers under his arm came into the store, crowded into the scene, looked at Ulysses, looked at the people, looked at Ulysses again, and then spoke.

"Hello, Ulysses," he said. "What you doing?"

"Hello, Auggie," Ulysses said. "Caught."

"What for?"

"Got caught."

The newsboy tried to help Big Chris, but only got in the way. He looked around, panic-stricken and paralyzed, but after a moment of confusion bolted for the street. He ran straight to the telegraph office. Homer wasn't there, so he ran into the street again, running one way and then the other, bumping into people and shouting the day's headline all at the same time.

A woman who had been bumped said to herself, "Crazy!—from trying to sell papers!"

Auggie ran a full block, got out into the middle of the street to look around in four directions for Homer. As luck would have it, Homer appeared around a corner on his bi- cycle. Auggie ran toward Homer, shouting at him with all his might.

"Homer! You've got to come right away!"

Homer got off his bicycle. "What's the matter, Auggie?"

"Something's happened!" Auggie shouted, even though Homer was right beside him. "You've got to come with me!" He took Homer by the arm.

"But what's the matter?"

"Over at Covington's. Hurry—you've got to come!"

"Ah," Homer said, "you want to show me some new fishing tackle or a rifle or something in the window. I can't go around looking at things any more, Auggie. I'm working now. I've got to go to work."

Homer got back on his wheel and began to ride away, but Auggie took hold of the bike seat and trotted beside him, pushing the bike toward Covington's. "Homer, you've got to come with me! He's caught—he can't get out!"

"What are you talking about?"

Now, they were across the street from Covington's. There was a small crowd in front of the store, and Homer began to be a little frightened. Auggie pointed at the people. The two boys pushed through the crowd into the store, to the trap. There in the trap was Homer's brother Ulysses, and around the trap were Big Chris, Mr. Covington, and a number of strange men and women and boys.

"Ulysses!" Homer shouted.

"Hello, Homer," Ulysses said.

Homer spoke to Mr. Covington. "What's my brother doing in *that* thing?" he said.

"He got caught," Mr. Covington said.

"What are all these people doing here? Go home," he said to the people. "Can't a small boy get caught in a trap without the whole world hanging around?"

"Yes," Mr. Covington said, "I'll have to ask you people to go, who are not customers."

Mr. Covington studied the people. "Mr. Wallace," he said, "you can stay. You trade here, and you, Mr. Sickert. George. Mr. Spindle. Shorty."

"I trade here," a man said. "I bought fish hooks here not more than a week ago."

"Yes," Mr. Covington said, "fish hooks. The rest of you will have to go." Only two people moved away a little.

"Don't worry, Ulysses," Homer said. "Everything's going to be all right now. It's a good thing Auggie found me. Auggie, run over to the telegraph office and tell Mr. Spangler my brother Ulysses is caught in a trap at Covington's and I'm trying to get him out. I'm late already, but tell him I'll be over as soon as I get Ulysses out of the trap. Hurry now."

Auggie turned and ran. He bumped into a policeman who was coming into the store and almost knocked the man down.

"What's all the commotion about?" the policeman said.

"We've got a small boy caught in a trap here," Mr. Covington said. "Can't get him out."

"Let me look into this," the policeman said. He looked at Ulysses, and then at the people.

"All right now," he said, "get along with you, all of you. These things happen every day. You've got better things to do than stand around and watch a small boy in a trap." The policeman moved the people out of the store and locked the front door. He went to Mr. Covington and Big Chris. "Now, let's get this boy out of this thing and send him home."

"Yes," Mr. Covington said, "and the sooner the better. You've got my shop closed at four-thirty in the afternoon."

"Well, how does this thing work?" Homer said.

"It's a new trap," Mr. Covington said— "just invented by Mr. Wilfred Safferty of Friant. He's asking twenty dollars for it and a patent's been applied for."

"Well, get my brother out of it," Homer said, "or get someone who *can*. Get Mr. Safferty."

"I've already tried to telephone Mr. Safferty, but the telephone is out of order," Mr. Covington said.

"Out of order?" Homer shouted. He was very angry about the whole thing. "What do I care if the phone's out of order? Get the man down here and get my brother out of the trap."

"Yes, I think you'd better do that," the policeman said to Mr. Covington.

"Officer," Mr. Covington said, "I'm trying to run a legitimate business. I'm a law-abiding citizen and I pay my taxes, out of which, I might say, you obtain your salary. I have already tried to reach Mr. Safferty by telephone. The telephone appears to be out of order. I cannot leave my shop in the middle of the day to go looking for him."

Homer looked at Mr. Covington straight in the eye and placed a wagging finger under his nose. "You go get the inventor of this torture machine," he said, "and get my brother out of it. That's all."

"It's not a torture machine," Mr. Covington said. "It's the most improved animal trap on the market. It holds the animal aloft without damage to fur or body. No squeezing, cutting, or crushing. It operates on the principle of dislocating the animal from its base and thereby rendering it powerless. Besides, Mr. Safferty may not be at home."

"Ah," Homer said, "what are you talking about?"

Now the policeman decided to study the trap. "Maybe," he suggested, "we'd better *saw* the boy out."

"Saw steel?" Mr. Covington said. "How?"

"Ulysses," Homer said, "do you want anything? Are you all right?"

Big Chris, working hard over the trap,

looked from one brother to the other, deeply moved by the calm of the boy in the trap and the furious devotion of his brother.

"Ulysses," Homer said, "can I get you anything?"

"Papa," Ulysses said.

"Ah," Homer said, "can I get you anything besides Papa?"

"Marcus," the boy in the trap said.

"Marcus is in the Army," Homer said. "Do you want an ice cream cone or anything like that?"

"No," Ulysses said, "just Marcus."

"Well, Marcus is in the Army," Homer said. He turned to Covington. "Get my brother out of this thing and hurry up about it, too!"

"Wait a minute," Big Chris said. "Hold your brother there, boy! Don't let him fall!" Big Chris was very busy with the trap now.

"You're *breaking* the trap!" Mr. Covington said. "It's the only one of its kind in the world. You mustn't break it! I'll go get Mr. Safferty. You're wrecking a great invention. Mr. Safferty's an old man. He may never be able to make another trap like this. The boy's all right. He's unhurt. I'll go get Mr. Safferty. I'll only be an hour or two."

"An hour or two!" Homer shouted. He looked at Mr. Covington with the most terrible contempt in the world, and then all around at the store. "I'll break this whole store," he said. He looked back at Big Chris. "Go ahead, mister. Break the trap—break it!"

Big Chris tugged at the trap with every muscle in his fingers, arms, shoulders and back, and little by little the trap began to give way to the force of his strength.

Ulysses twisted around to watch the man. At last Big Chris destroyed the trap.

Ulysses was free.

Holding him so that he would not fall on his face, Homer set his little brother on his feet. The crowd in front of the store cheered, but not effectively, as they were unorganized

and had no leader. Ulysses tried out his legs. As everything seemed to be all right now, Homer put his arms around his brother. Ulysses looked at Big Chris. The big man was almost exhausted.

"Somebody's got to pay for that trap," Mr. Covington said. "It's ruined. Somebody's got to pay for it."

Without a word, Big Chris brought some currency out of his pocket, counted out twenty dollars and tossed it onto the counter. He took Ulysses by the head and rubbed the boy's hair, as a father sometimes does. Then he turned and walked out of the store.

Homer talked to his brother. "Are you all right? How do you get into these terrible things?" Homer looked at the ruined trap and then kicked it.

"Careful there, boy," the policeman said. "That's some kind of a new invention. There's no telling what it's liable to do."

Mr. Covington went out into the street to speak to the people. "The store is open for business again. Covington's opens at eight every morning, closes at seven every night, except Saturdays when we are open till ten. Closed all day Sunday. Everything in the sporting line. Fishing tackle, guns, ammunition, and athletic goods. We're open for business, ladies and gentlemen. Come right in."

The people slowly walked away.

Homer turned to the policeman before leaving the store. "Who was that man that got my brother out of the trap?"

"Never saw the man before in my life," the policeman said.

"Big Chris," Ulysses said to Homer.

"Is that his name—Big Chris?"

"Yes. Big Chris."

Now, Auggie ran into the store. He looked at Ulysses. "Did you get out, Ulysses? How did you get out, Ulysses?"

"Big Chris," Ulysses said.

"How did he get out, Homer?" Auggie

said. "What happened? What happened to the trap? Where's the big man with the beard? What happened while I was gone?"

"Everything's all right, Auggie," Homer said. "Did you tell Mr. Spangler what I told you?"

"Yeah, I told him. What happened, Homer? Does the trap work? Will it catch animals?"

"Ah," Homer said, "that trap's a lot of hooey. What good is it to catch an animal if you can't get it out? Mr. Covington, you got a lot of nerve charging Big Chris twenty dollars for a piece of junk like that."

"Twenty dollars is the standard price," Mr. Covington said.

"Standard price?" Homer said. "What are you talking about? Come on, Auggie, let's get out of here." The three boys left the store and walked to the telegraph office. Mr. Spangler was leaning on the counter, looking out at the street. Mr. Grogan was sending a telegram. Homer was limping worse than ever now from his collision with Mr. Byfield in the two-twenty low hurdle race.

"Mr. Spangler," he said, "this is my brother Ulysses. We just got him out of some kind of a trap over at Covington's. Big Chris got him out. He had to break the trap. And then he had to pay for it—twenty dollars. This is Auggie. Did he tell you why I'm late?"

"Everything's all right," Spangler said. "A few telegrams have piled up that you've got to deliver, but it's all right. So that's your brother—Ulysses?" Ulysses was standing behind the telegraph operator, watching him work. In front of the telegraph operator, across the table, Auggie stood, listening to the telegraph box.

"A few calls have come in, too," Spangler said. "I took a couple of the near ones myself. The other two are on the call sheet. Take the calls first; then deliver the telegrams."

"Yes, sir," Homer said. "Right away. I'm awfully sorry about this, Mr. Spangler. Will you mind Ulysses until I get back? Maybe a little later when things are quiet I can take him home on my wheel."

"I'll mind your brother," Spangler said. "You go ahead."

"Yes, sir," Homer said. "Thanks very much. Ulysses won't be any trouble. He'll just watch. He won't *do* anything."

Homer left the telegraph office, limping in a hurry.

14 Diana

Ulysses moved closer to Mr. Grogan while Auggie listened to the clatter of the telegraph box.

"What's that for?" Auggie said to Mr. Spangler, indicating the box.

"Mr. Grogan's sending a telegram."

"Where's he sending it to?"

"New York."

"All the way to New York? How does it go?"

"It goes by wire."

"Wires on telegraph poles? Telegraph poles from here to New York? All the way from Ithaca to New York?"

"That's right."

"Who sends 'em?"

"All sorts of people."

The newsboy thought a moment and then said, "I never got a telegram in my life. How do you get one?"

"Somebody sends you one."

"I never got one. Who would send it?"

"Some friend or somebody."

"Everybody I know is right here in Ithaca." A green light went on, on the repeater rack. "What's that green light for?" Auggie said.

"It's a signal to us that the line is clear," Spangler said.

"What line?"

"The line to San Francisco."

"Oh," Auggie said. "How old do you have to be to be a messenger?"

"Sixteen."

"I'm nine. What do you have to wait so long for? You can enlist in the Navy when you're seventeen."

"It's a rule."

"What have they got all them rules for all the time?" Auggie said.

Spangler began to file a batch of outgoing telegrams into a block of pigeonholes.

"Well," he said, "*that* rule is to keep children from working."

"Why?"

"So they won't get tired. So they can play. That rule is for the protection of children."

"Protection from what?"

"Well," Spangler said, "protection from bosses who make kids do too much work for the money they're paid."

"Well, what if the kid doesn't want to be protected? What if he *wants* to work?"

"The rule protects him anyway."

"How old do you have to be not to be a child any more? How old do you have to be to protect yourself, or to do any kind of work you want to do?"

"Got to be sixteen to be a messenger."

"Homer's working, isn't he? Since when is Homer sixteen?"

"Well," Spangler said, "Homer is an ex-ception. He's only fourteen, but he's strong and he's intelligent."

"What do you mean—intelligent?" Auggie said. "Do you have to be intelligent to be a messenger?"

"No, but it helps. It helps to be intelligent no matter what you are."

"Well, how can you tell if a man's intelligent?"

Spangler looked at the newsboy and smiled. "By talking to him a few minutes."

"What are you putting those papers in there for?"

"These are telegrams that were sent yesterday. We file them in here, city by city, for our records and our bookkeeping. Now this telegram is to San Francisco, so I put it in here. All these telegrams in here are to San Francisco."

"I can do that," Auggie said. "I can ride a bike, too—only I haven't got a bike. If I get a bike, Mr. Spangler, can I be a messenger, too? Will you give me a job?"

Spangler stopped working to look at the boy. "Yes, I will, Auggie, but not just yet. Nine isn't quite old enough. Thirteen or fourteen—yes."

"Twelve maybe?" Auggie said.

"Maybe. What do you want to be a messenger for?"

"Learn things. Read telegrams. Find out about things." He paused a moment. "I won't be twelve for three years."

"Three years will go by in no time at all."

"Doesn't seem like it. I've been waiting a long time already."

"You'll find out," Spangler said. "You'll be twelve before you know it. What's your last name?"

"Gottlieb. I'm August Gottlieb."

The manager of the telegraph office and the newsboy looked at each other, each of them very earnest and very serious. "August Gottlieb," Spangler said, "I give you my word. When the time comes—"

Spangler stopped speaking to behold a young woman named Diana Steed who came galloping into the office. In front of the office in the street was the automobile that had brought her. At the wheel of the automobile sat a chauffeur in uniform. In a special, somewhat artificial yet attractive voice, she cried out to Spangler, "Oh, there you are, darling!" She charged upon him with a sweet fury of affection, threw her arms around him, and kissed him in a way that was so incredible it might have been real, or a little better than real.

"Wait a minute!" Spangler said. He held her back, and put the wire basket he was holding on the desk. The young woman came for him but again he warded her off. "Wait a minute," he said. "This is August Gottlieb!"

"How do you do, little boy?" the young woman said.

"August," Spangler said, "this is Miss Steed."

"Hello," August said. And then, not knowing what else to say, he said, "Paper, lady?"

"Why, yes, of course," Diana said. "How much is it?"

"Five cents," Auggie said. "Home edition. Race results, stock market closings, and the latest news of the War."

"I'll take one, please," Diana said.

Auggie accepted the nickel and handed Miss Steed a paper that he first folded in a very efficient and businesslike way, whacking the full paper on his knee, folding it in half, whacking the half paper on his knee again, folding that in half, and then, turning the result around neatly, somewhat like a magician doing an important trick. "Thank you, ma'am," he said. "Wednesdays I sell *The Saturday Evening Post*. I work the whole town."

"Well," Diana said, "I hope you make a lot of money."

"I average about forty cents a day, papers and magazines both. When the County Fair opens I sell soda pop."

"Well, you *do* keep busy, *don't* you?" Diana said in her bubbling cheerful voice.

"Yes," Auggie said, "and I learn things, too. I can figure people out pretty good." It appeared that Auggie had figured out Miss Steed and was pleased with his conclusions.

"Yes, you do," she said, "I'm sure you do." She turned to Spangler. "I waited for your call, darling. You *did* say you would call at five, didn't you?"

"Oh, yes," Spangler said. "I forgot. I was talking to Auggie here. He wants to be a messenger, and I've just told him when the time comes he's going to have a job."

"Well, thanks, Mr. Spangler," Auggie said. He moved to go. "I'll be seeing you. Goodbye, ma'am. Goodbye, Ulysses."

"Ulysses!" Diana said to Spangler. "My, what an appropriate name! Ulysses in Ithaca! Darling, I've only a moment. You will be out for dinner, won't you? You *must*, you know."

Spangler began to speak but the young woman stopped him. "No, you *promised!* Yes, you did! Mother and Father are dying to meet you! Seven o'clock sharp!"

"Now, wait a minute," Spangler said.

"Darling," Diana said, "you can't disappoint me again, can you?"

Spangler sighed. "I've been out to dinner twice in my life. I was scared to death both times, and I had no fun at all."

"You'll *love* Mother and Father. We're not dressing—just evening clothes."

"Evening clothes? I'm wearing the clothes I wear day and night both."

"Seven o'clock," Diana said. She noticed the hard-boiled egg on Spangler's desk. "Oh, darling, what a clever paper weight! What is it?"

"It's an egg. I keep it for luck."

"How sweet!" Diana said. "I've got to run, darling." She gave him a quick farewell kiss and left the office.

Mr. Grogan finished typing a telegram. Spangler led Ulysses over to the old man. "Willie," he said, "I'm going over to Corbett's. This is Ulysses Macauley, Homer's little brother. He's had an experience of some sort. Got caught in some kind of trap. Ulysses, this is Mr. Willie Grogan."

"Oh, we're old friends," Mr. Grogan said. "He's been watching me work."

"I'll be right back," Spangler said.

15 The Girl on the Corner

Spangler turned to go, but he was stopped by the working of the call box—by the message that simultaneously rang out and printed itself upon the ticker tape. He went to the instrument on the delivery desk and studied the marks on the tape. "That's a call from Ithaca Wine," he said to Grogan—"away out in the sticks. If Homer comes in, keep him here until we get the regular evening call from Sunripe Raisin. He's beat Western Union there twice in two tries. If he can make it again today, we may have a pretty good month of business after all. How many telegrams did we get from them yesterday?"

"Sixty-seven," Grogan said.

"Sixty-seven telegrams out of sixty-eight," Spangler said. "First boy there gets all the telegrams but one. Second boy gets one. Well, I'll go."

But now another call began to come in: *Dot dot dash dot dot dot.* When the manager of the telegraph office had heard only the first two dots, he knew the call was from Sunripe Raisin, and as Homer was not in the office to take the call, he shouted to Grogan. "*I'll* take the call. I'll get there first *myself.*"

By the time the call was repeated three times, Spangler was in the middle of the next block, moving through the people like an open field runner in a football game. On the corner before him, thirty yards away, stood a shy, lonely-looking girl of eighteen or nineteen—tired, hushed, and therefore beautiful. She was waiting for a bus to take her home, after work. Even though he was running, it was impossible for Spangler not to notice the girl's isolation—which seemed to him, even though he was in a hurry, like the isolation of *all* things, one from another. Not clowning, without any premeditation, swiftly and easily, he reached the girl, paused a moment, and kissed her on the cheek. Before he moved on, he told her the only thing it was possible to say: "You are the loveliest woman in the world!"

He ran on. When he was going up the steps of the Sunripe Raisin Association three at a time, the Western Union messenger, off to a slow start because the delivery clerk did not know the calls by heart as Spangler did, was just getting off his bicycle in front of the building, and when Spangler was going into the office, the Western Union messenger had only begun to wait for the elevator.

As if he were still a messenger, Spangler announced himself to the old woman at the desk of Sunripe Raisin. "Postal Telegraph!" he said.

"Tom!" the old woman said, pleased and

surprised. "Don't tell me you're a *messenger* now, too."

"Once a messenger, always a messenger," Spangler said, not at all embarrassed by the meaninglessness of the remark. He smiled at the old woman and then said, "But most of all I came to see *you*, Mrs. Brockington."

The Western Union messenger came into the office. "Western Union," he said.

"Well, Harry," Mrs. Brockington said, "you've been beaten again." She handed the messenger one telegram. "Better luck next time."

The Western Union boy, a little confused and embarrassed because he had been beaten again, this time not by another messenger but by the manager of the Postal Telegraph office, took the one telegram and said, "Thanks just the same, Mrs. Brockington," and left the office.

The old woman handed Spangler a whole bundle of telegrams. "Here you are, Tom. One hundred and twenty-nine night letters —all over the country—all paid. But where's the new messenger?"

"Homer?" Spangler said. "Homer Macauley? We got slowed down this afternoon on account of an accident that happened to his little brother, Ulysses. Got caught in some kind of a trap at Covington's. Homer had to go and get him out. But you'll be seeing him from now on." He smiled at the old woman. "Thanks for the telegrams."

When he reached the corner where the isolated girl had stood, he paused a moment. "It was right here that she stood. I'll never see her again, most likely, but even if I do, I'll never see her again as she was when I saw her this afternoon." He moved on down the street, whistling to himself. When he was across the street from Corbett's, he heard pianola music—the old waltz called *All That I Want Is You*. He moved to the swinging doors, listened a moment, then went in. Corbett himself was at the bar. He glanced over at the three soldiers listening to the player piano. "How is it going, Ralph?"

"Not bad," Corbett said. "Soldiers with a lot of time to kill and not very much money. I buy them three to their one."

"Can you afford to do that?" Spangler said.

"No, but what's the difference? After the War maybe I'll get some of it back. I just can't be a bartender. I'm Young Corbett."

The manager of the telegraph office and the former prize fighter talked for five minutes, and then Spangler went back to the office.

16 Going Home

At the delivery desk he saw the Macauley brothers, Homer and Ulysses—the messenger folding telegrams and putting them in envelopes, the younger brother watching with quiet admiration.

"Did *you* get Sunripe Raisin, Mr. Spangler?" Homer said.

"Yes, I did," Spangler said. "One hundred and twenty-nine telegrams." He showed the telegrams to the messenger.

"One hundred and twenty-nine! How did you get there first?"

"I ran."

"You beat Western Union to Sunripe Raisin *running?*"

"Sure. Nothing to it. I even stopped on the way—to pay tribute to beauty and innocence." Homer didn't understand, but Spangler went right on. "Take Ulysses home."

"Yes, sir," Homer said. "We've got a call from Guggenheim's. It's down our way, so I'll hike Ulysses home, then go to Guggenheim's, and from there I'll go to Ithaca Wine, then Foley's, and then I'll come right back. I'll be back in no time." The messenger left the office and carefully set his brother on the handlebars of his bicycle while Spangler watched. The older brother swung onto the bike and began to pedal down the street. When they were out of the town itself, Ulysses twisted around to look at his brother. For the first time that day his face broke out with the Macauley smile.

"Homer?"

"What?"

"I can sing."

"That's good."

Ulysses began to sing. "We will sing one song." He stopped and began again. "We will sing one song," but again he stopped.

"That's not a song. That's just a little part of a song. Now, you listen to me, and then sing with me." The older brother began to sing while the younger brother listened.

Weep no more, my lady, O weep no more today
We will sing one song for the old Kentucky home
For the old Kentucky home far away

"Sing it again, Homer," Ulysses said.

"OK," Homer said, and began to sing again, but this time the younger brother sang with the older; and as they sang, Ulysses saw the freight train again with the black man leaning over the side of the gondola, smiling and waving. That was one of the greatest things that had ever happened to Ulysses

Macauley in his four years of life in the world. He waved to a man and the man waved back to *him*—not once, but many times. He would remember that as long as he lived.

Homer got off his bicycle in front of the Macauley house and carefully set Ulysses on his feet. They stood together a moment, listening to the harp and piano of their mother and sister and the singing of their neighbor, Mary Arena.

"All right," Homer said, "you're home now. Go on in. I've got to go on to work."

"Going to work?" Ulysses said.

"Yes," Homer said, "but I'll be home tonight. Go on in, Ulysses."

The younger brother started up the front porch steps. When he got to the door, the older brother began to ride on down the street.

17 Three Soldiers

When the Steed family and their guests, including Thomas Spangler, sat down to dinner, a heavy rain was falling over Ithaca. Bess Macauley and Mary Arena, in raincoats and galoshes, walked to the telegraph office, bearing Homer's lunch-box. As they passed the Owl Drug Store, a young man standing in the doorway gave them the old wolf eye.

"Hi-ya, pretty," he said to Bess. "What's with?"

Bess ignored the young man and moved closer to Mary as they went up the street. Now, coming toward them were three young soldiers. They were sporting around in the street at a game improvised out of their happiness at being free for the night, and out of the refreshing rain. They pushed and chased one another, roaring with laughter, and calling out the nicknames they had given one another—Fat, Texas, and Horse. When the three boys saw Mary and Bess, they came to a worshipful halt. They bowed very low, one after another. The girls were pleased, but they weren't sure what they ought to do— what attitude they ought to take.

"They're just soldiers, Bess," Mary whispered—"away from home."

"Let's stop," Bess said.

The soldier called Fat stepped forward as the official representative of the group.

"American girls," he said, "we of the great Democratic Army, your humble servants, the soldiers—here today and, we hope, here tomorrow—thank you for your beautiful faces, in times of dryness no less than in times of rain, such as the present. May I present my comrades and your devoted admirers. This is Texas—he's from New Jersey. This is Horse —he's from Texas. And I'm Fat—I'm from hunger. Now, more than anything else I hunger for the companionship of beautiful American girls. How about it?"

"Well," Bess said, "we were going to the Kinema."

"To the Kinema!" Fat said dramatically. "May we—soldiers—whether here today or gone tomorrow—accompany you—American girls—to the Kinema? Tonight is tonight and tomorrow is tomorrow, but tomorrow

we return to barracks, to the awful but unavoidable business of war. Tonight we are your brothers—far from our firesides, and lonely, for Ithaca is not our native land. I have waddled into this costume of the American soldier from the side streets of the ferocious city of Chicago, of the old nation of Illinois. Restore me to that city and to that nation tonight in memory, and restore my good brothers each to his good place, for we are of one family, and except for the war we might never meet." The soldier who was called Fat bowed, then stood upright. "What is your decision?"

"Is he crazy?" Mary whispered.

"No," Bess said, "he's just lonely. Let's go to the movie with them."

"All right," Mary said, "but you *tell* him. I don't know what to say."

Bess smiled at the soldier. "All right," she said.

"Thank you, American girls," Fat said. He offered his arm to Bess.

"First, I've got to take my brother his lunch, at the telegraph office."

"Telegraph?" Fat said. "Then I shall send a telegram." He turned to the others. "How about you, Texas?"

"How much does it cost to send a telegram to New Jersey?" Texas said.

"Not nearly as much as it's worth," Fat said. "Horse?"

"Yeah," Horse said. "I think I'd like to send a telegram to Ma and Joe and Kitty— that's my girl," he said to Bess.

"Every girl in the world is *my* girl," Fat said, "and as I cannot send telegrams to each of them, I shall send a telegram to only one. I shall send millions of telegrams to the only one."

Willie Grogan was alone in the office when the two young women and the three soldiers walked in. The old man stood behind the counter.

"I'm Homer's sister Bess. I've brought his

lunch." She put the box on the counter.

"Your brother will be in soon, Miss Macauley," Grogan said. "I'll see that he gets his lunch."

"And these boys want to send telegrams," Bess said.

"Very well, young men," Grogan said. "Help yourself to telegraph blanks and pencils."

"How much does it cost to send a telegram to Jersey City?" Texas said.

"Twenty-five words for fifty cents, plus a small tax. But don't count the address or the signature. The telegram will be delivered tomorrow morning."

"Fifty cents? That's not bad at all." Texas began to write his telegram.

"How much does it cost to San Antone?" Horse said.

"Half as much as to Jersey City. San Antonio is nearer Ithaca than Jersey City."

The soldier called Fat who had been busy writing his telegram now handed it to the old man. Grogan read the telegram as he counted it.

EMMA DANA
C/O THE UNIVERSITY OF CHICAGO
CHICAGO, ILLINOIS

MY DARLING, I LOVE YOU, I MISS YOU, I THINK OF YOU ALWAYS. KEEP WRITING. KEEP STUDYING. KEEP WAITING. KEEP BELIEVING. DON'T FORGET ME. DON'T EVER FORGET ME BECAUSE I AM THE ONE WHO WILL NEVER FORGET YOU.

NORMAN

Next, the soldier called Texas handed Grogan *his* telegram.

MRS. EDITH ANTHONY
1702½ WILMINGTON STREET
JERSEY CITY, NEW JERSEY

DEAR MA. HOW ARE YOU? I AM FINE. I GOT YOUR LETTER AND THE BOX OF DRIED FIGS. THANKS. DON'T WORRY ABOUT ANYTHING. SO LONG. LOVE.

BERNARD

Then the soldier called Horse handed the old telegraph operator *his* telegram.

MRS. HARVEY GUILFORD
211 SANDYFORD BOULEVARD
SAN ANTONIO, TEXAS

HELLO MA. JUST WANT TO SAY HELLO FROM ITHACA IN SUNNY CALIFORNIA. ONLY IT'S RAINING. HA HA. GIVE MY REGARDS TO EVERYBODY. TELL JOE HE CAN HAVE MY GUN AND SHELLS. LOVE.

QUENTIN

The soldiers and the girls left the office, and Mr. Grogan went to his table to send the telegrams.

On the screen at the Kinema Theatre, as the three soldiers and the two American girls walked down the center aisle, Mr. Winston Churchill, Prime Minister of England in the year of our Lord 1942, appeared before the Canadian House of Parliament. By the time the young people were seated, Mr. Churchill had said three things, one after another, which had caused increasing delight both to the members of the Canadian House of Parliament and to the members of the audience at the Kinema Theatre in Ithaca. The soldier called Fat leaned over to Bess Macauley.

"There," he said, "is one of the great men of our time—and a great American, too."

"I thought Churchill was an Englishman," Horse said.

"Sure," Fat said, "but he's an American, too." He moved just a little closer to the girl on the other side of him, Mary Arena. "Thanks a lot for letting us come to the movie with you," he said. "It feels better to have girls near. It *smells* better than just soldiers."

"We were coming to the movie anyway," Mary said.

Now, the man named Franklin Delano Roosevelt, President of the United States, appeared in the newsreel, making a radio speech to the nation from his home in Hyde

Park. He spoke with his usual mixture of solemnity and humor. The five young people listened carefully. When the speech was over, the American flag appeared on the screen, and everybody in the theatre began to applaud.

"I get a lump in my throat every time I see the flag," Bess said. "It used to make me think of Washington and Lincoln, but now it makes me think of my brother Marcus. He's a soldier, too."

"Oh, you've got a brother in the Army?" Fat said.

"He was somewhere in North Carolina the last time we heard from him," Bess said.

At that moment Marcus stood at the bar in The Dive Bomber in a small town in North Carolina. His friend Tobey George and three other soldiers were at the bar with him. Marcus was playing a song called *A Dream*, and Tobey was singing. After the song, Tobey sat down beside his friend Marcus and asked him to talk some more about Ithaca and the Macauleys there.

As Marcus Macauley began to tell Tobey George about Ithaca, Thomas Spangler and Diana Steed came down the aisle of the Kinema Theatre. Now, the feature picture began to appear on the screen. When they were seated, the screen was filling with words, not pictures. These words named the picture and the people who had helped to make the picture. There were vast numbers of words, an enormous amount of credit given to enormous numbers of people. Accompanying these credits was a majestically inappropriate theme of music that had been especially composed for the occasion.

Spangler and Diana sat very close to the screen, in the third row, ten rows in front of Bess and Mary and the three soldiers. Their seats were at the very center of a row whose only other occupants were small boys.

Now on the screen appeared the spick and span linoleum-floored hall of a hospital. Over a loud-speaker at the end of the hall came the harsh voice of a bitter nurse who spoke over-emphatically.

"Dr. Cavanagh!" she cried. "Surgery! Dr. Cavanagh! Surgery!"

Immediately upon hearing these words Thomas Spangler got to his feet. The evening had been a rather difficult if pleasant one for him, full of complications and potentialities that were now working themselves out, it seemed, so that he felt no need at all not to carry on as if he himself were no older than the others in that row of seats.

"Ooop!" he said. "Wrong movie!" He took Diana's hand and said, "Come on."

"But, darling, the movie isn't over yet!" Diana whispered.

Spangler dragged her along. "It's over for *me.* Come on." Now, they were passing a small boy who was watching the screen with total fascination.

"*You'll* get to Heaven," Spangler said to the boy, and then to Diana, "Come on, don't stand in the boy's way."

"What did you say, mister?" the boy said.

"Heaven!" Spangler said. "I say *you'll* get there."

"Have you got the time?"

"No, I haven't, but it's still early."

"Yes, sir," the boy said.

Now, Spangler and Diana were in the aisle.

"We'll go to Corbett's," Spangler said, "listen to the pianola, and then you can go home." He turned to face the screen and began walking backward.

"Look at Dr. Cavanagh," he said. "He's going to pull out one of his front teeth with a pair of pliers."

In the lobby of the theater, Diana said, "You do love me, don't you?"

"Love you?" Spangler said. "I took you to a movie, didn't I?"

They went out to the street and began hurrying toward Corbett's, moving close to the buildings in order to keep out of the rain.

18 The Telegram

As Spangler and Diana ran through the rain towards Corbett's, Homer Macauley, soaking wet, brought his bicycle to a stop in front of the telegraph office and went in. He looked over the situation at the delivery desk. There were no calls to take, but there was one telegram to deliver.

Mr. Grogan finished a telegram he was typing and got up. "Your sister Bess brought your lunch, my boy."

"Ah, she didn't need to bring any lunch. I was going to get us two pies." Homer took the box and said, "There's *enough* of it. Will you have some lunch with me, Mr. Grogan?"

"Thank you, my boy, I'm not hungry."

"Maybe if you start to eat a little, your appetite will improve, Mr. Grogan."

"No. Thanks very much. But you're soaking wet. Look here, we've got raincoats."

"I got *caught* in the rain." Homer bit into a sandwich. "I'll eat this sandwich, and then I'll deliver the telegram." He chewed a moment and then looked over at the old telegraph operator. "What kind of a telegram is it?"

From the way that Mr. Grogan didn't answer, Homer knew the telegram was another death message. He stopped chewing and gulped the food down, dry. "I wish I didn't have to deliver telegrams like this," he said.

"Yes, I know," Mr. Grogan said. He didn't speak again for half a minute, while the messenger held the unfinished sandwich in his hand. "Your sister was with another very pretty girl."

"That's Mary. She's Marcus's girl. They're going to be married after the War."

"They were with three soldiers who sent telegrams."

"Is that so? Can I see the telegrams?"

Mr. Grogan indicated the hook on which dispatched telegrams were placed. Homer took the telegrams off the hook and one by one read them. After having read them, he looked at the old telegraph operator.

"If a fellow dies that way, Mr. Grogan," he said, "somebody you know, or somebody you don't know, somebody you've never even seen—they don't just die for nothing, do they?"

The old telegraph operator waited a moment before speaking, and then, as if there was so much to say that he wouldn't be able to make it, he went to his table, sat down, and tried to decide what to say.

"I've been a long time in the world," he said, "but I don't know the answer to that question, my boy. I'm not even sure there is an answer. It's a young question, and I'm an old man."

Mr. Grogan sighed deeper than ever now

and then after a moment brought out a slip of paper from his vest pocket, which he handed to the messenger. "Will you go on an errand for me again, to the drug store?"

Homer nodded, and hurried out of the office.

Mr. Grogan stood alone in the telegraph office, looking around at everything with a strange affection mixed with a kind of loving anger. Almost slowly he clutched at his collar, as if he had been waiting too long for the swift attack that could no longer surprise him. He moved back to his chair and sat in a terrible stiffness until the attack had spent its most extreme force.

The messenger returned from the drug store and handed the telegraph operator the small box.

"Water," the old man said.

Homer filled a paper cup full of water and took it to the old man, who dumped three of the pills out of the little box, tossed them into his mouth, took the cup from Homer, and swallowed the pills.

"Thank you, my boy."

Homer watched the old man to see if he was going to be all right, then went to the delivery desk and took up the telegram of death. He stood a moment holding the telegram and looking at it, and then he opened the envelope and took the message out of it, to read. He put the telegram back into a new envelope, sealed it, and then turned and walked out of the office into the rain. The old telegraph operator got up out of his chair and followed the boy into the street. He stood there on the sidewalk and watched the boy push against the wind and the rain. Inside the office the telegraph box began to rattle, but the old man didn't hear. The telephone rang, but again the old man didn't hear. He did not turn and go back into the office until the telephone had rung seven times.

19 Alan

Fifteen minutes later Homer got off his bicycle in front of a large fine old house where a party was in progress. Through the windows he could see four young couples dancing. The boy felt sick and terrified. He went up the walk to the door and stood listening to the music. He moved a finger toward the door bell and then let his hand drop.

"I'll go back to the office," he said to himself. "I'll quit."

He sat down on the steps of the house, to think. After a long time, he got up and went to the door again and pressed his finger against the button. When the door opened he saw a young woman, and before he knew what he was doing, he turned and ran to his bicycle. The young woman came out on the porch and called out, "Why, what's the matter, boy?"

Homer got off his bicycle and ran back to the porch. "I'm sorry," he said quickly. "I've got a telegram for Mrs. Claudia Beaufrere."

"Of course. It's Mother's birthday," the young woman said. She stepped back into the hallway. "Mother," she called out, "here's a telegram for you."

The girl's mother came to the door. "It's from Alan, I'm sure," she said. "Come in, young man. You must have a piece of my birthday cake."

"No, thank you, ma'am," Homer said. "I've got to go back to work." He held the telegram out to the woman, who took it as if it were nothing more than a birthday greeting.

"Not until you've had a piece of cake and a glass of punch." She tugged at Homer's arm and dragged him into the room to a table loaded with cake and sandwiches and punch. The music and dancing continued. "It's my birthday," she said. "Lord, I *am* old. Well, you must wish me happiness, boy." She handed Homer a glass of punch.

"I wish you—" Homer began to say, but he couldn't go on. He put the glass of punch on the table and bolted to the door. The mother looked around the room, then went to one side where she wouldn't be noticed; and the daughter, watching her, moved to the other side. Homer was on his bicycle racing through the rain back to the telegraph office. On the wall of the hall, in front of the mother, was a framed picture of a good-looking red-headed boy. Written on the photograph were the words, "To Mother with love from Alan on his twelfth birthday." The mother opened the telegram and read it, while the phonograph continued with a song called *Chanson pour Ma Brune,* and the happy people continued to dance. The daughter looked across the room at her mother in the hallway. Almost as if she had lost her reason, she rushed to the phonograph and turned it off.

"Mother!" she cried, and ran toward the woman in the hallway.

20 After the Movie

Now, the Kinema Theatre was letting out its visitors after the last show. In the street, Bess turned to the soldier called Fat and said, "Well, we must go home now."

"Thank you, American girls," Fat said. It was time to say goodbye, and yet somehow they stood together in the street, waiting, as if something wonderful but unknowable was on the verge of happening. The soldier called Fat looked from Bess to Mary, and then easily and innocently kissed Bess, and then Mary.

Now, the soldier called Horse shouted, "Well, what about us? We're somebody, too. We're in the Army, too." So this soldier kissed the girls, too. And after him Texas kissed them. A woman in the street watched with bitter distaste. The girls turned quickly and hurried down the street. The soldier called Horse jumped, and then pushed the soldier called Texas, who jumped and pushed the soldier called Fat. They moved down the side street, shouting at one another.

"Waaa-hooo!" Horse shouted.

"How you talk!" Texas shouted at Fat. "How you *do* talk!"

The soldier called Fat cackled with delight.

"Oh man!" he shouted. "When I get to Congress! I'll tell them a thing or two."

"Yippee-aye-ay," Horse shouted. *"Git along little dogies—it's your misfortune and none of my own."*

Now, the three soldiers began leaping over one another at a swift game of leap-frog, pushing down the dark, wet street nearer and nearer to whatever might be next for each of them, God-helping.

21 Valley Champion for Kids

By the time the messenger got back to the telegraph office from the Beaufrere home, the rain had stopped, the moon was shining, and an empty and exhausted cluster of clouds, now white, was being driven across the sky. The messenger was very tired when he came limping into the office.

"What's the matter with your leg?" Mr. Grogan said. "You've been limping all day."

"It's nothing," Homer said. "Any more telegrams?"

"All clear, and soon you can go home to bed. Now tell me. What happened to your leg?"

"I guess I twisted a ligament or something, running the two-twenty low hurdles this afternoon. Mr. Spangler was Valley Champion of that race, and I guess I'd like to be Valley Champion some day myself, too. I don't think I'll be able to make it this year, though." Homer flexed his leg a couple of times. "I'll rub some Sloan's Liniment on it tonight. Is the limp noticeable?"

"Well," Mr. Grogan said, "it's not *too* noticeable, but it is a *little*. Can you ride your bike all right?"

"Sure," Homer said. "It hurts a little when I get the hurt leg up, so I try to do all the pumping with my right leg. Sometimes I take the left leg off the pedal and let it hang. That way it rests. I guess something's happened to the ligament—I'll rub it with liniment."

There was a pause. Then the old telegraph operator said, "Keep talking, my boy."

"Oh, I *want* to, all right, but I don't know where to start," Homer said. "I didn't know *anything* until I got this job. I knew a lot of things, but I didn't know the half of it, and maybe I never will, either. Maybe nobody ever will. If anybody *should*, though, I should. I *want* to know, and I'll *always* want to know, and I guess I'll always keep trying, but how can you ever know? How can any man ever really get it all straight so that it makes sense?"

"Well," Mr. Grogan said, "I don't know, but I'm glad you've made up your mind to keep trying."

"I've *got* to keep trying," Homer said. "I

don't know how it is with other people, and I don't know whether I can tell you this or not, but I'm not just the guy people *see*, I'm somebody else besides—somebody better. Sometimes *I* don't even know what to make of it. I'd be ashamed to say this to anybody but you, Mr. Grogan, but some day I'm going to go to work and do something for the kids everywhere. All kinds of kids having all kinds of trouble. I don't know what it's going to be, but it's going to be *something.* Decent, I mean." Homer tested his leg to see if it had become healed as he had talked. It hadn't. "I don't like the way things are, Mr. Grogan. I don't know why, but I want them to be better. I guess it's because I think they *ought* to be better. At school I say a lot of funny things, but I don't do it to make trouble for the teachers. I do it because I've got to. Everybody's so mixed up, and everything's so wrong that I've just got to say funny things once in a while. I guess we ought to have some fun out of being alive. I don't think I could act refined even if I wanted to. I couldn't be polite if I didn't mean it."

He flexed his leg again and spoke of it as if it weren't his own. "Something's the matter with it." He glanced up at the clock. "Well, Mr. Grogan, it's five minutes after twelve. I guess I'll go home. I don't feel very sleepy, though, and tomorrow's Saturday. Saturday used to be the best day of all for me. No more, though. I guess I'll come down to the office. Maybe I can help out." He lifted the lunch-box off the delivery desk. "Wouldn't you like a sandwich now, Mr. Grogan?"

"Well," the old telegraph operator said, "come to think of it, my boy, yes, I would. I'm hungry now." Mr. Grogan took a sandwich out of the open box and bit into it. "Please thank your mother for me."

"Ah, it's nothing."

"No, please thank her for me."

"Yes, sir," Homer said, and left the office.

22 The Holdup Man

Alone in the telegraph office, Mr. Grogan, once young, once the fastest telegraph operator in the world, slowly began to clear off the work table. He hummed softly to himself a theme that had stayed in his memory from the earliest days of his life. As the old man did his work, Thomas Spangler, fresh from Corbett's and a little under the influence of a giddy and solemn happiness, came into the office and went to his desk. He glanced over at the old telegraph operator, but did not speak. They had an understanding. Very often it was no matter at all to be at work for an hour or two without exchanging one word. Spangler lifted the good-luck egg off a pile of telegrams and studied its amazing symmetry. Then he put the egg back on the pile of telegrams and remembering the girl pleasantly, he puckered up his lips in order to speak as she was given to speaking.

"*You do love me, don't you?*"

The old telegraph operator glanced at the manager of the office.

"What's that, Tom?"

"Willie, what would you think of a young woman who everytime she sees you tells you, '*You do love me, don't you?*'"

"I'd probably wonder how in the world she ever found out."

"It's the same with me." Spangler rubbed his face as if to get over his happiness and then said, "Anything doing tonight?"

"About the same, except for the rain."

"How's the new messenger? Is he all right?"

"The best *I've* ever seen. What do *you* think of him?"

"I liked him from the time he came up and asked for a job," Spangler said. "*You do love me, don't you?*" He couldn't get over the extraordinary way Diana Steed spoke the small words. "You can go home now, Willie. I'll close the office. I've got a little work to do."

"Home?" Mr. Grogan said. "If you don't mind, Tom, I'd like to sit around a little while with you. I've got nothing to do after work except sleep, and I can't sleep. I guess I'm scared."

"No need to be scared, Willie. I'd be helpless in this Office without you. You'll live to be a hundred, and you'll work every day of your life."

"Thanks," the old telegraph operator said. He paused and then said softly, "I had another little attack tonight. Oh, nothing serious. I felt it coming on for some time. The boy was here. I sent him for the medicine. I'm supposed to see the doctor every day, but I'm afraid to see him. And I'm supposed to rest."

"Doctors don't know everything, but maybe you ought to rest a little anyway."

"Oh, I'll rest, I'll take the great rest, Tom."

"Go to Corbett's on the corner. Listen to the pianola. Come back and we'll talk over old times—Wolinsky and Tomlinson and old man Davenport. Harry Bull the lineman, crazy Fred McIntyre, and wonderful Jerry Beattie. Go ahead now, Willie. When you come back, we'll kick around old times."

"All right, Tom," Mr. Grogan said, and left the office.

On the sidewalk for three or four minutes, a young man had passed the office several times, looking in. He came in at last and stood at the counter. Spangler noticed him and went over.

"How are you?" Spangler said, remembering the boy. "I thought you'd be on your way home to Pennsylvania long ago. Your mother sent you the money. You didn't need to come back to pay me."

"I didn't come back to pay you," the young man said. "I came back to get more, and I didn't come to beg it, either. I came to *take* it."

"What's the matter with you?" Spangler said.

"This is what's the matter with me," the young man said. From his right-hand coat pocket he brought out a revolver and held it in a trembling hand. Spangler didn't understand.

"Come on. Give me all the money you've got in this place. Everybody's killing everybody, so I don't mind if I kill you. And I don't mind if *I'm* killed, either. I'm excited and I don't want any trouble, so give me all the money, and hurry."

Spangler drew open the cash drawer and took the money out of the several compartments. He placed the money—currency, rolls of coin and open coins—on the counter before the boy.

"I'd give you the money, anyway," Spangler said, "but not because you're pointing a gun at me. I'd give it to you because you need it. Here. This is all the money there is. Take it and get on a train and go home. Go back where you belong. I won't report a theft. I'll make it good myself. There's about seventy-five dollars there."

He waited for the boy to take the money, but the boy wouldn't touch it.

"I mean it," Spangler said. "Take the money and go— you need it. You're no criminal, and you're not so sick you can't get well. Your mother's waiting for you. This money is a gift from me to her. You won't be a thief taking it. Just take the money, put that gun away, and go home. *Throw* the gun away— you'll feel better."

The young man put the gun back into his coat pocket. Over his trembling mouth he placed the hand that had held the gun. "I ought to go out and shoot myself," he said.

"Don't talk like a fool," Spangler said. He gathered the money together and held it out to the young man. "Now here. This is all the money there is. Take it and go home, that's all. If you like, leave the gun here with me. Here's your money. Yes, *yours*—it *is* yours, if you've got to take a gun out to get it! I know how you feel because I've felt the same way. We've all felt the same way. The graveyards and penitentiaries are full of good American kids who've had bad luck and hard times. They're not criminals. Here," he said gently, "take this money and go home."

The young man brought the gun out of his pocket and pushed it across the counter to Spangler, who dropped it into the cash drawer.

"I don't know who you are," he said, "but no one has ever talked to me the way you have. I don't want the gun, and I won't take the money, and I *am* going home. I bummed my way out here, and I'll bum my way back." He coughed a moment and then said, "I don't know where my mother got the thirty dollars. I know she has no money to spare. I spent some of the money."

"Come on in and sit down," Spangler said. After a moment the young man went to the chair beside Spangler's desk. Spangler sat down on the desk. "What's the matter?" he said.

"I don't know exactly," the young man said. "Maybe T.B. I'm not sure. If I haven't got it, I guess I *ought* to have it, the way I've been living. I don't like to complain. I've had a lot of bad luck, but I know it's my own fault. I'll go now. Thanks a lot—I'll try to remember you some day." The young man turned to leave the office.

"Wait a minute," Spangler said. "Sit down. Take it easy. You've got a lot of time—*now*. You're not rushing things any more. From now on, move a little slower. What's a fellow like you interested in?"

"I don't know. I don't know which way to go, or what to do when I get there, or what to believe, or anything. My father was a preacher, but he's been dead since I was three years old. I just don't know what to do." He looked at Spangler. "What *is* there to do?"

"Nothing in *particular*. Anything. It doesn't matter what a man does. Any good honest work."

"I've always been restless and dissatisfied. I don't know what it is. Nothing means anything to me. I don't like people. I don't like being near them. I don't trust them. I don't like the way they live or talk or the things they believe, or the way they push each other around."

"Every man in the world feels that way at one time or another."

"It's not that I don't understand *myself*. I guess I do. I've got no alibis. I'm responsible for everything. Now, I'm just tired and fed-up and sick. Nothing interests me. The whole world's gone crazy. I can't live the kind of life

I want to live and I don't feel like living any other kind. It's not money that I want or need. I know I could get a job, especially now. But I don't like the people you've got to get a job from. They're no good. I don't like being humble to them, and I can't let anybody push me around. I tried to hold a few jobs in York, Pennsylvania. I always had a fight and got fired. Three or four days, a week, or a week and a half. The longest I ever held a job was one month.

"I tried to enlist in the Army in York because I thought that might be a good thing to do—go somewhere—get killed maybe. If they boss you in the Army at least it's for something that's supposed to be halfway decent. I don't know whether it really *is* or not, but at least it's supposed to be. They turned me down. I couldn't pass the physical. It wasn't my lungs alone—it was other things, too. I didn't bother to find out." The young man began to cough again, but this time he coughed for almost a full minute. Spangler brought a small bottle out of the desk drawer.

"Here, take a drink of this."

"Thanks," the young man said. "I drink a little too much, but I *need* a drink now." He took a swallow from the bottle, then handed it back to Spangler. "Thanks," he said again.

Spangler decided he ought to urge the young man to go on talking. "What do you read?" he said.

"Oh, everything. At least I used to when I was home. My father had a lot of books— not religious books only—good books—by good writers. My favorite was William Blake. Maybe you know his stuff. I read every book my father had—some of them twice, a few three times. I used to like to read, but no more. Now I don't even want to look at newspapers. I *know* the news. Corruption and murder all over the place, every day, and not one man in the world able to do anything about it." He held his head in his hands and, speaking softly, he went on without looking up. "I can't thank you for what you've done and for the kind of human being you are, but I must tell you I would have shot you if you had been afraid of me, or unkind. Everybody in the world is afraid or unkind. I know now that I didn't come here with a gun for *money*. I don't know whether you will understand, but I came here with a gun to find out once and for all if the only man in the world I have ever known who has been decent to another man just to be decent—just for itself—was *truly* so. I came to find out if it wasn't an accident. I couldn't believe anybody could be really decent, because it made my whole feeling about everything and everybody untrue—the feeling I have had for a long time that the human race is hopeless and corrupt, that there isn't one man in the world worthy of another man's respect. For a long time I've had contempt for the pathetic as well as for the proud, and then suddenly thousands of miles from home, in a strange city, I found a man who was decent. It bothered me. It bothered me for a long time. I couldn't believe it. I had to find out. I wanted it to be true. I wanted to believe it, because I've been telling myself for years, 'Let me find one man uncorrupted by the world so that *I* may be uncorrupted, so that I may believe and live.' I wasn't sure the first time we met, but I'm sure now. I want nothing more from you. You've given me everything I want. You can't give me anything more. You understand, I know. When I get up it shall be to say goodbye. You needn't worry about me. I'm going home where I belong. I'm not going to die of this sickness. I'm going to live. And now I'm going to know *how* to live." The young man didn't lift his head for a moment. Then, he got up slowly and looked at Spangler. "Thanks a lot," he said.

Spangler watched him walk out of the office. He went to the cash drawer and put the money back where it belonged. He took the young man's revolver and unloaded it. He put the revolver back in the drawer and dropped the shells into his coat pocket. Then he went to the steel rack where each day's telegrams were tied into a bundle. In one bundle he found the telegram the boy had sent his mother. He took a fresh telegraph blank and began to write a telegram.

MRS. MARGARET STRICKMAN
1874 BIDDLE STREET
YORK, PENNSYLVANIA

DEAR MA: THANKS FOR THE MONEY. WILL BE HOME SOON. EVERYTHING FINE.

He read the words of the message and then decided to change "fine" to "OK." Then he remembered the young man a moment and added, "Love, John." He went to Mr. Grogan's place at the telegraph table and called for an operator. His call was answered after several moments, and then Spangler tapped out the telegram, after which he talked to the operator at the other end, smiling as he listened to the dots and dashes and made his answers. When he was through talking, he got up and went to his own desk.

Mr. Grogan came in and sat in the chair where the young man had been sitting.

"How do you feel now?" Spangler said.

"Better, of course," Mr. Grogan said. "I listened to the soldiers singing. They love that pianola and those old songs—songs they never heard before."

"*You do love me, don't you?*" Spangler said. "That's what she says, all the time, and that's the way she says it. I believe I'm going to marry her."

Spangler stopped dreaming of Diana Steed a moment to study the face of his old friend. "The old songs are OK."

"Tom," Mr. Grogan said, "remember the way old Davenport used to sing those ballads?"

"Sure," Spangler said, "as long as this office is here I'll hear him. I can hear him now. But not old ballads only—church songs, too. Don't forget the church songs old Davenport used to sing every Sunday."

"I haven't forgotten them. I remember every one of them. Of course, he liked to pretend he was an atheist, but all day Sunday he sang hymns—chewing tobacco, sending telegrams, singing, and squirting tobacco juice out of his mouth into the spittoon. First thing in the morning he'd start out with 'Welcome, delightful morn, thou day of sacred rest.' He was a great man, Tom. Then he'd holler out, 'This is the day of light. Let there be light today.' "

"I remember," Spangler said.

"Then, he would sing, 'Lord, God of morning and of night, We thank Thee for Thy gift of light.' The great unbeliever—and more than anything he loved light and life. And then at the end of the day he would get up from his chair slowly, stretch himself and sing very softly, 'Now the day is over, night is drawing nigh.' He knew all of the good old songs, and he loved every one of them. 'Saviour,' he would shout, pretending to be an atheist who was mocking, 'Saviour, breathe an evening blessing, Ere repose our spirits seal; Sin and want we come confessing, Thou canst save and Thou canst heal.' "

The telegraph operator became silent to remember his old friend who had been dead these many long years. "It's the truth, Tom. What he sang is the truth."

The manager of the telegraph office smiled at his old friend and patted him on the shoulder as he moved to turn off the lights and close the office for the night.

23 The Nightmare

Homer Macauley was in bed at last, tossing and turning. He dreamed he was running the two-twenty low hurdles again, but every time he got to a hurdle, Byfield was there to stop him. He hurdled anyway and they went down. At every hurdle Byfield was there. Finally the injury to Homer's leg was so painful that when he tried to run, he fell. He got up and pasted Byfield in the mouth. He shouted at the man, "You can't stop me! You can never stop me—low hurdles, high hurdles, any kind of hurdles!"

He began to run again, limping at first but soon running well, but the next hurdle was inhumanly high—eight feet—nevertheless, Homer Macauley, perhaps the greatest man in Ithaca, California, went over the hurdle with perfect form.

Next in the dream he was in his uniform riding his bicycle swiftly down a narrow street. Suddenly Byfield stood in the way. But Homer pushed toward the man more swiftly than ever. "I told you—you can't stop me!" He lifted upward on the handlebars, and the bicycle began to rise and fly. It flew directly over Byfield's head and came down lightly on the other side of him. But just as it reached the pavement, Byfield stood in the way again! Again the bicycle left the street and flew over the man. But this time it stayed aloft, suspended twenty feet over Byfield's head. The man stood in the street, amazed and displeased. "You can't do that!" he shouted. "You're breaking the law of gravity."

"What do I care about the law of gravity?" Homer shouted at the man in the street. "Or the law of averages, or the law of supply and demand, or any other law? *You can't stop me!* Worm, rust, and rot—I have no time for you." The messenger rode on through space, leaving the ugly man alone in the street, as inferior as any inferiority could ever be.

Now Homer flew high, among dark clouds. As the messenger rode through the sky, he watched another bicycle rider in a messenger's uniform very much like his own but moving even faster than himself, push out of black cloud. The second messenger, strangely, seemed to be Homer himself, but at the same time he seemed to be someone Homer feared. Homer raced after the second messenger to find out who he really was.

The two riders raced a good long distance before Homer began to catch up. Suddenly the other messenger turned, and Homer was amazed that the messenger looked exactly like himself, but at the same time was unmistakably—not so much in appearance as in feeling—the messenger of Death. The riders were swiftly coming to Ithaca. Homer raced after the messenger of Death, moving swifter than ever before. Far down in the distance he could see the lonely lights of the town and the lonely streets and houses.

Homer was determined to head off the other messenger, to keep him away from Ithaca. Nothing in the world was more important than to keep this messenger from reaching Ithaca.

The two riders raced hard and decently, with no tricks of any kind. They were both tiring now, but at last Homer was alongside the other rider, and was heading him away from Ithaca. Then, with a sudden burst of speed, the other messenger drew away and turned back toward the little town. Deeply disappointed in himself but still racing with all his might, Homer watched the other messenger ride on toward Ithaca, leaving Homer far behind. Now Homer could race no longer. There was no energy left with which to chase the messenger of Death. The boy almost collapsed on his bicycle, which began to fall, and Homer began to cry out to the other messenger, "Don't go to Ithaca! Leave them alone!"

The boy sobbed with terrible grief.

In the house on Santa Clara Avenue, the dreamer's little brother Ulysses stood beside Homer and listened. He went through the dark house to his mother's bed and shook her. When she sat up, he took her hand and without a word they went to Homer's bed. Mrs. Macauley listened to her son a moment, then put Ulysses back into his bed, tucked him in, and sat down beside the weeping boy. She spoke to him very softly.

"Be still now, Homer. Rest now. You are very tired. You must rest. Sleep now. Sleep peacefully." The messenger began to stop sobbing and soon his troubled expression went away. "Sleep now," his mother said. "Sleep peacefully."

The boy began to sleep. The mother looked over at her youngest son and he, too, was now asleep. In the corner of the room she thought she saw Matthew Macauley standing and watching, smiling. She got up

quietly, took the alarm clock, and went back to her own room.

The messenger's sleep moved from the realm of black terror to the realm of light and peace. Homer Macauley, in this new sleep, found himself lying on his back under a fig tree beside a brook. "This," he said to himself, "would be up by Riverview where I saw the fig tree by the lazy stream, under the sun that burned with a kind of laughter that made everything else laugh. I remember this place. It was last summer, and Marcus and I came here to swim; and then we sat on the bank of the river and talked about what we would do in the world." And now, knowing the pleasantness of the place he had reached and feeling the warmth of his memory of it, he stretched out comfortably on the grass under the tree—and forgot completely that he was asleep.

He was in the same old clothes he wore that summer day with Marcus. Before him, stuck into the soft earth, he saw the fishing pole; but this was not from that summer day —this was from a long, long time ago. Now, far away through the wilderness of grass and bough Homer Macauley beheld the beautiful Helen Eliot, barefoot like himself, and in a plain gingham dress, walking over a narrow path toward him. "That's Helen Eliot," Homer said to himself. "That's the girl I love." He sat up smiling, watched her walk, and then got to his feet and went to greet her. Without a word and with something like solemnity, Homer took the girl's hand and together they walked to the fig tree. There he removed his shirt and pants, and dived into the sweet water. The girl went behind a shrub and there she removed her dress. Homer watched her come to the riverbank, stand a moment, and then dive. They swam around in the gently flowing water, and then they left it together to lie on the sand in the sun, and sleep.

Chapters 13–23

Getting at Meaning

1. How is Ulysses caught in the trap? How do Ulysses, Big Chris, Mr. Covington, Auggie, and Homer react to this predicament?

2. Who is Diana Steed? How is she different from Spangler? Does he seem comfortable in their relationship? Why does he suddenly leave the movie theater?

3. Why does Spangler take the call for Sun-ripe Raisin? Why does he kiss the girl on the corner?

4. Bess and Mary ignore the young man in the doorway, but a few minutes later they agree to go to the movies with the three soldiers. Why?

5. Why does the Beaufrere family mistake Homer's death telegram for a happy one? How is Homer's experience with the Beaufreres different from his experience with Mrs. Sandoval? How are the two experiences similar?

6. What hopes for his life does Homer confide in Mr. Grogan after he returns from the Beaufrere home? What is Mr. Grogan's response? How do young and old contrast in this scene?

7. Why does the young man, John Strickman, return to Spangler's office? Why is he desperate? What does Spangler prove to him? How does Spangler help him?

8. What is the relationship between Spangler and Grogan? Cite specific incidents to illustrate your answer.

9. What two nightmares does Homer have the night he delivers the Beaufrere telegram? What real experiences are the basis for these dreams? How do the dreams relate to the struggles that Homer is facing?

Developing Skills in Reading Literature

1. **Character: Marcus.** Marcus has not actually appeared in the novel. Yet his presence is felt. How? What does the reader learn about him?

Spangler. The character of Spangler is developed in these chapters. What does the reader learn about him through his attitude toward Willie Grogan? Homer? John Strickman? the girl on the corner?

Ulysses. How old is Ulysses? Why is his young age surprising? What does his experience with Big Chris reveal about him? Why does he keep remembering the black man on the train? What is important to him? What other experiences in the novel support your view of his character?

2. **Theme.** In this novel, both young and old are touched by death. Consider the following; then try to explain Saroyan's message about death.

Homer's reaction to delivering the death telegrams

The reactions of the mothers to the telegrams

Homer's discussions of death with his mother and with Mr. Grogan

What other episodes in the novel support this theme?

The writer also presents a message about life, primarily through characters who embody certain values. What values do the following characters possess: Homer, Spangler, Miss Hicks, Big Chris? What values are reinforced through Spangler's conversation with John Strickman? What message about life emerges from the novel?

Developing Vocabulary

Root Words; Multiple Meanings of Words. The verb *mock* means "to make fun of" or "to imitate." It can be combined with other words and used as a noun or an adjective. Explain the use of *mock* in each of these sentences:

1. We had *mock* turtle soup.

2. The architects constructed a *mock-up* of the building for the committee.

3. The call of the *mockingbird* could be heard all through the forest.

4. The rain made a *mockery* of our plans for a picnic.

Developing Writing Skills

1. **Explaining an Idea.** In one paragraph, explain the meaning of Homer's statement, "... I'm not just the guy people *see*, I'm somebody else besides—somebody better."

2. **Combining Narration and Description.** Using vivid descriptions, write about a dream you have had. Try to recall the feelings associated with the dream. Were you frightened? excited? lonely? Through your choice of words, communicate these feelings in your paragraph.

24 The Apricot Tree

Ulysses Macauley was up very early, skipping through the morning's first light to the yard of a man who owned a cow. When he reached the yard, Ulysses saw the cow. The small boy stood and watched the cow a long time. At last the man who owned the cow came out of the small house. He was carrying a bucket and a stool. The man went straight to the cow and began to milk. Ulysses moved in closer until finally he was directly behind the man. Still, he couldn't see enough, so he knelt down, almost under the cow. The man saw the boy but did not say anything. He went right on milking. The cow, however, turned and looked at Ulysses. Ulysses looked back at the cow. It seemed perhaps that the cow did not like to have the boy so close. Ulysses got out from under the cow, walked away, and watched from near by. The cow, in turn, watched Ulysses, so that the small boy believed they might become friends.

On his way home, Ulysses stopped to watch a man who was building a barn. The man was high-strung, nervous, impatient, and should never have undertaken the work. He labored furiously, making all kinds of mistakes, while Ulysses watched and tried unsuccessfully to understand.

Ulysses got back to Santa Clara Avenue just in time to see Mr. Arena go off to work on his bicycle. Mary Arena waved to her father from the porch and then went back into the house.

It was Saturday morning in Ithaca. Out of a house not far away came a boy of eight or nine. Ulysses waved, and the boy waved back. This boy was Lionel Cabot, the neighborhood simpleton, but all the same a great human being, faithful, generous, and sweet-tempered. After a moment, Lionel looked over at Ulysses again, and, for want of something better to do, waved again. Ulysses waved back. This continued at frequent intervals until August Gottlieb came out of his house next door to Ara's Market.

Auggie had been the leader of the neighborhood boys since Homer Macauley had retired from that position at the age of twelve. The new leader looked around for his followers. He rejected Lionel as too dumb and Ulysses as too little, but waved a greeting to each of them nevertheless. He then went out to the middle of the street and whistled, newsboy style. It was a loud whistle, authoritative, commanding, and absolutely final. Auggie waited with the confidence of a man who knows what he is doing and what results he is going to get. Immediately windows were opened and replies were whistled. Soon a number of boys came running to the corner. In less than three minutes the gang was together—Auggie Gottlieb, the leader, Nickie Paloota, Alf Rife, and Shag Manoogian.

"Where we going, Auggie?" Nickie said.

"To see if Henderson's apricots are ripe."

"Can I come?" Lionel said.

"OK, Lionel. If they're ripe, will you steal some?"

"It's a sin to steal," Lionel said.

"Not apricots," Auggie said, making an important distinction. "Ulysses," he said, "you go home. This is not for little boys. It's dangerous."

Ulysses moved away three steps, stopped and watched. He wasn't hurt or offended by Auggie's orders. He understood the code. He was just not old enough yet, that's all. But while he respected the law, he couldn't resist wanting to be in the gang anyhow.

The boys started off for Henderson's. Instead of going by way of streets and sidewalks, they took alleys, crossed empty lots, and climbed over fences. They wanted to get there the hard way, the adventurous way.

Not far behind, at a safe distance, Ulysses followed.

"Ripe apricots are just about the best-tasting fruit in the world," Auggie said to the members of the gang.

"Do apricots get ripe in March?" Nickie Palotta said.

"It's almost April," Auggie said. "*Early* apricots get ripe in no time if the sun shines a lot."

"It's been raining lately, though," Alf Rife said.

"Where do you think apricots get their juice from?" Auggie said. "From rain. Rain is just as important as sunshine to apricots."

"Sunshine in the daytime, rain at night," Shag Manoogian said. "Warm them up, give them water. I'll bet there's a lot of ripe apricots on the tree."

"Boy, I hope so," Alf Rife said.

"It's too early for apricots," Nickie Paloota said. "They weren't ripe last year until June."

"That was last year," Auggie said. "This is this year."

From a distance of about one hundred yards, the boys stopped to admire the famous apricot tree—all green and pretty, very old and very big. It stood in the corner of Henderson's backyard. For ten years the boys of the neighborhood had raided old man Henderson's apricot tree. In the broken-down house every spring, Mr. Henderson had watched their coming with fascination and delight—always satisfying the boys by appearing at the last minute and scaring them away. Now, in the house at a curtained window, he looked up from his book.

"Well, look at that!" he said to himself. "Coming to steal apricots in March, in the dead of Winter." He peeked out at the boys again, whispering as if he were one of them. "Coming to get apricots off old man Henderson's tree. Here they come. Slowly, now. Hah-hah," he laughed, "look at them! And look at that little one! Surely not more than four years old. He's a new one. Come on, boys. Come to the wonderful old tree. If I could ripen them for you to steal, I'd do it—"

He watched the boys as Auggie instructed, directed, and led the attack. The boys surrounded the tree cautiously, with a mingling in their hearts of hope and fear. Even if the apricots were green, they were on Henderson's tree and belonged to him, and therefore their coming for the apricots was the same as if the apricots were ripe—therefore they *hoped* the apricots *were* ripe. But they were afraid, too. They were afraid of Henderson, they were afraid of sin, of capture and guilt, and they were afraid the apricots weren't ripe yet.

"Maybe he ain't home," Nickie Paloota whispered as the boys almost reached the tree.

"He's home," Auggie said. "He's *always* home. He's hiding, that's all. It's a trap. He wants to catch us. Careful, everybody. There's no telling where he'll be. Ulysses, you go home."

Obediently Ulysses retreated three steps and stopped to watch the magnificent duel with the magnificent tree.

"Are they ripe?" Shag said. "Do you see any color, Auggie?"

"Only green," Auggie said. "That's leaves. The apricots are underneath. Easy now, everybody. Where's Lionel?"

"Here I am," Lionel whispered. He was terribly afraid.

"Well," Auggie said, "be on your toes. If you see old man Henderson, run!"

"Where is he?" Lionel said as if Henderson might be invisible or no bigger than a rabbit, something likely to jump up suddenly out of the grass.

"What do you mean where is he? He's in the house, I guess. But you can never tell about Henderson. He might be hiding outside some place, waiting to take us by surprise."

"Are you going to climb the tree?" Alf Rife said.

"Who else?" Auggie said. "But let's see if the apricots are ripe first."

"Ripe or green," Shag Manoogian said, "we want to steal at least *some* of them, Auggie."

"Don't worry. We will. If they're ripe, we'll steal a *lot* of them."

"What are you going to say at Sunday School tomorrow?" Lionel said.

"Stealing apricots isn't stealing, like stealing in the Bible, Lionel. This is different."

"Then, what are you scared of?"

"Who's scared? We've just got to be careful, that's all. What's the use of getting caught if you can get away?"

"I don't see any ripe apricots," Lionel said.

"You see a tree, don't you?" Auggie said.

"I see a tree, all right. That's *all*, though—just a big tree—all green. It sure is pretty, too, Auggie."

Now, the gang was almost under the tree. Ulysses followed not far behind. He was absolutely unafraid. He didn't understand at all, but he was sure this was very important stuff—something about trees, something about apricots. The boys studied the branches of the old apricot tree, green with fine young leaf. The apricots were all very small, very green, and obviously very hard.

"Not ripe yet," Alf Rife said.

"Yeah," Auggie admitted. "I guess they need a couple more days. Maybe next Saturday."

"Next Saturday—*sure*," Shag said.

"There's a *lot* of them, though," Auggie said.

"We can't go back empty-handed," Shag said. "We've got to get at least *one* of them—green or ripe—*one* of them, anyway."

"OK," Auggie said. "I'll get it. Now, the rest of you be ready to run." Auggie dashed to the tree, swung up into it on one of its lower branches while the gang and Mr. Henderson and Ulysses watched with fascination, amazement, and admiration. Then, Mr. Henderson stepped out of the house onto the back-porch steps. All the boys went off like a school of startled minnows.

"Auggie!" Shag Manoogian shouted. "Henderson!"

Like a frightened orang-outang in the jungle, Auggie bounced around in the tree, hung from a branch, and then dropped to the ground. He was running almost before his feet touched the ground, but he noticed Ulysses and stopped suddenly, shouting at the boy, "Run, Ulysses! Run—run!"

Ulysses, however, didn't budge. He couldn't figure it out. Auggie rushed back to the small boy, lifted him off his feet, and ran with him while Henderson watched. When all the boys had disappeared and everything was quiet again, the old man smiled and looked up into the tree. Then he turned around and went back into the house.

25 Mr. Ara

One by one the members of August Gottlieb's Secret Society returned from their escape from old man Henderson and gathered in front of Ara's Market to wait there for the arrival of their leader. At last the great man was observed by his devoted followers coming around the alley, holding the hand of Ulysses Macauley. The members of the Society waited silently for the arrival of the leader, who was soon among them. The face of the leader was searched by each of the followers, and then the one named Alf Rife said, "Did you get an apricot, Auggie?"

The leader looked at this faithless one and said, "You don't have to ask that. You saw me in the tree. You *know* I got an apricot."

Now, all the members spoke in one voice. (All, that is, excepting Lionel, who was not really a member at all.) They said with great admiration, "Let's see it, Auggie. Let's see the apricot."

The little boy Ulysses watched everything, still completely unsure of the mysterious values involved but still certain that whatever these values might be, they were surely of greater importance than anything else in the world—at that moment, at any rate.

"Let's see the apricot you stole, Auggie," the members of the Society said again. "Come on, let's see it."

August Gottlieb quietly fished into the pocket of his overalls and brought out a clenched fist that he thrust before him. His followers gathered around and looked directly upon the fist. When everyone was appropriately quiet and respectful, August Gottlieb opened his fist.

There in the palm of his hand was a small green apricot the size of a quail egg.

The followers of the great religious leader smiled at the miraculous object in the palm of his hand, and Lionel—the kindest of them all, even though he was not a bona-fide member of the religious sect—lifted Ulysses so that he too could see the small green object. Having seen the green apricot, Ulysses squirmed, got down, and then ran for home, not disappointed, only eager to tell someone.

Now, out of his store, stepped Ara himself,

the man who had established Ara's Market in this neighborhood of Ithaca, California, seven years ago. He was a tall, lean-faced, melancholy yet comical man who wore a white grocer's apron over his plain business suit. He stood a moment on the small porch of the store to look down at the new Messiah and his disciples and to listen to their delighted expressions of adoration for the Holy Image.

"Auggie, you!" he said. "You, Shag! Nickie! Alfo, you! Lionel, you!—what you call this? United States Congress Washington? Go some odder place hold important meeting. This market, not Congress."

"Oh, sure, Mr. Ara," August Gottlieb said. "We'll go across the street to the empty lot. Do you want to see an apricot?"

"You got apricot?" the grocer said. "Where you get apricot?"

"Off a tree. Want to see it?"

"Is not apricot now. Apricot come in two more month. In Maytime."

"This is a March apricot," the leader of the whirling dervishes[1] said to the grocer. Again he opened his fist, revealing the small, hard, green object. "Look at it, Mr. Ara," Auggie said, and then paused. "Pretty?"

"All right, all right," Mr. Ara said. "Pretty. Very fine apricot. Now, go hold meeting United States Congress Washington some odder place. Today Saturday. Market open for business. Don't crowd small store first thing in morning. Give chance. Small store get scared, run away."

"OK, Mr. Ara," Auggie said, "we won't crowd your store. We'll go across the street now. Come on, you guys."

Mr. Ara watched the small migration of the religious fanatics. He was about to go back into the store when a small boy who resembled him came out of the store and stood beside him.

"Papa?"

"Hah, John?"

"Give me apple," the boy said to the man. He spoke earnestly, almost sadly.

The father took the son by the hand, and together they went into the store to the counter where the fresh fruit was stacked in piles.

"Apple?" the father said to the boy. He took an apple from the pile—the very best apple in the pile—and handed it to the boy. "All right, apple."

The father went behind the counter of his store to wait for a customer, and in the meantime to look upon his son, surely as melancholy as himself, even though there was a difference of at least forty years in their ages. The son took one enormous bite out of the apple, chewed it slowly, swallowed it, and then for a moment seemed to think about it, while the father himself thought about it, too. The apple did not make the boy happy. He put it down on the counter in front of his father, and then looked up at the man. There they were, in Ithaca, California, probably seven thousand miles from what had been for centuries their home in the world. Naturally there was a loneliness in each of them, but no one could know for sure that the same loneliness might not be in them had they been seven thousand miles away, back home. There on the floor of his store stood the father's son, and the father looked at the son —at his own face in the boy, his own eyes, and beyond the eyes surely his own character. There was the same man, only younger. The father took the rejected apple, attacked it with an enormous crackling bite, and stood chewing and swallowing. He might have been tragic Lear[2] himself, judging from the swiftness and noisiness of his stentorian chewing. An apple was too good a thing in

---

1. **whirling dervishes** (dɘr'vish iz) [Colloq.]: a Moslem order that practices whirling as a religious act.
2. **Lear** (lēr): the main character in a tragedy by William Shakespeare; a king who goes mad and dies brokenhearted.

the world to be wasted, and therefore if his son would not eat it, then he must eat it, even though he had no passion for apples or for their flavor. He simply knew that it was wrong to waste anything. He continued to bite into the apple, to chew, and to swallow, as if in dramatic soliloquy. At last, however, it was a little too much—there was a little too much apple. It would be necessary to waste *some* of it. With recklessness and perhaps a small amount of regret, he flung the remains of the apple into the garbage can.

Now, the son spoke again. "Papa?"

"Hah, John?"

"Give me orange."

The father selected the biggest orange in the neat pile of oranges and handed it to the boy. "Orange? All right—orange."

The boy bit into the peel of the orange, then began to finish the job of peeling with his fingers, working slowly but efficiently at first but after a moment accelerating his effort with such an intensity that even the father began to feel, as surely the son felt, that beneath the peeling of this growth of tree would be not simply the flesh of an orange but the heart's final fulfillment. The boy placed the peelings of the orange on the counter in front of the man, broke the orange in half, peeled off one section, put it in his mouth, chewed and swallowed. But alas, no. It was truly an orange, but it was truly *not* the heart's final fulfillment. The son waited a moment, then put the rest of the orange in front of his father. Again the father took up the unfinished work and silently began trying to finish it. But soon the limit was reached, and a little less than half of the orange went into the garbage can.

"Papa?" the boy said after a moment, and again the father replied, "Hah, John?"

"Give me candy."

"Candy? All right—candy."

From the candy showcase the father se-

lected the most popular five-cent bar of candy and handed it to the boy. The boy studied this manufactured substance, removed the wax paper, and took a big bite out of the chocolate-covered candy and again slowly chewed and swallowed. But again it was nothing—only candy—sweet, yes; otherwise, nothing, truly nothing. Once again the son returned to the father another substance of the world that had failed to bring him completion. Patiently the father accepted the responsibility—to avoid waste. He picked up the candy bar, started to bite into it and then changed his mind. He turned and flung the candy into the garbage can. He felt bitterly angry, and in his heart he cursed some people seven thousand miles away who had once seemed to him to be inhuman, or at least ignorant. *Those dogs!* he said.

"Papa?"

"Hah, John?"

"Give me banana."

The father sighed this time but did not abandon all faith. "Banana? All right—banana." He examined the bunch of bananas hanging over the piles of fruit and finally discovered what he believed to be the ripest and the sweetest banana of the bunch. He plucked this banana off the bunch and handed it to the boy.

At last a customer came into the store. The customer was a man Mr. Ara had never before seen. The storekeeper and the customer nodded to one another in greeting, and then the man said with an accent all his own, "You got cookies?"

"Cook-ies?" the grocer said eagerly. "What kind cook-ies you want?"

Another customer came into the store. This customer was Ulysses Macauley. He stood to one side, listening and watching, waiting his turn.

"You got cookies, raisins in?" the man said to the grocer.

"Cook-ies, raisins in?" the grocer said. This was a problem. "Cook-ies, raisins in," he said again, almost whispering. "Cook-ies, raisins in," he said still again. The grocer looked around the store. The grocer's son put the banana on the counter in front of his father —rejected.

"Papa?"

The father looked at the boy and then spoke very swiftly. "You want apple, I give you apple. You want orange, I give you orange. You want candy, I give you candy. You want banana, I give you banana. What you want *now*?"

"Cookies," the boy said.

"What kind cook-ies you want?" the father said to the boy, not forgetting the customer, and in fact, speaking *to* the customer, but at the same time speaking to his son, and at the same time speaking to everybody, everywhere—everybody wanting things.

"Cookies, raisins in," the boy said.

With furious restraint the father almost whispered his reply to his son, but instead of looking at his son he looked at the customer. "I got no cook-ies," he whispered. "*No* kind cook-ies. Why you want cook-ies? I got everything, but no cook-ies. What's cook-ies? What you want?"

"Cookies," the man said patiently, "for small boy."

"I got no cook-ies," the grocer said again. "I got small boy too." The grocer pointed to his own son. "I give him apple, orange, candy, banana, lots of good things." He looked the customer straight in the eye, and almost as if he were angry, he said, again, "What you *want*?"

"My broder's boy," the customer said. "He's got influenza. He cry—he want cookies. 'Cookies, raisins in,' he say."

But every man lives his own life and every life has its own theme, so that again the grocer's son looked at his father and said, "Papa?"

But now the father refused to look at the boy. Instead, he looked at the man whose nephew was ill and wanted cookies with raisins in them. He looked at the man with understanding, with sympathy, and yet with a kind of peasant rage, not against the man but against the world itself, against illness, against pain, against loneliness, against the heart wanting what it can never have. The grocer was angry at himself too, because even though he had established this market in Ithaca, California, seven thousand miles from home, he did not have cookies with raisins in them; he did not have that which the sick boy wanted. The grocer pointed at his son and spoke to the man.

"Apple," the grocer said, "orange, candy, banana—no cookies. He's my boy. Three years old. Not sick. He want many things. I don't *know* what he want. Nobody know what he want. He just want. He look at God. He say, Give me dis, give me dat—but he never satisfied. Always he want. Always he feel bad. Poor God has got nothing for such sadness. He give everything — world — sunshine — moder — fader — broder — sister — onkle — cousin — house, farm, stove, table, bed—poor God give everything—but nobody happy—everybody like small boy sick with influenza—everybody say give me cookies— raisins in." The grocer stopped a moment to take a very deep breath. When he exhaled he said very loudly to the customer, "*Is no cookies—raisins in.*"

The grocer began to move with an impatience and a fury that were almost majestic. First he took a paper bag and snapped it open. Then he began to toss things into the bag. "Here's orange, very pretty. Here's apple. Wonderful. Here's banana. Taste very good." Now, gently, and with great courtesy and sincere sympathy for the man and for the man's sick nephew, the grocer handed the bag to the customer. "Take to little boy. No pay. I no want money." And then again he said very softly, "Is no cookies, raisins in."

"He cry," the man said. "He feel very bad. He say, 'Cookies, raisins in.' Thank you very much, but we already give small boy apple, orange, odder things." The man put the bag down on the counter. "Sick boy say, 'Give me cookies, raisins in.' Apple, orange—no good. Excuse me, I go try chain store. Maybe *they* got cookies, raisins in."

"All right, my friend," the grocer whispered. "You go try chain store—but they no got cookies, raisins in. Nobody got."

Almost shyly the stranger left the store. For a full minute the grocer stood behind the counter staring at his son. Suddenly he began to speak in his own language, Armenian.

"The world's gone mad," he said. "In Russia alone, so near our own country, our own beautiful little nation, millions of people, millions of children, every day go hungry. They are cold, pathetic, barefooted— They walk around—no place to sleep—they pray for a piece of dry bread—somewhere to lie down and rest—one night of peaceful sleep. And what about us? What do we do? Here we are in Ithaca, California, in this great country, America. What do we do? We wear good clothes. We put on good shoes every morning when we get up from sleep. We walk around with no one in the streets to come with guns or to burn our houses or to murder our children or brothers or fathers. We take rides out into the country in automobiles. We eat the best food. Every night when we go to bed we sleep—and then what are we? We are discontented. We are *still* discontented." The grocer shouted this amazing truth at his little son with terrible love for the boy. "Apple," he said, "orange, candy, banana, for God's sake, little fellow, don't

do this! If I do it, you are my son, better than me, and therefore you must not do this. Be happy! Be happy! I am unhappy, but *you* must be happy." He pointed to the back door of the store that led into the house, and obediently, very sober-faced, the little boy left the store and entered the house.

Now the grocer spent a moment trying to compose himself. At last he believed he was calm enough to speak quietly to the customer in the store, Ulysses Macauley. He turned to the boy and tried to be cheerful. He even smiled. "What you want, little boy Ulysses?"

"Mush."

"What kind mush you want?"

"H-O."

"Two kinds H-O, little boy Ulysses. Regular kind, and quick-cooking kind. Two kinds. Slow, quick. Old, new. What kind your mama want, little boy Ulysses?"

Ulysses thought about this a moment and then said, "H-O."

"Old kind or new kind?"

But the little boy didn't know, so the grocer decided for him. "All right, new kind, modern. Eighteen cents, please, little boy Ulysses."

Ulysses open his fist and thrust his arm out toward the grocer, who took the quarter from the boy's hand. The grocer handed Ulysses the change, saying, "Eighteen cents, nineteen, twenty, and nickel—twenty-five. Thank you, little boy Ulysses."

"You're welcome, Mr. Ara," Ulysses said. He took the package of oatmeal and walked out of the store. It was very difficult to understand anything. First it was apricots on a tree, then it was cookies with raisins in, and then it was the grocer talking to his son in a strange tongue—but even so it was exciting. In the street the little boy kicked up his heel as he did whenever he was pleased, and began to run home.

26 Mrs. Macauley

Mrs. Macauley had the kitchen table set for one, waiting for her son Homer to come to breakfast. She was setting down a bowl of oatmeal when he came into the kitchen. Her glance at him was only fleeting, but even so she knew that the strange experience of his dream last night was still upon him. Even though he himself perhaps did not know he had wept in his sleep, his spirit seemed hushed, as the spirit of a man is hushed after grief. Even his voice seemed deeper and gentler.

"I didn't want to sleep this late," he said. "It's almost nine-thirty. What happened to the alarm clock?"

"You're working hard," Mrs. Macauley said. "You must rest, too."

"I'm not working so hard. Besides, tomorrow's Sunday." He said his morning prayer, only it seemed to last twice as long as usual. Then he picked up his spoon and was about to begin to eat when he stopped and studied the spoon strangely. He looked toward his mother who was busy at the kitchen sink. "Ma?"

"Yes, Homer?"

"I didn't talk to you last night when I came home, because it was like you said. I *couldn't* talk. All of a sudden on the way home last night I started to cry. You know I never did cry when I was little or at school when I was in trouble. I always felt ashamed to cry. Even Ulysses never cries. But last night I just couldn't help it, and I don't remember if I was ashamed, even. I don't think I was. And I couldn't come straight home, either. I rode out to Ithaca Wine and then I rode across town to the high school. On the way there I rode past a house where some people had been having a party earlier in the evening— the house was dark now. I took those people a telegram. You know the kind of telegram it was. Then, I went back to town and rode all around the streets looking at everything— all the buildings, all the places I've known all my life, all of them full of people. And then at last I really *saw* Ithaca and I really knew the people who live in Ithaca. I felt sorry for all of them and I even prayed that nothing would happen to them. After that I stopped crying. I thought a fellow would never cry when he got to be grown up, but it seems as if that's when a fellow *starts*, because that's when a fellow starts finding out about things." He stopped a moment, and then his voice became even more somber than it had been. "Almost everything a man finds out is bad or sad." He waited a moment for some word from his mother, but she didn't speak and didn't turn away from her work. "Why is that so?" he said.

Mrs. Macauley began to speak, still turned away from him. "You'll find out. No one can tell you. Each man finds out for himself, in his own way, because each man *is* the world."

"Why did I cry, and after I stopped crying why couldn't I talk? Why was there nothing for me to say—to anybody? To you, or to myself?"

"Pity—I suppose it was pity that made you cry. Unless a man has pity he is not truly a man. If a man has not wept at the world's pain, he is only half a man, and there will always be pain in the world. Knowing this does not mean that a man shall despair. A good man will seek to take pain out of things. A foolish man will not even notice it, except in himself. And the poor, unfortunate, evil man will drive pain deeper into things and spread it about wherever he goes. But each man is guiltless, I'm afraid, for he did not ask to come here and did not come brand new, from nowhere and nothing. He came from people. I really don't believe the evil know they *are* evil. It's just their bad luck, that's all. Eat your breakfast like a sensible fellow."

Suddenly he felt it was all right to eat.

27 Lionel

Ulysses Macauley and his best friend Lionel Cabot—the *great* Lionel—came into the Macauley kitchen. There was no mistaking this friendship, even though Lionel was a good six years older than Ulysses. They walked together and stood about together as only the very best of friends do, easily and with scarcely any need for one or the other to speak.

"Mrs. Macauley," Lionel said. "I came to ask permission—can Ulysses go to the pubalic liberry with me? I got to take back a book for my sister Lillian."

"All right, Lionel," Mrs. Macauley said. "But why aren't you with the others— Auggie and Alf and Shag and the other boys?"

"They—" Lionel began to say and then stopped, from embarrassment. After a moment he began again. "They chased me away. They don't like me because I'm dumb."

"You're no such thing, Lionel," Mrs. Macauley said. "You're the nicest boy in this neighborhood. But don't you be angry at the other boys, because they're all nice boys, too."

"I'm not angry," Lionel said. "I like every one of them. But every time I make a little mistake in a game they chase me away. They even swear at me. Every little mistake I make they get sore at me. 'That's all, Lionel,' they say. And when they say it, I know I've got to go. Sometimes I don't even last five minutes. Sometimes I make a mistake the *first* thing I do. And then they say, 'That's all, Lionel.' I don't even know what mistake I made. What do they want me to do? That's all I want to know, but nobody will tell me. Every Saturday they chase me away. Ulysses is the only one who sticks with me. He's the only partner I've got. But some day the others are going to be sorry. When the time comes and the others come to me and want me to help them—well, Mrs. Macauley, I'm going to help them, and then they're going to be sorry they chased me away all the time. Can I have a drink of water?"

"Of course, Lionel." Mrs. Macauley filled

a glass of water for the boy, and he drank it all quickly, making the kind of sound that boys make when water is still the most wonderful drink in the world.

"Don't you want a drink of water, too, Ulysses?" Lionel said.

Ulysses indicated by nodding that he would like a glass of water, too. After Ulysses had swallowed the water, Lionel said, "Well, I guess we'll go to the pubalic liberry now, Mrs. Macauley." The two friends walked out of the house.

When the two boys were gone, Homer said, "Was Marcus like Ulysses when he was little?"

"How do you mean?"

"You know, the way Ulysses is—interested in everything, always watching. Doesn't ever say anything but always gets a kick out of everything. Seems to like everybody, and everybody seems to like him. He doesn't know many words. He can't read, but you can almost always understand him by just looking at him. You can almost understand what he's telling you even if he doesn't say a word. Was Marcus like that, too?"

"Well, Marcus and Ulysses *are* brothers, so of course Ulysses is something like Marcus, but they're not *exactly* alike."

"Ulysses is going to be a great man some day, isn't he?"

"Perhaps not in the eyes of the world, but he is going to be great, of course, because he's great now."

"Marcus was great when he was little, too, wasn't he?"

"You've all a lot in common, of course, but not too much. Marcus was not restless, as you are. He was shy and would rather be alone than out looking for people to see, like Ulysses. Marcus liked to read and listen to music and just sit around or go for long walks."

"Well, Ulysses certainly *likes* Marcus."

"Ulysses likes everybody," Mrs. Macauley said. "He likes everybody in the world."

"Sure," Homer said, "but he likes Marcus *especially,* and I know why, too, because Marcus is still a child, even if he is in the Army. I guess a child looks for a child in everyone else he meets. And if he finds a child in somebody grown up, I guess he likes that person more than he likes the others. I wish I could begin to be grown up the way Ulysses is a child. I guess I admire him more than anybody else in the world outside of our family. Did he tell you what happened to him yesterday?"

"He didn't say a word about it. Auggie came and told us."

"Well, what did he say when he came into the house after I brought him home from the telegraph office?"

"He didn't say anything. He just sat down, listened to the music, and then we had supper. When I put him to bed he said, 'Big Chris.' That's all, and went to sleep. I had no idea who Big Chris was until Auggie told me."

"Who is Ulysses like—most of all?"

"Like his father."

"Did you know Papa when he was little?"

"Lord, no!" Mrs. Macauley said. "How could I? Your father was seven years older than me. Ulysses is like your father as your father was *all* his life. Oh, I've had good luck, thank God. My kids are human beings, besides being children. They might have been children only, and then my luck wouldn't have been so good. What's the matter with your leg?"

"Nothing," Homer said. "I took a little spill. I'm going to the telegraph office."

Homer left the house. His mother heard him bounce his bike several times to see if there was enough air in the tires, and then she saw him ride around the house headed for town.

28 At the Public Library

The good friends, Lionel and Ulysses, walked to the public library. On their way, a funeral procession emerged from the First Ithaca Presbyterian Church. Pallbearers carried a plain casket to an old Packard hearse. Following the casket, the two boys saw a handful of mourners.

"Come on, Ulysses," Lionel said, "it's a funeral!" They ran half a block, Lionel holding Ulysses by the hand, and very soon they were at the center of everything.

"That's the casket," Lionel whispered. "Somebody's dead in there. I wish I knew who it is. See the flowers. They give them flowers when they die. See them crying. Those are the people who knew him."

Lionel turned to a man who wasn't very busy. The man had just blown his nose and touched his handkerchief to the corners of his eyes.

"Who's dead?" Lionel asked the man.

"It's poor little Johnny Merryweather, the hunchback," the man said.

Lionel turned to Ulysses. "It's poor little Johnny Merryweather, the hunchback."

"Seventy years old," the man said.

"Seventy years old," Lionel said to Ulysses.

"Sold popcorn on the corner of Mariposa and Broadway for thirty years."

"Sold popcorn on the corner of—" Lionel stopped suddenly and looked at the man. He almost shouted. "You mean the popcorn man?"

"Yes, Johnny Merryweather—gone to his rest."

"I knew *him!*" Lionel shouted. "I bought popcorn off of him many times. Did *he* die?"

"Yes, peacefully. In his sleep. Gone to his Maker."

"I knew Johnny Merryweather!" Lionel said, almost crying. "I didn't know his name was Johnny Merryweather, but I knew him."

Lionel turned to Ulysses and put his arm around his friend. "It's Johnny," he almost wept. "Johnny Merryweather. One of my best friends, gone to his Maker."

The hearse drove away and very soon there was no one in front of the church except Lionel and Ulysses. Somehow it seemed wrong for Lionel to leave the place where he learned that the man who had died was a man he knew, even though he had never known that the man's name was Johnny Merryweather. At last, however, he decided he couldn't stand in front of the church forever, even if he *had* bought popcorn off of Johnny Merryweather many times—so, thinking of the popcorn, almost tasting it again, he went on down the street with Ulysses.

When the two boys entered the public library, they entered an area of profound and solemn silence, as if the funeral services were still going on. There were old men reading newspapers. There were town philosophers sitting over enormous books. There were high school boys and girls doing research, but everyone was hushed, because they were seeking wisdom. They were in the presence of books. They were trying to find out. Lionel not only whispered, he moved on tiptoe. Lionel whispered because he was under the impression that it was out of respect for books, not consideration for readers. Ulysses followed him, also on tiptoe, and they explored the library, each finding many treasures, Lionel—books, and Ulysses—people. Lionel didn't read books, and he hadn't come to the public library to borrow one. He just liked to *see* them—the thousands of them. He pointed out a whole row of shelved books to his friend and then whispered, "All of these—and these. And these. Here's a red one. All these. There's a green one. All these."

Finally Mrs. Gallagher, the old librarian, noticed the two boys and went over to them. *She* didn't whisper, however. She spoke right out, as if she were not in the public library at all. This shocked Lionel and made a few people look up from the pages of their books.

"What are you looking for, boy?" Mrs. Gallagher said.

"Books," Lionel whispered softly.

"What books are you looking for?"

"All of them."

"All of them? What do you mean? You can borrow only four books on one card."

"I don't want to borrow *any* of them."

"Well, what in the world *do* you want with them?"

"I just want to look at them."

"Look at them? That is not what the public library is for. You can look *into* them, you can look *at* the pictures in them, but what in the world do you want to look at the outsides of them for?"

"I like to," Lionel whispered. "Can't I?"

"Well," the librarian said, "there's no law against it." She looked at Ulysses. "And who's this?"

"This here's Ulysses. He can't read."

"Can you?"

"No, but he can't, either. That's why we're friends. He's the only other man I know who can't read."

The old librarian looked at the two friends. This was something brand new in all the years of her experience at the public library. "Well," she said at last, "perhaps it's just as well that you *can't* read. I *can*. I've been reading books for the past sixty years, and I can't see as how it's made any great difference. Run along now and look at the books all you like."

"Yes, ma'am," Lionel said.

The two friends moved off into still greater realms of mystery and adventure. Lionel pointed out more books to Ulysses. "These," he said. "And those over there. And these. All books, Ulysses." He stopped a moment to think. "I wonder what they say in all these books." He pointed out a whole vast area of them, five shelves full of them. "All these," he said—"I wonder what they say." Finally he discovered a book that was green, like fresh grass. "And this one, this one is pretty, Ulysses."

A little frightened at what he was doing, Lionel lifted the book out of the shelf, held it in his hands a moment and then opened it. "There, Ulysses! A book! There it is! See? They're saying something in here." Now he pointed to something in the print of the book. "There's an *A*. That's an *A* right there. There's another letter of some sort. I don't know which one that is. Every letter's different, and every word's different." He sighed and looked around at all the books. "I don't think I'll ever learn to read, but I sure would like to know what they're saying. Now, here's a picture. Here's a picture of a girl. See her?" He turned many pages of the book and said, "More letters and words, straight through to the end of the book. This is the pubalic liberry, Ulysses. Books all over the place." He looked at the print of the book with a kind of reverence, whispering to himself as if he were trying to read. Then he shook his head. "You can't know what a book says, Ulysses, unless you can read; and I can't read."

He closed the book slowly, put it back in its place, and together the two friends tiptoed out of the library. Outside, Ulysses kicked up his heel because it seemed he had learned something new.

29 At the Parlor Lecture Club

Homer Macauley got off his bicycle in front of the Ithaca Parlor Lecture Club, a white building that was an architectural cross between a Colonial house and a New England church. It was now two-thirty, and the Saturday afternoon lecture was about to begin. Consequently, many middle-aged ladies, most of them mothers, were cheerfully entering the building. The messenger took a telegram out of his hat and studied it. The telegram was addressed to Rosalie Simms-Peabody, Ithaca Parlor Lecture Club, Ithaca, California. Deliver in Person.

As the messenger walked into the hall, the President of the Club, a rounded lady in her early fifties, was beginning to introduce the lecturer, who was nowhere to be seen. The President of the Club pounded a small walnut-breaker on the table, and the audience in the hall began to quiet down.

"I've got a telegram for Rosalie Simms-Peabody," Homer whispered to a lady. "It's to be delivered to her *personally*."

"Rosalie Simms-*Pibity*," the lady corrected him. "Yes, Rosalie Simms-Pibity is expecting the telegram. You are to deliver it to her on the platform when she appears."

"When is that going to be?"

"In a moment now. Just sit down and wait. When Rosalie Simms-Pibity appears, run right up onto the stage and call out very clearly, 'Telegram for Rosalie Simms-Pibity!' Not *Peabody*, boy."

"Yes, ma'am." Homer sat down and the lady tiptoed away, smiling proudly at the important work she had done.

"Members of the Ithaca Parlor Lecture Club," the President of the Club said. "This afternoon we have in store a great treat. Our speaker is to be Rosalie Simms-Pibity." The President of the Club paused, so that there would be time for the customary applause. After the applause, she said, "I do not have to tell you who Rosalie Simms-Pibity is. She is internationally famous—one of the great women of our time. We all know her name and we all know she is famous. But do we, I wonder, know *why* she is famous." The President of the Club answered this question. "I am afraid not. The story of Rosalie Simms-Pibity," she said, as if she were telling a fable not unlike the fable of the Odyssey[3] itself, "is a story *especially* thrilling to women. Simms-Pibity—for that is how she prefers to be known—has lived a life brimming over with adventure, romance, danger, and beauty; and yet today she is scarcely more than a dashing handsome British *girl*—a girl hard as steel

---

3. **Odyssey** (ăd ə'sē): a poem about the wanderings of Odysseus, whose long journey brings many adventures.

and stronger than most men. In fact, there are few men who have lived a life as adventurous as the life of Simms-Pibity."

Now a note of tender sadness came into her voice. "As for us, the stay-at-homes, the mothers, the bringer-uppers, so to speak, of children, the life of Simms-Pibity is like a dream—*our* dream—the unfulfilled dream of each of us who stayed home, gave birth to our children, and looked after our houses. Hers is the beautiful life each of us would have *liked* to have lived if we had dared, but Fate, as it will, has not decreed such adventures for us, and in all the world there is only one Simms-Pibity. Only one!"

The President of the Club paused to look over the faces of her old friends in the audience. "What is it," she said, "that Simms-Pibity has done that has made her so rare among women? Well, the list of her adventures is staggering, and as I read the list, you will scarcely be able to believe any woman could do such things and still be alive; but alive she is, and *here*. Simms-Pibity is going to talk to us in plain language—language perhaps, to some of us, shocking. But first let me go over the adventures—only briefly—for a full recitation of them would take too long, as *every* day is a new adventure for Simms-Pibity. She *creates* adventure wherever she goes, and we may be sure that before she leaves our unknown little city, Ithaca, she will have discovered here things we ourselves do not know.

"From 1915 to 1917, Simms-Pibity drove an ambulance at the front—in the other war. During 1917 and 1918, she went around the world with another girl—on tramp steamers, cattle boats, walking and riding and living in many strange places—sometimes even in native huts. She visited twenty-seven different countries. She was captured by the Southern Army in China as she tried to go overland by river junk and sedan chair from Canton to Hankow." The President of the Club paused a moment to dwell on the magical words, and then repeated them. "Canton and Hankow. Simms-Pibity escaped her capturers by shooting the falls of the Sian River in the wet season when no other boat would go out on the perilous waters.

"In 1919, she went across North Africa from Morocco to Abyssinia. In 1920, she was employed in Syria in the secret service. In Damascus she met King Feisal, who helped her make the exploration of Kufara, never before visited by white people, the secret and sacred capital of the fanatic Senussi Sect, deep in the heart of the Libyan Desert. Simms-Pibity went disguised as an Egyptian woman, one thousand miles on camel-back, her only companions coarse, native men who could speak no English." The President of the Ithaca Parlor Lecture Club lifted her eyes after this remark and looked over at two of her most intimate friends. Homer Macauley wondered what she meant by that glance and then wondered how long she was going to talk about this incredible and wonderful person.

"During 1923," the speaker continued, "Simms-Pibity sailed a twenty-ton dhow with an Arab crew fourteen days down the Red Sea to land at the forbidden port of Jeizan. This time she was disguised as an Arab woman. In 1925, she climbed the Atlas Mountains of Morocco. In 1926, she walked one thousand miles through Abyssinia— perhaps a world record." And then with terrible scorn for herself and her friends, the President of the Ithaca Parlor Lecture Club said, "Do we, I wonder, ever walk with pleasure even so short a distance as the distance from Gottschalk's to Roeding Park?" She sighed and then, not knowing how to answer this question, she offered, "It might perhaps do us good." She returned to the matter of introducing the lecturer of the day, looking for her place in the booklet of notes she held in her hand.

"In 1928, Simms-Pibity covered the Balkans[4] for a London newspaper, disguised now as a native woman of one country, now as a native woman of another."

Getting bored, waiting impatiently, eager to get back to the telegraph office and his work, Homer wondered, "Why is she always disguising herself?"

"In 1930, Simms-Pibity made an exciting journey through Turkey and met Mustapha Kemal,[5] a Turk. There Simms-Pibity was disguised as a young Turkish girl from the hill country. She traveled nine thousand miles on horseback, moving all through the Near East. In Azerbaijan[6] she saw the uprising between the Communist Red Army and the Caucasian peasants. In 1931, she traveled through South America, exploring the jungles of Brazil with only native men for companions, one of whom was named, I understand—from Simms-Pibity herself—Max. But the adventures of Simms-Pibity are endless, and it is *her* you wish to see and hear, not *me*." This sweet modesty brought a nervous giggle out of the President of the Club, followed by sympathetic but hearty laughter from her friends. When a proper quietude had come over the audience, the President said in a firm and dramatic voice, "It gives me great pride, as President of the Ithaca Parlor Lecture Club, to present to you—Rosalie Simms-Pibity!"

The applause was swift and loud. The President of the Club turned toward the wings of the stage to greet the distinguished visitor, but she wasn't there. The audience, taking advantage of this delay, increased its applause and after perhaps two full minutes of steady hand-clapping—during which a number of women confessed that their hands were getting sore—the great lady finally presented herself.

Homer expected to see somebody unlike any woman he had ever before seen. He couldn't imagine what form this creature would take, but he felt certain that it would be at least interesting—and so it was. Rosalie Simms-Pibity was an old woman, horse-faced, dried-out, tall, gaunt, and sexless. Because the time had come for Homer to deliver the telegram, he got to his feet, but perhaps it was because he was amazed, for he did not run up onto the stage as he had been instructed to do.

Now, the nice lady who had given him his instructions came rushing over, and before he knew it, she was pushing him down the aisle and whispering loud enough for everyone to hear, "Now, boy! Deliver the telegram!"

On the stage the great lady pretended not to be aware of this commotion. "Ladies," she began to say. "Members of the Ithaca Parlor Lecture Club—" Her voice perfectly suited her appearance. It was high and shrill.

Homer hurried up onto the stage and in a very clear voice announced, "Telegram for Rosalie Simms-Pibity!"

The great lady stopped her speech and turned to the messenger as if his appearance was entirely unplanned. "Here, boy," she said. "I am Simms-Pibity!" She glanced back at the audience and said, "Excuse me, ladies." She signed for the telegram, took it from the messenger, and then offered him a dime, saying, "And that's for you, boy."

This was painful to Homer, but everything had been so ridiculous and confusing that he didn't care to bother about refusing it. He took the small coin, dropped it, picked it up, and, very much embarrassed, hurried down from the stage, as the woman began her speech.

"Now, in 1939," she said, "just before the

---

4. **Balkans** (bŏl'kənz): countries of the Balkan peninsula, including Yugoslavia, Albania, Bulgaria, Greece, and Romania.
5. **Mustapha Kemal** (moos'tä fä ke mäl'): the first president of Turkey.
6. **Azerbaijan** (ä'ər bī jän): a province near the Baltic sea, now a republic of the U.S.S.R.

outbreak of this new War, I chanced to be in Bavaria[7] on a secret mission, disguised as an Alsatian milkmaid."

In the street, seated on the sidewalk, Homer saw Henry Wilkinson who had lost both legs in a railway accident when he was a young man. Now, thirty years later, he had taken to holding a hat in his lap containing pencils. Homer did not know him by name but he had seen him all his life. Somehow or other, he had never gotten around to buying a pencil or dropping a coin into the hat. Therefore, upon seeing Henry Wilkinson, Homer dropped the dime into the man's hat and hurried to his bicycle.

30 Mr. Mechano

After their adventure at the public library, Lionel and Ulysses continued to explore Ithaca. At sundown they found themselves standing in a small crowd of idlers and passers-by, watching a man in the window of a shabby drug store. The man moved like a piece of machinery, although he *was* a human being. He looked, however, as if he had been made of wax instead of flesh. He seemed inhuman, and, in fact, he looked like nothing so much as an upright, unburied corpse still capable of moving. The man was the most incredible thing Ulysses had seen in all of his four years of life in the world. No light came out of the man's eyes. His lips were set as if they would never part.

The man was engaged in advertising *Dr. Bradford's Tonic*. He worked between two easels. On one easel was a sign on which the following message had been printed: "Mr. Mechano—The Machine Man—Half Machine, Half Human. More Dead Than Alive. $50 if you can make him smile. $500 if you can make him laugh." On the other easel Mr. Mechano placed pasteboard cards that he took in an extremely mechanical fashion from the small table in front of the easel. On these cards were printed various messages urging people to buy the patent medicine that Dr. Bradford had invented and thereby to become more alive. After each new card had been placed on the easel, Mr. Mechano pointed at each word of the message on the card with a pointer. When all ten of the cards had been placed on the easel, Mr. Mechano removed them all and put them back on the table and began the procedure all over again.

"It's a man," Lionel said. "I can see him. It's not a machine, Ulysses. It's a man! See his eyes? He's alive. See him?"

The card Mr. Mechano had just placed on the easel read: "Don't drag yourself around half dead. Enjoy life. Take Dr. Bradford's Tonic and feel like a new man."

"There's another card," Lionel said. "It says something on that card." Suddenly he was weary and eager to get home. "Come on, Ulysses, let's go. We've seen him go through all the cards three times. Let's go home. It's almost night now." He took his friend by the hand, but Ulysses drew his hand away.

"Come on, Ulysses! I've got to go home now. I'm hungry." But Ulysses didn't want

---

7. **Bavaria** (bə ver′ē ə): a region of Germany that is now a state of West Germany.

to go. It seemed that he didn't even *hear* Lionel's words.

"I'm going, Ulysses," Lionel challenged. He waited for Ulysses to turn and go with him, but the boy didn't budge. A little hurt and amazed by this betrayal of friendship, Lionel began to walk home, turning every three or four steps to see if his friend was not going to join him, after all. But no, Ulysses wanted to stay and watch Mr. Mechano some more. Lionel felt deeply wounded as he continued his journey home. "I thought he was my best friend in the whole world."

Ulysses stood among the handful of people watching Mr. Mechano until at last only he and an old man were left. Mr. Mechano went right on picking up the cards and putting them on the easel. He went right on pointing to each word on each card. Soon the old man went away, too, and then only Ulysses stood on the sidewalk looking up at the strange human being in the window of the drug store. When the street lights came on, Ulysses came out of the trance of fascination into which the vision of Mr. Mechano had placed him. It was almost as if he had become hypnotized by the sight of the man. Now, out of the trance, he looked around. Day had ended and everybody had gone—The only thing left anywhere was something for which he had no word—Death.

The small boy looked back suddenly at the mechanical man. It seemed then and for the first time that the man was looking directly at *him.* There was swift panic and terror in the boy, and then suddenly he was running away. The few people he saw in the streets now seemed full of death, too, like Mr. Mechano. Ulysses ran until he was almost exhausted. He stopped, at last, breathing hard. He looked around, feeling a deep, silent, steady horror about all things—the horror of Mr. Mechano—Death! He had never before really known fear of *any* kind, let alone fear such as this, and it was the most difficult thing in the world for him to know what to do. His poise was all gone—shattered by the fear of the horror catching up with *him,* and he began to run again. This time as he ran he said to himself, almost crying, "Papa, Mama, Marcus, Bess, Homer!"

The world had been wonderful and full of good things to see again and again, but now the world was a thing to escape, only he could think of no direction to take. He wanted swiftly to reach somebody of his family. He stood panic-stricken, and then began moving a few steps in one direction and then a few in another, feeling all around him a presence of incredible disaster, a disaster he could escape only by reaching his father, his mother, one of his brothers, or his sister. And then, instead of reaching one of these, he saw far down the street the leader of the neighborhood gang, August Gottlieb. The newsboy was standing on a deserted street corner, calling out the headline as if the area around him were full of people who must be told what had happened that day in the world. Hollering headlines had always seemed slightly ridiculous to August Gottlieb because, for one thing, the headlines were always about murder of one sort or another and, for another, it seemed somehow a thing of bad manners to go about among people in the streets of Ithaca lifting his voice. Consequently, the newsboy felt pleased when at last he discovered that the streets were deserted. Without even knowing that he was doing such a thing, whenever the streets had become empty of the people of Ithaca, August Gottlieb, as if grateful for his almost solitary inhabitance of the city, lifted his voice more powerfully than ever, calling out the day's miserable news. What could a man do about the news—sell a paper, and make a few pennies? Is that what he could do? Wasn't it foolish for him to cry out the daily message of mistake as if it were glad tidings? Wasn't it shameful for the people to be so steadily unimpressed by every day's new crimes? Sometimes even in his sleep the newsboy dreamed of calling out the headlines of the world's news, but there, in that inner area of experience, he felt contempt for the nature of the news; and when he shouted, it was always from a great height, and beneath him always were multitudes engaged in frantic activities of error and wrong-doing. But the minute they heard his voice, they stopped in their tracks to look up at him, and then he always shouted, "Now go back, go back where you belong! Stop your killing! Plant trees instead!" He had always loved the idea of trees.

When Ulysses saw August Gottlieb on the corner, some of the terror in his heart passed away. He wanted to call out to Auggie, but he couldn't make a sound. Instead, he ran with all his might to the newsboy and flung himself upon him in an embrace so forceful that it almost knocked Auggie down.

"Ulysses!" the newsboy said. "What's the matter? What are you crying about?"

Ulysses looked up into the eyes of the newsboy, but still he couldn't speak.

"You're scared about something. Well, don't be. There's nothing to be scared of. Now, stop crying." Auggie waited, and Ulysses tried very hard to stop. Soon the sobs came at infrequent intervals, each sob like a hiccup. Then Auggie said, "Come on, Ulysses, I'll take you to Homer."

At the sound of that name, the name of his brother, Ulysses smiled at last, and then hiccuped another sob. "Homer?"

"Sure. Come on."

It was almost too wonderful for the little boy to believe. "Going to see Homer?"

"Sure. The telegraph office is just around the corner."

August Gottlieb and Ulysses Macauley walked into the telegraph office. They found Homer seated at the delivery desk. When Ulysses saw his brother, a wonderful thing happened to his face. All the terror left his eyes, because now he was home.

When Homer saw his brother, he turned to Auggie. "What's Ulysses doing in town at this hour?"

"He got lost, I guess. He was crying."

"Crying?" Homer said, and then lifted and hugged his brother, just as Ulysses hiccuped another sob. "All right, I'll take you home on my bike."

From his desk, the manager of the telegraph office, Thomas Spangler, watched the three boys; and the old telegraph operator, William Grogan, stopped his work to watch them, too. They looked at one another several times. Homer put his brother down. He knew the boy was all right again when Ulysses went to the delivery desk to look at things there. Homer put his arm around August and said, "Thanks, Auggie."

Spangler got up and went to the boys. "Let me have a paper, Auggie."

"Yes, sir," Auggie said, and began to go through the routine of folding the paper and making the sale, but Spangler stopped him, so that he could hold the paper out before him. The manager of the telegraph office glanced at the headline, and then threw the paper into the wastebasket. "How's it going?"

"I've made fifty-five cents so far, but I started at one o'clock. When I make seventy-five cents I'm going home."

"Why?" Spangler said. "Why do you want to make seventy-five cents?"

"I don't know," Auggie said. "I just thought I ought to make seventy-five cents on a Saturday. There's nobody in town hardly, but I think I can sell the rest of my papers in another hour or two. Pretty soon people start coming back to town after supper—the movie crowd."

"Well, forget the movie crowd. Give me the rest of your papers and go home *now*. Here's a quarter."

Even though the newsboy felt grateful to the manager for this gesture, somehow it didn't seem right to him. What it came to was that you really had to sell papers one at a time and each one to a different person, and you had to stand on a street corner and holler the headline and make the people *want* to buy a paper and read the news. He was tired, and he wanted to get home to supper, and he never did know anybody like Spangler before, but it just didn't seem right, somehow.

"I don't want to make a quarter from *you*, Mr. Spangler."

"Never mind," Spangler insisted. "Give me the papers and go home."

"Yes, sir," Auggie said. "But maybe you'll let me do something for you some day."

"Sure," Spangler said, and threw the papers into the wastebasket.

Auggie turned to go home, but Homer stopped him. "Wait a minute, I'll hike you home. Is it all right, Mr. Spangler? I've got a pickup at Ithaca Wine, and it's on the way home. So if it's all right, I'll hike Ulysses and Auggie home and then go and get the pickup at Ithaca Wine. Is it all right?"

"Sure," Spangler said, and went back to his desk.

"You don't need to hike me home," Auggie said. "Hiking two people at one time is too much. I can walk it in no time."

"You can't walk it in no time. It's almost two miles. I can hike both of you very easily. You can sit on the frame and Ulysses can sit on the handlebars. Now, come on."

The three boys went out to Homer's bicycle. The load was a heavy one, especially for a man with one bad leg, but Homer got his passengers safely home. They stopped first at the little house next door to Ara's Market —Auggie's house. Ara himself was standing in front of the store, holding the hand of his little boy. They were looking up into the sky. Down the street, next to the empty lot, Mrs. Macauley stood in the yard under the old walnut tree, taking clothes off the line. Mary

and Bess were in the parlor playing and singing, and the sound of the piano and Mary's voice could be heard faintly.

Auggie got off the bicycle and went into his house. Homer stood a moment in the street, holding the bike and looking up at the sky and over at the Macauley house. Then, Auggie came out of the house and went up to Ara, the grocer.

"Did you do a lot of business today, Mr. Ara?"

"Thank you, Auggie, I am satisfied."

"I've got seventy-five cents I want to spend. I want to get a lot of things for tomorrow."

"All right, Auggie," the grocer said, but before turning and going back into the store, he pointed to the clouds in the sky and then looked at his son. "See, John? Nighttime come now—pretty soon we get in our beds, go to sleep. Sleep all night. When daytime come, we get up again. New day."

The grocer and his son and the neighbor boy went into the store. In the meantime, Ulysses, sitting on the handlebars of his brother's bicycle, was watching his mother. Now, Homer got back onto the bicycle and began to ride toward the house.

As they drew closer to the woman in the yard under the tree, the little brother's face filled with light, but at the same time there was now a deep sadness in the face.

Homer rode straight across the empty lot into the back yard, under the walnut tree. He got off the bicycle and set Ulysses down on his feet. Ulysses stood looking at his mother. Gone from him now almost as if forever was the terror that had come from Mr. Mechano.

"He got lost," Homer said. "Auggie found him and brought him to the telegraph office. I can't stay, but I'll go in and say hello to Bess and Mary."

Homer went into the house and stood in the dark dining room, listening to his sister and the girl his brother loved. When the song was over, he moved into the parlor.

The two girls turned. "I got a letter from Marcus today," Mary said.

"How is he?"

"Just fine. They're going away soon, but they don't know where. He says not to worry if we don't get any more letters for a while."

"He wrote to all of us," Bess said, "to Mama, and me, and even to Ulysses."

Homer waited a moment for the announcement of the arrival of *his* letter, afraid there might not be such an announcement. At last he said very quietly, "Didn't he send *me* a letter, too?"

"Oh, of course," Bess said. "Yours is the heaviest letter of all. I thought you'd *know* that if he wrote to all of us, he'd write to you, too."

Homer's sister lifted a letter off the table and handed it to him. Homer looked at the letter a long time, and then his sister said, "Well, why don't you open it and read it? Read it to us."

"No, Bess, I've got to go now. I'll take it to the office and read it there tonight when I've got a lot of time."

"We spent the whole day looking for a job," Bess said, "but we didn't find one."

"We had a lot of fun just the same," Mary said. "It was a lot of fun just going in and asking."

"Well, fun or no fun," Homer said, "I'm glad you didn't find a job. I make all the money this family needs, and Mary's father's got a good job at Ithaca Wine. You two don't need to go looking for a job."

"Yes, we do," Bess said. "And one of these days we're going to find one. Two places asked us to come back."

"Never mind finding a job," Homer said. He was angry now. "Any work that has to be done around here, men can do. Girls belong in homes, taking care of men; that's all. Just because there happens to be a war in the world isn't any reason for everybody to

go out of their heads. Just stay home where you belong and help Mama, and you help your father, Mary."

He was so bossy, his sister Bess was almost proud of him, because never before had she seen him so concerned about *anything*.

He went back to the dark dining room.

Bess began to play the piano, and soon Mary began to sing. The messenger stood in the dark room listening, but before the song was half finished, he went quietly out of the house. Now, in the yard, he found Ulysses standing over the hen nest looking down at one egg.

"Egg," Ulysses said as if the word were also the word for God, Himself.

Homer got onto his bicycle and began riding to Ithaca Wine.

31 On the Train

As Homer rode his bicycle, far away an American passenger train moved swiftly through the night. The train was filled with American boys in uniform.

Some of the boys were past forty, even, but most of them were kids—from big cities and little towns, from farms and offices, from rich families and poor families, some taken away from great dreams of achievement and some from humble dreams of peace—kids brilliant and swift in spirit and kids slow and steady. In the midst of the clamor, laughter, excitement, fear, doubt, confusion, eagerness, and the magnificent combination of profound ignorance and profound wisdom, Marcus Macauley and his friend Tobey George talked quietly.

"Well," Tobey said, "I guess we're on our way, at last."

"Most likely," Marcus said.

"I don't know about you, Marcus, but I feel lucky, because if it hadn't been for this War and the Draft, I wouldn't have run into you; and I would never have found out about your family."

Marcus felt embarrassed. "I feel the same way about you." He stopped a moment and then asked the question that every man exposed to unknown danger must ask himself again and again. "I want you to tell me the truth. Are you afraid of being killed?"

The other could not answer the question immediately, but at last he said, "Sure, I am. I *could* bluff, I guess, and *pretend* that I'm not. But I am. Aren't you?"

"Very afraid," Marcus said. "But if you're lucky, what do you want to get back to?"

"I don't know," Tobey said, because he didn't know. "I guess I want to get back to whatever it happens to be. I haven't got a family, as you have. I haven't anybody to go back to, but whatever it is, that'll be OK with me. I haven't got a girl waiting for me like you've got Mary, but I know I want to get back just the same—if I can."

"Right," Marcus said. "How does it happen that you like to sing?"

"How should I know? I just like to sing, that's all." They listened to the train and to the noise inside the train, and then Tobey said, "What do *you* think about?"

Marcus took a little time before trying to answer this question. "Ithaca," he said at last.

"It's a funny thing," Tobey said. "Maybe you won't understand a thing like this, but I feel that Ithaca is *my* home town, too. If we come out of this OK, will you take me to Ithaca?"

"Sure," Marcus said. "And I want you to meet my family. My father was some kind of a great man, I think. I don't mean successful or important or anything like that. He didn't even have a trade or a profession. He just worked for a living. Any kind of a job. He never made any more money than we needed, but I think he was great, just the same."

"Matthew Macauley?" Tobey said.

"He worked in the vineyards, in the packing houses, and in the wineries. Plain, ordinary, everyday work. If you saw him in the street you'd think he was nobody, but he was my father, and I know different. The only thing he cared about was his family—my mother, and his kids. He saved money for months and made a down payment on a harp—think of it, a harp. Nobody plays a harp any more, but that's what my mother wanted. It took him five years to pay for it. It was the most expensive harp you could buy. We used to think every house had a harp just because we had one. Then, he bought a piano for my sister Bess—that didn't cost so much. I thought everybody was like my father—until I got out and met some of the others."

"I wish I knew somebody like that," Tobey said. "He wouldn't have to be *my* father, he could be anybody, just so I *knew* him."

"Maybe your father *was* great."

"Maybe. Want to hear something funny? I didn't know kids had mothers and fathers until I went to school and heard the other kids talk about them. I thought every man was in the world alone—the same as me—to start out all by himself. I guess I felt bad for a long time, after I found out. Maybe *that's* the reason I like to sing. You don't feel so— out of everything—so alone when you're singing." Then shyly, almost timidly, he said, "What kind of a girl is Bess?"

Marcus knew his friend felt uncomfortable about asking the question. "You can ask me about my sister. I'd like you to meet her someday. I think she'll like you."

"Me?" Tobey said.

"Yes, I think she'll like you very much. I'd like you to stay at our house. If you like each other—well, I just think she'll like you very much, that's all."

Now, Marcus began to speak swiftly, because while he knew it was almost impossible to speak of such a thing at all, he also knew it was necessary to *try* to do so, at least. "If it happens that you like her, too—well, what I mean is, marry her and live in Ithaca. It's a good town. You can make a good life there. Now, here. I'm going to give you her picture —to keep." He handed Tobey a little snapshot of his sister. "Keep it in your identification folder where I keep Mary's picture. See?"

Tobey George looked at the snapshot for a long time, while Marcus looked at him. At last he said, "Bess sure is beautiful. I don't know if a guy can fall in love with a girl without meeting her, even, but I feel in love with Bess already. I feel sick. I'll tell you the truth. I was afraid to talk to you about Bess until now. But I figured, well, maybe as long as we're on our way, and there's no telling, you might not mind so much. I can't help it, but I always feel I haven't got the same kind of rights that other people have—you know, a guy who was given his name by an orphanage, not by his mother and father—who doesn't even know who his mother and father are—who doesn't even know what nationality they are—or what nationality *he* is. Some people say I'm Spanish and French, and some people say I'm Italian and Greek,

and some people say I'm English and Irish. Almost everybody gives me a different nationality."

"You're an American," Marcus said. "That's all. Any man can see that. Now keep that picture. We'll go back to Ithaca and you'll raise a family and I'll raise a family, and we'll visit each other once in a while, have some music and songs—pass the time of life."

"You know, Marcus," Tobey said, "I *believe* you. I swear to God I believe you. I don't think you're saying this just because we happen to be friends, on our way. I believe you, and more than anything else in the world I want to go to Ithaca. I want to live there and I want to do all the things you said." He stopped a moment to try to imagine what might go wrong to keep him from doing these things, and then he said, "If Bess doesn't like me—if she falls in love with somebody else—if she's married when we get there— I'm going to live in Ithaca, anyway. I don't know, but Ithaca seems to be *my* home now, too. For the first time in my life I feel that I belong somewhere and—I hope you won't mind—I feel that my family is the Macauley family, because that's the kind of family I'd want for myself if I could choose. I hope to God Bess does like me, or doesn't fall in love with someone else, because I *know* I like *her*." Now, he spoke very softly, and even though the train was full of noise, Marcus could hear the words, "Ithaca's my home. That's where I live. That's where I want to be when I die—if I can."

Now, the friends were greeted by other boys, and they shouted with the others, and even sang a song that several of the boys themselves had invented. And then in the midst of this singing, Tobey said, "At the orphanage, we were *forced* to pray. It was a rule there. Whether we wanted to or not, we prayed."

"That's not such a bad rule," Marcus said,

"but of course prayer is one thing you can't really force."

"I guess that's why I quit praying when I left the orphanage. I don't think I've said a prayer since I was thirteen years old. But I'm starting all over again, as of right now—and this is it." Tobey waited a moment and then, without closing his eyes, without bowing his head, without folding his hands, he began to pray, and what he said was unmistakably a prayer. "Just get me to Ithaca, if You can. Anything You say, but if You can, get me to Ithaca. Let me get home. Protect everybody. Keep everybody out of pain. Find homes for the homeless. Get the traveler safely home and get me to Ithaca. Amen!"

"That's a good prayer," Marcus said. "I hope it's answered."

Now, the soldiers were singing another song. This one had to do with the impermanence of all things, particularly a woman's love, and the boys delighted in the cynical wisdom of the song. Tobey and Marcus joined in the singing, and then suddenly Tobey said, "What do *you* pray for?"

"The same things you pray for—the very same things."

After the song everybody became silent. There was no reason for this silence, and yet every man on the train was suddenly unaccountably hushed. At last a soldier named Joe Higgins came to Marcus and Tobey and said, "What's the matter, what's everybody so quiet about? How about a *real* song, Tobey? How about playing for us on the accordion, Marcus?"

"What would you like to hear?" Marcus said.

"Oh, I don't know. We've sung all the new songs, maybe we ought to sing something old —you know, something *good!* Why don't we sing a good old-time church song—something we all know from when we were kids?"

"What church song do you know, Joe?"

"Well," Joe said. "Now don't you guys laugh. I know *Leaning*. You know—*Leaning on the Everlasting Arms.*"

"Do you know the words of that song, Tobey? If you don't, I can help you."

"Do I *know* them?" Tobey said. "I guess I sang that song almost every Sunday for ten years."

"All right," Marcus said, "let's do it for Joe. If you feel like joining in, Joe, you don't have to know how to sing. Just join in, that's all."

"Oh, I'm going to sing *that* song all right."

Marcus began to play the old hymn, and soon Tobey began to sing:

What a fellowship, what a joy divine,
Leaning on the everlasting arms;
What a blessedness, what a peace is mine,
Leaning on the everlasting arms.

Now, in a strong, unmusical but nevertheless pleasant voice, Joe began to sing with Tobey, and soon everybody in the train was listening. After a moment everybody gathered around Marcus and Tobey and Joe to be nearer the music, as Joe and Tobey sang:

Leaning, leaning, safe and secure from all
*   alarms;*
Leaning, leaning, leaning on the
*   everlasting arms.*

By this time everybody was singing.

32 Marcus

This Saturday was one of the longest and most eventful days of Homer Macauley's life. Little things began to take on fresh importance and to mean something he could understand. The sleep of last night, troubled and full of sorrow, was now forever a part of his wakefulness. He had tried with all his might to keep the messenger of Death from reaching Ithaca and its people. He had dreamed that, but now it was no longer a dream.

The letter from his brother Marcus was in the pocket of his blue messenger's jacket waiting to be opened and read.

He came into the telegraph office, limping, tired and eager to rest. He looked at the call sheet, and there were no calls to take. He looked on the incoming telegram hook, and there were no telegrams to deliver. All was clear. He went to the old telegraph operator and said, "Mr. Grogan, would you like to chip in for two day-old pies—apple and cocoanut cream?"

"I'll chip in, my boy, but I'll not have any of the pies—thanks just the same."

"If *you* don't want any of the pies, Mr. Grogan, I don't want any, either. I thought *you* might be hungry. I'm not hungry at all. I haven't had a chance to take it easy all day, but I'm not hungry. It seems funny. You'd think a fellow would get hungry working all day and all night, but sometimes he doesn't."

"How's your leg?"

"OK, I've forgotten all about it. I get around all right." He looked curiously at the old man and then said very softly, "Are you OK, Mr. Grogan?" He spoke earnestly.

"Yes, I am, my boy." Mr. Grogan went to his chair and sat down. After a moment he looked over at the boy across the table from him, not sitting but standing there. "You're getting around now, seeing a lot of things you never saw before. Well, let me tell you something. Anything that concerns people—be very careful about. If you see something you're sure is wrong, *don't* be sure. If it's people, be very careful. Now, you'll forgive me, but I must tell you, because you're a man I respect, so I don't mind trying to tell you that it's not right to criticize the way *any* people happen to be. As a man gets closer to the end of his time, he feels glad about the people he knows who're going to go on when he's gone. Can you understand what I'm saying?"

"I'm not sure, Mr. Grogan."

"I'm telling you this—be grateful for yourself. Yes, for *yourself*. Be thankful. Understand that what a man is is something he *can* be grateful for, and *ought* to be grateful for. Be thankful that the man you are will be trusted by total strangers. They will know you will not betray them or hurt them. They will know that you will not despise them. That you will see in them what everybody else has failed to see. You must know that about yourself. You must not be embarrassed by it. You are a man, fourteen years old. Who has made you such a man, I don't know; but as it's true, know that it's true, and be gratefull for yourself. Do you understand?"

The messenger gulped. "I guess so, Mr. Grogan."

"Then, I thank you. What's that you're holding—a letter? I have finished. Go ahead. Read your letter, boy."

"From my brother Marcus. I haven't had a chance to open it yet."

"Then, open it. Read the letter from your brother. Read it aloud."

"Aloud?"

"Yes, I'd like to hear it, if I may. Very much."

Homer tore open the envelope, brought out the letter, unfolded it, and began to read, speaking very slowly.

"Dear Homer: First of all, everything of mine at home is yours—to give to Ulysses when you no longer want them: my books, my phonograph, my records, my clothes when you're ready to fit into them, my bicycle, my microscope, my fishing tackle, my collection of rocks from Piedra, and all the other things of mine at home. They're yours because you are now the man of the Macauley family of Ithaca. The money I made last year at the packing house I have given to Ma of course, to help out. It is not nearly enough, though. I don't know how you are going to be able to keep our family together and go to high school at the same time, but I believe you will find a way. My Army pay goes to Ma, except for a few dollars that I must have; but this money is not enough, either. It isn't easy for me to hope for so much from you, when I myself did not begin to work until I was nineteen, but somehow I believe that you will be able to do what I didn't do.

"I miss you, of course, and I think of you all the time. I am OK, and even though I have never believed in wars—and know them to be foolish, even when they are necessary—I am proud that I am involved, since so many others are, and this is what's happening. I do not recognize any enemy who is human, for no human being can be my enemy. Whoever he is, he is my friend. My quarrel is not with *him*, but with that unfortunate part of him that I seek to destroy in myself first.

"I do not feel like a hero. I have no talent for such feelings. I hate no one. I do not feel patriotic either, for I have always loved my country, its people, its towns, my home, and my family. I would rather I were not in the Army. I would rather there were no War. I have no idea what is ahead, but whatever it is I am resigned and ready for it. I am terribly afraid—I must tell *you* this—but I believe that when the time comes I shall do what is right for me. I shall obey no command other than the command of my own heart. With me will be boys from all over America, from thousands of towns like Ithaca. I may be killed, of course. We all know that. I don't like the idea at all. More than anything else in the world I want to come back to Ithaca. I want to come back for Mary and a home and a family of my own. We leave soon—for action, but nobody knows where the action will be. Therefore, this may be my last letter to you for some time. I hope it's not the last of all, but if it is, hold us together. I have told my friend Tobey George about Ithaca and our family. Some day I hope to bring him to Ithaca. I am glad that I am the Macauley who is involved in this War, for it would be a pity and a mistake if it were you.

"I can say in a letter what I could never say in speech. You are the best of the Macauleys. Nothing must stop you. Now I will write your name here, to remind you: Homer Macauley. That's who you are. I miss you. I can't wait to see you again. God bless you. So long. Your brother, Marcus."

While he was reading the letter, the messenger sat down. He read very slowly, gulping and becoming sick many times, as he had become sick in the house of the Mexican mother. Now, he got up. His hands were trembling. He bit the corner of his lower lip and looked over at the old telegraph operator. He spoke very softly. "If my brother is killed in this stupid War, I shall spit at the world. I shall hate it forever."

Tears came to his eyes. He hurried to the locker behind the repeater rack, took off his uniform and got into his regular clothes. He was running out of the office almost before his clothes had been properly arranged.

The old telegraph operator sat a long time. It was very quiet when he shook himself at last, got up, and looked around the office.

33 At the Church

The pattern of life in Ithaca—of people everywhere in the world, for that matter—followed a design that at first seemed senseless and perhaps even crazy, but as the days and nights gathered together as months and years, the pattern was seen to have had some semblance of form and meaning.

Many times the telegraph box rattled, and Mr. Grogan sat at the typewriter and tapped out a message of love or hope, or pain, or death from the world to its children. "I am coming home." "Happy birthday." "The Department of War regrets to inform you that your son is dead." "Meet me at the Southern Pacific Depot." "Here is a kiss." "I am all right." "God bless you." Many times Homer Macauley delivered the messages.

In the parlor of the Macauley house, the strings of the harp were plucked and the message of song was heard. The soldiers moved on, over land, over water, through the air, under the water, into new places, new days, new nights, new sleep, and new and strange moments filled with incredible noises and dangers. The faces of the living changed, but imperceptibly—Marcus, Tobey, Homer, Spangler, Grogan, Mrs. Macauley, Ulysses, Diana, Auggie, Lionel, Bess, Mary, Rosalie Simms-Peabody, Mr. Ara, his son John, Big Chris, Miss Hicks, and even Mr. Mechano.

The freight train with the black man leaning over the side of the gondola moved on. The gopher peeked out of the earth. The apricots of Mr. Henderson's tree took on the smiling color of the sun and the freckles of the boys who came to steal them. The brooding hen came forth with her nation of chicks. Ulysses watched. The limp in Homer's leg healed. Easter Sunday came to Ithaca. And then the Sunday after Easter. And then another Sunday, and then another, and another, and another.

All of the Macauleys of Ithaca sat with Mary Arena on *this* Sunday in the First Ithaca Presbyterian Church. Ulysses sat on the aisle. Directly in front of him, by religious accident, sat a man with a bald head. This living ball which was the better part of a man was fascinating for Ulysses to behold: the shape alone was something to study, being not unlike the shape of the egg. The half dozen hairs of the head, growing in a lonely group, were unashamed and heroic. The wrinkle that divided the head as the equator divides the earth was a miracle of design.

Now, Reverend Holly and the congregation were engaged in a pious oral duel—on the theme of the Blessed Life. First, Reverend Holly read a verse, then, the congregation answered in one voice.

"And seeing the multitudes," Reverend Holly said, "He went up into a mountain, and when He was seated, His disciples came unto Him.

"And He opened His mouth," the congregation replied, *"and taught them, saying:*

"Blessed are the poor: for theirs is the kingdom of heaven.

"Blessed are they that mourn: for they shall be comforted.

"Blessed are the meek: for they shall inherit the earth.

"Blessed are they which do hunger and thirst after righteousness: for they shall be filled.

"Blessed are the merciful: for they shall obtain mercy.

"Blessed are the pure in heart: for they shall see God.

"Blessed are the peacemakers: for they shall be called the children of God.

"Rejoice, and be exceeding glad: Ye are the salt of the earth. Ye are the light of the world.

"Let your light so shine before men that they may see your good works and glorify your Father which is in heaven."

The responsive reading had begun while Ulysses was studying the bald head. Suddenly this object was decorated by a fly that began to explore the head, apparently looking for something recently lost. Ulysses watched the fly, and then reached out to catch it, but Mrs. Macauley took his hand and held it. Staring steadily at the bald head and the fly, thinking of nothing in particular, and then falling away into a daydream, Ulysses now saw the smooth skin of the head as a desert. He saw the wrinkle across the head as a stream, the group of seven hairs as palm trees, and the fly as a lion. Then he saw himself, in his Sunday clothes, on one side of the stream, with the lion on the other. He stood on the bank of the stream looking across at the lion, which in turn came directly opposite to look at *him.* The Scripture reading continued.

In the distance Ulysses saw an Arab, in flowing robes, lying asleep upon the sand. Beside the Arab was a mandolin, or some such musical instrument, and a pitcher of water. Ulysses saw the lion, in a peace and innocence not unlike the sleeping man's, move to the man's head and bend down to smell the man, but not to harm him. As a matter of fact, he had seen the picture in one of the books Lionel had opened at the public library.

The Scripture reading ended. The church organ breathed deeply, and the choir and the congregation began to sing a song in which Ulysses heard the words, "And he walks with me and he talks with me." The lion in the desert, of course. And then *Rock of Ages.*

The vision of the lion walking and talking in the desert vanished from the little boy's dream. In its place appeared an ocean. Clinging to a rock that rose several feet above the surface of this desolation of water was Ulysses himself. Only his head and hands were above water. He looked around for escape or rescue, but all that he could see was water. Even so, he was patient and full of faith. At last, far in the distance, walking on the water, Ulysses saw the great man, Big Chris. Big Chris came to Ulysses and without a word reached down to him, took him by the hand and lifted him out of the water onto the surface of it. After a moment, however, Ulysses fell back into the water, splashing, and once again Big Chris fished him out and set him on his feet. Holding the boy's hand, Big Chris went walking upon the water with Ulysses. Far away, the towers of a great white city became visible and around the city, earth and vegetation. The man and the boy walked toward the city.

The song ended. Suddenly somebody was shaking Ulysses. He woke with a start. It was Lionel—with a collection plate. Ulysses found his nickel, placed it in the plate, and passed the plate to his mother.

Lionel whispered to Ulysses, speaking with an air of piety and mystery. "Are you saved, Ulysses?"

"What?"

"Read this," Lionel said, and handed his friend a religious pamphlet.

Ulysses studied the pamphlet, but of course couldn't read the big letters that formed the following words: "Are you saved? It is never too late."

On the other side of the aisle, Lionel asked an elderly gentleman the same question. "Are you saved?"

The man looked at the boy severely and then whispered, "Go along, boy."

Before going, however, and somewhat in the manner of a missionary despised by an African tribal chief, Lionel offered the elderly gentleman one of the pamphlets. The elderly gentleman, irritated, grabbed the pamphlet out of Lionel's hands.

The elderly gentleman's wife whispered, "What is it, dear?"

"The boy asked me if I was saved. Then, he offered me *this*." The man handed the pamphlet to his wife who patted his hand and said, "How should the boy know you've been a missionary in China for thirty years?"

All during the ritual of taking collection, the organ played softly and a soprano sang. Lionel, Auggie, Shag, and a number of the other boys of Ithaca stood at the back of the center aisle, each holding a collection plate, until the music ended. Then, in ritualistic silence and earnestness the boys marched down the aisle to the table directly beneath the pulpit, where they put the collection plates one on top of the other, and then returned to their places beside their parents.

34 The Lion in the Net

After church and Sunday dinner, August Gottlieb was in his front yard patching an old tennis net into something he hoped might turn out to be useful. Enoch Hopper, a boy of Auggie's age, came by swiftly, stopped swiftly, and watched swiftly. He was the owner of an old baseball with the cover gone, which he slammed onto the sidewalk fiercely, making it bounce very high. He caught the ball and slammed it again. Enoch Hopper was the most high-strung boy in Ithaca, the most restless, the swiftest-moving, the most impatient, and the loudest-talking.

"What are you making, Auggie?"

"Net."

"What for? Fish?"

"No, animals."

Already Enoch was bored. "Come on, let's start a baseball game or go out to Guggenheim's water tank and climb it."

"Got to fix the net."

"Ah, what've you got to fix the net for?"

"Catch animals."

"Where do you see any animals around here? Come on, let's go. Let's go out to Malaga and go swimming."

"I'll catch animals in this net all right."

"Couldn't catch a *flea* with that tennis net. Come on, let's start a game. Let's go down and sneak into the Bijou, see a Tarzan picture."

"I'll catch a dog first, just to see how it works. And then, watch out!"

"Ah, that's an old tennis net, Auggie. You won't catch anything. Let's go down to the courthouse park, to the city jail there and talk to the prisoners."

"I've got to fix my animal net," Auggie said. "I'm only going to try it out today—and then oh, boy—tomorrow!"

"Oh, boy, *what?*" Enoch said. "There's no animals around here. A cow. A couple of dogs. Six or seven rabbits. A few chickens— what are you going to catch?"

"I got a good net here. Big enough for a bear."

"You couldn't catch a teddy-bear with that net. Let's go down to Chinatown and walk down China Alley."

August Gottlieb interrupted his work a moment to think about Chinatown and the Chinese. He looked up at Enoch Hopper and said, "You afraid of the Chinese?"

"Naaah," Enoch said truthfully. "I ain't afraid of nobody. Even if they were dangerous they couldn't catch *me*. Too fast on my feet."

"I bet a lion could catch you."

"Naah. I'm too fast. A lion couldn't get anywhere near me. Bears, tigers, Chinese—

I'm too fast for 'em. Come on, let's go over across the South Pacific tracks and get into a game with the Cosmos Playground gang."

"A trap could catch you."

"No trap in the world fast enough to catch me. Let's go out to the fair grounds and run around the mile track. I'll give you a hundred yards headstart."

"Your own father could catch you."

"Naah, couldn't come anywhere near me. I'd leave him in the dust."

Now, Lionel came along from his house. "What are you making, Auggie?"

"Net, to catch animals."

"Couldn't catch a flea with that net," Enoch said. "Come on, let's go out on the empty lot and play catch."

"*Me?*" Lionel said.

"Sure, Lionel. Come on. You throw 'em to me real hard. I'll throw 'em to you real easy. Come on, half the afternoon's gone."

"All right, Enoch," Lionel said, "but remember—throw 'em easy. I ain't so good at catch. Sometimes I miss and the ball hits me in the face. Hurt my eyes once, my nose twice."

"I'll throw 'em easy. Don't worry. Come on."

Enoch Hopper and Lionel Cabot moved across the street to the empty lot, and Auggie went ahead with his work. Soon he had all of the pieces of the old tennis net tied together, so that there was an almost square piece of netting. He stretched this netting out and attached each corner to a stick in the ground so that he could behold what he had made. Now, Shag Manoogian came over the backyard fence. "What's that?"

"Net, to catch animals. Want to help me try it out?"

"Sure. How does it work?"

"Well," Auggie said, "I'll hold the net and hide here behind Ara's store. You call Enoch. He's over there playing catch with Lionel.

Enoch is swifter and harder to catch than a lion. If this net can hold Enoch, it can hold anything. All right. I'm hiding. Call Enoch. Tell him you want to ask him something. I'm ready."

"OK," Shag said. He looked over at Enoch on the empty lot and then called out, "Enoch! Oh, Enoch!"

Enoch Hopper turned and shouted back, twice as loud, "What do you want, Shag?"

"Come here. I want to ask you something."

"What do you want to ask me?"

"I'll tell you when you get here."

"OK." Enoch began to run toward Shag, while Lionel followed, not quite sure whether he should run or walk.

"All right, Shag," Auggie whispered. "Duck back here and hide with me. Take hold of this end of the net. When he comes around the corner of the store, we'll jump on him and capture him. See?"

Running swiftly, Enoch shouted, "Let's go out to Malaga and swim. Half the afternoon's gone already. Let's do something. What are we waiting for?"

He came running around the corner of Mr. Ara's market. Auggie and Shag leaped out swiftly and spread the net over him. Sure enough, Enoch Hopper moved like an undomesticated animal, perhaps a lion. The two big-game hunters worked furiously, but the net wasn't quite strong enough, and soon Enoch Hopper was standing upright, completely unoffended by the unsuccessful experiment.

He slammed the baseball on the sidewalk. "Come on, Auggie, let's go! That net couldn't catch a flea! Come on! What are we waiting for?"

"OK," Auggie said, and threw the net into the yard. "Let's go to the courthouse park and talk to the prisoners."

Auggie, Enoch, Shag, and Lionel moved on down the street toward the courthouse park.

Soon Enoch Hopper was a block ahead of the others, shouting back at them, "Come on! What are you guys moving so slow for?" He slammed the baseball on the sidewalk.

35 Spangler

Thomas Spangler and Diana Steed were in the country for a Sunday afternoon drive around Kingsburg. The car was an old red roadster with the top down.

"Those," he said, pointing to a row of trees bordering a vineyard, "are fig trees. The vines beyond them are Muscat vines. There's some olive trees. That tree's a pomegranate. Those vines over there are Malaga vines. There's an orchard of peach trees. These are apricots. There's a walnut tree. There's a tree you don't see very often—persimmon. *Everything* grows in this valley."

"Oh, darling," Diana said, "you do love trees, don't you?"

"Yes, I do, and we're going to have ourselves at least two of each on our own little place, so the kids can climb them and take fruit off of them, and eat the fruit."

"Oh, darling, you are happy, aren't you?"

"Never been happier."

He put his arm around her. "I can't wait to see who it is. I'd like it to be a little girl. I'd like to hear the voice of a little girl like that. I used to think you were scatterbrained. Well, anybody who can do *that* can't be scatterbrained. And you *can* do it."

"Of course I can," Diana said. "It's perfectly natural, darling."

The little automobile moved along parallel with Kings River near the picnic grounds. On this Sunday afternoon five big picnics were going on—with music and dancing—Italians, Greeks, Serbs, Armenians, and Americans. Each group had its own kind of music and dancing. Spangler stopped the automobile at each group for a moment in order to be able to listen to the singing and to watch the dancing. "Those are Greeks over there. I used to know a family of Greeks. That's the way they dance in the old country."

The car moved on a short distance and stopped again. "Those people over there are the Armenians. I can tell from the bearded priests and the lively kids. That's what they believe in—God and kids." The car moved on and stopped near another group. "Those people are Slovenians and Serbs, and maybe a few other people from around in there."

The car moved a short distance and then stopped again. "Italians. Corbett himself is probably over there somewhere with his wife and kids."

Now, the automobile came to the last group. The music was loud swing, jive, and boogie-woogie, and the dancing was wild. "Americans! Greeks, Serbs, Poles, Russians, Mexicans, Armenians, Germans, blacks, Swedes, Spaniards, Basques, Portuguese, Italians, Jews, French, English, Scotch, Irish. You name it. That's who we are."

They looked and listened, and then the automobile slowly moved away.

36 Ithaca

The afternoon Santa Fe passenger train from San Francisco stopped at Ithaca and nine people got off, among them two young soldiers. But before the train moved on, a third soldier, with a limp in his left leg, got off and walked away, moving slowly.

The first soldier looked at his friend and said, "Well, brother, this is Ithaca. This is home."

"Boy, let me look at it," the second soldier said. "Just let me look at it." Now he hummed the delight he felt. "Ummmmmmm-man! My home, Ithaca! I don't know how *you* feel, but *this* is how I feel." He got down on his knees and began to kiss the brick of the walk again and again, like a Moslem bowing to Mecca.[8]

---

8. **Mecca** (mek'ə): the holy city for Moslems; the birthplace of Mohammed.

"Come on, man. People are looking. You want them to think soldiers are crazy?"

"No, I don't, but I can't help it. Boy, my Ithaca!" He got up at last and took his friend by the arm.

At length the two boys came up the street where Mr. Ara had his market. Suddenly they began to run, one boy running up onto the porch of one house and the other up onto the porch of the house next door. Alf Rife came running around one house and stood on the front lawn between the two houses, watching. The front door of each house opened at the same time. The women who opened the doors embraced the boys at the same time. And now men and boys and girls and women took turns embracing the soldiers. But there seemed to be a mistake. Alf Rife discovered the mistake and began shouting at the top of his voice.

"Wrong boy," he shouted, "wrong boy! It's Danny Booth, the neighbor's boy! He's come home. He lives next door. Came to the wrong house. We thought it was *our* boy. It's Mrs. Booth's boy. There's our boy over there kissing Mrs. Booth. Wrong boy, Ma, wrong boy!"

"Oh, hello, Danny," Mrs. Rife said to Danny Booth. "We thought you were Harry."

"Oh, that's all right, Mrs. Rife," Danny said. "I'll go over and kiss Ma, too. You come over, too."

On the porch of the other house Harry Rife said, "Hello, Mrs. Booth. Come on over to our house, *all* of you. It sure is good to see you, Mrs. Booth." He kissed her again. "Danny's over on my porch kissing my mother."

Now, the lawns of both houses filled with people going and coming in a kind of happy delirium, while Alf Rife shouted over and over again, "Wrong boy, wrong boy! He came to the wrong house! He lives next door. Hey, Harry—*here's* Ma! That's Mrs. Booth! Wrong house, Harry!"

37 The Horseshoe Pitchers

Homer Macauley, his sister Bess, his brother Ulysses, and their friend Mary Arena on a Sunday afternoon walk came to a lot of people standing in front of the Kinema Theatre, and among them Homer discovered Lionel.

"Going to see a movie?" he said.

"Haven't got any money," Lionel said.

"Then, what are you standing in line for?"

"Me and Auggie and Shag and Enoch," Lionel said, "we came to the courthouse park to talk to the criminals. Then, they chased me away. I didn't know where to go. I saw these people standing here, so I came and stood with them."

"How long have you been standing here?"

"About an hour, I guess."

"Well," Homer said, "do you *want* to see the movie?" He brought some money out of his pocket.

"I don't know," Lionel said. "I didn't have any place to go. I don't like movies very much."

"Well, come with us, then. We're only taking a walk, window-shopping. We'll walk around town awhile and then go home. Come on, Lionel." He lifted the rope and Lionel got out of the line.

"Thanks," Lionel said. "I sure was getting tired standing there that way."

As they walked, Ulysses stopped suddenly and tugged at Homer's hand. He pointed down at the sidewalk. There before the boy was a Lincoln penny, face up.

"A penny!" Homer said. "Pick it up, Ulysses, it's good luck. Keep it—always!"

Ulysses picked up the penny and looked around at everybody, smiling at his good luck.

They passed the telegraph office from across the street, and Homer stopped to look.

"That's where I work," he said. "That's where I've worked almost six months now." He stopped a moment, and then, as if talking to himself, he said, "It seems more like a hundred years." He looked far into the office and then said, "I think that's Mr. Grogan. I didn't know Mr. Grogan was working today." He turned to the others. "Wait here a minute, will you? I'll be right back."

He crossed the street and hurried into the office. The telegraph box in front of Mr. Grogan was rattling, but the old telegraph operator was not taking down the telegram that was being dispatched. Homer ran up to him and said, "Mr. Grogan, Mr. Grogan!" But the old man didn't wake up.

The messenger ran out of the office and across the street to the others. "Mr. Grogan's not feeling good. I've got to go back and take care of him. You go home. I'll be along after a while."

"All right, Homer," Bess said.

"What's the matter with him?" Lionel said, not even knowing who it was he was talking about.

"I've got to hurry back," Homer said. "Now go along. He's an old man, Lionel, that's all."

Homer hurried back to the telegraph office and shook Mr. Grogan several times. He ran over to the water jar and filled a paper cup, then splashed the water into the face of the old man. Mr. Grogan opened his eyes. "It's me, Mr. Grogan. I didn't know you were working today, or I would have come down long ago, like I always do when you work on Sundays. I was just passing by. I'll hurry and get the coffee."

The old telegraph operator shook his head, reached out to the telegraph key and interrupted the telegrapher at the other end. He put a telegram blank into the typewriter and began to type a message.

Homer ran out of the office to Corbett's on the corner and asked for coffee.

"He's making fresh coffee now," Pete, the bartender said. "Be a minute or two, Homer."

"Hasn't he got any, at all?"

"Fresh out. He's cooking a new pot now."

"It's very important. I'll go back to the office a minute and then I'll come back here. Maybe by that time the coffee'll be ready."

When Homer got back to Mr. Grogan, the old telegraph operator wasn't typing the telegram that was coming over the wire. Again Homer shook him. "Mr. Grogan, they're sending a telegram! They're making fresh coffee at Corbett's. I'll have a cup here for you in a minute or two. Stop them, Mr. Grogan! You're not getting the telegram."

Homer turned and ran out of the office.

The old telegraph operator looked at the telegram he had been typing, and read again what he had typed so far:

MRS. KATE MACAULEY
2226 SANTA CLARA AVENUE
ITHACA, CALIFORNIA

THE DEPARTMENT OF WAR REGRETS TO IN-
FORM YOU THAT YOUR SON MARCUS . . .

He tried to get up from his chair, but the attack came again and he clutched at his collar. After a moment he fell forward to rest upon the typewriter.

Homer Macauley came walking into the telegraph office as fast he could with a cup of hot coffee rattling in his hand. He came up to the old man and set the cup down on the table. Now, the telegraph box stopped its rattling and the whole office became very quiet.

"Mr. Grogan!" Homer said. "What's the matter?" He moved the old man back, away from the typewriter, to look into his face, and as he did so, he noticed the incomplete telegram in the typewriter. He read the words of the telegram, but refused to believe them. He stood as if paralyzed, holding the old man. "Mr. Grogan!" he said.

Felix, the Sunday messenger, came in and looked at the old man, and at the messenger. "What's the matter, Homer? What's wrong with the old man?"

"He's dead," Homer said.

"Ah, you're crazy," Felix said.

"No," Homer said. "He's dead. And maybe I am, too."

"I'll call Mr. Spangler," Felix said. He dialed a number on the telephone, waited, and then hung up. "He's not home. What are we going to do?" He went over to see what it was that Homer was staring at in the typewriter. After reading the telegram, Felix said, "It's not finished, Homer. Maybe your brother is only hurt or missing."

Homer looked at Mr. Grogan and then said, "No, *he* heard the rest of the telegram. He didn't type it out, because he *heard* it."

"Maybe he didn't," Felix said. "I'll tele-phone Mr. Spangler again. Maybe he's home now."

Homer Macauley looked around the telegraph office. Suddenly he spat, and then sat down, as if in a trance, looking straight ahead. There were no tears in his eyes.

Thomas Spangler drew up in his automobile in front of the telegraph office after the drive in the country. He sounded the horn and Felix ran out.

"Mr. Spangler," Felix said, "I've been trying to get you on the phone. Something's happened! It's Mr. Grogan! Homer says he's dead!"

"You go on home," Spangler said to Diana. "I'll be around later—but don't expect me for supper. Maybe you'd better go out and spend the night with your folks." He got out of the car and kissed her on the cheek.

Spangler hurried into the office. He looked at Mr. Grogan and then at Homer. "Felix, phone Dr. Nelson—1133. Tell him to come right down."

Spangler lifted the old man out of the chair and carried him to the couch at the back of the office. He came back and looked at Homer. "Don't feel bad, Homer. He was an old man. This is the way he wanted it to be. Come on, now, don't feel bad."

Now, the telegraph box rattled and Spangler went to answer the call. When he sat down in Mr. Grogan's chair, he saw the unfinished telegram. He looked at it a long time, and then he looked across the table at Homer. Spangler telegraphed the operator at the other end, asking questions about the unfinished telegram. The telegrapher at the other end tapped out the full message again. Spangler asked the other operator to postpone any more telegrams for a while. He then got up and went to his desk and sat down, looking at nothing. His hand fell idly on the hard-boiled egg which he kept for good luck. Without knowing what he was doing, he tapped the egg on the desk until the shell broke, and then slowly he removed all of the shell, looked at the peeled egg, and dropped it in the wastebasket.

"Felix," he said, "call Harry Burke, the day operator, 4241, and tell him to come right down. When the doctor comes, tell him to take care of everything. I'll talk to him later."

Homer Macauley got up, went to the typewriter and took the unfinished telegram out of it. He filed the carbon copy of the unfinished telegram in its proper place, folded the original and put it into an envelope. He put the envelope into his coat pocket. Spangler went to the messenger and put his arm around him. "Come on, Homer, let's go for a walk."

They left the telegraph office and walked two blocks in silence. At last Homer began to speak. "What's a man supposed to do? I don't know who to hate. I don't know what to do. How does a man go on living? Who does he love?"

Now, coming down the street toward them, Homer and Spangler saw Auggie, Enoch, Shag, and Nickie. The boys greeted Homer, and he greeted each of them by name. It was almost evening now. The sun was going down, the sky was red, and the city was darkening.

"Who can you hate?" Homer said. "Byfield knocked me down when I was running the low hurdles, but I can't hate *him*, even. That's just the way he happens to be. Who does it? I can't figure it out at all, but the only thing I want to know is, What about my brother? When my father died, it was different. He had lived a good life. He had raised a good family. We were sad because he was dead, but we weren't mad. Now I'm mad, and I haven't got anybody to be mad at. Who's the enemy? Do you know, Mr. Spangler?"

It was some time before the manager of the telegraph office decided that since there was

really nothing to say, it might be all right to try telling lies. "Well, I don't think the enemy is people," he said. "If people hate one another, it is themselves they hate. A man cannot hate others—it is always only himself. And if a man hates himself, there is only one thing for him to do—leave—leave his body, leave the world, leave the people of the world. Your brother didn't want to leave, he wanted to stay. He *will* stay."

"How?" Homer said. "How will he stay?"

"I don't know how," Spangler said, "but I've got to believe that he will stay."

"No," Homer said. "My brother's dead. He's dead, and all the rest of us aren't."

Now, they were walking through the courthouse park, past the city jail, to where horseshoes were being pitched.

Spangler knew he had failed, but he decided to try again, to keep trying—lies, truth, anything. "I'm not going to try to comfort you," he said. "I know I can't. Nothing can. But try to remember that a good man can never die. You will see your brother many times again—in the streets, at home, in all the places of the town. The person of a man may go, but the best part of him stays. It stays forever." But he knew it was useless, and he was embarrassed. "Are you any good at pitching horseshoes?" he said.

"No, sir," Homer said.

"Neither am I," Spangler said. "Would you care to pitch a game before it's too dark?"

"Yes, sir," Homer said.

38 The House

The limping soldier who got off the train that brought Danny Booth and Harry Rife home to Ithaca, began to walk around the town. He walked slowly, looking at everything, and talking to himself.

"There's the depot—the Santa Fé. There's the Kinema Theatre. The Public Library. The Presbyterian Church. There's Santa Clara Avenue. Ara's Market. And there's the house!"

The soldier stood staring at the house a long time. Then he moved on. "There's the courthouse park. The city jail with the prisoners at the windows. And two Ithaca men pitching horseshoes." The soldier walked slowly to the two men and leaned against the low picket fence.

Homer Macauley and Thomas Spangler pitched horseshoes in silence, not even counting points. It was too dark now for the game, but they went on pitching. Homer was a little startled when he noticed the soldier leaning on the fence. For an instant he thought it might actually be Marcus. He went

to the soldier and said, "Would you care to *pitch* a game?"

"No, thanks," the soldier said, "You go ahead. I'll just watch."

"I don't think I've ever seen you before. Is Ithaca your home?"

"Yes, it is."

"Are you on furlough?"

"No, they've sent me home—for good. I got off the train a couple of hours ago. I've been walking around the town, looking at everything again."

"Why don't you go home? Don't you want your family to know you're here?"

"More than anything in the world, but I think I'd better go home little by little. I want to see as much as I can, first. I can't believe I'm here. I'll walk around some more, and *then* I'll go home."

The soldier went off slowly, and Homer noticed his limp.

"I don't feel like pitching any more, Mr. Spangler; thanks very much." And then after a moment, "They're waiting for me at home. I told them I'd be home for supper. How am I going to go into the house and look at them? They'll know Marcus is dead the minute they see me."

"Wait," Spangler said. "Don't go home just yet. Sit down here. Wait awhile."

They sat quietly on a park bench, not talking. After a while Homer said, "What am I waiting for?"

"Well," Spangler said, not knowing for sure whether he was lying or telling the truth, "you're waiting for the part of *him* that died to die in you, too—the part that's only flesh —the part that comes and goes. That dying is hurting you now, but wait awhile. When the pain becomes total, becomes death itself, it will leave you. It takes a little time. Be patient with it; you will go home at last with no death in you. Give it time to go. I'll sit with you here until it's gone."

Now, from the Macauley house came the music of piano and harp and singing.

The young man sitting on the steps of the front porch, the soldier who had come home to a town he had never before seen, to a house he had never entered, to a family he had never known—listened with fear, doubt, and disbelief. What right had he to be there? And yet he knew that he *was* home. Ithaca *was* the place of his birth. This house *was* the house he grew up in. The family inside the house *was* his family.

Suddenly Ulysses Macauley was standing at the open front door, pointing. His sister Bess went over to see what it was. She turned to her mother. "Somebody's sitting on our front-porch steps."

"Well," Mrs. Macauley said, "ask him in, Bess, whoever he is."

Bess went out onto the porch. "My mother would like you to come in," she said.

The soldier turned slowly and looked up at the girl. He spoke very quietly. "Bess?" he said. "My legs are trembling, and if I try to stand, I'll fall. Please sit beside me."

The girl sat down beside the young man. "How do you know my name? Who are you?"

"I only know who *you* are, and who your mother is, and who your brothers are. Sit close beside me, Bess—until I quiet down inside."

"Do you know my brother, Marcus?"

"Yes, better than I know anybody else in the world. Yes, I know him."

"Where is Marcus?"

The soldier handed the girl a ring. "Your brother Marcus asked me to bring this to you."

Bess Macauley didn't speak for some time, and then she said, "Is Marcus dead?" Her voice was hushed, not excited.

Homer Macauley came walking down the street. Bess ran out to meet him. When they reached the soldier, she said, "He's come from Marcus. They were friends," and then she ran into the house.

"Tobey?" Homer said. "I thought I knew you when we talked in the park." He waited a moment, and then said, "The telegram came this afternoon. I have it in my pocket. What are we going to do?"

"Tear it up, Homer."

Homer brought the telegram out of his pocket and tore it up, but he put the small pieces back into his pocket—to keep, forever. "Let's go in."

Homer leaned down, and the soldier took his hands and slowly got to his feet.

Inside the house, incredibly, the music began again—piano, harp, and the voices of three women.

"Let me stand here a moment and listen," the soldier said.

Ulysses came out of the house and took the soldier by the hand. When the song ended, Mrs. Macauley and Bess and Mary Arena came to the open door. The mother stood and looked at her two sons, one on each side of the stranger, the soldier who had known her son who was now dead. Sick to death, she nevertheless smiled at the soldier, and said, "Won't you please come in and let us show you around the house?"

Chapters 24–38

Getting at Meaning

1. Why do the boys steal apricots from Mr. Henderson's tree? Which two children are not really a part of the group? Why? How does Mr. Henderson feel about the raid on his tree? How does he add to the sense of adventure felt by the boys?

2. What foods does John Ara request from his father? What does John do each time he gets what he wants? What does his father do? How does John's attitude toward the pieces of fruit contrast with the gang's attitude toward the one hard, green apricot?

3. Why does the customer in Mr. Ara's store want only "cookies, raisins in"? Why does Mr. Ara offer him a bag of fruit at no charge? Why does the customer refuse the gift? What does Mr. Ara mean when he tells the customer, "You go try chain store—but they no got cookies, raisins in. Nobody got"?

4. How is Mrs. Macauley's speech to Homer in Chapter 26 similar to Spangler's speech to John Strickman in Chapter 22?

5. How does Mrs. Macauley contrast her sons in Chapter 27?

6. Why is Lionel in awe of the library? What is the librarian's first reaction to Lionel and Ulysses? How does her manner toward them soften? What does she mean when she says, "I've been reading books for the past sixty years, and I can't see as how it's made any great difference"?

7. How is the appearance of Mrs. Rosalie Simms-Pibity different from Homer's expectations? Why do you think Homer was told to deliver the telegram to her personally on the platform? Why is the experience painful, ridiculous, and confusing to Homer?

8. Exactly what is Mr. Mechano? What makes him so fascinating to Ulysses? What fear does Ulysses experience for the first time?

9. How are the backgrounds of Marcus and Tobey different? Why is Tobey so interested in the Macauley family and in Ithaca? What plans do Marcus and Tobey make on the train?

10. What feelings does Marcus express in his letter to Homer? What responsibilities does he place on Homer? Why does Homer choose to read the letter at the telegraph office?

11. The passage of time is described at the beginning of Chapter 33. What incidents from preceding chapters are recalled in these paragraphs?

12. Who plays with Enoch while Auggie is fixing his net? How does Enoch react to Auggie's trick? What does Auggie do when his net fails to work?

13. What does the reader learn about Spangler and Diana Steed in Chapter 35?

14. Chapter 36 describes the homecoming of two soldiers. What mix-up occurs? How does this mix-up set the stage for Tobey's appearance at the Macauley house?

15. How does Mr. Grogan die? What does Spangler mean when he says, "This is the way he wanted it to be"?

16. Why does Spangler break his egg? How does he comfort Homer after the boy learns of his brother's death?

17. Why does Tobey say that he wants to "go home little by little"? How will he be able to become part of the Macauley household? How will Marcus continue to live?

Developing Skills in Reading Literature

1. **Mood.** The Macauley family is identified by the various musical instruments that they play; Mrs. Macauley plays the harp, Bess, the piano, and Marcus, the accordian. Homer sings, as does Tobey. The Macauley house is often filled with music. What kind of feeling does the music evoke in the reader? How does the feeling tie in with the feelings of the family members toward one another?

2. **Allusion.** The epic poem *The Odyssey*, at-

tributed to the poet Homer, recounts the adventures of Odysseus as he returns to his native land of Ithaca after fighting in the Trojan War. Odysseus, whose Latin name is Ulysses, travels for ten years on a wandering journey filled with hardship and adventure, before finally arriving at Ithaca. In the novel, who is the wanderer who arrives safely home? What is the connection between the character Homer and the poet of the same name? between the character Ulysses and the Greek adventurer? What do the classical allusions add to the novel?

3. **Theme.** The writer of this novel presents truths about human beings and about life and death. The following quotations relate to the themes of the novel. Explain the meaning of each quotation and identify the related theme, or message.

a. "Going home, boy—going back where I belong!" (black man, Chapter 1)

b. "There it was, all around him, funny and lonely—the world of his life. The strange, weed-infested, junky, wonderful, senseless yet beautiful world." (Chapter 1)

c. "The loneliness you feel has come to you because you are no longer a child." (Mrs. Macauley, Chapter 7)

d. "I wanted him to know that each of you will begin to be truly human when, in spite of your natural dislike of one another, you still respect one another. That is what it means to be civilized. . . ." (Miss Hicks, Chapter 12)

e. "I guess we ought to have some fun out of being alive." (Homer, Chapter 21)

f. "I thought a fellow would never cry when he got to be grown up, but it seems as if that's when a fellow *starts*, because that's when a fellow starts finding out about things." (Homer, Chapter 26)

g. "Each man finds out for himself, in his own way, because each man *is* the world." (Mrs. Macauley, Chapter 26)

h. ". . . a good man can never die. . . . The person of a man may go, but the best part of him stays." (Spangler, Chapter 37)

Developing Vocabulary

Words from Latin. Some Latin words have been incorporated into English without any change in their forms. The italicized words in the following sentences are examples of such words. Look up each word or phrase in a dictionary and record its definition.

1. Because she had bought the car through a *bona fide* business transaction, she was convinced that the dealer would honor the warranty.

2. I like my employer and *vice versa*.

3. John knew that he had to weed the garden, cut the lawn, trim the hedge, *et cetera*.

4. Because the drug was found to be dangerous, the company issued a *caveat* to all physicians.

5. We traveled to San Francisco *via* the Grand Canyon.

6. The campaign had been so successful that the company issued each employee a *bonus*.

Developing Writing Skills

1. **Analyzing Plot.** In Chapters 17 and 18 the writer interweaves several lines of action, all happening at about the same time. These lines of action might be summarized as follows:

Spangler and Diana dine with the Steeds, go to the Kinema, then leave the theater.

Bess and Mary meet three soldiers, go to the telegraph office, then go to the Kinema.

Homer returns to the telegraph office to find a death telegram; he talks with Mr. Grogan, then leaves the office.

Marcus and Tobey discuss Ithaca in a bar in North Carolina.

How does the weather unite the first three lines of action? How do all four lines of action relate to one another? How does the placement of each event add meaning to these chapters?

Choose one or two other chapters that have a similar convergence of events, and summarize the lines of action. Then write a paragraph explaining why the writer might have chosen to interweave these particular events.

2. **Analyzing Character.** Choose your favorite character, major or minor, and write a five-paragraph composition that explains in detail one quality the character possesses. Be sure to include specific examples from the novel in the body paragraphs.

Handbook of Literary Terms

Allegory. An allegory is a literary work that has a hidden meaning beneath the literal meaning of the story, poem, or play. Allegory usually relies heavily on symbolism to teach a lesson or to explain an idea. For example, the Bible recounts the story of Jacob who dreams that the sun and the moon and eleven stars bow down before him. The sun, moon, and stars symbolize his father, mother, and brothers. The allegorical meaning of the dream is that his family will come to him and beg for help.

The characters in an allegory often stand for abstract ideas or concepts. Sometimes the representation is obvious, as in certain medieval plays in which the characters are given names such as Patience, Purity, and Greed.

See *Fable, Parable*.

Alliteration. Alliteration is the repetition of consonant sounds at the beginnings of words. Alliteration occurs in both prose and poetry, as well as in everyday speech. The English language is filled with alliterative phrases such as "country cousins," "safe and sound," and "jumping jacks." Tongue twisters such as "Sally sells sea shells by the sea shore" also are good examples of alliteration.

Poets use alliteration to emphasize certain words, to create mood, to unify lines, to reinforce meaning, and to impart a musical quality to their poems. Notice the alliteration in the following poems and the way that the sounds relate to the other elements in each poem.

A tutor who tootled the flute
  Was teaching two tooters to toot.
Said the two to the tutor,
  "Is it harder to toot,
Or to tutor two tooters to toot?"
            CAROLYN WELLS
            "The Tutor"

There are plenty of sweeping, swinging,
  stinging, gorgeous things to shout about.
            VACHEL LINDSAY
            "Bryan, Bryan, Bryan"

Allusion. An allusion is a reference to a work of literature or to a person, place, or event outside of literature with which the reader is expected to be familiar. The title "Antaeus" is an allusion to a mythological character. The title of the poem "Be Daedalus" contains another allusion to classical mythology. The understanding of these allusions is important, if not vital, to the complete understanding of the selections. In the following poem, the poet assumes that her readers know the story of the "Three Little Pigs."

I told them a thousand times if I told them once:
Stop fooling around, I said, with straw and
    sticks;
They won't hold up; you're taking an awful
    chance.
Brick is the stuff to build with, solid bricks.
You want to be impractical, go ahead,
But just remember, I told them; wait and see.
You're making a big mistake. Awright, I said,
But when the wolf comes, don't come running
    to me.

The funny thing is, they didn't. There they sat,
One in his crummy yellow shack, and one
Under his roof of twigs, and the wolf ate
Them, hair and hide. Well what is done is done.
But I'd been willing to help them, all along,
If only they'd once admitted they were wrong.

SARA HENDERSON HAY
"The Builders"

Analogy. An analogy sets up a comparison between two things that may seem dissimilar but have important similarities. Analogies often include figures of speech such as simile, metaphor, and personification. Through analogies, readers can gain new insights into abstract ideas and complex processes.

In the following paragraph, a writer compares reading poetry to playing tennis, two things that are, on the surface at least, quite different.

An analogy can be drawn between reading poetry and playing tennis. Both offer great enjoyment if the game is played hard. Good tennis players must be constantly on the tips of their toes, concentrating on their opponents' every move. They must be ready for drives to the right or to the left, lobs overhead or drop shots barely over the net. They must be ready for top spins or underspins, balls that bounce crazily to the left or crazily to the right. They must jump for the high ones and run for the far ones. They will enjoy the game almost exactly in proportion to the effort they put into it. The same is true of poetry. Great enjoyment is there, but this enjoyment demands a mental effort equivalent to the physical effort one puts into tennis.

Readers of poetry have one advantage over tennis players. Poets are not trying to win matches. They may expect readers to stretch for their shots, but they *want* the readers to return them.

LAURENCE PERRINE
Sound and Sense

Aside. In a play, a remark spoken by one character to another that other characters on stage are not supposed to hear is called an aside. Sometimes an aside may be directed not to another character, but to the audience.

Assonance. Assonance is the repetition of a vowel sound within words. Examples of assonance are "free and easy," "love bug," and "windmill." Assonance often is used by writers to unify passages and to create a musical quality in both prose and poetry. Notice the repetition of vowel sounds in the following poem.

I've an ingle, shady ingle, near a dusky bosky
    dingle
Where the sighing zephyrs mingle with the
    purling of the stream.
There I linger in the jungle, and it makes me
    thrill and tingle,
Far from city's strident jangle as I angle, smoke
    and dream.

Through the trees I'll hear a single ringing
    sound, a cowbell's jingle,
And its ting-a-ling'll mingle with the whispers
    of the breeze;
So, although I've not a single sou, no potentate
    or king'll
Make me jealous while I angle in my ingle
    'neath the trees.

NEWMAN LEVY
"Midsummer Jingle"

See *Consonance.*

Autobiography. An autobiography is the story of a person's life written by that person, not by someone else. "I Know Why the Caged Bird Sings" and "A Christmas Memory" are both autobiographical selections. They focus on important experiences in the lives of the writers. Like most autobiographies, they are written from the first-person point of view.

Ballad. A ballad is a poem that tells a story, usually about ordinary people who have had unusual adventures or have performed daring deeds. Ballads differ from other narrative poems in that they are often written to be sung.

Most ballads have four-line stanzas, each with the same pattern of rhyme and meter. Often, ballads have a refrain, or repeated passage, at the end of each stanza.

Following is part of an English folk ballad called "Barbara Allen's Cruelty," revived in the present day by Joan Baez and other folk singers.

> In Scarlet town, where I was born,
>   There was a fair maid dwellin',
> Made every youth cry *Well-a-way!*
>   Her name was Barbara Allen.
>
> All in the merry month of May,
>   When green buds they were swellin',
> Young Jemmy Grove on his death-bed lay,
>   For love of Barbara Allen.
>
> He sent his man in to her then,
>   To the town where she was dwellin';
> "O haste and come to my master dear,
>   If your name be Barbara Allen."
>   ANONYMOUS

See *Narrative Poem.*

Blank Verse. Blank verse is unrhymed poetry written in iambic pentameter. This means that each line has five feet, or units of rhythm, and that each foot has an unaccented syllable followed by an accented syllable.

John Milton's famous English epic *Paradise Lost* is written in blank verse. The following final lines of the poem, which refer to Adam and Eve, illustrate the meter and the lack of rhyme in blank verse.

> The world/was all/before/them, where/to choose
> Thir place/of rest,/and Prov/idence/thir guide:
> They hand/in hand/with wand'/ring steps/and slow,
> Through E/den took/thir sol/itar/y way.

Character. Characters are the people (and occasionally animals) who carry on the action in a piece of literature. Characters are either main or minor, depending upon the extent of their development and on their importance in a narrative. A major challenge for the writers of novels, short stories, plays, and sometimes poems is the creation of full, interesting characters whose emotions and actions help a reader to understand people in the real world.

See *Characterization.*

Characterization. Characterization refers to the techniques that a writer uses to develop characters. The four basic methods of characterization are as follows.

1. Characters may be developed through physical description. Langston Hughes opens the story "Thank You, M'am" by identifying Mrs. Luella Bates Washington Jones as "a large woman with a purse that had everything in it but a hammer and nails." This statement points to Mrs. Jones's solid, practical character.

2. Characters may be developed through description of their speech and actions. When Mrs. Jones takes Roger, who has attempted to steal her purse, to her home and feeds him, the reader learns that she is compassionate and perceptive. When Mrs. Jones says to Roger, "You might run that comb through your hair so you will look presentable," the reader realizes that she understands Roger's need for structure and direction.

3. Characters may be developed through direct comments from the narrator, as in this passage about Roger.

    . . . the boy took care to sit on the far side of the room, away from the purse, where he thought she could easily see him out of the corner of her eye if she wanted to. He did not trust the woman *not* to trust him. And he did not want to be mistrusted now.

4. Characters may be developed through the speech and actions of other characters. The reader gains evidence of Mrs. Jones's unusual generosity when Roger cannot find words to express his appreciation.

The boy wanted to say something other than, "Thank you, m'am," to Mrs. Luella Bates Washington Jones, but although his lips moved, he couldn't even say that as he turned at the foot of the barren stoop and looked up at the large woman in the door. Then she shut the door.

Climax. The climax is the moment of highest intensity, or interest, in a work of dramatic or narrative literature. It is often the moment when the outcome of a story becomes clear. In "The Most Dangerous Game," for example, the climax occurs when the reader realizes that Rainsford has beaten General Zaroff at his own game. In dramatic literature the word *climax* often refers to the moment when the fortunes of the main character or characters are at their peak. In *Romeo and Juliet,* for example, the climax is the marriage of the main characters in Act III, after which circumstances begin to turn against them.

See *Conflict, Falling Action, Plot, Rising Action.*

Concrete Poem. A concrete poem is one in which the shape of the poem suggests something important about the poem's meaning. The following poem illustrates the relationship between shape and meaning in a concrete poem.

```
generation upon
generation upon
generation upon
generation upon
generation upon
generation upon
generation upon
generation upon
generation upon
generation upon
generation upon
generation upon
generation upon
generation upon
generation upon
generation upon
generation upon
generation upon
g neration upon
g neration up n
g nerat on up n
g nerat  n up n
g nerat  n  p n
g  erat  n  p n
g  era   n  p n
g  era   n    n
g  er    n    n
g   r    n    n
g        n    n
g        n
g
```

Edwin Morgan
"Archives"

Conflict. Conflict is the struggle between opposing forces, which is the most basic element of plot in dramatic and narrative literature. Conflict occurs in various forms. Sometimes two characters clash, as do Rainsford and General Zaroff in "The Most Dangerous Game." Sometimes conflict occurs between a character and society, as in "The Cave," in which George, the artist, retreats from the demands of society. Sometimes conflict is between opposing tendencies in a character's mind, as in "The Secret Life of Walter

Mitty." Sometimes conflict occurs between a character and nature, as in "The Sea Devil."

A longer work of literature may involve several conflicts. In *I Remember Mama,* for example, the family is in conflict over whether to kill Dagmar's cat; over whether to buy Katrin the dresser set for her graduation; over how to react to Mr. Hyde, their lodger who does not pay his rent.

See *Climax, Falling Action, Plot, Rising Action.*

Connotation. Connotation is the sum of the suggested meanings that surround the core, or literal, definition of a word. *Puppy,* for example, is defined as a young dog. To most people, however, the word connotes, or suggests, feelings of warmth, tenderness, and frivolity. This emotional response is the connotation of the word.

See *Denotation.*

Consonance. Consonance is the repetition of consonant sounds within and at the ends of words. Expressions such as "first and last" and "short and sweet" are examples of consonance. Writers use consonance along with alliteration, assonance, and rhyme to unify their works and to give their writing a musical quality. Notice the repetition of the final *s* sound in the following lines.

Praise the spells and bless the charms,
I found April in my arms.
OGDEN NASH
"Always Marry an April Girl"

See *Assonance.*

Couplet. A couplet is two consecutive lines of poetry that rhyme, as in the following poem.

By day the bat is cousin to the mouse.
He likes the attic of an aging house.

His fingers make a hat about his head.
His pulse beat is so slow we think him dead.

He loops in crazy figures half the night
Among the trees that face the corner light.

But when he brushes up against a screen,
We are afraid of what our eyes have seen:

For something is amiss or out of place
When mice with wings can wear a human face.
THEODORE ROETHKE
"The Bat"

A simple couplet may be written in any rhythmic pattern. The most common metrical foot is the iamb, in which an unaccented syllable is followed by an accented syllable.

See *Heroic Couplet, Stanza.*

Denotation. Denotation is the meaning of a word as defined in a dictionary.

See *Connotation.*

Description. Description is writing that helps a reader to picture scenes, events, and characters. For effectiveness, description usually relies upon precise adjectives, adverbs, nouns, and verbs; and on vivid, original phrases. This passage illustrates the use of colorful, interesting language in description.

The town itself seemed a negligible thing from such a distance. Were it not for the clutter on the shore, the flames and the tremulous pillars of heat that stood above the barrels, and of course the skaters who swooped and sailed and made bright, brave sounds, it would have been possible not to notice the town at all. The mountains that stood up behind it were covered with snow and hidden in the white sky, and the lake was sealed and hidden, yet their eclipse had not made the town more prominent. Indeed, where we were we could feel the reach of the lake far behind us, and far beyond us on either side, in a spacious silence that seemed to ring like glass.
MARILYNNE ROBINSON
Housekeeping

The final simile, "ring like glass," illustrates that imagery, too, is often important in successful description

Dialogue. Dialogue in literature is written conversation between two or more characters. The use of dialogue brings characters to life and gives the reader insights into the characters and their personalities.

Dialogue is used in almost all forms of writing. Plays rely on dialogue to tell the story. In scripts for plays, dialogue is indicated by the placement of words and sentences and by the appearance of the type in which the dialogue is printed. In other writing, dialogue is set apart according to special rules for punctuation and paragraphing; for example:

As soon as I got out of the plane, I smelled something peculiar.

"What's that smell?" I asked the man who met me at the plane.

"I don't smell anything," he replied.

"There's a definite odor that I'm not familiar with," I said.

"Oh, you must be talking about the fresh air. A lot of people come out here who have never smelled fresh air before."

"What's it supposed to do?" I asked suspiciously.

"Nothing. You just breathe it like any other kind of air. It's supposed to be good for your lungs."

"I've heard that story before," I said. "How come if it's air, my eyes aren't watering?"

"Your eyes don't water with fresh air. That's the advantage of it. Saves you a lot in paper tissues."

ART BUCHWALD
"Fresh Air Will Kill You"

Diction. Diction is a writer's choice of words. Writers use slang, informal expressions, and formal terminology, depending on their subjects, audiences, and purposes. For example, the writer of a humorous essay might refer to a young child as a "bundle of joy" or even a "kid." A doctor writing an article for a medical journal might use more formal words such as *baby* and *infant*.

By choosing their words with care, writers achieve the clearest and most effective writing possible. Their careful choices also contribute to their own unique writing style.

See *Style*.

Drama. Drama is literature that develops plot and characters through dialogue and action; in other words, drama is literature in play form. Dramas are meant to be performed by actors and actresses who appear on a stage, before radio microphones, or in front of television or movie cameras.

Playwrights usually include stage directions in their scripts. These instructions tell actors how to move and how to read certain lines. A playwright may also include suggestions for sound effects and music, as well as for the lighting and design of the stage set.

Most plays are divided into acts, with each act having an emotional peak, or climax, of its own. One-act plays, however, do exist, and "Trifles" is an example. Each act of a play may be divided into several scenes that represent changes in time or place.

Editorial. An editorial is an expression of opinion on a topic of social or political importance. An editorial may express the opinion of just one person or of a larger group. Oral editorials are presented on radio and on television. Written editorials appear in newspapers and magazines.

Essay. The essay is possibly the most versatile of literary forms. It is a brief composition that offers an opinion on any subject. Frequently the essayist tries to persuade the reader to accept a particular point of view.

Essays may be either formal or informal; they may be written for a general audience or intended for a small and specific group. "Whales for the Killing" and "Sleeping Arrangements" are both essays. The former is about a present-day problem; the latter is a humorous comment on the writer's youth.

Eulogy. A eulogy is a written or spoken tribute that praises a person's virtues and achievements. Often, though not always, a person is eulogized after his or her death. For example, in "The Washwoman" Isaac Bashevis Singer praises the laundress his family once employed.

Fable. A fable is a short, simple story that teaches a lesson. The fable is similar to the parable in that the most important elements are the conflict and the moral lesson. Unlike the parable, however, the characters in a fable are usually animals that act and talk like human beings.

The fables that are the most widely known are those of Aesop, a Greek slave who is supposed to have lived in the sixth century B.C.

THE FOX AND THE GOAT

By an unlucky chance, a Fox fell into a deep well from which he could not get out. A Goat passed by shortly afterwards, and asked the Fox what he was doing down there. "Oh, have you not heard?" said the Fox; "there is going to be a great drought, so I jumped down here in order to be sure to have water. Why don't you come down too?" The Goat thought well of this advice and jumped down into the well. The Fox immediately jumped on her back and, by putting his foot on her long horns, managed to jump up to the edge of the well. "Goodbye, friend," said the Fox, "remember next time,

NEVER TRUST THE ADVICE OF A
PERSON IN DIFFICULTIES."

Falling Action. The falling action in a dramatic or narrative work comes after the climax, or high point of intensity and interest. Thus, the falling action shows the aftereffects of the most important events and wraps up the loose ends in the plot. Acts IV and V of *Romeo and Juliet* are the falling action of the play, acquainting the reader with everything that happens after the ill-fated marriage of the lovers.

See *Climax, Conflict, Plot, Rising Action.*

Fiction. Fiction is the branch of literature made up of imaginative works of prose, including the novel and the short story. Although fiction is the product of a writer's imagination, it may have some basis in reality. For example, a writer might use a person in real life as the inspiration for a character in a short story, without trying to depict the real person accurately and faithfully. Similarly, a novelist might employ a real place as a setting and might even describe real buildings and monuments in that place. The narrative, however, will spring mainly from the writer's imagination.

See *Nonfiction.*

Figurative Language. Language that communicates ideas beyond the ordinary meanings of the words is figurative language. Figurative language is a way of being false and true at the same time. The words in a figurative expression are not literally true, but rather they stimulate vivid pictures and concepts in the mind of the reader. One poet describes snow this way.

The fenceposts wear marshmallow hats
On a snowy day;
Bushes in their night gowns
Are kneeling down to pray—
And all the trees have silver skirts
And want to dance away.
DOROTHY ALDIS
"Snow"

Obviously, no hats made of marshmallow rest on the fenceposts. The texture of the snow, however, suggests a marshmallow, and the shape of the snow suggests a hat.

Figurative language is used in poetry and prose, as well as in spoken language. The general term figurative language includes specific figures of speech. The most common are simile, metaphor, personification, and hyperbole.

See *Hyperbole, Metaphor, Personification, Simile.*

Flashback. A flashback is a conversation, a scene, or an event that happened before the beginning of a story, or at an earlier point in a narrative. Usually, a plot moves forward chronologically, beginning at one point in time and proceeding until the conclusion. When a flashback is included, it is generally because a writer believes that information from the past is necessary if the reader is to understand the present situation of a character or characters. The entire story "Marigolds" is a flashback, related by an adult narrator who is attempting to understand herself by examining an important moment from her past.

Foil. A foil is a character with qualities that contrast with those of another character. A writer might use a foil to emphasize a characteristic or to make that characteristic look more or less important. For example, in the story "The Elk Tooth Dress," Mary McTavish is a foil to Natalie. Her superficial attitude toward the traditional Indian ways makes Natalie by comparison seem even more genuine and sincere in her beliefs.

Foreshadowing. To foreshadow is to show beforehand, or to foretell. Thus, in literature, foreshadowing is a writer's use of hints or clues to indicate events that will occur later in the narrative. The usual reason for the use of this technique is to create tension and to make a reader curious about what is going to happen.

In Herman Melville's famous sea novel *Moby Dick*, the narrator Ishmael early in the novel clues the reader in to the approaching death of the character Queequeg. After Queequeg has performed a brave act, Ishmael says, "From that hour I clove to Queequeg like a barnacle; yea, till poor Queequeg took his last long dive."

Similarly, in Mark Twain's fascinating mystery novel *Pudd'nhead Wilson*, the main character, Dave Wilson, experiments with fingerprints long before they are an accepted form of courtroom evidence. The novel's many references to fingerprinting foreshadow the important role that fingerprinting plays in the spectacular ending of the novel, as do the mocking taunts of those townspeople who call Wilson a "pudd'nhead" because of the time he spends collecting fingerprints.

Free Verse. Free verse is poetry written without regular patterns of rhyme and meter. Like most poetry, free verse generally is more rhythmic than ordinary language. Much of the poetry written in the twentieth century is free verse.

The following poem illustrates the qualities of free verse.

I AM A
Cosmonaut
Cradled in dangers
Orbiting a garden universe
Snipping cosmos, probing Venus,
Sighting summer's end blindly,
Weightily weightless
Spinning out of reach,
    out
      of
        reach
Signaling strangers.
        LENORE MARSHALL

Hero and Heroine. A hero or heroine is the main character, or center of action, in a work of literature. In early literature, heroes and heroines exhibited great moral or physical strength, and often were blessed by and descended from the gods. These characters possessed traits such as courage, cleverness, honor, and intelligence. They were the protectors of their societies and the leaders who defended weaker human beings against the evils of the world. Siegfried, Ulysses, and

King Arthur are examples of early heroic figures.

In modern literature, the terms hero and heroine refer to the most important character in a short story, play, narrative poem, or nonfiction selection. The heroes and heroines of today are not always as courageous and honorable as the heroes and heroines in earlier literature. They may be devious, weak-willed, greedy, or jealous. Above all, they do not always emerge victorious. For example, Miss Strangeworth in "The Possibility of Evil" is self-righteous and is discovered and ultimately humiliated.

Heroic Couplet. A heroic couplet is two consecutive lines of poetry that rhyme and that are written in iambic pentameter. A line of iambic pentameter consists of five feet; each foot is made up of an unaccented syllable followed by an accented syllable. Heroic couplets usually can function by themselves as small units of meaning.

The following lines are heroic couplets.

All Nature is but Art, unknown to thee;
All Chance, Direction, which thou canst not see;
All Discord, Harmony not understood;
All partial Evil, universal Good:
And, spite of Pride, in erring Reason's spite,
One truth is clear, WHATEVER IS, IS RIGHT.
ALEXANDER POPE
"Essay on Man"

See *Couplet.*

Historical Narrative. A narrative is a fiction or nonfiction account of events and experiences. A historical narrative re-creates a particular time and place in history; it too may be fiction or nonfiction. "Pompeii" is a historical narrative, a nonfiction selection about events that occurred nearly 2,000 years ago.

Humor. Humor expresses what is funny or amusing. Sometimes, the purpose of humor is pure entertainment, but most often humor adds to a total effect or helps to make a serious point. "The World in a Wall," for example, is basically about a boy's experience with the animal life around his home. The attitudes of his family add humor to the account and also emphasize the boy's unique interest in nature by hinting at a long history of similar incidents.

Hyperbole. Hyperbole is a figure of speech in which the truth is exaggerated for emphasis. The statement "If I don't eat something right away, I'll starve" is an example of hyperbole.

The use of hyperbole is common in expressions of love. Romeo exaggerates Juliet's beauty when he says, "O, she doth teach the torches to burn bright!" A seventeenth century poet pays tribute to his love's beauty this way.

There is a garden in her face
Where roses and white lilies grow;
A heavenly paradise is that place
Wherein all pleasant fruits do flow.
THOMAS CAMPION
"There Is a Garden in Her Face"

Hyperbole can be used for a humorous effect, as in the following information for an almanac.

At the instance of several friends who feel a boding anxiety to know beforehand what sort of phenomena we may expect the elements to exhibit during the next month or two, and who have lost all confidence in the various patent medicine almanacs, because of the unaccountable reticence of those works concerning the extraordinary event of the 8th inst., I have compiled the following almanac expressly for the latitude of San Francisco:

NOV. 1 Terrific earthquake. This is the great earthquake month. More stars fall and more worlds are slathered around carelessly and destroyed in November than in any other month of the twelve.

NOV. 2 Spasmodic but exhilarating earthquakes, accompanied by occasional showers of rain and churches and things.

NOV. 3 Make your will.

NOV. 4 Sell out.

NOV. 5 Select your "last words." Those of John Quincy Adams will do, with the addition of a syllable, thus: "This is the last of earthquakes."

NOV. 6 Prepare to shed this mortal coil.

NOV. 7 Shed!

NOV. 8 The sun will rise as usual, perhaps; but if he does, he will doubtless be staggered some to find nothing but a large round hole eight thousand miles in diameter in the place where he saw this world serenely spinning the day before.

MARK TWAIN
"A Page from a Californian Almanac"

See *Figurative Language, Humor.*

Imagery. Imagery describes words and phrases that re-create sensory experiences for the reader. Because sight is the most highly developed sense, the majority of images are visual. They appeal to the sense of sight and thus create pictures in the reader's mind. The images in the following poem, for example, enable the reader to "see" the colors and contrasts of a mountain region.

Uganda mountains
Black soil
White snow
And in the valley
Zebra.

ALICE WALKER
"African Images"

Good writers often use images that appeal to several senses at the same time. The following paragraphs include images that appeal to the senses of sight, touch, and hearing.

One minute it was Ohio winter, with doors closed, windows locked, the panes blind with frost, icicles fringing every roof, children skiing on slopes, housewives lumbering like great black bears in their furs along the icy streets.

Then a long wave of warmth crossed the small town. A flooding sea of hot air; it seemed as if someone had left a bakery door open. The heat pulsed among the cottages and bushes and children. The icicles dropped, shattering, to melt. The doors flew open. The windows flew up. The children worked off their wool clothes. The housewives shed their bear disguises. The snow dissolved and showed last summer's ancient green lawns.

RAY BRADBURY
The Martian Chronicles

Irony. Irony is a contrast between what is expected and what actually exists or happens. When people say one thing and mean another, they are being ironic. For example, someone who has just tripped and fallen into the mud might say, "I certainly am graceful today."

Poets often use irony to communicate important ideas, as in this poem.

"A planet doesn't explode of itself," said drily
The Martian astronomer, gazing off into the
    air—
"That they were able to do it is proof that highly
Intelligent beings must have been living there."

JOHN HALL WHEELOCK
"Earth"

The poet means the opposite of what the Martian says. He believes that blowing up the earth shows no intelligence whatsoever.

Situations can be ironic too. In O. Henry's story "The Cop and the Anthem," for example, a man repeatedly tries to be arrested so that he can spend the winter in jail rather than on a cold park bench. When he hears an anthem coming from a church, he decides to reform his life and to make something of himself. At that moment, in an ironic turn of events, he is arrested for loitering.

Legend. A legend is a story passed down through many generations and popularly believed to have a historic basis. While the main character in a legend may have lived at one time, many of the stories associated with him or her are fictitious. The legend of King Arthur is an example of an old English legend. The stories of Paul Bunyon are modern legends. It is possible that both of these men did in fact live. It is highly unlikely, however, that all of the stories associated with them are true.

Metaphor. A metaphor is a figure of speech that makes a comparison between two unlike things that have something in common. Unlike similes, metaphors do not contain the words *like* or *as*; they make comparisons directly.

The poet Robert P. Tristram Coffin wrote, "A pheasant cock sprang into view,/ A living jewel, up he flew." The literal definitions of *pheasant* and *jewel* would show no similarities, but the bird and the gem do share the quality of brilliance. The poet leads the reader to see the pheasant's brilliance by comparing the bird to a jewel, an object more familiar to most readers. Following are additional examples of metaphors.

Love is a universal migraine,
A bright stain on the vision
Blotting out reason.
ROBERT GRAVES
"Symptoms of Love"

The red rose whispers of passion,
    And the white rose breathes of love;
Oh, the red rose is a falcon,
    And the white rose is a dove.
JOHN BOYLE O'REILLY
"A White Rose"

In extended metaphor two unlike things are compared in various ways. On occasion the comparison is carried throughout a literary selection, creating a strong image for the reader. The poem "I Like To See It Lap the Miles" by Emily Dickinson, for example, is an extended metaphor in which a train is compared to a horse. Following is another example of an extended metaphor in which a garden hose is compared to a snake.

In the gray evening
I see a long green serpent
With its tail in the dahlias.

It lies in loops across the grass
And drinks softly at the faucet.

I can hear it swallow.
BEATRICE JANOSCO
"The Garden Hose"

See *Figurative Language, Simile.*

Meter. Meter is the repetition of a regular rhythmic unit in a line of poetry. Each unit is known as a foot, with each foot having one accented and one or two unaccented syllables. Meter brings out the musical quality of language and often relates in some vital way to the subject matter of the poem.

In the following passage each line contains five feet. Each foot is made up of an unaccented syllable followed by an accented one, a foot known in English as the iamb. The iamb is the most common metric unit in English poetry.

$$
\begin{array}{ccccc}
1 & 2 & 3 & 4 & 5
\end{array}
$$

I stood/tip-toe/upon/a lit/tle hill,
The air/was cool/ing and/so ver/y still,
That the/sweet buds/which with/a mod/est
    pride
Pull droop/ingly,/in slant/ing curve/aside
JOHN KEATS
"I Stood Tip-Toe upon a Little Hill"

Mood. Mood is the feeling, or atmosphere, that the writer creates for the reader. Connotative words, sensory images, and figurative language contribute to the mood of a selection, as do the sound and rhythm of the language used.

Notice how Edgar Allan Poe creates a feeling of uneasiness in this paragraph from one of his chilling tales.

> Very suddenly there came back to my soul motion and sound—the tumultuous motion of the heart, and, in my ears, the sound of its beating. Then a pause in which all is blank. Then again sound, and motion, and touch—a tingling sensation pervading my frame. Then the mere consciousness of existence, without thought—a condition which lasted long. Then, very suddenly, *thought,* and shuddering terror, and earnest endeavor to comprehend my true state. Then a strong desire to lapse into insensibility. Then a rushing revival of soul and a successful effort to move. And now a full memory of the trial, of the judges, of the sable draperies, of the sentence, of the sickness, of the swoon. Then entire forgetfulness of all that followed; of all that a later day and much earnestness of endeavor have enabled me vaguely to recall.
>
> EDGAR ALLAN POE
> "The Pit and the Pendulum"

Myth. A myth is a traditional story, usually concerning some superhuman being or unlikely event, that was once widely believed to be true. Frequently, myths attempt to explain why the world is the way it is or why things in nature happen as they do. Because of this, myths were for earlier peoples both a kind of crude science and a religion. In addition, myths served as literature and as entertainment, just as they do for modern-day audiences.

The most famous myths, such as the stories of Theseus and Hercules, originated among the Ancient Greeks and Romans. Norse mythology, consisting of myths from Scandinavia and Germany, is also important classical literature, as the fame of the Siegfried story illustrates. On the continent of North America, many Indian tribes have produced fascinating myths of various kinds.

Narration. Narration refers to the process of telling a story. For both fiction and non-fiction selections, narration is either first-person or third-person.

First-person narration means that a character within a story tells the story in his or her own words. The character who narrates may be either a main character or a minor one. "Everyday Use" is an example of first-person narration. The mother in this story tells everything in the "I" voice, expressing her own views on her daughters and their lives. Because "The Ransom of Red Chief" is narrated by one of the kidnappers, it, too, is an example of first-person narration.

Third-person narration means that a story is told by a voice outside the action, not by one of the characters within the story. In third-person narration, characters are referred to by name or by the pronouns *he* and *she.*

If a story is told from an omniscient, or all-knowing, third-person point of view, the narrator sees into the minds of all the different characters. *The Human Comedy* is an example of omniscient narration.

If a writer uses a limited third-person point of view, it means that the narrator tells only what one, or perhaps two, characters think, feel, and observe. "The Secret Life of Walter Mitty," which reveals Walter Mitty's thoughts only, exemplifies limited third-person narration.

See *Narrator, Point of View.*

Narrative Poem. A narrative poem tells a story. "Lucy Gray" and "The Shooting of John Dillinger" are examples of narrative poems.

The ballad is a special type of narrative poem, often intended to be sung.

See *Ballad.*

Narrator. The narrator is the person who relates a story from his or her point of view.

The narrator of a short story or nonfiction selection may be the writer, a character within the selection, or even someone who is outside the action.

See *Narration, Point of View.*

Nonfiction. Nonfiction is prose writing that is about real people, places, and events. Unlike fiction, nonfiction is not the product of an author's imagination. Instead, nonfiction focuses on factual information and on true events and subjects. Biography and autobiography are types of nonfiction, as are editorials, essays, journals, news stories, and informative magazine articles. Historical accounts that resemble short stories or novels are nonfiction if they are factually accurate.

See *Fiction.*

Onomatopoeia. Onomatopoeia is the use of words that imitate sounds. Young children use onomatopoeia in its most basic form when they call a dog a "bow-wow" or a train a "choo-choo." Later, they might use words such as *plop, boom, dud,* and *pow.*

Onomatopoeia as a literary technique goes beyond the use of simple echoic words. Writers, particularly poets, choose words whose sounds suggest their denotative and connotative meanings; for example, *whisper, kick,* and *giggle.* Sometimes writers use the sounds of entire lines to reinforce a meaning.

In the following poem, the writer suggests the sounds of frogs and snakes and the rhythms of traditional cheers.

The frogs and the serpents each had a football team,
and I heard their cheer leaders in my dream:

"Bilgewater, bilgewater," called the frog,
"Bilgewater, bilgewater,
Sis, boom, bog!
Roll 'em off the log,
Slog 'em in the sog,
Swamp'em, swamp'em,
Muck mire quash!"

"Sisyphus, Sisyphus," hissed the snake,
"Sibilant, syllabub,
Syllable-loo-ba-lay.
Scylla and Charybdis,
Sumac, asphodel,
How do you spell Success?
With an S-S-S!"

EVE MERRIAM
"Cheers"

Parable. A parable is a short, simple story that teaches a moral or religious lesson. In a parable, the characters and setting are generally less important than the conflict that develops and the lesson that is taught. The conflict in the following parable is between the servant and Death. The moral might be expressed as "No one can escape death." As with many parables, the setting is the far distant past.

APPOINTMENT IN SAMARRA
Many years ago, there was a man in Bathsheba who asked his servant to go to market. His servant had known many years, and was faithful in service. Although his hair was white, he stood as tall as a young date tree in the autumn, whose leaves are beginning to fall, while the fruit of abundance draws to an end about it.

The servant went to market, and among the throng he saw Death, dressed in black and as pale as the moon that grows thin. Death made a gesture, and the servant grew frightened; for, although there were many people in the marketplace, who crowded to buy the things that would bring them joy while they lived, none of them heeded the lonely pair.

The servant ran home to his master, and he said, "Master, today I saw Death in the market amid the throng, and he made a threatening gesture to me. Master, I shall make haste and I shall ride like the wind to Samarra, for Samarra is many miles from here, and Death will not find me there."

So the servant rode away to Samarra, and his master was sorely troubled, as is the traveler in the desert who is called to the side of his dying father and his long journey draws to an end. The master went to the market and he sought out Death, whose dress was as dark as the sea at night when the fisherman is lost, and whose face was as pale as a grave on a frosty night.

The master said to Death, "Why did you make a threatening gesture at my servant? He has done me good service and is old in years."

Death replied, "I made no threatening gesture at your servant. That was a start of surprise, for I saw him this morning in Bathsheba, but this night I was to meet him many miles away in Samarra."

Paradox. A paradox is a statement that seems to contradict itself but is, nevertheless, true. Writers use paradox to emphasize an idea through contrast and to stimulate thinking among their readers.

In Act One, Scene 3 of *Macbeth*, Macbeth says, "So fair and foul a day I have not seen." On the surface, this line seems to contradict itself, for how can a day be both "fair" and "foul"? What Macbeth actually means is that, although the weather has been stormy, the battle has gone well for him.

Parody. Parody is a special kind of satire that mocks a specific literary work or type of literature. Like satire, the purpose of parody is to ridicule foolish ideas, customs, and traditions so that readers think about their foolishness and modify their behavior. Often the writers of parody use exaggeration and irony to achieve their goals.

In the following parody of a well known nursery rhyme, the poet wants the reader to think about the seriousness of nuclear war.

> Little Miss Muffet
> Crouched on a tuffet,
> Collecting her shell-shocked wits.
> There dropped (from a glider)
> An H-bomb beside her—
> Which frightened Miss Muffet to bits.
> PAUL DEHN
> "Little Miss Muffet"

Personification. Personification is a figure of speech in which human qualities are at-tributed to an object, an animal, or an idea. Like the simile and the metaphor, personification helps writers to communicate feelings and sensory images to their readers.

The personification in the following lines gives the reader a fresh look at the familiar phenomenon of leaves falling in autumn.

> The trees are undressing, and fling in many
>   places—
> On the gray road, the roof, the window sill—
> Their radiant robes and ribbons and yellow
>   laces;
> A leaf each second so is flung at will,
> Here, there, another and another, still and still.
> THOMAS HARDY
> "Last Week in October"

In this second example of personification, another poet re-creates his own particular view of a common scene.

> Outside my window
> two tall witch-elms
> toss their inspired
> green heads in the sun
> and lean together
> whispering.
>
> Trees make the world
> a proper place.
> ROBERT NYE
> "A Proper Place"

See *Figurative Language*.

Plot. Plot refers to the actions and events in a dramatic or narrative work. The characters are the agents who carry out the action.

Plot always involves some sort of conflict, whether it is between or among characters or within the mind of one character. The conflict nearly always builds to a climax, or turning point.

Long works of literature often have subplots in addition to their main plots. In *Romeo and Juliet*, for example, the main plot centers on the love, marriage, and eventual deaths of the two title characters. A subplot involves Mercutio and his death at the hands of Tybalt.

See *Climax, Conflict, Falling Action, Rising Action*.

Poetry. Poetry is language arranged in lines. Usually, poetry expresses meaning in a tighter, more compact way than prose. Because poetry frequently does not include the kind of detail and explanation common to the short story or the novel, poetry tends to leave more to a reader's imagination. Often poetry requires more from a reader's intelligence to unlock meaning. At one time, poets followed definite rules and patterns for rhyme and meter. Modern poets, however, often ignore these restraints and still produce what the reader recognizes as poetry.

Many poems are divided into stanzas, or paragraph-like groups of lines. The stanzas of a poem may have the same number of lines and the same meter, or they may vary. The lines may or may not rhyme, but there is generally a feeling of rhythm, even when the rhythm is not regular. The use of figurative language and imagery is a characteristic of poetry, with some poets relying more heavily on imaginative language than others.

Point of View. Point of view refers to how a story is narrated. If a character within a story describes the action, the story is told from the first-person point of view. If the writer or a character outside the story narrates, the story is told from the third-person point of view.

See *Narration, Narrator*.

Pun. A pun is a play on words. Puns involve words that sound the same but that have different meanings. The words need not be spelled the same way. Often, puns are a source of humor, as in this pun from an early American gravestone.

> Here lies Pecos Bill.
> He always lied and always will.
> He once lied loud.
> He now lies still.

Sometimes a pun deepens the meaning of a selection by making more than one interpretation possible. Notice the pun on the phrases "give a way" and "give away" in the following poem.

> The reeds give
> way to the
>
> wind and give
> the wind away
>
> A. R. AMMONS
> "Small Song"

Quatrain. A quatrain is a four-line stanza, or unit of poetry. The most common stanza in English poetry, the quatrain can have a variety of meters and rhyme schemes. The ballad stanza is one common quatrain.

Below are two quatrains from a poem about Abraham Lincoln.

> A bronzed, lank man! His suit of ancient black,
> A famous high top-hat and plain worn shawl
> Make him the quaint great figure that men love,
> The prairie-lawyer, master of us all.
>
> He cannot sleep upon his hillside now.
> He is among us: —as in times before!
> And we who toss and lie awake for long,
> Breathe deep, and start, to see him pass the door.
>
> VACHEL LINDSAY
> "Abraham Lincoln Walks at
> Midnight"

Refrain. In poetry, a refrain is part of a stanza, consisting of one or more lines or phrases that are repeated, sometimes with changes, at the ends of succeeding stanzas. Most ballads contain some sort of refrain.

The following stanzas from an English ballad illustrate the use of a refrain.

Love me little, love me long,
Is the burden of my song.
Love that is too hot and strong
   Burneth soon to waste:
Still, I would not have thee cold,
Not too backward, nor too bold;
Love that lasteth till 'tis old
   Fadeth not in haste.
     Love me little, love me long,
     Is the burden of my song.

If thou lovest me too much
It will not prove as true as touch
Love me little, more than such,
   For I fear the end:
I am with little well content,
And a little from thee sent
Is enough, with true intent
   To be a steadfast friend,
     Love me little, love me long,
     Is the burden of my song.
          ANONYMOUS
          "Love Me Little, Love Me Long"

Repetition. Repetition is a literary technique in which a word or phrase is repeated for emphasis. Notice the use of repetition in the following poem.

   Swing, Swing,
   Sing, sing
Hear! my throne and I am a king!
   Swing, sing,
   Swing, sing,
Farewell, earth, for I'm on the wing!

   Low, high,
   Here I fly,
Like a bird through sunny sky;
   Free, free,
   Over the lea,
Over the mountain, over the sea!

   Up, down,
   Up and down,
Which is the way to London Town?
   Where? Where?
   Up in the air,
Close your eyes and now you are there!

   Soon, soon,
   Afternoon,
Over the sunset, over the moon;
   Far, far,
   Over all bar,
Sweeping on from star to star!

   No, no,
   Low, low,
Sweeping daisies with my toe.
   Slow, slow,
   To and fro,
Slow-slow-slow-slow.
          WILLIAM ALLINGHAM
          "A Swing Song"

The repetition in each stanza gives the feeling of a swing moving back and forth. At the end of the poem, the swing and the reader begin to slow down with the repetition of "slow-slow-slow-slow."

Rhyme. Rhyme is the repetition of syllable sounds in poetry. When the sounds are repeated at the ends of lines, the rhyme is called end rhyme, as in this example.

I shall go
Up and down
In my gown.
Gorgeously arrayed,
Boned and stayed.
          AMY LOWELL
          "Patterns"

Rhyme that occurs within a single line, as in the following example, is called internal rhyme.

And all is seared with trade; bleared, smeared with toil. . . .
          GERARD MANLEY HOPKINS
          "God's Grandeur"

A rhyme scheme is the pattern of end rhyme in a poem. The pattern can be charted by assigning a letter of the alphabet, beginning with the letter *a*, to each line. Lines that rhyme are given the same letter. Notice the rhyme scheme in the following poem.

The rhino is a homely beast,	a
For human eyes he's not a feast,	a
But you and I will never know	b
Why nature chose to make him so.	b
Farewell, farewell, you old rhinoceros,	c
I'll stare at something less prepoceros!	c

OGDEN NASH
"The Rhinoceros"

Rhythm. Rhythm refers to the pattern or beat of accented and unaccented syllables in a line of poetry. Poets use rhythm to bring out the musical quality of language, to create mood, to emphasize ideas, and to reinforce content.

See *Meter.*

Rising Action. Rising action refers to the building complications in the conflict of a story or play. The climax is the highest point of the rising action. Thus, in *Romeo and Juliet,* all the events leading up to the marriage of the two title characters in Act III make up the rising action.

See *Climax, Conflict, Falling Action, Plot.*

Satire. Satire is a form of literature in which foolish ideas or customs are ridiculed through exaggeration. The purpose of satire is to get people to examine their foolishness and to change their ways or to prevent them from repeating the mistakes of the past.

The story "Everyday Use" satirizes people who feel that they have rediscovered their heritage. The author exaggerates and makes fun of Dee's adopted African name. Actually, Dee is responding only to the rekindled interest of society in her tradition. Maggie and her mother truly value their heritage and their forebears, as represented by the quilts.

See *Parody.*

Science Fiction. Science fiction is a form of fiction that draws imaginatively on scientific knowledge and theory in its plot, setting, and characters. Science fiction generally goes beyond technological truth into the realm of speculation, showing the reader what life could be like in the years to come. "Trurl's Machine," for example, is a fanciful story about a machine that can converse, move around at will, lose its temper, and hold a grudge.

See *Fiction.*

Sequence. Sequence is a series of events in the order in which they actually occur in a short story, play, narrative poem, or nonfiction selection. A term that means the same as sequence is *chronological order.*

Setting. Setting is the time and place of the action of a story. The importance of setting varies. In "Charles," for example, the writer gives almost no indication of where or when the action occurs. In "The Most Dangerous Game," on the other hand, the writer uses detailed descriptions of the setting to create the mood of the story. In stories of this type, the setting can be almost as important as the characters and events.

A writer might establish a setting with a brief, factual statement, as in the following sentence.

It began at three o'clock one October afternoon as I sat in the grandstand at the fall trotting and pacing meet at Sandusky, Ohio.
SHERWOOD ANDERSON
"I'm a Fool"

Another writer might describe a setting with rich detail, as in this paragraph.

The Virginia Preparatory School lies just off the Shirley Highway between Washington, D.C., and Richmond. It is a small Southern school with dull red brick dormitories and classroom buildings, quiet old school buildings with quiet old Southern names—Page House, Stuart Hall, Randolph Hall, Breckinridge, Pinckney, and Coulter. The high brick wall that surrounds the school is known as the Breastworks, and the shallow pond behind the football field is the Crater. V.P.S. is an old school, with an old school's traditions. A Virginia Department of Conservation sign commemorates the use of the school by Union troops as a military hospital in 1861, and every October the school celebrates "Liberation Day," in honor of the day in 1866 when the school reopened.

C.D.B. Bryan
"So Much Unfairness of Things"

Short Story. A short story is a work of fiction that can be read in one sitting. A short story usually contains a major conflict and at least one main character. Because it is fiction, the characters and events are largely products of the writer's imagination.

The four main elements of a short story are setting, character, plot, and theme. The setting is the time and place of the action; the characters are the people or animals that appear in the story; the plot is the story line, or the working out of the conflict. The three elements of setting, character, and plot usually combine to bring out the fourth element, the theme. The theme is the message that the writer wishes to communicate to the reader.

A short story must be unified; that is, all of its elements must combine to produce a total effect. This effect is reinforced through an appropriate title and through the use of symbolism, irony, and other literary devices.

See *Character, Plot, Setting, Theme.*

Simile. A simile is a stated comparison between two things that are actually unlike but that have something in common. Like metaphors, similes are figures of speech. Similes, however, contain the words *like* or *as.*

"Cool as a cucumber," "fresh as a daisy," and "stubborn as a mule" are similes used to describe people. A person and a mule, of course, are basically dissimilar, but they might both share the quality of stubbornness.

Writers use similes to give readers a fresh look at familiar things. Poets, in particular, make frequent use of similes, as in the following examples.

I spied a very small brown duck
Riding the swells of the sea
Like a rocking-chair.

Galway Kinnell
"Duck Chasing"

I heard a fly buzz when I died;
    The stillness in the room
Was like the stillness in the air
    Between the heaves of storm.

Emily Dickinson
"I Heard a Fly Buzz When I Died"

Arithmetic is where numbers fly like pigeons in and out of your head.

Carl Sandburg
"Arithmetic"

What happens to a dream deferred?

    Does it dry up
    like a raisin in the sun?
    Or fester like a sore—
    And then run?
    Does it stink like rotten meat?
    Or crust and sugar over—
    like a syrupy sweet?
    Maybe it just sags
    like a heavy load.

Or does it explode?

Langston Hughes
"Dream Deferred"

See *Figurative Language, Metaphor.*

Soliloquy. In drama, a soliloquy is a speech in which a character utters thoughts aloud. Generally, the character is on the stage alone, not speaking to other characters and perhaps not even consciously addressing the audience. Members of the audience feel as if they are overhearing a character talking to himself or herself.

Speaker. Speaker refers to the voice that "talks" in a poem. The ideas in a poem are presented through the speaker who is not necessarily the same as the poet. The speaker in poetry may be likened to the narrator in prose.

The writer of the following poem has chosen a phenomenon of nature as his speaker.

I can get through a doorway without any key,
And strip the leaves from the great oak tree.

I can drive storm-clouds and shake tall towers,
Or steal through a garden and not wake the
  flowers.

Seas I can move and ships I can sink;
I can carry a house-top or the scent of a pink.

When I am angry I can rave and riot;
And when I am spent, I lie quiet as quiet.
                                    JAMES REEVES
                                    "The Wind"

Stanza. A stanza is a group of lines that form a unit in a poem. Usually, the stanzas of a poem each have the same number of lines and often have the same rhyme and meter as well. Twentieth-century poets frequently experiment with the form of stanzas more than did earlier poets.

The following three-line stanzas were written by the poet Dylan Thomas as his father lay dying.

Do not go gentle into that good night,
Old age should burn and rave at close of day;
Rage, rage against the dying of the light.

Though wise men at their end know dark is
  right,
Because their words had forked no lightning
  they
Do not go gentle into that good night.

Good men, the last wave by, crying how bright
Their frail deeds might have danced in a green
  bay,
Rage, rage against the dying of the light.
    "Do Not Go Gentle into That Good Night"
See *Couplet.*

Structure. Structure is the way a work of literature is put together. In poetry, structure refers to the arrangement of words and lines to produce a desired effect. In prose, structure is the arrangement of larger units or parts of a selection.

The structure of a poem, short story, novel, play, or nonfiction selection usually relates to other elements. For example, in the poem "Training," the sounds and movements of the sea are reinforced by the arrangement of words and lines. In "The Secret Life of Walter Mitty," the interweaving of Walter Mitty's dream life with his real life reinforces the contrast between the actual Mitty and the imagined Mitty.

Style. Style is the way that a play, poem, or prose selection is written. Style refers not to what is being said but to how it is said. Many elements contribute to a writer's characteristic style. Sentence length, diction, tone, and imagery are only a few. A literary style might be described as heavy-handed, obscure, crisp, flowery, conversational, wordy, or elegant. The two passages below both describe unproductive land. Notice the difference in their styles.

To the red country and part of the gray country of Oklahoma, the last rains came gently, and they did not cut the scarred earth. The plows crossed and recrossed the rivulet marks. The last rains lifted the corn quickly and scattered weed colonies and grass along the sides of the roads so that the gray country and the dark red country began to disappear under a green cover. In the last part of May the sky grew pale and the clouds that had hung in high puffs for so long in the spring were dissipated. The sun flared down on the growing corn day after day until a line of brown spread along the edge of each green bayonet. The clouds appeared, and went away, and in a while they did not try any more. The weeds grew darker green to protect themselves, and they did not spread any more. The surface of the earth crusted, a thin hard crust, and as the sky became pale, so the earth became pale, pink in the red country and white in the gray country.

JOHN STEINBECK
The Grapes of Wrath

Where you stand the grass is rich and matted, you cannot see the soil. But the rich green hills break down. They fall to the valley below, and falling, change their nature. For they grow red and bare; they cannot hold the rain and mist, and the streams are dry in the kloofs. Too many cattle feed upon the grass, and too many fires have burned it. Stand shod upon it, for it is coarse and sharp, and the stones cut under the feet. It is not kept, or guarded, or cared for, it no longer keeps men, guards men, cares for men. The titihoya does not cry here any more.

ALAN PATON
Cry, the Beloved Country

Surprise Ending. A surprise ending is an unexpected twist at the end of the story, a twist that is not anticipated by the reader. The story "Charles," for example, ends with the surprise revelation that Laurie and Charles are the same boy.

See *Climax.*

Suspense. Suspense is the excitement that a reader feels about the outcome or resolution to the conflict of a story. Suspense makes the reader want to know what will happen next. Readers of "The Sea Devil," for example, are eager to find out if the fisherman will escape or will be pulled out to sea. They may feel their tension level build, and they may find themselves reading faster and faster as the fisherman tries repeatedly to free himself.

Symbol. A symbol is a person, place, object, or idea that stands for something beyond itself. The dove and the olive branch, for example, are symbols of peace. A wedding band symbolizes marriage, and a white flag symbolizes surrender. A king or a queen might symbolize patriotism for a country. Symbols can replace long explanations. Highway signs, for example, communicate directions through the use of symbolic pictures.

The use of symbols in literature is called symbolism.

Theme. The theme is the main idea in a work of literature. It is a writer's perception about life shared with the reader. Some stories and poems are pure entertainment and as such have no underlying message. In most serious writing, however, the writer makes one or more statements about life or the human condition. These themes are seldom stated directly and may reveal themselves only through careful reading and thought.

The theme of the poem "Dreams" is that dreams are necessary to life and make life richer and fuller. In "The Sniper" the theme is the cruelty and inhumanity of war, especially civil war. Both the climax and the ending of this short story bring out this theme.

Title. The name of a short story, novel, play, nonfiction selection, or poem is its title. A title is often carefully chosen. Novelist and playwright Paul Zindel, for example, believes that unusual titles generate reader interest. Thus, he has titled two of his books *The Pigman* and *My Darling, My Hamburger.* Some titles reinforce elements in a story. "Charles," for example, reinforces the irony of Laurie's true identity.

Tone. Tone is the attitude a writer takes toward a subject. All of the elements in a work of literature together create the writer's tone, which might be bitter, angry, detached, or playful. Tone is different from mood, which refers to the way a reader responds to a selection. For example, a story about three boys trapped in a cemetery for a night might have an eerie, frightening mood. The tone of the story, however, could reflect the writer's amusement at the predicament of the characters.

In "Sleeping Arrangements" Sam Levenson takes a humorous look at his youth. The tone of this selection is quite different from the serious recollections of Sherwood Anderson in "Discovery of a Father."

Tragedy. In broad terms, tragedy is literature, especially drama, in which actions and events turn out disastrously for the main character or characters. In tragedy the main characters, and sometimes other involved characters and innocent bystanders as well, end up being destroyed. Usually the destruction is death, as in *Romeo and Juliet*. Some tragedies, however, end with the main characters alive but in a devastated condition. Tragic characters generally evoke both pity and fear in readers or viewers: pity because they feel sorry for the characters and fear because they realize that the problems and struggles faced by the characters are perhaps a necessary part of human life.

Understatement. Understatement is the technique of creating emphasis by saying less than is actually or literally true. For example, on a scorching summer afternoon one athlete might say to another, "It's a bit warm today." When hard pressed, a suitor might say, "I think I like Sarah," when he is actually madly in love with her. Both the athlete and the suitor are expressing their ideas through understatement.

Biographies of the Writers

Nanina Alba (1917–1968) published her first collection of poems, *The Parchments*, at the age of forty-six. Her only other book, *The Parchments II*, followed soon after. Prior to the publishing of her work, Alba was a teacher of English, French, and music in various high schools and colleges.

Sherwood Anderson (1876–1941) was a professional writer from Camden, Ohio, who is famous for collections of short stories, such as *Winesburg, Ohio*. As a boy, Anderson moved from place to place with his family. He dropped out of school at fourteen and went to work to help support his six brothers and sisters. What he learned working on farms, in shops, and in livery stables later appeared in short stories that often dealt with the emotional problems of boyhood. At age thirty-six, Anderson seemed to be a typical, middle-class American. He had a wife, children, and a successful business partnership. During this year, however, Anderson left it all behind and traveled to Chicago where he began a new, and ultimately successful, career as a writer of novels and short stories.

Maya Angelou (born 1928). Few people are as multi-talented and as successful as Maya Angelou. She is, perhaps, best known for two autobiographical books, *I Know Why the Caged Bird Sings* and *Gather Together in My Name*. Angelou has also written poems, stage plays, screen plays, television specials, short stories, and magazine articles and has worked for newspapers in Egypt and Ghana. Angelou studied dance with Martha Graham, toured twenty-two countries in a production of *Porgy and Bess*, directed and acted in off-Broadway shows, and served as television narrator and interviewer. She has written and recorded songs and has composed musical scores for her screen plays. When time has permitted, Angelou has toured the country as a lecturer and visiting professor to various colleges and universities. During the 1960's, she worked with Dr. Martin Luther King, Jr. as a coordinator for the Southern Christian Leadership Conference and was appointed to the Bicentennial Council by President Ford.

Toni Cade Bambara (born 1939) has worked as a welfare investigator, project director for social programs, college instructor, and educational consultant for African-American studies. She has also studied dance for many years. As a writer she is known for her essays and articles on black Americans and as the editor of *The Black Woman* and *Tales and Stories for Black Folks*. Bambara urges young people to "read, read well, read everything in sight." She places special emphasis on the importance of listening to family elders.

Imamu Amiri Baraka (Leroi Jones) (born 1934) is a dramatist, music critic, theater director, social activist, and, most notably, a poet. He was raised in New Jersey, graduated two years ahead of his class, and studied religion and medicine before earning a B.A. degree in English. Jones spent three years in the Air Force and then began a career as a music critic and poet. By the end of the 1950's, his poetry began to attract attention. At this point his interests turned to drama. He wrote several short plays, including *Dutchman*, which won the Obie Award in 1964 as that year's best off-Broadway play. During these years he also received Whitney and Guggenheim fellowships and a grant from the National Endowment for the Arts. At the height of his popularity as a poet and dramatist, Jones became increasingly involved with social issues. He adopted an African name and retreated to the black communities of Harlem and Newark, using his talent to stir black audiences, to encourage black talent, and to stimulate social change.

Robert Benchley (1889–1945) was a kind, generous man, much loved by his friends and by the readers of his humorous essays. Actually, he managed to achieve success in three careers. Benchley published fourteen collections of light, witty essays, including *The Early Worm, From Bed to Worse,* and *Inside Benchley.* These comic pieces were peopled with vague, bumbling souls—the type who stumble over chairs and arrive at parties with unmatched shoes. Benchley also held important editorial posts at several newspapers and magazines, including *Vanity Fair* and *The New Yorker.* Benchley's third career was as an entertainer. He performed his humorous material on stage and on radio and appeared in the world's first all-talking motion picture. In all, he was featured in more than twenty-five short films and was honored with an Academy Award in 1936. Despite overwhelming praise from all sides, Benchley frequently described himself as a failure, one who had wasted his opportunities and talents. Serious or not, he claimed that what he really wanted was to be a social worker and to write a history of the Queen Anne period.

Elizabeth Bishop (1911–1979) spent a lonely childhood being passed from one relative to another. She entered Vassar College with a medical career in mind, but she graduated with a degree in English and a desire to write. Financial independence meant that she could travel extensively, and she lived for many years in Brazil, carefully crafting her own unique poetry as well as doing extensive translations of Brazilian poets. She returned to the United States in 1967, settled in Boston, and began teaching at Harvard University. Bishop's self-critical nature, along with her independent means, allowed her to publish only her best work. In thirty years as a poet, just five collections, a fraction of her writing, was printed. These books, however, received the highest critical acclaim, earning a Pulitzer Prize, a National Book Award, and the National Book Critics Circle Award. Her poems are known for their beauty, imagination, and detailed descriptions of nature.

Richard Brautigan (1935–1984) lived a secluded life, moving frequently between homes in San Francisco and Montana. Brautigan's first writings were poems. His unusual verse is filled with metaphors and similes, and his creative imagination often takes a humorous twist. His wit is evident in titles such as "Feel Free To Marry Emily Dickinson" and "Twenty-Eight Cents for My Old Age." Brautigan's novels, which have a wide following, include *A Confederate General from Big Sur* and *Trout Fishing in America.*

Robert Browning (1812–1889), a major English poet, grew up in a comfortable suburb of London. His parents passed on a love of art and music to their son, who received most of his education in his father's library of over 7,000 volumes. When Browning began to write poems and plays, he experienced slight success with the critics, but much favor with London's social set. He was a handsome, optimistic, intelligent young man and, therefore, was a favorite at dinners and parties. Unsatisfied with the results of his writing, Browning turned to the dramatic monologue, a poetic form in which characters speak about dramatic moments in their lives. Browning perfected this form, and his dramatic monologues are still popular with readers. In 1846, Browning met the frail poet, Elizabeth Barrett. Against the wishes of her domineering father, the couple secretly married and fled to Italy where they lived happily for sixteen years. After Elizabeth's death, a heartbroken

Browning returned to England. After recovering from his grief, he went on to write some of his finest poetry and in his later years gained critical as well as social popularity.

Truman Capote (1924–1984) spent his early years in the care of various southern relatives, including an elderly cousin, Miss Sook Faulk. She was the inspiration for his widely read story "A Christmas Memory." Capote was sent to New York for high school where he was a poor student, listless and uninterested in anything except writing. After graduation, he worked for *The New Yorker* as a glorified errand boy, occasionally publishing a short story. The winning of O. Henry awards in 1943 and 1946 allowed him to concentrate on writing. *Other Voices, Other Rooms* and *Breakfast at Tiffany's* were immediate successes, as were the books that followed. Capote spent six years on his most sensational book, *In Cold Blood*, which relates the true story of a mass murder in Kansas. His idea was to create a new literary form that combines fiction and journalism. He called his book a "nonfiction novel." Capote worked carefully, doing a great deal of rewriting. He was concerned with style and the rhythms and sounds of his prose. Capote himself was as unique and eccentric as the characters he created. When not writing, he often socialized with an exclusive international crowd.

Robert J. Casey (1890–1962) was a writer and editor with the *Chicago Daily News* for more than twenty years. During World War II he was a foreign correspondent, covering such events as the battle of London and the invasion of Normandy. Casey published more than thirty books. *The Cannoneers Have Hairy Ears* and *I Can't Forget* are two that deal with his war-time experiences.

Charles Causley (born 1917) is a teacher, editor, and poet from Cornwall, England. His collections of verse include *Farewell, Aggie Weston, Underneath the Water,* and *Figure of 8*. Although some of his collections have been published as children's books, Causley states that he does not begin with a particular age group in mind. His concern is "the problem of getting the poem on the paper as close as possible to what's in one's head. After the poem's written is the time to decide (if ever) what kind of audience it might reach."

Eugenia Collier (born 1928) started teaching college English in 1955 but did not begin writing until fourteen years later. One of her first efforts, "Marigolds," won the Gwendolyn Brooks short story award. Collier explains her new-found ability in this way: "After a conventional Western-type education, I discovered the richness, the diversity, the beauty of my black heritage. The fact of my blackness is the core and center of my creativity." Collier is making up for lost time with an outpouring of poems, stories, articles, and critical essays. Her work can be found in magazines, anthologies, and educational journals. Currently, she is at work on several projects that include a collection of poetry, more short stories, and a history of writing by black Americans.

Richard Connell (1893–1949) began his professional writing career at age ten by covering local baseball games for the newspaper his father edited. He attended Harvard University where he was editor of both the college newspaper and *Lampoon,* the school's humor magazine. After graduation, Connell worked for newspapers and advertising agencies before becoming a free-lance fiction writer in 1919. He wrote film scripts and published several short story collections and novels.

Edward Estlin Cummings (1894–1962) was an innovative modern poet whose work influenced many later writers. As a young man,

Cummings volunteered for duty in France during World War I. When the fighting ended, he stayed in Paris to study art. He was a talented painter, and his search for new methods of expression is evident in his art as it is in his poetry. Cummings—or as he wrote it, e.e. cummings—published his first book in 1923. In his poems, he ignored rules of punctuation, capitalization, and spacing, running several words together and stretching syllables out over several lines to create various rhythms and images. His intent was to coax meaning and dimension from the limitations of the printed word. At first, many critics condemned his work. Now, Cummings is accepted as one of America's major twentieth-century poets.

Borden Deal (1922–1985) worked at whatever jobs he could find—as a skip tracer, telephone sales representative, copywriter, circus performer, fire fighter—until he could afford to be a full time writer. From 1956 on he produced novels and short stories, all focusing on what he called "the new South." Deal portrays southern life since 1890, when that region began to renew itself after the physical and spiritual destruction of the Civil War. His books include *Walk Through the Valley*, *Dragon's Wine*, and *The Tobacco Men*. Deal's work has appeared in anthologies, textbooks, and magazines and has been translated into more than twenty languages.

Babette Deutsch (1895–1982) published her first book of poetry in 1919. During the next sixty years, she became famous for her poetry, and she wrote novels, books for children, and literary criticism as well. She also translated German and Russian verse. From 1944 until her death, Deutsch was a lecturer in poetry at Columbia University in New York City.

Emily Dickinson (1830–1886) lived her entire life in Amherst, Massachusetts. During her early years, she led the typical life of an upper-class young girl in small-town New England. At age twenty-six, however, she suddenly withdrew from the world and rarely appeared in public again. It is thought that an unhappy love affair caused the great change in her personality. Throughout the next thirty years, Emily spent long hours in her room, secretly writing poetry on envelopes, paper bags, and other scraps of paper. She wrote more than 1,700 poems of which only seven were published during her life. Although Dickinson used simple words and short stanzas, she was able to create strong, clear images. Her awareness of humanity and nature are amazing, given her limited experience.

Paul Laurence Dunbar (1872–1906) was the son of former slaves whose father escaped to freedom on the Underground Railroad. Unable to afford college, Dunbar abandoned thoughts of a career in law or the ministry. Instead, he worked as an elevator operator, writing poetry in his spare hours. His first collection, *Oak and Ivory*, was published in 1893 and was followed by a steady stream of novels, short stories, and more than 500 poems. Much of Dunbar's work is written in dialect. His subject matter includes the old plantation days, as well as the struggles and turmoil of emancipation. During his lifetime Dunbar's books were widely read by both black and white audiences, but he never achieved the financial success he thought his fame merited.

Gerald Durrell (born 1925) was born in Jamshedpur, India, of British parents. After a youth spent on the Greek island of Corfu, he studied in France, Italy, Switzerland, and Greece. Durrell collected pets wherever he lived, often to the dismay of his family. Their reactions to his hobby are described humorously in *My Family and Other Animals* and *Birds, Beasts, and Relatives*. After two years as a zookeeper in Great Britain, Durrell set off on a series of expeditions with the intent of forming his own animal collection. These expeditions produced not only animals, but also several books about his adventures. In 1959, Durrell founded a wildlife preserve on the Isle of Jersey, off the southeast coast of England. For more than twenty years, he has devoted himself to the protection and breeding of endangered species.

Dave Etter (born 1928) has a special feeling for the Midwest, which is evident in his many collections of poetry. He portrays the landscape, sounds, and temperaments of places such as Iowa, Illinois, Indiana, and, as he says, "my greatest passion, the Mississippi River." Etter's prize-winning books include *Go Read the River* and *The Last Train to Prophetstown*. His work has appeared in more than forty anthologies and 100 literary magazines. He has served as editor for Northwestern University Press, Encyclopaedia Britannica, and, currently, the Northern Illinois University Press.

Bernard Evslin (born 1922) is an award-winning producer of documentary films and a professional writer. Most of Evslin's film strips and books are based on Greek mythology and history. *Heroes, Gods, and Monsters of the Greek Myths, The Adventures of Ulysses*, and *The Trojan Wars* are three of his most popular titles.

Robert Francis (born 1901) has devoted his life to writing and teaching. In a small house called Fort Juniper on the outskirts of Amherst, Massachusetts, he lives a quiet life gardening, reading, and writing. His award-winning work consists of fiction, essays, autobiography, nonfiction and, most notably, poetry. Francis has published eight collections of poems, including *The Sound I Listened For, The Orb Weaver*, and *Come Out into the Sun*.

Robert Frost (1874–1963) was born in San Francisco. For eight generations, however, his ancestors had been New Englanders, and when Frost was ten, his family moved back to Massachusetts. As a young adult, he married and worked at odd jobs—as a mill hand, a shoe salesman, a farmer—to support his family. At thirty-eight his farm in New Hampshire failed, and he moved his family to England where he concentrated on writing poetry. Frost had been writing poems since the age of fifteen with no success whatsoever; but as he neared the age of forty, his work began to receive recognition. His first two collections were praised in both Britain and the United States, and he returned home to New England. With each succeeding volume his stature in the literary world grew, and for the last forty years of his life he was considered one of the world's most important living poets. Frost was issued a special congressional medal in 1960 and is the only American poet to win four Pulitzer Prizes. In 1961 he was asked to read his work at the inauguration of President John F. Kennedy. Most of Frost's poetry creates realistic pictures of New England and its people in an easy-going, conversational style. His seeming simplicity, however, can be deceiving. Frost himself once said that poetry is "saying one thing and meaning another."

Susan Glaspell (1882–1948) and her first husband, George Cook, were highly influential in changing the direction of American theater. In 1915, they founded the Provincetown Players, an experimental drama group through which new playwrights could present their work. Glaspell was an actress and a director, but more importantly, she wrote plays for the group. Best remembered are *The Inheritors* and "Trifles," which was based on a story that Glaspell covered while working as a reporter. *Alison's House*, which depicts a family's struggle over the publication of a dead member's poems, was based on the life of Emily Dickinson. It won the 1931 Pulitzer Prize. Most of Glaspell's novels and plays center around strong female characters. In some cases she portrays characters who possess the dignity and endurance of the pioneers. At other times she deals with the psychological tensions that result from woman's role in modern society.

Arthur Gordon (born 1912) was for ten years editor for two popular magazines, *Good Housekeeping* and *Cosmopolitan*. His career was interrupted during World War II by three years with the Air Force. After the war, Gordon became a free lance writer. Since then, he has published novels, biographies, nonfiction works, and more than 200 short stories and magazine articles. His hobbies, which include hunting, fishing, and boating, often provide subject matter for his writings.

Robert Graves (born 1895) grew up in London, England, and studied at Oxford University until the outbreak of World War I. His experiences in the war became the basis for much of his early poetry. Graves has published over twenty-five volumes of poetry, but he is best known for his prose writing. Because of his classical education, he is able to translate from French, Spanish, Latin, and Greek, and many of his books are based on Greek and Roman history and legend. His novel, *I, Claudius,* was adapted for a popular British television series. Although Graves is primarily a writer and scholar, he also has achieved the distinction of winning an Olympic medal. He is now the proprietor of a jazz club on the island of Majorca.

Eloise Greenfield (born 1929) has written children's books, novels, biographies, short stories, and poems. She has also written recollections of her childhood with the help of her mother, Lessie Jones Little. After growing up in North Carolina and attending Miner Teachers College, Greenfield worked at the U.S. Patent Office in Washington, D.C. for twelve years. She then joined the Black Writers Workshop, first as co-director of adult fiction, then as director of children's literature. Greenfield's own work was first published in 1970.

Lafcadio Hearn (1850–1904) has had a life more adventurous than most fictional characters. He was born on a Greek island of Irish-Greek parents and educated in France, England, and Wales. In 1869, he came to the United States, settling in New Orleans. He found work as a journalist and also began writing the strange, unconventional stories for which he became famous. Hearn's particular skill lay in searching out peculiar bits of life and describing them in vivid style. Of his writing he said, "I think a man must devote himself to one thing in order to succeed, so I have pledged myself to the worship of the odd, the strange, the exotic. It quite suits my temperament." After twelve years in New Orleans and the West Indies, Hearn set out for Japan, hoping to find material for more stories. He became fascinated with the country and spent the rest of his life there. Hearn married the daughter of a wealthy Samurai family, dressed in kimonos, practiced the Buddhist religion, and renamed himself Yakumo Koizumi. For ten years, Hearn taught at the Imperial University of Japan while writing books on the life, customs, and people of his adopted country.

W. C. Heinz (born 1915) dreamed about being Babe Ruth, Jack Dempsey, and Red Grange all rolled into one. When he realized that he lacked one basic quality—athletic ability—he decided that being a sports writer might be the next best thing to being a sports star. Heinz's journalism career has included assignments as a reporter, feature writer, war correspondent, and sports columnist for the *New York Sun.* He has written books, articles, and stories about sports and sports heroes.

His work has appeared in more than fifty anthologies. Heinz's other area of expertise is the field of medicine. His books, *The Surgeon* and *Emergency* are popular testimonies to his interest in medical matters.

Zenna Henderson (born 1917) has taught at a U.S. Air Force base in France and at a children's tuberculosis sanitarium in Connecticut. She currently teaches in her home state of Arizona. Henderson's science fiction and fantasy tales have appeared in many anthologies. Collections of her stories include *The Anything Box* and *The People: No Different Flesh*.

James Herriot (James Alfred Wight) (born 1916) is surprised and pleased by the success of his best-selling books based on his experience as a country veterinarian. "I suppose no one had thought of writing funny books about cows and pigs before," he says. Herriot began treating animals in 1940 after completing his veterinary training in Glasgow, Scotland. Although he is now a well known writer, he still lives and works in a quiet English town, enjoying the simple rural life. Despite the long hours and hard work, Herriot remains convinced that veterinary medicine is the finest possible profession. His books include *All Creatures Great and Small* and *The Lord God Made Them All*.

Max J. Herzberg (1886–1958) was a prominent educator and editor and was a teacher and principal in New Jersey for forty-four years. He also edited many textbooks and was influential in improving the position of American writers in school literature courses. Herzberg served as literary editor and critic for newspapers in Newark, New Jersey, for more than forty years. Five of those years were spent compiling and editing the *Encyclopedia of American Literature*, a widely used reference book.

Sandra Hochman (born 1936) often uses her poetry to explore the special problems and feelings of women. Much of her work is personal, based on her own lonely childhood and difficult relationships. Besides six collections of poems, including the prize-winning *Manhattan Pastures*, Hochman has written novels, plays, magazine columns, and a film script. At one time, she considered an acting career and appeared in a number of off-Broadway plays.

Langston Hughes (1902–1967) was the first black American to earn his living solely from writing. Before becoming established as a writer, he was a farmer, cook, waiter, sailor, and doorman and worked his way through more than eight countries. Hughes's first real recognition as a poet came to him when he was a hotel busboy. He left some of his poems at the table where poet Vachel Lindsay was dining. Lindsay was so impressed that he presented Hughes's work along with his own poetry readings. In addition to the poetry for which he is best known, Hughes wrote novels, short stories, plays, song lyrics, and radio scripts. In his writing, he described the common people of Harlem. He used their dialect and the rhythm of their blues music and dealt with the themes of racial prejudice and the struggle for equality. Hughes influenced young blacks to write about these and other relevant themes.

Shirley Jackson (1919–1965) claimed that she wrote "because it gave her an excuse not to clean out closets." Her work is unusual because it can be divided into two distinct categories. Jackson wrote many warm, lighthearted sketches about family life. *Life Among the Savages* and the story "Charles" are examples. At other times, however, Jackson turned her talents to chilling tales of horror. These tales include the famous short story "The Lottery" and the novels *The Haunting of Hill House* and *We Have Always Lived in the Castle*. Much of her work has been adapted for stage and screen.

Dorothy M. Johnson (born 1905) was made an honorary member of the Blackfeet tribe in Montana, probably due to her sympathetic portrayals of Indian life in the Old West. She has written many books about frontier life, including *Western Badmen*, *Lawmen of the Old West*, and *Warrior for a Lost Nation: A Biography of Sitting Bull*. A number of her short stories and articles have appeared in magazines and anthologies. Several have been adapted for radio and television. Three popular motion pictures, *The Hanging Tree*, *The Man Who Shot Liberty Valance*, and *A Man Called Horse*, are based on her work.

Hannah Kahn (born 1911) had little formal education as a child. She began working at the age of fifteen and eventually became an interior decorator. A childhood love of poetry continued to grow, and in spare moments, Kahn tried her hand at writing poems. In 1963, her first collection was published. Since then, hundreds of her poems have appeared in anthologies, magazines, and newspapers. Two of her books of poems are *Eve's Daughter* and *Ride a Wild Horse*. When Kahn was fifty, she began college classes at night. Twelve years later, she received a degree from Miami Dade Community College and became a faculty member there.

Richard Kell (born 1927) is an Irishman from County Cork who now resides and teaches in England. His first poetry collection, *Control Tower*, was published in 1962. His poems, short stories, and essays have also appeared in anthologies and magazines.

Stanislaw Lem (born 1921) is considered the leading science fiction writer in the Communist world. He is a native of Poland and has studied both medicine and philosophy. Lem's books have reached a world-wide audience with translations into more than fifteen languages. His works include *The Planet of Death*, *Book of the Robots*, and *Invasion from Aldebaran*.

Sam Levenson (1911–1980) was an entertainer and folk humorist who appeared on the most popular programs on radio and television for over thirty years. A homespun brand of humor characterized both his performances and his writings. Levenson's books, such as *In One Era and Out the Other* and *Everything But Money*, were filled with down-to-earth advice about family life and child rearing. He frequently concluded that old-fashioned methods were still the best. One of Levenson's typical comments was, "The Founding Fathers guaranteed only the pursuit of happiness, not happiness itself. Lots of kids today seem to want the happiness without bothering about the pursuit." His insight into the behavior of young people came not only from recollections of his own large family, but also from his early experience as a high school teacher.

Denise Levertov (born 1923) grew up in England in a strangely spiritual atmosphere. Her father, a converted Russian Jew, was an Anglican minister who filled the house with thousands of books and dozens of temporary refugees, artists, and literary exiles. Her mother, a descendent of a mystical Welsh preacher, read classics to the family and provided all of Levertov's education. When she was twelve, Levertov sent some of her poems to T. S. Eliot who thought them worthy enough to merit a long letter of advice. Her first collection was published in 1946. Her second did not appear until ten years later, after she had married an American soldier, moved to New York, and immersed herself in American culture. Levertov's many books include *Here and Now*, *The Sorrow Dance*, and *Footprints*. She is known for her fine craftsmanship and rich use of language.

Vachel Lindsay (1879–1931) used strong rhythms and chants in his poems and tried to blend music and poetry into a new art form. As a young man, Lindsay seriously disappointed his parents by refusing to follow his father into the medical profession. He studied art for twelve years, but it was poetry that made him famous. Filled with a great desire to awaken new interest in poetry, he became a wandering minstrel. For twenty years he criss-crossed the country reciting his poems. He gave his pamphlet, *Rhymes To Be Traded for Bread*, to those who offered him food and a place to sleep. Lindsay believed that poems should be performed, not merely read. Many of his poems include stage and movement directions. Some poems call for drum, flute, and banjo accompaniment.

Alonzo Lopez writes poetry in both English and his native Navajo language. His work attempts to describe the Navajo people, their culture, and their land. Lopez, a native of Arizona, attended the Institute of American Indian Arts, Yale University, and Wesleyan University. The latter provided him with advanced courses in American Indian studies.

Katherine Mansfield (1888–1923) spent her early years in her native New Zealand. Her writing talent became obvious with the publication of her first story at age nine. She was also a talented cellist and at one time considered a career in music. After attending school in England, Mansfield persuaded her parents to let her stay in London. There she lived a carefree life with other aspiring artists and writers. She sold an occasional story and earned small sums by writing book reviews. Mansfield suffered from ill health and criss-crossed Europe seeking cures and healthful climates. These travels provided the settings and experiences for most of her work. She published seven short story collections before her death at age thirty-four.

Mickey Mantle (born 1931) is one of America's greatest baseball heroes. As a boy, Mantle was coached and encouraged by his father who had named him after Mickey Cochrane, a catcher with the Detroit Tigers. After high school graduation, Mantle was signed by the New York Yankees for their farm club, and in 1951 he was moved to the major leagues. In all, he spent eighteen years with the Yankees, retiring from baseball in 1969. Mantle, a switch-hitter and center fielder, scored 536 home runs in regular season play and a record eighteen home runs during World Series play. Surprisingly, he also broke records for striking out more than any other player. Three times the American League named Mantle most valuable player. He was elected to the Baseball Hall of Fame in 1974.

William Matthews (born 1942) has been an editor for poetry journals and has taught at various colleges and universities. While working on a masters degree at the University of North Carolina, Matthews and some friends founded a publishing company, the Lillabulero Press. Included in the company's publications were a literary magazine and, in 1969, Matthews's first poetry collection, *Broken Syllables*. Several of his books have been published since then, and his poems are frequently included in anthologies.

Jean McCord (born 1924) has found time for writing even as she pursued forty-five different occupations, including time served in the Women's Army Corps. Among her novels are *Deep Where the Octopi Lie* and *Bitter Is the Hawk's Path*. Her short stories have been published in *Seventeen* magazine and in *Best American Short Stories*.

Phyllis McGinley (1905–1978) had a "wild and woolly" childhood in Colorado where she rode ponies to school and spent Sundays watching bronco-busting. She claimed to have "cut her teeth on a pencil" and began writing at age six. She became known for her poems, essays, and children's books. *Times Three: Selected Verse from Three Decades* won the 1961 Pulitzer Prize. McGinley considered herself a "housewife-writer," and much of her work deals with the problems and events of everyday life. McGinley used a light, witty style that often belied the serious undertones present in her writings. Her goal, she said, was "to narrow the gap between light and serious verse."

David Nava Monreal is a prize-winning poet who lives in California. His work has been anthologized in Chicano literature collections and in textbooks. "Moco Limping" is a poem that was written about his own dog.

Farley Mowat (born 1921) spent much of his youth exploring the Canadian Arctic wilderness and continues to prefer the life of a naturalist. "I am a simple fellow," says Mowat, "and I like simple things. Cities give me the pip. Civilizations scare me." Not surprisingly, Mowat writes about the land, people, and animals he loves. He is often highly critical of those forces that endanger the environment and its creatures. After living with the Ihalmuit Eskimos for two years, he wrote *People of the Deer* to protest the Canadian government's treatment of the vanishing tribe. *A Whale for the Killing* is another example of Mowat's concern over the destruction of the natural world.

Hector Hugh Munro (Saki) (1870–1916) was born in Burma of Scottish parents. Before he was two, Munro's mother died, and he was sent to England to be brought up and educated under the watchful eyes of two strict aunts. At twenty-two, his father arranged for his return to Burma and for a position with the Burma police. Munro endured thirteen months and seven bouts of fever before returning to London in pursuit of a writing career. There, he worked for several newspapers. He also published a novel

and short stories under the pen name "Saki," a character in a twelfth-century Persian poem. At the beginning of World War I, Munro enlisted as a private in the British army. He refused several offers of a commission and died on a battlefield in France. Munro has been called a master story teller. Critics praise his clever plots and his use of humor to point up human weaknesses.

Louis Nizer (born 1902) combines the careers of lawyer and writer and is well known for his work in both fields. Nizer was born in England, but at age three he moved with his family to the United States. He began his law practice in 1924 and since then has done much work for the film industry, serving as attorney for both the New York Film Board and the Motion Picture Association of America. Nizer's writing is based on his experiences as a lawyer. He has produced legal texts and best-sellers that highlight the drama and human emotion of the courtroom. *My Life in Court* and *The Jury Returns* are two of his most popular works. Nizer has also written a syndicated newspaper column and articles for legal journals and popular magazines.

Gloria Oden (born 1923) was a senior editor of math, science, and language textbooks before switching to a career of college teaching and poetry writing. Her work has appeared in numerous anthologies, and she has received two John Hay Whitney awards for creative writing. Her first book, *The Naked Frame: A Love Poem and Sonnets*, was published in 1952.

Liam O'Flaherty (1896–1984) was raised on the desolate Aran Islands off the west coast of Ireland. He was urged to become a priest, but O'Flaherty preferred the excitement of a military life. He signed up with the Irish Guards in 1915 but was discharged two years later after suffering severe shellshock. Returning to Dublin, O'Flaherty joined for a time in the Irish struggle for independence from Britain, then set out on a series of wanderings that took him around the world. He worked in a London brewery, signed on as a seaman bound for Brazil, lived in New York's Bowery, and worked in a Connecticut tire factory. Upon his return to Ireland in 1921, he began to write. The settings for O'Flaherty's novels and short stories are usually his native Aran Islands or Dublin. His characters are the peasant farmers and lower classes that inhabit these locales.

William Sidney Porter (O. Henry) (1862–1910) spent the first twenty years of his life in North Carolina. He left school at fifteen to clerk in his uncle's drug store. In 1882, he went to Texas where he worked as a ranch hand. His fellow cowboys must have thought him odd, as he carried a small dictionary in one pocket and a book of poetry in the other. Eventually, Porter found work as a journalist and also published his own humor weekly titled *The Rolling Stone*. When the publication failed, he was hired as a bank teller. Bookkeeping practices at the bank were careless and haphazard, and when a shortage was discovered, Porter was accused of embezzlement. He was almost certainly innocent and probably would have been acquitted, but he made the mistake of running away. Central and South America were his home for the next two years. When he returned to visit his dying wife, he was quickly arrested and sentenced to three years in prison. While serving his term, Porter wrote stories under the pen name O. Henry. Upon release he went to New York, where he remained for the rest of his life. Porter turned out stories at an amazing rate, often one a week. Several collections were not even published until after his death. Many of his stories are set in New York City. They present portraits of simple people caught in uncontrollable circumstances. The stories often have surprise endings.

Anthony Quinn (born 1915) is a native of Mexico with an Irish father and a Mexican mother. He tried boxing and painting before settling in Hollywood where he spent twenty years playing extras and bit parts. Quinn's vaguely foreign appearance has allowed him to play diverse nationalities. During his film career he has portrayed Latin Americans, Arabs, Greeks, Italians, Spaniards, American Indians, and even an Eskimo. After receiving two Academy Awards for best supporting actor in *Viva Zapata!* and *Lust for Life*, he began to be offered leading roles. Some of his best remembered films are: *Zorba the Greek*, *The Guns of Navarone*, *La Strada*, *The Shoes of the Fisherman*, and *The Secret of Santa Vittoria*.

Leroy Quintana is a native of New Mexico. He attended both the University of New Mexico and New Mexico State University where he later taught. Quintana now teaches at El Paso Community College. He recently published his first book of poetry, *Hijo del Pueblo*, (*Son of the Village*).

Marjorie Kinnan Rawlings (1896–1953) wrote short stories at night while working for a newspaper during the day. Finally, in 1928 she purchased an orange grove in Florida where she farmed and wrote in solitude for almost twenty years. *The Yearling*, her most popular book, tells of a fourteen-year-old boy's passage from childhood to manhood. It was awarded the 1939 Pulitzer Prize and was eventually adapted for the screen. Rawlings produced many other novels and short stories, most set in Florida's scrub-pine back country. *Cross Creek* is a collection of nonfiction sketches about Rawlings's farm life and neighbors.

Richard Rive (born 1931) lives in his native South Africa when he is not traveling or studying abroad. He has been awarded Fulbright and Heft scholarships and has done graduate work at Columbia University. In 1963, he received a fellowship from the Farchild Foundation, which enabled him to study contemporary African literature. Rive's writings include a collection of short stories, *African Songs*, and a novel, *Emergency*. He has also served as editor for several volumes of modern African literature. Rive is a former South African hurdles champion whose hobbies are mountain climbing and spear fishing.

Theodore Roethke (1908–1963) grew up in Michigan, where his father and uncle owned a greenhouse. As a young poet, he sold his poems for a dollar each. Eventually, though, he earned almost every honor a writer dreams of achieving—two Guggenheim Fellowships, a Pulitzer Prize, and two National Book Awards. Along with writing, Roethke taught at many universities and sometimes coached varsity tennis as well. Roethke is an original, imaginative poet. His work ranges from childlike nonsense rhymes to complicated metaphors. Many of his subjects are drawn from the world of nature.

Carl Sandburg (1878–1967) was born in Galesburg, Illinois, to Swedish immigrant parents who differed markedly in their attitudes toward the written word. His father was illiterate and "suspicious of books"; his mother encouraged her son to write, and saved wrapping paper for him to use. He left school at age fourteen to help support his family. Before he was twenty, he had worked as a truck driver, dishwasher, farmhand, janitor, and potter's apprentice. He served in the Spanish American War, studied briefly at Lombard College, then began a career in journalism. While working in Chicago, he published *Chicago Poems* and quickly found himself the center of a critical controversy. Critics praised and denounced his powerful free verse and the slang and street language in his poems. In 1950, his *Complete Poems*

won a Pulitzer Prize. A second Pulitzer was awarded for his four-volume biography of Abraham Lincoln. When Sandburg felt the urge to travel, he would sling his guitar on his back and set out across the country. During these travels, he collected native American folksongs, which he eventually published in *The American Songbag* and *New American Songbag*.

William Saroyan (1908–1981), the son of Armenian immigrants, grew up in Fresno, California. He left school after eighth grade to help support his family. His succession of odd jobs included newspaper boy, telegraph messenger, and vineyard worker. After his first book was published in 1933, Saroyan began writing full time. He produced an incredibly large body of work during his lifetime. In one six-year period he wrote more than 500 stories. One of his plays, *The Time of Your Life,* won a Pulitzer Prize. Saroyan refused this award, stating that he was opposed to the support of the arts by wealthy individuals. His most widely read work is the novel *The Human Comedy.* Saroyan wrote about ordinary, working-class people, praising their ability to survive in an often difficult world. Many of his stories are based on his own life. He used simple language, wrote quickly, and claimed that he never rewrote anything. Some critics have faulted him for not polishing his work. Saroyan has answered these critics by saying that he would rather come across to readers as a human being than a "fine piece of machinery."

Anne Sexton (1928–1974) began to write in high school, but soon stopped. She did not begin again until she was twenty-eight and a student of poet Robert Lowell. Sexton wrote personal and often painful poems that explore her feelings and events in her own life. Her first book, *To Bedlam and Part Way Back*, describes her stay in a sanitarium and her recovery from a nervous breakdown. After the success of this book, she continued writing and studying. She received the 1966 Pulitzer Prize for *Live or Die*. At various times during her life, Sexton was also a fashion model, a librarian, and a professor of creative writing.

William Shakespeare (1564–1616) is considered the greatest playwright and one of the finest poets of the English language. He was the third of eight children born to a glovemaker in Stratford-on-Avon, England. Shakespeare's father was a respected citizen who at one time served as mayor of Stratford. Little is known of Shakespeare's youth, but because of his father's position, he probably attended the local grammar school. There, children studied nine hours a day, year round. These classes most likely provided Shakespeare with the education necessary to become a writer. Official records show that he married Anne Hathaway when he was eighteen. They had three children, a girl and a set of twins, one boy and one girl. How Shakespeare supported his family during these early years is unknown, but ten years after his marriage, documents show that he was an established actor and playwright in London. Shakespeare's work was popular with both royalty and local audiences. His acting company owned two theaters, The Globe Theater and the Second Blackfriars Theater. When outbreaks of plague occasionally closed the theaters and reduced the demand for new plays, Shakespeare wrote poetry to maintain his income. Five years before his death, he retired to Stratford to live the life of a country gentleman. Thirty-seven plays have been attributed to Shakespeare. They usually are divided into three groups: tragedies, such as *Romeo and Juliet* and *Hamlet*; comedies, such as *A Midsummer Night's Dream*; and histories, such as *Richard III*. No other English writer has re-mained as popular as Shakespeare. His work continues to be produced, studied, and appreciated throughout the world. It endures mainly because of the author's profound understanding of human nature. His characters possess qualities and emotions that touch audiences today, just as they did over 300 years ago.

Robert Silverberg (born 1935) graduated from Columbia University in 1956 and immediately began to produce an avalanche of books. Time has not slowed his pace, and he continues to write and edit several volumes each year. Silverberg divides his work into two categories: science fiction and true-life scientific adventure. Some of his science fiction titles are *Revolt on Alpha C*, *Invaders from Earth*, and *Needle in a Timestack*. His nonfiction subjects include archeology, exploration, and ecology. He also writes biographies and underwater adventures.

Isaac Bashevis Singer (born 1904) came from a family of Jewish rabbis and studied at a rabbinical seminary, but finally decided on writing as a career. Although he has lived in the United States since 1935, Singer still writes in Yiddish, the language of his birthplace, Radzymin, Poland. Yiddish, says Singer, "contains vitamins that other languages don't have." Singer's work usually is set in nineteenth century shtetls (small Jewish villages in Poland). His stories are similar to folktales and are written in simple, clear language. A major feature of Singer's work is the casual blending of superstition and a supernatural world of imps and demons into the common routines of everyday life. In 1978 Singer received the Nobel Prize in recognition of more than forty years of writing novels and short stories.

Emma G. Sterne (1894–1971) worked as a teacher, editor, and free-lance writer. She wrote both fiction and nonfiction books including biographies of leaders such as Benito Juarez, Balboa, and Dr. Martin Luther King, Jr. Occasionally, she collaborated with her daughter, Barbara Lindsay. *King Arthur and the Knights of the Round Table* is one of their joint efforts.

Adrien Stoutenburg (born 1916) worked as a librarian, reporter, and editor before turning to writing as a full-time career. Since 1951, she has published more than thirty books, including poetry, short stories, biographies, and novels. One of her most popular books, *American Tall Tales,* is a collection of native folklore. Stoutenburg is also an accomplished artist, sculptor, and musician.

May Swenson (born 1919) often shapes her poems into typed pictures that enhance the sounds and subject matter of the verse. Swenson's style is unique, and she is regarded as a serious poet by critics who praise her fresh and unusual perception of ordinary things. Her numerous prizes and awards include a Guggenheim Fellowship. Her poems have been published in many magazines and anthologies; her books include *To Mix with Time* and *Half Sun Half Sleep.*

Hernando Tellez (born 1908) is a Colombian writer, chiefly known for his work as an essayist. A collection of his short stories, *Ashes for the Wind and Other Tales,* was published in 1950. One of these stories, "Lather and Nothing Else," has been widely translated and anthologized.

James Thurber (1894–1961) made a career out of poking fun at human beings and their complicated modern society. His humorous writings and cartoon drawings are peopled with small frightened adults bowing under the weight of life's pressures. Sad-looking dogs and unmannerly children also live in the Thurber world. Much of his work first appeared in *The New Yorker* magazine with which he was associated for more than

twenty-five years. Thurber's cartoons, essays, and short stories helped to give this publication its particular style. "The Secret Life of Walter Mitty" is one of the most popular of Thurber's short stories. His books include *The Thurber Carnival* and the autobiographical *My Life and Hard Times.*

J. R. R. Tolkien (1892–1973) was an English educator and writer. He was born in South Africa, orphaned at a young age, and raised under the guidance of Anglican priests. For thirty-five years, he was a respected professor at Oxford University. Literary experts praise his scholarly studies of Chaucer and Middle-English classics. To the general public, Tolkien is known as the creator of *The Hobbit* and *The Lord of the Rings.* These fantasies tell the story of a young hobbit from Middle-Earth and his perilous mission to destroy the evil Ring of Power. Although the books appeal strongly to youthful imaginations, they were not written for children. They began as a game for Tolkien, who enjoyed inventing new languages. Over a span of fourteen years, he created characters, countries, and histories, thus providing a complete world where his languages might be spoken. Other Tolkien books about Middle-Earth are *The Tolkien Reader* and *The Silmarillion.* His work has a devoted public following. Members of Tolkien Societies meet to discuss the intricacies of Middle-Earth and wear hobbit buttons, T-shirts, and other paraphernalia.

Jean Starr Untermeyer (1886–1970) began writing poetry secretly, several years after her marriage to poet and editor Louis Untermeyer. The poems were discovered by her husband, who submitted them to magazines and thus helped to launch her career as a writer. In the years that followed, she published several collections of poems, as well as autobiographical sketches, essays, and translations from German, French, and Hebrew.

She also taught at Olivett College and the New School for Social Research. Long before it was fashionable, Untermeyer proclaimed and defended a woman's need for private time and space for creative work.

John Updike (born 1932) originally hoped for a career as a cartoonist, but turned to writing after graduating from college. As a staff member of *The New Yorker* magazine, he contributed stories, poems, and essays. Although he has published several books of poetry, Updike is known mainly as a novelist. His best-selling trilogy, *Rabbit Run, Rabbit Redux* and *Rabbit Is Rich*, tells of one man's attempts to cope with modern society. The last of the series won the 1981 Pulitzer Prize. Updike uses a light, witty style as he explores human relationships and the problems of American life.

John Van Druten (1901–1957) was teaching law in England when his first play was accepted for staging in New York. He remained in the United States, eventually becoming a citizen. Although Van Druten was a successful novelist and theatrical director, he is best remembered for his work as a dramatist. Among the most popular of his twenty-eight plays are *The Voice of the Turtle, I Remember Mama*, and *Bell, Book, and Candle*. His Broadway hit *I Am a Camera* was the basis for the musical *Cabaret*. Van Druten had an ability to create memorable characters and realistic dialogue. His talents were recognized in Hollywood, where Van Druten worked on screen plays for major actors and top studios. He was largely responsible for creating the character of Paula Alquist in *Gaslight*, a role for which actress Ingrid Bergman won an Academy Award in 1944.

Kurt Vonnegut, Jr. (born 1922) once described a writer as "a person who makes his living with his mental disease." Whether the definition fits or not, Vonnegut writes wildly comic fiction about some of the blackest aspects of society. His concerns are the horrors of war, human brutality, and the crush of modern technology. Raised in the Midwest and armed with his father's advice to learn "something useful," Vonnegut went to college and studied biochemistry and anthropology. During World War II, he was captured by the German army. As a prisoner of war, he witnessed the Allied bombing of Dresden. The total destruction of the city and 135,000 of its citizens is a memory that haunts Vonnegut and that appears repeatedly in his work. His first attempts at writing were incorrectly labeled science fiction and were virtually ignored by critics. With the 1963 publication of *Cat's Cradle*, however, he experienced instant popularity with critics and the reading public. He has written many short stories and novels, including *Slaughterhouse Five, Breakfast of Champions*, and *Slapstick*.

David Wagoner (born 1926) combines the career of a college professor with that of a poet. He has taught at several colleges and universities and has published more than twenty collections of poetry. His work has received many prizes, including Guggenheim and Ford Fellowships.

Alice Walker (born 1944) has come a long way from the small Georgia farm where she was raised. She has worked her way through college, campaigned for welfare rights, helped in voter registration, and traveled to Kenya, Uganda, and the Soviet Union. She also has taught at Wellesley and Jackson State colleges and the University of Massachusetts. One book of Walker's poetry, *Revolutionary Petunias and Other Poems*, was a National Book Award nominee. A novel, *The Third Life of Grange Copeland*, and a collection of stories about black women have also received critical acclaim.

Margaret Walker (born 1915) won the Yale Younger Poets Award in 1942 for her first book of poetry, *For My People*. In 1966, she published *Jubilee*, a carefully researched novel of slavery and the Civil War. Besides being a writer, Walker has been a social worker, magazine editor, college English instructor, and mother to four children. In 1968, she was named director of the Institute for the Study of the History, Life, and Culture of Black Peoples. Walker, a native of Alabama and the daughter of a Methodist minister, holds a Ph.D. from the University of Iowa.

Robert Wallace (born 1932) has taught English at Bryn Mawr, Sweet Briar, and Vassar colleges. Currently, he is a professor at Case Western Reserve University in Cleveland, Ohio. Wallace's prize-winning collections of poetry include *Ungainly Things* and *Views from a Ferris Wheel*. His work has appeared in literary journals and in magazines such as *The New Yorker* and the *Atlantic Monthly*.

Walt Whitman (1819–1892) called himself the "people's poet," although the working class never claimed him as their own. After several years as a journalist, Whitman became a drifter, dressing in the rough clothes of a laborer, writing poetry, and taking whatever jobs he could find. With his own money, he published his poetry collection, *Leaves of Grass*. His free verse and championship of the common man did not impress the critics. Whitman spent the Civil War years nursing wounded soldiers in Washington, D.C. This experience inspired some of his finest poetry. In later years, Whitman peddled his books on street corners, appearing to be poverty-stricken. After his death, however, friends discovered his large bank account and the impressive tomb he had commissioned for himself. Although Whitman received little recognition during his lifetime, his original style influenced poets for years to come.

William Wordsworth (1770–1850), an English poet, is considered a founder of "Romanticism" in poetry. He believed that events in everyday life could be the subjects of serious poetry and that poems could be written in ordinary language, revolutionary ideas in the early 1800's. Wordsworth had a happy childhood, particularly enjoying the countryside of his native Cumberland. He was educated at Cambridge University and, after graduation, went to France where he became a fervent supporter of the French Revolution. As he grew older, his liberal political views gradually became more conservative. Wordsworth published hundreds of poems. His themes were nature, common people, and the idea that everything in the universe is somehow connected. One of his first books, *Lyrical Ballads*, was written with his lifelong friend Samuel Coleridge. Most popular among his poems are "Tintern Abbey," "The Daffodils," "Solitary Reaper," and "Lucy Gray." In 1843, Queen Victoria named Wordsworth Britain's poet laureate.

Elinor Wylie (1885–1928) was born into a prominent social and political family. She spent her youth in Washington, D.C., where she studied painting and secretly wrote poetry, wavering between the two as possible careers. After a socially correct but unhappy marriage, Wylie set out for Europe alone and began to write seriously. She returned to America in 1916, and her poems began to appear in magazines. Eight years later, she was a famous person, the author of two successful poetry collections and a novel. Her work includes *Nets To Catch the Wind, Black Armour,* and *Angels and Earthly Creatures.*

Glossary

The glossary is an alphabetical listing of words from the selections, along with their meanings. If you are not familiar with a word as you read, look it up in the glossary.

The glossary gives the following information:

1. **The pronunciation of each word.** For example, **turbulent** (tʉr′byə lənt). If there is more than one way to pronounce a word, the most common pronunciation is listed first. For example, **status** (stā′təs, stat′əs).

    A primary accent ′ is placed after the syllable that is stressed the most when the word is spoken. A **secondary accent** ′ is placed after a syllable that has a lighter stress. For example, **imitation** (im′ə tā′shən). The Pronunciation Key below shows the symbols for the sounds of letters, and key words that contain those sounds. Also, there is a short pronunciation key at the bottom of each right-hand page in the glossary.

2. **The part of speech of the word.** The following abbreviations are used:

adj. adjective	*conj.* conjunction	*pro.* pronoun
adv. adverb	*n.* noun	*v.* verb

3. **The meaning of the word.** The definitions listed in the glossary are the ones that apply to the way a word is used in these selections.

4. **Related forms.** Words with suffixes such as *-ing, -ed, -ness,* and *-ly* are listed under the base word. For example, **decisive** *adj.* . . . **decisively** *adv.,* **decisiveness** *n.*

Pronunciation Key

Symbol	Key Words	Symbol	Key Words	Symbol	Key Words	Symbol	Key Words
a	ask, fat, parrot	oi	oil, point, toy	b	bed, fable, dub	t	top, cattle, hat
ā	ape, date, play	ou	out, crowd, plow	d	dip, beadle, had	v	vat, hovel, have
ä	ah, car, father	u	up, cut, color	f	fall, after, off	w	will, always, swear
		ʉr	urn, fur, deter	g	get, haggle, dog	y	yet, onion, yard
e	elf, ten, berry			h	he, ahead, hotel	z	zebra, dazzle, haze
ē	even, meet, money	ə	a in ago	j	joy, agile, badge		
i	is, hit, mirror		e in agent	k	kill, tackle, bake	ch	chin, catcher, arch
ī	ice, bite, high		i in sanity	l	let, yellow, ball	sh	she, cushion, dash
			o in comply	m	met, camel, trim	th	thin, nothing, truth
ō	open, tone, go		u in focus	n	not, flannel, ton	*th*	then, father, lathe
ô	all, horn, law			p	put, apple, tap	zh	azure, leisure
o͞o	ooze, tool, crew	ər	perhaps, murder	r	red, port, dear	ŋ	ring, anger, drink
oo	look, pull, moor			s	sell, castle, pass	′	able (ā′b′l)
yo͞o	use, cute, few						
yoo	united, cure, globule						

A

abashed (ə bash'd') *adj.* Ashamed, ill at ease, embarrassed.

abdicate (ab'də kāt') *v.* To give up formally.

abrasive (ə brā'siv) *adj.* Causing scraping or rubbing off.

abruptly (ə brupt'lē) *adv.* Suddenly or unexpectedly.

accede (ak sēd') *v.* To consent, give in, or agree to.

accessible (ak ses'ə b'l) *adj.* That can be approached or entered.

accost (ə kôst') *v.* To approach and speak to, especially in a bold manner.

acolyte (ak'ə līt) *n.* An attendant or helper.

advisement (əd vīz'mənt) *n.* Careful consideration.

affable (af'ə b'l) *adj.* Easy to approach and talk to; friendly.

affluent (af'loo wənt) *adj.* Wealthy, rich.

affront (ə frunt') *n.* An open insult.

aghast (ə gast') *adj.* Horrified.

agile (aj''l) *adj.* Quick, keen, and lively.

agitate (aj'ə tāt') *v.* To disturb the feelings of.—**agitatedly** *adv.*

alibi (al'ə bī') *n.* An excuse.

alien (āl'yən) *adj.* Not natural; strange.

allay (ə lā') *v.* To calm or put to rest.

allegiance (ə lē'jens) *n.* Loyalty or devotion.

alliance (ə lī'əns) *n.* A union or association for a common goal.

allurement (ə loor'mənt) *n.* A temptation or attraction.

aloof (ə loof') *adj.* Distant in sympathy or interest.

amenity (ə men'ə tē) *n.* Pleasant quality; desirable feature.

amorphous (ə môr'fəs) *adj.* Vague or indefinite.

amphitheater (am'fə thē'ə tər) *n.* A round or oval building with an open space surrounded by rising rows of seats.

anguish (aŋ'gwish) *n.* Great suffering; agony.

animate (an'ə māt') *v.* To cause to act; inspire.

anomalous (ə näm'ə ləs) *adj.* Abnormal; not following the general rule.

anonymous (ə nän'ə məs) *adj.* Lacking in distinctive features.

antidote (an'tə dōt') *n.* Anything that works against an evil or unwanted condition.

antiquities (an tik'wə tēz) *n.* Relics or monuments of the distant past.

apothecary (ə päth'ə ker'ē) *adj.* Used in pharmacy.

apprehensive (ap'rə hen'siv) *adj.* Uneasy or fearful about the future.—**apprehension** *n.*

appropriation (ə prō'prē ā'shən) *n.* Money set aside for a specific use.

aptitude (ap'tə tood') *n.* A natural tendency or ability.

arbitrator (är'bə trāt'ər) *n.* A person chosen to decide a dispute.

arbor (är'bər) *n.* A place shaded by trees, shrubs, or vines on latticework.

arcane (är kān') *adj.* Understood by only a few.

arch (ärch) *adj.* Gaily mischievous.

ardent (är'd'nt) *adj.* Very enthusiastic or devoted.

arid (ar'id) *adj.* Dry and barren.

aristocrat (ə ris'tə krat') *n.* A member of the upper class.

armada (är mä'də) *n.* A fleet of warships.

artificer (är tif'ə sər) *n.* An inventor.

artisan (är'tə z'n) *n.* A skilled worker or artist.

ascetic (ə set'ik) *adj.* Self-denying and austere.

asinine (as'ə nīn') *adj.* Stupid, silly.

askance (ə skans') *adv.* With a sidewise glance.

aspiration (as'pə rā'shen) *n.* Strong desire or ambition.

assail (ə sāl') *v.* To attack with arguments or questions.

astrakhan (as'trə kən') *n.* A loosely curled fur from the pelt of lambs.

atavistic (at'ə vis'tik) *adj.* Having a characteristic found in an early ancestor but not in more recent ones.

atheist (ā'thē ist) *n.* A person who believes that there is no God.

atonement (ə tōn'mənt) *n.* Something done to make up for wrongdoing.

atrocity (ə träs'ə tē) *n.* Cruelty or brutality.

authoritative (ə thôr'ə tāt'iv) *adj.* Having or asserting power.

authorization (ô'thər i zā'shən) *n.* Legal power or right.

auxiliary (ôg zil'yər ē) *n.* Something additional or supplementary.

avenge (ə venj') *v.* To get revenge for.—**avenger** *n.*

avert (ə vurt') *v.* To avoid, prevent, or keep from happening.

awe (ô) *v.* To inspire deep respect mixed with fear and wonder.

awestruck (ô'struk') *adj.* Filled with wonder or respect mixed with fear.

B

banish (ban'ish) v. To send away or get rid of.

banshee (ban'shē) n. A female spirit believed to wail in warning outside a house.

banter (ban'tər) v. To tease in a playful way.

barbarous (bär'bər əs) adj. Uncivilized; cruel, brutal.

barnacle (bär'nə k'l) n. Any of a number of salt-water shellfish that attach themselves to rocks and ship bottoms.

barracks (bar'ikz) n. Buildings for housing soldiers.

barrage (bə räzh') n. A heavy attack of artillery fire.

barren (bar'ən) adj. Empty; not productive.

barter (bär'tər) v. To trade by exchanging goods.

battlement (bat''l mənt) n. A low wall, as on top of a tower, with open spaces for shooting.

bedlam (bed'ləm) n. Noise and confusion.

beguiling (bi gīl'iŋ) adj. Charming, delightful, alluring.

behemoth (bi hē'məth) n. A huge animal.

beleaguer (bi lē'gər) v. To attack by surrounding.

benediction (ben'ə dik'shən) n. A blessing.

besiege (bi sēj') v. To hem in with armed forces and keep under attack.

bestialize (bes'chə līz) v. To make like a beast.

betrayal (bi trā'əl) n. The act of being a traitor or breaking faith with.

bewilderment (bi wil'dər mənt) n. Hopeless confusion or puzzlement.

bifurcate (bī'fər kāt') v. To divide into two branches.

bilge (bilj) n. Dirty, stagnant water that gathers in a ship's hold.

billow (bil'ō) v. To surge or swell in a large wave.

blandly (bland'lē) adv. Smoothly, agreeably.

blather (blath'ər) n. Foolish talk.

blazon (blā'z'n) v. To portray in colors.

blithe (blīth) adj. Cheerful, carefree.

bluster (blus'tər) v. To speak in a noisy or bullying way.

boa (bō'ə) n. A woman's long, fluffy scarf, as of feathers.

boisterously (boi'stər əs lē) adv. Loudly and exuberantly.

bona-fide (bō'nə fīd') adj. Genuine, authentic.

bovine (bō'vīn) adj. Of an ox or cow.

bower (bou'ər) n. A place enclosed by overhanging boughs.

bravado (brə vä'dō) n. A pretending to be brave when one is really afraid.

brazen (brā'z'n) adj. Brassy, bold, showing no shame.

breaker (brāk'ər) n. A wave that breaks into foam.

brigand (brig'ənd) n. A bandit, usually one of a roving band.

bristle (bris''l) v. To become tense with fear or anger.

bureaucrat (byoor'ə krat') n. An official who follows fixed routines.

burgess (bur'jis) n. A citizen or freeman of a British borough.

burnish (bur'nish) v. To make shiny or glossy.

C

calamitous (kə lam'ə təs) adj. Causing deep trouble; disastrous.—**calamity** n.

calliope (kə lī'ə pē) n. A keyboard instrument like an organ, having a series of steam whistles.

callous (kal'əs) adj. Unfeeling, insensitive; lacking pity.

canine (kā'nīn) adj. Of or like a dog.

caper (kā'pər) v. To skip about.

caprice (kə prēs') n. A sudden change in thought that seems to have no reason; whim.

caricature (kar'ə kə chər) n. A poor imitation.

carnage (kär'nij) n. Bloodshed, massacre, bloody slaughter.

cataclysm (kat'ə kliz'm) n. Any great upheaval or sudden, violent change.

catastrophe (kə tas'trə fē) n. A terrible disaster.

cauterize (kôt'ər īz') v. To burn with a hot iron or needle so as to destroy dead tissue.

cavort (kə vôrt') v. To leap or romp about.

celluloid (sel'yoo loid') n. An artificial substance similar to plastic.

centrifugal (sen trif'ə gəl) adj. Moving away from a center.

cesspool (ses'pool') n. A center of moral filth and corruption.

---

fat, āpe, cär; ten, ēven; is, bīte; gō, hôrn,
tool, look; oil, out; up, fur; get; joy; yet;
chin; she; thin, then; zh, leisure; ŋ, ring;
ə for a in ago, e in agent, i in sanity,
o in comply, u in focus; ' as in able (ā'b'l)

chaff (chaf) *n.* The husks of wheat or other grain separated in threshing.

chalice (chal′is) *n.* A cup-shaped flower.

chaos (kā′äs) *n.* Extreme confusion or disorder.—**chaotic** *adj.*

chary (cher′ē) *adj.* Not giving freely; sparing.

chasm (kaz′′m) *n.* A gorge or deep crack in the earth's surface.

chastise (chas tīz′) *v.* To punish.

château (sha tō′) *n.* A large country house.

chink (chiŋk) *n.* A narrow opening; crack.

chintz (chints) *n.* A cotton cloth printed in colors and usually glazed.

chivalry (shiv′′l rē) *n.* The noble qualities desired in a knight such as courage, honor, and a readiness to help the weak and defenseless.

chloroform (klôr′ə fôrm′) *n.* A colorless liquid that changes into a gas, used to make people become unconscious.

christen (kris′′n) *v.* To give a name to.

clabber (klab′ər) *n.* Thickly curdled sour milk.

clamor (klam′ər) *n.* Uproar or loud noise.

claustrophobia (klôs′trə fō′bē ə) *n.* An abnormal fear of being in a closed or confined place.

cockleshell (käk′′l shel′) *n.* A small boat.

colossus (kə läs′əs) *n.* A gigantic thing.

commercial (kə mʉr′shəl) *adj.* Concerned with the making of profit.

commissary (käm′ə ser′ē) *n.* A store handling food and supplies.

communion (kə myōōn′yən) *n.* A close relationship with deep understanding.

compassion (kəm pash′ən) *n.* Sympathy, pity, or sorrow for the trouble of another.

concerted (kən sʉr′tid) *adj.* Done together.

conciliate (kən sil′ē āt′) *v.* To win over or make friendly; placate.

conclave (kän′klāv) *n.* A private or secret meeting.

concussion (kən kush′ən) *n.* A shock, as from impact.

condone (kən dōn′) *v.* To forgive or overlook.

confound (kən found′) *v.* To defeat or destroy.

conjurer (kän′jər ər) *n.* A magician.

conspiratorially (kən spir′ə tôr′ē ə lē) *adv.* As if plotting together.

constable (kän′stə b′l) *n.* A peace officer in a town.

construe (kən strōō′) *v.* To interpret or deduce the meaning of.

contemplation (kän′təm plā′shən) *n.* A thoughtful study; an intent gaze.

contemptuously (kən temp′chōō wəs lē) *adv.* With scorn or despising.

contiguous (kən tig′yōō wəs) *adj.* Near or adjacent.

contort (kən tôrt′) *v.* To twist or distort.—**contortion** *n.*

contrapuntal (kän′trə pun′t′l) *adj.* Using the principles of counterpoint, having one melody accompany another note for note.—**contrapuntally** *adv.*

contrition (kən trish′ən) *n.* A feeling of sorrow for wrongdoing; repentance.

convulsively (kən vuls′iv lē) *adv.* With a violent shaking.—**convulsion** *n.*

cosmic (käz′mik) *adj.* Of the universe.

cosmopolite (käz mäp′ə līt′) *n.* A person at home in all countries or places.

courtly (kôrt′lē) *adj.* Dignified, elegant.

covert (kuv′ərt) *adj.* Concealed, secret, hidden, or disguised.—**covertly** *adv.*

cower (kou′ər) *v.* To crouch or huddle up, as from fear.

crabbed (krab′id) *adj.* Hard to read; illegible.

craven (krā′vən) *adj.* Very cowardly.

craze (krāz) *v.* To produce small cracks in a surface.

creosote (krē′ə sōt′) *v.* To treat with an oily liquid, made from wood tar or coal tar, to preserve wood.

crescendo (krə shen′dō) *n.* A gradual increase in loudness or intensity.

crest (krest) *n.* The ridge of the neck of a horse.

crestfallen (krest′fôl′ən) *adj.* Made sad or humble.

crevice (krev′is) *n.* A narrow opening caused by a crack or split.

crochet (krō shā′) *n.* Needlework in which loops of thread are interwoven.

crone (krōn) *n.* An ugly, withered old woman; a hag.

crotchet (kräch′it) *n.* A queer or stubborn notion.

croup (krōōp) *n.* The rump of a horse.

cudgeler (kuj′əl ər) *n.* A person who beats with a club.

culprit (kul′prit) *n.* A person guilty of a crime or offense.

cultivated (kul′tə vāt′id) *adj.* Trained and developed; refined; cultured.

cunning (kun′iŋ) *adj.* Sly, crafty; skillful in deception.

curlew (kʉr′lōō) *n.* A large, brownish wading bird with long legs.

curtsy (kʉrt′sē) *v.* To make a gesture of greeting

characterized by a bending of the knees and a lowering of the body.

cynical (sin'i k'l) *adj.* Doubting the sincerity of people's motives and actions.—**cynically** *adv.*

D

damson (dam'z'n) *n.* A small, purple plum.

dank (daŋk) *adj.* Disagreeably damp; moist and chilly.

dappled (dap''ld) *adj.* Spotted.

dastardly (das'tərd lē) *adj.* Mean, sneaky, cowardly.

debacle (di bäk''l) *n.* An overwhelming defeat; a total collapse or failure.

deception (di sep'shən) *n.* A deceiving or misleading.

decree (di krē') *n.* An official order.

decry (di krī') *v.* To speak out against strongly and openly.

degrade (di grād') *v.* To disgrace, dishonor, or make lose respect.—**degradation** *n.*

delirium (di lir'ē əm) *n.* Uncontrollably wild excitement.

deluge (del'yōoj) *n.* A great flood.

demeanor (di mēn'ər) *n.* Outward behavior; conduct.

demonstrativeness (di män'strə tiv nəs) *n.* The act of showing feelings openly and frankly.

deplorable (di plôr'ə b'l) *adj.* Very bad; wretched.

deploy (dē ploi') *v.* To spread out troops so as to form a wider front.

depredation (dep'rə dā'shən) *n.* A robbing or laying waste.

derelict (der'ə likt') *adj.* Neglected.

derisive (di rī'siv) *adj.* Showing contempt or ridicule.—**derision** *n.*

derrick (der'ik) *n.* A large apparatus for lifting and moving heavy objects.

desecrate (des'ə krāt) *v.* To violate or insult, as with something sacred.—**desecration** *n.*

desolate (des'ə lit) *adj.* Lonely; very unhappy.—**desolation** *n.*

despairing (di sper'iŋ) *adj.* Feeling or showing a loss of hope.

deter (di tur') *v.* To keep or discourage a person from doing something.

devastate (dev'ə stāt) *v.* To make hopeless or overwhelm; to destroy.

diatribe (dī'ə trīb') *n.* Writing that attacks some person or thing in a harsh way.

diffuse (di fyōōs') *adj.* Spread out; not centered in one place.

disarming (dis är'miŋ) *adj.* Removing suspicions, fear, or hostility.

discern (di surn') *v.* To recognize or make out clearly.

disciple (di sī'p'l) *n.* A follower or pupil.

discomfit (dis kum'fit) *v.* To defeat or frustrate.

discourse (dis'kôrs) *n.* A formal treatment of a subject in a speech.

disdainful (dis dān'fəl) *adj.* Proud and feeling contempt for those beneath one.

disembark (dis'im bärk') *v.* To go ashore from a ship.

dislocate (dis'lō kāt') *v.* To put out of place.

dismay (dis mā') *n.* A loss of courage when faced with trouble.

disperse (dis purs') *v.* To break up and scatter in all directions.

disposition (dis'pə zish'ən) *n.* Arrangement.

disproportionate (dis'prə pôr'shən it) *adj.* Too great or too small.

dissentient (dis sen'shənt) *adj.* Disagreeing.

dissuade (di swād') *v.* To turn aside (from a course of action) by persuasion.

distaff (dis'taf) **1.** *adj.* Of the maternal side of a family. **2.** *n.* A staff on which wool is wound for use in spinning.

distaste (dis tāst') *n.* Dislike.

distraught (dis trôt') *adj.* Very troubled or confused.

diversion (də vur'zhən) *n.* A pastime or amusement.

docile (däs''l) *adj.* Easily managed; obedient.

dogged (dôg'id) *adj.* Not giving in readily; persistent.—**doggedly** *adv.*

doily (doi'lē) *n.* A small mat, as of lace.

domestic (də mes'tik) *adj.* Tame.

dominant (däm'ə nənt) *adj.* Ruling, prevailing.

dory (dôr'ē) *n.* A small, flat-bottomed fishing boat with high sides.

dowry (dou'rē) *n.* The property that a woman brings to her husband at marriage.

draught (draft) *n.* A drink.

---

fat, āpe, cär; ten, ēven; is, bīte; gō, hôrn,
tōol, look; oil, out; up, fur; get; joy; yet;
chin; she; thin, *th*en; zh, leisure; ŋ, ring;
ə for *a* in *ago*, *e* in *agent*, *i* in *sanity*,
o in *comply*, *u* in *focus*; ' as in *able* (ā'b'l)

droll (drōl) *adj.* Amusing in an odd or ironic way.

dun (dun) *adj.* Dull grayish-brown.

dwindle (dwin'd'l) *v.* To lessen or decrease.

dynamic (dī nam'ik) *adj.* Vigorous, forceful, energetic.

E

earnestness (ur'nist nis) *n.* Seriousness, sincerity.—**earnestly** *adv.*

ebb (eb) *v.* To recede or flow back.

ecstatic (ik stat'ik) *adj.* Feeling intense joy or delight.—**ecstatically** *adv.*

efficacious (ef'ə kā'shəs) *adj.* Effective; producing the desired effect.

egotism (ē'gə tiz'm) *n.* A thinking too much about oneself.

elemental (el'ə men't'l) *adj.* Of or like the forces of nature.

elusive (i lōō'siv) *adj.* Hard to catch, see, or discover.

embellish (im bel'ish) *v.* To decorate or adorn.

emblazon (im blā'z'n) *v.* To decorate with bright colors.

empathy (em'pə thē) *n.* The ability to share in another's emotions, thoughts, or feelings.

emphatically (im fat'ə kə lē) *adv.* Definitely, strikingly.

engulf (in gulf') *v.* To swallow up or overwhelm.

ensanguine (in saŋ'gwən) *v.* To stain with blood or make bloody.

entice (in tīs') *v.* To attract, lure, or tempt.

entomb (in tōōm') *v.* To bury.

entrails (en'trālz) *n.* Inner organs; guts.

equilibrium (ē'kwə lib'rē əm) *n.* A state of balance.

equine (ē'kwīn) *adj.* Of, like, or characteristic of a horse.

ermine (ur'mən) *n.* The soft, white fur of a weasel of northern regions.

erosion (i rō'zhən) *n.* A wearing away.

erratic (i rat'ik) *adj.* Irregular in action or behavior.

escapade (es'kə pād') *n.* A wild adventure or prank.

esoteric (es'ə ter'ik) *adj.* Beyond the understanding or knowledge of most people.

evade (i vād') *v.* To avoid answering directly.

evolution (ev'ə lōō'shən) *n.* A process of gradual change as something develops into a different form.

excavation (eks'kə vā'shən) *n.* Uncovering by digging.

exemplary (ig zem'plə rē) *adj.* Serving as a model; worth imitating.

exhilarate (ig zil'ə rāt') *v.* To make merry or lively.

expansively (ik span'siv lē) *adv.* Generously and sympathetically.

extemporaneous (ik stem'pə rā'nē əs) *adj.* Spoken without any preparation.

extraneous (ik strā'nē əs) *adj.* Not essential or not pertinent.

extricate (eks'trə kāt') *v.* To set free.

exuberance (ig zōō'bər əns) *n.* Action or speech showing high spirits.

F

facetiously (fə sē'shəs lē) *adv.* In a joking way.

fanatic (fə nat'ik) *n.* A person who is enthusiastic in an unreasonable or unbalanced way.

fancy (fan'sē) *v.* To think or suppose.

fastidious (fas tid'ē əs) *adj.* Daintily refined.

fathom (fath'əm) *n.* A unit of length, equal to six feet.

fatuous (fach'ōō wəs) *adj.* Stupid or foolish in a smug way.—**fatuously** *adv.*

fealty (fē'əl tē) *n.* Loyalty.

feline (fē'līn) *adj.* Of a cat; catlike.

ferocious (fə rō'shəs) *adj.* Fierce, savage.

festoon (fes tōōn') *v.* To decorate with.

fetid (fet'id) *adj.* Having a bad smell.

finale (fə nä'lē) *n.* The end, conclusion, or last part.

finery (fīn'ər ē) *n.* Showy, elaborate decoration.

firebrand (fīr'brand') *n.* A person who stirs up a revolt.

fiscal (fis'kəl) *adj.* Financial.

fissure (fish'ər) *v.* To crack or split apart.

fleeting (flēt'iŋ) *adj.* Passing swiftly; not lasting.

florid (flôr'id) *adj.* Flushed with red.—**floridly** *adv.*

flotilla (flō til'ə) *n.* A small fleet.

fluke (flōōk) *n.* Either of the two lobes of a whale's tail.

foil (foil) *v.* To keep from being successful.

foray (fôr'ā) *n.* A sudden attack or raid.

forbear (fôr'ber') *n.* An ancestor.

forebode (fôr bōd') *v.* To foretell or have a premonition.

forecloser (fôr klōz'ər) *n.* One who takes away the right to redeem (a mortgage).

foresight (fôr'sīt') *n.* A looking ahead and planning for the future.

fortissimo (fôr tis'ə mō') *adv.* Very loudly.

fortitude (fôr'tə to͞od') *n.* The strength to bear pain or misfortune calmly and patiently.

fraudulent (frô'jə lənt) *adj.* Based on deceit, trickery, or cheating.

frenzied (fren'zēd) *adj.* Characterized by frantic action or a wild outburst.

fulminate (ful'mə nāt') *v.* To explode or detonate.

furlong (fur'lôŋ) *n.* One-eighth of a mile.

furlough (fur'lō) *n.* A leave granted to a soldier.

furtive (fur'tiv) *adj.* Acting in a sly, sneaky way.

fusillade (fyo͞o'sə lād') *n.* A discharge of many firearms at the same time.

futile (fyo͞ot''l) *adj.* Useless, ineffective.

G

gaff (gaf) *v.* To strike with a barbed spear.

gallantry (gal'ən trē) *n.* A polite manner.

game (gām) *adj.* Having spirit.

gargoyle (gär'goil) *n.* The carved form of a fantastic creature.

garish (ger'ish) *adj.* Too bright or gaudy.

gaudily (gôd'ə lē) *adv.* Brightly and showily, but in bad taste.

gaunt (gônt) *adj.* Looking grim, forbidding, or deserted.—**gauntly** *adv.*

gauntlet (gônt'lit) *n.* Attack from both sides.

gecko (gek'ō) *n.* A soft-skinned, insect-eating, tropical lizard.

gibber (jib'ər) *v.* To chatter in a meaningless way.

gingerly (jin'jər lē) *adv.* Very carefully or cautiously.

girdle (gur'd'l) *n.* A belt.

gladiator (glad'ē āt'ər) *n.* In ancient Rome, a man who fought other men or animals in an arena as a public show.

glibly (glib'lē) *adv.* In a smooth, offhand way.

glower (glou'ər) *v.* To scowl or stare with anger.

gluteal (glo͞o tē'əl) *n.* The muscles of the buttocks.

gnarled (närld) *adj.* Knotty and twisted.

goad (gōd) *v.* To urge on or drive as with a sharp stick.

gondola (gän'də lə) *n.* A railroad freight car with low sides and no top.

graft (graft) *n.* A dishonest use of one's position to get money or property.

gravely (grāv'lē) *adv.* Solemnly and with dignity.

grisly (griz'lē) *adj.* Very frightening; horrible.

grovel (gruv''l) *v.* To crawl or behave in a humble way.

guerrilla (gə ril'ə) *adj.* Of or by a small defensive force of soldiers who are not part of a regular army and who make surprise raids.

H

haggard (hag'ərd) *adj.* Having a wild, wasted, worn look.

harangue (hə raŋ') *v.* To give a long, blustering or scolding speech.

haversack (hav'ər sak') *n.* A canvas bag for carrying food.

hermitage (hur'mit ij) *n.* A place where a person can live away from other people.

hircine (hur'sīn) *adj.* Of or like a goat.

hirsute (hur'so͞ot) *adj.* Shaggy or bristly.

holocaust (hal'ə kôst') *n.* Great destruction of life.

homage (häm'ij) *n.* An act done to show honor or respect.

homely (hōm'lē) *adj.* Not good-looking; unattractive.

hone (hōn) *v.* To sharpen as with a whetstone.

hubbub (hub'ub') *n.* A confused sound of many voices; uproar.

I

idleness (ī'd'l nəs) *n.* Laziness; inactivity.

illusion (i lo͞o'zhən) *n.* A misleading appearance or false impression.

illusive (i lo͞o'siv) *adj.* Unreal; caused by illusion.

imbecile (im'bə s'l) *n.* A foolish or stupid person.

imminent (im'ə nənt) *adj.* Likely to happen soon.—**imminence** *n.*

immortality (i'môr tal'ə tē) *n.* The state of living or lasting forever.

impale (im pāl') *v.* To pierce through with something pointed.

impart (im pärt') *v.* To give.

impeccable (im pek'ə b'l) *adj.* Perfect, flawless, without defect.

impede (im pēd') *v.* To bar or hinder the progress of.

impel (im pel') *v.* To force, compel, or urge.

impend (im pend') *v.* To be about to happen.

---

fat, āpe, cär; ten, ēven; is, bīte; gō, hôrn,
to͞ol, look; oil, out; up, fur; get; joy; yet;
chin; she; thin, *th*en; zh, leisure; ŋ, ring;
ə for *a* in *ago, e* in *agent, i* in *sanity,*
o in *comply, u* in *focus;* ' as in *able* (ā'b'l)

imperative (im per′ə tiv) *adj*. Absolutely necessary; urgent.

imperceptible (im′pər sep′tə b′l) *adj*. So small or slight that it is not easily noticed.—**imperceptibly** *adv*.

imperious (im pir′ē əs) *adj*. Arrogant or domineering.

imperishable (im per′ish ə b′l) *adj*. That will not die or decay; indestructible.

impermanence (im pʉr′mə nəns) *n*. The condition of being temporary and not lasting.

impertinent (im pʉr′t′n ənt) *adj*. Not showing proper respect.—**impertinently** *adv*.

implication (im′plə kā′shən) *n*. Something suggested; connection.

implore (im plôr′) *v*. To beg or ask with much feeling.

impotent (im′pə tənt) *adj*. Ineffective, powerless, or helpless.

impregnate (im preg′nāt) *v*. To fill, soak, or saturate.

improvise (im′prə vīz′) *v*. To compose and perform at the same time without any preparation.

imprudent (im prōōd′′nt) *adj*. Without thought of the consequences; rash.

impudent (im′pyoo dənt) *adj*. Shamelessly bold and disrespectful.

impulsively (im pul′siv lē) *adv*. Spontaneously; on impulse.

inaudible (in ô′də b′l) *adj*. That cannot be heard.

inaugurate (in ô′gə rāt′) *v*. To make a formal beginning of.

inconceivable (in′kən sē′və b′l) *adj*. That cannot be imagined or believed.

incongruency (in′kən grōō′əns ē) *n*. Lack of harmony, consistency, or appropriateness.

incontinently (in känt′′n ənt lē) *adv*. Without self-restraint.

incredulous (in krej′oo ləs) *adj*. Showing doubt or disbelief.—**incredulity** *n*., **incredulously** *adv*.

indelible (in del′ə b′l) *adj*. That cannot be blotted out or eliminated.

indeterminate (in′di tʉr′mi nit) *adj*. Indefinite, vague.

indifference (in dif′ər əns) *n*. A lack of concern or interest.

indignation (in′dig nā′shən) *n*. Anger at something that seems unfair.

indiscriminately (in′dis krim′ə nit lē) *adv*. Randomly; without making careful selections.

indolent (in′də lənt) *adj*. Lazy, idle.—**indolently** *adv*.

indomitable (in däm′it ə b′l) *adj*. Not easily discouraged or defeated.

indulgently (in dul′jənt lē) *adv*. Kindly or without strictness.

ineffable (in ef′ə b′l) *adj*. Too overwhelming to be expressed in words.

inert (in ʉrt′) *adj*. Without power to move or act.

inevitable (in ev′ə tə b′l) *adj*. Certain to happen.

inexplicable (in eks′pli kə b′l) *adj*. That cannot be explained or understood.—**inexplicably** *adv*.

infatuated (in fach′oo wāt′id) *adj*. Completely carried away by foolish love or attraction.

ingenious (in jēn′yəs) *adj*. Clever, resourceful, inventive.

ingot (iŋ′gət) *n*. A mass of metal cast into a bar or other shape.

inhabitance (in hab′i təns) *n*. A living in or occupying of a certain area.

inordinate (in ôr′d′n it) *adj*. Too great; excessive.

inquisitive (in kwiz′ə tiv) *adj*. Inclined to ask many questions or seek information.

inscrutable (in skrōōt′ə b′l) *adj*. Mysterious; that cannot be easily understood.

insinuatingly (in sin′yoo wāt′iŋ lē) *adv*. By hinting indirectly or implying in a sly way.

insolent (in′sə lənt) *adj*. Rude or boldly disrespectful.—**insolently** *adv*.

interdict (in′tər dikt′) *n*. A prohibition or restraint.

intimidate (in tim′ə dāt′) *v*. To make timid or afraid.

intolerable (in täl′ər ə b′l) *adj*. Unbearable; too painful to be endured.—**intolerably** *adv*.

intricate (in′tri kit) *adj*. Full of elaborate detail.

inversion (in vʉr′zhən) *n*. A reversal or change to the direct opposite.

invincible (in vin′sə b′l) *adj*. That cannot be defeated or overcome.

invulnerable (in vul′nər ə b′l) *adj*. That cannot be wounded or injured.

isinglass (ī′z′n glas) *n*. A thin sheet of a transparent mineral.

J

japonica (jə pä′ni kə) *n*. A flower in the rose family.

javelin (jav′lin) *n*. A light spear for throwing.

jeer (jir) *v*. To mock or make fun of in a rude, sarcastic manner.

joust (joust) *v.* To engage in combat between two knights on horseback.

juncture (juŋk′chər) *n.* A point of time or a critical moment.

K

kiosk (kē′äsk) *n.* A small structure, open at one or more sides, used as a newsstand.

L

laborious (lə bôr′ē əs) *adj.* Involving much hard work.

labyrinth (lab′ə rinth′) *n.* A maze or complicated arrangement.

lacerate (las′ə rāt) *v.* To tear jaggedly.

lackadaisical (lak′ə dā′zi k′l) *adj.* Showing lack of interest or spirit; listless.

lair (ler) *n.* A wild animal's den.

lament (lə ment′) *v.* To feel or express deep sorrow; mourn or grieve.—**lamentation** *n.*

languid (laŋ′gwid) *adj.* Without vigor or vitality; drooping, weak.—**languidly** *adv.*

languish (lan′gwish) *v.* To live under distressing conditions.

lascar (las′kər) *n.* An Oriental sailor, especially one who is a native of India.

lave (lāv) *v.* To wash or bathe.

lee (lē) *n.* Shelter or protection.

leer (lir) *v.* To look with a suggestive or wicked smile.

leper (lep′ər) *n.* A person with leprosy, an infectious disease that attacks the skin and flesh.

lethargic (li thär′jik) *adj.* Abnormally dull, drowsy, or sluggish.

liberate (lib′ə rāt′) *v.* To release or free.

limpid (lim′pid) *adj.* Perfectly clear.

lineage (lin′ē ij) *n.* Direct descent from an ancestor.

lithe (līth) *adj.* Bending easily; limber.

litter (lit′ər) *n.* A framework having long horizontal shafts near the bottom and enclosing a couch on which a person can be carried.

liturgical (li tʉr′jə k′l) *adj.* Relating to certain religious rituals.

loath (lōth) *adj.* Unwilling, reluctant.

loathsome (lōth′səm) *adj.* Disgusting, causing hatred.

loom (lōōm) *v.* To appear or take shape indistinctly, especially in a large or threatening form.

lope (lōp) *v.* To move with a long, swinging stride.

lugubrious (loo gōō′brē əs) *adj.* Very sad or mournful.

lupine (lōō′pīn) *adj.* Of a wolf; wolflike.

M

malicious (mə lish′əs) *adj.* Caused by or showing ill will; spiteful.—**malice** *n.,* **maliciously** *adv.*

mandolin (man′d′l in′) *n.* A stringed musical instrument with a deep, round soundbox.

maraud (mə rôd′) *v.* To make raids or rove in search of plunder.

marguerite (mär′gə rēt′) *n.* A daisy flower.

marinate (mar′ə nāt′) *v.* To steep in a pickling solution.

maudlin (môd′lin) *adj.* Foolishly and weakly sentimental.

meager (mē′gər) *adj.* Inadequate.

mediator (mē′dē āt′ər) *n.* A judge or go-between in trying to settle a dispute.

medieval (mē′dē ē′v′l) *adj.* Of or like the Middle Ages.

melancholy (mel′ən käl′ē) *adj.* Sad and depressed; gloomy.

melée (mā′lā) *n.* A noisy, confused hand-to-hand fight among a number of people.

menace (men′is) *v.* To threaten or be a danger.

mentation (men tā′shən) *n.* Thought.

Messiah (mə sī′ə) *n.* The Savior.

mid-Victorian (mid′vik tôr′ē ən) *adj.* Old-fashioned, prudish, morally strict.

minuscule (mi nus′kyōōl) *adj.* Very small.

mirage (mi räzh′) *n.* An optical illusion; something that seems to be real but is not.

modicum (mäd′i kəm) *n.* A small amount.

moor (moor) *n.* A tract of open, rolling wasteland, usually covered with heather and often marshy.

morass (mə ras′) *n.* A difficult or troublesome state of affairs; a swamp.

mottle (mät′′l) *v.* To mark with blotches or streaks of different colors.

multitude (mul′tə tōōd) *n.* A large number of people.

murky (mʉr′kē) *adj.* Dark or gloomy.

---

fat, āpe, cär; ten, ēven; is, bīte; gō, hôrn, tōōl, look; oil; out; up, fʉr; get; joy; yet; chin; she; thin, *th*en; zh, leisure; ŋ, ring; ə for *a* in *ago, e* in *agent, i* in *sanity, o* in *comply, u* in *focus;* ' as in *able* (ā′b′l)

mutiny (myo͞ot'ʼn ē) *n.* Forcible revolt against authority.

mystify (mis'tə fī') *v.* To puzzle or perplex.

N

naïve (nä ēv') *adj.* Simple in an unaffected way; unsophisticated.

nave (nāv) *n.* The main part of a church.

nectar (nek'tər) *n.* Any delicious beverage.

nimble (nim'bʼl) *adj.* Moving quickly and lightly.

noncommittal (nän kə mit'ʼl) *adj.* Not revealing one's opinion or purpose.

nostalgia (näs tal'jə) *n.* A longing for something far away or long ago.

O

oath (ōth) *n.* A curse or swear word.

oblivious (ə bliv'ē əs) *adj.* Forgetful or not noticing.

obscure (əb skyoor') *adj.* Not easily understood; vague, unclear.

obstinate (äb'stə nit) *adj.* Unreasonably determined to have one's own way; stubborn.—**obstinacy** *n.*

ogre (ō'gər) *n.* A monster or giant who eats people.

ominous (äm'ə nəs) *adj.* Threatening, sinister.—**ominously** *adv.*

omnipotent (äm nip'ə tənt) *adj.* All-powerful.

opaqueness (ō pāk'nis) *n.* A condition of not letting light through.

opiate (ō'pē it) *n.* Anything quieting or soothing.

oppress (ə pres') *v.* To keep down by the cruel or unjust use of power.

organdy (ôr'gən dē) *n.* A sheer, crisp cotton fabric.

organic (ôr gan'ik) *adj.* Organized.

orientation (ôr'ē ən tā'shən) *n.* A period of becoming adjusted to a situation.

ostensibly (äs ten'sə blē) *adv.* Seemingly, but not necessarily so.

ostentatious (äs'tən tā'shəs) *adj.* Showing off wealth.

outflank (out'flaŋk') *v.* To block or go around and beyond.

P

pagoda (pə gō'də) *n.* An Oriental temple that is a tapering tower.

painstaking (pānz'tā'kiŋ) *adj.* Using great care and effort.

palatable (pal'it ə bʼl) *adj.* Pleasant or acceptable to the taste.

palatial (pə lā'shəl) *adj.* Large; splendid, grand, magnificent.

palfrey (pôl'frē) *n.* A saddle horse.

pallet (pal'it) *n.* A small, crude bed or mattress used on the floor.

palpable (pal'pə bʼl) *adj.* That can be touched or felt.

paltry (pôl'trē) *adj.* Very small and almost worthless.

pandemonium (pan'də mō'nē əm) *n.* Wild disorder, noise, or confusion.

paranoia (par'ə noi'ə) *n.* A mental disorder in which a person thinks that others are persecuting him or her.

parapet (par'ə pit) *n.* A low wall.

paraphernalia (par'ə fər nāl'yə) *n.* Equipment; personal belongings.

paroxysm (par'ek siz'm) *n.* A sudden fit, spasm, or attack.

parry (par'ē) *v.* To ward off or turn aside.

parturition (pär'choo rish'ən) *n.* Childbirth.

pathetic (pə thet'ik) *adj.* Pitiful; arousing sympathy.

pathogenic (path'ə jən'ik) *adj.* Capable of causing disease.

pathos (pā'thäs) *n.* The quality in some happening or story that arouses feelings of pity, sorrow, sympathy, or compassion.

patronize (pāt'trə nīz') *v.* To be kind or helpful to, but in a snobbish way as if dealing with an inferior.—**patronizingly** *adv.*

peer (pir) *n.* An equal.

peremptory (pə remp'tər ē) *adj.* That cannot be denied or delayed.

perfunctory (pər fuŋk'tər ē) *adj.* Done merely as a routine.

peril (per'əl) *n.* Danger; exposure to harm or injury.—**perilous** *adj.*

permeate (pur'mē āt') *v.* To spread through; to pass into and affect every part of.

perplexity (pər plek'sə tē) *n.* The state of being confused or puzzled.

perverse (pər vurs') *adj.* Improper, wicked; turning aside from what is considered right or good.

petition (pə tish'ən) *v.* To ask for or appeal to.

petulant (pech'oo lənt) *adj.* Showing anger or annoyance over little things.

phobia (fō'bē ə) *n.* A strong, unreasonable, continuing fear of something.

phosphorescence (fäs'fə res'´ns) *n.* A giving off of light.

piety (pī'ə tē) *n.* Devotion to religious duties.

piling (pī'liŋ) *n.* Heavy beams driven into the ground to use for docks or bridges.

pinion (pin'yən) **1.** *v.* To bind firmly. **2.** *n.* A wing feather.

pious (pī'əs) *adj.* Having or showing religious devotion.

placidly (plas'id lē) *adv.* Calmly.

pliant (plī'ənt) *adj.* Easily bent; flexible.—**pliancy** *n.*

ply (plī) *v.* To work at.

pod (päd) *n.* A small group of animals, especially of seals or whales.

poignantly (poin'yənt lē) *adv.* Sharply, keenly, or painfully affecting the feelings.—**poignancy** *n.*

ponderously (pän'dər əs lē) *adv.* Heavily in a clumsy way.

porcine (pôr'sīn) *adj.* Of or like pigs or hogs.

portal (pôr t'l) *n.* A doorway, gate, or entrance.

porter (pôr'tər) *n.* A doorkeeper or gatekeeper.

portico (pôr'tə kō') *n.* A porch or covered walk, consisting of a roof supported by columns.

portly (pôrt'lē) *adj.* Large and heavy in a dignified way.

postern (pōs'tərn) *n.* A gate.

potent (pōt'n't) *adj.* Mighty, powerful, forceful.

prate (prāt) *v.* To talk on and on in a foolish way.

precarious (pri ker'ē əs) *adj.* Insecure; dangerous.—**precariously** *adv.*

predator (pred'ə tər) *n.* An animal that lives by killing and feeding upon other animals.

predicate (pred'ə kāt') *v.* To base on conditions.

predominance (pri däm'ə nəns) *n.* Superiority or authority over others.

preeminence (prē em'ə nəns) *n.* The state of standing high; outstanding in worth or rank.

premeditation (pri med'ə tā'shən) *n.* A thinking out or planning beforehand.

premonition (prē'mə nish'ən) *n.* A feeling that something bad will happen.

preoccupied (prē äk'yə pīd') *adj.* Wholly absorbed in one's thoughts.

presumptuousness (pri zump'choo wəs nəs) *n.* Extreme boldness or forwardness.

prevail (pri vāl') *v.* To be stronger or more widespread.

proclivity (prō kliv'ə tē) *n.* A natural or habitual tendency.

prodigious (prə dij'əs) *adj.* Wonderful, amazing, or impressive.

prodigy (präd'ə jē) *n.* A child who is amazingly talented or intelligent.

proffer (präf'ər) *n.* An offer or proposal.

profound (prə found') *adj.* Very deep; thoroughgoing.

profusely (prə fyōos'lē) *adv.* Freely and abundantly.

prologue (prō'lôg) *n.* Introductory lines spoken by an actor before a dramatic performance.

prophecy (präf'ə sē) *n.* A prediction.

prophesy (präf'ə sī') *v.* To predict.

prosaic (prō zā'ik) *adj.* Dull, commonplace.

proverbial (prə vur'bē əl) *adj.* Well-known because commonly referred to.

prowess (prou'is) *n.* Bravery or superior skill.

prudent (prōod''nt) *adj.* Sensible; using sound judgment.

pulsate (pul'sāt) *v.* To throb or vibrate rhythmically.

pulverize (pul'və rīz) *v.* To destroy completely.

pungent (pun'jənt) *adj.* Producing a sharp sensation of taste or smell.

putrefy (pyōo'trə fī') *v.* To become rotten and smelly.

pyre (pīr) *n.* A pile of wood for burning a corpse in a funeral rite.

Q

quarry (kwôr'ē) *n.* **1.** Anything that is being hunted. **2.** A place where stone is excavated.

quash (kwäsh) *v.* To overcome or put down as by force.

quaver (kwā'vər) *v.* To be shaky.

quay (kē) *n.* A wharf for loading and unloading ships.

quench (kwench) *v.* To overcome or subdue.

quietude (kwī'ə tōod') *n.* A state of being quiet; calmness.

---

fat, āpe, cär; ten, ēven; is, bīte; gō, hôrn, tōol, look; oil, out; up, fur; get; joy; yet; chin; she; thin, then; zh, leisure; ŋ, ring; ə for a in ago, e in agent, i in sanity, o in comply, u in focus; ' as in able (ā'b'l)

R

rakishly (rā′kish lē) *adv.* Done with a gay, careless look.

ramshackle (ram′shak′l) *adj.* Loose, rickety, and likely to fall apart.

rancor (raŋ′kər) *n.* A long-lasting and bitter hate.

rank (raŋk) *adj.* Growing vigorously and coarsely.

rapt (rapt) *adj.* Carried away with love or joy.

rapture (rap′chər) *n.* An expression of great joy or pleasure.

rash (rash) *adj.* Too hasty and careless; reckless.

rasp (rasp) *v.* To scrape or rub as with a file.

ravage (rav′ij) *v.* To destroy or ruin.

rebuke (ri byook′) *n.* A sharp scolding or reprimand.

recoil (ri koil′) *n.* A flying back when let go or fired.

recommence (rē′kə mens′) *v.* To begin or start again.

recompense (rek′əm pens′) *n.* Something done to make up for an injury; compensation.

recompose (re′kəm pōz′) *v.* To calm or quiet oneself again.

reconnoitre (rē′kə noit′ər) *v.* To make a survey or examination of.

refectory (ri fek′tər ē) *n.* A dining hall in a monastery, convent, or college.

reiterate (rē it′ə rāt′) *v.* To say again.

rejuvenate (ri joo′və nāt′) *v.* To bring back to youthful strength or appearance.

relentless (ri lent′lis) *adj.* Going on without stopping.—**relentlessly** *adv.*

reminiscent (rem′ə nis′′nt) *adj.* Given to a remembering of past experiences.

remorse (ri môrs′) *n.* A deep, torturing sense of guilt over a wrong.

rend (rend) *v.* To tear or split apart.—**rent** *n.*

renegade (ren′ə gād′) *n.* A person who abandons his principles to join the other side; a traitor.

renege (ri nig′) *v.* To go back on a promise.

reprehensible (rep′ri hen′sə b′l) *adj.* Deserving to be scolded or blamed.

reproach (ri prōch′) *v.* To blame or accuse.

reprove (ri proov′) *v.* To scold or express disapproval.—**reprovingly** *adv.*

resignation (rez′ig nā′shən) *n.* Patient acceptance of something.—**resigned** *adj.*

resolute (rez′ə loot′) *adj.* Showing a fixed, firm purpose; determined.

respite (res′pit) *n.* A period of temporary relief or rest.

retribution (ret′rə byoo′shən) *n.* Punishment that one deserves for a wrong he or she has done.

reveille (rev′ə lē) *n.* An early morning signal, as on a bugle, to wake soldiers or campers.

revel (rev′′l) *v.* To take much pleasure in.

reverberate (ri vʉr′bə rāt′) *v.* To echo back or resound.

reverie (rev′ər ē) *n.* Daydream or dreamy thinking.

rheumatism (roo′mə tiz′m) *n.* A painful condition in which the joints and muscles become inflamed and stiff.

righteous (rī′chəs) *adj.* Morally right; acting with justice or virtue.—**righteousness** *n.*

rime (rīm) *n.* A white frost on grass or leaves.

ritualistic (rich′oo wəl is′tik) *adj.* Done as a rite or formal ceremony.

roan (rōn) *n.* A horse of a solid color, as reddish-brown or black, with a thick sprinkling of whitish hairs.

robust (rō bust′) *adj.* Strong, sturdy, or muscular.

roe (rō) *n.* Fish eggs.

roil (roil) *v.* To stir up or agitate.

rollick (räl′ik) *v.* To play or behave in a carefree way.

rosette (rō zet′) *n.* An arrangement resembling a rose.

rotund (rō tund′) *adj.* Round, plump, stout.

rowel (rou′əl) *n.* A small wheel with sharp points, forming the end of a spur.

rueful (roo′fəl) *adj.* Feeling or showing sorrow or regret.—**ruefully** *adv.*

ruse (rooz) *n.* A trick or plan for fooling someone.

S

sacrilegious (sak′rə lij′′əs) *adj.* Misusing or violating what is thought to be holy.

sallow (sal′ō) *adj.* Having an unhealthy, pale-yellow look.

sanctified (saŋk′tə fīd′) *adj.* Pretending to be holy.

sarcastic (sär kas′tik) *adj.* Sneering or mocking in a way meant to hurt someone.—**sarcastically** *adv.*

saucy (sô′sē) *adj.* Lively and bold.

savor (sā′vər) *v.* To taste with relish; dwell on with delight.

scabbard (skab′ərd) *n.* A sheath or case to hold the blade of a sword.

scoffingly (skôf′iŋ lē) *adv.* In a mocking way.

scornfully (skôrn′fə lē) *adv.* With contempt.

scourge (skʉrj) *v.* To whip or punish severely.

scow (skou) *n.* A large flat-bottomed boat with square ends.

scruple (skrōō'p'l) *n.* An uneasy feeling about something one thinks is wrong.

scuttle (skut''l) *v.* To sink a ship.

seizure (sē'zhər) *n.* A sudden taking.

self-effacing (self'i fās'iŋ) *adj.* Keeping oneself modestly in the background.

semblance (sem'bləns) *n.* Outward look or seeming likeness.

seniority (sēn yôr'ə tē) *n.* The fact of being older or of higher rank.

sensuous (sen'shoo wəs) *adj.* Appealing or pleasing to the senses.

shackle (shak''l) *n.* A metal fastening device.

shard (shärd) *n.* A fragment or broken piece.

shrewd (shrōōd) *adj.* Keen-witted, clever, and sharp.

shroud (shroud) *n.* Something that covers, protects, or screens; a veil.

sibilant (sib''l ənt) *adj.* Making a hissing sound.

sidle (sī'd'l) *v.* To move sideways, especially in a shy or stealthy way.

siesta (sē es'tə) *n.* A brief nap or rest taken after the noon meal.

simper (sim'pər) *v.* To smile in a silly or self-conscious way.

simpleton (sim'p'l tən) *n.* A person who is stupid or easily tricked.

sinew (sin'yōō) *n.* A tendon.—**sinewy** *adj.*

sinister (sin'is tər) *adj.* Unfortunate or disastrous; threatening harm.

skein (skān) *n.* A quantity of thread or yarn wound in a coil.

skulk (skulk) *v.* To move about or hide in a sneaky or cowardly way.

slacken (slak''n) *v.* To become less intense.—**slack** *adj.*

slaver (slav'ər) *n.* Saliva drooling from the mouth.

slough (sluf) *v.* To shed or cast off.

smug (smug) *adj.* So pleased with oneself as to be annoying to others.

solicitous (sə lis'ə təs) *adj.* Showing care or concern.—**solicitude** *n.*

soliloquy (sə lil'ə kwē) *n.* Lines in a drama in which a character reveals thoughts to the audience by speaking as if to himself or herself.

somnolence (säm'nə ləns) *n.* Sleepiness, drowsiness.

sorcerer (sôr'sər ər) *n.* A person who practices black magic or witchcraft.

sordid (sôr'did) *adj.* Dirty, disgusting, low, or dishonorable.

spar (spär) *v.* To box with jabbing movements.

spasmodic (spaz mäd'ik) *adj.* In short, sudden bursts of activity.—**spasmodically** *adv.*

speculatively (spek'yə lə tiv lē) *adv.* By thinking about the various aspects of a subject; making guesses.

spendthrift (spend'thrift') *n.* A person who spends money carelessly.

spoor (spoor) *n.* The track or trail of a wild animal.

spume (spyōōm) *n.* Foam or froth.

squalor (skwäl'ər) *n.* Filth and wretchedness.

squander (skwän'dər) *v.* To spend or use wastefully.

squire (skwīr) *n.* A country gentleman who owns much land.

staccato (stə kät'ō) *adj.* Made up of short, sharp elements or sounds.

stalemate (stāl'māt') *n.* A deadlock; any unfinished situation in which further action is impossible.

stalwart (stôl'wərt) *adj.* Brave, strong, fearless.

stanch (stônch) *v.* To stop or cease flowing.

starboard (stär'bərd) *adj.* On the right-hand side of a ship as one faces forward.

stealthy (stel'thē) *adj.* Secret, sneaky, or quiet.

steed (stēd) *n.* A horse.

stentorian (sten tôr'ē ən) *adj.* Very loud.

stereopticon (ster'e äp'ti kən) *n.* A slide projector that allows one view to fade out while the next is fading in.

sterile (ster''l) *adj.* Not lively or interesting.

stoicism (stō'i siz'm) *n.* The state of being sternly unconcerned and unemotional about joy, grief, pain, or pleasure.—**stoical** *adj.*

stolid (stäl'id) *adj.* Showing little or no emotion.

stratagem (strat'ə jəm) *n.* A trick, scheme, or plan for achieving some purpose.

strop (sträp) *v.* To sharpen on a thick leather band.

stupefaction (stōō'pə fak'shən) *n.* Stunned amazement; astonishment; bewilderment.

---

fat, āpe, cär; ten, ēven; is, bīte; gō, hôrn, tōol, look; oil, out; up, fur; get; joy; yet; chin; she; thin, *th*en; zh, leisure; ŋ, ring; ə for *a* in *ago*, *e* in *agent*, *i* in *sanity*, *o* in *comply*, *u* in *focus*; **'** as in *able* (ā'b'l)

stupefy (stŏŏ′pə fī′) v. To stun or astound.

subjugate (sub′jə gāt′) v. To conquer or control.

submission (səb mish′ən) n. A giving up or surrendering.

subside (səb sīd′) v. To become quiet or less active.

subterfuge (sub′tər fyŏŏj′) n. Any action used to avoid a difficult situation.

suffuse (sə fyŏŏz′) v. To spread over so as to fill with a glow.

sullen (sul′ən) adj. Gloomy, somber, dull.—**sullenly** adv.

sultry (sul′trē) adj. Uncomfortably hot and moist.

supercilious (sŏŏ′pər sil′ē əs) adj. Proud and scornful; looking down on others.

supernatural (sŏŏ′pər nach′ər əl) n. Forces existing outside man's normal experience or the known laws of nature.

suppress (sə pres′) v. To keep back or restrain.

surreptitiously (sʉr′əp tish′əs lē) adv. In a sly, secret way.

swarthy (swôr′thē) adj. Having a dark complexion.

sylvan (sil′vən) adj. Of or characteristic of the woods or forest.

symmetrical (si met′ri k'l) adj. Balanced due to exact correspondence of opposite parts.

T

tableau (tab′lō) n. A striking, dramatic scene.

taint (tānt) v. To affect with something harmful.

tangible (tan′jə b'l) adj. That can be touched or felt; having actual form and substance.

tapestry (tap′is trē) n. A heavy cloth woven with decorative designs and pictures.

tarmac (tär′mak) n. A coal-tar material for paving roads.

tartar (tär′tər) n. A bad-tempered person who is difficult to deal with.

taunt (tônt) v. To drive or provoke by ridicule.

taut (tôt) adj. Tightly stretched.

tawny (tô′nē) adj. Brownish-yellow; tan.

teem (tēm) v. To be full; swarm.

telepathy (tə lep′ə thē) n. The supposed sending of messages from one mind to another by some means other than speaking or seeing.

tempest (tem′pist) n. A violent storm with high winds.

tenacious (tə nā′shəs) adj. Holding firmly; persistent, stubborn.—**tenaciously** adv.

tenement (ten′ə mənt) n. An apartment building that is in the slums and is run-down.

tentative (ten′tə tiv) adj. Done as a test; not definite.—**tentatively** adv.

termination (tʉr′mə nā′shən) n. An ending.

tersely (tʉrs′lē) adv. Using no more words than are needed to be clear.

tessellate (tes′ə lāt′) v. To lay out in a mosaic pattern of small, square blocks.

threadbare (thred′ber′) adj. That has lost freshness or novelty; stale.

throe (thrō) n. A spasm or pang of pain.

tippet (tip′it) n. A scarflike garment for the neck and shoulders, hanging down in front.

toady (tō′dē) v. To flatter others in order to get things from them.

toilsome (toil′səm) adj. Requiring hard work.

tragicomic (traj′ə käm′ik) adj. Combining tragic and comic elements.

trajectory (trə jek′tə rē) n. The curved path of something shot through space.

tranquil (traŋ′kwəl) adj. Calm, quiet, peaceful.—**tranquility** n.

transfix (trans fiks′) v. To make unable to move, as if pierced through.

translucent (trans lŏŏ′s'nt) adj. Letting light pass but spreading it so that objects on the other side cannot be clearly seen.—**translucency** n.

treacherous (trech′ər əs) adj. Seeming safe or reliable but not really so.—**treacherously** adv., **treachery** n.

tremor (trem′ər) n. A trembling or shaking.

tremulously (trem′yoo ləs lē) adv. Fearfully; with trembling.

trepidation (trep′ə dā′shən) n. Fearful uncertainty or worry.

triceps (trī′seps) n. A muscle at the back part of the upper arm.

trifle (trī′f'l) n. Something of little importance.

trippingly (trip′iŋ lē) adv. Lightly and quickly.

triumphantly (trī um′fənt lē) adv. Showing great joy in victory.

troubadour (trŏŏ′bə dôr′) n. A poet, musician, or singer.

tuffet (tuf′ət) n. A tuft of grass.

turret (tʉr′it) n. A low, armored structure for guns, as on a tank.

tycoon (tī kŏŏn′) n. A wealthy, powerful businessperson.

tyranny (tir′ə nē) n. Very cruel and unjust use of power or authority.

U

unaccountable (un′ə koun′tə b'l) adj. That cannot be explained; strange.—**unaccountably** adv.

unaffected (un ə fek′tid) adj. Sincere and natural.

unassuming (un ə soo′miŋ) adj. Not bold or forward.

uncanny (un kan′ē) adj. So remarkable or keen as to seem unnatural; strange.

undeleterious (un del′ə tir′ē əs) adj. Harmless; not injurious.

undeviating (un dē′vē āt′iŋ) adj. Not turning aside from a prescribed course.

undomesticated (un də mes′tə kāt′id) adj. Untamed, wild.

unduly (un doo′lē) adv. Beyond what is proper or right; too much.

unendurable (un in door′ə b'l) adj. Not able to bear or hold up.—**unendurably** adv.

unenterprising (un en′tər prī′ziŋ) adj. Not showing energy or initiative.

unerringly (un ur′iŋ lē) adv. Surely; without missing or failing.

ungainly (un gān′lē) adj. Awkward and clumsy.

unheralded (un her′əld id) adj. Not publicized; unannounced.

unicorn (yoo′nə kôrn′) n. A mythical horselike animal with a single horn growing from the center of its forehead.

unrelenting (un ri len′tiŋ) adj. Without mercy or compassion.

unrepentant (un′ri pent′ənt) adj. Not feeling sorrow or regret for wrongdoing.

unruly (un roo′lē) adj. Hard to control; disobedient, disorderly.

unwieldy (un wēl′dē) adj. Hard to handle because of large size or weight.

V

vagrant (vā′grənt) n. A person who wanders from place to place, especially one without a regular job.

valiant (val′yənt) adj. Courageous, brave.

valor (val′ər) n. Great courage or bravery.

vanquish (vaŋ′kwish) v. To conquer or defeat.

venerable (ven′ər ə b'l) adj. Worthy of respect.

vengeance (ven′jens) n. Revenge.

verandah (və ran′də) n. An open porch, usually roofed, along the outside of a building.

verisimilitude (ver′ə si mil′ə tood′) n. The appearance of being true or real.

vermilion (vər mil′yən) adj. Of a bright red color.

verve (vurv) n. Liveliness, spirit, energy.

vicissitudes (vi sis′ə toodz′) n. Ups and downs; changing circumstances.

victrola (vik trō′lə) n. A phonograph.

vindictive (vin dik′tiv) adj. Wanting to get revenge.

virile (vir′əl) adj. Strong, forceful, vigorous.

voluptuously (və lup′choo wəs lē) adv. Full of or characterized by sensual pleasures.

vulnerable (vul′nər ə b'l) adj. Open to attack; that can be wounded.

W

wanton (wän′t'n) adj. **1.** Without sense or mercy. **2.** Playful, lively.

warily (wer′ə lē) adv. Cautiously.

welter (wel′tər) v. To roll about.

whorl (hwôrl) n. Anything arranged in circles, as growths of hair.

wince (wins) v. To draw back slightly, usually twisting the face, as in pain.

wiry (wīr′ē) adj. Lean and muscular.

wither (with′ər) v. To make lose courage or be ashamed.

wont (wônt) n. Usual practice; habit.

wrest (rest) v. To pull or force away violently with a twisting motion.

wretchedness (rech′id nes) n. Unhappiness, misery.—**wretched** adj.

writhe (rīth) v. To squirm or make twisting movements.

Y

yeomanry (yō′mən rē) n. Landowners as a group.

Z

zealous (zel′əs) adj. Enthusiastic, eager.

---

fat, āpe, cär; ten, ēven; is, bīte; gō, hôrn, tool, look; oil, out; up, fur; get; joy; yet; chin; she; thin, *th*en; zh, leisure; ŋ, ring; ə for *a* in *ago*, *e* in *agent*, *i* in *sanity*, *o* in *comply*, *u* in *focus*; ' as in *able* (ā′b'l)

Index of Titles and Authors

Index of Fine Art

The Museum of Modern Art

Multiplication of the Arcs, 1954. Yves Tanguy.
Oil on canvas, 40 × 60".

Street Light, 1909. Giacomo Balla.
Oil on canvas, 68-3/4 × 45-1/4".

The Old Locomotive, 1906. Lyonel Feininger.
Lithograph, printed in black. Sheet: 11-1/6 × 15-3/4".
Composition: 6-1/4 × 12-5/8".

Gas, 1940. Edward Hopper.
Oil on canvas, 26-1/4 × 40-1/4".

Pierrot, 1918. Pablo Picasso.
Oil on canvas, 36-1/2 × 28-3/4".

Index of Skills

Reading and Literary Skills

Vocabulary and Language Skills

Writing Skills

Art Credits

Cover

Cin-Zin, Karl Knaths. The Phillips Collection, Washington, D. C.

Photographs

Arthur Daley/*Sports Illustrated,* 13; Joseph Martin/Scala, 16; Ralph Kleinhempel, 59; Robert E. Mates, 76; Malcolm Varon, N.Y.C. © M. Varon, 118, 180, 345, 386; Cliche Musees Nationaux Paris, 121, 282; John Tennant, 177, 381; *Sport* Magazine, 226; I. Hachette, 285; Scala/Editorial Photocolor Archives, 291; Michael Holford, 303, 308, 309, 310; Alfred J. Wyatt, 340; Joseph Szaszfai, 341; Eileen Tweedy, 369; Geoffrey Clements, 377, 406, 428; Carmelo Guadagno and Daniel Heald, 414; The Museum of Modern Art/Film Stills Archive, 431–482; Robert C. Ragsdale/Photos Courtesy of the Stratford Festival, 491–579.

Photo Researchers: Ken Biggs, 206; Charles A. Mann, 207, 253; William J. Jahoda, 209; M. E. Warren, 217; Mary M. Thacher, 222; Michael Philip Mannheim, 223, 225, 235; Chester Higgins, Jr., 228; Susan Kuklin, 234; Lowell J. Georgia, 236; Mary Ann D'Espo, 237; Rod Plank, 252; R. C. Hermes, 254; Angelina Lax, 255; Earl Roberge, 257; Tony Myers, 259; Russ Kinne, 260, 268; Carl Purcell, 262, 264; Tom McHugh, 263; Dick Rowan, 267; John G. Ross, 271; Davis Thomas, 273; John Verne, 276; Ronny Jacques, 277, 279; J. McCormick, 398.

Illustrations

Larry Frederick, 15, 185; Robert Baumgartner, 18; David Cunningham, 21, 129, 130, 199, 201, 203, 364, 379; James Watling, 29, 31, 133, 135, 140, 395; Elaine Kaneb, 34, 36, 37; Simon Galkin, 45, 47; Larry Raymond, 54, 56, 57; Robert Kosta, 63, 64; Jack White, 82, 84, 165, 167; B. J. Johnson, 89, 144, 146, 149, 192, 195, 385; Steven Schindler, 92, 365; Konrad Hack, 95, 97, 105, 107; Ben Otero, 152, 154; Betty Maxey, 158; Phill Reynaud, 188; James Thurber, 246, 247, 248; Richard Brown, 250, 251, 337; Kinuko Craft, 335; Charles McBarron, 350; Clifford Timm, 353; Jon Friedman, 354; Jean Helmer, 358, 359, 367; Dick Martin, 360, 370; Marie DeJohn, 585–675.

"Where the Rainbow Ends" by Richard Rive, from *Poems from Black Africa*, edited by Langston Hughes. Beatrice Janosco: For "The Garden Hose" by Beatrice Janosco; reprinted by permission of the author. Johnson Publishing Company and Eugenia Collier: For "Marigolds" by Eugenia Collier; copyright © 1969 by Johnson Publishing Company, Inc. Alfred A. Knopf, Inc.: For "Sixpence" by Katherine Mansfield, from *The Short Stories of Katherine Mansfield*; copyright 1924 by Alfred A. Knopf, Inc. and renewed 1952 by John Middleton Murry. For "Dreams" by Langston Hughes, from *The Dream Keeper and Other Poems*; copyright 1932 by Alfred A. Knopf, Inc. and renewed 1960 by Langston Hughes. For "Dream Deferred" by Langston Hughes, from *The Panther & The Lash* by Langston Hughes; copyright © 1951 by Langston Hughes. For "Velvet Shoes" by Elinor Wylie, from *Collected Poems of Elinor Wylie*; copyright 1921 by Alfred A. Knopf, Inc. and renewed 1949 by William Rose Benét. For "On the Inclusion of Miniature Dinosaurs in Breakfast Cereal Boxes" by John Updike, from *Midpoint and Other Poems*; copyright 1964 by John Updike. For "White Dwarf" from *Telephone Poles and Other Poems* by John Updike; copyright © 1962 by John Updike. For "Mother to Son," from *Selected Poems of Langston Hughes* by Langston Hughes; copyright © 1926 by Alfred A. Knopf Inc. and renewed 1954 by Langston Hughes. Little, Brown and Company: For "Southbound on the Freeway" and "Daffodils" by May Swenson, from *New & Selected Things Taking Place*; copyright © 1963, 1966 by May Swenson; first appeared in *The New Yorker*. For "Distance and a Certain Light" by May Swenson, from *New & Selected Things Taking Place*, copyright © 1963 by May Swenson. For "How Everything Happens (Based on a Study of the Wave)" by May Swenson, from *New & Selected Things Taking Place*; copyright © 1969 by May Swenson; first appeared in *The Southern Review*. For excerpts from *The Original Sin: A Self Portrait* by Anthony Quinn; copyright 1972 by Anthony Quinn. For excerpts from *A Whale for the Killing* by Farley Mowat; copyright © 1972 by Farley Mowat, Limited. Liveright Publishing Corporation: For "Spring Is Like a Perhaps Hand" by E. E. Cummings, from *Tulips & Chimneys*; copyright 1923, 1925, and renewed 1951 and 1953 by E. E. Cummings; copyright © 1973, 1976 by Nancy T. Andrews; copyright © 1973, 1976 by George James Firmage. Alonzo Lopez: For "Tears" by Alonzo López, from *The Whispering Wind*, edited by Terry Allen; © 1972 by The Institute of Indian Arts, Doubleday Company, Inc., Garden City, New York. Macmillan Publishing Co., Inc.: For "The Broncho That Would Not Be Broken," from *Collected Poems* by Vachel Lindsay; copyright 1917 by Macmillan Publishing Co., Inc., renewed 1945 by Elizabeth C. Lindsay. McIntosh and Otis, Inc.: For "The Elk Tooth Dress" by Dorothy M. Johnson, published in *Seventeen Magazine* of March, 1957; copyright 1957 by Dorothy M. Johnson. Scott Meredith Agency, Inc.: For "Pompeii," from *Lost Cities and Vanished Civilizations* by Robert Silverberg; reprinted by permission of the author and the author's agents, Scott Meredith Literary Agency, Inc., 845 Third Avenue, New York, N. Y. 10022. William Morris Agency, Inc.: For "One Throw" by W. C. Heinz; copyright 1950 by Crowell-Collier Publishing Co. New Directions Publishing Corp.: For "The Sharks" by Denise Levertov, from *Collected Earlier Poems: 1940–1960*; copyright © 1958 by Denise Levertov Goodman. For "Training" by Demetrio Herrera, from *An Anthology of Latin American Poetry*; copyright © 1970 by New Directions Publishing Corp. For "The Rainwalkers" by Denise Levertov, from *The Jacob's Ladder*; copyright © 1961 by Denise Levertov Goodman. New Mexico Magazine: For "Piñones" by Leroy Quintana, from *New Mexico Magazine*, Nov./Dec. 1974. Louis Nizer: For "An Editorial Lost in a News Item" by Louis Nizer, from *Between You and Me*. W. W. Norton & Company, Inc.: For "High Tide" by Jean Starr Untermeyer, from *Job's Daughter*; copyright © 1967 by W. W. Norton & Company, Inc. For "Small Song," from *Uplands, New Poems*, by A. R. Ammons; copyright © 1970 by A. R. Ammons. For "I Am a" by Lenore Marshall, from *Latest Will, New and Selected Poems*; copyright © 1969 by Lenore Marshall. Harold Ober Associates: For "Thank You M'am" by Langston Hughes, from *The Langston Hughes Reader*; copyright 1958 by Langston Hughes. For "Discovery of a Father" by Sherwood Anderson, from *Reader's Digest*; copyright © 1939 by the Reader's Digest Assoc., renewed 1966 by Eleanor Copenhaver Anderson. Gloria Oden: For "The Way It Is" by Gloria Oden, from *Poetry Is Alive and Well and Living in America*. The Organization of American States: For "Lather and Nothing Else" by Hernando Tellez, from *Américas*, bimonthly magazine published by the General Secretariat of the Organization of American States in English and Spanish. Penguin Books Ltd.: For "Sunset Colours" by Yoshino Hiroshi from *Post-War Japanese Poetry*, ed. and trans. by Harry and Lynn Guest and Kajima Shozo (The Penguin Poets, 1972), pp. 107–108; copyright © Harry Guest, Lynn Guest, and Kajima Shozo, 1972. Penn State Press of University Park: For "Dandelions" by Deborah Austin, from *Paradise of the World*; copyright © 1964. G. P. Putnam's Sons: For "Snow," from *Everything and Anything* by Dorothy Aldis; copyright © 1925, 1926, 1927, 1953, 1954, 1955 by D. Aldis. Random House, Inc.: For "A Christmas Memory" by Truman Capote, from *Selected Writings of Truman Capote*; copyright © 1956 by Truman Capote. For Chapter 1 from *I Know Why the Caged Bird Sings* by Maya Angelou; copyright © 1969 by Maya Angelou. For "Raymond's Run," from *Gorilla, My Love* by Toni Cade Bambara; copyright © 1970 by Toni Cade Bambara. For "The Cat" from *Sleek for the Long Flight* by William Matthews; copyright © 1972 by William Matthews. Rothco Cartoons, Inc.: For "Little Miss Muffet" by Paul Dehn; copyright © 1958 Punch/Rothco. St. Martin's Press, Inc. and MacMillan & Co., Ltd.: For Chapter 61 from *All Creatures Great and Small* by James Herriot. Estate of William Saroyan: For *The Human Comedy* by William Saroyan. Copyright © 1971 by William Saroyan, published by Dell Publishing Co. Saturday Review: For "Ride a Wild Horse" by Hannah Kahn, from *Into the Sun*, copyright © 1953 by *Saturday Review*, all right reserved, reprinted by permission. Scholastic Magazines, Inc.: For "Theseus" and "Daedalus" by Bernard Evslin, from *Heroes, Gods, and Monsters of the Greek Myths*; copyright © 1966, 1967 by Scholastic, Inc. Scott, Foresman and Company: For "Happy Birthday" by Toni Cade Bambara, from *What's Happening*; copyright © 1969 Scott, Foresman and Company. Charles Scribner's Sons: For "A Mother in Mannville" by Marjorie Kinnan Rawlings, from *When the Whippoorwill*; copyright 1936 by Marjorie Kinnan Rawlings; copyright renewed, copyright 1940, by Marjorie Kinnan Rawlings; copyright renewed, Charles Scribner's Sons, 1940. For "Earth," (copyright © 1936) by John Hall Wheelock, from *The Gardner & Other Poems*; copyright © 1961 by J. H. Wheelock. Simon & Schuster, a Division of Gulf & Western Corporation: For "Sleeping Arrangements" by Sam Levenson, from *Everything but Money*; copyright © 1949, 1966 by Sam Levenson. For Chapter 1, pp. 1–22 from *The Education of a Baseball Player* by Mickey Mantle; copyright © 1967 by Mickey Mantle. Mary Carter Smith: For "Jungle" by Mary Carter Smith, from *The Poetry of the Negro 1746–1970*, edited by Langston Hughes and Arna Bontemps. Texas Christian University: For "Everybody Knows Tobie" by Daniel Garza, from *Descant*, Spring, 1963. Mrs. James Thurber: For text and illustrations for "The Night the Bed Fell" by James Thurber, from *My Life and*

Hard Times; copyright © 1933, 1961 by James Thurber, published by Harper and Row. For "The Secret Life of Walter Mitty" by James Thurber, from *My World—and Welcome to It;* copyright 1942 by James Thurber, copyright © 1970 by Helen W. Thurber, published by Harcourt Brace Jovanovich. Viking Penguin, Inc.: For "Good Humor Man" from *Times Three* by Phyllis McGinley, originally published in *The New Yorker;* copyright 1947 by Phyllis McGinley, copyright renewed 1975 by Phyllis McGinley. For "The Elephant" from *Earthworks* by Sandra Hochman; copyright © 1970, by Sandra Hochman. For "The Story-Teller," from *The Short Stories of Saki* (H. H. Munrol); copyright 1931 by The Viking Press, Inc., copyright renewed 1958 by The Viking Press. The Viking Press Publishers: For "The World in a Wall" (Chapter 9) by Gerald Durrell, from *My Family and Other Animals;* copyright © 1956 by Gerald M. Durrell. Wesleyan University Press: For "Pigeons" by Richard Kell, from *Differences;* copyright 1969 by Richard Kell, by permission of Chatto and Windus with The Hogarth Press and Wesleyan University Press. For "The Base Stealer," from *The Orb Weaver* by Robert Francis; copyright © 1948 by Robert Francis; first appeared in *Forum.* Robert Wallace: For "The Double Play"; copyright © 1960 by Robert Wallace. Western Publishing Company, Inc.: For "The Sword in the Stone," "Excalibur," "Camelot," "The Gift of Leodegrance," "The Oath," "The Coming of Galahad," and "The Search for the Holy Grail," from *King Arthur and the Knights of the Round Table* by Emma Gelders Sterne and Barbara Lindsay; copyright © 1962 by Western Publishing Company, Inc.

The authors and editors have made every effort to trace the ownership of all copyrighted selections found in this book and to make full acknowledgment for their use.

Staff Credits

Editorial Director: Joy Littell
Managing Editor: Kathleen Laya
Associate Editor: Zana Courser
Rights and Permissions: Irma Rosenberg
Director of Design: Allen Carr
Associate Designer: Marcia Vecchione

Editor-in-Chief: Joseph F. Littell

85 86 87 / 9 8 7 6 5

Handbook:

How To Write
About Literature

Orange Level

McDougal, Littell & Company

Contents

ISBN: 0-88343-447-4

Copyright ©1985 by McDougal, Littell & Company
Box 1667, Evanston, Illinois 60204

Introduction

As you study the literature in this book you will be asked to write about what you have read. You will be assigned paragraphs and compositions, and you may be given essay questions to answer. You also will be directed to write poems, stories, letters, and accounts of your own experiences. When you are faced with the writing assignment, you may wonder where to begin and how to get your ideas down on paper. Later, you might ask: How can I tell if my writing is any good? The lessons in this handbook will help you solve these and many other problems connected with all writing.

The handbook is divided into three parts. Part 1 explains the process of writing. Each lesson in this part describes one step in the process and includes a sample that illustrates the direction. At the end of the lesson are exercises that will give you practice in using the process. After studying Part 1, you will be ready for any kind of writing assignment. You also will be able to refer to these pages whenever you need to review the writing process.

Part 2 provides help in writing about six major elements of literature. The lessons explain how to use the process of writing to analyze setting, character, plot, theme, tone and mood, and poetic language. Each lesson begins with suggestions for thinking about the element that is the subject of the lesson. Next, the lesson describes topics that you might be asked to write about. After this comes a list of points to keep in mind when completing an assignment. As in Part 1, the lessons in Part 2 include sample writing assignments and exercises.

Part 3 explains how to apply the process of writing when analyzing short stories and novels, nonfiction, poetry, and drama. Each lesson begins with suggestions for thinking about a selection, describes possible topics, and lists points to keep in mind when completing assignments. The lessons include samples and end with exercises that give you a chance to apply the process of writing and the suggestions in the lessons.

The lessons in Parts 2 and 3 are here to help you whenever you must write about a literature selection. Use the lessons first as a learning tool and later as a resource to help you improve your writing and analyzing skills.

LESSON 1 Pre-Writing: Setting a Clear Direction

The process of writing includes three stages: pre-writing, writing the first draft, and revising. During the pre-writing stage, you formulate a plan for writing. You decide what you are going to say and how you are going to say it. During the remaining stages, you put your pre-writing plan into action.

As you begin the lessons on the process of writing, choose a writing assignment from this book with the help of your teacher. Complete this assignment as you work through the lessons.

Analyzing an Assignment

When you are given a specific assignment or essay question, make sure that you understand exactly what you are being asked to do. Read the directions or questions several times. Read first for a general meaning. Then reread to identify key words, such as these common "direction" verbs:

discuss   describe   show   cite
compare   analyze   demonstrate   quote
contrast   explain   define   support

Other key words include the interrogative words *how, why, who,* and *where* and the nouns *effect, significance, example,* and *opinion.* Directions and essay questions also may contain literary terms such as *mood, tone, theme, imagery, character,* and *point of view.* If you are unsure of the meanings of these or other key words, consult a dictionary or the Handbook of Literary Terms in this book.

Many assignments in this book either tell you how much to write or imply the desired length in some way. Essay questions seldom include this kind of guidance. The length of your response depends on the question and, when taking tests, on the amount of time in the testing period.

Choosing a Topic

Sometimes you will be able to select your own topic. For example, you might be asked to write a poem about any subject, to describe an experience from your own life, to analyze a story or poem of your choice, to discuss a theme treated in several selections, or to write an original story. Each assignment presents its own special challenges. However, your basic approach should be similar to the following.

Steps in Choosing a Topic

1. List several possible topics. This is the beginning of your pre-writing notes.
2. Identify the topic that seems most workable and appealing.
3. Think about the final length of your work. Will it be a paragraph? A brief composition? A longer composition?
4. Limit your topic if it seems too broad. Broaden your focus somewhat if your topic seems too narrow.
5. Record your final topic in your pre-writing notes.

Knowing Your Purpose and Audience

Your purpose for writing and your audience affect both the details you select and the way you present them for your readers. Purpose and audience are interrelated, for the underlying reason for writing is to communicate something to a reader.

Purpose. From the key words in an assignment, you can determine your purpose for writing. Often, your purpose will be to present your conclusions about a work of literature. More specifically, you may write to define, to describe, to analyze, or to explain your topic.

When determining purpose, think about the effect that you want your writing to have on your audience. When writing an original poem or recalling experiences from your own life, for example, you may want to evoke a certain emotional response. When you are analyzing literary elements, you will want your readers to understand a selection in the same way that you do.

Once you have clarified your purpose in your own mind, record it in your pre-writing notes. Following is a sample statement of purpose: to explain the changes that take place in Squeaky as a result of her experiences.

Audience. Your audience generally will be your classmates and teacher. They, too, have read the literary selections that are assigned as subjects for analysis. For this kind of assignment, therefore, you do not need to summarize the content of the selection. Instead, you should refer to the literature to support your conclusions.

Many assignments in this book ask you to write about your own ideas and experiences. Keep in mind that your audience probably will be unfamiliar with your subject and that

you may need to do more explaining in this kind of writing.

Sample Writing Assignment

The following writing assignment is based on two short stories, "Charles," which begins on page 4, and "The Lie," which begins on page 40.

In "Charles" and "The Lie" the relationships between parents and children are strikingly similar. In one paragraph compare the relationship of Laurie and his parents with that of Eli and Dr. and Mrs. Remenzel. Use specific examples from each story to support your ideas.

EXERCISES   Applying the Process: Pre-Writing

1. Study the sample writing assignment. Then answer these questions:

What are the key words? Do you understand their meanings?

What length is specified?

What would be your purpose for writing?

What effect on your readers would you try to achieve?

Would your audience be familiar with your subject?

Read (or reread) "Charles" and "The Lie."

2. Analyze the **Developing Writing Skills** or **Unit Review** assignment on which you are working. Identify the key words and note any mention of length. Clarify the meanings of unfamiliar terms. Determine your purpose and think about your readers and the effect that you want your writing to have on them.

LESSON 2 Pre-Writing: Gathering and Organizing Ideas

Supporting details come from a variety of sources. When you are writing an original poem or story, details come from your imagination. When you are recalling your own experiences, you draw upon your memory for details. For a description, you generate details from observation, from your imagination, or possibly from a literary work. When analyzing literature, the selection or selections that are your subject are your source for details.

Details should be listed in your pre-writing notes. Be certain that each detail develops your topic in some way.

Gathering Details from Literature

When you are writing about a short story, an essay, a nonfiction excerpt, or a poem, it may be possible to reread the entire selection. However, for full-length novels and plays, you probably will choose to reread or examine closely only those portions that relate to your topic. As you read, take precise notes, keeping the following in mind:

Guidelines for Taking Notes

1. Copy accurately the lines and passages that you wish to quote. Give page or line numbers for all quotations.

2. Paraphrase, or put into your own words, important passages.

3. Summarize, or describe briefly, examples and incidents that relate directly to your topic.

4. Jot down ideas that occur to you as you read.

Grouping Details for Compositions

When you gather details for a composition, you most likely will end up with a long list of pre-writing notes. As a first step in organizing these details, identify three or four major ideas suggested by the details. Group your details accordingly, then identify each idea group with a word or phrase. As you form your idea groups, add details and delete any that do not seem to fit into your groups.

Some of the writing assignments for compositions suggest ways to organize your ideas. For example, a writing assignment may tell you what to discuss in the introductory paragraph, in the body paragraphs, and in the conclusion. Your idea groups should reflect any such guidance given in the assignment.

Organizing Details

Once you have grouped the details for a composition, your next step is to put the idea groups and the ideas within the groups into some logical order. If you do not have idea groups to work with, your approach is essentially the same. You will need to arrange the list of details into an order that suits the material. Number your details to show your final arrangement. Four common orders are described here.

Four Ways To Organize Details

Chronological Order. In this method, you present details in the order in which they occur. This method is useful when analyzing the development of character or plot and when writing original stories in prose and in poetry.

Spatial Order. In this method, details are organized in the order in which a viewer might notice them. This method generally is used in describing setting and the physical appearance of characters and of people in real life.

Order of Importance. This method can be applied in two ways: arranging details from least to most important or from most to least important. For example, if you are discussing a character, you might first note his or her least significant quality and then build to the most important quality. When analyzing the techniques used in a poem, you probably would discuss the most important techniques first and then mention others that are less significant but still contribute to the total effect.

Comparison and Contrast. This type of writing deals with two subjects. Statements about one are balanced with statements about the other. You might choose to analyze your subjects point by point, or you might discuss one subject and then the other. If you use this second approach, you probably will want to number your two groups of details separately.

Sample Pre-Writing Notes

Upon careful rereading of "Charles" and "The Lie," one writer took the following pre-writing notes.

Purpose: to show how the relationship between Charles and his parents is similar to that between Eli and his parents.

"Charles"

① ". . . my sweet voiced nursery-school tot replaced by a long-trousered, swaggering character. . . ." (p. 4)—mother's view different from what behavior shows

③ "At lunch he spoke insolently to his father, ~~spilled Jannie's milk~~. . . ." (p. 4)

~~"Laurie regarded his father coldly." (p. 4)~~

④ "I asked again, but Laurie slid off his chair, took a cookie and left, while his father was still saying, 'See here, young man.'" (p. 4)

~~Jokes with father (p. 4)~~

⑤ "He grinned enormously and said, 'Today Charles hit the teacher.'" (p. 4)—delights in Charles's antics

⑦ Mother wonders if kindergarten is "too unsettling for Laurie" (pp. 4-5)

⑥ Parents believe that all the children stayed after school with Charles—parents seem naive

~~Laurie did a Charles when he filled his wagon full of mud and pulled it through the kitchen (p. 5)—another example of bad behavior~~

② Mother: "Laurie usually adjusts very quickly." (p. 6)

"The Lie"

Behavior in the car:

① Adults don't notice the emptiness in Eli's voice; Doctor answers absently—absorbed in the building plans

② Eli "shrugged listlessly" in response to mother's questions

③ Parents make no attempt to find out what's wrong

⑥ "It was inconceivable to them that Eli could not go there, so they had no curiosity as to how Eli had done on the examinations. . . ." (p. 43)

⑤ Father suspects Eli didn't do well on the exam, but doesn't seem worried about rejection by school; Mother expects "a good strong medium"

④ ". . . Eli's grades in primary school . . . had ranged from medium to terrible." (p. 46)

~~Mother more sensitive to Eli's feelings, admittance to Whitehall seems more important to father~~

1. Study the sample pre-writing notes and the order in which the details will be presented. Notice that the details are numbered in two separate groups, one group for each story. Notice also that the writer crossed out several details. Be prepared to explain why she might have done this.

2. Gather ideas for the Developing Writing Skills or **Unit Review** assignment on which you are working. Develop pre-writing notes, and number the details to show the order in which they will appear in your paragraph or composition. If you are writing a composition, be sure to identify idea groups before you do any numbering. Cross out ideas and add new ones as you work.

LESSON 3   Writing the First Draft

During the pre-writing stage, you thought a great deal about your topic. As you write your first draft, you will put your ideas into more complete form. You then will be ready to finalize your writing so that it communicates your ideas as effectively as possible.

Writing a Topic Sentence

A topic sentence is a statement that introduces the idea to be developed in a paragraph or composition. Usually the topic sentence is the first sentence of a paragraph or composition. It presents the general idea that will be supported by specific details.

Sample Topic Sentence

This topic sentence is based on the sample pre-writing notes in Lesson 2. This is a first draft, not a final version.

There may be many differences between Laurie's parents and Eli's parents, but one similarity stands out—neither set of parents views its son realistically.

If you compare the sample topic sentence with the sample writing assignment in Les-

son 1, you will see that the topic sentence picks up the key words *Eli, Laurie, parents,* and *similar.* The sentence also presents the writer's conclusion about the major similarity between the two sets of parents.

Following is a summary of the steps to keep in mind when writing a topic sentence.

Steps in Writing a Topic Sentence

1. Study your pre-writing notes.
2. Identify any general ideas.
3. Draw conclusions.
4. Review the assignment or essay question.
5. Write a sentence that states a general idea that can be developed with specific detail.

Developing Paragraphs and Compositions

In a paragraph, the topic sentence is followed by several sentences that explain, reinforce, or extend the main idea. Each of these supporting sentences presents details from the pre-writing notes. In a composition, the topic sentence is expanded into an introductory paragraph, which introduces the ideas to be discussed in the next three paragraphs. Each of these body paragraphs supports one idea presented in the introductory paragraph.

A writing assignment for a composition may tell you what to talk about in each body paragraph. Without such specific directions, you will need to rely on the idea groups in your pre-writing notes. Combine idea groups, if necessary, so that you end up with three groups. Devote one body paragraph to each group, beginning the paragraph with a topic sentence.

For the concluding paragraph of a composition, you have several choices. You can re-state the main idea, summarize the ideas in the composition, or offer a final comment on the material. Just be sure that your final paragraph follows naturally from the paragraphs that come before it.

Completing the First Draft

Whether you are working on a paragraph, composition, story, poem, or another form of writing, use your pre-writing notes to complete your first draft. Concentrate on putting your ideas on paper. Add new details that occur to you as you write. Delete and rearrange details, too, always keeping your purpose in mind. Do not be concerned with the fine points of spelling, grammar, capitalization, and punctuation as you write your first draft. You will have time to perfect your writing during revision, the final stage in the process.

Sample First Draft

This first draft begins with the sample topic sentence presented earlier in this lesson.

There may be many differences between Laurie's parents and Eli's parents, but one similarity stands out—neither set of parents views its son realistically. Laurie's behavior clearly shows that he is not the angel his parents think. He swaggers, speaks insolently to his father, and "grins enormously" at Charles's antics. His parents are even naive enough to believe that all of the children choose to stay after school with Charles and of course the ultimate display of innocence is when Charles's mother wonders if kindergarden is "too unsettling" for Laurie and when she says "Laurie usually adjusts very quickly." (page 6) In Eli's case, his relationship with his parents has had several more years for the blindspot to grow. The Remenzels do not pay any attention to Eli as he listlessly responds to their questions. They are so preoccupied with their own observations that they make no attempt to see what is wrong with him and although they know that Eli's grades "had ranged from medium to terrible" it never occurs to them that he might not pass the entrance examinations. His father doesn't seem in the least bit worried about his being rejected, his mother expects a "good strong medium" score. It is inconceivable to them that Eli could not go to Whitehall, just as it is inconceivable for Laurie's parents to believe that he could act like a Charles.

EXERCISES Applying the Process: Writing the First Draft

1. Study the sample first draft, and answer these questions: Do the supporting sentences develop the idea stated in the topic sentence? Which details from the pre-writing notes have been deleted? Which details have been rearranged? Have any ideas been added? What kinds of errors need to be corrected during the revision stage? One problem with this paragraph is length. Where might cutting be done during revision?

2. Write the first draft of the Developing Writing Skills or Unit Review assignment on which you are working. If you are writing a paragraph or a composition, begin by writing a topic sentence, using the Steps in Writing a Topic Sentence. Then develop your idea, using the details in your pre-writing notes.

LESSON 4 Revising

Revision is the final stage of the writing process. It is your opportunity to get things "just right." During revision, you will look at the development of your ideas and at the technical aspects of your writing with a critical eye.

Begin revising by reading your first draft several times. With each reading, check a few elements and make any necessary changes. The following guidelines can be used for revising paragraphs and compositions and can be adapted for other kinds of writing as well.

Guidelines for Revision

1. Check to make sure that your writing accomplishes the purpose stated in your prewriting notes.

2. If you have a topic sentence, be certain that it states clearly the main idea of the entire paragraph or composition.

3. Make sure that you have included enough detail in your writing. If necessary, add details that will further develop or clarify your ideas.

4. If unnecessary details interrupt the flow of your ideas, delete them. Also cut and condense details if your writing seems too long.

5. Reread to make sure that you have maintained a logical order in presenting your details. Your writing should have a clear beginning, middle, and end.

6. Determine whether you have used the words that express your ideas exactly. Substitute new words for those that seem vague or imprecise.

Improving Transitions

As part of the revision process, add or refine the transitional words and phrases that connect your ideas and clarify their order. Among the most common transitional devices are those listed here.

Transitional Devices

Indications of Time. Time words are essential when presenting ideas in chronological order. These words include the following:

first	finally	afterwards	until
next	before	today	later
then	after	meanwhile	since

Indications of Relationships. These words are useful when explaining statements or supporting opinions. They include the following:

and	because	besides	similarly
also	therefore	moreover	unless

Indications of Opposites. Transitional words and phrases are used most often when contrasting two subjects. They include:

but	while	on the other hand
however	although	in contrast

Repetitions of Words and Phrases. This device can be used to reinforce important concepts and to remind the reader of your topic.

Synonyms and Definitions. To define a literary term, use a synonym or insert a definition after the term.

Finalizing Your Writing

After you have revised your first draft for content, proofread your writing for errors in grammar, and usage, spelling, punctuation, and capitalization. Refer to a dictionary or an English textbook for help in making corrections and for the proofreading symbols to use in indicating those corrections. Refer also to the **Checklist for Proofreading Titles and Quotations** on page 758. Then make a final, neat copy, using correct manuscript form.

Sample Revised Paragraph

~~There may be many differences between~~ *may be different in many ways ↗)* Laurie's parents and Eli's parents, but one similarity stands out— ~~neither set of~~ *these* parents ^ *do not* ~~views~~ *their 's* ~~its~~ son realistically. Laurie's behavior clearly shows that he is not the angel his parents think. He swaggers, speaks insolently to his father, and "grins enormously" at Charles's antics. His parents are even naive enough to believe that all of the children choose to stay after school with Charles and ~~of course the ultimate display of innocence is when Charles's mother~~ *to* wonders if kindergar~~d~~ten *t* is "too unsettling" for Laurie ~~and when she says "Laurie usually adjusts very quickly." (page 6) In~~ Eli's case, his relationship with his parents ~~has had~~ *are equally blind. In the car* ~~several more years for the blindspot to grow. The Remenzels do not pay any attention to~~ Eli ~~as he~~ listlessly responds to their questions, *but* They are ~~so~~ *too* preoccupied, ~~with their own observations that they make no attempt to see what is wrong with him and~~ *to notice* although they know that Eli's grades "had ranged from medium to terrible" it never *has* occurs *red* to them that he might *be* ~~not pass the entrance examination. His father doesn't seem in the least bit worried about his being~~ rejected, *by Whitehall* his mother *even* expects a "good strong medium" score, *on the entrance examinations* ~~It is inconceivable to them~~ *Eli's parents, like* ~~that Eli could not go to Whitehall, just as it is inconceivable for~~ Laurie's parents ~~to be-lieve that he could act like a Charles.~~ *see their son as they would like him to be, not as he really is.*

EXERCISES   Applying the Process: Revising

1. Study the sample revised paragraph, and make sure that you understand each change. Be prepared to identify changes made for these reasons:

  to correct an error in spelling, punctuation or grammar and usage

  to clarify an idea

  to eliminate a detail that does not fit with others

  to shorten the paragraph

  to improve the style

2. Revise the first draft of the Developing Writing Skills or Unit Review assignment on which you are working, and make a final copy.

Guidelines: The Process of Writing

Pre-Writing

1. Analyze the essay question or writing assignment.

2. Determine your purpose, and write it in your pre-writing notes.

3. Think about your audience.

4. Gather details listing them in your pre-writing notes.

5. Organize the details. For long lists of details, identify major idea groups, then orga-

nize the groups and the details within the groups. Use an order that suits the material, and number your details to show the order. Possible orders include the following:

Chronological order

Spatial order

Order of importance (most to least, least to most)

Comparison and Contrast

6. Add or delete details as necessary.

Writing the First Draft

1. For paragraphs and compositions, write a topic sentence that introduces the idea to be developed. Expand the idea with supporting detail.

2. Using your pre-writing notes, put your ideas into the required form.

3. Add, delete, or rearrange details.

Revising

Read what you have written. Answer the following questions:

1. Have you answered the question or fulfilled the requirements of the assignment?

2. Do all the sentences and paragraphs develop a main idea? Is that idea stated clearly in the topic sentence?

3. Have you included enough detail?

4. Have you deleted unnecessary details?

5. Are the details in logical order? Will this order be clear to your readers?

6. Have you used the precise words necessary to communicate your ideas clearly?

7. Have you achieved your purpose?

Checklist for Proofreading Titles and Quotations

1. Have you capitalized the first word and every important word in the titles of books, short stories, essays, articles, plays, and poems? For example, "The Secret Life of Walter Mitty" (a short story) and I Know Why the Caged Bird Sings (a book).

2. Have you used quotation marks to enclose the titles of chapters and other parts of books? The titles of short stories, poems, essays, and articles? For example, "The Ancient History Class" (a chapter in The Human Comedy), "The Most Dangerous Game" (a short story), and "Young" (a poem).

3. Have you underlined the titles of books and full-length plays? For example, Romeo and Juliet and The Human Comedy.

4. Have you used quotation marks to enclose the exact words of a writer? For example, in "Something Bright" Anna describes her reaction to the land of There by saying, "I felt tears burn out of my eyes and start down my cheeks, whether from brightness or wonder, I don't know."

5. Have you indented and set off quotations of four or more lines? For example, at the beginning of the famous balcony scene in Romeo and Juliet, Romeo greets Juliet with these words:

But soft! What light through yonder window breaks?
It is the East, and Juliet is the sun!
Arise, fair sun, and kill the envious moon,
Who is already sick and pale with grief
That thou her maid art far more fair than she.

6. Have you used a slash mark (/) to indicate the end of a line when quoting two or three lines of poetry? For example, the speaker in "Lineage" compares herself with her grandmothers in these lines: "My grandmothers were strong./ Why am I not as they?"

7. Have you indicated missing words from a quotation with an ellipsis (. . .)? For example, Robert Silverberg concludes "Pompeii" with a paragraph that begins, "To enter Pompeii is to step into the Rome of the Caesars. An entire city, forever frozen . . . awaits the visitor."

LESSON 5 Writing About Setting

Any kind of writing that tells a story has a setting, a time and place of the action. This includes novels, short stories, and plays as well as some poems and nonfiction selections. The development of the setting varies among selections. A short story set in a place or time unfamiliar to most readers, for example, would probably include more descriptive detail than a story set in a familiar time and place. The importance of setting also varies. In some stories, setting is a major element; in others, a minor one.

Setting may be presented directly through paragraphs or passages of description or indirectly through the observations of the characters or of the narrator or speaker. In either case, you should get a feel for the setting early in the story. As you form an impression, be aware of the figurative language and of the connotative words and phrases used by the writer. Ask yourself: How does the writer establish the setting?

A second question to keep in mind is: What is the time of the action? Some stories take place in an historically significant setting. Many science fiction stories are set in the future. The time of the setting also can be used symbolically. For example, spring is a time of rebirth, fall a prelude to winter and death. Likewise, morning is a time of awakening, while evening suggests the dying of the day and death in general.

A third question to consider is: What is the place of the action? Place can include details such as furniture, clothing, weather, sounds and smells, and the kind of society in which the characters exist. For example, one character might live in a society that is warm and family-centered. Another might live in a suspicious, hostile environment.

Once you discover the details of setting, you then can determine how the writer has used setting in developing the story. You might use questions such as these as a guide:

Does the setting trigger events in the story?

Does the setting change? Does this change signal a turning point in the action?

Do the characters interact with the setting? If so, how does the setting affect them?

What is the writer's message? How does the setting help to convey this message?

Considering the Assignment

An essay question or writing assignment about setting probably will ask you to describe a setting or to discuss the setting in relation to some other element in the selection. For instance, you may be asked to explain how setting reinforces the theme, or writer's message; develops a character; or builds a mood, or atmosphere. Occasionally, you may be asked to compare and contrast the settings of two or more selections.

Following the Writing Process

The best way to approach a writing assignment dealing with setting is to follow the process of writing presented on pages 750-757 and summarized on pages 757-758. Remember that each stage—pre-writing, writing the first draft, and revising—is important in developing a well written paragraph or composition.

Pre-Writing

After reading an assignment or question, you may find that you are able to form a generalization immediately. Do so, then go back to the selection to find support for your generalization. You also may begin with the selection. Identify the details that establish the setting, then examine the details and form a generalization.

Writing the First Draft

Organize your details so that one logically follows another. Spatial order is common for descriptions of setting. Chronological order often is used when tracing the development of setting in relation to another element.

When copying quotations from your pre-writing notes, pay attention to details such as word order, spelling, punctuation, and indications of missing words.

Revising

Be sure that all of the details in your paragraph or composition support your main idea and that you have included all the important details from your pre-writing notes.

Sample Writing Assignment

The story that is the subject of this sample begins on page 87.

In one paragraph explain how the setting of "Happy Birthday" reflects Ollie's feelings about life. In your topic sentence draw parallels between Ollie's life and the setting. Then present specific examples from the story to illustrate this idea.

Pre-Writing

Following is the beginning of one writer's pre-writing notes.

Purpose: to show how the setting in "Happy Birthday" reflects Ollie's feelings

Waited on the cellar steps; sat on the rail in front of The Chicken Shack Restaurant; pigeons on roof; "projects"—set in city, in run-down area

She goes from place to place—no one at home or interested in her

"Everything below was gray, as if the chimney had snowed on the whole block." (p. 88)—gray, empty, lifeless environment; a "gray" day in Ollie's life

Writing the First Draft

The writer made a generalization, then used this generalization as the basis for the following topic sentence.

Ollie's angry feelings and empty life are reflected by a hostile setting that lacks excitement and interest.

Studying the Sample

The sample topic sentence draws parallels between Ollie's angry feelings and the hostile setting and also between Ollie's empty life and the dull, uninteresting setting. The remainder of the paragraph should present details, organized in chronological order, to support this view of the setting. The paragraph also should include comments that point out the relationship between the setting and Ollie's life.

EXERCISES   Writing About Settings

1. Read (or reread) "Happy Birthday." Complete the sample pre-writing notes. Then expand the sample topic sentence with details that support the writer's generalization. Revise the entire paragraph and make a final copy.

2. Complete your current writing assignment dealing with setting.

LESSON 6 Writing About Character

Character is a basic element of fiction and of some kinds of nonfiction and poetry as well. Characters are the people or animals who take part in the action. Readers find out about characters through the writer's use of various characterization techniques. These include physical description, the words and actions of the characters, and the comments of the narrator, the person who tells the story. All characterization techniques have the same basic goal: to give the reader an impression of the characters that will help to communicate the writer's message.

Questions to consider when thinking about characters include the following.

Who are the main and minor characters? What qualities do they exhibit?

Does the main character change during the story? If so, how?

How do you learn about the characters? (See **Characterization** in the Handbook of Literary Terms.)

What does the writer seem to be saying about life or human nature?

Considering the Assignment

An essay question or writing assignment often will ask you to form a generalization about a character and then to support that generalization with details form the selection. You may be asked to identify a character's qualities, attitudes, or motivation. You may be asked to explain what a character has learned or how a character has changed as a result of his or her experiences. You may be directed to compare and contrast characters or to discuss the way that characters interact with setting and plot to convey a theme, or message.

Following the Writing Process

When writing about a character, you should complete each stage in the process of writing: pre-writing, writing the first draft, and revising. The process is explained on pages 750-757 and is summarized on pages 757-758. Certain aspects of the process are especially important to keep in mind when analyzing a character.

Pre-Writing

Reread the selection, if possible, to gather specific details concerning characters. Study your pre-writing notes to identify patterns and recurring ideas. These will form the basis for a generalization. In turn, the generalization will help you to evaluate your notes and to add or delete details.

Writing the First Draft

The generalization that you formed during pre-writing should be used as the basis for your topic sentence.

Provide explanations, if necessary, so that your readers will be able to understand the connection between your generalization and the details you cite. In other words, try to put what is in your own mind on paper.

Revising

Reread your paragraph or composition to be sure that your ideas flow smoothly. Check for logical organization, clear explanations, and effective transitions.

Sample Writing Assignment

The story that is the subject of this assignment is "Antaeus." It begins on page 25.

In one paragraph discuss some quality demonstrated by T.J. The topic sentence of the paragraph should make a general statement about T.J. The rest of the paragraph should cite specific incidents from the story to support the idea presented in the topic sentence.

Pre-Writing

Purpose: to discuss one quality demonstrated by T.J.

". . . T.J. kept plugging along on his own. . . ." (p. 27)—shows determination

"T.J. was smart enough to start in one corner of the building. . . ." (p. 27)

". . . his words shrewd and calculated toward the fulfillment of this dream. . . ." (p. 27)—shrewd

"He was smart. He knew where to give in." (p. 28) (about planting grass)

told factory owner that the gang was just trying to "pretty up" the roof—thinks quickly, deals well with adults

attachment to land—destroys the garden himself

Writing the First Draft and Revising

Following is the final, revised paragraph.

From T.J.'s own words and actions and through the narrator's observations, the reader learns that T.J. is smart. T.J. is the one who conceives the roof garden and who figures out how to build it. The narrator uses the word <u>smart</u> on two separate occasions. When the boys first start their project, the narrator says, "T.J. was smart enough to start in one corner of the building, heaping up the carried earth two or three feet thick, so that we had an immediate result to look

at. . . ." (page 27) Later, when the boys were deciding on a crop, T.J. agrees to plant grass, and the narrator comments, "He was smart. He knew where to give in." (page 28) In both of these instances, T.J. shows that he is "smart" in dealing with the other boys. He understands how to motivate them and when to compromise. He is equally smart in dealing with adults. When the factory owner threatens the boys with jail, T.J. first protests that the roof wasn't being used by the owner and then suggests that the boys actually were trying to "pretty up" the roof. He thus shows that he can think quickly and can present his actions in the most favorable light.

Studying the Sample

Several of the original pre-writing details were not included in the final paragraph. This "extra" information, however, was important for it helped the writer to identify several qualities and then to focus on one of them.

The assignment suggests that this paragraph begin with a general statement, followed by specific detail. Within this overall organization, the writer has cited examples in chronological order.

Notice that the writer cites examples and then explains how these examples support the generalization in the topic sentence.

EXERCISES   Writing About Characters

1. Read (or reread) "Antaeus." Choose two other qualities demonstrated by T.J.: for example, determination and sensitivity. Using the sample paragraph as a model, write a paragraph on each quality. Then combine the three paragraphs into a five-paragraph composition. Begin with an introductory paragraph that gives an overview of all three qualities. Conclude with a paragraph that tells how T.J.'s actions at the end of the story bring out the three qualities.

2. Complete your current writing assignment dealing with character.

LESSON 7 Writing About Plot

Plot refers to the actions and events in a short story, novel, play, or work of nonfiction that tell a story. Narrative poems, too, have plot. Plot always hinges on some kind of conflict: between or among characters; between a character and nature, society, or the supernatural; or within the mind of one character. The conflict usually builds to a climax, or turning point, the peak of highest dramatic intensity. At the climax, the outcome of the plot generally becomes clear. A long work may have subplots in addition to its main plot. Often, multiple plots are interrelated, which is true in *Romeo and Juliet,* for example. (For more information about plot see **Climax, Conflict, Falling Action, Rising Action, Surprise Ending,** and **Suspense** in the Handbook of Literary Terms.)

Questions to consider when thinking about plot include the following.

What major events and actions occur?

What kind of conflict is most important in the story? Are other conflicts present?

What is the climax of the story? Does it resolve the conflict? If so, in whose favor?

What purpose do the events after the climax serve?

If the narrative contains a subplot, how does the subplot relate to the main plot? What is the function of the subplot?

Considering the Assignment

An essay question or writing assignment may ask you to discuss different types of conflict or to pinpoint stages in the conflict, such as rising action, climax, and falling action. A common assignment for longer works is to write about the purpose of subplot. The ways in which events are unexpected, or ironic, is another common topic. How events shape character or reveal theme is yet another possibility.

Following the Writing Process

Writing about plot requires that you complete each stage in the writing process: pre-writing, writing the first draft, and revising. The process is explained on pages 750-757 and is summarized on pages 757-758.

Pre-Writing

Begin by thinking about the events and actions depicted in the selection. While answering the suggested questions about plot, jot down responses and ideas. This often will necessitate your rereading the work of literature or at least reviewing it closely. Your pre-writing notes may reveal patterns and insights that will form the basis for generalizations. Sometimes a generalization will occur to you before you take any notes, and your note taking will then be an attempt to support it.

Writing the First Draft

Begin with a generalization about your topic. Using this generalization as the main idea, expand the idea with the quotations and explanations that appear in your pre-writing notes and with additional details that occur to you as you write.

Revising

Be sure that you have used appropriate transitions when moving from one idea to another. Often, discussions of plot are arranged chronologically. The most common transitional devices used in such discussions are indications of time.

Sample Writing Assignment

The play that is the subject of this assignment begins on page 484.

In Shakespeare's *Romeo and Juliet,* one subplot concerns Mercutio and his death at Tybalt's hands. In one paragraph, discuss the way this subplot fits into the larger tragedy.

Pre-Writing

Purpose: to show how the subplot concerning Mercutio relates to the main plot

Mercutio is a friend to Romeo; Tybalt is Juliet's cousin; Tybalt hates the Montagues
The reader likes Mercutio and is shocked when he dies—thoughtful, clever, humorous, innocent, punning (p. 529), death scene (p. 531)
Tybalt is rash, like the lovers; stabs Mercutio in reaction to good-natured insults; feud becomes more serious
Mercutio's death leads Romeo to kill Tybalt, which leads to banishment; mix-ups lead to the deaths of the lovers
Mercutio and Tybalt both die, foreshadowing deaths of Romeo and Juliet—waste

Writing the First Draft and Revising

Following is a revised paragraph based on the writer's pre-writing notes.

In <u>Romeo and Juliet</u>, Tybalt's wasteful destruction of Mercutio, a promising young man, foreshadows the tragic and unnecessary deaths of Romeo and Juliet. In acts One and Two, Mercutio comes across as humorous and likeable, a person involved in the feud of the Montagues and the Capulets only as Romeo Montague's friend. He is pitted against Tybalt, Juliet Capulet's cousin, whose hatred for anyone associated with the Montagues is obvious from the first scene of the play, in which he says, "What, drawn, and talk of peace? I hate the word/ As I hate hell, all Montagues, and thee." (page 487) In Act Three Mercutio dies at Tybalt's hands. He has been teasing Tybalt, insulting him in a good-natured fashion, and Tybalt, hothead that he is, stabs Mercutio. Suddenly the Montague-Capulet feud has moved to a more serious level, which the dying Mercutio realizes when he says to Romeo, "A plague o' both your houses!/They have made worms' meat of me." (page 531) Romeo, angered by Mercutio's death, kills Tybalt and is banished from Verona. His exile greatly complicates the situation of the lovers, causing the mix-ups that lead to their deaths in Act Five. The sense of waste that the reader or viewer feels at these deaths was partially developed earlier, in Act Three, when Mercutio and Tybalt died for equally foolish reasons.

Studying the Sample

If you compare the pre-writing notes with the revised paragraph, you will notice that a few of the original details were not included in the paragraph, while other support was added. It is standard practice to add and eliminate in this way while you are writing. Why do you think that the writer did not mention more of Mercutio's good qualities? What might have prompted the writer to add the two quotations?

EXERCISES   Writing About Plots

1. Choose any story that you have read and identify the climax of the plot. Write a paragraph in which you answer these questions: What events make the climax believable? Why does the climax occur when it does? How does the climax resolve the conflict of the narrative? Be sure to begin with a general statement about the climax.

2. Complete your current writing assignment dealing with plot.

LESSON 8 Writing About Theme

Writing about theme in literature is as common as writing about character. This certainly is not surprising, for theme is in many ways the heart of literature, a writer's perceptions about life shared with the reader. Some literary works are pure entertainment, and as such they contain no real theme, or message. Most serious writing, however, contains one or more messages about the human condition. These themes usually are not stated directly; they are more apt to come to a reader only after careful reading and thought.

Theme is developed through other elements of literature. Therefore, any study of theme must begin with an understanding of these elements and of the way that they function within a particular selection. In narrative and dramatic works, the main elements include setting, character, and plot. In poetry, form, sound, language, and idea all combine to reveal theme. For more information about the different kinds of literature and their elements, see the Handbook of Literary Terms and introductions to Units 2, 3, 5, 6, and 7.

After you examine the various aspects of a selection, think about the theme, using questions such as the following as a guide.

Does the selection contain one theme or multiple themes?

How would you paraphrase each theme?

Is each theme simple or complex? Explain.

What implications for human life does each theme carry? What, if anything, does it ask of human beings? Of society?

Is the theme optimistic, pessimistic, or something in between?

Do you agree with the writer's message? Why, or why not?

Can you think of other works that develop an identical or similar theme?

Considering the Assignment

Most essay questions and writing assignments ask you to analyze one specific theme, usually the most prominent idea in the work. These assignments generally focus on the way that theme is developed. The questions given as guides for thinking about theme also are possible theme assignments, either singly or in combination.

Following the Writing Process

By now you should be accustomed to thinking of the writing process in three stages: prewriting, writing the first draft, and revising. If you feel uncertain about these stages, review pages 750-757, where each stage is explained fully, or pages 757-758, where the process is summarized.

Pre-Writing

Pre-writing is a crucial step in writing about theme, for without a clear plan you are likely to produce a paragraph or composition consisting of vague generalities. As you go over the suggested questions relating to theme, write our your answers, keeping these guidelines in mind.

Paraphrase theme precisely.

Be thorough in your examination of how theme is developed.

Record details that back up your paraphrase.

Change your paraphrase, if the evidence you accumulate warrants it.

Be sure to organize your notes in a logical order, perhaps making a brief outline before you begin to write. Ask yourself questions such as the following:

Which idea needs to come first? Why?

Are there connections between any ideas?

What idea ought to come last, perhaps as a summary comment?

Writing the First Draft

Although your pre-writing notes give you something concrete from which to work, remember that you are not bound by them. Alter your statements and your supporting evidence as you see fit.

Revising

Writing about theme requires you to dig below the surface and to draw inferences, coming to conclusions that rarely are expressed directly. As you revise your writing, be sure that your inferences and conclusions are based on the text.

Sample Writing Assignment

The story that is the subject of this assignment beings on page 187.

Write a well developed paragraph that answers the following questions: What message about war emerges in the short story "The Sniper" by Liam O'Flaherty? How is this theme established?

Writing the First Draft and Revising

One student wrote the following paragraph, using pre-writing notes that are not shown here.

The senseless destructiveness of war is the main theme in "The Sniper" by Liam O'Flaherty. Set in Dublin, Ireland, during a civil was, the story is filtered through the mind of a young sniper. As the reader learns about the sniper, it becomes clear that war is not glamorous and heroic, as people are often led to believe. At the beginning of the story, the sniper is tired and hungry, for "he [has] eaten nothing since morning." He kills an old woman who is an informer. Then, with his arm numb and in pain from an enemy bullet, he shams death and is able to kill his opponent. In killing this other human being, he ironically gives a "cry of joy." Afterwards, though, when the immediate threat is over, the soldier begins "cursing the war, cursing himself, cursing everybody." The sniper's final shock is yet to come, however, for in turning over the body of his enemy, he is confronted with the face of his own brother. What a pointless, twisted activity war is, the story proclaims, when it forces men to kill their brothers. The story also seems to suggest that all human beings are brothers, united in the human family. If this is true, is war ever justified?

Studying the Sample

Through specific details the writer shows not only what the story says about war but how the writer conveys this message. Notice the transitional words and phrases within the paragraph. What ideas are linked by these transitions? Why does the writer end with a question?

EXERCISES Writing About Theme

1. Choose a story in Unit 2 that you have already read. In one paragraph discuss its theme. Begin with a statement of theme. Then use specific details to show how the story develops this message.

2. Complete your current writing assignment dealing with theme.

LESSON 9 Writing About Tone and Mood

Tone is the attitude that a writer takes toward a subject. The tone of a literary work might be serious, humorous, bitter, nostalgic, angry, or any variation of these. Although a writer sometimes states his or her attitude directly—for example, "The entire situation made me very angry"—more often than not tone must be inferred. All of the elements of literature work to create tone. Word choice and imagery, however, are especially important contributors to tone.

Mood is the feeling, or atmosphere, that the writer creates for the reader. While tone and mood can be the same, they are not necessarily so. A writer may show a character in an embarrassing situation, creating a mood of tension. At the same time the writer's own attitude may be one of amusement or detachment. As with tone, mood often is created through connotative words and figurative language. The sound and rhythm of language help to create mood as well.

Consider these questions when thinking about the tone and mood of a selection:

Are the tone and the mood basically the same or different?

What words would you use to describe the tone? What elements, words, images, and so forth suggest the tone?

What words would you use to describe the mood? What elements, words, images, and so forth suggest the mood?

How do tone and mood contribute to your understanding of characters in the selection?

How do tone and mood reinforce the theme?

Considering the Assignment

Writing assignments related to tone and mood are among the most difficult to complete successfully. That is because determining tone and mood requires skill in making inferences and great sensitivity to the subtleties of language. Most questions and assignments concerning tone and mood ask you to describe the tone or mood and to discuss the way that the writer communicates that attitude or atmosphere. Sometimes you will be asked to relate tone to mood or theme and to back up your conclusion with evidence from the selection.

Following the Writing Process

To complete a writing assignment, go through the three stages of writing described on pages 750-757: pre-writing, writing the first draft, and revising. The process is summarized on pages 757-758.

Pre-Writing

Begin with a generalization about tone or mood, such as "The writer's tone in this story is humorous and courageous." Then examine the selection, keeping these questions in mind: What words and phrases suggest this attitude? What images convey the tone? How does the content of the selection reflect the tone? Jot down specific details to use as support in your paragraph or composition.

Organize your pre-writing notes, deleting any details that no longer seem necessary. Remember that you are not bound by your original generalization. If your details suggest that your idea should be modified or changed completely, by all means alter it to fit your material. You also may return to the selection to find evidence that does support your position.

Writing the First Draft

Before you begin to write your first draft, review the final generalization that emerged from your pre-writing notes. This statement generally can serve as the basis for your topic sentence.

Revising

At this stage your material already should be organized logically. Now, make sure that your organization is clear, and add transitions, if necessary.

Sample Writing Assignment

The selection that is the subject of this assignment begins on page 217.

Describe the tone of Truman Capote's "A Christmas Memory." Then analyze the way that Capote establishes this tone.

Pre-Writing

Purpose: to identify the tone of "A Christmas Memory" and to show how the writer communicates this attitude.

The writer's tone is warm and joyous (most of selection)
Images (sights, sounds, smells of holiday season); the "cheery crunch" of the pecan shells; "The black stove, stoked with coal and firewood, glows like a lighted pumpkin." (p. 220)
Characters embody holiday spirit—Haha Jones returns the money; "Inside myself, I feel warm and sparky as those crumbling logs, carefree as the wind in the chimney," (p. 220); When Buddy's friend feels "old and funny," he comforts her, saying, "Not funny. Fun. More fun than anybody." (p. 221); "We huddle in the bed, and she squeezes my hand I-love-you." (p. 223); great warmth and affection between them

The tone becomes sad; good times end and death is a reality
Predicts that Queenie will die: ". . . where, a winter hence, Queenie will be buried, too." (p. 224)
"This is our last Christmas together. Life separates us." (p. 224)
"Home is where my friend is, and there I never go." (p. 224); misses warmth of the past
Buddy's loss when his friend dies—loses "an irreplaceable part" of himself

Writing the First Draft

The following topic sentence is based on the sample pre-writing notes.

In "A Christmas Memory," Truman Capote's tone is warm and joyous as he recalls the Christmases of his youth; yet his attitude is also sad, for he knows that change and death are inevitable.

Studying the Sample

The pre-writing notes point out the contrast in tone within the selection This contrast is expressed in the sample topic sentence. Notice the many quotations in the pre-writing notes. These will be integrated into the paragraph to support the generalization in the topic sentence.

EXERCISES   Writing About Tone and Mood

1. Read (or reread) "A Christmas Memory." Then complete the sample writing assignment. Use the sample pre-writing notes and add new details as you wish. Begin your paragraph with the sample topic sentence.

2. Select a work of literature in which mood plays a dominant role. In a well developed paragraph describe the mood, and analyze how the writer achieves it.

3. Complete your current assignment dealing with tone or mood.

LESSON 10 Writing About Poetic Language

Poetic language refers to those words and phrases that evoke images in the reader's mind or that appeal to the reader's emotions. Poetic language is precise language. For example, instead of the general verb *run*, a writer might use the more poetic *dart, jog, scurry, race, sprint,* or *hasten*. Poetic language is also suggestive, having emotional overtones called connotations. The verb *bathe,* for example, suggests a much more soothing activity than the synonym *wash.*

Imagery is characteristic of poetry, although like all poetic language, imagery can be found in prose as well. Images are words and phrases that re-create sensory experiences for the reader. For example, the phrase "hands gnarled from work" stimulates a vivid mental image, as does "the sputter of fading fires."

Figurative language is writing that is not literally true but that sparks the reader's imagination. Hyperbole exaggerates reality; simile, metaphor, and personification compare unlike things. For example, "the sun round as an orange and orange as hot-weather moons" (similes).

Before writing about poetic language, be sure that you understand the terms *connotation, imagery, figurative language, hyperbole, metaphor, personification,* and *simile.* If necessary, review the definitions in the Handbook of Literary Terms. Then reread the entire selection two or three times. As you read, ask yourself questions such as these:

What feelings are evoked?

What mental image is created?

What words and phrases are especially striking?

What phrases suggest meanings that are imaginative rather than literal?

Why might the writer have chosen to use poetic language?

What effect is achieved through poetic language?

Considering the Assignment

An essay question or writing assignment may ask you to analyze the role of poetic language in creating the tone or mood of a selection or to discuss descriptive language in relation to another element such as setting, character, or theme. You may be asked to write about the language of a prose work or to focus on particular descriptive passages. One common writing assignment involves the analysis of a poem. For most poems, a major portion of such an analysis would be devoted to poetic language.

Following the Writing Process

As you work on an assignment concerning poetic language, complete each stage in the process of writing: pre-writing, writing the first draft, and revising. The process is explained on pages 750-757 and is summarized on pages 757-758.

Pre-Writing

It is especially important when examining the language of a literary work to understand both the denotative and connotative meanings of the vocabulary used. Be sure to consult a dictionary if you encounter any unfamiliar words.

You may need to narrow the focus of your topic to a few aspects of language or to specific parts of a selection. For instance, you might write about the use of similes and metaphors or about the way that the introductory paragraphs set the mood for a work.

When writing a paragraph, you probably will find that the best way to organize your details is chronologically. For a composition, you may choose to discuss the various kinds of poetic language in their order of importance within a selection.

Writing the First Draft

As you translate your pre-writing notes into a first draft, be alert for examples that do not relate directly to the generalization in your topic sentence. Do not include these examples in your paragraph or composition.

Revising

Check your paragraph or composition to be sure that you have supported your main idea adequately. Be certain that you have included several examples of poetic language, quoted from the selection.

Sample Writing Assignment

"The World in a Wall," which is the subject of this assignment, begins on page 252.

Gerald Durrell's use of vivid descriptive language helps the reader to visualize his environment and also to understand his feelings and attitudes. Durrell's powers of description are especially apparent in the paragraphs on the wall and its inhabitants. Reread these paragraphs. Then write one paragraph commenting on the descriptive language and on the qualities of the writer revealed by that language.

Writing the First Draft

Following is one writer's first draft, written in response to the sample assignment.

In the description of the wall and its inhabitants, Gerald Durrell offers the reader a long passage of imaginative prose and also reveals his fascination with this intricate little world. Durrell divides the description into two parts, first describing the wall, then its inhabitants. What might have seemed to be an ordinary wall comes alive through imagery and figurative language. The reader then meets the insect population, who also are portrayed in lavish detail. The richness of description is impressive, as is Durrell's keen observation. Clearly, he was an inquisitive child, appreciative of natural beauty, who has not lost these qualities as an adult.

Studying the Sample

The structure of the paragraph parallels somewhat the structure of the descriptive passage. The writer comments on the language used to describe the wall before noting the detailed description of the inhabitants.

One problem with the sample first draft is that the writer states several conclusions without providing adequate supporting detail. She has not included examples of the imagery and figurative language used to describe the wall or of the "lavish detail" used to portray its insect population. You will have a chance to correct this problem when you complete Exercise 1.

EXERCISES   Writing About Poetic Language

1. Read (or reread) "The World in a Wall." List examples that might be added to the sample first draft. Then revise the sample so that it contains adequate detail.

2. Choose a poem, and in one paragraph discuss the way that the poetic language establishes its tone. You might want to review the preceding lesson, Writing About Tone and Mood.

3. Complete your current writing assignment dealing with poetic language.

LESSON 11 Writing About a Short Story or a Novel

Any analysis of a short story or novel must begin with an understanding of the basic elements of fiction. These elements—character, setting, plot, and theme—are discussed in Lessons 5-8 on pages 759-766. Once you are familiar with the basic elements of a story or novel, you can examine other aspects of the work; for example, point of view, symbolism, style, and structure. (See the Handbook of Literary Terms for definitions.) The following questions can help you to apply your understanding of these terms in a selection.

Who tells the story?

How would the story be different if told from another point of view?

Is there a recurring person, place, or object that might function as a symbol?

How do the symbols relate to the writer's purpose?

How would you describe the style: straightforward, flowery, rambling?

How does the style suit the subject and theme?

Can the story be divided into parts or sections?

Is the story arranged so that one part parallels or balances another?

What effect has the writer achieved by the particular arrangement of material?

Considering the Assignment

An essay question or writing assignment often will ask you to analyze one or more elements of a short story or novel or to relate elements to each other. Another kind of assignment may ask you to evaluate the work or to discuss some problem related to the development of a character, theme, or other element. An assignment may ask you to consider one part of a novel and to discuss the relationship between that part and the rest of the work or to analyze the role of a subplot or a minor character within the work as a whole.

Following the Writing Process

When writing about a short story or novel, you should complete each stage in the process of writing: pre-writing, writing the first draft, and revising. Consult pages 750-758 for an explanation and summary of the process.

Pre-Writing

When you must choose a story to analyze, it is not always wise to choose your favorite story. Instead, select one that seems suitable for the assignment; for example, a story with strong characters or a clearly drawn setting.

When writing about a novel, be sure that your topic is narrow enough to be developed within the length specified in the assignment.

Writing the First Draft

Using the writing assignment or essay question as a guide, form a generalization from the evidence you have collected. This generalization should be stated in the topic sentence of your paragraph or composition. As you write, be sure to relate the examples and quotations to the generalization.

Revising

Check to be sure that all details support your main point. Also read to be sure that all of your sentences flow smoothly from one to another and that one point logically follows another.

Sample Writing Assignment

The theme of a short story is brought out through the character, setting, and plot. Choose a story from this unit, and in one paragraph analyze the way that one element relates to theme.

Pre-Writing

One writer chose "Raymond's Run," which begins on page 33, as the subject of his paragraph. Following are his notes on the character Squeaky.

Purpose: to show how the character Squeaky brings out the theme of this short story
Theme: human relationships are more important than winning

Throughout most of story, Squeaky's main concern is winning; ". . . no one can beat me, and that's all there is to it." (p. 33)
Other people seem to take second place to running ". . . he plays like he's driving a stage coach; which is OK by me so long as he doesn't run over me or interrupt my breathing exercises." (p. 34)
   "I'll high-prance down 34th Street like a rodeo pony to keep my knees strong, even if it does get my mother uptight so that she walks ahead like she's not with me. . . ." (p. 34)
   ". . . girls never really smile at each other because they don't know how and don't want to know how. . . ." (p. 35)
Just before race, Squeaky tells herself, "Squeaky you must win, you must win, you are the fastest thing in the world. . . ." (p. 37)
Becomes aware that Raymond is running too; realizes "that Raymond would make a very fine runner. . . ."; says, "and I'm smiling to beat the band, cause if I've lost this race, or if me and Gretchen tied, or even if I've won, I can always retire as a

runner and begin a whole new career as a coach with Raymond as my new champion. . . . I've got a roomful of ribbons and medals and awards. But what has Raymond got to call his own?" (p. 38)
At end of story, Squeaky can appreciate Gretchen's skill and dedication; they smile at each other; seems like the beginning of a friendship (see final paragraph)

Writing the First Draft

The writer used his sample pre-writing notes to write this topic sentence.

The change that takes place in Squeaky, the main character in "Raymond's Run," brings out the idea that human relationships are more important than winning.

Studying the Sample

The writer first identified the theme, then used it as a guide for taking notes. Notice that the notes include the writer's ideas as well as quotations to back them up.

The topic sentence names the story, the character, and the theme and introduces a conclusion about the relation between the character and the theme. The rest of the sentences must support this conclusion.

EXERCISES   Writing About Short Stories and Novels

1. Read (or reread) "Raymond's Run." Then complete the sample writing assignment, using the sample pre-writing notes and topic sentence.

2. In two separate paragraphs, analyze the setting and the plot of "Raymond's Run" in relation to its theme. Then join together all three paragraphs on this story. Frame the paragraphs with an introduction and a conclusion so that you end up with a five-paragraph composition.

3. Complete your current writing assignment dealing with a short story.

LESSON 12 Writing About Nonfiction

Nonfiction is prose writing that is about real people, places, and events. Biography and autobiography, accounts of people's lives, are types of nonfiction. So are editorials, essays, prose eulogies, journals, newspaper and most magazine articles, speeches, and historical accounts. (For more information see **Autobiography, Editorial, Essay,** and **Eulogy,** in the Handbook of Literary Terms.)

Questions to consider when thinking about nonfiction include the following.

How would you classify the selection? Is it an autobiography, historical account, eulogy, or essay? What characteristics enable you to label the work?

What is the tone of the selection?

Who is the writer's intended audience?

What appears to be the writer's purpose? What leads you to this conclusion?

What themes, if any, are brought out?

Considering the Assignment

Questions and writing assignments about nonfiction often involve one or more of the elements of fiction: setting, plot, character, theme, and point of view. Frequently, too, writing about nonfiction involves analysis of a writer's purposes and of how those purposes are achieved. Writing about style is always a possibility, as is commenting on a quotation from a work and discussing a work in a social, historical, or political light.

Following the Writing Process

As always, think of the writing process for any nonfiction assignment in three stages: pre-writing, writing the first draft, and revising. Review pages 750-758 if you feel uncertain about these stages.

Pre-Writing

If an assignment involves a quotation from the text, find the quotation and think about its relationship to the entire selection. If an assignment asks you to write about an element of literature—setting or character, for example—proceed as you would for an assignment on that element alone.

Writing the First Draft

As you write your sentences and paragraphs, remember that you are free to add and discard ideas, and that generally you should do so. This process of modifying and deleting is a vital part of producing unified writing.

Revising

Be sure that you have quoted accurately when incorporating quotations into a paragraph or composition. Also be sure that you have indicated clearly the location of each quotation by giving a page number in parentheses after the quotation and possibly by establishing the location in the sentence that introduces the quotation. For example, "After winning the race, Squeaky. . . ."

Sample Writing Assignment

The selection that is the subject of this assignment begins on page 234.

In Isaac Bashevis Singer's "The Washwoman," the old woman explains her recovery from serious illness, saying, "I could not rest easy in my bed because of the wash. . . . The wash would not let me die." In a paragraph explain how her statement reflects Singer's purposes for writing this selection.

Writing the First Draft and Revising

The following paragraph is based on pre-writing notes that are not shown here.

¶ In Isaac Bashevis Singer's "The Washwoman"

's statement

The old woman ~~says~~, "I could not rest easy in my bed because of the wash. . . . The wash would not let me die," *(page 237) indicates* Singer's

first

objective ~~is~~ to praise *[or eulogize]* this hard-working and honest person. ~~The washwoman worked for Singer's family in Poland early in the twen-tieth century,~~

Early in the selection ^ *describes*

Singer ~~discusses~~ how difficult

in the early twentieth century, before washing machines and dryers existed.

and exhausting it was to do laundry ~~back then.~~

It would have been easier for ... *to*

The old woman ~~could have~~ begged or

live[d] in a[n] old people's home, "But there was in her a certain pride and love of labor. . . . The old woman did not want to become a burden, so she bore her burden." (page 235)

As she says, "The wash would not let me die."

Her words suggest

Singer ~~has a~~ second purpose i[n] writing

for ... *about*

~~of~~ this person from his past[,] he wants his readers to see the washwoman as a symbol of human strength and perseverance, as well as of the need *[every]* human ~~has~~ for work and a sense of accomplishment. This larger purpose is summarized in the description of the washwoman's hands: "These hands

spoke of the stubborn[n]ess of mankind, of the will to work not only as one's strength permits, but beyond the limits of one's power."

In addition to her commitment to hard work, the old woman possessed deep honesty and integrity.

(page 236) When ~~the washwoman~~ *[she]* falls ill with the laundry of several families in her possession, ~~Singer describes her as~~ *[she is]* ". . . driven by an indomitable will to return the property to its rightful owners." ~~This shows that she is extremely honest.~~

Studying the Sample

The writer begins with the quotation given in the assignment and then relates this statement to Singer's main purpose. She includes specific detail that explains why Singer considers the old woman hard-working and honest and thus worthy of praise. She then goes on to explore Singer's second, less obvious purpose. Notice that part of the key quotation is repeated before this second purpose is explored. The writer ends the paragraph with another significant quotation, which summarizes this second purpose, an effective way to conclude a paragraph or composition.

EXERCISES   Writing About Nonfiction

1. Study the changes made in the sample paragraph and suggest a reason for each change.
2. Choose two of the "Essays of Social Commentary" in Unit 3. In two paragraphs discuss the purposes of the two writers in presenting their material. How are their purposes related? How are they different?
3. Complete your current writing assignment dealing with nonfiction.

LESSON 13 Writing About Poetry

Although poetry is difficult to define, certain characteristics are evident in most poems. In general, poetry is economical in expression, tending to be more compact than prose. The poet chooses each word carefully, often using language that evokes images in the reader's mind. The physical shape and the sound of a poem are important to communicating meaning.

The first step in writing about a poem is to reread it several times. You might use an approach similar to the following.

Read the poem aloud, forming a general impression and listing any unfamiliar words.

Read the poem again, noting lines and phrases that you do not understand.

Look up the definitions of the unfamiliar words.

Study the poem line by line and phrase by phrase. Keep these questions in mind: What is the literal meaning? What is the underlying meaning?

Ask yourself: Who "speaks" the poem? How does the speaker feel about the subject? How do you feel as you read the poem?

Write one sentence that summarizes the literal meaning of the poem.

Write one sentence that states the main idea, or theme, of the poem.

Considering the Assignment

A writing assignment or essay question may ask you to discuss one aspect of a poem, for example, the speaker, tone, rhythm and rhyme, or imaginative language. You may be asked to analyze the relation between one or more elements and the theme of the poem. You sometimes may be asked to react to a poet's message, offering your own views on the same subject.

Following the Writing Process

When writing about poetry, you will work through the same three stages as you do when writing about other kinds of literature. The stages, pre-writing, writing the first draft, and revising, are explained on pages 750-757 and summarized on pages 757-758.

Pre-Writing

An assignment dealing with a poem probably will contain one or more literary terms. Be sure that you know the exact meaning of each term. Use the Handbook of Literary Terms or another source to reinforce your understanding.

Sometimes an assignment will ask you to trace a technique or to explain the development of an idea. The details for such assignments generally should be organized chronologically.

Writing the First Draft

When working with notes, you may realize that you have too many details for a paragraph or brief composition. You can solve this problem by eliminating all but the most essential details, by narrowing your topic and using only those details related to your new main idea, or by writing a longer composition, with the approval of your teacher.

Revising

Check your writing for the characteristics of a well constructed paragraph or composition: a main idea clearly stated in the topic sentence, details that support the generalization in the topic sentence, and a clear relationship between each detail and the topic sentence.

Sample Writing Assignment

The poem that is the subject of this assignment begins on page 59.

In one paragraph explain how the figurative language and imagery in "The Fish" communicate the speaker's attitude toward the fish. Your topic sentence should connect the language of the poem with the speaker's attitude. The rest of the paragraph should support your generalization with references to the poem.

Writing the first Draft and Revising

The pre-writing notes for the following revised paragraph were not shown here.

~~At the end of~~ *Throughout* "The Fish" the speaker ~~lets~~ *describes* the fish ~~go. This shows~~ admiration ~~and~~ re~~- ~~ *in* ... *ying* *ful terms, building to the moment when he or she makes a final gesture of respect by releasing the* (spect) ~~for the fish which is hinted at~~ *fish.* ~~throughout the poem.~~ *From the beginning* The speaker sees the fish as "venerable" ~~and~~ worthy of respect. *In the first half of the poem* The fish, though "battered" and "homely," *iful flowers ⊙ The pattern of its brown* is compared with ~~natural~~ beauty. ~~Its~~ skin ~~is~~ *recalls* "shapes like full-blown roses" (line 14), its barnacles ~~like~~ *are* "fine rosettes of lime" (line 17), its pink swim-bladder *is* "like a big peony" (line 33), *Even* its "shiny entrails" are *described as* "dramatic reds and blacks." (lines 30 and 31) The speaker's admiration increases when he *or she* notices *the fish's lips:*

"that from his lower lip

—if you could call it a lip—

grim, wet, and weaponlike,

hung five old pieces of fish-line,

(lines 48-51)

Finally, Admiration triumphs over desire to keep the fish *as* The speaker sees the hooks and lines as "medals, *...* a five-haired beard of wisdom."

(line 63) ~~All of the description evokes a positive feeling in the reader, who sees the fish through the speaker's eyes.~~

Studying the Sample

The revised topic sentence makes a generalization about the speaker's feelings and the language in the poem. The organization of the paragraph is generally chronological, which emphasizes the speaker's growing respect for the fish. Each quotation from the poem demonstrates the connection between the speaker's admiring attitude and the positive language used to describe the fish.

EXERCISES   Writing About Poetry

1. Study the changes made in the sample revised paragraph. Be ready to suggest a reason for each change.

2. Study "The Fish." Then in one paragraph discuss the way that the sound of the poem helps to communicate its meaning. Consider the sounds of individual words and phrases and the overall rhythm of the poem.

3. Complete your current writing assignment dealing with poetry.

LESSON 14 Writing About Drama

Drama is literature in play form, literature that develops plot and character through dialogue and action. Dramas, although they are read as scripts, are written primarily to be seen and heard.

Drama has a great deal in common with narrative writing. Like the short story and the novel, drama includes the elements of setting, plot, character, and theme. What sets drama apart is the way that the elements are developed. Drama consists almost entirely of dialogue. However, a reader does get some information, usually about setting and characters, in the stage directions. These are the playwright's instructions for how the set should look and how the actors should look, move, and read lines. They also may include suggestions for sound effects and lighting.

When thinking about a play, begin by examining the setting, characters, plot, theme, tone, mood, and language. You may use the questions suggested in Lessons 5-10, pages 759-770. Then focus on the following questions, which will help you to understand what makes drama unique.

How is the play put together? How many acts does it have? Are the acts divided into scenes? What happens in each "unit" of the play? (See **Drama** in the Handbook of Literary Terms.)

Where is the turning point in the play? What interesting events take place after it?

Study the stage directions. What information do they give you?

What would be especially entertaining about this play in performance?

What problems would exist in staging?

Considering the Assignment

An essay question or writing assignment may ask you to write about setting, plot, character, theme, or mood. Assignments often involve writing about irony, or writng about the symbols in a play and sometimes involve writing about the characteristics of comedy or tragedy. With a longer play you may be asked to write about dramatic structure: to discuss what happens when or where the tension peaks. You might even be asked to explain how you would stage a particular play, answering questions such as these:

What kind of set would you create? How would you achieve required special effects?

Following the Writing Process

Drama assignments require you to apply a three-stage writing process: pre-writing, writing the first draft, and revising. Pages 750-758 explain and summarize these stages.

Pre-Writing

As you read a play, try to imagine it performed. Visualize the setting and the movements of the characters. Imagine the sound effects and the voices of the characters. Also, be aware of changes in the characters and emerging patterns of action.

The amount of detail that you include in your pre-writing notes depends on the length of your assignment. When you are writing only one paragraph, include only details that could properly be included in that paragraph.

For longer compositions you may find it helpful to organize your pre-writing notes in outline form, taking care to order the ideas logically and to look for natural connections among ideas. As you develop your outline, do not hesitate to delete ideas that turn out to be repetitive or off your topic. If necessary, dig deeper for additional ideas.

Writing the First Draft

Although the dialogue in a play is not enclosed in quotation marks, be sure to use quotation marks when quoting lines of dialogue within a paragraph or composition.

Revising

When reviewing your first draft, you may find that your paragraph or composition is too long. A paragraph of eighteen sentences, for example, probably should be divided into two or three shorter paragraphs or condensed into one well developed paragraph of eight or nine sentences. If you cannot decide how to fix an overly long piece of writing, ask your teacher for help.

Writing the First Draft

Using the sample pre-writing notes, one writer began the following first draft.

In Susan Glaspell's one-act play "Trifles," Minnie Wright's canary is a symbol that functions three ways. First, the bird clearly represented beauty and companionship to Mrs. Wright. In her lonely farmhouse, the bird's singing must have cheered her, especially in the face of her husband's frequent absence and constant silence. The reader knows that Mrs. Wright must have loved the bird, because she wraps its tiny dead body in silk and places it in a "pretty box." Second, the canary functions as a symbol of Minnie Wright herself.

Sample Writing Assignment

The play that is the subject of this assignment begins on page 419.

In one paragraph analyze the symbolism of the bird in Susan Glaspell's play "Trifles."

Pre-Writing

Purpose: to discuss the symbolism of the bird in "Trifles"

Bird a symbol of Minnie Wright; before her marriage: "She used to sing real pretty herself." (p. 424); ". . . she was kind of like a bird herself—real sweet and pretty, but kind of timid and—fluttery." (p. 425)

Bird a symbol of beauty and companionship to Minnie Wright; husband frequently absent, silent; no children; isolated on farm

Wright killed the bird (physically) and Minnie (mentally and spiritually); "No, Wright wouldn't like the bird—a thing that sang. She used to sing. He killed that, too." (p. 426)

Minnie wrung husband's neck—bird's death reflects Wright's death

Studying the Sample

Compare the pre-writing notes and the beginning of the first draft. Notice that the writer has chosen to discuss the idea of beauty and companionship first. Next, he will talk about the bird as a symbol of Minnie Wright and then as a symbol of the dead John Wright. Is this order of development logical? Why, or why not?

EXERCISES   Writing About Drama

1. Read (or reread) "Trifles." Then complete the sample paragraph, using the sample pre-writing notes. First, support the idea that the canary symbolizes Minnie Wright. Next, write a transition sentence similar to this one: Finally, the canary in its dead state symbolizes John Wright in his dead state. Follow with details that support this idea.

During revision, be sure that your paragraph is not too long. If it is, delete all details except those needed to explain each symbolic function.

2. Complete your current writing assignment dealing with drama.